FROMMER'S

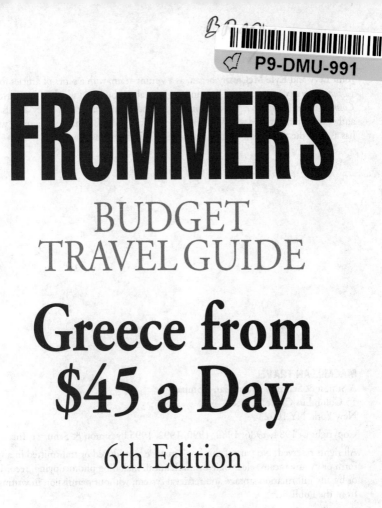

BUDGET
TRAVEL GUIDE

Greece from $45 a Day

6th Edition

by John Levy & Kyle McCarthy
assisted by John Bozman

MACMILLAN • USA

ABOUT THE AUTHORS

John Levy and **Kyle McCarthy** began, as a writing team, with a series of articles for the *China Daily* newspaper; they have since written about budget and adventure travel for *Cosmopolitan, Backpacker, Connections,* and several airline magazines. They are also the authors of Frommer guides to Thailand and Bangkok. **John Bozman,** also a travel writer, has assisted the authors on their Bangkok and Thailand guides as well.

MACMILLAN TRAVEL
A Simon & Schuster Macmillan Company
15 Columbus Circle
New York, NY 10023

ISBN 0-02-860464-4
ISSN 1042-8410

Editor: Theodore G. Stavrou
Map Editor: Douglas Stallings
Design by Michele Laseau
Maps by Geografix Inc. and Ortelius Design

Manufactured in the United States of America.

Contents

8 Crete 215

SPECIAL FEATURE

9 The Cyclades 275

SPECIAL FEATURE

10 The Dodecanese 375

SPECIAL FEATURE

List of Maps

What the Symbols Mean

★ **FROMMER'S FAVORITES** Hotels, restaurants, attractions, and entertainments you should not miss

$ **SUPER-SPECIAL VALUES** Really exceptional values

Abbreviations in Hotel and Other Listings

The following symbols refer to the standard amenities available in all rooms:
A/C air conditioning
MINIBAR refrigerator stocked with beverages and snacks
TEL telephone
TV television

The following abbreviations are used for credit cards:

AE	American Express	ER	enRoute
CB	Carte Blanche	JCB	(Japan)
DC	Diners Club	MC	MasterCard
DISC	Discover	V	Visa

Trip Planning with This Guide

USE THE FOLLOWING FEATURES:

What Things Cost To help you plan your daily budget

Calendar of Events To plan for or avoid

Suggested Itineraries For seeing the regions or cities

What's Special About Checklist A summary of each region's highlights—which lets you check off those that appeal most to you

Easy-to-Read Maps Walking tours, city sights, hotel and restaurant locations—all referring to or keyed to the text

Fast Facts All the essentials at a glance: currency, embassies, emergencies, safety, taxes, tipping, and more

OTHER SPECIAL FROMMER FEATURES

Cool for Kids Hotels, restaurants, and attractions

Did You Know? Offbeat, fun facts

Impressions What others have said

Acknowledgments

This is the sixth edition of our guide to Greece, revised and, we hope, made even more user friendly. We are especially grateful to the Greek National Tourist Organization, in New York and throughout Greece, and Tassoula Christofidis.

Once again we are deeply indebted to our helpful and informative friends in Greece, Peter and Dimitri Cocconi, Vassiliki Bali, John Polychronides, and Kim Sjogren. A special *efcharistó* also to Eleni and Dimitris Sarlas, Tony and Nick Droseros, Sotiris and Marianne Nikolis, Yanna and Dimitris Skalidis, Soula and Dimitris Ghikas, the Diareme family, Dorina Stathopoulou, Rena Valyraki, Rena Papademetriou, Susan Spiliopoulou, Nikos Antonopoulos, George Nomikos, Manolis Grillis, Michalis Valaris, Alexis Zikas, Kathy Gavalas, Lia Mathioudakis, Vassilis Vassilatos, Despina Kitini, Ares Talares, Lefteris Trakos, Theo Spordilis, Michael Kolokythias, Eleni Boliako, and last but certainly not least, the ever gracious Thanos and his excellent staff.

Many thanks to our exhaustive (and sometimes exhausted) researchers M. J. Nolan Kelly and Ariel Zeitlin, for their tremendous input into this edition. And our continuing gratitude to the staff at Macmillan Travel who put everything together, our current editor, Theodore Stavrou, and our past editor, Marilyn Wood.

Invitation to the Reader

In this guide to Greece, we have selected what we consider to be the best of the many wonderful establishments we came across while conducting our research. You, too, in the course of your visit to Greece, may come across a hotel, restaurant, shop, or attraction that you feel should be included here; or you may find that a place we have selected has since changed for the worse. Let us know of your discovery. Address your comments to:

John Levy & Kyle McCarthy
Greece from $45 a Day
c/o Macmillan Travel
15 Columbus Circle
New York, NY 10023

Disclaimers

We have made every effort to ensure the accuracy of the prices as well as of the other information contained in this guide. Yet we advise you to keep in mind that prices fluctuate over time and that some of the other information herein may also change as a result of the various volatile factors affecting the travel industry. The wise traveler will add 15% to 20% to the prices quoted throughout.

The authors and the publisher cannot be held responsible for the experiences of the reader while traveling.

Safety Advisory

Whenever you're traveling in an unfamiliar city or country, stay alert. Be aware of your immediate surroundings. Wear a moneybelt and keep a close eye on your possessions. Be particularly careful with cameras, purses, and wallets—all favorite targets of thieves and pickpockets. Although Greece is comparatively safe, you should nevertheless bear in mind that every society has its criminals. It is therefore your responsibility to exercise caution at all times.

Greek Street Names

Most signposts in Greece, especially in the cities and larger towns, have street names in English as well as Greek. For an explanation of abbreviations, however, see the note on page 46. For possible variations in spellings, see the discussion of transliterating Greek in Appendix A.

Accent Marks

To aid the reader in the pronunciation of Greek words, we have added an accent mark to indicate where you should put the stress. Getting the right pronunciation *can* be important, especially if you are asking for directions or are buying, say, a train or bus ticket (see page 50). Thus, for example, in Leofóros Vassiléos Konstantínou (King Constantine Avenue, in Athens), the accents tell you that the words should be pronounced Leh-oh-*FOH*-rohs Vah-ssee-*LEH*-ohs Kohn-stahn-*TEE*-noo.

Getting to Know Greece

1

MOST READERS WHO PICK UP THIS GUIDE ALREADY HAVE AN IMAGE OF GREECE shaped by childhood memories of the *Iliad*, the music and dance of *Zorba the Greek*, personal journeys inspired by the *Odyssey*, slide shows of the *Venus de Milo*, and the myths of centaurs, muses, and Olympian gods. Although there are tangible symbols such as the Acropolis in Athens and many other ruins scattered about the country, it's the sun, the deep blue of the Aegean Sea, and the blinding white of cube-shaped houses that stir the traveler's imagination. When friends return from Greece they always look healthy and alive, revived by the most basic physical and spiritual pleasures.

Even now, after many months of research, after hopping from island to mainland and back again, the memories we recall most vividly are elemental to the Greek lifestyle: calm seas dotted with bright-colored fishing boats, octopuses drying outside portside tavernas, silvery-green leaves of a million olive trees shimmering in the summer breeze, barren cliffs traversed by goatherds and their flocks, smiling mammas whitewashing doorsteps in preparation for Easter, time-worn pebbles warming our feet after a dip in crisp, clear water.

We hope our readers will seek out their own combination of Greece's sensual and intellectual pleasures. We urge you to explore the famous ancient sites that chronicle the country's long history and its role in the rise of Western civilization. The history section below, by no means exhaustive, serves to put into context the events, speculative tidbits, and mythological tales discussed later in our book, as we consider the country region by region.

But don't become overwhelmed by antiquity's many silent and majestic monuments. Enjoy what Greece is today: the European sophistication of its cities, myriad islands offering sun and fun, watersports and hiking, international nightlife, inexpensive accommodations, and healthy dining. It's a country whose spirit is as bright and lively and colorful as its landscape, and whose people continue the tradition since Homer's time of welcoming guests with enthusiasm, and even have a word to describe it—*philoxenía.*

1 Geography, History & Politics

Geography

Greece (Hellás or, in modern Greek, Ellás), officially known as the Hellenic Republic, comprises the mainland on southeastern Europe's Balkan peninsula, the Peloponnese peninsula, and almost 6,000 small islands, only about half of which are inhabited. With an area of 50,961 square miles, this country of approximately 11 million is a little smaller than the state of Alabama. Greece is bordered by Albania, Yugoslavia, and Bulgaria to the north, the Ionian Sea to the west, and the Aegean Sea and Turkey to the east.

The islands are divided into eight major groups: the Ionian Islands west of the mainland; the Saronic Gulf islands south and east of the Peloponnese; Évvia and the Sporades off the east coast; the Cyclades and Crete in the central Aegean; the northeastern Aegean islands to the south of Thrace; and the Dodecanese group in the eastern Aegean bordering Turkey.

IMPRESSIONS

We are all Greeks.
—Shelley, *Preface to Hellas,* 1821

After 4,000 years of deforestation (for shipbuilding and firewood), and many decades of overdevelopment (for tourism), much of the country is too arid for cultivation. Tanker boats and desalination plants must supply water for many of the inhabited islands. Yet, as recently as 1984, 28% of the population was engaged in farming 30% of the land; the main products are grains, fruits, vegetables, olives, and livestock (goats for milk and sheep for meat). In 1991 the European Community (now European Union) placed two popular Greek exports, the anise-flavored liqueur called ouzo and feta cheese, on its protected-products list.

History

According to archeological finds, Greece had a long prehistory that extended back into the Neolithic Age (at least 6000 B.C.). Its earliest history, beginning some 3,000 years later, can be divided into three main periods: the Minoan, the Mycenaean or Helladic, and the Classical. The years 2600 to 1500 B.C. were dominated by the Minoan culture, which flourished on Crete and,

Dateline

- **3000–1400 B.C.** *Minoan Period:* Knossós (Crete); King Minos; Theseus slays the Minotaur in his Labyrinth. ➤

Did You Know?

- In 1991, Greece celebrated 25 centuries of democracy. The official ceremony, attended by prominent world figures, was held in Athens, at the *bema* (forum) atop Pnyx Hill from where, in the 6th century B.C., the statesman Cleisthenes exhorted the Athenian assembly to accept his democratic reforms.
- In 500 B.C., Athens opened the first municipally run garbage dump, decreeing that all waste had to be disposed of one mile outside the city walls.
- Among the engineering feats of ancient Greece was a tunnel built on the island of Sámos by Eupalinos, a Megarian architect, in the 6th century B.C. to bring water from nearby mountain springs to the island's capital, Pythagorio. The tunnel was dug some 1,000 yards through the mountain by workers who started at both ends and met in the middle, only about one inch off their marks.
- The gleaming marble stadium in the middle of Athens was built in 1896 for the first of the modern Olympic Games, which took place in Greece. It occupies the site of a 4th-century B.C. stadium where the quadrennial Panathenaic Games were held. Like the original, of which it is a faithful copy, the stadium is one stade (about 606 feet) long, the standard measure of the Olympic foot race.
- Some 40% of Greece's approximately 11 million people live in and around Athens.
- Greece has the highest rate of traffic accidents in Europe, averaging seven deaths per day.
- In addition to exports and tourism, Greece's economy depends on remittances from the approximately 5 million Greeks living abroad. In 1991 those remittances amounted to $948 million.
- Flokáti, the shaggy woolen rug made in Greece, is actually handwoven from wool imported from New Zealand. Greece's many sheep are bred for their meat rather than their wool.

Dateline

- **1400–1150 B.C.** Agamemnon; Jason and the Argonauts; Achilles; the battle of Troy.
- **1200–1100 B.C.** *The Dark Ages.*
- **800–600 B.C.** *Aristocratic Age:* Athens unites with towns of Attica; Draco proclaims severe laws; Solon reforms constitution; Homer composes the *Iliad* and the *Odyssey.*
- **520–430 B.C.** *Persian Wars.* Themistocles fortifies Piraeus.
- **492 B.C.** Pheidippides runs 26 miles from Marathon to Athens to announce Athenian victory.
- **480 B.C.** Aeschylus wins Athens drama festival.
- **480–430 B.C.** *Classical Age:* Parthenon built; Pericles in power; Aeschylus, Sophocles, and Euripides at work.
- **430–400 B.C.** Peloponnesian War. Naval battle of Syracuse; Erechtheum on Acropolis completed; Aristophanes writes comedies; Pericles dies; Socrates drinks hemlock; Sparta triumphs over Athens.
- **360–300 B.C.** *Macedonian Age:* Alexander the Great conquers; Aristotle founds school.
- **200 B.C.–A.D. 300** *Roman Period:* Rome sacks Corinth.
- **31 B.C.** Octavian crowned first emperor of Rome.
- **A.D. 300–1200** Constantine builds Constantinople; Crusaders build forts. ➤

archeologists speculate, on the Aegean island of Thera (present-day Santoríni), near settlements of the lesser-known Cycladic civilization. The Mycenaean civilization, which lasted from about 1600 to 600 B.C. (including a 400-year period, 1200 to 800, that is referred to as the Dark Ages), was centered in the Peloponnese. The Classical era, so called because the arts, culture, and democracy of the Greeks reached their peak at this time, spans the years from 600 B.C. to the death of Alexander the Great in 323 B.C.

EARLIEST SETTLERS

Pottery dating from as early as 6000 B.C., found in Macedonia, Thessaly, and the Cyclades confirms the existence of agricultural and livestock-breeding settlements that later developed into a primitive Neolithic culture. About 2600 B.C., a wave of emigrants from what we now know as the Middle East brought copper to Greece. Archeologists have found traces of another race at Phaistós, on Crete, from about 2300 B.C.; several sites abandoned about 2000 B.C. suggest that northern invaders overran Greek settlements about this time. After this transitional period, Minoan culture became predominant during the middle Bronze Age (2000–1580 B.C.).

MINOAN CIVILIZATION

Around 1900, Sir Arthur Evans, a British archeologist who had been conducting excavations on a Cretan hillside near Iráklio, came upon the remains of what appeared to be an enormous structure. The discovery of the royal palace at Knossós, Crete's ancient capital, caused a sensation; for the complex of multistoried buildings, many of them now partly restored, proved the existence of a civilization more advanced than hitherto supposed.

Indeed, not only in architecture but also in physical works, commerce, and the arts, the Minoans achieved a rare degree of sophistication. They were gifted artisans, producing beautiful frescoes for the Cretan palaces and, probably for homes in their colony at Akrotíri, on the southwestern coast of Thera. (The best-preserved of these frescoes are on display in the archeological museums of Iráklio and Athens.) By the 16th century B.C. the Minoans had founded colonies at Miletos, on the coast of Asia Minor near Sámos, and on Kalymnos (Kálimnos), Rhodes, and Kythera (Kýthira). Goods from as far away as Egypt and

Syria have been excavated at Minoan sites, and the eggshell-thin, multicolored Kamáres ware they produced has been found throughout the Mediterranean (Kamáres is the village where they were first discovered). The most fascinating find may be a collection of tablets, thought to be royal records, written in syllable symbols and numerals that have not yet been fully deciphered. In a kind of archeologists' shorthand, the symbols are referred to as Linear A.

Almost as intriguing as the culture of the Minoans is the mystery surrounding the disappearance of their civilization. The late Greek archeologist Spyrídon Marinátos, who headed the excavation of Akrotíri, and other archeologists have postulated that a severe volcanic eruption on Thera at about 1500 B.C. caused a tidal wave that wiped out Knossós and Crete's northern shore (the theory is very popular with those who believe that Thera was the mythical Atlantis). Other scholars conclude from tablets written in a script later used at Mycenae (and dubbed "Linear B") that invaders from the north destroyed this society. It was about this time that a new race was prospering in the Peloponnese, in the towns of Pilos, Tiryns, and Mycenae.

MYCENAEAN CIVILIZATION

As early as 2600 B.C., Asian tribes, later called Pelasgians, were settling in the Peloponnese. Their pottery and sculpture, found in Asia Minor, Egypt, the Cyclades, and on Crete, indicate that the Minoans had direct contact with their eventual successors. It took the hard work and imagination of Heinrich Schliemann, the 19th-century German amateur archeologist, to forge the link. In 1870, in a quest to prove the veracity of Homer's *Iliad,* Schliemann began excavating at Hissarlik, on the northwestern coast of modern Turkey. After six years of exploring the multilevel ruins of ancient Troy, he continued to the eastern coast of the Peloponnese, searching for evidence of Homer's Greek heroes. The royal shaft graves he uncovered at Mycenae, filled with gold masks, jewelry, and pottery, convinced him, albeit wrongly, that he'd found King Agamemnon's tomb. Nevertheless, the graves, which clearly show Minoan influence, indicated that here was a culture that had supplanted the Minoan.

These people, centered in Mycenae (see Chapter 7, "The Peloponnese"), achieved new heights in architecture and bronze work. By the 14th century B.C., shaft

Dateline

- 1204–1797 Venice rules duchies in the Ionian Isles, the Peloponnese, and other isles.
- 1453 Fall of Constantinople.
- 1453–1821 *Period of Turkish rule.*
- 1821–1829 Greek War of Independence.
- 1833 Prince Otto of Bavaria appointed first king of Greece.
- 1863–1913 Prince William of Denmark rules as King George I. A liberal constitution is adopted; Greece regains much of its territory from the Turks; economy flourishes.
- 1917 Greece joins Allies during World War I.
- 1923 League of Nations organizes massive resettlement of Muslim and Greek Orthodox citizens.
- 1940–1941 Italians and Germans invade Greece; King George flees; resistance forms.
- 1944 British and Greek forces liberate the country.
- 1944–1949 Civil war occurs between Communist and progovernment forces in the north.
- 1948 Dodecanese Islands returned to Greece.
- 1951 Greece joins NATO.
- 1952 Women get the right to vote.
- 1967 Military junta takes over; King Constantine flees country.
- 1973 Monarchy abolished.
- 1974 Junta yields power; democracy restored.
- 1975 New, republican constitution adopted.

➤

Dateline

- **1981** Greece becomes 10th member of the European Community.
- **1991** Athens celebrates 2,500 years of democracy.

graves had evolved into *thóloi,* beehive-shaped burial vaults cut into the mountainside, a significant engineering feat for that time. Nestor's palace at Pilos displays another Mycenaean invention. Unlike other Minoan palaces, it was built around a *megaron,* a reception hall with a central hearth and columned portico at one end, the forerunner of the classic Greek temple. Linear B tablets found at Pílos (deciphered in 1953 by Michael Ventris) tell us that their syllabic script was an early form of ancient Greek. Then, a more militaristic mood prevailed in the Mycenaean centers. Cyclopean wall fortifications (so called because only huge monsters could stack the tremendous boulders seen today) began appearing about 1300 B.C., the same time that smaller villages were falling to outside invaders. Decadence accompanied the declining civilization. Once used only commercially, Mycenaean trading ships ran pirate raids against other Mediterranean sailing ships. Archeologists think it was the Dorians (from the Balkans) who eventually destroyed this civilization. Although the Dorians were Greek-speaking, they were barbarians, and Greek history plummeted into the Dark Ages.

The only archeological finds from the period 1100 to 750 B.C. come from the Keramikós Cemetery in Athens. Old-fashioned cist graves, not seen for a millennium, and new iron jewelry pieces indicate that culture retrogressed. Scholars think that bronzeworking may have lapsed because trade restrictions made it difficult to obtain tin, a component. However, many associate the use of iron for metalwork with Anatolian and Middle Eastern tribes and believe that these peoples were related to the Dorians. Historians think this was the period of the Trojan War, which Homer chronicled in his *Iliad* nearly 500 years later. The first Greek colonies were established in Asia Minor, and the Phoenicians dominated commerce in the Aegean.

Art historians call this the protogeometric period because the pottery found from Athens was decorated with concentric circles or painted geometric forms. Many examples are on display at the National Archeological Museum in Athens. Trade with other, more sophisticated cultures seems to have resumed after 900 B.C. Skillfully crafted geometric period vases have been excavated in Phoenicia and Egypt, indicating that a new, broader range of trading partners helped pull Greece from the Dark Ages.

CLASSICAL CIVILIZATION

The Classical period, from about 600 to 300 B.C., is considered Greece's Golden Age. In three centuries the Greeks left an unrivaled cultural legacy. Some examples: the democratic government of Solon and Pericles; the natural science of Pythagoras and Hippocrates; the poems of Homer, the historical writings of Herodotus and Thucydides, and the drama of Sophocles, Euripides, and Aristophanes; the philosophy of Socrates and Plato; the art of Phidias and Praxiteles, and the work of countless others. Several factors contributed to this cultural flowering.

Growth of the City-State The mountainous, inhospitable Greek terrain made the city-state (*pólis*) a practical social unit. By 800 B.C. the barbaric tribes who had overrun Greece during the Dark Ages were settling into agricultural communities. The economy had decentralized; inhabited settlements, isolated from their neighbors by mountain barriers, clustered into fertile valleys. Homes were built upon any plateau (*acrópolis*) that could be easily safeguarded from invaders. As trade increased, agriculture became more specialized. The city-state of Athens, for example, planted its farmland with vineyards and olive groves, not only for their export value but because of the crops' suitability to the arid terrain. The once fertile inland was being eroded by overforesting (to build ships) and overgrazing. In the 4th century, Plato wrote of the region: "What now remains, just as on small islands, compared with what used to be, is like the body of a sick man, with all the rich and fertile earth fallen away." The lack of arable land to satisfy an increasing population forced the city-states to found colonies abroad. Greece was now entering what archeologists call the Archaic Age. About 750 B.C. the colony of Cumae (north of Naples) was founded by Greeks from Kými, Chalkís, and Erétria on Euboea (Évvia). Soon after, Syracuse in Sicily, Messalía (Marseilles), and Byzántion (Istanbul) were settled by Greeks. By 600 B.C., there were 1,500 overseas colonies linked to mainland Greece by language, custom, and religion. All others in the ancient world were considered *barbaroi.*

The largest-growing city-states were Corinth and Megara on the Peloponnese, Aegina and Athens in Attica, and the islands of Rhodes and Sámos. The responsibility of maintaining their colonies forced these city-states to expand commercially and industrially. Metal tools and weapons, pottery and textiles were heavily traded, so much so that even small neighboring city-states became rivals. The wealth amassed through the lower-class pursuits of trade, commerce, and craftsmanship began to equalize society. The army, once the exclusive province of the landed gentry, now recruited *hoplites,* soldiers who could pay for their own armor. Usurers began to prey on small farmers, who were hard hit by the growing specialization in food for trade. Social upheaval in every class generated changes in government.

First Democracy At the dawn of the Classical period some city-states attempted democratic governments, where popular assemblies ruled; and some established oligarchies, where aristocratic councils ruled. All governments had similar precepts: a magistracy (which evolved from the old tribal kings) led by a religious, military, or judicial figure; a council or senate made up of elder advisers, often the aristocracy; and an assembly of the people, who could act on the council's recommendations.

In 594 B.C., Solon established a code of laws and a democratic framework for Athens. He canceled farmers' debts and attempted to restore an egalitarian social order. He also established public works programs, festivals, and athletic events. Later, under Pericles, civil servants would collect salaries, so that none were prevented from participating in the democratic process. Taxes came from voteless foreign residents, customs, and allied city-state "protection" revenues. The rich in Athens were always "supertaxed"; financing the equipping of a trireme or the staging of a play or chorus rehearsal was their tax burden.

The next government reform in Athens (510 B.C.) came from the tyrant Cleisthenes, after he acceded to revolutionary demands made by the aristocratic council (*Areopagus*). Now citizenship depended on being a member of a *démos,* or civil parish; there were 168 in Athens. These were divided into groups of ten and then mixed so that a geographic and ethnic blend of tribal members would be achieved. A Supreme Court of nine representatives from the council was voted on annually, and the people's assembly was increased to 500 members. A president was elected by the assembly on a rotational basis from among tribal leaders.

ALBANIA
FORMER YUGOSLAV REPUBLIC OF MACEDONIA
Adriatic Sea
Kilkís
Giannítsa
Édessa
Kastoriá
Mt. Olympus
Kalpaki
Elassona
GREECE
Ioánnina
Corfu
EPIRUS
Tríkkala
Lárissa
Karditsa
THESSALY
Páxos
Arta
Préveza
Karpeníssi
Vónitsa
Lamía
Lefkáda
CENTRAL GREECE
Agrínio
Mt. Parnassós
Astakós
Messolóngi
Livadiá
Delphi
Ithaca
Kefalonia
Pátra
Ionian Sea
IONIAN ISLANDS
Kyllíni
PELOPONNESE
Corinth
Zákynthos
Pírgos
Mycenae
Argos
Olympía
Trípoli
Náfplio
Andrítsena
Megalópolis
Mistrá
Sparta
Kalamáta
Mediterranean Sea
Pílos
Gýthio
Areópolis
Sea of Crete
CRETE
Aghios Nikólaos
Réythymno
Iráklio
Aghía Galíni
Ierápetra
9608

BULGARIA
Black Sea
Dráma
Xánthi
THRACE
Komotiní
TURKEY
Istanbul
Alexandroúpoli
Sea of Marmara
Stratóni
Thássos
Samothráki
Dardanelles
Mt. Athos
Límnos
Aegean Sea
NORTHERN SPORADES
Alónissos
Lésvos
Skýros
SOUTHERN SPORADES
TURKEY
Paralía Kímis
AEGEAN ISLANDS
Izmir
Chíos
Kárystos
Sámos
Ándros
Tínos
Sýros
Délos
Mýkonos
Sérifos
Páros
Náxos
Antípaxos
Sífnos
CYCLADES
Mílos
Íos
Santoríni
DODECANESE
Rhodes
0
50 mi
81 km
N

Athenian leaders dispensed with their critics through the process of *ostrakismós,* whereby each winter the assembly would be asked to vote on whether there was anyone worthy of expulsion. Affirmative answers would lead to a spring vote, in which members wrote the undesired person's name on a discarded pottery fragment (*ostrakós*). The top scorer would be banished for 10 years, but without loss of property or status.

Aristotle summed up democracy this way: "You can't have a state of 10 citizens. But when you have 100,000, it is no longer a polis. [It should be small enough for] the citizens to know each other's characters. Where this is not the case, both elections and decisions at law are bound to suffer." The Greeks were very proud of their political democracy; in fact, it was in defense of their political system in the Ionian colonies that Greece faced its first great challenge, the Persian Wars.

Persian Wars The mighty Persian Empire had long kept a watchful eye on Greece, targeting it as a potential conquest. Emperor Cyrus consolidated the Greek colonies in Asia Minor under Persian rule in 546 B.C., but not until 499 B.C. did the Ionian cities, now under Darius, openly revolt. Aristagoras, the tyrant of Miletos, went first to Sparta, then to Athens to plead for help against Darius. The following year, 20 ships from Athens and five from Eretria sailed for Ephesus. After four years of battle the Persians prevailed, but Darius was determined to punish Athens for its aid. In 492 B.C. his first naval expedition was shipwrecked by a storm off Mt. Athos on the easternmost tip of Chalcidice (Chalkidhikí), but he soon sent another, this time to the Bay of Marathon. The Athenian general Miltiades and his troops, together with their Plataean allies, camped at Marathon to await requested Spartan reinforcements. The messenger Pheidippides ran 150 miles to Sparta in less than two days, but found the willing Spartans unable to march before the lunar holiday. Miltiades was forced to attack and boldly defeated the enemy by concentrating on the vulnerable Persian wings. Darius's troops fled back to their ships and sailed immediately for Cape Sounion, hoping to find an unguarded Athens. Miltiades' men rushed back by land to defend their city. The following day the Spartan reinforcements arrived; they were so delighted at the Athenians' victory that they marched north to Marathon to see the Persian dead for themselves. By the way, it was Pheidippides' 26.2-mile run to Athens to announce victory that gave us our modern-day marathon.

The Persians did not take well to their defeat at Marathon. Under Darius's son, Xerxes, two pontoon bridges were constructed across the Hellespont (Dardanelles), and a canal was dug through Chalcidice to prevent the possibility of another storm from delaying Persian revenge. In May of 480 B.C., Xerxes set off with about 180,000 troops, including exotic Indian, Ethiopian, Egyptian, and Phoenician infantry and Arabs on camelback. Countless tales are told of collapsed bridges, Persian stupidity, and needless naval losses. The Greeks had their naval defense at Cape Artemisium, north of Euboea, and a land defense at the Thermopylae Pass. After several days of intense battle at sea, the Greeks were chased south to Salamis. The Spartan general Leonidas and 7,000 men were guarding Thermopylae, a natural land barrier preventing the Persians from reaching southern Greece. After three days of fighting, a traitor, Ephialtes, led the Persians over another mountain pass and Leonidas's troops were surrounded. Aware of the hopeless situation, Leonidas chose to remain behind with his 300 Spartans and Boeotian soldiers to guard the others' retreat. Herodotus has immortalized their bravery in battle; they fought till none were left. Their epitaph, still seen at Thermopylae, reads: "Passerby, go tell the Spartans that here in obedience to their laws we lie."

The Greek navy managed an astonishing victory after this crushing land defeat. At Salamis the Athenian leader, Themistocles, heeding the Delphic oracle's prophecy that "wooden walls" would save Athens, ordered all the city's warships manned. He then sent a Greek slave in traitor's guise to encourage Xerxes to attack immediately. The Persians were lured into a narrow bay, where the much smaller Greek navy easily defeated them. Stunned, Xerxes withdrew to the Hellespont. In the following spring, the Persian general Mardonius recaptured Attica, inflicting heavy damage. Then the Spartan leader Pausanias rallied his troops to battle the Persians at Plataea, near Thebes; the Persians were defeated, and soon after the remaining Persian fleet was burned off Cape Mycale, on the coast of Asia Minor. The Persian invasions made clear to the Greeks that they had to organize a common defense.

Athens took the lead by founding, in 478 B.C., the Delian League, so called because its administrative center was on the sacred island of Delos. Some 200 city-states in the Aegean, in Thrace, and on the Asia Minor coast joined the league, contributing ships and funds to remain under the protection of Athens. In turn, Athens used the league to augment its own power in the region. As military strength became the city's primary concern, the Athenians elected a brilliant general (*strategós*), Pericles, to lead them.

Athens Under Pericles During Pericles' rule (461–429 B.C.), Athens prospered and achieved cultural preeminence in the Greek world. Its democracy was strengthened. The state now began to pay those who served it, thus allowing a greater number of citizens to enter public service. Magistrates had to be elected, and government operations were centralized in the *tholos,* next to the council in the Agora. All business was screened by the council before it went to the people's assembly, but any citizen could bring a grievance before the assembly.

Because there were 250 council seats and members could hold only two, nonconsecutive, terms in a lifetime, many Athenians became involved in the political process. Wealthy landowners and the military had traditionally controlled local politics; now a new breed of orators (demagogues) rose to represent the naval and civilian working class. Slaves were still common but many were skilled, had the right to vote, and kept their own businesses, paying their owners a royalty on earnings.

Pericles himself came from an aristocratic background but was a staunch supporter of democratic government. Even though his enemies called him a dictator, he reaffirmed his rule over Athens in regular and fair elections. Contemporary writers describe him as an intelligent, skillful orator and a brilliant military strategist. Lesser politicians conceded that he was uncorrupted by his almost total power over the city, yet they used his highly publicized affair with a courtesan against him in his declining years.

In 447 B.C., as part of a major public-works program, Pericles ordered construction to begin on the Parthenon. For the project, he used funds from the Delian League's coffers, dismissing objections by other members. In 437 B.C. the Propylaea and a new odeum, or covered theater, were added to the Acropolis. Pericles also commissioned several temples—of Poseidon at Cape Soúnio, Nemesis at Rhamnous, and Hephaestus in Athens, overlooking the Agora—as well as the Hall of Mysteries at Eleusis.

Plutarch, in his *Parallel Lives of Greeks and Romans,* writes that Pericles was an avid enthusiast of the arts. His politically astute social programs also served to promote his personal interest in the performing and visual arts. In 460 B.C. he commissioned his friend Phidias to sculpt a huge chryselephantine (gold-and-ivory) statue of

Zeus for the sanctuary at Olympia. Phidias was already known to Athenians for his *Athena Promachus,* a huge bronze statue of the goddess constructed on the Acropolis to celebrate Athens's victory over the Persians. When the architects Ictinus and Callicrates began designing the Parthenon, Phidias was put in charge of all its sculptural ornamentation.

During Pericles' time the theater flourished. The first dramatic diversion from the solemnity of religious rituals came in 520 B.C., when Thespis introduced a *hypokrítes,* or play actor, reciting narratives. In 477 B.C., Aeschylus, Greece's first major tragic poet, added a second actor and further dialog, in his play *The Persians,* to create a more complex plot. After him the young Sophocles, who won the Athens drama competition in 468 B.C., introduced a third actor, as well as painted scenery. Best known for his *Antigone* and *Oedipus Rex,* Sophocles wrote more than a hundred popular dramas. They were presented three at a time, followed by a farce, or so-called satyr play, as was the custom. The third great tragedian, Euripides (b. 480 B.C.), wrote realistic, often politically controversial plays. Among them are *Medea, The Trojan Women,* and *The Bacchae.* He made use of the *deus ex machina,* the intervening god lowered by contraption on stage to influence the plot.

Comedy, too, was very popular. The leading comic poet was Aristophanes, whose witty social and political commentaries enjoyed great success. Despite his plays' often burlesque nature, they contained many fine lyrical choral passages. In *The Knights, The Wasps, Lysistrata,* and a handful of other surviving comedies, Aristophanes satirizes politicians, Athenian courts, modern music, Athens's imperial policies, even the battle between the sexes. In *The Clouds* he mocks the great philosopher Socrates, for running "a logic factory for the extraclever." At the factory, says one of the characters, "they teach you (if you pay enough) to win your arguments whether you're right or wrong." Some historians believe that Aristophanes' play led the Athenians to condemn Socrates, the perennial gadfly, to death in 399 B.C.

Athens's unique Golden Age under Pericles was short-lived. In 430 B.C., the first of two devastating plagues struck the city, killing nearly a third of its population. Many felt that the gods were indicating their displeasure with Pericles, whose aggressive attempts at land expansion were opposed by some of the other city-states, particularly Sparta, Athens's chief rival. When Athens was at its weakest, its unbridled urge for conquest led to the first major inter-Greek conflict, the Peloponnesian War.

Peloponnesian War Sparta was the mainstay of the Peloponnesian League, a powerful military alliance. Pericles' initial forays outside of Attica had angered Sparta and its allies, but it was not until Athens began meddling in Corinth's affairs in the Ionian Sea (431 B.C.) that war was declared. Pericles directed Athens's offense at sea and was usually victorious. Spartan land raids into Attica were ineffective; Athens defended itself by remaining safely behind its fortifications and the "Long Walls" that connected the city with Piraeus and Phalerum. The war was devastating to both sides; in the captured colonies, men were killed and their wives and children sold off into slavery. After Pericles died, in 429 B.C., a disorganized Athenian leadership chose a bolder offensive. Political greed motivated most of the Athenians' forays, and the resultant anger of many Delian League allies only accelerated Athens's downfall. After inconclusive fighting, a truce was declared in 421 B.C.; it was to last only three years.

Athens then turned a covetous eye on the prosperous colony of Sicily. A huge fleet was sent to capture the island but failed; the Sicilian expedition marked the second phase of the war. Thucydides, the great historian, blames Athenian arrogance for the humiliating naval defeat; only a few sailors escaped after the last great battle at

Syracuse harbor, in 413 B.C. Alcibiades, the nephew of Pericles, first betrayed Athens in the Sicilian fiasco by turning to Sparta, then betrayed Sparta by joining the Athenian fleet off Samos for the last phase (412–404 B.C.) of the war. By this time, Sparta had traded in its Ionian colonies for Persian support. After years of battling in the Ionian and the Aegean, the Athenian fleet was defeated. Xenophon, another historian of the war, writes that Athens's Long Walls were immediately torn down "to the music of flute-girls and with great enthusiasm" and the victors required surrender of all but 12 ships. Perhaps the greatest tragedy of this outcome was that Athens, fit to rule and at its prime culturally, was denied the only chance it had ever had to unite all Greece under its aegis.

Sparta The dictionary defines *spartan* as "warlike, hardy, disciplined," adjectives that the ancient world also used to describe the inhabitants of Sparta (see Chapter 7, "The Peloponnese"). In the 7th century B.C., under the leadership of the legendary Lycurgus, the Spartans decided to make their city-state a model of disciplined life and martial training.

According to Plutarch, a committee of elders judged babies at birth and left weaklings on the slopes of Mt. Taygetus to die. Hardier infants were bathed in wine (which was thought to bring out the "fits" in sickly ones) and raised to be unafraid of the dark, tolerant of all foods, and uncomplaining. At the age of seven, the state took all boys for athletic training and basic education. They were underfed so that they might resort to stealing, which was believed to foster cunning and resourcefulness, two qualities especially prized in battle; if caught, they would be punished *for being caught.* Violent team games and long, solo wilderness missions developed endurance. At 20, young men attempted to win election to a *syssition,* a military unit in which they lived out their adulthood. Women lived at home but received rigorous physical training as well, to ensure that they would bear strong children. Wives could meet their husbands only secretly at night; if their husbands were sterile, they would be lent to other men so that they could bear children.

The government of Sparta was run by two kings, who kept a check on each other. There was no political unrest among the citizenry because Spartiates (land-owning, full-blooded descendants of Spartan parents) lived without class distinctions and left all necessary work to their *helots* (state-owned slaves). Thucydides describes their city as "formed of villages in the old Greek manner," indicating that in architecture, as in the other arts, the strict Spartan life-style discouraged creative expression. Nevertheless, the Spartans were extremely patriotic, brave, and proud of their city's achievements, and their political stability was the envy of many of their contemporaries.

Decline of the City-States Nearly 30 years of conflict was devastating for every city-state involved in the Peloponnesian War. There was rampant inflation, widespread unemployment, and constant food shortages. There was no work for slaves, the poor sought jobs as mercenary soldiers, and the rich sustained the farmers with subsidies. In 399 B.C. war broke out again. This time the Persians were asking Sparta to support them against the Asian Greek colonies. Within four years, an alliance of erstwhile enemies was formed to resist Sparta and Persia. It was composed of the Boeotian League (a confederation of central Greek city-states), Thebes, several Peloponnesian League members that had been betrayed by Sparta, and Athens. The Persian king, Artaxerxes, became concerned with rebel forces fighting in the Persian colonies of Egypt and Cyprus. Fearing a protracted and costly war on Greek soil, Artaxerxes demanded that Sparta make peace with the other Greek city-states.

From 378 to 371 B.C., Thebes, under the leadership of the brilliant King Epaminondas, was the major power on the Greek mainland. After the Theban victory at the Battle of Leuctra, in which the Spartans were crushed, Epaminondas led his troops on a conquest of the Peloponnese, liberating Messenia and founding the model city of Megalopolis. Athens was so alarmed by Thebes' growing power that it sided with Sparta. The struggle came to a climax at Mantinea in 362 B.C. Epaminondas fell in battle. It is said that his death so disheartened the Boeotians, who were winning, that they lost all interest in fighting and retreated. In less than a generation, the Greek city-states, now in hopeless disarray, would be united under Philip of Macedonia.

Philip of Macedonia After the Battle of Leuctra, Athens regained political stability under the leadership of Demosthenes, its greatest orator. Sensing, however, a growing Macedonian threat, it undertook, along with Thebes, a series of preemptive incursions into Thessaly and Macedonia itself. During a Theban-led raid, Macedonia's young Prince Philip was taken hostage; he was later released and assumed the throne in 359 B.C. Seeking to unite the Greek city-states, Philip embarked on a conquest of the mainland by making forays of his own into Chalcidice and Thessaly, while proclaiming his friendship for Thebes and Athens.

Suspicious of Philip's intentions, Demosthenes warned the Athenians that they should strengthen their fleet to protect Athens's interests in northeastern Greece as a first step to meet the challenge of Philip, whose ambition was sure to lead him to attack Athens sooner or later. In yet another kaleidoscopic shift of alliances, Persia joined Athens, Thebes, and other Greek cities to form a united front against Philip. In 338 B.C., at the Battle of Chaeronea, Philip defeated the combined Greek forces and emerged as the undisputed leader of Greece. He dealt sternly with Thebes but leniently with Athens, after forcing Demosthenes into exile.

In 336 B.C., Philip was assassinated. He was succeeded by his son, Alexander, who carried the campaign of Greek unity beyond the mainland.

Alexander the Great The intellectual climate in Greece was consonant with Alexander's ideals. Two great thinkers were very influential in the 4th century. Plato, a free-thinking tutor hired to teach the son of a Sicilian tyrant, was so outspoken that his boss sent him to the slave market. Luckily, Plato was bought by a Greek and freed to found a school (348 B.C.) in a local Athenian park, under a statue of Akademos. His philosophy was based on truth as a way of life; nothing disgusted him more than imitation in art or life. His *Republic* mocked democratic politics and his *Laws* condemned religion. Plato wrote the definitive treatise on Socrates' ideas, but never formalized his own in writing. Nevertheless, the Academy he started continued to draw the top Greek minds until A.D. 529, when Emperor Justinian put an end to all pagan institutions.

The scholar Aristotle was born in Chalcidice, but went to Athens as a young man to join its respected academic community. Philip brought him to Macedonia to tutor young Alexander, who surely benefited from his teacher's vast knowledge of the natural world, logic, and rhetoric. When, in 335 B.C., Aristotle left Alexander's court, he founded a school in Athens, near the temple of the Apollo Lykeios. His Lyceum offered courses in rhetoric, logic, ethics, politics, and biology; and his research was financed by Alexander. Although Aristotle was greatly admired, he was forced to flee Athens after Alexander's death because of the ill will toward anyone with Macedonian ties. Alexander's breadth of interest and his commitment to unifying all the known races of the world in one kingdom was greatly influenced by the far-thinking Plato and Aristotle.

So many legends surround the life and death of Alexander the Great that our whole book could be devoted to him. It is said of the young man that every time he heard of his father's military victories, he complained that Philip would leave him nothing to conquer. Plutarch recounts the story of Boucephalas, an unmanageable horse that Philip and his elder trainers rejected. When Alexander succeeded in mounting him, Philip reportedly said, "My son, look for a kingdom big enough for yourself. Macedonia is too small." Alexander served as a general in the Battle of Chaeronea and learned many effective military maneuvers from Philip. After his father's death, Alexander took over the Macedonian throne and also Philip's position as general of the League of Corinth.

In 334 B.C. Alexander began his conquest of Persia, ostensibly to avenge past invasions of Greece (more likely to replenish Macedonian coffers). At Troy, Alexander made sacrifices to Athena in imitation of his hero Achilles (he reportedly carried a copy of the *Iliad* with him throughout his Asian campaign.) During the first two years of his campaign he captured Miletos, Tyre, Phoenicia, Palestine, and Egypt, after difficult fighting, personal injuries, and great hardship for his troops. Darius fled eastward, leaving behind his mother, wife, and daughters, whom Alexander took captive. Alexander spent the winter of 332–331 B.C. in Egypt, founding the city of Alexandria, the first and greatest of the 16 Alexandrias he would found along his route of conquest. Later in 331 B.C. he routed Darius at Gaugamela, but refused Darius' attempt at a settlement. He continued east instead to Babylon, Sousa, and Persepolis, where he burned down the old palace of Xerxes in revenge for the slaughter at Thermopylae. Darius, now left with minimal troops that he had great trouble controlling, was killed at Ecbatana by Bessos, the murderous satrap of Bactria, who hoped to impress Alexander by the deed. Alexander, however, gave Darius a royal funeral and had Bessos executed. Alexander continued east until all opposition in the rugged, inhospitable eastern mountains had been crushed. In 327 B.C. he decided to invade India.

About this time Alexander began emulating Persian ways, including having his many new Persian advisers prostrate themselves on the ground before him. His Greek troops, who would bow only before the gods, were offended by his behavior. Most were anxious to return to their homeland and felt that they'd accomplished all they had set out to do. Despite his dealing with any signs of discontent harshly, Alexander's troops continued to follow him because of personal loyalty and respect. Within the year, Alexander and his army crossed the River Indus (now part of Pakistan), but the seasonal monsoon vanquished his troops' morale. They refused to continue across the Hyphasis River. After fruitless pleading, Alexander agreed to turn back. But nearly a year of arduous trekking, hunger, thirst, and natural disasters passed before Alexander arrived back at Sousa. There, he celebrated by marrying a Bactrian princess and presiding at a ceremony in which some 10,000 of his men married Asian women. He retired thousands of Macedonian soldiers and tried to replace them with Persian recruits, angering many loyal troops, who felt betrayed.

Alexander was planning to conquer Arabia when he fell ill (some say from malaria, others poisoning, alcoholism, or venereal disease) and died in Babylon in June of 323 B.C. This brilliant military tactician and charismatic ruler contributed much to the knowledge of natural sciences and exposed the known world to Greek culture. Unfortunately no one else was capable of governing his unwieldly empire and it was split into four parts, all of which grew again under the influence of Hellenistic civilization.

HELLENISTIC ERA

From Alexander's death (323 B.C.) to the crowning of Octavian as the first Roman emperor (31 B.C.), Greek culture dominated, remarkably, a world where Greeks had little political control. A common form of the Greek language, *koiné,* spread throughout the Mediterranean (the New Testament was later written in it) as individual city-states and colonies were absorbed by and influenced large kingdoms. The increase in worldwide trade and travel also integrated Greeks with other races. By the Roman era a very cosmopolitan and sophisticated whole had evolved from the mixture of new cultures and traditions.

After Alexander's death Greece itself united into the Hellenic League, in order to win its freedom from Antipater, the Macedonian leader. After the Hellenic League's defeat at Lamia, Antipater's navy soundly defeated the Athenian navy at the Dardanelles. Athens surrendered. Antipater's policies of disenfranchising any citizen without the requisite minimum of property, abolishing democracy, and offering land to anyone who would resettle in Thrace so weakened the city that Athens never regained her former status.

For 20 years the rest of Alexander's empire was at war. Antipater's son, Cassander, ruled Macedonia and installed Demetrius to rule over Athens. Alexander's former bodyguard, Ptolemy, headed the Hellenistic Empire from Alexandria, Egypt. He worked to sustain Alexander's ideals, and even smuggled Alexander's corpse into Alexandria so that a tomb could be built for him. Ptolemy's empire flourished until 31 B.C., when Cleopatra and Mark Anthony were defeated. The leader of Alexander's footguards, Seleucus, consolidated his Asian holdings along the lines of the old Persian Empire and established his capital at Antiochus (named after his son) in Syria. The Seleucid Empire was the most visible remnant of Alexander's former glory, but it, too, slowly dwindled in strength since no effort was made to unite its diverse people.

GREECE UNDER THE ROMAN EMPIRE

Greece and Carthage allied themselves against the Romans for the first Macedonian War in 215 B.C. Troops under King Philip V resisted the Romans through another war, but in 205 B.C. Greece fell. Not until the Romans defeated the combined forces of the Achaean League (146 B.C.), however, was Greece made a province, subjected to Roman laws and forced to pay tribute. In 146 B.C. Corinth was leveled, and in 86 B.C. rebelling Athenians were massacred by Sulla. Ruthlessly putting down the rebellion of the poorer classes, the Romans rewarded some property holders with positions as local magistrates. Roman civil wars fought on Greek soil also caused much damage to Greece and its economy.

After the 2d century A.D. when little of value was left in Greece, the Romans became more lenient with their Greek subjects. They began building public works, restored some cities, and brought Greeks into local government. Hadrian revived old religious festivals and founded a new Panhellenic League. The Romans enthusiastically adopted the Hellenistic culture and its artisans. In this period of "antiquarianism," early masterpieces were reproduced, old dramas were restaged, and classical philosophies and old dialects were revived. The writer Plutarch (A.D. 46–120) stirred Roman interest by praising Greek heroes, ethics, religion, and philosophy in his series of biographies, *The Lives.* In the mid-2d century Pausanius wrote a scholarly account of Greece's archeological history that not only helped sustain Roman interest in Greek culture but also contributed to educating the Western world about Greece's past.

BYZANTINE ERA

In Greece the 3d century A.D.was marked by invasions of European barbarians that caused great destruction. Although the declining Roman Empire couldn't afford to repair the damage, Emperor Claudius II did guarantee the Greeks' physical safety. Christianity had now grown into a powerful force within the Roman Empire. At the end of the 3d century, Diocletian divided Greece into several dioceses, with Constantinople as the capital. Greek art and goods were shipped to the Asian city, increasing trade and bolstering local Greek communities. In 394, Emperor Theodosius I abolished the Olympic Games and all "pagan" rituals, but many Greeks continued to follow their old beliefs.

Under the Isaurian dynasty (8th century) the country was divided into *themes,* many of which prospered as the wealth of the Byzantines grew. The *themes* became feudal principalities after the fall of Constantinople to the Crusaders in 1204. New Latin conquerors and old Byzantine rulers, notably the Venetians, French, Aragonese, Sicilians, and Catalans fought over and traded the principalities. A Frank, Geoffroy de Villehardouin, administered the principality of Morea, one of the most prosperous of its day. The Palaeologoi, Byzantine rulers, retook Morea in 1262, renamed it the Peloponnese, and made Mystra their capital (see Chapter 7).

From 1204 to 1797, Venice held many Greek duchies, leaving an architectural legacy still admired today. The Ionian Islands; Methóni, Koróni, Argos, Monemvassiá, and Náfplio on the Peloponnese; and Crete, Évvia, Náxos, and other islands still bear evidence of this heritage. Overall, the ecclesiastical rule of the Byzantine Era provided a period of self-confident growth for Greece from its state of neglect at the end of the Roman period to the nationalistic spirit and strength it would need to defend itself against its next conqueror.

TOURKOKRATIA

This Greek word, *tourkokratía,* for the period of history when Greece was under the rule of the Ottoman Empire (1453–1821) is still said today in pensive tones. Much of the Greek mainland had already been taken when Constantinople (now Istanbul) fell to Sultan Mohammad II in 1453. Although some individual islands resisted annexation to the Empire for years, many Greek cities found Ottoman rule preferable to that of the Franks or Venetians. In theory, the Greek Orthodox religion was tolerated so long as it permitted political loyalty to the Ottomans. Under Suleiman the Magnificent the Greeks also enjoyed freedom of trade and language; and strong Ottoman forces protected the mainland from attack by its former feudal overlords and extended a small amount of autonomy to local governments.

For the Greeks, of course, life without freedom was intolerable. They were obligated to pay a per capita tax for the "privilege" of living under Ottoman rule, real estate and commerce were taxed, and, worst of all, about 20% of the male children were sent to Istanbul for training as *janissaries,* servants to the sultan. The janissary system was abolished in the 1600s, but until then some Greeks actually took advantage of its educational opportunities to rise within the ranks of Turkish government. (When the revolution came, the "Turkish" Greeks did not forget their homeland.) In the 18th century Catherine the Great, empress of Russia, encouraged rebellion among her Orthodox brethren. The first uprising, centered in the Peloponnese in 1770, was forcibly put down with no Russian intervention. When Catherine tried to stir up trouble in 1786, most of the Greeks ignored her, although in Epirus there was an unsuccessful revolt against the local Sultan, Ali Pasha.

The next few decades were inspirational for the oppressed Greeks: They witnessed the French Revolution, the American Revolution, the fall of Napoleon, and other nationalist rebellions. Ali Pasha had eroded Ottoman rule in the north by annexing all of the neighboring territories. In response, the Greek aristocratic and intellectual classes contemplated revolt, while Greeks in Europe sought support for their cause. When Ali Pasha decided to split from the Empire in 1820, it provided a perfect opportunity for the Greeks to demand their freedom. The War of Independence (1821–29) eventually won liberation for the Greeks, but the fledgling nation's fragmented forces, conflicting allegiances, and disparate goals gave the new government a rough road to traverse.

During the two years between the decisive Battle of Navarino (which granted Greece independence under the Treaty of London) and Russia's war on Turkey (settled by the Treaty of Adrianople), Greece had extended its boundaries north and south of the originally negotiated borders. Alexandros Mavrokordatos and Dimitrios Ypsilantis, who consolidated this expansion, played an important part in foreign policy. Ioánnis Capodístrias, a noted leader in foreign affairs, took office as president on January 18, 1828. During his presidency, the European powers tried to install a king, Prince Leopold of Saxe-Coburg. The wealthy Greeks thought Capodistrias's democratic reforms were excessive, while liberals felt he was autocratic and too willing to accept a king. Capodistrias was assassinated by an aristocratic dissident in Náfplio in 1831, leaving the government in chaos. An ineffective government coalition, including Capodistrias's brother and Theódoros Kolokotrónis, was created. While awaiting a policy decision, the European powers took action to support the weakened democracy by sending in French troops to keep order. Under their auspices, the hastily convened Conference of London finally proclaimed Greece an independent kingdom.

MODERN HISTORY

The establishment of a monarchy is one hallmark of Greece's modern history; territorial disputes is another. At the Conference of London, Greece was granted the Peloponnese, the mainland north to the Árta-Vólos line, and some of the Aegean Islands (but not Crete or Sámos), all to be guarded by Britain, France, and Russia. Greece's first monarch, Prince Otto (Othon) of Bavaria, arrived in 1833. Two issues caused resentment among the country's former war heroes: Greece had yet to expand to its previous boundaries, and all positions in Othon's government were held by Bavarians. In 1843, Greek wartime leaders and rebel forces stormed the royal palace, demanding the removal of foreign rulers and a new constitution. Othon complied and a National Assembly, including representatives from the still unliberated areas of Macedonia, Thessaly, and Epirus, drafted a new constitution. For the next 20 years Othon ruled over the *Voulí* (Lower House) and the *Gherousía* (Senate). His increasingly autocratic rule, however, caused popular resentment. In 1862 minor mutinies led to a full-scale revolt in Athens, ending in Othon's fall. While the Europeans quickly searched for a new king, Britain voted to cede the Ionian Islands to Greece. In 1863 young Prince William of Denmark accepted the Greek throne under the name of George I.

During his long reign (1863–1913), Greece flourished. Thessaly, Macedonia, Epirus, and most of the Aegean islands were reunited. In 1896 a major uprising occurred in Crete, leading to a war between Turkey and Greece. A peace treaty was arranged by the European powers in 1897 and in 1898 the Turks left Crete. The Europeans, instead of allowing Crete's union with Greece, installed Prince George of

England as High Commissioner under the sultan's suzerainty. The compromise was actively opposed by Elefthérios (Eleutherios) Venizélos, a prominent Cretan who led the struggle for union. Because of his effective leadership, the European powers withdrew their troops in 1908.

The Balkan Wars In 1909, Venizelos was summoned to Athens by the military, who sought political reform, and made prime minister. He revised the constitution and effected social and financial reforms. At the same time he pressed for the independence of the rest of Greece. In 1912, Greece joined the Balkan League in a war against Turkey, winning back Epirus, Macedonia, Sámos, and Crete. An unexpected event, however, shook Greece's fragile order: The military hero Constantine had to assume the throne when his father, King George, was assassinated.

The Treaty of London abolished the Turkish Empire and returned occupied lands to the Balkan League. Disputes over their disposition led to the Second Balkan War, in which Serbia and Greece were allied against Bulgaria. The Truce of Bucharest, signed in 1913, left Bulgaria a small part of Macedonia and access to the Aegean, and created Albania from part of Epirus. However, the Turks and Italians refused to leave their occupied positions on the Aegean and Dodecanese islands. World War I put an end to this shell game.

World War I The war provoked division in Greece. King Constantine favored neutrality (many felt he really sided with Germany). Prime Minister Venizelos sided with Britain and France. Venizelos was dismissed, and Constantine maintained Greece's neutrality until June 1917, when the Allies demanded Greek participation in the war. Constantine left the country in protest, and Venizelos returned as prime minister. Military successes in Macedonia strengthened Venizelos's bargaining position with the Allied powers at the Versailles peace conference in 1919.

In 1919 the Allies encouraged the Greeks to retake Smýrna (now Izmir). The Greco-Turkish War that ensued was disastrous for the Greeks. In 1923 the League of Nations insisted on the resettlement of Muslim and Greek Orthodox citizens; half a million Greeks in Turkey emigrated to Greece. Because of the Greeks' Asia Minor fiasco, Constantine was relieved of his throne, but his successor, George II, reigned for only a year.

In 1924, Admiral Pávlos Koundouriótis was proclaimed first president of the new Republic of Greece. The republic lasted only 11 turbulent years. Venizelos, as leader of the antiroyalist Liberal Party, reappeared several times in an effort to take control. Panayiótis Tsaldaris headed the royalist Popular Party, which stepped in after one of Venizelos's failed coups and restored the monarchy of George II in 1935.

The first general election showed that the Greek people were bitterly divided between Venizelists and monarchists. In 1936, King George permitted a military takeover by General Ioánnis Metaxás. Metaxas, citing a Communist threat, imposed a quasi-fascist dictatorship that lasted until World War II.

World War II and Civil War Greece entered the war in October 1940. Until then it had been neutral, but when Italy demanded that Italian troops be allowed to cross into Greece from neighboring Albania, the Metaxas government responded with a firm *"Óchi!"* (no). (*Óchi* Day, October 28, is now a national holiday.) The Italians invaded but were forced back into Albania. The British sent troops to assist the Greeks, but in 1941 the German army struck through Yugoslavia and occupied Greece until 1944. Meanwhile, the king had gone into exile.

During the war a heroic resistance movement sprung up throughout the country, consisting of Communist-organized forces (EAM-ELAS) and democratic rebel forces (EDES). The two fought the Germans as well as each other. By the summer of 1944, the Communists, having consolidated their power, formed a provisional government in the north. Liberal Greeks, with British help, attempted to unite the guerrilla forces, but at the end of the year bloody incidents in Athens between EAM-ELAS supporters and opponents sparked the beginning of civil war. It lasted five years, ending with the defeat of the Communists. During that time, the United States, under the Truman Doctrine (1947), provided extensive military and economic aid to Greece. The psychological damage caused by the civil war left a greater mark on Greek politics than did any other conflict since the Peloponnesian War.

Postwar Greece In 1946 a plebiscite returned George II to the throne. He died a year later, however, and was succeeded by his brother, Paul. In 1952, after a series of unstable coalition governments, Field Marshal Alexander Papágos formed a government headed by his Greek Rally party. In the intervening period, Greece regained the Dodecanese islands (1948) and joined the North Atlantic Treaty Organization (1951).

Under a newly adopted constitution, Greek women were given the right to vote in 1952. A program of national reconstruction was put into effect by Papagos and continued by his successor (1955), Constantine Caramanlís. The country allied itself firmly with the West and tried to settle some of its differences with its neighbor and NATO ally, Turkey. In 1959 the issue of Cyprus's sovereignty was resolved by the Zurich Accord between Greece, Turkey, and Britain (which ruled the island); it granted Cyprus independence and provided for the sharing of power between the island's Greek and Turkish communities.

Caramanlis remained in power until 1963, when a left-of-center coalition led by George Papandréou narrowly defeated the ruling conservative party. In 1964, after new elections in which the left increased its hold on Parliament, King Paul died and was succeeded by his son, Constantine II. A battle of wills between the elderly Papandreou, a veteran Venizelist, and the young monarch soon led to Papandreou's resignation and a protracted period of political instability as one government succeeded another. Finally, in April 1967, a group of colonels, headed by George Papadópoulos, seized power, dissolving Parliament and banning political activity.

In 1973 the military junta, after having earlier forced the king and his family into exile, abolished the monarchy, and Papadopoulos proclaimed himself president of the new republic. He promised to restore civil liberties and to schedule national elections the following year. But he was soon ousted by hard-line officers. In July 1974, in the wake of an Athens-inspired coup in Cyprus that led to a Turkish invasion of the island, the military junta yielded power to civilian leaders. Caramanlis, who had gone into exile in France after his 1963 defeat, returned to head an interim government.

In late 1974 a plebiscite rejected the return of the monarchy, and the following year Parliament ratified a new constitution providing for a republican form of government. Caramanlis and his New Democracy party won a majority in national elections; they were returned to office in 1977. In 1980, Caramanlis stepped down as prime minister to become president of the republic; as such, he presided over Greece's entry into the European Community (now European Union) as a full-fledged member in 1981. That same year, Greek voters elected the country's first socialist government, headed by Andréas Papandréou, the Harvard-educated son of George Papandréou. In 1985 strains between the conservative Caramanlis and the leftist Papandreou, reelected, led to the election of a new president, Chrístos Sartzetákis.

In 1989 charges of corruption brought down the Papandreou government, and the Panhellenic Socialist Movement went into opposition. The new prime minister, Constantine Mitsotákis, and his New Democracy majority in Parliament elected Caramanlis to a new five-year term as president in 1990.

The conservative government set about to reverse many of the Socialists' free-spending policies, which had led to high inflation and a crippling national debt. It reduced outlays for social services, limited public-employee raises, and increased public-utility rates—measures that, as expected, touched off a series of labor strikes. The austerity program had been mandated by the European Union as a condition for further EU aid to Greece.

The government lost its popularity because of its economic policies, and it lost its parliamentary majority because of a foreign-policy issue that had aroused nationalist passions—the dispute with the neighboring Former Yugoslav Republic of Macedonia (FYROM) over that state's adopted name, "Macedonia," and national symbols (among them the star of Vergina, identified with Alexander the Great), which Greece regards as inherently Greek. Foreign Minister Antónis Samarás, accusing Mitsotakis of being too eager to settle the issue "against Greece's interests," resigned, bolted from New Democracy, and formed his own rightist group, Political Spring. Others defected from the governing party also, and in 1993 new elections were called.

The Socialists, under Papandreou, returned triumphantly to power. They moderated their socialist program (although they renationalized public transportation and slowed down the previous government's privatization program); but they exacerbated the "Macedonia" issue by imposing an economic embargo on FYROM, which depends heavily on trade through the port city of Thessaloníki, until the two sides resolved their dispute. Meanwhile, New Democracy chose a new leader, Miltiádes Evert, former mayor of Athens, who, with Samaras, represented a younger generation of Greek politicians.

POLITICS

According to the constitution adopted in 1975, Greece is a parliamentary republic, with a president as head of state. Under a constitutional amendment approved in 1985, authority to name and dismiss cabinet ministers, veto legislation, dissolve Parliament, and proclaim a state of emergency was taken from the president and given to the prime minister. Legislative responsibility resides in a unicameral Parliament (Voulí) of 300 members, elected by the people to a four-year term; 288 are elected from the 56 districts into which the country is divided, while 12 seats are reserved for deputies of state, apportioned according to the total national vote. In the 1990 election this system of representation was simplified to reflect more accurately the percentage of votes received by each political party.

The two major parties since the restoration of democracy in 1974 have been the Panhellenic Socialist Movement (abbreviated PASOK in Greek), which is dominated by its founder, Papandreou, and the right-of-center New Democracy party, established by Caramanlis. The parties' rivalry, rooted in the troubled period before 1974, has been as much over personalities (the animosity between Papandreou and Mitsotakis is legendary) as it is over ideology and policy. A third force in Greek politics is Political Spring, a recently formed rightist group that is attracting young people with its appeals for a new approach in the conduct of the nation's affairs, consonant with the post–cold war changes in Europe. There are also several smaller parties on the left, including a surviving Communist Party that still looks to Lenin for inspiration.

2 Art, Architecture & Archeology

Art & Architecture

Ancient Greek art and architecture had a profound influence on the Western world's esthetic sensibilities. From the "Grecian bend," coined to describe the forward-leaning gait so fashionable in 19th-century England, to the timeless images of Isadora Duncan's graceful dancing on the steps of the Parthenon, to the bold "Greek profile" universally praised as beautiful, we have absorbed certain principles of classic Greek style into our common language.

The Greek art we consider classical is traced by art historians directly from the Mycenaean empire. The large amount of pottery found (much of it made in Athens) had simple geometric patterns applied in black paint to a terra-cotta ground, thus giving the era (1100–700 B.C.) the names protogeometric and geometric. The Lion Gate at Mycenae, the best known example of stone construction from the Bronze Age, dates from 1250 B.C. The huge, irregular, hand-hewn building stones (the gate's lintel is carved from one 10-foot-by-12-foot block, sculpted with bas-relief lions) were typical of those stacked into cyclopean walls widely seen in Peloponnesian architecture from this era.

After the 8th century, potters began to incorporate friezes of sticklike figures, chariots, and animals in their designs. Soon, Greek sailors introduced metalware and ivory to Cyprus and Asia Minor. Artisans began carving more voluptuous people and animals, hammering bronzes, and doing filigree and granulation work in gold. Vase painting soon reflected these new undulating forms from the East. Trade with Egypt sparked an interest in monumental sculpture and architecture, and by the 6th century many Greek outposts in Italy and along the Mediterranean shore were constructing huge stone temples.

Corinth's temple of Apollo (mid-6th century) is the oldest extant Doric temple in Greece. The baseless fluted columns end in simple round "cushion" capitals similar to but more graceful than the cigar-shaped Doric columns of the temple of Hera in Paestum, Italy, also from this period. Doric columns typically supported a frieze divided into triglyphs (vertical bands), separated by metopes (often sculpted areas) in a style derived from both Mycenae and Egypt. The basic temple hall was the cella, surrounded by a colonnaded stoa. The eastern Greek settlements and Aegean islands were influenced by the Near East and Oriental cultures with whom they traded, so they adapted the Ionic column as the basic element in building. The temple of Artemis at Ephesus, Turkey, with its multitiered and sculpted bases, slender fluted columns, and double volute capitals, is one of the earliest examples.

During this period, bold stone male (*kouros*) and, less often, female (*kore*) statues, their feet firmly planted in a frontal stance, were created as attendants to the gods or memorials over graves. The National Archeological Museum in Athens has an excellent collection of these monumental figures and examples of the more naturalistic sculpture that developed. By the time construction began in the 5th century on Athens's Acropolis, Phidias and his team of extraordinary sculptors were working on the lush, naturalistic figures that decorated the Parthenon frieze. The Acropolis's decorative sculptural elements are considered among the finest classical-era art ever produced.

The monuments of the Acropolis are considered among the greatest architectural achievements of all time. The Doric temple of Athena Parthenos (Virgin)—the

Parthenon—designed by Mnesicles, was built between 447 and 433 B.C. with plans by Ictinus and Callicrates. Ictinus's other great work, the temple of Vassae in the Peloponnese, introduced the Corinthian capital (a crown of acanthus leaves under two Ionic volutes) to the Greeks' building vocabulary. The Erechtheum (421–405 B.C.) is the Acropolis's most unusual structure, with its Porch of Maidens and ornate Ionic columns. After the Acropolis, construction flourished throughout Attica: Public buildings, courts, and markets were designed in what would be known as the "classical" style.

As classical artists developed more skill and their work became more sophisticated, many were given free rein to create for beauty's sake rather than for functional or religious purposes. Bronzes, now made by the lost-wax casting process, began to rival marble sculpture in detail and the figure's ease of movement. Intricately sculpted folds of transparent drapery revealed the muscles and flesh of male statuary, and the sensuous female anatomy. The 4th century brought us the bronze Marathon Boy; Praxiteles' marble Hermes with Dionysos (from Olympia) and his Aphrodite of Cnidos; and the graceful circular *tholos* temple at Delphi. Lysippus, the favored sculptor of Alexander the Great and another star in the art world, is primarily known from later Roman copies of his work.

Although the huge tomb of Mausolus (mausoleum) at Halicarnassus (now Bodrum, in Turkey) dates from the late 4th century, within Greece monumental architecture was still limited to public buildings, particularly theaters. They were typically designed with a large *orchestra* for the actors and chorus, surrounded by tiers of marble seats built into a hillside. The theaters at Delphi, Delos, Megalopolis, and Epidaurus are typical examples.

As Alexander the Great (336–323 B.C.) carved out his empire, he brought the Greek arts and culture to the people of Asia, as far east as the Indus River in Pakistan, north to southern Russia, and south to Egypt. The eastern and Asian influences that Greeks were exposed to in their turn, and the gifts of tribute and royal patronage that flowed back to the country, catapulted the classical period of art and architecture right into the Hellenistic. The blossoming of Greco-Buddhist art in Gandhara (now the Swat Valley of Pakistan) is one of the most beautiful offspring of this cultural marriage.

The overornate works from the Hellenistic era, such as the Acropolis at Pergamum, Turkey; the stoa of Attalos, still seen in Athens; the temple of Didyma in Miletos, Turkey; the *Winged Victory of Samothrace* and the *Venus de Milo* (both seen in the Louvre); and the Colossus of Rhodes: All reflect a new interest in overscale figures, intense movement and emotion, softly blurred details, and mannered, dramatic expressions. Simultaneously, techniques of glassblowing were refined, and portrait painting on murals and vases became more common. Though some earlier works had been polychrome, we have very few examples of paintings. The art of mosaic with tesserae (cubes of glass or stone) flourished; some particularly beautiful examples can be seen at Alexander's capital at Pella in northern Greece.

After the Romans sacked Corinth in 156 B.C., pure Greek art and architecture began its decline. The Romans were great admirers, however, and commissioned Greek artists to copy the well-known classics and create new works. We begin to see a nostalgia for the classical period alongside the flourishing of the more ornate style preferred by the Romans. As their conquest of the East continued, the Romans spread Greek ideals of esthetic beauty throughout the Western world, establishing for us this artistic and cultural legacy.

Archeology

Ever since the amazing discovery of the tomb of King Philip of Macedonia at Vergina in the late 1970s, there has been a rekindled interest in Greek archeology. The spectacular traveling museum show "The Search for Alexander" in the 1980s, and the highly acclaimed restoration of the Parthenon taking place in the 1990s have received tremendous publicity around the world. New excavations and older digs (those going on for more than 100 years!) are attracting the greatest interest in decades. A complete description of Greece's innumerable sites goes far beyond the scope of this book. We recommend using one of the fine books written by such qualified Greek archeologists as Manólis Andrónicos, Spíros Marinátos, and J. A. Papapostólou (all published by Ekdotikí and sold at bookstores and museums) as companion guides in your rubble explorations.

3 Myth & Folklore

The vast majority of literature, mythology, and folklore from classical Greece revolves around the Greek gods, those celebrated residents of Mt. Olympus. Here's a brief glossary to acquaint you with their areas of influence; many legends revolving around their carryings-on are sprinkled throughout this guide.

Aphrodite Goddess of love and beauty; mother of Eros, messenger of love.
Ares God of war.
Artemis Goddess of the hunt and of the moon; twin sister to Apollo.
Asclepius God of medicine and healing.
Athena Goddess of wisdom and patron of the arts and crafts; daughter of Zeus and protectress of Athens.
Cronus The most powerful god during the Saturnian Age. Zeus took his place as leader on Mt. Olympus.
Dionysus God of wine. The performance rituals honoring him were the basis for all Greek drama.
Hades God of the Underworld.
Hephaestus God of fire and metalwork. He made the armor that protected Achilles throughout the Trojan War.
Hera The beautiful but jealous and exacting wife of Zeus.
Hermes Messenger of the gods. He led the dead to the Underworld.
Hestia Goddess of the hearth and family life. She was honored throughout Greece in homes and public buildings with a flaming altar.
Poseidon God of the sea and fresh waters. His symbol, the three-pronged trident, was a powerful weapon.
Zeus Father of the gods and all men. His symbol and weapon was the thunderbolt.

4 Performing Arts & Evening Entertainment

Music

The familiar melody that Zorba danced to in the movie *Zorba the Greek* is typical of *bouzouki* music, a traditional folk music still heard at social gatherings or sung by old-timers. The bouzouki "sound" (or *rebétika,* as the Greeks know it) actually began in the 1920s in the back streets of Piraeus. The port of Athens was filled with rebetes—

down-and-out prostitutes, druggies, and a wave of impoverished immigrants from Asia Minor, who brought with them a Turkish musical heritage. They began playing soulful folk music on their acoustic bouzoukis (a mandolinlike instrument) in the smoky dives on the harbor.

Mános Hadjidákis, one of the greats of modern Greek music, composer of the film score for *Never on Sunday* (his recent death saddened us and the whole nation), has been quoted on the subject of rebétika: "[I was] dazed by the grandeur and depth of the melodic phrases . . . I believed suddenly that the song I was listening to was my own—utterly my own story."

A style of music developed in much the same way the blues did in America, and by the 1950s these tunes had caught the fancy of well-to-do Greeks, who empathized with their lyrics of lost love, unemployment, death, family squabbles, sunken ships, and other crises. Popular musicians added a rhythm section, amplification, and often piano accompaniment to create the lively, spirited sound we now associate with Greek films and modern bouzouki clubs. Whereas once in *Zorba* Anthony Quinn was carried away and danced a *zeibékiko* (an intensely personal expression of feeling) to Mikis Theodorakis' haunting music, tourists now leap up en masse to join hands in the *syrtáki,* one of the simpler folk dances taught by light-footed waiters. So, the next time you see a Greek transported in dance or caught up in the frenzy, look for the tears behind the smiles and the laughter.

Theater

The Greeks, of course, invented drama, and outdoor performances of classical Greek comedies and tragedies (usually given in modern Greek) abound during July and August. In Athens, performances are held at the Herod Atticus Odeum, at the foot of the Acropolis, and in an amphitheater at the top of Lykavittós Hill. Also popular are the performances given at Epidaurus, Greece's largest ancient theater, in the Peloponnese. For more information about these and other performances in Greece, contact the Greek National Tourist Organization (see Chapter 2, section 1, for addresses). For schedules, in Greece pick up the current issue of *The Athenian* magazine or a copy of the daily *Athens News* (both are in English).

5 Sports & Recreation

ADVENTURE TRAVEL, HIKING & TREKKING

This is a new area of travel for Greece. Nevertheless, we found a terrific group that organizes sea kayaking journeys, hikes across the Víkos Gorge in the Víkos-Aóos National Park, ascents of Mt. Olympus, mountain hiking in northern Greece, and zodiac inflatable boat trips around Crete. The company also rents out most of the equipment you'll need for an adventure trip, including sleeping bags and tents. Contact **Trekking Hellas,** Odós Filellínon 7, Athens 10557 (☎ **01/32-34-548,** telex 226040 HIM, fax 01/32-51-474) for more information.

SKIING

Most visitors don't associate Greece with winter pleasures, but, in fact, many Greeks enjoy hurtling down the (relatively small) slopes at Mt. Parnassos, about a 2½ hour drive north of Athens. At Fterolaka and Kellaria, the Greek Tourist Organization has opened the full-service **Parnassos Ski Centre** to manage 20 ski slopes, chair lifts, tow bars, a ski school, snack cafés and restaurants, equipment rental service, child care center, and First Aid department. Contact the Greek Tourist Office (EOT) or the Parnassos Ski Centre, Arachova Viotias 32004 (☎ **0234/22-689** or **22-493,** fax 0234/22-695) for more information.

WINDSURFING

Windsurfing is one of Greece's most popular watersports and can be enjoyed on most islands. On the most touristed ones, even the less-frequented beaches have gear for rent and virile young locals waiting to teach you. Rates vary, but lessons run about 1500 Drs ($8.30) to 1800 Drs ($10) per hour. The Dodecanese island of Kos and the Ionian island of Ithaca both have windsurfing schools with week-long packages organized by European tour operators. For more information, see Chapters 10 and 14, respectively, or contact the **Greek Windsurfing Association,** Odós Filellínon 7, 105 57 Athens (☎ **01/32-30-0330** or **01/32-30-068**).

YACHTING

Is there anything more romantic or glamorous than chartering a yacht to sail the Greek islands? Information and a listing of yacht brokers can be obtained from your nearest office of the Greek National Tourist Organization. For information on special rules and regulations governing yachting and the chartering of these boats (rates range from $90–$7000 per day) in Greece, contact the **Greek Yacht Brokers and Consultants Association,** P.O. Box 30393, Athens 100-33 (☎ **98-16-582**). **Ghiolman Yachts, Travel and Aviation** is one long-established yacht broker; contact them at Odós Filellínon 7, Athens 10557 (☎ **01/32-30-330,** telex 222065, fax 01/32-23-251) for information. **Acoskar Hellenic,** P.O. Box 10, Spetses 18050 (☎ **0298/72-464,** telex 226086 SKAR GR, fax 0298/73-707) specializes in Saronic Gulf charters. Our budget suggestion for sampling the high life: contact the **Greek Islands Cruise Center,** 50 Post Road West, Westport, CT 06880 (☎ **203/226-7911,** fax 203/226-2765; or ☎ **01/89-80-879,** fax 01/89-40-952 in Athens), to find out about their low-cost cruise packages through the islands.

YACHT RACING

For those of you passing through Greece at the highest possible velocity, consider pitting your skills against the locals in the popular sport of yacht racing. For more information, contact the **Hellenic Yachting Federation,** Odós Santaróza 23, 185 34 Piraeus (☎ **01/41-37-351** or fax 01/41-31-191).

6 Food & Drink

Food

MEALS & DINING CUSTOMS

Greece is definitely a three-meals-a-day kind of country. The emphasis is on a big midday lunch (about 2pm), followed by a siesta, a reviving coffee or snack at 6pm, and then a light dinner around 10 or 11pm. If you can work yourself into this schedule (easy to do when the sun doesn't set until 9:30 or 10pm), you'll see and enjoy the best of Greek dining.

GREEK CUISINE

Most of us are familiar with souvlaki, moussaka, Greek salads, and baklava pastry, but in Greece a wide variety of other foods (usually prepared with vegetables, meats, fish, and olive oil) will keep you trying something new for weeks.

Breakfast Our pet peeve is the usual pension "brekfest complet": an awful serving of dried-out bread or packaged toast, Nescafé, and an airline packet of butter and marmalade. However, now that hoteliers realize they can charge you $5 for something more substantial, many of our favorite small inns have added eggs, cheese, yogurt, biscuits, and cake to their buffet tables. On the islands and in small towns, your best bet is the local *kafenío* (they are increasingly difficult to find), where you can order a fresh-brewed Greek coffee, bread, and sometimes eggs, yogurt, or cheese pie.

Lunch Lots of options here, from retsina and fish to toast, at those uniquely Greek sandwich shops where your combination of fast eats is pressed onto a roll or hero with a waffle iron.

Dinner This is the time to let loose, sample everything, drink some wine, and stroll it off. There's a list of menu items in the appendix. Don't worry about pronouncing them: Most tavernas welcome you right into the kitchen to peek, sniff, and point out what you want. The only rule of thumb about Greek restaurants is that if there are tablecloths instead of plastic sheets, it's going to cost you more.

Drinks

Although tap water on the mainland and on most islands is potable (on some islands water comes from desalination plants and tastes terrible), most locals and visitors prefer bottled water (widely sold, both within restaurants and at news kiosks and markets). Major international-brand sodas and Greek-produced juices are also readily found.

Beer and wine (the latter produced throughout the country), are readily available and inexpensive. Henniger is the most popular beer, and some of the favorite bottled wines include Nykteri from Santoríni, Samiana from Sámos, Robola and Gentilini from Kefalonía, Ligeri from Páros, and Aghio Ritiko from the Mt. Athos region of northern Greece. In many wine-producing regions ask for *krassi,* the locally aged house wine, whenever you dine out.

Less expensive but more potent drinks are retsina, an often home-brewed wine flavored with pine resin, and ouzo, an anisette liquor usually drunk mixed with water.

7 Recommended Books & Films

Books

Greece has produced or inspired some of the greatest literary works ever created. The following is a sampling of books that we've enjoyed during our travels and that would make worthy companions on any journey through Hellas.

GENERAL

Over the years more people have become Grecophiles after reading Mary Renault's books than from just about anything else—including traveling to Greece. Renault, who died in 1983, wrote more than a dozen books, mostly historical novels, that breathe life into the ancient Greek past. Among her best-known books are *The King Must Die, The Mask of Apollo,* and *Fire from Heaven.*

If you haven't already done so in school, you should read Homer's *Odyssey* and *Iliad,* the blind poet's mythological and historical epics. The translations by Robert Fitzgerald capture more of the original spirit than Edith Hamilton's more widely read versions. Hamilton's *Mythology,* however, is a good reference book and makes for lively reading.

Many other writers have used Greece as the setting for their tales: Gore Vidal's *Creation,* Thornton Wilder's *Woman of Andros,* and Irving Stone's *The Gold Treasures of Iris Leaman* are entertaining reading.

Finally, one of our favorite books on Greece is a book that uses the ancient Greek alphabet to describe some of the more remarkable aspects of ancient Greek life, all the while winding you around the authors' etymological finger. The name of this fascinating volume is *From Alpha to Omega (The Life and Times of the Greek Alphabet),* by Alexander and Nicholas Humez.

THE ARTS & ARCHITECTURE

Art and architecture buffs should bring along John Boardman's classic *Greek Art* (Oxford University Press), then shop in one of Athens's fine bookstores for the excellent Ekdotikí collection of museum and archeology guides. The color reproductions make a delightful souvenir of your travels.

FICTION

Henry Miller's *The Colossus of Maroussi* and the novels and travel books of Lawrence Durrell (*The Alexandria Quartet* and *Prospero's Cell*) are fine works by modern writers. *The Magus,* which takes place on Spetses, is one of John Fowles's best, and is a perfect book to read while lying on the beach.

No list of suggested books about Greece would be complete without some by the country's national writer, Níkos Kazantzákis: *Zorba the Greek* and *A Modern Sequel to the Odyssey* (which is 33,333 lines long) capture the essence of the Greek soul. The poems of C. P. Caváfy (translated by Rae Davin), Greece's most important modern poet, are to verse what Kazantzakis is to prose. Byron is one of the most famous European poets to glorify Greece; Elizabeth Langford's *Byron's Greece* retraces his journeys and includes artwork illustrating his love affair with the country.

TRAVEL

Literary buffs should get Richard Stoneman's *Literary Companion to Travelling in Greece,* and the accidental tourist can read Helen Miller's *Greece Through the Ages.* The armchair traveler will relish Patrick Fermor's personal journeys in *Mani: Travels in the Southern Peloponnese* or his *Roumeli: Travels in Northern Greece.* Romantics have long been wooed by Lawrence Durrell's guide, *The Greek Islands.* For in-depth information, good color photography, and lively folk and historical lore about many of the Greek islands, look for the individual guides published by Lycabettus Press and sold on the islands in souvenir shops, news kiosks, and book shops.

Films

A tremendous number of films have been shot in Greece over the years. Some of the best-known examples:

Zorba the Greek (1964), with Anthony Quinn dancing around Crete.
James Bond's *For Your Eyes Only* (1981), shot in Corfu and Metéora.
Paul Mazursky's version of Shakespeare's *The Tempest* (1982), filmed in Gýthio on the Peloponnese and in Corfu.
Every teen's favorite, *Summer Lovers* (1982), filmed on Santoríni.
Every woman's favorite, *Shirley Valentine* (1989), filmed on Mýkonos.
John's favorite, *Mediterraneo* (1991), an Italian film about soldiers stationed on an outer island during WWII.

The Francis Ford Coppola segment of *New York Stories,* where Giancarlo Giannini conducts his orchestra in front of the Parthenon.

Melina Mercouri's unforgettable *Never on Sunday* (1959), filmed mostly in Piraeus.

Paschali's Island (1988), James Dearden's BBC docudrama about the Turkish occupation, starring Ben Kingsley and filmed in Rhodes.

Carl Foreman's *Guns of Navarone* (1961), starring Anthony Quinn, with a famed naval battle staged for film off the island of Rhodes.

By the way, the film of Nicholas Gage's novel Eleni (1985), starring John Malkovich in a moving tale about the civil war in northern Greece, was actually filmed in Algeria. Costa-Gavras's famed thriller from the Vassílis Vassilikós novel *Z* (1969) was shot in France. Both shifts of location were made for political reasons.

2 Planning a Trip to Greece

ASIDE FROM THE ELEMENTAL APPEAL OF SUN AND SAND, VISITORS COME TO GREECE with many fantasies of what there is to see and do. Some arrive by ship to enjoy the luxury of sailing on a fully outfitted cruise vessel; for them relaxing on deck with an occasional stopover at an interesting port is heavenly. Others arrive by train and ferry, armed with a EurailPass, backpack, and a keen instinct for hunting down the best beach and the wildest party. Most bring suitcases, cameras, and a desire to touch a little bit of Greek magic wherever it is found: archeological sites, bouzouki clubs, tavernas, open-air markets, museums, beaches. It's for these people that our guide has been written.

1 Information, Entry Requirements & Money

Sources of Information

Before you go to Greece, you can obtain travel information as well as basic information about the country and its various points of interest from the **Greek National Tourist Organization (GNTO).** The GNTO has offices in the following major cities:

UNITED STATES **New York:** 645 Fifth Ave., 5th Floor, New York, NY 10022 (☎ **212/421-5777,** fax 212/826-6940). **Chicago:** 168 North Michigan Ave., 4th Floor, Chicago, IL 60601 (☎ **312/782-1084,** fax 312/782-1091). **Los Angeles:** 611 West 6th St., Suite 2198, Los Angeles, CA 90017 (☎ **213/626-6696,** fax 213/489-9744).

CANADA **Toronto:** 2 Bloor St. West, Cumberland Terrace, Toronto, ON M4W 3E2 (☎ **416/968-2220,** fax 416/968-6533). **Montréal:** 1233 Rue de la Montagne, Suite 101, **Montréal,** QC H3G 1Z2 (☎ **514/871-1535,** fax 514/871-1498).

UNITED KINGDOM **London:** 4 Conduit St., London WIR DOJ (☎ **071/734-5997,** fax 071/287-1369).

AUSTRALIA **Sydney:** 51–57 Pitt St., Sydney, NSW 2000 (☎ **2/241-1663,** fax 2/235-2174).

GREECE **Athens:** In Greece the GNTO is known simply as the Greek Tourist Organization, or *Ellinikós Organismós Tourismoú (EOT).* Its information office in Athens (☎ **322-2545** or **323-4130**) is right on Sýntagma Square, the city's main quadrangle, at Odós Karagheórghi tís Servías 2 (2 Karageorges of Serbia Street), in the National Bank of Greece. The head administrative office (☎ **322-3111**) is a few blocks away, at Odós Amerikís 2 (2 America Street).

CUSTOMS

Greece permits you to bring in most personal effects and the following items duty free: two still cameras with 10 rolls of film each, one movie or video camera, tobacco for personal use, one bottle of wine and one bottle of liquor per person, a portable radio, a tape recorder, a typewriter, a bicycle, golf clubs, tennis racquets, fishing gear, skis, and other sports equipment.

Visitors arriving from most countries outside the European Union (EU), of which Greece is a member, may import up to 200 cigarettes (300 from the EU), 50 cigars (75 from the EU), 250 grams of tobacco (400 from the EU), 1 liter of alcohol or 2 liters of wine or liquor (1.5 liters of alcohol or 5 liters of wine or liquor from the

EU), 50 grams of perfume (75 grams from the EU), 500 grams of coffee and 100 grams of tea (one kilogram of coffee and 400 grams of tea from the EU). Adults may bring in gift items worth up to 9,000 drachmas or $38 (up to 40,000 drachmas, or $167, if coming from an EU country). The importation of plants with soil is prohibited. Cats and dogs may be brought into Greece with a health and rabies inoculation certificate, issued not more than 12 months and not fewer than 6 days prior to arrival.

There's no restriction on the number or value of traveler's checks on either entry or exit. Be very careful about antiques that you buy in Greece; the laws protecting Greek antiquities are very strict, and no genuine antiquities may be taken out of the country without prior special permission from the Archeological Service, at Odós Polygnótou 3 (3 Polygnotus St.), in Athens.

In the U.S. Returning to the United States from Greece, American citizens may bring in $400 worth of merchandise duty free, provided they have not made a similar claim within the past 30 days. Remember to keep receipts for purchases made in Greece. For more specific guidance, request the free pamphlet "Know Before You Go" by writing to the U.S. Customs Service, P.O. Box 7407, Washington, DC 20044.

In Canada For total clarification, Canadians can write for the booklet "I Declare," issued by Revenue Canada Customs Department, Communications Branch, Mackenzie Avenue, Ottawa, ON K1A OL5. Canada allows its citizens a Can$300 exemption, and they can bring back duty free 200 cigarettes, 2.2 pounds of tobacco, 40 ounces of liquor, and 50 cigars. In addition, they are allowed to mail unsolicited gifts (but *not* alcohol or tobacco) into Canada from abroad at the rate of Can$40 a day. On the package, mark "UNSOLICITED GIFT, UNDER $40 VALUE." All valuables you own and take with you should be declared before departure from Canada on the Y-38 form, including serial numbers. **Note:** The $300 exemption can be used only once a year and then only after an absence of seven days.

In the U.K. & Ireland Members of European Union countries do not necessarily have to go through Customs when returning home, providing all their travel was within EU countries. Of course, Customs agents reserve the right to search if they are suspicious. However, there are certain EU guidelines for returning passengers, who can bring in 400 cigarillos, 200 cigars, 800 cigarettes, and 1 kilogram of smoking tobacco. They can also bring in 20 liters of fortified wine, 90 liters of wine, and 110 liters of beer. Persons exceeding these limits may be asked to prove that the excess is either for one's personal use or gifts for friends. For further details, contact **HM Customs and Excise,** Excise and Inland Customs Advice Centre, Dorset House, Stamford Street, London SE1 9NG (☎ **071/202-4227**).

In Australia The duty-free allowance in Australia is Aus$400 or Aus$200 for those under 18. Personal property mailed back from Spain should be marked "AUSTRALIAN GOODS RETURNED" to avoid payment of duty. Upon returning to Australia, citizens can bring in 200 cigarettes or 250 grams of loose tobacco and 1 liter of alcohol. If you're returning with valuable goods you already own, such as foreign-made cameras, you should file form B263. A helpful brochure, available from Australian consulates or Customs offices, is *Customs Information for All Travellers.*

In New Zealand The duty-free allowance is NZ$500. Citizens over 16 can bring in 200 cigarettes or 250 grams of loose tobacco or 50 cigars, 4.5 liters of wine or beer, or 1.125 liters of liquor. New Zealand currency does not carry restrictions regarding import or export. A Certificate of Export listing valuables taken out of the country allows you to bring them back without paying duty. Most questions are answered in a free pamphlet, *New Zealand Customs Guide for Travellers,* available at New Zealand Consulates and Customs offices.

Money

CASH & CURRENCY

The unit of currency in Greece is the **drachmaí (Dr),** in the form of a coin or bill. (The drachma—called *drachmi,* plural *drachmaí* or *drachmés,* in Greek—was also in use in ancient Athens; see the coin exhibits in the city's Numismatic Museum.) As of this writing, US$1 = 240 Drs. Because of constant fluctuations in the exchange rate, however, and also because of possible increase in prices since the European Union inaugurated a single market, you should *use the figures in these pages as a guide only.*

The drachma is made up of 100 **leptá;** a single *leptó* is worth less than a penny. There is a new gold coin for 100 Drs, and coins for 1, 2, 5, 10, and 20 Drs. Bills are worth 50 Drs (blue), 100 Drs (red), 500 Drs (green), 1,000 Drs (brown), and 5,000 Drs (blue). There always seems to be a shortage of (or a reluctance to make) change in many places. If you know that you're going to be making inexpensive purchases or paying low tabs, ask for 1,000 Dr bills when you exchange currency.

Some coins may seem to be worth peanuts, but you'll need them for tipping, telephones, and trolleys.

Note: In the following pages, the dollar equivalents have been rounded off to the nearest dollar for the sake of simplicity.

TRAVELER'S CHECKS

Traveler's checks are the safest way to carry cash while traveling. Before leaving home, purchase traveler's checks and arrange to carry some ready cash (usually about $250, depending on your habits and needs). In the event of theft, if the checks are properly documented, the value of your checks will be refunded. Most large banks sell traveler's checks, charging fees that average between 1% and 2% of the value of the checks you buy, although some out-of-the-way banks, in rare instances, charge as much as 7%. If your bank wants more than a 2% commission, it sometimes pays to call the traveler's check issuers directly for the address of outlets where this commission will be less.

Issuers sometimes have agreements with groups to sell checks commission free. For example, the Automobile Association of America (AAA) sells American Express checks in several currencies without commission.

American Express ☎ toll free **800/221-7282** in the U.S. and Canada) is one of the largest and most immediately recognized issuers of traveler's checks. No commission is charged, as mentioned above, to **AAA** members and holders of certain types of American Express charge cards. The company issues checks denominated in U.S. or Canadian dollars, British pounds sterling, Swiss or French francs, German marks, and Japanese yen. The vast majority of checks sold in North America are denominated in U.S. dollars. For questions or problems that arise outside the U.S. or Canada, contact any of the company's many regional representatives.

IMPRESSIONS

Marvelous things happen to one in Greece—marvelous good *things which can happen to one nowhere else on earth.*
Henry Miller, *The Colossus of Maroussi,* 1942

Citicorp (☎ toll free **800/645-6556** in the U.S. and Canada, or **813/623-1709,** collect, from anywhere else), issues checks in U.S. dollars, British pounds, German marks, and Japanese yen.

Thomas Cook (☎ toll free **800/223-9920** in the U.S., or **609/987-7300,** collect, from anywhere else) issues MasterCard traveler's checks denominated in U.S. dollars, French francs, German marks, Dutch guilders, Spanish pesetas, Australian dollars, Japanese yen, and Hong Kong dollars. Depending on individual banking laws in each of the various states, some of the above-mentioned currencies might not be available in every outlet.

Interpayment Services (☎ toll free **800/221-2426** in the U.S. or Canada, or **800/453-4284** from most anywhere else) sells Visa checks sponsored by Barclays Bank and/or Bank of America at selected branches around North America. Traveler's checks are denominated in U.S. or Canadian dollars, British pounds, Swiss or French francs, German marks, and Japanese yen.

The Greek Drachma

For U.S. Readers At this writing, $1 = 240 Drs (or 1 Dr = $0.004). This was the rate of exchange used to calculate the dollar values given in the table below and throughout this edition.

For U.K. Readers At this writing, £1 = 370 Drs (or 1 Dr = £0.002). This was the rate of exchange used to calculate the pound values in the table below.

Note International exchange rates fluctuate from time to time and may not be the same when you travel to Greece. Therefore, this table should be used as a guide for approximate values only.

Drs	US$	UK£
5	0.02	0.01
10	0.04	0.03
25	0.10	0.07
50	0.21	0.14
75	0.31	0.20
100	0.42	0.27
125	0.53	0.34
250	1.04	0.68
1,250	5.21	3.38
2,500	10.42	6.76
5,000	20.83	13.51
7,500	31.25	20.28
10,000	41.67	27.02
12,500	52.10	33.78
15,000	62.50	40.54
17,500	72.92	47.30
20,000	83.33	54.05
22,500	93.75	60.80
25,000	104.17	67.57

CREDIT & CHARGE CARDS

You'll find that carrying credit and charge cards is useful in Spain. **American Express, Visa,** and **Diners Club** are widely recognized. If you see the Eurocard or Access sign on an establishment, that means it accepts **MasterCard.**

Credit and charge cards can save your life when you're abroad. With American Express and Visa, for example, not only can you charge purchases in shops and restaurants that take the card, but you can also withdraw drachmas from bank cash machines at many locations in Greece. Check with your card company before leaving home.

Keep in mind that the price of purchases is not converted into your national currency until notification is received in your home country, so the price is subject to fluctuation. If your national currency—be it dollars, pounds, or whatever—declines by the time your bill arrives, you'll pay more for an item than you expected. But those are the rules of the game. It can also work in your favor if your national currency should rise, against the drachma.

CURRENCY EXCHANGE

Many Athens hotels will simply not accept a dollar- or pound-denominated check, and if they do, they'll almost certainly charge for the conversion. In some cases, they'll accept countersigned traveler's checks or a credit card, but if you're prepaying a deposit on hotel reservations, it's cheaper and easier to pay with a check drawn on a Greek bank.

This can be arranged by a large commercial bank or by a specialist such as **Ruesch International,** 825 14th St. NW, Washington, DC 20005 (☎ **202/408-1200,** or toll free **800/424-2923**), which performs a wide variety of conversion-related tasks, usually for only $2 U.S. per transaction.

If you need a check payable in drachmas, call Ruesch's toll-free number, describe what you need, and note the transaction number given to you. Mail your dollar-denominated personal check (payable to Ruesch International) to the office in Washington, DC. Upon receiving this, the company will mail a check denominated in drachmas for the financial equivalent, minus the $2 charge. The company can also help you with many kinds of wire transfers and conversions of VAT (value-added tax, which is known as IVA in Greece), refund checks, and also will mail brochures and information packets on request. Britishers can go to Ruesch International Ltd., 18 Saville Row, London W1X 2AD (☎ **0171/734-2300**).

What Things Cost in Athens	US$
Taxi from the airport to the city's center	10.00
Local telephone call	.02
Double at a B-class hotel	96.05
Bathless double in a pension	26.80
Lunch for one at a taverna	8.75
Dinner for one, with wine, at a restaurant	32.50
Bottle of beer	1.25
Soda	1.00
Cup of Greek coffee	.83
Roll of ASA 100 Kodacolor film, 36 exp.	8.40
Admission to National Archeological Museum	6.25

What Things Cost in Corfu (Expensive Island)	US$
Taxi from the airport to the city center	4.60
Local telephone call	.02
Double at a B-class hotel	90.30
Bathless double in a pension	34.40
Lunch for one at a taverna	8.80
Dinner for one, with wine, at a restaurant	35.85
Bottle of beer	1.66
Soda	1.25
Cup of Greek coffee	1.05
Roll of ASA 100 Kodacolor film, 36 exp.	9.75
Admission to Archeological Museum	2.10

What Things Cost in Póros (Inexpensive Island)	US$
Local telephone call	.02
Double at a B-class hotel	56.85
Bathless double in a pension	24.45
Lunch for one at a taverna	6.30
Dinner for one, with wine, at a restaurant	22.25
Bottle of beer	1.25
Soda	1.05
Cup of Greek coffee	.95
Roll of ASA 100 Kodacolor film, 36 exp.	9.20

Mutual of Omaha/Travelex, 1225 Franklin Ave., Garden City, NY 11530 (☎ toll free **800/377-0051** in the U.S.) provides foreign currency exchange at 30 U.S. airport locations or through the mail. With exchanges of $500 or more, they will guarantee to exchange back up to 30% at the same rate you originally exchanged with no service fee. Annual or short-term flight insurance policies are available starting at $5.

2 When to Go—Climate, Holidays & Events

Climate

Greece has a generally mild climate: cool winters (that hover around 55° to 60°F in Athens and the south and 45° to 50°F in Thessaloníki and the north) and *meltémi* breeze-cooled summers (about 85° to 95°F throughout the country). The Greek National Tourist Organization claims that Greece has 3,000 hours of sunshine each year! The best seasons to visit are spring (late April to June) and fall (mid-September to November) when the sun is less intensely blinding, the wildflowers are out, and the tourists are gone. However, when there are fewer tourists there are also fewer facilities open, particularly on the islands. Many places are closed from mid-September to mid-May.

Holidays & Special Events

The following are legal national holidays in Greece:

New Year's Day January 1
Epiphany January 6
Shrove Monday Occurs 41 days before Easter
Independence Day March 25
Good Friday through Easter Monday
May Day May 1 (Labor Day)
Whitmonday Occurs 50 days after Easter
Assumption of the Virgin August 15
***Óchi* Day** October 28 (see page 19)
Christmas December 25–26

On these days, government offices, banks, post offices, and most stores are closed. Various museums and attractions, however, may be open to the public. Some restaurants also remain open. For further information, inquire at your hotel or consult the English-language publications (such as *The Athenian,* a monthly) available in Athens and elsewhere.

Hundreds of special events—folkloric, religious, festive, and cultural—take place throughout the year all over Greece. For a complete list, contact the Greek National Tourist Organization. The major events are given in the calendar below.

Greece Calendar of Events

January

- **Feast of St. Basil** A national holiday, celebrated with traditional New Year's pie, or *pita,* and with an exchange of gifts. January 1.
- **Epiphany** The Blessing of the Waters, a religious ceremony celebrating Christ's Baptism held throughout Greece, although the most spectacular spot to visit is Piraeus. January 6.

February

- **Carnival time throughout Greece.** Pátra has one of the largest and most gala parades. Midmonth.

April

- **Nightly, sound-and-light performances,** begin in Athens and Rhodes and continue through October.
- **Anniversaries dedicated to St. Spyrídon,** patron saint of Corfu. Midmonth.

May

- **Flower Festival** May 1.
- **Anniversary of the Ionian Islands' union with Greece in 1864.** Celebrated mostly on Corfu. May 21.
- **Nightly, sound-and-light performances,** begin in Corfu. Continue through mid-September.
- **Navy Week Festival** Celebrated throughout Greece. In Vólos, there's a reenactment of the sailing of the Argonauts' expedition; on Hydra the event is turned into a celebration of Admiral Andréas Miaoúlis (1769–1835), a hero of the War of Independence. End of month.

June

- **Wine festivals,** at Dafní, about 10 kilometers outside Athens, on Rhodes, and in other locations. Free wine-tasting, as well as dancing at outdoor tavernas. Midmonth.
- **Athens Festival** Featuring music, drama, and dance. Begins at the Herod Atticus Theater, at the foot of the Acropolis, and on Lykavittós Hill. Performances until the end of September.

July

- **Wine Festival at Alexandroúpolis** Begins mid-month and runs for four weeks.
- **Epidaurus Festival of ancient Greek drama.** Held in ancient amphitheater. Performances continue through early September.
- **Northern Greece National Theater,** performs ancient Greek drama in the open-air theaters at Philippi and on the island of Thássos. Performances continue through August.
- **"Dionysia" Wine Festival,** on island of Náxos. Midmonth.
- **Wine Festival,** Réthymno, Crete. Throughout month.

August

- **Ancient Greek dramas,** performed in the open-air theater at Dion, near Mt. Olympus, and at the ancient theater at Dodóna. Midmonth.
- **Art exhibition,** on Skýros island. First week of month.
- **Hippokrateia Festival,** featuring ancient drama, musical performances, and a reenactment of the Hippocratic Oath, on the island of Kos. Midmonth.

September

- **Thessaloníki International Trade Fair.** Midmonth.
- **Thessaloníki Film Festival and Festival of Popular Song.** End of month.

October

- **Demetrius Festival,** featuring music, opera, ballet. Held in Thessaloníki.

November

- **St. Andrew's Day,** celebrating the patron saint of Pátra. November 30.

3 Health & Insurance

Health

You will encounter few health problems traveling in Greece. The tap water is safe to drink, the milk pasteurized, and health services are good. Occasionally the change in diet may cause some minor diarrhea, so you may want to take some antidiarrhea medicine along.

Carry all your vital medicine in your carry-on luggage and bring enough prescribed medicines to last you during your stay. Bring along copies of your prescriptions that are written in the generic—not brand-name—form. If you need a doctor, your hotel can recommend one or you can contact the American embassy or consulate. You can also obtain a list of English-speaking doctors before you leave, from the **International Association for Medical Assistance to Travelers (IAMAT)** in the United States at

417 Center St., Lewiston, NY 14092 (☎ **716/754-4883**); in Canada at 40 Regal Road, Guelph, ON N1K 1B5 (☎ **519/836-0102**).

If you suffer from a chronic illness, talk to your doctor before taking the trip. For such conditions as epilepsy, diabetes, or a heart condition, wear a Medic Alert identification tag, which will immediately alert any doctor to your condition and provide the number of Medic Alert's 24-hour hotline so that a foreign doctor can obtain medical records for you. For a lifetime membership the cost is $30. Contact the **Medic Alert Foundation,** P.O. Box 1009, Turlock, CA 95381-1009 (☎ toll free **800/344-3226**).

Insurance

Before purchasing any additional insurance, check your homeowner's, automobile, and medical insurance policies as well as the insurance provided by credit-card companies and auto and travel clubs. You may have adequate off-premises theft coverage or your credit-card company may even provide cancellation coverage if the ticket is paid for with a credit card.

Remember, Medicare covers only U.S. citizens traveling in Mexico and Canada.

Also note that to submit any claim you must always have thorough documentation, including all receipts, police reports, medical records, and so forth.

If you are prepaying for your vacation or are taking a charter or any other flight that has cancellation penalties, look into cancellation insurance.

The following companies will provide further information:

Travel Guard International, 1145 Clark St., Stevens Point, WI 54481 (☎ toll free **800/782-5151**), which offers a comprehensive policy that covers basically everything, including emergency assistance, accidental death, trip cancellation and interruption, medical coverage abroad, and lost luggage, based on the cost of the trip. There are restrictions, however, that you should understand before you accept the coverage.

Travel Insurance Pak, Travel Insured International, Travelers Insurance Co., P.O. Box 285568, East Hartford, CT 06128 (☎ **203/277-2318,** or toll free **800/243-3174**), offers illness and accident coverage, costing from $10 for 6 to 10 days. For lost or damaged luggage, $500 worth of coverage costs $20 for 6 to 10 days. You can also get trip-cancellation insurance for $5.50.

Mutual of Omaha (Tele-Trip), 3201 Farnam St., Omaha, NE 68131 (☎ **402/345-2400,** or toll free **800/228-9792**), charges $3 a day (with a 10-day minimum) for foreign medical coverage up to $5,000, which features global assistance and maintains a 24-hour hotline. The company also offers trip-cancellation insurance, lost or stolen luggage coverage, the standard accident coverage, and other policies.

Wallach HealthCare Abroad (MEDEX), 107 W. Federal St., P.O. Box 480, Middleburg, VA 22117 (☎ **703/255-9800,** or toll free **800/237-6615**), offers a policy, good for 10 to 120 days, costing $3 a day, including accident and sickness coverage up to $100,000. Medical evacuation is also included, along with a $25,000 accidental death or dismemberment compensation. Trip cancellation and lost or stolen luggage can also be written into this policy at a nominal cost.

4 What to Pack

Look at the sheer, flowing robes enveloping the Venus de Milo statue and you'll get a sense of what's appropriate attire in this country. Light, casual clothing is the best defense against Greece's intense summer heat; if you're sensitive to the sun, we recommend long-sleeve garments and a lightweight hat. Breathable cottons or linens are far preferable to synthetics. Although most budget hotels don't offer laundry service, you can handwash casual cottons, which dry quickly in your room or on your balcony.

Skirts, sleeveless dresses, slacks, long shorts, and T-shirts are acceptable in any but the most formal situation. Men may want a short-sleeve dress shirt and summer sportcoat for the fanciest resort restaurants. Although topless and nude sunbathing are common on remote beaches, you must use a cover-up when swimming near towns or religious buildings. Black, though fashionable elsewhere in Europe, is a color worn only by widows in Greece. Bring a light sweater, a windbreaker, or light jacket for the cooler spring or fall weather and for those unexpected late-night ferries. Last, but most important, bring comfortable lace-up shoes for exploring archeological sites and hiking the hills, and water-resistant sandals or shoes for your beach outings.

If you wear contact lenses or eyeglasses, bring along an extra pair, even though there are skilled opticians in all the major resort areas. A small flashlight may come in handy for exploring archeological sites or taking seaside strolls at night. Hostel-goers should bring a towel and soap, as those items are rarely provided; everyone may want to bring a favorite beach towel. Common prescription and over-the-counter American- and European-made drugs and toiletries are widely available. **Sunscreen** up to SPF8 is sold everywhere; bring a stronger product if you need one. Mosquito repellent will come in handy on some of the islands in July and August. Kyle loves premoistened towelettes; they're refreshing and handy, especially in the many tavernas with no napkins!

5 Tips for the Disabled, Seniors, Singles, Families & Students

For the Disabled

Before you go, there are many agencies that can provide advance-planning information.

For example, contact **Travel Information Service,** Moss Rehabilitation Hospital, 1200 West Tabor Rd., Philadelphia, PA 19141-3099 (☎ **215/456-9900**). It charges $5 per package, which will contain names and addresses of accessible hotels, restaurants, and attractions, often based on firsthand reports of travelers who have been there.

You may also want to subscribe to ***The Itinerary,*** P.O. Box 2012, Bayonne, NJ 07002-2012 (☎ **201/858-3400**), for $10 a year. This travel magazine, published bimonthly, is filled with news about travel aids for the handicapped, special tours, information on accessibility, and other matters.

You can also obtain a copy of ***Air Transportation of Handicapped Persons,*** published by the U.S. Department of Transportation. It's free if you write to Free Advisory Circular No. AC12032, Distribution Unit, U.S. Department of Transportation, Publications Division, M-4332, Washington, DC 20590.

You may also want to consider joining a tour for disabled visitors. Names and addresses of such tour operators can be obtained by writing to the **Society for the Advancement of Travel for the Handicapped,** 347 Fifth Ave., Suite 610, New York, NY 10016 (☎ **212/447-7284,** fax 212/725-8253). Annual membership dues are $40, or $25 for senior citizens and students. Send a stamped, self-addressed envelope.

The **Federation of the Handicapped,** 211 West 14th St., New York, NY 10011 (☎ **212/206-4200**), also operates summer tours for members, who pay a yearly fee of $4.

For the blind, the best information source is the **American Foundation for the Blind,** 15 West 16th St., New York, NY 10011 (☎ toll free **800/232-5463**).

For Seniors

Many senior discounts are available, but note that some may require membership in a particular association.

For information before you go, write to **"Travel Tips for Senior Citizens"** (publication no. 8970), distributed for $1 by the Superintendent of Documents, U.S. Government Printing Office, Washington, DC 20402 (☎ **202/783-5238**). Another booklet—and this one is distributed free—is called **"101 Tips for the Mature Traveler,"** available from Grand Circle Travel, 347 Congress St., Suite 3A, Boston, MA 02210 (☎ **617/350-7500,** or toll free **800/248-3737**).

SAGA International Holidays, 222 Berkeley St., Boston, MA 02116 (☎ toll free **800/343-0273**), runs all-inclusive tours for seniors, 50 years old or older. Insurance is included in the net price of their tours. Membership is $50 ($80 per couple) a year.

In the United States, the best organization to join is the **American Association of Retired Persons (AARP),** 1909 K St. NW, Washington, DC 20049 (☎ **202/872-4700** or toll free **1-800-424-3410**), which offers members discounts on car rentals, hotels, and airfares. AARP travel arrangements, featuring senior citizen discounts, are handled by American Express; ☎ toll free **800/927-0111** or **745-4567.**

Information is also available from the **National Council of Senior Citizens,** 1331 F St. NW, Washington, DC 20004 (☎ **202/347-8800**), which charges $12 per person to join (couples pay $16) for which you receive a monthly newsletter, part of which is devoted to travel tips. Discounts on hotel and auto rentals are available.

Elderhostel, 75 Federal St., Boston, MA 02110 (☎ **617/426-7788**), offers an array of university-based summer educational programs for senior citizens throughout the world. Most courses last around three weeks and are remarkable values, considering that airfare, accommodations in student dormitories or modest inns, all meals, and tuition are included. Courses include field trips, involve no homework, are ungraded, and emphasize liberal arts.

Participants must be over 60, but each may take an under-60 companion. Meals consist of solid, no-frills fare typical of educational institutions worldwide. The program provides a safe and congenial environment for older single women, who make up some 67% of the enrollment.

For Single Travelers

Unfortunately for the 85 million single Americans, the travel industry is far more geared toward couples, and singles often wind up paying the penalty. It pays to travel with someone, and one company that resolves this problem is **Travel Companion,** which matches single travelers with like-minded companions. It's headed by Jens Jurgen, who charges between $36 and $66 for a six-month listing in his well-publicized records. People seeking travel companions fill out forms stating their preferences and needs and receive a minilisting of potential travel partners. Companions of the same or opposite sex can be requested. For an application and more information, contact Jens Jurgen, Travel Companion, P.O. Box P-833, Amityville, NY 11701 (☎ **516/454-0880**).

Singleworld, 401 Theodore Fremd Ave., Rye, P.O. Box 1999, NY 10580 (☎ **914/967-3334**, or toll free **800/223-6490**), is a travel agency that operates tours for solo travelers. Some, but not all, are for people under 35. Annual dues are $25.

For Families

Advance planning is the key to a successful overseas family vacation. If you have very small children, you should discuss your vacation plans with your family doctor and take along such standard supplies as children's aspirin, a thermometer, and Band-Aids.

On airlines, a special menu for children must be requested at least 24 hours in advance, but if baby food is required, bring your own and ask a flight attendant to warm it to the right temperature. Take along a "security blanket" for your child—a pacifier, a favorite toy or book, or, for older children, something to make them feel at home in different surroundings—a baseball cap, a favorite T-shirt, or some good luck charm.

Make advance arrangements for cribs, bottle warmers, and car seats if you're driving anywhere.

Ask the hotel if it stocks baby food, and, if not, take some with you and plan to buy the rest in local supermarkets.

Draw up guidelines on bedtime, eating, keeping tidy, being in the sun, even shopping and spending—they'll make the vacation more enjoyable.

Baby-sitters can be found for you at most hotels, but you should always insist, if possible, that you secure a baby-sitter with at least a rudimentary knowledge of English.

Family Travel Times is a newsletter about traveling with children. Subscribers to the newsletter, which costs $35 for ten issues, can also call in with travel questions, Monday through Friday only, from 10am to noon eastern standard time. Contact **TWYCH,** which stands for Travel With Your Children, 80 Eighth Ave., New York, NY 10011 (☎ **212/206-0688**).

For Students

The largest travel service for students is the **Council on International Educational Exchange (CIEE),** 205 E. 42d St., New York, NY 10017 (☎ **212/661-1414**), providing details about budget travel, study abroad, working permits, and insurance. It also sells a number of helpful publications, including the *Student Travel Catalogue* ($1), and issues International Student Identity Cards (ISIC) for $10 to bonafide students.

For real budget travelers it's worth joining the **International Youth Hostel Federation (IYHF).** For information, write AYH (American Youth Hostels), P.O. Box 37613, Washington, DC 20013-7613 (☎ **202/783-6161**). Membership costs $25 annually, except that under-18s pay $10.

6 Alternative/Adventure Travel

Educational/Study Travel

Some travelers arrive in Greece searching for the new culture, not the ancient one, and find that a command of modern Greek is an essential clue to this thriving civilization. There are several good schools. The **Athens Center,** Odós Archimídous 48, 116 36 Athens (☎ **01/70-12-268**), comes highly recommended. You can write to the school for more information. Language courses (both modern and ancient Greek) run from three to ten weeks and are offered year round; they start at about $300.

Homestays

You should contact the Greek National Tourist Organization for information about rooms to let and about the few remaining "traditional settlements" where you can live in a Greek home. However, these accommodations are often used for rental income only, with the proprietors living in an adjoining space. The island of Lésvos (also called Mytilíni), in the northeast Aegean), has an organized program to place visitors in farmhouses in its villages. You can study cooking and farming with your host family. See Chapter 16 for more information.

Adventure/Wilderness

Some of you may not consider Greece the most adventurous destination in the world, but several tour operators and academic groups offer trips to the mainland and the islands for those looking for something different. One of our favorite expedition leaders, **Mountain Travel-Sobek Inc.,** often leads summer treks through the Pindos mountain range of Macedonia or through the Zagória region of northern Greece. Contact the agency at 6420 Fairmount Ave., El Cerrito, CA 94530 (☎ **510/527-8100** or toll free **800/227-2384**), for more information. Another fine expedition leader is **Exodus Expeditions,** 9 Weir Rd., London SW 12 OLT, United Kingdom (☎ **081/675-5550,** fax 081/673-0779). In 1994, Exodus offered several different treks through northern Greece, some including backpacking and camping; the treks ranged in price from £580 to £650.

Ornithologists and general nature buffs should contact **World Nature Tours, Inc.,** P.O. Box 693, Silver Spring, MD 20918 (☎ **301/593-2522**). They offer an annual birding trip to northern and northeastern Greece, in conjunction with the University of Thessaloníki, that sounds fascinating. In 1991 the 14-day package departed in June and cost $1,650.

Hikers should contact the **Appalachian Mountain Club,** 5 Joy St., Boston, MA 02108 (☎ **617/523-0636**), regarding the many members who organize and lead annual hiking and sailing trips to Greece. In 1992 the cost for two-week hiking, sailing, and sightseeing vacations around the country ranged from $2,300 to $2,500.

For information about trekking, windsurfing, and yachting vacations offered by tour operators within Greece, see our section on "Sports & Recreation" in Chapter 1. Also, contact your travel agent or the nearest branch of the Greek National Tourist Organization for more information on special-interest and adventure trips.

7 Getting There

Two common ways of getting to Greece are by ferry, from Italy, and by air. Airports greet the greatest number of visitors. Considering the multitude of price breaks, promotions, and charters available, traveling by air can be a real bargain. There is also inexpensive express-train and bus service from the major European cities to Athens and Thessaloníki, but the EurailPass is valid only on ferry service from Italy.

By Plane

Our strategy for securing the best airfare is to shop around. Most airlines offer an assortment of fares—first class, business class, and economy class; the lowest-priced regular airfare carries no special restrictions or requirements. Most airlines also offer heavily discounted promotional fares, which carry stringent requirements—

such as advance-purchase, minimum-stay, and cancellation penalties—but are an excellent value. Obviously, the prices quoted below are subject to change.

Lufthansa German Airlines ☎ **718/895-1277** or toll free **800/645-3880**) provides extensive service to Athens, Thessaloníki, and Crete from the United States, Canada, and points in Europe via their Frankfurt hub. Daily nonstop flights leave from 10 U.S. cities to Frankfurt, a convenient stopover for those touring elsewhere in Europe on their way to or from Greece. From Frankfurt, there are direct daily connections to Athens and Thessaloníki (three times weekly to Crete). During the high season, a round-trip, economy-class ticket from New York to Athens costs from $1,125, based on a 30-day advance purchase and a stay of 7 to 21 days in Greece. During the fall "shoulder" season and winter "low" season, fares drop by $150 to $225.

Lufthansa also provides exceptional service in its business-class and super-deluxe first-class sections; tickets in business class are $4,390 round-trip year round and in first class $7,785 round-trip. For schedule and fare information from other cities, contact Lufthansa or your travel agent. Most other major scheduled carriers, including **Delta** (☎ toll free **800/241-4141**), **TWA** (☎ toll free **800/892-4141**), **British Airways** (☎ toll free **800/247-9297**), and **KLM** (☎ toll free **800/882-4452**), provide service to Greece from North America. Fares are comparable to Lufthansa's, but these carriers provide fewer direct flights.

Olympic Airways ☎ **212/838-3600** or toll free **800/223-1226**) is the national carrier of Greece and has daily nonstop flights from New York to Athens, as well as twice-weekly flights from Boston to Athens. Olympic also offers weekly flights from Montréal and Toronto to Athens. During the high season, a round-trip economy ticket from New York to Athens costs from $1,070 to $1,291 (tickets must be purchased in advance, and there are other restrictions). Olympic offers lower fares in the low season. The airline's comfortable business class costs $1,284 each way throughout the year.

DOMESTIC AIR TRAVEL Olympic Airways is the primary carrier servicing domestic routes. Tickets for flights within Greece can be purchased outside Greece (in conjunction with your international ticket); fares, however, may be somewhat higher if the exchange rate fluctuates during your visit. To obtain a copy of Olympic's *Summer Timetable,* contact the airline's offices at 647 Fifth Ave., New York, NY 10022 or in Athens at Odós Óthonos 6, near Sýntagma Sq. (☎ **01/92-92-111**). See "Getting Around" below for sample airfares.

Southeast European Airways (SEEA), an affiliate of Virgin Atlantic, Odós Voulís 7, Athens (☎ **01/3310100-9,** fax 01/3250260, offers less-expensive fares to Corfu (Kérkyra), Mýkonos, Santoríni, Rhodes, Thessaloníki, Alexandroúpoli, and Iráklio (Crete), with plans for expanded service.

Cretan Airlines (☎ **081/288108,** fax 081/287975, has daily flights between Athens and Iráklio, as well as service linking Corfu, Thessaloníki, and Athens with Europe.

CHARTERS Every year different companies offer charter flights to Athens. Generally, you must book a seat a month or so in advance to get on a flight in June, July, or August; the prices depend on how many days you intend to stay, what day of the week you're leaving, and at what time of year you plan to go. **Homeric Tours** (☎ **212/753-1100** or toll free **800/223-5570**) is one of the established charter companies. In 1995 they charged as low as $549 for round-trip flights departing from New York in the winter and from $765 to $899 for round-trip flights during the spring and summer. They offer several flights a week from New York between June and September, but only one flight a week during the rest of the year. **Tourlite International** (☎ **212/599-3355** or toll free **800/272-7600**) charges similar rates for its flights from New York to Athens. Both companies offer low-cost tours, car rental, cruises, and hotel packages. Several British and German tour operators offer inexpensive but restrictive charter packages from points in Europe direct to many islands.

Warning: Since 1985 a long-ignored airline regulation regarding charter flights has been enforced by Greece. Charter flights are legally restricted to providing transportation at discount fares between two countries only. Tickets are not supposed to be used to facilitate travel to a third country; thus, those flying by charter between New York and Athens may not ferry over to Turkey during their holiday. We strongly urge all readers possessing charter air tickets to consult with their travel agency or charter airline before departure regarding the policy on travel to a third country.

BUCKET SHOPS The stringent rules and regulations governing airfares in the United States make us hesitant to recommend any of the so-called bucket shops that advertise discounted airfares in the Sunday travel section of many urban newspapers. However, if you're in London in search of some of those legendary cheap flights to the continent, try the **Travel Arcade** (☎ **01-734-5873**) at Triumph House, Suite 305, 189 Regent St. The company advertises in the back of *Time Out,* along with many other so-called bucket shops, but we have found this one to be particularly reliable and inexpensive.

FLIGHTS TO EUROPE Many people want to visit other parts of Europe, then arrive in Greece by train, bus, or ferry. **Icelandair** (☎ toll free **800/223-5500**) has long been a budget favorite. In 1994 the airline charged between $398 and $608 and during the low season and between $598 and $798 during the high season for a round-trip ticket from New York to Luxembourg. There are no restrictions on stays within Europe for up to one year, and (this may appeal to somebody out there) you're entitled to a stopover in Iceland! Icelandair normally has daily flights to Europe from New York, with additional departures from Baltimore/Washington, D.C., and Orlando, Fla.

It's also possible to fly to Europe on lower-cost airlines like **Virgin Atlantic** (☎ **212/242-1330** or toll free **800/862-8621**). Virgin Atlantic flies daily from New York (JFK Airport to London's Heathrow Airport) or from Newark Airport, in New

Frommer's Smart Traveler: Airfares

1. Keep calling the airlines; if you can wait till the very last minute and your flight is not fully booked, an airline may discount tickets to achieve full capacity.
2. Check the weekend travel section of your local newspaper, plus the Sunday edition of the *New York Times* or the *Los Angeles Times* for advertised discount fares and charter operators. London's *Time Out* also advertises many discount vendors or bucket shops.
3. Call around to consolidators (discount air-ticket sellers who profit by buying unused seats in bulk from various airlines) and be prepared to leave on short notice. Some recommended consolidators are **Council Charter** (☎ toll free **800/223-7402**), **Travac** (☎ toll free **800/872-8800**), and **Unitravel** (☎ toll free **800/325-2222**).

Jersey) for $499 to $599 round-trip, depending on the season. It also flies daily from Los Angeles, and several times weekly from San Francisco, Milwaukee Boston, Orlando, and Miami, to London. The airline often has substantially lower promotional fares.

Again, all these fares change with the wind. Check your newspaper or travel agent for current details and special fares.

By Train

A EurailPass offers unlimited travel in first or second class on trains throughout Europe. It also enables you to ride the ferryboat, on the Hellenic Mediterranean Lines (the Eurail correspondent company), that links Bríndisi, Italy, and the island of Corfu (Kérkyra) as well as the cities of Igoumenítsa and Pátra on the Ionian coast. Once in Greece, EurailPass holders can use the country's network of trains and buses that are part of the Railway Organization of Greece (**Organismós Sidirodrómon Elládos,** or **OSE**).

Contact the **Council Travel Service,** a subsidiary of the Council on International Educational Exchange, at its head office, 205 East 42d St., New York, NY 10017 (☎ **212/661-1450**), or your local university or travel agent for information on obtaining a EurailPass, which must be purchased in the United States. A special Eurail Youthpass (second class only, $578 for one month) is available for travelers under 26; call **Rail Europe** at **800/438-7245**. An InterrailPass can be obtained by European residents outside the United States for unlimited travel through Greece; the requirement, again, is that the purchaser should be under 26.

OSE's Venezia Express runs from Thessaloníki to Belgrade, Budapest, Kiev, and Moscow as well. Contact the railway organization's main office, at Odós Károlou 1, Athens (☎ **01/82-13-882**), for information. (**Note:** As of this writing, service has been suspended because of the conflict in Yugoslavia.)

By Bus

Those once indomitable overlanders **Magic Bus International** no longer operate their own bus service, but they still have an office in Athens, at Odós Filellínon 20, near Sýntagma Sq. (☎ **01/323-74-71,** fax 01/322-02-19), and book seats for a twice-weekly London-Athens express bus (and other nondomestic points) for about $150 one way; they also offer cheap airfares. If you're heading north, check fares also

Street Names

The Greek word for Street is *Odós.* The word for Avenue is *Leofóros,* abbreviated *Leof.* In this guide, the Greek words are used in full addresses.

Street names appear in the genitive case. Thus, *Leofóros Vassilíssis Sofías,* in Athens, should be read "Avenue of Queen Sophia." The words for Queen (*Vassílissa,* gen. *Vassilíssis*) and King (*Vassiléfs,* gen. *Vassiléos*) appear in the city's major thoroughfares abbreviated in both cases "*Vass.*"

The names of squares are kept in the nominative case in this guide. Thus, instead of *Platía Syntágmatos* (Square of the Constitution), the main square in Athens, we say simply Sýntagma Square. If you were to ask for directions to Sýntagma, you would be readily understood.

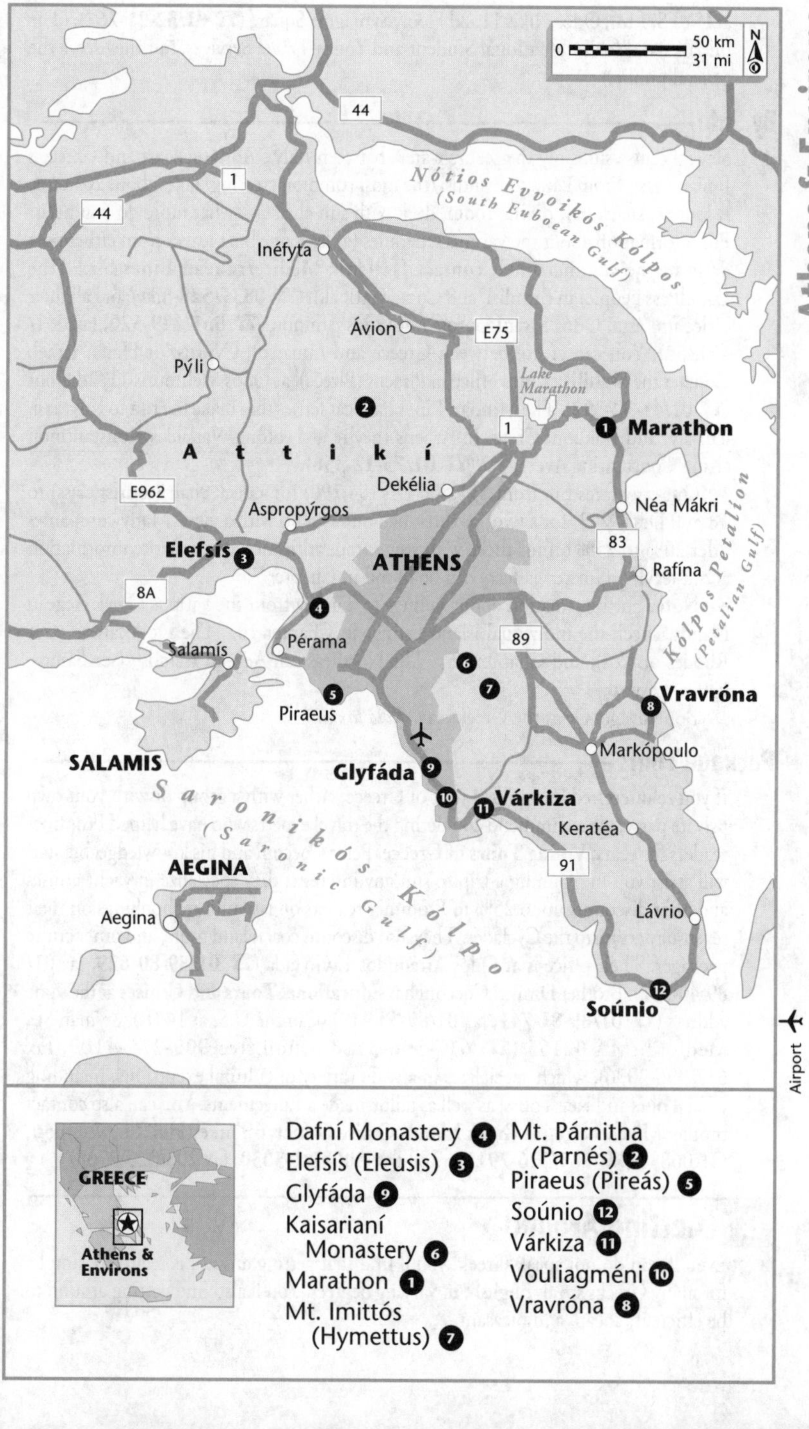
0
50 km
31 mi
N
44
1
44
Nótios Evvoikós Kólpos
(South Euboean Gulf)
Inéfyta
Ávion
E75
Pýli
Lake Marathon
2
1
1 Marathon
A t t i k í
E962
Dekélia
Aspropýrgos
Néa Mákri
83
Elefsís 3
ATHENS
Rafína
Kólpos Petalion
(Petalian Gulf)
8A
4
Pérama
89
Salamís
6
7
5
Piraeus
8 Vravróna
Markópoulo
SALAMIS
Glyfáda 9
10
11 Várkiza
Saronikós Kólpos
(Saronic Gulf)
Keratéa
AEGINA
91
Aegina
Lávrio
12
Soúnio
Airport
GREECE
Athens & Environs
Dafní Monastery 4
Elefsís (Eleusis) 3
Glyfáda 9
Kaisarianí Monastery 6
Marathon 1
Mt. Imittós (Hymettus) 7
Mt. Párnitha (Parnés) 2
Piraeus (Pireás) 5
Soúnio 12
Várkiza 11
Vouliagméni 10
Vravróna 8

at **ISYTS, Ltd.,** Odós Níkis 11, 2d Floor, Sýntagma Square (☎ **01/32-21-267**). (The initials stand for International Student and Youth Travel Services, but they serve the general public.)

By Ship

Several cruise ships ply the scenic waters between Italy's Adriatic coast and Greece's Ionian coast. From Pátra to Bríndisi (the most common crossing) takes about 20 hours. A lounge, snack bar, dining room, deck with sun chaises—what more do you need? For information about the various schedules (at least one boat leaves from either port daily in the summertime), contact **Hellenic Mediterranean Lines** S.r.l. (the EurailPass people) in Brindisi, at 8 Corso Garibaldi (☎ **0831/528-531**), or call their office in Pátra, Odós Sarantapórou 1 at Odós Athinón (☎ **061/429-520,** fax 061/421352). You can cruise between Greece and Limassol, Cyprus, or Haifa, Israel. Contact the **Stability Lines** office in Piraeus (Pireós), at Odós Sachtoúris 11, 2d Floor (☎ **01/41-32-392**). The **Minoan Lines** have car ferries that make the run to Kuşadasi, Turkey, and Iráklion, Crete. In Athens they're at Leofóros Vassiléos Konstantínou (King Constantine Avenue) 2 (☎ **01/75-12-356**).

One-way fares run from $11,500 Drs ($4,790) for a deck chair (tourist class) to 48,500 Drs ($202) for a two- or three-bed outer cabin with a view. Many companies offer 20% to 25% off for those with student identification cards. More information about leaving Greece via ferry can be found in Chapter 7.

Note: For information about sailings to Turkey from the various Greek Aegean islands, check the individual island listings in Chapter 10, "The Dodecanese" (see Rhodes or Kos), and Chapter 16, "The Northeastern Aegean Islands" (see Sámos, Chíos, Lésvos).

Bon voyage! Or as the Greeks say, *Kaló taxídi!*

Package Tours

If you're interested in a guided tour of Greece, either with a group or with your own private party, we recommend contacting the travel experts who have helped Frommer readers for years: **Viking Tours of Greece.** Peter Cocconi and his knowledgeable staff will assist you in planning a trip to suit any interests; they specialize in yacht cruises and offer discounts up to 25% to Frommer readers on last-minute bookings on their seven-day cruise to the Cyclades. They also discount coach land tours, and other cruise packages. Their office is at Odós Artemídos 1, Glyfada (☎ **01/89-80-829,** fax 01/89-40-952). Brother Dimitri Cocconi has **Educational Tours and Cruises** at the same address (☎ **01/89-81-741,** fax 01/89-55-419) or in the U.S. at 14 (R) Wyman St., Medford, MA 02155 (☎ **617-396-3188** or toll free **800-275-4109,** fax 617-396-3096), which specializes in a wide variety of cultural excursions, including Chat Tours and Key Tours, as well as tailor-made arrangements. You can also contact brother Mike Cocconi at **Greek Islands Cruise Center,** 6 Turkey Hill Rd., Westport, CT 06880 (☎ **203/226-7911** or toll free **800-341-3030,** fax 203/226-2765).

8 Getting Around

Even if you do not speak Greek, you'll find that getting around is relatively simple, for many Greeks speak English, in varying degrees. You'll also find getting around to be efficient, cheap, and pleasant.

By Plane

Airplanes make it possible to fly between islands directly (for example, Crete to Santoríni or Rhodes to Mýkonos) or hop between them via Athens. However, in the high season doing so is more of an ordeal than it should be; bumped passengers, delayed flights, and incorrectly written tickets are common. We suggest, therefore, that you make your reservation as far in advance as possible, and that you then confirm them within 24 hours of your flight. Be sure to get to the airport at least an hour before departure time.

Note that if you decide to change or cancel your reservation on a domestic flight, you may have to pay a penalty: as much as 30% if you change or cancel within 24 hours of departure time; as much as 50% if you do so within 12 hours of departure time.

Some sample airfares to the islands are listed below; all fares are one way from Athens:

Chíos	12,000 Drs ($50)
Lésvos (Mytilíni)	11,500 Drs ($48)
Crete (Iráklio) 12,200 Drs ($67.80)	19,440 Drs ($81)
Rhodes	24,000 Drs ($100)
Corfu	18,000 Drs ($75)
Skíathos 8800 Drs ($48.90)	13,920 Drs ($58)
Kos	18,700 Drs ($78)
Santoríni	17,750 Drs ($74)
Mýkonos	15,840 Drs ($66)
Páros	15,600 Drs ($65)

By Train

The slow but pleasant and efficient railroad system in Greece is under the care of the Railway Organization of Greece (OSE). The OSE maintains railroad and bus stations side by side in Athens. The main bus stations for travel to other parts of the country are Stathmós Laríssis (Lárissa Station) for northern Greece and Stathmós Peloponnísou (Peloponnese Station) for southern Greece. For most intra-Greece trains, you can purchase tickets a half hour before departure time from the ticket window at the train station (open 6am to 11pm). For international journeys or for information, contact any of the OSE offices, located at Odós Siná 6 (☎ **36-24-402**), off Akadimías St. near Omónia Sq.; at Odós Károlou 1 (☎ **52-22-491**), near Omónia Sq.; and at Odós Filellínon 17 (☎ **32-36-747**), Sýntagma Sq. Tickets can be purchased for all international buses and domestic or international rail trips. All offices are open from 8:30am to 6pm Monday through Saturday.

By Bus

Public buses are a cheap and easy way to travel around Greece. In Athens and other cities, kiosk news vendors sell tickets and are a good source of **local bus** information. Have a ticket ready to cancel when you hop on.

Long-distance buses usually leave from one of the convenient central stations; check with the Greek National Tourist Organization for current schedules. (**Note:** Inside Greece itself, the Greek National Tourist Organization is known simply as the Greek Tourist Organization, *Ellinikós Organismós Tourismoú*, abbreviated EOT.) EurailPass holders are entitled to use the OSE train network free of charge, but may find sometimes that a bus belonging to KTEL, the privately run bus network, is worth the drachmas for its more direct and convenient service. Make sure you know the correct pronunciation of your destination (a friend of ours who sought to buy a ticket to Mycenae, pronouncing it *Maïsíne* instead of *Mikíne,* was sent by mistake to the town of Messíni, at the southern end of the Peloponnese); then try to sit near the driver, so that he can tell you when to get off. Fares are usually paid to the ticket collector on board. Express buses from major centers (Athens, Pátra, Thessaloníki) usually sell reserved seat tickets for long trips; determine your seat and the bus's comfort (is it air-conditioned?) before you pay for a ticket! Buses can be noisy, hot, crowded, and smokey, but they're usually fun.

By Car

CAR RENTALS Renting a car in Greece is an extremely expensive proposition, but one that makes sightseeing much easier and more pleasurable. Try to pick up other tourists to car-pool and share expenses. Driving can be very adventurous; Greece has the highest accident rate in Europe. So, drive cautiously and make sure you've purchased the maximum insurance plan available. Most car-rental companies require that drivers have a valid driver's license, are at least 21 years old (24 years old for some models), and leave a cash deposit if they don't have a major credit card.

The major rental companies in Athens are: **Interrent Europcar** (☎ **92-33-452,** fax 92-21-440), **HellasCars** (☎ **92-35-353,** fax 92-35-397), **Hertz** (☎ **92-20-102,** fax 93-33-970), **Avis** (☎ **32-24-951,** fax 32-30-811), and **Budget** through its licensees (☎ **92-14-771,** fax 92-24-444); all have several offices throughout the mainland and the islands and will book cars in advance. The smaller, Greek-owned companies tend to have lower rates. **Viking Tours** (☎ **89-80-879**) and many hotels can also arrange car rentals at discount rates. Daily rates start at $55, plus 36¢ per kilometer; weekly rates start at $515, with unlimited mileage for the smallest Suzuki. Remember that gas (*venzína,* sold by the liter) costs almost $3 per gallon, and that you can save by booking at home in advance.

DRIVING RULES An international driver's license is recommended, but all valid U.S., Canadian, European, and Australian licenses will be accepted for one year after your arrival in Greece. To obtain an international driver's license, in the United States apply to the **American Automobile Association (AAA);** you must provide two 2-by-2-inch photographs, a photocopy of your state driver's license, and a $10 fee. For a list of the AAA's local branches, contact its national headquarters at 100 AAA Drive, Heathrow, FL 32746 (☎ toll free **800/AAA-HELP**). Canadians can get the address of the nearest branch of the **Canadian Automobile Club** by calling its national office (☎ toll free **800/336-HELP**).

The Greek Automobile and Touring Club, **ELPA,** can extend your license. It will also provide you with maps and information.

Two important telephone numbers to bear in mind are **104** for **emergency road service** and **171** for **tourist information.**

By Taxi

Our least favorite mode of transportation is the taxi. In Athens taxis are virtually impossible to find. Either they have an odd number on a day when only even numbers are allowed to enter certain areas, or they're already carrying a local who's not going in your direction (group rides are sanctioned because of a taxi shortage; each passenger pays the difference between the final meter reading and the reading when he or she entered); or, if empty, they refuse to pick you up when they realize you're a tourist (it's usually because they have so many communication problems with them!). On the islands, they're no better.

Beware of the following typical taxi tricks:

- Some taxi drivers will pick up a group of tourists and insist (illegally) that every passenger pay the full metered fare.
- Some taxi meters include a decimal point for the obsolete *leptó* ($^1/_{100}$ of a drachma), and drivers often don't speak up when unwitting tourists pay 12,000 Drs instead of 1,200 Drs for their ride.
- Late at night, taxis at airports, ferry piers, and train and bus stations refuse to use their meters and demand a flat rate, usually 100% to 300% higher than normal.
- Taxis at airports often overcharge tourists for the nominal additional fees (see Chapter 3, "Athens," section 2, "Getting Around," for more information.)
- Drivers often adjust their meter, so that it counts at twice the speed, even though your destination is not outside the city limits, where this practice is authorized. Check the small window to the right of the drachma display on the face of the meter; it should read "1" in town and "2" only if you're leaving the city limits.
- Another trick is when the driver tells you the hotel you want to go to is fully booked and he knows another with a room (where he can get a commission).

Outside Athens, the government has tried to set a standard rate for taxis, which are the primary mode of transport for older tourists heading to the islands' more suburban resorts. Rates are 75 Drs per km for a one-way fare and 125 Drs per km for someone going round-trip, within a 280-km radius. For example, to visit an ancient temple 10 km outside of Réthymno, Crete, would cost 750 Drs ($3.15) one way or 1,250 Drs ($5.20), plus 750 Drs ($3.15) per hour waiting time if the taxi waited to bring you back to Réthymno.

Now that you've gotten the picture, let us say that New York cabbies may be worse, that taxi rides are usually cheap anyway, and that there are some wonderful Greek drivers filled with good-natured advice, news, and gossip. Try to determine from a local what the approximate fare should be before entering a taxi, so that you'll have some basis for judgment—we want to warn you, not make you totally paranoid.

By Ferry

Most readers will sample the ferryboats, either the large ships leaving from Piraeus and other ports or the smaller, interisland boats. What can we say? They're unreliable, and subject to weather and personal calamities; they're also fun and a great way to meet people. The best way to plan your island itinerary is to get a map from the National Tourist Organization (EOT), that indicates by dotted lines most of the routes between islands, and their weekly schedule of departures from Piraeus (the major port) and Rafína (a nearby Attica port that services the Cyclades more quickly and more cheaply than Piraeus). Remember that these ferries run less frequently between September and May; plan your vacation time accordingly. Also, every travel agent sells tickets for different lines. Shop around for prices and ask to see a photo of your vessel when traveling between islands; a larger ship makes a big difference in rough seas.

Arrive at least one hour before departure time (interisland boats often depart before their scheduled time) to purchase tickets from dockside agents. In Athens you can purchase ferryboat tickets and book cabins (great fun!) on night ferries in advance at **Galaxy Travel Bureau,** Odós Voulís 35, at Apóllonos, Sýntagma Square (☎ **01/32-29-761,** fax 32-29-538); it's open daily except Sunday.

HellasTours, a Thomas Cook representative, at Odós Karagheórghi tís Servías 4, Sýntagma Square (☎ **32-20-005,** fax 32-33-487) is a full-service agency that changes money without commission for its clients. The nearby **Summertime Tours,** in the arcade at Odós Karagheórghi tís Servías 10 (☎ **32-34-176**), offers discounts on its services.

In each chapter on an island group, we've tried to indicate the frequency and variety of sailings and have suggested that you talk to the local tourist office or port authority or to travel agents for schedule information. **Note:** Those taking ferries from the Dodecanese Islands to Turkey will need to submit their passport and payment one day in advance of departure.

Here are sample tourist-class fares from Piraeus (Pireás) to some **Aegean** points. The embarkation tax and value-added tax (VAT) will add a few hundred drachmas for all classes. Fares should be about 10% less in the low season.

Tourist-Class Fares from Piraeus

Destination	Fare
Iráklio (Crete)	5,511 Drs ($23)
Rhodes	7,320 Drs ($30.50)
Mýkonos	3,370 Drs ($14)
Sámos	5,060 Drs ($21)
Íos	4,300 Drs ($18)
Náxos	3,440 Drs ($14.30)
Pátmos	5,300 Drs ($22)
Monemvassiá (Peloponnese)	3,350 Drs ($14)
Santoríni	4,300 Drs ($18)
Lésvos (Mytilíni)	5,050 Drs ($20)
Kos	6,600 Drs ($27.50)

From Vólos, in central Greece, to the nearby Aegean island of Skíathos, the fare is 4,260 Drs ($17.75).

In the **Ionian,** some sample fares are: from Igoumenítsa to Corfu, 840 Drs ($3.50) from Pátra to Kefalonía, 2,885 Drs ($12).

HYDROFOILS

Hydrofoils are now a basic, but expensive, part of the Greek sea scene. They can save you a great deal of time (they're about twice as fast as ferries) and seasickness. They currently service the Sporades, the Cyclades, Crete, the Dodecanese, the Saronic Gulf islands, and some coastal cities in the Peloponnese (see relevant chapters for more information).

By Moped

Mopeds are probably the most common form of private tourist transportation. They're a fun, practical, and cheap way (about $15 to $30 per day) to sightsee in the islands. Before renting one, though, make sure you feel comfortable about riding along steep, sand- or gravel-strewn roads where cars know no speed limit. Since no tourist ever accepts a helmet from the few vendors who offer one (you could be the exception!), choose a slower, easier-to-balance moped rather than a small 125cc motorcycle. Organize your possessions so that luggage straps are secure. And *take a close look at your moped* before driving off. Check especially for faulty brakes. Also, since many tourists have accidents and fail to report them to the rental shops, their successors end up with bent frames that make steering and balancing the bikes difficult and unpredictable.

9 Suggested Itineraries

The idea of including suggested itineraries is to recommend certain destinations in a reasonable order. You may wish to depart from these plans, however, to satisfy your own interests, needs, and desires.

Searching for Greekness

We've become increasingly frustrated with the effects of industrial tourism, represented by the blight of group-oriented tour companies on the Greek landscape. To cater to these groups, what were once genuinely Greek destinations have become international-style apartment towns, always near a beach, peppered with bars, discos, and motorcycle rental shops. The traditions and customs that we seek have largely disappeared in these areas, which are unfortunately the very sites that most tourists are eager to visit. They hope to find the Greece that they've always imagined, but the reality is usually disappointing.

To help those, therefore, who wish to discover something more than the beach/disco/bar version, we have taken a new look at Greece. Kyle calls this look a "search for Greekness."

Our tour begins in Rafína, a port near Athens. Piraeus can be a difficult and intimidating place, so why not leave from a more congenial town? The first stop is the Cycladic islands, but instead of visiting Mýkonos, Páros, and Santoríni, we suggest touring the less-developed and less-known islands of Tínos, Náxos, Sífnos, and Folégandros. There, you'll find various aspects of contemporary Greek culture that still feel authentic. As with all of these destinations, we suggest that you read about them in the appropriate chapters to see if they meet your ideas about traveling through Greece. Crete, an island that has undergone some of the heaviest development in the last few years, is worth a visit for Iráklio (to see the archeological museum and nearby Knossós), the mountain village of Spíli, and Chaniá in the west. A journey through the Dodecanese usually entails a visit to Rhodes and Kos, ending in the Northeast Aegean island of Sámos. On the searching-for-Greekness route, we suggest visiting Sými and Pátmos, and if you can make it, Kárpathos. On Sámos visit the old town in Vathí and the village of Manolátes, then head for Chíos or northern Lésvos (did you know that you can cross to Turkey from these islands?). In the Sporades, we like northern Skópelos (around Glóssa) and especially the island of Skýros; in other words, consider passing up a stay on Skíathos.

The mainland of Greece, particularly the north, is the country's least explored and most ethnically compelling region. Among our favorite areas are the monasteries on Mt. Áthos (unfortunately, for men only), Kastoriá, and north to the Albanian border; the lovely rural mountain villages of Epirus; the Zagoria region; the outcrop-topped monasteries of Metéora and across the mainland to Mt. Pílio. No trip to Greece should exclude a visit to Delphi and the Peloponnese peninsula; however, after visiting the archeological sites, why not head west to Andrítsena or south to the Máni (southern Peloponnese). Finally, if you have the time to explore the Ionian islands, instead of touring Corfu, consider a minicruise from Kefalonía to Ithaca and Páxos (including a beach stop on Antipáxos). We're confident that if you explore these areas you'll be amply rewarded with an exciting journey.

Itinerary Choices

If You Have One Week

Since most travelers begin their trip in Athens, explore the fascinating capital first. The main places to see are the Acropolis, National Archeological Museum, Museum of Cycladic and Ancient Greek Art, and Plaka, the city's lively, characteristic quarter. Try to fit in a day trip to the temple of Poseidon at Soúnio, at the tip of Attica. On the fourth day, head west to the Peloponnese to ancient Corinth, the theater at Epidaurus (especially during the summer, when the theater offers a full schedule of classical Greek plays), the extensive excavations at Mycenae, south to beautiful Nafplio, then west to the elegant museum and site at Olympia. If you still have the energy (or, in lieu of the Peloponnese, if you only have the stomach for one archeological site) head north to Greece's premier destination, Delphi. All these moves are more easily accomplished by joining a group tour.

If You Have Two Weeks

Follow our itinerary for the first week (above). The second week should be spent island hopping. It's much better to limit your travels to one particular island group, so as to ease potential transportation problems.

The two most varied and easily accessible island groups are the Cyclades and the Sporades. Consider the Cyclades: maybe Mýkonos (and by all means Délos), Páros, and Santoríni, with an excellent combination of archeological sites, fine beaches, a sophisticated resort and shopping scene, and classic island architecture. The best of the Sporades include Skíathos, Skópelos, and Skýros, all three of which are slightly less crowded and less expensive, but with sensational beaches and a more traditional Greek life-style (especially on Skýros).

If You Have Three Weeks

You can follow the two-week itinerary above and spend your third week exploring northern Greece (particularly for hikers and nature buffs) or moving on to lesser-known island groups (see "Searching for Greekness" above).

THEMED CHOICES

GREEK ARCHEOLOGY These destinations concentrate on archeological excavations, museums, and medieval cities. This cross-country trip will take between three weeks and one month.

Start at Athens (Acropolis, National Archeology Museum, Museum of Cycladic and Ancient Greek Art, Soúnio, Dafní, and Aégina). Head east to the Cyclades: Mýkonos (Délos and Maritime Museum), Ándros (Museum of Modern Art and Archeological Museum of Ándros), Santoríni (Akrotíri).
South to Crete Iráklio (Knossós and Archeology Museum).
East to the Dodecanese Rhodes (Líndos), Kos (Asklepiíon), Pátmos (Chóra).
North to the northeast Aegean islands Sámos (Eupalinius Tunnel, the Heraion, and the Archeology Museum), Lésvos (Theóphilos Museum).
North, back to the mainland Thessaloníki (Archeology Museum, walking tour of churches, Philippi, Vérgina), Metéora.
South to the Peloponnese Olympia (optional trip to Vássae and Místra if traveling by car), Mycenae, Epidaurus, ancient Corinth.
North to central Greece Delphi (and Óssios Loukás).
Return to Athens.

BEACH AND ISLAND HOPPING Instead of giving you an itinerary here, we'll mention some of our favorite beaches and party spots, not in any particular order. We love the many beaches on Mýkonos, Milópotas Beach on Íos, Mátala on Crete, the sandy strips of southeastern Kos, Embório on Chíos, several beaches on Skíathos, the island of Antipáxos, Mýrtos on Kefalonía, and the newly accessible beaches on Lefkáda. There are many other smaller beaches in more remote locations, but those mentioned above are all of sufficient quality to warrant a special visit if you're longing for a place in the sun.

If you want to escape the hordes of summer tourists, there are a few out-of-the-way locations where you're bound to find that empty beach you've dreamed about or that perfect Greek fishing village that seems to have disappeared. Try the Cyclades (especially the western Cyclades, including Sífnos and Folégandros) and Sporades (northern Skópelos, Alónissos, and Skýros). We particularly enjoy the Dodecanese and the Ionian islands. In the Dodecanese, can one journey not only to a large resort island like Rhodes or Kos with its ancient ruins, but also to such smaller gems as Sými and Pátmos. The Ionians offer Corfu, but more intrepid island hoppers make stops on Páxos, Antipáxos, and Kefalonía.

A note on seasickness: This unpleasant subject is not often discussed, but it is very much a part of island hopping, particularly in May and August when seas can be rough. Consult a doctor, who may prescribe medication, possibly a new patch called Transderm-Scop. If you're reading this while bobbing around on a ferry boat: Don't stay inside (unless there's a threat of being washed overboard!); get fresh air; focus on the horizon (the only unmoving thing around); and breathe deeply. If you haven't gotten sick yet, eat dry soda crackers and don't drink fluids. A doctor friend from Harvard suggests taking a Dramamine or Bonine the night before a cruise; this technique is supposed to work without making you drowsy.

10 Enjoying Greece on a Budget

The $45-a-Day Budget

We've tried hard in this book to keep costs down for the budget traveler. By $45 a day we mean spending that much per person for food and lodging—about $25 a hotel room (usually either in a Class C or D hotel or in a first-class pension, with private toilet/shower facilities plus continental breakfast) and about $20 a day for three meals (dining in the Greek style: a big meal at midday, a snack about 6pm, and a light supper). You won't live like a jet-setter on this sum, but you can be quite comfortable. Needless to say, if you insist on doing things American style, it will cost you more.

The limit of $45 a day does not cover transportation, admission to museums or historic sites, souvenirs for your friends back home, a night out to check out the local after-dark activities, and so on. However, we have listed the best budget choices for transportation, sightseeing, shopping, nightlife, and excursions, so that in these categories, too, you'll get the most for your drachmas.

There are a few caveats regarding the $45-a-day figure. Individual travelers should expect to spend approximately $55 to $60 a day for the same accommodations and dining suggestions that couples follow. If you plan to travel to the more upscale islands, such as Corfu, Mýkonos, Santoríni, Rhodes, and Crete, prices are likely to be higher than in the less-developed destinations; again, consider increasing your budget to $50 or $55 a day per person. If you want to visit Greece on the cheap, it's best to plan your journey during spring or fall, or totally off-season in winter (see "Seasonal & Other Discounts" below).

Saving Money on Accommodations

In Greece, particularly during the high season (mid-June to mid-September), single travelers are often forced to pay the same hotel rate as two do. Therefore, our $45-a-day formula works best for two, three, or more people traveling together. Couples may even find that by taking the "single" room with a matrimonial (double) bed they can save over the "double" twin-bed rate. Our prices are always high-season rates, unless otherwise noted.

Seasonal & Other Discounts

You can really save by traveling during the months other than June through September, but be aware that on most of the islands nearly all the hotels and restaurants are open only from late April/early May to late September/late October.

From early May to the beginning of July, you can save from 20% to 45% over high-season room rates, and from the beginning of September till the autumn closing you can usually save at least 20%. Greece is much more beautiful in the spring or fall, and much less crowded than during the hysterically busy months of July and August (August is the worst). The weather is cooler, more temperate, and somewhat more stable, and the strong northern *meltémi* winds are not blowing. Each year, as more and more people discover this about the climate, the crowds reach their favorite islands earlier in the season. You'll find that at the most popular resorts (Mýkonos, Santoríni, Rhodes, Corfu, Crete) hoteliers have begun to develop a "shoulder," or middle, season, when they feel they can charge a little more for their rooms because of the increased demand. Nevertheless, it's still the best time to visit, and the season for which we'd urge you to plan your trip.

Other Money-saving Strategies

A trend on the islands has been to bypass Greek government regulations (and restrictions on new hotel construction) by putting up small "apartment" buildings along the coast. These usually consist of studio and one-bedroom apartments, with fully stocked minikitchens, linens, and periodic maid service. They have become popular with Europeans, who frequently travel with their families and prefer to stay on one island for their two- or three-week vacation. As rooms to let and older family hostels are being modernized, Greek owners opt for reception-free apartments where they don't have to bother manning a switchboard or serving breakfast. We have noted some of the better-value apartments where relevant; most of them, however, are booked by local travel agents and you cannot make a reservation by writing or calling.

Our reviews generally concentrate on the small hotels and pensions that we prefer, so a brief note about them is in order. First, Greece is not a "fancy" place; in fact, its elegant style is based on simplicity and sparseness of design. Government ratings (deluxe and Class A, B, C, D, and E hotels or first-, second-, and third-class pensions) and loose price controls are based on facilities, size of rooms, number of bureaus, and the like, not on whether there are carpets, chandeliers, and VCRs in each room. Rooms to let in private homes, or guesthouses, though licensed, are not rated.

We have concentrated on reviewing the Class C and D hotels and first-class pensions (which generally run $30 to $70 for a double, often with continental breakfast, in the high season) but have thrown in a Class A or B splurge (with all the amenities of an American hotel) when we felt you'd treat yourself like royalty for only a lord's ransom.

The majority of newer hotels are nondescript Class C ones, usually with an elevator, private bathrooms, sometimes air conditioning (for an extra fee), telephones, a TV lounge/bar, and a breakfast room. To us the best pensions are older, converted mansions, villas, or restored portside hotels with frescoed ceilings, winding staircases, wrought-iron balconies, and marble floors. (Living with a Greek family is becoming a thing of the past, except in the less-visited inland villages.) We rank cleanliness and character at the top; of lesser concern is the size of the room and whether it has a bathroom (you'll pay much less for a room that has only a sink, with a toilet/shower directly across the hall).

If you intend to travel to any of the popular island resorts during the high season, you should make reservations as far in advance as possible. You can write directly to any of the hotels we recommend, or you can write to the Hellenic Chamber of Hotels, Odós Stadíou 24, 10564 Athens, Greece (☎ **32-21-410** or **32-37-193,** fax 01/32-25-449). The chamber will expedite your reservation, for a 10% commission; it can also suggest alternative accommodations in a similar category if your first choice is not available. If you're traveling without reservations, the local tourist office, tourist police, or travel agents may help you find a hotel or private room upon arrival.

Fast Facts: Greece

Business Hours The Greek system of business hours takes some acclimatization, but once you've been there awhile, you'll want to take it home. The typical six-day week for most vendors and service businesses consists of the following hours: Monday and Wednesday, 8:30am to 3pm; Tuesday, Thursday, and Friday, 8:30am to 2:30pm, then again 5 to 8:30pm; Saturday, 8:30am to 3:30pm. The afternoons are for siestas. Many businesses catering to tourists forgo the nap and have expanded hours, from 8am to 10pm daily. Most government offices are open Monday through Friday, 8am to 3pm, and are closed Saturday and Sunday. We suggest that you call ahead to check the hours of any business you will be dealing with.

Climate See "When to Go" in this chapter.

Crime See "Safety" below.

Currency See "Information, Entry Requirements & Money" in this chapter.

Customs See "Information, Entry Requirements & Money" in this chapter.

Documents Required See "Information, Entry Requirements & Money" in this chapter.

Driving Rules See "Getting Around" in this chapter.

Drugstores Drugstores (*farmakía,* singular *farmakío*), your first source of medical help, are found all over Greece; they rotate their schedules so that a drugstore is almost always open in each neighborhood. Check with your hotel for one nearest you.

Electricity Electric current in Greece carries 220 volts at 50 cycles. Some of the larger, deluxe hotels have 110 volt outlets in the bathrooms for electric shavers.

Embassies and Consulates See "Fast Facts: Athens" in Chapter 3.

Emergencies See "Police" below.

Film See "Photographic Needs" below.

Holidays See "When to Go" in this chapter.

Information See "Information, Entry Requirements & Money" in this chapter, as well as individual city chapters for local tourist information offices.

Language Greek is one of the oldest languages in the world and belongs, as does English, to the Indo-European family of languages. Ancient Greek had three main dialects: Ionian (spoken in Asia Minor and on many of the Aegean islands), Attic (spoken mostly in Athens), and Doric (spoken in Sparta and other cities in the Peloponnese). In the time of Alexander the Great, Attic became the dominant dialect, and from it, later, derived an idiom known as *koiné,* which served for many centuries as a "common" language in the eastern Mediterranean region and what is now the Middle East. (The New Testament, for example, was written in *koiné.*) From it developed modern Greek, which retains much of the vocabulary of ancient Greek but differs from it in grammar and pronunciation. Modern Greek has absorbed many foreign words—Turkish, Italian, Slavic, and now English—and has itself contributed to many other languages; some 15% of English words (largely scientific) are of Greek origin.

Although Greek has a different alphabet, it is not difficult to pronounce (see Appendix A, "Basic Greek Vocabulary"). You may want to learn a little Greek before your trip. There are several excellent phrasebooks, such as Berlitz's *Greek for Travellers,* which comes with an audiocassette. Don't be shy, once you get to Greece, about using the expressions you have learned; your effort alone, however faltering, will draw an appreciative response.

Laundry All the big cities and major island resorts have small commercial laundries where your clothes can be done, at a reasonable rate, within 48 hours. A few resorts even have self-service *lavomatiques,* with several coin-operated washers and dryers. If you're on the go as much as we are, bring maintenance-free cottons and hand wash them; things dry quickly in the Greek sun.

Mail As in most countries, you can receive mail addressed to you, c/o Poste Restante, General Post Office, City (or Town), Island (or Province), Greece. You will need a passport to claim your mail. American Express card holders can receive mail for a nominal fee at any American Express office or agent throughout Greece.

Measurements Greece uses the metric system (see Appendix C, "Metric System"). It also, however, has an additional unit of weight—the oke (*oká*), which is equal to about 2.8 pounds.

Passports See "Information, Entry Requirements and Money" in this chapter.

Photographic Needs Cameras, accessories, and film are readily available, though more expensive, in Greece. A 36-exposure roll of Kodacolor Gold (100 ASA) costs about 2,000 Drs ($8.40).

Police Wherever you are in Greece, first contact the local tourist police (local phone numbers are noted in each chapter) for assistance with tourist information, crime reports, or medical emergencies. There will usually be an English-speaking officer available. If not, contact the local police.

Restrooms Let's start with Greek toilets. For the most part, they're clean and they work, even in public parks and museums. Carry tissues with you, and pay attention to the signs you see everywhere: don't try to flush the tissues down the toilet—put them in the bin, as the signs ask. Even if there's no sign, don't put any paper products in the toilets (the old, narrow pipes can't cope!). Believe us, it's much easier to find a trash bin than to explain in Greek that the toilet has just flooded.

With a little patience you'll soon learn to use and appreciate a "Danish" shower. (Believe those signs saying "Greece is going dry." Pátmos has to have its water shipped in from Sámos; on Santoríni it's trucked from the springs at Kamáres; and in even the most fortunate places it's scarce and expensive.) Grasp the nozzle in one hand and turn the water on long enough for it to get warm and to soak yourself, then turn it off while you lather up; turn it back on to rinse. Standing or sitting with your back to the corner and directing the spray carefully will minimize the water in the rest of the bathroom when there's no curtain. (Yes, we know it doesn't sound like a lot of fun, but you can find luxury elsewhere, and you'll be conserving a precious resource.)

Safety Crime is not a serious problem in Greece. Pickpocketing and purse snatching, however, do occur in tourist areas. Wear a moneybelt or place your wallet in an inside pocket. Don't sling your camera or purse over your shoulder; instead, wear the strap diagonally across your body. Every society has its criminals; just be aware and alert at all times, even in the most heavily touristed areas.

Service Charge and Tax Unless otherwise noted, all hotel prices include a service charge, usually 12%, and tax; the latter consists of a 6% value-added tax, or VAT, and a 4.5% community tax. In most restaurants, a 13% service charge is added, along with an 8% VAT (in Athens, there is also a 5% city food tax). Rental-car rates are charged an 18% VAT.

Telephones Pay telephones require a 10-Dr coin. After depositing the coin, you'll hear an irregular beeping sound. That's your dial tone. A regular beeping sound indicates that the line is busy. You'll notice that the full-length telephone booths come in different colors: The silver-and-blue ones are for local calls, and the silver-and-orange ones are for long-distance calls (outside Athens and international). Telephones using the new card-phone system are becoming increasingly common; cards can be purchased at OTE (see below) and news kiosks. (Kiosks usually still let you use their telephone for 20 Drs and in remote areas may even let you make a long-distance call.)

Long-distance calls, whether within Greece or international ones, can be made from almost any hotel, but you'll find that the surcharges add between 50% and 100% to your telephone bill. The alternative is to make your calls from any of the conveniently located centers of the national telephone system, OTE (Organismós Tilepikinonión Elládos, or Telecommunications Organization of Greece). At OTE centers, you can dial long-distance calls directly and pay for them in cash; you can also make collect calls, but they may require up to an hour's wait, as may credit-card calls.

Be warned: The cost of a long-distance call can be high, even at OTE. On our last visit, a call to the United States cost 750 Drs ($3.15) per minute. But there is an alternative: If you have a **telephone credit card** from AT&T, MCI, or Sprint, you can access that company's international network and have your calls billed directly to your card. For AT&T service dial **00800-1311;** for MCI service dial **00800-1211;** for Sprint dial **00800-1411.** When you use your credit card, you can reduce the cost of calling home by more than 50%; a service charge, however, is attached by the telephone company to each call. You can make credit-card calls from any OTE center for a small fee or from your hotel for no fee. The larger OTE centers usually have a fairly recent collection of international telephone books.

In making long-distance calls, you must use the appropriate **area codes.** Within Greece, area codes always begin with a zero. In our guide, we've included the area codes of all accommodations, except those in Athens; to call a number in Athens from outside the city, use the area code **01**. To make a call to the United States, first dial the country code **001,** then dial the local area code and the number itself.

Time Greece is two hours ahead of Greenwich mean time. With reference to North American time zones, it is ahead seven hours of eastern standard time, eight hours of central standard time, nine hours of mountain standard time, and ten hours of Pacific standard time.

In Greece the European system of a 24-hour clock is used officially, so that, for example, noon is 1200, 4pm is 1600, and 11pm is 2300. Popularly, however, expressions such as "2 in the afternoon" and "8 at night" are used.

Tipping A 10%–15% service charge is included in most restaurant bills and is reflected in the two columns of prices next to menu items. Nevertheless, it's customary to leave an additional 5%–10% for the waiter. Often, on small bills, change up to the nearest 100 Drs is left. This rule applies to taxi fares as well. (Greeks, by the way, do not usually tip taxi drivers, but tourists are expected to do so.) Small tips to chambermaids and porters (200–500 Drs) are always appreciated.

Tourist Offices See "Information, Entry Requirements & Money" in this chapter and also discussions of specific cities in other chapters.

Visas See "Information, Entry Requirements & Money" in this chapter.

3

Athens

ATHENS IS UNIQUE AMONG THE GREAT CAPITALS OF EUROPE. TO SEE THE GOLDEN marble columns of the Parthenon crowning the rocky slope of the Acropolis is an awe-inspiring experience that has brought travelers to this capital of the ancient world for more than 2,000 years. Yet Athens's renown as the birthplace of democracy and its rich store of antiquity's finest art and architecture represent just two aspects of this fascinating city. Side by side with the remnants of the great Classical Age, today's visitors find intriguing evidence of Athens's Byzantine heritage in its tiny, old churches and in its bustling Eastern-style markets. And a reminder of the centuries of Turkish rule are the city's many coffeehouses, exuding the pungent aroma of what we know as Turkish coffee but the Greeks call Greek coffee. Put all this in the midst of a sprawling, fast-growing city of four million people and you'll have some idea of the vibrancy and excitement that infuse contemporary Athens.

Some big-city problems have come to Athens in recent years. Congestion is one, aggravated by a recent influx of Eastern European refugees, many of them wandering the city's streets in search of lodging and work. Traffic and noise are another—the city has more than a million automobiles. A third problem—which stubbornly persists despite efforts by one government after another to solve it—is pollution. The city's noxious smog, called *néfos* by the Athenians, clouds the air on many days, especially during the summer.

Yet, serious as these problems are, they have not dampened the energy and vibrancy of Athens, which is at its liveliest when other cities are fast asleep—early in the morning and late at night. The shops and markets and vegetable stalls, particularly those in Monastiráki and around Omónia Square, open almost at the crack of dawn. By 8am traffic is already heavy, with taxis weaving in and out of the paths of tethered trolley buses, which are filled with Athenians on their way to work, as the sound of car horns blaring impatiently signals the start of another day. The cafés downtown are abuzz with activity as bleary-eyed office workers jostle each other for a quick cup of coffee while scanning their favorite newspaper for the latest political gossip.

At 2 or 3pm most businesses shut their doors for the officially sanctioned siesta, a period of rest and fortification, especially during the summer, at the height of the midday heat. The whole city, it seems, heads home for lunch (the biggest meal of the day) and an hour or two of sleep.

Beginning around 9 or 10pm, the city gets its second wind. Crowds pour into Athens's tavernas, restaurants, and bars, filling them until well past midnight. Sometime around 2am, Athenians wander home for a few hours of shut-eye before they begin anew.

IMPRESSIONS

Athens, the eye of Greece, mother of arts and eloquence.
—Milton, *Paradise Regained*, 1671

In Athens I saw . . . a spirit . . . which a thousand years of misery had not squelched.
—Henry Miller, *The Air-Conditioned Nightmare*, 1945

Athens leaves me cool.
—Henry Adams, 1898

What's Special About Athens

Architecture

- The Parthenon on the Acropolis, one of the architectural highlights of the world.
- The Agora, the ancient marketplace, whose ruins lie in the shadow of the Parthenon.
- Temple of the Olympian Zeus and Hadrian's Arch, two relics of ancient architecture standing alone near Sýntagma Square.
- The Herod Atticus Odeum, a gem of a theater dating from the 2d century A.D., still used for concerts and theatrical productions.

Museums

- The National Archeological Museum, with endless rooms filled with treasures of antiquity.
- The Museum of Cycladic and Ancient Greek Art, with its stunning collection of Cycladic statuary.

Garden

- The National Garden, in the heart of the city, with miles of footpaths and a small zoo.

Neighborhoods

- Pláka, one of the oldest neighborhoods in the city, now a warren of shops, bars, and restaurants.
- Anafiótika, a neighborhood in the upper back streets of Pláka settled by immigrants from the island of Anáfi, still feels like a rural Cycladic village.

Festivals

- The Athens Festival, a diverse cultural and arts program of dance, music, and theater, with performances from Pavarotti to Aristophanes, during the summer and early fall months.

1 Orientation

Arriving/Departing

If you haven't been to Greece before, you may be surprised at what a big city Athens is. It is a sprawling metropolis; and as a result most transportation terminals lie outside the heart of the city.

BY PLANE

There are two terminals at **Ellinikón International Airport,** located in the eastern suburb of Glyfáda. The East Terminal (*Anatolikó*) handles international flights of all scheduled and charter airlines other than Olympic Airways. The West Terminal (*Dytikó*) handles only Olympic flights, both domestic and international. A shuttle service operates between the two terminals every hour between 8:30am and 8:30pm.

Arriving travelers will find the same services at each terminal. There are foreign-currency exchange booths offering the same rates as downtown banks; luggage carts for 200 Drs (change money before collecting your baggage); a booth of the national telephone system, OTE, offering international telephone and fax service; tourist information centers (inside the departure area of the East Terminal and across the street at the West Terminal); cafés and restaurants. The airport's only luggage storage facility is located outside the East Terminal.

Transportation into Athens To reach downtown Athens from Ellinikón International Airport, you have several alternatives that vary in cost and speed, in the usual inverse relationship. There are taxi queues at both the East and West Terminals. From the airport to Sýntagma Square should cost 2,000–2,500 Drs ($8.30–$10.40). Without traffic the trip from the airport should take 20–30 minutes, but during rush hour it could take 1–1½ hours.

From the West Terminal only, the **Olympic Airways bus** leaves every half-hour from outside Olympic's international terminal (adjacent to the domestic terminal) and takes Olympic passengers to the airlines' office at Leofóros Syngroú 96 (in Koukáki) or to Sýntagma Square (where there are buses to many other parts of the city). The Olympic buses run regularly between 6:30am and 10:30pm; the fare is 190 Drs ($1.06), and you must have exact change. You can catch the airport-bound bus at Amalías Avenue on the northeast corner of Sýntagma Square or at the Syngroú Avenue Olympic office.

A second choice for Olympic passengers at the West Terminal—and the only express choice for everyone else (that is, passengers at the East Terminal)—is the blue-and-yellow, double-decker **express bus** that runs every 20 minutes from 6am to 11pm, every 30 minutes from 11pm to 2am, and hourly from 2am to 6am, taking passengers to Sýntagma Square or Omónia Square, also for 200 Drs (80¢) with a 25% night premium from midnight to 6am. This bus leaves Amalías Avenue at Sýntagma Square or Stadíou Street at Omónia Square for the return trip.

If you're really on a budget and have the time, you can take public bus no. 133, which plies the coastal route and stops at Posidónos Street outside the airport grounds. For 80 Drs (33¢) it, too, will take you to Sýntagma Square. However, you must buy a ticket from the bus kiosk or a newsstand before boarding and then have the ticket stamped after boarding.

Transportation to Piraeus (Pireás) If you're skipping Athens and heading straight for the island boats, take a taxi to Piraeus; the fare for the half-hour trip is

Taxi Caveats

1. Make sure that the meter is on. Some drivers will try to make a "special" off-meter price (a fare of 5,000–10,000 Drs or $20.80–$41.70, is not uncommon). Don't accept it under any circumstances; stop the cab and call for a policeman before you leave the airport.
2. If you've won that battle, check the meter as you drive away; drivers must keep it on the single-fare counter, indicated by a "1" in a small window on the meter. A "2," indicating double fare, is acceptable only for out-of-town or midnight-to-5am trips. Be bold—question any discrepancy immediately.
3. Drivers may add an airport charge of 250 Drs ($1.38), plus 100 Drs (42¢) for every piece of luggage over 22 pounds. It's customary to add a small tip, 10%–15%.

1,500–1,800 Drs ($6.25–$7.50). Budget travelers at either terminal can take public bus no. 19 to Karaïskáki Square in Piraeus for 300 Drs ($1.25).

To those travelers who imagine returning from the islands on an overnight boat with a neat connection to an early morning homeward flight, we can only say *Good luck!* Some may succeed, but many have been foiled by delayed boat arrivals and Athens's early-morning gridlock. You're better advised to allow a buffer day. You'll also face a conspiracy of taxi drivers, who meet the boats and have one fare—4,000 Drs ($16.66)—to go anywhere. Pass them by and walk to the nearest major street, where you'll probably find an honest taxi driver. Or catch the same bus no. 19 at Karaïskáki Square.

Airline Offices Most international carriers have ticket offices in or near Sýntagma Square. The **Delta Airlines** office is at Odós 4 Óthonos (☎ **32-35-242**). The **Lufthansa Airlines** office is at Leofóros Vassilíssis Sofías 11 (☎ **77-16-002**). The **TWA** office is at Odós Xenofóntos 8 (☎ **32-26-451**).

Olympic Airways is the national carrier and offers both international and domestic service. For information on schedules and fares, visit either Olympic's Sýntagma Square office, at Odós Óthonos 6 (☎ **92-92-555**), or its main office, at Leofóros Syngroú 96 (☎ **92-92-251**). The main reservations number is **96-16-161.**

For general and flight information at the East Terminal (non-Olympic flights), call **96-99-466.** For Olympic flights at the West Terminal, call **98-92-111.**

BY TRAIN

If you're arriving from Northern Europe or the north of Greece, your train will pull into the main station, StathmósUeríssis, near Karaïskáki and Omónia Squares. Trains coming from the Peloponnese arrive and depart from the ornate old station next door. The beaux-arts Stathmós Peloponnisou has smoked-glass panes, crystal-and-gilt chandeliers, and a marvelously carved wooden ticket booth with graceful wrought-iron dividers (a treat for the train buff). **Note:** The Baríssis station has a bank booth (open from 7:30am to 10pm Monday through Saturday, from 11am to 10pm on Sunday) and an OTE center for local and long-distance telephone calls (see "Telephones" in "Fast Facts: Greece," in Chap. 2). Across the street there's a police station.

Taxis are available at all hours from the parking area outside the train stations and should cost less than 900 Drs ($3.75) to Sýntagma Square. Trolley no. 1 (in front of Laríssis) goes to Sýntagma Square and Koukáki, passing through Omónia Square. (Catch it on Amalías Avenue in front of the Parliament building at Sýntagma.) Trolley no. 405 is an alternative route to Sýntagma Square. The fare is 80 Drs (33¢). You must purchase a ticket before boarding the trolley, either from a transit kiosk near the bus stop or from a newsstand.

You can purchase train tickets through a travel agent or at the Omónia Square ticket office, at Odós Károlou 1 (☎ **52-40-647**). The office at Odós Filellínon 17 (☎ **32-36-747**) is more convenient to Sýntagma.

BY BUS

The two nationwide bus networks in Greece, KTEL and OSE, operate buses in Athens and throughout Greece. Fares on the two may vary.

KTEL BUSES There are two principal KTEL bus stations. The terminal at Odós Kifíssou 100 handles buses to Pátra, the Peloponnese, the Ionian islands, and all points south and west. Public bus no. 51 will take you from this terminal to the corner of Zínonos and Menándrou Streets, near Omónia Square; from there you can catch a

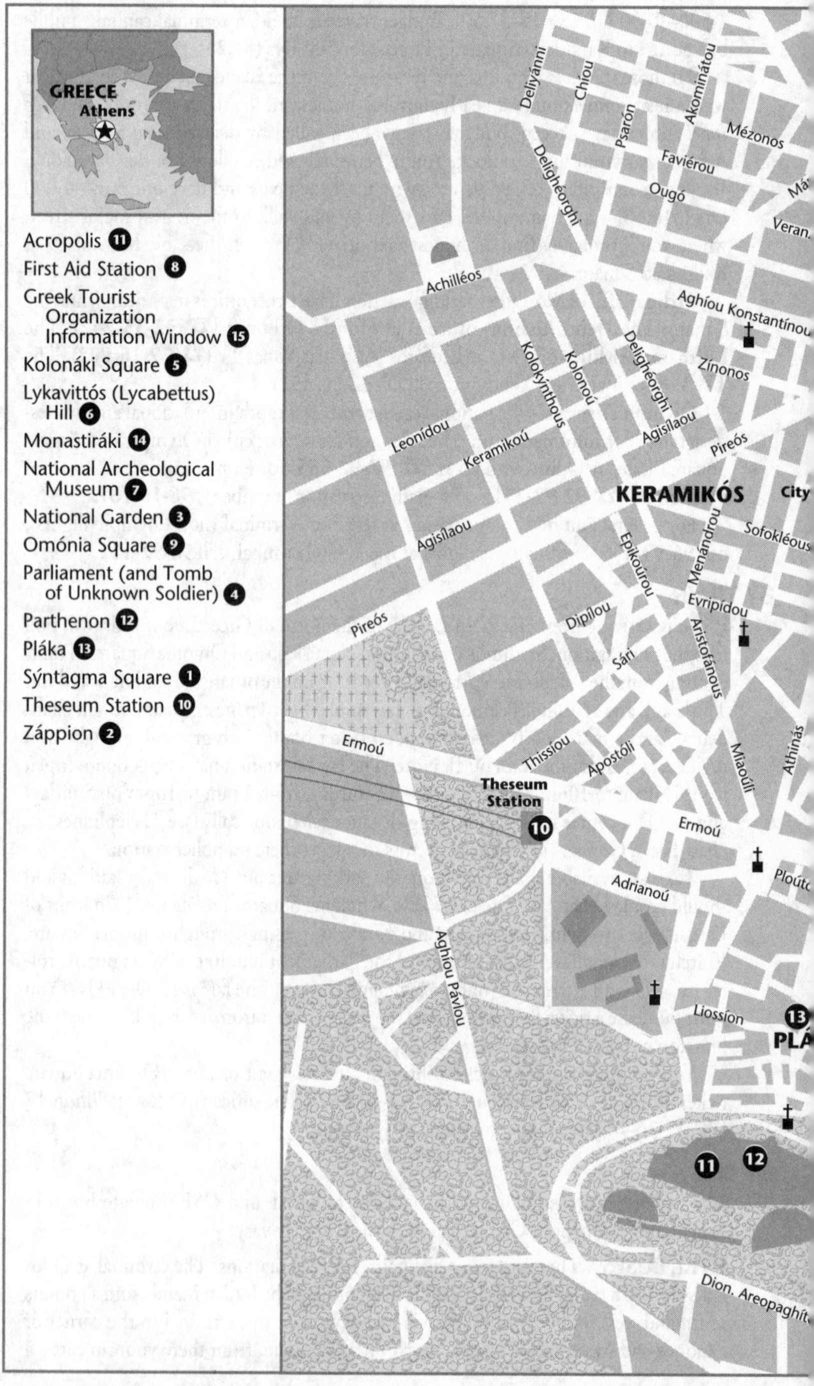
GREECE
Athens
Acropolis 11
First Aid Station 8
Greek Tourist Organization Information Window 15
Kolonáki Square 5
Lykavittós (Lycabettus) Hill 6
Monastiráki 14
National Archeological Museum 7
National Garden 3
Omónia Square 9
Parliament (and Tomb of Unknown Soldier) 4
Parthenon 12
Pláka 13
Sýntagma Square 1
Theseum Station 10
Záppion 2
Deliyánni
Chiou
Psarón
Akominátou
Mézonos
Deligheórghi
Faviérou
Ougó
Veran.
Achilléos
Aghíou Konstantínou
Kolokýnthous
Kolonoú
Deligheórghi
Zínonos
Leonídou
Keramikoú
Agisílaou
Pireós
KERAMIKÓS
City
Agisílaou
Sofokléous
Epikoúrou
Menándrou
Evripídou
Pireós
Dipílou
Sári
Aristofánous
Ermoú
Thissíou
Apostóli
Miaoúli
Athinás
Theseum Station
10
Ermoú
Adrianoú
Aghíou Pávlou
Liossíon
13
11
12
Dion. Areopaghít

Athens Orientation

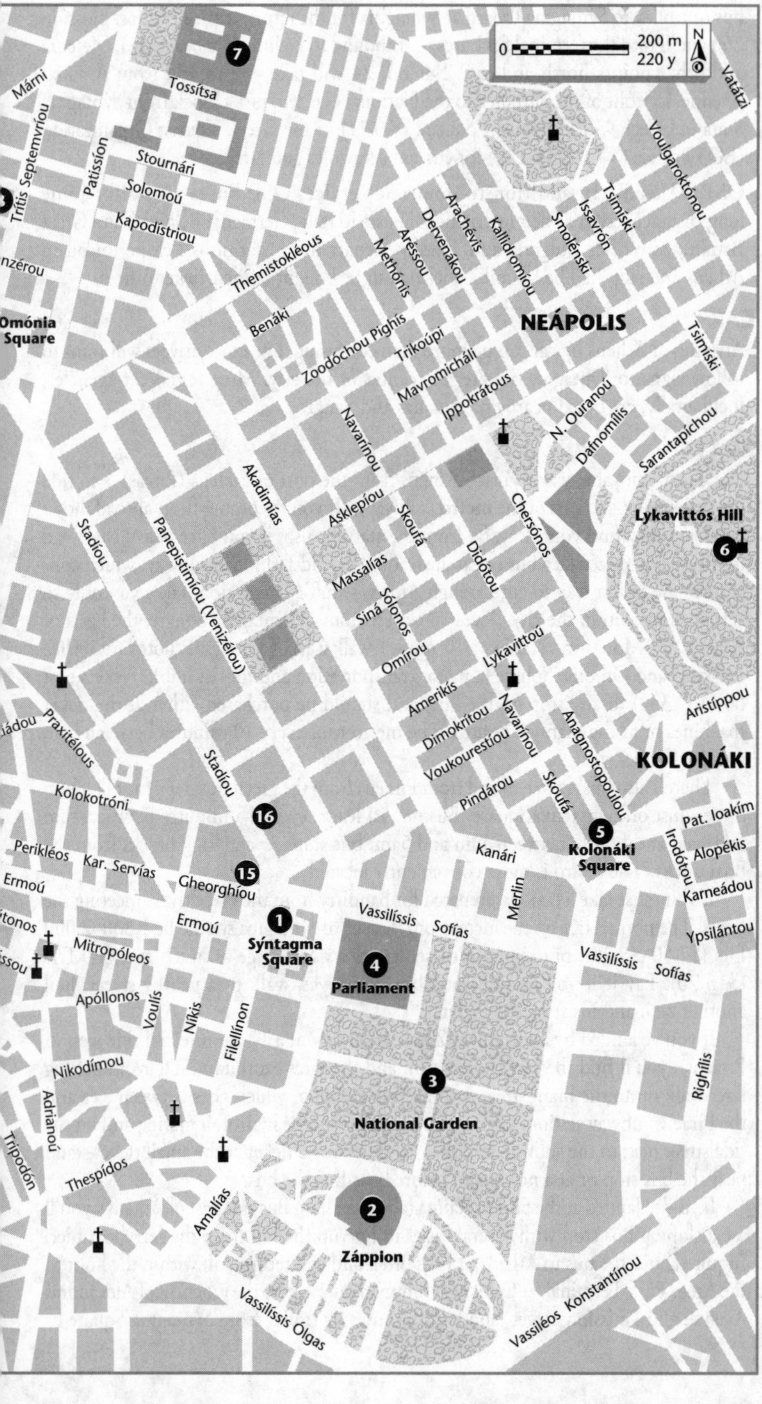

0
200 m
220 y
N
NEÁPOLIS
KOLONÁKI
Omónia Square
Lykavittós Hill
Kolonáki Square
Sýntagma Square
Parliament
National Garden
Záppion
Márni
Tossítsa
Trítis Septemvríou
Patissíon
Stournári
Solomoú
Kapodístriou
Themistokléous
Benáki
Zoodóchou Pighís
Arachévis
Dervenákou
Arèssou
Methónis
Kallidromíou
Tsimíski
Issavrón
Smolénski
Voulgaroktónou
Vatátzi
Trikoúpi
Mavromicháli
Ippokrátous
Navarínou
N. Ouranoú
Dafnomílis
Sarantapíchou
Akadimías
Asklepíou
Skoufá
Chersónos
Stadíou
Panepistimíou (Venizélou)
Massalías
Didótou
Sólonos
Siná
Omírou
Lykavittoú
Amerikís
Dimokrítou
Voukourestíou
Anagnostopoúlou
Aristíppou
Pindárou
Praxitélous
Kolokotróni
Periklėos
Kar. Servías
Gheorghíou
Ermoú
Kanári
Merlin
Irodótou
Pat. Ioakím
Alopékis
Karneádou
Ypsilántou
Vassilíssis Sofías
Mitropóleos
Apóllonos
Voulís
Níkis
Filellínon
Nikodímou
Adrianoú
Tripodón
Thespídos
Amalías
Vassilíssis Ólgas
Vassiléos Konstantínou
Righílis

Church
Post Office
Information

bus or trolley to Sýntagma (board at Sýntagma for the return trip). At Odós, Liossíon 260 you'll find the terminal for buses northbound to Delphi, Thebes, Evvia, Metéora and other points north and east. Bus no. 24 will take you to and from Amalías Avenue, in front of the entrance to the National Garden, just a block from Sýntagma Square. Check with the tourist police (☎ **171**) or the Greek Tourist Organization (EOT) office (☎ **32-34-130**) for current schedules and fares.

OSE BUSES In addition to domestic service, OSE buses also offer some long-distance service. Their international buses to Italy, Germany, Belgium, and Great Britain, as well as Bulgaria and Turkey, depart from Stathmós Peloponnísou in Athens and stop in Thessaloníki. Tickets can be bought at their ticket offices.

BY CAR

Arriving in Athens by car can be more than confusing, but most drivers will want to follow signs to Sýntagma Square, the center of the city. Most rental-car agencies, incidentally, are based nearby on Amalías and Syngróu.

BY BOAT

The most enjoyable way to reach Athens from the port of Piraeus (Pireás) is to ride the yellow-and-red cars of the **metro** (subway). (If you're coming from abroad, however, you may find your dock far from the station; also, if you have heavy bags, you may be advised to take a bus or cab instead.) This old-fashioned subway, which constitutes the fastest way to cut through Athens's traffic congestion, takes you only to certain stops within the city. The two closest stops to Sýntagma Square, the heart of Athens, are Monastiráki (about a 10-minute walk west of Sýntagma, noted for its flea markets) and Omónia Square (a major transportation and tourist hub). Tickets cost 60 Drs (33¢) to any stop on the line, and should be purchased either at the ticket machines or at the manned booths. The metro runs every 10 minutes between 5am and 12:10am.

There's also bus service to and from Piraeus from the green bus depot at Filellínon Street, just off Sýntagma Square. Bus no. 40 leaves every 15 minutes between 5am and 1am and hourly between 1am and 5am, but stops several long blocks from the boat docks. The metro is more conveniently located.

If you must take a taxi, be prepared for banditry from the taxi drivers meeting the boats. The normal fare on the meter from Piraeus to Sýntagma should be 1,800–2,000 Drs ($7.50–$8.30), but many of these drivers try to charge as much as 4,000 Drs ($16.70). Pay it if you're desperate, but better yet, walk to a nearby street, hail another taxi, and insist on the meter.

If you've landed by hydrofoil at Zéa Marina (about a 10-minute taxi ride west of Piraeus), you'll find the taxi choices slim and the rates exorbitant. To avoid the big fare, walk up to the main street and take bus no. 905, which goes between Zéa and the Piraeus subway station. Catch it up the hill from the hydrofoil marina and on the side street next to the subway station. You must buy a ticket at the small ticket stand near the bus stop or at a newsstand before boarding the bus.

If you've landed at the port of Rafína (about an hour bus ride east of Athens), you'll see a sloping bus stop with several buses in line up the hill from the ferryboat pier. Inquire about the bus to Athens; it runs often and will return you within the hour to the Áreos Park Terminal, at Odós Mavrommatéon 29, near the junction of Alexándras Avenue and Patissíon Street (about 25 minutes by trolley from Sýntagma Square or one block from the Victoria Square metro stop). From the terminal, there are buses to Rafína every half hour.

Tourist Information

The most convenient source for a wide range of tourist information is the **tourist police.** They offer 24-hour service in English, as well as other languages, and you can reach them by dialing **171.** The tourist police are also the ones to call with problems or emergencies.

The **Greek Tourist Organization (EOT)** has an information desk in the arrival area of the East Terminal of Ellinikón International Airport, open daily. Tourist information at the West Terminal is provided by the tourist police.

The most convenient EOT office in Athens is at Sýntagma Square: at the National Bank of Greece branch at Odós Karagheorghítis Servías 2 (☎ **32-34-130**), open Monday through Thursday from 8am to 2pm and 3:30 to 6:30pm; Friday from 8am to 1:30pm and 3 to 8:30pm; Saturday from 9am to 2pm; Sunday and holidays from 9am to 1pm. It has a wide range of brochures, bus and train schedules, hotel listings, and an excellent (and free) map of Athens and Greece. There is also an EOT office at Zéa Marina; ask at the hydrofoil office for directions.

City Layout

It's hard to imagine that only about 150 years ago Athens was little more than an obscure outpost with fewer than 10,000 inhabitants. Period engravings show shabby, single-story wooden homes flanking the Acropolis and Agora. Beyond them the barren hills and plains of the Attica peninsula spread far into the distance. Today, metropolitan Athens revolves around the center city, with Sýntagma Square as its hub and the surrounding suburbs of Kifissiá to the north, Kaisarianí to the east, Piraeus to the southwest, and Glyfáda (adjacent to the airport) and Vouliagméni to the south. Athens's approximately four million people live within a 150-square-mile area that's rapidly bumping up against the mountains and the sea. The city is such a magnet that roughly 40% of the entire population of Greece lives within its borders!

NEIGHBORHOODS IN BRIEF

Most of the sites and services of interest to tourists are in the center city, within a triangle defined by Sýntagma Square to the east, the Acropolis (including the neighborhood of Koukáki) to the southwest, and Omónia Square to the north. The neighborhood of Monastiráki, with its flea market and ruins, is near the center of the triangle.

Sýntagma Square Draw a straight line between the Acropolis and Lykavittós, Athens's two major hills, and you will note, with a geometrician's delight, that the midpoint is Sýntagma Square—the tourist, government, and business center. The old royal palace stands guard over the landscaped square on the east side, and is now home to the Greek Parliament and the Tomb of the Unknown Soldier. A fun event is the delightfully theatrical changing of the guard by white-skirted, pompom-shoed *évzones.* Behind and beside the Parliament building are the verdant acres of the National Garden, an oasis of quiet greenness in the bustling city. The exclusive neighborhood of Kolonáki lies northeast from here, Omónia Square northwest, Monastiráki west, and Pláka and the Acropolis southwest.

In Sýntagma Square you'll find the queen of Athens hotels, the Grande Bretagne. Walking counterclockwise around the square, you'll come to two banks with foreign-exchange services, each containing a required stop on your travels—an EOT office and an American Express office. Cafés once lined the west side and filled the center of the square. Now only a limited number remain. On the south side you'll find Olympic Airways and on nearby side streets many of the other airline offices, as well as travel agents, foreign-exchange offices, bookstores, and numerous tourist-oriented shops. The airport buses leave from the southwest corner of the square, on Amalías Avenue. Public buses leave from various parts of the square to almost anywhere you'd want to go. Check with the bus ticket booth near the General Bank of Greece office.

Mets A residential area south of Sýntagma Square, between the temple of Zeus and the First Cemetery and next to Ardítos Hill, Mets is noted for its many fine old garden houses, which give it a villagelike aspect reminiscent of Old Athens. Named after a popular café, Metz, that once flourished here, it has become a favorite of the city's literati. Mets has several stylish boutiques and art stores as well as bars and a famous taverna along Moussoúri Street. The nightlife reflects the understated tone of its residents, many of whom are young professionals.

Kolonáki Kolonáki, the chic shopping district at the base of Lykavittós Hill, is a 10-minute walk northeast of Sýntagma Square. Although it has lost some of its glamour to the nouveau suburbs, Kolonáki remains Athens's best in-town address. Lykavittós Hill offers a stunning view (when the smog clears) of the entire metropolitan area, and a contemporary outdoor theater with a diverse program of music and theater. There's a funicular railway that runs up the hill from the upper streets of Kolonáki, leading to an expensive restaurant and a moderately priced snack bar on top. We like the walk up and a funkier, cheaper restaurant midway up (see "Where to Eat" in Chapter 4).

Pláka Pláka, a tourist favorite, is located just a few blocks to the southwest of Sýntagma and extends to the base of the Acropolis and around to the Agora. It was settled in the 19th and early 20th centuries by wealthy merchants. They built luxurious multistory wood-and-marble mansions with finely crafted interiors. Today, some of those mansions remain as homes, but most have been transformed into bars, bouzouki clubs, restaurants, and shops. Yet, despite the rows of T-shirt and souvenir shops, the back lanes of this old neighborhood retain a charm that leads us to recommend a number of hotels and restaurants in the area.

Koukáki Koukáki is one of Athens's best-kept secrets, a quiet middle-class neighborhood hidden behind the southern flank of the Acropolis. The streets are a mix of early 20th-century and modern town houses; the restaurants are little frequented by tourists; and there's nary a souvenir shop to be found. We like several small, well-priced hotels and pensions in the area, in which we include Makriyiánni. Buses and trolleys run frequently from Koukáki's main streets, making stops at Sýntagma (only a short walk away), and other parts of town. Syngroú, the wide boulevard leading toward Piraeus, Glyfáda, and the two terminals of Ellinikón International Airport, runs along the edge of the neighborhood, near which you'll find most of the car-rental agencies, the public bus to Piraeus, and Olympic Airways' main office (where the airport bus arrives and departs after leaving Sýntagma).

Monastiráki This is a small neighborhood west of Sýntagma Square on the north side of the Acropolis, next to the Agora. Its name, "Little Monastery," derives from a monks' abode that was once there. There is a very convenient metro stop that leads south to Piraeus and north to Omónia Square and all the way up to suburban Kifissiá. It is home to an extensive labyrinth of shops and to a world-famous weekend flea market. On its north edge, merging with the Omónia Square area, you'll find some good, reasonably priced small hotels.

Omónia Square If you look at a map of Athens, you'll come to the conclusion that all roads lead to Omónia Square. Two parallel streets connect Omónia with Sýntagma Square: Panepistimíou, along which lie the university, the National Library, and the Academy; and Stadíou, with Kolokotróni Square and the main OTE (public telephone) office.

There are many hotels, office buildings, and markets, as well as several modes of transportation, including the metro (subway) to Piraeus, around the square. The square was for many years the commercial and tourist center of Athens. Today, however, after many businesses have moved out of the precinct and the hotels have gone downhill, it strongly resembles New York's Times Square, complete with homeless refugees from Eastern Europe's recent turmoils, and we no longer recommend hotels there. Yet, while not the safest or most attractive part of town, it certainly remains one of the most interesting. There are meat and vegetable markets and huge department stores, and the National Archeological Museum is only a short walk away.

Exárchia Exárchia, the neighborhood around Exárchia Square, is about a 15-minute walk north of Omónia Square. For many years it was lost in the shadow of its famous neighbor, the National Archeological Museum. Now it's a lively hangout of urban professionals, students, visiting intellectuals, and local families. Residents and Athenians who flock to the cafés and tavernas around its mimosa-filled square wonder a bit about rumors of drug-dealing nearby, but you'd never guess that there was a problem while enjoying a cup of Greek coffee at one of the cafés.

The Suburbs As elsewhere in the world, in Athens the suburbs are not the most interesting part of the city, although, as elsewhere, the middle-class keeps flocking to them. About the ritziest suburb of all is Kifissiá, to the north of downtown Athens, where houses are big and modern. A stroll down one of Kifissiá's nicer streets will remind you of an American neighborhood. Farther north is pine-covered Drossiá, a suburb that has the distinction of being always 10 degrees cooler than Athens and serving the best *penirlí* (boat-shaped cheese bread) in Greece. Glyfáda, to the south of Athens, is home to the airport and is the residential area for many diplomats. The people and shops are cosmopolitan and chic. Farther south on the coast is Vouliagméni, noted for its beach. One of Greater Athens's best hotels, the Astir Palace, is located in Vouliagméni.

STREET MAPS

The Athens map given out free at the offices of the Greek Tourist Organization is very good. The best commercial map is called *Athens, Piraeus, Salonica* and is published by John Glavas; it's available at newsstands everywhere in those cities.

2 Getting Around

The area that most tourists travel in is small enough so that we recommend walking as the best mode of locomotion, but we suggest navigating the smaller streets parallel to the big avenues to avoid some of the stifling pollution that often fills the air. For longer trips, taxis are so inexpensive—usually less than the 500 Drs ($2.10) minimum—that we recommend you take them everywhere, when you can get one.

By Subway (Metro)

One of Athens's great surprises is its clean, quiet, and efficient subway system. Though consisting of only one line, with a second line being constructed, the metro (as the Greeks call it) is a great way to get from Sýntagma Square (the nearby Monastiráki stop) or Omónia Square to Piraeus, or from Sýntagma to the National Archeological Museum. Other stops include Néo Fáliro, which is good for diners heading to Mikrolímano; Victoria Square, near the Green Park bus or railroad station; Monastiráki, for sightseeing in Pláka or the Agora or for shopping in the flea market; and Kifissiá (a prosperous outer suburb). Subway tickets can be purchased from ticket machines or at booths in the station, with fares of 75–100 Drs (31¢–42¢) each way, depending on destination. The metro operates every 10 minutes between 5am and midnight. The trip from Monastiráki to Piraeus takes about 15 minutes. *Validate your ticket.*

By Bus/Trolley

Trolleys and local buses are among the most convenient ways to get around the city. Trolleys no. 1 and 5 go almost everywhere the tourist needs: to Sýntagma Square, the National Archeological Museum, Omónia Square, the train station of Stathmós Laríssis, and the Koukáki region behind the Acropolis. At every stop (signposted with a yellow triangle), notices list the trolleys' numbers and final destinations.

You must buy tickets before boarding, either at the small transit ticket booths near some stops or at most news kiosks. The fare is 75 Drs (31¢). Once on board, you must have your ticket stamped by the small machines at the front and back. *Failure to do so may result in a citation.* Always check your route with local passengers waiting at the stop or with your hotel reception desk, as route numbers change frequently. Call the tourist police if you're uncertain.

Many trolley lines run from 5am to midnight. Athens buses often coincide with trolley routes or partially overlap them and then take off on their own. Main routes are noted on the free EOT map.

By Taxi

Traveling by taxi in Athens is an adventure and not always a good one. We've noted the problem with taxis from the airport (see "Orientation" in this chapter); similar ones face you in the city. Although we met some wonderful drivers who play strictly by the rules, we also ran into a few who do not. They are a minority, yet you should be wary of them. Some dishonest drivers will try to set a fixed price rather than going by the meter. Do not allow it and leave the cab if they insist. This is particularly prevalent at the boat and hydrofoil docks in Piraeus and Zéa Marina, where the fixed price is 4,000 Drs ($16.65), *twice* the proper fare. Your only alternative is to walk to a nearby street and look for a more honest man.

There are taxi stands scattered throughout Athens, but more often you'll end up hailing one. Taxis are required to pick up as many additional passengers as possible going in the same direction, so don't give up if the rooftop light is turned off. Keep waving—one may stop to pick you up! Then check the meter to see that it's registering properly; except for out-of-town trips and in the hours between midnight and 5am, there should be a number "1" in the small box. Double fare is valid only in those first-mentioned cases. If the taxi picks up other passengers, everyone will end up paying the fare on the meter up to the point when he gets off; if you are the last in and the first out, you may try to negotiate your part of the fare.

The surest way to get a taxi (and the only way in the wee hours) is to call one or, preferably, have the concierge at your hotel, or the maitre d' at the restaurant call one. There is a radio surcharge of 500 Drs ($2.10) added to the meter, but it's worth it.

There are legal surcharges allowed for pickups from the airport (500 Drs or $2.10) and from the train or bus station (200 Drs or 85¢), plus baggage charges (80 Drs or 35¢). Waiting time is charged at 1400 Drs ($5.85) per hour. If you're suspicious of any charges, ask to see the official rate sheet that all taxis are required to carry. If you've been gouged, get the taxi number and call or write to the tourist police.

By Car

We can't recommend that you drive yourself around Athens. The streets are confusing and parking difficult to find. If you want to hire a car and driver, check with the desk at your hotel or a travel agent. For rental car information, see "Getting Around" in Chapter 2.

Fast Facts: Athens

American Express The main office is on Sýntagma Square, at the corner of Ermoú Street (☎ **32-44-975,** fax 32-27-893). If you're going to be receiving mail there, the mailing address is Odós Ermoú 2, Sýntagma Square, 102 25 Athens, Greece. American Express will cash and sell traveler's checks, accept claims for lost and stolen credit cards and traveler's checks, store luggage for 300 Drs ($1.25) per day, make travel arrangements or book tours, accept mail for card members (others pay 500 Drs, or $2.10, per collection) and package and send parcels. Office hours are 8:30am to 4pm Monday to Friday, 8:30am to 1:30pm on Saturday. The office closes 1 hour earlier in winter, and mail service ends at 4:30 weekdays. Don't forget your passport. During off-hours, for lost or stolen credit cards and checks, call collect to the American Express office in London (☎ **0044/273/675-975**).

Area Code The country code for Greece is **30.** The area code for Athens is **01.**

Babysitters Baby-sitting service is available through some hotels, with advance notice.

Banks The National Bank of Greece on Sýntagma Square (☎ **32-22-255**) is open Monday through Thursday from 8am to 2pm and 3:30 to 6:30pm, Friday from 8am to 1:30pm and 3 to 8:30pm, on Saturday from 9am to 3pm, and on Sunday and holidays from 9am to 1pm. The extended evening and weekend hours are for foreign exchange only and are shorter from October to April. (This branch has the added bonus of having an EOT office inside for tourist information.) Official banking hours throughout Greece are 8am to 2pm Monday through Thursday and 8am to 1:30pm on Friday. The General Bank across the street has similar hours. International banks with local offices include Citibank, Odós Othonos 8 (☎ **32-27-471**); Bank of America, Odós Panepistimíou 39 (☎ **32-44-975**); and Barclays Bank, Odós Voukourestíou 15 (☎ **36-44-311**). Americans with Cirrus cards may be able to access automatic cash machines, if they have a special four-digit PIN code. Check with your local bank.

Bookstores The biggest of the foreign-language bookstores in Athens is Eleftheroudákis, at Odós Níkis 4 (☎ **32-22-255**), just behind Sýntagma Square. Its collection is enormous, especially good on guidebooks! Also good is Pandelídes, at Odós Amerikís 11 (☎ **36-23-673**), which accepts second-hand books for credit. Another personal favorite (with a much more eclectic, student bent) is Compendium, at Odós Níkis 28 (☎ **32-21-248**); it also buys used books in return for store credit. For a look at the many fine guides and art books, as well as the photography-filled books about Greece, go to the retail store of Ekdotiki (Ekdotike), at Odós Omírou 11 (☎ **36-08-911**). For stationery supplies, head straight to the best: A. Pallis, at Odós Ermoú 8, on the corner of Voulís (☎ **32-31-128**), near Sýntagma Square.

Car Rentals See "Getting Around" in Chapter 2.

Credit Cards See "Fast Facts: Greece" in Chapter 2.

Climate See "When to Go" in Chapter 2.

Crime See "Safety" below.

Currency See "Information, Entry Requirements, and Money" in Chapter 2.

Currency Exchange In Greece, banks, post offices, and even travel agencies are authorized to change money at government-posted rates of exchange. Hotels will often change traveler's checks for guests, but at rates lower than those offered by banks. The maximum commission is 4%. Several travel agents near the National Bank of Greece on Sýntagma Square offer foreign exchange late into the evening; their rates, however, can be less than competitive. Because of bank holidays and erratic labor strikes, you may suddenly find banks in Greece closed for a day or several days; we recommend, therefore, that you always have some extra drachmas on hand.

Dentists and Doctors Most embassies or consulates can provide a list of recommended dentists and doctors. Call the Citizens Services section during business hours. In an emergency, call the main number anytime.

Drugstores Most drugstores (*farmakia*) around Sýntagma Square have personnel who speak English. Every pharmacy has a list posted on its door indicating where the nearest all-night pharmacy is located (see also "Fast Facts: Greece" in Chapter 2). The *Athens News* also lists pharmacies open after normal hours.

Embassies and Consulates The embassy of the United States is at Leofóros Vassilíssis Sofías 91 (☎ **72-12-951**). Hours for its Citizens Services section are 8:30am to 5pm Monday through Friday. (There is also a U.S. consulate in Thessaloníki.) The embassy of Canada is at Odós I. Ghennadíou 4 (☎ **72-54-011**). The embassy of the United Kingdom is at Odós Ploutárchou 1 (☎ **72-36-211**). There are also British consular offices in Crete (Iráklio), Corfu, Pátra, Rhodes, Sámos, and Thessaloníki. Australia has a consulate located at Odós D. Soútsou 37 (☎ **64-47-303**).

Emergencies In an emergency call the tourist police at **171**. An English-speaking police officer is on duty 24 hours a day. If that line is busy, dial **166** for an ambulance and **199** for the fire department. The general police emergency number is **100** (you may not, however, reach an English-speaking officer). Check with your embassy for advice on medical assistance.

For lost-and-found information, call the traffic police (☎ **52-30-111**). For lost passports, contact the alien police (☎ **36-28-301**).

Any theft should be reported immediately to the tourist police, since all insurance policies require a police report for reimbursement. A police report is also required when you're replacing a lost passport or airline ticket. You'll need an English translation, as well, if the report is in Greek.

Film See "Photographic Needs" below.

Holidays See "When to Go" in Chapter 2.

Hospitals There are many hospitals in the Greater Athens area, but the only one that can be fully recommended is the Hygeia (pronounced *Yghía*) Diagnostic and Therapeutical Center, Odós Erythroú 4 at Kifissiás Street, north of Sýntagma Square, toward the Olympic Stadium, near the suburb of Filotheï (☎ **68-27-940**). It is a private hospital and will require proof of payment before admission (credit cards are accepted).

In an *emergency,* dial **171** or **166** for information to the nearest hospital. You'll likely be sent to a government hospital, but may not want to stay. Even at a government hospital, you will be expected to pay for any treatment (Blue Cross or other American insurance policies are not accepted). Citizens of the European Union, however, will not have to pay.

Hotlines For the local chapter of Alcoholics Anonymous, call **96-27-122** or **96-27-218.**

Laundry/Dry Cleaning The National Dry Cleaners and Laundry Service, Odós Apóllonos 17 (☎ **32-32-226**), is next to the Hermes Hotel and is open from 7am to 4pm Monday and Wednesday, 8pm Tuesday, Thursday, and Friday. Laundry costs 1,500 Drs ($6.25) per kilo. Dry cleaning runs 1,500 Drs ($6.25) for a dress and 2,500 Drs ($10.40) for a man's suit. There's a self-service laundry in Pláka, at the corner of Afrodíti Street and Odós Herefóntos 10.

Libraries The best library for those interested in reading more about modern Greek civilization and culture is the American Library at the Hellenic American Union, Odós Massalías 22 (☎ **36-38-114,** fax 36-42-981). The seventh-floor Clary Thompson Reading Room is open Monday and Thursday from noon to 7:30pm; Tuesday, Wednesday, and Friday from 10am to 2:30pm. The British Council Library, with more than 13,000 English-language volumes, is at 17 Kolonáki Square (☎ **36-33-215**).

Lost Property Call the tourist police for lost or stolen property. Also check with your embassy, as lost items are often returned there. If you leave valuables in a taxi or bus, call the General Lost Property Office (☎ **77-05-711**). See also "Emergencies" above.

Luggage Storage/Lockers Many hotels (and, surprisingly, hostels as well) will store your excess luggage for you while you cavort in the islands or wherever. Some will accept it for free; others charge 300–500 Drs ($1.25–$2.10) per day per piece. The Pacific Ltd. Travel office (☎ **32-41-007**), Odós Níkis 24 off Sýntagma Square, has a formal luggage-storage system. Each piece costs 500 Drs ($2.10) per day, 1,000 Drs ($4.15) per week, 2,500 Drs ($10.40) per month. Hours are 7am to 8pm Monday through Saturday, 7am to 2pm Sunday and holidays.

In Piraeus there is luggage storage inside the subway terminal, but it's costly. Both railway stations (StathmósUeríssis and Stathmós Peloponnísou) have luggage-storage facilities.

Mail See "Post Office" below.

Newspapers/Magazines The *Athens News* is a daily newspaper published locally in English; it's available at kiosks everywhere for 150 Drs (63¢). The *International Herald Tribune* hits the newsstands after 7pm each day. *Athenscope* is a weekly magazine that's full of information, restaurant reviews, and cultural and recreational listings, as well as articles of interest to English-speaking tourists; it's available at most news kiosks for 300 Drs ($1.25). *Athens Today,* available free at most hotels, has much the same information, plus a good map of the downtown area and more specifics on transportation.

Photographic Needs For one-hour processing, try Fotofast, Odós Níkis 14 (☎ **32-29-135**), open Monday through Saturday from 8am to 8pm.

Police See "Emergencies" above.

Post Office The general post office (GPO) is a half block from Omónia Square at Odós Eólou 100. It's open Monday through Friday from 7:30am to 8pm, Saturday from 8am to 3pm, and Sunday from 8am to 2pm. There is also a branch at Mitropóleos Street, just off the square, with the same hours. *Poste restante* mail can be directed either to Omónia Square (where anything marked "GPO" will go) or to Sýntagma Square. (Bring your passport when picking up *poste restante* mail.) The post office for sending parcels (surface mail is painfully slow and not much cheaper than air mail) is at Odós Stadíou 4. Leave any internationally bound parcels unwrapped until they've been inspected there. Post offices also offer outbound fax service; some offer foreign-currency exchange. A first-class letter or postcard costs 100 Drs (55¢), while express mail service costs 3,400 Drs ($18.90) for 500 grams (approximately one pound).

Religious Services For Roman Catholic services, contact St. Denis Church, Odós Venizélou 24 (☎ **36-23-603**). For interdenominational English-language services, contact St. Andrew's Protestant International Church, Odós Siná 66 (☎ **65-21-401**). For Anglican services, contact St. Paul's Church, Odós Filellínon 29 (☎ **72-14-906**). Athens's only synagogue is the Beth Shalom Synagogue, Odós Melidóni 5 (☎ **32-52-823**).

Safety Athens rates among the safest capitals in Europe. There are few reports of violent crimes. Pickpocketing, however, is not uncommon, especially in Pláka and the Omónia Square area, on the metro and buses, and in Piraeus. We advise travelers to avoid the back streets of Piraeus at night. As always, leave your passport and valuables in a security box at the hotel. Carry a photocopy of your passport, not the original.

Shoe Repairs Shoe repair shops are fairly common, especially in the Sýntagma and Omónia Square areas. Ask the concierge at your hotel for the nearest one.

Taxis See "Getting Around" in this chapter.

Telephones/Telefaxes/Telegrams The main office of the Telecommunications Organization of Greece (OTE) is Odós Stadíou 15 (two blocks from Sýntagma Square). This and the Omónia Square branch are open from 8am to 10pm. The OTE office at Odós Patissíon 85 (near Victoria Square) is open 24 hours. There are other, smaller OTE exchanges in Athens; they generally have more limited hours of operation.

Telegrams, telexes, and telefaxes can also be sent through the OTE offices. Some post offices also have fax service.

Tourist Information See "Tourist Information" earlier in this chapter. *Athens Today,* available free at most hotels, is an excellent source of the very latest information.

Transit Information For bus routes, ferry schedules, and other transit information, call the Tourist Police at **171.**

Weather Weather forecasts can be found in the daily edition of the *Athens News.*

4

Where to Stay & Eat in Athens

Almost every neighborhood in central Athens has some reasonably priced hotels. You should familiarize yourself with the various areas. Many tourists have complained that it's impossible to find a room quiet enough to get a good night's sleep. You'll want to avoid hotels on major streets and next to bouzouki clubs, but beyond that you'll probably be happy at most of the hotels we recommend. If you've never stayed in a Greek hotel, don't expect high style and ornamentation. They are most often plain and unadorned but should be clean and comfortable.

Omónia Square was once the favorite area for tourists, but in recent years the neighborhoods around Sýntagma Square, including Pláka, Koukáki, and Monastiráki, have become more popular. We especially recommend Koukáki for its quiet residential back streets and the feeling it offers of a real Greek neighborhood; although it's not as conveniently situated as Pláka or Sýntagma Square, it's only a short walk or bus ride from those areas. For pure convenience, the Sýntagma hotels—as well as those in the lively Pláka area—can't be beaten.

Note: We strongly advise that you write or fax ahead of time to the lodging that interests you for reservations, because the best-value hotels sell out in the summer.

1 Where to Stay

IN PLÁKA

Pláka has once again become a terrific place in which to stay, being in the midst of all the nightlife and shops. If your hotel is not adjacent to a major music source, you'll probably get a good night's sleep—when you're not up taking part in the nocturnal activity.

Many of our choices in this section are small hotels that have been created from the old villas and mansions in this area.

Dioskouros Guest House, Odós Pittakoú 6, Pláka, 105 58 Athens. ☎ **32-48-165.** 12 rms (none with bath).

Rates: 6,440 Drs ($26.85) single; 8,050 Drs ($33.55) double. No credit cards.

The Dioskouros Guest House, off Amalías Avenue, is an old home with a dramatic, winding staircase. Many rooms overlook an attractive, tree-filled courtyard, which brings blessed quiet. The rooms are private and somewhat shabby but bright.

★ **Hotel Acropolis House,** Odós Kodroú 6–8, Pláka, 105 58 Athens. ☎ **01/32-22-344.** Fax 01/32-44-143. 25 rms, 4 suites (15 with bath). A/C TEL

Rates: 7,800 Drs ($32.70) single without bath; 9,450 Drs ($39.35) double without bath; 14,400 Drs ($60) suite. Add 1,600 Drs ($6.65) for rooms with bath. V.

This is our first choice of the inexpensive hostelries, with more old-world charm than most in the budget category. Panos and members of the Choudalákis family are the friendly and helpful hosts who've restored this 150-year-old villa, located at the end of Voulís Street, opposite the Adónis Hotel. The original classical architectural details, the molding, and a decorative frieze combine with lace curtains and traditional two-tone painted walls to re-create an era. The Choudalakises have added a "newer" wing (it's 60 years old) that's not as special, but it's clean and the toilets (there's one to a room, but across the hall) are fully tiled and modern. The best views are from rooms 401 and 402. Breakfast costs 1,100 Drs ($4.60).

Hotel Adonis, Odós Koudroú 3, Pláka, 105 58 Athens. ☎ **01/32-49-737.**
Fax 01/32-31-602. 25 rms, 1 suite (all with bath). TEL

Rates (including breakfast): 8,165 Drs ($34) single; 11,500 Drs ($39.35) double. No credit cards.

This quiet, clean, class B hotel, near Voulís Street, has central heating, an elevator, and a pleasant roof garden with great Acropolis views. The rooms, however, are rather plain. Ask for one of the rooms with a balcony, which is large enough for sunbathing. Breakfast is served on the roof.

Hotel Ava, Odós Lysikrátous 9–11, Pláka, 105 58 Athens. ☎ **32-36-618.**
Fax 01/32-31-061. 11 rms, 6 suites (all with bath). TEL

Rates (including breakfast): 8,625 Drs ($35.95) single; 12,535 Drs ($52.25) double; 14,200 Drs ($59.15) efficiency apartment for two. Rooms with air conditioning 1,200 Drs ($5) extra. AE, MC, V.

Planning a lengthy stay in Athens? The Hotel Ava, a half block from Hadrian's Arch, off Amalías Avenue, may be just the thing. The Ava's well-equipped, comfortable utility apartments are for those who like a bit of home life during their visit. Write ahead to Mr. Fissendjidis or call for reservations.

Hotel Byron, Odós Vironos 19, Pláka, 105 58 Athens. ☎ **01/32-30-327.**
Fax 01/32-30-327. 20 rms (all with bath). MINIBAR TEL

Rates (including breakfast): 10,500 Drs ($45) single; 13,800 Drs ($57.55) double. No credit cards.

The rooms here are neat and cheerful. The six front ones are a tad noisy, but they have balconies and a view of the Acropolis. The rooms in the back are quieter and overlook nearby rooftops and gardens.

Hotel Nefeli, Odós Iperídou 16, Pláka 105 58, Athens. ☎ **32-28-044.**
18 rms (all with bath). TEL

Rates (including breakfast): 10,900 Drs ($45.40) single/double. No credit cards.

The small, charming Hotel Nefeli, at the end of Voulís Street, is the perfect place for getting away from the bustle and noise of the city. Its rooms are spotless, though small, and its marble-floored hallways are lined with botanical prints. We like it for its central location, the quiet street, and the old-fashioned ceiling fans in some of the rooms.

★ **Hotel Plaka,** Odós Kapnikaréas 7, Pláka, 105 56 Athens. ☎ **01/32-22-096**
Fax 01/32-22-412. 67 rms (all with bath). A/C TEL

Rates (including breakfast): 12,450 Drs ($51.75) single; 14,900 Drs ($62.10) double. For air conditioning, add 1,500 Drs ($6.25). AE, MC, V.

IMPRESSIONS

We are lovers of the beautiful yet simple in our tastes, and we cultivate the mind without loss of manliness.

—Pericles, in Thucydides, *The Peloponnesian War,* ca. 430 B.C.

The climate and country [of Greece] were such as to gratify every appetite for pleasurable sensation, without enervating or relaxing the frame or allowing the mind to sink into an Asiatic torpor.

—J. C. and A. Hare, *Guesses at Truth,* 1847

If you want to spend a few drachmas more for a step up in hotel living, try the Pláka, at the corner of Mitropóleos Street. Its bright, spotless white lobby sets the tone. The fresh and clean rooms and bathrooms, as well as the hallways, are in shades of blue. We think this higher-priced alternative is a good value in a great location. Request a rear, Acropolis-facing room for a better view and a more peaceful night's rest, although street-facing rooms have double-glazed windows and private balconies.

KOUKÁKI

Art Gallery Pension, Odós Erechthíou 5, 117 42, Athens. ☎ **01/92-38-376.** Fax 01/92-33-025. 22 rms (all with bath). TEL

Rates: 9,200 Drs ($38.30) single; 10,575 Drs ($44) double. No credit cards.

As you might expect, the Art Gallery Pension, three blocks south of the Acropolis, has an artistic bent. Bright orange awnings open over the balconies adjoining the rooms. Polished hardwood floors, ceiling fans, and a tiny cage elevator add a warm, homey feeling to a house whose old parlor has French doors, and doubles as a rooftop breakfast room and bar. Owner and architect Yannis Assimacopoulos told us that this 40-year-old family house had been home to several artists, who left behind a legacy of paintings that are now displayed everywhere (hence the name).

Hotel Acropolis View, Odós Webster 10, 117 42, Athens. ☎ **01/92-17-303.** Fax 01/92-30-705. 32 rms (all with bath). A/C TEL

Rates (including breakfast): 13,900 Drs ($58), single; 18,700 Drs ($78) double. AE, EC, MC.

There is one of the high-end accommodations in Koukáki worthy of mention for the splurge urge in some of our readers, a lovely hotel in the truly "classic" Athens setting, though readers complain its upkeep has slipped. It's on a quiet, winding lane, between Propiléon and Rovértou Gálli Streets, and has rooms and a rooftop bar that overlook the Acropolis. In the summertime the rooftop bar becomes an elegant barbecue with a perfect sunset view. The rooms are small but filled with the most modern amenities and private bathrooms.

Hotel Austria, Odós Moussón 7, 117 42, Athens. ☎ **01/92-35-151.** Fax 01/90-25-800. 37 rms (all with bath). TEL

Rates (including breakfast): 13,600 Drs ($56.75) single; 18,350 Drs ($76.50) double. AE, CB, DC, EC, MC, V.

This hotel, next to Pnyx Hill by the Acropolis, is a little above our price category, but merits mention for its quiet location, clean but spartan decor, and well-kept facilities. The rooms in the front look out over a park, with Acropolis views from the expansive roof garden that are postcard beautiful. Hotel Austria, which opened in 1989, is owned by an Austrian-Greek family.

Hotel Hera, Odós Falírou 9, 117 42, Athens. ☎ **01/92-36-682.** Fax 01/92-47-334. 49 rms (all with bath). A/C TEL

Rates: 13,200 Drs ($55) single; 18,800 Drs ($78.35) double. No credit cards.

The Hera, off Makriyáni Street, near Pláka, is an attractive, modern hotel with large, arcaded picture windows, and a slate-tiled rooftop bar overlooking the Acropolis. The spacious, double-height lobby includes a coffee shop and a breakfast lounge and bar with a view of the back garden. The compact rooms are simply furnished and carpeted, with piped-in music and private facilities.

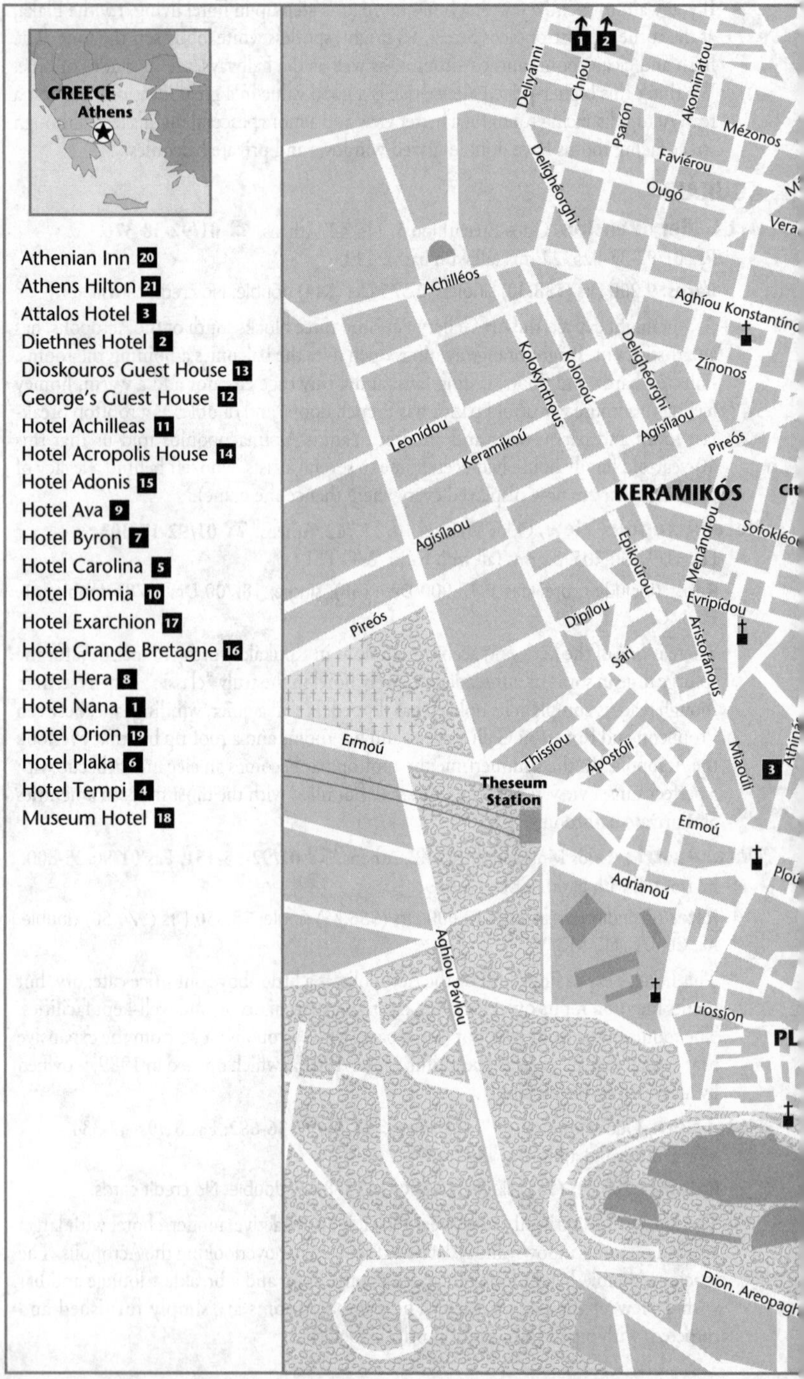
GREECE
Athens
Athenian Inn 20
Athens Hilton 21
Attalos Hotel 3
Diethnes Hotel 2
Dioskouros Guest House 13
George's Guest House 12
Hotel Achilleas 11
Hotel Acropolis House 14
Hotel Adonis 15
Hotel Ava 9
Hotel Byron 7
Hotel Carolina 5
Hotel Diomia 10
Hotel Exarchion 17
Hotel Grande Bretagne 16
Hotel Hera 8
Hotel Nana 1
Hotel Orion 19
Hotel Plaka 6
Hotel Tempi 4
Museum Hotel 18
Deliyánni
Chíou
Psarón
Akominátou
Mézonos
Faviérou
Ougó
Delighéorghi
Achilléos
Aghíou Konstantíno
Kolokýnthous
Kolonoú
Delighéorghi
Zínonos
Leonídou
Keramikoú
Agisílaou
Pireós
KERAMIKÓS
Agisílaou
Epikoúrou
Menándrou
Sofokléou
Evripídou
Dipílou
Pireós
Sári
Aristofánous
Ermoú
Thissíou
Apostóli
Miaoúli
Theseum Station
Ermoú
Adrianoú
Aghíou Pávlou
Liossíon
Dion. Areopagh

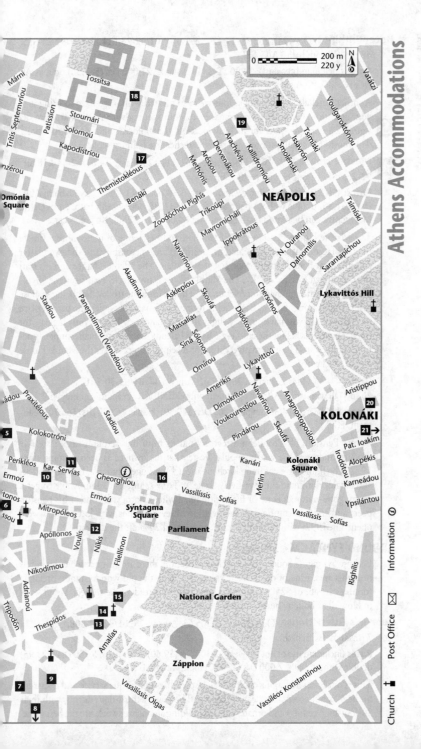

Athens Accommodations

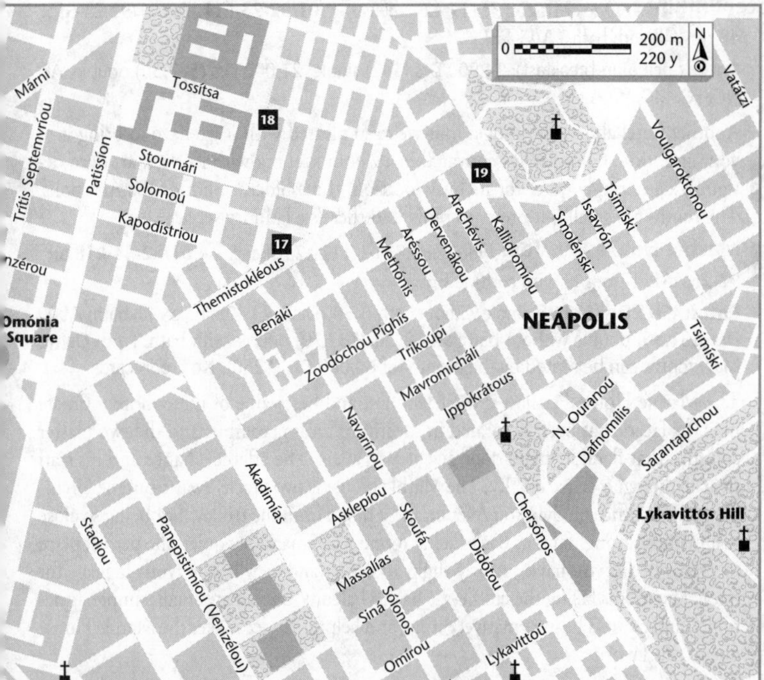

Church
Post Office
Information

Hotel Phillipos, Odós Mitséon 3, 117 42 Athens. ☎ **01/92-23-611.** Fax 01/92-23-615. 48 rms (all with bath). A/C TEL

Rates (including breakfast): 14,900 Drs ($62) single; 21,000 Drs ($87.50) double. AE, DC, EC, MC, V.

$ Another hotel above our budget, but we're so pleased with it we have to bring it to your attention. Completely renovated in 1994 in keeping with its sleek art deco design, it's amazingly quiet for its busy location, three blocks south of the Acropolis. The rooms are small but pretty in pink, and there's a laundry service.

★ **Marble House Pension,** Odós Zinní 35A, 117 42 Athens. ☎ **01/92-34-058** or **92-26-461.** 17 rms (9 with bath). TEL

Rates: 4,375 Drs ($18.25) single without bath; 5,600 Drs ($23.40) single with bath; 7,000 Drs ($31.50) double without bath; 9,000 Drs ($37.70) double with bath. From Oct to May, rooms can be rented by the month for 60,000 Drs ($250). No credit cards.

The Marble House Pension is the friendliest and best value of these more intimate inns. Its facade has been decorated in sheaths of creamy marble, and the two plaster columns that flank its main door give it a regal air. The affable Thanos and his staff treat all their guests like royalty. The Marble House is two blocks away from the Olympic Airways office on Syngroú Avenue and a block from the trolley. For being so close to a major thoroughfare, its back-facing rooms are remarkably quiet, the perfect place to grab a bed if you have an early flight to catch (and they'll store your luggage for free). The rooms facing the cul-de-sac have a balcony, and all are small, simple, functional, and clean. The informative, caring, and helpful service makes the Marble House one of our favorites.

Tony's Pension, Odós Zacharítsa 26, 117 42, Athens. ☎ **01/92-30-561.**
26 rms (all with bath). A/C (in apartment only) MINIBAR (in apartment only) TV TEL

Rates: 8,250 Drs ($34.30) single; 9,800 Drs ($40.80) double; 16,000 Drs ($66.70) apartment. EC, MC.

Tony's Pension, off Propiléon Street, six blocks from the Acropolis, is a tastefully modern update of the wildly popular hostel that the owner has been running since 1972. The floors have common kitchens and a TV lounge. Students, fashion models, and singles dominate the ever-lively scene at Tony's, and if it's impossible to get a room, good-natured Tony or his multilingual wife, Charo, will contact his pension peers and try to accommodate the overflow. Eleven studios with kitchenettes were opened in 1992, with monthly rentals discounted 20% off the day rate.

AROUND SÝNTAGMA SQUARE

Because Sýntagma Square is such a choice location, there are only a few budget hotels near this area. One of our favorite splurges is here, the old-world Grande Bretagne (doubles are about $250)—fun for a look, but most readers, we suspect, won't want to blow their holiday budget in one night.

George's Guest House, Odós Níkis 46, 105 63, Athens. ☎ **01/32-44-808.**
7 rms (none with bath).

Rates (including use of hot showers): 2,300 Drs ($9.60) dorm beds; 5,750 Drs ($23.95) double without bath; 7,000 Drs ($29.20) triple without bath.

This is our lesser Sýntagma choice, which specializes in brusque service and is spartan to the max but acceptably clean and cheap. The hostel's third-floor dorms, with their 20-foot-high ceilings and ornate, painted molding and plaster work, are the best value.

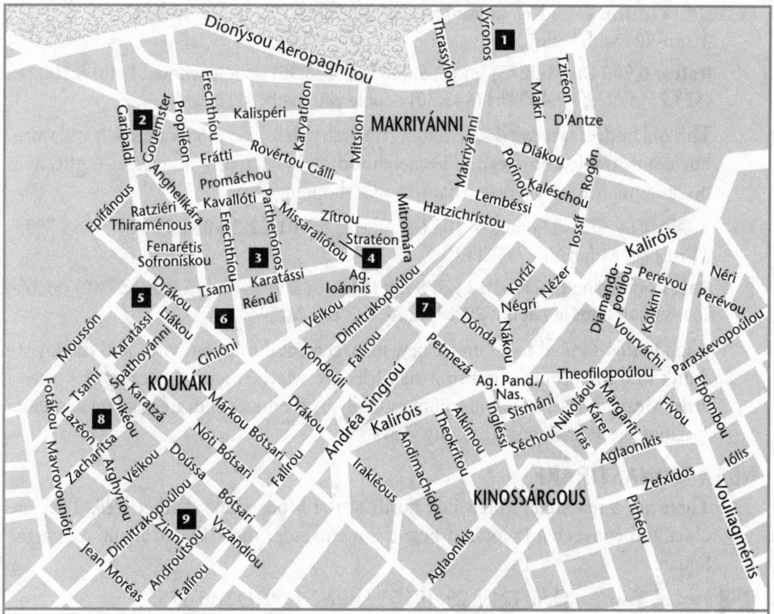

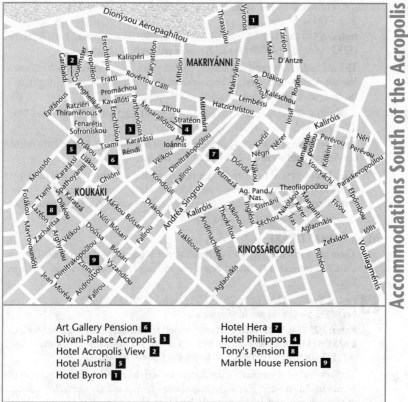

Art Gallery Pension **6**
Divani-Palace Acropolis **3**
Hotel Acropolis View **2**
Hotel Austria **5**
Hotel Byron **1**
Hotel Hera **7**
Hotel Philippos **4**
Tony's Pension **8**
Marble House Pension **9**

9611A

By the way, George's glorious villa was built by Hádji Nikólas, a war hero in the 1821 struggle for liberation from the Turks. Check in early if you hope to get a room in this popular hostel. George's also has bathless doubles and triples and free luggage storage. George closes the house in January and February.

$ Hotel Achilleas, Odós Lekká 21, 105 62 Athens. ☎ **01/32-333-197.** Fax 01/32-41-092. 32 rms (29 with bath) A/C TEL

Rates (including breakfast): 7,800 Drs ($32.50) single with shared bath; 10,600 Drs ($44) single with private bath; 11,250 Drs ($47) double with shared bath; 14,000 Drs ($58) double with private bath. For air conditioning, add 1,200 Drs. Twin rooms with shared bath. 18,000 Drs ($75). AE, V.

We recently discovered this little budget favorite, owned by the same family that operates Hotel Pláka. The Achilléas is on a quiet side street a short walk from Sýntagma Square. Well-priced rooms (slated for a 1995 renovation) are spacious and bright, all with sitting rooms, and several with a flower-filled balcony. Families will welcome the twin bedrooms, which share a common sitting room and bath. Breakfast is served in the first-floor dining room. Don't be discouraged by the dim off-street entrance—good value awaits you inside.

Hotel Carolina, Odós Kolokotróni 55, 105 60 Athens. ☎ **01/32-40-944.**
32 rms (24 with baths). TEL

Rates: 6,900 Drs ($28.75) single, 9,200 Drs ($38.30) double without bath; 8,100 Drs ($33.75) single; 10,400 Drs ($43.30) double with bath. AE, EC, MC, V.

This old budget favorite is still holding up pretty well. The rooms are small and worn, but comfortable and clean. The neighborhood is actually quieter at night, as it becomes increasingly a pedestrians-mostly shopping area.

Hotel Diomia, Odós Diomías 5, 105 63, Athens. ☎ **01/32-38-034.** Fax 01/32-48-792.
71 rms (all with bath). A/C TEL

Rates (including breakfast): 11,375 Drs ($47.40) single; 16,650 Drs ($69.40) double. Low-season rates are about 20% less. AE, EC, DC, MC, V.

The Diomia seemed to be under new management during our visit, and frankly we didn't find the people who run it very friendly. Maybe they'll spruce up the place a little. Meanwhile, choose your room carefully, as the upper ones are brighter and more spacious, some with good balcony views.

NEAR MONASTIRÁKI

There are a few small hotels just north of the Monastiráki market area. They are quiet and conveniently located near the metro stop, the Pláka area, and Sýntagma Square.

$ **Hotel Tempi,** Odós Eólou 29, 105 51 Athens. ☎ **01/32-13-175.**
Fax 01/32-54-179. 24 rms (6 with showers).

Rates: 1,750 Drs ($7.30) bed and cover on roof; 3,500 Drs ($14.60) single without bath; 6,675 Drs ($27.80) double without bath; 7,150 Drs ($29.80) double with shower; 7,820 Drs ($32.60) triple with shower. All rooms share toilets. AE, MC, V.

This low-budget alternative for the student crowd is located three blocks north of the Monastiráki metro stop. Pleasantly situated across from placid, car-free St. Irene Square, this is a well-managed, freshly painted Class D lodging that's clean and friendly, though a bit worn. The homey touches include hallway murals of Greece, a laundry room with ironing facilities, free luggage storage, and a paperback-lending library.

$ **Attalos Hotel,** Odós Athinás 29, 105 54 Athens. ☎ **01/32-12-801.**
Fax 01/32-43-124. 80 rms (all with bath). TEL

Rates: 7,500 Drs ($31.25) single; 9,775 Drs ($40.75) double. V.

This excellent-value lodging, two blocks north of the Monastiráki metro stop, has been popular with past readers and grows steadily in our estimation. It is a large, multistory building with comfortable, clean, quiet rooms, an accommodating staff, and a grand, beautifully landscaped rooftop bar with a drop-dead view of you-know-what. The Attalos also offers free luggage storage and a discount for our readers.

AROUND EXÁRCHIA SQUARE

There are three decent hotels situated in Exárchia, a neighborhood near the National Archeological Museum. It's the right place to stay if you've come to Athens to spend time with this extraordinary collection of ancient art.

Hotel Exarchion, Odós Themistokléous 55, 106 83 Athens. ☎ **01/36-01-256.**
Fax 01/36-03-296. 49 rms (all with bath). TEL

Rates: 6,900 Drs ($28.75) single; 8,050 Drs ($33.55) double. No credit cards.

The modern Hotel Exarchion has comfortable rooms, most of which have a balcony. The lobby is artfully decorated, and there is a large rooftop, where you can eat or drink while you watch students debate in the square below.

Hotel Orion, Odós Emmanouíl Benáki 105, 114 73 Athens. ☎ **01/36-27-362.** Fax 01/36-05-193. 20 rms (10 with bath).

Rates: 5,060 Drs ($21.10) single without bath; 6,325 Drs ($26.35) single with bath; 6,900 Drs ($28.75) double without bath; 9,200 Drs ($38.35) double with bath. No credit cards.

The Oríon is a quiet little hotel set on a green hillside above Stréfi Park, near Anexartisías Street, about a 15-minute walk from the celebrated Benaki Museum. Breakfast is served on a neat, skyline-view terrace. Call to double-check the route, as even cab drivers may have trouble.

Museum Hotel, Odós Bouboulínas 16, 106 82 Athens. ☎ **01/36-05-611.** 58 rms (all with shower). TEL

Rates (including breakfast): 5,175 Drs ($21.50) single; 7,130 Drs ($29.70) double. AE, DC.

This bright, clean hotel is so close to the National Archeological Museum that all of its balconies overlook the museum's tree-filled park. It's a good value in a good location far from the madding crowd.

KOLONÁKI

Kolonáki is one of the most sophisticated, elegant, and expensive neighborhoods in Athens. It rises up a slope of Lykavittós Hill and commands an imperial view of the city.

Athenian Inn, Odós (C)háritos 22, 106 75 Athens. ☎ **01/72-38-097.** Fax 01/72-42-268. 28 rms (all with bath). A/C TV TEL

Rates (including breakfast): 15,350 Drs ($64) single; 22,900 Drs ($95.50) double. AE, DC, V.

This is one of the few hotels in this area, one of those hideaway places that veteran travelers love to know about. The international clientele prizes its quiet location (three blocks east of Kolonáki Square), spacious and clean accommodations, and friendly, informative staff. (A quote from the guest book: "At last the ideal Athens hotel, good and modest in scale but perfect in service and goodwill. Hurrah. Lawrence Durrell.") Many of the rooms have balconies that look out to Lykavittós Hill. You can have breakfast in the cozy lounge (decorated with a fireplace, piano, and two Mexican sombreros). The rates drop about 20% in the low season.

NEAR THE RAILROAD STATION

The only reason to stay near the railroad station is to make a convenient overnight connection between trains, saving time and taxi fare.

Diethnes Hotel, Odós Paioníou 52, Athens. ☎ **01/88-32-878.** 22 rms (none with bath).

Rates: 4,000 Drs ($16.75) single; 5,750 Drs ($23.95) double. No credit cards.

This aging, three-story, pale-blue house with white trim has at least one thing going for it—it's within sight of the Baríssis station. It is a cleanish, reasonably well-managed place, where you can pick up tips on student discounts, cheap restaurants, bargain air fares, and behind-the-scenes Athens.

Hotel Nana, Odós Metaxá 27, Athens. ☎ **01/88-42-211.** Fax 01/88-23-220. 50 rms (all with bath). A/C TEL

Rates: 10,350 Drs ($43.10) single; 12,650 Drs ($52.70) double. No credit cards.

This hotel is just south of the park across from the Laríssis station and is probably the best value in the area. The Nana's clean and well-maintained rooms have all the Class B amenities, including air conditioning. Request rear-facing rooms for a quieter sleep. There is 24-hour room service, from the downstairs Nana Café, a popular local hangout.

NEAR THE AIRPORT

There are no good budget hotels near the Ellinikó International Airport, so if you're faced with a layover, your best bet is to grab a bus or taxi into Athens and enjoy an evening on the town. Two of the best choices are in suburban Glyfáda, but they're neither bargains nor free of the noise of thundering planes. They're **Hotel London,** Leofóros Vassiléos Gheorghíou 38, Glyfáda, Athens (☎ **01/89-46-738**), and **Hotel Golden Sun,** Leofóros Metaxá 72 (☎ **01/89-55-218**). Both have pools (the London's is better) and rates starting at 16,500 Drs ($68.75). The hotels are within walking distance of the beach. The London is definitely the nicer and quieter choice.

YOUTH HOSTELS

There are several lodgings in Greece that belong to the Greek Youth Hostel Federation (GYHF). For a complete listing, contact the Greek Tourist Organization (EOT) or, for further information, the Greek Youth Hostel Federation, Odós Dragatsaníou 4, 105 59 Athens (☎ **01/32-34-107** or **32-37-590**).

YWCA, Odós Amerikís 11, Athens. ☎ **01/36-24-291.**

Rates: 4,000 Drs ($16.70) single without bath; 5,500 Drs ($22.90) single with bath; 6,250 Drs ($26) double without bath; 7,800 Drs ($32.50) double with bath; 7,995 Drs ($33.30) triple without bath. **Closed:** Dec 1–Jan 15. No credit cards.

Women will find spotless lodging at bargain prices at the YWCA (XEN in Greek), which is located a block off Panepistimíou Street. There are a few rooms available for married couples. Call or write ahead, as this is a convenient and popular place.

YMCA. ☎ **01/36-26-970.**

The YMCA (XAN in Greek) has closed its hostel.

Annabel's Youth Hostel. Odós Koumoundoúrou 28, Athens. ☎ **01/52-45-834.**

Rates: 1,750–2,600 Drs ($7.30–$11). No credit cards.

This reliable establishment was about to be taken over by new management during our visit, and given the deteriorating neighborhood we can't promise you anything except reasonably low prices.

Hostel Aphrodite, Odós Einárdou 12 & Michaíl Vodá, near Laríssis Station. ☎ **01/22-66-686,** Fax 01/82-20732.

Rates: 3750 Drs ($15.60) single without bath to 11,250 Drs ($46.85) for four with bath.

This clean, well-maintained place was the best hostel we found in Athens. Its location a few blocks northwest of Victoria Square is fairly central, and they have hot showers, a safe for valuables, an information desk, a sun roof, and free luggage storage.

SPLURGE CHOICES

★ **Divani-Palace Acropolis,** Odós Parthenónos 19-25, Makriyáni, 117 42 Athens. ☎ **01/92-22-2945.** Fax 01/92-14-993. 242 rms, 11 suites (all with bath). A/C MINIBAR TV TEL

Rates: 40,000–51,500 Drs ($166.60–$214.60) single; 46,000–62,000 Drs ($175–$258); suites from 63,000 Drs ($263). AE, DC, MC, V.

For luxury, comfort, and location you'd have a hard time beating this recently renovated beauty, just three blocks south of the Acropolis. The rooms are quietly elegant; service is friendly but professional; the spacious modern lobby is appointed with copies of classical sculpture—sections of the actual walls built by Themistocles during the Persian Wars are exhibited in the basement! The hotel has a small, handsome pool and a bar, a good restaurant, large meeting facilities, and a lovely roof garden with the view you expect.

Hotel Grande Bretagne. Sýntagma Square, 105 63 Athens. ☎ **01/32-30-251.** Fax 01/32-28-034. 365 rms, 33 suites (all with bath). A/C MINIBAR TV TEL

Rates: 48,875–97,175 Drs ($204–$405) single; 54,625–109,250 Drs ($228–$455) double; suites from 74,750 Drs ($311). AE, CB, DC, MC, V.

This grande dame is our favorite splurge hotel for old-world elegance. Built in 1864, it remains a venerable institution, its beaux-arts design without equal in all of Greece. The polished marble floors and classical pillary of the lobby, with its ornately carved wood panelling and soaring ceilings, lend a true continental air to the Grande Bretagne, a feeling that the clientele only enhances. Yet, the Greek flavor prevails, as the movers and shakers of Greek society pass through for power lunches at the popular GB Corner.

Softly lit hallways with marble wainscotting lead to old-fashioned rooms with 12-foot ceilings and wall-to-wall coziness. The Sheraton hotel chain has assumed management of the Grande Bretagne, so you can expect a continuing renovation to smarten the slightly worn edges of the guest rooms. Very little is needed, however, to maintain our long-standing affection for this gem of a hotel.

Athens Hilton, Leofóros Vassilíssis Sofías 46, 115 28 Athens. ☎ **01/72-20-301.** Fax 01/72-13-110. 427 rms, 19 suites (all with bath). A/C MINIBAR TV TEL

Rates: 48,000–121,000 Drs ($200–$505) single; 57,500–121,000 Drs ($240–$505) double; suites from 135,000 Drs ($565). Plaza Executive rates: 85,800 Drs ($358) single; 101,800 Drs ($424) double. AE, DC, EC, MC, V.

The Athens Hilton, near the U.S. Embassy, is something of an institution in the capital. Not only is it home to many an international businessperson or diplomat, but for years it has been a place to meet for a swim or a drink or to dine in one of its many restaurants. Because it is the Hilton flagship in Greece, it is only appropriate that everything should be quietly elegant and of polished marble. The lobby and other public spaces glisten and guest rooms are comfortable, with marble bathrooms and a pleasantly neutral style. Hilton often runs promotional sales, so check with your travel agent about special weekend rates before booking. For those on business, there is the Plaza Executive floor of executive rooms and suites, a separate business center, and a higher level of service. Sports options include a great pool and a health club. The lobby Polo Club and top-floor Galaxy Roof Terrace, with stunning city views, are fine venues for a drink.

2 Where to Eat

This section is divided into geographic regions of the city, making it easy to find an eatery right nearby when you're hungry. All establishments are open for lunch and dinner unless otherwise noted; most are open year-round, but some of the best are closed in August. If you want to plan a night on the town, turn directly to the section "Splurge Restaurants," which recommends fine restaurants of several cuisines, regardless of locale. If you're hankering after a particular taste, the following is a quick index to recommended restaurants by specialties.

Of the **tavernas,** the most expensive (good too) is Myrtia, near the Olympic Stadium. The best combination of food and Acropolis view is Taverna Strofi, in Koukáki. For music and a good casual Greek place, try Taverna Xinos in Pláka. The last two are open evenings (closed Sunday). Good, moderately priced food, and a young and lively crowd can be found at Socrates' Prison in Koukáki.

The most expensive **continental cuisine** is found at Boschetto Ristorante, in Evanghelismós Park; it offers an excellent taste of Italy in the heart of Greece. The best of the less formal, moderately priced continental/Greek restaurants is the Ideal Restaurant in Omónia Square. The best European old-world ambience with an exquisite menu of light snacks and desserts is found at To Tristrato in Pláka.

A good **vegetarian** restaurant is hard to find. Most tavernas, however, serve a variety of vegetable dishes.

Ouzerís, casual bars, are a superb Greek invention, a place to nurse an *ouzo* (a strong, anise-flavored liquor) and munch on varied appetizers (*mezédes*). Our favorite Athens ouzerí is Yiali Kafines in Kolonáki. Sadly, it's closed in the summer, so Kouklis Ouzerí is a lesser, though acceptable, backup.

For a midday break, midafternoon lift, or late-night treat of **dessert and coffee,** try Dionysos-Zonar's near Sýntagma Square, a typical ice-cream and confection parlor. The most mind-boggling display of sweets is undoubtedly at Select on Fokíonos Négri Street. For stand-up coffee and sweets, we like the murals and 1930s brass decor and great java blends of the Brazilian off Sýntagma Square.

PLÁKA

Pláka has been Athens's "Restaurant Row" for decades. In every corner of its narrow streets you'll find a lively taverna, fast-food snack stand, or raucous bouzouki joint.

Grill House Plaka, Odós Kydathinéon 28. ☎ **32-46-229.**

Cuisine: GREEK. **Reservations:** Not required.

Prices: Light meals 800–1,500 Drs ($3.35–$6.25)

If you're not in the mood to sit down and make a big production of a meal, this simple, clean, family-run gyro joint in the heart of Pláka is a good choice. For 1,500 Drs ($6.25) you get a full savory plate with two skewers of souvlaki or chicken, pita bread, fresh greens, fries, and some tzatzíki.

Kouklis Ouzeri (To Gerani) Odós Tripodón 14. ☎ **32-47-605.**

Cuisine: GREEK. **Reservations:** Not required.

Prices: Appetizers 350–700 Drs ($1.45–$2.90). No credit cards.

Open: Daily 11am–2am.

In summer, small wrought-iron tables are moved from within this classic two-story town house to the rooftop terrace and the sidewalk. Diners are presented with a dozen plates of *mezédes:* appetizer portions of fried fish, beans, grilled eggplant, taramosalata, cucumber-and-tomato salad, olives, fried cheese, and other seasonal specialties. With a liter of the house *krassí* (wine) (750 Drs or $3.15), you can dine on a budget at Kouklis.

Palia Plakiotika, Odós Lissíou 26. ☎ **32-28-722.**

Cuisine: GREEK. **Reservations:** Required on weekends.

Prices: Appetizers 800–1,500 Drs ($3.35–$6.25); main courses 1,400–3,335 Drs ($5.85–$13.90); fixed-price dinner 3,750 Drs ($20.80). No credit cards.
Open: Daily 7pm–2am.

T. Stamatopoulos's taverna, Palia Plakiotika, is, as the name implies in Greek, one of the oldest in Pláka. This beautiful split-level garden, with vines tumbling down its trellised walls, provides a refreshing sanctuary on a hot summer's night. The typical taverna fare is a bit more expensive than what is offered by some of the competition, but the highlight is not the food but the Greek music and the lively local crowd that frequently joins in song.

Taverna Ta Bakaliarakia, Odós Kydathinéon 41. ☎ **32-25-084.**

Cuisine: GREEK. **Reservations:** Not required.
Prices: Appetizers 460–700 Drs ($1.90–$2.90); main courses 1,300–2,070 Drs ($5.40–$8.60). No credit cards.
Open: daily 7pm–12am; closed July–Sept.

Ta Bakaliarakia (also known as Damigos), in the heart of Pláka, has been in the Damigos family since 1865. A marble column, antique rifles, and framed family photos fill the walls of this underground taverna. Fried foods—codfish, potatoes, zucchini slices, small fish—and piquant dips, such as *skordaliá* (garlic sauce) and *tzatzíki* (garlic, cucumber, and yogurt) are the house specialties. Bakaliarakia has been famous for this fare since long before anyone knew cholesterol existed. After sampling the terrific house retsína (resin-flavored white wine), you'll want to wander upstairs to the colorful and original Brettos Bottle Shop. Its candy selection is a treat, too.

$ **Taverna Platanos.** Odós Dioghénous 4. ☎ **32-20-666.**

Cuisine: GREEK. **Reservations:** Not required.
Prices: Appetizers 500–920 Drs ($2.10–$3.85); main courses 1,300–2,000 Drs ($5.40–$8.35). No credit cards.
Open: Mon–Sat noon–4:30pm; 8pm–midnight.

This is one of the last of a vanishing species—a taverna in Pláka that is still truly "Greek." The food is traditional and free of tourist-oriented shortcuts, like frozen vegetables and microwave moussaká. Tables are scattered around a shaded bend in this quiet back lane near the Agora, and time seems to stand still with the rhythmic sounds of cicadas under the noonday sun. We like Plátanos for the hearty fare and, especially, for the timeless atmosphere.

★ **Taverna Xinos,** Odós Anghélou Ghéronta 4. ☎ **32-21-065.**

Cuisine: GREEK. **Reservations:** Recommended.
Prices: Appetizers 920–1,725 Drs ($3.85–$7.20); main courses 1,725–2,350 Drs ($7.20–$10.55). No credit cards.
Open: Mon–Fri, 8pm–12:30am. **Closed:** Sat–Sun and all July.

This is one classic that's worth making reservations for (but make them for *after* 9pm). Tucked in back of a narrow, pebble-paved lane near Iperídou Street, its walls graced with Dionysian folk-art murals, Xinos offers superb food to the accompaniment of live music. Its informal atmosphere draws guests in aloha shirts as well as the suit-and-tie crowd. It is highly recommended by Greeks, who consider it one of the finest restaurants in Athens (some readers, however, have complained about the service). Try the excellent lemony stuffed grape leaves, the tasty moussaká with fresh ground spices, the lamb fricassee in an egg-lemon and dill sauce, or the veal stew with tomatoes and potatoes in rich olive oil. You can't go wrong with any course at Xinos. If you don't have reservations, you may wait an hour. Walk around Pláka until your turn comes.

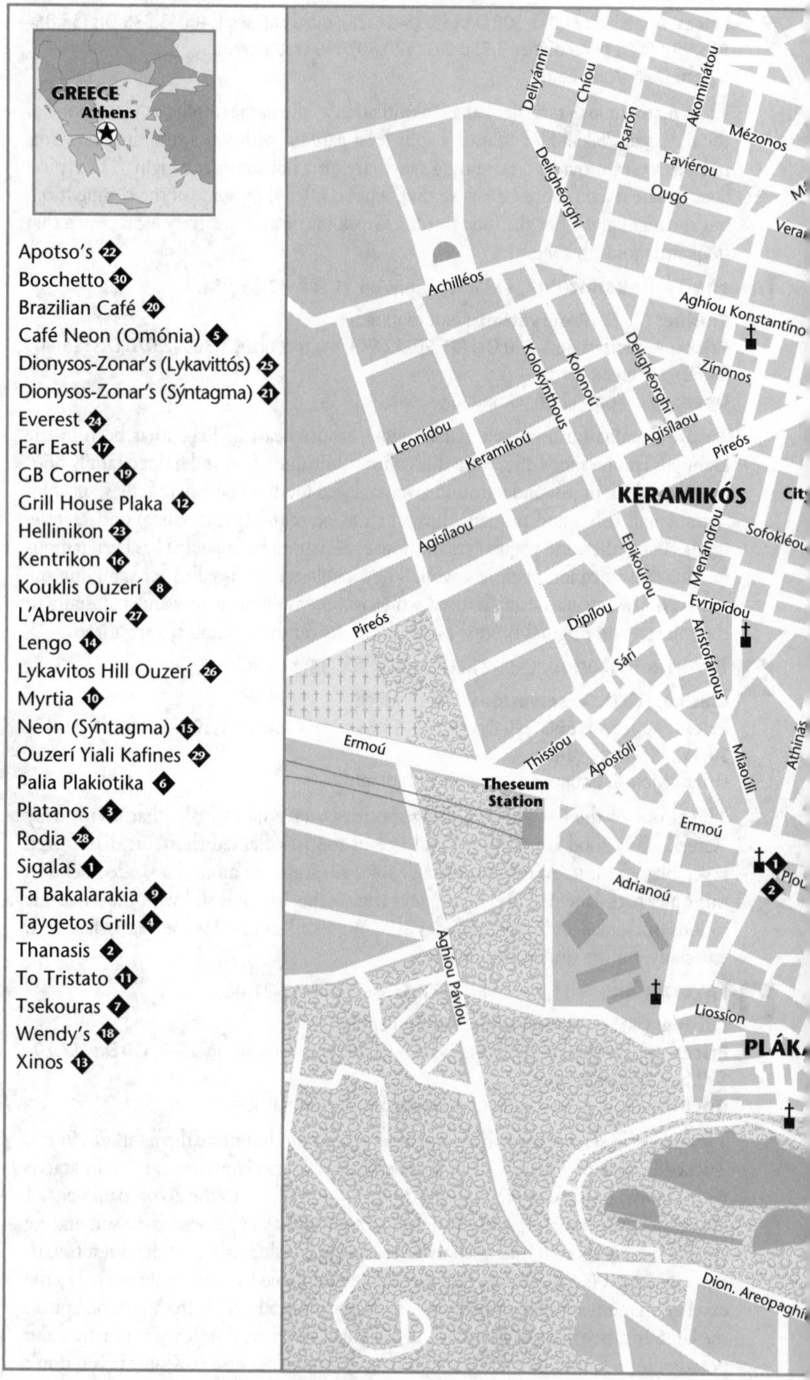

GREECE
Athens
Apotso's 22
Boschetto 30
Brazilian Café 20
Café Neon (Omónia) 5
Dionysos-Zonar's (Lykavittós) 25
Dionysos-Zonar's (Sýntagma) 21
Everest 24
Far East 17
GB Corner 19
Grill House Plaka 12
Hellinikon 23
Kentrikon 16
Kouklis Ouzerí 8
L'Abreuvoir 27
Lengo 14
Lykavitos Hill Ouzerí 26
Myrtia 10
Neon (Sýntagma) 15
Ouzerí Yiali Kafines 29
Palia Plakiotika 6
Platanos 3
Rodia 28
Sigalas 1
Ta Bakalarakia 9
Taygetos Grill 4
Thanasis 2
To Tristato 11
Tsekouras 7
Wendy's 18
Xinos 13
Deliyánni
Chíou
Akominátou
Psarón
Mézonos
Faviérou
Ougó
Delighéorghi
Achilléos
Kolokýnthous
Kolonoú
Delighéorghi
Zínonos
Agisílaou
Pireós
Leonídou
Keramikoú
KERAMIKÓS
Agisílaou
Epikoúrou
Menándrou
Evripídou
Dipílou
Pireós
Sári
Aristofánous
Ermoú
Thissíou
Apostóli
Theseum Station
Miaoúli
Ermoú
Adrianoú
Aghíou Pávlou
Liossíon

Athens Dining

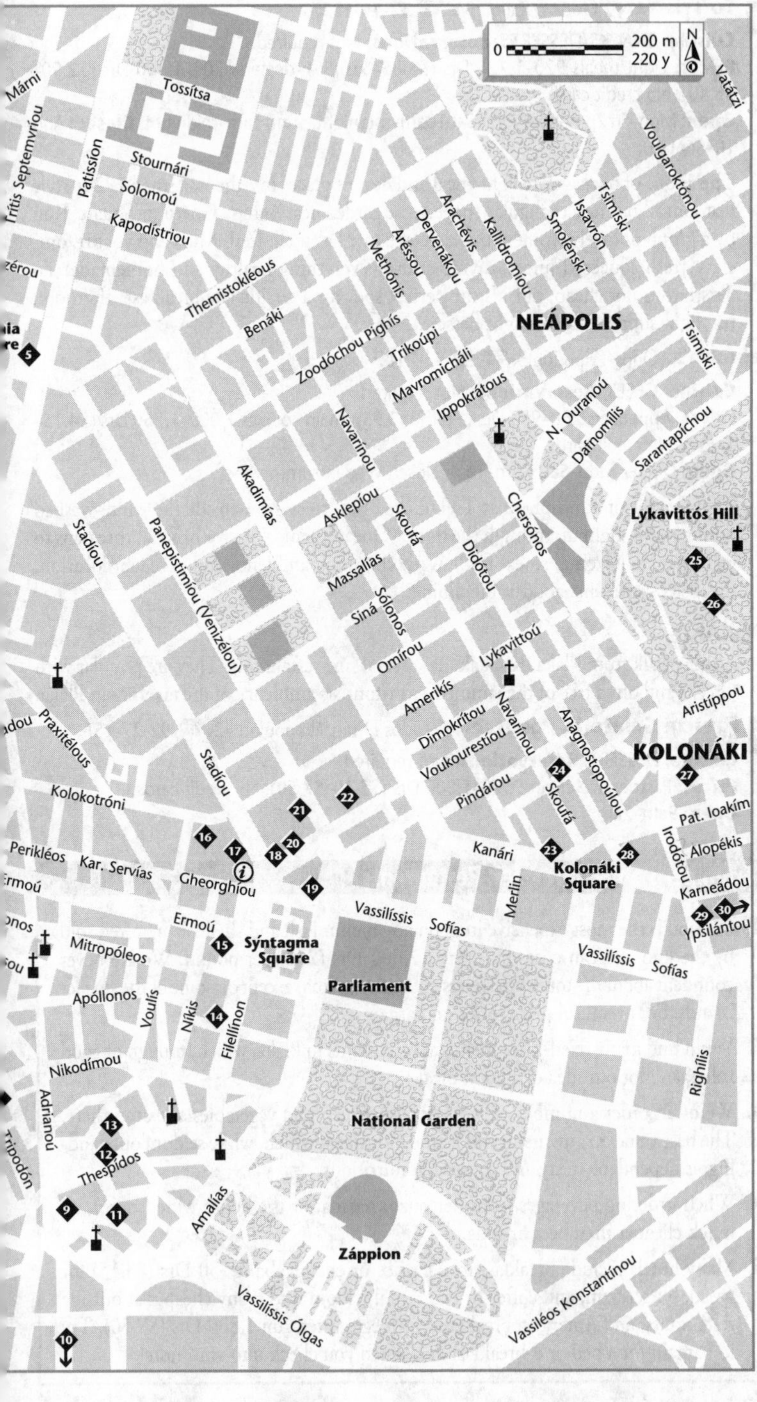

Church
Post Office
Information

★ **To Tristrato,** Odós Dédalou 34. ☎ **32-44-472.**

Cuisine: SNACKS/DESSERTS. **Reservations:** Not required.
Prices: Light meals 920–1,725 Drs ($3.85–$10.55); desserts 700–1,300 Drs ($2.90–$5.40). No credit cards.
Open: Mon–Fri 2pm–midnight; Sat 10am–midnight, Sun 11am–midnight. **Closed:** Aug 10–Sept 10.

This is one of our favorite light-meal and dessert places in Athens, a small 1920s-style tearoom adjoining a triangular-shaped rose garden near Aghíou Ghéronta Square. Run by a group of lovely women, this new-age café has it all: fresh fruits and yogurt, omelets, fresh-squeezed juices, divine cakes—everything healthy and homemade. To Tristrato is not cheap, but it's the perfect spot for a terrific late breakfast, afternoon tea, light supper, or late-night dessert.

Tsekoura's, Odós Tripodón 3. ☎ **32-33-710.**

Cuisine: GREEK. **Reservations:** Not required.
Prices: Appetizers 280–950 Drs ($1.15–$3.95); main courses 1,000–1,750 Drs ($4.15–$7.30). No credit cards.
Open: Dinner Mon–Sat, 7pm–1am; closed Wed in summer.

There's a lot of atmosphere at Tsekoura's. Two trees grow inside the white-washed dining room, right up through the floor. (One of them, a fig tree or *sikiá,* threatens to take over the taverna, so eat fast!) With charming ambience and excellent location, this place represents good-value dining.

KOUKÁKI

A short walk from Pláka, Koukáki has several fine restaurants. They are popular with Greeks and often free of the jammed-with-tourists ambience of the tavernas in Pláka.

★ **Firenze Gelateria Pasticceria,** Odós Dimitrakopoúlou 42. ☎ **92-27-156.**

Cuisine: DESSERT. **Reservations:** Not required.
Prices: Pastries, ice cream: 500–1,800 Drs ($2.10–$7.50). No credit cards.
Open: 9am–2am.

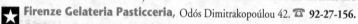

Frommer's Smart Traveler: Restaurants

1. Seafood is the most expensive item on any menu. Fish and shellfish are often sold by the kilo and can cost you up to 12,000 Drs ($50) per pound. We are never confident about the touted freshness of the day's catch, except on some of the smaller islands. So, premium prices offer no bargains.
2. You'll find many fixed-price menus at restaurants in Pláka, which, though of good value, are not our idea of a good meal.
3. We often order a number of *mezédes* (appetizers) and vegetables and stop there. The best value on any menu will be the moussaká, which, while seldom outstanding, is dependably tasty and somewhat nutritious.
4. When ordering beverages, consider ouzo, retsína, or the house wine (*krassí*), all much cheaper than beer or soda.
5. Many hotels include breakfast in the price or charge about 750 Drs ($3.15) for bread, butter, jam, and coffee or tea. You'll seldom find it any cheaper at outside restaurants, and American breakfasts with eggs often run 1,800 Drs ($7.50). Try to bargain for a bed-and-breakfast deal when you check into your hotel.

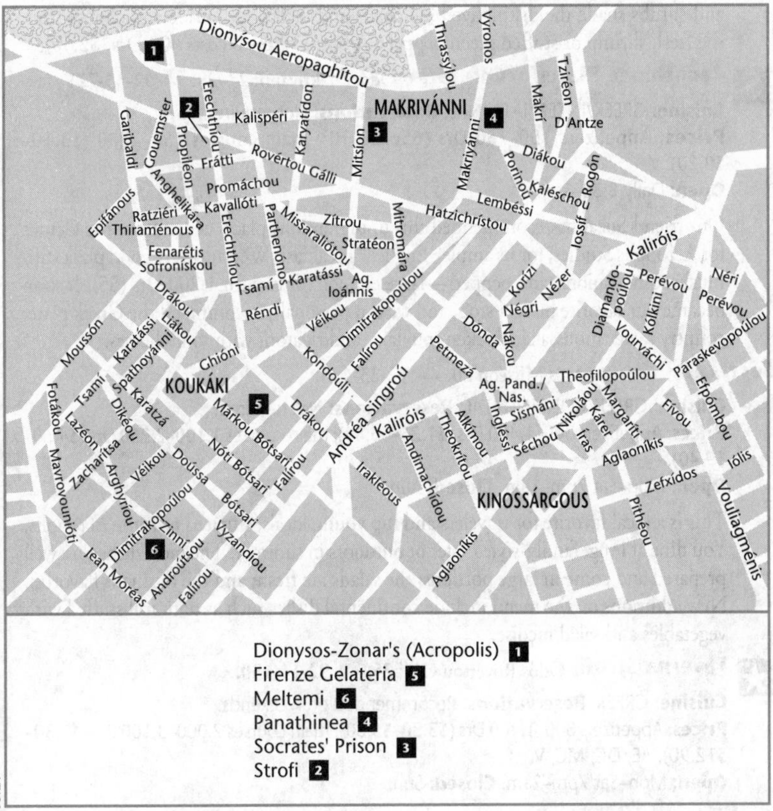

In your Athens travels you'll pass an endless stream of cafés serving coffee and desserts (most of which, we think, are made in the same subterranean kitchen and beamed all over the city). Pass them all by and take a short walk into Koukáki to this comfortable and hip spot on shady Drákou Street, at the corner of busy Dimitrakopoúlou Street. Ice-cream lovers will embrace the superb *gelati* and *graniti* (sorbets), with fruit flavors of strawberry, melon, banana, kiwi, and more, as pure and fresh as can be. The pastries—tarts, cheesecakes, rich cream cakes—are superior, with cappuccino and espresso that are the best in town. Outdoors under the trees or in the marbled modern indoor space, you'll find it well worth the walk. If you want to combine your dessert with a reasonably decent pizza, walk across the plaza to Gargareta Pizza, pick up a slice and enjoy it at the outdoor tables before moving on to the sweet stuff.

Meltemi, Odós Zinní 26. ☎ **90-28-230.**

Cuisine: GREEK. **Reservations:** Not required.
Prices: Appetizers 350–1350 Drs ($1.50–$5.65). No credit cards.
Open: Mon–Sat noon–1:30am.

If you are arriving or leaving from the Olympic Airways office on Syngroú Avenue, the Meltemi is a nearby ouzerí that is a good stopover for a light meal or drink. Trees and shrubs shade the distinctive blue chairs and tables. Go inside and choose from the fresh shrimp or stuffed green peppers. A bottle of ouzo costs 600 Drs ($2.50).

$ **Panathinea Pizzeria/Cafeteria,** Odós Makriyánni 27–29. ☎ **92-33-721**

Cuisine: GREEK/INTERNATIONAL. **Reservations:** Not required.
Prices: Appetizers 150–750 Drs (65¢–$3.10); main courses 750–2200 ($3.10–$9.20). V.
Open: Daily 8:30–1am.

Our friend Suzanna recommended this unpretentious place, across from the Center for Acropolis Studies, for its ample "English" breakfast. We had a very good pizza with mushrooms, onions, and peppers—large enough for two for 1,200 Drs ($5). It soon became our favorite budget stop, and we can personally recommend the Greek plate, country salad, moussaká, chicken souvlaki, and rigatoni with four cheeses.

Socrates' Prison, Odós Mitséon 20. ☎ **92-23-434.**

Cuisine: GREEK/CONTINENTAL. **Reservations:** Not required.
Prices: Appetizers 300–1,400 Drs ($1.25–$5.85); main courses 1,100–2,250 Drs ($4.60–$9.40).
Open: Mon–Sat 7pm–1am. **Closed:** Aug.

This is a local favorite for travelers and hip young locals, situated near the Acropolis. You dine at long, family-style tables or outdoors in summer. The meat dishes are well prepared and come in large portions; the salads are fresh; and the retsína is flavorful. New additions on the menu include continental dishes such as pork roll stuffed with vegetables and salad niçoise.

★ **Taverna Strofi,** Odós Rovértou Gálli 25. ☎ **92-14-130.**

Cuisine: GREEK. **Reservations:** Recommended on weekends.
Prices: Appetizers 800–1,400 Drs ($3.30–$5.80); main courses 2,000–3,100 Drs ($8.30–$12.90). AE, DC, MC, V.
Open: Mon–Sat 7pm–2am. **Closed:** Sun.

The stunning Acropolis vista from the rooftop garden of this longtime favorite is one of the best in town. Run by Vassilis and Damiano Manologlou, Taverna Strofi offers a varied cuisine, marked by interesting cheeses, fine olive oils, and the freshest of ingredients. Every dish is well presented and served. We especially like the superb *mezédes* (appetizers) and the excellent lamb and veal courses. In the winter, the Manóloglous add a Saturday brunch with 20 *mezédes* and ouzo.

SÝNTAGMA SQUARE

You'll find many good eating choices in this area, which is in the center of Athens. They range from fast food to fine Chinese cuisine.

Apotso's, Odós Panepistimíou 10. ☎ **36-37-046.**

Cuisine: GREEK. **Reservations:** Not required.
Prices: Appetizers 320–1,700 Drs ($1.35–$7.10). No credit cards.
Open: Mon–Fri 11am–5pm; Sat 11am–4pm.

This classic, high-ceilinged taverna, decorated with old tin signs, wine and ouzo bottles, and tiny marble-top tables, is tucked away at the end of a cul-de-sac between some of Sýntagma Square's best shops. Apotso's provides good, moderately priced food in an authentically Athenian environment, drawing lots of shoppers and midtown businesspeople at lunch. Dining is on the ouzerí model, where *mezédes* (appetizers), delicious plates of fresh salad, small fried fish, *keftédes* (meatballs), and regional cheeses are served.

Brazilian, Odós Voukourestíou 1. ☎ **32-35-463.**

Cuisine: COFFEE BAR. **Reservations:** Not required.
Prices: Coffee 250–600 Drs ($1.05–$2.50); pastries 200–400 Drs (85¢–$1.70).
Open: Mon–Fri 7am–8:30pm, Sat 7am–4pm (until 9pm in winter).

Turn right at the Wendy's on Sýntagma Square, walk a half block and find the bustling Brazilian on the left, a 1930s-style coffeehouse filled with working Athenians, newspaper-reading travelers, or shoppers deep in conversation. There are no tables or chairs inside, yet it's a popular spot to stand and drink a quick espresso or grab a pastry or sandwich. You can sit outside. It's our favorite breakfast-on-the-run spot.

Dionysos-Zonar's, Odós Panepistimíou 9. ☎ **32-30-336.**

Cuisine: GREEK. **Reservations:** Not required.
Prices: Appetizers 1,100–2,400 Drs ($4.60–$10); main courses 1,400–3,200 Drs ($5.85–$13.35); pastries from 700 ($2.90). AE, DC, MC, V.
Open: Daily noon–11pm.

Dionysos-Zonar's is the quintessential *zacharoplastíon,* the Greek term for pastry shop, coffee bar, candy store, and bakery all rolled into one. This is the Sýntagma Square branch (you can't miss the huge awning and the bright sidewalk tables filled with travelers gorging on ice-cream sundaes). Dionysos-Zonar's also serves good Greek food. It's not cheap, but it's worthwhile for a splurge.

GB Corner, Hotel Grand Bretagne, Sýntagma Square. ☎ **32-30-251.**

Cuisine: INTERNATIONAL. **Reservations:** Required for lunch.
Prices: Appetizers 3,000–7,000 Drs ($12.50–$29.20); main courses 3,500–8,300 Drs ($14.60–$35.60). AE, CB, DC, EC, MC, V.
Open: Daily 6:30–11am, noon to 1am.

This exclusive corner of the elegant Grande Bretagne hosts Athens's highest power-lunch crowd of major politicians and businessmen. The atmosphere is more British men's club than Athens taverna, with dark leather booths and hunting pictures on the walls. The menu has a full international/continental range, as well as breakfast and late-night offerings.

★ **Kentrikon Restaurant,** Odós Kolokotróni 3. ☎ **32-32-482.**

Cuisine: GREEK/INTERNATIONAL. **Reservations:** Not required.
Prices: Appetizers 450–900 Drs ($1.90–$3.75); main courses 1,350–3,500 Drs ($5.65–$14.60). AE, DC, EC, MC, V.
Open: Mon–Fri noon–6pm.

Many travelers try to put aside a lunch hour for this spacious, air-conditioned upscale eatery. Service is prompt and polite—a great combination when you're waiting for a delectable lamb ragout with spinach, chicken with okra, or the Kentrikón's special macaroni. Don't be afraid to walk into the kitchen and peek into the pots; it is, after all, the Greek way.

Lengo Restaurant/Bistro, Odós Níkis 22. ☎ **32-31-127.**

Cuisine: GREEK/CONTINENTAL. **Reservations:** Not required.
Prices: Appetizers 850–4000 Drs ($3.55–$16.70); main courses 1,100–3,200 Drs ($4.60–$13.35). AE, EC, MC, V.
Open: Daily noon–1am.

The menu at the pricey but popular Léngo includes grilled specialties, fluffy omelets, a variety of continental courses, such as filet mignon with mushrooms and wiener-schnitzel. The air-conditioned taverna has a quiet side patio that is, for many sightseers, a priceless midday haven in this busy shopping district. It's found two blocks east of Sýntagma Square, at Xenofóntos Street.

Neon, Odós Mitropóleos 3. ☎ **32-28-155.**

Cuisine: INTERNATIONAL. **Reservations:** Not required.
Prices: Snacks 185–525 Drs (80¢–$2.20); sandwiches 400–750 Drs ($1.70–$3.15); main courses 900–2,150 Drs ($3.75–$9). No credit cards.

This brand-new addition to the Neon chain offers yet another choice for this busy area. The sleek art deco style is perfect for the no-nonsense food and cafeteria service. You're sure to find something to your taste—maybe a Mexican omelet, a Green Forest salad, spaghetti Bolognese, or sweets ranging from Black Forest cake to tiramisú.

Wendy's, Odós Stadíou 4. ☎ **32-39-421.**

Cuisine: FAST FOOD. **Reservations:** Not required.
Prices: Main courses 350–1150 Drs ($1.50–$4.80). No credit cards.
Open: Daily 8–2am.

We were loathe to give space to Athens's first American fast-food eatery, but Kyle's husband insisted that you can't argue with success—and where better to take the kids who can't stand Greek food? It's true—the place is packed around the clock not only with American families but with Athenian ones as well.) You'll swear you are in Peoria.

KOLONÁKI

As is to be expected in an upscale area, most of Kolonáki's restaurants are more expensive; some are also a bit snobby. The real problem is that few are open in August and early September. Nevertheless, we've listed those that are open year-round.

Everest, Tsakálof Street at Iraklítou Street. ☎ **36-22-116.**

Cuisine: FAST FOOD. **Reservations:** Not required.
Prices: Sandwiches: 180–440 Drs (75¢–$1.85); stuffed croissants 200–400 Drs (85¢–$1.70). No credit cards.
Open: Daily 24 hours.

The bright, modern, red-and-white facade of Everest masks its long history of providing several generations of Athenian families and teenagers with Greek fast food. For years, locals have stopped at its counters and barstools for *spanakópita* (spinach

Frommer's Cool For Kids: Restaurants

Café Neon (see page 99) For its varied and tasty choices, quick service, and reasonable prices, this cafeteria is a good place to relax after a full morning of shopping or sightseeing.

Wendy's (see page 98) A touch of home. Need we say more?

Everest (see page 98) For good fast food the Athenian way. Try the spanakópita (spinach pie) and treat the kids to their favorite flavor of ice cream while you cool off with some coffee frappé.

Dionysos-Zonar's (see pages 97 and 100) A must stop at Lykavittós Hill, if only for the spectacular view of Athens. Take the funicular or walk up the hill (good exercise for the whole family) and reward yourself with some (overpriced) snacks. Try the Zónar's off Sýntagma Square for some good desserts in a more convenient location.

pie) or *tirópita* (cheese pie) or for coffee frappé or ice cream. The contemporary Everest also serves burgers, sandwiches, and stuffed croissants.

Hellinikon, 19–20 Kolonáki Square. ☎ **36-01-858.**

Cuisine: GREEK. **Reservations:** Not required.
Prices: Appetizers 600–1,575 Drs ($2.50–$6.60); main courses 1,400–4,400 Drs ($5.85–$16.70). No credit cards.
Open: Daily 8am–1am.

The perimeter of Kolonáki Square is lined with sidewalk cafés where the upper-middle-class kids and young adults come to see and be seen over coffee and pastries. The attitude at some of the newer "hip" establishments is so thick you need a chainsaw to get through it, so it's refreshing to find a quiet, understated restaurant in this great shopping area. The Hellinikon serves an older, more elegant crowd in a nicely upscale, if smoke-filled, environment. Food covers both Greek and continental territory, with offerings ranging from spinach croquettes to burgers. A reader introduced us to this one and recommended a stop just for the fine pastry selection.

★ **Ouzerí Yiali Kafines,** Odós Ploutárchou 18. ☎ **72-25-846.**

Cuisine: GREEK. **Reservations:** Not required.
Prices: Appetizers 525–2,550 Drs ($2.20–$10.60). No credit cards.
Open: Mon–Sat 12:30–5pm, 8pm–2am.

Like most of upscale Athens, the owners of Yiali Kafines (the name is Turkish but everything else is Greek) head for the islands in the summer, so many readers will miss this great little treat. If you get lucky, try the *seftaliés* (Cypriot meatballs), cod-fish croquettes with skordaliá, and tabbouleh salad. Sit outside on the quiet side street and knock down a few ouzos; you'll go away happy.

Rodia Taverna, Odós Aristípou 44. ☎ **72-29-883.**

Cuisine: GREEK. **Reservations:** Not required.
Prices: Appetizers 425–1,250 Drs ($1.80–$5.20); main courses 450–2,100 Drs ($1.90–$8.75). No credit cards.
Open: Mon–Sat 8pm–2am.

This is a romantic, old-fashioned taverna below street level in one of Kolonáki's oldest homes, at the foot of Lykavittós Hill. In the winter, dining is in Rodiá's dark interior, where patterned tile floors, lace curtains, and kegs of the house *krassí* (wine) are the decoration. At other times, the small tables are put in the vine-shaded back garden. Specials include octopus in mustard sauce; oregano or lemon beef; fluffy, divine *bourékkis;* and, for dessert, fresh halvá.

OMÓNIA SQUARE

Café Neon, Odós Dórou 1. ☎ **52-36-409.**

Cuisine: INTERNATIONAL. **Reservations:** Not required.
Prices: Main courses 900–2,150 Drs ($3.75–$9). No credit cards.
Open: Daily 8am–2am.

Readers first turned our attention to the restored Kafeníon of 1924 that has reopened as this exciting new "free-flow" restaurant. In the air-conditioned comfort of one of Omónia Square's grandest old edifices, workers in sailor suits help customers through several self-service stations. You can choose from the salad bar (our favorite, at 850 Drs or $3.55 for a bowlful), the omelet kitchen, the hot-entrée counter, or the pastry counter. Everything seems freshly made, tasty, and a good value. Vegetarians will appreciate the cold and hot vegetable dishes, and all will enjoy the breakfast choices.

Taygetos Grill, Odós Satovriándou 4. ☎ **52-22-392.**

Cuisine: GREEK. **Reservations:** Not required.
Prices: Appetizers 350–650 Drs ($1.25–$2.70); main courses 1,100–2,100 Drs ($4.60–$8.75). AE, DC, V.
Open: Daily 9am–1am.

The Taygetos Grill, which opened in 1925, sports a bright striped canopy, shading the outdoor café tables on a quiet pedestrians-only side street, two blocks north of Omónia Square. Inside, the whirling spit groans with sizzling chicken and lamb. A satisfying meal for two, including moist grilled lamb, a grilled quarter chicken, fresh Greek salad, beer or chilled retsína, can be had for a very reasonable price.

MONASTIRÁKI

Taverna Sigalas, 2 Monastiráki Square. ☎ **32-13-036.**

Cuisine: GREEK.
Prices: Appetizers 400–750 Drs ($1.70–$3.15); main courses 900–1,500 Drs ($3.75–$6.25). No credit cards.
Open: Daily 7am–2am.

This worthy taverna holds its own opposite the delightful Monastiráki flea market and metro station (the station nearest Pláka and Sýntagma Square). It's housed in a vintage 1879 commercial building, with a newer outdoor pavilion. Its lively interior has huge, old retsína kegs in the back and dozens of black-and-white photos of Greek movie stars on the walls. After 8pm nightly there's Greek Muzak. At all hours, Greeks and tourists are wolfing down large portions of stews, moussaká, grilled meatballs, baked tomatoes, gyros, and other tasty dishes.

Thanasis, Odós Mitropóleos 69. ☎ **32-44-705.**

Cuisine: GREEK. **Reservations:** Not required.
Prices: Main courses 300–1,500 Drs ($1.25–$6.25). No credit cards.
Open: Daily 8:30am–1am.

Thanasis is probably the hottest souvlaki stand in town, conveniently located near the Monastiráki metro station. Locals flock here for the take-outs, and taxi drivers stopping for a quick snack block the street during the day. The grill is smoking as flea marketeers and tourists chow down the delicious souvlaki and excellent french fries. The atmosphere is informal, and the price is right. A great budget choice.

SPECIALTY DINING

Dining with a View

We must mention two Dionysos restaurants with unforgettable views, but let us advise you that better food at better prices can be had elsewhere. Our favorite in the food-with-view department is Taverna Strofi (reviewed above in the Koukáki section).

Dionysos-Zonar's, Dionysíou Aeropaghítou Avenue, at the Acropolis. ☎ **92-31-936.**

Cuisine: CONTINENTAL. **Reservations:** Recommended.
Prices: Appetizers 950–3,500 Drs ($4–$14.60); main courses 2,200–6,000 Drs ($9.20–$25). AE, DC, MC, V.
Open: Daily noon–11pm.

On the side of Philopáppou Hill, commanding a magnificent view of the Acropolis, is one of the branches of Dionysos. The decor is modern and not very interesting, and the international menu is high priced (there's an undistinguished coffee shop on the lower level). But nothing can detract from the view of the Parthenon, especially after 9:30pm, when its facade is mottled by the dramatic lighting of the sound-and-light display.

Dionysos-Zonar's, atop Lykavittós Hill. ☎ **72-26-374.**

Cuisine: CONTINENTAL. **Reservations:** Recommended.
Prices: Appetizers 950–3,500 Drs ($4–$14.60); main courses 2,200–6,000 Drs ($9.20–$25). AE, DC, MC, V.
Open: Daily noon–11pm.

This Dionysos (open from March 1 to January 30) can be reached by the funicular that begins at the head of Ploutárchou Street above Kolonáki Square. The funicular deposits you at the top of Athens's highest peak, just perfect for an overview of the glittering city, especially at sunset. This branch of Dionysos also features an international menu but is less overpriced and at lunch offers salads and sandwiches from 900–2,800 Drs ($3.75–$11.70).

Lykavaitos Hill Ouzerí, Lykavittós Hill, above Kolonáki Square.

Cuisine: GREEK. **Reservations:** Not required
Prices: Appetizers 400–1,150 Drs ($1.70–$4.80); main courses 650–2,000 Drs ($2.70–$8.35). No credit cards.
Open: Daily 11am–midnight.

This magical little place is one of our favorite spots in Athens. It's about halfway up the hill by car or foot. It's a popular bar for the leisurely enjoyment of a glass of ouzo or wine, with a wide variety of well-priced and reasonably tasty *mezédes* (appetizers). The *tirópita* (cheese pie), *saganáki* (fried cheese), and chicken and lamb souvlaki are all good. The view from here, over the city to Piraeus and the distant Saronic Gulf, is best at sundown.

SPLURGE CHOICES

Whenever we ask our Greek friends for recommendations to the most expensive Greek restaurants, they reply that the best Greek food is to be found in simple tavernas. Fancy Greek restaurants don't impress them. So, our splurge choices include only one Greek establishment. You'll find fine food choices in other sections. What unites the restaurants listed in this section is the trinity of cost, quality, and ambience.

L'Abreuvoir, Odós Xenokrátous 51. ☎ **72-29-106.**

Cuisine: FRENCH. **Reservations:** Recommended.
Prices: Appetizers 1,500–6,500 Drs ($6.25–$27.10); main courses 3,900 Drs–7,200 Drs ($16.25–$30). AE, DC, MC, V.
Open: Daily 12:30–4:30pm, 8:30pm–midnight.

For a romantic, candlelit evening under a mulberry-tree canopy, there's no better choice than this longtime favorite, in Kolonáki. L'Abreuvoir (which means "watering hole") has a comfortable, welcoming ambience that's suited to a dress-up evening or a gourmand's casual night out. It's frequented by wealthy Athenians and resident expatriates longing for a European feast. Most of L'Abreuvoir's specialties are French; all are excellently prepared and artistically presented. From the fluffy spinach tart or smoked trout to the steak au poivre, entrecôtes Provençales (a filet cooked in a marvelous garlic, mushroom, and parsley sauce) to the soufflé au Grand Marnier or chocolate mousse, it's all a delight. L'Abreuvoir has all the attributes of a perfect splurge evening: a quiet, elegant setting, wonderful food, and superb service. For such gourmet fare and first-class treatment, the prices are reasonable.

Boschetto Ristorante, Evanghelismós Park. ☎ **72-10-893.**

Cuisine: ITALIAN. **Reservations:** Recommended.

Prices: Appetizers 1,800–4,000 Drs ($7.50–$16.70); main courses 2,800–9,000 Drs ($11.70–$37.50). AE, V.

Open: Mon–Sat 9pm–1am, summer; 8:30pm–12:30am, winter.

The fairy-tale Evanghelismós Park, its leafy bowers lit with Christmas tree lights and its resident cicadas drowning out the drone of nearby traffic, is the setting for Athens's most acclaimed Italian restaurant. Excellent food and attentive, but not fawning, service have made Boschetto the favorite venue of the city's well-dressed elite for several seasons. At our unforgettable visit, *la cucina divina* began with imaginative antipasti, such as the terrine of tomato, mozzarella, and zucchini, and smoked fish served with capers and grapefruit. The insalata of chicken breast and gorgonzola, served with seasonal greens, was delightful. Of the many *primi piatti,* we sampled spaghetti with bountiful seafood and pappardelle (lasagnelike noodles folded into triangles) with fresh lotte fish in a puréed asparagus sauce. The favorite *secondi piatti* included the carpaccio of beef fillet grilled with prosciutto and the tender prawns wrapped in crisp-fried tagliatelle, grilled with garlic and butter, all delicately prepared and carefully served. We somehow found room for fresh peach sorbet, creamy tiramisù, and the super-rich crème brûlée. With several bottles of the good house wine, the bill came to about $60 per person, a bargain compared with a similar meal in New York or Rome, and a special way to end our journey. In the winter, tables are moved inside and the crowd becomes a little dressier.

Far East, Odós Stadíou 7. ☎ **32-34-996.**

Cuisine: CHINESE/JAPANESE/KOREAN. **Reservations:** Recommended.

Prices: Appetizers 1,200–3,000 Drs ($5–$12.50); main courses 700–6,000 Drs ($2.90–$25). AE, EC, DC, MC, V.

Open: Daily 11:30am–2am.

Several Oriental restaurants have recently opened in central Athens, but this is the only one we can fully recommend. Though expensive, it turns out the town's best chicken and beef dishes, some tofu and mixed-vegetable dishes, and light, steamed dumplings. The decor is 1960 Chinatown, with teak paneling and floral patterns and with waitresses (some even Chinese) in classic cheongsam. If you've the taste for Chinese, consider the Far East a splurge and go for it.

Myrtia, Odós Trivonianoú 32-34. ☎ **92-47-175.**

Cuisine: GREEK. **Reservations:** Recommended.

Prices: Fixed-price menus from 9,000–14,000 Drs ($37.50–$58.30). AE, DC, EC, MC, V.

Open: Mon–Sat 8:30pm.–2am. **Closed:** Aug.

Myrtia, located up the hill behind the Olympic Stadium, in the Mets area, is the most famous of the fixed-menu tavernas in Athens, providing an unforgettable gastronomic bacchanalia that's as much a part of the Greek experience as is your first sight of the Parthenon. The atmosphere is meant to transport you to the world of a Greek village. Landscape murals, shiny brass lamps, worn ceramic pottery, and thatched straw matting all contribute to achieving the effect. A trio of strolling musicians tops it off. They weave in and out of the paths of the waiters, who are burdened with large trays of *mezédes* (appetizers), jugs of wine, select dishes of roast chicken or lamb (the best!), fruits and sweets, and more wine. You'll need to take a cab, and you should dress well, but we guarantee that your evening will not be easily forgotten. Dinner is served in the garden from mid-May to October.

5

What to See & Do in Athens

AFTER THREE DAYS OR SO, MOST VISITORS TO ATHENS, ESPECIALLY FIRST-TIMERS, SEEM to have had enough of the congested capital. The smog, the heat (in July and August), and the noise become too oppressive for them to bear. So, before you, too, begin to falter, aim straight for the heart of the city—the ancient Acropolis, high above the frenetic activity of a constantly expanding and developing modern metropolis. There, amid the silent ruins, you'll find tranquility, cool breezes, and the inspiration of 2,500 years of history.

The magnificent achievements of the 5th century B.C., concentrated on this 512-foot-tall limestone mound, still dominate the cityscape. No matter how far the bounds of Athens press, the Acropolis remains the storehouse of the city's soul. And for good reason. The Athens of Pericles was a historical epiphany: The idea of political democracy, the outpouring of revolutionary forms of drama, poetry, philosophy, and science, the creation of extraordinary works of art and architecture set off an explosion that, within a century and a half, would shake the world as far away as China.

A visit to the Acropolis, the Herod Atticus Odeum at the foot of the hill, and the nearby Agorá (the ancient marketplace, or *archéa agorá* in Greek) will jolt you with the power and nobility of the ancient buildings that still stand there, albeit in various states of ruin. For amid their walls and columns, in this city that Pericles called the "school of Hellas," there once flourished some of the greatest poets and thinkers of Western civilization: the philosophers Socrates, Plato, and Aristotle; the dramatists Aeschylus, Sophocles, and Euripides; the comic poet Aristophanes; the historians Herodotus, Thucydides, and Xenophon; the orators Lysias, Isocrates, and Demosthenes. Their tragedies and comedies are still performed today; their philosophical and historical works are still studied and debated; their speeches—on liberty and freedom of thought and the importance of each citizen's taking part in the affairs of his state—are still a source of inspiration.

Suggested Itineraries

If You Have One Day

If you have only one day in Athens, visit the National Archeological Museum after your communion with the Acrópolis. Then, go hear bouzouki or rebetika at night.

If You Have Two Days

Visitors with only two days to spend can see the other archeological sites, stroll through Pláka, and take in another museum (we recommend the Goulandrís Museum of Cycladic and Ancient Greek Art).

If You Have Three Days

A visit of three days will enable you to be more leisurely. Try the cafés in Mitropóleos Square or the National Gardens for people-watching. Sample different kinds of Greek foods and wines, shop for trinkets in the flea market or for Parthenon ashtrays in Omónia Square.

If You Have Five Days or More

Add day trips to Cape Soúnio, Delphi Aegina, or a day cruise through the Saronic Gulf.

1 The Top Attractions

Every year or so, the closing days and the hours of museums and sights are changed, so check with your hotel desk or with the Greek Tourist Organization (EOT) for current schedules.

THE ACROPOLIS

Many of the ancient city-states in Greece were built around a high promontory of land. Called an acropolis, it was the highest place in the city and was fortified with ramparts, for it was often used as the last refuge from marauding forces. Being the closest spot to the gods, the acropolis, in prehistoric times, was home to the rulers of the city-state but later evolved into a place of worship. The Acropolis of Athens was considered a sacred spot even in Neolithic times. Archeological evidence suggests that mystical cult worship was practiced on this ledge as long as 5,000 years ago.

Beginning in the 7th-century B.C., monumental temples and sacred buildings were constructed. In 480 B.C. the Persians invaded Athens and burned the city and the Acropolis structures. After the Greek naval victory at Salamís and land battle at Plataea, the returning Athenians swore that they would leave the temples in ruins as an eternal reminder of the barbarity of the invaders. What archeologists uncovered in the excavations between 1885 and 1891 was the "Persian Deposit," pits filled with sculptural and architectural fragments that had been carefully buried after this destruction. The Athenians soon reconsidered their pledge, and under Pericles the wealthy, newly democratic, and invigorated city-state began an intensive rebuilding program.

Only four major buildings remain: though in ruins, they still convey the grace, style, and technical achievement of the Golden Age. The **Propylaea,** a grand entryway that led worshippers from the temporal world into the spiritual atmosphere of the sanctuary, was begun in 437 B.C. The architect Mnesicles' graceful structure introduced a revolutionary design concept: the mixture of Doric and Ionic principles. The Propylaea has an outer and an inner facade of six Doric columns, which created five entryways on both sides of the building. To support the massive roof, columns in the lighter, more graceful Ionic style were installed inside as well.

To the right of the Propylaea, dramatically visible from the upper staircase to the Acropolis plateau, is the temple of Athena Nike. This elegant, white-marble monument was built over the site of an earlier altar dedicated to the goddess of Victory for the Panathenaic Festival almost 150 years before. Pericles commissioned the architect Callicrates to build a new temple at a time when Athens was about to embark on the Peloponnesian War. In 425 B.C. an additional protective parapet, decorated with a sculptural frieze expressing the Athenians' hope for final victory, was added to the temple. Fragments of this frieze can now be seen in the Acropolis Museum (at the site). One in particular is the lovely 5th-century "Nike Unlacing Her Sandals."

As you pass through the Propylaea, you'll see the **Erechtheum** on your left, on a site where once stood the Ancient Temple, dedicated to Poseidon, god of the spring that bubbled up life-giving water to previous generations of Acropolis inhabitants, and to Athena, goddess of the sustaining olive tree. Pericles had ordered the building of a new temple to replace the one burned by the Persians. Work on the temple was halted by the Peloponnesian War and by Pericles' sudden death in a plague but was resumed in 421 B.C.

The Erechtheum has three basic parts: the main temple, the northern extension, and the famous Porch of the Maidens. The main temple is divided so as to accommodate both deities; the eastern half is dedicated to Athena and the western half to

Poseidon. The covered porch, used in rituals, had graceful stone maidens, called Caryatides, instead of columns. The original five maidens have parted ways: One sailed with Lord Elgin to London in the early 19th century and is now in the British Museum; her four sisters recently have been removed, because of Athens's corrosive pollution, to the Acropolis Museum. The fat and frumpy cement copies thrown up in their place don't deserve a second glance.

Finally, you'll turn to the **Parthenon,** the most magnificent of structures, which is sadly suffering from the effects of Athens's *néfos,* the cloud of sulfur dioxide that often hangs over the city; the *néfos* combines with rain and dew to create an acid rain that dissolves the marble first into plaster and then into dust. Fortunately, the Greek government, with the assistance of the United Nations, has committed restoration funds and the talents of an international advisory committee of architects and scientists to try to preserve what's left.

The Parthenon is the largest Doric temple ever completed in Greece, and it's the only one made entirely of marble, shipped from Mt. Pentelicus. Most of it was built in nine years (447–438 B.C.). It's been estimated that the Parthenon cost over $150 million!

Pericles commissioned architects Ictinus and Callicrates to design a temple that would give Athenians "eternal honor." The sculptor Phidias insisted that it be wide enough and tall enough to house his planned 12-meter-high statue of Athena Parthenos (Virgin), to be made of gold and ivory. The design followed much of the floor plan of the original temple but was expanded to include eight columns on its shorter sides and 17 on its longer sides, thereby meeting the classical requisite that the long sides must be twice as long, plus one column more to add grace. Every stone in the structure was trapezoidal in shape and cut to fit its own unique position. Iron support beams, where needed, were sheathed in flexible lead to allow for expansion and prevent corrosion. Phidias is credited as master of the Parthenon for the huge amount of sculptural work he did ornamenting the facade. He carved all 92 metopes that circled the building, depicting scenes from mythology. Fragments of Athena's fight against the Giants (Gigantomachy), from the building's eastern side, can be seen in the Acropolis Museum.

The famous frieze of the Parthenon (constituting the bulk of the Elgin Marbles now in the British Museum in London) depicted the Panathenaic Procession, the annual event that drew hundreds of thousands of worshippers to the Acropolis, wending their way up the hillside, bearing gifts, children, and the aged in hand. The individualism and expressiveness of these Athenians is an incredible feat; even the worn and pollution-eroded frieze left in place on the western side of the Parthenon evokes a feeling for the beauty that must have been.

IMPRESSIONS

Above the low roofs of Athens the Acropolis rises on its pedestal of rock: astonishing, dramatic, divine, with at the same time the look of a phantom.

—Edmund Wilson, *Europe Without Baedeker,* 1947

Since 146 B.C. Greece has been selling foreigners the Age of Pericles, and this is what meets the traveler on arrival.

—Kevin Andrews, *Athens,* 1967

In the early Christian era, the Parthenon was turned into a church by the Byzantine Emperor Theodosius II. Later, the Franks had its wall crenelated and constructed a tower in the Propylaea. In the 15th century it became a mosque for Turkish conquerors, who kept a harem in the Erechtheum. Turned into a powder store, it was hit in 1687 by a Venetian bombardment, which caused 28 columns to fall, along with most of the interior cella; much of the frieze of Phidias was also destroyed. The Turks masked the disfigurement with the trappings of a mosque, replete with minaret. Earlier, the Propylaea, also filled with gunpowder, had been almost completely destroyed when lightning struck it.

After the Turks left, in 1834, efforts began to restore some of the ruins. Many were missing: Several years before, Thomas Bruce, earl of Elgin and ambassador to the sultan, obtained permission from the Turks, to diagram, analyze, and finally take away, for "safekeeping," the carved stones and masonry that remained on the Acropolis. They are now in the possession of the British Museum. The Greeks deeply resent that some of their finest artifacts from antiquity are housed in a foreign land, and they've been trying to repatriate them. In 1981 the Parthenon was jolted more than an inch off its base by an earthquake.

The entrance to the Acropolis is on the west end, and it can be approached from the north by bearing south from Monastiráki past the Roman Forum or from the south via Dionýsou Areopagítou Street from near the theater of Herodes Atticus.

Acropolis Museum

Housed in a discreet white building just below the Parthenon, this small collection of finds from the Acropolis contains some superb sculpture, including the Gigantomachy pediment from the Ancient Temple to Athena that stood before the Erechtheum. There are a few extraordinary Classical-era sculptures attributed to Phidias, which do justice to his reputation. The large collection of *korae* (statues of the young women in attendance on Athena) are particularly beautiful. In their strong faces, bright eyes, and robust figures we can trace the lineage of many of the Greeks we see today. Some coloration is still preserved on their pure marble surface—how horrified we might be if we were to see the Acropolis and its statuary painted in their original, vivid, primary colors!

One of the best guides to the site is *The Acropolis* (Ekdotiki), written by the late Greek archeologist Manolis Andronikos. It includes illustrations that attempt to re-create the Acropolis as it once was.

Admission: 1,750 Drs ($7.30) adults; students half price.

Hours: Mon–Fri 8am–6:30pm, Sat–Sun 8:30am–2:45pm.

The **Acropolis Museum** is open from 11am to 6:30pm on Monday, 8am to 6:30pm from Tuesday to Friday, 10am–2pm Saturday and Sunday. Check with the Greek Tourist Organization (EOT) for shortened hours during the winter months.

AUTHORS' NOTE

Readers from Tennessee certainly know that Nashville boasts the world's only life-size replica of the Parthenon. For the rest of you, let us say that this concrete, full-color copy, made from an 1897 model and built to commemorate the Nashville centennial, is quite a sight. A 42-foot-high quasireplica of the missing statue of Athena Parthenos is also in the works.

- Academy 25
- Acropolis 10
- Acropolis Museum 12
- Aghios Gheorgios 22
- Ancient Agora 3
- Athens Cathedral 18
- Benaki Museum 28
- Byzantine Museum 29
- Hadrian's Arch 14
- Hadrian's Library 6
- Monastiraki Church 5
- National Archeological Museum 21
- National Garden 17
- National Historical Museum 19
- National Library 23
- National Picture Gallery 30
- Omónia Square 20
- Parliament Building 27
- Parthenon 11
- Presidential Palace 16
- Roman Market 7
- Stoa of Attalos 4
- Stoa of Zeus 2
- Sýntagma Square 26
- Temple of Olympian Zeus 14
- Theater of Dionysus 13
- Herod Atticus Odeum 9
- Theseum (Hephaestium) 1
- Tower of Winds (Aerides) 8
- University 24
- Zappion 15

9610

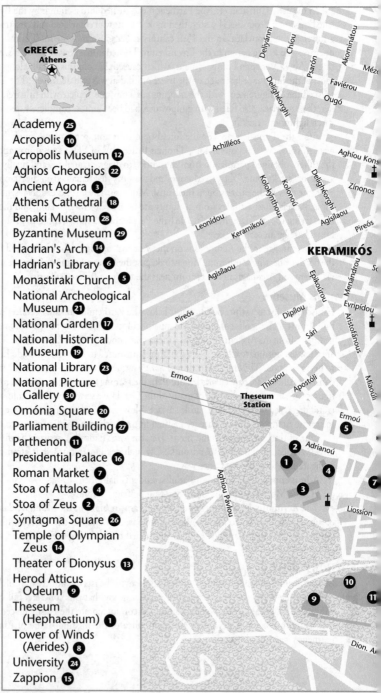

Athens Attractions

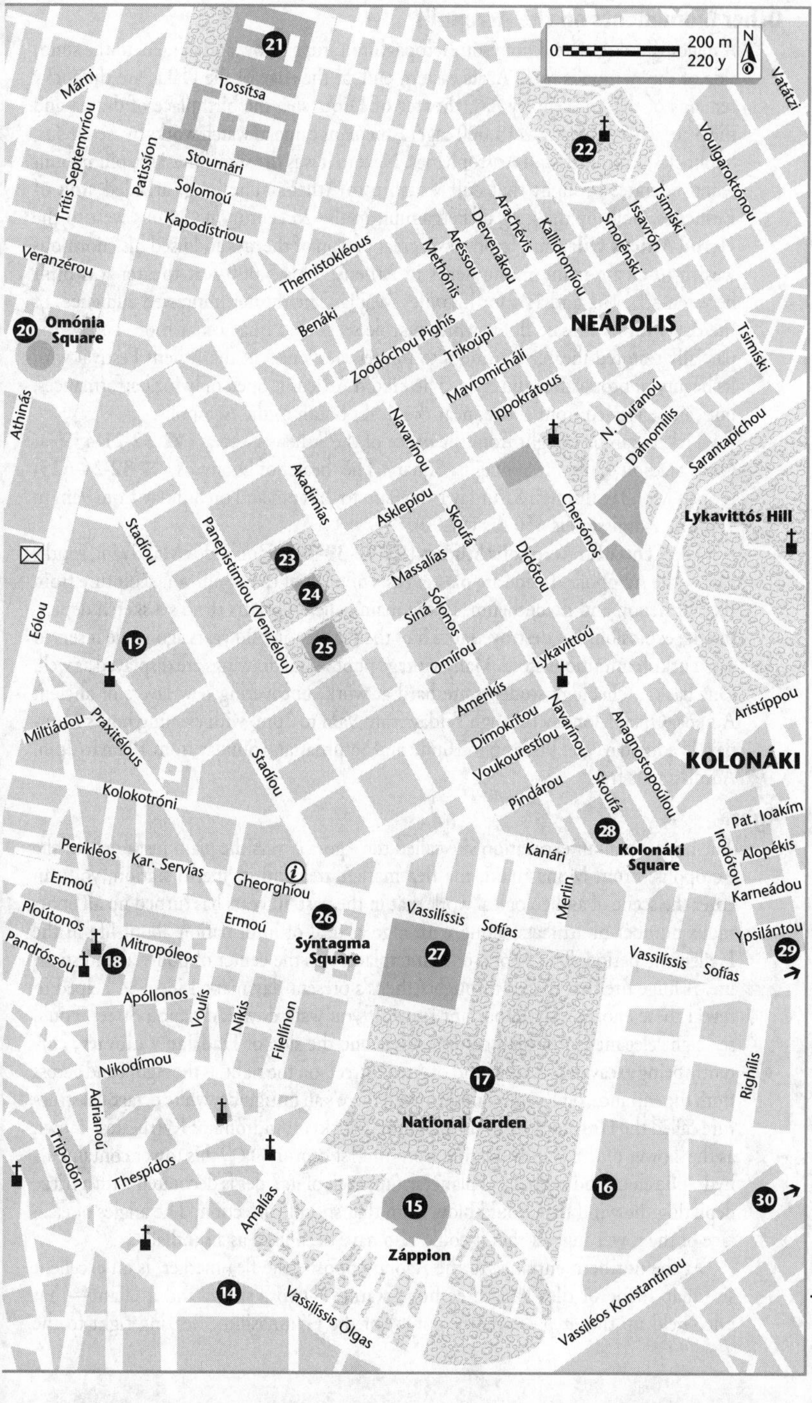

Church
Post Office
Information

Other Monuments on the Acropolis

A major thoroughfare, Dionýsou Aeropaghítou, runs below and parallel to the south side of the Acropolis rock. At its eastern end, at the edge of the Pláka, are the rocky remains of the 5th-century B.C. **theater of Dionysos,** the birthplace of drama and the place where as many as 13,000 eager Athenians came to watch works by Aeschylus, Sophocles, Euripides, and Aristophanes. Next to it was the site of the Asclepium, built when Socrates brought that cult worship to Athens. The long, arcaded **stoa of Eumenes,** built by the king of Pergamum in the 2d century B.C., runs west to the **Herod Atticus Odeum.** Herod was a great patron of the arts and used his enormous wealth to create many monuments in Athens. This 5,000-seat theater was built between A.D. 161 and 174 for his wife, Regilla. The theater impressed audiences of the day with its mosaic floor, white-marble seats, and huge cedar roof. Today, the partially restored theater continues to impress audiences at the Athens Festival with its beauty of proportion and style. The Herod Atticus is open only for performances, but can be viewed from above, near the ticket booth to the Acropolis.

Tickets can be bought from the office of the Athens Festival (☎ **32-21-459**) at Odós Stadíou 4, just off Sýntagma Square. The theater of Dionysos (☎ **32-24-625**) is open Monday through Saturday from 9am to 2:45pm and on Sunday from 9am to 1:45pm. Admission is 450 drs ($1.90).

The **Center for Acropolis Studies** (☎ **92-39-381**) is on Odós Makriyáni, southeast of the Acropolis. Inside are plaster casts of most of the significant sculpture from the Parthenon and Erechtheum. In the main gallery upstairs there's a sketch depicting the explosion that destroyed much of the Parthenon 300 years ago while it served as a Turkish munitions store. Many vintage photos and drawings are displayed as well. Out back, archeology students are hard at work, uncovering new layers of ancient Athens. Open Monday through Friday from 9am to 2pm, with evening hours Monday, Wednesday, and Friday 6 to 10pm; and Saturday and Sunday from 10am to 2pm. Admission is free.

Agora

The huge, open-air excavation site called the Agora covers the plain just north of the Acropolis. From Monastiráki, the flea market area and its metro station, you can enter the scene of archeological work that in the past 50 years has turned up an enormous number of artifacts, along with a great deal of information about life in the Hellenistic period. The Agora, or marketplace, was the center of political and social life. A huge fire that roared through Athens's present-day market in 1884 helped to reveal these enormously important ruins. If you walk down Adrianoú Street, you'll see eight elegant Corinthian columns that line the side of **Hadrian's Library,** currently being excavated. At the head of Áreos Street, on the right, is the Agorá and across from the entrance, on Epaminóndou Street, there's an intriguing, white octagonal structure called the **Horologion** or Horologium (Clock) of Andrónikos Kyrrhéstes, known as the Tower of the Winds. Dating from the 1st century B.C., this tower contained a hydraulic clock and probably a planetarium; each of its sides is decorated with a frieze depicting the wind that would blow from that specific direction. The angles of each face of the tower suggest that it could also have been used as a sundial.

At the northern entrance to the Agora, opposite the flea market, is an excellent site map made of tiles and three huge statues—two Tritons and a Giant—that once held up the *propylon* (entry porch) of the Gymnasium. Bearing right to the spectacular Theseum, you'll pass a bold, headless sculpture of the Emperor Hadrian (reigned A.D. 117–138).

The **Theseum** (*Thissíon* in Greek) is also known as the temple of Hephaestus and Athena, or the Hephaístion, because of its location on Ághios Kolonós Hill, site of the ancient iron and metal works over which these patrons presided. Built between 449 and 444 B.C., the Theseum is the best-preserved temple in all Greece (because of its conversion to a Christian church dedicated to St. George). The Theseum was the work of the architectural genius who created the temple of Poseidon at Cape Soúnio (Sunium) and the temple of Nemesis near Marathon. You can still appreciate the friezes under the portico on the eastern and western sides.

The huge, red-tile-roofed building across the open Agora from the Theseum is the stoa of Attalos, now the **Agora Museum** (**☎ 32-10-185**). Constructed of marble, the stoa has 134 columns arranged in double rows of Doric, Ionic, and Aeolic capitals to form two stories. It's thought to have been a shopping bazaar in the Hellenistic era.

The Agora Museum that's been created in the renovation is quite interesting; the range of scientific inventions, tools, games, and machinery makes this the Smithsonian of the ancient world. Of particular interest to us is a display of artifacts from the Neolithic period to the 1st century B.C., among them pottery, pottery-making tools, and bronze-casting and ceramic molds. A display of antique wine jugs and their identifying stamps colorfully depicts the history of wine making and the jugs used to contain the wine. Also found is a 2d- or 3d-century B.C. *klerotérion*—a slotted marble rock that held name plates for choosing chairmen of the Twelve Tribes and worked with balls that dropped and kept score. The clepsydra was a six-minute water clock used to limit the speeches given in court. A double-layer wine cooler, from the 8th century B.C., was stored in cold water. There's also a collection of Roman theatrical masks and charming toys and a pretty ivory statuette of the Apollo Lykeios, a replica of a work by Praxiteles.

The hardy can wander up the few paving stones that remain of the Panathenaic Way, which leads directly up the hill to the Acropolis, for more sightseeing. This is the shortest route to the Parthenon.

Open: The Archeological Site daily 8:30am–3pm. Agora Museum Tues–Sun 8:30am–2:45pm.

Admission: 900 Drs ($3.80) adults; students half price.

Olympium

At the foot of busy Amalías Avenue, just before it reaches the even busier Syngroú Avenue, you'll find two lonely monuments to antiquity: the temple of Olympian Zeus and Hadrian's Arch.

The **temple of Olympian Zeus** (Naós Olympíou Diós), begun under Peisistratus in 515 B.C., is the largest temple to the father of the gods ever built in Greece. Work on it was discontinued after the fall of Peisistratus's tyranny but commenced again under the Syrian King Antiochus IV Epiphanes. A Roman architect, Cossutius, was brought in to complete the temple according to the original plans but added a new Corinthian flair of his own. When Antiochus died, work was halted once more. Finally, in Hadrian's reign (about A.D. 131), the temple's 104 Corinthian columns were raised to the god. Of them, only 15 tall columns still stand, together with the base of the colossal structure; one column, felled by an earthquake, lies in fluted segments among the wildflowers, as if to demonstrate its grandeur close up.

The squat archway overlooking the site, **Hadrian's Arch** (Pýli Adrianoú), was built to honor the emperor during his reign, perhaps in congratulations for the completion of Zeus's temple. The arch symbolically separates Hellenic Athens (Theseus's city) from Roman Athens (Hadrian's city).

Open: Tues–Sun 8:30am–3pm.

Admission: 450 Drs ($1.90). Hadrian's Arch is always open.

2 More Attractions

ATHENS'S "LITTLE" SIGHTS

The **Panathenaic Stadium,** behind the National Garden at King Constantine Avenue, is a re-creation in solid white marble of the original stadium at Olympia, now over 2,000 years old. This 60,000-seat theater was opened for the 1896 Olympic Games, the first held since antiquity, and is still in use today. Pause and think of what an immense accomplishment the event must have been in 1896, and then imagine such an event in ancient times!

The neoclassical **Parliament Building,** located at the head of Sýntagma Square, is guarded by two stiff-faced young men (*évzones*) in traditional garb. You can watch the Changing of the Guard ceremony at 6pm daily in front of the Tomb of the Unknown Soldier. Go early and buy chick-peas 150 Drs (65¢) from any of the many vendors to feed the hordes of pigeons that know supper's coming. Then stick around for the formal marionette march as the guards' pompomed red-leather shoes clomp in unison across the marble square.

The **National Garden** is one of the most civilized places in Athens: several square blocks without traffic, noise, or heat. It is also the feline capital of Greece, with hundreds of stray cats all looking for love and food. It's open sunrise to sunset, and the many entrances include those on Amalías Avenue at Sýntagma Square, on Amalías Avenue at Hadrian's Arch, and on King Constantine Avenue opposite the Panathenaic Stadium. Joggers will find the city's freshest air within its confines, with several paths of packed gravel weaving in and out of the exotic plantings. Food kiosks, birds, haggard tourists, and smiling Greeks abound. There's even a small zoo.

The **Záppion** is a large, neoclassical building used primarily for exhibitions and international conferences. It's usually closed to the public, but if you're strolling through the National Garden, take a minute to peek in and admire the fine entranceway and interior columns.

Another side of Athens rarely seen is expressed vividly in **Anafiótika,** a small quarter of island-style whitewashed homes built high up on the Acropolis hill by immigrants from Anáfi. This volcanic Cyclades isle sent many workers to Athens in the 19th century, and the low-slung stucco homes, built around large courtyards filled with caged birds, reflect the traditional Cycladic architecture of that time.

In Pláka, next to the monument of Lysikrates at Epimándou and Býronos Streets (pronounced *Výronos* in Greek), is a perfect example of a midcity **excavation in progress.** The Athens law requiring that all contractors with building permits submit to an archeological review of the planned site before construction begins has indefinitely postponed more projects than you can imagine. This site spans the Classical, Roman, and Byzantine eras; pottery shards, jewelry, and coins have already been found. Renovation on this square began in 1982, when the site was discovered.

MUSEUMS/GALLERIES

National Archeological Museum, Odós Patissíon 44. ☎ **82-17-717.**

This museum, a ten-minute walk from Omónia Square, contains one of the most exciting collections of antiquity in the world. If not for its checkered history, this treasure trove of Greek finds might indeed be the world's best. Unfortunately, during the centuries of foreign domination many other countries had their chance to pick and choose among the antiquities. The Louvre may have the *Winged Victory of Samothrace* and the *Venus de Mílo,* the British Museum may have the Elgin Marbles, the Arsenal of Venice may be guarded by a Lion of Délos, and the New York Metropolitan Museum of Art may have the largest collection of Greek ceramics, but in Athens there remain works of art of such caliber that we will label them "must sees."

It wasn't until 1866 that the Greek government settled on building a central museum to house the scattered collections of archeological societies, scholars, and wealthy patrons. Years of cataloguing and organizing were interrupted by World War II, when every art work in the building was removed and buried underground. After 1945, Marshall Plan aid from the United States and other funds enabled the Greeks to dig out their collection and renovate their museum, yet until 1964 there was no unified plan for the exhibition space. As other countries move rapidly into contemporary design schemes and high-technology preservation techniques, the National Archeological Museum seems more and more behind the times. Nevertheless, its collection is an unparalleled legacy; to forgo a personal encounter with some of these masterworks is to miss one of traveling's rare privileges.

"Must Sees"

Room 4 The Mycenaean Room includes gold jewelry, artifacts, and masks from the shaft graves discovered by the German amateur archeologist Heinrich Schliemann. The famous *Mask of Agamemnon* brings to life Homer's words from the Iliad: "He was the King of Men . . . distinguished among many and outstanding among heroes."

Room 6 The Cycladic Room contains marble figurines (mostly of women) from the 3d millennium B.C.

Rooms 7–11 The Archaic Sculpture Rooms hold a collection of huge *koúroi,* stylized statues of male youths, which once filled the great temples.

Room 15 The Poseidon Room houses bronze sculptures and the 6½-foot-tall bronze statue of the sea god himself, poised gracefully, (once) trident in hand, arms and legs outspread, sensuous curls weaving through his hair and beard. The hand of this masterpiece was discovered off Évvia (near Artemísion) in 1926; two years later divers found the rest of the body.

Room 47 The Bronze Room contains the handsome *Marathon Boy,* a bronze Hermes from the school of Praxiteles, found in 1926 off the coast of Marathon. His eyes are limestone with pupils of glass; his nipples were inlaid with copper.

Room 48 The Fresco, or "Thera," Gallery, at the top of the stairs, displays the reconstructed frescoes found at Akrotíri, a Minoan city on the island of Santoríni (Thera).

Rooms 49–56 The Vase Galleries contain an incredible range of sophisticated and folk ceramics from throughout the Greek world.

Admission: 1,725 Drs ($7.20) adults; 850 Drs ($3.60) students. One-hour tours 3,500 Drs ($13) for 1–10 people.

Open: Mon 12:30–7pm, Tues–Fri 8am–7pm, Sat–Sun 8:30am–3pm. **Trolley:** No. 1 or 3 from Sýntagma Square.

Nicholas Goulandris Museum of Cycladic and Ancient Greek Art, Odós Neophýtou Douká 4. ☎ **72-28-3213.**

In 1986 the Nicholas P. Goulandrís Foundation gave Athens a new museum, filled with the earliest sculpture, pottery, and bronzes from the Cycladic, Minoan, and Mycenaean civilizations (3000 B.C.–A.D. 300). This collection, distinguished by the early Cycladic pieces, is one of the most impressive in the world. The marble figurines, their physical attributes so simply defined, are superbly displayed and informatively labeled. Their new white-marble home is as simply elegant as are the works it contains. A new wing added in 1992 will house temporary exhibits.

The Museum of Cycladic and Ancient Greek Art is located near the National Garden, off Queen Sophia Avenue. To leave Athens without seeing it would be to miss a rare glimpse at an ancient art that speaks eloquently of Western civilization's beginnings.

Admission: 290 Drs ($1.20).

Open: Mon, Wed–Fri 10am–4pm, Sat 10am–3pm.

Benaki Museum, Leofóros Vassilíssis Sofías at Odós Koumbári 1. ☎ **36-11-617.**

Unfortunately the private collection of the late Anthony Benáki, a wealthy Greek from Alexandria, Egypt, will be closed for restorations till the summer of 1996. This eclectic display of Hellenic, Byzantine, and post-Byzantine art objects is delightful to some and totally unappreciated by others. There is a rich collection of ecclesiastical art, including some fine icons and several rare illustrated manuscripts and an interesting collection of Greek folk art, embroidery, and costumes, which appeals to many visitors interested in traditional handicrafts.

National Gallery and Alexander Soutzos Museum, Leofóros Vassiléos Konstantínou 50 at Leofóros Vassilíssis Sofías. ☎ **72-11-010.**

The National Gallery and Alexander Soútzos Museum opened in 1976 with a commitment to display modern work by Greek artists. On the first floor you'll find four El Grecos and some Byzantine icons among the Renaissance through impressionistic paintings of other Greek artists. The Greek artists Konstantínos Parthénis and Níkos Hatzikyriákos Ghíkas are well represented.

Admission: 575 Drs ($2.40).

Open: Mon–Sat 9am–3pm, Sun 10am–2pm.

Byzantine Museum, Leofóros Vassilíssis Sofías 22. ☎ **72-31-570.**

The Byzantine Museum is housed in an 1840 mansion built by an eccentric French aristocrat, the duchess de Plaisance. Beyond the open-air court is an interesting reproduction of a Byzantine domed-cross-in-square Orthodox church from the 12th or 13th century. The well-labeled architectural details and sculptural fragments provide an excellent introduction to Byzantine architecture, one of Greece's best-represented art forms. To the right of the entry is a reconstruction of an early Christian basilica with sculptures (5th–7th century A.D.) brought from many parts of Greece and reassembled here. After walking clockwise through chronologically progressing displays, you'll arrive at a chapel (late 17th to 19th century) lit by an exquisite carved wood chandelier. The floor above has a fine collection of Byzantine and post-Byzantine icons, frescoes, jewel-encrusted vestments, and other ecclesiastical memorabilia.

Admission: 575 Drs ($2.40).

Open: Tues–Sun 8:30am–3pm.

Museum of Greek Folk Art, Odós Kydathinéon 17, Pláka. ☎ **32-29-031.**

The Museum of Greek Folk Art celebrated its 70th anniversary in 1988 with a commitment to renovate and expand its already excellent exhibitions. Elaborate embroideries from several islands, ceramics, original costumes, jewelry, silverwork, and traditional leather shadow puppets are only some of the museum's highlights. We love the plate collections from Skýros and the photo blowups illustrating the context in which many of these goods were used. This museum is a real must for anyone interested in the roots of contemporary Greek culture.

Unfortunately the nearby **Center of Folk Art and Tradition,** at Odós Hatzimicháli 6 (☎ **32-43-987**), will be closed for renovation until summer, 1996.

National Historical Museum, Odós Stadíou 13. ☎ **32-37-617.**

This museum is housed in the old Greek Parliament building. In its collection of Greek and Athenian historical items are portraits of heroes from the 1821 War of Independence (for those who've often wondered whom or what many of the squares and streets are named after). A small but charming aspect of this museum is the collection of 12 watercolors by 19th-century artist Panaghiotis Zographos, depicting famous battles from the War of Independence.

Admission: 250 Drs ($1.40).

Open: Daily, 9am–2pm.

Numismatic Museum, Odós Tossítsa 1. ☎ **82-17-769.**

The Numismatic Museum contains a collection of Greek, Roman, Byzantine, medieval, and modern coins, lead seals, weights, and engraved stones. The museum, however, will be closed until 1996, so that the collection can be moved from its former home in the Archeological Museum to the restored mansion of Heinrich Schliemann on Odós Panepistimíou (also known as Venizélou).

Beth Shalom Synagogue, Odós Melidóni 8. ☎ **32-52-773.**

The Beth Shalom Synagogue and Jewish Museum, off Odós Ermoú near Sýntagma Square, is a living testament to the tenacity of a people and the perseverance of their faith. Prior to World War II there were more than 77,000 Jews living in Greece. After the Holocaust there were fewer than 11,000. A fascinating account of one man's survival in the Nazi death camps is told in *Athens to Auschwitz* (Lycabettus Press).

Beth Shalom was built in 1939 and underwent extensive renovation in the 1970s. The white-marble facade in modern style is reason enough to make a visit, but also notice the copper pulpit, or *bema* (pronounced *víma*), in similar period design. Across the street, above the synagogue offices, is a reconstruction of the interior of an older synagogue.

Open: Daily 9am–1pm; services Mon and Thurs at 8am, Fri evening, Sat morning.

Jewish Museum, Leofóros Amalías 36. ☎ **32-31-577.**

The Jewish Museum is located across from the temple of Zeus. A small, though expanding, collection, it presents a fascinating story of the region's once flourishing Jewish culture. Few, if any, museums in Greece present objects with more care and understanding than does this dedicated staff. Along with excellent changing exhibitions, the museum publishes a newsletter of great interest. Although most of the community disappeared during World War II, the Jewish Museum chooses to celebrate the spirit and proud history of Jews in both Turkey and Greece rather than create a memorial for those who died in the Holocaust. Allow time to visit; we stayed here for about two hours. The museum has a small selection of gift items and books for sale.

Admission: Free.

Open: Sun–Fri 9am–1pm.

Ion Vorres Museum, Paianía. ☎ **66-44-7710.**

The small Ion Vorrés museum contains a fascinating folk art collection.

Admission: 345 Drs ($1.45).

Open: Sat–Sun 10am–2pm.

Natural History Museum, Odós Levídou 13, Kifissía. ☎ **80-86-405.**

This is a wonderful small museum, devoted to natural history. It was founded by the Goulandrís family, whose collection forms the basis of the Museum of Cycladic and Ancient Greek Art.

Admission: 460 Drs ($1.90).

Open: Sat–Thurs 9am–3pm. **Closed:** Fri.

There are many other small museums, such as the Train Museum, the Theater Museum, the Museum of the History of the Greek Costume, the Philatelic Museum, and the War Museum. You can obtain information about these museums at any office of the Greek Tourist Organization (EOT).

Walking Tour 1
Sýntagma Square & Pláka

Start: Sýntagma Square

Finish: Pláka, at foot of the Acropolis

Time: Allow approximately $2^1/_2$ hours, not including museums or shopping stops.

Best Times: Weekdays at dusk or weekends.

Worst Times: Weekday rush hours or the midday heat.

Sýntagma (Constitution) Square is the heart of the city, where you'll find government offices, places of international commerce, tourist services, and elegant shops. From here, a brief walk will take you to the cobblestone lanes of Pláka, as timelessly Greek a neighborhood as you can hope to find in this bustling city.

At the northern corner of the recently landscaped Sýntagma Square you'll see the venerable:

1. **Grande Bretagne,** visit the lobby for a taste of old-world luxury. To the right (east), across heavily trafficked Leofóros Amalías, is the:
2. **Tomb of the Unknown Soldier,** and behind it is the Parliament Building, guarded by colorfully clad *évzones.* Walk south to the corner of Óthonos and Filellínon Streets (Olympic Airways is on Óthonos) and head away from the square along Óthonos Street (this is where it joins Mitropóleos Street). The first left will be Níkis Street; turn here to the first right, which is Apóllonos Street, and follow Apóllonos down past six small quiet streets till you reach the wider, brighter Adrianoú. To your left are:

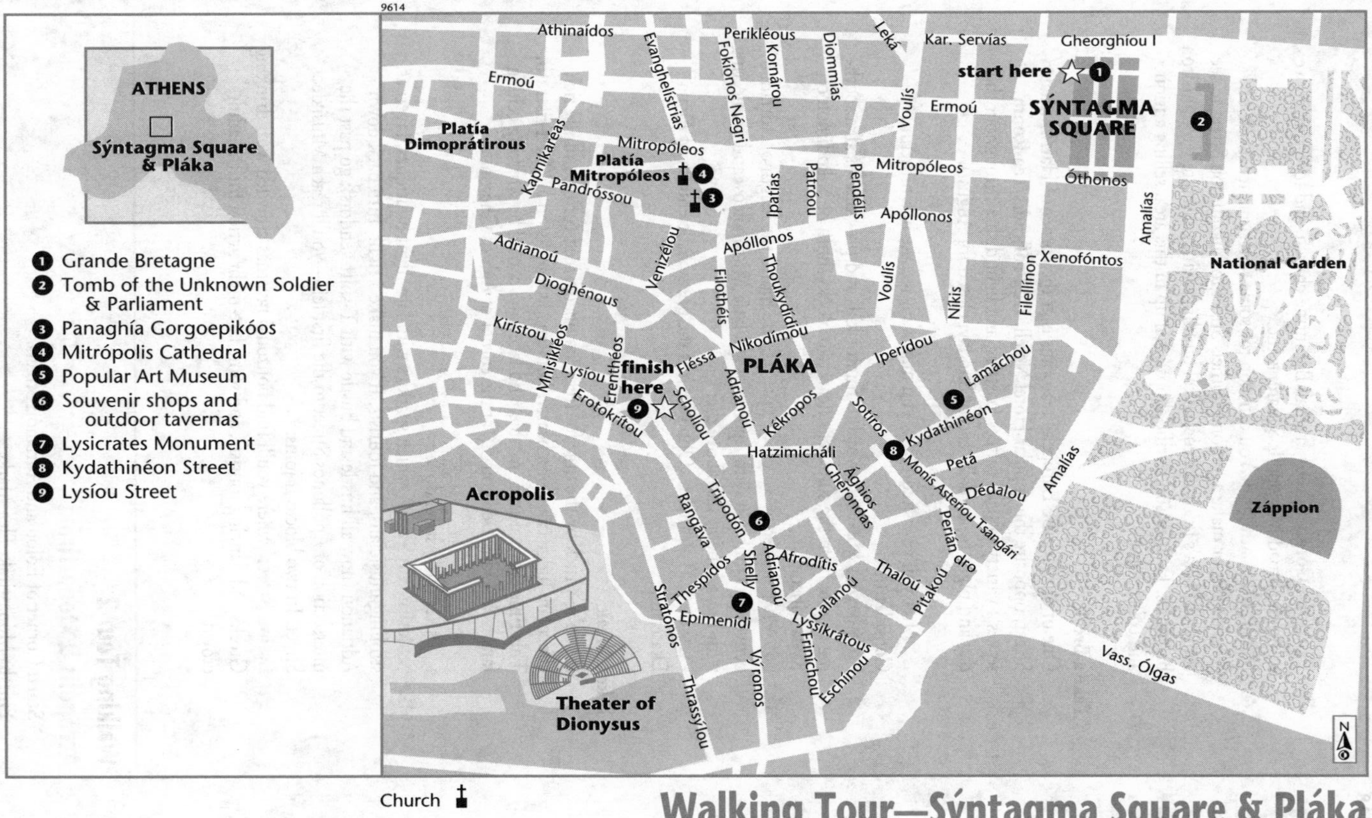

Walking Tour—Sýntagma Square & Pláka

3. **Panaghía Gorgoepikóos,** a small Byzantine church, and towering above it, on the broad Mitrópolis Square, is the:
4. **Mitrópolis Cathedral.** You can stop for some refreshments at one of several cafés or make a left on Filothéis Street to Nikodímou Street to see some of Pláka's fine old neoclassical buildings with elaborate wrought-iron balconies. Each season terrific shops open up in this area, selling antiques and collectibles.

Take a Break

One of our favorite European tearooms is at the corner of Hatzimicháli Street, opposite the popular Hotel Neféli. **De Profundis Tea Room** serves a variety of teas, coffees, pastries, and light dishes throughout the day and night (open daily except Sunday; closed for August).

After you've visited Pláka, you may want to take in a museum. Consider the:

5. **Popular Art Museum,** which is fun for kids and provides for all a soothing respite from the summer's heat, two blocks south of Nikodímou on Kydathinéon.
6. **Souvenir shops** and **outdoor tavernas** are found the length of Adrianoú, between its junction with Apóllonos at Platía Mitropóleos, and its meeting with Kydathinéon just above the:
7. **Lysicrates Monument.** Opposite it is the pretty little church of Aghía Ekateríni.

Take a Break

If you're struck by the urge for fresh lemonade, iced coffee, sinfully rich chocolate fudge cake, or a hearty, homemade soup, stop at: **To Tristrato.** This time-worn stucco, marble, and lace café, cooled by whirring ceiling fans, is at Odós Dédalou 34, at the corner of Ághios Ghérondas.

After dusk, stroll down:

8. **Kydathinéon Street,** which sparkles with late-night boutiques, tavernas, strolling musicians, and tourists. If you make a right, turn back down Adrianoú (now all hustle and bustle with T-shirt vendors); go past the intersection of Apóllonos Street to the first left—you'll reach Mnisikléos Street. In two blocks it joins:
9. **Lysíou Street,** where you'll find bouzouki tavernas crowded with drinking Greeks and dancing tourists, and some late-night action for the adult crowd.

Walking Tour 2
Acropolis & Monastiráki

Start: Corner of Eólou and Adrianóu Streets.
Finish: Monastiráki Flea Market.

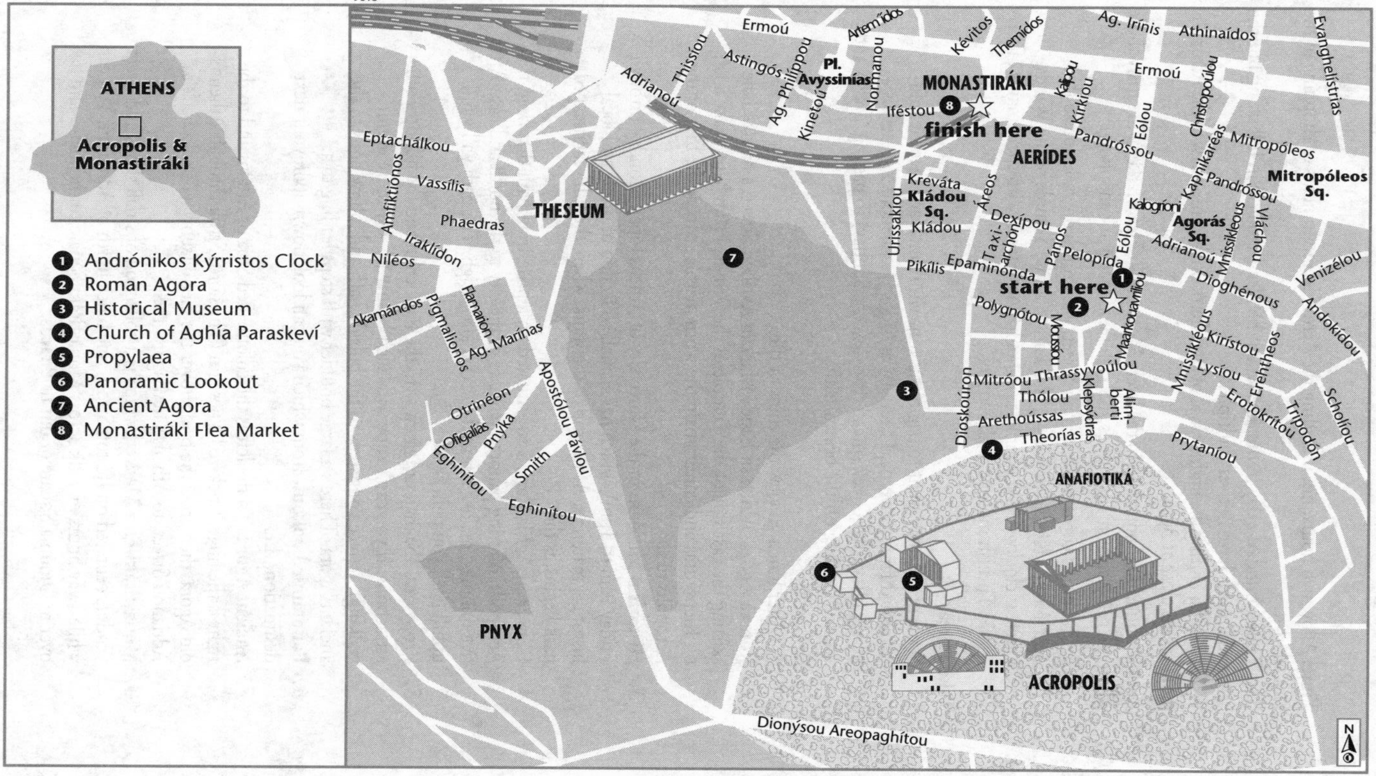

Walking Tour—The Acropolis & Monastiráki

Time: Allow two hours, not including the Acropolis monuments or shopping in the Flea Market.
Best Times: Sunday, early in the day, when the Flea Market is in full swing but the heat and crowds have not yet multiplied.
Worst Times: During the midday heat or late afternoon, because many of the Acropolis monuments close at 3pm.

A walk around Acropolis Hill to the lively Monastiráki Flea Market will satisfy those who prefer to glance at antiquities and save their energy for shopping.

From the corner of Adrianoú Street, walk south down Eólou to the:

1. **Andrónikos Kýrristos Clock,** also known as the Temple of the Winds. Circle it clockwise. At your left is Dioghénous Street, with the remains of an old Turkish mosque at the corner.

Take a Break

Some of you may want to begin this tour with lunch at a favorite, old-fashioned family taverna: **Platanos,** at Odós Dioghénous 2. It serves a hearty but casual Greek spread daily (except Sunday) to passing Greeks and tourists straying off the beaten path.

After lunch go view the ruins of the:

2. **Roman Agora,** which sit beside Márkou Avrilíou Street, a narrow lane skirting the east side of the Temple of the Winds. From here, make a left on Klepsýdras and continue up the worn marble stairs at the foot of the Acropolis to the:
3. **Historical Museum** of the University of Athens (open Monday through Friday 9am to 1pm), which has a small collection of prints and local historical materials. At the top of the stairs, where the hill's landscaped park begins, is the:
4. **Church of Aghía Paraskeví,** situated on a pedestrian path that rings the Acropolis, offering panoramic views of the city to the north and east. After five minutes, make a left at the CLOAK ROOM sign. The path will wind uphill until you're in sight of the:
5. **Propylaea,** the majestic gateway to the Parthenon and the hilltop's other attractions. If you can't cope with such beauty (or any more uphill walking), retrace your steps to the hillside path and follow signs to the ancient Agorá. There's a large boulder with steps leading to a:
6. **Panoramic Lookout,** from which you can look down upon your next destination, the:
7. **Ancient Agora.** To the left is the colonnaded Stoa of Attalos and to the right is the huge, brick-red Theseum (Thissíon). Stroll through Athens's old Agora, then cross the bridge over the metro (subway) tracks back to Adrianoú Street, to Athens's new agora, the:
8. **Monastiráki Flea Market,** which is a collection of small shops and street vendors centered on Iféstou Street, one block north of Adrianoú. You can while away hours or walk across Monastiráki Square to the metro and head over to Omónia Square or out to Piraeus.

ORGANIZED TOURS

For readers who are more comfortable in a tour bus, several companies offer organized sightseeing tours of Athens. The half-day version hits the high spots of the sights, for a price of approximately 7,000 Drs ($29.20). There are several night versions, which range from the basic sound-and-light shows, combined with Greek folk dancing at the Dóra Strátou Folk Dance Theater, to dinner and Greek dancing afterward. Prices range from 6,000 to 9,000 Drs ($25–$37). Day tours to Delphi, Cape Soúnio, and Corinth-Mycenae-Epidaurus are also offered, at prices ranging from 4,500 to 14,000 Drs ($18.75–$58). Several tour companies offer day trips to the nearby islands of Aegina, Póros, and Hydra in the Saronic Gulf.

Tours can be arranged through your hotel or by calling **Viking Tours** at **89-80-729.** Viking can also arrange customized individual tours, with emphasis on historical and educational aspects of Athens, one of its specialties.

3 Special/Free Events

ATHENS FESTIVAL

Since 1955 the Athens Festival, held in one of the world's most beautiful ancient theaters, the Herod Atticus Odeum (built in A.D. 161 and reconstructed after World War II) has entertained international audiences with theater, ballet, and musical performances by acclaimed traditional and modern artists. Martha Graham's and Maurice Béjart's companies have performed in a revival of the Dionysia performances begun by Peisistratus, ruler of Athens during the 6th century B.C. In addition, the Bolshoi and Kirov ballets, the London Philharmonic, and the Deutsche Staatsoper Berlin, among many other internationally known groups, have appeared, along with the celebrated National Theater of Greece, which stages classical Greek dramas in modern Greek. Performances are also held in the open-air theater on Lykavittós Hill, as well as at the ancient theater at Epidaurus, in the Peloponnese.

Performances are held frequently (almost daily) and are often sold out far in advance. Contact the Greek Tourist Organization (EOT) for the current schedule or call the Athens Festival at **32-32-771** or **32-23-111** for information. Tickets go on sale two weeks prior to the performance, at the **Athens Festival Box Office,** Odós Stadíou 4 (in a pedestrian shopping mall off Voukourestíou Street near Sýntagma Square); the box office is open daily from 8:30am to 2pm and from 5 to 7pm. Tickets for the *Epidaurus Theater Festival* (see Chapter 7, "The Peloponnese") can also be purchased here. Athens Festival tickets cost from 800 to 9,500 Drs ($3.30–$39.60); remaining seats can be purchased from the Herod Atticus Odeum box office between 6:30 and 9pm on the day of the performance. Check with the EOT or *Athens Today* (at most hotels) or *Athenscope* (at newsstands) for festival information.

LYKAVITTÓS FESTIVAL

A lesser known but equally delightful open-air festival is held each summer at the theater on top of Lykavittós (Lycabettus) Hill. A funicular running from the top of Ploutárchou Street in Kolonáki will sweep you up to a restaurant from which a short walk leads to the panoramically situated modern bowl, where contemporary dance, music, and theatrical performances are given several evenings each week. Past performers included the Kronos Quartet, the pop group Tangerine Dream, Nina Simone, Jan Garbarek, and many notable Greek composers. For schedule and ticket information, contact the

EOT at **32-23-111** or the **Lykavittós Theater** (☎ **32-21-459**). Tickets can be bought at the Athens Festival box office or at the gate. Ask about free transportation for ticket holders. Otherwise, you'll have to take a taxi or the funicular.

4 Sports & Recreation

SPECTATOR SPORTS

SOCCER The Greeks love soccer and follow it with a passion. You'll be lucky if you can get tickets to any game, but try it through your hotel. The **Karaïskáki Stadium** is in Fáliro, near the metro stop on the way to Piraeus (☎ **481-2902**).

HORSE RACING The **Hippodrome** is the major racetrack in Athens, located near the soccer stadium in Fáliro (☎ **94-17-761**). Races are held Monday, Wednesday, and Friday from 2:30 to 6pm in the winter and from 6 to 10pm in the summer.

RECREATION

GOLF The most convenient golf course is the **Glyfáda Golf Club** (☎ **89-46-820**) in the nearby suburb of Glyfáda, south of the airport.

TENNIS Try the **Athens Tennis Club,** Leofóros Vassilíssis Ólgas 2. (☎ **92-32-872**), not far from Sýntagma Square, or the **Attica Tennis Club** (☎ **68-12-557** or **68-27-408**) in the suburb of Filothéi.

HORSEBACK RIDING The **Riding Club of Athens** (☎ **66-11-088**) is located in the suburb of Gérakas.

WINDSURFING Contact the **Greek Windsurfing Association,** Odós Filellínon 7, 105 57 Athens (☎ **32-30-068**).

SCUBA There are many limitations on scuba diving in the Greek islands, due to the fragility of the environment and archeological treasures. For information, contact the **Scuba Club** (☎ **67-25-357**), in the suburb of Kifissiá.

5 Savvy Shopping

THE SHOPPING SCENE

Shopping Around Sýntagma Square

Just off Sýntagma Square, northeast of Panepistimíou Street is elegant little Voukourestíou Street, which has become a high-fashion international shopping mall. You'll find jewelry and haute-couture boutiques featuring such acclaimed designers as Ungaro, Yves St. Laurent, Pierre Cardin, and Ted Lapidus. Unfortunately, these imported fashions cost as much as, if not more than, they do in the United States. Better menswear can be found along Akadimías Street, near Amerikís and Pindárou Streets. Again, the most fashionable garments will probably be of Italian or French design and thus very expensive.

Surprisingly enough, designer shoes by such names as Charles Jourdan, Bally, and Valentino cost about half of what they do in New York! Why? Because although they're not labeled as such, many of these shoes are actually manufactured in Greece, where the labor is cheaper. Check out the high-fashion shoe shops on Ermoú and Mitropóleos Streets, among them **Rollini** at Ermoú 16 (☎ **32-34-838**), **Studio Mocassino** at Ermoú 2 (☎ **32-34-744**), and **Bournazos** at Ermoú 3 (☎ **32-23-938**).

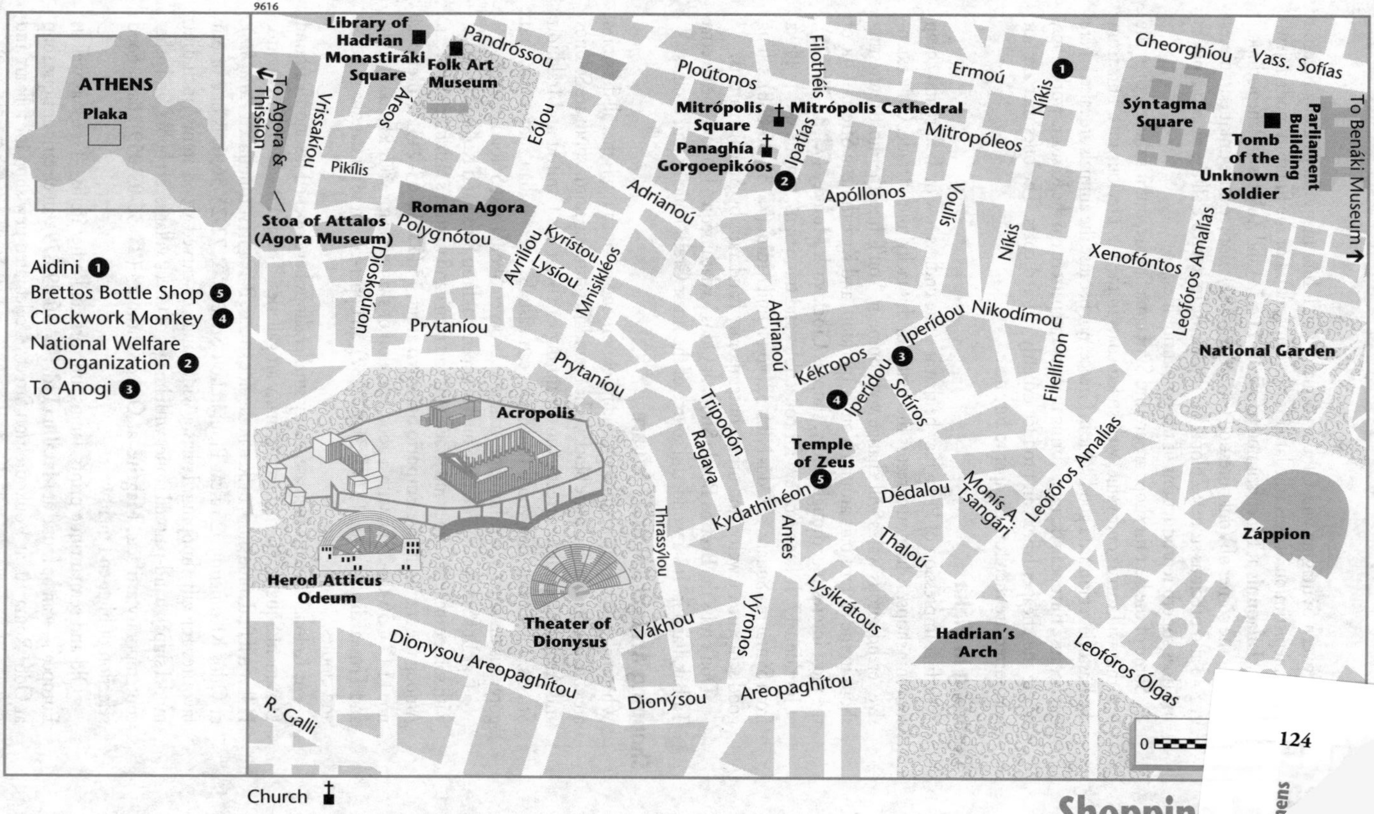
9616
ATHENS
Plaka
Aidini 1
Brettos Bottle Shop 5
Clockwork Monkey 4
National Welfare Organization 2
To Anogi 3
Church
To Agora & Thissíon
To Benáki Museum
Library of Hadrian
Monastiráki Square
Folk Art Museum
Pandróssou
Ploútonos
Filothéis
Ermoú
Níkis
Gheorghíou
Vass. Sofías
Sýntagma Square
Parliament Building
Tomb of the Unknown Soldier
Mitrópolis Square
Mitrópolis Cathedral
Panaghía Gorgoepikóos
Ipatías
Mitropóleos
Apóllonos
Voulís
Níkis
Xenofóntos
Leofóros Amalías
Vrissakíou
Áreos
Eólou
Pikílis
Adrianoú
Roman Agora
Stoa of Attalos (Agora Museum)
Polygnótou
Avrilíou
Kyrístou
Lysíou
Mnisikléos
Dioskoúron
Prytaníou
Prytaníou
Adrianoú
Iperídou
Nikodímou
National Garden
Kékropos
Iperídou
Sotíros
Filellínon
Acropolis
Tripodón
Ragava
Temple of Zeus
Kydathinéon
Dédalou
Monís A. Tsangári
Leofóros Amalías
Antes
Thaloú
Thrassýlou
Herod Atticus Odeum
Theater of Dionysus
Vákhou
Výronos
Lysikrátous
Hadrian's Arch
Záppion
Leofóros Ólgas
Dionysou Areopaghítou
Dionýsou
Areopaghítou
R. Galli
0

Between Sýntagma and Omónia Squares you'll find many shops along Stadíou and Panepistimíou Streets (the latter is more upscale). For the finest in modern jewelry, try **Lalaounis** at Panepistimíou 6 (☎ **36-11-371**) and **Zolotas** at Panepistimíou 10, near the corner of Voukourestíou (☎ **36-13-782**). Both feature unique art pieces in gold and precious stones; Zolotas has the license to re-create all the museum pieces and does superb reproductions of the best antiquities.

Some of the best fur shops are around Sýntagma Square, but it's the less than the best that will carry good-value, well-styled coats in the less precious furs. Furs from the Kastoriá region are a good value in Greece, not because the animals are raised there but because European designers bring in skins and patterns to the Kastoriá workshops, where the cheaper labor can produce expertly tailored coats. The ones that are not reexported are therefore cheaper to buy here.

Shopping in Pláka

Your first impression of Pláka may be that it's one endless row of T-shirt and cheap souvenir shops. Adrianoú Street is the center of this tacky tourist trade. Only extensive serendipitous walks will change your opinion. You'll find the most interesting shops in the eastern part around Voulís, Iperídou, and Kydathinéon Streets. One of the most interesting, though pricey, shops is **Clockwork Monkey** (☎ **32-28-321**), at Iperídou 17. It has a fine eye for collectibles and trade signs. On the way to Pláka from Sýntagma Square, at Odós Níkis 32, you'll find **Aidini** (☎ **32-26-088**), selling good sculpture, jewelry, and other contemporary handcrafts by Athenian artists.

Don't miss the **Brettos Bottle Shop,** at Odós Kydathinéon 41, above the taverna Tá Bakaliarákia. It's a wonderful source of the finest Greek liqueurs and candies.

Shopping Around Kolonáki Square

What makes shopping in this high-end neighborhood so much fun is that all the stores are concentrated in six square blocks. The boundaries running north-south are Sólonos and Anagnostopoúlou Streets; those running east-west are Omírou and Iraklítou Streets. Inside this area you'll find European casuals, great Italian sportswear, and gorgeous designer-wear shops, on Iraklítou between Skoufá and Sólonos Streets.

Tsakálof Street is a pedestrian mall between Iraklítou Street and Kolonáki Square, with some excellent leather and shoe shops and men's and women's fashion resort wear. Among the standouts are **Emporio Sportivo** at no. 15 (☎ **36-45-943**); **Balletto** at no. 11 (☎ **36-00-251**), with a good selection of swimwear for your island sojourn; and **Trussardi** also at no. 15 (☎ **36-07-282**), an upper-end store for handbags, belts, and clothes.

As Kolonáki's rents increase, many smaller shops have opened just north around Dexamení Square, where there are many art galleries. Toward the base of Lykavittós Hill you'll find some shops tucked in the side streets. **Panagiri** (pronounced *Panaghíri*), at Odós Kleoménous 25 near Ploutárchou Street (☎ **72-25-369**), is one of our favorites for gift shopping. It has a wide range of carved wood items (including model ships), hand-painted stones with images of Greek villages, art books, and other contemporary artifacts. **Magrite,** at Odós Xánthou 3 (☎ **36-03-059**), has a good selection of high-end menswear.

Old and semiantique prints, lamps, mirrors, and other items—Greek as well as European—can be found at **Macalina Ltd.** (☎ **36-09-879**), an electric antique shop at Odós Roma 10, at Voukourestíou Street. A celebrated new shop for folk art and recent antiques, all top quality, is **Archipelagos,** Odós Iássou 6 (☎ **72-27-308**), at Moní Patráki.

For very fine hand-crafted jewelry, try the shop of **Nikos Nafpliotis,** at Odós Loukianoú 21B (☎ **72-29-277**).

These shops are not, of course, budget finds. For budget shoppers, a good small department store has arrived in the form of the French chain **Prisunic,** at Odós Kanári 9. You'll find good prices on underwear, cosmetics, and a small line of clothing.

Shopping Around Omónia Square

Omónia Square is definitely the workers' part of town, and the big, efficient department stores and budget boutiques reflect the market. There are three main departmentlike stores: **Lambropouli Bros.** is at Eólou and Lykoúrgos Streets; **Athenee** is at Odós Stadíou 33; and **Minion,** the largest and most varied, is at the corner of Veranzérou and Patissíon Streets (a continuation of Eólou Street).

BHS (British Home Stores), two blocks south of Omónia, at Efpolídos and Athinás Streets, has an excellent self-service restaurant (open 9am–8:30pm), on the 8th floor, with indoor and outdoor seating and fabulous views.

Omónia Square has several small fruit-and-nut stores, a whole-wheat macrobiotic bakery (at Stadíou and Eólou Streets, next to the main post office), and many souvenir stands in narrow arcades off Stadíou Street and in the underground metro stop. Souvenirs are also sold at streetside kiosks and by mobile vendors.

BARGAINING

The first rule of bargaining is: "Take yourself seriously." Really believe that you're going to pay only a certain amount and not more and be prepared to walk away if the vendor doesn't meet your price (in fact, walking away seems to reduce the price a lot!). Carry small bills as evidence of your limited budget, always use cash, and talk fast and firm. Remember, too, that someone else has the same merchandise, and that you can always come back the next day to buy it because no one will remember the scene you created.

BEST BUYS

The best values in Athens are items that are uniquely Greek—folk arts or internationally designed merchandise that's been manufactured in Greece. What's cheaper than what you get back home? Shoes, furs, and bathing suits. What's uniquely Greek? Hand-knit woolen sweaters, flokáti rugs, cotton embroideries from the islands, and some museum-reproduction ceramics. What are the best souvenirs? Copper trinkets from the flea market, *kombolóia* (worry beads), sponges, and the things you find in the small towns, villages, or islands you'll visit.

Crafts

We like several stores for their still original, handmade crafts and goods. The **Greek Women's Institution,** at Odós Kolokotróni 3 (☎ **32-50-524**), specializes in embroidery from the islands, as well as replicas of Benáki Museum embroideries. The **National Welfare Organization** (Ethnikí Pronía), at Odós Ipatías 6, off Apóllonos Street in Pláka (☎ **32-40-017**), carries the woven goods, ceramics, copperware, and jewelry produced by local craftspeople. This store features a fine stock of tapestries, rugs, and small goods guaranteed to delight.

Reader Christy Buck of Grand Rapids, Mich., recommended **To Anogi,** Odós Sotíros 1, across from the Hotel Nefeli (☎ **32-26-487**). Kati Epostolos paints the luminous icons she sells in her shop. She also has hand-painted eggs, traditional pottery, weaving, and ceramics from other artists on the mainland and the islands.

Museum Shops

The **Museum of Cycladic and Ancient Greek Art,** at Odós Neophýtou 4; the **Benáki Museum,** at Odós Koumbári 1; and the **National Archeological Museum,** at Odós Patissíon 4, sell reproductions of items in their collections. The Benáki also sells other items, such as scarves, needlepoint kits, and linens whose designs were inspired by traditional Greek motifs. The National Archeological Museum also sells castings of items exhibited in other Greek museums and copies of paintings and murals.

Flea Markets

Monastiráki is a daily market area radiating from a picturesque old square below Pláka. If you're walking, the easiest way to get there is to go parallel to Mitropóleos Street, down Pandróssou Street. The metro will take you right there; when you exit you'll find Pandróssou Street on the right and Iféstou Street on the left, both of them filled with knickknack displays when the Sunday flea market is held. Try to get there on a Sunday (hours are from 8am to 2pm), when the park behind the Theseum (Thissíon) is filled with young and old alike "walking" their canaries. The flea market is a great place for campers. You'll find plates, kitchen utensils, jars, flashlights, gas burners, cotton underwear (the Greek sizes are very narrow), watches, new and used music cassettes and records, Chinese alarm clocks, punk clothes and Sears coveralls, leather goods, wispy cotton Isadora Duncan dresses, and ***kombolóia,*** among many other items for sale. Dig deeper.

Hephaistos, at Odós Iféstou 12, is filled with old and new copper and brass products. Remember, though: You can't cook in copper pots that are unlined, but you can serve in them. (By the way, *Iféstos* is the modern Greek pronunciation of Hephaestus, the god of fire and metalworking.)

A few doors away at Iféstou 5, **Iakovos Antiques** (☎ **32-10-169**) offers an interesting collection of Greek and European collectibles, including porcelains, brass products, and paintings. The merchandise is high quality, with prices to match.

Next door, at Iféstou 6, you'll enjoy the handmade bouzoukis and guitars of **Vasilios Kevorkian** (☎ **32-10-024**). Theater and folk-art buffs will be intrigued by **Studio Kostas Sokaras,** at Odós Adrianoú 25 (☎ **32-16-826**). It sells a wonderful variety of puppets from the Greek shadow theater, along with folk costumes, jewelry, and textiles. For an interesting collection of art-nouveau lamps and glass shades, visit **E. & P. Sokara Antiques,** at Odós Níssou 1 (☎ **32-54-051**).

At the edge of Pláka, at Odós Pandróssou 89, is the leather shop of **Stavros Melissinos** (☎ **32-19-247**), resident bard to the flea market, acclaimed poet, celebrity, and shoemaker to the stars (Robert Wagner and Barbra Streisand). For 4,000–8,625 Drs ($16.75–$35.95), you can walk away in a pair of sandals that may be similar to those (reputedly) once ordered by Jacqueline Onassis, the Beatles, or Rudolf Nureyev (who knew good shoes).

You may find some bulk-knit homespun wool sweaters here or in Pláka, at one of the pricier tourist-only shops. If you're off to the islands soon, you can probably find better designed and more finely knitted ones; if you're off to Crete or to Delphi and points farther north, you can find equally folksy ones at better prices.

The **Piraeus Flea Market** is a worthwhile Sunday excursion (open 8am to noon), when the enclosed, older market heads outdoors. It's located off Ippodámou Street, near the metro terminus, and specializes in old ship bric-a-brac, lamps, hand embroideries, and whatever else gets washed ashore.

Shopping Around Om

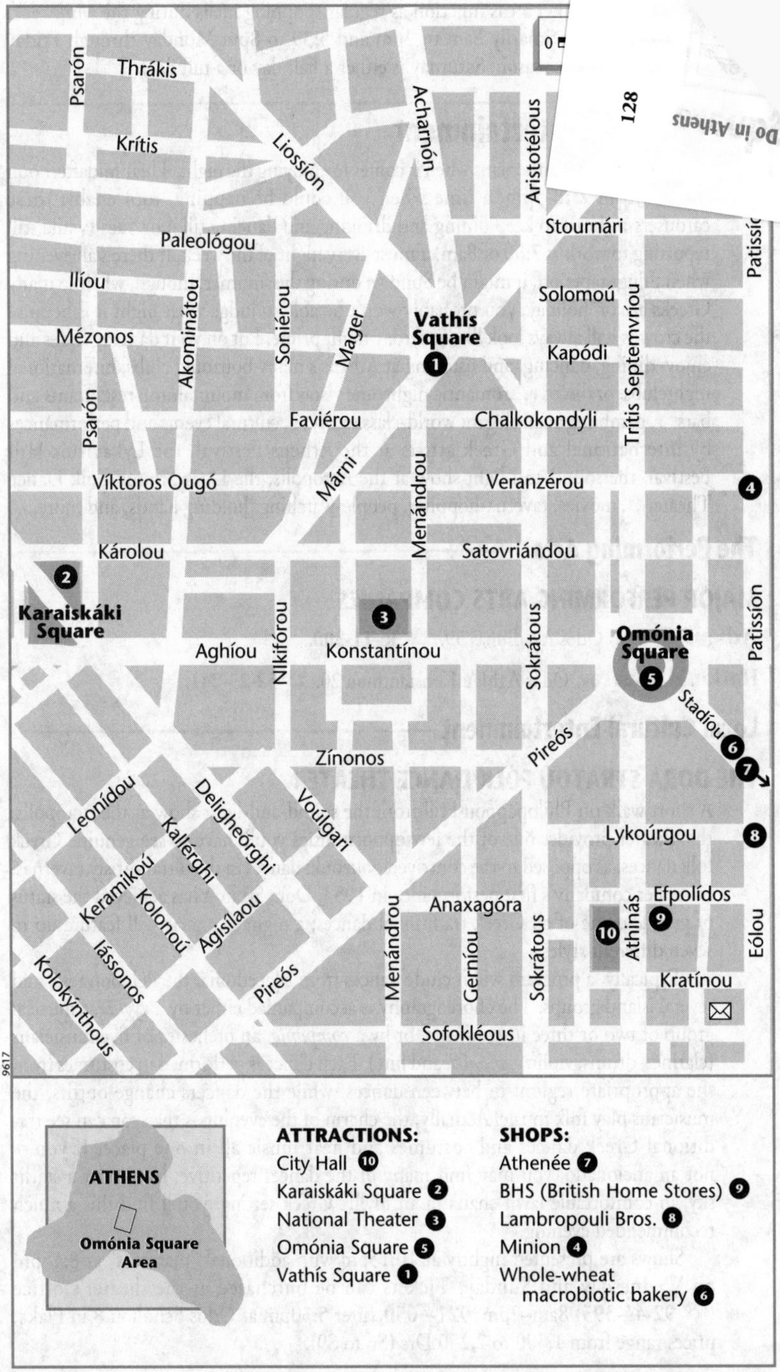

Both flea-market areas function as regular shopping malls during the workweek. Their hours are primarily 8am to 2pm and 5:30 to 8pm Monday through Friday (depending on the season, Saturday is either a half day or a full day).

6 Evening Entertainment

No one can match Athenians when it comes to enjoying the night. Their midafternoon siestas (from 2 to 5pm, a time when you could be napping, too) enable these carousers-at-heart to keep dining and drinking and dancing till 4 or 5am (while still reporting to work at 7:30 or 8am) almost every night of the week. If there's an evening when things taper off, it might be Sunday; during the summer, though, when so many Greeks are on holiday, you probably won't be able to judge what night it is because the crowds will always look like Saturday night prime. Put on your dancing shoes and enjoy: dining, dancing, and listening at Athens's many bouzouki clubs, international nightclubs, or discos . . . romantic nighttime vistas from mountaintop restaurants and bars . . . gambling at an elegant world-class resort . . . cultural events and performances by international and Greek artists at the Athens Festival, the Lykavittós Hill Festival, the sound-and-light show at the Acropolis, the Dora Stratou Folk Dance Theater . . . movies, taverna-hopping, people-watching, holding hands, and more. . . .

The Performing Arts

MAJOR PERFORMING ARTS COMPANIES

Athens Opera, Odós Akadimías 59. ☎ **36-11-300.**

National Theater, Odós Aghíou Konstantínou 20. ☎ **52-23-241.**

Local Cultural Entertainment

THE DORA STRATOU FOLK DANCE THEATER

A short walk on Philopáppou Hill from the sound-and-light show at the Acropolis, this theater provides one of the few opportunities you'll have to see genuine Greek folk dances, as opposed to the contrived bouzouki dances in the ultratouristy tavernas. Since her company's first performance in 1953, Dora Stratou has achieved the status of grande dame of all Greek traditional dances; a night's concert will feature up to seven different styles.

Typically, a program will include dances from Macedonia, the Peloponnese, and several island groups. The choreography is accompanied either by a *zyghiá,* a musical group of two or three instruments, or by a *companía,* an orchestra of five musicians (clarinet, drums, violin, *santoúri,* and lute). Each dance is performed in costumes from the appropriate region; in between dances, while the dancers change outfits, the musicians play folk music. Actually, the charm of the evening is that you can see traditional Greek dances and costumes and hear music all in one place. If you're not an aficionado, you may find many of the dances repetitive; but under a starlit sky, in comfortable lawn chairs in an idyllic Greek setting, you'll find this a much recommended evening.

Shows are presented nightly at 10:15pm with additional "matinees" at 8:15pm on Wednesday and Sunday. Tickets can be purchased at the theater's office (☎ **92-44-395**) 8am–2pm, **921-4650,** after 5:30pm at Odós Scholíou 8 in Pláka; prices range from 1,500 to 2,250 Drs ($6 to $9).

The Club & Music Scene

Your choices range from classic Greek bouzouki clubs to international-style discos. Athens has a fine selection of both.

BOUZOUKI CLUBS

If you visit Greece, you can't avoid the lure of the bouzouki clubs, those noisy nightspots where free-flowing wine, an amplified band, and willing guests join to dance up a storm. Plate-smashing, the accepted method of showing appreciation, has been outlawed, but the tradition persists in some clubs; check with the management before you join in, because you'll be charged by the plate! (If you really get into it, they're sold before the show begins, by the dozen.) Then go to it.

Pláka has always been the center of the tourist-oriented bouzouki clubs, an area where a few key streets are just wall-to-wall sound and the clubs have only pink or blue neon signs to differentiate them. Many of the tavernas with musicians or elaborate floor shows serve a high-priced meal beforehand to get you in the mood; count on spending at least 6,000 Drs ($25) a head.

Note: Those readers who are serious about bouzoukiing should consult their hotel receptionist or the current issue of *Athenscope* magazine (in English and available at newsstands) to find out which clubs are featuring the best performers. The really "Greek" clubs are a distance from the Sýntagma/Pláka area, so budget another 2,500–4,000 Drs for round-trip taxi fare. If you want some background, buy a copy of *Greek Dances* (Lycabettus Press), by Ted Petrides, available at many bookstores for 1,000 Drs ($4.20); it has a lively, informative introduction to the country's various dances, accompanied by explicit foot diagrams, so that even a klutz can learn the *syrtáki*, one of the easiest dances.

Taverna Kalokerinos, Odós Kékropos 10, Pláka. ☎ **32-32-054.**

Music usually begins at about 9pm, and heavy singing and dancing begin after 10pm; call ahead to make reservations. Dinner is forgettable and expensive, but the tour groups usually go for it. If you want to come at 10pm for the show only, there's a minimum

Major Concert/Performance Halls

Mégaron, Queen Sophia Avenue. ☎ **72-90-391.**

Athens is more than proud of this state-of-the-art concert hall, which opened in 1991 to rave reviews. The Mégaron is one of the newest and finest halls in all Europe, and hosts opera, theater, and classical as well as modern music performances.

Odeum of Herod Atticus, Dionýsou Areopaghítou Street, below the Acropolis. ☎ **32-32-771.**

This is among the most ancient (A.D. 161) and most dramatic of all performing venues in the world. At the odeum (*odíon* in Greek), the Athens Festival presents a wide range of theatrical, dance, and music performances during the summer and early fall. It's an easy taxi or bus ride from Sýntagma Square, beyond the Hilton Hotel and next to the U.S. Embassy.

Pallas Theatre, Odós Voukourestíou 1. ☎ **32-28-275.**

Most of the major jazz and rock concerts are held here, as well as classical music performances.

of 4,000 Drs ($16.70), which you'll quickly leave in the dust with a few drinks. But as the owner told us, Kalokerinós is "the only club where you can break dishes every night." (By the way, it's 100 Drs or 40¢ per plate.)

Open: Daily 8pm–2:30am.

Admission: 4,000 Drs ($16.70) minimum.

Palia Taverna Kritikou, Odós Mnisikléos 24, Pláka. ☎ **32-22-809.**

The marble staircase intersection of Lysíou and Mnisikléos Streets, about two blocks from the Tower of the Winds, sings at night with revved-up tourists and aggressive taverna hawkers. This is one of the many simple but expensive touristy tavernas, and one of the oldest in Pláka, as its name—*Paliá* (old) Taverna Kritikou—suggests. We like its open-air, casual feel—a good place to enjoy an orchestra with singers and folk dancers, and some lively dancing by a mixed Greek-and-tourist clientele.

Open: Daily 8:30pm–2:30am.

Admission: No cover charge.

Leoforos, Leofóros Syngroú 251. ☎ **94-28-237.**

This is one of the more expensive and ritzier Greek cabaret/bouzouki clubs. Watch yourself here; a drink can cost as much as 5,000 Drs ($21), and a bottle of whisky starts at 20,000 Drs ($83). Known singers and Greek superstars on the order of Frank Sinatra appear at clubs like Leoforos; the Greeks who come here expect to pay well for the quality entertainment they'll get.

Open: Daily 8:30pm–2:30pm; shows start at 10pm. Reservations required.

Admission: 3,500 Drs ($14).

DISCO, POP & ROCK

Athens's nightlife grows ever livelier, more various and variable—so variable that all our suggestions in the last edition were gone or changed greatly during our most recent visit. Also, the distinctions we commonly make between various forms of popular music aren't quite so clear-cut, and clubs are rather mercurial. Do be careful in the area just south and east of Sýntagma Square, as clip joints abound there. Nothing beats word-of-mouth on the current in places, so ask, or at least check *Athenscope* for information, even about these suggestions.

The hip local young people were seeking musical entertainment and social interaction in Kifissiá (a northern suburb rather distant from our usual haunts) and near Exárchia Square, at **Rhythm 'N' Blues,** Odós Tossítsa 11 (☎ **822-8870**). We trust our younger readers will be resourceful enough to find the current hot spots.

In Makriyáni, just southeast of the Acropolis, **Avant Garde,** Odós Lebési 19 (☎ **924-2737**), was loud and crowded. Across the street, at Lebési 20, **Granazi** (☎ **325-3979**) was a popular gay hangout, though the best-known alternative place is the nearby **E . . . Kai** ("So What?"), Odós Iossíf ton Rogón 12 (☎ **922-1742**). Pub lovers should drop by **Pano Kato,** Odós Fratti 1 (☎ **902-8172**). A little farther south, at Odós Syngroú 49, **Mad Club** (☎ **922-6694**) was doing its best to live up to its name.

Those willing to part with a little more money may want to hit fashionable Kolonáki to check out **City,** Odós Cháritos 43 (☎ **722-8910**); **Fun O Mania,** Odós Spefsíppou 11 (☎ **723-1463**); **Memphis,** Odós Ventíri 5 (☎ **722-4104**), with live music, more or less, as its name implies; and **Nick's Place,** Odós Spefsíppou 26 (☎ **724-1235**).

JAZZ & PIANO BARS

Our readers with more sedate tastes will likely find their cup of tea in Kolonáki, especially near the Hilton. We suggest the **Jazz Club Diva,** Odós Antinóros 42 (☎ **729-0322**); **Lord Byron Bar,** at the Caravel Hotel, Leof. Vass. Alexándrou 2 (☎ **725-3744**); or the **Polo Bar,** at the Hilton (☎ **722-0201**).

Evening Stroll (*Volta*)

Perhaps the best entertainment is the street life of Athens at night: Watch the glee and exuberance with which Athenians soak up the night air, go for a stroll (*vólta*) along the seafront, overtake a sidewalk café table, devour a taverna feast.

The narrow, winding streets, cobblestone footpaths, and uneven stonesteps of **Pláka** never fail to delight the first-time visitor. Refer to "Walking Tours" (pages 116–20) for guidance, or just set out and follow the crowds. For a close-up look at the under-30 crowd, there's no better place than **Fokíonos Négri,** a long, broad pedestrian mall of cafés north of the Archeological Museum. The chic crowd strolls over to **Kolonáki Square** (a short walk from Sýntagma Square), to any of the jam-packed cafés that overlook the little planted green. Around sundown, the **top of Lykavittós Hill** is particularly special. At the head of Ploutárchou Street you can catch the funicular that speeds you up or back. Check out the "Dining with a View" section in Chapter 4; our favorite spot is a little ouzerí halfway back down on the easy trail. For those wanting a **seaside stroll,** we suggest a taxi or metro ride (from the Néo Fáliro stop) to Mikrolímano, a neighborhood built around a natural yacht harbor. Seafood restaurants line this basin, and though we don't recommend eating here, it's a picturesque venue for a sundown stroll.

More Entertainment

SOUND-AND-LIGHT SHOW AT THE ACROPOLIS

Sound-and-light shows can be one of the most effective ways to bring an architectural monument to life. From the top of Philopáppou Hill (grab the seats farthest away from the public-address system) you can let yourself imagine the flawless grandeur that was. The silhouettes of the Parthenon, the Erechtheum, and particularly the Acropolis walls are enhanced by the ever-changing light. For those who are disappointed by their daytime view when scaffolding and the effects of pollution on the temples are so obvious, a distant examination of the glowing gem perched above a twinkling Athens skyline may be the cure. If you insist on listening to the melodramatic delivery, have a few glasses of retsína before the show. It's a skimpy review of the Acropolis's history; the program, which costs 400 Drs ($1.65), will enable you to read it later on.

Performances are given from April 1 to October 31 in several languages: *English* daily at 9pm; *French* daily, except for Tuesday and Thursday, at 10pm; and *German* on Tuesday and Thursday at 10pm. Bring a sweater and a camera (if you have high-speed film) and wear your good walking shoes. The price is 1,200 Drs ($5) adults, students 600 Drs ($2.50). Call **32-24-128** for information.

MOVIES

The old outdoor cinemas we used to enjoy are disappearing, being shouldered aside by modern facilities not much different from what you find elsewhere in Europe. We counted 70 cinemas showing "foreign" films—mostly in English, with a few French thrown in; 55 of these had Dolby stereo, though only the Alexandra, Odós Patissíon

79 (☎ 95-60-306), and the Apollon, Odós Stadíou 19 (☎ 32-36-811), were air-conditioned. What was even more amazing was the number of quality first-run and even classic American films—a couple of dozen; so, if you're hungry for a movie, you won't have any trouble finding one to your liking. See *Athens News* or *Athenscope* for the current schedule.

CASINOS

Casino Mont Parnes, Párnitha. ☎ **24-69-111.**

In addition to the Achilleion on Corfu and the Astir Grand Palace on Rhodes, Greece has a third major casino. It's part of a complex, which includes a nightclub and a restaurant, on top of Mount Párnitha (Parnés) (about 35 km out of town). There's bus service; call **142** for the schedule. If you're driving (we wouldn't want to imagine the cab fare to get there!), you can shave off the last 8 km by taking the Parnés cable car directly to the hotel's front door. Proper dress required. The complex itself is part of a resort. Open: Mon–Tues and Thurs–Sun 8pm–2am.

ADULTS ONLY

After-hours company can be found in several areas of Athens. Near Omónia Square, try Sokrátous, Sofokléous, and Menándrou Streets; near Pláka, try Androútsou and Byzantíou Streets, off Syngroú Avenue (behind the Olympic Airways terminal). Try also the bars by the large hotels on Aghíou Konstantínou Street (near Omónia) and on Ermoú and Karagheórghi Streets (near Sýntagma).

Warning: The police have asked us to warn readers about the scam that's most often reported to them by tourists. This is how it goes: A young woman will approach a man either inside or outside one of the bars, bouzouki clubs, nightclubs, or cafés frequented by tourists and will ask him to buy her a drink. The drink is almost always "champagne" (usually just a carbonated beverage or a supercheap local brew) that she'll consume while the man nurses his own drink. When the bill comes, it runs from 10,000 to 30,000 Drs ($40 to $125) a bottle for the "champagne"! The bartender gets his money, the girl gets her cut, and the victim gets another blow: Too embarrassed, drunk, or mad to think of it, he walks out without asking for a receipt; and when he goes to the police, he is told that an investigation cannot proceed without such proof. *Caveat emptor!*

7 The Ports—Piraeus & Rafína

Piraeus

Piraeus (*Pireéfs* or, more commonly, *Pireás* in Greek) has been the port of Athens since antiquity. Although the Greek maritime industry isn't what it once was, the thousands of tourists who board ferries bound for the Aegean islands each day contribute to maintaining Piraeus's position as the number-one port in the Mediterranean. As a city it has the conveniences and amenities of Athens, but not the charm; as a port it has the seamier sides of a sailors' lair but also all the color and life of an active harbor.

Piraeus is one of the most seen, least appealing places on the Greek itinerary. If you're trying to visit almost any of the islands by boat, you'll have to pass through Piraeus. Nighttime visitors should confine their wanderings to the port if they're waiting for a ferryboat or to Mikrolímano's expensive but scenic harborside taverns.

Ferry tickets can be purchased at a ticket office up to one hour before departure; after that they can be purchased on the boat. For booking first-class cabins or for advance-sale tickets, see one of the harborside travel agents (around Karaïskáki Square by the domestic ferries and along Aktí Miaoúli Street, opposite the Crete ferries). Most open at 6am and will hold your baggage for the day (but there is no security). The Greek Tourist Organization, EOT, publishes a list of weekly sailings, but the **tourist police** (dial **171**) or the **Port Authority** (☎ **45-11-311**) can provide you with schedule information.

If you need a travel agency to make reservations or to recommend a particular service, try **Explorations Unlimited** (☎ **41-16-395** or **41-11-243**), at Odós Kapodistríou 2 just off Aktí Posidónos Street near the metro station. Michális (Mike) Hadgiantoníou and his English-speaking staff are helpful, particularly with making ferry and hydrofoil arrangements as well as hotel bookings. Open Monday through Friday from 8am to 7pm; Saturday 9am to 2pm.

The port spreads along the waterfront for quite a distance, so be sure to know the boat you are taking and ask for directions. Opposite the metro station are the boats to the islands. Both normal boats to the Saronic Gulf and hydrofoils (Flying Dolphins) to Aegina are found opposite and to the left of the metro station; the hydrofoils leave from the foot of Goúnari Street. Boats to the other islands are around to the right and away from the station. Boats to Italy and Turkey are found a mile or so to the left. Hydrofoils to other destinations leave from Zéa Marina, a separate harbor some three miles southeast of the metro station.

GETTING THERE

Getting to Piraeus is easy from any of Athens's centers. The fastest and easiest way, from Omónia Square or Monistaráki (a short walk from Sýntagma Square), is to take the metro to the last stop (75 Drs or 31¢), which will leave you one block from the domestic port. From Sýntagma Square take the Green Depot bus no. 40 from the corner of Filellínon Street; it will leave you one block from the international port, about a 10-minute walk along the water from the domestic port. A taxi from Sýntagma Square will cost up to 1,800 Drs ($7.50). From the airport, bus no. 19 goes to Piraeus; the fare is 300 Drs ($1.25). A taxi from the airport to the port costs about 1,500 Drs ($6.25).

Unfortunately, getting back to Athens can be more difficult. The easiest way is to take the metro to central Athens, to either Monastiráki or Omónia Square. Taxi drivers have a conspiracy to overcharge tourists disembarking from the boats. They charge 4,000 Drs ($16.70), two or three times the legal fare. If you stand on the dock, you'll get no mercy. The only option is to walk to a nearby street and hail a cab.

INFORMATION

For boat schedules, transit information, and other tourist information, dial **171;** the line is open 24 hours. The closest EOT office (☎ **45-37-107**) is inconveniently located on the street above Zéa Marina (the hydrofoil port) on the second floor of a shopping arcade stocked with yacht supplies. It is open weekdays from 9am to 2:30pm, but its limited resources probably won't warrant the 20-minute walk from the ferry piers. If you really need information, go straight to Sýntagma Square in Athens.

There are several banks in Piraeus along the waterfront. The **National Bank,** on Ethnikí Antistáseos Street, has extended hours in summer. A portable **post office** branch opposite the Aégina ferry pier also offers currency exchange; it's open Monday through Saturday from 8am to 8pm and Sunday from 8am to 6pm. The main post office is at Ethnikí Antistáseos and Dimitríou Streets. The phone center, EOT, is a block away from the post office. There is another branch by the water, on Aktí Miaoúli Street at Merarchías Street, open daily from 7am to 9:30pm. You'll find secure but expensive **luggage storage** in the metro station, at the Central Travel Agency (☎ **41-15-611**); the cost is 1,000 Drs ($4.10) per piece per day.

WHAT TO SEE & DO

On midsummer evenings, open-air theatrical performances are given at the Kastélla Theater, a few blocks inland from Mikrolímano. In the wintertime performances are staged indoors, at the Public Theater, on the green at King Constantine Avenue (where you can also catch the bus to Sýntagma Square). The Piraeus Archeological Museum (☎ **45-21-598**) is at Odós Trikoúpi 31, near the Zéa Marina; it's open Tuesday through Sunday from 8:30am to 3pm; admission is 500 Drs ($2.10). The Hellenic Maritime Museum (☎ **45-16-822**) is at Aktí Themistokléous and Freatída Streets, near the hydrofoil pier at Zéa Marina; it's open Tuesday through Saturday from 8:30am to 1pm and closed in August; admission is 150 Drs (60¢).

WHERE TO STAY

We're not great fans of an overnight stay in Piraeus, but if it makes sense in your travel plans, here are some decent choices. The best of all is the Mistrál, in the Kastella neighborhood behind Mikrolímano and Zéa Marina. In any case, be careful walking around at night.

Elektra Hotel, Odós Navarínou 12, 18531 Piraeus. ☎ **01/41-77-057.**
19 rms (none with bath).

Rates: 4,875 Drs ($20.30) single; 8,125 Drs ($33.85) double. No credit cards.

The Eléktra is a budget-conscious, older, but reasonably maintained choice, located on a noisy street a block behind the domestic port. The high-ceilinged rooms have some semblance of charm. Nearby bathrooms are freshly painted, one to a room.

Lilia Hotel, Odós Zéas 131, Passalimáni 18534 Piraeus. ☎ **01/41-79-108.**
Fax 01/41-14-311. 20 rms (all with bath). TEL

Rates (including breakfast): 10,350 Drs ($43) single; 13,800 Drs ($57.50) double. AE, V.

This is a better choice in a more savory district. Moderately priced, it offers clean, bright, and comfortable rooms with ceiling fans. The Lília is a 20-minute walk from Passalimáni, the small boat harbor fed by Zéa Marina (a taxi ride costs 600 Drs or $2.50). The neighborhood is good for strolling; it has some authentic ouzerís that are just great for a sunset drink and contemplation of the pleasure boats.

Ideal Hotel, Odós Notara 142, 18531 Piraeus. ☎ **01/45-11-727.** 29 rms (all with bath). A/C TEL

Rates: 8,050 Drs ($33.55) single; 10,350 Drs ($43.15) double. AE.

If you absolutely want to stay close to the port, the Ideal is just two blocks inland from the waterfront, opposite the international ferries. It is a clean, pleasant Class C hotel that's air-conditioned and well maintained.

Hotel Mistral, Odós Vassiléos Pávlou 105, Kastella 18533 Piraeus. ☎ **01/41-21-425.**
Fax 01/41-22-096. 100 rms, 3 suites (all with bath). A/C TEL

Rates (including breakfast): 17,250 Drs ($72) single; 22,425 Drs ($93.45) double. AE, EC, MC, V.

The modern Hotel Mistral is only two blocks inland from the lively seafood dining capital of Mikrolímano. Spacious rooms have radio and other amenities and views of the Aegean from sunny balconies. Best yet, there's a nice roof garden; plans still call for the swimming pool to reopen.

WHERE TO EAT

Boat-bound travelers should get to Piraeus early enough to buy their tickets, find their ferry, and have time to walk into the market area behind Aktí Posidónos and the Aégina hydrofoils. There are a lot of outdoor fruit vendors, dried fruit-and-nut shops, bakeries, and knickknack traders. The port of Mikrolímano is a high-end dining area that we've removed from our recommended listings due to hugely overinflated prices.

Be warned: As seafood has become increasingly expensive, we've received a proportionately larger number of letters complaining of rip-offs, especially in Piraeus. Make sure of the price. Insist on a receipt, and take any complaints immediately to the Tourist Police.

Rio-Antirio, Odós Merarchías 14. ☎ **45-14-583.**

Cuisine: GREEK. **Reservations:** Not required.
Prices: Appetizers 350–520 Drs ($1.45–$2.20); main courses 650–1,500 Drs ($2.70–$6).
Open: 8am–1am.

Rio-Antirio is a very clean, modern taverna with good salads, souvláki, pasta, and chicken. You can peek around the display case till you're sure you understand what you're eating. Everything is tasty, freshly prepared, and inexpensive.

Da Nicola Pizzeria, Odós Merarchías 8. ☎ **45-19-623.**

Cuisine: ITALIAN. **Reservations:** Not required.
Prices: Appetizers 350–1,200 Drs ($1.45–$5); main courses 1,250–2,400 Drs ($5.20–$10). V.
Open: Mon–Sat 11:30am–11pm.

Just before the Fos cinema (soft-core and violent movies) is this moderately priced ristorante and snack café that's a good dining alternative in the area. Da Nicola is quite large, air-conditioned, and comfortable, with a pizza oven in the front window. There are tables indoors or outside on the bustling street.

Tzaki Grill, Odós Goúnari 7. ☎ **41-78-932.**

Cuisine: GREEK. **Reservations:** Not required.
Prices: Appetizers 220–850 (92¢–$3.55); main courses 700–2,100 Drs ($2.90–$8.75).
Open: Daily 8am–2am.

Near the Aégina hydrofoil pier and the ticket agents' offices you'll find the unpretentious but clean Tzaki Grill. The octopus hanging out to dry marks the spot for inexpensive and delicious charcoal-grilled fresh fish or chicken specialties. Don't miss the octopus, either.

Ariston, Odós Bouboulínas 415.

Cuisine: DESSERTS. **Reservations:** Not required.
Prices: Pastries: 120–900 Drs (50¢–$3.75).

This excellent *zacharoplastío,* which lives up to its name (*áriston* means "excellent"), sells great sweets, miniature cheese pies, and rich *spanokópitas* (spinach-filled pies) to take for your voyage.

Rafína

One way to beat the high cost of ferries is to start your trip to the Cyclades from Rafína. Buses leave Athens from Áreos Park, Odós Mavromatéon 29 (☎ **82-10-872**), at 6am daily and continue every 30 minutes till 10:15pm, crossing the 27 km to this Aegean port through Athens's urban sprawl and vineyards. Once there, you'll find that boats run daily (twice a day in summer) to Ándros, Tínos, and Mýkonos (call the port police at **0294/22-300** for specific sailing times); four or five times weekly to Sýros, Páros, and Náxos (daily in summer); thrice weekly to Kos and Rhodes; and once a week to Níssiros, Tílos, Kálymnos, and Astypálaia in the Dodecanese or Límnos and Kavála. You'll find a savings of 20%–40% over the fares from Piraeus. **Ilios Lines** (☎ **0294/25-100** or **23-500**) also runs daily hydrofoil service to Stýra, Marmári, and Kárystos on Évvia.

In 1991 Ílios started hydrofoil service from Rafína to the Cyclades, serving Ándros, Tínos, Mýkonos, Páros, and Náxos twice daily in July and August (several times a week in low season) and continuing on to the little visited (except by wealthy Greeks with villas) Schinoússa, Koufoníssi, and Amorgós twice weekly. Call the **Rafina Travel Company** in Rafína (☎ **0294/22-888**) or **Explorations Unlimited** in Piraeus (☎ **01/41-16-395**) for schedule information.

WHAT TO SEE & DO

You'll notice many small beaches near Rafína. Villas and condos dot the coastline, and big resort hotels for Athenian weekenders crowd Golden Beach, the stretch south from Néa Mákri. A large joint U.S.-Greek naval base gets the prime beachfront here, leaving tourists with an incredibly diverse selection of junk-food parlors and cheap motels along the coastal highway until the more charming Marathon Beach. Although Rafína doesn't have a good beach of its own, the small harbor and sea breezes compensate by making it a refreshing change from the *néfos* (pollution) of the Greater Athens region. Life centers around the large *platía* (square), whose elevated position gives it an air of small-town dignity quite different from the dockside hustle that goes on at sea level below.

In contrast to the commercialized shipping industry in Piraeus are the casual car ferries to Évvia and the steamers and hydrofoils that run to the Cyclades from Rafína.

This easygoing fishing port is about one hour by bus north of Athens; it's a refreshing drive and an instant change of pace once you reach the harborside. Everything seems much more manageable in Rafína; those readers heading to the Cyclades or the Dodecanese might want to sail from this calmer port and save some money in the bargain.

WHERE TO STAY

Spending a night in Rafína is a pleasant alternative to an early-morning schlep to steamy Piraeus. Because many budget-tour groups use Rafína as their base for day trips, the hotel scene is dominated by a few huge Class C places.

A note on camping: The immaculate Kókkino Limanáki Campgrounds (☎ **0294/31-603**) are in nearby Kókkino Limanáki (the name means "little red port"), a multitiered site that sits above a beautiful red-cliff cove with a pebble beach. Rates are only 950 Drs ($4) per sleeping bag, with hot showers and a laundry room. It may be worth your while to check in just for a swim, if you have a long wait for the ferry.

Hotel Akti, Odós Vithinías 14, Rafína 19009 Attica. ☎ **0294/24-776.**
20 rms (none with bath). TEL

Rates: Summer 5,000 Drs ($20.83) double. No credit cards.

The friendly Hotel Akti is a simple place with small, clean rooms featuring partial sea views. It is freshly painted in pale blues, has a popular café, and is well run. Open only from June 1 to September 15.

Hotel Avra, Rafína 19009 Attica. ☎ **0294/22-781.** Fax 0294/23-320.
96 rms (all with bath). A/C TEL

Rates: 11,700 Drs ($48.75) single; 18,400 Drs ($76.70) double. No credit cards.

The Avra is by far the most full-service place, with well-kept, balconied rooms (some with a sea view) and a well-informed, multilingual staff. Best yet, the hotel is open year-round.

WHERE TO EAT

There are two general areas to grab a bite in Rafína, either up around the *platia* or down by the car-ferry pier. Colorful, awning-shaded cafés, banks, and other tourist essentials surround the spacious square. Of the cafés, Diagalákis Pizza is the best bet for reasonably priced pizza, spaghetti, great cakes, or a nightcap.

On the east end of town (a two-minute walk) a road slopes down to sea level, bearing the weight of cars that will soon be loaded onto ships bound for the Cyclades, Évvia, or the Dodecanese. Interspersed with the ferryboat ticket agencies are several seafood tavernas. At lunchtime or suppertime watch out for the gregarious restaurateurs who'll try to rope you in for an expensive (though certainly scenic) fish fry. Try Kalá Krasiá, which is on the near end, with street and rooftop dining. Its excellent fried calamari, *mezédes* (appetizers), *skordaliá* (garlic dip), and fresh galeos (an inexpensive, tasty white fish) cost us about 2,000 Drs ($8.50). These tavernas are great fun when the ships are pulling in—you're far enough away to eat peacefully, yet close enough to enjoy the scene and activity.

8 Easy Excursions from Athens

It's sometimes hard to take the midsummer heat in Athens (in July and August temperatures can actually exceed 120°F!). Our first recommendation for getting away is to head south to the beaches; all along the "Apollo Coast" between Piraeus and Cape Soúnio are resorts, beaches, tavernas, nightlife, and a relaxing change of pace. Your day could begin at the beautiful-to-behold temple of Poseidon at Soúnio and stretch into an afternoon of beach sampling, an easy thing to do by public bus. (At the temple of Poseidon, by the way, look for the name "Byron" carved into one of the marble columns by the English poet more than 170 years ago!)

A cool, forested retreat that's very popular with Athenians is the Kaisarianí Monastery, located on the verdant slopes of Mt. Imitós within a half hour of the urban center. Archeology buffs will enjoy an opportunity to head west to Dafní (with its wine festival and beautiful monastery) and then on to Elefsína (ancient Eleusis), site of the fascinating Eleusinian mysteries of antiquity. Archeologists have uncovered an incredible variety of remains in a spot once considered sacred but today is fit only for heavy industry. The east coast of the Attic peninsula features the Plain of Marathon, site of the famous battle against the Persians. The museum and tombs uncovered here, combined with a lighthearted dip in the nearby bay, make a very interesting minijourney. North of Marathon is the temple of Nemesis (goddess of vengeance), while south of Marathon is the temple of Artemis (goddess of fertility and hunting), at Brauron (Vravróna).

Several tour operators offer one-day excursions to Epidaurus (see Chapter 7, "The Peloponnese"), Delphi (see Chapter 11), and the Saronic Gulf islands of Aégina, Hydra, and Póros (covered in Chapter 6). We think these sights deserve more than one day of your time, but if you're pressed, contact **Viking Tours,** Odós Artemídos 1, Glyfáda (☎ **01/89-80-829** or **01/89-80-729**), for more information about the budget-wise packages they offer.

"Apollo Coast"

The 65 km of coastline curling around the Saronic Gulf between Athens and Cape Soúnio is known fondly by travel agents as the Apollo Coast. In actuality, the first 20 km are just an indistinguishable outgrowth of Athens. The first city south of Athens is Glyfáda, best known as home of the airports.

WHAT TO SEE & DO

Glyfáda is a well-to-do but hardly quiet suburb. The streets are lined with cafés, restaurants, and chic sportswear shops. There are many expatriates and members of the military and diplomatic corps who make Glyfáda their home, and the style and taste of the area reflect this foreign presence. The one bizarre and noisy aspect of life in this suburb is that jets from the nearby airport seem to hover over the avenues on their way in or out of Greece.

Other than the occasional rattle of windows, life in Glyfáda is lots of fun. It's a great place to visit for those of you who may be homesick. The main drag, King George Avenue, is lined with cafés and restaurants, but for serious eating go around the corner from the Bank of Greece to Konstantinópoulos Street. There are several eateries, sophisticated pizza parlors, steak restaurants, and bars.

Some readers enjoy spending the night in Glyfáda, in full view of the sea, especially on their last night in Greece. It's just 10 minutes south of Ellinikón Airport's Eastern Terminal, and the Glyfáda Golf Course (☎ **89-46-875**) is nearby. The neighborhood offers much more than the streets around the airport hotels.

If you have time to spare, explore the collection of modern Greek art found at Glyfáda's Pierídis Gallery (☎ **89-48-287**), at Leofóros Vassiléos Gheorghíou 29. It's open Monday through Friday from 6 to 9pm and Saturday and Sunday from 1am to 1pm.

If you're after a beach, head south to Várkiza, about 30 km away. The Várkiza beach operated by the Greek Tourist Organization (☎ **89-72-102**) has small bungalows that rent for 5,280 Drs ($22), but admission is only 500 Drs ($2.10) for adults, half price for children. The nice public beach will be packed on summer weekends but at other times it makes a good day trip. When you're there, you can walk or take the bus the 2 km to Vári, a small town north of Várkiza known for its grilled lamb. Around the small square are several barbecues, serving private-label retsína and lamb on a spit. For those of you who are missing the Greek Easter feast, this is a way to experience every Greek's favorite meal. Several blue public buses leave Athens from Queen Olga Avenue south of the Záppion and the National Garden. Take the Soúnio coastal route bus and get off at Vótsala/Lagoníssi.

The beaches improve in direct proportion to their distance from Athens. As you continue to Cape Soúnio, stop at Lagoníssi or at the small beach opposite the Eden Beach Hotel. Depending on crowds and season, seaside hotels may claim rights to the sand in front of their cafés and will extract 500–1000 Drs ($2.10–$4.20) from you for placing your towel there.

WHERE TO STAY

We've listed two Glyfáda hotels in the previous chapter (see the section "Near the Airport" under "Where to Stay" in Chapter 4). They are **Hotel London,** at Leofóros Vassiléos Gheorghíou 38 (☎ **01/89-46-738**), and **Hotel Golden Sun,** at Leofóros Metaxá 72 (☎ **01/89-55-218**). Both offer good service but at nonbudget rates.

Soúnio

Our first-choice day trip would begin with a visit to the temple of Poseidon at Cape Soúnio(n) (Sunium). The temple's 15 sun-bleached columns stand out starkly against the Mediterranean sky, their power enhanced by the hilltop placement overlooking the sea. Their bold Doric design (no entasis, or bulging effect at the midriff, and only 16 flutings instead of 20) comes from the same master hand that designed the Theseum in the Agorá. Scholars believe that this 5th-century B.C. temple was built over the remains of an earlier Poseidon and Athena temple as part of Pericles' master plan.

Very little remains of the propylon (entryway) or the stoa (covered arcade) that protected worshippers from the blazing sun. Yet the temple's strong columns (the square one which is engraved with Lord Byron's name is inside the southeast corner) and the solid base, which you can still walk on (this is one of the few temples in Greece that can be entered), convey an immediate sense of the respect felt by the architect and the worshippers for the god Poseidon. From his height only can you look straight out to the sea; the fortress walls that once surrounded it defended this strategic highpoint over the Saronic Gulf and the shipping lanes to Évvia. Northeast of Poseidon's sanctuary was the temple of Athena Sounias, but little of it remains today.

We recommend coming first thing in the morning so that you can have some time alone with this unforgettable monument. The temple of Poseidon (☎ **0292/39-363**) is open Monday through Saturday from 9am to sunset and Sunday from 10am to sunset. Admission is 800 Dr ($3.35) for adults, half price for students.

After your first visit, walk down the hill to the tempting Hotel Aegaeon (☎ **0292/39-200**). On its beach, notice the hollowed-out storage niches in the encircling cliffs, where the Athenians drydocked their triremes. You can picnic, eat at one of the tavernas, or have lunch and change clothes at the Aegaeon's great café. Make sure to wander into the lobby to admire the barnacle-crusted amphorae and gemstones found in the seas below the temple.

Don't leave without returning to the temple of Poseidon to admire it in the waning light of sunset. Looking west over the blue Aegean, your view framed by the majestic white columns nearly 2,500 years old, is an experience that every traveler should have.

READERS RECOMMEND

Varkiza. *"We stayed here the last two nights of our trip and found it the ideal place to wind down, very picturesque, with lots of activity along the waterfront and a good choice of restaurants. It's convenient to Cape Soúnio and an easy (15-km) trip to the airport.*

"We highly recommend the ***Stefanakis Hotel*** *at Odós Aphroditis 17, a few blocks up from the main street, by far the best C-Class hotel we saw during our visit. The staff is very friendly, the breakfast is superior, and there's a very nice pool. A double with a real tub and shower curtain costs 11,000 Drs ($45.85)."*—Hope and Vern Boothe, Don Mills, Ontario.

KTEL (☎ **82-13-203**) buses leave Athens for Soúnio from Odós Mavromatéon 14, at Areos Park, every hour between 6am and 6pm for the 90-minute ride; the fare is 900 Drs ($3.75). Public (blue) buses leave from Queen Olga Avenue, south of the Zappion and the National Garden.

Mount Imittós & Kaisarianí Monastery

A refreshing half-day trip for tourists weary of the Big City is to the Kaisarianí Monastery, just 7 km east in a cool, bird-infested forest at the foot of Mt. Imittós (Hymettus). The healing spring waters pouring forth from the marble goat's head at the monastery's entrance have distinguished this as a holy site for centuries. Kaisarianí, dedicated to the Presentation of the Virgin, was built over the ruins of a 5th-century Christian church, which in turn probably covered an ancient Greek temple.

The small church is constructed in the form of a Greek cross, with four marble columns supporting the dome. The lovely frescoes date from the 16th century, with the exception of those in the narthex, signed "Ioánnis Hýpatos, 1689." On the west side of the paved, flower-filled courtyard are the old kitchen and the refectory, which now houses some sculptural fragments. To the south, the old monks' cells and a bathhouse are being restored (exploration at your own risk is permitted).

The Kaisarianí Monastery (☎ **72-36-619**) is open Tuesday through Sunday from 8:30am to 3pm; admission is 600 Drs ($2.50). Bus no. 224 leaves from Venizélou Street and Queen Sophia Avenue every 20 minutes to the monastery.

Mt. Imittós offers beautiful prospects over Athens, Attica, and the Saronic Gulf (try to come up here on a smogless day). At every scenic parking spot you'll find men playing backgammon, couples holding hands, and old people strolling. After sunset Imittós becomes Athens's favorite lovers' lane. The road winds around these forested slopes for nearly 18 km, and the choice of sun, shade, cool breezes, and picnic spots is unlimited.

In antiquity, Mt. Imittós is believed to have been crowned with a statue of Zeus Hymettios, and ancient caves (including a 6th-century B.C. altar) have been found near the summit. More recently the mountain was cherished by Athenians for the honey produced by bees that fed off the mountain's fragrant flowers and herbs. Most of the bees have migrated now, although a few apiaries still exist for heather-fed bees.

Monastery of Dafní

The recently restored 11th-century monastery, one of the finest examples of Byzantine mosaics, architecture, and design in all Greece, is situated off the main Athens-Corinth highway about 10 km west of Athens. Dafní Monastery (☎ **58-11-558**) is open daily from 8:30am to 3pm. Admission is 600 Drs ($2.50). From mid-August to mid-September an annual wine festival is usually held on the grounds; open 8pm to midnight, entrance is 600 Drs ($2.50), for 1,500 Drs ($6) you can sample many different kinds of wine. Check with the Athens Festival box office (☎ **32-27-944**) for information regarding the wine festival. Public bus no. 873 leaves from Delighiórghi Street near Eleftheria (Freedom) Square in Athens every 30 minutes.

Elefsís

In the modern industrial town of Elefsís (also Elefsína in modern Greek, Eleusis in ancient Greek), farther west on the Athens-Corinth highway, you'll find the site of the most famous and revered of all the ancient mysteries, Eleusis. We probably owe the word "mystery" itself to the place. The names of the famous people initiated into the sacred rites here would fill the rest of this chapter, yet we know almost nothing for certain about those ceremonies.

We do know that they were bound up in one of the most important myths: Demeter, the goddess of agriculture who had given humanity the gift of grain (our word cereal comes from her Roman name, Ceres), had a beautiful daughter, Persephone, whom Hades, god of the Underworld and lord of the dead, fell in love with and abducted. Demeter could hear her daughter's cries for help coming from the cave you see immediately upon entering the site, which the ancients believed was connected to the Underworld and called the Ploutonion (Pluto was the Roman name for the proprietor of Hell). She was unable to find her, despite the cries. At the Kallichoron (Callichorum) Well, to the left across the courtyard, she wept bitterly for her only child and, giving in to grief ,let the earth grow cold and all vegetation wither.

Eventually, she went to Mt. Olympus to plead for her daughter. Zeus declared that if the girl's grief had been equal to her mother's and she had eaten nothing, she could return. But Hades had given Persephone a pomegranate and urged her to eat it. She swallowed six seeds. So, for six months she was compelled to remain as queen of the Underworld, during which time Demeter grieved and allowed winter to come. For the remainder of the year, Persephone could return to her mother, who then, in her happiness, gave the earth the flowering of spring and the bounty of summer.

We surmise that the mysteries, celebrated in two degrees in the large central temple, the Telesterion (Telesterium), which was built about 600 B.C. over a Mycenaean temple, honored Demeter as the source of fertility and Persephone as the embodiment of spring. Scholars believe that these mysterious ceremonies were part purification, and part drama. It is thought that priestesses promised immortality to the initiated. Homer, in the *Odyssey,* says that the initiated go to "the Elysian Plain and the world's end . . . where life is easiest for men. No snow is there, or great storm, or any rain." Herodotus tells us: "Every year the Athenians celebrate a festival in honor of the Mother and the Maid (*Kore*), and anyone who wishes, from Athens or elsewhere, may be initiated in the mysteries."

On the right, after entering the site, behind the labeled temple of Artemis is the Eschara, a Roman-era pit where sacrificial victims were burned. To the left of the huge, sculpted marble medallion of Antonius Pius (its builder) is the Greater Propylaea, from the 2d century A.D., modeled after the Propylaea of the Acropolis. Built on top of a 5th-century B.C. version, this entrance to the Sacred Way had balustrades to curb the flow of devotees to the sanctuary behind it. To the left of the Greater Propylaea can be seen one of two triumphal arches dedicated to the Great Goddesses and to the Emperor Hadrian. This arch inspired the Arc de Triomphe, which caps the Champs-Elysées in Paris.

Nearby, the pit (Kallichoron Well) marks the area where the Eleusinian women danced and chanted in praise of Demeter. Turning back, up the marble-paved Sacred Way is the Ploutonion (Plutonium), the sacred cave where Persephone disappeared with Hades to the Underworld. Climbing up beyond this will bring you to roofed-over areas where walls of several eras have yet to be fully excavated. On the right, the small carved stone steps are thought to have led to a terrace altar to worship the goddesses. Behind the church is the Telesterium, a large square with rows of seats carved in the stone embankment. This was thought to be the Hall of Initiation (designed by Ictinus, of Parthenon fame), where devotees would gather to receive their mysterious rites.

In the small museum you can find the greater part of a famous Demeter statue by Agoracritus and several *korae,* or maidens. There are also various remains from the site, as well as Roman statues.

The site and archeological museum (☎ **55-46-019**) are open Tuesday through Sunday from 8:30am to 3pm. Admission is 600 Drs ($2.50). Public bus no. 853 or 862 leaves Elefthería Square regularly for the one-hour trip to Elefsína.

Marathon

The bravery of the Athenians who defeated the invading Persian hordes at Marathon in 490 B.C. has been heralded since as one of history's greatest testimonies to the spirit of freedom and democracy. An archeological museum, the tomb of the Plataeans, and the tomb of the Athenians mark the spot of the battle, but the realization that this scrub-brush, rocky plain and the clear blue bay beyond it were the site of such a momentous event transforms this day trip into an elevating experience. No one tells the story of the Battle of Marathon (pronounced *Marathón* in Greek) better than Herodotus. You may want to read it in his *History* before you visit the site (the Penguin Classics series has a good translation). Public (orange) buses to Marathon leave Athens from Odós Mavromatéon 29 at Áreos Park; call the **tourist police** at **171** for information and schedules. The nearby town of Marathon Beach (Paralía Marathónos) offers the closest accommodations and restaurants. Its pleasant beach, however, can get very crowded.

WHAT TO SEE & DO

TUMULUS OF THE PLATAEANS Near the base of Agrielíki Hill, the command post for the Athenians and their allies, a large grave site (tumulus) was discovered. The tumulus has been rebuilt so that you can enter and see the opened graves of the Plataean warriors. Herodotus tells us that Plataea contributed 1,000 troops to fight alongside the Athenians at Marathon. They've been laid to rest about 200 meters from the archeological museum.

TOMB OF THE ATHENIANS Located across the highway and about 3 km south of the archeological museum turnoff is the tomb of the Athenians at Marathon, where the cremated remains of the 192 Athenian soldiers who died defending Hellas from the Persians are buried. The site is marked with a simple stele (dating from 510 B.C.) carved with the likeness of Aristion, a strategós (general) who led the Athenians. The tomb of Miltiades has been found near the site of the present-day museum.

ARCHEOLOGICAL MUSEUM Marathon's archeological museum (☎ **0294/55-155**) is next to the recently restored tomb of the Plataeans, 2 km west of the highway turnoff marked "Marathon." The museum is well worth a visit. It's well organized (labels are in English as well as Greek) and features Neolithic to Byzantine-era finds from throughout the Marathon region. The small courtyard, filled with bitter orange and kumquat trees, has a large Ionic capital thought to be the top of a huge pedestal that supported a trophy honoring the victorious soldiers at Marathon. Archeologists think this column is similar in purpose to that of the Naxian Sphynx at Delphi.

The museum is open Tuesday through Sunday from 8:30am to 3pm. The tumulus of the Plataeans and the tomb of the Athenians are open during the same time. Admission is 600 Drs ($2.50).

THE ATHENS OPEN INTERNATIONAL MARATHON Held every October since 1972, this race commemorates the run of Pheidippides to announce the Athenian victory over the Persians at the Battle of Marathon (490 B.C.). The race begins outside the village of Marathon and continues along Pheidippides course for exactly 42.195 km (26.2 miles) to the Panathenaic Stadium built for the first modern Olympic Games (1896) in Athens. There is no qualifying time to enter the race. Applicants should contact SEGAS, Leofóros Syngroú 137, 17121 Athens (☎ **01/93-20-636** or fax 01/93-42-980) for information.

AN EXCURSION TO THE TEMPLE OF NEMESIS

A possible excursion from Marathon is to the temple of Nemesis (goddess of vengeance) at the nearby acropolis of Rhamnous. It's accessible most easily by taxi (the fare is 900 Drs or $37.50) or by car from Marathon Beach. Little is left of the graceful work of the unknown architect who designed the temple of Poseidon at Soúnio and the Theseum in the Agora. The beautiful wildflowers that blanket the site are painful; Rhamnous means "place of spiny buckthorn." Nemesis wasn't kidding.

But the Greeks have had the last laugh. The impressive three-tiered base of the goddess's temple is scarred with graffiti, particularly feet pointing in opposing directions. As an ironic touch, a smaller temple of Themis (the goddess of eternal justice) was constructed behind that of Nemesis; its ruins are more impressive. The beautiful promontory was once lined with white marble towers guarding the Euripus Channel. It's now a scrub-brush slope, blocked off with fencing, but still offers a beautiful view of Marathon Bay and, beyond, the island of Évvia. The temple of Nemesis site in Káto Soúli is open Tuesday through Sunday from 8:30am to 3pm; admission is free. Cars should follow road signs to the ferry at Aghía Marína, then bear left up the road toward the hills.

Temple of Artemis at Brauron

In the small village of Vravróna (also Vráona, variants of ancient Brauron) stands a temple of Artemis that's a fabulous surprise. Not well known or frequented, because bus service is inconvenient, this lovely site is dedicated to the goddess of fertility (who was also the patroness of unmarried girls and chastity). Apollo's twin sister, Artemis was the protective mistress of all beasts; her role as goddess of the hunt was often chronicled in mythology.

Scholars believe that the temple was constructed in the Middle Helladic era (2000–1600 B.C.) to appease Artemis's anger over the killing of a bear. The bear was her favorite animal; and after the sanctuary was built, it was decreed that in the spring all the young girls from neighboring towns should dress like bears to serve Artemis. Every five years the Brauronia Festival was held, and girls between the ages of five and ten would come in yellow *chitons* (full-length garments) and dance like bears in the sanctuary grounds. Many young women remained to grow up there, creating what might be called the first "feminist cell." King Agamemnon's daughter Iphigenia remained at Brauron when she returned from Tauris with Orestes to become a priestess. While Artemis was venerated in gratitude for motherhood and good health, Iphigenia was brought votive offerings at the death of a baby or a woman in childbirth.

The best-preserved part of the site is the stoa, a colonnaded way once called the Parthenon, perhaps because the young devotees of Artemis lived there during festivals ("Parthenon" derives from the word *parthénos,* "virgin"). These ruins date primarily from the 5th century B.C. and cover earlier shrines at this site. The proportions of the temple are square; the squat Doric columns end abruptly on the limestone terrace and appear more primitive than the graceful supports of the famous Doric temples at Soúnio or on the Acropolis.

The archeological museum of Vravróna is a kilometer away from the site, along the main road that winds through vineyards and grazing fields. Inside are 4th-century B.C. votive reliefs and friezes from the sanctuary, geometric-era ceramics from early tombs, and other finds from a prehistoric settlement discovered on a hill above the temple. The most interesting displays are those that illuminate the activities of temple inhabitants; there are terra-cotta plaques carved in relief and depicting Artemis in her many incarnations, gold jewelry and ornamental objects found in the silty deposit from the sacred spring, and charming ceramic statuettes of the young girls who came to perform and worship here.

The museum (☎ **0294/71-020**) and the archeological site are open Tuesday through Sunday from 8:30am to 3pm; admission to each is 600 Drs ($2.50). During our last visit, Vavróna, 35 km east of Athens, could not be reached directly by public bus. An overnight in Markópoulou (not our idea of a lovely place) would be required to catch the early (school) bus on to the site; the only return bus was in the afternoon. (There are a few small hotels in Vavróna, a couple of kilometers away through the countryside.) We hope transportation improves; call **142** for domestic bus schedule.

6

The Saronic Gulf Islands

THE BODY OF WATER SEPARATING ATTICA FROM THE PELOPONNESIAN COAST HOSTS the island chain closest to Athens, the Saronic Gulf islands of Aegina, Póros, Hydra, Spétses, and Salamís. Each has its unique identity. Above **Aegina's** pine-covered hills stands the graceful temple of Aphaia, one of Greece's best-preserved Doric structures. Below the temple are groves of pistachios and coves for swimming. **Póros** is an island for dancing, wandering the town's terraced back streets, and visiting nearby Lemonodásos, a giant lemon grove adjoining a fine sandy beach. Visiting **Hydra** is a sublime experience; the entire island has been declared a national monument because of its wealth of elegant stone mansions, monasteries, and natural harbors and coves. **Spétses** offers wonderful architectural sights, long walks through pine forests, and lovely beaches. The large island of **Salamís,** visible from Piraeus, has been marred by heavy industry and construction projects, and it's no longer a tourist destination. However, it's famous in history as the birthplace of Euripides, the classical tragic poet, and as the site, in 480 B.C., of a sea battle between the Athenians and the Persians, who were roundly defeated in its narrow strait.

The Saronic Gulf islands are preferred by Athenians as weekend destinations. From Friday through Sunday during the summer, these islands take on a carnival atmosphere, with festivals, parades, and a giant influx of visitors from around the world. During midweek the ports and beaches return to relative calm; it's the only time when restaurants and hotels have vacancies and the best time to see the sights. The Saronic Gulf islands can be treated as day trips from Athens or can be visited on a three-isle day cruise; Hydra is our favorite for a stay of more than two or three days. Any way, each is a perfect getaway destination for those who've been beaten by the rigors of sightseeing in Athens.

Seeing the Islands

One of the joys of touring the Saronic Gulf is that, with few exceptions, you can go to any island from any other island at almost any time of day. Car ferries, excursion boats, and hydrofoils run constantly; rarely in July and August will you have to wait more than an hour.

This efficient state of affairs is bolstered by the operation of the **Flying Dolphins,** a fleet of yellow-and-blue, Russian-built hydrofoils that fly on the surface of the water at more than twice the speed of a normal ferry. The Ceres Company's huge new **Black Cat** hydrocatamarans are even more comfortable and faster! The cabin is laid out like the interior of an airplane, with bucket seats, fore-and-aft sections, and even food and beverage service in first class.

Generally, a hydrofoil takes half the time of a regular ferry and costs about 35% more. Most depart from Zéa Marina in Piraeus; the car ferries, excursion boats, and most Aegina-bound hydrofoils leave from the main Piraeus docks. All begin operating at 6am and continue service until the late evening, stopping at Aegina, Póros, Hydra, Spétses, Kyrapássi, Hermióne, Leonídion, Pórto, Céli, Monemvassiá, and, in the high season, Týros, Tólo, Neápolis, Náfplio, and Kýthira.

Another popular and interesting way to see the Saronic Gulf islands is on a three-isle day cruise aboard the **Epirotikí Lines** (☎ **36-01-919**). These cruises, which can be booked through **Viking Tours** (☎ **89-80-829**) or through many hotel reception

IMPRESSIONS

The isles of Greece, the isles of Greece!
—Byron, *Don Juan,* 1819–24

What's Special About the Saronic Gulf Islands

Architecture

- The classic rusticated stone mansions of Hydra's main port are part of a national historic-preservation program that severely restricts further development.
- Aegina's temple of Aphaia, situated on a hilltop, devoted to a goddess regarded as a protector of women.

Literary Shrines

- John Fowles's novel *The Magus* is set on Spétses, where he once taught.

desks, make stops on Hydra (for swimming and shopping), Póros (for lunch and sightseeing), and Aegina (to see the temple of Aphaia or to go swimming). Lunch is served on board; there's also a small pool. Epirotiki provides transportation to and from the ship from your Athens hotel. Cost of the one-day cruise is about 14,300 Drs ($59.60). It's a wonderful introduction to the luxury of traveling by cruise ship.

1 Aegina

17 nautical miles SW of Piraeus

ARRIVING/DEPARTING • Ferry and excursion-boat tickets can be purchased at the pier; call the **Piraeus Port Authority** (☎ **45-11-311**) for schedule and departure pier information. Flying Dolphin tickets can be purchased in advance at the **Ceres Hydrofoil Joint Service** office (☎ **42-80-001**), at Aktí Themistokléous 8, along the Piraeus waterfront, or at the pier.

ESSENTIALS There are several tours on the island. **Pipinistours** (☎ **0297/24-456**), one block inland opposite the hydrofoil pier, is extremely helpful and also serves as the Ceres Hydrofoil agent. **Aegina Island Holidays** (☎ **0297/25-860**) is another good agent, at Odós Dimokratías 47, on the port. For **foreign exchange**, there's the National Bank of Greece on the waterfront street, although both travel agents exchange currency during extended hours.

The island **hospital** (☎ **22-251**) is on the northeast edge of town, for medical emergencies. The telephone center (**OTE**) is five blocks from the port, on Aiákou Street. The **police** (☎ **22-391**) are on Odós Leonárdou Ladá, about 200 meters from the port. The **post office** is off to the left and around the corner as you disembark from the ferry. An excellent guide is Anne Yannoulis's *Aegina* (Lycabettus Press).

Aegina (Aíghina, also Eyina) is the largest of the Saronic Gulf islands and close to Piraeus, making it a convenient and pleasurable day-long introduction to the Greek islands. Many people even treat it as an extension of the capital (in fact, Aegina was the capital in the early years of the modern Greek nation), commuting on the Flying Dolphins as if taking the train to work. An even-larger group visit Aegina on weekends.

Despite the pressures of tourism and development, Aegina manages to maintain its identity. The countryside supports the usual Greek staples (olives, figs, and almonds), but in between are strangely gnarled pistachio trees. Farmers set up temporary booths along the road to peddle these exotic nuts.

Most people come to Aegina to visit the temple of Aphaia, one of the best-preserved sanctuaries in Greece, on a par with the temple of Poseidon at Soúnio. If you take binoculars, you can see the Parthenon and the temple of Poseidon; the ancients built the three temples in an equilateral triangle in sight of each other, for communication with signals made by fires and reflecting glass.

Orientation

Both the ferry and the Flying Dolphin dock at Aegina town, on the northeast coast, where the Gothic-shaped breakwater creates calm waters for mooring the many visiting yachts. The port is a comfortable village, with big, crowded family beaches north and south of the harbor. The harbor is busy: Merchants sell fresh fruit and vegetables brought over from the mainland; signs on the bobbing fishing boats advertise prices for the day's catch; farmers from the cooperative shovel pistachios into paper bags (1,650 Drs, or $6.90, for 500 grams) to sell to groups of tourists; and bicyclists roam up and down the waterfront road.

Aegina's erratically sculpted coastline is a terror to sailors and a delight to swimmers, with rocky coves on nearly every inch of the perimeter. Pérdika, on the southwest side, is the favored beach. Set on a pine-covered crest above Aegina's dramatic shoreline is the noble temple of Aphaia. Island buses travel as far as the east coast honky-tonk beach town of Aghiá Marína, where groups of German and British tourists annually lay siege.

The bus station is off to the left and around the corner as you disembark from the ferry. A bakery, cafés, markets, hotels, and nearly anything you'll need are on the long waterfront street, Dimokratías.

Getting Around

The bus to the temple of Aphaia and Aghía Marína runs every hour during the summer; the fare is 300 Drs ($1.20). Taxis are available next to the bus depot; expect to pay 2,200 Drs ($9.20) for the half-hour ride to the temple site. Bicycle-rental stands and moped dealers are located on the other side of the *paralía* (beachfront), near the southern beach. Watch out—some of the shops have been known to charge tourists outrageous prices! The daily rate for a bicycle should be around 800 Drs ($3.35) and for a moped 3,000–5,000 Drs ($12.50–$20.85).

What to See & Do

The **town of Aegina** has a good feeling about it. Wander down the back streets of the port and you'll get a hint of yesteryear on the island, especially in one of the horse-drawn carts (about 3,500 Drs ($14.60)). On our last visit, we enjoyed visiting the restored Markélos Tower, a squat, 15th-century structure in the middle of town. Just past the north side beach is the hill of Kolóna, where a sole Doric column stands above the remains of ancient Aégina. The **archeological museum** in town (open Tuesday through Sunday from 8:30am to 3pm) contains objects dating from prehistoric times and includes a good collection of 5th-century B.C. sculpture.

From town, the road winds through hilly terrain up to the graceful **Temple of Aphaia.** The sanctuary we see now is the second stone structure built on the site and dates from 490 B.C. It was dedicated to Aphaia, a Cretan goddess connected with Artemis and worshipped as a protector of women. When the temple was excavated, archeologists found numerous statues done in the Archaic style. Only a few sculptures remain on Aegina (in the museum); the others were removed to Athens and also sent to Munich. The temple is one of the finest examples of Archaic architecture in the Hellenic world, with many of its 6-foot-by-12-foot Doric columns preserved. The site is open Monday through Friday from 8am to 7pm and on the weekend from 8am to 3pm. Admission is 660 Drs ($2.75) for adults, half price for students.

Either a long walk down the donkey path or a short bus ride will lead you to the unappealing village of **Aghía Marína,** a group-tourist resort that has defaced what was otherwise a perfectly lovely stretch of sandy beach. Far preferable is the beach community at Pérdika, where boats ply the water to Moní Island, an ideal camping spot only 10 minutes away.

For those who want to leave the group scene behind, head over to the nearby island of Anghístri. Small boats make the 20-minute commute every couple of hours—or whenever the boat is filled with passengers (340 Drs, or $1.40). You'll find tavernas, rooms for rent, and one of the few nudist beaches on the Saronic Gulf, Skála Liminária. The services, however, are pretty basic.

Where to Stay

Pipínistours (☎ **0297/24-456**), one block inland, opposite the hydrofoil pier, and **Aegina Island Holidays** (☎ **0297/25-860**), on the portside Dimokratías Street, are both good sources for rooms to let around the island. Doubles with private bath start at about 7,150 Drs ($29.80) per night.

Hotel Brown, Aegina 18010. ☎ **0297/22-271.** Fax 0297/23-586.
28 rms (all with bath). TEL

Rates (including breakfast): 7,700 Drs ($32.10) single; 10,450 Drs ($43.50) double. No credit cards.

The elegant, neoclassical facade of this older hotel overlooks the harbor. Facilities are basic but well maintained, with distinguished common spaces and a garden in the original building. There's a cheerful breakfast room, and in the adjoining new bungalow complex there are brightly tiled rooms with patios.

Eléni Rooms to Let, Odós Káppou 5, Aegina 18010. ☎ **0297/26-450.**
7 rms (4 with bath).

Rates 6,160 Drs ($25.70) single/double without bath; 7,700 Drs ($32.10) single/double with bath. No credit cards.

Our top choice is the Eléni Rooms in part of a house built in 1888. Cool, quiet rooms are spotlessly clean, with refinished pine floors and whitewashed walls. Each room is different, but we preferred those with private baths on the second floor. In the downstairs area are a small lobby and courtyard and a kitchen, where hostess Annerose Moe and host Marinos Gheorghios frequently cook a meal for their guests.

Traditional Hostel, Aegina 18010. ☎ **0297/24-156.** 14 rms (all with bath).

Rates: 7,920 Drs ($33) single; 11,275 Drs ($47) double. No credit cards.

The classical building housing the Traditional Hostel is located at the corner of Aghíon Nikoláou and Thomaídou. This converted mansion was restored in 1982, but few of the smallish, modern rooms have anything left of the original grandeur. Nevertheless, it is a pleasant place with a comfortable lobby area downstairs.

Where to Eat

Day-trippers will probably not wander any farther than the *paralía,* but here are a few good choices in town. Don't leave without trying some of the delicious local pistachios!

Estiatórion Económou, Dimokratías St. ☎ **25-113.**

Cuisine: GREEK. **Reservations:** Not required.

Prices: Appetizers 385–1,650 Drs ($1.60–$6.90), main courses 1,070–1,980 Drs ($4.45–$8.25). No credit cards.

Open: Daily 11am–1am.

A reader wrote to us about the excellent food he found at this blue-canopied portside taverna. The lemony fish soup, grilled sfirída (a local fish), and tender lamb kebab with chips we tried were very tasty. Estiatórion Económou also serves locally caught lobster grilled to order, but it's a real splurge at 12,100 Drs ($50.40) per kilo.

Maridaki Cafe, Dimokratías St. ☎ **24-014.**

Cuisine: INTERNATIONAL. **Reservations:** Not required.

Prices: Appetizers 1,320 Drs ($5.50), main courses 880–1,100 Drs ($3.70–$4.60). No credit cards.

Open: Daily 8am–midnight.

Like many of the newer portside cafés, this lively place, near the Port Police station, serves a little bit of everything to please the day-trippers. In fact, the food at Maridaki is pretty good, with a variety of fresh *mezédes,* grilled octopus, and okra stewed in tomatoes topping our list.

Taverna Vatsoúlia, Ághii Assómati St. ☎ **22-711.**

Cuisine: GREEK. **Reservations:** Not required.

Prices: Main courses 550–880 Drs ($2.30–$3.70). No credit cards.

Open: Wed, Sat, and Sun 6pm–1am.

Many island residents swear by this taverna, which is located about a ten-minute walk from the center of town. We contend that it's both the best and the cheapest on the island, with rabbit as its specialty. Vatsoúlia is rustic, with traditional cuisine. The only drawback is its erratic schedule; call before heading there.

Evening Entertainment

At sunset, Aegina's port comes alive with waterside strollers, yachtsmen showering on their decks, and European holidaymakers descending from their studio apartments. We found two places for a drink and some action: **Kanella's Piano Bar,** where nightly entertainers perform pop music; and **N.O.A.,** a traditional portside ouzerí, where retired sailors and visiting Athenians nurse ouzo and octopus. Motion-buffs should try the **Inoi Disco** in Fáros for Greek music, or **Disco Elpianno** in Aegina town. Bar-hoppers will also enjoy the **Rainbow Bar** on Mitrópolis for a nightcap.

2 Póros

31 nautical miles S of Piraeus

ARRIVING/DEPARTING There are two ways to get to Póros. Most people arrive by ferry or hydrofoil, originating in Piraeus or on one of the other Saronic Gulf isles and landing at the port in Póros town. Call the **Piraeus Port Authority**

The Saronic Gulf Islands

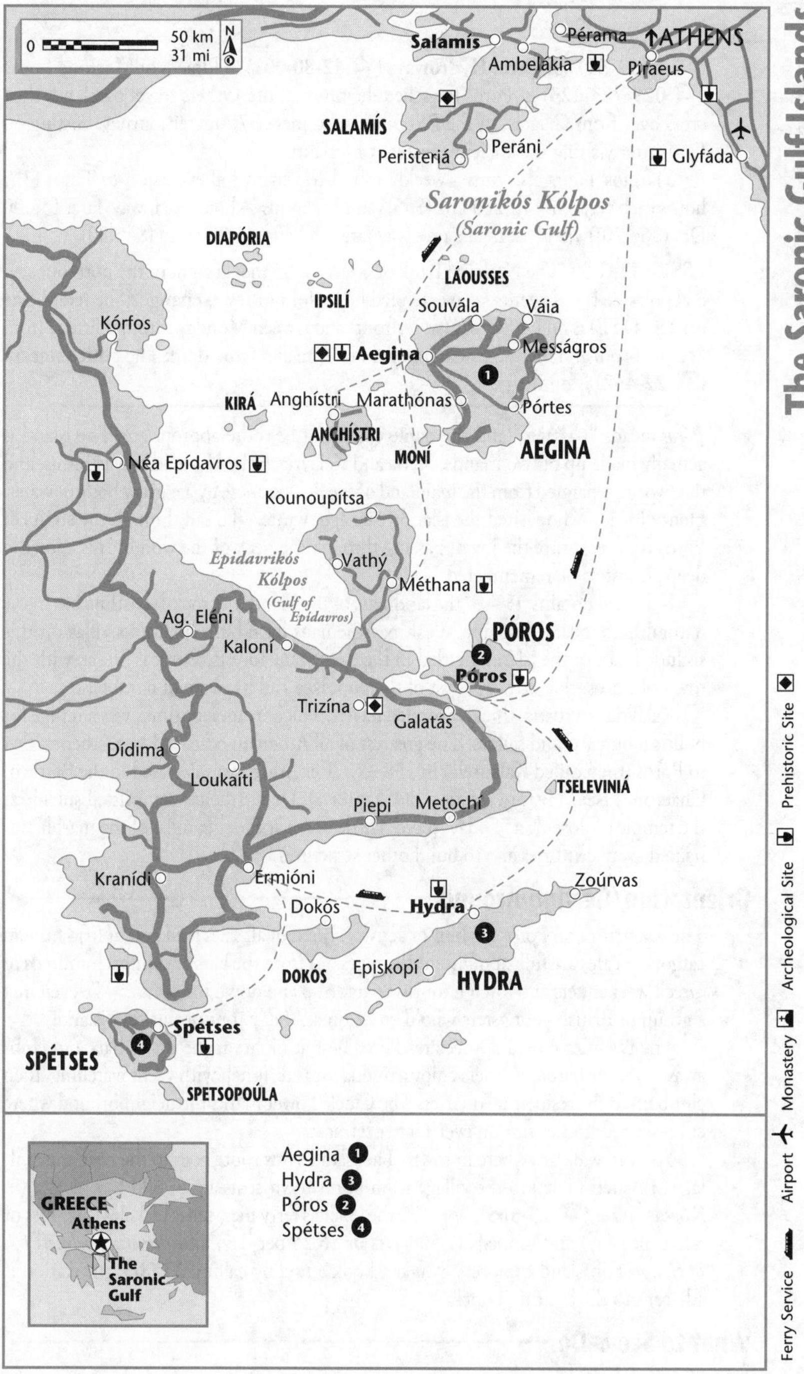

(☎ **45-11-311**) or **Ceres Hydroways** (☎ **42-80-001**) in Piraeus or **Marinos Tours** (☎ **0298/23-423**) in Póros for schedule information. Others travel overland, then cross over from Galatás, in the Peloponnese (a mere 370-meter journey, costing 50 Drs), after visiting the ancient theater at Epidaurus.

Marinos Tours also runs a weekly round-trip hydrofoil excursion to Tínos ($3^1/_2$ hours each way; fare: 13,200 Drs ($55)) and Mýkonos (4 hours each way; fare: 15,400 Drs ($64.20)) via Hýdra. The one-way fare is a hefty 11,000 Drs ($45.80).

ESSENTIALS The National Bank of Greece is on the far right of the port, but several portside travel agents keep extended hours for **money exchange.** The **telephone center (OTE)** is on the *paralía* (waterfront) and is open Monday through Friday from 8am to 11pm and on weekends from 8am to 1pm and 5 to 10pm. The **police station** (☎ **22-462**) is on the port.

Póros means "passage," and the name could not be more appropriate. The island is actually made up of two islands, Sfería and Kalávria, linked by a narrow isthmus, and the two are separated from the mainland of the Peloponnese by a narrow body of water. Henry Miller, who visited the island years ago, wrote: "To sail through the straits of Póros is to recapture the joy of passing through the neck of the womb. It is a joy too deep almost to be remembered."

Kalávria contains 95% of the landmass of the island; the rocky coastline has many natural harbors and beaches. Wealthy Athenians have built luxurious villas on this secluded part of the island, nestled in the dense pine forests. But it is Sfería, with the town of Póros, that attracts most of the populace and has a small naval base.

Kalávria is a rustic, thickly wooded haven, which in ancient times was a refuge for political outcasts and sailors. The greatest of all Athenian orators, Demosthenes, fled to Póros (then called Kalaureia) in 338 B.C. after Athens was defeated in the Battle of Chaeronea (see "History" section in Chapter 1). Demosthenes committed suicide at the temple of Poseidon. Today, there is little to see at the site; most of the marble was hauled away centuries ago to build other structures.

Orientation/Getting Around

The waterfront on Póros is a blur of activity. Boats of all sizes load and unload human cargo; the cafés are full; at night music pours out from the bars and clubs; hundreds of Greek weekenders and foreign tourists parade up and down the *paralía.* We even met a group of British youngsters who'd come on a *14*-day tour of this tiny island!

The twenties crowd appreciates Póros best at night, at the many bars and clubs away from the harbor. Others enjoy a midday seaside lunch with yacht watching, then climb up to the residential quarter. The Clock Tower marks the neighborhood where cube-shaped houses rest on ever-higher terraces.

You can walk anywhere in town. The island's bus route goes to the beachside village of **Askéli** (a taxi to the village from Póros town costs about 600 Drs or $2.50). **Kóstas Bíkes** (☎ **23-565**), opposite the Galatás ferry pier, rents bicycles (500 Drs or $2.10 per day) and mopeds (1,500 Drs or $6.25 per day) and *dispenses helmets free of charge!* For island explorers, you can book a **taxi** by calling **23-003**; the station is adjacent to the hydrofoil dock.

What to See & Do

Unfortunately, the two most often suggested excursions on the larger part of the island are pretty much a bust. The **temple of Poseidon** is really nothing more than rubble on a picturesque plateau, while the **monastery of Zoödóchos Pighí** is just another monastery. (Still, you may find the Lycabettus Press guide *Póros,* by Níki Stavrolákes, an interesting introduction to the area.)

Instead of touring Kalávria, head over to the mainland. If you visit **Galatás** in the middle of June you may be lucky enough to witness the annual Flower Festival, a cornucopia of parades, floats, marching bands, and floral arrays. (Did you know that Greece exports flowers to Holland?) A bus from Galatás runs 8 km to the village of **Troizéna,** thought to be the birthplace of Theseus (certainly the birthplace of Theseus's son, Hippolytus) and site of the ancient temple of Asclepius. There is a lovely walk, along the Devil's Gorge (so named because of a face that looks like you-know-who on one of the walls), which leads to the site. Again, there isn't much to see, but it's a pleasant stroll through fields of carnations and will be of interest to those who enjoyed Mary Renault's novel *The King Must Die.*

Far more sensual is **Lemonodásos,** a 25,000-tree lemon grove that was planted after Greece's War of Independence. This is one excursion that's hard to resist: a walk through a citrus grove whose fragrant flowers and fruit will send your nose into ecstasy. After a long hike, like an oasis, the **Kardassi Taverna** (with some of the grumpiest Greeks) comes into view. It dispenses freshly squeezed lemonade for 440 Drs ($1.80) and a retsína so strong that an entire Australian rowing team was brought to its knees at our visit. On the far side of Lemonódasos is a sandy beach called Alíki.

Póros is a dancer's island. You're sure to find a club where people will be doing the steps to a fast-paced *chasápiko* (a regional dance that must have been designed for weight loss). As for where *you* can dance—the best disco is still **Scirocco,** about 1 km south of town, where every Tuesday night is "Rock 'n' Roll Competition." In Askéli the white marble–sheathed music bar **Artemis,** an elegant nightspot, draws the yachting crowd.

Where to Stay

For more selections than those described below, contact **Marinôs Tours** (☎ **23-423**) on the harbor; manager Marinos Chatzipetros speaks good English and is very helpful. Marinos handles more than 450 rooms and apartments, in addition to booking local hotels. Count on spending 6,600–13,200 Drs ($27.50–$55) per night for two, depending on location and facility.

Hotel Latsis, Odós Papadopoúlou 74, Póros 18020, Trizinías. ☎ **0298/22-392.**
36 rms (some with bath). TEL

Rates: 4,400 Drs ($18.30) without bath; 7,700 Drs ($32.10) double with bath. No credit cards.

This blue-shuttered hotel is on the north side of the port, opposite the Galatás ferry pier, so it offers a scenic but somewhat quieter location. Worn but clean rooms, with balconies overlooking the Peloponnese, are good value. The Látsis has a restaurant downstairs.

Maria Christofa Rooms to Let, Póros 18020, Trizinías. ☎ **0298/22-058.**
6 rms (none with bath).

Rates: 5,500 Drs ($22.90) single/double. No credit cards.

The home of Maria Christofa can be found in the narrow lanes at Póros town's highest point. Many of her simple rooms have breathtaking views of the town and harbor. We enjoyed staying in her high-ceilinged space, really the bargain of the island.

Hotel Sirene, Askéli, Póros 18020, Trizinías. ☎ **0298/22-741.** Fax 0298/22-744.
120 rms (all with bath). TEL

Rates: 15,400 Drs ($64.15) single; 25,630 Drs ($106.80). Half-board optional. MC.

If you're looking for top-of-the-line accommodations, you'll like this Class B hotel situated on the road leading to the monastery, on the southern coast of Kalávria. (To get there, take the bus or a taxi from port; the bus fare is 165 Drs (70¢) and a taxi costs 660 Drs ($2.75). At the modern six-story building, all spacious rooms face the sea. This exquisite view is complemented by a lovely private beach and swimming cove as well as a swimming pool built hard on the water's edge. We enjoyed sitting on the long wrap terrace on the top floor, adjacent to the popular bar. The Sirene is tightly booked with Euro-groups, so reservations are a must.

Where to Eat

Lucas Restaurant, Paralía, Póros Town. ☎ **22-145.**

Cuisine: GREEK. **Reservations:** Not required.
Prices: Appetizers 330–660 Drs ($1.40–$2.75); main courses 880–3,300 Drs ($3.70–$13.75). No credit cards.
Open: Daily 7pm–1am.

The outdoor Lucas Restaurant is located about 550 yards from the center of town, opposite the private yacht mooring. It's a pleasant walk to this casual place run by a Greek dancer and his English wife, Susie. Their fresh seafood and typical taverna fare is good and well priced for this upscale side of town.

Caravella Restaurant, Paralía, Póros Town. ☎ **23-666.**

Cuisine: GREEK. **Reservations:** Not required.
Prices: Appetizers 550–1,320 Drs ($2.30–$5.50); main courses 1,100–3,300 Drs ($4.60–$13.75). No credit cards.
Open: Daily 10am–1am.

This portside taverna specializes in fish entrées and other traditional dishes such as veal stifádo (veal with onions) and moussaká. We particularly liked the Caravella's octopus salad, stuffed eggplant, and roast souvlaki, and enjoyed gossiping with owner Takis Makris.

Padelis Taverna, Paralía, Póros Town. ☎ **22-581.**

Cuisine: GREEK. **Reservations:** Not required.
Prices: Main courses 1,100–1,650 Drs ($4.60–$6.90). No credit cards.
Open: Daily Mon–Sat 7am–5pm.

Padelis holds a special place in our gastronomic universe. The main dining room, located one block inland (near the market), is spacious and homey, but we prefer sitting outside in a skinny alleyway whose five tables make it the narrowest "taverna" in Greece. The food is traditional and not at all bad, as the band of happy, singing seamen we dined with agreed.

3 Hydra

35 nautical miles S of Piraeus

ARRIVING/DEPARTING Several car ferries and excursion boats make the 4-hour journey from Piraeus daily; contact the **Piraeus Port Authority** (☎ **45-11-311**) or the **Hydra Port Authority** (☎ **52-279**) for schedules. Several hydrofoils (both the

Flying Dolphin and the super new Flying Cat) leave Piraeus's Zéa Marina harbor for the 75-minute trip daily; contact **Ceres Hydroways** (☎ **42-80-001** in Piraeus or **52-019** in Hýdra) for schedules and reservations (recommended weekends).

Among the Aegean islands, Hydra (Ýdra) stands out like a jewel among gems. Nature's scenic elegance has been matched by man's handiwork; grand domestic architecture wrought a century ago by Italian architects is well preserved and a nationally recognized monument. Best of all, Hydra has banned all motorized vehicles. Pedestrians peacefully strolling the port's back lanes encounter only donkeys and, occasionally, the island's lone garbage truck. Nary a moped to be found.

The slate-gray town of Hydra rises up a natural amphitheater from the port; to appreciate its peacefulness, just take a short (but challenging) walk uphill. Follow the worn cobblestone steps up to the stone wall, which surrounds a whitewashed monastery and local cemetery. At this distance, the sounds of the town and land wash over you in a flood of fresh sensations. The tinkle of goat bells, the braying of donkeys, and the chatter of children float up from below, joining the singsong chant of a monk above you.

To avoid the distracting crush of day-cruise visitors (from 11am to 3pm), plan to stay overnight. In midweek, when the Athenian weekend crowd is busy at work and rooms are easier to find, the island is a virtual paradise. If you can, come for Greek Easter, to share in the colorful Good Friday ceremonies, or come toward the end of June for the special Miaoúlis Festival. The festival celebrates a famous naval victory during the War of Independence, in which the Hydriot Admiral Andréas Vókos, known as Miaoúlis (1769–1835), defeated the superior Ottoman fleet. The battle is re-created each year, complete with the burning of a fireship, exploding cannons, and fireworks.

History

The most important migration to Hydra took place in the 1600s, when Orthodox Albanians, on the run after the fall of Mistras to the Turks, took refuge on the island. Over the years these mountain people became excellent sailors, hired by other nations to run blockades and fight in foreign wars. The island amassed tremendous wealth and avoided the burden of taxation by the Turks in exchange for training the Ottoman navy. When the winds of revolution swept over the nearby islands, Hydriots were a little reluctant to join forces, not wanting to upset a favorable relation with the occupying Turks. As it turned out, Hydra joined in the War of Independence and under Admiral Miaoúlis won several stunning victories.

Today, the major migration consists of glitzy Athenian and international jet-setters (among them Joan Collins) who weekend on this special island. After tourism, Hydra's main business must be training real-estate agents, because prices for houses on the island are astronomical. In 1994, restored homes with port views began at 70,000,000 Drs ($291,667)!

Fast Facts: Hydra

Banks The National Bank of Greece and the Commercial Bank both have offices on the harbor. They're open Monday through Thursday from 8am to 2pm, Friday from 8am to 1:30pm, and Saturday (high season only) from 11am to 2pm.

Currency Exchange Several travel agents, including Saitis Tours, exchange money at bank rates daily from 9am to 8pm.

Newspapers/Magazines A small store on the central *paralía* sells English-language periodicals and a small selection of books.

Police The tourist police (☎ **52-205**) are at Odós Votsí 9, two lanes up from the waterfront. They will provide copies of the free publication *This Summer in Hydra,* with a list of rooms for rent.

Post Office The post office is just off the *paralía* at Tombázi Street and is open Monday through Friday from 7:30am to 2:15pm. It will exchange money.

Telephones The telephone center (OTE) is across the street from the police station. It's open Monday through Saturday from 7:30am to 10pm and Sunday from 8am to 1pm and from 5 to 10pm. The **area code** for Hydra is **0298.**

Tourist Information At Saitis Tours (☎ **0298/52-184** or fax 0298/53-469), we found Theofilis, Sotiris, and their poodle, Lady D., to be very helpful with long-distance calls, money exchange, information about rooms and villas, and ferry schedules.

Orientation

Your boat, whether ferry or hydrofoil, will dock on the left (north) side of the port, a jumble of gold shops, cafés, and boutiques. Hydra town curls around the busy waterfront, spreads inland for several nameless lanes, then climbs steeply uphill. Don't worry about street names; addresses are given in relation to hotels located on each lane, so just ask a local when you get lost.

Though small and rocky, the island beaches provide the favorite daytime activity. Leaving the town, a pleasant hike south will bring you to the popular sand-and-single beaches at **Kamínia** (20 minutes away) and **Vlichós** (45 minutes away). A wonderful stroll to this lovely spot (there is a taverna/bar, noted under "Where to Eat") is to walk up to the top of Hydra town and take the upper trail west past a small monastery and graveyard. The trail continues through hilly farmland and winds down to remote Vlichós.

Mólos, Palamída, and **Bísti** are beaches even farther away on the western coast. To the east of the town, at Mandráki (a 20-minute walk), is **Miramáre Beach,** a busy sand-and-shingle beach dominated by the hotel of the same name and a water-sports center.

GETTING AROUND

Walking will be your only choice of transport within Hydra town. However, each of the island's beaches is serviced by regular caiques from the port (fares run from 190 Drs (80¢) to 1,980 Drs ($8.25), or by private water taxis. The water taxis are a great way to travel to far-off restaurants in the evening; they charge an extra 550 Drs ($2.30) one way, per boat, when booked by phone.

What to See & Do

Hydra is a small island, but there's enough for a visitor to do to keep busy for several days. A brief walking tour of the town is a good introduction to the island's architectural splendor; a fine companion guide is *Hydra,* by Catherine Vanderpool (Lycabettus Press).

Beginning at the north end of the port, the Tsamádos mansion is now the National Merchant Marine Academy, the oldest in Greece. Next door is the site of Hydra's **archeological museum,** where renovations should be completed by 1993. If you carefully ascend the worn stairs, you'll find the fortress and cannons that once protected the harbor.

Walk west, along the waterfront, to the **Clock Tower** and the **Monastery of the Assumption of the Virgin Mary.** Today, it houses the island's administrative offices, but in the courtyard you'll feel the serenity of an isolated mountain retreat. There is a small chapel with precious Byzantine art (the attendants ask for a donation of 125 Drs or 50¢, for which you also get a postcard).

Continue down the *paralía;* up the hill to the right is the most impressive of all the Hydriot mansions, built by the Tombázis family. This four-story slate villa is now an annex of the School of Fine Arts of the Athens Polytechnic. Each year students from the school and artists from around the world stay at the Tombázis mansion to study and pursue art. Call the mansion in Hydra (☎ **52-291**) or the Athens Polytechnic (☎ **01/61-92-119**) for information about the mansion's program and summer exhibits.

At the far western edge of the port is a three-story stone mansion owned by the Ecónómou-Miriklís family. Around the other side of the port, above the rocks, is the gigantic mansion of George Koundouriótis, the largest on Hydra. The closest swimming area is immediately below the mansion, where you can just dive off the rocks into the crystal-clear sapphire sea.

If you feel like stretching your legs, consider ascending the trail that leads from Miaoúli Street to the monastery of Prophet (Profítis) Ilías and the convent of Aghía Efpraxía. Both communities are active, and from the top you'll have a fabulous view of the town and beyond. Walk farther south beyond these compounds to the convent of Ághii Taxiárchi, and you will have reached the south coast of the island. The trails are rewarding but rugged, so wear good shoes. **Warning:** Men and women in shorts and tank tops will not be allowed into the monasteries.

If you hate the idea of walking, try shopping in the myriad portside boutiques. We always hesitate to recommend particular shops, but one that we found to our tastes was **Louláki** (☎ **52-292**), at Odós Miaoúli 22, a combination gallery and boutique that carries many objets d'art in the local shade of *louláki* (or indigo).

On an island known as an artists' colony, there are, of course, many galleries. The fascinating **Studio Véritas** (☎ **52-668**) is a small, ground-floor atelier, opposite the Hotel Orloff, owned by Rachel Williamson and Michel Le Goff. Rachel is an art historian, whose passion for collecting and restoration led to a special sales business. On their walls you might find a naif Greek folk piece or a painting by Raphael. If you're really into art, drop by to peruse the collection and enjoy a chat with these intriguing proprietors. If you can't tear yourself away, talk to Michel, one of the island's high-end real-estate dealers.

In the evening, everyone turns out for a *vólta* (a stroll along the *paralía*) or a nightcap at one of the portside cafés (we like **To Roloi**). Hikers in this crowd will be pleased to know that Hydra has several discos; all of them, however, are low-key and are usually open only June to September. The favorites are **Cavos** (☎ **52-416**) a 10-minute walk west of the port, and **Heaven** (☎ **52-716**), on the west side of town up the hill. As for bars, the **Pirate** (☎ **52-711**) on the *paralía,* near the Clock Tower, is still the spot for Hydra's celebrants. We also liked **Veranda,** with bright blue accents and a view of the harbor, on the balcony of Savvas Rooms to Let, near the Hotel Hydra.

Where to Stay

All the hotels and rooms to let mentioned below are open from March to late October unless otherwise noted. Low-season prices (for the months other than July and August) are 20% to 30% less, often including breakfast. During summer and weekends, reservations are a must.

DOUBLES FOR LESS THAN 24,000 DRS ($100)

Hotel Greco, Kouloúra St., Hydra 18040. ☎ **0298/53-200.** Fax 0298/53-511. 19 rms (all with bath). A/C TEL

Rates (including breakfast): 11,000 Drs ($45.80); 14,300 Drs ($59.60) double. AE.

This hotel, in a quiet neighborhood away from the tourist center, has a slick, modern interior built inside a traditional stone fishing-net factory. All rooms are spotless and done in designer-print fabrics with blue tile floors. The taverna on the large, enclosed stone patio is a pleasant venue for fresh grilled meats and Greek fare in the evening.

Hotel Hydra, Hydra 18040. ☎ **0298/52-102.** 13 rms (8 with bath). TEL

Rates (including breakfast): 6,490 Drs ($27) single or 11,880 Drs ($49.50) double without bath; 8,910 Drs ($37.10) single or 13,860 Drs ($57.75) double with bath. MC, V.

This is another Hydriot mansion now open to visitors, a two-story, gray-stone hotel on the western cliffs (to the right as you depart from the ferry). The building was purchased from the National Tourist Organization by Dimitri Davis and has been beautifully restored. The rooms are carpeted, high-ceilinged, and simply furnished; many have balconies overlooking the town and harbor. One of the best values in the port if you don't mind a hike; open mid-April to October.

Hotel Leto, Hydra 18040. ☎ **0298/53-385.** Fax 01/36-12-223 in Athens. 24 rms and 6 suites (all with bath). A/C MINIBAR TEL

Rates (including breakfast): 14,685 Drs ($61.20) double. Suites 19,800 Drs ($82.50) for three or four persons. No credit cards.

The recently upgraded Leto (pronounced *Litó* in Greek) has been remade in an old stone home, and its bright, contemporary furniture and collection of modern-art posters are some of the most tasteful in town. The hotel's garden is a delight. An American-style breakfast buffet is presented by the eager-to-please staff in the basement lounge. Though not an architectural classic, the Leto is a good place.

★ **Hotel Miranda,** Hydra 18040. ☎ **0298/52-230.** Fax 0298/53-510. 16 rms (all with bath). TEL

Rates (including breakfast): 16,720–21,560 Drs ($69.60–$89.80) single/double; 26,290 Drs ($109.50) suite. AE, V.

You may consider this a splurge hotel, but it deserves exceptional mention. Set in a sea captain's mansion dated 1810, the Miranda is eclectically decorated with Oriental rugs, tattered wooden chests, marble tables, contemporary paintings, and period naval engravings. Most of the renovated rooms are extremely spacious; some have lovely painted ceilings and antique wooden furniture. Hosts Yannis and Miranda are as gracious as one can hope for, transforming their mansion into a casual, homey abode. If you can manage it, we suggest that families stay in the "suites," which are stylish three-bedded accommodations with Greek country antiques and oversize balconies with harbor views.

Mistral Hotel, Hydra 18040. ☎ **0298/52-509.** Fax 0298/53-411.
20 rms (all with bath). TEL

Rates (including breakfast): 10,500 Drs ($41.30) single, 14,300 Drs ($59.60) double, 15,950 Drs ($66.45) double with A/C. AE, V.

The three-story Mistral (named for those strong August winds) is newly built in an old house and belongs to the same family that owns Saitis Tours. It features a spacious stone courtyard with flowers, a bar and comfy rattan chairs shaded by a bamboo pergola. The rooms are distinctive, suffused with the charm of hostess Sofia. Only guests can take advantage of dinner in the courtyard—a chance to sample the freshest seafood at bargain prices. Open February to November.

★ **Hotel Orloff,** Hydra 18040. ☎ **0298/52-564.** Fax 0298/53-532.
10 rms (all with bath). A/C TEL

Rates: 23,980–29,480 Drs ($99.90–$122.80) room. AE, DC, MC, V.

A short walk from the port will bring you to this delightful, 200-year-old Hydriot mansion, recently restored. The entire place is decorated with prints, lace curtains, and old furnishings. The hotel's cozy bedrooms, among the best the island has to offer, are priced in accordance with size, location, and facilities. Breakfast is one of the real treats here. There's an elegant basement lounge with a bar, and another wonderful bar in the hidden back garden, especially beautiful when illuminated in the evening. The Orloff is professionally and graciously managed by Irene Trageas and Pierre Cladakis.

$ **Hotel Aggelika,** Odós Miaoúli 42, Hydra 18040. ☎ **0298/53-202.**
22 rms (all with bath).

Rates (including breakfast): 8,250 Drs ($34.40) single; 13,200 Drs ($55) double. No credit cards.

The Pension Aggelika (pronounced *Angélika*) is a friendly place about a 10-minute walk from the ferry pier. Its rooms are simple, clean, and a good value. All overlook a quiet arbor courtyard (where breakfast is served). Rooms 6, 8, 9, and 10 even have large rooftop terraces with panoramic views.

Pension Efi, Sachíni St., Hydra 18040. ☎ **0298/52-371.** 15 rms (all with bath).

Rates: 7,700 Drs ($32.10) single/double. No credit cards.

Éfi is a new pension, offering good views of the harbor or the town's rooftops from its modern, simple rooms. You'll find the affable proprietor at a tourist shop opposite the Clock Tower. Although his English is limited, his hospitality is forthcoming.

Savvas Rooms to Let, Odós Antoníou Lychnoú 13, Hydra 18040. ☎ **0298/52-259.**
5 rms (none with bath).

Rates: 7,150 Drs ($29.80), 8,250 Drs ($34.40) triple. No credit cards.

Near the Hotel Hydra is this gray-stone home with the sign SAVVAS ROOMS TO LET outside, run by the gregarious Kechaghioglou brothers. Unlike most recently built rooms to let, these are spacious and handsomely furnished, with two clean bathrooms outside in a plant-filled courtyard. Climbing up the steep wooden stairs with the narrow pipe handrail may remind some of their sailing days. The china cupboards, the sofas with flower-print cushions, and the old sloping floors leave no doubt that you're in their home. The brothers have also turned their balcony into **Veranda,** one of the most pleasant spots in town to sip a glass of retsína or a café frappé and watch the sun set over the harbor. Open from March to September.

Where to Eat

As usual, the waterfront taverns are to be avoided for anything but coffee or a quick snack (exception: **To Roloi,** with its great, friendly waiters). Head into the back lanes of town for a better meal and deal. In fact, two of our favorite places are at nearby beach areas to the west of town. Worth a special mention is the family-run **Taverna Cristina and Vagelis** (pronounced *Vanghélis*), where simple fare, mostly fish, achieves heights of greatness.

$ **Barba Dimas,** Hydra. ☎ **53-166.**

Cuisine: GREEK. **Reservations:** Not required.
Prices: Appetizers 550–790 Drs ($2.30–$3.30); main courses 935–2,475 Drs ($3.90–$10.30). No credit cards.
Open: Daily 6–11:30pm.

For one of Hydra's few typical tavernas, try Barba Dimas, a tiny (six-table) place, with a blue-and-yellow facade, behind the Amaryllis Hotel. Chef Yannis turns out wonderful *salingária* (snails with garlic and onion) and *souzoukákia* (lamb meatballs in tomato sauce). You won't know what's for supper until you examine his kitchen, but it's guaranteed to be fresh and cooked with loving care.

Taverna the Garden, Hydra. ☎ **52-329.**

Cuisine: GREEK. **Reservations:** Not required.
Prices: Appetizers 450–800 Drs ($1.90–$3.35); main courses 1,400–2,300 Drs ($5.85–$9.60). No credit cards.
Open: Daily 7pm–midnight.

One of our longtime favorites is located several blocks inland from the hydrofoil ticket office, behind tall, whitewashed walls in a tree-filled garden. On a July or August evening you'll know this grill restaurant by the line waiting to get in. The meat is superb and the swordfish souvláki divine; don't pass up the *exochikó* (lamb wrapped in phyllo leaves).

Marina's Taverna, Vlichós. ☎ **52-496.**

Cuisine: GREEK. **Reservations:** Not required.
Prices: Appetizers 330–990 Drs ($1.40–$4.15); main courses 880–2,750 Drs ($3.70–$11.50). No credit cards.
Open: Daily noon–11pm.

For a special occasion or even just for fun, take a 45-minute hike (1,800 Drs or $7 for a water taxi ride) west beyond Kamínia to the best sunset view in Greece. Perched high above the small pebble beach, this stunning spot offers a fine meal cooked by the lovely Marína. The menu is basic, hand-crafted and fresh; her *kléftiko,* an island specialty of pork pie, is superb. Marina's Taverna—also called, appropriately enough, **Iliovasílema** or Sunset—is our favorite dining experience on the island.

To Steki, Miaoúli St., Hydra. ☎ **53-517.**

Cuisine: GREEK. **Reservations:** Not required.
Prices: Appetizers 110–1,100 Drs (45¢–$4.60), main courses 3,300–6,600 Drs ($13.75–$27.50). Daily specials 2,200–3,575 Drs ($9.20–$14.90). No credit cards.
Open: Daily noon–11pm.

Locals favor this small, blue-shuttered taverna for its simple fresh food and reasonable prices. The interior, where clients dine in the chilly winter months, has some wonderful folk murals of Hydriot life. The fare is basic but very good. We hate the idea of fixed-price menus, but To Steki offers four or five daily, some including locally caught fish; all dishes come with salad and dessert.

Ouzeri Strofilia, Miaoúli St., Hydra. No phone.

Cuisine: GREEK MEZÉDES. **Reservations:** Not required.
Prices: Appetizers 330–2,860 Drs ($1.40–$11.90). No credit cards.
Open: Daily summer noon–3am; winter 6pm–3am.

This is our favorite ouzerí for a drink and appetizers (or a grazer's full meal). Where else can you choose from 48 *mezédes*—among them a superb mussels *saganaki, fasólia* (black-eyed peas), *kreatopitákia* (lightly fried mini–meat pies), seven cheeses, and three types of olives. Strofilia also has a good, well-priced wine list.

4 Spétses

53 nautical miles from Piraeus; 1.5 nautical miles from Hermióni, Peloponnese

ARRIVING/DEPARTING Several car ferries and excursion boats make the five-hour journey from Piraeus daily; contact the **Piraeus Port Authority** (☎ **45-11-311**) for schedules. Several hydrofoils (among them the Flying Dolphin and the supernew Flying Cat) leave Piraeus's Zéa Marina harbor for the 90-minute trip daily; contact **Ceres Hydroways** (☎ **428-00-01** in Piraeus) or **Bardákos Tours** (☎ **73-141**) in Spétses for schedules and reservations (recommended weekends).

ESSENTIALS Currency **exchanges** can be made at the portside banks or at the nearby travel agencies, which are open daily from 9am to 8pm. There's a **medical clinic** (☎ **72-201**) inland from the east side of the port. The local **police** and the **tourist police** (☎ **73-100**) are near the harbor, on Bótsari Street. The **post office** is up the lane from the police station, and the **telephone center (OTE)**, open daily from 7:30am to 3:10pm), is behind the Hotel Soleil. **Pine Island Tours** (☎ **0298/72-464** or fax 0298/73-255), across from the water taxi stand, can help you with ferry tickets, travel plans, yacht charters, and day tours. The manager, Kostas, knows the island exceedingly well.

Spétses (also Spétsai), the farthest island from Athens in the Saronic group, was once (after Hydra) the "in" weekend destination for tourist-weary Athenians. However, the tourists have caught up with them, and groups from Great Britain, Italy, France, and the United States now inundate the island. There are still many reasons to visit the island (its museum, pine forests, and wonderful beaches), but the tranquillity of yesteryear has been disturbed by the proliferation of mopeds and cars. Still, Spétses' horse-drawn carriages can take you away from the crowds at the port and into the quiet of the old port or the nearby forests.

Orientation

Spétses is oval shaped; the ferry and hydrofoil dock at Dápia, on the northeast coast, which is a 20-minute walk east of **Paleó Limáni,** the picturesque old harbor. Most visitors prefer to sleep in the nightlife capital of Dápia. The lush interior is covered with Aleppo pines and fragrant spices. Of Spétses' beaches, Aghía Paraskeví and Ághii Anárghiri, both on the southwest coast, are the best; neither is sandy, but the scruffy foliage and casual feeling make for pleasant swimming and sunning. Locals also recommend Zogeriá, farthest from town, but circled by a pine forest. To the southeast is Spetsopoúla, the island domain of the wealthy Niarchos shipping family.

Getting Around

Despite a tradition of horse-drawn carriages, Spétses has succumbed to the motorized demons from Tokyo. Mopeds can now be rented everywhere, starting at 2,250 Drs ($12.50) per day. Mountain bikes have also become popular; new, 21-speed models rent for 2,000 Drs ($11.10) per day, and several shops rent 3-speeders for 1,000 Drs ($5.60) per day.

Speaking of horses, there are still two kinds of carriage drivers. The first is polite, drives slowly, and is usually talkative and hospitable. The second doesn't say a word but is a terror on wheels; just sit back and you'll get to where you want to go. Rides from Dápia to the old harbor cost 1,650 Drs ($6.90).

Another way to see the island is by water taxi. An around-the-island tour costs about 4,000 Drs ($16.70), while shorter trips, such as the Dápia–Old Harbor run, cost 1,980 Drs ($8.25). Group taxis for beach hopping cost less (schedules are posted at the pier).

What to See & Do

Most people stay in Dápia and from there take walks and day trips. We think the two most interesting sights are the Mexís and Bouboulína museums. The **Mexís Museum** is housed in the family home of Hatziyannis Mexis, an island celebrity. Walking through this small collection, you'll see the usual unspectacular artifacts, archeological relics, and recent folk objects. The Mexís Museum also pays homage to the island's great lady, the indomitable Laskarina Bouboulina, with a bunch of bones in an aging casket. Open daily from 9:30am to 1:30pm; admission free.

When she was better fleshed, Bouboulina was a terror on the open seas. Born in prison of Hydriot parents, she was rumored to be half-pirate, half-revolutionary, serving the cause against the Turks during the War of Independence. With her powerful fleet, she sealed off the harbor at Náfplio, in the eastern Peloponnese, to defeat the Turks. The **Laskarína Bouboulína House** (☎ **72-077**) in Pefkákia, just off the port, has recently been restored and opened to the public. If you're intrigued, you can join an English-speaking guide for a half-hour tour of her stately home. Open from 10am to 5:30pm Monday through Saturday; admission 770 Drs ($3.21) adults, 330 Drs ($1.40) children.

On a rainy day, you can go shopping in town. We particularly liked the shop **Pityoussa** (no phone), just behind the portside Hôtel Soleil, for its collection of decorative folk paintings, ceramics, and interesting gift items made by an English artist, David Weber.

On a sunny day, head straight for Spétses's sand-and-shingle beaches. The best, **Aghía Paraskeví** and **Aghii Anárghyri,** are on the opposite coast from Dápia and can be reached by bus, caique, moped, or bicycle (lots of hills), or, for the fit, by foot. Paraskeví is bordered by pine trees and is favored for its setting and privacy (at one point it's a nude beach), while Anárghyri is a longer, more spacious, yet busier beach on a perfect C-shaped cove. **Kósta** beach, on the Peloponnese, is a popular day trip by caique.

Set in between Paraskeví and Anárghyri beaches is a large, white house known in fictional accounts as Villa Bourani. This location is the setting for John Fowles's novel *The Magus.* Fowles taught on Spétses at Anarghyrios and Korghialénios College (the Eton of Greece) from 1951 to 1952; he returned later to write this famous work.

Where to Stay

Finding a good-quality, quiet, and inexpensive room is difficult, so start at **Pine Island Tours** (☎ **0298/72-464**). Try to avoid the group "villas"; they're often the noisiest and least attractive accommodations. Expect to pay 6,600–7,700 Drs ($27.50–$32.10). As for hotels, we think that our recommendations, a little removed from the main streets, are the best value. All are open from late April to mid-October unless otherwise noted.

Anna Maria Hotel, Dápia 18050, Spétses. ☎ **0298/73-035.**
20 rms (all with bath). TEL

Rates: 6,600 Drs ($27.50) single; 9,900 Drs. ($41.25) double. No credit cards.

This bright new lodging seems more like a pension than a hotel, with a second floor reception and breakfast lounge, above the village's post office (breakfast is 725 Drs or $3 extra). If the Anna Maria isn't overrun with British tour groups, check out the clean, simple rooms.

Hotel Faros, Kentrikí Platía, Dápia 18050, Spétses. ☎ **0298/72-613.**
40 rms (all with bath). TEL

Rates: 7,700 Drs ($32.10), single, 9,900 Drs ($41.25) double. No credit cards.

The older Hotel Faros overlooks a busy square filled with Taverna Faros, Faros Pizzeria, and other dining establishments whose tables and chairs curb the flow of vehicular traffic. (*Fáros,* by the way, means "lighthouse.") Take the elevator to the top floor, where simple, comfortable, twin-bedded rooms offer the quietest, balconied views of the island.

★ **Hotel Poseidon,** Dápia 18050, Spétses. ☎ **0298/72-006** or **72-308.**
Fax 0298/72-208. 55 rms (all with bath). TEL

Rates (including breakfast): 15,400 Drs ($64.20) single with garden or sea view; 23,100 Drs ($96.25) double with garden or sea view. AE, DC, MC, V.

The Poseidon (pronounced *Posidón* in Greek) is a grand, gracious hotel that dates from 1911 but is well maintained. This belle époque classic, which boasts two grand pianos, is a landmark for many Spetsiots—a handsome bronze statue of Bouboulína guards the harbor from the plaza at the Poseidon's front door. High-ceilinged rooms are spacious and sparsely but elegantly furnished; old-fashioned bathrooms have large bathtubs. It's not cheap, but it's a treat.

Star Hotel, Dápia 18050, Spétses. ☎ **0298/72-214** or **72-728.** Fax 0298/72-872.
50 rms (all with bath). TEL

Rates: 7,500 Drs ($41.70) single; 10,000 Drs ($55.60) double. No credit cards.

This five-story hotel—luckily situated on the *votsalotá* (native-style pebble-mosaic reminiscent of Rhodian work) pavement that's off-limits to vehicular traffic—is the best of the older establishments. All rooms have a balcony; the blue-shuttered front ones command a view of the harbor. Large bathrooms contain a bathtub, a Danish shower, and a bidet. Breakfast is available à la carte in the large lobby.

Where to Eat

Consistent with an island that is known for good living, Spétses has its share of fine restaurants. Most are open from March to October, and really get packed on weekend evenings. To avoid the Greek crush, try to be seated before 9:30pm. Spétses also has some of the best, and probably the most numerous, bakeries in the Saronic Gulf. All serve an island specialty called *amigdálato;* as Andrew Thomas describes it in his guide *Spétses* (Lycabettus Press), it is "a small cone-shaped almond cake covered in icing sugar and flavored with rosewater." Don't miss it.

The Bakery Restaurant, Dápia. No phone.

Cuisine: CONTINENTAL. **Reservations:** Not required.
Prices: Appetizers 539–1,320 Drs ($2.25–$5.50), main courses 990–2,585 Drs ($4.10–$10.80). EC, MC, V.
Open: Daily 6:30pm–midnight.

The Bakery, located on a deck above one of Spétses's more popular *pâtisseries,* reminded us of summer dining in Berkeley, Calif. The food is prepared fresh, cooked with very little oil, and served piping hot. The chef, who obviously understands foreign palates, prepares smoked trout salad, grilled steak, and roasted lamb with peas, as well as moussaká and other taverna favorites.

★ **Exedra Taverna.** Paleó Limáni. ☎ **73-497.**

Cuisine: GREEK/SEAFOOD. **Reservations:** Not required.
Prices: Appetizers 375–625 Drs ($2.10–$3.50); main courses 880–2,640 Drs ($3.70–$11). No credit cards.
Open: Daily noon–3pm and 7pm–midnight.

This is our favorite island eatery, known to locals as both Exedra and **Siora's,** after its proprietor. The keystone of the old harbor, it's where yachts from all corners of Europe pull in and out. The specialties are fish Spetsiotá, a tasty broiled-fish-and-tomato casserole, and Argó, a shrimp-and-lobster casserole baked with lots of tangy feta cheese. Exedra's freshly cooked zucchini, eggplant, and other seasonal vegetable dishes are also excellent. If you can't find a table at supper, you may try the nearby Ligeri Taverna (pronounced *Ligheri*), also popular for its seafood.

Lazaros Taverna, Dápia. No phone.

Cuisine: GREEK. **Reservations:** Not required.
Prices: Appetizers 550–880 Drs ($2.30–$3.70), main courses 890–2,200 Drs ($3.70–$9.20). No credit cards.
Open: Daily 6:30pm–midnight.

Another Dapian favorite, where good food mixes with a normally lively local crowd, is Lazaros. It's our kind of traditional place, decorated with potted ivy and family photos; huge kegs of homemade retsína line the walls. Lazaros's menu is small and features daily specials (goat in lemon sauce was a tasty, unusual choice when we ate there), plus mostly grilled meat dishes. Everything's fresh and reasonably priced.

Evening Entertainment

There's a lot of nightlife on Spétses, with bars, discos, and bouzoúki dancing from Dápia to the old harbor, and even more at a few far-flung beaches. Among the **bars,** there's Socrates in the heart of Dápia. The Anchor is more upscale, but don't overlook the Brachera Music Bar on the yachting marina, which attracts the boating set. To the west of the town, in Kounoupítsa near the popular Patralis Fish Taverna are the nicer, up-market bars Zorba's and Kalia.

For **discos,** there's Figaro, around the old harbor, as well as the Delfina Disco, located opposite the Dápia town beach on the road to the old harbor, which has been quite popular the last few seasons.

7

The Peloponnese

THOUGH FAMOUS CHIEFLY FOR ITS UNFORGETTABLE ARTIFACTS FROM GREECE'S classical era, the Peloponnese today has some of the most picturesque rock beaches and mountainous terrain Greece that has to offer. This peninsula, separated from the mainland by the Corinth Canal, is the ideal place to start your love affair with the glory that is Greece. In the high season, it's much less crowded than the island resorts, allowing residents to maintain their traditional hospitable ways.

The archeological sites at Corinth, Mycenae, and Olympia are expressive ruins of ancient times, leaving visitors with a tangible feeling of life as it must have been more than 3,500 years ago. In fact, the rural Peloponnese is one of the few places left with a tangible feeling of Greek life today.

Seeing the Peloponnese

There are five convenient points of entry to the Peloponnese: From Athens a bus will take you into Corinth; from Italy you can ferry to Pátra; boats to and from Crete and Piraeus leave and arrive at Gíthio and Monemvassía; and several port towns in the Argolid are serviced by ferry. There are daily flights to Kalamáta (southwest) from Athens.

Once you arrive in the Peloponnese, a car combined with foot power can give you the maximum in sightseeing; however, all the major areas of interest are serviced regularly by public bus. Even though those tough-to-get-to gems, like the Máni, have poor service, this is offset by the fact that most can be seen in a day or less using another Peloponnese town as a home base. (The larger towns also have train service that can be combined with buses for the most efficient touring.) **Note:** Pick up the printed bus and train schedules from the Greek Tourist Organization (EOT) before you leave Athens so that you can plan ahead.

If you visited the places that we liked best it would take you about a week by car. The thought of that much driving may not appeal to you; neither might the patience you will need at some of the bus stops. If you want the comfort and ease of a tour, **Viking Tours,** Odós Artemídos 1, Glyfáda (☎ **01/89-80-729**), books other companies' tours (principally the excellent Chat Tours). Viking offers a four-day tour of the Peloponnese and Delphi; the best of the classical sites for $365 (first-class hotels), including a professional guide. Their tour goes from Delphi to Antirio, where you ferry over to the Peloponnese at Río; then to Pátra, Olympia, Tripolis, Mycenae, Náfplio, Epidaurus, Corinth, and back to Athens. Viking offers discounts to senior citizens, professors and students, and military personnel, and can often sell this package at a discount if reservations are made a day or so before departure.

NORTHEASTERN PELOPONNESE (ARGOLID)

In the Argolid, this cradle of western civilization, with magnificent ruins all about you, you feel a quality of timelessness. Surrounded by mountains on the west and north and by the sea on the east and south, relics of the past blend with the enduring beauty of nature's bays, rocky slopes, and plains.

Archeological evidence now dates the first inhabitants of the Argolid back to 3000 B.C. Some 1,500 years later, around 1450 B.C., it was the heart of the Greek Empire. Every aspect of Greek life was influenced by the Mycenaeans, especially so in the Argolid.

Although this region never became a united state (factions were always at war with each other), it has always been considered a single geographical unit, with the plain of Argos as its center. Around the 12th century B.C., Dorians established themselves at

What's Special About the Peloponnese

Archeological Sites and Museums

- The most extensive, important, and best-preserved ruins are in a line between Athens and Olympia: Athens, Corinth, Mycenae, Tiryns, Epidaurus, Náfplio, Olympia.
- Some of the finest antiquities unearthed in Greece are in the museums at Epidaurus and Olympia.
- The Corinth Canal, completed in A.D. 62, makes the Peloponnese Greece's largest island.

Architecture

- The fully restored amphitheater at Epidaurus seats 14,000 spectators at annual performances of classic Greek drama.
- The temple of Apollo at Vassae is the oldest extant Doric-style temple in Greece.
- The fortified stone towers built by feuding families of the Máni region have been restored and converted into hotels.

Film Locations

- The cast and crew of Paul Mazursky's film *The Tempest,* starring the late Raul Julia and Susan Sarandon, lived in Gíthio while filming on a small island off the south coast.

Argos, which became their official capital until the Romans subjugated the Peloponnese. At the beginning of the 13th century A.D. the Franks occupied the Argolid region, which in turn was occupied by the Venetians. In the revolution of 1821 the Argolid was the major battleground, and after the cessation of hostilities Náfplio became the capital of all Greece, to be replaced by Athens in 1834.

History was made again when a German archeologist, Heinrich Schliemann, discovered a tomb in 1876 in Mycenae. His discoveries of gold masks and other antiquities alerted the world to this region once more. If you only have time to sample the Peloponnese, head here first.

1 Corinth

55 miles W of Athens

GETTING THERE • By Train Daily train service is slow and erratic from Athens's Peloponnísou Station to Corinth. Call **01/51-24-913** for schedules and information.

IMPRESSIONS

Corinth, the Gibraltar of the Peloponnesus.
—E. D. Clarke, *Travels in Various Countries,* 1818

When God finished making the world all He had left was stones, and He made . . . Mani last of all.
—Greek Old Man, in Kevin Andrews, *The Flight of Ikaros,* 1959

• **By Bus** Fifteen buses a day leave from the Athens Terminal at Odós Kifíssou 100. Call **51-29-233** for schedules and information.

• **By Car** From Athens, the excellent, but ugly, seven-lane Corinth highway follows the winding southern coast of the mainland along the Saronic Gulf.

ESSENTIALS • **Getting Around** Athens and local buses (from new to Ancient Corinth [Archéa Kórinthos] leave from Ermoú and Koliátsou Streets, east of Corinth's park, every hour between 7am and 8pm, with returns on the half hour. It's a pleasant 15- to 25-minute ride. The buses that run to Náfplio, Mycenae, and Árgos leave every hour from the corner of Konstantinou and Aratou Streets.

• **City Layout** The railway station is at Pirínis and Damaskinoú Streets on the east side of town. There are two banks on King Constantine Avenue. You could also catch a Greek movie at one of the two theaters on Damaskinoú Street, one near the Ephira Hotel, the other near the Bellevue Hotel.

Corinth is the gateway to the Peloponnese. As a city it's not very interesting; in its present form it has existed only since 1928, when an earthquake leveled the town for a second time. Even then the ruins of "New Corinth" were no match for those of Ancient Corinth, and today Corinth is still primarily a stop on the way to the wonderful ruins five miles out of town.

You can break up the 3½-hour drive from Athens to Corinth with a morning stop at the monastery of Dafní; 6½ miles farther west is Elefsís, site of the ancient Eleusinian mysteries (see Chapter 5, for more information). The next 38 miles offer some sumptuous vistas of the gulf and a much truck-filled superhighway. When you reach the Corinth toll, admire the canal as you cross the bridge.

In ancient times Corinth was a wealthy precinct because of its location as the "middleman" between the Ionian and Aegean seas. As early as A.D. 62 Nero saw the wisdom of building a **canal** across Corinth to save ships from the dangerous 185-mile detour around the peninsula. He personally dug the first clod of earth with a gold shovel and carried it away on his back—more, some say, a mark of his love of theatricality than of his energy! Although 6,000 Jewish prisoners continued to dig, it was never finished, languishing for nearly 2,000 years. Work began again in 1881, and it was completed in 1893 by a French company. The beautiful four-mile waterway is only 30 yards wide, its smooth, flat rock sides 270 feet straight up.

Ancient Corinth

On a plateau at the base of the Acrocorinth mountain stands the remains of the ancient city of Corinth, all that's left of what once was the most powerful precinct in all Greece. It occupied the land bridge between the mainland and the Peloponnese, a position it took full advantage of by charging exorbitant tolls to those who would cross the isthmus in order to trade. To defend itself, Corinth became a great maritime power, able to dominate both the Corinth and Saronic gulfs because of its ability to move ships overland to the sea almost immediately.

Corinth reached its zenith in the 5th century B.C. In 44 B.C. it became a Roman colony. Archeologists who started digging in 1896 have so far found only Roman remains. Under Roman rule the name of Corinth became synonymous with luxury and pleasure to excess, an image it shared with Spartan women, said to be the most pampered and glamorous of all. One of the Roman ruins found so far is the Peirene Fountain, an enclosed-courtyard type of area with a central "pool" that looks about the size of an Olympic pool, now overgrown with flowers, and arched entryways flanked by pieces of columns.

What to See & Do

One of the very few remains from the Greek period, and the most outstanding, is the **temple of Apollo,** built in the 6th century B.C. One of the oldest in Greece, it stands on a bluff overlooking the ancient marketplace, with 7 of the original 17 columns still standing. Each column was entirely carved from a single piece of stone. Next door is the **museum** (☎ **31-207**), filled with sculpture, friezes, and other relics found during the digs. The display next to the museum shows the evolution of Greek columnar architecture, culminating in the highly decorative Corinthian style. With its Roman mosaic floors the museum is the perfect place to come in out of the sun during the summer; you can also picnic in the inner courtyard. Admission is 600 Drs ($2.50), half price for students. The site is open Monday through Friday 8am to 7pm (8:45am to 3pm during the off-season), and weekends from 8:30am to 3pm. From Corinth, the site and museum are 7 kms south on the Árgos road.

At the top of the Acrocorinth, overlooking the site, is the **Fort of Acrocorinth,** a huge fortress with foundations dating from ancient times. The rest was built and rebuilt by various other groups, including the Byzantines, Franks, and Turks. The uppermost part was originally the temple of Aphrodite.

If you haven't brought a picnic, there's the **Taverna Acrocorinth,** open daily from 8am to 10pm. It features a great view, cool drinks, and souvenirs. Lunch will run about 1,350 Drs ($5.60) per person. An ancient fountain at the first bend of the unpaved road has modern plumbing to provide you with cool running water.

To get to the Acropolis, continue past the entrance to Ancient Corinth, and make a left at the sign (you can hire a taxi shuttle for 460 Drs or $1.90 per person, each way) and continue for 2 km, or hike up to the site, a one- to two-hour trip up an unpaved road. The reward for this sacrifice is the many gorgeous vistas you'll see at every bend in the road. The site is open Tuesday through Sunday from 8:30am to 3pm; admission is free.

Where to Stay

Hotel Apollon, Odós Pirínis 18, Corinth, 20100 Peloponnese. ☎ **0741/22-587.** 18 rms (all with bath).

Rates: 4,600 Drs ($19.15) single; 6,900 Drs ($28.75). No credit cards.

The first floor has been remodeled with wood paneling and all-tile bathrooms; so, if you need a quick bed, try for this hotel. Many rooms have a small balcony, and though they may be a little noisy, the friendly English-speaking owner, George Katmis, makes up for it.

Bellevue, Odós Damaskinoú 41, Corinth, Peloponnese. ☎ **0741/22-068.** Fax 0741/22-019. 17 rms (2 with bath).

Rates: 4,000 Drs ($16.75) single/double without bath; 4,800 Drs ($20) single/double with bath. No credit cards.

Our favorite hotel is the Bellevue. The owners have tried hard to give the old Bellevue a new look, and their efforts have given the city a good-value Class-C pension with some charm, but it's often booked by groups.

The Peloponnese

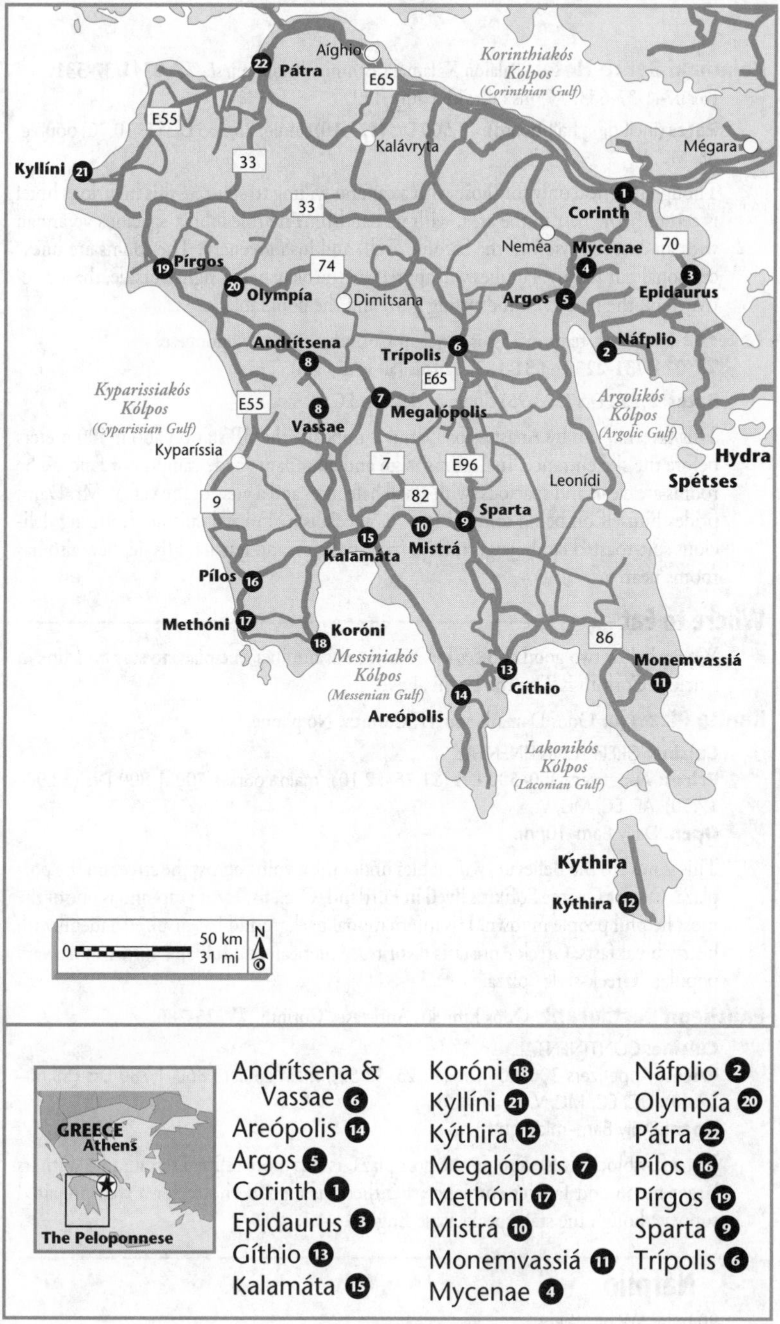

9619

Kalamaki Beach Hotel, Palaión Kalamáki Isthmia, Peloponnese. ☎ **0741/37-331.** Fax 0741/37-653. 75 rms (all with bath). TEL

Rates (including half-board): 18,500 Drs ($77.10) single; 26,565 Drs ($110.70) double. AE, MC, V.

Though practical only for those with a car and willing to splurge, this luxurious hotel is certainly the best in the area, with its handsome marble lobby, spacious verandah with an excellent view of the Saronic Gulf, and lush greenery. The rooms are unexceptional but roomy; families will appreciate the okay beach right outside, the attractive pool, the rentable windsurfing gear, and the pool table.

Taverna Dafni, Estiatório Tássos, Ancient Corinth, 20007 Peloponnese. ☎ **0741/31-225** and **31-183.** 12 rms (all with bath). TEL

Rates: 5,750 Drs ($23.95) single or double. EC, V.

This taverna, run by Anastassios Dafni, is opposite the BP station about 500 meters before the site entrance. Its "rooms" sign and abundant shade caught our fancy. The rooms are clean and spacious, with small balconies and a view of the valley. Mr. Dafni prides himself on being something of a "specialista" in local cuisine, featuring delicious spit-roasted lamb, yogurt, fresh fruit, pastries, and retsína. His nephew also has rooms nearby.

Where to Eat

We list below two good choices in Corinth; our number one place to stay *and* dine in Ancient Corinth is Taverna Dafni above.

Kanita Pizzeria, Odós Damaskinoú 41, Corinth. No phone.

Cuisine: GREEK/CONTINENTAL.
Prices: Appetizers 300–500 Drs ($1.25–$2.10), main courses 700–1,800 Drs ($2.90–$7.50). AE, EC, MC, V.
Open: Daily 8am–10pm.

This is next to the Bellevue, with tables under the awning across the street on the port plaza. Owner George Sofikitis lived in Portland, Ore., for eight years and is one of the most helpful people in town. His international background has inspired a menu with hearty breakfasts, Greek Antístasis favorites, American and Italian courses, and a very popular "Greek-style" pizza.

Pantheon Restaurant, Odós Ethnikís Antístasis, Corinth. ☎ **25-780.**

Cuisine: CONTINENTAL.
Prices: Appetizers 300–600 Drs ($1.25–$2.50), main courses 860–1,780 Drs ($3.60–$7.40). DC, EC, MC, V.
Open: Daily 8am–midnight.

Just a few blocks west, also on the port plaza, is this more refined restaurant. With its larger menu and fancier ambience, Pantheon is a good choice for a well-prepared supper, though the staff speaks little English.

2 Náfplio

90 miles SW of Athens

GETTING THERE • By Train There is no train service to Náfplio(n), so you'll have to get off in nearby Argos. It's about 5 hours from Athens, 2½ hours from Corinth.

• **By Bus** Fourteen buses a day leave from Athens's Odós Kifissoú 100 terminal; call **51-34-588** for schedule information.

• **By Boat** One hydrofoil leaves Monday through Saturday from Piraeus' Zéa Marina port to Náfplio. Contact **Ceres Flying Dolphins** for information (☎ **32-42-281** or **45-36-107**); it's a 3½-hour trip.

• **By Car** For the scenic route, drive south from Corinth, past Epidaurus, on the coast road. The quick route is the new Tripolis-Argos highway.

ESSENTIALS • Information The local Greek Tourist Organization (**EOT**) information office (☎ **24-444**) is in the town hall, a three-story building on Iatroú Square, across from the monument in the park. At the bus station buy the best regional map, *Pelopónnisos,* published by F. Láppas in English, French, and German; it also has street plans for six of the most important towns in the Peloponnese.

• **Getting Around** Within Náfplio, you can walk everywhere. The bus station is at Nikitára Square: local buses for Argos leave every half hour, and the bus to Mycenae and other towns goes three or four times a day. You can book cruises or day trips, or rent a car for about $75 per day from **Staikos Travel,** on the *paralía* (☎ **0752/27-950,** fax 28-000). **Kalkanakos Panagiotis Motor Technik** (☎ **27-183**) rents bicycles and motorcycles. **Hikers** should call **01/32-34-555** for information about nearby mountain huts.

Náfplio (Nauplion) is a city of Venetian fortresses, an ancient harbor, and an almost idyllic serenity. Flower gardens are scattered throughout. If the resonance of the city's church bells don't wake you in the morning, then the assorted street noises will. This place is so inviting that you might consider taking a breather from the usually "If this is Tuesday it must be Sparta" program that most travelers adhere to. Náfplio is the ideal base for visits to Corinth, Argos, Mycenae, Epidaurus, and the rest of the Argolid.

In antiquity Náfplio was a great naval power. In the 3rd century B.C. fortifications on the southern side of town were built on a clifftop rising straight up from the sea. One fort, the Palamidi, still towers over the town.

What to See & Do

Although its geographical location is enough to recommend it as a base for sightseeing, Náfplio is itself a treat. Two blocks from the waterfront is **Sýntagma (Constitution) Square,** the perfect small-town square, with several cafés, a bookstore with some titles in English, a bank, and the Hotel Athena.

The light brick Byzantine-style building with red-tiled dome that dominates the west corner of Sýntagma Square is a 19th-century **Turkish mosque** that was once the palace of the Turkish governor. Today, it's used for music recitals and other local events.

The **Xenia Palace Hotel,** high on the hillside just below the fortress, offers one of the best views of Náfplio. Take the several flights of stairs from where the road diverges from the *paralía,* and follow the long entrance tunnel to elevators that ascend to a terrace built on the site of the Venetian-era fortifications. The ancient Cyclopean walls are still evident.

The **Public Square** (Kolokotróni Square and Matsíkas Street) has a park (with a children's playground), an outdoor taverna, some cafés, a fountain, and fast food! It's somewhat of a local hangout—a lot of life, a lot of color. The prices are better here in the shops and cafés than at other squares.

SIGHTS

Popular Arts Museum, Sofróni and Ypsilántou Streets. ☎ **28-379.**

The Popular Arts Museum, one of the best of its kind, is just off the square. Its shady courtyard is a great place to have morning coffee and the gift shop has replications of costumes, music, tapes, and posters for sale. Clothing from many regions of Greece is displayed (even the earliest animal hide garb), and the gold embroidery done by men is very impressive. Admission is 500 Drs ($2.10), students half price. It's open Wednesday through Monday from 9am to 2:30pm (and is closed for the month of February. The Peloponnesian Folklore Foundation recently opened **Stathmós,** a museum of children's folk artifacts, with displays of birthing rituals, toys, puppets, christening items, and school things. It's located in the imaginatively restored old railway station (*stathmós*) of the city, in Kolokotronis Park.

Admission: Free.

Open: Mon–Sat 4–9pm.

Archeological Museum, Sýntagma Square. ☎ **27-502.**

On the west side of the main square is a three-story Venetian barracks with a small symbol of St. Mark, the patron saint of Venice, gracing the facade. There is an excellent collection of early and late Hellenic pottery here, as well as finds from several Mycenaean sites, and a remarkably well-preserved 15th-century B.C. Mycenaean suit of armor.

Admission: 500 Drs ($2.10) adults; 250 Drs ($1.05) students.

Open: Tues–Sun 8:30am–3pm.

Military Museum, Odós Amalías. ☎ **25-591.**

A look at Greece at war since its independence in the 1820s, through photographs, old prints, and weapons of various sorts.

Admission: Free.

Open: Tues–Sun 9am–2pm.

Palamidi Castle, Náfplio. ☎ **28-036.**

To get to the Palamidi Castle, perched on a crag over 700 feet high, you can walk the 857 steps, or take a car, taxi, or bus up the mile and a half. The seven forts inside the blindingly beautiful palace were built by the Venetians in the early 18th century. You'll enjoy the expansive view of the Argolid Gulf, while the shade of the ramparts is an inviting spot for a picnic lunch.

Admission: 500 Drs ($2.10) adults, 250 Drs ($1.05) students.

Open: Mon–Fri 8am–7pm, Sat–Sun 8am–3pm.

Pasqualigo Castle, Island of Bourdzi, Náfplio Harbor. No phone.

Below the Palamidi Castle, guarding the entrance to the harbor, is a medieval castle on tiny Bourdzi, best admired from afar. The Palamidi executioners lived here, because they weren't allowed to live in the town.

SHOPPING

Of the many stylish boutiques and junky souvenir stores, we very much liked the shop owned by Yiorgos Agathos and Sigrid Ebeling, called **Camara** (☎ **24-093**) located at Odós Spiliádou 11, near the *paralía.* This fascinating emporium sells contemporary silver jewelry and a wide assortment of antiques, rugs, and other Greek objets d'art. (Open daily 10am–10pm, Sunday 2–10pm; AE, DC, EC, MC, V.) Sigrid has recently opened a new store at Odós Vassiléos Konstantínou 10 (☎ **26-077**), which showcases their unique jewelry designs.

Where to Stay

There's a fine variety of hotels within the town (perfect for the stroller and action-lover), a few fancy places on the edge of town, and a few on the nearby beach at Tolo(n) for you sunworshippers. Buses going from Náfplio to Tolo and back leave every hour from 7am to 7pm daily; the 11 km trip takes 20 minutes. Campgrounds are to be found about 2 km out of Náfplio on the road to Argos. These are European-style "carparks" and should be passed by; you'd do better to find a room near the harbor or Square.

IN NÁFPLIO

Hotel Byron, Odós Plátonos 2, Aghíou Spyrídonos Square, Náfplio 21100, Peloponnese. ☎ **0752/22-351.** Fax 0752/26-338. 13 rms (all with bath).

Rates: 8,800 Drs ($36.65) single; 12,600 Drs ($52.30) double.

Shirley Nelson of Ottawa, Canada, wrote to alert us about this special hotel beneath the clock tower near the historical church of St. Spyridon in the old city. Aris Papaioannou has beautifully restored an 18th-century home, appointing the small rooms with marble-topped, wrought-iron tables, oriental rugs, and lace curtains.

Hotel Dioscouri, Odós Zygomála 6, Náfplio, 21100 Peloponnese. ☎ **0752/28-550.** 49 rms (all with bath). TEL

Rates: (including breakfast): 10,350 Drs ($43.15) single; 14,200 Drs ($59.15) double. No credit cards.

Hotel Dioscouri has Class C prices with a Class A view! You'll find this very popular place by walking up the same steps as to the Leto Hotel (see below) and turning right, for one more block. Its rooms are standard, but those views from the front and side rooms make it worthwhile.

Hotel Epidaurus, Odós Kokkinou 1, Náfplio, 21100 Peloponnese. ☎ **0752/27-541.** 28 rms (5 with bath).

Rates: 6,325 Drs ($26.35) single without bath; 7,475 Drs ($31.15) double without bath, 8,625 Drs ($35.95) single/double with bath. No credit cards.

The Hotel Epidaurus, at the quiet corner of Bikáki and Lambropoúlou Streets, has ten bright rooms with small terraces overlooking the town, and ten new rooms across the street (these, all handsome and comfortable, offer the best value in town). The pension offers similar clean accommodations, with baths across the hall. Highlighting the classic detailing of this old house is a spiral staircase winding up to gray eight-foot double doors framed in fresh sky-blue enamel paint.

Leto Hotel, Odós Zygomála 28, Náfplio 21100, Peloponnese. ☎ **0752/28-093.** 11 rms (7 with bath).

Rates: 7,590 Drs ($31.60) single without bath; 9,200 Drs ($38.35) double without bath, 11,400 Drs ($47.50) double with bath. No credit cards.

While the Leto is not a classic, its charm is in its quiet location. Follow Farmakopoúlou Street past the Otto to the end of the street and walk up the three flights of stairs. On both sides you'll see the back streets of Náfplio, and they're wonderful. The rooms in the front have the best view; the rest are rather nondescript. Breakfast is served on a veranda that has a view of the city's graceful harbor, mountains, and roof tiles.

SPLURGE CHOICES

Hotel Agamemnon, Aktí Miaoúli 3, Náfplio 21100, Peloponnese. ☎ **0752/28-021.** 40 rms (all with bath). TEL

Rates (including half-board plan): 12,650 Drs ($52.70) single; 20,700 Drs ($86.25) double. No credit cards.

This large establishment has a spacious, pretty lobby with huge picture windows, as well as a rooftop terrace, where you can sit and watch the harbor. Half board is compulsory here in high season, but the hotel is open all year and rates drop considerably in the low season. Though they may cost lots of drachmas, the large doubles have gorgeous marble terraces that hang out over the port.

Hotel Xenia Palace, Akronáfplia, Náfplio, 21100 Peloponnese. ☎ **0752/28-981.** Fax 0752/28-987. 48 rms, 54 bungalows, 3 suites in Palace; 58 additional rooms in Xenia Hotel (all with bath). TEL

Rates (including half-board): 22,920–28,750 Drs ($95.50–$119.80) single; 34,850–43,450 Drs ($145.20–$181) double depending on facility. AE, EC, MC, V.

Of the newer regional resorts, we much prefer the splashy (yes, there's a pool) Xenia Palace, the latest in understated elegance. Created from finely finished wood and marble, rooms have spacious bathrooms with full bathtubs and shower curtains, and comfortable beds—not to mention the views! There are also private bungalows and the less sumptuous Xenia Hotel, plain in name only, a little farther down this road. If you don't mind the relative isolation (see "What to See & Do," above), we couldn't imagine a more relaxing base. Open year round.

IN TOLO(N)

Hotel Artemis, Leofóros Bouboulínas 7A, Tolo 21056, Náfplio, Peloponnese. ☎ **0752/59-458.** Fax 0752/59-125. 19 rms (all with bath). TEL

Rates: 8,050 Drs ($33.55), 9,200 Drs ($38.35) double. V.

You'll find this hotel on a small beach overlooking the Gulf of Argos. Seaside rooms have large balconies, and there are clean, comfortable air-conditioned rooms on the street-facing side. The Artemis is known locally for its good Greek/continental food restaurant.

★ **Hotel Tolo,** Leofóros Bouboulínas 15, Tolo 21056, Náfplio, Peloponnese. ☎ **0752/59-248.** Fax 0752/59-689. 59 rms (all with bath). TEL

Rates (including breakfast): 9,430 Drs ($39.30) single; 12,650 Drs ($52.70) double. EC, V.

The best place to stay is the Hotel Tolo, conveniently located on the main street, with clean, modern rooms facing the beach. The charming Dimitris Skalidis and his family make all their guests feel special. His lovely wife, Yanna, runs **Tolon Tours** (☎ **59-686**), which handles day cruises to Hydra and Spetses, once weekly day sails to Monemvassía, car rentals, bus tours to the major archeological sites, tickets to Italy, and Olympic Airways flights. The Skalidises also have 14 fully equipped, air-conditioned apartments, in a quiet neighborhood 250 meters off the main drag, for 14,200 Drs ($59.15) for two and 17,250 Drs ($71.85) for four. This is an ideal spot to unload your bags and make day trips to the rest of the Peloponnese.

Where to Eat

Be careful of the restaurants on Sýntagma Square; most are tourist traps. However, on the right-hand side of the harbor, looking out across the gentle waters of the Gulf of Argolis to the island castle of Bourdzi, are several popular cafés where both locals and tourists can sit or swing (yes, big swinging love-seats!) and admire the views. If you want to escape the more touristy restaurants, head for the ouzerís along the *paralía* (waterfront) below the fortifications (all offer protected swimming areas open to the public). The first waterside south is **Banieres** (☎ **28-125**), where ouzo and a tasty selection of *mezédes* (appetizers) await you at lunch or dinner. A great meal of ouzo, *saganáki* (fried cheese), octopus, and salad will run about 1,800 Drs ($7.60).

Aktaion Cafe, Aktí Miaoúli 3, Náfplio. ☎ **27-425.**

Cuisine: SNACKS/PASTRY.
Prices: Snacks and desserts 180–1,375 Drs (76¢–$5.75). No credit cards.
Open: Daily 7am–3am.

This local landmark is next door to the Agamemnon Hotel, where the *paralía* turns. The innovative new owners have refurbished it but kept its classic quality, and along with its famous dessert called *galaktaboúreka* (350 Drs or $1.45), it serves several kinds of excellent coffee, a luxurious tropical breakfast with fresh fruit (1,375 Drs or $5.75), and beautiful ice cream concoctions that taste even better than they look. Don't miss this special treat.

Old Mansion Taverna, Siókou and Ypsilántou Streets, Náfplio. ☎ **22-449.**

Cuisine: GREEK. **Reservations:** Recommended in July.
Prices: Appetizers 300–400 Drs ($1.25–$1.65); main courses 1,100–1,400 Drs ($5.40–$6.70)
Open: Daily 7pm–2am.

Tassos Koliopoulos and his lovely wife, Anya, run this homey taverna a couple of blocks from the *paralía* near the Folk Museum. The portions are generous and the menu changes daily. Delicious local wines are available by the liter.

Savouras Psarotaverna, Leofóros Bouboulínas 79, Náfplio. ☎ **27-704.**

Cuisine: SEAFOOD.
Prices: Fish from 1,150–10,350 Drs ($4.80–$43.15) per kilo. No credit cards.
Open: Daily 11:30am–11:30pm.

Several readers recommended this seafood eatery, east of the port and next to the Customs House on the *paralía*. It's a favorite with locals for its freshly made seasonal appetizers, top-quality olive oil, and excellent preparation of the day's catch. A kilo of fish can feed four; two should spend about $30 for a medium-grade grilled fish, vegetables, and a salad.

3 Epidaurus

39 miles S of Corinth; 25 miles E of Náfplio

GETTING THERE • By Bus Two buses leave daily from the Athens terminal at Odós Kifissoú 100 to make the three-hour trip to Epidaurus; three local buses leave daily between the site and the port of Náfplio, where you'll find a wide range of accommodations. (Palaiá Epídavros is about 12 miles away and has several hotels, but it is just not as interesting as Náfplio.) An extra late-night bus (after performances) runs on Saturday and Sunday to Náfplio or Palaiá Epídavros.

• By Car Take the scenic coastal highway south from Corinth. Follow signs to the ancient theater of Epídavros, rather than to Néa Epídavros (the dull new town) or Palaiá Epídavros (the old town).

ESSENTIALS Epidaurus is best known today for the Epidaurus Festival, superb productions of classical Greek theater held each summer in its beautifully restored amphitheater. Tickets to the same night's 9pm performance can be purchased at the site box office after 5pm (usually sold out by 8pm); prices range from 1,800–3,250 Drs ($7.50–$13.50), students 900 Drs ($3.75). They can also be purchased in advance in Athens at the **Athens Festival Box Office,** Odós Stadíou 4, in the arcade off Sýntagma Square (call **01/32-21-459** for information). Performances are given Saturday and Sunday nights between the end of June and September; check with the Greek Tourist Organization (EOT) for the summer's schedule. Programs sold beforehand have an English translation of the entire play and cost 600 Drs ($2.50).

If you decide to stay overnight at Epidaurus, the tourist pavilion at the site houses the **Epidaurus Xenia Hotel** (mailing address: Ligourio, Nafplias, Peloponnese; ☎ **0753/22-005**). Of their 26 units, 12 have private bathrooms. Clean, quiet bungalows of hewn stone are neatly tucked behind the pines and olive trees so as not to intrude on the classical setting, or let the mass of day-trippers intrude on you. It's a popular weekend excursion with Athenians, so book early. Rates (including breakfast) are 9,540 Drs ($39.75) single and 12,075 Drs ($50.30) double, with or without bath. No credit cards are accepted.

Today the name of Epidaurus (Epídavros) is associated with its celebrated amphitheater; yet to the ancient Greeks, the place was home to the most renowned Asclepion (center of healing arts) in the Hellenic world.

What to See & Do

ASCLEPION

The sanctuary to the god of healing, Asclepius, was built over a 7th-century B.C. shrine to Apollo Maleatas. Historians believe that Asclepius was a Thessalian king blessed with a talent for healing who eventually became deified for his abilities, the myth developing that he was in fact a son of Apollo who was trained in the healing arts by the wise centaur Chyron. Even the oracle of Delphi, when prompted, assured the questioners that Asclepius had come from the town of Epidaurus and that a sanctuary there to him would be most important. By the 5th century B.C. the sanctuary, located near the villages of Ligoúrio and Palaiá Epídavros, drew the infirm from all parts of Greece. Within a century the Asclepion reached its peak. Most of the buildings (in ruins) that can be seen date from this period. Belief in cult practices was diminishing at this time, so the priests were training physicians, called *Asclepiadae,* who could treat patients in a more organized manner. Worshippers would come for a miracle cure, but stay for a longer period to rest, exercise, go to the theater, take mineral baths, and diet—then depart, probably healthier.

ARCHEOLOGICAL MUSEUM & SITE

The **museum** at Epidaurus is more than you could want. Tall Corinthian columns grace a facade trimmed with fragments of ancient sculptural frieze. Inside, bright galleries are lined with statuary and sculpture found at the Asclepion sanctuary. Most of the male figures, many with snakes, represent Asclepius; most of the female figures are of Hygeia, goddess of health. Snakes were symbols of regeneration connected to the underworld and the fertility of the earth.

Crude medical instruments, similar to the drill used by Hippocrates for brain surgery, are displayed in the front room. Many of the ancient cures meted out at the Asclepion were based on natural herbs and flowers, much like herbal medicine today. However, some cures were purely spiritual. A terra-cotta plaque with two ears on it was intended for patients who wanted to ask the god directly for their cure.

The architecture of the site is quite fascinating. Plans and watercolors, coupled with reconstructed facades and pediments, give a vivid picture of the scope of the sanctuary. The **tholos** was an especially noteworthy construction because of its shape, patterned floor, and interior maze design. Notice the beautiful carved lilies and acanthus flowers that bloomed from the coffered ceilings.

The archeological site, which is still undergoing excavation, can be reached by a path behind the museum. The many stones in disarray represent the remains of the **Propylaea,** an Ionic-columned entryway; the **Abaton,** or Dormitory of Incubation, where patients slept so that Asclepios could come to cure them in their dreams; and a temple dedicated to **Artemis,** Asclepius's aunt. Nearby was the two-story **Katagogion,** a full-amenities, 160-room guesthouse! The stadium to the west was the site of the Panhellenic Games, held every four years. The huge temple of Asclepius (380–375 B.C.) was designed by the architect Theodotos, and once held a gold-and-ivory statue of the god seated with his snakes and a dog by his side that has never been recovered.

The archeological museum (closed for repairs at our last visit) and site are open Monday through Friday 8am to 7pm, and Saturday through Sunday 8:30am to 3:15pm. Admission is 1,200 Drs ($5) for adults and half-price for students.

THEATER OF EPIDAURUS

"I never knew the meaning of peace until I arrived at Epidaurus," wrote Henry Miller. Only in 1900 did archeologists (who began working at the site in 1881) uncover the magnificent amphitheater that's come to symbolize the majesty of ancient Epidaurus. Carved into the side of Mt. Kynortio, just east of the Asclepion, it once seated 14,000 healthy and recuperating spectators. Polycleitus the Younger is credited with designing this architectural masterpiece, with its scenic landscaping, excellent acoustics, orchestra (more than 22 yards in diameter), and well-arranged seating; even the poorest spectators enjoyed good sightlines and fine sound. (Strike a match above the stone podium and listen.) The theater's excellent state of preservation when found enabled the Greek government to begin presenting the modern *epidauria* (drama festivals) there in 1954. Classic works by Aeschylus, Sophocles, Euripides, Aristophanes, and others are presented in modern Greek but are staged with an eye to their original production.

4 Mycenae

71 miles SW of Athens; 31 miles S of Corinth.

GETTING THERE • By Bus Take the Athens long-distance buses for either Corinth or Náfplio (see above) and change. There are three buses daily from both towns to Mycenae, a pleasant one-hour ride.

• By Car Take the Corinth-Argos highway south from Corinth for 30 miles, then follow signs east to the site.

Some of you may remember the name Mycenae (Mykíne or *Mykínes* in modern Greek) from school. Several famous plays were written about its king, Agamemnon, and his unhappy family, giving life to such characters as Orestes, Electra, and Iphigenia. On our most recent trip, our excellent guide, Myrto, had everyone inspect the mountain range on the road out of Mycenae. She challenged us to find the silhouette of Agamemnon in the sleeping rocks, a king still humbled by the misery he wreaked on so many lives. Today, Mycenae is visited for its truly magnificent archeological site. There's little happening, but archeology buffs or those stranded by the public bus system enjoy passing a night in the tiny commercial town.

What to See & Do

In 1841 excavations were begun here, but it wasn't until some 33 years later that the German amateur archeologist Heinrich Schliemann took an interest in Mycenae. He unearthed tombs, pieces of palaces, and aqueducts, and other relics that had been mentioned by Homer, thus establishing that Homer's writing was based on fact. The most famous of his finds is the **Acropolis;** its noted **Lions Gate,** on the newer western wall, was the first discovery made. The gate (from 1250 B.C.), once closed by two wooden and bronze doors, is capped by an 18-ton lintel supporting the famous lions, their front paws perched on pedestals. These cats announced to the world that within these walls was the mighty kingdom of Atreus.

On your right as you pass through the Lions Gate is the **Royal Cemetery,** the burial ground of 16th-century B.C. Mycenaean kings. These six "shaft" graves (so named because the kings were buried standing up) held many of the most important ancient Greek artifacts; some of these exquisite gold and silver artifacts—including the famous gold face mask that Schliemann thought was Agamemnon's—can be seen today in the National Archeological Museum in Athens.

At the top of the Acropolis are the few remnants of the **Grand Palace,** which included a throne room, a great court (its foundations still remain), and the megaron, the official reception hall, whose frescoed walls can be reconstructed, from the fragments on display in Athens, by the imaginative visitor. Behind the Acropolis is the rear gate of the fortress. This was Orestes' escape route after he had killed his mother to avenge his father Agamemnon's death by her hand. The Acropolis is two miles away from the national Corinth-Argos road and is open Monday through Friday 8am to 7:30pm, and on Saturday and Sunday until 2:45pm. Admission is 750 Drs ($3.10) for adults, half-price for students.

Keep your ticket from the main site and take yourself over to the **Treasury of Atreus,** known also as the Tomb of Agamemnon. It's a huge, magnificent empty cone with extraordinary acoustical characteristics and is the coolest spot to be found during the hot Mycenaean summer. The dromos (corridor) approach to the tomb is nearly 100 feet long, and the interior of the tholos (a beehive-shaped tomb) was once entirely decorated in bronze. The cavity at the right is believed to have been used to store excess skeletons, since the main chamber was filled steadily over generations. Shepherds often used this tomb as a shelter for their flocks (notice the smoke-blackened ceiling). Several tholos have been excavated in the vicinity of the Mycenae mound, and because of their scale and grandeur, names of the principal members of the House of Atreus (Agamemnon) have been assigned them. All the great funerary objects discovered here come from the circular grave mounds mentioned above.

Where to Stay

For campers, there are two possibilities: Camping Atreus, the first campground as you enter the city (☎ **0751/66-221**), which is 1,100 Drs ($4.60) per person; and Camping Mycenae (☎ **0751/66-247**), opposite the Belle Hélène. This campground has 10 sites for pitching tents and 20 for bus groups for about the same sum. The hotels below are closed from December to March.

Hotel Agamemnon, Odós Tsoúnta 3, Mycenae, Argolis 21200. ☎ **0751/76-222.**
8 rms (all with bath).

Rates (including breakfast): 9,200 Drs ($38.35) single; 10,900 Drs ($45.40) double. AE, DC, EC, MC, V.

This small hotel may well be a bargain in this very heavily touristed area. The modern, grand facade hides ordinary but comfortable rooms, some of which even have air conditioning. Yet inside there's a huge, sunny day-trippers' dining room seating 600! The restaurant has set breakfast and dinner menus for guests.

Dassis Rent Rooms, Mycenae, Árgolis. ☎ **0751/76-123.** Fax 0751/76-124.
10 rms (all with bath).

Rates: 6,000 Drs ($25) single; 9,000 Drs ($37.50) double. AE, DC, EC, MC, V.

Several readers have highly praised this place. Lovely, spacious rooms have pine furniture, big, American-style bathrooms, and balconies with a countryside view. Marion Dassis is Canadian and multilingual; her travel agency next door is a handy information source for travelers.

La Belle Hélène, Mycenae, Árgolis. ☎ **0751/76-225.** 8 rms (none with bath).

Rates (including breakfast): 7,280 Drs ($30.35) double. EC, V.

George Dasis's La Belle Hélène has a welcome sign reading HEINRICH SCHLIEMANNS HAUS, ERBAUT 1862. Even if you're not German or an archeology student (take a look at their guest book, dating from 1878, for the list of luminaries), you'll be interested in this charming inn. Take the plank-wood stairs up to Room 3, where Schliemann himself slept; its windows open out onto a view of one of his greatest accomplishments.

Hotel La Petite Planète, Mycenae, Árgolis. ☎ **0751/76-240.**
30 rms (all with bath). TEL

Rates (including breakfast): 10,350 Drs ($43.15) single; 12,650 Drs ($52.70) double. AE, EC, V.

Run by the ebullient Dimitrios Dasis, this is a bright, sunny, clean, and spacious hotel high enough on a hill to catch the breeze. You'll have a wonderful view from either the front or back rooms. There is also a swimming pool and a bar/restaurant under a shaded verandah. Open only from March to October; in the summer make a written reservation at least one month in advance.

Where to Eat

There are several places to eat, all surprisingly similar and with easy-to-understand names: the **Achilleus, Menelaos,** the **Electra Café,** the **Iphigenia Restaurant.** Our favorite, the Achilleus, is reviewed below. Also on the main road near the archeological site, with inexpensive hostel beds and some rooms to let, are the Electra and Iphigenia. These two, plus the Menelaos, serve pretty decent food but specialize in fixed-price lunches 2,500–3,500 Drs ($10.40–$14.60 per person) aimed at bus tours.

Achilleus Restaurant, Main Street, Mycenae. ☎ **76-027.**

Cuisine: GREEK/CONTINENTAL.
Prices: Appetizers 400–920 Drs ($1.90–$3.85), main courses 920–2,070 Drs ($3.85–$8.60). AE, V.
Open: Daily 11am–10pm.

This friendly place, run by a nice woman who is known as the best cook in town, has the widest range of food. Besides the usual Greek fare, you'll find spaghetti, seafood, veal, and the occasional beef goulash.

5 Argos

8 miles S of Mycenae.

GETTING THERE • **By Bus** Five buses leave daily from the terminal at Odós Kifissoú 100 in Athens; call **51-34-588** for schedule information. 25 local buses leave daily from Náfplion for the 30-minute ride. There are also frequent local buses from Mycenae.

• **By Car** Drive 36 miles southwest of Corinth on the Corinth-Argos highway.

Argos is home of the (surprise!) Argonauts, who actually sailed from Vólos in Central Greece on their quest for the Golden Fleece. According to legend, Argos is the oldest town of the Argolid, dating from prehistoric times. Around the end of the 6th century B.C. the name Argos became synonymous with fine pottery and sculpture, particularly metal and bronze work, at which Hageladas and Polycleitus excelled to such an extent that their names were known throughout the Hellenic world and still survive today.

When you arrive in Argos you'll notice the hills of **Lárissa** and **Aspída.** On top of Lárissa (the higher hill), watching over the strategic plains of the Argolid, sits a Venetian fortress on the site of an original acropolis, to which Byzantine and Turkish fortifications were later added. It remained in such good condition that its use in the 1821 War of Independence turned the tide for the Greeks (who held the Peloponnese against the Turkish onslaught). The low-to-the-ground white houses of the modern town are on the same site as the ancient city. Today the town has about 16,000 inhabitants, a lively public market, and a yearly fair that takes place on October 1.

What to See & Do

At the southeast foot of Lárissa Hill lies the **Amphitheater of Argos.** Even larger (though now less impressive) than the one at Epidaurus, this theater has 81 tiers cut from rock and was designed to seat 20,000. It was remodeled twice, the second time, in the early 4th century B.C., in order to turn the orchestra into a water tank where nautical combat would be performed! To make it watertight, the floor was paved with blue-and-white marble. Excavations continue at the site on the lower levels. You can find it a little over half a mile from the main square on the road to Tripolis; it is open Monday through Saturday 9am to 6pm and 10am to 3pm on Sunday; there is no admission fee.

Next to the theater are the ruins of the **Roman baths,** with a crypt containing three sarcophagi, a frigidarium (the cold-water room), and three pools, dating from the 2d century A.D. The tall red-brick structure in front of the theater is what remains of the **aqueduct** that serviced the city of Argos and fed the baths and swimming pool.

Just off the southwest corner of Argos's main square is the **Archeological Museum** (☎ **28-819**); the big St. Peter's Church there is also worth a visit. As you enter the museum's flower-filled garden, turn left and under the covered colonnade (stoa) you will see superb Roman mosaic floors from private homes, found during various excavations. Inside, glimpse paganism transforming into Christianity through their impressive collection, most of which was found by the French School of Athens. On the first floor there's a suit of bronze armor and helmet (probably from the 8th century B.C.) that the museum is rightly proud of. Downstairs you'll find a terra-cotta female figurine from about 4500 B.C.; there's a gracefully strong Hercules at the top of the stairs. Don't miss the three-foot-tall image of Dionysos and a goat, taken from the theater in Argos. The museum is open Tuesday through Sunday 8am to 3pm; the admission fee is 500 Drs ($2.10), half-price for students.

Where to Stay & Eat

If you decide to stay overnight, there are some small hotels in town, several acceptable Greek tavernas, and a few lively cafés on the Argos main square. The **Mycenae Hotel,** Platía Aghíou Pétrou (St. Peter's Square) 10, Argos 21200 (☎ **0751/28-569**), has 27 rooms with private facilities on the west side of the square. It's older, but recently renovated. The **Theoxenía,** Odós Tsokrí 31, Argos 21200 (☎ **0751/27-370**) has 18 bathless, simple but homey rooms. It's just 327 yards west of the square and quiet. Bed and breakfast singles run 9,250 Drs ($38.55) and doubles run 12,250 Drs ($51.05) at the Mycenae Hotel; rates without bath or breakfast are half that price at the Theoxenia.

An Excursion to Tiryns

Seven and a half miles from Argos, reached by a road with mountains on one side and sea on the other, are the ruins of the Mycenaean acropolis of **Tiryns,** with its walls of Cyclopean masonry (so called because the ancients believed Cyclops himself built them to protect Proteus, the king of Tiryns). Tiryns was fortified back in the 13th century B.C., at least two generations before Mycenae. This royal vacation palace by the sea is a great treat for the modern visitor, with its upper level, or palace site, surrounded by huge, handmade walls. Although the chariot-width entrance is identical to the one at Mycenae, these ruins are in much better shape. Excavation at the lower level is slowly uncovering the foundations of several dwellings, among them the Lower Castles. These were rebuilt after a 13th-century B.C. earthquake and survived well into the Mycenaean age. The site is open Monday through Friday from 8am to 5pm and 8:30am to 3pm on Saturday and Sunday; admission is 500 Drs ($2.10), half price for students.

Central Peloponnese (Arcadia)

The central Peloponnese, an immensely mountainous region of great beauty, remains as it must have been thousands of years ago. Its inhabitants were thought by Herodotus to be the oldest residents of the Peloponnese. The original Arcadians consisted of several different tribes, who united for the first time when they fought in the Trojan War. Arcadian independence began on September 23, 1821, with the capture of Tripolis,

READERS RECOMMEND

Arcadian train trip. *Rail enthusiasts might be interested in a trip through the central Peloponnese from Argos to Kalamáta. The trip takes about four hours. The ride through central Arcadia is spectacular, over precipices and deep gorges, with hairpin curves. The scenery is magnificent. Get a first-class ticket to ensure a seat. There are only snacks on these trains, so it would be wise to bring a loaf and a bottle.*—Helen and Stuart Landry, Endwell, N.Y.

today the capital of the central Peloponnese. Tripolis itself was leveled in 1825 and then completely rebuilt.

Several small towns circle Tripolis: Nestani and Mantinea are north of the capital, and both have interesting ruins and monasteries. Farther north is Levidio, with its temple to Artemis Hymnia. To the southwest is Vytina, a popular Greek winter ski resort. Megalopolis lies 34 miles southwest from Tripolis, surrounded by mountains and remnants of its rich past. Nearby is the temple of Apollo at Vassae (which you will see spelled as "Bassae"). This temple is so extraordinary that we urge you to see it; even if the thought of another ruin makes you wince, let the magic of this Doric masterpiece fill your senses.

All the towns are served well by public transport, but traveling is slow. Drivers making an arc through the northern Peloponnese can cut across and see these sites between Náfplio and Olympia. The landscape changes steadily, from the low, dry hills of the Argolid to the often snow-capped peaks of the Taigetos and Parnon mountains that surround Sparta.

6 Trípolis

120 miles SW of Athens; 37 miles SE of Argos.

GETTING THERE • By Train Several trains a day leave from Athens's Peloponnísou Station. Call **51-31-601** for information.

• By Bus Eleven buses a day leave from Athens's Odós Kifissoú 100 terminal. Frequent local buses run from Náfplio (about 1½ hours) or Argos (2 hours).

• By Car Take the Athens-Corinth highway west, then the Corinth-Argos highway south to the Tripolis highway, then west to Tripolis.

ESSENTIALS The local **tourist police** (☎ **071/223-030**) are at Odós Spetseropoúlou 20, at the northeast corner of Ághios Vassílios Square.

Tripolis is the capital of Arcadia, its chief industrial city, and a transportation hub for the Peloponnese. After the Turks destroyed it, Tripolis was rebuilt along more modern lines, so the streets are unusually wide and regular, and there are public parks and gardens. An altitude of 2,160 feet makes it particularly cool for the region, and a pleasant respite if you're between buses.

What to See & Do

If you have some time, take a stroll around the town. Readers have written us about their visit here: "There are some beautiful public parks and gardens full of shady trees and roses, and grand cafés, where you can while away a few hours." The central *platía,* **Ághios Vassílios** or St. Basil's Square, can be reached from the bus station (located at Kolokotrónis Square) by walking west along Gheorghíou Street. The exterior of **St. Basil's Church** is currently being restored, but inside it's a real beauty—cool, dark, and mysterious with three chandeliers for soft illumination. A right turn up Konstantínou Street will take you past the **Tripolis Theater** to the edge of the attractive city park. Or, you can walk a few blocks from the bus station to the **Archeology Museum** on Spiliopoúlou Street. It has a wide range of artifacts, with good marbles, bronze vessels and implements, coins, even glassware, from the Neolithic to 3d century A.D. Items are particularly well labeled in English with maps and color photographs of sites. The museum is open Tuesday through Sunday from 8:30am to 3pm; admission is 500 Drs ($2.00), half price for students.

Where to Stay

Galaxy Hotel, Ághios Vassílios Square, Tripolis, Peloponnese. ☎ **071/225-195.**
80 rms (all with bath). TEL

Rates: 6,380 Drs ($26.60) single; 8,610 Drs ($35.85) double. No credit cards.

This Class-C establishment has spacious clean rooms, piped-in Muzak, and small balconies overlooking St. Basil's Church. Even the single rooms have double beds, making the Galaxy a better bet than you'd think if you judged it by its small, spare lobby.

Arcadia Hotel, Kolokotrónis Square, Tripolis, Peloponnese. ☎ **071/22-55-51.**
45 rms (all with bath). TEL

Rates (including breakfast): 8,970 Drs ($37.35) single; 11,500 Drs ($47.90) double. No credit cards.

This place is not only convenient, it's choice. Rooms are freshly wall-papered, light and cheerful, with pleasant, light furniture and carpeting. Bathrooms are large and clean, with shower curtains!

Where to Eat

Park Chalet Cafe, Áreos Square. No phone.

Cuisine: CONTINENTAL.

Prices: Appetizers 250–500 Drs ($1.05–$2.10), main courses 850–2,200 Drs ($3.55–$9.15). V.

Open: Daily 8am–1am.

This café at Konstantínou and Dimitrakopoúlou Streets would be a treat even if the food and service weren't so superb. Their menu has a surprising range and depth, from fine pastas to filet mignon. The Park Chalet cake is a dessert-lover's dream, and their are five kinds of coffee to wash it down with.

Taverna Konati, Odós Petropoúlou 3. No phone.

Cuisine: GREEK.

Prices: Appetizers 220–480 Drs (90¢–$2), main courses 680–1,600 Drs ($2.85–$6.65). No credit cards.

Open: Daily 6pm–midnight.

This distinguished taverna, off the eastern corner of Ághios Vassílios Square, is considered the best and most traditional; meats, liver, sausage, and wild game are featured in their glass case. Pick your supper (little English is spoken) and lounge over a drink while it's prepared fresh. At our visit, the party of young cyclists in town for a rally stood and cheered the chef after their meal.

7 Megalópolis

21 miles SW of Tripolis

GETTING THERE Several local buses run daily from Tripolis, Sparta, or Kalamáta.

Megalopolis today is a large, modern town that stands near the remains of the ancient town of the same name. The 4th-century B.C. ruins of Megalopolis are in such a picturesque setting that they're well worth the minor detour if you're en route from Tripolis, Sparta, or Kalamáta to Olympia.

An optimistic Epaminondas (famed for his leadership of Thebes) founded Megalopolis ("large city") as a planned Utopian community during the years 371–368 B.C. Hoping to create cities (including Messene and Mantinaea) to contain the aggressive Spartans, he convinced 40 smaller cities to unite into one huge capital. Villagers from all parts of Arcadia emigrated to Megalopolis. Unfortunately, dissension among the relocated inhabitants and the city's forced entry into a coalition against Sparta brought about a very swift decline. Though the town was rebuilt several times, by the time it was visited by Pausanias in the 2d century A.D. it lay in ruins.

What to See & Do

ARCHEOLOGICAL SITE

The **amphitheater** (☎ **23-275**) of Megalopolis was the largest in all of Greece, seating nearly 20,000 people. There was a water channel that encircled the stage to allow for enhanced acoustics, so the actors' voices could be heard in the last row! These same rows are now filled with evergreens, which make the bleachers a great spot for a picnic lunch.

Behind the stage, to the north of the site, are the column remains of the **Thersilion,** a congress hall that seated 6,000 and had standing room for an additional 10,000 people. It was built to ensure that the Arcadian Confederacy had a meeting place, and if you've ever been involved with "government by committee," you can understand why Megalopolis wasn't around for long. North across the river, shamefully neglected and barely accessible, are the ancient **agora** and a **temple of Zeus.**

The site, found about a mile north of the modern city on the Andritsena road, is open daily from 9am to 3:30pm. There is no admission fee.

Where to Stay & Eat

If you want to stay over in Megalopolis there are two hotels, both located just off the main square. The **Achillion Hotel** (☎ **0791/22-311**), is west of the square at Odós Papaioánnou 67, Megalopolis, and has 28 clean and comfortable rooms with phone and private shower. Every Friday, there is a great produce market out front! Rates, including breakfast, are 5,175 Drs ($21.55) for a single, 8,000 Drs ($33.35) for a double, and AE, EC, MC, and V are accepted. The simpler, but certainly clean and acceptable, **Pan Hotel** (☎ **0791/22-270**) is east of the square at Odós Papanastassíou 7. They charge about 20% less for 15 bathless rooms.

There are several acceptable restaurants around the main square, and prices are reasonable. The **Deli Jiannis Christos** at Odós Papanastassíou 10 serves moist, light, and flaky pastry and delicious *spanakópita.* Just northwest off the square is **Super Market,** a real-life American-style food shop with myriad picnic supplies.

En Route from Megalopolis to Andrítsena

On the road from Megalopolis to Andritsena there is a fork on the right that leads to Karítena; take it. **Karítena** is a picture-perfect medieval town perched on the slopes of adjoining hills. From the town there's a wonderful view of the Alfios River as it winds through the Likeo Valley below. The bus to Andrítsena stops in Karítena, turns around and goes back downhill. If you've been riding too long, get off at the fork, where there's an ouzerí, and wait the 15 minutes for the bus to return, after which you continue on to Andrítsena.

8 Andrítsena & Vassae

Andrítsena

This is a lovely mountain village with hillside homes, foliage, and an old church, all of which make it a worthy stop on the way to Vassae. The best thing is the air; in the deep summer it's crisp and light, in winter invigorating. If you've ever been to India, summer here will remind you of the imperial retreats to which the British escaped during the summer months, only less luxurious.

Where to Stay & Eat

If you want to stop in Andrítsena for the night (and bus riders may have to), there are two places we can recommend, both open from April to November if the season has been busy. The **Hotel Pan** (☎ **0626/22-213**), at the north end of town has seven small and neat guest rooms (five with shower). Their small marble staircase is lined with voracious plants. Rates are 4,600 Drs ($19.15) for a single, 3,680 Drs ($15.35) for a double. The **Theoxenia Hotel** (☎ **0626/22-219**, fax 0626/22-235), at the south end of town, is somewhat bigger with 45 rooms, and also more expensive. The rooms (all with shower and private phone) are clean and spacious, and have a great view of the mountains. The hotel's public spaces feature a weird collection of needlepoint, including Greek, European, and Walt Disney pieces! Rates, including breakfast, are 5,865 Drs ($24.45) for one, 7,820 Drs ($32.60) for two. Neither hotel accepts credit cards.

The Theoxenia has its own restaurant with pretty good food, including some quasicontinental choices. The best café in town, which doubles as the bus station, is across the street from the Hotel Pan.

Vassae

Vassae (Bassae), or more commonly Vassés, is located 14 miles outside of Andrítsena, at the end of a winding, mountainous, and dusty road that offers a fine view of the village and the Alpheus Valley. At the top is one of mankind's greatest works of art, the temple of Vassai (also called the temple of Apollo Epicurion).

Set on a rocky plateau nestled in the highlands (and oaks) of Arcadia, this inspiring temple stands alone, aware of its own grace and majesty. This isolation served well the Phygalians, who hid in the hills around Vassai during their retreat from the Spartan army. They erected the temple to thank their god for saving them from a plague that descended during the Peloponnesian War.

The Vassai temple was built by the famed architect Ictinus. Unlike his more famous Parthenon, Vassai is made of limestone hewn from the huge deposits in the area. It is much studied because it encompasses the three great Greek architectural traditions: Doric, Ionic, and Corinthian. Ictinus's genius was in integrating these three differing styles into one cohesive whole; fortunately, it remains one of the best preserved temples in Greece. Unfortunately, you will have to go to London to see the exquisite frieze that once adorned it, for, like its more renowned Athenian cousin, the sculptures are on display at the British Museum.

Because of its location the temple is not a common stop for tourists, but those who go will be well rewarded. You'll have to take private transport as there's no public transportation; a taxi from Andritsena costs about 3,200 Drs ($13.50) per person and includes one hour waiting time.

9 Sparta

153 miles SW of Athens; 36 miles S of Tripolis.

GETTING THERE • **By Bus** Seven buses a day leave from Athens's terminal at Odós Kifissoú 100; call **01/51-24-913** for schedule information.

• **By Car** It is a 2½ hour trip along mountain roads south from Tripolis.

ESSENTIALS **Tourist information** (☎ **0731/24-852,** fax 0731/26-772) can be found at Town Hall, Lykoúrgou Street, central square. The local **tourist police** (☎ **26-229**) are at Odós Hilonos 8, just east of the main square.

Ancient Sparta was a mélange of five communities within four villages built on six hills under one set of laws. This curious experiment was launched in the 9th century B.C., when a race of Dorians invaded the Laconian plain and subsequently settled there to mix with the locals. These four villages were brought together by a man who is both a historical and a legendary figure, the legislator Lykourgos, who set down the laws and principles of this new state, Sparta. He felt that three classes of inhabitants, two kings, and one senate were needed to ensure stability. The constitution he drafted was so strong that this new state remained intact for centuries.

After the Persian war Sparta became increasingly jealous of Athens's influence. This led to the bloodbath known as the Peloponnesian War, which lasted nearly 30 years. Sparta emerged the victor, but her dominance in Hellenic affairs was diminished by the toll the fighting had taken, and the decline continued. From the 6th century B.C. on, austerity was Sparta's modus operandi, and since this applied to architecture and the arts as well as to daily life, even its ruins are disappointing. So ended an experiment in urban development that left its mark on history.

What to See & Do

Modern Sparta (Spárti) is a prosperous town with much construction and lively, gregarious people. You can join these less austere Spartans at the bustling produce market in the Kleomvrotoa pedestrian mall (Wednesday or Saturday mornings), or in their nightly *volta* around the main square.

Just about two blocks east of the central square, on Dionysos Dafnou Street, is the **Museum of Sparta** (☎ **28-575**). It houses a small but interesting collection of marbles (including the famous *Spartan Soldier* thought to be Leonidas), friezes, mosaics, pottery, and even jewelry ranging from the 6th century B.C. to the 2d century A.D. These items, all from local excavation sites, offer much insight into the character of ancient Sparta. There's also a fragrant, charming garden in the front laden with shaded benches for contemplation of the statuary that surrounds you. The museum is open Tuesday through Sunday from 8:30am to 3pm; admission is 500 Drs ($2.10).

At the north end of the city (about a ten-minute walk from the Hotel Apollon) is the site of **Ancient Sparta.** To visit this site, leave town by the Tripolis road until you reach Leonidas Street; turn left, and about 300 yards farther down the road you'll see the "tomb" of Leonidas. Up a dusty road and through a grove of olive trees you'll find five column bases, some old stones, the echo of a theater, and a very nice vista of the city. Beyond are the ruins of two Byzantine churches and a Roman portico. Little remains of such a great power except the legendary dedication of its men, who left their homes when they were seven years old to live by the river, read Homer, and harden themselves to become warriors.

Where to Stay

Hotel Cecil, Odós Paleológou 125, Sparta, 23100 Laconia. ☎ **0731/24-980.**
13 rms (3 with bath). TEL

Rates: 4,000 Drs ($16.75) single; 5,675 Drs ($23.65) double without bath; 6,325 Drs ($26.35) double with shower. No credit cards.

Mr. Tzanetakis is your host, and he presides over a Class D establishment close to the central square. It tends to be a little noisy, but is otherwise attractive, with clean baths and showers on each floor.

Hotel Maniatis, Odós Paleológou 72, Sparta, 23100 Laconia. ☎ **0731/22-665.**
Fax 0731/29-994. 80 rms (all with bath). A/C TEL

Rates: 8,625 Drs ($35.95) single; 10,900 Drs ($45.40) double. EC, MC, V.

This is our favorite hotel in the center of town. The Maniatis is popular with groups since it has so many clean, air-conditioned rooms. It also has a large, comfortable TV lounge and restaurant. Its moderate prices also help to make it a popular Class-C spot for singles, too.

Where to Eat

Dias Restaurant, Odós Paleológou 72. ☎ **22-665.**

Cuisine: GREEK/CONTINENTAL.
Prices: Appetizers 500–1,050 Drs ($2–$4.40); main courses 650–2,000 Drs ($2.65–$9.15). EC, MC, V.
Open: Daily 12:30–4pm, 7pm–midnight.

Next door to the Maniatis Hotel, this smart new art deco restaurant is appealingly decorated in various pastels. The food is up-to-date, quite good, and reasonably priced.

Diethnes Taverna, Odós Paleológou 105. ☎ **28-636.**

Cuisine: INTERNATIONAL.
Prices: Appetizers 600–1,050 Drs ($2.50–$4.40), main courses 1,100–1,600 Drs ($4.60–$6.70). V.
Open: Daily 8am–midnight.

At this popular old restaurant, near the central square, you can choose your food cafeteria-style from a wide selection (the name "*diethnes*" actually means international and the range reflects it). The friendly staff will seat you under the colorful streetside awning, or under fragrant lemon and orange trees out back in the lovely garden.

Elysse, Odós Paleológou 113. ☎ **29-896.**

Cuisine: CONTINENTAL.
Prices: Appetizers 460–1,050 Drs ($1.90–$4.35), main courses 980–1,400 Drs ($4.10–$5.85). V.
Open: Daily 11am–1am.

This place looks as French as its name, but in fact owners Stavros and Katarina spent 20 years in Canada and welcome their diners in fluent English. The large and eclectic menu features charcoal-broiled chicken and meats, and chicken Bardouniotiko, a Spartan specialty sautéed with onions and tomatoes, topped with feta cheese. Elysse also features daily specials made with seasonal produce.

10 Mistrá

2.7 miles W of Sparta.

GETTING THERE • By Bus The easiest way to Mistrá is via Sparta; the bus leaves from the corner of Leonídou and Lykoúrgou, three blocks west of the central square, every 1½ hours. From Mistrá's Xenia Restaurant stop it's a hearty uphill walk.

• By Car Drivers leaving Sparta should follow the signs west off Paleológou along Lykoúrgou Street, and up toward the Taygetos mountains.

ESSENTIALS The town of Mistrá (Mystrá) itself, about 1½ miles below the ancient city, exists (like many others) solely to service the vast hordes of tourists that pass through, but there is one hotel. The **Byzantion** (**☎ 0731/93-309**), Mistrá, Sparti 23100, Laconia, is a Class-B hotel with 22 plain, clean rooms, all with bath; bed and breakfast singles cost 7,130 Drs ($29.70); doubles 10,900 Drs ($45.40). AE, EC, MC are accepted. There's an excellent new campground within a 15-minute walk of the monastery called **Castle View Camping** (**☎ 0731/93-303,** fax 20-028), run by a Greek-American couple. The grounds include hot showers, snack bar, mini-market, information center, and a sparkling swimming pool. Rates start at 1,300 Drs ($5.40) per adult; open April through October.

Diners might try the **Taverna To Kastro** (**☎ 93-526**) across from the hotel, a good choice at dinnertime. Just below the site and in a gorgeous setting is **Restaurant Marmara,** one of the better cafés in the area for lunch. Hostess Ann grew up in New Jersey and prepares fine Greek cuisine. Note the mineral springs behind the restaurant, which fed the marble bath that Emperor Constantine used to bathe in!

The Byzantine ghost town that lies in the foothills of Mt. Taygetos is populated today by birds, wildflowers, and rabbits. Mistrá was a site of great learning, a Byzantine retreat where Theophilus tried to reconcile the precepts of ancient Greek philosophy with the new religion of Christianity.

What to See & Do

If you visit Mistrá in spring you'll see the wildflower population running wild on the hills and in the cracks of the ruins. An equally colorful variety of birds and insects have also made Mistrá their home. Hike up the worn stairs and crisscross the paths of this solitary spot, hearing the donkeys' bells and studying the abstract shapes of the ruined buildings as you ascend. Then rest in the shade of a tree (older than most countries) and you will be transported to a world, ascetic and removed, where you can coexist with the spirits of those monks who inhabited this place 500 years ago.

The spirit of old Mistrá is reflected in her beautiful churches, which include **Peribleptos,** with its wall paintings; the **Evangelistria,** which boasts sculptured decor; the **Monastery of Pantanassa** and its frescoes; and **St. Demetrios Church,** in the lower city, whose architecture, paintings, and mosaics are expert examples of Byzantine art.

At the summit is **St. George's Church,** which is in the best condition and whose assorted emblems testify to the Franks influence. The double-headed eagle marks the exact spot where the last Byzantine emperor was crowned in Mistrá's long-ago heyday. Admission to this church is 1,250 Drs ($5.20), half-price for students, and free Sunday and holidays. It is open daily from 8:30am to 3pm. Wear suitable clothing (no shorts or halter tops, and so on); cloth aprons or shawls may be provided by the nuns who live in the convent.

SOUTHERN PELOPONNESE

Most tourists concentrate their travels on the Peloponnese in the more historic north. However, for those in search of striking scenery, out-of-the-way places, and some interesting sites, the south has much to offer.

11 Monemvassía

210 miles SW of Athens; 57 miles SE of Sparta.

GETTING THERE • By Bus Seven buses leave daily from the Athens terminal at Odós Kifissoú 100 to Sparta (6-hour trip), then change for the bus to Monemvassía; or take the morning bus that goes directly to Monemvassía (8-hour trip) Call **51-24-913** for schedule information.

• By Boat The car-ferry to Kýthira from Piraeus makes calls at Monemvassía two times weekly; check with the Port Authority in Piraeus (☎ **45-11-311**).

• By Hydrofoil You can catch a hydrofoil twice daily from Zéa Marina in Piraeus, to whisk you to Monemvassía. The **Ceres Flying Dolphin** (☎ **61-219** or **32-42-281** in Athens) saves you almost three hours over the ferry's travel time.

ESSENTIALS Most tourist services and the local police are in the mainland village of Monemvassía, near the causeway/bridge crossing to the island rock ("Monemvassía Castle").

The most helpful and knowledgeable person around is Peter Derzotis at **Malvasia Travel** (☎ **0732/61-432,** fax 61/432), at the bus station, who sells ferry tickets and arranges accommodations, car, and motorbike rentals.

Go two miles out of the port town of Monemvassía, over a narrow stone causeway to the "Gibraltar of Greece," and you'll find the real Monemvassía, one of the most beautiful spots on the Peloponnesian coast. It's a 13th-century Byzantine village, more complete than Mistrá architecturally, yet more overrun by flowers too. Tucked away on the south face of a hill, shadowed by an imposing fort, is a tiny bit of Paradise.

When you enter the vaulted gates to this walled community, you'll be delighted by the charm and tender beauty of the vehicle-free village. Hordes of day-trippers mob the few cafés and souvenir shops nestled in grottoes of the original Byzantine dwellings, but at dusk peace returns. On top of the hillside is the 13th-century **Aghía Sofía,** similar in style to the Byzantine church at Dafní. The crystal-clear, inviting Aegean below you can be reached by the paths that corkscrew down the hill.

Where to Stay

There's one special hotel within the island castle; other mainland listings are for the convenience of those who must overnight here.

Aktaion Hotel, Monemvassía 23070, Peloponnese. ☎ **0732/61-234.**
18 rms (all with bath). TEL

Rates (including breakfast): 5,175 Drs ($21.55) single, 7,475 Drs ($31.15) double. No credit cards.

The Aktaion is located near the village's waterfront and is housed on the second floor of a popular restaurant. Many of the simple rooms have balconies from which you can see a yacht basin and the headland rock. It's the best value on the mainland.

Glyfada Apartments, Monemvassía 23070. ☎ **0732/61-445.** Fax 0732/61-432. 9 apts (all with bath). TEL

Rates: 5,750 Drs ($23.95) single; 9,200 Drs ($38.35). V

These apartments are a bargain. A ten-minute walk from the town in a quiet neighborhood, they are comfortable and well furnished; each one has a balcony. There's a small beach in front of the hotel. Next door, Pericles Labrakis, who spent many years in the States, has the inexpensive **Glyfada Taverna.** His wife, Evangela, is a renowned cook in the area.

★ **Hotel Malvasia,** Castle of Monemvassía, 23070 Peloponnese. ☎ **0732/61-113.** Fax 0732/61-722. 28 rms (all with bath).

Rates: 7,475 Drs ($31.15) Drs ($49.30) single; 10,350 Drs ($43.15) double; 17,250–51,570 Drs ($71.85–$215.65) suite. EC, MC, V.

One of the greatest assets on this mesmerizing rock is the Hotel Malvasia, which occupies three separate restored locations in the old castle. Some have handcrafted suites complete with living rooms decorated in woven flokotis, kitchenettes, solid-marble bathrooms, and beautiful bedrooms. To find it, leave your vehicle outside the castle gate, and, wearing sturdy shoes, proceed to the reception area to the left of the entrance. It's a marvelous vacation resort, a romantic port, or an idyllic retreat for the weary traveler, especially after most tourists depart at day's end.

Minoa, Odós Spártis 14, Monemvassía 23070, Peloponnese. ☎ **0732/61-209.** Fax 0732/61-040. 25 rms (all with bath). TEL

Rates: 7,475 Drs ($31.15) single; 12,420 Drs ($43) double. V.

The Minoa is situated a stone's throw from the harbor, with well-kept rooms that all have balconies. The lobby has beautiful floors of colorful inlaid stone and adjoins a good pâtisserie and café.

Where to Eat

There are some good places to eat in the mainland village, and several pricier snack cafés on the island rock. Most open only for the April–October tourist season.

Restaurant Kypros, Monemvassía village. ☎ **61-477.**

Cuisine: GREEK.

Prices: Appetizers 500–920 Drs ($2.10–$3.85), main courses 1,050–1,725 Drs ($4.35–$7.20). AE, EC, MC, V.

Open: Daily noon–4pm; 6pm–12:30am.

This is another nice place, located two blocks south of the main street on the waterfront. Fortunately, it's far enough removed from the causeway scene to avoid the musical din that has engulfed other eateries. The fresh fish is simply prepared from the day's catch, but we preferred their moist grilled chicken served with French fries. The grilled lamb is also very good.

To Canoni, Castle of Monemvassía. ☎ **61-387.**

Cuisine: GREEK/CONTINENTAL.
Prices: Breakfast 460–1,050 Drs ($1.90–$4.35); appetizers 600–1,400 Drs ($2.50–$5.85); main courses 1,400–1,800 Drs ($5.85–$7.50). AE, DC, EC, MC, V.
Open: Daily 8am–midnight.

Adonis Yovannis is the owner of this pleasant taverna, a few doors down from the Hotel Malvasia. You can dine inside, which is decorated with red-and-white checked tablecloths and crocheted lace curtains, or outside on one of three patios. Delicious food and classical music will soothe the weary traveler.

12 Kýthira

108 nautical miles S of Piraeus.

GETTING THERE • By Air There are two flights daily from Athens.

• By Ferry Miras Ferries (☎ **41-27-225** in Piraeus, 33-490 in Kýthira) has two boats daily from Neápolis and one from Gíthio.

• By Hydrofoil Ceres Flying Dolphins (☎ **45-47-107** in Piraeus) has service five times weekly from Zéa Marina.

ESSENTIALS Conomos Travel, run by the knowledgeable Lia Megalokonomos, books accommodations and sells ferry and Olympic airline tickets. The **police** are in Chóra (☎ **31-206**) and Potamós (☎ **33-225**); the **harbor police** are in Aghía Pelaghiá (☎ **33-280**). There's a **medical center** (☎ **33-203**) and a post office in Potamós. The National Bank of Greece has branches in Chóra and Potamós.

GETTING AROUND There is one bus daily in summer from Aghía Pelaghía to Chóra via local stops; the fare is 400 Drs ($1.65). Motorbike and car rentals are available.

Hesiod, in *Theogonia,* says that Aphrodite was born in the sea foam off Kýthira, and she is revered by the Kythirians.

It is believed that the Minoans had a trading post on Kýthira, off the Peloponnese's southernmost coast, as early as 2000 B.C. Over the centuries the island followed closely the development of the peninsula, with the Achaeans, Dorians, and Argives all in their turn taking over and settling in before being displaced by someone else. During the Peloponnesian War it was held by Athens and used as a base from which the Athenians could raid the Laconian Plain. They located themselves at the ancient capital (Kýthira), which occupied the southern hill of the island on top of which was a fortified acropolis.

Today, the capital city is Chóra, an ingratiating village, with cobbled lanes and crooked streets, that faces south toward the Cretan Sea and has, like Mistrá, many Byzantine churches. Chóra's neighbor to the south is the active port of Kapsáli, which contains the relics of an ancient Venetian fort perched 900 feet overhead on a hill.

Kýthira, because of its unspoiled beauty, is home to many villa-owning Greeks and an extensive community of friendly Greek-Australians. It is renowned for its honey, olive and almond groves, the bright yellow semperviva that grows in abundance, and the hospitality of its residents. It's worth a visit for its natural beauty, unchanged small villages, and general lack of tourists.

The comfortable **Hotel Kytheria** in Aghiá Pelaghía (☎ **0735/33-321,** fax 33-825) has 10 rooms, all with bath, for 5,750 Drs ($23.95) a single and 9,775 ($40.70) a double. It's presided over by Frieda Megalokonomos, a genial Australian Greek, and is a stone's throw from the town beach.

There are two tavernas and an ouzerí on the "strip." We recommend the **Faros,** next door to the hotel, where main courses run about 1,000–2,000 Drs ($4.15–$8.35).

Seven kilometers north of Aghía Pelagía is the sandy stretch of Platiá Ámmos, with a taverna open in summer. To the south along a paved five-kilometer road are three good beaches: Firi Ammos, Kalamátis and Kako Lagádi, where there is a lake and a gorge. From Potámos, the central market town, you can visit Diafkóti beach and the church of Ághios Gíorgos, noted for its mosaics. Continue south to reach Ághios Nikólaos Bay, where there are three beaches: Asprogas, Kastraki (with the remains of a Minoan settlement nearby) and Avlémenos, where there is a campsite and Sotiros Taverna.

The west side of the island is accessible only by boat—except for Milopótomos, site of a ravine and waterfall, and the Cave of St. Sofia, half a kilometer west. Farther south is Myrtidia and the Church of Our Lady of the Myrtle, patron saint of the island, whose festival is held on the 15th of August.

If you're an islandaholic there's Antikýthira, a smaller island just off the coast that's quite the place for explorers. Art buffs may enjoy scuba-diving off its coast, where in 1900 divers found a wrecked ship full of sculptures in marble and bronze and fragments of superb relief work. In 1802 nearly 20 crates filled with the Parthenon's sculptural frieze (on their way to London under the aegis of the notorious Lord Elgin) "fell" off their freighter and into the deep seas (the Kýthira Triangle?) off Kýthira.

MÁNI

There are three peninsulas on the southern tip of the Peloponnese. The middle one is referred to as Máni, but its history and people have also influenced the western peninsula.

13 Gíthio

186 miles SW of Athens; 27 miles S of Sparta.

GETTING THERE • By Bus Four buses leave daily from Athens's Odós Kifissoú 100 terminal; call **51-24-913** for information. Local buses leave every hour for Sparta (to connect to other Peloponnese destinations).

• By Boat Two car-ferries leave weekly to and from Kissamos (Kastelli), Crete, or the island of Kýthira. Call **0733/22-207** for information.

• By Car From Monemvassía, follow the scenic coast road 42 mi west around the Gulf of Laconia, or head due south from Sparta on the faster highway.

ESSENTIALS Perivoláki (Public Garden) Square is the heart of Gíthio; the bus station is across from it on the north side. As you face the square from the water, walk up the first street on your left (Vassiléos Pavlou Street) and you'll find most hotels and tavernas. The **police station** is at Odós Vass. Pavlou 21 near the harbor (☎ **22-271**). Ferry tickets to Monemvassía, Kýthira, Crete, Piraeus, and so forth can be bought at the **Rozákis Agency,** Odós Vassiléos Pávlou 5 (☎ **0733/22-455**); boat schedules are posted daily on the front door.

Gíthio (Gythio) is a small coastal town on the Gulf of Laconia that was known as Cranae in antiquity, the port of Sparta. This was the first refuge of the lovers Paris and Helen when they eloped over the Taygetos mountains from her home in Sparta and set off by ship to Troy. Today, Gíthio is the capital of the Máni, the isolated southern fringe of the Peloponnese named after Maina Castle, built by William de Villehardouin in the 13th century, the same gentleman who gave us the castles at Monemvassía and Mistrá.

Gíthio is noteworthy only as a driving point between Sparta and Monemvassía or Areópolis. Tall old houses along the seafront overlook a lighthouse on the tiny island of Marathoníssi, now connected by a roadway to the mainland. Several faded tavernas, rooms to let, and tourist-worn shops line the seafront to Perivoláki Square, all catering to those who await the twice-weekly ferries to Kýthira or Crete. However, Gíthio is the octopus capital of Greece, and most seaside cafés serve this tasty denizen of the Gulf. By all means, try it!

Where to Stay & Eat

Hotel Kranai, Odós Vassiléos Pávlou 17, Gíthio, Peloponnese. ☎ **0733/24-394.** 22 rms (all with bath). A/C TEL

Rates: 6,325 Drs ($26.35) single; 7,475 Drs ($31) double. EC.

This is an older hotel, but it's very well kept and has surprisingly modern amenities. The high-ceilinged rooms have clean tile floors; many have balconies overlooking the harbor. Nick, the friendly manager, speaks good English and is a willing source of local information and sightseeing advice.

Hotel Pantheon, Odós Vassiléos Pávlou 31, Gíthio, Peloponnese. ☎ **0733/22-289.** Fax 0733/22-284. 57 rms (all with bath). TEL

Rates (including breakfast): 10,350 Drs ($43) single; 14,200 Drs ($59.15) double. AE, DC, V.

The hotel has a distinctly 1960s look, with a spacious modern lobby and attractive carpeted rooms. Many have balconies jutting over the boardwalk; it is peaceful in the low season, potentially noisy in the summer. The place to be if you want to be in the center of things.

Pension Kondoyiannis, Odós Vassiléos Pávlou 19, Gíthio, Peloponnese. ☎ **0733/22-518.** 7 rms (none with bath).

Rates: 5,175 Drs ($21.55) single/double. No credit cards.

Matina Kondoyiannis makes you feel at home, on the second floor above her own cozy home, right up the stone stairs (first door on left) next to the town police station. The rooms are homely but clean, and for 500 Drs ($2) more, guests can make use of a kitchen. This pension is open year round; and Mrs. Kondoyiánnis is a patient and attentive hostess (though not fluent in English).

We didn't think much of the portside cafés within the village, at least not for a full meal, but don't overlook the traditional ouzerís where grilled octopus is a specialty. For better meals, follow the Skála highway (the route heading to Monemvassía) out just past Perivoláki Square to our pick, **O Kóstas Taverna,** on the left just past the medical office, which offers classic Greek food, well prepared and reasonably priced.

Kostas Vrettos has a treasure chest of an antique shop, **Paliazures,** next to the Pantheon Hotel, with all sorts of "old things"—pots, furniture, lamps, paintings, pottery, guns, farm implements, and coins—all legally exportable.

14 Areópolis

16 miles SW of Gíthio; 49 miles SE of Kalamáta.

GETTING THERE • By Bus Ten buses leave Athens for Kalamáta from the terminal at Odós Kifissoú 21; call **51-24-913** for schedules. There are several local buses daily from either Kalamáta or Gíthio.

• By Car The highway west from Sparta to Kalamáta, then the coast road from Kalamáta south to Areópolis, is the quickest route there.

ESSENTIALS You'll find the local Greek Tourist Organization (**EOT**) office (☎ **51-239**), the **police station** (☎ **51-209**), and the Gíthio bus station all on the main square.

The first village of the traditional Máni lands is Areopolis, known in the old days as Tsimova. The enclosed courtyards, small cobbled lanes, and housing give the impression that Areopolis was probably at one time a heavily fortressed place in which to live.

What to See & Do

The best thing to do (easily accomplished for those with a car) is to visit one of the restored Máni towers; several are described in "Where to Stay" below. The Towers Kapetanákos, restored by the Greek government as part of their laudable Traditional Settlements program, is within a brief walk of the village square, and is well worth a visit by even those passing through.

About five miles south of Areópolis are the famous Caves of Pírgos Dirou. They're part of an underground river, and the 5,000 meters that have been exposed are fascinating. From the entrance, skillful, whistling gondoliers steer small boats through narrow passageways, around beautiful formations of stalagmites and stalactites, their colors created by rain water penetrating the calcium carbonate in the rock. The caves have served as places of worship in Paleolithic and Neolithic times, as hiding places during the Resistance movement, as cold storage for local cheesemakers, and as refuge for weary sheep; they are thought by many to be connected to the Underworld.

The 39 caves are a cool place to visit in summer (averaging 50°–70°F), but you can wait up to two hours for a boat, unless you go early. (The damp, close quarters are not for the claustrophobic.) Admission is 1,500 Drs ($6), half price for children and students; call them (**0733/52-222**) for the hours and days of operation, which depend on the time of year.

For you museum mavens there's the popular **Historical Museum of Máni** (☎ **74-414**), located at Koutifari (Thalames). This museum is housed in a Máni dwelling restored by a local Mániot, Níkons Demanghelos. The collection of artifacts (unlabeled), lithographs, and costumes is sure to interest those who have become Máni-acs. The loom on display is the actual one used to make the multicolored weavings that you'll see in all the area's shops and hotels. The museum is open daily from 9am to 7pm April through September; admission is 500 Drs ($2.10)—no student discount.

Where to Stay & Eat

The hotels below are open April through October only, unless otherwise noted.

Hotel Mani, Areópolis 23062, Laconia. ☎ **0733/51-269.** 18 rms (all with bath). TEL

Rates (including breakfast): 8,050 Drs ($33.55) single; 9,430 Drs ($39.30) double. No credit cards.

As you pull into town, you can't miss the Máni, with its new, clean rooms. Because of its nondistinctive hotel style, we hope you'll be flush enough to stay at one of the restored Mániot dwellings.

Towers Kapetanakos, Areópolis 23062, Laconia. ☎ **0733/51-233.** 6 rms (2 with bath).

Rates: 5,750 Drs ($23.95) single, 7,625 Drs ($31.75) double without bath; 8,250 Drs ($34.40) single, 10,875 Drs ($45.30) double with bath. AE, EC, V.

This 1820 tower, surrounded by a beautiful garden, was reconstructed in 1979. Today it has four tower rooms, which share a common bath and excellent views over the countryside, and two suites, with private bath, around the ground floor courtyard. The walls are over three feet thick (you urbanites will appreciate this) and the furnishings are all traditional, employing old Máni motifs throughout. It is open all year.

Traditional Tower Hotels of Vathia, EOT Paradosiakós, Ikismós, Vathia. ☎ **0733/54-244.** 12 rms (all with bath).

Rates (including breakfast): 13,810 Drs ($57.55) single; 17,990 Drs ($74.95) double. No credit cards.

During the 1980s the Greek Tourist Organization (EOT) opened another Traditional Settlement in Vathia, which consists of well-furnished rooms decorated in the Máni style, and fitted into the tall, imposing stone towers once used to fortify this small Máni hill village. An interesting place to spend the night for those with their own transport.

★ **Tsitsiris Castle,** Stavri, Gherolinénas 23071, Laconia. ☎ **0733/56-297.** Fax 01/64-20-429 in Athens. 20 rms (all with bath). A/C

Rates (including breakfast): 7,370–10,640 Drs ($30.70–$44.30) single; 10,125–14,200 Drs ($42–$59) double, according to season. No credit cards.

An incomparable experience: a 200-year-old guest house lovingly restored in harmony with the environment by a local family. It is traditionally furnished but with modern comfort and convenience; rooms have private bathrooms with tubs and shower curtains. Views are of the wild beauty and timeless serenity of the Máni. Excellent food is served in a picturesque wine cellar, both to guests and the gracious, charming family who live and work here. The other towers in Stavri are only sparsely populated with the elderly of the Máni, and deserve the new lease on life that this place has received.

Don't think you've come as far as Areópolis to discover a great taverna. Instead, we found good, solid taverna fare at most of the hotels, and particularly fine food in wonderful company at the **Tsitsiris Castle** (see above). Another fine choice is **Georgios Taverna,** on the main platía of Areópolis, convenient for those passing through. The **Diron Taverna,** at the site of the caves of Pírgos Dirou, is also popular.

15 Kalamáta

171 miles SW of Athens; 36 miles W of Sparta.

GETTING THERE • By Plane There is one flight from Athens daily on Olympic Airways; call **96-16-161** in Athens or **22-376** in Kalamáta for information. A bus goes to and from the Kalamáta Airport to meet flights; cost is 250 Drs ($1.05).

• **By Train** There's slow daily train service from Athens's Stathmós Peloponnísou (train station); call **51-31-601** for information.

• **By Bus** Ten buses leave daily from the terminal at Odós Kifissoú 100 in Athens; call **51-34-293** for information. Several local buses run daily from either Sparta or Areópolis to Kalamáta.

• **By Car** Taking the highway from Athens to Corinth, then south to Argos and Tripolis, then southwest to Kalamáta, is the fastest route.

ESSENTIALS **Tourist information** is available at the town hall (no phone) on Thoukidídou Street, or at the Office of Tourism Development, Odós Pháron 221 (☎ **0721/22-059;** fax 0721/21-959). Additional branches are open from July to September at the riverside Makedonías Street and at the airport. The **tourist police** (☎ **23-187**) are at Odós Aristoménous 46, off central square. One travel agent was recommended to us: John Trigilidas, Odós Policharous 4 (☎ **0721/20-777;** fax 0721/26-293). He offers day trips through the Máni to the Pírgos Dirou caves, and trips to Pílos and Methóni, among others.

Kalamáta, "the southernmost city in Europe" seems almost tropical—green and abundant with bougainvillea, geraniums, and hibiscus. There's little to remind you of the earthquake that devastated the city in 1986, except ubiquitous construction and many new buildings. This large city's streets are regular (except near the citadel), following the Nedon River and then opening onto a long central square. Most readers will be content to pass through Kalamáta; you'll find the train station just south of the square and the bus station to the north of it.

The region's main business, agriculture, has fully recovered from the earthquake. Luckily for travelers, Kalamáta continues to be famous for its olives, fine olive oil, and excellent figs.

Where to Stay

The recent beachfront development of Kalamáta means that many hotels, busy tavernas, cafés, and nightclubs line Navarínou Street, the waterfront named after the big naval victory.

Hotel Plaza, Odós Navarínou 117, Kalamáta 24100. ☎ **0721/82-590.**

20 rms (none with bath). TEL

Rates (including breakfast): 6,325 Drs ($26.35) single; 9,200 Drs ($38.35) double. MC, V.

This is the best value in Kalamáta, with clean and comfortable balconied rooms, and capably managed by the charming and helpful Irene Papademetriou. It's in the heart of dining and nightlife possibilities, with swimming available in the Bay of Messinia across the street.

Hotel Filoxenia, Paralía, Kalamáta 24100. ☎ **0721/23-166.** Fax 0721/23-343.
398 rms (all with bath). A/C TV TEL

Rates: 15,300 Drs ($63.75) single; 23,000 Drs ($95.85) double. AE, DC, EC, MC, V.

The Class-B Filoxenia is another choice on the *paralía*, one that was totally renovated after recent events. There's a satellite feed for their TV, and many of the modern rooms overlook a large pool. This last item will probably make this splurge worthwhile if you're stuck in Kalamáta for any length of time.

Where to Eat

As for dining, the harbor has several cafés and tavernas where you'll find souvlaki, pastries, retsína, and so on. Fresh produce, including the famous local figs, can be found in the New Market north of the main square on Aristomenous, near the bus station.

Village Tavern [to Kastraki], Berga. ☎ **41-331.**

Cuisine: GREEK.
Prices: Appetizers 400–980 Drs ($1.65–$4.10), **main courses** 980–1,725 Drs ($4.10–$7.20). AE, EC, MC, V.
Open: Daily 6pm–midnight.

Actually, the best place for a meal in Kalamáta isn't in town, but on the hillside east of town at the so-called "tavern on the hill." Two miles off the road to Areopolis, in the village of Berga, you'll find this pretty taverna built into the side of a hill. It certainly serves some of the best food in these parts, with a wonderful specialty of tender baby goat baked in foil.

16 Pílos

196 miles SW of Athens; 67 miles W of Sparta.

GETTING THERE • By Bus Two buses leave daily from the terminal at Odós Kifissoú 100 in Athens; call **51-34-293** for schedule information.

• By Car Drive for about three hours west of Sparta, via the highway through Kalamáta to get to Pílos.

ESSENTIALS There is no local Greek Tourist Organization (EOT) office, but **M Travel** (☎ **0723/22-356**; fax 0723/22-676) at Odós Filellínon 11 (on the main street two blocks past central square) is extremely helpful for making travel plans.

"Sandy Pílos," Homer called it, the home of the venerable King Nestor. Yet, the long and interesting history of Pílos (Pýlos) came from its situation as one of the finest natural harbors in the world. In 425 B.C., the island of Spacteria, across the mouth of the bay, was held for months by 400 Spartans against 14,000 Athenians during a critical engagement of the Peloponnesian War. A Byzantine-era fortress there attests to Venice's former hold over the bay, which they named Navaríno. The Turks built the new castle (Neókastro) on a hill south of Pílos in 1573, which Ibrahim Pasha made his headquarters for Turkish forces trying to quash Greece's rebellion. When the pasha unwisely attacked a fleet of English, French, and Russian vessels in the bay in 1827, he was soundly defeated, losing 58 of 87 warships and nearly 6,000 troops. The so-called Battle of Navaríno inadvertently won Greece her independence!

Today, Pílos is occupied by tourists, but it somehow manages to get on with its shipping trade and still seem serene. Fishing boats and the occasional yacht bob up and down in the marina, while farther out in the gulf of Kiparíssia a tanker sits idle. There's a pleasant, tree-shaded central square and a scenic harbor with some cafés.

What to See & Do

In town is the **Neókastro,** the Turkish fortress built in 1573. The other castle, **Paleókastro,** is also well worth exploring. It's the property of the city, which in turn leases part of it out to experienced innkeepers who maintain it. There's also an archeological museum at the site, two blocks off the *platia,* with memorials from the War of Independence. Museum hours are Tuesday through Sunday 8:30am–3pm; admission is 500 Drs ($2.10).

More interesting is **Nestor's Palace** (the palace of Pílos), a 30-minute drive heading northeast. The excavations that unearthed the largest palace yet discovered in Greece were begun by the University of Cincinnati in 1939. Archeologists estimate that Nestor, the wealthy king of Pílos, founded this capital in 1300 B.C. After the fall of Troy (to which his fleet had greatly contributed) Nestor returned to settle in Pílos. His fabulous palace has been reconstructed in prints drawn by Piet de Jong (reproduced in the local guidebook); some say the palace itself fell prey to fire in a Dorian attack around 190 B.C.; other scholars credit a 12th-century fire. The site is hard to appreciate, despite what was obviously a painstaking effort. Nonetheless, standing on the hilltop site and surveying the as-yet-undeveloped natural beauty of the Peloponnese as a whole and the Gulf of Kiparíssia (over which Nestor reigned) left us spellbound.

To get there, take Kalamátas Street, which rises at the north end of the harbor, and follow the signs to Kiparíssia. After about a mile and a half, go left on the coast road; after six miles you'll hit Korifas (Romanou). Here the unmarked right fork will lead you (after another six miles) right to the site, which is open Tuesday through Sunday from 8:30am to 3pm daily; admission is 500 Drs ($2.10) for adults, half price for students, plus video camera fees.

The **archeological museum** is located two miles beyond the site, in Chóra. There are several three-handled pithoid jars used for burying the dead, and a good collection of many artifacts uncovered at the palace site (many others are in the National Archeological Museum in Athens). Museum hours are the same as those at the site; admission is 500 Drs ($2.10).

Where to Stay

Karalis Beach Hotel, Pílos 24001, Messinia. ☎ **0723/23-021.** Fax 0723/22-970.
14 rms (all with bath). TEL

Rates (including breakfast): 14,950 Drs ($62.30) single; 18,400 Drs ($77) double. AE, EC, MC, V.

Our number-one place to stay opens in April and closes at the end of October: the Karalis Beach Hotel just off the waterfront. It has spacious rooms with clean, modern facilities. We love the afternoon breezes that blow in from the harbor. The Hotel Karalis, Odós Kalamátis 26, is also recommended.

Hotel Miramare, Pílos 24001 Messinia. ☎ **0723/22-751.** Fax 0723/22-226.
25 rms (all with bath). TEL

Rates (including breakfast): 6,900 Drs ($28.75) single; 11,500 Drs ($47.90) double. AE, DC, EC, MC, V.

This is a nice hotel, which a reader led us to. It offers sea views, and half the spacious rooms have balconies. Above all, there's a friendly atmosphere. It is open year-round.

Nilief Hotel, Odós René Payot 4, Pílos 24001 Messinia. ☎ **0723/22-575.**
20 rms (all with bath).

Rates (including breakfast): 8,050 Drs ($32.55) single; 10,350 Drs ($41) double. No credit cards.

This former pension has become a fine small hotel. The attractive rooms are quite large, and its inland location makes it a quiet choice in the evening. It is open all year.

Where to Eat

Agilos Karabatsos Bakery, Odós Pissistratou 2. No phone.
Cuisine: SNACKS/DESSERTS.
Prices: Snacks/Pastry 250–600 Drs ($1–$2.50). No credit cards.
Open: Mon–Sat 7am–2pm, 5–8pm.

There's a terrific bakery in town—just walk up the stairs on the west side of the platía to their balcony and sample their wares. Try their fresh-made *spanokópita*! We each bought one, plus a donut twist, then two large, fresh-baked cookies, and devoured them all before we were halfway to Methóni.

Philip Restaurant, on the Pílos-Kalamáta Rd. ☎ **22-741.**
Cuisine: GREEK/CONTINENTAL.
Prices: Appetizers 350–700 Drs ($1.45–$2.90), main courses 920–2,875 Drs ($3.85–$11.95). MC, V.
Open: Daily 7:30am–midnight.

We agree with our Pílos buddies that this place, set in the first house on the left as you enter Pílos from Kalamáta, is the best around. The menu is mixed Greek and elegantly continental; the ambience is absolutely local. Try their super grilled swordfish or veal cutlets. Upstairs you'll find seven rooms to rent at prices comparable to the hotels above but, of course, with a deluxe breakfast thrown in.

17 Methóni & Koróni

248 miles SW of Athens

From Kalamáta you'll cross inland to Methóni or tour the east coast to Koróni. This part of the western Peloponnese has a wild, superlative beach along the Gulf of Messinia. Koróni and Methóni are the two principal ports for this region, known as the "Two Eyes of Venice" because of their respective Venetian fortresses (or lighthouses).

Methóni

Methóni is an out-of-the-way treasure, far from the well-known tourist stomping grounds. You're more likely to run into wealthy Greeks yachting around Methóni's glistening harbor than German tour groups just in for a weekend romp. Like Koróni, Methóni is a medieval town, but it's much less claustrophobic than its neighbor. The Venetians fought long and hard to capture Methóni, and when they eventually succeeded they were less than delighted—the entire town was devastated. Starting with a fresh canvas, these Renaissance men constructed a superb fortress and lighthouse, both of which stand today as a testament to their skill and taste. The castle site has a marvelous moat and a series of well-preserved walls that are beautifully engineered; the wall extends out into the harbor, culminating in the medieval lighthouse that is known in these parts as one of the "eyes of Venice." Site hours are Tuesday through Saturday from 8:30am to 3pm and Sunday from 9am to 3pm.

WHERE TO STAY

Methóni is a very comfortable seaside resort with many room to let signs all over town, offering the least expensive accommodations.

Alex Hotel, Methóni, Messinia 24006. ☎ **0723/31-219.** 20 rms (all with bath).

Rates: 8,625 Drs ($35.95) single; 10,925 Drs ($45) double. No credit cards.

This Class-C inn is near the Methóni Beach Hotel, and of more recent vintage. It's a personable, full-service place with clean, modern rooms, a restaurant, and the town beach about 78 yards away.

Finikas Hotel, Methóni 24006, Messinia, Peloponnese. ☎ **0723/31-390.** 10 rms (all with bath).

Rates: 7,550 Drs ($31.45) single; 10,000 Drs ($41.65) double.

Rooms are basic and clean here, but we can't vouch for the management yet. Let us know what you think.

Galini Hotel, Methóni 24006, Messinia, Peloponnese. ☎ **0723/31-467.** 11 rms (all with bath).

Prices: 11,500 Drs ($47.90) single; 14,200 Drs ($59) double.

A somewhat superior hotel for its class, with a few extra touches. There's parking for those with their own wheels.

WHERE TO EAT

George's Cafe, Central Square. ☎ **31-640.**

Cuisine: SNACKS/DESSERTS.
Prices: Snacks/desserts 350–1,050 Drs ($1.45–$4.35). No credit cards.
Open: Daily 7am–midnight.

This is a big place for so small a town, but it's friendly and has good casual fare. Their full breakfasts (500 Drs/$2.80) are particularly good, especially with one of the imported coffees. Upstairs, George keeps some simple rooms with private showers. Both establishments are open all year.

Taverna Klimateria, Methóni town. No phone.

Cuisine: GREEK.
Prices: Appetizers 600–820 Drs ($2.40–$3.85), main courses 980–1,725 Drs ($4.10–$7.20). EC, MC, V.
Open: Daily noon–3:30, 6:30pm–12:30am.

This quiet, walled garden under a grape arbor is found just a few blocks south and east of central square (ask the locals). It's probably the best restaurant in the southern Peloponnese; just go in and *look* at the food displayed and try to resist sampling all the delectables. Between mid-May and mid-October, Klimateria's owners grow all their own vegetables and even raise rabbits, which they make into a fabulous stew.

EN ROUTE TO KORÓNI

Traveling directly between the west and east coastal towns can be a jarring experience—the roads are in poor condition for more than half the journey. If you're busing it, then you may have to go from Methóni, via Pílos and Kalamáta, to Koróni, just ten miles if you went direct! Try to negotiate a shared taxi; it's faster and easier. Those who undertake the trip will be amply rewarded by some of the sights.

About ten miles from Koróni, not long out of Methóni, is the tiny beach town of **Finikóundas,** where you can discover something akin to the "soul of Greece." The **Finikounda Hotel** (☎ **0723/71-208**)), has 30 cheerfully furnished rooms with private showers, phones, and views over the peaceful village. It's open year round, with doubles from 8,000 Drs ($33.35) and EC, MC, V are accepted. There are also many rooms-to-let, and the town square makes a comfortable eating area, with food available. Along the road as you head out of town you'll see cypress trees, vineyards, and rows of tomatoes and vegetables growing under Long Island–style plastic canopies.

Koróni

This small, medieval coastal town is set on the hilly western side of the Messinian Gulf near a 13th-century Venetian fortress: in short, another Greek port-and-fort town. Its compact three- and four-story buildings have wrought-iron "lace" balconies, and the stairways and streets are all narrow and worn. The entire town is built amphitheatrically—spread out at the highest hill, then angled down to the harbor below. Thousands of years of foreign armies have marched in and out, obliterating what came before them and then leaving their own brand on the town. Today's Koróni has a small protected harbor that makes for a pleasant visit, but not much else.

WHERE TO STAY & EAT

There are many rooms-to-let above the various tavernas and restaurants on the waterfront. The Class-E **Diana** (☎ **0725/22-312**), Koróni, Messinia 24004, is both hotel and taverna. Mr. Sipsas runs a clean, simple eight-room place that has bathless single rooms for only 5,060 Drs ($21.10), doubles for 6,325 Drs ($26.35). The **Hotel Flisvos** (☎ **0725/22-238**) is another eight-roomer on the waterfront. It's clean and charges (for a single or double with bath) 6,900 Drs ($28.75); neither establishment accepts credit cards.

WESTERN PELOPONNESE

It was to Elis, this most western part of the Peloponnese, that the inhabitants of the Máni migrated to pursue agriculture and livestock breeding. However, because of the heavy immigration from other areas of Greece to the west, feuds over the use of the land were constant and ongoing, to the point where Maniots became known as "pirates on the sea and robbers on land." Their homes in the village of Pírgos, the modern capital of this area, were virtual minifortresses.

18 Pírgos

190 miles W of Athens; 13 miles W of Olympia.

GETTING THERE • By Train There are daily trains from Athens's Stathmós Peloponnísou (railroad station) to Pírgos; call **51-31-601** for schedules.

- **By Bus** Buses leave ten times daily from Athens's Odós Kifissoú 100 terminal; call **51-34-110** for schedules and information. There are hourly local buses between Pírgos and Olympia.
- **By Car** Take the Athens-Corinth highway west to the Pátra highway, then the coast highway south to Pírgos.

ESSENTIALS • Getting Around The **tourist police** (☎ **23-333**) are at Odós Karkavítsas 4, off the Pátra highway and a few blocks northwest of the main square. Local buses to Athens, Olympia, and Pátra leave from Manolopoúlou Street. Pírgos town buses leave from Ypsilándou Street; the train station is at the foot of the same street. If you want a tour to Olympia, **Achtypis Tours,** Odós 28th October 26 (☎ **0621/26-301;** fax 0621/22-200) offers excursions there and to other regions.

Pírgos (Pýrgos) is a transportation center where many find themselves changing trains or buses on the way to Olympia or Athens or anyplace other than Pírgos. From here you head north to Pátra for the ferry to Kefalonía or Italy, south to Kiparíssia, or east to Tripolis in order to connect with Sparta or Náfplio or . . . we'll spare you the rest.

Where to Stay & Eat

If you plan to stay in Pírgos for the night, there are some places we can recommend to ensure that you'll have a nice time. Most hotels have restaurants in them, and just by walking around you'll find lots of options when it's time to munch.

Ilida Hotel, Odós Patrón-Deliyiánni 50, Pírgos 27100, Elis. ☎ **0621/28-046.**
35 rms (all with bath). A/C TEL

Rates: 10,900 Drs ($45.40) single; 2,420 Drs ($51) double. No credit cards.

The Ilida is also about two blocks from the railroad station, a quick right off Ethnikís, Antístasis Street. The lobby is modern and might remind you of an airport waiting lounge, with plenty of thriving plants. All the rooms are fine; air conditioning will be turned on if requested for an additional fee of 1,200 Drs ($4.70) per day.

Hotel Marily, Odós Deliyánni 48, Pírgos 27100, Elis. ☎ **0621/28-133.**
27 rms (all with bath). TEL

Rates: (including breakfast): 7,360 Drs ($30.65) single; 9,200 Drs ($38.30) double. AE, DC, EC, MC.

This hotel is a quick left off broad Ethnikís Antístasis Street; you can't miss their orange sign on the left. Though its proximity to the train tracks makes this not the most scenic neighborhood, the Marily boasts an attractive lobby with wood-paneled walls, maroon marble floors, and big cushy chairs. Rooms are small, but clean and nicely furnished, with balconies overlooking the area.

Olympos, Odós Karkavítsa 2, Pírgos 27100, Elis. ☎ **0621/23-650.**
37 rms (all with bath). TEL

Rates: 6,900 Drs ($28.75) single; 8,625 Drs ($35.95) double. EC, MC, V.

The Olympos, five blocks up Ethnikís Antístasis Street from the railroad station, is a comfortable, clean place run by friendly people. In fact, your hosts speak English about as well as anyone in Pírgos. Rooms have balconies and are neatly furnished; many have big, old bathtubs in the private bathrooms.

19 Olympía

199 miles W of Athens; 13 miles E of Pírgos.

GETTING THERE • By Train Daily trains leave from Athens's Stathmós Peloponnísou (railroad station) to Pírgos; call **51-31-601** for schedules. From Pírgos, you'll have to change to the spur line to Olympia.

• By Bus Buses leave three times daily direct to Olympia from the terminal at Odós Kifissoú 100 in Athens; call **51-34-110** for schedules and information. There are also hourly local buses between Pírgos and Olympia.

• By Car Take the Athens-Corinth highway west to the Pátra highway, then the coast highway south to Pírgos, then turn east (inland) to Olympia.

ESSENTIALS • Information The city of Olympia operates an excellent tourist information (EOT) office (☎ **0624/23-100** or **23-125,** fax 0624/23-173) right on the main street, Praxitélous, near the ancient site. It is open from 8am to 10pm in summer, and from 11am to 6pm daily in winter. They can exchange traveler's checks and provide a city map and brochures, plus lists of rooms and camping and hotel facilities in the area. The Olympia tourist police (☎ **22-100**) are at Odós Ethnossineléfseos 6. The OTE (Telecommunications Organization of Greece), also on Praxitélous near the site, is open Monday through Friday only, from 7:30am to 10pm. Most of the town's banks, as well as the bus station, are on the main street. The train station is off Kondýli Street, on the north end of town.

Today's modern Olympia is a half-mile tourist strip, overflowing with very commercial cafés, shops, and hotels. The prices everywhere in town are high, but if you slip off the main drag, either one block up or down, you'll find that hotels and tavernas tend to be less expensive and better.

Olympia is at its best in the early spring before the tourist hordes descend. If you have no car, you can hoof it, take the bus, or call a taxi (☎ **22-580**) to pick you up. It's an easy 15-minute walk to the site and museum.

What to See & Do

The first Olympic Games were held in 776 B.C. By 576 B.C. the games had been restructured as a footrace held every four years for five days, during the summer full moon. At this time messengers would travel to announce a sacred truce, and athletes from all over Greece would stop fighting to compete in the games.

The original Olympic event, a run down the length of the stadium (142.25 meters), was soon expanded to include multilap races, the pentathlon (running, wrestling, discus, jumping, and javelin), boxing, chariot races, and contests of strength. To preserve the integrity of the athletes, strict rules were imposed and stiff fines were levied against offenders. Anybody who bore arms at the sanctuary during the period of this sacred truce was fined, and bronze casts of Zeus were made and displayed from these earnings. Marble bases from these casts still exist and dot the site.

Women were not allowed to watch the competitions, primarily because the participants were nude. However, one priestess, representing Demeter, the goddess of fertility, was always present. Women did participate in the chariot races and had their own Olympics at another time, the Heraea, in honor of Zeus's wife, Hera.

As Greek civilization declined, so did the allure of the laurel wreath (with which winners were crowned), and subsequently corruption and vice plagued the sanctuary at Olympia. In A.D. 393 the Emperor Theodosius banned the games by decree; 30 years later his son ordered all the temples at the sanctuary destroyed.

The games were revived in 1896, when the first modern Olympiad was held in Athens. In 1936 the tradition began of bearing a flame from the original sanctuary at Olympia to the site of the new Olympiad. The five entwined circles symbolize the unity of the five continents that participate. Today, the flame is lit by focusing the sun's rays through a magnifying glass located at the temple of Hera. The lit torch is then conveyed by a "priestess" through the arched entrance to the stadium and then to the field, where the first runner in the relay to the site starts the journey that the whole world watches. Olympic competitors always ran toward the temple of Zeus; start your race at the far end. (We have fun picking olive branches and making "Olympic" wreaths after our modest marathon jog.) The site is open Monday through Saturday from 8am to 7pm, and from 8:30am to 3pm Sunday. You can take a donkey ride around the site, but bargain with the wranglers until it's down to 1,150 Drs ($4.20) for the journey.

For the utmost appreciation of this site, go to the nearby **archeological museum** (☎ **22-529**). Superb pediments from the temple of Zeus have been reconstructed and displayed in a room of the same spatial dimensions as its original setting. The statuary from them is remarkable for the attention to anatomical detail and the fluid facial expressions. After seeing this, you develop a respect for the word "monumental," and it drives home the religious aspect of the original games. The other great treasure here is the statue of Hermes by Praxiteles, which was discovered amid the ruins of the temple of Hera; notice how the archeologists have reconstructed the legs from the knees down, with only the right foot to work from. Finds from continuing excavations at the site are often moved to the museum; the most interesting dig is at the monument of Pelops. This is really a one-of-a-kind museum.

Signs for the museum are at the site entrance and on the road. The hours are 8am to 5pm weekdays (Monday noon to 6pm) and 8:30am to 3pm on Saturday and Sunday. Admission is 1,250 Drs ($5.20), half-price for students. Flash pictures and video cameras require additional permits at high fees.

The **Museum of Olympic Games** is in town, about three blocks north of the bus station. The hours are 8am to 3:30pm Monday to Saturday, 9am to 4:30pm Sundays. It costs 600 Drs ($2.50).

Where to Stay

Olympia is the most popular archeological site on the Peloponnese; tour buses and individuals pass through town all summer long. If you're traveling between July and the middle of August, call ahead for reservations. Hotels noted below are open from late May to late September unless otherwise noted.

DOUBLES FOR LESS THAN 10,000 DRS ($42)

Pension Achilleus, Odós Stefanopoúlou 4, Ancient Olympia 27065, Peloponnese. ☎ **0624/22-562.** 7 rms (none with bath).

Rates: 4,000 Drs ($16.75) single; 5,750 Drs ($23.95) double.

The Pension Achilleus has clean, large rooms above a snack bar, about two lanes up from the busy main street. Inquire out front about available rooms; the keeper often tends the store downstairs. There's a shower down the hall for guests.

Hotel Phedias, Odós P. Spiliopoúlou 2, Ancient Olympia 27065, Peloponnese. ☎ **0624/22-667.** 9 rms (all with bath).

Rates: 5,750 Drs ($23.75) single; 6,900 Drs ($28) double. AE, MC, V.

The Class-C Hotel Phedias is down the block from the easily visible Hotel Hercules, and opposite one of Olympia's pretty churches. The charming owner, George Bournas, has provided the nicest bathrooms in Olympia; the showers are also half-tubs! All the rooms have a balcony.

Pelops Hotel, Odós Varéla 2, Ancient Olympia 27065, Peloponnese. ☎ **0624/22-543.** Fax 0624/22-213. 25 rms (all with bath).

Rates: 5,950 Drs ($24.90) single; 9,085 Drs ($37.85) double. AE, EC, MC, V.

This is the best value in this price range, with more than a few touches of distinction. Susan Spiliopoulou, the lovely owner/manager, is an Australian experienced in travel, the perfect hostess, and a joy to talk with. She keeps her rooms spotless, and is constantly making improvements, according to the two happy couples we met there.

Pension Posidon, Odós Stefanopoúlou 9, Ancient Olympia 27065, Peloponnese. ☎ **0624/22-567.** 10 rms (4 with bath).

Rates: (including breakfast): 5,175 Drs ($21.58) single, 5,720 Drs ($23.95) double without bath.

This pension is located two lanes up from the main street and is comparable to the Achilleus nearby. Though rooms are not quite as large, they're cleaner and quieter, and the common showers were better at our visit.

DOUBLES FOR LESS THAN 30,000 DRS ($125)

Hotel Europa, Ancient Olympia 27065, Peloponnese. ☎ **0624/22-650.** Fax 0624/23-166. 42 rms (all with bath). A/C TEL

Rates: 18,900 Drs ($78.75) single; 27,350 Drs ($113.95) double. AE, DC, EC, MC, V.

The most luxurious hotel in town is high above it, and at once modern and traditional, open and spacious, and beautifully decorated. Rooms are very comfortable, with peaceful vistas from each balcony. The public spaces are equally fine; the top floor dining room has a roof terrace, and facilities include an outdoor pool, tennis courts, and horseback riding. Two big surprises for Greece: 24-hour room service and laundry service! The Europa is open year-round. (Call Best Western **1-800-528-1234** for reservations.)

BUDGET BETS

Camping Diana, Kalamáta Highway, Ancient Olympia 27065, Peloponnese. ☎ **0624/22-314.**

Rates: 800 Drs ($3.36) per person; 625 Drs ($2.65) per tent site. No credit cards.

This campground is near the Museum of Olympic Games in a quiet, shady spot. It's very homey, with solar-powered showers, a swimming pool, facilities for washing clothes and dishes, and a small grocery store.

Camping Alphios, Ancient Olympia 27065, Peloponnese. ☎ **0624/22-950.** Fax 01/34-65-262.

Rates: 1,000 Drs ($4.20) per person; 800 Drs ($3.20) per tent. No credit cards.

On Drouva Hill, just below the Hotel Europa, the site has glorious views of the town and hills. There's a pool, mini-market, snack bar, and restaurant.

Where to Eat

George Bourna's Pastry Shop. ☎ **22-548.**

Cuisine: BREAKFAST/DESSERTS.
Prices: Breakfast 700 Drs ($2.90); desserts 460–700 Drs ($1.90–$2.90). No credit cards.
Open: Daily 7am–noon.

A half block up from main street near the Olympic Games museum, next to the Phedias Hotel, is this delightful bakery. George is charming and a terrific cook. There's good pastry, hearty breakfasts, yogurt with honey, and lots of goodies at much higher quality and lower prices than found in the myriad fast food shops.

Taverna Klimataria, Main Street, Koskiná. ☎ **22-165.**

Cuisine: GREEK.
Prices: Appetizers 350–600 Drs ($1.45–$2.50); main courses 1,050–1,400 Drs ($4.35–$5.85). No credit cards.
Open: Mon–Sat dinner 7pm–12:30am.

About a mile and a half out of town in Koskiná is the Taverna Klimataria, an old-style place with homemade wine, where we had a very tasty dinner. It's worth the pleasant walk (especially on a moonlit night) to try their *soutsoukákia* and *bekrís mezés,* but even the fresh vegetable dishes are well prepared. It is closed the month of June.

Pete's Den, Stefanopoúlou Street. ☎ **22-066.**

Cuisine: GREEK/GERMAN.
Prices: Appetizers 350–860 Drs ($1.45–$3.60); main courses 800–2,000 Drs ($3.35–$8.35). AE, MC, V.
Open: Lunch Mon–Sat noon–3pm; dinner daily 6:30pm–12:30am.

Run by a friendly Greek named Pete, Pete's Den reflects a superb melding of cooking styles. The *saganáki* (fried cheese), for example, is served sizzlingly hot and, at the table, doused with cognac and set ablaze. Zucchini pie and various salads are served on an appetizer plate that will easily satisfy two. Follow that with lamb oreganato or beef and bacon shish kebab and a carafe of homemade retsína. Pete's is open from February to December.

Taverna Praxitelis, Odós Spiliopoúlou 7. ☎ **23-570.**

Cuisine: GREEK.
Prices: Appetizers 460–860 Drs ($1.90–$3.60); main courses 1,050–1,600 Drs ($4.35–$6.70) No credit cards.
Open: Daily 11am–3pm, 6pm–1am.

Next door to the police station, this taverna owned by Saris Floras enjoys the best reputation among the locals for traditional Greek cuisine at moderate prices. Daily

READERS RECOMMEND

Restaurant Bel Ami, Main Street, Olympia. *"On the chilled rainy night we entered, it was a refuge of warmth and friendliness, as its name suggests, away from the congested town center, toward Pírgos-Pátras. We accepted the recommendation of the attentive proprietor, Leonidas Tzoulakis, and chose the moussaká and stifado accompanied by a distinguished Greek salad and the very palatable local white retsína. We stayed for a dessert of very smooth crème caramel and conversation with other contented guests."*—Robert C. Huber, Winston-Salem, North Carolina.

specials include fresh seafood, game such as rabbit and quail, and grilled chicken and meats.

Evening Entertainment

If you're not too tired from jogging around Olympic Stadium, consider the **Touris Club** (☎ **23-001**), on the hill north of town near the Olympic Games museum. Several travelers we met really enjoyed the mix of modern and traditional entertainments. There's a good-sized pool (lounge there while sampling the fixed-price lunch of 3,400 Drs or $14.30), and after 9:30pm nightly, a floor show (dinner is optional). Two dance groups composed of talented, enthusiastic locals perform at least a dozen folk dances, after which they teach spectators; then they expect you to join in. After you're warmed up, the P.A. system plays "Good Golly, Miss Molly" and "Let's Twist Again," after which the place starts apoppin'.

George Vikatos, formerly an engineer in Texas, returned home with big ideas and know-how to open the popular **Stadium Club,** one block up from the National Bank. The music moves from rock to reggae to rebetika.

20 Kyllíni

181 miles SW of Athens; 47 miles SW of Pátra; 23 miles NW of Pírgos.

GETTING THERE • **By Bus** Buses leave ten times daily from the terminal at Odós Kiffísoú 100 in Athens; call **51-34-110** for schedules and information. There are frequent local buses between Pátra, Pírgos, and Kyllíni.

• **By Car** Take the Athens-Corinth highway west to the Pátra highway, then the coast highway and local roads south to Kyllíni.

ESSENTIALS You should count on having cash, as the tiny port of Kyllíni has no bank or American Express offices, and few tourist services! Ferry departures for the Ionian isles are three times daily to Zakynthos (1 1/2-hour trip) and twice daily to Kefalonia (3 hours). Confirm departure times by calling **0623/92-211.**

The area of Loutrá Kyllíni (Kyllíni Hot Springs) is home to a hydropathic spa shrouded in eucalyptus trees. The excellent public beach and hot mineral springs (especially famed for curing respiratory ailments) are open May through September to tempt you.

Kyllíni proper is a small port with a skinny stretch of dirty beach on either side of the busy ferry terminal that services the Ionian Islands. Plan ahead so that you will have only a little time to kill, and walk the side streets till the boat arrives. If you're going to be in Kyllíni overnight, we must warn you that the whole region is infested with mosquitos; bring a garlic necklace and repellent for a good night's rest.

Where to Stay & Eat

If you have to be in this neighborhood, there is a special place in Kástro, 6 miles south of Kyllíni (see below). However, there are acceptable hotels within sight of the port, a mouthwatering bakery up from the village post office, and a half dozen cafés in the car ferry terminal. The café next to the ticket booth is so big you can sit in the shade and never have to purchase anything as you people-watch.

Hotel Ionian, Kyllíni, Iliás. ☎ **0623/92-318.** 22 rms (all with bath). TEL

Rates: 8,165 Drs ($34) single; 10,350 Drs ($62.30) double. No credit cards.

If you don't have your own transport, and you happen to miss the last boat, the Hotel Ionian is next door to the port, but far enough away to enjoy some quiet. Rooms are average but clean, and you can swim on the sandy beach across the road.

Xenia Hotel, Loutrá Kyllíni, Iliás. ☎ **0623/96-440.** Fax 0623/96-474.
80 rms (all with bath). TEL

Rates: (including half-board): 14,240 Drs ($59.35) single; 17,800 Drs ($95.85) double. AE, EC.

Near the hot springs, a little farther back in the gardens, is the Xenia Hotel with well-kept undistinctive rooms. The hotel's facilities include volleyball, basketball, and tennis. To unwind, you can lower yourself into a spring-water thermal bath (600 Drs or $2.50), famous since antiquity for its curative powers.

CAMPING

At Loutrá Kyllíni, in the Xenia Hotel compound, there's a campground (☎ **0623/96-270**) with four-person bungalows for 6,000 Drs ($25) a night. Tent sites go for 900 Drs ($3.75), and you can park and star-gaze for free. The setting makes this one of the best camping spots we know, with great beaches close at hand.

NEARBY IN KÁSTRO

Chrissi Avgi Hotel, Odós Loutropóleos 9, Kástro 27050, Ilias. ☎ **0623/95-224.**
10 rms (all with bath). TEL

Rates: 7,935 Drs ($33) single/double. No credit cards.

This is the place to stay at—if you can get a room—in all the north Peloponnese. It's convenient for drivers visiting Olympía, Pátra, and the Ionians, with excellent beaches just minutes away. A London reader told us about charming host Christos Lepidas and his lovely French wife, Catherine, who make all guests feel at home. This is a clean and quiet lodging with fine meals served in the evenings. To find it, turn south at Lehena and continue through Neochóri (the *kástro,* or fortress, is up ahead of you); you'll find it in the village, on the right behind two magnificent, centuries-old olives trees.

If you don't dine with the Lepidas family, try the **Taverna Apollon** (☎ **95-302**) on the main street of Kástro. It's open evenings and offers fresh fish or locally raised meats, fresh from the refrigerator and cooked to order.

21 Pátra

128 miles NW of Athens

GETTING THERE • By Train There is daily service from Athens's Peloponnísou Railroad Station (☎ **51-31-601**). Call for schedule information.

• By Bus There are 15 buses daily from Athens's Odós Kifssoú 100 terminal; call **51-24-914** for information.

• By Car Take the Athens-Corinth highway west to the Pátra highway, continuing west along the Gulf of Corinth.

ESSENTIALS • Information The national tourist office EOT Polytechníou in Pátra (☎ **061/420-305**) is at Odós Iróon Polytechníou 1, at the New Port by the entrance to Gate 6. It has the largest collection of free brochures in the entire country, so try to stock up! Vassiliki Báli and the terrific staff help all from 7am to 9:30pm weekdays, and 2 to 9:30pm weekends or holidays. The **tourist police,** among the most helpful we've encountered, are at Odós Patreos 53, a block west of the main square (☎ **220-902**).

The American Express office is at Odós, Othonos-Amalías 48 (☎ **061/220-993** and **224-609**) with daily hours. The Óthonos-Amalías branch of the National Bank of Greece is open 8am to 2pm weekdays (Saturday until 1pm), 10am to 1pm on Sunday, and from 5:30 to 8:30pm every day.

• **Getting Around the Greek Mainland** You can hire a car at one of several agencies or avail yourself of public transportation. There are two **bus companies:** the privately operated KTEL (☎ **222-164**) at Zaïmí and Óthonos-Amalías Streets, which services Athens, Pírgos, Kalamáta, and Thessaloníki; and the government-run OSE (☎ **273-694**) at Óthonos-Amalías and Arátou Streets. Both KTEL and OSE service parts of the Peloponnese. The bus to Athens costs 3,400 Drs ($14.15) and takes about 3 hours; the train takes longer (about 4½ hours) but costs only 1,750 Drs ($7.25) and you can use your EurailPass. The **train station** (☎ **273-694**) is on the port and services Athens, Pírgos, and Kiparíssia. If you want to book a flight or just confirm one, the Olympic Airlines office (☎ **222-901**) is at Odós Ághiou Andréa 16 (near the Hotel Astir), at the corner of Arátou Street. The main **post office** is at Zaïmí and Mezón Streets, and the telephone center (OTE) is at Dimitriougoúnai and Kanakári Streets; both have New Port branches.

• **Boat Trips from the Greek Mainland** If it's the Ionian Islands you want, call **Ionian Cruise Lines** (☎ **061/336-130**) or the **Tsimara Shipping and Travel Office** (☎ **061/277-783**) at Odós Óthonos-Amalías 14 down the street from the National Bank. If it's **ferries** to Italy, there are 15 boats a day to Brindisi, Ancona, or Bari. Brindisi is serviced by the Adriatica, Libra, Fragline, and Hellenic-Mediterranean Attica lines; Ancona by the Anek, Marlines, Strintzis, Kargeorgiou, and Minoan lines; and Bari by the Arkadia and Ventouris lines. The Hellenic-Mediterranean Lines transport EurailPass holders free; their office (☎ **429-520**) is at Odós Sarantaporou 1 at Athinon Street.

The modern city of Pátra (also Pátrai in Greek, Patras in English) stands just below the site of the ancient city where, according to legend, St. Andrew preached Christianity and was crucified for his efforts, later being buried here. Capital of Achaea (the northwest part of the Peloponnese), it derived its name from its founder Patreus, the leader of the Achaeans who drove out the Ionians. This area is very mountainous, yet ruins indicate that it has been settled since the Paleolithic Age.

The ancient acropolis was capped with a Byzantine castle that still dominates the city. Pátra is the third-largest port in Greece, and the hub of the business world in the Peloponnese. The city's heart is Platía Gheorgíou (George tou Protou Square).

What to See & Do

The city's arches are the first sight many travelers see of Greece, for Pátra is where thousands of Europeans disembark from ferries arriving from Brindisi, Ancona, or Bari, Italy, or from the Ionian isles of Corfu and Kefalonía, or the northern mainland at Igoumenítsa. As you might have guessed, Pátra is always crowded with visitors. There's actually plenty to see, including the biggest cathedral (though not a great beauty) in all of Greece, St. Andrew's.

The Pátra International Festival occurs in July and August, featuring concerts, art shows, and the usual hoopla. The festival is a terrific venue for artists. Young Greek directors like Victor Arditti have presented experimental theater; even Bob Dylan played there in 1989! Call **061/336-390** for schedule information. Annually, between May and September, there is the Pátra Summer Festival (☎ **061/272-911**), a smaller performing arts festival.

Pátra is also the home of **Archaia Clauss** (☎ **325-051**), one of the largest Greek manufacturers/exporters of wine. Every year, for two weeks at the end of August, there is the Pátra Wine Festival, where wine sampling and entertainment are offered nightly. Call **061/279-866** for information on the festival, and the Achaia Clauss winery directly for information on tours. Once a year, for three weeks during February or March (ending the night before Lent), the annual Carnival featuring a chariot parade, traditional Greek theater, and pre-Lenten feasting takes top priority over other gala events.

At Odós Maízonos 42, you'll find the archeological museum (☎ **275-070**), with its fragments of sculpture, bronzes, clay vases, gold and ivory work, jewelery and mosaic; it's open Tuesday through Sunday from 8:30am to 3pm. And, needless to say, Pátra has its quota of Byzantine and Turkish and Frankish architecture and ruins if you still haven't had enough.

The modern city is best seen receding in the distance, but if you're caught here, begin by taking a stroll around Platía Gheorghíou. We probably won't have to bring your attention to the lively nightlife the locals enjoy on the west side. Continuing south up Gherokostopoúlou, you'll find fast food places and some stairs leading to several bistros and all-night cafés. Keep climbing and you'll come upon the ancient odeum, built during the Roman period and razed in the 3d century A.D., and still used for concerts and theater performances. Farther up Pantokrátoros Street, you'll pass the handsome church that gives the street its name (well worth a peek inside). A left beside the church leads to the acropolis and the old Turkish-built towers of the kastro for a bird's eye view.

Where to Stay

Hotel Acropole, Odós Óthonos-Amalías 39, Pátras 26223, Peloponnese.
☎ **061/271-809.** Fax 061/221-533. 33 rms (all with bath). TEL

Rates: 5,750 Drs ($23.95) single; 8,050 Drs ($33.55) double. EC, MC, V.

Centrally located, just across from the port and railway station, and one block from the bus station. We met fellow travelers who were stopping there for the sixth time. The gracious Charmaine and Perikles Foundas are certainly part of the reason. The front rooms face the port and are surprisingly quiet, due to recently installed thermopane windows. The adjoining Acropole Restaurant is also good.

Hotel Adonis, Odós Zaïmí 7 at Kapsáli St., Pátra 26223. ☎ **061/224-213.**
Fax 061/226-971. 56 rms (all with bath). A/C TV TEL

Rates: (including breakfast): 11,400 Drs ($46) single; 14,145 Drs ($78.45) double. AE, EC, MC, V.

A typical-American style hotel, completely refurbished in 1994, the Hotel Adonis is a pleasant, quiet place. Modern rooms have very firm beds, piped-in classical Muzak on the radio, and even TVs. It's also close to the city center, bus depot, and ferry ticket offices.

Astir Hotel, Odós Aghíou Andréa 16, Pátra 26223. ☎ **061/277-502** Fax 271-644.
121 rms (all with bath). AC TV TEL

Rates: 18,400 Drs ($76.65) single; 22,080 Drs ($92) double. AE, MC, V.

This is a spacious and modern hotel that would rank as a worthwhile splurge if the attention paid to service and maintenance were a bit higher. Nonetheless, rooms are vividly decorated (ours was shades of sea foam, loden, olive, and chartreuse green with a turquoise phone) and the bathrooms are tiled in black marble.

Hotel El Greco, Odós Aghíou Andréa 145, Pátra 26223. ☎ **061/272-931.**
24 rms (8 with bath).

Rates: 4,625 Drs ($18.25) single; 6,325 Drs ($26.35) double. No credit cards. This is the best budget choice in town as the cheaper hotels are pretty awful. George Vlachoyianis, the friendly manager, speaks English, and the rooms are clean and comfortable.

A YOUTH HOSTEL

GYH Hostel, Odós Iróon Polytechníou 62, Pátra 26441. ☎ **061/427-278.**
7 dorms (none with bath).

Rates: 1,725 Drs ($7.20) bed. No credit cards.

This hostel is located about 872 yards east of the Pátra ship terminal. It's in a handsome old villa along the coast road that served as a German barracks during World War II. Within its enclosed courtyard, the hostel offers hot showers and laundry facilities and is very clean. Definitely one of the best GYH facilities in Greece.

CAMPING

For those who like to camp, there are several campgrounds outside of Pátra, the closest in Aghía Pátra about a mile and a half east of the city. It's called **Ávia Patrón Camping** (☎ **061/424-131**) and it can hold 800 people, 250 cars, and 50 trailers! Call for current rates, as they fluctuate seasonally. It should run about 750 Drs ($3.15) per person, 350 Drs ($1.45) for a small tent. **Campsite Rio George** (☎ **061/991-323**), which also has a taverna, is about 4 miles east, near the port of Rion. Fees here are a little less: 700 Drs ($2.90) per person, with children under 10 free, and 300 Drs ($1.45) per tent.

Where to Eat

As many hotels as there are in Pátra, restaurants outnumber them. Most of these places are tourist traps, and we hope you can spot them by their telltale tailoring, and avoid them. Sweet tooths should make a beeline a half block west of the main square to the new pâtisserie **Zacharoplastiki,** at Odós Maízonas 46 for some fresh bread, cookies, or incredible pastries.

Issimo Bistro, Odós Gherokostopoúlou 53. ☎ **222-627.**

Cuisine: INTERNATIONAL.
Prices: Snacks 400–920 Drs ($1.90–$3.85); main courses 800–2,070 Drs ($3.35–$8.60). No credit cards.
Open: Daily 9am–2am.

The name means "most" in Italian, but in any language this is obviously the largest and hottest of the many bistros on the "new" stairs above Platía Gheorghiou. Grab a table—if you're lucky enough to get one—on the pedestrian-only street, inside the contemporary dining room, or in one of the *intimo* side alcoves. Beverages are the priority with most diners, but the good food ranges from sandwiches and snacks to filet mignon and Greek favorites.

Tricoyia Brothers Restaurant, Odós Óthonos-Amalías 46. ☎ **279-421.**

Cuisine: GREEK.

Prices: Appetizers 500–980 Drs ($2–$4), main courses 1,000–2,400 Drs ($4.15–$10). AE, DC, MC, V.

Open: Daily 10am–11pm.

Our favorite dining room is the lively Tricoyia Brothers across from the train station. Among the many dishes that we tried, John particularly liked the beef with zucchini, carrots, and potatoes, while Kyle went for the lamb with vegetables in a creamy lemon sauce. You'll find all the waiters are nice, too.

Easy Excursions to Rio & Antirio

Rio's claim to fame is that it's the port city (5 miles north of Pátra) that connects the Peloponnese to the mainland at Antírio. The curious and museum-happy crowd will want to head over to the pier to see the ruins of **Morea Castle** (built in 1499 by the Sultan Beyazid); the let's-get-on-with-it crowd will make a beeline to the souvlaki trucks and the small and sometimes expensive markets.

If you have a car, the 15-minute ferry ride across this mile-wide divide will cost you 810 Drs ($4.50); tickets are sold on board. Bus riders crossing to and from the Peloponnese will find themselves changing buses before the ferry and paying the 100 Drs (55¢) fare, the same as their noncar companions. When you reach the other side, you will be greeted by the fortress ruins of Roumelia, built by the Turks to fortify the strait. In ancient times a temple to Poseidon stood at both ports, checking out all those who sailed through the Gulf of Corinth.

Crete

8

THE NATURAL RESOURCES AND ARTISTIC RICHNESS OF CRETE (KRÍTI) HAVE MADE THE island coveted by every Mediterranean culture in history, and today's traveler will find it just as desirable.

Nature lovers make the pilgrimage around the perimeters and through the mountainous heartland of Crete unparalleled for its variety of scenic beauty. The island is the longest link in a geological chain stretching from the mountainous Peloponnese through Kýthira to Rhodes and beyond to Asia Minor; its terrain reflects these different landscapes, particularly on the eastern and western coasts. Crete's developed northern coast is defined by a national highway linking several harbors on the azure Aegean. Once-great centers of the ancient maritime powers have become overdeveloped beach resorts and picturesque fishing ports. The untamed rugged southern coast curls lazily along the Libyan Sea, facing the tropical coast of Africa across the Mediterranean. Crete's wealth comes from the south's thriving year-round agribusiness—tomato hothouses line the roads curved above huge canyons and rocky gorges; date palms and vineyards are interspersed with placid, sandy beach coves and dense banana plantations.

The culture that many consider the mother of all Greek civilization originated on Crete. The variety of archeological treasures from the Minoan civilization will delight even visitors bored with "old stones." The great palaces at Knossós, Mália, and Phaistós are only the first leg of a historical odyssey that leads to Hellenic, Byzantine, and Venetian sites throughout the island.

Whether you're interested in a motor-coach tour of historical sites or an overland expedition to unexplored beaches, Crete has it all.

Seeing Crete

Crete has been discovered by group tours in a big way, but it's still Greece's single most fascinating island, especially if you're willing to explore the less obvious destinations. Try to allow at least one week to sample its many pleasures.

The northern coast has been developed for tourism, to the detriment of most of its once picturesque fishing ports, especially Ághios Nikólaos. We'd recommend Sitía as a base for exploring the eastern part of the island and Chaniá for exploring the central and western part.

Of the southern coast beaches, Sougiá is perhaps the quietest. Mátala is our preference for its not insane development (it is still very built up) and good beach in town. Árvi is a choice (with a poorer beach) that makes a good, tranquil base for beach seekers with cars or hikers with strong legs.

Cretans consider their tourist season to extend only from April 1 through October 31 on the northern coast, after which many accommodations and restaurants close. The southern coast advertises itself as a year-round resort because of its mild climate, but here, too, many accommodations are seasonal. We recommend that visitors planning an extended winter holiday on Crete contact a local travel agent.

Suggested Itineraries

If you treat Crete as a stopover only on a race-around-Greece tour, plan on spending at least one day in Iráklio, at Knossós and the Archeological Museum. If you have an additional day, consider taking an excursion to Phaistós and on for an afternoon on

What's Special About Crete

Archeological Sites and Museums

- The world-renowned Minoan ruins at Knossós and the Archeological Museum (with its graceful frescoes) in nearby Iráklio are a highlight on any tour of Greece; both are popular with kids who'll settle for nothing less than the spectacular.
- The Palace of Phaistós, a Minoan site accessible from Iráklio, Mátala, and Réthymno, is equal to the grandeur of Knossós but is in a less rebuilt style of excavation.
- Réthymno's fortress and harbor are picturesque reminders of the Venetian occupation.
- Chaniá, another Venetian-era settlement, is Crete's most attractive city and is a fine base for exploring Crete's southern and western shores.

Beaches

- Mátala's caves and beaches make this southern coast resort one of the most attractive on the island.
- The western coast beach at Fallasarna (south of Kastélli) and the exquisitely remote beaches on the southwestern Elafonísi island are among the least visited and most alluring on Crete.

Villages

- Visiting the mountain village of Élos, on the western side of the island, or the rural towns of Gavalochóri and Xirostérni, or the monasteries northeast of Chaniá will give you a taste of the traditional patterns of life in the heart of Crete.
- The Lassíthi Plains town of Psychró provides a breathtaking view of thousands of working windmills.

Natural Sight

- The Samariá Gorge, sometimes referred to as the Grand Canyon of Greece, is a rugged one-day trek from the craggy center of the island down to the south coast town of Aghía Roúmeli.

the beach at Mátala. Alternatively, you could visit Réthymno and Chaniá, returning to Iráklio on the following day.

For those with at least one week, we suggest renting a car—if it's within your budget—and following this course:

Day 1 Arrive in Iráklio and visit the Archeological Museum and Knossós.

Day 2 Continue to Chaniá, passing through Réthymno and nearby rural villages.

Day 3 Hike the Samariá Gorge and either return to Chaniá or stay in one of the southern coast beach towns (Aghía Roúmeli or Chóra Sfakiá, or take an extra day and go to Sougiá).

Day 4 If you return to Chaniá, travel southeast, back through Sfakiá, and continue on to Frangokástello; otherwise, continue to the ruins at Phaistós and spend the rest of the day on Mátala's beaches.

Day 5 Travel east, through Ierápetra and head north, stopping overnight in Sitía.

Day 6 If you have sufficient time, visit the palm beach at Vái or, even better, visit the Gorge of the Dead and the nearby beaches at Káto Zákros or Itanós.

Day 7 Stop in Mochlós for a quick seaside lunch and swim, and return to Iráklio.

History

Crete is known to have been inhabited since the 7th millennium B.C., but it was not until about 2600 B.C., when immigrants from Asia Minor and Africa arrived with bronze tools and implements, that we see the beginnings of the first distinct civilization, dubbed "Minoan," after the island's legendary King Minos. The most exciting archeological finds date from 1900–1700 B.C., when large palaces were founded at Knossós, Phaistós, and Mália. In the Archeological Museum there's a collection of faience plaques in the shapes of two- and three-story local houses that indicate the high level of sophistication the Minoan builders achieved.

About 1700 B.C. a disaster befell the Minoans (either an earthquake or a massive invasion), and the palaces were destroyed. Over their rubble rose magnificent new palaces, which have been partly restored and can be seen today. Some two centuries later, another cataclysmic event occurred that destroyed the Minoan civilization. Some archeologists believe it was a huge tidal wave caused by a volcanic eruption on the island of Thera (Thíra; now called Santoríni), just 60 miles north. Spýridon Marinátos arrived at that conclusion after his excavation at Amnissós revealed layers of volcanic ash; his later work at Akrotíri, on Santoríni, proved that this Minoan-like civilization had been destroyed by the eruption as well. Yet, within the last few years new excavations on Crete's northeastern quarter have revealed highly developed Minoan centers, such as that at Móchlos and Paleókastro, that postdate the Santoríni eruption.

By 1000 B.C. the Dorians had invaded Crete, establishing a new aristocratic government while adopting many Minoan legal precepts as the foundation for their new Spartan state on the mainland. Under the Dorians a militaristic mood predominated in Crete. Cities that had flourished while united under Minos became rivals. Successful trading continued with Asia Minor and Africa, introducing Oriental styles to an island mostly isolated from mainland Greece. After several thwarted attempts, the Romans finally took over Crete in A.D. 67 and chose Górtyn as their capital. For 800 years under Roman rule, Crete was a prosperous colony, which saw the arrival of Christianity in the 5th century.

In A.D. 826 the Saracens invaded, destroying Górtyn (Górtys), and inhabiting the newly fortified port of Candiá (Khandak), present-day Iráklio. Nikephóros Phokás retook Crete from marauding pirates in 961, and from Byzantine hands it was purchased by Venice.

Candiá was now the artistic and political center of an island settled by Greek and Venetian nobility. Scholars speak of the Cretan Renaissance during the 16th and 17th centuries, when local poetry, architecture, and painting flowered. Iráklio's loggia, Réthymno's fountain, and Chaniá's stately homes all date from this period. The only extant works from the Cretan School of Painting, which produced several artists (including Doménikos Theotokópoulous, known to the world as El Greco), are displayed in the church of Aghía Eateríni, a Venetian monument in Iráklio.

The Venetians had architect Michele Sammicheli refortify the ramparts of Iráklio's fortress, and it withstood the Turkish onslaught for 21 years. In 1669 the last free

9620

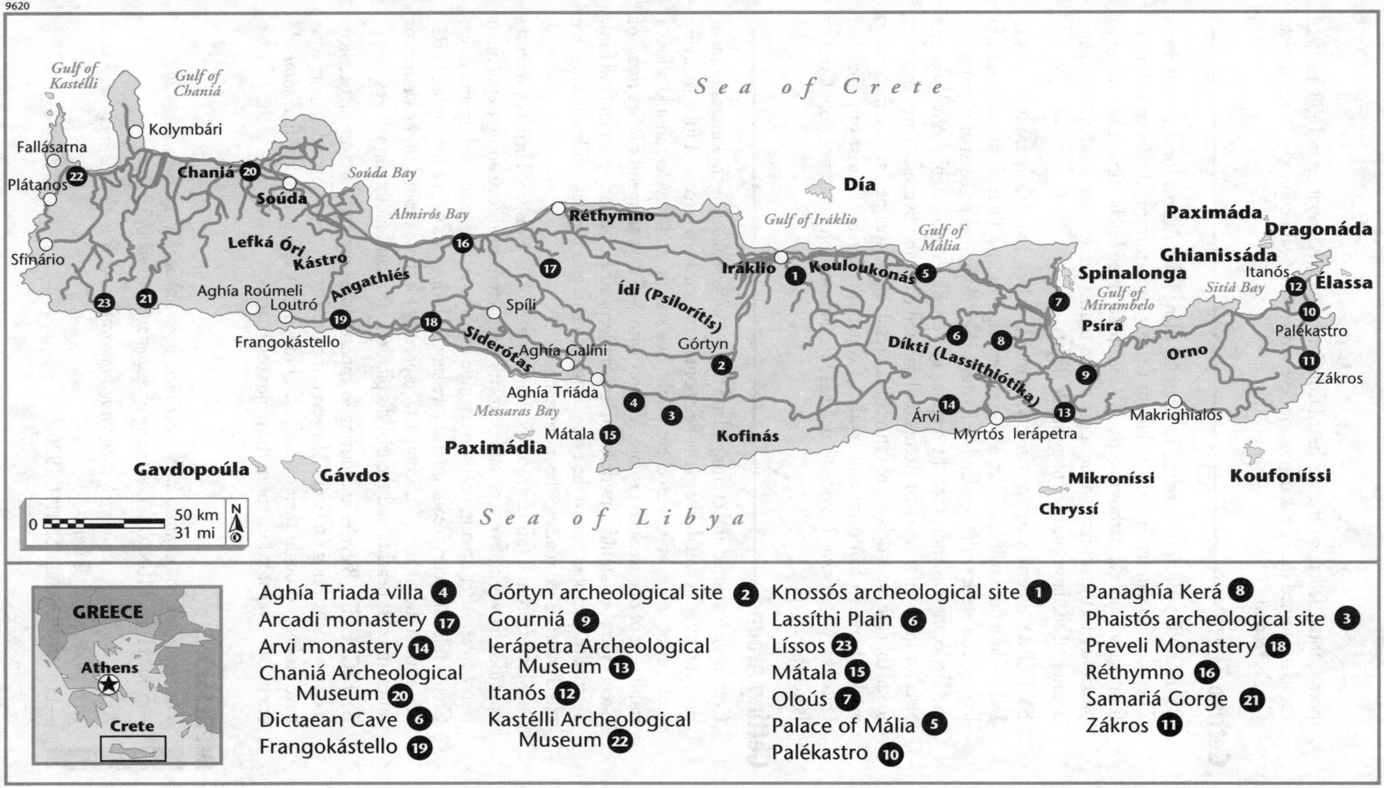
Sea of Crete
Gulf of Kastélli
Gulf of Chaniá
Kolymbári
Fallásarna
Plátanos
Sfinário
Chaniá
Soúda
Soúda Bay
Almirós Bay
Lefká Óri Kástro
Angathiés
Aghía Roúmeli
Loutró
Frangokástello
Réthymno
Spíli
Siderótas
Aghía Galíni
Aghía Triáda
Messaras Bay
Mátala
Paximádia
Gavdopoúla
Gávdos
Ídi (Psiloritis)
Górtyn
Kofinás
Día
Gulf of Iráklio
Iráklio
Kouloukonás
Gulf of Mália
Díkti (Lassithiótika)
Árvi
Myrtós
Ierápetra
Makrighialós
Spinalonga
Gulf of Mirambelo
Psíra
Orno
Paximáda
Dragonáda
Ghianissáda
Itanós
Sitiá Bay
Élassa
Palékastro
Zákros
Mikroníssi
Chryssí
Koufoníssi
Sea of Libya
0
50 km
31 mi
N
GREECE
Athens
Crete
Aghía Triada villa 4
Arcadi monastery 17
Arvi monastery 14
Chaniá Archeological Museum 20
Dictaean Cave 6
Frangokástello 19
Górtyn archeological site 2
Gourniá 9
Ierápetra Archeological Museum 13
Itanós 12
Kastélli Archeological Museum 22
Knossós archeological site 1
Lassíthi Plain 6
Líssos 23
Mátala 15
Oloús 7
Palace of Mália 5
Palékastro 10
Panaghía Kerá 8
Phaistós archeological site 3
Preveli Monastery 18
Réthymno 16
Samariá Gorge 21
Zákros 11

Crete

port, Candiá, fell, and little was heard from Crete until its liberation in 1898. In 1912 the island joined the Greek nation, but even today you hear people say, "Cretans first, Greeks second."

Getting There

BY PLANE Visitors traveling to Crete by plane from Athens (once a week from Thessaloníki) can fly into the Iráklio or Chaniá airport, from Rhodes to Iráklio, or from Kassos and Kárpathos to Sitía. We recommend the Iráklio airport because of its proximity to the capital, where most of the tourist services are located, and hence because of the large number of available flights.

BY FERRY Ferries service Crete year-round at least twice daily from Piraeus to Iráklio, and once daily to Chaniá. A steamer originating in Piraeus connects Crete at least once a week with the island of Ký́thira, the Peloponnesian coast at Gýthio, and the Dodecanese islands. (See the sections on Kastélli, Iráklio, Ághios Nikólaos, and Sitía for more information.) Excursion boats sail daily and hydrofoils are scheduled to sail (but are often delayed or canceled as a result of bad weather) at least three times weekly between Santoríni and Iráklio. Contact the Greek Tourist Organization (*Ellinikós Organismós Tourismoú,* or EOT) for information on cruises from Crete to Israel and Egypt.

Getting Around

Crete is such a varied and exciting island that we suggest allotting the same amount of time and interest you'd give to the Peloponnese or northern Greece. A fully satisfying tour can be made by the excellent public bus system, and travelers should allow a minimum of one week to explore. Visitors with 3–5 days to spend can see many of Crete's sites, but should consider renting a car. Jeeps are particularly popular (and fun), because they expose you to the ever-changing scents and breezes, while allowing free travel on unpaved roads to the more remote areas.

Moving around this large, scenic island is part of its pleasure. There is a recently upgraded network of very passable but still treacherous roads extending to the main resort areas. After driving nearly every mile of highway and local road up and down Crete's hilly and curvaceous interior, we suggest hiring cars with a little more horsepower than the smallest "subcompact," especially for those headed to the western or southern coast beaches and the island's picturesque inland mountain villages.

BY BICYCLE Bicycles are starting to appear more frequently and are an excellent means of sightseeing on Crete. However, the tourists you see in Spandex sportswear have probably brought their own bikes. Throughout Crete you'll only find some old one-speeds available for rent in the major resort areas.

IMPRESSIONS

The people of Crete unfortunately make more history than they can consume locally.
—Saki (H. H. Munro), *The Jesting of Arlington Stringham,* 1911

Knossos is of course immensely interesting historically, but it is all on a small scale, and gives no aesthetic pleasure.
—Logan Pearsall Smith, 1926

BY BOAT The Sofia Company has developed a network of caique shuttles between nearly all of the southern coast towns and Elafonísi island. During the summer, service is generally on a daily basis; during the cooler winter months, it is usually weekly.

BY BUS Public bus service is frequent, pretty inexpensive, and, when not in the middle of the summer, comfortable; most sites of tourist interest are easily reached from nearby resorts. In general, there is far more frequent service between the northern coast towns than between towns on the southern, eastern, and western coasts.

BY CAR Cars and Jeeps are affordable for those traveling in small groups and can greatly simplify south coast travel. Rental car companies such as **Hertz** and **Avis** have offices and representatives in nearly every major tourist center; however, we have found the best prices in locally owned outlets, such as **Caravel** and **Motor Club** in Iráklio (see below). As with mopeds, be sure to either buy or carry insurance.

BY MOPED Mopeds are inexpensive and easy to rent, but be sure to buy insurance and wear a helmet. Even Crete's newest paved roads can disintegrate to gravel paths after sudden rains or harsh weather.

BY TAXI Metered taxis are widely available for sightseeing and for group transport to sites outside the main towns. However, if you plan to do any sightseeing for more than one day, a rental car is cheaper and offers a greater degree of independence. There are taxis available at fixed-rate prices at the Iráklio airport that will take you to nearly any of the established resort towns.

1 Iráklio

If you have only one or two days to devote to Crete, you must spend them in Iráklio(n) (Herakleion), the largest city and principal port. This busy capital is graced with a cosmopolitan air and such superb artistic and cultural treasures that it's a vital stopover for any visitor to Greece. A visit to the nearby palace of Knossós and to Iráklio's world-class Archeological Museum is an absolute must. (There's hope that new runway construction will put an end to aircraft taking off and landing over the city, which is many people's chief complaint.)

Getting There

BY PLANE Iráklio Airport is serviced by direct charter flights from all over Europe. Otherwise, **Olympic Airways** handles most flights from within Greece; their office is at Eleftheria (Liberty) Square (☎ **229-191**). There are several flights daily from Athens to Iráklio, three times daily from Athens to Chaniá, two times a week from Athens and once a week from Kárpathos and Kássos to Sitía; and three times a week between Iráklio and Rhodes, and two times a week to Thessaloníki (Salónica). **Cretan Airways** has daily flights from Athens. **Southeast European Airways (SEEA)** also has service from Athens.

Iráklio Airport is 15 minutes outside the city. City buses leave every 15 or 20 minutes from the center (several stops) on the way to the airport and cost 200 Drs (83¢). Taxis cost approximately 1,000 Drs ($4.20). There is a **tourist information desk** run by the Civil Aviation Authority at the Iráklio Airport and also a board to make free phone calls for different tourist information.

As for buying air tickets, we found the **Blavákis Travel** office at 8 Kalargón Square (☎ **282-541**), near Fountain Square, to be helpful and efficient.

BY BUS The bus stations for the northwest, east (including Chaniá and Réthymno), and southeast of Crete and Mália are 436 yards from the ferry quay, under the red canopy (☎ **282-637**). Buses to Mátala, Phaistós, and Aghía Galíni leave from the terminal at Kalokerinoú and Makaríou Streets (☎ **283-073**), in the west-central part of town, opposite the Chaniá Gate. There is frequent bus service to all parts of the island, and a complete schedule is available from the National Tourist Office (EOT). There is frequent public bus service between the airport and central Iráklio for 200 Drs (83¢).

BY FERRY Ferryboats depart daily from Piraeus for Iráklio and Chaniá, and three times weekly for Ághios Nikólaos. The most convenient steamers leave at 6:30 or 7pm and arrive at Iráklio or Chaniá the following morning after a 12-hour ride. The steamers that service Ághios Nikólaos directly are most often local boats, which make stops throughout the Cyclades, then at Ághios Nikólaos and Sitía, and then continue on to Kássos, Kárpathos, and the other Dodecanese islands. For more information on schedules, contact **Tourist Information** in Athens (☎ **143**) or the Piraeus Port Authority (☎ **45-11-311**).

Excursion boats and scheduled ferries ply the popular Iráklio-to-Santoríni route at least five days weekly. Tickets are available from local travel agents for 2,300 Drs ($9.60) for the 5½-hour trip. When it's operating on a regular basis, you can go in 2½ hours by hydrofoil (5,200 Drs or $21.70); for information, contact nearly any travel agent, such as **Arabadzóglou Travel** (☎ **226-697**) or **Blavákis Travel** (☎ **282-541**) near Fountain Square.

Getting Around

BY CAR **Hertz** (☎ **081/229-702** in Iráklio at the airport) has several Crete offices and offers the convenience of reserving your car in advance worldwide. **Avis** (☎ **081/225-421**) and **Hellascars** (☎ **081/223-240**) also have Iráklio offices, as well as the flexibility of having additional offices on the island. As always, it's much cheaper to make your rental-car arrangements outside of Greece than to reserve a car in the country. If you reserve a small Nissan in Iráklio, for example, you'll pay upward of 125,000 Drs ($520) per week for unlimited mileage!

Some of the cheapest rental deals can be made by the week with companies such as **Caravel** (☎ **081/288-060**; fax 220-362) and **Motor Club** (☎ **081/222-408**; fax 018/222-862). On our last trip we drove an excellent little Fiat Panda with a sun roof from Motor Club for about 75,000 Drs ($312.50) a week. It's often difficult to book a car from any of the small companies during the high season (June to September); calling ahead for reservations is recommended. Remember to carry insurance on any rental.

BY MOPED During the high season, automatic 50cc mopeds, rented everywhere, average 6,000 Drs ($25), including insurance and taxes. **Motor Club,** with its central office in Iráklio at no. 1, 18 Ánglon Square (☎ **081/222-408**), has an office in all the main tourist cities on Crete.

BY TAXI Taxis cruise the city of Iráklio and can be booked by dialing **210-124** or **210-102.** There is also a taxi stand across the street from the Archeological Museum. The taxi problems of Athens also abound in Iráklio. Drivers tell you the hotels you ask for are booked and insist on taking you elsewhere. If you have reason to be suspicious, stand up to the driver or insist on getting out of the cab. At the airport you will find posted long-distance prices to different parts of Crete. For example: 14,000 Drs ($58.30) to Réthymno or Aghía Galíni. It might be worth it if you belong to a group of three or four; in Iráklio there is a minimum charge of 500 Drs ($2.10); there is a surcharge of 350 Drs ($1.50) for trips to the airport.

Fast Facts: Iráklio

American Express The American Express agent for Crete is the **Adámis Travel Bureau,** Odós 25 Avgoústou 23, Iráklio (☎ **246-202,** fax 224-717). It's open Monday through Saturday from 8am to 5pm, and Sunday from 10am to noon and 6 to 8:30pm for emergency traveler's check services; they handle mail during these hours.

Area Code When calling from outside the various towns, use area code **081** for Iráklio, **0821** for Chaniá, **0831** for Réthymno, **0841** for Ághios Nikólaos, and **0842** for Ierápetra. Many smaller districts that have their own district codes are also noted in the text.

Car Rentals See "Getting Around" in this section.

Climate See "When to Go" in Chapter 2.

Crime See "Safety" below.

Currency Exchange A Bank of Greece and an Ionian Bank on Odós 25 Avgoústou are open the standard banking hours: Monday through Thursday from 8am to 2pm and Friday from 8am to 1:30pm. The National Bank of Greece, at Odós 25 Avgoústou 35, is open Monday through Friday at the same hours. The post offices, some EOT offices, and many of the larger hotels throughout Crete will cash traveler's checks at extended hours for a nominal fee.

Doctors/Dentists Refer to your hotel reception desk or to the local EOT office (☎ **081/228-203**).

Emergencies In case of emergency, contact the local police (☎ **081/283-190**) at Venizélos Square. There is usually an English-speaking officer on duty.

Film See "Photographic Needs" below.

Holidays The island whose most famous native son is Níkos Kazantzákis's fiercely individualistic Zorba the Greek is certain to celebrate many unique holidays. Before departure from Athens you can get information on national holidays such as **Naval Week,** celebrated mid-July at the port of Soúda near Chaniá; **Greek Easter;** the **Wine Festival,** held in August in Réthymno; the government-sponsored arts festivals, such as the **Iráklio Festival.** Don't forget to check with the local tourist office or with the police for information on Sitía's **Sultana Raisin Festival** in September; **Kritsa's Folk Festival,** where a mock wedding is performed; **Elos's Chestnut Festival;** and Aghía Galíni's **Sheep Shearing Festival.**

Hospitals Venizélio Hospital (☎ **237-502**) is on Knossó's Road, Iráklio. For general first-aid information, call **222-222.**

Laundry/Dry Cleaning **Lavomatique,** at Odós Merabelou 25, near the Archeological Museum in Iráklio, is one of several self-service laundries, open from 9am to

8pm daily, except holidays. Wash costs 1,400 Drs ($5.80). Bring your own soap or pay 200 Drs (83¢) extra. There's a dry cleaners on Dikeosínis Street providing one-day service.

Luggage Storage/Lockers **Left Luggage** (☎ **250-714**), at Odós 25 Avgoústou 48, is perfectly located (across the street from the Bank of Greece) and the ideal solution for excessive or cumbersome luggage. Each piece of luggage costs 400 Drs ($1.70) a day to store (compared to 800 Drs at the airport); the cost includes insurance on your stuff. Left Luggage is open daily from 7am™ to 11pm and provides man-on-duty security daily between April 1st and October 31st.

Photographic Needs Camera repairs, photographic supplies, and film processing are available at **Iokimides,** Odós Dikeosínis 33 (☎ **283-245**), and at several shops in the town center.

Police See "Emergencies" above.

Post Office The main post office is on Dascaloyánnis Square, in Iráklio. It's open Monday through Friday from 8am to 8pm. The portable branches at El Greco Park and the port are open Saturday from 8am to 8pm and Sunday from 9am to 6pm.

Religious Services The church of Ághios Ioánnis Vaptistís (St. John the Baptist), at Antoníou Street in Iráklio, has Catholic services twice a day Tuesday through Sunday. Call the Greek Tourist Organization (EOT) for the hours.

Safety Iráklio is a relatively safe city, and is well suited for late-night walks. Nevertheless, there are basic precautions you should take whenever you're traveling in an unfamiliar city or country. Stay alert and be aware of your surroundings. Wear a moneybelt and keep a close eye on your possessions. Be especially careful with cameras, wallets, and purses—all favorite targets of pickpockets. For extra safety, leave your passport and other valuables in your hotel safe-deposit box.

Taxis See "Getting Around" in this section.

Telephones/Telegrams/Telexes The central telecommunications office, OTE, is over and down one street from the back of El Greco Park in Iráklio. It is open daily from 7:30am to 11pm, with limited services after 8pm. There is a mobile OTE on Elefthería Square, it's open Monday through Friday from 8am to 11pm and closed Saturday and Sunday. The OTE at the airport never closes (theoretically).

Tourist Information The Greek Tourist Organization (EOT), at Odós Xanthoudídou 1, off Elefthería Square in Iráklio (☎ **081/228-203**), is open Monday through Friday from 8am to 3pm and has a very helpful and knowledgeable staff; it's closed Saturday and Sunday. There is also a Civil Aviation Authority information office (no telephone) at the Iráklio airport; it's open daily from 7:30am to 4:30pm.

One of the most helpful travel offices in Iráklio is **Arabadzóglou Travel,** at Odós 25 Avgoústou 54 (☎ **226-697,** fax 222-184).

What to See & Do

Iráklio has several major historical sites from throughout Crete's colorful past. The Minoan Palace at Knossós is just three miles south of the heart of the city. Within walking distance of the ferry are several fascinating Venetian and Byzantine remains.

A WALKING TOUR

Ferries from Piraeus arrive daily between 7 and 8am, a perfect time to explore the still-quiet city. From the new harbor, turn right and continue along the waterfront to the old Venetian Arsenal, an arcaded storage area awaiting development. New historical-preservation laws have been effected in Iráklio to ensure restoration rather than destruction of its historic monuments.

At the tip of the old port is the "Koules," a wonderfully preserved 14th-century fortress, rebuilt between 1523 and 1540. A Lion of St. Mark proudly guards the doorway. Each morning the old harbor comes alive, with brisk trading in red mullet, *chopis* (a local fish), and swordfish brought in by the fishing boats. If you continue along the waterfront (Makaríou Street) and uphill, you'll soon see the West bus station, and behind it the small Historical Museum of Crete, Odós Kalokerinoú 7 (☎ **283-219**). It houses a private collection of Cretan folk art, Venetian and Turkish antiquities, memorabilia of Crete's celebrated son, author Níkos Kazantzákis, and an El Greco painting. The museum (☎ **246-211**) is open Tuesday through Sunday 8:30am–3pm. Admission is 500 Drs ($2.10).

If you turn left opposite the old port at Odós 25 Avgoústou, you'll be on Iráklio's travel agent/ticket office/rental-car row. Behind the first small square on your left is the church of Ághios Títos, built in the 16th century and dedicated to Títos, who first brought Christianity to Crete (at the city of Górtyn). Just past the Knossós Hotel is the lovely Venetian Loggia and, farther up, the church of San Marco (from 1303, converted into a mosque by the Turks and now used as an exhibition hall). Across the street is the Lion, or Morosíni, Fountain, built by the Venetian general Francesco Morosini and dedicated in 1628. The lion support, thought to have come from another 14th-century fountain, dominates Venizélos Square, named for Elefthérios (Eleutherios) Venizélos, a Cretan revolutionary and later premier of Greece. The popular square is now more commonly called the Fountain Square. Stop at one of the many cafés for a breakfast of Crete's flavorful bread with local jams or honey. To avoid problems, be sure to ask the prices in advance if a set menu is not offered. As you revive, you can watch the pace of the city quicken.

A few blocks down Katekháki Street is the cathedral of Ághios Mínas. On the right side of the transept are four icons credited to Michael Damaskinós, a master of the Cretan School (and perhaps teacher of El Greco). At the nearby church of Aghía Ekateríni is a collection of icons by members of this same school. Other Venetian monuments, such as the Porta Chaníon (near the bus station for Phaistós), the Bembo Fountain on Kornáros Square, and the Martinengo Ramparts, along the Venetian enclosure wall at the southern tip of the city, are recommended for those with an abundance of time.

GUIDED TOURS

Many of Iráklio's visitors arrive on cruise ships in the morning and depart the same evening, so tourist services are geared to catch these hit-and-run sightseers. One of the biggest tour operators is the **Creta Travel Bureau,** Odós Epiméndou 20–22 (☎ **081/22-70-02**), with offices also in Ághios Nikólaos and Réthymno.

To get the most from a visit to Iráklio's two greatest sites, the Archeological Museum and the palace of Knossós, we recommend purchasing the excellent guidebook *Crete* (in the Greece Museums and Monuments series), by J. A. Papapostólou, for 1,500 Drs ($6.25), especially if you'd like to go on your own. Otherwise, a guided tour of what remains of the fascinating Minoan culture is strongly recommended. Half-day guided bus tours to Knossós and the museum are offered daily by several travel agents, either as separate sites—at 4,500 Drs and 3,250 Drs ($18.75 and $13.50), respectively—or as a combined tour for 6,000 Drs ($25), not including entrance fees.

A popular way of touring is by horse-drawn cart or on horseback. This pastime is offered by *Heraklion Riding Centre*, **Finikia Stables** (☎ **253-166,** fax 250-781). Guides lead riders through the surrounding hill villages for a look at the way things used to be.

Archeological Museum

The Archeological Museum, on Xanthoudídou Street (☎ **226-092**) opposite the national tourist (EOT) office, merits at least two hours of close examination by anyone interested in the Minoan civilization. The labeled ground-floor exhibits are grouped chronologically in 15 galleries. The museum includes Neolithic, Hellenic, and Roman finds from throughout Crete, but is unique in the world for its comprehensive Minoan collection. Superb examples abound of terra-cotta icons and ceramic ware, decorated in typically Minoan black swirls and spirals. There are marble, bronze, ivory, and stone figurines worshipping, fighting with bulls, dancing, making music, and performing acrobatic feats. Precious faience plaques depict styles of housing, clothing, sports, and worship. Several pieces of exquisite gold jewelry are displayed. There are drawings, sculptures, reliefs, and seals representing every aspect of the bull in secular and religious terms. The spirit of the Minoans, their love for natural and physical beauty, their delight in depicting the wonders of the world around them, are to be seen everywhere in this exquisite collection.

Upstairs on the first floor is the marvelous collection of frescoes from the palaces of Knossós (copies have been installed at the site), Mália, and Phaistós, and the smaller villas of Amnissós and Aghía Tríada. Erect, lean young men with long curls; buxom, topless maidens; graceful lilies and dolphins; bulls and ornate, multicolored decorative patterns bring the Minoan culture back to life.

Admission: 1,250 Drs ($5.20) adults, students half price; free on Sunday. (If you insist on using your video camera, expect to pay a whopping 11,250 Drs or $46.90.)

Open: Monday 11am–5pm, Tues–Fri 8am–5pm (daily till 3pm from October–March) and Sat–Sun 8:30am–5pm.

Knossós

The archeological site at Knossós, three miles south of Iráklio, contains the Central Palace, which dominated Minoan civilization from 2000 to 1400 B.C. The remarkable excavation of ruins by British archeologist Sir Arthur Evans includes an elaborate recreation of large parts of the original palace.

Evans began his work in 1900 (after some 1878 finds by a local scholar); as his dig progressed, he steadily bought up the land behind the growing port of Iráklio. He found that a town had existed before Minos built his palace, so he conjectured that the king (and spiritual leader of the Minoans) may have been a wealthy landowner. The huge complex (over four acres in area) is thought to have had 1,400 rooms, on many levels; it's known that the east wing of the palace had five stories and the west had three.

Evans used lots of cement and a color code to evoke images of the original structure. The round red columns were painted wood, used in building because their tensility made them earthquake resistant. Column bases and the lower portion of walls were covered in marble or alabaster, in contrast to the stuccoed top half, decorated with lively, multicolored frescoes. Wood was used in the brick walls and for door and window frames; the panes were alabaster. Remember that the fabulous frescoes have been removed from the site and can be found at Iráklio's Archeological Museum.

Eighteen storerooms were uncovered containing 150 *pithoi* (large urns) holding liquids (perhaps olive oil) used to light lamps. Evans believed that the palace was finally destroyed by a fire that roared through its wooden structure, fueled by lamps overturned in an earthquake. The little that remains of the palace is still a marvel.

Most of the lower flights of the original, expertly crafted stairs are still used, and near the queen's megaron is what's considered to be the first flush toilet! Horizontal and vertical clay pipes (proof of the Minoans' expert sewage system) can still be seen. In the administrative wing of the palace, a wooden throne, thought to have belonged to Minos, has been re-created from a void fused in some volcanic ruins by a casting process. Outside the palace buildings are the paved stones of Europe's oldest road and the collapsed steps of Europe's first theater.

Evans also found the remains of what may have been an area (outside the palace grounds) for the celebrated bull dances, part of the mysterious religious cult surrounding this animal. If the colorful restoration of Knossós is too much for your historical sensibilities, at the knee-high ruins of Mália and Phaistós you can imagine what the palaces must have looked like all by yourself.

Admission: 1,250 Drs ($5.20) for adults, students half price; free on Sunday. (If you use your video camera, expect to pay a whopping 11,250 Drs—$46.90.)

Open: Mon–Fri 8am–5pm; Sat–Sun 8:30am–3pm. Try to come before 9:30am or after 11:30am (before the half-day tours from the cruise ships arrive and after they have departed) so you'll have space to explore. **Bus:** Bus no. 2 runs to Knossós every 20 minutes from outside El Greco Park. It can also be picked up at Elefthería (Liberty) Square. The fare is 250 Drs ($1).

SHOPPING

Iráklio has some very Greek shopping opportunities. There's a daily meat and produce market at the head of Odós 25 Avgoústou, along 1866 Odós, a few blocks inland from the Morosíni Fountain. It's best in the early morning, but always a lot of fun.

Several shops carrying souvenirs, tape cassettes of Cretan music, photo greeting cards, and kitschy worry beads are found around Eleftheria Square, along Dikeosínis Street and, parallel to it, along the pedestrian mall of Daedalou Street. Eléni Kastrinouyanni has a weaving, handcraft, jewelry, and museum-reproduction shop on Eleftheria Square, across from the Archeological Museum at Odós Íkarou 3 (☎ **245-040**). Elegant European sportswear is found on Chandákos Street, off Morosíni Fountain Square, as well as on Koraí Street, another pedestrian mall parallel to Daedalou.

Where to Stay

Many of the Class C hotels originally built to handle Iráklio's tourist boom now find themselves in the middle of a noisy, crowded city. Some of the best of the newer lodgings are located outside the city center, but we've also included many of the older pensions, whose remnants of European charm make up for their area's big-city drawbacks.

BY THE NEW PORT

$ **Hotel Poseidon,** Odós Posidónos 46, Póros (New Harbor area). ☎ **081/245-360** or **222-545.** Fax 081/245-405. 26 rms (all with bath). TEL

Rates (including breakfast): 10,000 Drs ($41.70) single; 14,000 Drs ($58.35) double.

The outstanding choice here is the Hotel Poseidon (located at the end of the street), because of the hospitality, warmth, and helpfulness of its staff. The owner, John Polychronides, is sophisticated and well traveled and keeps up-to-date on tourists' needs. He and his staff are knowledgeable about historical sites and the ever-changing resorts on Crete. All the Poseidon's rooms (spotless, with plenty of hot water) have balconies overlooking the port or face west with a view of the Stroumboúlis mountains (ensuring a welcome breeze in Crete's hot summer). Breakfast is served in a lounge decorated with embroidery and local handicrafts. (**Note:** The hotel may be too close to the airport for some.)

BY THE OLD PORT

Ilaira Hotel, Odós Ariádnis 1, Iráklio 71202. ☎ **081/227-103.** Fax 081/227-666. 20 rms (all with bath). TEL

Rates (including breakfast) 11,180 Drs ($46.60) single; 14,820–15,780 Drs ($61.75–$65.75) double. AE, V.

Several blocks above, and commanding a somewhat obscured view of, the Venetian harbor is the Ilaira, which has modern, whipped-stucco-walled rooms. This establishment is an acceptable alternative, but we found it in need of some freshening up.

$ **Kris Hotel,** Odós Bofor 2, Iráklio 71202. ☎ **081/223-211** or **223-944.** 12 rms (all with bath). MINIBAR

Rates: (including breakfast) 9,100 Drs ($37.90) single; 11,700 Drs ($48.75) double.

The first choice in this part of town for value is the Kris Hotel. The wonderfully friendly Maria rents single and double occupancy rooms with kitchenettes and balconies in this converted apartment building. The rooms have some homey touches (flowering vines, for instance) and are spacious.

Lato Hotel, Odós Epimendou 15, Iráklio 71202. ☎ **081/228-103.** Fax 081/240-350. 54 rms (all with bath).

Rates: 11,960 Drs ($49.85) single: 16,120 Drs ($67.20) double. AE, DC, MC, V.

Readers Joel and Nili Goldschmidt of Red Bank, New Jersey, recommended this hotel just above the old harbor. We found it modern enough, clean and comfortable, though some of the bathrooms have been added outside on the balconies. There's a nice little café-bar downstairs, and room service is offered 7am to 11pm for a 20% surcharge.

Marin Hotel, Odós Bofor 10, Iráklio 71202. ☎ **081/220-737.** 48 rms (all with bath). TEL

Rates (including breakfast): 8,340 Drs ($34.75) single; 12,785 Drs ($53.30) double. AE, EC, MC, V.

The Marin Hotel is another choice on the block. Several of its rooms have large balconies overlooking the harbor, and there's a bar, open evenings, on the roof garden.

DOWNTOWN

Hotel Daedalos, Odós Daedalou 15, Iráklio 71202. ☎ **081/224-391.** 60 rms (all with bath).

Rates: 8,500 Drs ($34.40) single; 13,250 Drs ($55.20) double.

Our friend Suzanna stays here on the busy pedestrian shopping lane when in town, and we found it attractive enough but full on both our most recent visits—not a bad sign. Check it out.

Hotel Lena, Odós Lachaná 10, Iráklio 71202. ☎ **081/223-280.** 18 rms (9 with bath).

Rates: 4,550 Drs ($18.95) single; 7,800 Drs ($32.50) double with bath, 5,850 Drs ($24.40) without bath. V.

The Hotel Lena, off Výronos Street, is well run by the Manganas family. The Lena has freshly painted, bathless rooms (five have showers) that are bargain priced. The accommodations represent a major step up from the more budget oriented hostels in the area but are still quite modest.

Mirabello Hotel, Odós Theotokopoúlou 20, Iráklio 71202. ☎ **081/285-052.** 25 rms (7 with bath).

Rates: 7,540 Drs ($31.40) single with bath, 6,000 Drs ($25) single without bath; 10,150 Drs ($42.30) double with bath, 8,990 Drs ($37.45) double without bath.

The Mirabello occupies an attractive old building, and its balconies overlook the neighborhood's quiet residential streets. Host Costas Kamaratakis, ex-captain in the Greek Merchant Navy, runs a tight ship here, and is renovating the hotel.

NEAR THE MUSEUM

$ **Rea Pension,** Kalimeráki and Chandákos Streets, Iráklio 71202. ☎ **081/223-638.** 16 rms (5 with bath).

Rates: 6,370 Drs ($26.55) single with bath, 4,550 Drs ($18.95) single without bath; 7,540 Drs ($31.40) double with bath, 5,655 Drs ($23.55) double without bath.

Rea Pension has spare, spotless rooms, some with balconies. Compared with others in this price range in the center of Iráklio, the guest rooms and facilities are a tad cleaner and better maintained. A good value.

Pension Vergina, Odós Hortatson 32, Iráklio 71202. ☎ **081/242-739.** 8 rms (none with bath).

Rates: 3,200 Drs ($13.35) single; 4,720 Drs ($19.65) double.

Pension Vergina is a calm place behind the historical museum. All eight old-fashioned, bathless rooms are clean and spacious. The Vergina's lovely garden with banana trees is a real bonus, especially after a long day of touring.

YOUTH HOSTELS

GYH Youth Hostel, Odós Výronos 5, Iráklio 71202. ☎ **081/286-281** or **222-947.** 5 rms (all with bath) and 100 beds.

Rates: 1,400 Drs ($5.80) bed; 3,900 Drs ($16.25) family room.

The GYH Youth Hostel has about 100 beds in dorm-style rooms, plus 40 beds on the roof, as well as a limited number of double private "family" rooms. There is a spacious sitting/dining/breakfast room where hostess Irene is reputed to make the best Greek salad on the island (375 Drs or $2.10) as well as tasty omelets.

A SPLURGE CHOICE

★ **Galaxy Hotel,** Odós Dimokratías 67, Iráklio. ☎ **081/238-812.** Fax 081/211-211. 140 rms (all with bath). A/C (in summer only) TV TEL

Rates (including breakfast): 24,895 Drs ($103.75) single; 32,500 Drs ($135.40) double. AE, DC, EC, MC, V.

The starkly modern design of this cast-concrete hotel, considered one of Iráklio's better inns, gives a hint of the many high-end facilities found within (sauna and cappuccino bar are but two). The Galaxy is a 15-minute walk away from the center of town. All rooms are spacious and paneled in cane matting; they have the latest amenities and, best of all, have views of the fabulous pool and sun deck below. Because of its orientation to groups and business travelers, the Galaxy is busy year-round.

Where to Eat

Iráklio boasts some excellent restaurants. Their special dishes are attributed to the variety of fresh produce (grown year-round in the south) and the Cretans' special flair for cooking. Crete is also known for its subtle wines—the rich, dry Minos Cava white and the Cava Lato reds.

Daedelou Street, a pedestrian mall running between Elefthería and Fountain squares, is lined with restaurants that are great for people-watching.

$ **Ippocampos Ouzeri,** Odós Mitsotáki 3. ☎ **282-081.**

Cuisine: CRETAN.
Prices: Appetizers 525–1,000 Drs ($2.20–$4.15); main courses 1,000–2,100 Drs ($4.15–$8.75).
Open: Mon–Sat 1–3:30pm and 7pm–midnight; closed Sun.

Three seahorses identify the small Ippocampos Ouzeri on a hill, near the foot of August 25 Street, a perfect introduction to the finery of Cretan cusine. Sample any of its long list of *mezédes* (appetizers) with a carafe of the tasty house white wine, and enjoy the cruise ships pulling into the harbor. We liked the small, fried whole fish, fresh shrimp veal meat balls, petite rice-stuffed dolmádes, large tender calamari with lemon, fried sliced potatoes, and smooth mashed eggplant.

★ **Kyriakos,** Odós Dimokratías X-51. ☎ **224-649.**

Cuisine: CRETAN. **Reservations:** Required.
Prices: Appetizers 500–1,400 Drs ($2.10–$5.85); main courses 1,225–3,100 Drs ($5.10–$12.90). AE, DC.
Open: Thurs–Tues noon–4pm and 7pm–midnight; closed June 15–July 15 and Sun July 16–Sept 30.

Many residents consider Kyriakos the finest restaurant in town and definitely worth the 15-minute walk south of the Archeological Museum. You'll find seating indoors and out at tables with lively pink tattersall cloths, a wine display, and a largely Greek clientele. Try the lamb fricassee or the veal with onions and the piquant taramosaláta. **Note:** If you can't get in (it's often booked up), consider going to nearby Tartufo for fine pizzas.

Minos Taverna, Odós Daedelou 10. ☎ **244-827.**

Cuisine: CRETAN.
Prices: Appetizers 600–1,500 Drs ($2.50–$6.25); main courses 950–3,600 Drs ($3.95–$15). AE, MC, V (commissions added to bill).
Open: Lunch and dinner Mon–Sat 11am–3pm and 6–10pm; closed every other Sunday.

Minos Taverna is favored by locals for its special Cretan veal with onions, the seasonal stuffed zucchini flowers, the house wines, and the exotic lamb-baked-in-yogurt dishes. Harris runs the show here and makes sure that the service is attentive, if sometimes too rushed in summer; don't expect to be allowed to linger after your meal. The Minos is one of the few eateries in Iráklio open year-round. (We also recommend the Klimataria next door.)

Baritis Taverna, Póros (New Harbor area). ☎ **225-859.**

Cuisine: CRETAN/SEAFOOD.

Prices: Appetizers 260–1,400 Drs ($1.10–$5.85); main courses 700–3,000 Drs ($2.90–$12.50).

Open: Mon–Sat noon–2:30pm and 7pm–2am; Sun 7pm–2am.

A fig tree grows in Iráklio—that is, if you're in the lovely garden taverna run by the Baritis family. The taverna's specialty is fish (although there is a varied menu). A canopy of grape vines shades the dining area where locals (with a scattering of tourists) leisurely sup while Greek tunes waft through the warm summer air. We sampled and enjoyed grilled octopus, calamari, salad, and crisply fried potatoes, and had a wonderful time of it in this most sublimely simple setting.

Taverna Faros, Póros (New Harbor area). ☎ **243-233.**

Cuisine: SEAFOOD.

Prices: Appetizers 525–1,000 Drs ($2.10–$4.15); main courses 1,000–2,600 Drs ($4.15–$10.85).

Open: Dinner only Mon–Sat 7pm–2am; closed Sun.

Taverna Faros offers some of the freshest fish and seafood we encountered in the Iráklio area. It is popular with residents, who seem to seek this lesser-known eatery for its fresh seafood as well as its friendly and caring hosts. Prices are midmarket, falling somewhere between those of Kyriakos and Ippocampos.

Evening Entertainment

If you're still sampling Cretan wines or need some coffee, stroll over to the Lion Fountain and grab the nearest empty chair. This is where the action is. For international diversion, try the **Apollo Cinema** off Daedalou Street for showings of imported B-pictures and an occasional French classic.

A quieter, more intimate venue is **Pub La Palma,** at Odós Idomenéos 14, where you can have a drink on the comfortable patio under Bob Marley and James Dean banners. For a similarly mellow atmosphere there is the **Dore Piano Bar and Castro.** Opposite the old Venetian port, at the foot of Odós 25 Avgoústou (across from the Ippocampos Ouzerí), is **To Trata,** a pleasant outdoor café cooled by the sea breezes that swirl around the fortress. It's a very nice spot to while away the cocktail hour and watch the cruise ships. Among the best of the lesser-known café/pubs is **Guernica,** located along Psaromiligon Street. **Theasi** and **Glow** are two popular bars located just off Elefthería Square on Ginari Street. We hung out at **Onar,** at Odós Chandákos 36 (☎ **288-298**), listening to Greek rock 'n' roll, sipping coffee, playing a terrible game of backgammon, and enjoying the scenic outdoor area; it's open daily from noon to 1am.

When you're ready to bash heads (or merely rock), try the dynamic duo **Scala** and **Trapeza** on Bofor Street. They open at 10pm, and the entrance fee is 1,500 Drs ($6.25), which includes a free drink. Just past the bend in the road, at Odós Íkarou 9, is **Disco Athina** (☎ **282-242**), a steady standby on the Iráklio club scene, where things start popping at 10:30pm; admission is 1,500 Drs ($6.25).

One-Day Excursions

The region south of Iráklio is similar to California's Napa Valley or France's Bordeaux region. Low, rolling hills and gently shaded valleys are resplendent with groves of trellised grapes cultivated for many of Crete's fine wines and powerful *rakí.* Sun worshippers should try the long Thombrouk beach east of the city in Amnissós.

ARCHÁNES

If you want to experience the full sensuality of this region, drive or take one of the frequent buses to Archánes (9.3 miles south of Iráklio) and walk to some of the nearby vineyards. You'll be saturated with the fragrance of the air as you behold the exquisite vistas. Stop by a vineyard during August or September (depending on the weather) and you can watch the harvest. Each year several visitors hire themselves out as day laborers during the harvest period. Most vineyards pay about 5,000 Drs ($22) a day, and it really is tough, back-breaking work. But there's nothing like jumping in and taking part in a tradition that dates back thousands of years.

A delightful stop in Páno (Upper) Archánes is the shaded ouzerí Miriófito, located at the base of the hill on which the village is built. Miriófito serves local drinks and light food, and you can watch the goings-on from under the cool of the trees.

The region has a long history of wine growing. At Vathypétro, three miles south (you must walk), excavations have unearthed a Minoan palace (from about 1600 B.C.) with facilities for pressing grapes. Olive presses and kilns for firing pottery have also been found. Nearby, archeologists have uncovered what they believe are the remnants of an early, important center of worship. Traces of blood have led researchers to the conclusion that sacrifices (animal and human) took place near the palace.

Southeast of Archánes is the town of Thrapsánou, where local craftsmen still make the huge ceramic urns *(pithoi)* that have been made since Minoan times. Paradosiakí Keramikí (☎ **0891/41-374**), 7/10 of a mile outside Thrapsánou, is an ideal place to watch the age-old method of pottery making. The potter's small shop has some tantalizing bargains, like glazed espresso cups at 1,000 Drs ($4.15) for a set. Open Monday to Saturday.

SPÍLI

Spíli is the perfect antidote to the Dionysian revelries of Crete's beach resorts. Imagine a hillside village of grapevines and roses and cherry trees where the old stone houses, built generations ago, are linked by winding, pebble-strewn paths wide enough only for donkeys; where the immaculate courtyards are filled with geraniums and drying herbs left for the family goats to nibble on; where the whitewashed terraces are covered with grape-filled trellises, palms, and a variety of fragrant flowers; where the square has a fountain that spouts mountain spring water from 19 stone lions' heads.

The charmingly bucolic character of this community, its chief attraction, seems somewhat threatened as Spíli gains popularity as an excursion site and its inhabitants, mostly farmers and their families, attune themselves to today's world. Serving the village and its steady stream of visitors, for example, are seven nearby cafés, two gas stations, a video store, two banks, a post office, a dry cleaner, a "supermarket," and a small hotel. But you can easily lose the crowds by abandoning the main street and striking out on Spíli's back lanes.

To get there, take the bus from Réthymno to Aghía Galíni and tell the driver to let you off at Spíli (in Greek: *Thélo ná katevó stí Spíli*).

Where to Stay & Eat

Green Hotel, Spíli 74053. ☎ **0832/22-225.** 15 rms (all with bath). TEL

Rates: 6,000 Drs ($25) single; 7,500 Dr ($31.25) double.

John has dubbed it the "Green House," for besides the plants that have overtaken the hotel's light natural-wood interior, every one of the rooms has a balcony filled with potted geraniums and overlooking flower-covered houses on the main street or the valley below. George Maravelakis, its owner, claims to speak a "Greek salad" of English, French, and German, but he just couldn't understand our praise for his "green thumb." Stay and you'll have the opportunity to try his yogurt (drenched in home-grown honey and nuts) for breakfast. George's brother, Giannis, runs **Gianni's Restaurant** (☎ **22-707**), a fairly new one near the fountain square, heartily recommended for its two specialties, pork gyros and lamb with vegetables. It is open daily 7am to midnight; closed November to February.

What to See & Do

GÓRTYN

Górtyn (Górtys) (☎ **081/226-092** is one of Crete's most important archeological sites because of the excellent ruins from several eras found there, among them the remains of the three-aisled basilica of Ághios Títos, dedicated in the 6th century A.D. to a pupil of Saint Paul (Titus) who founded the first Christian community on Crete at this site in A.D. 65. It's considered Crete's finest Christian monument. The basilica is at the foot of the ancient acropolis of Górtyn, which served as the capital of Crete during the Roman period. Surrounding the basilica are the remains of a 2d-century Roman odeum. Across the highway, enter the olive grove past the Metropolis road to see the remains of a 2d-century praetorium (governor's house), a nymphaeum that the Byzantines converted into a fountain, and a temple dedicated to the Egyptian gods Isis and Sarapis; there's even a temple to the Pythian Apollo. Farther back are remains of a small amphitheater.

The earliest settlement dates from post-Mycenaean times (10th century B.C.), and almost every succeeding generation has used materials from existing temples to construct edifices of its own. The best evidence of this is the Code of Górtyn, written in an ancient Doric dialect, that designated the rights and property of man. It's carved in stone blocks that make up part of the much later odeum. You'll see the stone tablets in the reconstructed facade behind the theater.

Admission: 500 Drs ($2.10).

Open: 8:30am–3pm daily.

PHAISTÓS

If you've come to see the fascinating ruins of Crete's second-largest Minoan palace (☎ **0892/91-315**), we hope you've purchased the guidebook *Crete,* by J. A. Papapostólou (which has excellent drawings and maps of Minoan sites). The palace of Phaistós (Festós) is every bit as grand as that at Knossós. Excavations were begun in the same period that the British archeologist Sir Arthur Evans was working at Knossós, but it wasn't until 1950 that a systematic examination of the site was completed.

As you walk down the stairs to the site, you'll be in the middle of the court from the older palace (from about 2000 B.C.). On your right, the grand stairs mark the entrance to the newer palace built on the earthquake-shattered remains of the older one, in about 1750 B.C.—a grand Minoan palace dominating the Messará Plain, where civilization flourished until 1450 B.C.

To the 20th-century traveler the highlights of the palace are the royal apartments, found under protective plastic canopies on the northern side of the site. In the first apartment, the remains of four columns make it easy to envision the arched roof they supported over the perimeter of the room, and the well of the light created in the courtyard. The benches and flooring that have survived in places at the western end of the room are still sheathed in alabaster slabs, mortared with red plaster. A staircase between the royal suites led up to the palace's second story.

Phaistós is still an active archeological site. We managed to visit the lower part of the site, where a team was uncovering a vast new section of the palace. Those with a serious archeological interest may obtain permission to consult with on-site scholars of the Italian Archeological School from the director of antiquities at the Archeological Museum in Iráklio.

Admission: 1,000 Drs ($4.20).

Open: 8am–5pm daily.

Aghía Triáda

Near the palace at Phaistós is the villa of Aghía Triáda (☎ **0892/91-360**), a small Minoan palace dating from 1700 B.C. It's believed to have been the summer home of the king who resided at Phaistós, and makes a refreshing side trip at midday because of the cool breezes blowing off the Libyan Sea, just 6.2 miles south. The Archeological Museum at Iráklio contains two carved vases, incredible sculpture with reliefs depicting boxers and harvesters, and beautiful frescoes found at this site.

Admission: 500 Drs ($2.10).

Open: 8:30am–3pm daily.

CHERSÓNISSOS

The tourist developments along Crete's northern coast emanate in both directions from Iráklio. The satellite cities of Néa Kydoniá, Aghía Mariná, Arína, and Thémis Beach are full-service resorts housing budget-tour groups who've jumped on charters in Brussels or Frankfurt for a "Week at the Beach" package that's cheaper than staying at home. TOGA PARTY TONIGHT signs abound.

Chersónisos is the first major autonomous town, although the hundreds of white prefab Mediterranean-style hotels, boutiques, and scooter-rental outfits must have been cloned from the model issued at the Bureau of Greek Hotel Standards. For miles along the island side of the road, big, small, elegant, and ugly homes sprout "villas to let" signs. About 1 1/2 miles past the main street is **Caravan Camping** ☎ **0897/22-025** where you can share the narrow sand-and-pebble beach with thousands of others. Believe us, you don't want to visit Chersónisos.

Continuing east, you'll reach Stális, a much smaller development of the same ilk, and then Mália.

Mália

On the way through, stop to see the palace of Mália, an interesting Minoan site just outside this uninteresting, unappealing beach resort. Buses run from Iráklio every

30 minutes; they turn off the main highway to leave you at the foot of the public beach in town, or continue to the site.

If you feel compelled to stay in Mália, you'll find several cheap accommodations along the Chersónisos model. The **Grammatikakis Pension** (☎ **0897/31-366**), with rooms right on the beach, has a café with outdoor showers for day-trippers. There are dozens of clean rooms, with "cottage-cheese" stuccoed walls and newly tiled private bathrooms, above the shops on the main street. At 6,825 Drs ($28.45) they're a good value.

Just two miles outside Mália are the ruins of a Minoan palace, the **Palace of Mália.** Greek archeologist Joseph Chatzedakis first conducted excavations here in 1915 and found the ruins of what was probably the Minoan city of Míletus. The simple remains of Crete's third Minoan palace (from about 1700 B.C.) give the visitor a good impression of what the palace at Knossós might have looked like before Sir Arthur Evans's extraordinary restoration. There the comparison ends. Archeologists think the lack of frescoes and the simple style of the Mália palace indicate that it was a provincial outpost.

The site (☎ **0897/31-597**) is open Tuesday through Sunday from 8:30am to 3pm; it's closed Monday. We were asked to inform readers that "proper" attire is required; admission is 500 Drs ($2.10).

Lassíthi Plain

A visit to the mountainous inland region of the Lassíthi Plain can be made as a day trip from Iráklio. Tour guides have earmarked Psychró as the best vantage point for clear views over the Lassíthi Plain, a sight to see in midmorning, when the thousands of white sailcloth windmills are spinning wildly, pumping water to irrigate the lush wheat fields. It is breathtakingly gorgeous.

Nearby is the Dictaean Cave (Diktaíon Ántron), where Rhea gave birth secretly to Zeus (she was seeking to save him from the fate of his brothers and sisters, who were eaten at birth by their father, Kronos). Legends say that Zeus was suckled by the goat Amalthea in the cave; archeologists have uncovered many icons and votive symbols, confirming that the cave was an important worship area during the Minoan era. The Dictaean Cave can be visited via donkey or well-shod feet. If you join a tour or go by public bus, you'll exit the northern coast highway just before Mália and head south through the fertile Mochas area, past the villages of Potamiá and Kéra.

A more dramatic mountain road, practical only for tourists with wheels, leads from the mountain town of Neápolis. This small city, on a plateau west of the Dikti range, offers its own view of windmills. The left side of the road is covered by the tall stone towers of now idle, traditional windmills, while the right, or valley, side of the drive is filled with bright aluminum ones, with spinning cloth-covered blades. It seems that most of Crete's 30-million olive trees are clinging to the hillsides here, vigorously nurtured by the continuous flow of water.

Just after Neápolis, a left turn off the highway at the flower-filled village of Kastélli will bring you along the more scenic, original road to Ághios Nikólaos. You can go left at the coast up to Pláka, a fishing village whose two tavernas overlook the tip of Spinalonga Island. From the dock, skillful negotiation can provide you with a private boat trip to the island.

Bearing right will bring you to the once equally appealing, though now very developed, port at Eloúnda. We recommend that you approach Ághios Nikólaos, the megaresort of this sparkling coastline, via the new highway, with its impressive vistas, rather than the resort hotel strip that's been developed from its northern end toward Eloúnda. As you approach Ághios Nikólaos you pass by Ístron Bay, a beautiful stretch of beach that has also been tremendously developed.

2 Ághios Nikólaos

The once sleepy little port town of Ághios Nikólaos was a well-kept secret for many years, but now the local publicity hawkers proudly dub it the "St-Tropez of Crete." It took years to spoil one of Crete's most ideal vacation spots. When the summer season cranks up and tourists pour in, discos, loud tavernas, overcrowding, and moped madness make Ághios Nikólaos an oppressive environment. This is no place to visit between May and September if you don't want to be disappointed.

Ághios Nikólaos has developed around the Gulf of Mirabello, so named by Venetian conquerors for its "beautiful view." When its sheltered cove protected Cretan rebels from the Turkish navy, the port was renamed for the church of St. Nicholas, which stood on its shore. In 1867 governor Kostas Adosidis Pasha built a canal to link the village's stagnant pond with the nearby sea, and created the picturesque harbor so admired today.

Getting There

BY BUS Ághios Nikólaos is well connected to the main centers of Crete. Buses run every half hour from 6:30am to 8:30pm for the 1½-hour trip to Iráklio; the fare is 1,500 Drs ($6.25).

BY TAXI Expect to pay about 12,000 Drs ($50) from central Iráklio or the airport to Ághios Nikólaos.

BY FERRY Ferryboats arrive three times weekly from Sitía.

Orientation

The town is built on a couple of low hills and centered around this small pond—the locals and all of the maps refer to it as a "lake." It's one of the most tranquil places to while away the hours at a café and watch the little fishing caiques pull in.

The lake meets the sea under a small bridge that divides I. Kondoúrou, the seaside street and focus of all development, roughly into two halves. The southeast end is the older and quieter part of the village, where hotels and pensions, built on a bluff high above the sea, are reached by stairs from the harbor. This location puts them somewhat above the noise. The northwestern half of the port is called Aktí Kondoúrou, but here the parade of bars and cafés faces to the beach. This town beach has steep stairs leading to the water, where concrete piers encourage sunbathing and swimming. The mopeds that eternally ply this beach route make it difficult to find nocturnal repose.

Our Greek friends don't think the town beach is clean enough. Instead, they head two miles south to Almirós, to a pebble beach whose chilly water is said to come from fairies bathing there at night. Two other beaches are closer: Kitroplatía beach is just south of the western spit of land and Ammoúdi beach (the most crowded) is $^{6}/_{10}$ of a mile north on the Eloúnda road, but both are very crowded.

Three commercial streets (one of them R. Koundoúrou, a very popular local name) run perpendicular to the port, alongside the lake, and provide anything a tourist can imagine. (Our applause to the news kiosk at the corner of October 28 Street that advertises condoms with the sign YOU KNOW IT'S SAFER.)

Getting Around

Stathis, which is near the tourist office (EOT) (at the bridge between the lake and the port) rents bicycles, for 1,000 Drs ($4.15) per day.

Fast Facts: Ághios Nikólaos

Banks All town banks are open Monday through Thursday from 8am to 2pm and Friday from 8am to 1:30pm. The Commercial Bank is also open Saturday, from 9am to 1pm. You can also change money at the tourist information office daily from 8:30am to 9:30pm.

Ferries **Massaros Travel** (☎ **0841/22-267**) sells tickets for the ferries that head three times a week to Sitía, Kássos, Kárpathos, and Rhodes and twice weekly to Mílos and Piraeus.

Hospitals The new Ághios Nikólaos General Hospital (☎ **0841/25-221** or **22-537**) is located next to the old one on Lasithíou Street.

Police The tourist police (☎ **0841/26-900**) are open Monday through Friday from 8:30am to 2pm and closed Saturday and Sunday. They're located at the intersection of Látous and Kondoyánni Streets.

Post Office The post office is on October 28 Street. It's open Monday through Friday from 7:30am to 8pm and Saturday and Sunday from 9am to 1pm. The postal code is 72100.

Religious Services There is a Greek Orthodox church, Ághios Charálambos, on the top of Messologíou Street. It has Roman Catholic masses during the summer season only (every Sunday at 6pm).

Telephones, Telegrams, Telexes The central telecommunications office, OTE, is open daily from 6am to midnight and is located south of the post office, on March 25 and Sfakináki Streets.

Tourist Information At the bridge between the lake and the port is the office of the Greek Tourist Organization (EOT) (☎ **0841/22-357;** fax 26-398). It's open daily from 8:30am to 9:30pm. The staff is fairly well informed and will change traveler's checks during normal hours.

What to See & Do

There are many wonders to admire in the naturally beautiful and scenic port. Just 1.3 miles from the village is a little-known Byzantine church, Ághios Nikólaos, with fine frescoes; it gave the town its name. The church is normally closed, but you can get the keys next door from the reception desk at the Minos Palace Hotel; you'll likely have to leave your passport or credit card as a deposit.

A church devoted to the Virgin, Panaghía Brephotróphou, dating from the early 12th century, is on Meletíou Street, near the bus station. The fine archeological museum is at 17 Paleológou Street (☎ **22-462**) and has finds from this district, particularly from the ancient towns (now beach resorts) of Mochlós, Mýrtos, and Kritsá. It's open Tuesday through Sunday from 8:30am to 3pm and closed Monday; admission is 500 Drs ($2.10), half price for children. A small but fun Museum of Popular Art is tucked in the same building as the tourist office, next to the bridge. It's open Sunday through Friday from 10am to 1:30pm and from 5:30 to 9pm, closed Saturday; admission is 300 Drs ($1.25).

At sunset, there's a greater variety of activity. The northwest side of the harbor buzzes with popular bars, such as **Aquarius** (advertising drinks like the Fuzzy Navel, Monster, and Chi-Chi) and **Oasis,** where a huge neon martini glass and loud Eurodisco music lure young men and women to outdoor tables.

At night, Ághios Nikólaos sizzles. The southeast side of Kondoúrou Street is a cacophony of bass notes emanating from discos such as Banana, the Bora Bora Video Disco, and the Lipstick. The above-20 crowd goes downstairs to the Candiá Café for ouzo and espresso—and to look cool and gossip, but there's no way they can hear themselves talk. Bemused elders choose the Asteria or one of the other cafés that flank the bridge between both parts of the harbor, where the competing din becomes an almost soothing white noise.

Where to Stay

Both the southeast, or village area, and the northwest, or beach area, of Ághios Nikólaos have good accommodations. The trick is finding one that's retained some of the magic that made this such a popular tourist destination in the first place. Another difficulty is that most hotels are often fully booked by groups throughout the season.

The number-one selections above the east side of the port are the Hotel Odysséas and the Pension Mílos. Those readers who want to be in closer proximity to swimming and nightlife might try the Hotel Linda. It's on the west side, sandwiched between the much larger and more expensive hotels Coral, Hermes, and Rea (see below). On the low end, Evans Street, which runs inland from the southeastern part of the harbor just after you pass all three commercial streets, has several buildings offering rooms to let at about 7,000 Drs ($29.20) for two.

Most of our readers wouldn't be interested in the dozens of luxury-class resorts that line the coast above and below Ághios Nikólaos village; those who are should book accommodations through a travel agent before departure.

Readers visiting in winter should contact the **Municipal Tourist Office** (☎ **0841/22-357**) regarding which facilities are open. The small Hamburg Pension, at Odós Látous 2 (☎ **0841/28-639**), near the town hall, is one of the few.

Pension Istron, Odós Sarolídis 4, Ághios Nikólaos, 72100. ☎ **0841/23-763.**
9 rms (none with bath).

Rates: 3,450 Drs ($14.35) single; 5,200 Drs ($21.65) double.

The Pension Istron, run by the Dachis family, is a reasonably attractive choice, with rooms enlivened by fresh-cut flowers and crisp new paint.

Linda, Odós Salamínas 3A, Ághios Nikólaos 72100. ☎ **0841/22-130.** Fax 0841/24-955.
22 rms (all with bath). TEL

Rates: 8,580 Drs ($35.75) single; 9,325 Drs ($38.85) double.

We found the Linda both clean and attractive. The decor of the rooms is what we refer to as "Hessian Greek moderne" but the bougainvillea-covered, trellised canopy over the breakfast patio is lovely. Open year round.

Pension Marilena, Erythroú Stavróu (Red Cross) 4, Ághios Nikólaos 72100. ☎ **0841/22-681.** 14 rms (all with bath).

Rates: 5,200 Drs ($21.65) single; 9,000 ($37.50) double. AE, MC, V.

We met the friendly owner and her baby granddaughter on the street, just up from the Linda and Hermes Hotels, when we asked for directions. First we tried the food in her small café, where her son is the cook, then we looked at her clean, comfortable rooms. We recommend them both.

$ **Pension Milos,** Odós Sarolídis 24, Ághios Nikólaos 72100. ☎ **0841/23-783.** 10 rms (5 with bath). TEL

Rates: 6,500 Drs ($27.10) single or double with bath, 9,100 Drs ($37.90) single or double without bath.

Pension Milos is a spotless pension that has fine views of the sea. The two sisters who run it, Maria and Georgia, will greet you with their warm and generous Cretan hospitality. A stay in one of the rooms above theirs will make you feel as if you're visiting a Greek family.

Hotel Odysseas, Aktí Themistokleos 1 Ághios Nikólaos 72100. ☎ **0841/28-440.** 27 rms (all with bath). TEL

Rates (including breakfast): 5,980 Drs ($24.90) single; 8,450 Drs ($35.20) double.

The Hotel Odysseas is where many longtime English visitors choose to stay. It has a "homely" feel (as the English like to say) but is often filled with guests who are up for a good part of the day and night. Recently it has hosted several tour groups, who completely buy out the hotel.

Hotel Vasilia Inn, Odós Ariádnis 5, Ághios Nikólaos, 72100. ☎ **0841/23-572.** 9 rms (all with bath).

Rates: 3,850–5,440 Drs ($16–$22.65) single; 4,550–7,920 Drs ($18.95–$33) double.

Near the seaside bluff is quiet Ariádnis Street, where you'll find the small Hotel Vasilia Inn. Paintings, Cretan weavings, embroidered curtains, mismatched upholstery, and a friendly staff give it a comfortable feeling. (On our last visit, however, we noticed that it could still use some improvement.)

A SPLURGE CHOICE

★ **Elounda Bay Hotel,** Ághios Nikólaos 72100. ☎ **0841/41-580,** or **01/32-43-961** in Athens. Fax 0841/41-783. 300 rms (all with bath). A/C MINIBAR TEL

Rates: 39,500 Drs ($164.65) single half board; 58,250–75,000 Drs ($242.70–$312.50) double half board.

The Elounda Bay Hotel, formerly called the Astir Palace Elounda, has hosted Prime Minister Andréas Papandréou, and many other Greek notables, as well as international celebrities. The Elounda is known for fine service and excellent cuisine, and draws an elite, somewhat older, crowd. Although the facilities are similar to those of the Eloúnda Beach Hotel, its neighbor under the same management, we found the staff more accommodating and the setting more private. The large, deluxe rooms have balconies or terraces overlooking the manicured grounds, flagstone sun decks, a huge outdoor pool, and the beautiful bay itself. But the true splurges here are the private bungalows, many with hideaway decks that jut over the water for an instant swim. This high-priced resort has a full complement of water sports (including parasailing) and tennis courts.

Where to Eat

Aouas Taverna, Odós Paleológou 44. ☎ **23-231.**

Cuisine: TAVERNA/GRILL.
Prices: Appetizers 520–1,300 Drs ($2.15–$5.40); main courses 1,000–2,600 Drs ($4.15–$10.85).
Open: Daily 6pm–1am.

This large outdoor taverna/grill is popular with a local crowd and specializes in grilled food as well as the usual taverna dishes. We particularly liked the grilled lamb and chicken, but found their garden a bit crowded.

Klimataria, Odós Ethnikís Antistáseos 3. ☎ **28-687.**

Cuisine: TAVERNA/GRILL.
Prices: Appetizers 400–1,200 Drs ($1.65–$5); main courses 1,000–2,400 Drs ($4.15–$10).
Open: Daily 6pm–1am.

We're sure that Ghiórgos, Ghiórghia, María, and Tonia, the talented family behind the Klimataria, will be sure to make yours a special dining experience. We savored a meal of veal yuvétsi, pork cooked in wine, and cheese balls accompanied by a sweet mountain wine from Agrilos, near Sitía. The restaurant is set in a lovely garden off the northeast corner of the lake.

DINING OUT OF TOWN

Dionyssos, Límnes. ☎ **33-401** or **28-321**.

Cuisine: CRETAN.
Prices: Fixed-price menu 7,000 Drs ($29.15).
Open: Dinner only Thurs–Sun in high season (call for hours).

In the village of Límnes, at the Dionyssos, pros and amateurs join in the fun. Four nights a week waiters will show off a variety of Greek specialties, then leap onto the dance floor, pounding to the beat of live musicians. Dionyssos is closer to an authentic bouzouki club, has better food, and is reasonably priced.

FAST FOOD

Fast food and takeaway food have become the nightmare following Americans to Greek resorts, and Águios Nikólaos is no exception. For breakfast, though, consider tiny **Glaros Fast Food,** on Paleológou Street, where omelets start at 350 Drs ($1.45). Nescafé alone at the portside cafés will cost twice that. The **Candiá Café,** at Odós I. Koundoúrou 12 (☎ **26-355**), serves very nice cakes and Cretan desserts daily from 7:30am to 3am.

DINING WITH A VIEW

A view certainly has its price. We liked the **Blue Lagoon Taverna** on the paved pedestrian walk on the east side of the lake. Two can dine well for about 9,000 Drs ($37.50) and up. There are other scenic options on the beach side of Aktí Kondoúrou. For those who want the Riviera ambience of the busy beach-coast promenade, try **Zefiros,** at Odós Aktí Koundoúrou 1 (☎ **28-868**); it's open daily from 8am to 2am. Even though you'll pay more here, you'll be getting a very fine meal.

Excursions

ORGANIZED TOURS

Creta Tours on Aktí Koundoúrou (☎ **0841/28-496,** fax 0841/23-879) and several other agents offer motor-coach tours around Crete originating in Ághios Nikólaos and local boat excursions. Taxis can be used for day trips, but charge from 9,000–29,000 Drs ($37.50–$120) depending on the distance and time needed for your excursion. Consult with the taxi office (☎ **24-000** or **24-100**) for suggested fares to different sites.

Spinalonga Island is one of the most popular destinations from Ághios Nikólaos, and boat tours cost about 3,500 Drs ($14.60); but small boats can be hired for much less from the ports at Eloúnda and Pláka for short visits. Check with the **Massaros Travel Agency** (☎ **0841/22-267,** fax 0841/23-077), at Odós R. Koundoúrou 29, open seven days a week. They've got all the info on various trips, sell ferry tickets, and even list villas to rent. Spinalonga was a peninsula until the Venetians built a powerful fortress over the ruins of the ancient city of Olonte. The Venetians restored their bastion in 1526 and reinforced it by cutting a canal through the peninsula. This insular fortress was one of the last three on Crete (along with the fortresses at Grambousse and Soúda Bay), providing the Venetians with an impregnable stronghold against the Turks for 50 years, until 1715. In modern times (until 1958) Spinalonga was the site of a leper colony, earning the poignant nickname "Island of Pain and Tears," but it's now extremely picturesque and inviting.

EXCURSION TO ELOÚNDA AND PLÁKA

Just 6½ miles north of Ághios Nikólaos, along a resort-encrusted road, is the once-sleepy port of Eloúnda, now awakened by the avalanche of tourist drachmas. Your first sight of it will be the land bridge that stretches out to meet the island of Spinalonga, forming a natural lagoon. Straddling this spit of land is a solitary, graceful Venetian fortress in ruins.

Eloúnda is the perfect example of a "picturesque fishing village nestled in a sheltered cove" swallowed whole by tourism. Its pretty harbor can provide respite from the midsummer crowds. One of the overlooked highlights of Eloúnda is the underwater ancient city of Oloús. This Minoan town can be seen from the land only when the water is perfectly calm and clear. If you have snorkeling gear, you may obtain permission from the police station in Eloúnda to explore underwater.

Where to Stay and Eat in Eloúnda/Pláka

Taverna & Rooms Spinalonga, Pláka, Lissithi 72953. ☎ **0841/41-804.**
9 rms, 4 apts (all with bath).

Rates: 6,000 Drs ($25) double; apartments 7,200–9,000 Drs ($30–$37.50). No credit cards.

We suggest you continue on through Eloúnda another seven kilometers north to quiet Pláka, where you'll find a new all-purpose place. Friendly Evangelia can provide you with very attractive accommodations and serve you good Cretan food, including fresh fish caught by her husband John, who can also take you out to Spinalonga island. There's good swimming nearby on a clean, smooth-stone beach.

Taverna Vritomartis, Eloúnda. ☎ **41-325.**

Cuisine: FISH.
Prices: Appetizers 500–3,000 Drs ($2.10–$12.50); main courses 1,500–3,500 Drs ($6.25–$14.60). AE, DC, EC, MC, V.
Open: Daily 9am–2am.

The small Taverna Vritomartis occupies the most scenic spot in town, at the end of the short breakwater that juts into Eloúnda Bay. At bayside tables under a bamboo canopy you can enjoy cool breezes. We really enjoyed a combination of grilled swordfish with special salad and a plate of creamy hummus. The owners of this always crowded eatery operate a couple of fishing boats that supply the fish on a daily basis.

EXCURSION TO KRITSÁ

The hill town of Kritsá is located 6½ miles south of the main north-coast highway, and provides a welcome glimpse of the way life used to be in this well-touristed part of Crete. The traditional weavings seen throughout the island provide much of the village's income, and the small handicraft shops on the main street offer many good buys. The town is known for its almond juice drink, Soumada, drunk cold in summer and hot in winter.

Just before you arrive in town is the celebrated 14th-century Byzantine church of Panaghía Kerá, with well-preserved remains of religious frescoes. The style of the renderings is comparatively primitive and is marked by decorative elements (from nature), somber colors, and the brooding expressions of saints, villagers, and kings. The church is open daily from 9am to 3pm; the admission fee is 500 Drs or $2.10. It is a wonderful place to experience the religious devotion once expressed in this isolated village and confirms the town's past as one of the most important centers of Byzantine art during the Venetian period. There are also beautiful frescoes at the church of Ághios Gheórghios Kavousiótis.

EXCURSION TO GOURNIÁ

The superbly restored remains of the village of Gourniá (14 miles east of Ághios Nikólaos) are unique on Crete because this is the only settlement dating from the earliest Minoan period, before the earthquake of 1450 B.C. From the road, the rough stone walls and even the plan of Gourniá's "streets" could be mistaken for a well-organized olive grove, minus the trees. If you climb up the 3,500-year-old main street to the top of the mound, where there once stood a modest palace, you'll enjoy a wonderful view of the houses, back alleys, and agora, as well as the Bay of Istron beyond. There's no fee to enter the archeological site of Gourniá, which is open Tuesday through Sunday from 8am to 3pm, closed Monday. Regular public bus service from Ághios Nikólaos will cost 400 Drs ($1.70).

EXCURSION TO MOCHLÓS

We really don't want to say too much about this exquisitely simple fishing port (and thus spoil one of the island's last quiet places) except to point out that one of the most important newly excavated archeological sites on Crete is located just 100 yards off shore on a rocky island. Here is evidence of a post-volcano/Minoan settlement. Finds from Mochlós are on display in the museums in Ághios Nikólaos and Sitía. If you decide to stay, you'll find a scattering of rooms to rent, a couple of waterfront cafés, a tiny pebble beach, and not much to do at night.

3 Sitía & The Northeast

Sitía was a Venetian stronghold until the Turkish pirate Barbarossa laid siege to the fort in the late 16th century. The Kazarma (from Casa di Arma) Fortress is one of the few legacies of the Venetians' stay. Once only a way station between Ághios Nikólaos and the palm-lined beach at Vái, or an embarkation port for the once weekly ferries to the Dodecanese and Cyclades, Sitía has grown from a quiet port into a bustling seaside town built amphitheatrically on a hill. The new Sitía overlooks a newly renovated and enlarged harbor, now lined with hotels and cafés. We recommend it mainly as a base for sightseeing.

Getting There

The bus to Sitía follows the highway, the only road extending to the eastern tip of Crete at Vái. Beyond the clutter of development from Kaló Chorió until Ístron (a secluded spot where you might consider stopping for the rest of your life) you will be witness to the most exquisite vistas of mountain and sea on the whole island. The scent of pressed olives wafts through the air, mingling with the sweet flowers in sensual confusion.

As the road climbs, cascades of yellow tumble down the hillside, where olive trees grow at an alarming 45° angle. Donkeys burdened with herbs and grape leaves are led by old farmers in their traditional baggy black pants, and you often see Crete's unique kris-kris, a curly-horned goat, nibbling at the road's shoulder.

Almost 6.2 miles before you reach Sitía is a turnoff for the "Minoan House of Chamaizi," a site for avid Minoanphiles. A 1,100-yard walk along the stone road leading down from the highway will take you to the ruins of this old home, safely settled among olive groves. In the nearby hamlet of Hamésio you can see local finds at the Cretan Home Museum.

Orientation/Information

A portable **tourist information** trailer (☎ **0843/24-955**) is on the central harbor. The bus station is on Itanós Street, which runs perpendicular to the harbor on the east end of town. In the high season there are six daily buses to Ierápetra, six daily to Ághios Nikólaos and Iráklio, and hourly buses to the popular hamlet of Palékastro (and on to Vái). **Tzortákis Travel,** on the port (☎ **0843/28-900,** fax 0843/22-731), sells ferry boat tickets for the weekly daytime sailings to Kássos, Kárpathos, Chalkís, and Rhodes, and for the thrice-weekly night sailings to Ághios Nikólaos, Mílos, and Piraeus. There is an **Olympic Airways** office (☎ **22-270**) at Odós Venizélos 56. Sitía is connected by infrequent flight with Kárpathos, Kássos and Athens. The airport is quite close, about a 10-minute walk up the hill; you can take a taxi for about 600 Drs ($2.50).

What to See & Do

Sitía is an entertaining place for Minoanphiles; plan on spending a minimum of one night. You'll want to see the remains of the palace at Zákros (maybe take the hike through the Gorge of the Dead leading to Káto Zákros), perhaps visit the archeological site at Palékastro and tour the new archeological museum, 109 yards south of town on the Ierápetra road. The core of this splendid small collection has been culled from the most recent excavations in the eastern end of Crete, including the exciting finds that postdate the earthquake that was thought to have brought an end to the Minoan culture. Proof of the vitality of this "post-Minoan" work is a delicately crafted ivory sculpture that greets you as you enter the exhibition space. The museum (☎ **23-917**) is open Tuesday through Sunday from 8:30am to 3pm, closed Monday; the admission fee is 500 Drs ($2.10).

Sitía also boasts an interesting Museum of Folklore above Arkadíou Street. It also has a not too appealing two mile stretch of beach just east of town; swimmers will find that the cleanest water is at its far east end.

The seaside has several cafés, providing tables for excellent *zacharoplastía* (*pâttiseries*). The central square on the harbor is Platía Polytechníou, where you'll find a friendly and photogenic pelican, a portable post office, and a taxi stand. Venizélos Street runs parallel to this square, one block in, and has the greatest number of commercial services.

Don't miss **Sitian Arts** (☎ **22-600**), two blocks from the port, at Odós Vitséntsou Kornárou 148. Jane Kafetzákis, formerly of the Isle of Man, is a wonderful painter who sells watercolors, painted bags and scarves, decorated stones, jewelry, and other excellent gift items. Her shop is open daily from 9am to 1pm and from 2:30 to 8pm.

Where to Stay

Arhontiko Hotel, Odós Kondilákis 16, Sitía 72300. ☎ **0843/28-172.**

10 rms (none with bath).

Rates: 4,500 Drs ($18.75) single; 5,200 Drs ($21.70) double.

Among pensions, the Arhontikó Hotel, which is up the steps toward the cathedral, is redolent with atmosphere. Its spacious, well-maintained, and clean rooms are in an early 1900s wooden house, with slightly sloped wooden floors, surrounded by an orange and a lemon tree. Hosts Apostolis Kimalis and Brigitte Hurdalek are as hospitable as can be. Apostolis also has three rooms attached to his home, each with private facilities (7,000 Drs or $29.15 for single or double).

El Greco Hotel, Odós Arkadiou 13, Sitía 72300. ☎ **0843/23-133.**

15 rms (all with bath). TEL

Rates (including breakfast): 8,450 Drs ($35.20) single; 9,750 Drs ($40.60) double.

The El Greco Hotel, owned and operated by the professional Manuel Tzikelakis, is up the central steps from the harbor and left of the main church. The large, balconied rooms offer a wonderful vista of the harbor and the Gulf of Sitía. Cretan weavings and dark wood decor give the El Greco the homey feel of a mountain lodge. Another fine choice.

A YOUTH HOSTEL

GYH Youth Hostel, Odós Theríssou 4, Sitía 72300. ☎ **0843/22-693.**

Rates: 1,000 Drs ($4.15) bed.

The GYH Youth Hostel, up the hill from the bus stop, is a great stop for budget tourists. Lakis and his helpful manager will do everything to make your stay in Sitía pleasant and cheap.

Where to Eat

$ **Kali Kardia Taverna,** Odós Foundalídou 22. ☎ **22-249.**

Cuisine: TAVERNA.

Prices: Appetizers 250–600 Drs ($1.05–$2.50); main courses 700–1,800 Drs ($2.90–$7.50).
Open: Daily 8am–1am.

This is a wonderfully local Greek space: Grizzled elderly men sit frozen in an "ouzoed" state; rifles, carved walking sticks, and scythes compete with impossible beach and mountain oil paintings for wall space, while 1940s American standards drone on the radio. *Kalí Kardiá* means "Good heart," and we can only surmise that the patron here feels there's a connection between his food and the name. Everything we sampled was superb—not fancy mind you, but absolutely delicious. Start with an ouzo and a few *mezédes* (appetizers), then move on to a house specialty, *tiropitákia* (small cheese pies), and to any of the daily specials. Kardiá is a bargain, with prices one notch lower than those at the portside eateries. Our favorite.

$ **Mihos Taverna,** Odós Vitséntsou Kornárou 117. ☎ **22-416.**

Cuisine: TAVERNA.
Prices: Appetizers 500–1,200 Drs ($2.10–$5); main courses 1,000–1,800 Drs ($4.15–$7.50).
Open: Daily dinner only 6pm–midnight.

Mihos Taverna, another fine back-street eatery, presents an ascetic interior. Two spacious, whitewashed rooms are linked by a simple arched doorway. Fortunately, all the flair goes into the food. We dined on an excellent variety of traditional taverna cuisine: octopus, tirópita, dolmádes, stuffed zucchini flowers accented with cumin, *kotópoulo* (chicken), and lamb prepared on the spit, all tasty and low priced. An excellent choice.

Zorba's, Platía Kosmazótou, Sitía. ☎ **22-689.**

Cuisine: GREEK/CONTINENTAL.
Prices: Appetizers 400–950 Drs ($1.70–$3.95); main courses 600–1,600 Drs ($2.50–$6.65). AE, EC, MC, V.
Open: Daily 8am–2am.

This large, pleasant taverna and its brother minitaverna, Zorba's II, a few cafés away, have an extraordinarily varied menu that's reliable, good, and priced for the harbor views. Whereas the original possesses an enviable site, overlooking the harbor, Zorba's II will appeal to those who appreciate grilled food. There, you can sample chicken or lamb on the spit as well as other meat specialties. Our only complaint at both places is the harried, verging on rude, service during the busy summer season.

Excursions

VÁI

Vái is a highly touted destination 17 miles northeast of Sitía. Cretans and Europeans take this palm-lined, sand-beach inlet very seriously, and those of you who've enjoyed Florida or California beaches will be amused by the ecstatic Germans and Italians who pose for photos under the seaside palm fronds (now fenced in!). This place is very out of the way for a beach excursion, but a large parking lot, a cafeteria, and (best of all) private showers ensure its popularity year-round.

The hardy who scale the hill beyond the tourist restaurant will descend to an out-of-sight cove sanctioned for nude sunbathing. If you really want to test the farthest-out beaches, continue straight for 1.24 miles, past the right turnoff for Vái.

ITANÓS

At the northeastern tip of the island near Ermoúpolis is the ancient city of Itanós, uncovered by French archeologists. The remains of the eastern acropolis indicate that this picturesque promontory was inhabited from the Geometric period. On the taller, western acropolis the remains date from the 3d century (the height of city's naval power). The Byzantines occupied the land between the acropolises. Of interest to the modern visitor are two isolated sandy coves easily viewed from the height of either acropolis, which provide superb swimming and sunbathing without the Vái crowds.

PALÉKASTRO

The remains of a Minoan port found at Roussolákos, 12.4 miles east of Sitía, mark the site of ancient Palékastro (Palaíkastro), an active archeological excavation that is producing spectacular finds. However, the newer village of Palékastro, on the road between Sitía and the major Minoan site at Káto Zákros, is what draws visitors today. This popular town is still somewhat typical of old Crete, despite its hotels, rooms to let, and two discos.

From Palékastro, surrounded by olive groves, it's a short commute to nearby beaches. Besides the swimming at Vái or Itanós, there is Agathía, a smaller, traditional village east of Palékastro that provides access to a popular beach called Shona. Those drawn to peaceful Palékastro will find the 32-room **Marina Village** (☎ **0843/61-284**; fax 0843/61-285), a small resort with a pool and tennis courts outside the town; doubles run 15,200 Drs ($63.35), singles 11,200 Drs ($46.65). The **Hellas Pension** (☎ **0843/61-240**), and several *domátia* (rooms to let) offer lower-cost accommodations above the shops off the main square.

ZÁKROS

Some of the most magnificent Minoan artifacts have been unearthed at Káto Zákros, located 23 miles from Sitía, on Crete's far east end, south from the exotic beach at Vái. Zákros is the fourth Minoan palace, and archeologists have determined that its location was of major strategic and commercial import for the Minoan empire. The palace gave the Minoans a base for trading and keeping tabs on the other major powers of antiquity: Syria, Egypt, and the whole of Asia Minor.

Excavation began in the early 1960s and continues, with the major discovery of remarkably carved stone vases excavated from the only unplundered Minoan tomb on Crete. Some vessels are in the Archeological Museum of Sitía. The best of them are among the highlights of the Archeological Museum in Iráklio. The site, like the other Minoan palaces, was built about 1700 B.C. on top of the remains of an earlier palace. Unfortunately, the palace at Zákros is not as well preserved as those at Knossós and Phaistós, but it is certainly worth a visit for those fascinated by Minoan culture and history. The site is open daily from 8:30am to 3pm; admission is 750 Drs ($3.15).

The town of Zákros (five miles from the site) has the Class-C **Hotel Zákros** (☎ **0843/93-379**), with bed and breakfast for two at 7,500 Drs ($31.25), and rooms to let. There is a good beach at Káto Zákros; so, if the heat of ancient stone gets to you, cool off in the sea. Hikers should inquire about exploring the nearby Gorge of the Dead, the site of an ancient necropolis.

For the truly intrepid, there is the usually deserted and totally wonderful beach at Xerokámpos, located south of Zákros, via a very funky, winding road.

4 The South—Ierápetra to Aghía Galíni

To Cretans, Ierápetra is the star of the southern coast, the next willing victim of tourist inundation (because of its sandy beaches and clean waters). Fortunately for Crete, it is already the wealthiest city (in terms of per capita income) because of its thriving agricultural industry. From here, tomatoes, eggplants, cucumbers, herbs, and raisins are exported to other parts of Greece and to Northern Europe. The hothouses seen on both sides of the road as you approach from Sitía keep those ripe tomatoes coming for Greek salads in Athens year-round. Unfortunately for the hoteliers, the plants and offices that service this vital cash crop have made Ierápetra a rather homely, bustling seaside city.

Nonetheless, Crete's southern coast along the Libyan Sea boasts the clearest waters and warmest climate in Europe, and the national highway system has made Ierápetra one of its gateway cities. The small beach communities at Mýrtos, Árvi, and Mátala are overnight options on the way west to the resort of Aghía Galíni.

Ierápetra

For those who need activity and want to sightsee along Crete's beautiful southern coast, Ierápetra's long harbor, pleasant cafés, and urban activities make a fairly nice base. For advice on local sightseeing, contact the staff of the Ierápetra **Express Tourist Office** (☎ **0842/28-123** or **22-411;** fax 0842/28-330), Platía Eleftheria, opposite the National Bank. The multilingual guides and group representatives who share the space are available daily from 8am to 1:30 and from 4:30 to 9pm to book tours and rooms and exchange money.

WHAT TO SEE & DO

If you're interested only in the beach, backtrack east for about 17 miles to Mávros Kolimbos at Makrighialós, a small fishing village with a long public beach. Staying in one of the few spartan rooms to let above the main street will give you solo time on the beach before the day-trippers arrive.

From Ierápetra's harbor, three 60-passenger cruise boats depart daily April through October for an excursion to the tiny uninhabited Chryssí Island (5,500 Drs or $22.90 round-trip). Its sand beaches are considered among the finest in Crete. There's only one taverna, so bring a picnic, or adequate supplies if you plan to rough-camp in this nearly African isle.

An easier (and less expensive) excursion is to the less frequented beach at Aghía Fotía, 12.4 miles east of town. The privately run KTEL buses to Sitía, leaving from the central square, will drop you there. Between Aghía Fotía and Makrighalós you can climb down to Galíni Beach, near Koutsoúras, where snorkeling is popular. Recent development has made all beaches more crowded.

Within Ierápetra town there's a small archeological museum (open Tuesday through Sunday from 8:30am to 3pm). For one of the most pleasant evening activities, take a sunset stroll, or *vólta.* We recommend starting at the central part of the harbor down from Elefthería Square. Turning right, you'll pass an old, official-looking iron building. A stroll past the drydocked fishing boats and worn hulls in the midst of repair will lead into taverna row, where you can judge the local action, and then on past the town beach. At the west end of the harbor is a Venetian fortress and a mosque. Contact the **Ierápetra Express Tourist Office** (☎ **28-123** or **22-411**) for information about organized tours.

WHERE TO STAY

Heightened tourist (or should we say tour operator?) interest in Ierápetra has led to increased prices at all the official hotels, but there are many alternatives. We preferred places along the quieter east end of the harbor (where cars are turned back and pedestrians take over the flagstone promenade), although cheaper rates can be found at several pensions on Ioanídou Street or inland from the central square.

Hotel Castro, Odós Stratigoú Samouíl 54, Ierápetra. (☎ **0842/23-858.**) 7 rms (5 with bath).

Rates: 4,875 Drs ($20.30) single; 6,250 Drs ($26.05) room with twin beds.

At the far west end, where things are a bit quieter, the Hotel Castro stands above the Cretan Arts Tourist Shop. Twin-bedded rooms in this clean pension have minifridges, but share bathing facilities.

Pension Diagoras, Odós Kyrvá 1, Ierápetra. ☎ **0842/23-898.** 9 rms (all with bath).

Rates: 4,375 Drs ($18.25) single; 6,875 Drs ($28.65) double.

Behind the city hall and toward the beach end of the harbor is the Pension Diagóras, where clean doubles with a Danish shower and a good view nestle above the inexpensive and old-style café/bar of the same name. Front-facing rooms may be quieter.

El Greco Hotel, Odós Michaíl Kothrí 40, Ierápetra. ☎ **0842/28-471.** Fax 0842/26547. 34 rms (all with bath). TEL

Rates: 9,000 Drs ($37.50) single; 11,250 Drs ($46.90) double. MC, V.

The El Greco has a front door on the street and a seaside back door on the east end of the harbor. Its rooms are clean and pleasant; many of them have great views from their balcony. The seaside rooms not only command a better view but tend to be quieter also. Hotel guests receive a 15% discount on meals taken in the downstairs restaurant.

$ **Hotel Katerina,** Michaíl Kothrí St., Ierápetra. ☎ **0842/28-345.** 16 rms (all with bath).

Rates: 7,000 Drs ($29.15) double or single. V

Almost next door to the El Greco, on the harbor, just before the eastern stretch of sand begins, is the delightful Hotel Katerina, run by the friendly and accommodating Katerina. Walk up to the reception desk and check out the small but clean balconied doubles with private showers.

WHERE TO EAT

Since Ierápetra has a life beyond tourism, there are several good and inexpensive tavernas inland from Venizélou Street. If you've come for the view (as we did), try the beachside tavernas. **Konaki Restaurant,** at Odós Stratigoú Samouíl 32 (☎ **24-422**) is good, with a grilled shrimp, fresh *barboúnia,* or a mixed-seafood meal costing about 4,500 Drs ($18.75) per person. You can also eat meat or vegetable specialties for half that price. They're open daily from 8am to midnight. The pedestrian promenade on the eastern end of the harbor has the best cafés for a sunset drink or *après-diner* dessert and coffee.

Mýrtos

Mýrtos appears, from the road, like one of the many "hothouse" towns on Crete's attractive southern coast. Walk into town and you'll see lovely gardens in small homes and grapevines creeping up rickety trellises. If you continue walking, you'll come to Mýrtos's black-sand and pebble beach, which, unfortunately, is more likely than not to be strewn with trash (the western side of the town beach is much cleaner).

Mýrtos is a pleasant town, with a few narrow streets squeezed between the highway to Ierápetra (only 10.5 miles away) and a concrete promenade (really a bulkhead) that prevents the seaside tavernas from being swept away. It is quiet, picturesque, and clean (in your walks you'll probably encounter black-dressed old women busily sweeping the sidewalk). It is also not quite overrun yet with tourists—an attribute that may appeal to some of you.

WHERE TO STAY & EAT

If you decide to stay, try the ten-room **Villa Mare Pension** (☎ **0842/51-274;** fax 0842/51-328), near the church on the western side of town; it has good seaviews from its top-floor rooms and roof garden. Single or double rooms run 8,200 Drs ($34.15). Superior but more expensive lodgings are found at the crenellated pseudotowers of the 13-room **Kastro Studios** (☎ **0842/51-444**) and at the slick eight-room **Myrtini Apartments** (☎ **0842/51-386**) on the vanguard of Mýrtos's development. Doubles cost about 10,000 Drs ($41.65) for both places.

The newest and nicest place in town is **Mertiza Studios and Apartments** (☎ **0842/51-208,** fax 0842/51-036,) with spacious studios from 8,200 Drs ($34.15) and apartments from 11,250 Drs ($46.90).

If the above establishments are booked, another alternative is the older, but still attractive 21-room **Hotel Mirtos,** Odós Main 140, 72056 Mýrtos (☎ **0842/51-266**), where a double costs 5,250 Drs ($21.90). There are also clean, newer rooms to let above the supermarket, near Mýrtos's church, and above several *kafeneia.* These newer rooms usually have Danish showers in private-stall bathrooms, and small balconies with views over the nearby tomato greenhouses and construction sites (by the way; you haven't eaten unless you've tried some of the luscious tomatoes of southern Crete!).

Rates are readily bargained down by half for two anytime other than June through September. The off-season is also the best time to appreciate the "Greekness" still left in the town.

During the day, **Katerina's Taverna** serves a respectable *choriátiki saláta* (what we call "Greek salad") and stewed beef dish, and is popular for town watching. At night, **Eros,** on the beach promenade, beckons the beer and Deméstica-wine crowd with its live bouzoukia.

Mýrtos boasts three beachfront cafés. Our favorites are **Taverna Votsal** and **Aktí.**

Árvi

After overcoming the initial shock of Crete's sprawling northern coast developments, the truly committed beach seeker inevitably opens up the map in search of less inhabited shorelines. The tiny south coast village of Árvi, once unknown to all but a few, has become one of the favorites.

Like other points on the island, Árvi's natural surroundings reflect Crete's close proximity to Africa and Asia Minor. Its long, thin beach is within 109 yards of banana plantations and melon groves; there's also a spectacular gorge facing Árvi, 15–20 minutes' hiking distance from the town. The path (delightfully void of signs, guard rails, and tourists) leads through tilled fields of bananas, cucumbers, and grapes. You'll probably run across farmers bringing goods from town, laborers working on the water pipes, goats, and a stray dog or two. The path parallels a small stream; at the mouth of the gorge you have to wade in knee-deep water. The sinewy curves of the rock there were formed by thousands of years of rushing water.

Árvi also has a 300-year-old monastery that is a moderate walk from town. From its hillside perch you have a good view of Árvi's unusual layout. Most people come to Árvi for the beach, but unfortunately it isn't the paradise one might imagine. In fact, locals prefer the wider beach 1.2 miles west of the town. The town beach is certainly adequate; but with the number of tourists who take refuge here in the summer months, it tends to crowd up.

WHERE TO STAY

As for hotels, there is a pension, the 17-room **Hotel Gorgona,** Árvi 70004 (☎ **0895/71-353**), charging 9,000 Drs ($37.50) for two, and a Class-C hotel, the 14-room **Ariadni** (☎ **0895/71-300**), where doubles run 9,950 Drs ($39.60) and singles go for 8,500 Drs ($35.40). The pension, run by the elderly Aliki Christaki, is small, spotless, and a bit homey.

The **Adriadni** (situated right on the shore) is a bit beach-worn but offers a discount to students, which tends to make it a great congregating place. There are also numerous rooms to let (about 5,000 Drs or $20.85 for two with private bath) both above the shops along Main Street and along the shore (such as Arvi Villa Apts., (☎ **0895/71-324**), but Árvi remains relatively tranquil. Unfortunately, the tourists who do come for its scenic pleasures tend to pass through on motorcycles, so choose your room carefully.

WHERE TO EAT

Of the half-dozen family-run tavernas in the village, we found the **Taverna Diktines** (☎ **71-249**), on the eastern end, to be the most popular, open daily from 7am to 1am. Our favorite dining room, run by **Avios Dias** (☎ **71-256**), is located in the center of town with outdoor tables overlooking the water. We especially enjoyed locally caught grilled fish with vegetables, served *zestó* (hot), a real rarity in these parts. Maria is the voluble hostess and cook; her eatery is open daily from 8am to 1am.

If Árvi isn't to your taste and you don't mind an even bumpier road, visit the quiet fishing port of Tsoutsoúros. It has a wide beach, some of the best fishing on Crete, and lower-priced rooms to rent.

Mátala

One of Crete's southernmost beach communities, Mátala is known for the cave dwellings carved by early Christian refugees in the cliffs that encircle its beach. Cretan resistance forces hid in them centuries later, during World War II, and young foreigners inhabited them during the 1960s and '70s. The town boasts several of the best fine-pebble beaches on Crete, and the natural cove, formed by a horseshoe of sandstone cliffs, has perfectly clear warm water. Busloads of very young vacationers pour in every day.

Beach aficionados should make sure to climb the hill behind the pensions or take the new street in town to Red Beach (expect to walk about 20 minutes), where some of Mátala's visitors sun in blissful seclusion; there's a drink stand there if you need to quench your thirst. If you climb over the tourists gaping at the once-inhabited caves (on the opposite side of the cove, fenced off but still explored by the public), you'll get to Komo Beach, another five-mile-long stretch of sand. The less hardy can take the hourly bus or drive and then walk for about ten minutes back through town; take the first unpaved road on the left for 2½ miles. There are a few tavernas and restaurants on the beach.

Because of the most pleasant year-round weather, several hundred Europeans have made Mátala their permanent abode. During the winter, most residents of the seaside town migrate just a few miles north to the less touristed village of Pitsidia. You, too, can stay here during the busier season and usually for a lot less in a private room.

WHERE TO STAY

The quality and price of sleeping facilities in Mátala varies according to season and location more than in other coastal villages. Returning New Age hippies and their families come in the off-season, and the "sun-and-fun" budget-tour groups come in July and August. Available housing depends on the success of presold tours, but since even the curious still grab the frequent KTEL buses from Iráklio to Mátala, it sometimes seems easier to sleep in a cave than to find a free room.

Nikos Hotel, Mátala. ☎ **0892/42-375** or **42-765.** Fax 0892/42-120.
25 rms (17 with bath).

Rates: 6,250 Drs ($26) single without bath, 6,875 Drs ($28.64) single with bath; 7,500 Drs ($31.25) double without bath, 8,750 Drs ($36.45) double with bath. **Closed:** Nov–Mar 15.

The best choice of the lot is Nikos Kefalakis's hotel, which is near the beach on an unnamed street. Friendly and charming Nikos and his geranium-filled courtyard draw some of Mátala's nicest regulars, many of whom have been visiting since the 1970s. Call ahead, as reservations are often tough to come by in the high season.

Just up the road from Nikos are a host of perfectly acceptable guesthouse/pensions that we've stayed in over the years. The **Pension Fantastic** (☎ **0892/42-362**) is another in the price range of Nikos Pension. It has nine neat rooms (all with bath) and charges 7,500 Drs ($31.25) for a double, 5,600 Drs ($23.40) for a single. Rates are similar at the nearby guesthouse of **Silvia Spinthákis** (☎ **0892/42-127**) and at **Antónios' Rooms** (☎ **0892/42-123**). Antonios is a talented and diligent gardener, as evidenced by his self-proclaimed "paradise," a small flower garden with bananas and pomegranates. Be aware, if coming without reservations, that many hotels and even small pensions deal exclusively with groups and are fully booked in the high season. Mátala's few bigger hotels differ by offering views over the town parking lot (to the beach cove beyond) and balconies over the moped-filled main street.

WHERE TO EAT

Just below the portable post office on the shopping street, under a blue-striped awning, is the **Blue Restaurant** (☎ **42-107**), specializing in pizza and souvlaki. We loved the pizza pies, with fresh vegetables and salami (veg versions are also available). Expect to pay about 1,200–1,500 Drs ($5–$6.25) for a one-person pizza. Open daily from 11am to 11pm. The **Corali** (☎ **42-744**), on the main square in the center, serves traditional Greek fare, with an emphasis on grilled meats. Appetizers run 500–800 Drs ($2.10–$3.30), and main courses are 800–1,400 Drs ($3.30–$5.85); the hours are 8am to 1am daily.

Budget watchers should sample the souvlaki at **Gyros Nasos** near the main steps leading to the beach.

Kókkinos Pírgos

This village has recently developed a reputation among wandering adventurers. Kókkinos Pírgos ("Red Castle") is less than six miles from Aghía Galíni on the southern coast highway. It has a small caique port on the western end and a scruffy pebble beach on the eastern end. However, water views from the main coastal street are blocked by several tavernas and souvlaki stands that are built on the rocks or bulkheading above the narrow sand-and-stone shore.

On our last visit, we were struck by the large number of new hotels, pensions, and rooms to let, especially since the villager's long beach seems so unattractive in comparison with those at other nearby beach towns.

WHERE TO STAY

As mentioned, there are several *domátia* (rooms to rent) above storefronts. The small **El Greco Hotel** (☎ **0892/51-182**) is also a possibility, but we can't even imagine why anyone would want to stay in Kókkinos Pírgos overnight!

Aghía Galíni

The locals tell of a Byzantine emperor who set sail in quest of the Holy Grail. After months of difficult travel he met with a great storm at sea and took refuge in a quiet cove at the Bay of Messará. He prayed fervently for the storm to end, and when it did he built a small church on the nearest shore, dedicating it to Aghía Galíni, "Holy Peace."

A small, overbuilt beach community has sprung up at this once peaceful spot. The narrow streets, packed with shops and cafés, provide a lively, informal resort atmosphere. Unfortunately, the massive overbuilding of the past few years has managed to spoil Aghía Galíni's pretty port. We can't imagine coming here during the high season when the place is a total zoo. We were here last September and couldn't wait to move on. Before setting out for Aghía Galíni, therefore, make sure you're up to a heavy crowd scene.

ORIENTATION

The steep hill overlooking the port is tiered with hotels (which fill up in July and August). From the plusher Class-C hotels, there is a terrific view of the placid Libyan Sea. If you do decide to stay here, we recommend choosing a smaller hotel or rented room off to the side yet closer to the port; there you still have a view, it's less noisy, and you're a little closer to the activity (it's also less legwork walking up the switchback road after a few glasses of wine at night!). Below the lowest level are the busy tavernas around Fountain Square (now a quiet pool). This is the town parking lot and main bus stop (buses leave once daily at 8:30am to Iráklio, five times daily to Réthymno, three times daily to Plakiás). One lane above the fountain are the post office and National Bank. Pebble beaches are a short walk east around the point.

WHAT TO SEE & DO

If you're starting to feel that Aghía Galíni is well set up for tourists, you've gotten the point. It's a popular base for budget-charter groups that come from Germany and Great Britain for a week in the sun, and is therefore not very well organized to assist independent travelers who want to explore Crete's south coast from an inexpensive and comfortable resort.

The knowledgeable **Candia Tours** office (☎ **91-278,** fax 91-174; in Iráklio, **226-168**) rents cars, exchanges money, and offers trips to all of Crete's outstanding sights. Hours are 8:30am to 1pm and 5 to 9pm. Day trips include a visit to Samariá Gorge for a hike at 9,000 Drs ($37.50), several cruises to nearby Libyan Sea beaches, a tour to the Minoan palace at Phaistos, ruins at Gortyn, and the lovely beach at Mátala for 4,500 Drs ($18.75). In fact, many visitors pass up Aghía Galíni's clean pebble beach, hop on the frequent local bus, and head for the exceptionally scenic Mátala or the just slightly quieter fishers' beach at Plakiás (see the section below).

WHERE TO STAY

The 11-room **Hotel Selena,** Aghía Galíni 74056 (☎ **0832/91-237**), has spotless doubles, nearly all with baths as well as showers, and an excellent view from the common breakfast terrace. Prices run 6,875 Drs ($28.65) for two, 4,950 Drs ($20.65) for one, including a hearty breakfast. The Selena is managed by the friendly Eleni Mavroghiorghi (a former English teacher) and is open year-round. Nearby are two smaller pensions.

The nautical-style design of the **Ariston Pension** (☎ **0832/91-285** or **91-122** in the Ariston Taverna) drew us to it. Helen Mougarakis runs a tidy ship, with five spic-'n'-span doubles with bath for 5,850 Drs ($24.40), 4,875 Drs ($20.30) for a single. A budget alternative is run by Helen's mother. The **Acropol** (☎ **0832/91-234**) has doubles without bath for 3,900 Drs ($16.25); showers are 600 Drs ($2.50) extra.

The **Dedalos** (☎ **0832/91-214**) and the 12-room *Hotel Candia* (☎ **0832/91-359**) are both quiet and a good value.

Camping

Camping Aghía Galíni (☎ **0832/91-386**) is situated in an olive grove by the sea, just two miles south of town. It's on a beach, and it has 45 spaces and a restaurant and market.

WHERE TO EAT & DANCE

In the cluttered pedestrian main street, the choice for pizzas and for good-value, tasty Greek dishes is the **Libya Sea**, and **Thessaloniki** for good snacks. At **Bozos,** on the port, they serve a great Greek salad (*choriátiki saláta*) and many seafood dishes. The nearby **Whispers Bar** and **Jazz in Jazz Bar** are fairly priced and popular. **Sweet Bar** is the café spot for Greek coffee and pastry while you pore over the *International Herald Tribune* (purchased at the foreign-language bookshop next to Libya Pizza). Among establishments open year-round are the **Steki** and the **Acropol.**

The tiny **Onar Taverna** has a narrow stairway entrance off the main street, in keeping with this village's theme. Its three-story perch above two other, less distinctive, cafés offers great vistas, and the small menu represents carefully prepared food.

For some *après-diner* dancing, try the loud disco **Soroco Le Club,** on the beach, and the **Disco Juke Box.** Both open nightly at 9:30pm.

5 Réthymno

The port of Réthymno, dominated by the impressive Venetian Fortezza (fortress) of 1574 on a peninsula at its western end, has retained more of a medieval flavor than the port of Iráklio. It has become Crete's newest stylish resort. Réthymno played a historic role as capital of the province under the Venetians and the Turks, and it carried on an active trade with the Orient.

Getting There

Located 49 miles west of Iráklio on the northern coast, Réthymno can be visited as a day trip from Iráklio or Chaniá or used as a lively and pleasant vacation base. Buses from Iráklio run daily every half hour from 5:30am to 8:30pm for 1,650 Drs ($6.90) there is also frequent service from Chaniá.

One-way taxi fares from Iráklio are 14,000 Drs ($58.30) and from Chaniá 9,200 Drs ($38.30). Every Sunday and Tuesday in the high season there is an excursion ferry to Santoríni. Tickets are sold by several travel agents.

Orientation

The old quarter of the city, surrounding the Fortezza and bordered by the rocky sea coast, is made up of two-story stucco houses, whose Turkish wooden balconies shade narrow, twisting lanes. Small, typical churches, *kafenía* (coffeehouses) filled with locals, and nesting sparrows crowd this tranquil quarter. The two small museums that record Réthymno's intriguing history are both in this area.

East is the Customs House on Neárchos Street, and the charming, old fishermen's harbor. From the Old Harbor, the main commercial waterfront road broadens to become Venizélou Street, along which the government has created a pleasant sandy beach. Arkadíou Street runs parallel to the waterfront, one block in. Most small hotels, rooms to let, and shops are located on Arkadíou between the old port and the newly built jetty that marks the beginning of Réthymno's startlingly modern apartment and beach hotel row.

If you're staying in Réthymno for a while, pick up the excellent book *Rethymno,* by A. Malagari and H. Stratidakis, sold at the comprehensive International Press bookstore, one block from the Archeological Museum and Venizélou Street. It's open daily from 9am to 11pm.

Getting Around

The Dimokratías **bus station** (☎ **0831/22-212**), on Moátsou Street, has daily buses every half hour to Iráklio 1,650 Drs ($6.90) and Chaniá 1,500 Drs ($6.25) between 5:30am and 7:30pm. The station is a 10-minute walk south of the public beach at Venizélou.

There is a taxi stand opposite the tourist office.

Fast Facts: Réthymno

Hospital The state hospital (☎ **27-814**) is on Trantallídou Street.

Laundry There is a laundry next to the Youth Hostel, on Tombázi Street, open Mon–Sat 8am–8pm.

Olympic Airways The Olympic Airways office (☎ **0831/27-353**) is behind the city park, on Koumoundoúrou Street.

Police The tourist police station (☎ **28-156**) is on Platía Iróon (Heroes' Square).

Safety Réthymno is relatively safe. Nevertheless, there are basic precautions you should take whenever you're traveling in an unfamiliar place, since every society has its criminals. Stay alert and be aware of your surroundings. Wear a moneybelt and keep a close eye on your possessions. Be especially careful with cameras, wallets, and purses—all favorite targets of pickpockets. Leave your passport and other valuables in your hotel safe-deposit box.

Telephones The national telecommunications system, OTE, has a main branch on Kountounóti Street and a kiosk station on Venizélou Street. The main branch is open daily from 7:30am to midnight; the kiosk's hours are Monday through Saturday from 8am to 11:30pm and Sunday from 9am to 2pm and 5 to 10pm.

Tourist Information There is a municipal **tourist information office** (☎ **0831/24-143**) on Venizélou Street along the public beach. It's open Monday through Friday from 8:30am to 8pm, Saturday and Sunday from 8:30am to 2pm. (Next door is the local branch of the **Sea Turtle Protection Society of Greece,** open daily from 11am to 2pm and 8 to 11pm.)

What to See & Do

Sightseers should start from the sheltered end of the harbor and turn left. A four-minute walk up Paleológou Street will take you to the lovely 17th-century **Rimondi Fountain,** also called *Mégali Vryssi.* A block away is the **Neratzés Mosque,** with its minaret—one of the many signs of Turkish occupation that give Réthymno so much color. There's also a fine (now empty) mosque near the Great Gate to the Fortezza. On Arkadíou Street is the early 17th-century **Venetian Loggia,** once used as a clearinghouse by local merchants. Near the Fortezza is the **Archeological Museum** (☎ **29-975**), open Tuesday through Sunday from 8:30am to 3pm, closed Monday; admission is 500 Drs ($2.10), free on Sunday.

During the last half of July, go straight past the Neratzés Minaret to the flower-filled, well-groomed public park, where the annual **wine festival** is held. Behind the old port on Mesologíou Street is the **Historical and Folk Art Museum,** a private collection of Cretan folk art that's well worth seeing. The museum is raising funds to move into a restored Venetian villa, so double-check the address with the Greek Tourist Organization (EOT) before visiting; on our last visit, the museum was open Monday through Saturday from 9am to 1pm and 7 to 9pm. Admission is 300 Drs ($1.25).

Now that you've had a land tour, return to the Venetian Fortezza for an aerial one. It was built of thick, low stone walls to deflect cannon fire. From its parapets you can see Réthymno and imagine what the Venetians saw nearly 400 years ago. Inside its 1,131 yards of wall are water wells, the remains of a prison, a Greek Orthodox chapel and a mosque, and several small buildings. Open daily from 8:30am to 5pm; the admission fee is 500 Drs ($2.10).

With Réthymno's newfound resort status have come the tour operators. The excellent **Creta Travel Bureau** (☎ **0831/22-915**) has opened an office at Odós Venizelou 3, offering day trips to Iráklio's Archeological Museum and the palace of Knossos (11,250 Drs or $46.90), and to most other sites of tourist interest on Crete. **Nias Tours,** Odós Arkadíou 94 (☎ **831/23-840**), offers boat excursions to nearby beaches and an evening cruise to see the "lights of Rethymnon . . . dancing over the waters."

The lights also glisten at night at the **Fortezza Disco,** on the old port, where the action peaks about 11:30pm. A cover charge of 1,200 Drs ($5) includes the first drink. The Fortezza is being besieged by the newer **Sound Motion,** on the newly constructed Beach Road. Luckily for pedestrians, street traffic is barred from the harbor promenade at night, ensuring large sunset crowds for the nightly *vólta.*

Head east along the new port if you're interested in things bigger and more expensive or into the Old Quarter in search of more intimate venues, such as **Apple, Galero, Cinema,** and **Opera.** To find the best traditional Cretan music, continue along Paleologou past the Church of the Annunciation and along P. Coroneou to **Nikolaou Gounaki.**

Shoppers will find lots of new kitsch in the recently tourism-happy boutiques that line Arkadíou Street, but there are some fun handcrafts, gifts, and attractive, reasonably priced sportswear, especially up Souliou Street. More fashionable European styles and imports can be found inland on Varda Kallergí Street.

Hikers may want to find the **Happy Walker** (☎/fax 52-920) on Odós Tobazi, which offers daily guided hikes through various local areas. Horses can be found at the **Riding Center** (☎ **289-07**), Odós N. Fokeas 39, Platanias, southeast of town.

Where to Stay

Réthymno has a wide range of accommodations in the busier new section of town by the sand beach, and just a handful in the more tranquil and picturesque old quarter by the fort. In each area, we've recommended a worthy splurge choice as well as several budget-priced lodgings. Most facilities are open only between April or May and October.

IN THE OLD QUARTER

The back streets encircling the fort are the city's prettiest and hark back to the port's former days of glory under the Venetians. Both a splurge hotel and budget pension reflect this time.

Pension Anna, Odós Georghíou Katacháki 5, Réthymno 74100. ☎ **0831/25-586.** 7 rms (all with bath). MINIBAR

Rates: 7,150 Drs ($29.80) without kitchen single or double, 7,800 Drs ($32.50) with kitchen single or double.

Flanking the steps leading to the Fortezza are two buff-colored, restored houses. On the right is Anna's family house and on the left is her inn, the Pension Anna. The renovated rooms offer guests a small kitchenette, several others have minifridges, and all are spotless.

★ **Fortezza Hotel,** Odós Melisínou 16, Réthymno 74100. ☎ **0831/55-551.** Fax 0831/54-073. 54 rms (all with bath), including 3 suites. TEL

Rates (including breakfast): 15,700 Drs ($65.65) single; 24,500 Drs ($102.10) double; 26,750 Drs ($111.50) suite for four. AE, EC, MC, V.

The recently built Fortezza Hotel blends in admirably with its historic setting. The pink stucco, traditionally styled building has parquet marble floors, a large lounge off the lobby with a huge fireplace and TV, and a large pool surrounded by a private, tiled sun deck with snack bar. The Fortezza's rooms, decorated in contemporary pastel colors, are carpeted, spacious, and modern. Most have balconies overlooking the pool or Fortezza. This hotel is closed in the winter and recommends reserving high-season rooms at least one month in advance.

Since the beach isn't as good as those near Vái or along the south coast, we'd spend our hotel money at an older lodging within the narrow twisting streets behind the Venetian port. If you do want to stay to the west of the new jetty (northeast of the Fortezza), along the rocky seaside coast road, there are many rooms to let including the 14-room **Lefertis Pension,** Odós Plastira 26 (☎ **0831/23-803**), contained within three linked buildings; doubles run 4,650–7,275 Drs ($19.40–$30.30), singles range from 4,000–7,000 Drs ($16.70–$29.20). Another decent place to stay is the nine-room **Kastro Hotel,** Odós Plastira 15 (☎ **0831/24-973**), also built overlooking the scruffy pebble beach. Here doubles with breakfast cost 9,750 Drs ($40.65), singles are half that.

IN THE HEART OF TOWN

The modern part of Réthymno is roughly the area south (inland) from the sandy beach. (The newest, most recently developed beachside strip to the east is usually booked by package tours, so it isn't covered by this guidebook.) Choose your hotel room carefully because the portside cafés and broad avenues of this active city can be very noisy, day and night.

Kyma Beach Hotel, Platía Iróon, Réthymno 74100. ☎ **0831/55-503.**
Fax 0831/27-746. 34 rms (all with bath). A/C TEL

Rates (including breakfast): 12,870 Drs ($53.65) single; 19,240 Drs ($80.15) double. Rates negotiable in low season. AE, EC, MC, V.

The modern and stylish Kyma Beach Hotel is an altogether different choice. It's located at Platía Iróon (Heroes' Square), on the beach east of the tourist office. You can't miss its au courant Santa Fe–cum-art-deco styling, or the broad white Japanese umbrellas that shade its chic, beachside Station Café. Rooms are small but very tasteful, with balconies, marble floors, and furnishings, some with loft beds and simple Greek watercolors on the walls. Reservations at least one week in advance are recommended.

Hotel Minoa, Odós Arkadíou 62, Réthymno 74100 ☎ **0831/22-508.**
32 rms (all with bath). MINIBAR TEL

Rates: 6,800 Drs ($27.10) single; 7,150 Drs ($29.80).

Turning your back to the fortress behind the marina, walk along Arkadíou Street, and up the block you'll find the older Hotel Minoa. The Minoa is one of the few older inns whose bright, creamy-colored rooms are spotlessly maintained: all this plus inexpensive rates and a family-based staff, both helpful and hospitable. The twin rooms offer shared balconies.

Hotel Valari, Odós Kountouríotou 86-88, Réthymno 74100. ☎ **0831/22-236.**
Fax 0831/29-368. 35 rms (all with bath). TEL

Rates (with breakfast): 10,125 Drs ($42.20) single; 13,750 Drs ($57.30) double.

Our first choice is the friendly Hotel Valari, three blocks inland from the tourist office. It's well maintained with fresh paint and carpeting in all rooms. All rooms have balconies, but we liked the back rooms that overlook the small pool and snack bar. The Valari also has a roof garden where you can sunbathe and get a view of the harbor.

Zania Hotel, Odós Pávlou 3, Réthymno 74100. ☎ **0831/28-169.**
5 rms (none with bath). TEL

Rates: 5,850 Drs ($24.40) single; 10,950 Drs ($45.65) double.

Nearby the Hotel Minoa is the totally captivating Zania Hotel, run by Miss Foni Psarokalou. In excellent French, she'll describe the history of this 150-year-old house. The prices are high for sharing a huge old bathroom with others, but the Zania's specialness should sway some readers.

A YOUTH HOSTEL

From the central taxi square in front of the Church of the Fours Martyrs go through the Porta Guora arch and take the first street on the right to find the welcoming Réthymnon Youth Hostel at Odós Tobázi 4 (☎ **0831/22-848**), where you'll find 82 beds, plus 30 on the covered roof, for 1,200 Drs ($5), hot showers, three lounge areas, breakfast and inexpensive snacks.

Where to Eat

$ **Restaurant Apostolis,** Odós Kallirons Siganou 10. ☎ **24-401.**

Cuisine: TAVERNA.

Prices: Appetizers 250–600 Drs ($1.05–$2.50); main courses 875–1,500 Drs ($3.65–$6.25).

Open: Daily 6am–11pm.

This 60-year-old, family-run establishment is the perfect spot for that moussaká or beef stifado for which you've been longing. Just a 10 to 15 minute walk away from the tourist zone in a quiet residential neighborhood, the Apostólis is as unassuming as one can imagine, which is why it makes our short list of "real" places. Oh, yes, the food is terrific, and Géorghios and Nikólaos are your friendly hosts.

Famagusta, Odós Plastíra 6. ☎ **23-881.**

Cuisine: CRETAN/CONTINENTAL.

Prices: Appetizers 500–1,400 Drs ($2.10–$5.85); main courses 1,200–3,200 Drs ($5–$13.30). AE, DC, MC, V.

Open: Mon–Sat 9am–midnight; closed Sun.

On the beach road between the harbor and the fortress is a perpetual favorite with a lovely view of the sea. Diners can eat various local specialties prepared in the Cretan style or sample Famagusta's expanding menu of continental dishes, including steaks and an assortment of pasta dishes.

Go through the arch of the Rimondi Fountain and turn right to find the best budget choice we know of, **Kyria Maria** (☎ **29-078**), where you can have traditional Greek food serenaded by a couple of dozen songbirds; a vegetarian plate costs 850 Drs ($3.55), 1,500 Drs ($6.25) with meat.

There are a few other notable eateries in the old quarter. **Ovelistirion** is the name of Stelios' taverna on Theo. Arambatzoglou Street, just a block from the Fortezza's entrance. Its simple tables overlook the Orthodox Church of the Annunciation that dominates the quiet square. Typical Greek dishes are served in the old style; fried calamari, rich moussaká, a country salad, and retsína will satisfy two for 27,500 Drs ($11.50).

Nearby at Odós Nikiforou Foka 93 is the **Germaniki Bakery,** ☎ **28-084,** a traditional shop with brick ovens that turns out crusty loaves in the shape of chickens, baskets, geese, rabbits, and other prize-winning decorative baked goods, open daily 8am–3pm and 5–8pm. On the sea side of the Fortezza, on the road leading to the Chaniá Gate, is **Iliovasilirata,** an ouzerí popular with locals for its large variety of appetizers and the sunset view.

For desserts and snacks, there are several appealing but costly seaside cafés and inexpensive souvlaki and pizza places, all inland along Arkadíou Street.

6 Excursions South to Plakiás

One-day Excursions

Among the most popular excursions for fit travelers to Crete is the hike down the Samariá Gorge, the so-called Grand Canyon of Europe. We've covered it in the section 7, "Chaniá & the Southwest Coast," but it can be made as a full-day trip from Réthymno; nearly every travel agent in town offers just such an excursion.

Two other excursions that are possible from Réthymno include a visit to Crete's famous **Monastery of Arcadi,** a 16th-century Venetian work with a lovely church within. Its Renaissance-style door and elaborate columns and arches were not badly damaged in the Turkish siege of 1866, during which the Abbott Gabriel chose to ignite the monastery's store of powder kegs—killing 800 refugees and attacking soldiers—rather than surrender to the Turks. There are four buses daily to the Monastery of Arcadi; the last one returns to Réthymno at 4pm.

Another excursion is to the nearly perfect mountain village of **Spíli** (discussed in "Day Trips from Iráklio"), which is 18.6 miles south of the national highway. On the way you'll pass by the old church on the square in the village of **Arméni,** a pretty town filled with outspread fan cacti and dripping with bougainvillea.

For the truly adventurous, a full-day trip, camping expedition, or hitchhiking foray should be made to the coast due south of Réthymno. Head for Plakiás and stop at the **Preveli Monastery** and Frangokástello along the way.

The Preveli Monastery has long been a stronghold of Greek nationalism, a base for resistance against hostile armies. Its remarkable location, high on the rocks overlooking the blue Libyan Sea, is both remote and strategic. For the monks who live here, it's a sanctuary of calm and beauty. For the Greek Resistance it was a base for counterattack against both the Turks and, during World War II, the Germans.

The monastery was built in 1836 and contains several panels painted in the 1600s; a carved crest above the medieval marble fountain bears a Crusader cross. The monastery maintains a small museum that exhibits priests' vestments, religious symbols, and ornaments. It is open from sunrise to sunset daily. The sign at the gate says: "No shorts." Dress accordingly.

To reach the monastery, take the infrequent Plakiás bus and get off where the north-south road and south coast highway intersect. It's a $2^1/_2$-mile walk from there.

Also at the Preveli Monastery is a plaque commemorating the British, Australian, and New Zealand forces that took part in the Battle of Crete.

The week of May 21 marks the anniversary of these events, and is duly noted by the people of Crete. Full details are available in *Greece and Crete 1941,* by Christopher Buckley, published by the Efstathiádis Group of Athens.

Excursion to Frangokástello

A dominating presence over a wide, gray sandy stretch of coastline, the 14th-century Venetian Fortress of Frangokástello will impress all but the most blasé tourists. The fort is totally intact, with flowers growing inside and outside its massive walls. The worn sign of Saint Mark (the Lion of Venice) is still visible over the southern portal. Buses run once a day from Chaniá to Frangokástello (2,000 Drs or $8.35 each way); you have to exit at the castle.

Today, the most vital part of Frangokástello is its haunting legend, the story of Fata Morgana. During the War of Independence in 1821 a small battalion of Greek soldiers was hopelessly outnumbered by fierce Turkish forces who moved in and massacred the Greeks. Since that time local inhabitants swear that late at night when the sea is calm (at the end of May or September), a ghostly image of the gallant battalion appears, hovering above the ocean. The visitation of the restless souls of the soldiers reminds the locals of the terrible day when Frangokástello was the scene of this region's most ghastly event. (A coterie of young Greeks and foreigners return annually to camp out at Frangokástello's pensions and await Fata Morgana.)

Tourist development elsewhere has made this once mystical spot somewhat of a miniresort, with about two dozen new rooms to rent and apartment complexes springing up along the south coast highway. Their presence has diminished the power once radiated by this isolated, majestic fortress. Among them is **Apartments Castello,** Frangokástello, Sfakiá (☎ **0825/92-068**), an 11-apartment complex. The decorative crenellations of the castle have found their way across the road and down some (about a quarter mile), to this tidy and tastefully furnished lodging. Apartments with kitchenettes can accommodate either 2 or 4 people; rates are 8,000 Drs ($33.35) for 2, or 15,500 Drs ($64.60) for 4; DC and V are accepted. Mr. Giannarakis rents 8 rooms attached to his taverna (0825/92-137), on the bluff above the beach and no more than 109 yards from the castle, for 6,750 Drs ($28.15) a double, 4,875 Drs ($20.30) a single.

Excursion to Plakiás

Plakiás is a burgeoning southern coastal fishing town, whose attractive sand-and-pebble beach and year-round warm water have been thoroughly discovered by tourists, especially charter group vacationers. It's still a fine place for those who enjoy hiking and climbing over rocks. On the far-left side of the beach is a series of caves, and on either side of the cove are many more isolated beaches.

Since the completion of the new roads from Réthymno to the north, and from Sfakiá (Chóra Sfakiá) to the west, Plakiás has developed at a rapid pace but with some planning. The dozens of two-story pensions that have sprung up along its beach and on a newly built back lane are supported by European tour operators who buy out their rooms from mid-June to September.

Plakiás's prominence has earned it a mobile post office (open Monday through Saturday from 8:30am to 2pm and Sunday from 9am to 1pm; they also change money), moped dealer, supermarket, several minimarkets, some souvenir and sunblock shops, and a self-serve laundromat (☎ **31-471;** open daily except Sunday; 1,800 or $7.50 for a wash and dry). There is also a branch of Candia Tours (☎ **0832/31-571,** fax 0832/31-433), which offers weekly trips to most of Crete's archeological sites, to Ághios Nikólaos, and even to Réthymno and Chaniá.

GETTING THERE

Getting to Plakiás is a snap in the high season and a chore in the off months. Buses run eight times a day from Réthymno to Plakiás and twice a day from Sfakiá. The roadway from Réthymno (23 miles north) winds up and down hills until just a few miles outside of the town, and the more scenic bus route passes through the rugged but beautiful Kourtaliótiko Gorge and the lovely mountain village of Mirthios, where there are a few rooms to let, a good youth hostel, and a couple of tavernas.

WHERE TO STAY

The low season is the best time to visit, because there are some good deals in the few older hotels or rooms to let above the small row of storefronts, and good rates in the newly built pensions.

Alianthos Beach Hotel, Ághios Vassílios, Plakiás 74060. ☎ **0832/31-280.** Fax 0832/31-282. 150 rms (all with bath). TEL

Rates (including breakfast): 8,450 Drs ($35.20) single; 12,870 Drs ($53.65) double. AE, DC, EC, MC, V.

The recently enlarged Alianthos Beach Hotel is the fanciest establishment and especially popular with Eurogroups. Large, front-facing, bright rooms, their balconies dripping with geraniums, overlook the central part of the cove, while the newer rooms, behind the original building, face the interior. The large pool and sun deck, small kiddy pool, and TV lounge make it perfect for kids who tire of frolicking on the beach across the road.

Flisvos Hotel, Plakiás 74060. ☎ **0832/31-421.** 11 rms (all with bath).

Rates: 5,625 Drs ($23.45) single; 7,500 Drs ($31.25) double.

When we visited the Flisvos again last spring, this sparkling white inn was still the cleanest place in town and the management was the friendliest. They also have a good snack bar downstairs.

There are rooms to rent between 5,000 Drs ($20.85) and 8,000 Drs ($33.35) for two anywhere, depending on the season. Our favorites are on the far northwestern end of Plakiás, beyond the main strip. For example, we liked the **Aponimos Rooms** (☎ **0832/28-813**) and the next door **Rooms on the Rocks** (no tel.). These informal inns have only a handful of doubles located above two tavernas; ask for the top floor rooms that rent for 8,000 Drs ($33.35) and come with extra large balconies and terrific views. Back in town is the lively 27-room Class C **Hotel Lamon** (☎ **0832/31-279;** fax 0832/31-424), located next to the Candia Tours office on the waterfront. Basic accommodations with breakfast run 7,500 Drs ($31.25) for two, 5,625 Drs ($23.45) for a single. A second choice is the 16-room **Hotel Livykon** (☎ **0832/31-216**). The rooms are clean if spartan and not a bad deal at 7,500 Drs ($31.25) or 5,125 Drs ($21.35), double or single, respectively, if you take breakfast at the bakery next door.

A Youth Hostel

The brand new purpose-built **Plakias Youth Hostel,** secluded five minutes from the beach, is the best we found on our last trip. It has 80 beds (1,125 Drs or $4.70), very nice bathroom and handwashing facilities, mosquito screens, a snack bar, volleyball court, and plans for more.

WHERE TO EAT

Petit Plakiás has a large number of eateries, many of which are snack/toast/café bars, but one can still find some outlets serving excellent, locally caught seafood. Best among them is the **Sofía Grill** where tender, freshly grilled octopus, a large *choriátiki saláta* with Crete's famous tomatoes, and a glass of the local rosé will cost 2,750 Drs ($11.45); the Sofía is located on the central part of the *paralía.* Next door is the **Corali Restaurant,** another all-year-round place and popular with Plakiasotis; prices are similar to the Sofía Grill. **Taverna Christos,** on the west side of the port at the caique harbor, is yet another of our favorites. Two can eat healthy portions of stuffed vegetables, *pastítsio,* or gigantes, prepared with that special Cretan flair, for under 3,500 Drs ($14.60). Their moussaká is especially popular.

The cafés on the central part of the beach alternate between bars that fill up at sunset, like **Ostrako,** and the hip late-night cafés that serve drinks, ice cream, and popular music. The high-tech gray, pink, and mirrored **Swing** is, as of our last visit, still the most popular of these cafés.

Plakias has a few inexpensive places still left, which are frequented by the locals. **Platia** is an overgrown souvlaki stand that's good and cheap and therefore very popular. If you're up for an evening walk, hike to Lefkogia, the tiny village three miles east of Plakiás and try the **Stelios Taverna,** whose Greek specialties are very good and inexpensive.

Night owls should try the **Meltémi Dance Club** on the road leading into town or the **Hexagon,** behind the cafeteria of the same name.

7 Chaniá & the Southwest Coast

The city of Chaniá bears the stamp of its Renaissance-era Venetian occupants more than any other city on Crete. Narrow streets with 600-year-old slender wood and stone houses still grace the old city, and thick stone walls fortify the small, secluded harbor. A solitary lighthouse stands watch at the port point.

Surrounding this historic center is a modern vibrant city. Like Iráklio, there are large areas of little interest to tourists, busy market sections with trucks bringing produce in and out amid the endless buzzing of motorbikes and compact cars.

The comparison with Iráklio is a popular sport on Crete, where boosters of each city claim their own to be the island's "Number One." Although the capital was moved from Chaniá to Iráklio, and the latter is more economically developed, Chaniá wins hands-down for sheer architectural elegance. This intraisland competition goes back perhaps as far as the 2d century B.C., when ancient Chaniá (called Kydoniá in those days) battled against its less powerful adversaries at Knossós. Chaniá was occupied by the Venetians (who built the walls, harbor, and nearby residential area) during the 14th and 16th centuries, then, for over 200 years, by the Turks. The Germans moved into Crete during World War II and damaged or flattened much of the old city.

Today, the physical vestiges of Venetian rule are seen around the port, its fortifying walls and the graceful stone mansions that tower over the narrow-paved lanes of the old quarter. The best hotels, restaurants, and shops are found here. Unfortunately, Chaniá's recent popularity as a group tour destination has greatly diminished the appeal of the newer city surrounding this quarter. We recommend strongly that you try to visit this picturesque and intriguing city in the off season. That's the best time to find rooms in one of the lovely restored mansions of the old quarter and to experience the charms of a bygone era.

Getting There

BY AIR Chaniá is connected to Athens via Olympic at least three times daily in the high season. There is also a weekly flight to Thessaloníki.

BY BOAT Ferry tickets for the nightly Piraeus boats departing from Souda (15 minutes from the market by bus) are sold by several travel agents for 5,500 Drs ($22.90) for the 12-hour voyage.

BY BUS Buses run from Iráklio and Réthymno every half hour between 5:30am and 8:30pm; fares are 3,000 Drs and 1,500 Drs ($12.50, $6.25), respectively.

Getting Around

Chaniá is definitely a walking town and nearly all of the areas that you'll want to explore are within a fairly small area. If you intend to tour in the vicinity, there are many taxis available.

Orientation/Information

There may be a temporary Tourist Information Office of Chaniá at Odós Sífaka 22 (☎ **0821/59-990**). It's supposed to be open Monday through Saturday from 8:30am to 8:30pm, and closed 2 to 3pm for lunch; however, when we visited recently, nothing was certain. The less conveniently located but more helpful EOT office, at Odós Kriari 40, on the 4th floor (☎ **92–943**), is open Monday through Friday from 8am to 3pm.

The **post office,** open 8am to 8pm weekdays, is behind the agorá on Tzanakaki Street. There's a **laundry** on Tzanakaki Street opposite the post office, as well as one on Kanevarou Street opposite the taxi stand. The local **Chaniá Hospital** (☎ **27-231**) is off Venizélou Street.

Stavros Paterakis and the helpful staff of **Spa Tours** (☎ **0821/21-327**, fax 0821/55-283), at Odós Mihelidaki 10, can take care of all your tour and travel needs. You can also make travel arrangements through **InterKreta;** their office is at Odós Kanevaro 9 (☎ **0821/52-552**).

Olympic Airways, Odós Stratigou Tzanakaki 88 (0821/27-701), offers bus service 90 minutes before departure time to Chaniá Airport from their office; the fare is 500 Drs ($2.10).

What to See & Do

A walking tour of old Chanía should be the first activity for new arrivals, followed by some interesting shopping.

A WALKING TOUR

Begin with a stroll around the cobbled old **Venetian Harbor.** Behind the "white" **Tzamasi Mosque** is **Kastélli,** the oldest part of the city, where you can glimpse the remains of several cultures, particularly the Venetian and Turkish. Right (east) along the harbor will bring you to the **Venetian Arsenals** so often featured in photos of Chaniá, now used as meeting and exhibition space. Across the harbor the **Lighthouse** and **San Salvatore** guard the entrance to the harbor. Turn and walk back around the harbor to the opposite rampart to visit the **Naval Museum of Crete** (☎ **91-875**), with interesting artifacts and displays chronicling the island's deep connection with the sea; it's open Tuesday through Sunday 10am to 2pm (4pm May through October), admission is 400 Drs ($1.65), half price for students.

Make your way through the maze of charming streets back south along the still imposing western **Wall.** The large round hill at the southwest corner of the Old City is **Bastion Siavou,** constructed as a vantage point and damaged by recent erosion. Eventually you'll find yourself on busy Odós Hálidon, a major commercial street, and near the harbor you'll find the **Archeological Museum** (☎ **20-334**), with finds from the area; open Tuesday through Sunday 8:30am to 3pm, 500 Drs ($2.10). A couple of streets behind it you'll find a ruined synagogue, waiting for restoration since the

German occupation during World War II. The **Catholic Church,** with its pretty pink interior, is just south on Hálidon, and not far away across the street is the **Orthodox Cathedral.**

Turn left after the Cathedral on Odós Skridlóf, famous for its leather, and after a few blocks you'll reach the large **Municipal Market,** built about a century ago in the shape of a Greek cross, well worth a visit and a good place to buy fresh produce and other comestibles, as well as souvenirs. South and west from the market takes you into the modern commercial and official center. South and east along Odós Dimokratías will lead you to the lush **Municipal Garden,** begun in 1870, and the nearby stadium. Head north again to find the **Venetian Rampart** or wander through the labyrinth of streets where you'll find no end to sights and delights, including several old churches and a minaret.

SHOPPING

There are dozens of souvenir and jewelry shops on the side streets off the old port, particularly on Halidon Street up to Platía 1866, and along the pedestrian mall on Skridóf Street. The **Chaniá District Association of Traditional Handicraft,** Odós Afendoúli 14, has a cooperative store at Tombazi Street on the harbor, filled with the ceramics, paintings, and crafts of local artists. Next door are a few small souvenir shops with a collection of *mati,* those blue glass eyes thought to ward off evil.

Chaniá also has an old bronze and brass foundry at Odós Halidon 35 housed in a Turkish-style building that is run by the metalsmith Apostolos Papadakis.

For the discerning, there's an incredible selection of old and antique Cretan blankets and kilims at Odós Anghélou 5 (near the Naval Museum). Kostas Liapakis (☎ **98-571**) claims that his embroideries and weavings are about 100 years old and made from old, local dowry fabrics. The rich red background and decorative geometric patterns in the fabrics are quite stunning, and you might be seduced into spending around $200 for a 3-by-5-foot souvenir. The shop is open Monday through Sunday from 9am to 8pm.

One of the coolest shops in Chaniá is **Anatolia,** Odós Halídon 5, (☎ **41-218**), run by Juliette and Patrick Fabre, a boutique specializing in Asian antique (and near antique) jewelry. The shop is open Monday through Saturday from 10am to 9:30pm. We also liked **Carmela,** next to Kostas Liapakis' rug shop (see above), at Odós Anghélou 7 (☎ **90-487**) Carmela Iatropoulou has put together a stylish collection of contemporary (there are also a few older pieces) silver jewelry designed and made throughout Greece. Prices are very reasonable and when we returned from our last trip, laden with presents, those bought from Carmela's shop were a hit. Carmela's is open daily 10am to 9:30pm; AE, MC, and V are accepted. Across the street is **Ornatus Jewellery Work Shop** at Odós Agélou 12 (☎ **55-538**), another interesting jewelry boutique, open 10:30–11pm.

Where to Stay

One of Chaniá's most appreciated features is its wonderful offering of hotels, many of which are converted 14th-century Venetian homes and boarding houses. Chaniá is the place for a special splurge.

★ **Amphora Hotel,** Odós Párados Theotokopoúlou 20, Chaniá 73131.
☎ **0821/93-224.** Fax 0821/93-226. 20 rms (all with bath). TEL

Rates (including breakfast): 14,950 Drs ($62.30) single; 20,800 Drs ($86.70) double. EC, MC, V.

The white-and-blue Amphora Hotel, behind the Amphora Restaurant on the east side of the Old Harbor, is a converted 600-year-old Venetian villa with unique rooms. Extremely high ceilings, French doors opening on harbor views, simple furnishings, and modern private bathrooms grace each one. Room no. 7 is especially romantic, with its matrimonial bed, a single bed behind a curtain, and working fireplace. The Amphora is open year-round, although you should contact the hotel if you plan to come during the off-season.

Hotel Contessa, Odós Theofánous 15, Chaniá 73131. ☎ **0821/98-565.**
6 rms (all with bath). TV TEL

Rates (including breakfast): 13,650 Drs ($56.90) single; 20,475 Drs ($85.30) double. AE, EC, MC, V.

To call the Hotel Contessa venerable is an understatement. Housed in a 300-year-old Venetian-era home across the lane from the Amphora, with antiques decorating the lobby, it reeks of old Chaniá. We think that the high tariff is worth it for the treat of basking in such old-world elegance.

★ **Doma,** Odós Venizélou 124. Chaniá 73133. ☎ **0821/51-772.** Fax 0821/41-578.
28 rms (all with bath), 1 suite. TEL

Rates (including breakfast): 16,625 Drs ($69.25) single; 22,500 Drs ($93.75) double; 47,500 Drs ($197.90) suite. DC, MC, V.

Doma, a stately neoclassical mansion, is a converted family home situated on the edge of the Haleppa district. This elite 19th-century neighborhood is where the Greek statesman Elefthérios Venizélos lived and where many regal homes can still be seen. The owner and gracious proprietoress, Ms. Irene ("Rena") Valyraki, has tastefully decorated the inn with family photos and heirlooms. We have yet to find such a comfortable space in any other lodging on Crete. The parlor, for example, is filled with distinctive Cretan embroideries, copper pots, and ancient marbles. A tiny elevator leads to the homey third-floor dining room, where gourmet cuisine is served in full view of the Gulf of Chaniá; be sure to take your breakfast here, as it easily ranks among the best we've sampled anywhere in Greece. Doma's rooms are large and *gemütlich.* (If you like to sleep with your windows open, choose a quieter back-facing room.). There's even laundry and room service. All in all, the Doma rates as our favorite lodging on Crete.

El Greco Hotel, Odós Theotokopoúlou 63, Chaniá 73131. ☎ **0821/918-829.**
Fax 0821/95-566. 25 rms (all with bath).

Rates: 8,450 Drs ($35.20) single; 11,050 Drs ($46.05) double. AE, MC, V.

Several readers recommended this hotel on the quiet street behind the harbor next to the west Wall, and we're glad to say it's as charming and friendly as they assured us. Some of the upper rooms even have good views.

Maria Studios, Kalamáki 189, Chaniá 73100. ☎ **0821/31-870.** 7 rms (all with bath).
MINIBAR TEL

Rates: 10,625 Drs ($44.25), single/double, 12,125 Drs ($50.50) on the beach west of town.

The friendly owners at Maria Studios, Charlie and Maria, speak excellent English (they lived for about 15 years in Philadelphia). The place is newish, and each room includes a small kitchenette and a shower. The Studios should be open during the off-season at prices about 30% less than in the summer.

If these sound inviting but you're running low on drachmas, try one of the three pensions housed in 600- to 700-year-old homes next to the Naval Museum on Angélou Street. The one closest to the harbor is the **Meltémi** (no tel.), and is followed by **Theresa, Ekati** and **Stella** (☎ **0821/43-756**). The Theresa (☎ **0821/92-798**) at no. 8 is by far the nicest (and most expensive). Doubles go for about 9,375 Drs ($39.10) for two, including shower and harbor views from the roof terrace; expect to pay 5,500 Drs ($22.90) single or double at the other guesthouses without private facilities. A stay in any of these homes is enjoyable for the portside atmosphere, winding creaky stairs, and high, decorative ceilings.

A YOUTH HOSTEL

There is also a GYH Youth Hostel inconveniently located at Odós Drakonianoú 33 (☎ **0821/53-565**). Call for directions. It's open year-round; the 60 beds in dorm rooms cost 875 Drs ($4.90) each.

Where to Eat

Chaniá's lovely harbor has been somewhat overrun by ice cream cafés and loud music bars, where tourists on cheap packaged holidays and sailors from the nearby Greek and U.S. Navy bases congregate to have a good time. Nevertheless, in the quieter spring and fall months it is a pleasant place to dine. We recommend the **Amphora Restaurant.** Most of our favorites are set away from the central waterfront scene, in and around the quiet eastside residential neighborhood of Haleppa.

Aeriko, Aktí Miaoúli. ☎ **59-307.**

Cuisine: OUZERÍ/TAVERNA.
Prices: Appetizers 440–1,100 Drs ($1.85–$4.60); main courses 925–2,700 Drs ($3.85–$11.25). V.
Open: Dinner only 6pm–1am daily.

Aeriko is a well-designed waterside ouzerí/taverna that attracts a sophisticated Greek and Eurotourist crowd. Owner Stelio Blazakis (formerly of To Carneyo) opened this attractive eatery in 1990, and since then we've come to appreciate it for its fairly unusual Greek mezédes (appetizers), especially stuffed calamari and green peppers with cheese. Among the most popular dishes is veal with mushrooms, but we prefer the Greek favorites such as chicken souvlaki and fried zuccini.

Doma, Odós Venizélou 124. ☎ **0821/21-772.**

Cuisine: CRETAN. **Reservations:** Necessary one day in advance.
Prices: Appetizers 750–2,000 Drs ($3.15–$8.35); main courses 940–4,900 Drs ($3.90–$20.40). DC, MC, V.
Open: Dinner only 6:30–11pm daily.

Although we have reviewed the Doma as the city's top lodging alternative, it should also be considered for dinner as one of the more attractive dining rooms. Here one can sample traditional Cretan cuisine made in the style one might be served at home instead of a larger, tourist-oriented restaurant. Among the top dishes are an excellent Cretan style cheese pie, marrows pie, lamb cooked with herbs in wine, and all of the veal dishes. We also can't stress enough how much we enjoyed our breakfast at the Doma, and would heartily recommend stopping here for an exceptional offering of freshly made yogurt, homemade quince jam, spices, dried fruit, and nuts.

★ **Thalasino Ageri Fish Taverna,** Odós Viviláki 35, Haléppa. ☎ **56-672.**

Cuisine: FISH/SEAFOOD. **Reservations:** Recommended.

Prices: Appetizers 350–1,800 Drs ($1.45–$7.50); main courses 800–3,000 Drs ($3.35–$12.50).

Open: Dinner only 8:30pm–midnight daily.

To give you an idea about the owner's care about the cuisine, we were told that Falasin Ageri ("The Sea Breeze") only closes if there is no fresh fish. Nektarios and Maria Lionaki opened this little known waterside haunt (past a long row of leather workshops) in 1990; we made our first visit in 1991 and have enjoyed it ever since. The setting is both secluded and attractive, making it a wonderfully romantic escape from the in-center food outlets, and the fish is as fresh and as well prepared as you'll find. There is a limited menu for non-seafood eaters. As with some of our other Haleppa selections, make sure that you have directions or you'll likely get lost.

To Carneyo, 8 Katecháki Square. ☎ **53-366.**

Cuisine: TAVERNA.

Prices: Appetizers 550–2,600 Drs ($2.30–$10.85); main courses 1,100–3,400 Drs ($4.60–$14.15).

Open: Daily 7am–midnight.

To Carneyo is a fine choice for authentic taverna fare in a relatively tranquil environment. Their grilled chicken, zucchini bourekis, and baklava are sure to be as good. Gregarious host Dimitris does his best to keep the food up to the highest level and has succeeded on our visits.

Our favorite find on our last trip was **Rudi's Beer House,** Odós Sífaka 24 (☎ **50-824**; Rudi, a friendly Austrian, and his lovely Greek wife, Elpída, serve 58 kinds of beer and excellent snacks—we particularly liked their tuna salad—at budget prices. Nearby at Odós Sifaká 37 is **Anaplous** (☎ **41-320**), the only vegetarian restaurant we know of on Crete; they also serve simple traditional food at uncommonly low prices.

Evening Entertainment

We know that we're not much fun at night anymore (maybe because we've left our teenage years behind or quite possibly it's the job), but we've never found a whole lot to do other than the traditional waterside *vólta* (stroll) in Chaniá. We know, however, that there are a few of you who long for that late-night activity and we've searched high and low just for you.

On the far east end of the Venetian Harbor you'll find the area known as *Dio Lux* (after some old gas lamps that were once there) where the local young people go to mingle. **Pyli,** atop the Rampart, is the bar with the most spectacular setting, a place to savor a drink to soft rock under trees and the stars. Across the Old Town near the Catholic Church you'll find three somewhat more sophisticated places: **Ideon Andron** (after the cave where Zeus was born), Odós Hálidon 26, is probably the most inviting, but if it doesn't appeal to you, stroll around the block and check out **Anagenesis** ("Born Again") and **Babel** (no translation necessary, we hope). Midway on the harbor **Ariadne Disco** is still holding her own against **Scala.** Jazz connoisseurs will want to visit **Fagotta,** favorite of local artists and literati, at Odós Angélou, near the Naval Museum. If a cold brew and conversation is more your speed, find **Rudi's Beer House,** Odos Sífaka 24.

The **Attikon II Cinema,** Odós Venizélou 118, plays American films in English in the open air June through September every night at 8:45 and 11; admission is 1,200 Drs ($5).

One-Day Excursions

Among the most popular excursions is the full-day trek down the Samariá Gorge and back, via Aghía Roúmeli. This is most often done as a day trip and is covered fully below.

Save some of that shopping money for a boat cruise around **Souda Bay,** an evening barbecue and cruise, or a swimming excursion offered by Domenico Tours, Odós Kanevaro 10 (☎ **53-262**; fax 53-262). The tours are priced from 4,000 to 9,000 Drs ($16.65–$37.50); check their office for information.

Diktynna Travel (☎ **41-458**) is one of many along Hálidon Street that offer day trips to **Elafonísi,** our favorite unspoiled beach on the west coast. Buses stop at the Chryssoskalitissas Monastery on the way; bring a picnic and count on a long day. The tour costs 6,000 Drs ($25).

Chaniá's well-organized taxi drivers have published their own brochure advertising day trips to all of Crete's major sites. Call them at **28-288** or **54-747** for information and fares. The most popular excursion from Chaniá is a hike through Europe's largest canyon to Crete's south coast.

Excursions to the Southwest Coast

The prefecture of Chaniá is the least developed part of Crete, due to its poor infrastructure. The snow-capped inland mountain ranges, fertile valleys, and startling palisades that tumble into the navy-blue Mediterranean make it impossible to link the isolated beaches and villages to the national highway system. To reach most of the west's idyllic beaches takes time, patience, a boat or Jeep, or an invigorating hike through the Samariá Gorge (see below).

We were tipped off about a detour to **Élos,** on the road that links Kastélli to Paleochóra. This tiny mountain gem is little more than a bakery, taverna, and a few houses, but, oh, does it feel like a timeless place. We know that it's pretty far out of the way and that you'll likely pass by it, but if you despair about the commercialization of Crete, the insanity of its resorts and overly developed cities, take the time to visit Élos. If you're there in late September to early October, you'll likely be there for the chestnut harvest.

An Excursion to the Samariá Gorge

The Samariá Gorge (often referred to as the Grand Canyon of Greece) connects the small inland mountain hamlet of Omalós to the southern coast beach town of Aghía Roúmeli. An 11-mile footpath leads through the narrow canyon and is the only passage in or out of the area.

The rigorous hike takes about four to five hours. You don't have to be in mountaineer condition (the hikers we met were all ages), but you should feel comfortable with the idea of walking (albeit downhill) for 11 miles and have stamina. Wear light hiking boots or sneakers, and bring food for a picnic and a towel and swimsuit for the post-descent dip.

The trail begins at a well-marked entrance at Omalós, at the *kosokolon* ("wooden steps"). The path drops steeply for the first 1.9 miles with lots of switchbacks and loose stones. Good views of the gorge are within less than a mile, so if you decide that the full trek isn't your style, you can still witness the 654-yard drop to the bottom of the canyon. A multitude of wildflowers line the path, giving the impression of a predetermined design. The trail continues to drop (it's downhill the entire way) until it levels out at the deserted town of Samariá, 4$^1/_2$ miles into the Gorge. The inhabitants of Samariá were forced to leave in 1962 after the gorge was declared a national park. They were relocated quite conveniently at the end of the trail (6$^1/_2$ miles away), where they now own and service the lucrative tourist concession. As at many points along the trail, there is an abundant supply of fresh mountain water.

The second segment of the journey is the real payoff. The trail finally hits the river bottom, then meanders through the rocky bed. The deep gorge becomes narrower; and the water-eroded striations and patterns on the rocks and walls are exquisite. The river-cut trail passes through a chasm for about 2$^1/_2$ miles; then, in the more scenic part of the canyon, fast-running, turquoise-hued water suddenly emerges, enticing more than a few to a quick swim, which unfortunately is strictly forbidden. At the end of the official park boundaries the gorge is only nine feet wide (and at its most dramatic). The canyon widens after that, and after 2$^1/_2$ miles leads to the great black pebble beach at Aghía Roúmeli (see below). Cold drinks, restaurants (our favorite was the Taverna Tara; try their tasty dolmádes!), and the inviting water of the Libyan Sea make the end of this journey particularly pleasurable.

Although there are many conveniently packaged tours for visiting the Samariá Gorge, they all tend to arrive at the same time, clogging up the trail and forcing hikers to stay more or less in line instead of just experiencing the canyon. A better, and less costly bet, is to sleep in Chaniá and take the early-morning (6:15am) public bus to Omalós. This will get you into the gorge well before the crowds descend. At our visit, there were three morning buses leaving Chaniá for the one-hour trip. The gorge is normally open (depending on the weather) from April 1 to October 30; there are many restrictions, including NO CAMPING and NO SINGING).

AGHÍA ROÚMELI

If you enjoy the beach at Aghía Roúmeli after your hike through the gorge, you might consider staying overnight. There is the small **Aghia Roumeli Hotel** (☎ **0825/91-293**) and several spartan and some newly constructed rooms-to-let at the **Livikon, Tara, Stratos,** and **Kri-Kri guesthouses.** There is an even better beach at St. Paul's (a one-hour walk east). Simple, bathless, beach-shack rooms rent for 3,800 Drs ($15.85) for two, including the occasional hot shower.

The only way out of Aghía Roúmeli, short of hiking in reverse, is the Sofía Company ferry to Chóra Sfakiá. Boats run six times a day from May to October, once daily in April, and cost 1,550 Drs ($6.45). The ferry makes a brief stop at Loutro, a small cove with plenty of rooms, a beach, a few places to eat, and a few too many tourists for our taste. As always, check the schedule. Daily ferry service is also available to Paleochora from April to October, costing 2,000 Drs ($8.35) each way.

CHÓRA SFAKIÁ

Chóra Sfakiá (Sfakion) has become one of the most popular south coast beach towns, both because it's the bus take-out point for the popular Samariá Gorge trek and because it's linked by a paved road to the north coast highway at the yogurt capital, Vrýssi (do stop for that lovely 750 Drs ($3.15) plate of the village specialty). Such a privileged position unfortunately subjects the tiny village to the mad crush of exhausted tourists who arrive between 3 to 7pm each evening to meet return buses—we counted over *50* on our last visit!—after having hiked the 11 miles through the Samariá Gorge and taken the five times daily caique shuttle from Aghía Roúmeli. In addition to those who come by bus from Iráklio, many hikers passing through decide to stay, straining the tiny town. Although the town is jammed until about 7pm, during which time the swarms depart for Chaniá and points north, Sfakiá returns to a semblance of calm. It stays that way until early afternoon when the parade begins anew.

In 1941 courageous citizens from this tiny port evacuated Australian and New Zealand troops after the famous Battle of Crete. The spirited Sfakiots have changed little, although the traditionally clothed men sitting in the kafeneions have been shunted to the back lanes. The dozen portside tavernas are reserved for the tourists who watch the parade of bikinis and hiking shorts from their shaded tables.

INFORMATION Tiny Chóra Sfakía has its share of tourist services. There is a **police station** at Odós Martiou 25, which is also the town bus parking lot. A **post office** that exchanges money (open Monday through Friday from 7:30am to 8pm; Saturday from 7:30am to 2pm, and Sunday from 9am to 1:30pm), some souvenir shops, a moped dealer, a bakery, and a market are all on the skinny lane behind the main coast street; the OTE is on the *platia.* There are taxis for transport and bus service to and from Chaniá three times daily, once a day to Plakiás and Frangokástello. The 2-hour bus trip to Chaniá costs 1,500 Drs ($6.25), 14,000 Drs ($58.35) by taxi. There is boat service to Loutro, Aghía Roúmeli, Sougiá, Paleochora, and Elefonísi.

WHAT TO SEE AND DO After a long hot walk, it's easy to become enchanted with Sfakiá's diminutive gray pebble beach lying idly below the tour-bus parking lot. There are still some days (other than June through September) when Chóra Sfakiá is a great place to get away from it all. We must issue a *warning about wind:* When we were there in September, there was a veritable gale, spoiling any hopes of a tranquil beach day.

If you take any of the local caique trips to Sweetwater Beach or to the tranquil island of Gavidos, you'll find their more natural state a stark contrast to the whitewashed domatia that are creeping up Sfakiá's steep hillside.

WHERE TO STAY The 34-room **Hotel Stavris (☎ 0825/91-220,** fax 0825/911-52) is on a quiet lane above the port. Clean rooms with private shower and balcony cost 6,875 Drs ($28.64) for two, 5,625 Drs ($23.45) for a single. The Perákis brothers also run a traditional kafeneion downstairs.

The pricey 12-room **Xenia Hotel** (**☎ 0825/91-238**), on the west side tucked away innocuously behind geraniums, runs 9,750 Drs ($40.65) for a double, but any of the locals' rooms-to-let run only 3,800–7,000 Drs ($15.85–$29.15) for a double, most including private baths. They're above the few tavernas and up on the hillside along the road out of town, where you'll also have the benefit of superb views looking out over the Libyan Sea.

WHERE TO EAT For dining, we preferred **Limani** on the west end of the port (next to the Xenia) and, on the east side, **Samariá.** Their grilled fish is delicious, if rather expensive, but fish fetches a premium everywhere now that many fishermen have turned their caiques into "buses" for coastal day trips. These two normally alternate as to which will stay open during the winter months.

LOUTRÓ

If Sfakiá's trekker-bus scene is too busy for you, jump on one of the caiques to Loutró, a just slightly sleepier port west along the coast. It's also the destination of those who seek unsanctioned camping in the many nooks and crannies of this lovely coast.

Loutró's fine, small beach is named Phoeníkia after the nearby ancient city of Phoenix, though the local Turkish-era castle is a much better preserved historical site. This fast-growing fishing village is connected by a terrible winding road to Chóra Sfakiá, and by the Sofía Company's caique shuttle (480 Drs or $2) that runs seven times daily in the summer between the busier ports of Aghía Roúmeli to the west and Chóra Sfakiá to the east. As do her sister ports, Loutró has a few hundred room selection of inexpensive accommodations to let and a few tavernas; expect to pay 4,500–7,800 Drs ($18.75–$32.50) for a double with private facilities.

8 Western Crete

At our last visit, Crete's west coast, west and south of Chaniá, was taking the heat of new resort development. Since the north coast highway would collapse under the weight of any further construction to the east (a 21st-century Atlantis?), small developers fueled by European tour operators have set their sights on once-boring Réthymno, once sleepy Chaniá, and now, Kissamos (Kastélli).

Kastélli

Modern-day Kastélli ("Kissamos" is the official name and refers to the region) is built on the site of the ancient city of Kissamos. Today, it retains that lazy seaside feeling of a charmless port that receives only two big steamers per week. A rush of backpackers from the Peloponnese briefly descends on the small main square, but then most catch the first bus to other beaches or urban centers.

Kissamos has a **post office** (they change money), a bank, and some shops on the main square where the privately run KTEL buses arrive. About 50 meters off the northeast corner of the main square toward the water is another smaller square with a fountain where you'll find a couple of travel agencies, a hotel, a restaurant, a café, a news kiosk, and a bakery. During our last visit the first office, that of Manolis Xirouchakis (☎ **0822/22-655**), sold tickets for Minoan Lines and rented bicycles, while two doors north the Iris Travel Agency (☎/fax 0822/23-606) sold tickets for Anek Lines and rented cars.

Those interested in purchasing a ferry ticket to the Peloponnese—Kalamata (three times a week), Githio (twice a week), Kýthira (3), Antikythira (3), or Neópoli (2)—had to hie themselves about a hundred meters east (left) of the fountain square to Horeftakis Tours (☎ **23-250**).

The small but very pleasant 11-room **Castell Hotel** (☎ **0822/22-141**), run by the knowledgeable Michális Xirouchákis, is on the fountain square. Large, comfortable doubles with balconies and private showers cost 6,250 Drs ($26.05); singles are 3,750 Drs ($15.65). There is a good unnamed restaurant next door. Another fine eatery, the fish taverna **Stimadoris** (☎ **22-057**), named for its owner, is located just before the small fishing harbor, less than a mile west of the town. It's open daily for lunch and dinner.

The rocky but long and quiet beach is a five-minute walk through cultivated fields. There you'll find several rooms to let and more under construction.

East of Kastélli, the narrow, winding but well-paved road leads north to Kolymbári, 12 miles away. Here is a small pottery school for the preservation of traditional Cretan arts, the Orthodox Academy of Crete for religious training, and the monastery of Gonía, a lovely Venetian-style building from the 17th century.

The Beaches

Beach seekers should head seven miles south of Kastélli to Plátanos, a village with access to the beach (some say this is Crete's best) at Fallasarna; locals advised us that it's best appreciated from April to June and in late September. There are the ruins of an ancient city here, some tavernas, a few rooms to rent, some tar washed up from passing steamers, and a long, stretch of rocks, pebbles, and fine sand. It's so isolated that nude swimming is tolerated. However, it does get many adventurous visitors in the summer season who reportedly leave their camping litter behind.

Returning to Plátanos and continuing south, you'll find another remote beach enclave in tiny Sfinarion, where there are a few rooms to let. Heading south on this dizzyingly curvaceous north-south road, you pass a few inland villages and come to a fork in the road. Bear east (left), and the road connects to the slightly wider route to very popular Paleochóra.

Paleochóra

This once quiet fishing village was always known as another mystery stopover on the Sofía Company's south coast caique shuttle, a route used primarily for its stops at Aghía Roúmeli and Chóra Sfakiá (covered under the section "Chania & the Southwest Coast"), but now Paleochóra is also connected by the picturesque but winding road to the north coast highway, resulting in its recent development. Time and a paved road have changed Paleochóra in a big way.

There are now enough tourists to justify the caiques for hire that make day trips to the ancient city of **Lissos,** where there are ruins of some houses, a theater, faded mosaics, government buildings, a partially excavated temple of healing, and an Asclepion. There is also a small, quiet, and clean beach if you visit when the boats aren't running—plan on hiking there some 1½ hours.

GETTING THERE Paleochóra has a six-times-daily bus connection to Chaniá, 48 miles to the northeast, and coaches running on the half hour to Iráklio. Taxis can be booked by calling **41-140.** The Sofía Company boats run daily in the summertime from Aghía Roúmeli, at a cost of 1,900 Drs ($7.90), as well as daily to Sougiá and Elafonísi.

INFORMATION A Municipal Tourist Information office at 43 Main Street (no tel.) open Wednesday through Monday from 10am to 1pm and from 5 to 8pm; it is closed Tuesday. The **National Bank of Greece** has normal hours and is nearby at Odós Main 51. A **health clinic** is open Monday through Friday from 8:30am to 2:30pm and 5:30 to 9pm, and for emergencies at other times. The **post office,** located along the sandy beach side of town, sells stamps and changes money; it is open Monday through Saturday from 7:30am to 2pm and 9am to 1:30pm on Sunday. There is a **movie theater,** the Attikon, that often shows films with English subtitles. Mrs. Vou Politopoulou at **Interkreta,** Odós Kontekaki 4 (☎ **0823/41-393;** fax 0823/41-050), books rooms and hotels as well as sells air, boat, and bus tickets. Interkreta also offers a thrice-weekly Samariá Gorge day trip for 5,500 Drs ($22).

WHERE TO STAY & EAT

If you want to make Paleochóra your base (a great many students and '90s tie-die hippies do), plan on looking around since we found many of the proprietors grumpy, and their places pretty basic. Among the best (and most expensive) of them is the 50-room, beachfront-facing **Pal Beach Hotel,** 73001 Paleochóra (☎ **0823/41-512**), which has simple Class-B rooms with private showers and air conditioning for 14,750 Drs ($61.45), including breakfast; singles run 10,500 Drs ($43.75). A good mid-price option is the very clean **Polydóros Hotel** (☎ **0823/41-068**) where doubles run 9,750 Drs ($40.65). One of the best low-cost deals are the 7 rooms at the **Eleni** (no tel.; contact Interkreta at **0823/41-393**) where doubles and singles cost a very reasonable 3,750–5,850 Drs ($15.65–$24.40). For those who have sleeping bags there is a camping site (☎ **0823/41-120**).

The **Wave Restaurant,** a seaside eatery, has a small menu but good food, and it's run by a friendly bunch. The **Galaxy,** next to the post office on the sandy beach, is excellent for fish; it is open daily from noon to 1am. For taverna fare, try the **Dionysos** next to the National Bank. If you're in the mood for grilled lamb chops or souvlaki, head over to **Akrogiali** by the stone beach; it is open daily.

FOR THE EXPLORER

Within a long hiking or brief caique distance from Paleochóra is the port of Sougiá. A cistern, a tomb, and some house foundations provide evidence of the ancient city of Syia, perhaps another settlement of ancient tourists attracted by the long beaches, striated pebbles, and calm Libyan Sea. Even in the height of summer the long pebble- and smooth-black-stone beach was relatively free of throngs. Sougiá is our favorite out-of-the-way beach resort on the southern side of Crete.

The daily boat from Paleochóra costs 1,000 Drs ($4.15); there is twice-daily bus service to Chaniá for 1,650 Drs ($6.90). **Syia Travel,** along the river (☎ **0823/41-198**), can arrange rooms, exchange money, and issue tickets; it is open Monday through Saturday from 8:30am to 12:30pm and 5 to 9pm. Sougiá already boasts the nine-room, well-kept **Pikilasos Pension** (☎ **0823/51-242**) and several rooms-to-let where you can stay for 3,750–5,200 Drs ($15.65–$21.65) a day.

In Sougiá there are a couple of basic beachside tavernas—we like the **Galini Restaurant/Bar**—where you can dine for about 2,200 Drs ($9.15) per person.

If Sougiá isn't remote enough, you can always catch a caique to the heavily wooded, sparsely populated island of Gavidos. This point is the southernmost point in Europe and is rumored to be the island where Calypso seduced Odysseus. Gavidos can be reached from Chóra Sfakiá or from Paleochóra by caique; it's a two-hour ride south into the crystalline Libyan Sea.

Backtrack inland and then cut over due west (you deserted-beach seekers had better get a good map) to come to the monastery of Chryssoskalitissas, in the southwestern corner of the island. It is said that one of the 90 steps leading up to this nunnery (dress modestly for your visit, please) was made of solid gold.

You've come all the way to Chryssoskalitissas to walk through the shallow waters to Elafonísi, a once-deserted, pure-sand nirvana where Cretans say "the sun sets like on no other place on earth." The island hasn't yet attracted thousands, but it does have free campers and some simple tavernas. Several tour operators are offering weekly day trips to Elafonísi by bus from Chaniá and Réthymno. About half of the 12-hour excursion is spent in a bus, and you have to bring a picnic to stave off starvation. In July and August a public bus makes the three-hour trip from Kastélli daily to the end of the narrow road leading south to the monastery of Chryssoskalitissas.

The Cyclades

9

STILL SPIRALING AROUND DÉLOS, GREECE'S SPIRITUAL CENTER IN CLASSICAL TIMES, the Cyclades (in Greek *Ky-klá-des*, or "Circular Islands") today are a blend of ancient and modern. From the abstract white marble sculpture of a harpist carved nearly 4,000 years ago to the billowing sails of a windmill, snow-white village churches, brilliant blue sky, and a hammy pelican or two, the Cyclades are the quintessential Aegean islands.

Mýkonos is known the world over for its extraordinary beaches, postcard-perfect villagescapes, and wild nightlife. It's miraculous that with all of the island's development so much of its original beauty and appeal survives. **Délos** is a short commute from Mýkonos. The entire island is a vast archeological treasure; the French have been excavating the site for 100 years and they're still going. **Sýros** is the untouristy, administrative capital of the Cyclades, and its wealth is evidenced by the lavish neoclassical mansions that grace its port, Ermoupolis. Another star in this chain of islands is **Páros**—a destination with all of the attractions of Mýkonos, including the nightlife, and several villages to choose from. **Náxos** is directly across from Páros. It's the largest of the Cyclades, and its mountains and steeply terraced villages make it one of the best islands for hiking and camping. **Íos** is a party island—a popular hangout for American, British, and European students since the 1960s, with one of the best beaches in the country. **Santoríni** is a volcanic paradise complete with black-sand beaches, astonishing excavations, and donkeys that transport visitors up the switchback trail to the picturesque town of **Firá. Oia,** a recently restored village on the northern tip of Santoríni, offers a breathtaking view of the rest of the island and adjacent moaning volcanos. Each year Greeks in the tens of thousands descend on **Tínos** to visit the Church of the Panagia Evangelistria in hopes of receiving a cure or blessing. It's hard to miss **Ándros,** the Cyclades' second-largest island and the site of excellent ancient and modern art museums. Soon more tourists will visit this pine-covered island. Even more overlooked are the western islands, **Sérifos, Sínos—Mílos** and **Folégandros,** which are ideal destinations for those who cherish a solitary beach and rural village life.

Getting to the Cyclades

There are few island chains easier to get to than the Cyclades. Car ferries leave every day from both Piraeus and Rafína, a port north of Athens. You can knock off an hour or so on sailing time—and about 20% of the ticket price—if you depart from Rafína instead of Piraeus. Excursion boats (risky in rough weather) and catamaran hydrofoils operate almost daily between nearly all the islands. Hydrofoils, though twice the price, are twice as fast (a real savings when coming from Piraeus). Some travelers don't like their indoor seating and cramped feel, but they can provide a far more stable ride on the high meltémi-blown seas. Olympic Airways has service, often several flights a day, to Mýkonos, Páros, Santoríni, and Mílos.

Interisland Travel

There is frequent and extensive ferry service between the Cycladic isles and occasional service between the Cyclades and the Dodecanese or Northeast Aegean island groups. See the "Arriving/Departing" section for each island for more specifics; schedules change dramatically before and after the high season.

What's Special About the Cyclades

Beaches

- The fine gold sand of Mýkonos's Paradise and Super Paradise beaches make them among Greece's most beautiful.
- Kolimbithres, on Páros's north coast, is a beachscape broken by weird black rocks that jut up from the sea.
- Milopótas on Ios, one of the longest fine sand beaches in the Aegean, ranks among our Top Ten beaches of Greece.

Archeological Sites

- The entire island of Délos, reputed birthplace of Artemis and Apollo, is a fantastic archeological preserve.
- The 7th-century B.C. monumental kouros, left unfinished in a marble quarry on Náxos, is a fun sculpture to play on.
- The Minoan-era city of Akrotíri, preserved under volcanic ash on the island of Santoríni, is thought by some to be the legendary city of Atlantis.

Architecture

- Mýkonos's whitewashed, sculpted stucco Paraportianí Church is one of the finest examples of Cycladic religious style.
- The 13th-century Venetian *kástro* in Náxos's Chóra is a delightful pedestrian maze of traditional housing.
- The main towns of several islands—Pláka on Mílos, Appolonía on Sínos, Chóra on Mýkonos, the agora in Paroikía, on Páros—are picture-perfect enclaves of traditional Cycladic architecture.
- Páros's Ekatontapylianí Church, known for its 100 doors, is a celebrated example of Byzantine-era architecture.
- The north coast village of Oia on Santoríni, the only one to survive the 1953 earthquake that levelled the island, is a classic example of antiseismic Cycladic architecture.

The easiest way to island hop is on a chartered yacht cruise; you don't have to worry about hotel reservations, ferry connections, or life in general. **Viking Tours and Yacht Cruises** (☎ **01/89-80-729**; fax 01/89-40-952) at Odós Artemídos 1, Glyfáda 16674 Athens, can customize a tour through the Cyclades for you or a group (they can often pair individual travelers with an organized group to reduce costs) at a price far below what comparable companies offer. **Viking Tours** also has an office in Connecticut (☎ toll free **800/340-3030** or **203/226-7911**).

IMPRESSIONS

I found [Santoríni] a fantastic spot. Picturesque, or romantic, is too mild a term; the cliff scenery and the colors of the sea and land made one catch one's breath.
—Norman Douglas, *Looking Back,* 1933

The island [of] Páros, celebrated by poets for the fine marble growing there.
—Fynes Moryson, *An Itinerary,* 1617

Seeing the Cyclades

If you have one week to "do" the Cyclades, this would be our version of their "greatest hits":

Days 1–3 Fly to Mýkonos from Athens (or Crete or Rhodes), sample the beaches, take a day trip to the archeological site on the island of Délos, shop, see the museums, enjoy the nightlife.

Day 4 Take the ferry to Páros, find accommodations in Paroikia, sightsee and spend the evening in the agora.

Day 5 Head to Páros's north coast beaches and dine in Naoussa.

Day 6 Take the ferry from Paroikía to Santoríni, visit the site of Akrotíri and swim/dine at Kamári beach.

Day 7 Shop and sightsee in Fira, visit the coast village of Oia, and return to Fira for sunset and an evening meal. Fly back to Athens tonight or in the morning.

1 Mýkonos

96 nautical miles E of Piraeus

ARRIVING/DEPARTING • By Air **Olympic Airways** flies seven to ten times daily from Athens; once daily from Iráklio (Crete), Rhodes, and Santoríni; and thrice weekly to Chíos, Lésvos, and Samós. It's very difficult to get a seat on the planes that fly in and out of Mýkonos, so make reservations early and reconfirm them at Olympic Airways in Athens (☎ **01/96-16-161**) or Mýkonos (☎ **22-490**).

• By Sea From Piraeus, the **Ventouris Lines** have departures at least once daily, usually at 8am; a second, afternoon ship is added in summer. Check schedules in Athens at 171, or at 45-11-311. There are daily ferryboat departures from Rafína on the **Strintzis Lines**; schedules can be checked at 0294/25-200. Daily ferries leave from Mýkonos to Ańdros, Páros, Sýros, and Tínos, and five to seven times a week to Íos, Náxos, and Santoríni; four times a week they go to Iráklio, Crete, and twice weekly to Ikaría, Sámos, Skíathos, Skýros, and Thessaloníki.

Check each travel agent's current schedule; most ferry tickets are not interchangeable on different ships. **Sea & Sky Travel** (☎ **0289/22-853,** fax 24-753) on Taxi Square represents the Strintzis Lines, Flying Dolphins, Agapitos Lines, and the catamaran to Crete, also changes money at good rates, and offers excursions in five languages to Délos and a beach party on the island of Rhenia. Takis and Sally Manesis have an excellently trained staff who are knowledgeable about all schedules. The **Veronis Agency** (☎ **0289/22-687,** fax 23-763), on Taxi Square, also offers information, safekeeping of baggage, and other services.

Fast hydrofoil (catamaran) service to Crete, Íos, Náxos, and Santoríni is still irregular. For schedules, call the Port Authority in Piraeus at **45-11-311,** Rafína at **0294/23-300,** or Mýkonos at **22-218.**

Nearly everyone planning a trip to Greece dreams of visiting Mýkonos—an island of universal appeal that is the most accessible of all the Greek islands. Its special blend of simple and sophisticated pleasures attracts a wide range of visitors. Whether you've come to look or be looked at, the Mýkonos scene is a delightful introduction to the latest trends in fashion, music, and lifestyles.

First-time visitors will be pleased to know that even after years of popularity, the island's unique gifts remain unspoiled. The five bold-white windmills that have greeted

The Cyclades

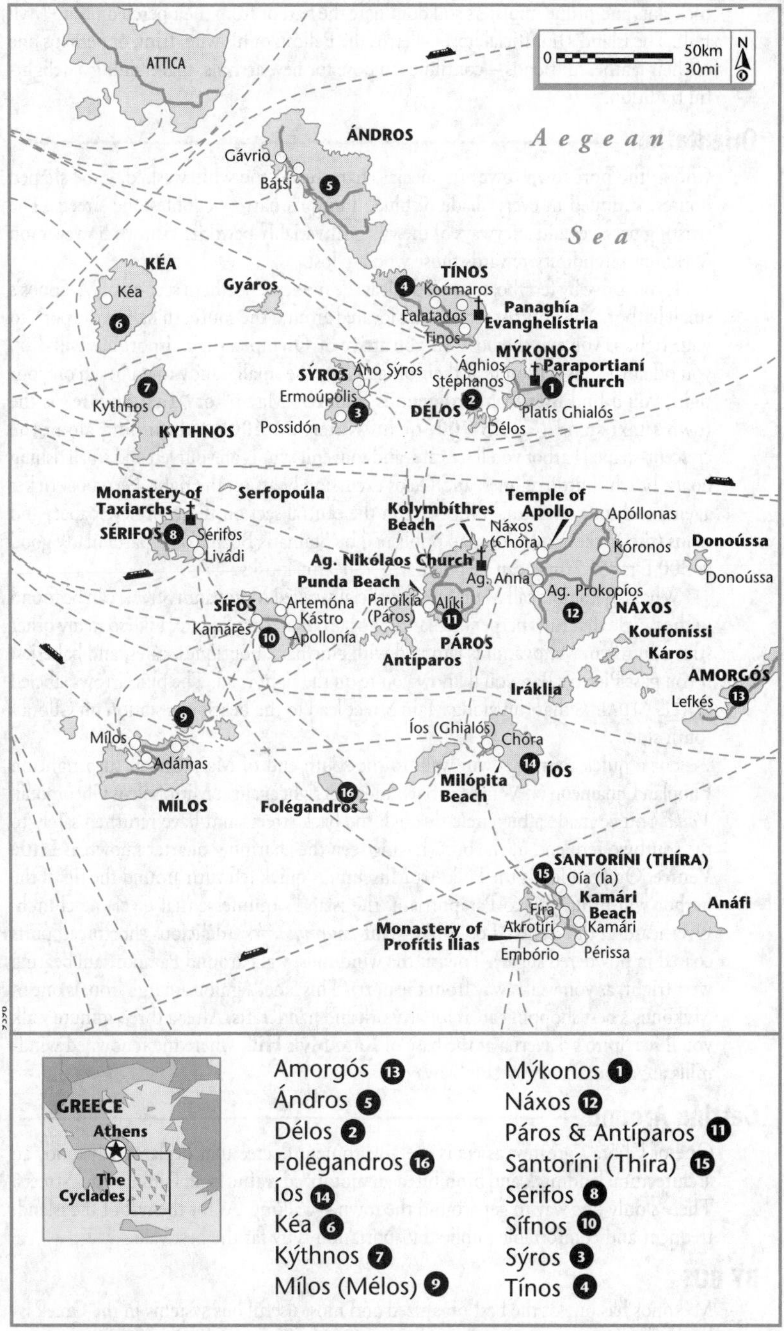
ATTICA
0
50km
30mi
N
Aegean
Sea
ÁNDROS
Gávrio
Bátsi
KÉA
Kéa
Gyáros
TÍNOS
Koúmaros
Falatados
Tínos
Panaghía
Evanghelístria
MÝKONOS
Ághios
Stéphanos
Paraportianí
Church
SÝROS
Áno Sýros
Ermoúpolis
Possidón
DÉLOS
Délos
Platís Ghialós
Kythnos
KYTHNOS
Monastery of
Taxiarchs
Serfopoúla
SÉRIFOS
Sérifos
Livádi
Kolymbíthres
Beach
Temple of
Apollo
Náxos
(Chóra)
Apóllonas
Kóronos
Donoússa
Ag. Nikólaos Church
Ag. Anna
Ag. Prokopíos
Punda Beach
SÍFOS
Artemóna
Kástro
Kamáres
Apollonía
Paroikía
(Páros)
Alíki
PÁROS
Antíparos
NÁXOS
Koufoníssi
Káros
AMORGÓS
Lefkés
Iráklia
Mílos
Adámas
MÍLOS
Íos (Ghialós)
Chóra
ÍOS
Milópita
Beach
Folégandros
SANTORÍNI (THÍRA)
Oía (Ia)
Kamári
Beach
Kamári
Fíra
Akrotíri
Monastery of
Profítis Ilias
Embório
Périssa
Anáfi
GREECE
Athens
The
Cyclades
Amorgós 13
Ándros 5
Délos 2
Folégandros 16
Íos 14
Kéa 6
Kýthnos 7
Mílos (Mélos) 9
Mýkonos 1
Náxos 12
Páros & Antíparos 11
Santoríni (Thíra) 15
Sérifos 8
Sífnos 10
Sýros 3
Tínos 4

Ferry Route

rock stars and prime ministers still dominate the harbor from their perch on Kato Myli Hill. The island's unofficial host—Pétros the Pelican or his wife, Irini, or perhaps one of their feathered friends—continues to pose for new arrivals, maintaining a delightful tradition.

Orientation

Chóra, the port town, owes its special character to the whitewashed, cube-shaped houses, trimmed in every shade of blue, lining its narrow cobblestone streets. The twisting passages and alleyways of the village invariably bewilder visitors; however, on Mýkonos serendipity rewards those who are lost.

If you arrive by ferryboat, you'll dock at the modern, northern section of Mýkonos's small harbor. Most tourist services are located around the southern half of the port, to your right as you exit the boat. (If you arrive by Olympic, their airport bus will drop you off at the bus station near their office.) Past the small, sandy town beach on your right, you'll find **Manto Mavrogenous Square.** "Mavro" or **"Taxi Square"** is the town's taxi stand (☎ **23-700,** or in winter, **22-400**). Continuing along the crescent-shaped harbor you'll see cafés and souvenir stands on your left and small fishing boats, beach shuttle caiques, and Délos excursion boats on the right. Ferryboat ticket agents and tour operators' offices are in the central section. Foreign newspapers and maps (the Mýkonos-Délos map published by Stamatis Bozinakis is particularly good at 300 Drs ($1.70); it can be purchased at nearby kiosks.

What Mykoniots call Main Street (officially called Matoyánni Street) can be found in the tangle that runs perpendicular to the harbor at Taxi Square. Like so many other streets in town, Matoyánni is jammed with chic bars, boutiques, cafés, and bakeries; if you pass Pierro's Bar, you'll know you're on the right road. The blue arrows labeled PLATIS GHIALOS that run along Main Street lead to the beach bus station on Chóra's south side.

For a quick tour of town, walk to the south end of Main Street, turn right on Enoplan Dinameon (at Vengera's Bar), and turn right again at Mitropóleos Gheorgoúli. *Voilà!* You've made a big circle through the back streets and have returned safely to the southwestern end of the port, having seen the charming quarter known as **Little Venice.** On your left is the Folk Art Museum. A quick left turn around the tip of the harbor will bring you to Paraportianí, the island's quintessential Cycladic church. Overheard at the scene: "Looks like giant *kourambiédes*" (delicious shortbread puffs coated in powdered sugar). To visit the windmills, walk around Paraportianí bearing west (right, as you walk away from the port). This lane, Aghíon Anarghýron, is one of Mýkonos's best shopping areas for artwork and handcrafts. After a three-minute walk you'll see Spiro's Taverna at the base of **Káto Mýli Hill,** where the renowned windmills are a short stairway climb away.

Getting Around

One of Chóra's greatest assets is the government decree that declared Mýkonos an architectural landmark and prohibited all motorized traffic from Chóra's back streets. There's only one way to get around the town—walking. As for the rest of the island, frequent and comfortable public transportation is by far the best value.

BY BUS

Mýkonos has one of the best organized and most useful bus systems in the Greek islands; the buses run frequently and cost 200 Drs (83¢) to 600 Drs ($2.50) one way.

There are two bus stations in Chóra: the **Leto Hotel bus station,** by the pier, has buses leaving for Ághios Stéphanos beach, northwest coast hotels, the inland village of Áno Méra, and the far east coast beaches at Elía and Kalafátis; the airport bus stops at the far side of the Hotel Leto, across from Olympic Airways. Schedules are posted, though subject to change. Ask your driver when buses return if you're planning a trip far from Chóra.

The **"beach" bus station** is on the south side of town, about a ten-minute walk from the harbor. Follow those helpful blue arrows on Main Street and you won't get lost. These southbound buses go to Ornos/Ághios Ioánnis and Platís Ghialós/Psárou beaches. To get to the island's best sandy stretches (called Paradise and Super Paradise), take the Platís Ghialós bus. From the pier, shuttle caiques run continuously. (In the high season, day trips by caique often leave from Chóra's port and Ornos Bay.) Although there are posted departure times for the beach buses, they often leave as soon as they're full. If you miss the last bus, you can always walk or call a taxi. **Beware:** Cab rides cost about five times the one-way bus fare.

BY MOPED, CAR & TAXI

Since public transportation to the principal tourist sites is excellent, it's not necessary to spend your drachmas on any motorized transport. However, for those who haven't tried them, **mopeds** can be a fun way to get around. Mopeds and motorcycles (too dangerous for the novice) are available at shops near either bus station. Expect to pay 2,800–8,600 Drs ($11.65 to $35.85) daily during the high season, depending on machine size. Explorers should gather in groups of four to rent Jeeps, available from travel agents for 17,250 Drs ($71.85) per day, including full insurance.

Getting a taxi in Chóra is easy; either walk to Mavro (Taxi) Square and line up or telephone **23-700**. If you're outside of Chóra and call a taxi, you'll be charged from Chóra to your pickup point, plus the fare to your destination. Before calling, try to find a taxi returning empty to Chóra from the village you're in, or flag one down along the road. The driver will be happy to make a few extra drachmas—be sure you know the set price before you take off, though. Another budget tip: Many of the posh out-of-town hotels have private shuttle service back to Chóra. A friendly request to the concierge may get you a free ride.

Fast Facts: Mýkonos

Area Code The telephone area code for Mýkonos is **0289.**

Banks The Commercial Bank and the National Bank of Greece conveniently located on the harbor a couple of blocks west of Taxi Square; both are open from 8am to 2pm and 6 to 8:30pm Monday through Friday. The National Bank is open for exchange only on Friday from 8am to 1pm, Saturday from 9am to 12:30pm and 5:30 to 8:30pm, and Sunday from 5:30 to 8:30pm. Traveler's checks can also be cashed at the post office, as well as at many tourist agencies and hotels, at less-than-bank rates.

Laundry Self-service Laundry is on Ághios Anargyron at Scarpa, about four "blocks" off Main Street southwest of the harbor, between the Popular Arts and the Folklore Museum. Apollon Laundry (☎ **24-496**) is at Odós Mavrogenous 17, near Taxi Square.

Medical Center The Mýkonos Health Center handles minor medical complaints (☎ **23-944**). The hospital (☎ **23-994**) offers 24-hour emergency service and is open for general visits from 9am to 1 and 5 to 10pm.

Police Call **22-235** or **22-482**. The tourist police (☎ **22-482**) are near OTE.

Post Office On the harbor two blocks west of Taxi Square, the post office is open 7:30am to 2pm Monday to Friday.

Telephones The OTE office (☎ **22-499**) is on the west end of the harbor, open daily from 7:30am to 10pm.

Tourist Information Office The office is at the northeast end of the harbor near the ferries. Call 0289/23-990. There's a desk at the airport during the summer.

What to See & Do

BEACHES

Despite what many regard as vast overdevelopment in comparison with Mýkonos's virgin years, the island's gorgeous sandy beaches and fresh, clear water remain unspoiled by tourist hordes. The erratically shaped coastline offers several secluded stone-and-sand beaches; we'll review the better-known ones accessible by foot, bus, moped, or caique.

Note: Mýkonos has learned to accommodate every type of tourist—family, single, gay, straight, backpacker, and jet-setter. Each beach draws its own crowd with their own unwritten rules for wardrobe and conduct, but in the high season, anything goes anywhere.

NEAREST TO TOWN **Megáli Ámmos** is a pleasant family beach about ten minutes south of the Theoxenia Hotel. This is strictly a family beach, with some topless activity at off-hours on the fringes. Megáli Ámmos is too accessible to the cruise-ship day-trippers to even be considered by those in search of peace and quiet.

From the southside bus station behind the Theoxenia you can catch a ride or walk the two miles south to **Ornos Beach,** on calm and shallow Ornos Bay. Ornos is preferred by families and bathtub bathers who relish its still, tepid clean water. If Ornos becomes too crowded, due west of it on a small peninsula facing the sacred island of Délos is the placid stretch at **Ághios Ioánnis.** Bus service from Chóra was recently begun to accommodate the hotels that have sprung up nearby, but Ághios Ioánnis remains relatively secluded. It's a casual family beach with some watersports and tavernas. The restaurants fill up at sunset, when romantics come for the splendid view.

There are two more sand beaches, both accessible by poor-quality roads or on foot from Ághios Ioánnis. To the north is **Kapári,** and on the southeast side of the peninsula, **Glyfádi.** Both of these are places where you'll have some breathing room in summer.

Readers Recommend

The Bodywork Gym, Chóra, Mýkonos (no telephone). "As a serious fitness buff, it is important for me to maintain my workout routine while traveling. During our recent visit to Mýkonos, I discovered a great fitness center—it's well equipped, clean, inexpensive, and seems to be the most popular place on the island for serious weight trainers and body builders. The owner/manager, Ankie Feenstra, is a friendly and professional trainer who runs an excellent gym that I heartily recommend."—James M. Berg, Buettelborn, Germany

If you hop on the alternative southbound bus, you have a choice of several other beaches. From the waterfront bus stop you'll find **Psárou Beach** on your right, a popular family beach with diving, waterskiing, and windsurfing facilities, and a water slide. To the left is busy **Platís Ghialós,** lined with multicolored striped umbrellas, bright windsurfers, and a mixed bag of sun worshipers. Topless women are not unheard of here.

Many visitors stepping off the ferry grab the nearest bus to the popular **Ághios Stéphanos,** two miles north of Chóra. Unfortunately, this mediocre beach, crowded with guests from nearby hotels, isn't really worth the trip. Most watersports facilities are available.

All of these beaches are within a half hour's walk from Chóra, but we wouldn't recommend attempting it in the midday heat of July and August. Transport from the southside bus station is frequent. Buses to Ornos run hourly from 8am to 11pm and to Ághios Yiannis five or six times daily for 220 Drs (92¢). Buses to Platís Ghialós and Psárou begin at 8am and run every 15 minutes till 8pm, then half-hourly until midnight, for 180 Drs (75¢). Schedules for both are posted on the small snack shop at the near side of the square. Buses to Ághios Stéphanos leave from the Leto Hotel near the ferryboat pier and run hourly between 8am and 10pm, for 180 Drs (75¢).

AROUND THE ISLAND From the Platís Ghialós pier or, less frequently, from Ornos you can catch caiques to other beaches. One of Mýkonos's unforgettable sights has to be the fat old fishermen with twinkling eyes calling out "Paradise and Super Paradise" as if heaven was only a boat ride away. Between 9:15am and 6:30pm their brightly colored caiques shuttle eager tourists back and forth to the pristine, fine sand beaches of Paradise, Super Paradise, and Elia.

As you'd expect, **Paradise** is crowded with blissful souls, mostly bared, who treasure its pure gold sand and crystal-clear water. This was the original nude beach, and today it's still where the action is, in addition to having an excellent taverna. **Super Paradise** is not quite as attainable, and so less crowded. The beach is predominantly gay and bare, and has a cafeteria-style taverna playing nonstop pop music. Clothed sunbathing is condoned and some watersports are available.

Paradise and Super Paradise are also accessible by road with private transport, though the road to Super, in particular, is of dubious quality. Paradise can be reached in a 30-minute hike from Platís Ghialós. This walk is highly recommended to the lover of anonymous beaches, who will find many semi-private niches along the way. **Paranga** is a tiny cove that is popular with nudists and is usually not too crowded; there's a large camping area nearby.

Caiques from Platís Ghialós take about 45 minutes to get to **Elia Beach,** so it's much less crowded than Paradise or Super. Throughout the day some wealthy guests from the hilltop Hotel Ano Mera are shuttled down to Elia for a brush with the sand. It's a clean, pale sand beach, one of Mýkonos's largest, with two good tavernas. If Elia becomes too busy, head west to Agrári, another quiet south-coast beach. **Agrari** is sheltered by lush foliage, so all types of apparel and nonapparel are accepted. It seems that only a peaceful few are willing to walk the 15 minutes from Elia to this lovely cove. If you've come this far, stay for a lunch of homemade taverna fare at the beach's only eatery.

An amusing sight along this coast is the local shepherds washing their goats and sheep. From atop the cliffs, they toss the burly animals into the pure Aegean below.

Every time the matted creatures clamber back onto the slippery rocks, they are mercilessly shoved in again for another rinse.

The village of **Áno Méra** is worth a stop on the way to get a tan somewhere else. It's the transportation hub for the central, northern, and eastern parts of the island, with about 200 inhabitants and much of its original character. Once a community of farmers, most now work in the booming construction trade. Besides the remains of a Venetian-era fortress, ancient ruins show that Áno Méra was once the capital (with a harbor at Panormos Bay) of ancient Mýkonos. Nearby is the **Tourlianí Monastery,** with a collection of baroque woodcarvings, marble sculpture, and ecclesiastical vestments.

Around the Cape of Kalafáti is another long, sandy stretch. The beach that beckons sunbathers is actually near the port of the most ancient citadel of Mýkonos (about 2000–1600 B.C.), which crowned the peninsula between here and the Bay of Aghía Anna. Kalafáti is now dominated by a new citadel, the **Paradise Aphroditi Beach Hotel** (**☎ 0289/71-367**). A large pool, two restaurants, and 150 large rooms with balconies march down the gentle, rocky slope to the shore. May, June, and October rates are the best deal here, at 23,000 Drs ($95.85) for two with breakfast. Buses run regularly to Kalafáti from the Hotel Leto bus stop in Chóra.

Those with more time and stamina should check out some of the less-frequented beaches around the island. Some of our recommendations require private transportation for access, and some, up to a few miles of walking from public bus stops.

West of Kalafáti is the little-known sand beach at **Aghía Anna,** reached by a terrible road off the paved road (due west of it) that leads to popular **Kaló Livádi Beach.** East of Kalafáti, and reached by a direct, passable road, is **Lia Ammoudia**—a favorite for its fine sand and small taverna.

The north coast beaches get even fewer crowds because they are often buffeted by strong Aegean winds. If you take the bus to Áno Méra and get off at the road for the Ághios Pateléimon Monastery, you'll be within two miles of **Panormos,** a sand beach in the cove below the Ághios Sóstis church. About 2.8 miles east of town on the Áno Méra road is a Jeep-passable road to the north, and a half mile farther, a footpath that will put you within a 15-minute walk of **Ftelias beach.** Ftelias is excellent for windsurfing because its recessed cove creates strong cross currents, and its sandy sea bottom helps prevent accidents.

ATTRACTIONS

On Mýkonos, a "What to See" section should be called "what to do when it rains." For those who are determined, there are a few nonhedonistic pursuits of interest. First and foremost, of course, is a day trip to the sacred island of **Délos,** a marvelous island/museum with vast archeological ruins of great beauty and interest. This island site, open Tuesday through Sunday, is completely amazing and so important that it's treated separately in this chapter.

For those going to Délos, a visit to the archeological museum may be of interest. The **Mýkonos Archeological Museum** (**☎ 22-325),** northeast of the harbor near the bus station, has a lot of ceramic pieces and some interesting 6th-century B.C. Cycladic finds. It's open Monday and Wednesday through Saturday from 9am to 3:30pm, Sunday and holidays from 10am to 3pm. Admission is 700 Drs ($2.90).

The lovely **Paraportianí (Our Lady by the Port) Church** on the southwest side of the port is considered by architects around the world to be a superb example of the Cycladic style. The sloping, whitewashed stucco exterior are reminiscent of the sensual adobe churches of Taos, New Mexico. Hidden within its organically shaped walls are four small chapels, each of which are oriented toward a point on the compass. It's not uncommon to see artists of all ages sketching, painting, or maneuvering to photograph this Cycladic landmark. Don't leave until you've walked completely around this amazing building to see it from every angle.

Next to the church on the square is the **Folk Museum,** which has a fun collection of local handcrafts, furniture, silver figurines, and ship memorabilia. Outstanding in this large collection are some petrified bread samples, baked in braided shapes with red Easter eggs, and the wax life-size sailor who stands beside the huge model of a warship from 1821. The Folk Museum is open from Monday through Saturday 4 to 8pm and Sunday from 5 to 8pm.

There is an **Aegean Maritime Museum** (☎ **22-700**) halfway into town off Main Street. Even if it's sunny every day you're on Mýkonos, don't miss it. This small collection of old maps, prints, coins, and seafarer's memorabilia is delightful and very informative. You can use the 19th-century English prints to identify the notables for whom every platía and odós are named, or study the excellent ship models to learn how the Athenian navy defeated the Persians. Make sure to get to the back garden, where you can climb up a reconstructed Armenistis lighthouse tower from 1890, with its prisms and globe still intact. It's open daily from 10:30am to 1pm and 7 to 9pm; the fee is 300 Drs ($1.25).

Next door, the **House of Helena** is an homage to Mýkonian daily life. In an original, middle-class 19th-century home, furnishings, housewares, and utensils typical of the period have been preserved. It's a wonderful contrast to the international style commonly seen today. It's open daily from 7 to 9pm.

If you haven't climbed to **Káto Mýli** you'll be wondering why we said there were five windmills, when only three tall whitewashed ones are visible from a distance. If you go up to explore, wait until early evening, when the windmill closest to the stairs is open for viewing.

For those interested in acquiring or just admiring the best of local art we recommend **The Studio** (no phone), two streets up after a left turn off Main Street at the Vengera Bar, which features Monika Derpapas's neo-Byzantine mosaics (which grace the residences of many local connoisseurs) and Richard James North's mythical, magical painted-wood objects that give new meaning to the term "flight of fantasy." There are also hand-painted T-shirts that are last word in body art fantasy—and washable! Whether or not you are interested in buying jewelry, don't miss the Lalaounis Gallery, just up from Taxi Square.

SUNNY SOLUTIONS (☎ **0289/28-640,** fax 28-642), operated by Mýkonos and travel veterans Vassilis Plakotaris and Anita Godiker, is across from the antique shop on the way to the windmills from the bus station at LAKA. In addition to full accommodation and travel services, they excel in special events such as weddings and corporate meetings and offer walking tours, gallery and shopping tours, and island exploration by Jeep.

Our two favorite cinemas al fresco have been reborn as restaurants. However, change is always possible on Mýkonos, so check the tourist office if you're interested in this experience.

Where to Stay

Mýkonos is probably Greece's best-known island, and what qualifies as the low season here (April to June 15 and October, with most places closed all winter) would look overcrowded on most other islands. The many visitors who've been enchanted in past years return annually, while neophytes arrive daily, increasing the pressure on hotel rooms that are often booked a year in advance.

Most of the hotels and rooms listed below will accept reservations one to three months in advance only if accompanied by a deposit equal to one-third of the fee for your total stay; and this only after their past customers have been accommodated. If at all possible, visit in the low season, when sky-high prices are slightly lower and you have a good chance of finding a bed.

For those determined to be in the hottest spot at the hottest time, we have one suggestion: make a reservation early and plan your trip around it. If you don't get any response from these hotels, try an outfit that's the best thing that's happened to Mýkonos in years: the **Mýkonos Accommodations Center (MAC).** The parent company, **Accommodation Centers Greece** has offices at Odós Voulis 7 in Athens (☎ **01/322-0000** or **322-3400,** or fax 01/324-9204) and at Odós Matoyánni Street 46; ☎ **0289/23-160** or **23-408,** fax 0289/24-137) on Mýkonos. Their multilingual and helpful staff will correspond, talk by phone, or meet with you to determine the best accommodation for your budget (and they're not stuffy about booking cheap rooms in local houses, though of course there aren't many on Mýkonos). Mýkonos is one of Greece's most expensive islands, and MAC offers a very wide range of Class C and D hotels—from 11,000 Drs ($45.85) to 17,000 Drs ($70.85)—and some private rooms. For ensuring you an affordable bed they charge 15% of the rental or a 4,500 Drs ($18.75) minimum fee, which may be worthwhile to those who can only visit in the peak season. MAC will book rooms at other islands for the same fees (lower if the hotel pays a commission, too). The center is pricey but John van Lerberghe and his staff do come through for you and can spare you disappointment and heartache.

If you haven't made reservations or talked to MAC, we strongly recommend that you do not go to this island in the high season.

If you're reading this in the low season while sunbathing on a ferry speeding toward the island, don't despair. You may find a room in one of the in-town hotels (discussed below), which are all within minutes of the port. If anyone offers you a private room as you disembark, grab it and be grateful if it's affordable and nice (you can always move the next day). Be prepared to accept lodging in another community outside of Chóra, whose old hotels sell out to regulars every year.

IN CHÓRA

Hotel Apollo, Paralía, Chóra, Mýkonos 84600. ☎ **0289/22-223.** 20 rms (8 with bath).

Rates (including breakfast): 18,400 Drs ($76.70) double with bath. No credit cards.

The harborside Hotel Apollo, one of the island's oldest and best-value hotels, has a carefully maintained 19th-century facade that blends in with the neighboring commercial establishments in the central section of the port. The rooms are simply furnished, a little worse for wear, but clean and comfortable.

Hotel Delphines, Mavroghénous Street, Chóra, Mýkonos 84600. ☎ **0289/22-292.** 7 rms (all with bath).

Rates (including breakfast): 15,730 Drs ($65.55) single; 19,678 Drs ($82) double. No credit cards.

Located near the Hotel Manto is this older, more homey, blue-shuttered hotel. The seven doubles are cozy, and the singles are not a bad deal in this crowded port, considering that many hotels on Mýkonos charge a single person the price of a double.

Edem House Hotel, District Road, Chóra, Mýkonos 84600, ☎ **0289/22-855.** Fax 0289/23-355. 24 rms (all with bath). TEL

Rates (including breakfast): 23,040 Drs ($96) single; 27,648 Drs ($115.20) double.

This brand new hotel has spacious, comfortable, well-furnished rooms as well as a bar.

Maria Hotel, Odós Kalogherá 18, Chóra, Mýkonos 84600. ☎ **0289/24-212.** Fax 0289/24-213. 10 rms (all with bath). TEL

Rates (including breakfast): 20,000 Drs ($83.35) double. V.

Around the corner from Marios below—and much like it—the Maria's rooms are as clean and modern, just a little sunnier.

Marios Hotel, Odós Kalogherá 24, Chóra, Mýkonos 84600. ☎ **0289/22-704.** 12 rms (all with bath).

Rates (including breakfast): 21,190 Drs ($88.30) single or double. No credit cards.

The quaint Class C Marios Hotel, located across from the small Zorzis, is distinguished by its dark wood-beamed ceilings. The Marios has spotless doubles with modern facilities, some with balconies overlooking a garden.

Hotel Matina, Odós Fournakíon 3, Chóra, Mýkonos 84600. ☎ **0289/22-387** or **24-501.** 14 rms (all with bath).

Rates (including breakfast): 17,680 Drs ($73.65) single; 23,660 Drs ($98.60) double. No credit cards.

The Hotel Matina is another good choice, with small modern rooms. A real plus here: it's ideally situated inside a large garden, which insulates it from the noise of its central location.

Hotel Matogianni, Matoyánni Street, Chóra, Mýkonos 84600. ☎ **0289/22-217.** 22 rms (all with bath). TEL

Rates (including breakfast): 14,950 Drs ($62.30) double.

The Matogianni has modernized doubles with private phones—an unnecessary convenience that shouldn't seduce you into avoiding the OTE, where metered long-distance calls are much cheaper. Although the Matogianni is on swinging Main Street, the rooms overlooking their pretty garden are quiet.

Hotel Philippi, Odós Kalogherá 32, Chóra 32, Chóra, Mýkonos 84600. ☎ **0289/22-294** or 22-295. 12 rms (all with bath).

Rates: 15,340 Drs ($63.90) double. No credit cards.

Located on the first right off Main Street past Matogianni, is this homey hotel. Flower-print wallpaper or ruffled bedspreads create the cozy decor unique to each room. The Philippi's owner, Angelique Kontiza, also tends a lush flowering garden that is set behind her son's restaurant. Many evenings these flowers grace the tables of Philippi's—an elegant eatery widely proclaimed as Mýkonos's best.

PENSIONS AND ROOMS TO LET Since the local government stopped issuing hotel building permits, the big news on Mýkonos is that many of the pensions, rooms-to-let, studios, and villas are larger, more comfortable, and offer better views than the small, older hotels mentioned above. Most of the pensions and rooms don't serve breakfast on the premises but they can be a very good deal; at this writing no rooms had been consigned to tour operators.

If the tourist office (☎ **0289/23-990**) is open, check with them first to see what's available. Otherwise, the two best areas to find rooms are along Main Street, between the Hotel Matogianni and Kalogherá Street, and along Kalogherá Street between Aghíon Saránta and Aghíou Gherasímou Streets.

If you're not carrying a lot of luggage, follow the blue arrows southwest away from the port that direct you to PLATIS GHIALOS. There are several tour operators' villas near the southside bus stop, and the odd rooms that remain empty are rented out by the group's booking agent, who's usually on the premises.

Maria and Mike Mitropia, Laka Square, Chóra, Mýkonos 84600. ☎ **0289/23-528.** 20 (13 with bath).

Rates (including breakfast): 12,500 Drs ($52.30) double without bath, 14,300 Drs ($59.60) double with shower. V.

This couple keeps very tidy and comfortable rooms above Mike's locksmith shop on Laka Square, near the town police station and opposite the Mýkonos Market. Try to reserve one of their quiet, good-value rooms.

$ **Pension Stelios,** Chóra, Mýkonos 84600. ☎ **0289/24-641.** 12 rms (all with shower).

Rates (including breakfast): 16,900 Drs ($70.40) double. No credit cards.

This whitewashed, blue-shuttered addition to the hill behind the OTE office, on the northeast end of the harbor, is close to the Piraeus/Rafína ferryboat pier. It is easily reached by broad stone steps above the road, making it a quiet, scenic, and convenient place to stay. The clean, modern, twin-bedded rooms have small balconies with good views and a common lounge.

ON THE EDGE OF TOWN Most of the new construction has been built along Aghíou Ioánnou Street, the road that circles the pedestrian-only older Chóra. In addition, the south beach road that begins at Xenías Street in the southwest part of Chóra, intersects with Aghíou Ioánnou Street, and then runs south to the beaches at Platís Ghialós, has also seen much recent development. Both are good areas, with great views of old Chóra and the sea, and easy access by vehicle, though they are within a ten-minute walk of the nightlife. Many of the newer places boast a swimming pool, larger rooms, private telephones, breakfast terraces, balconies or patios, and the buzz of a larger hotel.

Pension Giovanni, Odós Giovanni 3, Chóra, Mýkonos 84600. ☎ **0289/22-485.** Fax 22-485. 9 rms (all with bath).

Rates (including breakfast): 16,500 Drs ($67) single; 20,700 Drs ($86.25) double. EC, MC, V.

Rena Giovanni runs this whitewashed, brown-shuttered pension across from the Marina Pension with a personal touch. It was converted from a medical clinic, so all the rooms are quite large.

Hotel Ilio Maris, Despotiká, Mýkonos 84600. ☎ **0289/23-755.** Fax 24-309. 26 rms (all with bath). TV TEL

Rates (including American breakfast): 26,000 Drs ($108.35) single; 32,500 Drs ($135.40) double. AE, V.

Built on a slope down from the south beach road, this attractive hotel has balconied rooms with a view of their pool and the sea beyond. Their comfortable bar, lounge, and rooms are tastefully decorated with traditional Greek art—a small touch that adds style to the surroundings. Some rooms are air conditioned.

K Hotels, P.O. Box 64, Mýkonos 84600. ☎ **0289/23-435** or **23-431.** Fax 23-455. 135 rms (all with bath). A/C

Rates (including breakfast): 28,470 Drs ($118.60) single; 29,640 Drs ($123.50) double. AE, EC, MC, V.

The Four K Hotels (Kalypso, Kohili, Korali, and Kyma) form a complex just off the south beach road. Clean, modern air-conditioned rooms are stacked on two levels to offer views of the sea, the hills, the pool, or tennis courts. Each building has a small bar and breakfast lounge, and there's a common restaurant.

Pension Marina, Aghíou Ioánnou and Laka Streets, Chóra, Mýkonos 84600. ☎ **0289/22-441.** 6 rms (all with bath).

Rates (including breakfast): 18,270 Drs ($76.15) double. No credit cards.

Like the Pension Giovanni, this small pension is very close to the edge of Chóra on the west side. It's next to the church and just behind the minimall, which contains a butcher, baker, souvlaki shop, rent-a-car, and travel office. The friendly owner, George Athimaritis, and his manager, Tom, maintain spic-and-span, twin-bedded rooms with bureaus, chairs, and good lighting. There is also a patio for sunning or snacking.

Hotel Poseidon, Chóra, Mýkonos 84600. ☎ **0289/24-441.** Fax 23-812. 41 rms (all with bath).

Rates (including breakfast): 24,700 Drs ($102.90) double. Parking. AE, EC, MC, V.

Hotel Poseidons A and B have attractive surroundings, a pool, and particularly attentive service. Poseidon B has air conditioning. They're located near the sea on the road to Ornos.

$ **Hotel Rochari,** Ághios Ioánnou Street, Rochari, Mýkonos 84600. ☎ **0289/23-107** or 0289/22-379 in winter. 53 rms (all with bath). TEL

Rates: 14,690 Drs ($61.20) single; 25,740 Drs ($107.25) double.

This hotel is on a hill in the quarter known as Rochari. Regular guests who like the homey ambience, TV lounge, and comfortable rooms with terraces book most of the rooms by late March (the hotel is closed from November to March), but do try them!

AROUND THE ISLAND

There are hotels clustered around many popular beaches on the island, but most people prefer to stay in town and "commute" to the exquisite beaches of Paradise and Super Paradise. For those who need to curl their toes in the sand before breakfast, a few selections follow.

There are private studios and very simple pensions at both Paradise and Super Paradise beaches, but rooms are almost impossible to get, and prices more than double in July and August. Contact **M.A.C.** (☎ **0289/23-160**), or for Super Paradise, **GATS Travel** (☎ **0289/22-404**), for information on the rooms they represent. The tavernas at each beach may also have leads.

AT COSTA ÍLIOS This village nestled atop a small cove on Ornos Bay is considered by many to be one of the most beautiful spots on the island. Private homes, in the traditional style, of course, with accommodations for two to six people and with twice-weekly maid service, can be rented by the week for 198,000–300,000 Drs ($825–$1,250; DC, MC.). The village has its own beach, tennis court, swimming pool and children's pool. Contact: **LEMA,** Odós Makrás Stoás 1, Piraeus 18531,

☎ **41-75-988** or **41-76-741,** fax 41-79-310; or write Maria Koulalia, Cósta Ílios, Mýkonos 84600. ☎ **0289/24-522.**

AT ORNOS BEACH This beach on calm Ornos Bay is particularly recommended to families, who will appreciate its watersports facilities, tavernas, and shallow waters. **Club Mýkonos Hotel** (☎ **0289/22-600,** fax 24-560). Two stories of spacious bungalow-style rooms, suites, and studios (plus time-share units) are contained within the long sleek lines of this modern hotel. Double rooms overlooking the water, breakfast, and transportation to and from the airport cost 30,375 Drs ($128.10) and studios are 33,345 Drs ($138.95); AE, EC, MC, and V are accepted. The family-owned, comfortable **Hotel Asteri** (☎ **0289/22-715**) is near the beach; a double with breakfast goes for only 20,800 Drs ($86.65), no credit cards.

AT PLATÍS GHIALÓS Fifteen minutes by bus or 30 minutes on foot south of Chóra is the sandy, crescent-shaped beach of Plati Yialos, better known as the caique stop for shuttles running to Paradise and Super Paradise beaches. There are several excellent hotels, most very similarly named.

Nissaki Hotel, Platís Ghialós, Mýkonos 84600. ☎ **0289/22-913.** Fax 23-680.
14 rms (all with bath). TEL

Rates (including breakfast): 21,450 Drs ($89.40) single; 24,700 Drs ($102.90) double. AE, EC, V.

On a slope not far from the beach, this Petinos-owned hotel has good, nicely furnished rooms and patios with beach views.

Hotel Petassos Bay, Platís Ghialós, Mýkonos 84600. ☎ **0289/23-737.**
21 rms (all with bath). A/C MINIBAR TEL

Rates (including breakfast): 28,000 Drs ($117) single; 29,900 Drs ($124.60) double. AE, V.

Large air-conditioned rooms with phones, personal Muzak, and balconies overlook the beach, which is only 33 yards away. They have a good-sized pool and sun deck and offer free transfers to and from the airport or ferry pier.

Hotel Petassos Beach, Platís Ghialós, Mýkonos 84600. ☎ **0289/22-437.**
64 rms (all with bath). A/C MINIBAR TV TEL

Rates (including breakfast): 29,600 Drs ($123.35) single; 31,000 Drs double. V.

This place next door to the Petassos Bay and under the same management. The rooms and facilities are quite similar, but there is no air conditioning.

Hotel Petinos, Platís Ghialós, Mýkonos 84600. ☎ **0289/22-127.** Fax 23-680.
66 rms (all with bath). A/C TV TEL

Rates (including breakfast): 23,400 Drs ($97.50). V.

Here you'll find good, clean, attractive rooms with large balconies shaded by an arcaded facade.

Petinos Beach Hotel, Platís Ghialós, Mýkonos 84600. ☎ **0289/24-311** or **24-310.**
Fax 23-680. 19 rms (all with bath). A/C TV TEL

Rates (including breakfast): 39,936 Drs ($166.40) single; 49,800 Drs ($207.50) double. AE, EC, V.

This small Class-A hotel has spacious rooms with exposed-beam ceilings, each distinctively furnished in traditional style and with private phone. There's a handsome pool for guests right on the beach and a small chic bar.

AT ÁGHIOS STÉPHANOS About 2 1/2 miles north of Chóra is the popular resort of Ághios Stéphanos. The several hotels, pensions, tavernas, and a disco that make up this village are within reach of a pleasant, though crowded, sandy beach. Near the coast, the best Class C choices are the **Hotel Artemis** (☎ **0289/22-345**), 32 yards from the beach, near the bus stop, with 23 rooms (all with bath) for 16,900 Drs ($70.40), breakfast included; and the **Hotel Panorama** (☎ **0289/22-337**), 76 yards from the beach, with 27 rooms (all with bath) for 14,900 Drs ($62.30). The small **Hotel Mina** (☎ **0289/23-024**) is uphill behind the Artemis and offers 15 double rooms with private bath for 10,400 Drs ($43.40).

CAMPING

Paradise Camping, Paradise Beach, Mýkonos 85600. ☎ **0289/22-852** or **22-9375.** Fax 24-350.

Rates: 1,900 Drs ($8) per person; 1,170 Drs ($4.85) for tent. MC, V.

The official campground on Mýkonos is at Paradise Beach. The fee includes the use of all facilities: showers, a bar, restaurant, minimarket, and transportation to and from the port and town. They offer rooms and bungalows as well at one of the loveliest spots on the island. How could a night in any hotel or villa compare to sleeping under the stars at the edge of Paradise?

Paranga Beach Camping, Paranga Beach, Mýkonos 85600. ☎ **0289/24-578.**

Rates: 1,900 Drs ($8) per person; 1,170 Drs ($4.85) for tent.

This newer and even nicer facility a few miles east offers all Paradise can and more—including cooking and laundry facilities.

Where to Eat

Mýkonos is famed for its restaurants, and the fashionable ones change as rapidly as the value of the drachma. Nevertheless there are several favorites that have stood the test of time. **Note:** Wait until 9:30 or 10pm to begin supper. It's the Greek way and everything's much livelier at this hour.

LIGHT SNACKS

For breakfast or snacks, there is a classic bakery just off the harbor. (The harbor itself is lined with expensive cafés, where an early-morning or late-night coffee is the best value.) The **Andreas Pouloudis Bakery,** Odós Flórou Zuganéli 3 (☎ **22-304**), off Mavro Square in the tiny lane behind the gold store can be identified by the contented weight-watchers outside eating cheese pies. It's run by a grumpy, talented baker. Andreas offers a variety of *"kookis," "caik,"* and "*tutti frutti* pies" as well as yummy cheese, spinach, and zucchini pies for 400–600 Drs ($1.88–$2.50). In the square is **Alexis Snack Bar,** open at all hours, which features a salad bar, as well as good, inexpensive burgers, gyros, and other snacks and refreshments.

On Kalogherá Street near the Hotel Philippi is the more refined **Hibiscus Croissanterie,** offering a large variety of croissants plus fluffy quiche Lorraine and other authentic delights created by its French owner, Anna.

Unfortunately, Chóra's mass-market popularity has spawned mass-market eateries. You can easily find full-color photo displays of pizza, hamburgers, souvlaki, club sandwiches, ice cream, and other international junk food in many back lanes.

Antonini's, Taxi Square, Chóra. No telephone.

Cuisine: GREEK.
Prices: Appetizers 585–1,170 Drs ($2.45–$4.85); main courses 1,200–1,820 Drs ($5.00–$7.60). No credit cards.
Open: Daily 11am–3pm, 7pm–1am.

Located next to the Alexis Snack Bar, this casual, inexpensive taverna favored by Mykonians serves typical, yet satisfying Greek peasant fare.

Delphines, Odós Matoyánni, Chóra. ☎ **24-269.**

Cuisine: GREEK
Prices: Appetizers 520–1,430 Drs ($2.15–$6); main course 1,040–2,600 Drs ($4.35–$10.75).
Open: Daily noon–midnight.

Irini, the cook at this small, family-owned spot on "Main Street," runs the kitchen like a grandmother feeding her only grandchild. The food is delicious and the portions are generous. Makis, the charming owner, has decorated the taverna in antiques with a maritime theme and advises you not to miss the special dessert, *prálina,* made from his mother's secret recipe. Take his advice!

El Greco/Giorgos, Tría Pigádia, Chóra. ☎ **22-074.**

Cuisine: GREEK/CONTINENTAL.
Prices: Appetizers 650–1,690 Drs ($2.70–$7.05); main courses 1,750–3,250 Drs ($7.30–$13.55). AE, DC, EC, MC, V.
Open: Daily 7pm–1:30pm.

Located on a square next to Mýkonos's Tría Pigádia (Three Wells), El Greco is a traditional taverna with a large patio and a sophisticated menu. Start with El Greco's mixed plate of tzatzíki (garlic-flavored dip), *taramasaláta* (fish roe mix), and *melitzanosaláta* (eggplant mix), or their unusual and delicious eggplant *boureki.* El Greco specializes in grilled meats. You can splurge on chateaubriand at dinner and easily spend 4,000 Drs ($16.60) each, or have a well-prepared and simpler meal for less than half that price.

$ **Niko's Taverna,** Chóra. No phone.

Cuisine: GREEK/CONTINENTAL.
Prices: Appetizers 520–780 Drs ($2.15–3.25); main courses 1,100–2,340 Drs ($4.60–$9.75); fresh fish 10,400 Drs ($45.35) per kilo.
Open: Daily noon–11pm.

Bustling Niko's Taverna spans a narrow lane near Paraportianí Church, and is quite popular with locals. It's one of the few good places that's also open for lunch and has a varied, inexpensive taverna menu and a very friendly staff.

Sesame Kitchen, Tría Pigádia, Chóra. ☎ **24-710.**

Cuisine: GREEK/CONTINENTAL.
Prices: Appetizers 700–1,900 Drs ($2.95–$7.85); main courses 1,750–2,340 Drs ($7.30–$9.75); meal for two 5,500 Drs ($22.90). V.
Open: Daily 7pm–12:30am.

Next to the Aegean Maritime Museum is a popular, new, partly vegetarian and health food, taverna. Fresh spinach, vegetable, chicken, or cheese pies are baked daily.

The Sesame Kitchen serves a large variety of salads, brown rice, and soya dishes—even a vegetarian moussaka—and some lightly grilled and seasoned meat dishes. Daily specials are healthy, typical continental courses. Local wine is available.

To Steki Manthos, Tourlós Beach, Chóra. ☎ **23-435.**

Cuisine: INTERNATIONAL.
Prices: Appetizers 520–2,200 Drs ($2.15–$9.20); main courses 1,170–2,860 Drs ($4.85–$11.90). No credit cards.
Open: Daily 9:30am–3pm, 7pm–1am.

Drive, take the bus (to Gephiráki stop), or walk (it's worth the 15 minutes) north toward Águios Stephanos to find this fine place with a large and varied menu, an excellent chef, and a wonderful view of the sea and the nearby cruise-ship docks.

SPLURGE CHOICES

Having surveyed all manner of elegant eateries, we've come up with three that fit our criteria of more formal dining, attentive service, interesting menus with Greek specialties, and great food (not necessarily in that order). We would be remiss if we didn't also mention the town's most lavish restaurant, **Katrine's.** Its dark, intimate interior is filled with the rich and near-rich, enjoying excellent seafood—at Paris prices!

Edem Restaurant, Odós Kaloghéra, Chóra. ☎ **22-855** or **23-335.**

Cuisine: GREEK/CONTINENTAL. **Reservations:** Recommended during July–Aug.
Prices: Appetizers 1,100–3,250 Drs ($4.60–$13.55); main courses 2,600–5,200 Drs ($10.85–$21.65). AE, MC, V.
Open: Daily 7pm–1am.

Superb food is the attraction of this casual garden restaurant with plenty of elbow room. Edem is famous for its meat dishes, but it has a wide range of continental and Greek specialties on its menu. The service is second to none.

Philippi, Main Street, Chóra. ☎ **22-294.**

Cuisine: GREEK/CONTINENTAL. **Reservations:** Recommended during July–Aug.
Prices: Appetizers 1,690–3,250 Drs ($7.05–$13.55), main courses 4,290–7,670 Drs ($17.85–$31.95). AE, MC, V.
Open: Daily 7pm–1am.

Long a favorite with locals and tourists, Philippi is set in an enchanting olive tree garden. Woven fabrics cover the tables and banquettes, which are spaced to provide intimate, romantic dining by candlelight. When you step down into the garden off the busy Main Street, you'll enter a quiet European world where elegant dining prevails. The continental menu includes French classics, curry, and many elaborately prepared traditional Greek dishes. There is a sizable wine list.

Yves Klein Blue, Odós Kaloghéra, Chóra. No telephone.

Cuisine: ITALIAN.
Prices: Appetizers 1,040–1,950 Drs ($4.35–$8.25); main courses 1,820–3,900 Drs ($7.55–$16.25). AE, DC, EC, MC, V.

This elegant trattoria, just up from the Credit Bank, named after the French painter from the Sixties, who used the indigo that dominates the interior, is our favorite of the many Italian restaurants. The food is classical northern Italian, superbly prepared. When the diners thin out later in the night, it becomes a piano bar.

Evening Entertainment

Mýkonos really sparkles at night, so whatever your budget, plan on dressing up for the evening and walking the streets to admire everyone else admiring you.

BARS

For early drinks, try the **Lotus** (☎ **22-181**) on Main Street—good food, good music, and a great place to watch people—or head west to **Little Venice.** At sunset the intimate **Kastro,** behind the Paraportianí Church, and the rocking **Caprice Bar,** down the block on Scarpa, are perfect for chillier evenings, when the rosy reflection on the calm Aegean can be admired from their picture windows. Both profit from the sea spray splashing on the edge of Little Venice to enhance the dramatic setting. For a quiet, civilized drink, try the **Montparnasse** (☎ **23-719**), on the same lane, a cozy bar where Toulouse-Lautrec posters are complemented by classical music. The hipper **Argo** (☎ **24-674**), a favorite of our Mykoniot friends, is at Three Wells, just down the street from the Maritime Museum. Look for Richard James North's "Cowboy Boot" on Matoyannia Street; **Uno** (☎ **22-365**) is a hot (cool) new addition to the scene.

The longtime "king of the scene" in Mýkonos, **Pierro's,** on Main Street just a mob scene away from the harbor, is an elegant old bar that's seen so many fads and celebs come and go it's a wonder it's still around, but it's still *ne plus ultra* and a must-see for everyone. You may have to go into **Mantos Bar** next door to buy a beer, because you can't squeeze through the flesh out front, but then you're set for the best people-watching and pickup action on the island—some would say, in all of Greece. Pierro's is in full swing after 11pm.

Just down from Paraportianí Church, near Niko's, you'll find **Stavros Irish Bar** (☎ **23-687**), the wildest place on the island: English girls dancing on the bar miming Madonna, outside a table of Italian models, and inside all hell breaking loose.

If it's true that blondes have more fun, the hotter spot is the **Scandinavian Bar,** in a narrow lane behind Nikos Taverna. Two indoor bars draw such a huge, mixed crowd with cheap drinks and an "anything goes" policy that you'll have to fight your way through to the nearby **Windmill Disco,** where the drinks are less expensive and foreign under-twenties consort with Mykoniot under-twenties.

If you're ready for some authentic Greek dancing, try **Thalami** (☎ **23-291**), a small underground club near Nikos Taverna underneath the Town Hall on the port. You can push your way through the beaded curtains to see fine, authentic dancing by local men and visiting professionals. The **Mykonos Club** (☎ **23-529**), opposite the Caprice Bar in Little Venice, is a bouzouki nightclub that's frequented by locals and tourists in search of the road to *rebétika* (Greek blues).

AFTER-HOURS CLUBS & DISCOS

We're always surprised that our favorite places survive the waves of faddism to remain consistently popular. Now, some of the best happy-hour bars have become night owl refuges. A still current, longtime favorite frequented by Mýkonos's older and classier crowd is **Vengera's** (☎ **22-800**), on Main Street near Kalogherá. This same crowd moves on to the chic **Mercedes** or the even more sophisticated **Remezzo Disco,** near the telephone center (OTE) on the port, to party on under the stars into the morning, or to the more laid-back **Nine Muses,** near Taxi Square.

Newer bars include the **Anchor Club,** on Main Street near Pierro's, which is stylishly spare with just enough lighting and volume from its jazz, blues, and 1960s rock repertoire to earn a devoted mid-30s clientele; the already- mentioned Argo, which turns into a rappin' and rockin' disco with great music after midnight; and the **Astra** near the Three Wells (only 20 years ago they were Chóra's only water source!), which is more high-tech, hard-edge rock.

Another after-1am hotspot is **MADD,** on Taxi Square, where a super DJ plays jumpin' music, the drinks are good, and the view of the port is fabulous.

2 Délos

95 nautical miles E of Piraeus

ARRIVING/DEPARTING • By Sea Organized guided and nonguided excursions leave Tuesday through Sunday for the 40-minute ride to the island, and cost 2,200 Drs ($9.20) round trip for transportation alone or 6,650 Drs ($27.70) for the guided tour run by **Yiannakakis Tours (☎ 22-089)**. Boats depart the harbor at 9 or 10am and return at 12:30 or 2pm—ample time for most visitors to explore.

This tiny island where Apollo and Artemis were born was considered by the Greeks to be the holiest of sanctuaries, the sacred center around which the Cyclades circled. The entire island of Délos, off-limits to all but day-trippers, is now an archeological museum that's one of the best sites in Greece.

What to See & Do

The three hours on Délos allotted by excursion boats should allow even avid archeology buffs enough time to explore the principal sites. To the left of the new pier where you'll dock is the partially filled-in **Sacred Harbor,** where pilgrims and traders from throughout the ancient world used to land. At the ticket kiosk—the site is open daily from 8:30am to 2:30pm for a fee of 700 Drs ($2.90)—site plans and picture guides are for sale, and even the cheapest is adequate enough to serve as your guide. Our favorite, with an excellent text, good pictures, and a foldout map in the back, was *Délos: Monuments and Museum,* by P. Zaphiropoúlou (Kreve Edition).

Proceed up past the **Agora,** where festivals were celebrated by the freed men and traders on the island. Bear right up the hill to explore the south side of the site dominated by **Mt. Kynthos,** which the hardy may want to ascend for its fine views over the sanctuary. Along the way, a maze of ruined warehouses will be on your right. Be sure to check out the various houses, or "Maison," once inhabited by wealthy Athenians, where some exquisite mosaics have been found. Most of the mosaics on Délos were designed and installed by artists brought in from Syria.

The large, roofed **House of Masks** contains a superb colored mosaic of Dionysus on a panther (Délos's best-known treasure) in the room at right and some geometric patterned borders in the central room, where also the tiles of five elaborate masks depicting a range of theatrical expression have been taken up for reconstruction. The bright color of these Syrian works, now over 2,000 years old, is astounding.

From the summit of Mt. Kýnthos there's a spectacular view of the entire site of Délos, as well as the nearby islet of Ekáti, the Delian burial ground of Rhenia, and beyond them, Siros. Coming down, you'll cross the **Sacred Way** and the Egyptian **temple of Isis** and other foreign gods.

If you head back down toward the lush palm groves (the filled-in Sacred Lake, where it's thought Leto gave birth to Apollo) you'll soon come across the famous **Delian Lion Walk.** These six skinny guardians, left from the original sixteen, are from the second half of the 7th century B.C. and face east to the Lake. Continuing along this path you'll see the large **Poseidoniasts of Beirut** building—a sort of merchant's club for Mideastern traders. Beyond, several rooms of elegant houses line the stone-paved route. Fragments of painted stucco on the brick walls and some ornate mosaics are sure proof that trading at this port was lucrative for many. Don't forget to look at the bases and their fragments; some bear writing that looks as if it were carved yesterday! Since 1873, when the French School began their excavations, work has continued each summer at Délos.

3 Sýros

78 nautical miles E of Piraeus

ARRIVING/DEPARTING • By Air One to three flights go out daily from Athens. Call **Olympic Airways** at their Ermoupolis office (☎ **81-244**) or in Athens (☎ **96-16-161**) for reservations.

• By Sea Sýros is connected twice daily by ferryboat to Piraeus, Tínos, and Mýkonos; four times weekly to Páros, Íos, Santoríni, and Náxos; and once a week to Mílos, Sínos, and Sérifos. The F/B *Kímolos* has three weekly sailings to Síkinos and Folégandros. All schedules should be checked with a local travel agent; **Sýros Travel** (☎ **0281/23-338**) is one on the harbor. There are also daily ferries from Rafína (avoid the slow cargo boats).

ESSENTIALS The city of Ermoúpolis **Tourist Information Office** (☎ **0281/27-027**) is on the second floor of the Town Hall, open 8am to 2:30pm Monday–Friday. The **police** (☎ **22-610**) and the **post office,** open 7:30 to 3pm weekdays, are opposite the Town Hall; the **port police** (☎ **22-690**) are nearby. Just west is the Telecommunications Organization of Greece **(OTE),** open 6am to 11pm daily. For **medical emergencies** call 22-555.

Teamwork Holidays (☎ **0281/23-400,** fax 23-508) is on the *paralía* (harbor front), at Odós Rálli 10, and is open daily to book rooms, handle travel plans, change money, sell Olympic Air Ways tickets, arrange rental cars, and offer a round-the-island half-day bus tour or a full-day beach tour by motor boat.

AA Sýros (☎ **0281/27-711,** fax 23/508) at the New Port sells boat tickets and changes money.

Only ten years ago, Sýros, the administrative capital of the Cyclades, was also its shipping capital—the hub for passengers switching ferry lines to other island chains. Since Páros became the new tourist transport hub, few stop here anymore, yet the islanders' off-handed style with foreigners and the lack of tourist savvy can be rather refreshing. Sýros offers a rare opportunity to vacation as the Greeks do, on an island whose lack of beautiful sand beaches, archeological wonders, and discos has spared it rampant overdevelopment.

Since antiquity Sýros's central position has made it a prosperous trading and shipping port. Excavations at Chalandriani have revealed the existence of an early Cycladic civilization from the 3d millennium B.C. The northern tip of the island is said to have been the home of the philosopher Pherecydas. His best pupil, Pythagoras, was a brilliant mathematician who went to Sámos to help build an engineering marvel, the Eupalinius Tunnel, which brought water underground for over a mile. After the Greek Liberation of 1821, the northern Aegean islanders who'd been driven out by the Turks sought refuge on Sýros. Throughout the 19th century Sýros flourished as a maritime center, becoming the most important port in Greece.

Today the affluent Syrians do not rely on tourism as the mainstay of their economy. Besides the huge shipping industry, textiles and inland greenhouses are main sources of revenue. Most visitors would swear the economy turns on *loukoúmia,* the locally produced Turkish delights that look like Jell-O cubes in powdered sugar and taste like . . . well, you'll have to try them yourself. *Halvadópita,* a locally made nougat sold in tissue-covered pancake slabs, is also extremely popular.

Orientation

Ferryboats dock at **Ermoúpolis** (our recommended base for visitors), which served as the island's major port in ancient times. Today, Ermoúpolis is a busy harbor, enlarged by a huge modern breakwater that provides anchorage for many tankers and container cargo ships. Still lovely in their fading glory are the large neoclassic mansions overlooking the water, vestiges of Sýros's prosperous past. The city appears to be spread over three hills; the hill to the east above the new town is topped with the blue-domed Greek Orthodox church of the Resurrection. This area, known as **Vrontado,** was built up after the Greek immigration of 1821, and its narrow streets, large marble-paved squares, and dignified mansions lend a certain old-world charm to the bustling inner city.

Back at midport is Venizélou Street, which shortly leads inland to the marble-paved **Platía Miaoúli** (Miaoúlis Square), the city's true heart. Platía Miaoúli is dominated by the buff-colored classic town hall, designed in 1876. If it's closed, check out the grand interior of the **Roma Café** below it.

Two streets from the port is Protopapadáki or Proíou Street, which is open to car traffic and chock full of shops. Inexpensive sandals, espadrilles, costume jewelry, cotton sportswear sought after by vacationing Greeks, well-priced fashionable bathing suits, children's clothes, you name it, are all here. Chíos Street (the west side of Platía Miaoúlı) is the location for the town produce market.

Getting Around

Getting around is easy. Buses circle the southern half of Sýros about eight times a day between 10am and 8pm, and more frequently in summer. The route goes to Possidónia/Dellagrazia, Fínikas, and Galíssas. Buses to Vari and Megálos Ghialós, the south coast beaches, run six times a day from Ermoupolis, between 6:45am and 2:30pm, making late sunbathing an option only for those with mopeds or cabfare.

Midway along the *paralía,* or Aktí Rálli, you'll find the bus station, in front of a snack bar whose owner has a vague idea of the schedules.

What to See & Do

ERMOÚPOLIS

The **Sýros Archeological Museum** is on the west side of Town Hall, beneath a clock tower. Its small collection includes some fine Cycladic sculptures from the 3d millennium B.C., two beautiful miniature Hellenistic marble heads, and Roman-era sculpture from Amorgos. It is open daily 8:30am to 3pm; and there is no admission charge. The late **Apollo Theater,** a 19th-century miniature of Milan's La Scala, is being totally rebuilt thanks to funding from the European Union; work may be completed by your visit.

AROUND THE ISLAND

The northwest hill of Ermoúpolis (to the left, looking from the water) is the town of **Áno Sýros,** which is a Christian medieval town built by the Venetians in the 13th century. Áno Sýros originally spread across the summit of both hills, where its inhabitants were protected from pirate raids. Several Roman Catholic churches still stand, the most important of which is the **Church of San Giorgio.** The large buff-colored square building on the hilltop is the medieval **Monastery of the Capuchins.** Remnants of castle walls, stone archways, and narrow lanes will delight visitors. Áno Sýros can be visited by climbing up the old stairs from Ermoúpolis or by local bus.

Around the teardrop-shaped island there are quiet beaches at Megálos Ghialós, Possidónia, and Fínikas (or Phoenix), which are great for those bored with seeing other tourists but probably unsatisfactory for true connoisseurs. Most bathing is off the rocky bluffs that jut from the tree-lined shore into the many bays and inlets on the south and west coasts.

Sýro's 20,000 inhabitants support themselves by both land and sea. The island's east coast south of Ermoúpolis is lined with large and small piers. The huge **Neorion Boatyards** handle the construction and repair of vessels as large as 80,000 tons! In between their piers are the tiny caiques and larger fishing boats that supply tavernas around the island. The southern half of the island, particularly between **Áno Mána** and **Dellagrazia** (the Venetian name for the village dominated by the Madonna of Grace Church), or the beach of **Possidón,** is neatly terraced with vineyards, wheat fields, tomato greenhouses, and fruit trees. Syriot vegetables are exported to Athens. In the more mountainous north, dairies produce the popular St. Michali cheese, milk, and butter that visiting Greeks love to take home

Where to Stay

ERMOÚPOLIS

Europe Hotel, Odós Stam Proíou 24, Ermoúpolis, Sýros 84100. ☎ **0281/28-771.** Fax 23-508. 28 rms (all with bath).

Rates: 8,750 Drs ($36.45) single; 11,500 Drs ($47.90) double. No credit cards.

This pleasant hotel, converted from a circa-1823 hospital, a five-minute walk west of Platía Miaoúli, was closed for renovations during our last visit. We hope it will be open again in 1995 and recommend you have a look. The Church of the Assumption (Kimisis), where you can see an El Greco icon when the church is open, is nearby.

★ **Ipatia Guesthouse,** Odós Babaghiótou 3, Ermoúpolis, Sýros 84503. ☎ **0281/23-575.** 8 rms (5 with bath).

Rates: 6,325 Drs ($26.35) double without bath, 8,050 Drs ($33.55) double with bath. No credit cards.

This lovely restored Syriot mansion dating from 1870 is uphill from the Ághios Nikólas Church. If you walk up the east side of the Platía Miaoúli and bear right, you'll soon have a wonderful prospect over Vaporia, the quarter whose homes abut the rocky Asteria beach on the first cove east of the port. Rooms at the Ipatia share this view; stone steps across from it lead to concrete bathing platforms and a waterside taverna. But what's truly special about the Ipatia is the family who runs it—the Lefebvre family from Philadelphia, who, several years ago, were steered to rooms at the aging Ipatia, fell in love, and bought it. They now open it to guests and friends every June to September. High-ceilinged rooms have brass beds, stone floors, and simple Syriot furnishings. Frescoed ceilings, carved wood doors, spotless rooms, and sloping stairs add enough charm to compensate for a little wear, though all is being continually updated. This place is truly a home away from home. (In the winter you can contact the Lefebvres at 45 Tookany Creek Parkway, Cheltenham, PA 19012.)

Hotel Kymata, Platía Kanári, Ermoúpolis, Sýros 84100. ☎ **0281/22-758.** 8 rms.

Rates: 7,935 Drs ($33.05) single/double. No credit cards.

There's another restored neoclassic home on Platía Kanári, across from the beautiful (but bad value) Hotel Hermes. The Kymata has a simple style, highlighted architectural details, scalloped stucco ceilings (an old anti-earthquake reinforcement technique), and great port views from its front rooms. Spacious, bright rooms are spotless, with modern showers tucked away inside. Open year round.

AROUND THE ISLAND

Those drawn to the outer villages will find the most happening (it's still not much) at Galíssas, which is a beach town 5½ miles southeast of Ermoúpolis. In Galíssas, there is **Camping Yianna,** Galíssas (☎ **0281/42-447**), about 109 yards from the beach. It has its own open-air disco—something to weigh carefully before unfurling your sleeping bag!—minimarket, snack bar, restaurant, and exchange, transportation and information service. Rates are 1,000 Drs ($4.15) per person; 700 Drs ($2.90) per tent. The **Hotel Françoise** in Galíssas (☎ **0281/42-000**) has 34 rooms with private facilities on the roadside, about five minutes from the beach. Their reasonable rates are 6,800 Drs ($28.50) for single; 8,500 Drs ($42.70) double. The **Maistrali Pension** (☎ **0821/42-059**) is another choice, with balconied rooms only 76 yards from the beach. Singles pay the same here as at the Françoise; doubles will pay 12,650 Drs ($52.70). None of these places accept credit cards.

READERS RECOMMEND

Dendrinos' Rooms-to-Let, Galíssas, *Sýros. "I find the sandy bottom bay and beach at Galíssas to be the best on the island of Sýros and one of the best in Greece. I also have found a wonderful place to stay, close to the bus stop. Nana and Takis Dendrinos are wonderfully hospitable and the rooms are spotlessly clean. In addition, there is a great taverna,* **Nikos' Restaurant,** *where the Kapellas family has delicious food and very good prices."*— Rev. Martin A. Peter, Indianapolis, Ind.

Finikas is a few miles south of Galíssas. A ten-minute walk south from here brings Italophiles to Possidón or Dellagrazia. Here, too, are some hotels, a tiny rocky beach, and a neat pier and sand beach on an off-limits spit of land. The attractive, 60-room Class B **Posidonion** (☎ **0281/42-100**) has the best facilities for those who want to hike the area; doubles cost 15,300 Drs ($63.75). Search for neoclassic mansions with Turkish-inspired wooden balconies and gingerbread trim; they can be spotted occasionally between the modern homes and rolling hills.

Where to Eat

Kyle's favorite dining in Ermoúpolis is at the numerous *zacharoplastía* (pâtisseries), many featuring homemade *loukoúmi* and serving café frappé to idlers. In fact, a kindly Orthodox priest showed us to one sweet shop off Platía Miaoúli that he claimed had the best *loukoúmia* on the island. We found the Mavrákis dealer in a shop on the west side of the port, tucked in a recess behind some cafés and a minimarket. Gift-wrapped boxes with photos of Sýros's scenic highlights come flavored with rosewater, mint, mastic, or almond and cost about 700 Drs ($2.90) per pound (500 grams).

The **Pyramid Pizzeria** (☎ **24-295**) on the Platía Miaoúli is a fashionable, more casual, and inexpensive choice. Sunsets are particularly fine when viewed from **Tramps,** a snack bar and café on the east side of the *paralía.* There is also a very popular late afternoon and evening café next to the tourist office in the wonderful **Customs House,** by the ferry at Platía Évripos, the place to celebrate the comings and goings of friends.

Eleana Restaurant, Platía Miaoúli, Ermoúpolis. No telephone.

Cuisine: GREEK/INTERNATIONAL.
Prices: Appetizers 400–800 Drs ($1.65–$3.35), main courses 920–1,400 Drs ($3.85–$5.85). No credit cards.
Open: Daily 11am–3pm, 7–11pm.

Eleana has a varied taverna menu of vegetable dishes and meat casseroles. The interior is air-conditioned and the exterior opens onto the picturesque square.

Cavo d'Oro, Paralía, Ermoúpolis. ☎ **81-440.**

Cuisine: SEAFOOD.
Prices: Appetizers 350–800 Drs ($1.45–$3.35), main courses 1,150–2,070 Drs ($4.80–$8.60). No credit cards.
Open: Daily 11am–midnight.

More serious diners should turn to seafood, served very fresh, grilled or fried, at Cavo d'Oro at the center of the *paralía.* It's a clean, comfortable restaurant with indoor and outdoor seating and a large selection of fish, squid, and octopus dishes. The chef makes a piquant *skordaliá* (garlic dip that goes very well with fish), *taramosaláta, chórta* (greens), and other typical dishes to please the Greek clientele.

4 Páros

91 nautical miles SE of Piraeus

ARRIVING/DEPARTING • By Air Olympic has ten daily flights to Páros. For schedule information and reservations, call Olympic Airways (☎ **01/96-16-161** in Athens, or **21-900** in Paroikía).

• By Sea The major port, **Paroikía,** is serviced at least once daily (six-hour trip) from Piraeus. Schedules should be confirmed with tourist information in Athens

(☎ **171**) or by dialing **45-11-311.** The **Ventouris Lines** leaves three times a week from Piraeus via Sýros to Páros; call **0294/25-200** for schedules. **Strintzi Line's** *Ionian Sea* (☎ **42-25-000**) sails three times weekly from Piraeus via Sýros. **Ilio Lines** (☎ **42-24-772**) has hydrofoil service almost daily from Rafina. Paroikía is linked to the other Cyclades via daily ferry service to Náxos, Íos, and Santoríni (Thíra). The F/B *Golden Vergina* has overnight service to Ikaría and Sámos four times a week. From Sámos you can arrange a next-day excursion to Éphesus, Turkey. The F/B *Margarita* runs three times a week (daily in summer) to Sínos. Cruise excursions leave daily from Paroikía or Náoussa (the north coast port) to Mýkonos.

For many years, Páros was known by only a small coterie of European travelers in search of a quiet island retreat. Several bought villas in the countryside and settled here. Since becoming the transportation hub of the Cyclades, thousands have passed through Paroikía's caged-in piers on their way to other Cyclades islands, Sífnos, or faraway Crete and Sámos. Inevitably, many visitors—those whom Mýkonos can no longer accommodate or those looking for an alternative Greek Isles experience—disembark.

Paroikía, the island's major port, is actually most alluring in the narrow, stone-paved back streets of the agorá section, where the enveloping and often disorienting white-washed walls block off all connection with the sea. The north coast port of Náoussa, once a sleepy fishing village, hosts gourmet restaurants and stylish hotels, making it one of the island's most understated resorts.

In the last few years, fine beaches and reasonable prices have also lured young visitors and charter flight groups who settle into Paroikía for a summer of sun and discos, or head to the coastal developments to camp or stay in private rooms.

Fortunately, Páros's high season doesn't begin until school is out, so that travelers searching for the island's more subtle charms have from April until late June and September through October to explore Paroikía and the island more intimately. Those arriving in July and August will probably prefer to make Náoussa their base.

Orientation to Páros

If you've come to Páros to party, meet young people, or luxuriate over a glass of Crevellier wine, then Paroikía's the spot for you. Paroikía is the island's capital—a sophisticated resort with a diverse selection of restaurants and discos, comfortable hotels, and excellent shops. You can easily explore the island's sights by moped or by joining one of the many excursions offered by local travel agents. Pleasant beaches are within a half hour's walk to the south. (The beaches in town are crowded but acceptable.)

Náoussa offers a sizable selection of good restaurants and shops, most tucked into the pedestrian lanes off the town's main square. Within 40 minutes' walk of the Náoussa Square are the island's most exquisite **beaches,** nestled in the nooks and crannies of the jagged northern coastline. Many of the better hotels are scattered across the rolling hills and narrow, unpaved coastal paths leading to these beach coves. Because of this, Náoussa appears less developed than it actually is.

Getting Around Páros

A stroller's pace is appropriate for this serene isle; there are many scenic attractions within an hour's walk of both Paroikía and Náoussa. But there are many options when you want to cover more territory.

BY BUS

The **public bus** provides hourly service between Paroikía (leaving on the hour from 8am to 8pm) and Náoussa (leaving on the half hour from 8:30am to 8:30pm). The other public buses from Paroikía run hourly from 8am to 9pm in two general directions: south to Alíki or Pounda and southeast to the beaches at Píso Livádi, Chryssí Aktí, and Dríos. Schedules are posted at the stations, or call **21-133.**

BY CAR & MOPED

An easy and adventuresome alternative is to rent a **moped.** There are several moped dealers along the harbor (between the windmill and the yacht marina to the north). It's a seller's market on Páros in July and August, and most of the rental shops stand firm on their prices. Mopeds, as we've said before, can be dangerous, so check them out carefully before deciding on a rental. Depending on size they will cost 3,500 Drs to 4,500 Drs ($14.60–$18.75). Another alternative is a Jeep or dune buggy. After comparing vehicle quality, the best bets were **Rent-A-Car Acropolis** (☎ **21-830,** fax 23-666), run by the good-natured Boyatzis Brothers and **Budget Rent-a-Car** (☎ **22-302**), along the harborfront. Groups of three or four might enjoy renting one of the Acropolis's wildly painted buggies at 14,000 Drs ($58.35) per day or a Suzuki Jeep, which costs 21,850 Drs ($91) per day. Full insurance, which we recommend, is an additional 2,875 Drs ($12) per day.

BY TAXI

Taxis can be booked (☎ **21-500**) or hailed at the windmill taxi stand. If you're coming off the ferry with lots of luggage and a hotel reservation in Náoussa, it's worth the 1,700 Drs ($7.20) to take a taxi directly there.

BY BICYCLE

Bicycles, which can be rented for about 1,750 Drs ($7.30) per day, are another popular alternative for exploring the island; rolling hills provide just the right amount of workout for weekend bicyclists. Páros has some difficult-to-navigate pebble-and-dirt roads, so don't forget to check your tire pressure if you rent a bike.

Paroikía

ORIENTATION

Ferryboats land at Paroikía, site of the ancient capital and the largest village on Páros. In front of the pier is Paroikía's best-known landmark, a squat, whitewashed **windmill.** If you turn left and follow the bay, you'll hit the bus station (schedules are posted on their kiosk) and a very handy luggage storage (hours are 8am to midnight) at a cost of 250 Drs ($1.40) for each piece until midnight. With the windmill as a handle, imagine Paroikía's four main streets spreading out like the delicate frame of an open rice-paper fan. To your right, the road curves out of sight and follows the rock and sand coastline around the telephone center (OTE) to the old *kastro.*

Directly in front of the windmill (facing inland) is **Mavroghénous Square.** Ms. Mavroghénous, whose surly-faced bust is in the middle of this garden setting, has been commemorated on Páros and on Mýkonos (her birthplace) for her heroism during the War of Independence. In the 1820s, Mavroghénous successfully quelled a band of Algerian pirates, then led her resistance fighters against Ottoman soldiers in Évvia, Thessaly, and Turkey itself. After liberation, she settled on Páros, where she died, impoverished and forgotten, in 1848.

On the left side of the square are travel agents, ferryboat-ticket vendors, round-the-island excursion operators, and many offices that help with accommodations. The lane that runs straight back through the square, between the two banks, leads to the enticing and picturesque **agorá** (market) section, which is concentrated in a relatively small area of town.

Returning to the harbor, you can't help noticing the graceful lines of the bright white **Ághios Nikólaos Church,** on its own tiny traffic island. This street leads past the public gardens to the church called **Ekatontapylianí** (Church of 100 Doors), which is considered the most superb example of Byzantine architecture in the Cyclades. Many of Paroikía's hotels lie in the hidden alleyways that snake between Mavroghénous Square and the Ekatontapylianí Church.

To the extreme left of the windmill is the waterside road, which runs northwest, past the bus station, the post office, the yacht marina, and a slew of new hotels.

Fast Facts: Páros

Area code The telephone area code for Páros is **0284.**

Banks There are three banks on Mavroghénous Square, open weekdays 8am to 2pm, and evenings and Saturday in the high season.

Emergencies Call the **national police** (☎ **21-221**).

Ferryboat Tickets Tickets are sold by several agents around Mavroghénous Square. We recommend the **Vintzi Agency** at the other end of the port for the best service. Schedules are posted along the sidewalk. Day excursions to Mýkonos, Santoríni, Náxos, and Sínos cost from 4,875–9,750 Drs ($20.30–$40.60) and are widely sold.

Laundry/Dry Cleaning There's dry cleaning at **Laundry Ostria** (☎ **22-492**) on Ligaria Square behind the Kontes Hotel. (In Náoussa, there's a self-service laundry near the bus station.)

Medical Clinic The Páros Clinic, down the road from Ekatontapylianí, can be reached at 22-500. (In Angeria call **22-2690;** Antíparos, **61-219;** Marpissa, **41-205;** Náoussa, **51-216.**) There's a new private **Medical Center** (☎ **24-410**) in Paroikía.

Police Call **23-333.** (In Antíparos call **61-202;** Marpissa, **41-202;** Náoussa, **51-202.**) For information, find the helpful tourist police on the port, ☎ **21-673.**

Post Office The post office (☎ **21-236**) is on the road to Livádi; it is open Monday through Friday 7:30am to 2pm, with extended hours in July and August. They now offer public fax service, 22-449. (There's a branch on Main Street in Náoussa.)

Telephones The telephone center (OTE) is located at the head of the southbound coastal road near the windmill; its long hours (daily from 7:30am to midnight) help to offset crowding by the midday throng. If the front door is closed, go around to the back; wind direction determines which door is left open! (There's also a branch in Náoussa with similar hours.)

Tourist Information The Páros Tourist Information Bureau (☎ **22-079**) is inside the windmill on the harbor. It's open from 9am to 11pm daily, June through September, and the staff speaks English and French; they also provide local schedules and change traveler's checks.

WHAT TO SEE & DO

Paroikía features excellent **shopping,** particularly in the agorá. The wide range of galleries, handcrafts boutiques, clothing shops, and food markets make Páros one of the best spots in all of Greece for memorable souvenir and folk-art shopping. Just off Market Street, almost at its end, you'll find the **Aegean Center for the Fine Arts,** founded by the late American artist Brett Taylor. A highly regarded painter who passed away in 1983, Taylor left behind an enduring arts institution where artists, photographers, and writers come to study year-round. Contact the current director, John Peck, at the center, Paroikía, Páros 84400, Cyclades (fax 0284/23-287).

A unique shop in the agorá directly across from the Levantis Restaurant is **The Teapot** (☎ **21-177**), filled with teas, spices, herbs, henna, and folk art; its assorted packaged herbs and potpourri of local Greek wildflowers make inexpensive and easy-to-carry gifts. There's also great shopping (particularly for "hippie" memorabilia) along the *paralía* at night, when traveling European artists and vendors display their wares for passersby.

The site that draws thousands of pilgrims annually to Páros is its famous church, the **Panaghía Ekatontapylianí.** Located just off the private boat harbor, it's a large, graceful example of Byzantine church architecture. The name means "100 Doors," but those who try to count will find only 99. There's a legend that if the 100th door is found, then Constantinople (the holiest Greek Orthodox city, known now as Istanbul) will be returned to the Greek nation. The Ekatontapylianí was constructed in the 6th century and rebuilt in the 10th century. Of special note is the ornately carved iconostasis of luminescent Parian marble. The swing doors that lead to the altar are carved wood painted to resemble marble. The marble floors and columns add lightness and grace to the stone walls. At one time the ceiling and walls were covered with frescoes, and remnants can still be seen. Behind the main basilica on the right is the baptistry, now restored and occupied by several doves. The best time to visit Ekatontapylianí is on August 15th, the Feast of the Assumption, when great festivities are held at the site. The church is open for viewing daily from 8am to 1pm and 5 to 8pm.

Behind the baptistry of the Ekatontapylianí is the **Páros Archeological Museum** (open Tuesday through Sunday from 8:30am to 3pm). The museum contains finds from the 3d millennium B.C. at Saliágros to the 1st century B.C. In the room to the right of the entrance is a fragment of the Parian Chronicle (no. 26), an important tablet from which many events in ancient Greek history were dated, including the birth of Homer (the larger portion of the Parian Chronicle is in England, at Oxford University). The museum also contains a 3d-century plaque inscribed with a biography of Archilochus, a famed 7th-century B.C. lyric poet and one of Páros's most famous native sons. His poetry reflects a thoroughly 20th-century mentality: "What breaks me, young friend, is tasteless desire, dead iambics, boring dinners." Admission to the museum, which may be expanded by the time you visit, is 500 Drs ($2.10).

Another neighborhood of great interest to those who delight in the architectural wonder of the agorá is the **kástro,** about a ten-minute walk south of the windmill on the seaside road. The remains of the 13th-century Venetian fortifications are all the more interesting because of the marble fragments from the ancient temples of Demeter and Apollo that were incorporated into the *kástro* walls. Traditional Cycladic housing clings to the old Venetian tower and ramparts in a fascinating mélange of architectural styles that spans nearly 3,000 years.

WHERE TO STAY

The port of Paroikía has three basic hotel zones: the agorá, the harbor, and the beach. Because of Páros's immense popularity most hotels now require reservations for July and August, and these should be made at least one month in advance. All written requests must be accompanied by a deposit equal to one night's rent. Once you arrive in Greece, a follow-up phone call is highly recommended for those who haven't received a written confirmation.

In the Agora

The agorá is the heart of Paroikía—its pulse beating 24 hours a day. This neighborhood is the most intriguing in which to stay, though it can get noisy! Note that accommodations are available on the outskirts of the agorá in the quiet back streets, where the tourist presence is less pervasive.

★ **Hotel Argonauta,** Agorá, Paroikía, Páros 84400. ☎ **0284/21-440.** Fax 0284/23-422. 15 rms (all with shower). TEL

Rates (including breakfast): 7,360 Drs ($30.60) single; 9,200 Drs ($38.30) double. EC, MC.

The rustic stone façade and second-floor inner courtyard of this comfortable hotel fit in well with the traditional architecture found behind the Emborikí (Commercial) Bank and above the very good taverna of that name, overlooking Mavroghénous Square. Soula and Dimitris Ghikas own and operate modern, well-equipped rooms that draw a tamer crowd than many of Paroikía's hostels, so it's refreshingly quiet.

$ **Hotel Dina,** Market Street, Pariokía, Páros 84400. ☎ **0284/21-325.** 8 rms (all with bath).

Rates: 9,200 Drs ($38.33) double. No credit cards.

Our favorite small lodging in Paroikía would be indistinguishable from its pure-white neighbors if not for the discreet sign mounted outside. When you enter the long, narrow hallway the first thing you'll see are attractive plantings; then, you'll probably find the friendly proprietor, Dína Patélis, relaxing over a Greek coffee in the back garden. All the simply furnished, spotless rooms with blue-tiled bathrooms sparkle.

Floga Hotel, Paroikía, Páros 84400. ☎ **0284/22-017.** 12 rms (all with bath).

Rates: 6,900 Drs ($28.75) single; 8,625 Drs ($35.95) double. V.

The Floga began as rooms-to-let above the Lobster Restaurant near Livádi. Niko and his wife, Anna, turned their clean, twin-bedded rooms into a small hotel with views over the surrounding fields. It's a block beyond Mrs. Mavro's, and, unless there's a lobster party below, it's very quiet.

Hotel Platanos, Paroikía, Páros 84400. ☎ **0284/24-262.** 11 rms (all with bath). TEL

Rates: 14,950 Drs ($62.30) double. No credit cards.

Located 350 meters south of the windmill and one block in from the *paralía,* the Platanos comes highly recommended by reader Garry Wabba. The neighborhood is quiet, the rooms comfortable. Ursula Antionou is a most gracious hostess.

Mrs. Zambia Mavro, Paroikía, Páros 84400. ☎ **0284/21-628.** 6 rms (none with bath).

Rates: 4,600 Drs ($19.15) double without bath. No credit cards.

Mrs. Mavro's large home and two-story pension is in front of a vineyard off the road leading to the Hotel Galinos-Louiza. She speaks very little English, but the buzzing, salon-style hair dryers operating in her living room betray her main occupation! Even after coiffing hair all day, Mrs. Mavro manages to keep six neat rooms.

Pension Vanguelistra, Paroikía, Páros 84400. ☎ **0284/21-482.** 6 rms (all with bath), 2 apartments.

Rates: 9,200 Drs ($38.35) double; 10,350 Drs ($43.15) apartment. No credit cards.

Definitely the coziest and most attractive lodging in the neighborhood down the lane across from the Hotel Louiza. You can't miss its flower-covered veranda, which brightens the whole street. Ghiorgos and Voula Maounis and their outgoing, English-speaking kids make every guest feel welcome. The rooms are spotless and four have balconies.

At the Harbor

The harborside nearest the windmill is a convenient and lively place to spend your evenings, and at sunset the views are magnificent.

Hotel Georgy, Platía Mavroghénous, Paroikía, Páros 84400. ☎ **0284/21-667.** Fax 0284/22-544. 38 rms (all with shower).

Rates: 9,230 Drs ($39.30) single; 14,200 Drs ($59.15) double. No credit cards.

The Kontostavros family takes pride in providing good service to their guests. You have a choice of views over a richly planted inner courtyard or out toward lively Mavroghénous Platía (Square). Continental breakfast in their café costs 350 Drs ($1.90).

Hotel the Kontes, Platía Mavroghénous, Paroikía, Páros 84400. ☎ **0284/21-096.** 27 rms (all with bath).

Rates: 6,900 Drs ($28.75) single; 8,625 Drs ($35.95) double. No credit cards.

One of the best values nearest the windmill is this oddly named—and sometimes oddly run—older inn with a broad, arched doorway that faces toward Mavroghenous Square. The balconied second-floor rooms have great views of the windmill and the sea; the first-floor rooms, with shuttered French doors, open onto a large, pleasant sun deck. A well-maintained, stylish building where cleanliness more than makes up for a little peeling paint.

Hotel Kypreos, Paroikía, Páros 84400. ☎ **0284/21-383** or **22-448.** 5 rms (all with shower).

Rates: 6,000 Drs ($25) single; 8,000 Drs ($33.35) double.

Just north of the windmill, Anne, the warm and helpful hostess, offers neat, simple rooms that include double beds and balconies that shade her husband's car-rental shop below. (A night's stay at the Kýpreos might get you a discount on a car rental.)

At the Beach

The strip of hotels that line Livádi Beach (about a ten-minute walk north of the windmill) have three common features: bland Class C decor, proximity to the crowded town beach, and Aegean sea views. We'll review a few of them briefly, in order of their proximity to the ferryboat pier.

Hotel Paros, Paroikía, Páros 84400. ☎ **0284/21-319.** 15 rms (all with bath).

Rates: 8,625 Drs ($35.95) single; 11,500 Drs ($47.90) double. MC, V.

This older hotel on the beach street has good-value rooms with Aegean views. A good continental breakfast costs 550 Drs ($2.20), and Peter, the friendly owner, and his family will help make your stay pleasant.

Hotel Argo, Paroikía, Páros 84400. ☎ **0284/21-367** or **21-207.**
45 rms (all with bath). TEL

Rates: 8,625 Drs ($35.95) single; 11,500 Drs ($47.90) double. No credit cards.

The Hotel Argo is a bit farther from the pier, but also on the beach strip. Its cozy, overfurnished lobby reminded us of our grandmothers' homes, but there is an elevator and the balconied rooms are spacious. However, breakfast is not available.

Hotel Asterias, Paroikía, Páros 84400. ☎ **0284/21-797** or **22-171.** Fax 0284/22-172.
36 rms (all with shower). TEL

Rates: 12,420 Drs ($51.75) single; 15,640 Drs ($65.15) double. EC, MC, V.

The white stucco Asterias is the best bet. This attractive Cycladic-style hotel is the closest to the beach, and it has a front-facing, flowering garden. Spacious rooms include wooden-shuttered doors that open onto balconies, all with sea views.

Villa Ragousi, Paroikía, Páros 84400. ☎ **0284/21-671.** 10 rms (all with shower).

Rates: 11,500 Drs ($47.90) single/double. No credit cards.

Recommended by readers, this modern three-story house up the hill from the Taverna Skouna has good clean rooms, some with balconies overlooking the bay. Gavrilla Ragousi speaks English and drives a cab during the day; ask for him at the taxi stand.

Camping

Northwest of the harbor, about 872 yards from the ferry pier, is **Camping Koula** (☎ **0284/22-082**); 700 Drs ($2.90) per person. Because of its site on Livádi Beach, Koula is the area's first-choice campground, but in the summer it gets so busy that most find it unpleasantly noisy.

Parasporos Camping (☎ **0284/21-944**) is a newer facility south of Paroikía on the road to Eloúnda. It has all the amenities on large, well-landscaped grounds, and the breathing room and quiet they ensure, even in busy July and August. At both places, the fee is 1,050 Drs ($4.35) per person; tent sites are free.

WHERE TO EAT

Since a large number of foreigners have taken up residence on Páros, their presence has become apparent in the quality restaurants (where foreign employees are critical to success) as well as the informal places (where foreign foods are the appeal). If nothing below appeals, you'll see the dozens of souvlaki/pizza/burger joints with neon lighting and a knack for catering to college kids that have overtaken sections of the agora and the *paralía.*

$ **Aligaria Restaurant,** Aligaría Square, Paroikía. ☎ **22-026.**

Cuisine: GREEK.

Prices: Appetizers 500–1,150 Drs ($2.10–$4.40); main courses 1,100–2,000 Drs ($4.60–$8.35). EC, MC, V.

Open: Daily 9am–midnight.

Owner Elizabeth Nikolousou really knows her way around a kitchen! Her zucchini pie is light as a feather, and the chicken cooked in beer and potato balls is superb; furthermore, the portions are generous! She also has one of the best selections of Greek wines we've come across.

Dionysos Taverna, Agorá, Paroikía. ☎ **22-318.**

Cuisine: GREEK/INTERNATIONAL. **Reservations:** Recommended during July–Aug.
Prices: Appetizers 400–980 Drs ($1.65–$4.10), main courses 1,100–2,400 Drs ($4.60–$10.05). AE, EC, MC, V.
Open: Daily 6pm–midnight.

This popular taverna has most of its seating outdoors, in a pretty garden filled with bright red geraniums. Inside, a flaking fresco depicts mortals frolicking around Dionysus, who oversees the sale of the Parian favorites: Lagari, a strong red wine, and Kavarnis, a dry white.

Hibiscus Cafe, Platía Valentza, Paroikía. ☎ **21-849.**

Cuisine: GREEK/PIZZA.
Prices: Appetizers 460–700 Drs ($1.90–$2.90); main courses 860–1,725 Drs ($3.60–$7.20). No credit cards.
Open: Daily noon–midnight.

Located on the *paralía,* about 109 yards south of the port, this is one of the few casual yet stylish places. It's inexpensive, with seaview tables, a wide snack menu, and brick-oven pizza.

Levantis Restaurant, Agorá Street, Paroikía. ☎ **23-613.**

Cuisine: GREEK/EASTERN MEDITERRANEAN. **Reservations:** Recommended July–Aug.
Prices: Appetizers 600–780 Drs ($2.50–$7.40), main courses 1,600–2,600 Drs ($6.70–$10.85). AE, DC, EC, MC, V.
Open: Wed–Mon 7pm–2am.

Dinner is served under grapevines that some of the older citizens remember being there when they were young. Vivacious Mariana is happy to recommend her favorite of the day, and her husband Nikolas offers a friendly glass of wine. We ate there late, and suddenly Vassili, who choreographed *Zorba,* came in and tables were quickly moved aside and the dancing began! Wonderful!

Ouzerí Albatross, *paralía,* Paroikía. ☎ **24-265.**

Cuisine: GREEK.
Prices: Appetizers 400–750 Drs ($1.70–$3.15); main courses 900–1,850 Drs ($3.75–$7.70). No credit cards.

Our friend Stergios led us to this inconspicuous place about half a kilometer right from the port. We had a feast of *barbounia* (red mullet), *saganaki,* charcoal-grilled octopus, *skordalia,* country salad, fried zucchini and ouzo, topped off with apple rings sprinkled with cinnamon, for less than $15 per person.

$ **Poseidon Grill,** Livádi Beach. ☎ **22-667.**

Cuisine: GREEK.
Prices: Appetizers 350–600 Drs ($1.45–$3.60), main courses 920–1,725 Drs ($3.85–$7.40). No credit cards.
Open: Daily 8am–midnight.

Across from the Stella Hotel near the beach is the Poseidon Grill, a fancier taverna with a wide range of vegetable entrées and excellent fish. Share a swordfish, grilled calamari, some *mezédes* (appetizers), salad, and a bottle of Nissiotissa wine.

EVENING ENTERTAINMENT

Warning: Several places on the strip offer very cheap drinks or "buy one, get one free"—usually locally brewed alcohol the locals call *"bomba."* It's illegal, and it makes one intoxicated quickly and very sick afterward.

Just behind the windmill is another Paroikía landmark, the **Port Café.** This basic kafenío, lit by bare incandescent bulbs, is filled day and night with tourists waiting for the ferry, bus, taxi, or just waiting. The Port Café serves coffee, drinks, and pastry, and you can pass the time kibbitzing with a wide variety of fellow travelers.

The **Saloon d'Or** (☎ **22-176**), south of the port, is the most popular place for starting the evening with fairly inexpensive drinks, and on good nights gets the liveliest young crowd around. Continue south along the coast road, turn left at the bridge and about a 109 yards on you should have no difficulty finding a complex with the **Dubliner** (☎ **22-759**), which has live Irish music several nights a week, **Down Under** (Australian, mate), and the **Hard Rock Café** (☎ **21-113**).

If partying's not your thing, Paroikía offers several elegant alternatives. The **Pirate Bar,** a few doors away from the Hotel Dina in the agorá, is a tastefully decorated bar whose stone interior is braced with dark wooden beams. Mellow jazz, blues, and classical music accompany the slightly more expensive drinks.

Back at the bustling *paralía* there's a more sophisticated choice with wonderful Aegean views. The **Evinos Bar** is above the three-tiered retaining wall south of the OTE, high enough above the din that you can appreciate the music streaming subtly from the bar speakers and take in the lovely scenery.

For you party types, there's the **Rendezvous,** down from Evinos, with pretty good pop music. **Black Bart's** (☎ **21-802**) is midway on the *paralía*—a good spot for very loud rock music and a boisterous, big-drinker clientele.

The outdoor **Ciné Rex** (☎ **21-676**), with two nightly B-pictures (usually dubbed in Greek), is very close by. This night outing may be more to your taste, and is a good, amusing way to rest up for dancing.

There are enough discos tucked in the back lanes of the agora and at the far end of the *paralía* that it would be futile to recommend one over another.

Náoussa

Náoussa is perched on Páros's north coast, in the middle of two fat peninsulas lined with rocky coves and sandy beaches. Fortunately, recent tourist development has focused on the beach areas, keeping the village relatively unspoiled. Despite a major construction boom, and the recent onslaught of younger tourists, this is a small active port where fishermen still fish and the gnarled, whitewashed back lanes still give Náoussa some charm.

ORIENTATION

If you're coming the seven miles north from Paroikía, you'll know you're approaching Náoussa by the hotels and restaurants that line the paved roadway. After crossing a street-level bridge, Archilochus Street and Náoussa's main square will be on the right. The square, shaded by tall eucalyptus trees, marks the bus station and the taxi stand.

If you continue across the square to an arched entryway, you'll be at the medieval gates of the old city. Within are the fascinating back alleys of Náoussa; they are best explored in midafternoon, when the inhabitants retire inside for siesta. Walking softly along the cobblestone paths and peeking into the geranium-filled gardens provides an undisturbed view of Greek life.

Beyond the National Bank is the busy harbor at **St. Demetrios Bay.** It's most active at sunrise and late afternoon, when the fishers are setting out or returning home with the day's catch. From the portside cafés you can watch the nets being spread out on the dock, then carefully folded for the next day's outing. The blue, green, orange, and yellow caiques are scrubbed, rinsed, and fixed to their moorings. Across the way, the small whitewashed **Ághios Nikólaos Church,** dedicated to the patron saint of sailors, stands out strikingly in a sea of primary colors. A legacy of the 15th-century Venetian occupation of this tiny port is the old stonework of the breakwater on the eastern side. Divers will find ruined ramparts submerged throughout this part of the harbor.

INFORMATION

Tucked in a storefront off the main square, just opposite the pastry shop, is the indispensable **Nissiótissa Tours** office (☎ **0284/51-480** or **51-094**, fax 51-189), known locally as Gavalas Travel. Cathy and Kostas Gavalas, Greek-Americans who returned to Náoussa, know this area better than anyone and are experts at helping you find a hotel, room-to-let, apartment, or villa. The Gavalases also book Olympic flights and arrange other plane, ferryboat and excursion tickets, island tours, and rental cars (EC, MC, V are accepted). They also have a book exchange as well as used books for sale. They can even arrange two-hour horseback riding tours with experienced guides (9:30am and 5pm), 6,900 Drs ($28.75).

The town **police** (☎ **51-202**) are on the road to Paroikía, across from the **OTE.** (You can also use metered phones at travel agencies.) The **post office** is 600 meters out on the road to Ambelas. The town medical **doctor** is on the main square, on the right before the church. There's a **foreign periodicals shop** on the square.

GETTING AROUND

Náoussa's sudden growth in popularity has meant expanded transportation connections to other Páros villages and Cyclades islands.

Buses run between Paroikía and Náoussa approximately every half hour between 8am and 10pm. The fare for the 15-minute trip is 250 Drs ($1.05). Bus service to Santa Maria beach is twice daily; to other island villages it runs on poorly paved or narrow dirt roads, and is infrequent.

Because there are so many excellent beaches within 12½ miles of Náoussa village, a **moped** is an expedient way to sample them at your own pace. There are several moped dealers on the square; prices are comparable to those in Paroikía and bargaining is unlikely in the peak-demand summer season.

Nissiotissa Rent-A-Car rents Renault Jeeps for about 19,000 Drs ($79.15) daily in the high season, negotiable in the low.

Taxis are an expensive alternative for beach hopping and cannot easily be found outside the village, but, for getting to and from Paroikía, they're often worth the 1,800 Drs ($7.50) tariff. Luggage costs about 100 Drs (42¢) per bag extra.

Daily **excursion boats** leave from the Náoussa harbor for Mýkonos and Délos. The two-hour journey can be taken one way for 4,600 Drs ($19.15); the full-day, round-trip excursion costs 9,200 Drs ($38.35). Also in summer, daily excursions can be made to Náxos and Santoríni; round-trip fares are 4,600 Drs ($19.15) and 10,350 Drs ($43.15) respectively, though one-way tickets are sold for half price. Local caiques make day trips to the beach of Santa Maria, about four miles away around the eastern peninsula, for about 1,500 Drs ($6.25) round trip. There's also round-trip caique service to Kolymbíthres Beach (on the west peninsula)/Monastery Beach/Laggeri Beach for 600 Drs ($2.50).

WHERE TO STAY

In the quiet back streets surrounding the Hotel Minoa—and in the whole area behind the Sagriótis Monument—you'll find a scattering of whitewashed abodes sporting ROOMS, CHAMBRES, and ZIMMER signs. If you haven't made high-season reservations and are unable to find a hotel room, try **Gavalas Travel (☎ 0284/51-480)** just off the square.

Hotel Fotilia, Náoussa, Páros 84401. **☎ 0284/51-480.** Fax 0284/51-189.
14 rms (all with bath). TEL

Rates (including breakfast): 16,100 Drs ($67.10) single; 19,550 Drs ($81.45) double.

Climb to the top of the steps at the end of town and to the left of the church you'll see a restored windmill behind a stone archway. Here the companionable Michael Leondaris greets you with a glass of wine or a cup of coffee. The rooms are spacious and furnished in an elegant country style. Crisp blue-and-white-striped curtains open to balconies that overlook the old harbor and bay.

$ **Kalypso Hotel,** Aghii Anárghyri Beach, Páros 84401. **☎ 0284/51-488.**
Fax 0284/51-607. 40 rms (all with bath).

Rates (including breakfast): 11,730 Drs ($48.85) single; 17,900 Drs ($60) double. EC, MC, V.

This is a very nice beachside hotel built around a cobblestone courtyard, although many of the outer, balconied rooms overlook the sea. The upper-floor rooms, quite spacious, are reached via an ornately carved wooden mezzanine that overlooks the Kalypso's bar.

Papadakis Hotel, Náoussa, Páros 84401. **☎ 0284/51-643.** Fax 0284/51-643.
16 rms (all with bath).

Rates (including breakfast): 15,640 Drs ($65.15) single/double. No credit cards.

If you like hillside locations, the friendly Papadakis offers the best views over the village and bay. After a brisk five-minute walk from the square, you'll arrive at their sunny breakfast lounge, where fresh carnations grace every table. Their large, newly built rooms have balconies overlooking the bay and village or open out onto a common patio; those who climb the steps to the highest balconied rooms are most rewarded.

Hotel Petres, Náoussa, Páros 84401. **☎ 0284/51-480.** Fax 0284/52-467.
16 rms (all with bath). A/C MINIBAR TEL

Rates: 11,500 Drs ($47.50) single; 16,100 Drs ($67.10) double.

Enter a charming reception area furnished with antiques. Claire Hatzinkolakis has decorated her rooms with loving care: handsome woven covers on the beds, hand-crocheted lace draped over the lamps, and prints from the Benaki Museum on the walls. A kitchen and barbeque are available to guests. Her "honeymoon suite" has her grandmother's marriage bed in it.

Apartments

There are a number of newly built apartments and studios in this area, at Ághii Anárghyri Beach. Most function like small hotels, with a manned reception desk, common switchboard, lounge, and sometimes, breakfast service.

Batistas Apartments, Náoussa, Páros 84401. ☎ **0284/51-058** (or Athens **01/97-57-286**). 8 apts.

Rates: 14,400 Drs ($60) for two; 23,000 Drs ($95.85) for four.

Mrs. Batistas's homespun lace, crochet, and needlework give these handsome apartments an extra feeling of home.

Kapten Nikolas Apartments, Ághii Anárghyri, Páros 84401. ☎ **0284/51-340.** Fax 0284/51-519. 17 apts. TEL

Rates: 14,400 Drs ($60) for two; 23,000 Drs ($95.85) for four.

Located near the Hotel Calypso, these apartments are handsomely furnished with marble-top tables and colorful furniture. The neighborhood is quiet and the sea views are lovely. The larger apartments have two bathrooms. (Contact Nissiotissa Tours for reservations.)

Lily Apartments, Náoussa, Páros 84401. ☎ **0284/51-377.** Fax 0284/51-716. (Athens, ☎ or fax **01/95-89-314.**) 17 apts.

Rates: 14,400 Drs ($60) for two. EC, MC, V.

Lily Ananiadou has our favorite apartments: simple, pleasantly modern, fully equipped—with kitchens, telephones, and balconies overlooking dry, scrub-brush hills.

Two Splurge Choices

Astir of Páros, Kolymbithros Beach, Páros 84401. ☎ **0284/51-797.** Fax 0284/51-985. 15 rms (4 with handicapped access), 42 junior suites, 4 executive suites. A/C MINIBAR TV TEL

Rates: 26,450 Drs ($110.20) single; 46,000 Drs ($191.65) double; suites from 56,350 Drs ($234.80). AE, DC, EC, MC, V.

Built like a traditional Cycladic village, this hotel has sumptuous gardens, a pool, three-hole golf course, jacuzzi, tennis court, gym, and art gallery. The elegant reception area displays contemporary Greek art. The staff is attentive, the rooms are spacious, and there's a private beach.

Hotel Contaratos Beach, Ághii Anárghyri Beach, Náoussa, Páros 84401. ☎ **0284/51-693** or **01/49-13-530** in Athens. Fax 0284/51-740. 33 rms (all with bath). TEL

Rates (including breakfast): 17,800 Drs ($74.40) single; 26,575 Drs ($110.70) double. EC, MC, V.

One of the best on Páros, with rooms (most with balconies) that have large bathrooms with bathtubs, good reading lights, and views to Ághii Anárghyri beach. There's a large swimming pool and sun deck, a tennis court, a private beach, and water sports.

WHERE TO EAT

Náoussa's main square has most of the casual eating establishments in the area. Go past the church near Christo's Taverna to find the village's **bread bakery.** The **Náoussa**

Pâtisserie has moved across the street. Delicious snacks of cheese pies, biscuits, espresso, and pastries can be consumed in the shaded outdoor café, often for less than 550 Drs ($2.30). Unfortunately, the fast-food-pizza-sandwich–ice cream shops have proliferated in Náoussa as elsewhere, so you'll have plenty of choices for a snack or breakfast.

Taverna Christo's, Archilochus Street, Náoussa. ☎ **51-442.**

Cuisine: EURO-GREEK. **Reservations:** Recommended during July–Aug.
Prices: Appetizers 350–1,050 Drs ($1.45–$4.35), main courses 980–2,875 Drs ($4.10–$11.95). No credit cards.
Open: Daily 7:30–11:30pm.

Taverna Christo's is known for its eclectic menu and Euro-Greek style. Dinner is served in a beautiful garden filled with red and pink geraniums. The trellised roof is dripping with grape clusters whose dark purple color in late August is unforgettable. You can listen to classical music while dining on elegantly prepared, freshly made veal, lamb, or steak dishes.

Barbarossa Ouzerí, Náoussa. ☎ **51-391.**

Cuisine: GREEK.
Prices: Appetizers 450–1,050 Drs ($1.90–$4.35). No credit cards.
Open: Daily 1pm–1am.

Right on the harbor, this local *ouzerí* is proof that there are still enough local Greek citizens in town to support an authentic *ouzerí*. Old, windburned fishers sit for hours nursing their milky ouzos (this clear firewater turns white when you add water) and their miniportions of grilled octopus and olives. Try it, if you haven't had time in your busy schedule for an afternoon or evening lounging at an *ouzerí*.

★ **Kavarnis Bar,** Archilochus Street, Náoussa. ☎ **51-038.**

Cuisine: CONTINENTAL.
Prices: Crêpes 860–1,725 Drs ($3.60–$7.20), pasta 1,050–2,300 Drs ($4.35–$9.60). No credit cards.
Open: Daily 7:30pm–2am.

This beautiful bar, just around the corner from the post office, has an interior that reminds you of another time, of Paris in the 1920s or an American private clubhouse from the 1940s. The menu is crêpes stuffed with everything from fruit to meat to ice cream! Try the famous Cognac Crêpe. The restaurant also serves elaborate cocktails with some modern jazz.

Lalula, Náoussa. ☎ **51-547.**

Cuisine: GREEK/VEGETARIAN/MEDITERRANEAN. **Reservations:** Recommended during July–Aug.
Prices: Appetizers 920–1,600 Drs ($3.85–$6.70), main courses 1,600–2,875 Drs ($6.70–$11.95). No credit cards.
Open: Daily 7–11:45pm.

Down from the Minoa Hotel is this venture of two chefs favored by past readers who loved their Tria Asteria Restaurant. Ruth and Siggi, skillful German restaurateurs, feature a more health-conscious, vegetarian-oriented menu than one usually finds in Greece. Their specials change daily to reflect what's fresh at the market. Two daily soups, Greek *mezédes* (appetizers), vegetable quiche, sweet-and-sour chicken with rice and ginger chutney, and fish steamed in herbs are some of the regular items.

Minoa Restaurant, Minoa Hotel, Náoussa. ☎ **51-309.**

Cuisine: GREEK.
Prices: Appetizers 300–800 Drs ($1.25–$3.35), main courses 980–2,875 Drs ($4.10–$11.95). No credit cards.
Open: Daily 7:30am–midnight.

Located uphill from the village square, the Minoa is actually one of Náoussa's best tavernas. A feast of rich, old-fashioned Greek fare steeped in olive oil and oregano, with fresh bread and wine will cost about $20 for two.

Pervolaria, Náoussa. ☎ **51-721.**

Cuisine: GREEK.
Prices: Appetizers 350–1,100 Drs ($1.45–$4.60), main courses 1,100–3,100 Drs ($4.60–$12.95). AE, V.
Open: Daily 7pm–midnight.

About 109 yards from the port are tables set in a lush garden of geraniums and grapes, or inside a whitewashed stucco house decorated with local ceramics. Favorite courses here include the schnitzel à la chef (veal in cream sauce with tomatoes and basil) and the tortellini Pervolaria (with pepperoni and bacon), both original, but the Greek plate with souvlaki and varied appetizers is also popular.

EVENING ENTERTAINMENT

If holding hands while strolling under the stars doesn't fill up your evening, you can take in an outdoor B-picture at the **Makis Cinema** (☎ **21-676** or **22-221**). Nightly shows are usually at 10pm and midnight and cost 1,000 Drs ($4.15). If you had something a little more active in mind, try the **Paracato Disco** (☎ **51-108**) or the **Banana Moon.** Both are a ten-minute walk up the hill on the main street of Náoussa and they are right next door to each other.

Around the Island

If your time is limited, rent a moped or car pool for a one-day, around-the-island tour. Single travelers may find it more economical to book one of the bus tours offered by several local travel agents for 2,500 Drs ($10.40). **Páros Travel** (☎ **0284/21-582,** fax 22-582) is one choice with a variety of tours that cost from 1,700 to 3,400 Drs ($7.20–$14.35).

WHAT TO SEE & DO

A day of sightseeing around the island of Páros should begin in Paroikía, include Petaloúdes and a visit to a beach such as Kolymbíthres on the way north, then a stop in Náoussa for a seafood lunch at the picturesque harbor. From Náoussa, the tour continues south to one of the finest east coast beaches, such as Ormós Mólos. On the return trip across the heartland of Páros to Paroikía, stops should be made at Lefkés, the medieval capital, and at the marble quarries of Maráthi.

PETALOÚDES The valley of Petaloúdes (butterflies) is a lush oasis of pear, plum, fig, and pomegranate trees four miles from Paroikía. Taking the beach road out of town, continue for about 2½ miles until the left-hand turnoff for the monastery of Christos tou Dassous (Christ of the Forest), which has been a nunnery since 1805. Then, head a little over a half mile downhill to what Greeks call *Psychopiana*—the place to lighten the heart and mind—and we couldn't have put it better. Kóstas Graváris opens his home daily from 8am to 8pm, closing it for siesta from 1pm to 4pm.

He recommends coming in the early morning or evening, when the butterflies leave the ivy leaves they cling to and fly around. The butterflies, genus *Panaxia quadripunctaria poda,* look like black-and-white-striped arrowhead flowers when they relax in the shade. When they fly, you can see their bright-red undersides. As at Petaloúdes in Rhodes, the butterflies are born and die here (they're most numerous from July 15 to August 15). The unique combination on this arid island of a freshwater spring, dense foliage, flowering trees, and cool shade is what has lured the butterflies here for at least 300 years (since the Gravaris family has had this property). They run a small snack bar at the site; the butterfly keeper's fee is 700 Drs ($2.90). Donkey trips to Petaloúdes cost 1,700 Drs ($7.20).

LEFKÉS Head south from Náoussa to Marpissa, then take the westward inland road to Paroikía, a pleasant change from the hot and dusty coastal route. After winding through ancient olive groves and well-tended farmland, it begins to ascend steep hills. When the road levels out, you've come to the perimeter of Lefkés. The amphitheatrical tiers of whitewashed houses with red-tiled roofs surround a central town square. It's said that Lefkés, medieval capital of Páros, was built in the hills so that if pirates ever reached Lefkés, its sharply angled, narrow streets and confusing levels would thwart them. Even today, trying to reach the famed Aghía Triáda (Holy Trinity) Church, whose carved marble towers are easily visible from a distance, is a feat.

MARBLE QUARRIES AT MARÁTHI Parian marble, prized for its translucency and soft, granular texture, was used by ancient sculptors for their best works, including the *Hermes* by Praxiteles and the *Venus de Milo.* The marble quarries at Maráthi are the last stop on the return trip to Paroikía; to reach them, take the winding mountain roads about three miles west of Lefkés, where the tiny farming community of Maráthi lives on a plateau. From the road, walk up to the left beyond the few farmhouses toward the deserted buildings that once belonged to a French mining company. In 1844, the firm had brought out enough marble from this site to construct Napoleon's tomb. If not for the prohibitive cost, modern-day sculptors could still work with this incomparable material.

Continue 1.3 miles farther to the village of Kóstos; perched above it you'll find **Studio Yria (☎ 29-007)**, where local craftsmen Stelio and Monika Ghikis produce functional earthenware incorporating the octopus motif (John loved the large serving platters with this abstract pattern) and other indigenous designs, as well as weaving and objects of cast bronze, forged iron, and Parian marble.

WESTERN COAST BEACHES South from Paroikía, along the west coast, which faces the island of Antíparos, are several fine beaches. Just two miles from the port is **Aghía Iríni.** This secluded sandy beach cove is visible from the elevated main road just before the turnoff for Petaloúdes. At Aghía Iríni you'll find a taverna, the **Aghía Iríni Campgrounds (☎ 0284/22-340)**, and a handful of palm trees. Another ten minutes south by moped is the turnoff for **Pounda,** a popular sandy beach with many rental rooms that gets crowded in July and August. Pounda is located at the narrowest stretch of the Aegean between Páros and Antíparos. Here you can sit in a café and examine Antíparos's main port.

About 12½ miles south of Paroikía is **Alíki,** a charming fishing village turned tourist resort. Tucked around a large clean sandy beach cove are discos, cafés, and many new, prefab buildings (with more to come). Yet, many hand-built caiques are moored in the small natural harbor.

There are many rooms by this friendly port. (Buses run hourly from Paroikía, but they're sometimes unreliable.) The first choice would be the **Hotel Angeliki** (☎ **0284/91-235**), a 13-room Class C place at the far end of the town's pier. Doubles with private bath are 6,500 Drs ($26.95) in the summer; singles are 5,200 Drs ($21.55). All the balconies have beautiful views of the busy port and beach.

Alíki's other pension is the **Aphroditi** (☎ **0284/91-249**) on the road into town and managed by the friendly Aliprantis family. Their 20 modern spacious rooms with balconies are spotless and simply furnished; doubles with bath are 6,900 Drs ($28.75).

Many shops and the **general store** (where you park your vehicle, since you have to walk through most of the town) also have rooms to let.

NORTHERN COAST BEACHES The north coast beaches, hugging the two peninsulas that jut into St. Demetrios Bay around the village of Náoussa, are the best on the island. To the west of Náoussa, 600 Drs ($2.50) for a caique or about ten minutes by moped, is the picturesque **Kolymbíthres Beach.** Small sandy coves are punctuated by smooth, giant rocks, which must be scaled or swum around to reach the next cove or the open sea. Reminiscent of the weird rocks that jut forth into the air above Metéora, this lunar seascape is well worth a visit even for those who can't stand sparkling azure water and golden sand. Nearby is the very attractive **Hotel Kouros** (☎ **0284/51-565,** fax 51-000). Its 55 spacious, full-amenity rooms are often booked by German tour groups, but it's very close to a narrow beach (about a ten-minute walk from the lunarscape of Kolymbíthres). Doubles rent for 13,750 Drs ($57.30) per night; AE, EC, MC, V are accepted. For eating we recommend the **Dolphin Taverna,** about 109 yards from the Kouros; it's open from 7am to 2am for traditional Greek food; dinner for two with wine will cost about 6,000 Drs ($25). **Camping Naoussa** (☎ **0284/51-595**) has amenities 54$^1/_2$ yards from the beach; tent sites are free and camp guests pay 1,100 Drs ($4.60) each; tents can be rented for 700 Drs ($2.90).

North of Kolymbíthres, by the Ághios Ioánnis Church, is **Monastery Beach,** the north coast's nudist beach, and the new **Monastiri Beach Club.** In this secluded cove bathers clothed and unclothed enjoy the calm waters. West of Náoussa beaches are often more populated because of new hotels along the roads of this peninsula. **Ághii Anárghyri** is a good example; it's a well-maintained beach but the hotels that border it provide daily crowds.

About 2$^1/_2$ miles north of Náoussa on a poorly paved road is the popular **Lageri Beach.** Before you reach Lageri, the road forks to the right. Bearing right will bring you to **Santa Maria Beach,** perhaps the most beautiful one on the island because of its purity. Shallow sand dunes (very rare in Greece) line the broad banks of fine sand that curve around the irregular coastline. Although Santa Maria is only about 20 minutes from Náoussa by public bus or moped, most tourists don't make it that far. Those who do can't miss **Aristophanes Taverna,** which now has villas for rent. In a simple, shaded outdoor deck behind the dunes, you can have grilled fish (particularly good are the foot-long *barboúnia,* red mullets) or meats, and in the cooler spring and fall weather, a daily soup. A lunch feast of fresh grilled astakos (local lobster) with wine, cheeses, and a salad will cost about 11,400 Drs ($47.50) for two of you, but you'll never forget the experience.

Nearby, the **Santa Maria Surf Club** provides windsailing gear and lessons. Check here or at Aghía Iríni, Kolymbíthres, or Logares on windsurfing lessons and equipment rental.

Southeast of Náoussa, and connected by public bus, is the beach town of **Ampélas.** Several rooms to rent are now available at this small beach, plus some inexpensive tavernas.

EASTERN COAST BEACHES The east coast beaches, equidistant from Paroikía or Náoussa, can be reached by private transport or public bus. Buses leave hourly in the summer from either village.

The east coast roadway runs about a third of a mile inland from the sea, so a window check from a moving bus can't give you a status report on crowd conditions at the beach. Choose wisely; once you've disembarked, it's several miles to the next beach. (The local beach-bum grapevine in either port town will provide the latest update.)

The beautiful beach at **Ormós Mólos,** on a small peninsula near the village of Marpissa, is the closest, and therefore the most crowded. **Píso Livádi,** about six miles from either Paroikía or Náoussa, is a small sandy beach cove surrounded by hotels and pizza parlors; the village feels crowded even when there's no one in sight. The shallow harbor makes an unappealing swimming hole in full view of the overtouristed town. The next cove south, **Logares,** has started to feel Píso Livádi's crowds. **Camping Kafkis** (☎ **0284/41-479**) is the closest tent rest to these small beaches.

There is a universal consensus on the best beach-for-beach's sake: **Chryssí Aktí,** (Golden Coast) on Páros's east coast, is 15 1/2 miles south of Náoussa. The community is about half a mile off the paved main road, with a parking lot at the end for beach commuters. At the parking lot, the **Golden Beach Hotel** (☎ **0284/41-194,** fax 41-195) has 35 Class C rooms with views over the almost mile and a half stretch of fine golden sand; doubles run 12,000 Drs ($50.30). Next door is the newer, 38-room **Amarilis Hotel** (☎ **0284/41-410,** fax 41-600), where private-bath doubles cost 15,000 Drs ($63.75). There are tavernas and rooms-to-let near the beach, but most visitors head south 1 1/2 miles to the newly created village of **Drios,** which has sprung up just to deal with tourists. The **Julia Hotel** (☎ **0284/41-494**) has 12 rooms with doubles for 6,400 Drs ($26.85) near the small pebble beach. The very nice **Hotel Annezina** (☎ **0284/41-037**) has 13 double rooms with bath, at 6,900 Drs ($28.75) each, and a good restaurant in the center of tiny bustling Dríos. It's wedged in next to a good supermarket, by the bus stop, and near the popular **Anchor Tavern.** Buses run to Dríos from Paroikía five times daily, hourly in the summer.

AN EXCURSION TO ANTÍPAROS

A visit to Antíparos is popular with today's tourists who want to get away from all the crowds in Paroikía. This seven-mile-long island, just anti, or "opposite," the western coast of Páros, was once connected to it by a natural causeway. For centuries its huge cave drew distinguished tourists who otherwise had little reason to go to Páros. King Otto of Greece and Lord Byron visited the cave and carved their names in the many stalagmites and stalactites.

Tourists who arrive on the excursion caiques from Paroikía no longer descend the 98 yards into the cave by rope—a safer cement staircase has been built. Nonetheless, an hour spent in the dark, echo-filled cave trying to decipher some of the inscriptions is a lot more adventuresome than sitting on a beach (and makes for good storytelling long afterward).

Excursion caiques leave the port of Paroikía regularly beginning at 8am for the 45-minute ride to the busy port of Antíparos. Round-trip excursions that include a visit to the caves (about a two-hour walk from the village of Antíparos) cost 2,750 Drs ($11.40) from Paroikía, and 1,375 Drs ($5.70) from Náoussa. When you dock, you'll have to climb the hill to the church of St. John of the Cave. From here you'll have an excellent view south to Folégandros (farthest west), Síkinos, and Íos, with a bit of Páros to your left. There are also local shuttle boats ferrying the channel between Pounda and Antíparos continuously from 9am. The fare is 250 Drs ($1.10).

WHERE TO STAY There are two flights daily from Athens. Besides the several pensions and rooms-to-let, the newer **Hotel Artemis** (☎ **0284/61-460,** fax 61-472) at the end of the *paralía,* has 30 comfortable rooms; a double with breakfast is 11,500 Drs ($47.90). The **Mantalena** (☎ **0284/61-206**) has 35 rooms, with doubles from 6,325 Drs ($26.35). There's also a **campground** (☎ **0284/61-221**) with full facilities about a ten-minute walk north from the port. The official campground is on an excellent beach, but free camping (if litter-free) is condoned on all the beaches at the north tip of the island. Another popular beach, small but well protected, is at Apantima opposite Alíki on Páros's western coast.

5 Náxos

103 nautical miles SE of Piraeus

ARRIVING/DEPARTING There is one boat daily to and from Piraeus, Santoríni, Íos, Páros, and Mýkonos, as well as once daily catamaran service to Piraeus. You can connect to Rafína by car ferry Tuesday through Sunday. There are three ferries weekly to Sýros, twice to Amorgós, and four weekly ferries to Ághios Nikólaos, Crete. The Crete-bound boat continues on to Kássos, Kárpathos, and Rhodes. The sea can be choppy; we prefer the faster, thrice-weekly hydrofoils. Call 22-993, the Piraeus (☎ **01/45-11-311**), or the Náxos Port Authority (☎ **0285/22-340**) for information.

ESSENTIALS There's no official tourist information; the commercial **Náxos Tourist Information Center** (☎ **0285/22-923** or **24-525**, fax 25-200), across from the ferry pier, is run by Despina and Kostas Kitini. Their informative office (bus and boat schedules are posted outside) makes them the most reliable and helpful information service on the island. They sell Olympic Airways and ferry boat tickets, book island excursions, make hotel and villa reservations, exchange money, hold luggage, and will help you make card and collect phone calls!

The Telecommunications Organization of Greece **(OTE)** is at the south end of the port; summer hours are daily 7:30am to midnight. Turn inland at OTE, take the first right and find the **post office** on the left; it's open 8am to 2:30pm. The **tourist police station** (☎ **22-100**) is two blocks behind the Panatanassa Church, about 200 meters from the dock; there's a list of hotels and private rooms there, and they'll make reservations for you. Náxos has a **medical clinic** (☎ **22-356**), but for serious problems contact the police. Banks all keep the same hours—8am to 2pm Monday through Thursday, 8am to 1:30pm Friday—but travel agents change money during extended work hours. Newspapers can be found on the street behind the *paralía* (harbor front).

You can attack Náxos in two ways. If you relish verdant valleys, craggy peaks, and isolated mountain villages, hike along the island's trails and backcountry roads. If you're an inveterate café hopper, museum hound, or shopper, center your activities around the port and the lovely walled Venetian *kástro* (fortress) that overlooks the harbor and sea.

To learn more about the island, read John Freely's *Náxos* (Lycabettus Press), a short, colorful account with excellent descriptions of walking tours. Also, be sure to try three of Náxos's specialties: *kefalotíri,* a superb sharp cheese, *graviera,* a milder one, and *citron,* a sweet liqueur made from oranges and lemons.

Orientation

Boats arrive at the harbor on the northern end of Náxos in the main town, called **Náxos,** or **Chóra.** Along the harbor are two of the town's most notable landmarks. South of the pier, built on a tiny islet nestled in the harbor, is the whitewashed **Myrtidiótissa Church.** On the north side of the port, to the left as you disembark, is the unfinished yet perfect **temple of Apollo.** The temple is built on another islet and is connected to the mainland by a narrow causeway. Rising from this rocky site is the Portara (which means "Great Door"), a gargantuan post-and-lintel opening made of tan-colored Naxian marble. This ancient portal, practically all that's left of the temple, is Náxos's best known monument—a grand doorway that has welcomed visitors to the island for over 2,500 years.

If you set off in an easterly direction you'll visit Grotta, Bourgo, and Fountana, which are the oldest quarters in Náxos town. **Grotta** abuts the northern coast of Chóra. This section has just undergone a major transformation, from a sleepy neighborhood to a resort hosting a fresh crop of oceanfront villas and hotels. **Bourgo** and **Fountana** are picturesque districts filled with two- and three-story homes covered in gardenias and bougainvillea. These two areas surround the island's most captivating structure—the 13th-century Venetian **kástro.** Isolated from the town below by an imposing wall, the *kástro* is a magnificent medieval town-within-a-town.

The southern half of Chóra, leading down to the beachfront resort of **Ághios Gheórghios,** is where you'll find most of the town's hotels, restaurants, and tourist services. The most direct way to reach Chóra's south side is to walk down the *paralía,* the café- and souvenir-lined lane that overlooks the Náxos harbor.

Getting Around

Walking Náxos's trails and back roads brings you face to face with the island's hospitable inhabitants. Exchanging a simple *mera* (shortened form of *kaliméra,* "good day") with a passing farmer, listening to the metallic clanging of a goat's bell, or breathing the lemon-scented air from a nearby grove is what visiting Greece is all about. Náxos is ideal for this kind of travel, because the most interesting parts of the island are no more than a half-day walk from Chóra. And the scenery within this relatively small area is remarkably varied.

If you plan to walk around the interior section of the island, particularly in the Traghea region, conserve your energy by taking a short **bus trip** from Chóra to Chalkí, Filóti, or Apíranthos. There's service five to six times daily; check with the helpful KTEL office at the north end of the port. Buses leave from the nearby terminal. There's hourly service to Ághios Prokópios and the beach at Aghía Anna. Fares run from 230 to 400 Drs (95¢–$1.70). Most other destinations have buses running only two or three times a day. One of the most popular day trips is a visit to Apóllonas on the northern end of the island. However, the bus travels this route only twice a day, and a one-way journey takes 2¼ hours. Competition for seats on the Apóllonas-bound bus is fierce, so your best bet is to get on the bus as early as possible. It's a long ride, especially if you have to stand the entire way.

Although it's possible to tour the island by bus, you may find its inefficiency more than you can bear, particularly if you intend to visit fairly remote spots. A **moped** or **motorcycle** is an ideal way of getting around. **Stelios Rent-A-Bike** (☎ **24-703**), near the police station, has a good selection; rates are 3,500–6,900 Drs ($14.60–$28.75) per day, including insurance. Remember to check that your bike is in good running order before taking it. Náxos has some major mountains to cross, requiring a strong motor and good brakes.

Those traveling in a group of three or four, or with a few drachmas to burn, might consider exploring the island by Jeep. Most travel agents rent them; we recommend **ZAS Travel** (☎ **23-330,** fax 23-419), near the ferry dock, rents buggies, cars, and Suzukis for 9,200 to 15,650 Drs ($38.30–$65.20) per day. For this price you get full insurance, free mileage and road service, a map, and good advice.

If you're on Náxos for only one day and you want to see everything, consider hiring a **taxi,** ☎ **22-444.** Náxos is filled with cabs, and you can hire one for a half-day-around-the-island tour for about 12,500 Drs ($52.10), less than a full-day car rental—and a guide is included. Make sure you bargain with the cabbie and set a price. Each taxi can hold up to four people.

What to See & Do

Náxos is renowned for its scenic treasures. The Traghéa region and Apóllonas have been so celebrated throughout time that only the Olympian gods could have created such a wondrous landscape. There are equally beautiful beaches. However, the island's two most fascinating sights are located right in Chóra.

ATTRACTIONS IN CHÓRA

Chóra's most exquisite monument is the Venetian kástro, a medieval citadel that overlooks, and is quite separate from, the town below. The kástro's once-secure walls are crumbling in spots, but even their modest deterioration lends a sense of aged grandeur. Behind these ramparts is a maze of rising and falling streets. Narrow alleyways and whitewashed steps, long ago attached to shops and homes, now lead only to the sky.

Artists, writers, craftsmen, as well as the descendants of the kástro's original Venetian occupants, live in majestic Renaissance-era mansions—many still bear the crest of the family that built them. The kástro was built on what was probably the ancient Mycenaean acropolis. In the 13th century, Marco Sanudo, nephew of a Venetian doge, made Náxos the capital of the duchy of the Archipelago—Venice's claim to the Aegean islands. The kástro was established as the seat of power and from there St. Mark's Republic ruled the islands for more than 300 years.

Wandering through the dizzying array of streets will invariably bring you past the kástro's major buildings, all built during the Venetian and Turkish occupations. One of the most interesting is the so-called French School, founded in 1627 for both Roman Catholic and Greek Orthodox students. Among them was the Cretan writer Nikós Kazantzákis, who studied there in 1896. Nikós's studies were cut short when his father pried him out of the school, fearing that his son was being indoctrinated by "papist dogs."

The school is no more, having been converted into the island's **archeological museum** (open from 8:45am to 3pm daily, 9:30 to 2:30 Sunday, closed Tuesday); admission is 250 Drs ($1.10). The museum is a treasury of early Cycladic pottery, sculpture, and religious knickknacks. A short walk around the corner will bring you to a 13th-century Roman Catholic church, and farther on, to the main tower of Sanudo's original fortress/palace.

The **temple of Apollo** is Chóra's second grand attraction. Archeologists assume that the temple is dedicated to Apollo from only a scant reference in the Delian Hymns. If you visit the temple on a very clear day, Délos will be visible far to the north. For hundreds of years it was thought that the temple was dedicated to Dionysus, the island's patron deity.

BEACHES

Some of Náxos's best beaches are near the main town. **Ághios Gheórghios,** a ten-minute walk from Chóra, is considered the town beach, lined with hotels and restaurants and jammed with tourists. These days, most people head south via foot, bus, or caique for the clean sandy beaches at **Ághios Prokopios** and **Aghía Anna.**

Ághios Prokopios is a broader, cleaner, longer, fine sand beach with many pensions and tavernas built along the road, away from the sand. The **Hotel Kavoúras** (☎ **0285/23-963**) is one of the many rooming options. A double with private bath is 7,000 Drs ($29.15), and studios for four are 9,000 Drs ($37.50). The lovely new **Ostria Hotel** has 16 studios, 12,000 Drs ($50) for a double. **Kavouras Restaurant,** open 8am to midnight, at the town bus stop, has good food at reasonable prices.

Aghía Anna, the next cove south, is much smaller, with a small port for the colorful caiques that transport beachgoers from the main port. **Hotel Kapri** (☎ **0285/23-799,** fax 24-736) has 36 rooms and 12 studios; doubles with private bath are 6,900 Drs ($28.75) and studios are 9,200 Drs ($38.33). Minibus service to Náxos town is available several times a day. The **Iria Beach Hotel** (☎ **0285/24-022,** fax 24-656) has 21 apartments at 8,050 Drs ($33.55) for two, 9,200 Drs ($38.35) for three; there's also a restaurant, minimarket, and change bureau. **Taverna Gorgona** (☎ **23-799**), at the pier where the caiques dock, has an excellent buffet dinner daily, with fresh grilled fish and meat, salads, vegetables, and complimentary wine.

Midway (16km from Náxos town) is Kastráki Beach, with waters recently rated the cleanest in the Aegean and a 7km stretch of beach. The **Summerland Complex** (☎ **0285/75-461,** fax 75-399) has 12 studios for 17,135 Drs ($71.40) and three apartments for 23,000 Drs ($95.85), a pool, snack bar, tennis courts, workout rooms, and minimarket.

Both beaches have windsurfing and are ideal day trips, but not for those seeking nighttime activities. **Camping Maragas** (☎ **24-552**) is a good facility at Aghía Anna. **Camping Apollon** (☎ **24-117**) is closer to Chóra and inland, but has modern facilities and space for RVs.

Both Ághios Prokopios and Aghía Anna are accessible over dirt roads by public bus in the high season, when school-year buses take over summertime vacation routes. They run almost hourly from Chóra and cost 290 Drs ($1.20). Aghía Anna, which has a pier, is also serviced by caiques from the small caique port in Chóra. They run hourly from 9:30am to 5:30pm and cost about 600 Drs ($2.50) each way. From Aghía Anna it's a ten-minute walk north to Ághios Prokopios.

For the true connoisseur the best beach on the island is south of Aghía Anna, known by Naxians as **Pláka beach.** To get there, take the summer-only caique from the harbor in Chóra, or from its stop at Aghía Anna, and instead of walking north (toward Ághios Prokopios), head south. There you'll find a 5-km stretch of almost completely uninhabited shoreline. It's ideal for nude sunbathing.

The large protected bay at **Pyrgáki** and **Agiassos,** about 20 km south of Chóra, is considered the best swimming area on Náxos. There's no local transportation, so you'll have to take a moped or private car.

ATTRACTIONS AROUND THE ISLAND

Although many tourists travel the distance to **Apóllonas** (especially to stay overnight), it's a wearing journey if you're traveling by bus or moped. A more civilized day trip is to visit Traghéa, a region including the inland villages of Chalkí, Filóti, and especially Apíranthos. The busy road leading from Chóra to Chalkí bisects well-cultivated farmland shrouded by bamboo windbreaks. Horn-tooting taxis and buses speed out of town, often narrowly missing an overloaded donkey and its master.

TRAGHÉA The road continues past **Káto Sangrí,** a small village distinguished by an abandoned Venetian mansion that stands high on a barren hill. From Káto Sangrí to Chalkí, marking the beginnings of the Traghéa region, the landscape takes on a surreal quality. Mésa Potamiá, a series of dangerous-looking spiked peaks, lie to the north, and huge, flat stones shaped like cut tiles line the valley floor. The landscape looks decidedly Martian in the glow of the pink late-afternoon light. The blazing summer sun drives up temperatures to extremes, so the approach to **Chalkí** comes as a relief (particularly for those traveling by foot or moped). The outskirts of town are resplendent with sweet-smelling lemon and shady olive trees, highlighted by the chanting cicadas hidden in flowering oleanders.

Chalkí was the region's commercial center and features two 18th-century Venetian *pírgoi* (a cross between a stately mansion or castle and a fortified outpost). Turn right at Panaghía Prothónis, a lovely church that's almost always closed, and walk along the ancient cobblestone road. The first *pírgos* is to your right, a white marble crest advertising the year it was built, 1742. Be sure to climb the worn marble steps. There's a picture-perfect view of the Filóti, one of the largest inland villages, which sweeps down the mountainside like an overturned can of whitewash. Chalkí's other *pírgos* is on the far end of town (toward Filóti), behind a grove of olive trees.

As you head to Filóti, near the hamlet of **Keramio,** atop an anonymous peak, sits a lone whitewashed church, small and round in form, perfect in relation to man, mountain, and sky.

Filóti has classically Cycladic cube-shaped homes with pastel shutters and red tiled roofs. The town rises steeply from the *platía* (square) along the road to the silver-domed church, with its primitive-style figures adorning a three-pronged steeple. If you climb a few steps beyond the church and turn right, you'll tour the upper town and dead-end at a pirgos dated 1718. Filóti has two tavernas and many private rooms to rent.

If there were a beauty contest among the inland towns of Náxos, **Apíranthos** would win hands down. This richly endowed hill town overlooks perfectly stepped vineyards and deep green valleys. The houses, dating from the 18th and 19th centuries, combine Venetian and Cycladic styles. If the homes strike you as ornate, it's because Apíranthos was once home to Náxos's wealthiest class, emery-mine owners. Most of the mines have closed and many of the houses are deserted, but the town maintains a regal air. There's a small museum near the central *platía* containing early Cycladic marble idols and some very old and primitive folk ceramics.

The road from Apíranthos to Apóllonas is curvy in the extreme. **Koronos** and **Skado** are both gorgeous mountain villages and are the only towns of note along the way. The road is lined on both sides with honeysuckle-scented yellow broom that grows so thickly that it brushes passing cars like towels at a car wash.

APÓLLONAS A motor-coach view of Traghéa can be had throughout the course of a visit to Appollonas. A day trip to this northern coast port, 54 km from Náxos town, is a popular excursion because it gives you ample introduction to the scenic wonders of the island's interior on the way to an interesting archeological site. Many of the small mountain villages along the route have their own points of interest, principally from the Venetian period, but the island's historical highlight is at Apóllonas. Here, in an abandoned marble quarry about a 15-minute walk above town, lies a famous 30-foot-tall statue sculpted in a rigid frontal pose that was never completed. Archeologists date it to the 7th century B.C. and some presume that he was intended for the huge temple of Apollo which stood at this tip of the island. He is sometimes simply called a *kouros* (young man) but his beard indicates that he is neither, but probably the island's patron, Dionysus. He lies lifeless in the chiseled marble rock face from which he was hewn—the long crack across his nose is possibly the reason why he was left here—and with his eroded strong torso and flexed feet he looks like Frankenstein awaiting the breath of life.

The petit fishing port of Apóllonas has a sandy cove and a larger pebble cove ideal for swimming and bathing, which are, however, in full view of the modest town. The friendly villagers offer rooms to let, many with private baths, for about 6,000 Drs ($24). The **Hotel Kouros** (☎ **0285/81-340**) is a hospitable, well-maintained hotel on the pebble beach at the far end of town; doubles are currently 7,500 Drs ($31.15).

With so many day-trippers the port has a profusion of restaurants, cafés, and snack bars. At the café on the corner along the harbor they serve locally brewed *citron* as well as *kefalotíri,* the hard, sharp cheese we recommend.

Where to Stay

Chóra's long, broad *paralía,* so popular for an evening *vólta* (stroll), is traffic-filled, overrun by cafés, and overpriced. Instead, we've recommended some hotels in other areas, all within a ten-minute walk of the port. Grotta, the cliffside area northeast of the port that's becoming very developed, offers tranquility, wonderful views of Chóra and the sea, and a small pebble beach for swimming. The picturesque Bourgo quarter below the Kástro has a few smaller hotels nestled in its winding back streets. Ághios Gheórghios, the town's sand beach south of the port, has many recently built hotels that are a good value, though this area gets very busy with day trippers, especially in July and August.

IN GROTTA

Hotel Anna, Chóra, Náxos 84300. ☎ **0285/22-475.** 9 rms (all with bath). MINIBAR

Rates: 9,200 Drs ($38.35) double. No credit cards.

The tiny Class E Hotel Anna is across from Panaghía Chryssopolítissa. Each of the hotel's homey rooms has a unique character—the result of hostess Anna Glezos and daughter Eleni's loving hands.

$ **Hotel Grotta,** Chóra, Náxos 84300. ☎ **0285/22-215.** Fax 0285/22-000. 20 rms (all with bath). TEL

Rates (including breakfast): 8,800 Drs ($36.65) single; 13,000 Drs ($54.15) double.

This modern hotel overlooking the bay of Grotta on the coast road is an excellent value. The host, Mr. Lianos, is gracious to a fault, and he and his family run a sparkling inn. And if you call ahead the owner will pick you up at the ferry. Spotless rooms have polished marble floors and large balconies. Even if you go just to look at a room, you'll have a hard time leaving without accepting Mr. Lianos's offer of a shot glass of *citron.*

IN BOURGO

Our Bourgo district recommendations are most easily reached by following the arrows to the Anixis Hotel, once you've left the port by the lane next to the small square with the Port Authority building on it.

Hotel Anixis, Chóra, Náxos 84300. ☎ **0285/22-112.** 16 rms (12 with bath).

Rates: 5,175 Drs ($21.55) single/double without bath, 8,600 Drs ($35.95) single/double with bath. No credit cards.

Located one block east of the kástro's large Venetian tower, the Hotel Anixis deserves praise for its effective signage. It's a contemporary-looking place with comfortable, twin-bedded rooms on two levels sharing a long balcony. The common facilities are clean.

Hotel Panorama, Chóra, Náxos 84300. ☎ **0285/24-404.** 16 rms (10 with bath).

Rates (including breakfast): 5,200 Drs ($21.55) single, 8,000 Drs ($33.55) double without bath; 9,200 Drs ($38.35) double with bath. No credit cards.

Just across the lane from the Anixis, this stone-and-stucco hotel is a good, family-run choice for those who want to stay in Chóra's most atmospheric neighborhood, below the kástro amid whitewashed homes and twisting lanes.

★ **Chateau Zevgoli,** Chóra, Náxos 84300. ☎ **0285/22-993** (Athens, ☎ **01/65-15-885**). Fax 0285/24-525. 14 rms (all with bath).

Rates (including breakfast): 15,000 Drs ($62.50) double. V.

The recently restored Chateau Zevgoli is Bourgos's most attractive hotel. In a Naxiot fashion, the cozy rooms are built around a marble-tiled courtyard smothered in potted plants. Stucco and blue-trimmed rooms with ornately carved wood furnishings, lace curtains, and modern tiled bathrooms offer the best of both worlds.

IN ÁGHIOS GHEÓRGHIOS

From the edge of the port all the way down to the end of the sandy Ághios Gheórghios is an endless strip of hotels, bungalows, private rooms, discos, bars, and restaurants. New hotels, legal and not, are being built every day, so if you can't find a room at one of the suggested places (all near the beach), be assured that there'll be a spanking-new inn to welcome you.

Hotel Galini, Ághios Gheórghios, Chóra, Náxos 84300. ☎ **0285/22-114.** Fax 0285/24-916. 30 rms (all with bath). TEL

Rates (including breakfast): 9,000 Drs ($37.50) single, 10,800 Drs ($45) double. No credit cards.

The Galini and its sister, the **Sofia,** are both run by the wonderful Sofia (who has a great green thumb) and her amiable son George. Quiet, spotless rooms have marble floors, and balconies with sea views and cooling breezes. Transportation is provided to and from port if you have a reservation.

Hotel Glaros, Ághios Gheórghios, Chóra, Náxos 84300. ☎ **0285/23-101.** Fax 0285/24-877. 13 rms (all with bath).

Rates (including breakfast): 13,200 Drs ($55.10) single/double. AE, V.

A distinctive hotel with comfortable, shuttered rooms with balconies overlooking a pretty rock-strewn beach. Mr. Franjescos, the friendly owner, will pick you up at the port if you have a reservation.

Hotel Nissaki, Ághios Gheórghios, Chóra, Náxos 84300. ☎ **0285/25-710.** Fax 0285/23-876. 40 rms (all with bath). TEL

Rates (including breakfast): 12,800 Drs ($53.35) single; 16,000 Drs ($66.65) double. AE, DC, EC, MC, V.

The Papadopoulos family owns and operates this comfortable hotel, which has a pool and is a pleasant exception to the blur of beach hotels. Many of its large, well-furnished rooms have balconies with beach and sea views. Its large restaurant serves three meals a day at the edge of the sand, and its gift shop sells plenty of sunblock.

A SPLURGE CHOICE

Mathiassos Village Bungalows, Chóra, Náxos 84300. ☎ **0285/22-200** (in Athens, **01/29-18-749).** Fax 0285/24-700. 110 bungalows (all with bath). TV TEL

Rates (including breakfast): 15,000 Drs ($62.50) double. AE, DC, MC, V.

This resort complex provides amenities not common on Náxos. In lushly landscaped grounds, there are semiattached but private bungalows, a large swimming pool and sundeck, a tennis court, cafeteria, a taverna restaurant, and an ouzerí with gaming tables. Large bungalows come with patios, radio, and the option of TV and refrigerator; some are two-story units to accommodate families. Mathiassos Village doesn't have sea views, but there's a bus to the beach; so it's an ideal getaway vacation spot.

Where to Eat

Although Náxos isn't the wildest island in the Cyclades, there are enough excellent eateries and nightspots to satisfy gourmands and night owls alike.

Christos' Grill, Chóra. ☎ **23-072.**

Cuisine: GREEK.
Prices: Appetizers 400–920 Drs ($1.65–$3.85); main courses 1,300–2,530 Drs ($5.40–$10.55)

This small family-run taverna is one street up from the *paralía,* just off the district road (next to the church that was once a synagogue). Christos and his wife serve fresh grilled fish and meat with a large assortment of side dishes. We recommend their delicious fried Náxos potatoes!

Nikos, Paralía, Chóra. ☎ **23-153.**

Cuisine: GREEK.
Prices: Appetizers 575–1,500 Drs ($2.40–$6.30), main courses 900–2,300 Drs ($3.75–$9.60). MC, V.
Open: Daily 8am–2am.

Located above the Commercial Bank is the most popular restaurant in town, and justifiably so. The recently expanded dining room is so enormous that it resembles a suburban country-club banquet hall with a view of the harbor on one side and the old town on the other. Don't be put off though, because the real star at Níkos is the food. Try the *exochikó,* fresh lamb and vegetables cooked with fragrant spices and wrapped in crispy pastry leaves (phylla), or the barbecued fish—(the red snapper and swordfish are perfect)—lightly topped with oil and locally grown lemon. Nikos Katsayannis is himself a fisherman. Don't overlook the delightful ice-cream desserts.

Manolis Taverna, Chóra. ☎ **23-619.**

Cuisine: GREEK.
Prices: Main courses 900–1,400 Drs ($3.85–$5.85). No credit cards.
Open: Daily 6pm–1am.

Continue past the post office about 40 meters, near the Galini and Sofia Hotels, to find this casual place for good Greek fast food (very tender lamb and crisp french fries) at budget prices. It's refreshingly unpretentious.

Pizzaria Grill, Chóra. ☎ **22-083.**

Cuisine: INTERNATIONAL.
Prices: Main courses 600–1,600 Drs ($2.50–$6.70); pizza for two 1,600 Drs ($6.70). No credit cards.
Open: Daily 11am–1am.

One street back from the port, near the international newsstand, you'll find this good place for pizza, baked spaghetti, roast chicken, pork chops, stuffed eggplant, and shrimp.

Evening Entertainment

Apostolis, an ouzerí on the port near the ferry pier, is the place for a superb sunset and a leisurely sip. There are many bars and cafés, and the loud ones are, of course, easiest to find. We liked **Dolphini**—a multitiered café in Bourgo behind the Panteboy Fast Food shop on the port, where the evening begins with classical music and segues into rock easy enough for conversation. Layers of seating have been created in the hillside and landscaped with flowers. Downstairs from Florins, at the south end of the port, is the equally sophisticated **Veggera's** cocktail bar and garden (☎ **23-567**), which opens at 9pm but gets livelier nearer to its 3am closing. The **Island Bar** (☎ **22-654**), on the south end of the port, offers good rock and soul from 10pm to 3am.

The **Pâtisserie Aktaiou** on the *paralía* is the best for late-night coffee and dessert, but you'll have to fight with the hundreds of locals who come to watch the evening *vólta* (stroll) and eat their special *citron* desserts and puddings.

Dancers can try the **Ocean Club** on the road to Ághios Gheórghios, which is considered to be the best of the indoor discos. Farther down, at the south end of the beach, is **Flisvos** (☎ **22-919**), a casual surf-and-sand joint open during the day for drinks and snacks, which becomes a nightspot where volume and youth know no bounds.

6 Íos

107 nautical miles SE of Piraeus

ARRIVING/DEPARTING There are two daily boats from Piraeus; for specific departure times call the Port Authority in Piraeus (☎ **45-11-311**) or Íos (☎ **0286/91-264**). Íos is well connected to the surrounding Cycladic islands with daily service to Náxos, Páros, Mýkonos, and Santoríni; sailing three times a week to

Sýros; twice a week to Mílos and Sífnos; and two or three times a week to Folégandros, Síkinos, and Anáfi.

There is hydrofoil service daily (except Sunday) in summer connecting Íos to Mýkonos, Páros, Santoríni, and Crete. Tickets for the catamaran *Nearchos* are sold by travel agents, but if the seas are rough, it doesn't always run.

ESSENTIALS The calm, good-natured **Íos Tourist Information Office** (☎ **0286/91-028**) is a godsend. The main office at the bus stop in Chóra will help with rooms and hotels, has posted ferry schedules, sells tickets for all boat lines, and will even help you make a collect call; it's open 6am to 2am in summer. There's also an office at the port of Ghialós (☎ **0286/91-029**) open daily in the summer from 7am to 2am.

The **police station** (☎ **91-222**) is conveniently located across from the bus stop. The **post office** (open from 8am to 2pm, Monday through Friday) is a couple of blocks south of the main square; the new telephone center **(OTE)** is farther south, off the road to Milopótas Beach, up from the police station. Both keep extended summer hours. If you want to make collect calls, be aware that you can only book them through OTE 7:30am to 1pm Monday through Friday, though the OTE office is open until 10pm. For medical emergencies call **91-227.** There are three banks—all open from 8am to 2:30pm weekdays, with extended summer hours. The tourist office, most travel agencies, and many shops are also authorized to change money.

The most knowledgeable and helpful travel agents on Íos are at **Acteon Travel** (☎ **0286/91-343** or **91-318**, fax 91-088), the American Express agent located on the port square and at Milopótas beach. They usually stay open daily until 10:30pm, and will assist you with information and maps, in making calls, changing money, finding a room, booking tickets (they have an electronic airline link) and storing luggage.

Íos is an island with a reputation that it is trying hard to change. Since the 1960s, hundreds of thousands have made a pilgrimage here for the sun and sea, music and dancing, and cheap carefree living. The revelers who participate in this modern-day Dionysian carnival make Íos the celebrated Island of Youth, an electric, plugged-in rock in the Aegean.

We were dreading our last visit, having outlived our wilder days, but were pleasantly surprised to find the inhabitants responsibly involved in cooperative efforts to save their lovely island from the party animals. The quality of accommodations and food has definitely improved. The cheap (and illegal) locally brewed booze that has intoxicated and sickened so many young guests will no longer be countenanced. That doesn't, of course, mean that it will entirely vanish, so *be careful in those joints where the prices seem too good and your fellow drinkers are getting too merry too fast,* unless you're fond of throwing up or waking up with a raging hangover.

Orientation

Like many of the Cyclades, Íos is a barren, rocky island that suffers from a lack of fresh water. Today, the only foliage is in the center of the island and in the extreme north, although Homer once wrote that he'd like to be buried here, one of the most verdant of isles.

All boats dock at **Ghialós,** the port city of Íos. To the left of the pier as you alight from the ferry is a beach that tends to collect debris from the harbor, but it is certainly acceptable, especially if you're stuck in the heat waiting for a ferry. Ghialós itself has little to offer; most of the action is up the hill in **Chóra,** where you'll probably want to stay. On the other side of Chóra is highly regarded **Milopótas Beach,** far and away the most popular beach on the island. Long-term tourists quickly discover that Íos has beaches on almost every cove, indentation, or stretch of coastline; each with its own character. The biggest problem is transportation. Other than Milopótas, most other beaches must be reached by foot, moped, or caique. (Bus service is on the horizon.)

Getting Around

There is excellent bus service between the port, Chóra, and Milopótas Beach—cheap, at 150 Drs (63¢) from Ghialós to Chóra, and frequent (approximately every half hour from 8am to midnight). You can walk to these same points, but it can be very hot, especially up to Chóra from the beach (about a 30-minute walk). If you plan to walk after dark, bring a flashlight as the path is poorly lit. The island's only other bus route crosses from the port to Aghía Theodóti on the east coast; it's infrequent and runs only during July and August. Travel agents also offer a daily private red bus that conveys visitors round trip to Aghía Theodóti for 1,500 Drs ($6.25). Again, walking is an alternative, although it's about two hours away by foot.

For many years, no one wanted to or could afford to rent a moped on Íos, but that's changed. Now a small percentage of visitors pick up a moped (about 4,000 Drs or $16.70 a day) or 50cc motorbike (about 5,000 Drs or $20.80) and tear across the gravel and dirt to Ághia Theodóti, Plakátos, or the beaches at Psáthi and Maganári. **Rent A Reliable Car** (☎ **91-047**) on the south side of the port is the biggest outfit. Their rates include a tankful of gas, third-party insurance only (if you damage the bike, you pay), and an optional helmet. On an island where bars boast ONE DRINK FOR THE ROAD you should drive with extreme caution.

Kritikákis Tours (☎ **91-395**) runs a boat trip, twice daily in July and August, to Maganári beach on the south coast. Round-trip tickets cost 1,875 Drs ($7.80).

What to See & Do

The nighttime party is in Chóra's back streets. The daytime party is on **Milopótas Beach,** one of Greece's longest sandy beaches. The water is clean, and notwithstanding the usual mob scene, it's a fabulous place to spread out a towel or mat to bake under the strong Aegean sun. Perhaps 90% of those visiting Íos go no farther than Milopótas, yet the whole island is ringed with beaches. **Manganári,** on the extreme south coast, has a sandy beach, rooms to rent, a taverna, and even deluxe accommodations. You can explore the other beaches by foot or by moped. A 1½-hour walk northeast from Manganári is the lonely **Three Churches beach,** a haunt of those looking for undisturbed, private bathing. On the east coast are **Psáthi** (an hour away by moped-able dirt road) and **Aghía Theodóti,** both with beaches, food, and camping.

Of some historical interest are the swimming cove and caves at **Plakátos,** which archeologists incorrectly claimed to be Homer's tomb. You'll have to hire a boat to visit the caves at Plakátos.

Where to Stay

Íos is a mob scene in the summer: Visitors outnumber islanders 14 to 1. Literally, there used to be days when the Port Police would not allow ferry passengers to disembark on the island. The hotel scene isn't totally hopeless, for on Íos, as on most of the islands during the high season (here, a particularly apt term), you can always go to the tourist office or local travel agency to inquire about a private room. The other alternative is, of course, to make reservations; it may violate the free spirit of life on Íos but at least you'll know that you have a room. Most places open only from June to mid-September, and most charge the same for single or double rooms!

The regular police (☎ **91-222**) have a complete list of private rooms and hotels, as well as official prices for all accommodations. The friendly force is acutely aware of pricing violations, and they encourage tourists who have been overcharged to report the problem.

AT THE PORT

Now that group tours have struck Ghialós, some of the better hotels fill up early or don't even open until July when their travel agents' contracts begin. The port has one official camping spot—though people are known to camp all over when rooms are occupied—**Íos Camping Porto** (☎ **0286/91-329**). It's near the small, south side beach and fully equipped. Andréas Apostolákis, the manager, loves to exchange "real life" views and charges 750 Drs ($3.10) a night for his space by the water.

Acteon Hotel, Ghialós, Íos 84001. ☎ **0286/91-343.** Fax 0286/91-088. 15 rms (all with bath).

Prices: 6,500 Drs ($27.10) single; 8,200 Drs ($34.15) double. AE, MC, V.

Conveniently above the ever-helpful Acteon Travel agency, you'll find these good, clean, reasonably priced rooms. These rates are a bargain for last-minute arrivals, but the late-night ferries and nearby cafés can sometimes be noisy.

Hotel Mare-Monte, Ormós, Íos 84001. ☎ **0286/91-564.** 30 rms (all with bath).

Rates (including breakfast): 16,000 Drs ($66.65) single/double. V.

One of the best conventional hotels, it has double rooms with balconies and sea views, right on the town beach to the left (south) of the pier. Everything is kept clean, and the breakfast lounge is very pleasant.

Golden Sun, Ghialós-Chóra Road, Íos 84001. ☎ **0286/91-110.** 17 rms (all with bath).

Rates: 9,000 Drs ($37.50) single/double. V.

This new hotel 300 meters up from the port was the nicest, quietest place we found on our last visit. The hospitable John and Koula Kladis recently moved back home from New Jersey and wisely built this handsome place off the road and above the clamor of the port, 10 minutes along the pedestrian path from Chóra.

IN CHÓRA

In the village (which locals call "the jungle"), you can choose between a few hotels and hundreds of rooms. Visit the tourist office or police for a current "Rooms to Let" list and official prices.

Hotel Aphroditi, Chóra, Íos 84001. ☎ **0286/91-546.** 12 rms (all with bath).

Rates: 8,700 Drs ($36.25) single; 10,650 Drs ($44.40) double. No credit cards.

This hotel, on the west side of town, has modern, clean rooms, and its all marble floors lend a touch of elegance. Íos's only year-round hotel is in the middle of a hill neighborhood (opposite the big church hill) that is undergoing a lot of construction.

Francesco's, Chóra, Íos 84001. ☎ **0286/91-223.** 35 rms (30 with shower).

Rates: 2,500 Drs ($10.40) single without shower; 4,050 single with shower; 8,000 double with shower.

Francesco has renovated the "last" house in town, a 300-year-old mansion into a charming collection of rooms with a bar and several gathering places, some with splendid views. A little above the "jungle," though certainly not isolated, it made us fondly recall our first big trip to Europe.

The Hill, Chóra, Íos 84001. ☎ **0286/91-481.** 18 rms (all with bath).

Rates: 4,000 Drs ($16.75) single; 8,000 Drs ($33.35).

Some very nice, and completely sober, young Americans on their way home from Israel were pleased to show us their place across from the village, up left of the museum, police station and Rock Café 7–11 (which we heard is a good, cheap place to eat, near the OTE). New, simple, clean, and quiet. The family who owns it didn't speak much English, but they were friendly and hospitable.

AT MILOPÓTAS BEACH

Milopótas Beach is an increasingly popular place to stay, with new hotels going up at an amazing rate. Perhaps the most popular place for rock-bottom accommodations is the campground **Stars** (☎ **0286/91-302**). Petros runs this place, decked out with all the facilities any camper could possibly need: a restaurant, snack bar, disco, bar, and small market, showers, and lockers—all inexpensive! It's situated close to the beach, and the price is right, 1,200 Drs ($5) per person, 500 Drs ($2.10) per tent. They accept AE, MC, V. There's also the excellent new **Far Out Camping** (☎ **0286/91-468**) at Milopótas Beach, which has an air-conditioned restaurant and bar minimarket, kitchen facilities, handicapped-access toilets, a swimming pool, watersport facilities, an athletic center with regulation tennis, volleyball, basketball squash courts, and free transfer from the port. Waste water is treated by a state-of-the-art system and recycled to new plantings of trees and shrubs, which will beautify and cool. All this costs only 1,100 Drs ($4.60) per person, 350 Drs ($1.45) per tent; comfortable bungalows are 3,500 Drs ($14.60) per person; AE, MC, V accepted. If you find better camping facilities anywhere in Greece, please write us.

Hotel Acropolis, Milopótas, Íos 84001. ☎ **0286/91-303.** 14 rms (all with shower).

Rates: 6,750 Drs ($28.15) single/double. No credit cards.

At the top of the donkey path above the beach. All the very simple rooms have showers, and most have balconies with great views of the beach below.

Hotel Aegeon, Milopótas, Íos 84001. ☎ **0286/91-008.** Fax 0286/91392. 16 rms (all with shower).

Rates: 8,625 Drs ($35.95) single/double. V.

All the rooms have balconies and patios and are kept spotless by Elisabet and her friendly family. Rooms are simply furnished but comfortable.

Elpis Hotel, Milopótas, Íos, 84001. ☎ **0286/91-243.** 17 rms (all with shower).

Rates: 6,900 Drs ($28.75) single/double. V, MC.

At the base of the path, on the stretch of beach where New Age capitalists give hair cuts and massages, this hotel has perfectly comfortable rooms. It's in the heart of the action, therefore potentially noisy!

Far Out Hotel, Milopótas, Íos 84001. ☎ **0286/91-446** (in winter ☎ **0286/91-560**). 45 rms (all with shower). TEL

Rates: 17,250 Drs ($71.90) single/double. AE, MC, V.

Don't be put off by the name; it's only five minutes from the beach, with comfortable, beautifully appointed rooms, all with seaviews, a swimming pool, a friendly, helpful staff, and transportation to and from the port. Quite luxurious for this island.

A SPLURGE CHOICE

Hotel Íos Palace, Milopótas, Íos 84001. ☎ **0286/91-269** (in Athens **0141/37-406**). Fax 0141-37-591. 64 rms (all with bath). A/C TEL

Rates (including breakfast): 19,200 Drs ($80) single; 25,000 Drs ($104.15) double. AE, MC, V.

The island's greatest anomaly is this palatial hotel built on terraces on the steep hillside on the north end of the beach with modern, built-in furnishings, marble tile bathrooms, excellent Aegean views from private balconies, private phones, geraniums cascading down from hidden planters, and a large pool with flagstone sun deck and poolside bar. The rooms (whose rates vary according to season) get snatched up one month in advance of busy July and August; a one-night's deposit will guarantee you this bit of luxury.

Where to Eat

Food is cheaper here; restaurateurs are forced to keep prices low because so many visitors shop at grocery stores and bakeries. Anyway, most places serve pretty mediocre fare to crowds who couldn't care less. A few exceptions are:

CHÓRA

Kalypso Restaurant, Chóra. ☎ **91-120** or **91-377.**

Cuisine: GREEK/CONTINENTAL.
Prices: Appetizers 120–650 Drs (50¢–$2.70), main courses 600–1,250 Drs ($2.50–$5.50). No credit cards.
Open: Daily 5pm–1am.

Below the bend in the main road you can eat outdoors or on the more pleasant roof garden across the pedestrian lane.

The Nest, Chóra. No telephone.

Cuisine: GREEK.
Prices: Appetizers 290–520 Drs ($1.20–$2.15); main courses 600–1,400 Drs ($2.50–$5.85). No credit cards.
Open: Daily 12:30–3:30pm, 5pm–midnight, all year.

Northeast of the main square, across from the pharmacy, you'll find one of the best budget places, with big portions of well-prepared typical Greek and a little Italian food. It consistently wins approval from locals and tourists.

Pinocchio Restaurant, Chóra. ☎ **91-470.**

Cuisine: ITALIAN.
Prices: Appetizers 450–1,000 Drs ($1.90–$4.15); pizza 1,000–1,750 Drs ($4.15–$7.30); pasta 800–1,750 Drs ($3.35–$7.30). AE, MC, V.
Open: Daily 6pm–1am.

This new and rather *nouvelle* bistro is in the maze of streets between the main square and Áno Piáza. A young Scandinavian and his Greek wife bring their international experience to the meticulous preparation of Italian food.

Romantica Patisserie & Snack Bar, Chóra. ☎ **91-506.**

Cuisine: CONTINENTAL.
Prices: Snacks 80–850 Drs (45¢–$4.70). No credit cards.
Open: Daily 8am–11pm.

Two blocks over from the vehicle street, opposite a heavenly aromatic bakery, and sort of romantic; good breakfasts and snacks are served on outdoor tables.

The Mills Taverna, Chóra. ☎ **91-284.**

Cuisine: GREEK.
Prices: Appetizers 200–800 Drs (85¢–$3.35), main courses 800–2,500 Drs ($3.35–$10.40). No credit cards.
Open: Daily 6pm–midnight.

Opposite the windmills on the highest point in Chóra is where you'll find classic Greek food at its best. The salad is made with *misithra* or *xinó* cheese, a delicious alternative to feta. The goat meat and *kontosoúvli* are tender and savory. Some swear by the pork souvlaki surrounded by ripe tomatoes, but our favorite is stuffed eggplant.

GHIALOS

Enigma Cafe-Bar, Ghialos. ☎ **91-047.**

Cuisine: FAST FOOD.
Prices: Breakfast 700–1,400 Drs ($2.90–$5.85); pizza 1,000–1,600; main courses 800–1,900 Drs ($3.35–$7.90). No credit cards.

There's plenty of fast food at the port, but the best selection and quality is on the far right of the plaza.

Ouzerí 33, Ghialos. No telephone.

Cuisine: SEAFOOD.
Prices: Appetizers 550–900 Drs ($2.30–$3.75); main courses 900–2,300 Drs ($3.75–$9.60). No credit cards.

The best place on the island for fresh fish, according to locals, is this homely place left of the port before the town beach.

At Koumbara Beach, across the little penisula east of the port overlooking the beach, you'll find **Polydoros Taverna** (☎ **91-132**), a place recommended by our Greek friends where hearty traditional cooking is served native-style, evenings only, and one can feast for about 2,500–3,000 Drs ($10.40–$12.50).

At Milopótas Beach we recommend **Drakos Taverna**–no. 1 at the north end of the beach (open 9am–midnight) and no. 2 at the south end (open 11am–midnight), where you'll find fresh fish and meat nicely grilled for about 2,500–3,000 Drs ($10.40–$12.50) per person.

Evening Entertainment

Imagine a giant all-night street party of intoxicated teenage nomads—this is night-time on Íos. Chóra is the epicenter.

Clubs and discos there are aplenty. A casual stroll up Chóra's twisting lanes and main street will take you past at least ten good danceterias. You don't even have to poke your head in to hear what kind of music they play—it'll be obvious. The clubs change names and musical styles even more frequently than on Mýkonos, but below are recent favorites.

On the main street, below the stairs, is **Disco 69,** where there are cheap drinks and up-to-date tunes. **Underground** is just that, off Chóra's right-hand lane, a bar where drinks are less expensive during their happy hour from 9pm to midnight! Old Dylan tunes (new to most of the clientele) were packing 'em in at the **Parachute Club,** while the **Tropicana** was an early boogy bar with rap music and contemporary top-40. **Taboo,** the **Blue Note,** and **John's Electric** are all on or near the main square, where the clash of musical styles creates a cacophony that was heretofore deemed scientifically impossible. Fringe clubs (in location, not style) include the **New Look,** especially hot after 2am, and **Scorpion,** one of the oldest but still hopping. The newest hot spots are **The Dubliner,** where dancing on the tables is acceptable, and **Sweet Irish Dream,** both behind the big church on the east side of town, where people gather to rev up for the night's revelry.

7 Santoríni

126 nautical miles SE of Piraeus; 75 nautical miles N of Crete

ARRIVING/DEPARTING • By Air There are six flights direct from Athens daily to the "international" (they receive European charters) airport at Monólithos. There are three flights per week from Iráklio, Crete; four from Rhodes; and one daily flight from Mýkonos. For schedule information and reservations, check their Fíra office (☎ **22-493**), or call **01/96-16-161** in Athens.

• **By Sea** Santoríni is serviced at least twice daily from Piraeus by several maritime companies. The trip takes 10 to 12 hours. There are daily **ferries** to Sýros, Páros, Náxos, Íos, Folégandros, Síkinos, and Anáfi, and four ferries weekly to Mýkonos. Schedules should be confirmed with Tourist Information in Athens (☎ **171**) or the Piraeus (☎ **45-11-311**) or Thíra Port Authority (☎ **0286/22-239**). Once-weekly ferry service from the Dodecanese calls first at Rhodes, Kárpathos, Kássos, and Crete. From Crete, there are almost daily excursion boats leaving Iráklio that offer one-way transport for 4,000 Drs ($16.70). (Beware of this open-sea route in stormy weather—six hours of nausea may make the airfare seem cheap.)

The high-speed hydrofoil *Nearchos* connects Santoríni with Íos (2,850 Drs/$11.85), Parós 5,700 Drs ($23.75), Mýkonos (6,400 Drs/$26.65), and Iráklio, Crete (7,800 Drs $32.50) three times weekly in the low season, almost daily in the high season, *if the winds are not too strong.* Contact a travel agent for schedule information.

Most ferry tickets are handled by **Nomikos Travel** (☎ **0286/23-660**) with offices in Fíra, Kartaradoes, and Périssa. Almost all the ferries now dock at Athínios. Buses to Fíra, Kamári, and Périssa Beach meet the ferries; Oia-bound travelers should go to Fíra and change buses there. Taxis are also available from Athínios but are about ten times the price.

The exposed port at Skála (below Fíra) is too unsafe for the larger steamships; often the small ferries that do dock there have to shuttle passengers in to shore on small caiques. If you dock at Skála you can choose between a tough 45-minute hike uphill around 250 pushy mules; a 900 Drs ($3.75) mule ride, including luggage (negotiate in low season); or the 750 Drs ($3.10) cable-car ride to reach Fíra town. We recommend donkey up and cable car down.

Santoríni (Thíra) is unique among the arid, whitewashed, rocky Cyclades for its dramatic volcanic landscape. Visitors arriving by sea are stunned by the sheer black cliffs that stretch around a fantastic cauldron-shaped bay, the Caldera. Deep red soil and long streaks of white pumice stripe the cliffs, which are white-capped 250 meters above sea level by the capital city of Fíra. Besides the breathtaking first impression, Santoríni's black sand beaches, good cheap wine, and folktales linking it to the legendary Atlantis lure American tourists in droves.

History

The geology of Santoríni separates it visually and historically from the other Cyclades isles. In ancient times this volcanic island was called Strongylé ("round," pronounced *Stronghili*), a reference to the almost perfect semicircle that remained after this volcano's eruption and subsequent collapse. The fishers living in traditional villages on nearby Thirasia inhabit mountaintops of Strongylé that remained above water. In fact a land bridge is submerged between the two islands. To the southwest, the tiny Aspronísi is another peak in the Strongylé ring.

The two islets in the center of the Caldera bay are the original lava cones. The smaller one, Paleá Kaméni, emerged after an eruption in 197 B.C. and grew, then shrank and grew again, to its present size, during 700 turbulent years. In 1707 a mild earthquake caused the larger islet, Néa Kaméni, to rise. It's been an active volcano ever since, last erupting in 1950. Brave souls can take boat tours to both islands, bathe in the hot springs created off their coasts, and peer down into the sizzling inferno within.

The volcanic eruption between 1647 and 1628 B.C., according to the most recent information, that caused the collapse of Strongylé was so forceful that archeologists think it caused tidal waves that totally flattened Crete and touched the shores of Africa. The fascinating city of Akrotíri, uncovered on Santoríni by Professor Spyridon Marinatos in 1967, was apparently an ally or member of the Minoan kingdom that flourished on Crete until 1500 B.C., and may have been the legendary Atlantis. The ruins of Akrotíri, well preserved under lava and volcanic ash, have been immensely important in understanding Minoan culture. The exciting excavations continue today in the "Pompeii of the Aegean" and should not be missed by even the one-day visitor.

In time, the no-longer-round Strongylé was renamed Kálisti, "Fairest One." In the 10th century B.C. it was renamed Thíra, after a Dorian ruler from Sparta who invaded the island and settled seven villages. The ruins of Ancient Thíra, the Dorian hilltop capital, also reflect the later presence of Roman and Byzantine conquerors. The Venetian crusaders occupied Santoríni (European sailors named it after its patron, St. Irene, who died in exile here in A.D. 304) from the 13th to the 16th century. In the village of Embório you can see several hillside homes built within the only Venetian fortress walls that remain.

In 1956 an earthquake registering 7.8 on the Richter scale destroyed about two-thirds of the housing on the island. Because it struck early in the morning, when most of Santoríni's residents were working in the fields or on their boats, only 40 people were killed. Many homeless islanders, unable to secure government loans to rebuild, fled to other Greek ports, the United States, and Australia to begin new lives. Now Santoríni's 11,000 inhabitants subsist principally on tourism and the thriving wine industry. Vines hooped in coils over low supports (to protect grapes from the extreme heat and *meltémi* winds) grow everywhere in the rich, volcanic soil.

Orientation

In recent years Santoríni's spectacular west coast cliffs have been marred by the extraction of pumice to use in the manufacture of high-quality cement. For centuries, to the tourists' delight, mules were used to make the steep ascent from the old port at Skála to Fíra. The hardy beasts are now augmented by a Doppelmayer cable car that makes the lava rock cliff look like an Austrian ski resort, and adds 800 tourists per hour to the capital city. Unfortunately, almost all ships now dock at the colorless port of Athínios, south of Skála. However, the cable car, which runs every 20 minutes between 8am and 9pm, has found a new life as a sightseeing attraction. You can marvel at the island's geography for only 750 Drs ($3.10).

After the port, your first stop will be the hilltop, shopping-mad capital of **Fíra,** the central bus station for around-the-island and beach bus connections. A ten-minute walk along the cliff north from Fíra will lead you to **Firostepháni,** where the hotels are a better value and the view back to Fíra breathtaking. If you've come for more than two days (or in the height of the season) consider a room in one of the smaller villages. The pace is a little less tourist-oriented and nearby local beaches are less congested.

Because no rivers or lakes appeared on this volcanic island after its eruption, Santoríni's development has depended on water supplied by the few springs discovered at **Kamári Beach.** Kamári's black sand beaches and natural water supply guaranteed it would be the first resort to be fully developed by charter-tour packages. Off-season, Kamári Beach is one of the island's highlights (as is the nearby black sand **Périssa Beach**), but during July and August it's a place you'll want to stay away from. Instead, there are several small inland villages, where hotels, pensions, and rooms to let won't be group-booked.

Getting Around

BY BUS OR TAXI

Santoríni is one of the few Cycladic islands with acceptable bus service. The square in Fíra serves as the island's **central bus station.** The drivers speak some English and can provide information on return departures. If you're unfortunate enough to miss the last bus (most routes are serviced every half hour from 7am to 11pm) you'll be at the mercy of Fíra's too few taxi drivers. All taxis must be booked by phone (☎ **22-555**) and base their rates from Fíra. A cab ride from Oia to Fíra can cost 2,200 Drs ($9.15); from Kamári Beach, 1,800 Drs ($7.60).

BY MOPED & CAR

Santoríni's young crowd seems to prefer transportation on two wheels; it's not uncommon to see young men in varsity sweatshirts leaning on their mopeds outside the post office or snack shops, waiting to offer some fair damsel a ride. **Moped** dealers are ubiquitous and offer single-person mopeds for 2,500 Drs ($10.40) to 4,800 Drs ($20) per day, depending on the season and duration of rental. There is limited medical treatment on the island; wear a helmet and drive carefully!

Visiting Europeans prefer rental cars. Most travel offices can provide them, or you can contact **Budget Rent-A-Car** (☎ **22-900,** fax 22-887), a block below the Fíra bus stop square. A four-seat Fiat Panda will run you 17,500 Drs ($72.90) a day, with unlimited mileage.

What to See & Do

A visit to Santoríni would not be complete without a stop at the archeological site of Akrotíri. The impact of this startling 1960s find has been compared to the discovery of King Tut's tomb in the 1920s. Those without an archeological background should take advantage of the many excellent local tours and see the site with a knowledgeable guide. The standard around-the-island day tour will also include a visit to the Monastery of Profítis Ilías, reviewed below. A personal favorite was a self-guided tour of Ancient Thíra.

AKROTÍRI

The Minoan satellite city of Akrotíri is an outstanding monument to that culture and to the efforts of the archeologist who discovered it far below layers of volcanic ash. Since the early 1930s, Minoan expert Spyridon Marinatos devoted his life to the search for Akrotíri. The findings from Akrotíri have provided the world with some of the most beautiful Minoan stone artifacts and the most impressive frescos of the prehistoric world. The high artistic quality of the finds suggests that Akrotíri was a city of wealthy merchants and ship captains.

As you enter the covered site you'll be walking on the main street. Most of the remains on either side were stores or warehouses for Akrotíri commercial trade. In one room 400 clay pots were found, all stacked according to size. Another room held large urns with traces of olive oil, onion, and fish inside. Continuing down the street, you'll come to a "square" in the shape of a triangle, and in front of you is the West House. This multistoried home is also called the Captain's House because of the richly decorated fresco of Minoan and Libyan sea battles unearthed on the second floor.

Continuing along the main street, you'll see many more houses where remarkably preserved frescoes were discovered. Unfortunately, the best works from Akrotíri were carted away to Athens and are on view at the National Archeological Museum. (A museum is being built in Fíra, however, and it is hoped that eventually the frescoes will be housed there.)

Akrotíri can be reached by public bus or private bus tours. Cost of admission is 1,250 Drs ($5.20) for adults, half price for students. Hours are 8:30am to 3pm daily, but it's hot and crowded at midday. Arrive first thing in the morning, if possible, then hike over to the pebbly Red Beach for a good seafood lunch and a swim.

MONASTERY OF PROFÍTIS ILÍAS

The monastery of Profítis Ilías (Prophet Elijah), built by two monks from Pýrgos in 1711, is well worth a morning away from the beach. Part of the chapel and the monastery museum were added when King Otto, impressed by the monastery's work, asked the Greek government for funds to enlarge it. From this period come the many small rooms, clustered in a maze around the chapel, which now house fascinating exhibits of local culture. The monastery has always been cherished by the people of Santoríni for its role during the Turkish Occupation (1453–1821). The few monks who inhabited it opened a "secret school," where they taught the island's children the Greek language and traditions outlawed by the Turks. In the museum, a model secret school has been created in a monk's cell. By the 1800s its instruction and care for the needy earned Profítis Ilías the support of wealthy benefactors. Many of the monastery's fine religious items and valuable gifts were sold off to raise funds for the War of Independence, but the remaining sets of porcelain, silver, and ecclesiastical items are displayed.

The old hostelry and dining quarters of the enlarged monastery were converted into a museum of Thíran culture by the three monks who remained when the monastery's fortunes dwindled. They still offer a glass of *tsikouthiá* (Santorinian firewater) and a candy to all who come to visit—but, please, don't take their picture! The folksy museum is in contrast to the classic chapel, which contains a portrait of Ilías from 1500 done in the Cretan style. It's on the far right of the altar; you can notice the similarities to the later work of El Greco, the best-known exponent of this school. The cultural museum's workshops include displays of tools, grains, candlemaking supplies, and other implements of local cottage industries.

Several companies offer this as part of a half-day tour. Striped cotton coveralls are provided for those who arrive in shorts. Usually open Monday through Saturday from 8am to 1pm and 2:30pm to sunset, but check whether it's closed for repairs before you plan your excursion.

ANCIENT THÍRA

The acropolis of the island's ancient capital, now called Archéa Fíra, was inhabited by Dorian colonists from the 9th century B.C. Its impressive remains are situated on the hill towering 1,200 feet above Kamári Beach. Make sure to check out the springs in the cliff. Most of the buildings on the acropolis date from the Ptolemaic period (300–145 B.C.).

After entering the site, follow the path on the left. Carved in the rocks at a small shrine are the eagle symbol of Zeus, the lion of Apollo (you can sit on his throne and put your foot in his imprints) to the left, the dolphin of Poseidon, and a portrait of a Dorian admiral. Just south is the open Agorá, and behind it the hewn stone ruins of the Governor's Palace. On the southern tip is a terrace thought to be the center of religious practices; stone tablets found here told of naked young boys who would frolic in homage to Dionysus. From this point you have a fantastic aerial view of the ancient port at Kamári and the long black sand streak of Périssa, and a clear sense of how valuable this acropolis was to the defense of the ancient capital. Behind this point there's a partially shaded, smooth stone sanctuary of the Egyptian gods, ideal for picnicking. Nearby is an underground sanctuary, whose Doric columns still support a stone canopy for an alternative shaded picnic spot.

Getting to Ancient Thíra demands some forethought: Wear good shoes, bring water, and by all means a picnic. At the nearest bus stop, you can negotiate for half-day excursions by mule up the stone path (cost: 3,500 Drs or $19.40). It's possible to arrange a round-trip taxi tour from Fíra, which costs about 6,000 Drs ($25), including waiting time. Ancient Thíra is open from 9am to 2:30pm Tuesday through Saturday, and to 1pm on Sunday and holidays.

VILLAGES

The large southern village of **Embório** is at the turnoff for Périssa Beach, and still displays aspects of traditional Greek life that have long been lost at the beach resorts. Second in size to Fíra, it has some unusual houses built inside the ruins of a large Venetian fortress. In the sign-posted TRADITIONAL AREA, stuccoed homes and closed blue-wood shutters lend an air of perpetual siesta. Our friend George Kokkinis at Kamari Tours told us that Jean-Paul Sartre spent six months in a castle here, writing *The Flies.* Scale the hillside to the windmills and imagine the solitude a writer can find today.

Pýrgos is another pretty inland village, the oldest and highest one on Santoríni. There are several small churches to see and the crumbling stucco and exposed stone of original Cycladic houses clinging to remnants of a Venetian-era kástro. From Pýrgos, it's a demanding hour hike to the **Monastery of Profítis Ilías.** Then, head west and you can catch a bus to **Kamári.** On the way, stop at the **Canava Roussos** (☎ **31-278**). This winery is open to wine tasters, who can sample the Roussos reds, rosés, and white wines (a Santorinian specialty) for a nominal fee. Of course, wine is packaged for sale as well.

As tourism eradicates the last vestiges of whatever traditional village life the people of Thíra had, tour operators have begun to package these inland communities as "typical villages." Day trips often include Embório, Pýrgos, the earthquake-devastated Mésa Goniá (where unrestored ruins give a hint of the quake's effect more than 30 years ago), Éxo Goniá, and Kartarádos, but we prefer to hike, take a bus, or drive to these villages to find more of the flavor we came for.

PORT OF ATHÍNIOS

Compared with the old port at Skála, the new port at Athínios lacks interest. A one-lane town with a few snackbars, ferry ticket agents, bad shops, and rooms at the Motel A, the best thing about it is that it's very easy to avoid being stuck there. Buses meet each ferry and wait to take arrivals to Fíra (400 Drs or $1.65), to Oia (650 Drs, or $2.70 and change at Fíra), Kamári Beach (350 Drs, $1.45), or Périssa Beach (280 Drs or $2). To catch your ferry, check returning bus schedules or book a taxi (☎ **22-555**)– they cost a few hundred drachmas more if reserved for you. Standard taxi fares are 2,800 Drs ($11.65) to or from Fíra, 5,000 Drs ($20.85) to Oia, 4,300 Drs ($17.90) to Kamári, and 3,200 Drs ($13.35) to Périssa.

Fíra

Most first-time visitors stay in super-touristy Fíra, where the majority of services are located, even if only for a day or two. Its boutique-lined pedestrian lanes are filled with the hundreds who arrive daily on cruise ships. They pause briefly to admire the scenery and then gallop up on mules to buy gold, furs, and ceramics that are no better value here than almost anywhere else in Greece.

ORIENTATION

Fíra is a confusing maze of narrow lanes off three basic main streets. After your ascent from the port, the taxi, bus, mule, or cable car will leave you at **Nomikós Street,** which becomes **Aghía Mína.** This pedestrian street runs along the cliff wall and offers beautiful views of the Caldera. Scenic dining spots, discos, and boutiques line **Aghía Mína.** If you walk the other way (north) on Nomikós Street, you'll reach **Firostepháni.**

Fíra's second street, **Ypapántis** (also known as Gold Street), is crammed full of jewelers, clothes boutiques, souvenir stands, and restaurants. In the central core you'll find most tourist services and the archeological museum (☎ **22-217**), which is open 8am to 3pm daily; closed Monday. Admission is 500 Drs ($2.10). There is also an international bookshop on the near end.

The third street through Fíra is **25 Martíou,** which is open to cars and leads north to Oia. In the center of things here is **Platía Theotokopoúlou,** the main square, from which the buses depart. On both sides of the street are travel agents, tour operators, ticket salesmen, tourist information offices—you get the picture.

Fast Facts: Fíra

American Express **X-Ray KiloTravel Services** (☎ **0286/22-624**, fax 0286/23-600), on the main square, is the American Express representative on Santoríni.

Area Code The telephone area code is **0286.**

Banks The National Bank (open weekdays 8am to 2pm) is at the south end of the cliff path, near the post office. Many travel agents also change money during working hours (for most, daily 8am to 9:30pm).

Hospital Fíra's small hospital is also on 25 Martíou (☎ **22-237**).

Laundry Miele Laundry (☎ **23-514**), open daily 8am–10pm, next door to the Pelican Hotel, northeast of the main square, has self-service and assisted laundry for 3,000 Drs ($12.50) a load (5 kilos or less). The Penguin Laundromat (☎ **22-092**), open daily 9am–11pm, on the left 200 meters up on the road to Oia, offers two-hour service at the same price.

Police The police station (☎ **22-649**) is on 25 Martíou south of the bus station. The port police can be reached at **22-239.**

Post Office The post office (☎ **22-238,** fax 22-698), open 8am to 1pm Monday to Friday), is next to the bus station.

Telephones The telephone center (OTE), up from the post office, is open from 8am to 11:30pm Monday through Friday. Santo Volcano (☎ **0286/22-127,** fax 0286/22-955), on the main square, will help you send a fax or make a phone call.

Tourist Offices There is no official government tourist office but we found the **Kamari Tours** office (☎ **0286/22-666,** fax 0286/22-971), two blocks south of the square, particularly helpful. If you're stuck for a room or a moped, they'll do what they can. Kamari Tours also offers day trips to most of the island's sites. **Damigos Tours** (☎ **22-504,** fax 22-266), on the main square, was the first established in Fíra and also offers excellent guided tours, at slightly lower rates. **Nomikos Tours** (☎ **0286/23-660,** fax 0286/23-66), has three offices in Fíra.

WHERE TO STAY

First, a word of warning: Santoríni is densely populated in July and August, and travelers without sleeping bags should make a reservation, accompanied by a deposit, at least two months in advance of arrival. Otherwise, head straight from the ferry and catch the bus into Fíra's bus stop square and ask one of the travel agents to help you find a room. If anyone offers you one along the way, take a long look before you turn it down. You can always move the next day if you find something better.

IN FÍRA Most of the Fíra hotels with views of the spectacular Caldera charge a premium that puts them way beyond our budget. Fortunately, there are a few good-value choices that offer quiet, comfort, and that wonderful view. Since Santoríni's mostly young tourists prefer to live in a real Greek home, rooms-to-let has become such a big business that most families just build impersonal multiroom additions to their charming and homey residences. Nonetheless, many have modern private facilities and hotel amenities at a better price than the hotels.

Between April and mid-June and in September and October, double rooms can be had from 5,000 to 8,000 Drs ($20.85 to $33.35), while in July and August the prices soar to 9,000 to 12,000 Drs ($37.50 to $50). Very few establishments are open year round.

International Youth Hostel Kamares, Fíra, Santoríni 84700. ☎ **0286/23-142.**
66 beds, 80 more on roof, 14 showers.

Rates: 1,500 Drs ($6.25). No credit cards

This IYHF hostel, 200 meters north of the bus station on the left, is newer, cleaner and better managed. There are separate dorms, with bunk beds, for male and female, but there's no curfew.

Kontohori International Youth Hostel, Fíra, Santoríni 84700. ☎ **0286/22-722.**
48 beds (24 female, 24 male).

Rates: 1,000 Drs ($4.10). No credit cards.

This hostel is about 400 meters north of the bus stop, right off 25 Martíou Street. They offer clean dorm beds, hot showers, advice, and ferry tickets at a discount to their guests.

Doubles for Less than 21,000 Drs ($87.50)

Hotel Asimina, Fíra, Santoríni 84700. ☎ **0286/22-989.** Fax 22-155.
14 rms (all with bath).

Rates: 9,840 Drs ($41) single; 16,160 Drs ($67.35) double. AE, MC, V.

This newer Class E hotel, run by Mendrinos Tours, is located in a quiet spot next door to the Archeological Museum. Belying its hotel classification, rooms all have private facilities and adequate, if simple, furnishings. We've received complaints about mosquitos.

Pension Blue Sky, Fíra, Santoríni 84700. ☎ **0286/23-400.** 25 rms (all with bath).

Rates: 7,800 Drs ($32.50) single; 10,400 Drs ($43.35).

Several readers wrote to recommend this excellent new hotel with a swimming pool. Go northeast off the main square past the Pelican Hotel, turn left at the supermarket, take the next right and find it about 100 meters down on the right. If they're full, ask about the Pension Soula across the street.

$ **Loucas Hotel,** Fíra, Santoríni 84700. ☎ **0286/22-480.** Fax 0286/22-880.
25 rms (all with bath). TEL

Rates (including breakfast): 15,900 Drs ($66.25) single; 20,750 Drs ($86.45) double. MC, V.

Our first choice inn has operated on Santoríni's cliffs since 1959. Each of its rooms are unique "caves" with vaulted ceilings built to prevent collapse during an earthquake. They are basically furnished, with no frills, some a bit worn but well kept; and they have private facilities. Best of all, they share a tiered stone terrace tacking like a sailboat down the steep cliff, and have recently added a new bar, the Renaissance, with a great view of the Caldera. (The Loucas is open March 1 to November 30, longer than most of Santoríni's hotels.)

Doubles for Less than 27,000 Drs ($112.50)

Pelican Hotel, P.O. Box 5, Fíra, Santoríni 84700. ☎ **0286/23-113.**

18 rms (all with bath). A/C TV TEL

Rates (including breakfast): 21,335 Drs ($88.90) single; 26,600 Drs ($110.85) double. AE, DC, MC, V.

This newer hotel, on the central square just north of the central square, is a plush addition to the Class C accommodation scene in Fíra. Its large, spotless rooms come with refrigerators, and the breakfast includes fresh orange juice.

OUTSIDE FÍRA You may not want to live in fast-paced Fíra, but most visitors will want to visit the capital city for an infusion of society. Sleeping in a nearby village may be the solution.

Just a ten-minute walk north is the community called **Firostepháni,** which, to our minds, offers the loveliest view of the Caldera and the active volcano at Néa Kaméni. There are many rooms to let in the area but the **Hotel Galíni** (☎ **0286/22-336**) in the center stands out for its modern, tiered architecture, which assures that all 15 rooms with private bath have a fabulous view and the privacy of separate entrances off a common veranda. Doubles run 12,650 Drs ($52.70); AE, MC, and V are accepted. A little north of these on the cliffside path is the **Hotel Heliovassílema** or **Sunset Hotel** (☎ **0286/23-046**), a contemporary interpretation of the island's traditional houses. Stucco, curving lines and some details found in the original Oia dwellings make these comfortable double rooms with telephones a little more special than most. In the high season they cost 15,000 Drs ($62.50), plus 1,000 Drs ($4.15) each to breakfast on their Caldera view terrace.

Nomikos Villas (☎ **0286/23-887,** fax 23-66) is our first choice among the luxury apartments and studios in Fierostepháni. Eighteen traditional cave houses have been thoroughly modernized without a loss of charm, complete with bath, telephone, and television; some even have kitchens and their own private terrace. Breakfast or a drink on the large common terrace with its great view is a very special experience. Doubles start at 25,000 Drs ($104.15), apartments for four cost 45,000 Drs ($187.50), and six can share a villa for $58,500 Drs ($243.75); AE, MC, V accepted. The **Grotto Villas** (☎ **0286/22-141,** fax 22-187) has 12 similar units, each with its own private terrace; studios for two start at 25,000 Drs ($104.15). There are also 12 **Vallas Apartments** (☎ **0286/22-050,** fax 22-142), recommended by a reader, with doubles from 19,500 Drs ($81.25).

Make reservations for the high season, but if you arrive in the off season, you can stroll along the cliffwalk and examine the many small traditional-style pensions and villas, in search of a bargain.

Imerovigli, named for the "day watch" kept for pirates from the highest point on the Caldera, is the next village north. Outstanding among the accommodations there is **Heliotropos** (**0286/23-670,** fax 23-672 or 01/93-83-059 in winter), a perfect place for a honeymoon, a beautiful secluded traditional complex with eight studios (50,000 Drs $208.35) and two suites 39,000 Drs ($162.50), each distinctively configured and decorated; all major credit cards accepted. The dining grotto is especially charming, and the breakfast is one of the best. Nearby **Remezzo Villas** (☎/fax **0286/23-030**) has eight units with kitchen and bath from 26,000 Drs ($108.35), three bedrooms for 32,500 Drs ($135.40). AE, MC, V accepted.

For those who shun the singles pubs, discos, and jewelers of main-street Fíra, there are rooms to let and some hotels in the attractive, whitewashed village of **Kartarádos,** 1 1/4 miles south of Fíra. Here several of the village women offer rooms attached to their homes at 7,000–11,000 Drs ($29.15–$45.85) per double to help offset the cost of water, which is brought everywhere on the island by tanker trucks from the springs at Kamári.

A few minutes from Kartarádos's main square, near the bus station, the **Hotel Palladion** (☎ **0286/22-583**) has simple doubles with bath and telephone for 11,500 Drs ($47.90). The treat here is breakfast in the marvelously decorated ground floor, which is cluttered with lace, flowers, and embroidery in traditional—and rarely seen—Santorinian fashion. Farther up the same road is the whitewashed **Hotel Cyclades** (☎ **0286/22-948**), which looks like your rich Greek aunt's private villa. Stathis Sigalas has 26 double rooms for 10,000–15,000 Drs ($41.65–$62.50) with breakfast.

One pension comes recommended by readers who loved their stay at the **Pension George** (☎ **0286/22-351**) because of its gregarious host, George Halaris, whose wife, Helen, is English. For a clean room with private bath, just a quick walk from the Kartarádos square, expect to pay 8,125 Drs ($33.85) single, 11,250 Drs ($46.90). Two hotels were also suggested by readers: the **Hotel Olympia** (☎ **0286/22-213**), which has a pool and 25 rooms—all with bath—singles for 11,250 Drs ($46.90), doubles for 15,600 Drs ($65); and the **Villa Odyssey** (☎ **0286/23-681**), with 17 rooms, all with bath, 10,000 ($41.65) single; 13,750 Drs ($57.30) double.

Also, you can visit the helpful **Nomikos Tours** office (☎ **0286/23-660**), where George Nomikos and his generous staff will find you a room, exchange traveler's checks, and arrange ferry tickets. They're on the main square. If you're only passing through, take time to explore Kartarádos's still-original and very much traditional village centered around the old Cathedral just below the square.

Kartarádos has a few unremarkable tavernas; a pleasant exception is the **Coral no. 2 Taverna,** where a hard-working family serves up spaghetti, barbecued pork, lamb on a spit, and other traditional Greek foods with gusto. For the island's only good bread you'll have to go to the bakery in nearby **Messaria.** This little village, crowded with the hotels Apollon, Messaria, Andreas, Margariti, and Artemidoris, is at the busy crossroads connecting the Fíra road to almost every site and beach on the island. When the moped smoke clears you'll see several pleasant tavernas on the main square.

Just before entering the village of **Akrotíri** you'll find the place most frequently recommended by locals, **Villa Mathios** (☎ **0286/81-152**), which has a swimming pool, restaurant, and 25 rooms, all with bath: 14,500 Drs ($60.40) for singles; 16,250 Drs ($67.70) for doubles, including breakfast and transport.

Splurge Choices

Hotel Aressana, Fíra, Santoríni 84700. ☎ **0286/23-900.** Fax 0286/23-902. A/C TEL

Rates (including breakfast): 33,800 Drs ($140.85); 50,000 Drs ($208.00); suites from 52,000 Drs ($216.65). AE, DC, MC, V.

This new hotel has almost everything we would ask except for a Caldera view, though it's only a block away, just beyond the Cathedral, across a small plaza from the Hotel

Atlantis. The rooms are large, nicely furnished, and very comfortable; but the big pluses are the large swimming pool and its proximity to the action and views.

★ **Santoríni Tennis Club Apartments,** Kartarádos, P.O. Box 39, Santoríni 84700. ☎ **0286/22-122** (in Athens ☎ **01/86-57-157**). Fax 0286/23-698.
9 villas. TEL

Rates (including breakfast): 21,500 Drs ($119.40). AE, MC, V.

The Santoríni Tennis Club is a particular favorite, a complex of restored early 19th-century Cycladic homes in the village of Kartarádos. Nine vaulted-roof dwellings have been created from abandoned villagers' homes nestled in the soft stone cliffs. Units sleeping from two to five people are all whitewashed stucco and stone inside, with carved-in furniture, tiny shuttered windows, and niches filled with ceramics. Fully stocked kitchenettes are for those who never want to leave; breakfast is brought daily into each home or served outside on the bluestone patio. True to its name, the Tennis Club has two porous concrete courts, plus a large swimming pool and sunbathing deck.

WHERE TO EAT

There are restaurants aplenty to cater to those with a bit more money, those with sophisticated tastes who are tired of Greek food, and those young enough to live on French fries and pizza. Unfortunately, few places stand out.

Be careful: *We've had numerous reports of exorbitant charges for seafood and wine in several of the newer restaurants.*

Aris Restaurant, Odós Aghíou Miná, Fíra. ☎ **22-840.**

Cuisine: GREEK/INTERNATIONAL.
Prices: Appetizers 250–1,200 Drs ($1–$5); main courses 1,000–2,400 Drs ($4.15–$10). MC, V.
Open: Daily noon–1am.

On the lower pedestrian street, south of the donkey path down to Skala, below the Loucas Hotel you'll find Aris Ziras's new restaurant. The chef was formerly with the Athens Hilton, and, though the dishes are mainly Greek, the cooking is somewhat updated and better presented than you usually find. The *mezédes* are excellent and the moussaka is among the best we've ever had. Try the white house wine.

Barbara's Café-Brasserie, Fabrica Shopping Center, Fíra.

Cuisine: INTERNATIONAL.
Prices: Breakfast 500–1,200 Drs ($2.10–$5); sandwiches 600–1,200 Drs ($2.50–$5). No credit cards.
Open: Daily 9am–1am.

One of the best places for breakfast or a light lunch is a couple of blocks up from the bus station toward the Cathedral. After 7pm it becomes one of the least expensive bars in town, with beer for 400 Drs ($1.65), wine by the glass for 500 Drs ($2.10).

Canava Cafe/Art Gallery, Cliffside, Fíra. ☎ **22-565.**

Cuisine: INTERNATIONAL.
Prices: Brunch 1,000 Drs ($4.15) and up. AE, MC, V.
Open: Daily 8am–2am.

Above the Loucas Hotel with a great Caldera view, a beautiful spot to sip a cool drink and watch the sunset. Even better in the morning for a thoroughly civilized breakfast or brunch of bread, fruit, and pastry.

Creperie House, Theotokópoulos Square, Fíra. No telephone.

Cuisine: INTERNATIONAL.
Prices: Croissants 250–450 Drs ($1.05–$1.90); crêpes 500–1,000 Drs ($2.10–$4.15). No credit cards.
Open: Daily 9am–3pm, 8pm–3am.

On the north side of the central square you'll find this good place for breakfast, light meals, and drinks.

★ **Meridiana Restaurant Bar,** Fabrica Shopping Center, Fíra. ☎ **23-427.**

Cuisine: INTERNATIONAL. **Reservations:** Recommended for dinner.
Prices: Appetizers 900-2,300 Drs ($3.75–$9.60), main courses 2,300–6,200 Drs ($9.60–$25.85). AE, MC, V.
Open: Daily 11am–3pm, 7pm–1am.

Near the Cathedral with a great panoramic view, this upscale, sophisticated place is one of the best and most popular. Hosts Angelo and Barbra genuinely enjoy food and their enthusiasm is evident in the varied menu. They serve a piquant paella, chicken curry made with spices from London, pasta from Italy, Teriyaki beef, or a complete typical Santoríni dinner. Even the more commonly seen courses are well prepared and a bit off-beat. In the evenings a lively, mixed clientele, many of them regulars, come as much for the gregarious hosts as for the excellent cooking.

Nicholas Taverna, Erythroú Stavroú Street, Fíra. No telephone.

Cuisine: GREEK.
Prices: Appetizers 240–1,000 Drs ($1–$4.15), main courses 800–2,100 Drs ($3.35–$8.75). No credit cards.
Open: Daily 12pm–11pm.

For the closest thing to authentic taverna fare try the atmospheric Nicholas in the heart of town, on Red Cross Street. Their fava-bean dip is an island specialty that's prepared very well. We find their authentic daily specials and untrendy decor a relief. You may appreciate the brisk service.

Sphinx Restaurant, Mitropóleos Street, Fíra. ☎ **23-823.**

Cuisine: INTERNATIONAL. **Reservations:** Recommended.
Prices: Appetizers 900–1,800 Drs ($3.75–$7.50); main courses 1,500–4,500 Drs ($6.25–$18.75). AE, DC, MC, V.
Open: Daily noon–3pm, 7pm–2am.

In a restored old mansion near the Atlantic Hotel you'll find one of the finest restaurants on the island, appointed with antiques, sculpture, and interesting ceramics by local artists. (Competing with the art may make you want to get gussied up.) Julia, the owner, is friendly and attentive and takes care that every meal is fresh and superbly

READERS RECOMMEND

Restaurant Nefeli, Fíra. ☎ **22-557.** *"We found a restaurant along the main road to Kartarádos that was excellent and reasonable. The food was fabulous and there was a large variety."*—Susan and Neville York, North Vancouver, British Columbia.

Several readers wrote to recommend the budget ***Delfi Restaurant,*** *one block east of the main square in Fíra, and the* ***Pyrgos Taverna,*** *in Pýrgos, for a touristy but fun evening of traditional Greek food and music.*

prepared. Their seafood specials and imaginative preparations of typical Greek fare are wonderful.

Taverna Poseidon, Desigala Street, Fíra. ☎ **22-841.**

Cuisine: GREEK/SEAFOOD.
Prices: Appetizers 200–1,200 Drs (85¢–$5), main courses 900–2,500 Drs ($3.75–$10.40). No credit cards.
Open: Daily 8am–4pm, 7pm–2am.

The Poseidon, just below the bus stop square, serves grilled mullet, stuffed vegetables, and rich soups every day. It's great at lunch, a bit too fluorescent for our taste at dinner, but an authentic place where couples can eat heartily and enjoy a bottle of Santoríni Boutari at moderate prices.

EVENING ENTERTAINMENT

Fíra's evening scene is one of her lures, a bubbling maelstrom that satisfies both the young looking for quick action and those who prefer to while away the night in communion with the island's natural gifts.

If you're looking for some jovial company, try **Bon Jour,** north of the main square, or cruise the inner pedestrian lanes filled with boutiques and you'll find that several discreet storefronts burst to life after 9pm. The **Kirathira Bar** draws jazz devotees and those interested in conversation; the **Town Club** packs in a clean-cut rock crowd; and the **Two Brothers,** the chummiest, largest, and most casual young drinking crowd in the Cyclades. The parrot-crowned, outdoor **Tropical Bar,** which attracts a loud party gang, is on the cliff road, a bit north of the restaurant and café strip.

Discos are a tough call on Fíra, where trendy spots change more rapidly than the style of beachwear, but one of the newest, loudest, and therefore most popular, discos is **Hysteria,** below the bus stop square. In the height of summer, when there are enough movers and shakers on the island to crowd every dancehall, the old-time **Enigma** is still in with those interested in good music. They're all easy and fun to check out, and free—you don't pay until you start ordering the 1,500 Drs ($6.25) drinks. The **Koo Club** has replaced the old Dionysos Disco, enlarged the garden, and added a fountain and tropical bar.

In Fíra, those who are visiting in August or September can enjoy classical music at the new **Santoríni Festival.** International singers and musicians perform at the open-air amphitheater over a two-week period. (Call **22-220** for details.)

Despite many distractions, Fíra's unique attribute is her remarkable natural beauty. One of the best places to savor the sunset over the Caldera while enjoying a fairly inexpensive drink is the **Renaissance Bar,** below the Lucas Hotel.

From the few tavernas below Aghía Mina on the cliff we'd recommend **Franco's Bar,** whose view over the Caldera is unbelievably beautiful, particularly at the magic sunset hour. You can unwind to classical music, sip local wines, and admire the stylish crowd. Franco's is expensive, but highly recommended because the charming Italian host has combined his native flair for food with a wonderful esthetic sensi-bility to create a delightful, elegant, and totally Cycladic café.

Many visitors with their own transport or cab fare enjoy a seaside stroll in the evening. Kamári Beach's promenade is the best suited for this as the ugly port of Athínios is no place for a moonlit *vólta.* Instead, you can stroll past the many cafés and tavernas, take in the glinting black pebble beach, and pause for a glass of wine or even a dinner at **Camille Stephani,** one of Kamári's more formal restaurants (see below), which serves such good European food that it alone would justify an excursion.

Kamári

Kamári Beach is Santoríni's most popular destination because its beautiful black pebble beach, 8 km long, was long ago discovered and exploited by tour operators. Each week, 17 planeloads of Europeans land directly at Santoríni's airport for a packaged vacation at this unique resort. For those of you able to visit Kamári in the spring or fall, it is possible to find a room at prices comparable to those in Fíra or the less attractive Périssa Beach.

There is little to do but dance, dine, drink, or soak up the sun at Kamári Beach. The local **Kamári Tours** office (☎ **0286/31-390** or **31-455**) runs excursions to all of Santoríni's sites, in addition to booking most of Kamári's rooms as well as cruises to other islands. When you're ready to leave, buses for Fíra (where you can change for transport to other villages) leave nearly every half hour between 7am and 11pm. For spontaneous types, a taxi can be ordered (☎ **31-668**, or from Fíra at ☎ **22-555**) but the ten-minute ride will cost about 1,800 Drs ($7.60).

WHERE TO STAY

Almost all hotels and rooms work with travel agents. You can contact the local **Kamári Tours** office (☎ **0286/31-390**) to get an affordable beachside room (the hotels pay them a commission; guests don't), or walk to the south end of the beach and into the little village, where you'll find these other choices.

Doubles for Less than 19,500 Drs ($81.25)

Kamári Camping, Kamári Beach, Santoríni 84700. ☎ **0286/32-452** or **31-453.**
590 camping sites.

Rates: 1,500 Drs ($6.25) per person.

An attractive site 800 meters from the beach with a tourist information center, restaurant, cafeteria, minimarket, laundry, hot showers, public telephone, and bus service.

Akis Hotel, Kamári Beach, Santoríni 84700. ☎ **0286/31-670.** Fax 31-423.
18 rms (all with bath).

Rates: 15,500 Drs ($64.60) single; 19,500 Drs ($81.25) double. AE, MC, V.

The Akis Hotel, on the main street, is the closest—just 30 meters—to the black beach. It has a cafeteria/café downstairs with good food and a local clientele.

Rooms Hesperides, Kamári Beach, Santoríni 84700. ☎ **0286/31-185.**
17 rms (all with bath).

Rates: 10,000 Drs ($41.65) single/double. No credit cards.

This is a recently opened pension that delighted us with its "Greekness." It's a collection of neat, modern rooms in a pistachio grove. The owner and his wife are a friendly older couple who wonder when they'll get their front yard back. Excavations around their pistachio trees have revealed a buried Byzantine city, whose ruins are open for exploration as you walk to your room. How much more Greek can you get?

Doubles for Less than 27,300 Drs ($113.75)

Kamári Beach Hotel, Kamári Beach, Santoríni 84700. ☎ **0286/31-216** or **31-243**. Fax 0286/31-243. (In Athens, call **01/48-28-826**). 92 rms (all with bath).

Rates (including breakfast): 27,300 Drs ($113.75) double. AE, DC, MC, V.

This hotel has the best beachfront location. All the Kamári's spacious, balconied rooms take advantage of the view over the Aegean and the lovely pool down below.

Korali Hotel, Kamári Beach, Santoríni 84700. ☎ **0286/31-904.** 9 rms (all with bath), 2 apts.

Rates: 18,000 Drs ($75) single/double. MC, V.

About 50 meters behind the Korali Taverna, the owners have built a very handsome small hotel, each room with its own private entrance. It wasn't quite finished during our visit, but we feel fairly certain it will be comfortable, quiet, and a good value.

Matina Hotel, Kamári Beach, Santoríni 84700. ☎ **0286/31-491.** Fax 31-860. 27 rms (all with bath).

Rates (including breakfast): 18,850 Drs ($78.55) single/double; 14,950 Drs ($62.30) single/double without breakfast in pension annex. AE, EC, MC, V.

A thoroughly modern hotel a two-minute walk from the beach. The spacious, airy rooms are often group-booked, but try them, or their nearby annex, Pension Matina.

Venus Hotel, Kamári Beach, Santoríni 84700. ☎ **0286/31-183.** 60 rms (all with bath).

Rates (including breakfast): 19,500 Drs ($81.25) single/double. MC, V.

Another plush hotel has sprung up next to the Kamári Beach. The Venus has white-on-white, marble-floored bedrooms with flashes of tasteful pastel to break up the coolness. Rooms have central heating (the Venus is open year round) and radio.

WHERE TO EAT

Kamári has been a popular beach resort for so many years that the beach road is jammed with moderate-priced restaurants. We suggest:

Agiris Taverna, Kamári village. ☎ **31-795.**

Cuisine: GREEK.
Prices: Appetizers 180–800 Drs (75¢–$3.35), main courses 900–3,200 Drs ($3.75–$13.75). V.
Open: Daily 6pm–midnight.

The best Greek food in Kamári is actually in the village opposite the main church. This old family-run taverna caters to the locals and a few tourists looking for an authentic Greek meal. Stuffed chicken is an unusual and delicious specialty. Everything has mom's personal touch.

Alex's Grill, Kamári Beach. No telephone.

Cuisine: GREEK/INTERNATIONAL.
Prices: Appetizers 150–900 Drs (63¢–$3.75), main courses 650–2,400 Drs ($2.70–$10). No credit cards.
Open: Daily 11am–3pm, 7pm–1am.

No shirt, no shoes, no hassle. In the pine grove on the north end of the beach—just as you'd suspect, charcoal-grilled chicken, lamb chops, souvlaki, fish at reasonable prices.

★ **Camille Stephani,** Kamári Beach. ☎ **31-716.**

Cuisine: GREEK/INTERNATIONAL. **Reservations:** Recommended during July–Sept.
Prices: Appetizers 750–2,000 Drs ($3.15–$8.35), main courses 1,800–4,200 Drs ($7.50–$17.50). AE, DC, MC, V.
Open: Daily 1pm–4pm, 6:30pm–midnight.

Camille Stephani, formerly one of our favorites in Fíra, has brought excellent continental cuisine and more formal dining to the north end of the beach, 500 meters from the bus stop. The special is a tender beef filet with green pepper in Madeira sauce.

Irini Restaurant/Cafeteria, Kamári Beach. ☎ **31-246.**

Cuisine: GREEK.
Prices: Appetizers 600–1,200 Drs ($2.50–$5), main courses 900–3,000 Drs ($3.75–$12.50). No credit cards.
Open: Daily 8pm–midnight.

On the south end of the beach you can have an evening meal of stuffed tomato or souvlaki and the couple of beers favored by so many beachers for about 1,500 Drs ($8.30).

Korali Taverna, Kamári Beach. ☎ **31-904.**

Cuisine: GREEK.
Prices: Appetizers 500–1,500 Drs ($2.10–$6.25), main courses 900–3,600 Drs ($3.75–$15). MC, V.
Open: Daily 8am–1am.

Another casual place in the pine grove on the north end of the beach. Here you can get the usual Greek dishes at fairly reasonable prices and an excellent fresh-grilled daily catch—priced according to supply and demand.

EVENING ENTERTAINMENT

Nothing much was shaking during our last meeting, but our friends assured us that **Valentino's,** a chic open-air place on the beach near the bus stop, was a sure bet, as was the nearby **Mango's.** The old Sail Inn, on the beachside promenade, was being transformed into **Persephone,** though no one knew for sure what she would be after her emergence from the underworld.

There's an outdoor cinema on the main road next to Kamári Camping that gets popular American flicks about a year after their initial release; 900 Drs ($3.75) per seat.

Périssa

Périssa is Santoríni's other beach resort area, a much smaller enclave of pensions, group tour hotels, and cafés near a wide, long beach of black pebbles on the southeast coast. In the summer, Périssa's cheaper lifestyle ensures its popularity with backpackers fleeing high-priced Fíra, Kamári, or Oia. The beach gets very noisy, crowded, and badly littered. Those who can afford it should consider staying elsewhere.

Buses run from Fíra to Périssa every half hour between 7am and 11pm. On the **Timíou Stavroú (Holy Cross)** you'll find public showers (400 Drs or $1.60), a worn miniature golf course with video games, a few markets, a moped dealer, and a branch of the **OTE** (open 8am to 1pm and 6 to 9pm Monday through Saturday, 8am to 1pm Sunday). Both **Kamari Tours** (☎ **0286/81-127**) on the road, and **Nomikos Travel** (☎ **0286/23-085** or **81-060**) on the beach, can change traveler's checks, help book rooms, and handle problems.

WHERE TO STAY

Périssa is still a fledgling resort and there are many lodgings comparable to those below, nearby. Doubles at most of these hotels (usually booked by groups) will run 7,200 Drs ($29) with bath.

Perissa Camping (☎ **0286/81-343**), right behind the beach, has sites from 750 Drs ($3) per person; a tent is 300 Drs ($1.25) extra. It's also the nude sunbathing center of Périssa and has free hot showers for guests, a minimarket, a bar, a snack bar, and a very active canteen with great music.

There are two youth hostels across the main road from each other about 100 meters from the beach. The **International Youth Hostel Perissa** (☎/fax **0286/81-639**) is better managed, offers hot showers, a friendly atmosphere and 40 beds for males, 42 for females, at 2,200 Drs ($9.15) per person. The **Youth Hostel Anna** is trying hard, doing as well as it can on its limited means, has a friendly management and enjoys a good local reputation; it should cost slightly less.

Marco's Rooms, our best recent find, can be found by inquiring at Marco's Taverna. This spotless new family-run pension is a five-minute walk from the beach; all 12 rooms have baths, marble floors, and balconies and rent for 8,500 Drs ($35.40) for two; MC and V are accepted. **Darzeda Pension** (☎ **0286/81-236**), just 60 meters from the beach at the bus stop on the north end of town, is a good value, with 13 clean simple rooms, all with bath and refrigerator, some with balconies, that cost 7,400 Drs ($30.85).

The modern **Meltemi Hotel** (☎ **0286/81-119** or **81-325,** fax 81-139), which has its own pool, is presently the only hotel that wins our approval. It has 47 fresh new rooms, all with private phones and baths; singles for 8,000 Drs ($33.35), doubles for 10,500 Drs ($43.75), AE, MC, V are accepted. They've recently added air-conditioned Class A apartments that rent for 16,500 Drs ($68.75) for two, 4,000 Drs ($16.65) for each additional bed.

WHERE TO EAT

Périssa's best beachside eatery is **Marco's Taverna** (☎ **81-205**), located on the north end of the beach by the rock. You'll find it open noon to midnight, serving a wide selection of food, all well prepared and costing 900–1,600 Drs ($3.75–$6.65) per main course, MC and V are accepted. **Makedonia,** on the main road, open 8am to midnight, is very popular for its inexpensive pizza.

The party crowd should try **Taboo,** with live music from 7pm, then either or both branches of the **Florida Disco,** with music from 10pm to 3am, all on the main vehicle street into town.

Oia

Ascending the steps from the fishing port of Armeni, 1,200 Drs ($5) by donkey, or 15 minutes on foot, the village of Oia (pronounced *Ía*) appears as a thin white icing of traditional Cycladic homes atop the dark black and red cliffs that rise from the Caldera. From this northernmost tip of the island you can admire the mist-shrouded, volcanic rock islands that break the gently rippling surface of the Aegean.

Those readers who stay will want to touch base with Oia's goodwill ambassadors, Marcos and Manolis Karvounis, at **Karvounis Tours** (☎ **0286/71-290** or **71-209,** fax 0286/71-291). Their office has a metered phone for long-distance calls (it's very difficult to call in or out of Oia); they change money, book wonderful villas and rooms, find taxis, book island day trips, and do ferry and plane tickets, accepting AE, MC, and V. In fact, after someone sent them a story from the *New York Times* about an American couple's trials and tribulations in planning a wedding in Oia, they urged us to let you know they arrange weddings (not marriages!) as well. They also offer special monthly rentals on island homes in the winter ($300–$500) for those seeking peace, quiet, and real village life. Go see them if you need anything.

Oia is basically a two-street community: the west-facing vehicle road that leads into the bus stop and, almost parallel to it, Nikólaos Nomikós Street, the pedestrian-only, marble-paved walkway along the east-facing cliff. The Karvounis Tours office and most services are located off the cliffwalk near the village's main church.

GETTING THERE

From Fíra hordes climb onto the group tour buses at midday for some village sightseeing and transport to Oia (about 2,500 Drs or $10.40). If you don't have wheels, and you don't want to join a group tour, try to round up a few other people to taxi-share for your sunset excursion to Oia. Hitchhiking is very difficult because the fuel shortage keeps the few locals off the roads and most tourists rent mopeds. Public buses run from Fíra to Oia about ten times a day between 8:30am and 8pm; the last bus for sunset watchers leaves Oia at 9pm. Taxis from Fíra to Oia cost 2,200 Drs ($9.15); from Oia to Fíra they sometimes have to be booked by phone (☎ **22-555**) and so cost 3,200 Drs ($13.35).

WHAT TO SEE & DO

In the village there is a small **marine museum,** open 9am to 12:30pm and 4 to 7pm daily. There are a few shops, many pleasant tavernas, and a vigorous walk down the cliffside to the fishing port of **Armeni.** The nearest sand beach is **Baxedes,** partially accessible by bus from the town square. A 1 km walk over the black sand will bring you to a relatively isolated, undeveloped bathing area. Oia's overnight guests walk north and down to the beach at **Ammoudi** or down the west side of the island (a gently banked, cultivated area) to **Kolumbus Beach.** Back in the town are the ruins of **Lontza Castle,** the best place to station yourself for views of the setting sun.

If you think you've seen enough gold in the shops in Fíra, rest your eyes on gorgeous antique jewelry and vintage watches—at reasonable prices—at **Dolphin of Santoríni,** on the main street between the church square and the high view down to the port. Angelo also sells museum copies of classic Greek antiquities.

WHERE TO STAY

As more traditional houses are restored to meet increased tourist interest, it's become possible for visitors in almost any budget range to use Oia as their home base to explore the island. Information and bookings are available from **Cycladic Environments,** P.O. Box 382622, Cambridge, MA 02238, ☎ **800-719-5260,** fax 617-492-5881.

The restored villas accommodate from two to seven people; rates begin at 15,000 Drs ($62.50) a night for two up to 31,500 Drs ($131.20) for six.

Karvounis Tours (☎ **0286/71-209,** fax 0286/71-291) books the **Armenaki Villas,** a more contemporary choice overlooking the village and Caldera, that rent for 32,000 Drs ($133.35) for two, as well as other villas and private apartments.

There are a few rooms to let as well, but prices run about 25% more than rates in Fíra. For conventional accommodations we recommend:

Oia Youth Hostel, Oia, Santoríni 84702. ☎ **0286/71-292.** Fax 0286/71-291.

Rates (including breakfast): 3,250 Drs ($13.55) single.

The Karvounis Brothers have constructed an international youth hostel about 50 meters north of the bus stop square. The rooms are comfortable, traditional-style dormitories, and the complex includes a minimarket, bar, restaurant, as well as telephone, postal, and travel service.

Hotel Anemones, Oia, Santoríni 84702. ☎ **0286/71-220.** 10 rms (all with bath).

Rates: 10,000 Drs ($41.65) single/double. No credit cards.

Good accommodations at a good price, with a fabulous view from the breakfast room. Modern rooms are comfortable, but without much traditional Cycladic style.

Hotel Finikia, Finikia, Santoríni 84702. ☎ **0286/71-373** (or Athens **01/65-47-944**). Fax 0286/71-338. 15 rms (all with bath).

Rates: 10,500 Drs ($43.75) single; 13,500 Drs ($56.35) double. MC, V.

This new sparkling white Cycladic complex has a good pool. Each room has its own personality and a small front patio garden.

Hotel Fregata, Oia, Santoríni 84702. ☎ **0286/71-221.** Fax 71-333. 19 rms (all with bath). TEL

Rates (including breakfast): 14,850 Drs ($61.90) double.

This is less costly than a villa, but is one of Oia's better hotels, another contemporary lodging with little traditional style. Yet how many hotels have this fantastic view, a plant-filled breakfast room, plus a giant chess game on the rooftop terrace?

Laokasti Villas, Oia, Santoríni 84702. ☎ **0286/71-343.** Fax 71-116. 8 units (all with bath). TEL

Rates (including breakfast): 24,000 Drs ($100) double; 4,000 Drs ($16.65) extra per person. AE, MC, V.

Eight small villas on the west side of the vehicle road, fashioned and fully furnished in the typical style. Kitchenettes and space to accommodate three or four in some rooms, add a homey feel. Laokasti, though, has the amenities of a hotel—a swimming pool, a reception room with fireplace, a cafeteria, cozy bar, and breakfast room with a panoramic view toward the beach and coast.

Lauda Rooms & Houses, Oia, Santoríni 84702. ☎ **0286/71-204** or **71-157.** 16 rms (2 with bath).

Rates: 12,700 Drs ($52.90) single/double without bath. 15,000 Drs ($62.50) single/double with bath; 20,000 Drs ($83.35) house with kitchen.

These are charming traditional rooms on the cliff side of Oia's only street, and we found them equally pleasant with or without a private bathroom. The Caldera view is priceless, making them a very good value.

A Splurge Choice

Perivolas Traditional Guesthouses, Oia, Santoríni, 84702. ☎ **0286/71-308** (in Athens ☎/fax **01/62-08-249**). Fax 0286/71-309. 14 rms (all with bath).

Rates: Beginning at 48,000 Drs ($200) for two and 74,000 Drs ($308.35) for four. EC, MC, V.

Of the privately run villas, the Perivolas Traditional Guesthouses are among the most beautiful. They are superbly restored, cavelike wineries with a rustic elegance, domed bathrooms, kitchenettes, patios, and a nice new pool.

WHERE TO EAT

Snackers can try the **Minute,** a small snackbar for ice cream or juices, or the bakery next to the bus stop. **Zorba's** is one of the better cliffside pubs for happy-hour or after-hour drinks.

Finikia Restaurant, Finíkia. ☎ 71-373.

Cuisine: GREEK/INTERNATIONAL.
Prices: Appetizers 480–1,000 Drs ($2–$4.15), main courses 1,400–3,200 Drs ($5.85–$13.35). MC, V.
Open: Daily 11am–1am.

In the village of Finíkia, on the bus road a ten-minute walk south of Oia, even the finicky will find something to their taste—hamburgers, soups, fried squid, chicken Kiev, meat casseroles, veal chops, fillets—on a lovely veranda with flowers on the tables.

Giorgios Taverna, Finíkia. ☎ 71-382.

Cuisine: GREEK.
Prices: Appetizers 220–1,000 Drs (92¢–$4.15), main courses 1,100–3,000 Drs ($4.60–$12.50). No credit cards.
Open: Daily 7pm–1am.

You'll also find good traditional Greek cooking in Finíkia village at this charming taverna; the stuffed vegetables and lamb dishes are particularly fine. (Giorgio can also help you find a room.)

Koletta Restaurant, Port of Oia. ☎ 71-280.

Cuisine: SEAFOOD.
Prices: Appetizers 180–960 Drs (75¢–$4), main courses 1,000–2,800 Drs ($4.15–$11.65).
Open: Daily 9am–1am.

Locals consider Katina Pagoni's the best place to eat in Oia, though it isn't in town, but down at the port of Ammoudi—best reached by donkey. It's very romantic on moonlit nights when the Aegean glitters at your feet.

Neptune Restaurant, Oia village. ☎ 71-294.

Cuisine: GREEK.
Prices: Appetizers 400–960 Drs ($1.65–$4), main courses 900–2,200 Drs ($3.75–$9.15). MC, V.
Open: Daily 7pm–1am.

A solid, modern Greek eatery with a rooftop garden—with a partial sunset view—near the church square. The Neptune enjoys a good local reputation for moderately priced, typical Greek dishes. We suggest their vegetable specials, always made with the season's best pick.

8 Tínos

87 nautical miles E of Piraeus; 66 nautical miles E of Rafína

ARRIVING/DEPARTING There are three or four **ferries** daily from Piraeus and three daily from Rafína; schedules should be confirmed with Tourist Information in

Athens (☎ **143**) or the Piraeus Port Authority (☎ **45-11-311**). Information and departure times from Rafína can be checked at 0294/25-200. There are several sailings daily from nearby Mýkonos, Sýros, and Ándros, and several daily excursions to Mýkonos and Délos, at 8,500 Drs ($35.40).

ESSENTIALS **OTE,** open from 8am to midnight, is on the corner of the main street (leading to the church of Evanghelístria) and Lazárou Dóchou Street. The **post office** is on the port next to the Hotel Tinion. Opposite the waterfront are several banks (open 8am to 1:30pm) and ferry ticket agents; we recommend **Nicholas Information Center** (☎ **24-142,** fax 24-049), open from 6:30am to midnight, for tickets, information, and rooms. There's a **first-aid center** (☎ **22-210**) and the **police** can be reached at 22-255.

Many visitors find Tínos the least commercial of all the Cyclades and enjoy a visit for exactly that reason. Tínos has some beautiful beaches, an attractive port town, traditional hill villages where little English is spoken, and a green landscape dotted with dovecotes from the Venetian period. The most heavily visited island in Greece, more than 90% of the tourists are Greeks themselves. Many people go on a day trip only to visit Tínos's famous site of religious pilgrimage at the port called Tínos town.

Church of Evanghelístria

Its church of Evanghelístria draws thousands of pilgrims annually, making Tínos the second "holy island" after Pátmos. The spiritual and national life of the Tinians has been centered around Panaghía Evanghelístria ("Our Lady of Good Tidings") since 1823. In 1822, Pelághia, a nun from the Kechrovouniou Nunnery, had a dream that an icon was buried on a nearby farm. She summoned her neighbors to help excavate, and they soon found the foundation of a Byzantine church. There, a workman found a gold figure of the Madonna, an icon thought to have been sent by the Virgin Mary to cure the faithful of Tínos. Work began immediately on the elegant, traditional-style Greek Orthodox church that can be seen today.

On August 15 (Feast of the Assumption) and on March 25 (Feast of the Annunciation), the faithful, and particularly the handicapped, infirm, and sick, make a pilgrimage to kiss the holy icon of the Madonna, hang their tin votive representations on her picture, and await a miracle cure.

From the ferry port, take the street on the left (where the Tínos Tours office is), Leofóros Megalochάris. The walled-in church is just a few minutes' walk away. You'll pass several shops selling candles (up to 6 feet long!), incense, medallions, books, and silver and gold votive offerings.

The church, built on two levels, is of Parian and Tinian marble—notice the prized green-veined marble from Tínos. The bottom level (always crowded with Greek children dressed in white) has small chapels and a baptismal font filled with gold and silver offerings. Around the Rhodian-style pebble-paved courtyard are galleries housing other icons, religious artifacts, and the painting and sculpture of some of the famous Greek artists from this island.

Continue up the grand marble stairs to the main chapel. To the left of the central isle is the Sacred Icon of the Madonna, so covered in gold and diamonds that it's hard to discern. The priests conduct services regularly. Outside the main chapel are a few galleries of ecclesiastical art.

The hours for the church and galleries are noon to 6pm year-round, increased to 8am to 8pm in summer, but the posted hours are not always adhered to. Some galleries are closed on certain days. To enter, you must be properly attired: long pants for men, long skirts for women.

Orientation

If you've seen enough tourists to last you a lifetime on other Greek islands, you might find Tínos town, the pleasant port, a refreshing change. Hotels, shops, and restaurants are accustomed to serving only Greek vacationers. Although few locals speak English, their enthusiasm and hospitality overcome any language barrier.

Getting Around

There are several shops renting **mopeds** (at 3,500 Drs or $14.60 a day)—we recommend Nicholas (☎ **24-142**) and Moto Mike (☎ **23-304**)—or **cars** (at 13,500 Drs or $52.25 with insurance). The **taxi stand** and **bus station** are at the harbor; you can check at the KTEL office there for schedules and rates.

What to See & Do

AROUND THE PORT

A half day can be spent exploring the **church of Evanghelístria** and its many museums. About half a block below the church on Leofóros Megalocháris is the **Archeology Museum,** open Tuesday through Sunday 8am to 1:30pm; admission is 500 Drs ($2.10). The small collection includes finds from the ancient sanctuary of Thesmophoríon (in the Exobourgo region). Of note are some 8th- to 7th-century B.C. red clay vases. In the museum's courtyard are marble sculptures from the 2d-century A.D. site at Kidomie, the Sanctuary of Poseidon and Amphitrite.

There's a fun **flea market** region behind the port that's easily found if you turn up the street where the Ferry Boat Naias ticket office is. Besides the huge variety of candles and religious paraphernalia, you can find embroideries, weavings, and the wonderful local nougat and Sýros-made *loukoúmia* (Turkish delights), along with typical Greek souvenirs at lesser prices. Ceramic shops on the waterfront, **Margarita** and **Bernardo** and **Manina,** also have particularly fine pottery, jewelry, and copperware at moderate prices.

Don't miss the shop of **Harris Prassas Ostria–Tinos** Odós Evanghelístrias 20 (☎ **23-893**, fax 24-568). He has a fabulous collection of gold and silver jewelry in contemporary or classical styles, silverwork, and beautiful religious icons. It isn't a place for bargains, but it's very fine work and credit cards are accepted.

AROUND THE ISLAND

The 800-odd **dovecotes** scattered throughout the island are one of Tínos's most picturesque assets. Many date from the 17th century, when proud Venetians built towers with ornate latticework tiles on top for their doves to sit on. The lazy man's way to see some of these dovecotes is to take about a half-hour walk west from town. Follow the waterfront around the Aigli Hotel and you'll find the west road that takes you by some small breakwaters. As you see the dark sand-and-rock Stavrós beach come into view, below you on the left will be a charming blue-domed church that has a small ouzerí below it, right at the water's edge. This spot can be lovely or perilous, depending on the *meltémi* winds.

From the coast road you can see the large Tínos Beach Hotel, which has two authentic dovecotes (behind the tennis courts) on its property. Past the hotel, on the coast road, you'll find the minimal ruins of the excavated temple of Poseidon and Amphitrite.

A pleasant day trip from Tínos to Pýrgos will take you through many inland villages to the region of green marble quarries and local sculptors. From Pýrgos you can go to Tínos's best beach (at Panormos), where there are rooms to rent. Buses leave the port five times a day beginning at 6:30am for the one hour trip; check the schedule at the stop in Pýrgos for return times. For dovecote fans, a short detour would include **Tarampados** or **Koumaros.** These villages are in the Exbourgo region, the old acropolis of Tínos where the ruins of a Venetian castle can be seen. Every two hours a Tínos bus runs the route through the villages of **Steni** and **Mesi,** then up to **Falatados,** a typical hill village. Ornithologists should purchase the white-covered map that gives the bird types found in each region of Tínos (found at any of the harbor newsstands).

BEACHES **Ághios Fokás** is just south of town, but seekers of isolated beaches should try **Kolymbíthra** on the better-protected northern coast. Local buses run six times daily to **Kómi** from Tínos, a beautiful ride through the hills. From here it's only a 3 km walk to the dark sand beach, and there's a campsite nearby. Since there is no public transport, only a moped will give you access to the little-known **Lychnaftia** and **Porto** beaches on the southeast coast.

Where to Stay

You'll have no problems finding a room if you avoid the Panaghía festivities in March and August; however, hotels often become crowded in July, when most Greeks vacation.

On several streets behind the port you can find rooms-to-let from 4,500 to 6,500 Drs ($18.75–$27.10) for two. Next to the Hotel Oceanis on Gkízi Street we found rooms to let at **O Giannis** (☎ **0283/22-515**) in a wonderful old house with green shutters and balconies. Large, high-ceilinged, very homey rooms with spotless shared facilities cost 4,600 Drs ($19.15) for two—a fair price for such a warm, friendly environment. **Stratis Keladitis** (☎ **0283/24-142**), who runs the Nicholas Information Centre at Odós Evanghelístrias 24 (the main market street perpendicular to the port), keeps ten broom-clean, old, sloped-floor rooms in a pension above the shop. He's friendly and filled with advice, has cheap moped rentals, postcards, and so on. The rooms with shared shower cost 4,350 Drs ($18.15) for two. Both places are within a five-minute walk of the ferry pier.

Avra Hotel, Tínos town, Tínos 84200. ☎ **0283/22-242.** 14 rms (all with bath).

Rates: 7,150 Drs ($29.80) single; 10,695 Drs ($44.55) double. No credit cards.

East on the waterfront is the 112-year-old Avra, whose simple, old-fashioned, high-ceilinged rooms are very spacious. They're built off a common hallway circling a plant-filled tiled courtyard.

Hotel Eleana, Platía Ierarchón, Tínos town, Tínos 84200. ☎ **0283/22-561.** 17 rms (all with bath).

Rates: 5,750 Drs ($23.95) single, 7,475 Drs ($31.15) double. V

Tínos's best-value hotel is on the pretty Platía Ierarchón (behind the Hotel Posidonios). The small Eleana doesn't have harbor views, but the rooms are large and sunny and have balconies.

Hotel Tinion, Odós Alavánou 1, Tínos town, Tínos 84200. ☎ **0283/22-261.** 20 rms (all with bath).

Rates: 9,200 Drs ($38.35) single; 11,500 Drs ($47.90) double. EC, MC.

This hotel—first and foremost in our minds—is immediately striking in its old-world air, with lace curtains, marble floors, and hand-polished wood. Its rooms have 14-foot ceilings, a huge terrace, and old tilework floors.

Where to Eat

Tínos has some particularly good restaurants, probably because their customers are most often other Greeks.

Lefteris, harborfront, Tínos. ☎ **23-013.**

Cuisine: GREEK.

Prices: Appetizers 150–800 Drs (65¢–$3.35), main courses 700–2,300 Drs ($2.90–$9.60). No credit cards.

Open: Daily 11am–midnight.

Hidden near the harbor, Lefteris is identifiable by a blue neon sign over an arched entranceway that opens to a huge garden court decorated with fish plaques on the walls. The grilled sea bass, veal *stifádo* (with onions), and lemon-coated *dolmádes* (stuffed grape leaves) are especially recommended from the varied menu. A large open area behind the tables invites dancing by enthusiastic tourists and waiters!

O Kipos, Tínos. ☎ **22-838.**

Cuisine: GREEK.

Prices: Appetizers 140–720 Drs (60¢–$3), main courses 800–2,100 Drs ($3.35–$8.75). No credit cards.

Open: Daily noon–midnight.

A small taverna run by the friendly Yannis Krontira that's very popular is located almost four lanes inland from the taxi stand (turn left after the Posidonios Hotel). In this quiet, residential section of town you'll see the bright lights of O Kipos (The Garden). Behind the kitchen area is a lush garden, where you can eat simple and good taverna fare and consume light white retsina at very reasonable prices.

★ $ **Peristerionas,** Odós Paksimádi Fraiskóu 12, Tínos. ☎ **23-425.**

Cuisine: GREEK.

Prices: Appetizers 460–1,000 Drs ($1.90–$4.15), main courses 1,400–1,750 Drs ($5.85–$7.30). No credit cards.

Open: Daily 12–3pm, 7–11:30pm.

Our favorite is Peristeriónas ("Dovecote"), which is decorated to resemble one of the Venetian towers built as dove perches that are found all over Tínos. The restaurant is found on a small lane uphill and left behind the Lido Hotel, and its outdoor tables and chairs fill the walkway. The Dovecote's special courses are grilled meats and fish. Their delicious contribution to Greek cuisine is the wonderful dill, onion, and vegetable fritters called *marathotiganítes*.

9 Ándros

43 nautical miles E of Rafína

ARRIVING/DEPARTING Ándros can only be reached by ferry from Rafína, but is connected twice daily to Tínos or Mýkonos, and once daily to Sýros. Contact

George Batis Travel (☎ **0282/71-489**) at the port of Gávrio or the Strintzis Lines in Gávrio (☎ **0282/71-235**), or at their Rafína office (☎ **0294/25-200**) for schedule information. For the Ándros Port Authority call **0282/71-213.**

ESSENTIALS The telephone center (OTE), the *post office,* the *taxi station,* and a bank are on the main square, Platía Goulandrís, in the inland capital, Chóra. There are several ferry ticket offices in Batsi and Gávrio. The *police* can be reached at **23-300**; **41-204** in Batsi; **71-220** in Gávrio. For *medical emergencies* call **41-326.**

At the port of Gávrio *Achivida Tourism Office* (☎ **71-556,** fax 71-571), above the Ydroussa Bar, exchanges money, sells ferry tickets, and arranges accommodations.

Evergreen-covered Ándros, the second-largest island in the Cyclades, has long been cherished by Greek tourists for its pine-shaded beaches, old-fashioned family values, and uninflated prices. After centuries in which the mercantile trade made Ándros one of the few islands that prospered without foreign tourism, economic realities are slowly changing. The fabulously wealthy Goulandris family, shipping magnates and global jet-setters, have given sleepy Ándros international cachet with enormous gifts: Chóra's stunning museum of modern art and the excellent archeological museum next door are both courtesy of Basil and Elise Goulandris. Their grand entry into the international art scene has done more to popularize the island than any travel agency and has assured that foreign tourism will continue to develop.

Ándros's earlier moment in the spotlight was in 1833 when archeologists unearthed two statues, the *Hermes of Ándros* and another that was the likeness of a woman from Iráklio. All the furor was over the artist, thought to be Praxiteles; later, however, scholars concluded he must have been a 1st-century B.C. sculptor from a little-known Parian workshop. Both figures were on display in the National Museum in Athens until 1981, when Elise Goulandris persuaded the Greek government that two of its finest treasures should be returned to the new museum home that she'd created for them.

Orientation

Most foreign tourist activity is centered in Batsi, a small village with an ordinary sand beach just 6 km south of the ferry port at Gávrio. The main town, Ándros or Chóra, is on the north coast, where strong winds make its beaches less pleasant for swimming. However, this pretty hilltop town filled with narrow steps, winding lanes, and some fine neoclassic mansions has two museums that are the island's newest attractions.

In the high season the frequent ferries to and from Tínos and Mýkonos mean you can take an extended day trip just to visit the museums. If you plan to stay overnight, we'd recommend Batsi as your base, so you can squeeze in a refreshing swim at the beach. If you're looking for a very Greek experience, make Chóra your home.

Gávrio

Your first stop will be the island's only active port at **Gávrio,** where three lines servicing Ándros from Rafína call. (You can't get there from Piraeus.) Ticket offices are opposite the ferry pier at the north side of the small C-shaped fishing cove. In the center of Gávrio is the local's favorite, **Valmas Taverna.** The small pebble and sand beach at Gávrio's south end is reserved for the fishers, some wild ducks, a few chickens, stray cats, and odd litter. Buses leave five times daily from the ferry pier to Batsi, and cost 180 Drs (75¢) versus 2,500 Drs ($10.40) taxi fare; call **22-316** for information. To Chóra the fare is 420 Drs ($1.75); versus 3,500 Drs ($14.60) taxi fare.

Batsi

Batsi is built amphitheatrically around a C-shaped cove with a small caique port at its south end. There is a portable post office, an OTE (telephone) center, and a moped rental shop near the Hotel Scouna. The **police** can be reached at **41-204.**

Heading south from Batsi to Ándros town or Chóra, you'll come to **Paleopolis,** site of an ancient acropolis 300 meters above sea level. Many beautiful Hellenistic sculptures, including the *Hermes of Ándros,* came from this site and can be seen in the Archeological Museum. At Stavrópeda you turn east over Ándros's tall central mountains to Messaria, with its noted Byzantine-era **Church of the Taxiarchis.**

Where to Stay

Dimitris and Thanie Marousas (☎ **0282/41-080**) have spacious comfortable apartments in a quiet location 150 meters from the bus stop, a five-minute walk from the center of town; doubles are 14,200 Drs ($51.15).

If they or the central Chryssi Akti Hotel (see below) are full, head to the **Andrina Tours** office (☎ **0282/41-064,** fax 41-620), where between May and October, Ulli, Giannis, or Theo will help you find a place to stay, exchange money, and arrange car or motorbike rental or a bus tour around the island for 5,500 Drs ($22.90). Batsi's few other hotels consign all their rooms to travel agents and won't deal with individual tourists, so Ulli can get you a studio with kitchenette in one of the area's many private lodgings. They typically cost 7,500 Drs ($31.25) for one, 10,000 Drs ($41.65) for two, or 12,500 Drs ($52.10) for three per night. Long-term stays, private villas, and other accommodations are negotiable. There is camping outside Gávrio at **Camping Ańdros** (☎ **0282/71-444**).

Chryssi Akti Hotel, Batsi, Ándros 84503. ☎ **0282/41-236.** Fax 0282/41-268.
61 rms (all with bath). MINIBAR TV TEL

Rates: 8,000 Drs ($33.35) single; 10,000 Drs ($41.65) double. No credit cards.

If the central Chryssí Akti Hotel, located across from the town beach, has available rooms, grab one. Their older doubles are a bit worn, but are clean and have big balconies and private showers.

Where to Eat

Batsi has several sweet shops and markets, and some good restaurants.

O Ti Kalo, Batsi. No telephone.

Cuisine: SEAFOOD.

Prices: Appetizers 150–850 Drs (65¢–$3.55), main courses 800–2,800 Drs ($3.35–$11.65). No credit cards.

Open: Daily noon–3pm, 7pm–1am.

This small place one level up from the caique port is great for fish; check out the day's catch. They also offer a popular combo platter of lobster, *barboúni* (red mullet), and red snapper called "Georgy Porgy."

Rainbow Restaurant, Batsi. ☎ **41-467.**

Cuisine: INTERNATIONAL.

Prices: Appetizers 350–750 Drs ($1.45–$3.15), pasta 850–1,200 Drs ($3.55–$5), pizza 1,400–2,000 Drs ($5.85–$8.35). No credit cards.

Open: Daily 6pm–3am.

A ten-minute stroll up from the beach is this delightful new sparkling-white place with spacious seating in the garden or inside under flickering chandeliers with fountains splashing. The food is widely varied in style and interesting, and the staff is friendly and attentive.

Taverna Oasis, Batsi. ☎ **41-590.**

Cuisine: GREEK.
Prices: Appetizers 300–700 Drs ($1.25–$2.90), main courses 800–1,300 Drs ($3.35–$5.40). No credit cards.
Open: Daily 7pm–1am.

On the hillside next door to the Rainbow is this less formal taverna that serves grilled fresh meat and chicken specialties under a vine-covered pergola. There's plenty of room to dance to the Greek music.

The **Gallery Coffee Bar,** near Andrina Tours on the beach, is a good place to watch the sun set and enjoy a cocktail or ice cream concoctions. There are plenty of bars for later hours and two popular discos, the **Blue Sky,** on the hillside road above the Chryssi Akti, and **Sunrise,** just off the same road, toward Batsi. If you have your own transport, try the **Marabout Pizza Disco,** halfway between Batsi and Gávrio on the main road.

Chóra

Platía Goulandrís is the heart of Chóra, with the bus and taxi stations, post office, and an OTE (telephone) center. Goulandrís Street is the main pedestrian thoroughfare. Ańdros's capital is built on a promontory with houses tumbling down both sides to sandy beaches (too rough for swimming because of the north winds). Steep stairs and narrow lanes are the only way to navigate the back streets.

On Main Street above the Ionian Bank is the old **Egli Hotel** (☎ **0282/22-303**), one of the early Class C places with 15 double rooms renting for 7,500 Drs ($31.25) per night. You'll find many *zacharoplastía* (pâtisseries), each selling the island's own *loukoúmia* (Turkish delights), and its special sweet, the ground-almond *amygdalota.* The monumental marble **Kambanis Fountain** is the centerpiece of **Platía Theofílis Kairí,** the central square with a good taverna overlooking the sea and these two museums.

The **Archeological Museum of Ándros** features sculpture from the archaic through Roman periods (700 B.C.–A.D. 330) on the ground floor. These modern, well-lit galleries include the beautiful *Hermes,* thought to be a marble copy of a bronze by Praxiteles. There is also a gallery of marbles from many of the island's Byzantine- and Venetian-era sites. The museum is open Tuesday through Sunday from 10am to 2pm; admission is 500 Drs ($2.10).

Down the steps from the archeological museum is the **Goulandrís Museum of Modern Art,** with a separate **Museum of Sculpture** across the lane. Both contain a remarkable collection of contemporary Greek and European art. Unfortunately, they're open only from May through September, Wednesday through Monday, from 10am to 2pm and 6 to 9pm.

Buses run from Gávrio to Chóra four times daily, passing through Batsi; it's a one-hour trip. Just north of Chóra is Stenies, an older village known for the **Bistis Mouvelas Tower,** one of the few remaining 17th-century fortified homes left on the island. This village has been well preserved by the merchant seamen who still live here and in Chóra.

10 Sérifos, Sífnos, Mílos & Folégandros

None of the western Cyclades is nearly as developed for tourism as their more publicized cousins, though they are beginning to receive the overflow from the hugely popular islands of Mýkonos, Páros, Íos, and Santoríni. Sérifos is the island for those who want to lose the crowd completely. Sínos is a gorgeous island, with an equally attractive beach, that's beginning to become popular, while Mílos offers the most interesting archeological sites and striking scenery.

Sérifos

Sérifos ("Bare One") is one of the most untouched places in Greece. It derives its name from its rocky landscape. According to mythology, when Perseus (son of Zeus) and his mother, Danae, were cast into the sea off the coast of Árgos, they drifted for a very long time until they washed ashore on Sérifos. Here, they lived happily for many years. When the young Perseus matured, King Polidectus of Sérifos ordered him to kill the snake-haired monster Medusa. The king hoped that in Perseus's absence he could woo Danae. Perseus, to everyone's amazement, returned home with the Medusa's head and, learning of the king's plot, turned him and the court into stone. The legacy of these stones is the bare island we see today.

ARRIVING/DEPARTING There are departures five times weekly (daily in summer) from Piraeus on the Sérifos-Sínos-Mílos route. Sérifos is also connected to Kýthnos, Íos, and Santoríni, although only once or twice a week. Check with the Port Authority in Athens (☎ **143** or **45-11-311**) or in Livádi (☎ **0281/51-470**) for schedules.

ESSENTIALS The **Sérifos Travel and Tourist Office** in Livádi behind the market will change money, give information, and help you find a room—if they're open. Otherwise, see Mr. Bouris at the Hotel Areti. There are **ferry ticket agents** near the port, but no banks. The telephone center **(OTE)** and the **post office** are up the hill in Chóra, just off the main square. OTE is open daily from 7:30am to 12:30am. The post office will change money and is open Monday through Saturday from 7:30am to 2:30pm. The **police** can be reached at 51-300. There's a **medical clinic** and a doctor can be reached at 51-202.

ORIENTATION

Livádi ("meadow") lies in a small relatively verdant lowland, where family farms grow apricots, figs, grapes, beans, and tomatoes in a helter-skelter fashion. Mosquitos abound, so repellant may be necessary. Some hotels have screens or repellant systems. You may want to purchase one of those inexpensive small electrical devices that burn an odorless tablet, a good investment.

Ferries land on the south side at a modern pier, yachts and caiques moor in the middle, and a narrow, pebble and sand beach with rooms-to-let extends to the north.

On a barren rock above Livádi is Chóra or Sérifos, a startling image of whitewashed houses and churches clinging like melted ice cream to the peak at Kástro. Hand-hewn rock steps wind their way up the steep hillside from Livádi (the car road is 5 km) to Chóra. On this centuries-old path you'll pass donkeys carrying old women to the port, men on their way to the farms, and children rushing uphill to school. In Chóra, the village elders calmly wash oregano to fix lunch or pluck weeds from between the marble tiles outside their homes. If you look in the cracks of walls and stone you'll find a rare pink flower that's known to grow only on the island.

GETTING AROUND

The island's two **buses** run several times daily between Livádi and Chóra from the ferry pier. (Like much of Sérifos, they are somewhat erratic; sometimes they meet the boat, sometimes they run hourly, and sometimes they're not seen for hours.) You can rent cars and mopeds at **Blue Bird Rentals** (☎ **51-511**).

WHAT TO SEE & DO

Beetle-shaped Sérifos is the third-largest of the western Cyclades, with most development on its southeast side, facing toward Sínos. **Chóra** is a must-see for anyone visiting the island. There's a direct cobblestone donkey path much of the way. If you decide to climb it, go early in the day and wear good shoes for the 45-minute climb up the moderate slope, or take the bus up and walk down. Just as you enter the town there's a small **Folk Art Museum** up on the right. From the bus stop there are a few signs, some of them in white on the pavement, that lead you to the central square and the handsome if faded yellow and red neoclassical **Town Hall,** which has a small collection of marbles in its basement, entered from the street on its left, that barely qualifies as an **Archeological Museum;** admission is free. Continue through the square and up to reach the Kástro.

Parts of the ancient fortress of the **Kástro** are said to date from Roman times, but it was left in its present state of ruin after a pirate raid in the 13th century. The small chapel of **St. John Theológos** is at its peak, on the site of an ancient temple of Athena. Downhill from here, through lanes of crumbling stone houses flanked by pristine white-and-blue Cycladic restorations, are homes with Venetian medallions over their doors or ancient marble steps.

It's a brief walk to the square, where Kýklopos Street and the car route meet, site of a few coffeehouses and tavernas, which offer a view of old windmills. Their disabled spokes used to drive huge grinding stones to mill flour from wheat brought to Chóra by the island's farmers.

Just a ten-minute walk over the hill above Livádi's ferry pier on the southwest side of town is **Livadákia,** a popular family beach community. There is a very nice coarse sand beach lined with tamarisk trees, some snack bars, pedal boat rentals, lots of rooms-to-let, and the aptly named Relax Pub. Isolated **Karávi Beach,** a 20-minute walk from Livadákia (the road is only partially passable by moped), is a favorite spot for nude sunbathing.

Northeast of Livádi, a 3-km walk or moped ride from the town beach to the next cove, is **Psilí Ámmos,** one of Sérifos's best sand beaches. You'll find some rooms to let here, and snack cafés on the way. A bit farther is the smaller but pretty **Ághios Sostis** beach, south of the promontory with the church of this name.

About 6 km west is **Koutalas,** an old iron-ore mining village whose now devastated buildings are very picturesque. There is a small snack bar in the village, and a narrow road leading to the tree-lined, sand beach at Ganema. An unpaved road leads east to **Méga Livádi,** and in this small sheltered cove you'll find another beach.

In northern Sérifos, near Galaní, is the grand **monastery of the Taxiarchs,** built in 1600 in dedication to Sérifos's patron saints, Michael and Gabriel. Unfortunately, if any of these excursions interest you, you'll have to rent a moped or car to see them.

WHERE TO STAY

Most of the island's hotels and pensions are in Livádi, the main port.

Hotel Areti, Livádi, Sérifos 84005. ☎ **0281/51-479.** Fax 51-547. 12 rms (all with bath).

Rates: 9,200 Drs ($38.35) single; 10,350 Drs ($43.15) double. No credit cards.

This excellent pension up the stairway closest to the ferry pier is the best value on the island, and you'll be close to Livadákia Beach, just over the hill. The Areti is built on a hill and offers great views, especially from its top-floor, balconied rooms. Breakfast at the pleasant snackbar downstairs is only 800 Drs ($3.35) per person.

Maistrali Hotel, Livádi, Sérifos 84005. ☎ **0281/51-381** or **51-220.** Fax 0281/51-298. 19 rms (all with bath).

Rates: 16,000 Drs ($66.65) single/double. Back-facing rooms are about 20% less. No credit cards.

This attractive hotel with clean modern rooms is midway on the port beach (called Avlomonas). It's the closest hotel to the nearby, much nicer, sand and swimming beach at Psilí Ámmos, and it has its own restaurant.

Sérifos Beach Hotel, Livádi, Sérifos 84005. ☎ **0281/51-209.** Fax 0281/51-209. 40 rms (all with bath).

Rates: 9,000 Drs ($37.50) double. AE, DC, MC, V.

The older Sérifos Beach Hotel is one lane back from the beach. The tall tamarisks in front block the view, but it's a comfortable if somewhat homely choice. The Sérifos Beach is open year-round.

WHERE TO EAT

Livádi has most of the island's eateries, most of them fronting along the beach. On the first stairway up on the left as you leave the ferry pier you'll find **Ta Skalakia,** which according to Robin, a Scottish travel writer, has "seriously good gyros."

Taverna O Mokkas, Livádi. ☎ **51-242.**

Cuisine: GREEK.
Prices: Appetizers 250–1,200 Drs ($1.05–$5); main courses 900–2,500 Drs ($3.75–$10.40). EC, MC, V.
Open: Daily noon–midnight.

One of the first places on the town beach is also one of the best. Standard Greek fare is well prepared and the service is prompt and friendly. We particularly liked the moussaká, *yemistá* (stuffed tomato), and french fries.

Taverna Stamatis, Livádi. ☎ **51-309.**

Cuisine: GREEK.
Prices: Appetizers 290–740 Drs ($1.20–$3.10), main courses 750–2,000 Drs ($3.15–$8.35). No credit cards.
Open: 7pm–midnight.

On the far side of the beach around Livádi's broad bay, with a red neon sign on its roof, is this typical taverna with good, inexpensive Greek fare. It's a favorite of locals for fresh fish, 6,500–8,000 Drs ($27.10–$33.35) per kilo.

Sífnos

One of the best-kept secrets in the Cyclades, Sífnos is a favorite destination for Greeks who want to escape the hordes of tourists on the other islands. Like Sérifos, the island was famed in antiquity for its mines, but in Sífnos's case the ore that was extracted was gold. Each year, the islanders sent a solid-gold egg to Delphi as a tribute to Apollo. But one year they succumbed to their greedier instincts and substituted a gilded egg. Apollo, incensed, sank the mines deep into the Aegean. Since that time no gold has been found on the island, giving meaning to its name—Sífnos, "Empty One."

ARRIVING/DEPARTING There is at least one boat daily from Piraeus, in addition to daily connections to the other western Cyclades, Sérifos and Mílos. The small F/B *Margarita* makes a three-hour crossing from Kamáres to Paroikía, on Páros, every Monday, Wednesday, and Friday (daily in summer), and returns the same day. There is also a ferry four times a week to Íos and Santoríni, and a ferry once a week to Crete. Contact the **Port Authority** in Piraeus (☎ **143** or **45-11-131**) or in Sífnos (☎ **0284/31-617**) for information.

ESSENTIALS Your first stop should be the excellent **Aegean Thesaurus Travel and Tourism** office on the port (☎ **31-804**) or **Siphanto Travel** (☎ **32-034,** fax 31-024), where you can book a room, buy ferry tickets, rent a car or motorbike, arrange excursions, and leave your luggage.

Tourist services are centered around the main square, Platía Iróon, in Apollonía. The **post office** (☎ **31-329**) is open weekdays from 8am to 3pm, Saturday and Sunday 9am to 1:30pm in the summer. The National Bank (☎ **31-237**) is open Monday through Thursday from 8am to 2pm, Friday 8am to 1:30pm. The telephone center (OTE), just down the vehicle road, is open daily from 8am to 3pm, and in summer 5 to 10pm. (The news kiosk on the square has a metered phone for after-hours calls.) The **police station** (☎ **31-210**) is just east of the square, and a first aid station is nearby; for **medical emergencies** call **31-315.**

The main office of **Aegean Thesaurus** (☎/fax **0284/311-145**), 20 meters north of the square up the pedestrian lane, is a one-stop help center, where you can cash traveler's checks, pick up a bus schedule and a good map of the island for 600 Drs ($2.50), book a flight, and avail yourself of their other services every day from 9am to midnight; all credit cards accepted.

ORIENTATION

To ferry passengers, almond-shaped Sífnos appears to be a barren rock stretched lazily across the western Aegean. In fact, the island's west coast, dominated by the port at Kamáres, is much drier than the east. Most visitors arriving during the cooler weather (facilities are open from mid-April to late September) will want to base themselves at Apollonía, the island's inland capital. It's the most interesting village and just 5 km northeast of the port.

In the high season things get very busy. A room at the east coast beach resort at Platís, Ghialós is most highly prized, but the yachting crowd and lively cafés of Kamáres give it appeal also. If you're not a dedicated sun worshipper, head to Apollonía or the picturesque village of Artemóna.

From Apollonía's **Platía Iróon,** site of a monument to Sífnos's World War II veterans, gently sloped, winding pedestrian paths of flagstone and marble lead through this beautiful Cycladic village. Along the village's only car route are a few shops, a small market with island maps,and everyone's favorite hangout, Lakis Kafeneion.

GETTING AROUND

Getting around Sífnos is one of its pleasures; many visitors come for the wonderful hiking and mountain trails. We didn't think a car or moped was necessary. Apollonía's

Platía Iróon is the main taxi stand and island bus stop. The bus system is fairly efficient, and can be combined with delightful walks up and down the cultivated hillsides, so that they're not too tiring. Apollonía does have a few moped dealers; try **Yoni's** (☎ **31-155**) on the main square or **Easy Rider** (☎ **31-001**) on the road circling the village. Cars can be rented at **FS** (☎ **31-795**) and **Aegean Thesaurus** (☎ **31-145**) in Apollonía or in Kamáres at **Siphanto Travel** (☎ **32-034**) or **Sífnos Car** (☎ **31-793**).

WHAT TO SEE & DO

In Kamáres, the town beach is the focal point of most people's day, unless you're out polishing the hull of your yacht. When you levitate from the sand, explore the shops filled with the island's best-known contemporary commodity: ceramics. Sifniot ceramics and everyday pottery are exported throughout Greece and are still in wide use because of their durability and charming folk designs. One of the most interesting shops is the ceramics workshop of **Antonis Kalogirou** (☎ **31-651**) on the main harborside lane. Antonis sells folk paintings of island life and the typical pottery of Sífnos, which is manufactured in his showroom from the deep gray or red clay mined in the inland hill region. Most of the pottery sold is usable and inexpensive, but there are also decorative pieces.

From the Kamáres pier you can hire a caique to **Vathí,** a small coastal village due south, with a good sandy beach. Vathí's twin-domed **monastery of the Taxiarchs** watches over the skimpily clad bathers. Vathí is also the site of some old potteries, which can be explored, and has several tavernas. **Chersónissos** is an even better beach on the north coast that's accessible by a new unpaved road or by caique from Kamáres. In the summer season, travelers gather at the caique port and bargain with fishermen, who usually charge about 6,000 Drs ($25) each way for a boat seating ten.

In Apollonía, there's a small **Popular and Folk Art Museum** on Platía Iroon, open July–Sept 15, 10am–1pm, 6–10pm, 300 Drs ($1.25). Left of it on the pedestrian lane, **Cheronissos** (☎ **32-209**) has a choice selection of contemporary jewelry and ceramics. There are several other contemporary ceramics galleries featuring the excellent work of Greek artisans in the winding back streets, as well as **Mouses** (☎ **32-165**) 50 meters north of the main bus stop on the road to Artemona.

Kástro is a beautiful east coast village, just 3 km south. Enter through either of the carved marble loggias; well-preserved and decaying whitewashed houses adjoin each other in irregular chains circling the sheer cliff. The Venetians took Sífnos in 1307 and built this fortress on the foundation of the ancient acropolis. Venetian coats-of-arms are still visible above the doorways of the older houses that abut the fort. Kástro is built overlooking the sea, with a small pebble swimming beach at sea level. Within this maze are a few shops, rooms-to-let, and a small **Archeological Museum,** open daily from 10am to 2pm.

WHERE TO STAY

Apollonía

Many young Athenians vacation on Sífnos, particularly on summer weekends, and it can be very difficult to find a room. **Aegean Thesaurus** (☎/fax **0284/32-190**) can place two in a room in a private house with your own bathroom for 6,000 to 7,000 Drs ($25–$29.15), in a studio with a kitchenette for 9,750 Drs ($40.65), or in other accommodations ranging up to a stylish villa and sleeping six for 50,000 Drs ($208.30) per night.

Hotel Anthoussa, Apollonía, Sífnos 84003. ☎ **0284/31-431.** 7 rms (all with bath).

Rates: 9,200 Drs ($38.35) single; 10,350 Drs ($43.15) double. MC, V.

This hotel is above the excellent and popular Gerontopoulos café–pâtisserie. Although the streetside rooms offer wonderful views over the hills, they overlook the late-night sweet-tooth crowd and in the high season can only be recommended to night owls. The back rooms are quieter and overlook a beautiful bower of bougainvillea.

★ **Hotel Sífnos,** Apollonía, Sífnos 84003. ☎ **0284/31-624.** 9 rms (all with bath).

Rates: 7,130 Drs ($29.70) single, 10,500 Drs ($43.75) double. AE, EC, MC, V.

This is the best in the village, located southeast of the main square, on the pedestrians-only street to the cathedral. The hotel's manager, Helen Diareme, and her son Apostolos will do their best to make your stay comfortable. The Sífnos is open year-round and is the most traditional choice in terms of island architecture.

Hotel Sofia, Apollonía, Sífnos 84003. ☎ **0284/31-238.** 11 rms (all with shower).

Rates: 5,320 Drs ($22.15) single; 7,445 Drs ($31) double. No credit cards.

This recently built hotel is on the road circling the town, a two-minute walk from the square. Most of the rooms are large with private shower, many with balconies overlooking the town roofs, and a supermarket on the ground floor.

Hotel Artemon, Artemóna, Sífnos 84003. ☎ **0284/31-303** or **31-888** in winter. Fax 0284/32-385. 24 rms (all with bath). TEL

Prices (including breakfast): 11,960 Drs ($49.85) single; 15,870 Drs ($66.15) double. AE, EC, MC, V.

This quiet, comfortable hotel is on the road just before the *platia.* Patios or balconies show off the pastoral view of wheat fields and olive groves sliding slowly to the sea. The Artemon has a large terrace restaurant shaded by grape vines, and a lobby lounge that is spacious enough for families to play in.

Kamáres

Though it has the biggest concentration of hotels and pensions on the island, make reservations by May if you plan to be in Kamáres during the high season.

Hotel Boulis, Kamáres, Sífnos 84003. ☎ **0284/32-122; 31-640** in winter. Fax 0284/32-381. 45 rms (all with bath). TEL

Rates (including breakfast): 6,920 Drs ($28.80) single; 10,640 Drs ($44.30) double. AE.

This recently built hotel is right on the port's beach and has many amenities, including large carpeted rooms with beach-view balconies and a spacious marble-floored reception.

Hotel Kamari, Kamáres, Sífnos 84003. ☎ **0284/31-709.** Fax 0284/31-709. 18 rms (all with bath). TEL

Rates: 6,635 Drs ($27.65) single; 9,780 Drs ($39.50) double. AE, MC, V.

This is a clean, attractive lodging with balconied rooms at the quiet end of town, where the road and beach meet. The friendly and attentive management also offers car rental and transfer to other villages by minibus.

Hotel Stavros, Kamáres, Sífnos 84003. ☎ **0284/31-641.** Fax 0284/31-709. 14 rms (10 with bath). TEL

Rates: 5,585 Drs ($23.25) single/double without bath, 8,000 Drs ($33.35) double with bath. AE, MC, V.

The same friendly management who runs the Hotel Kamari also tends this simple place on the paralia next to the church. Kyle found it quiet, and the spartan rooms and common showers are kept very clean.

Platís Ghialós

July and August bring the stormy *meltémi* winds and the many Greek and European tourists who return annually to this resort's few pensions and hotels. The new **Community Camping** (☎ **31-786**), just 600 meters from the beach, costs 650 Drs ($2.70) per person, with free showers for guests.

Hotel Benakis, Platís Ghialós, Sífnos 84003. ☎ **0284/32-221.** 24 rms (all with bath).

Prices (including breakfast): 9,200 Drs ($38.35) single; 16,000 Drs ($66.65) double. No credit cards.

This small hotel is run by the friendly, helpful Benakis family. We're happy to report that it's fine, with a lovely sea view from its perch on the main road.

Hotel Philoxenia, Platís Ghialós, Sífnos 84003. ☎ **0284/32-221.** 9 rms (all with bath).

Prices (including breakfast): 11,250 Drs ($47) single/double. No credit cards.

This small, simple hotel on the main street has large, clean rooms, some with balconies offering sea views.

★ **Hotel Platis Gialos,** Platís Ghialós, Sífnos 84003. ☎ **0284/31-324** or **0831/22-626** in winter. Fax 0284/31-325 or 0831/55-049 in winter. 26 rms (all with bath). A/C TEL

Prices (including breakfast): 22,750 Drs ($94.80) single; 27,600 Drs ($115) double. No credit cards.

The island's best hotel is ideally situated overlooking the beach from its perch on the west side of the cove. A recent renovation has added modern bathrooms with tubs and tiling throughout, large private patios to the ground-floor rooms and wonderful ceramics, painted tiles, and small paintings as a final touch. The Platis Gialos's flagstone sun deck extends from the beach to a diving platform at the end of the cove, with a bar and restaurant sharing the same Aegean views.

WHERE TO EAT

Apollonía

Apostoli's Koutouki Taverna, Apollonía. ☎ **31-186.**

Cuisine: GREEK.
Prices: Appetizers 340–900 Drs ($1.40–$3.75), main courses 1,100–2,800 Drs ($4.60–$11.65). No credit cards.

There are several tavernas in Apollonía, but this is the best for Greek food, though the service is usually Greek slow. Any of the vegetable dishes, most made from locally grown produce, are delicious.

Sifnos Cafe-Restaurant, Apollonía. ☎ **31-624.**

Cuisine: GREEK.
Price: Appetizers 300–800 Drs ($1.25–$3.35); main courses 1,000–2,400 Drs ($4.15–$10). AE, EC, MC, V.
Open: Daily 8am–midnight.

On the main pedestrian street up to the cathedral, between the Sifnos Hotel and a quiet plaza, under a grape arbor, you'll find the best all-around place to eat in town.

Breakfast includes fresh fruit juice and a dozen coffees. Choose from a variety of snacks, light meals, and desserts during the day. Have ouzo and *mezédes* for a mellow sunset. Go in and check out the refrigerator case when you're ready for a big evening meal.

Artemóna

★ $ **To Liotrivi (Manganas),** Artemóna. ☎ **32-051.**

Cuisine: GREEK.

Prices: Appetizers 200–800 Drs (85¢–$3.35); main courses 800–2,800 Drs ($3.35–$11.65). No credit cards.

Open: Daily noon to midnight.

The island's favorite taverna has a handsome new building, with dining inside, down in a charming cellar, on the roof or streetside. Taste for yourself why the Sifnians, who pride themselves on their fine, distinctive cooking, consider Yannis Georgoulis one of their finest cooks. Try his delectable *kaparosaláta* (minced caper leaves and onion salad), *povithokeftédes* (croquettes of ground chick-peas) or *ambelofásoula* (crisp local black-eyed peas in the pod). Or go for something ordinary: even the beef fillet with potatoes baked in foil is a mouth-watering delight!

Kamáres

Pothotas Taverna [O Simos], Kamáres. No telephone.

Cuisine: GREEK.

Prices: Appetizers 300–1,100 Drs ($1.25–$4.60), main courses 700–1,800 Drs ($2.90–$7.50). No credit cards.

Open: Daily 11am–midnight.

This unobtrusive portside place has a basic Greek menu, but everything is well done. The bread brought to your table is sprinkled with sesame seeds, and their choriatiki salad is made with locally aged *mizíthra* cheese. Fish is fresh and not expensive; the individually baked pots of moussaka are delicious.

Captain Andreas, Kamáres. ☎ **32-356.**

Cuisine: SEAFOOD.

Prices: Appetizers 300–1,200 Drs ($1.25–$5), main courses 900–1,400 Drs ($3.75–$5.85); fish 2,000–14,000 Drs ($8.35–$58.35) per kilo. No credit cards.

Open: Daily 1–5pm, 7:30pm–12:30am.

The favorite place for seafood, with tables right on the town beach. Andreas the fisherman serves the catch of the day, usually simply cooked but terrific with chips or a seasonal vegetable dish.

READERS RECOMMEND

Themonia Restaurant, *crossroads of Káto Petáli and Kástro* (☎ **31-866**). *"We discovered a restaurant on the beautiful island of Sífnos so special we thought we'd spread the word. This family operation (Smaragda Georgouli doesn't speak much English but is a perfect hostess) uses only the freshest local ingredients. It offers a truly unbeatable combination: delicious home cooking, generous portions, and inexpensive prices. And in case your stomach is beginning to overdose on taverna dishes drowning in oil, you'll find the fare tasty but light. What's more, it's probably the cleanest restaurant anywhere in the islands."* —Aspassia Yaga and Daniel Tai, New York, N.Y.

Platís Ghialós

Ampari Café, Platís Ghialós. No telephone.

Cuisine: BREAKFAST/SNACKS.
Prices: Snacks 350–1,200 Drs ($1.45–$5). No credit cards.
Open: 9am–1am.

The "Ship's Hold," on the central beach, has two decks, cozy indoor and outdoor spaces, and a beach bar, where you can enjoy breakfast, light snacks, salads, and fresh fruit. It's a popular café/bar on weekends, when two Sifniot musicians bring out a violin and a 200-year-old *láouto* to play indigenous folk music.

Sofia Restaurant, Platís Ghialós. ☎ **31-890.**

Cuisine: GREEK.
Prices: Appetizers 150–800 Drs (65¢–$3.35), main courses 700–2,400 Drs ($2.90–$10). No credit cards.
Open: Daily 9pm–1am.

At the east end of the beach is the best restaurant for Greek peasant fare, popular for its outdoor terrace and large wine list. For many in Apollonía, the casual seaside ambience warrants an evening outing.

EVENING ENTERTAINMENT

In Apollonía the **Argo Bar, Botzi,** and **Volto** on the main street are good for the latest European and American pop at very loud volumes. In summertime, the large **Dolphin Pub** becomes a lively and elegant nightspot, closing in mid-September.

Even if you're sleeping in Apollonía, consider the cab fare to Kamáres for a special evening. At sunset, you can seek relative tranquility near the beach at the picturesque **Old Captain's Bar** or join the yacht set drinking Sífnos Sunrises and admiring the gang at the rival **Collage Club** above it. Later, the **Mobilize Dance Club** and the more elegant **Follie-Follie,** right on the beach, start cranking up the volume to become seaside discos.

AROUND THE ISLAND

Kamáres, on the island's west coast, will be most visitors' introduction to **Sífnos.** If you explore a little, you'll find some old pottery kilns under the watchful eyes of the **Aghía Marína** and **Aghía Anna** churches that cling to the port's north banks. The central part of Kamáres cove is a sandy beach lined with tamarisk trees and dune grass, and there are some fine, isolated beaches north and south of it that can be reached by boat.

The 5-km drive between Kamáres and Apollonía reveals the island's agricultural heart and almost obsessive neatness. Every hillside is impeccably terraced with walls of schist and flagstone slabs. Rocky surfaces, delineated by higher walls, serve as footpaths over the hills; carved stone and marble steps between the olive and almond trees are common. Small Cycladic farmhouses with the occasional ornamental dovecote are scattered throughout, most supporting a bevy of geraniums, hibiscus, or apricot trees. Apollonía is spread over three mounds in the foothills of Mt. Profítis Ilías, site of an 8th-century Byzantine monastery.

Pretty **Artemóna** fans over a hillside crowned by two blue-domed windmills and the remnants of others, just a 2-km walk from Apollonía. Some impressive neoclassic mansions belonging to the island's oldest families are on its borders near the encircling outer vehicle road.

Platís Ghialós is the biggest and most southern of the west coast beaches. It's a long stretch of fine suntanned sand lining a shallow cove that's perfect for swimming laps, and is a great place for beach bums, particularly in late May, June, and September when the sea is warm but calm. From here, it's a half-hour walk through the olive groves and intoxicating oregano and thyme patches over the hill to **Chryssopighí,** for another good beach.

The Apollonia-bound bus stops at **Panaghía Chryssopighí,** near the village of **Apókofto,** a remarkably sited monastery built on a sacred rocky promontory. The double-vaulted whitewashed church is built on a rock that was split after two women prayed to the Virgin Mary for protection against a band of pirates. The icon inside the church was said to have radiated light when it was discovered. There is good swimming immediately below the monastery and along the coast where secluded bays protect swimmers from rough water.

From this sheltered cove you can scale the point crowned by the **Charálambos Church** to the twin coves at **Fáros.** You'll pass a stone and metal structure below the pathway, the remains of a chute that once brought iron ore from a mine above you to the cargo ships anchored below. The path behind the south cove beach leads to an enclave of rooms to let, a seaside taverna, and a small fishing-boat port.

Mílos

Known primarily for the *Venus de Milo,* the 4th-century B.C. statue of Aphrodite that was found in an island cave and spirited away by the French (it's on display in the Louvre), Mílos is the site of one of Greece's oldest civilizations. During Minoan times, Mílos became one of the richest islands in the Aegean as a result of its obsidian trade. A particularly dark moment in the island's history took place during the Peloponnesian War, when Athens, angry with the Milians for siding with Sparta, wiped out the male population. Mílos is still a prosperous island and has little inclination to exploit its natural beauty for tourism, although the recently constructed airport promises to increase its flow of tourists.

ARRIVING/DEPARTING • By Air There is one flight daily to Athens. Call **Olympic Airways** at their Adámas office (☎ **22-380**) or in Athens (☎ **96-16-161**) for reservations.

• By Sea Mílos is served by daily ferries from Piraeus (four times weekly in the low season); the trip takes 5 to 7 hours. The F/B *Ierápetra* makes the 8-hour voyage from Mílos to Ághios Nikólaos and Sitía, on Crete, every Monday, Wednesday, and Friday night; these sailings are subject to change.

There are connections twice weekly to Kímolos, Folégandros, Íos, and Santoríni (Thíra); boats leave daily for nearby Sífnos and Sérifos. Check with the **Port Authority** in Athens (☎ **143** or **45-11-311**) or in Mílos (☎ **0287/22-100**) for information.

ESSENTIALS Tourist services are found along the *paralía* (harbor front) in the port of Adámas. The town-run **Mílos Tourist Information Centre** (☎ **0287/22-286** or **22-287**) is near the pier. The helpful and knowledgeable **Milos Travel** (☎ **0287/22-000**, fax 22-688), nearby, will store your luggage and exchange currency. Their staff sells ferry tickets and books a daily round-the-island boat tour that makes stops for swimming and costs 4,000 Drs ($16.75). The telephone center **(OTE)** is open weekdays from 7:30am to 3pm; the **post office** is open weekdays from 7:30am to 1:30pm.

The **police** can be reached at ☎ **21-204.** The **Health Center** (☎ **22-700** or **22-701**) in Pláka can deal with medical emergencies. The town **bus stop** is on the main road about 200 meters east of the pier; schedules are posted.

ORIENTATION

Mílos is the largest of the western Cyclades. Most tourist activity is concentrated around Adámas on the east side of the port, where the ferryboats dock. The island's capital, Pláka or Mílos (just 3 km north and inland), is well worth a visit for its authentic, decorative Cycladic architecture and its archeological and folk-art museums. On the road between Adámas and Pláka are catacombs carved in the soft rock by early Christians.

The Mílos Airport is at Alíkes, 8 km south of Adámas on the port's coastal road. Most of Mílos's industrial development is in this vicinity. The island is rich in ores and minerals. Although mining has scarred the landscape, it has made Mílos prosperous and independent of its tourist trade.

The best-known beaches are on the outer coasts and are reached in an hour by car or moped, or by the infrequent buses. The western half of the island is more mountainous and is traversed by small, often unpaved roads.

GETTING AROUND

Speed Rental (☎ **22-440**) is just east of the pier. The friendly Dimitrios Kassis, a former Houstonite, rents cars and Jeeps starting from 9,000 Drs ($37.50) per day plus 1,700 Drs ($7.10) insurance. He also rents mopeds starting at 2,850 Drs ($11.90) a day, including liability, and has helmets available—take one.

WHAT TO SEE & DO

Two of the most interesting sites on Mílos are within 4 km of Adámas. The island's capital, **Pláka** or **Mílos,** is one of the best preserved Cycladic villages in Greece. Gently sculpted, whitewashed houses lean side by side on narrow pedestrian lanes. Old marble and bluestone paving tiles, even where patched by concrete, are neatly outlined in both white and blue. Pots of geraniums and flowering succulents are put on the stucco windowsills to catch the afternoon sun.

From the bus stop (buses run every half hour between 7:30am and 11:30pm) follow signs through the car-free lanes to the **Folk and Arts Museum** (☎ **21-292**). A small but fine collection of old photographs, ceramics, traditional Milian costumes, and embroidery are housed in an old building opposite one of the many churches of Pláka. From this square, you'll have the most striking vista of mountains, sea, and sky. This museum is open daily from 10am to 1pm and 6 to 9pm, Sunday from 10am to 1pm only; closed Monday.

After touring Pláka, head to the village of Trypití (a ten-minute walk) where you'll find the **Archeological Museum.** It has a good collection of Hellenistic-era sculpture and finds from Milian archeological sites. In the foyer is, of course, a French-made reproduction of the Louvre's *Venus de Milo;* the original was found in a cave nearby. The museum is open from 8:30am to 3pm Tuesday through Sunday, and admission costs 500 Drs ($2.10).

Within walking distance, in **Klíma,** the Roman-era capital, are fantastic **Katakómbes** (catacombs) dug by Christians in the 1st century A.D. (open 8:30am to 3pm, closed Wednesday, admission is free). Ancient inscriptions are etched into the walls—along with modern graffiti—and burial crypts that once held a half-dozen bodies are now fully excavated. You'll have to walk through very narrow corridors and low tunnels to see the full extent of the catacombs, so if you're claustrophobic, beware! There are remains of a Roman theater and temple within a 15-minute walk of the Trypití bus stop. Downhill is the present-day Klíma, a picturesque fishing village with old houses built on the water's edge.

Apollonía (or Polonía) is the most popular beach on Mílos, a sheltered sandy strip on the north coast, away from the winds that sometimes bombard the Adámas beach. There are some pensions in this small community and more catacombs to explore nearby. You can take the same bus to Fylakopí, one of Mílos's most important archeological sites.

The excavations at **Fylakopí,** 4 km west of Apollonía, show the influence of both the Minoans and mainland Greeks on this Middle Cycladic (2000 B.C.) settlement. Many obsidian tools were found here that actually date from pre-Minoan times.

Caiques leave from Apollonía three times daily in summer for the trip to the nearby island of **Kímolos.** The whole island is built on a foundation of chalk; absolutely everything is a dusty grayish white. There's a great beach and some interesting archeological finds dating from Mycenaean times.

Paleochóri is the most popular of the south coast beaches, but buses from Adámas through the village of Zefiría run only three times daily. A small village of rooms-to-let and tavernas caters to beach folk, who have unofficially divided Paleochóri's two coves into a family beach (with the tavernas) and a nude beach.

WHERE TO STAY

There are many rooms-to-let above the businesses along the *paralía,* **Aktí Pávlou Damouláki.** Take a moment to inspect any rooms before you take them—just imagine what a moped might sound like at 2am! Private rooms with attached bathrooms should cost about 8,500 Drs ($35.40) for two. Mílos Travel (☎ **22-000**) also rents apartments on the hill above Adámas for about 12,000 Drs ($50) for two.

Hotel Corali, Adámas, Mílos 84001. ☎ **0287/22-204** or **22-216.**
16 rms (all with bath). TEL

Rates: 11,250 Drs ($46.95); 13,800 Drs ($57.50) double. No credit cards.

Over the hill behind the ferry pier, just beyond the church clock tower, is a comfortable place—quiet, but quite a hike if you have luggage. They have good-quality rooms, so if you're not afraid of commitment, make a reservation and their minivan will pick you and your luggage up at the pier.

Hotel Delfini, Adámas, Mílos 84001. ☎ **0287/22-001.** 17 rms (all with bath).

Rates: 6,200 Drs ($25.85) single; 10,120 Drs ($42.15) double. No credit cards.

Our favorite local lodging is this small tranquil hotel run by the gregarious John Mathioudakis. The balconied side-facing rooms have views around the large Venus Village complex, to the sea. Back rooms overlook an olive and citrus grove.

Hotel Milos, Adámas, Mílos 84001. ☎ **0287/22-087** or **22-306.** Fax 0287/22-306.
31 rms (all with bath). TEL

Rates: 11,440 Drs ($47.65) single; 13,800 Drs ($57.50) double. No credit cards.

The Hotel Milos is a slightly more expensive option, and its location off the road to Apollonía isn't ideal, but the rooms are attractive. Breakfast is an additional 1,000 Drs ($4.15) per person.

WHERE TO EAT

O Flisvos, portside, Adámas. ☎ **22-349.**

Cuisine: GREEK.

Prices: Appetizers 150–700 Drs (65¢–$2.90); main courses 700–2,100 Drs ($2.90–$8.75). No credit cards.

Open: Daily 11am–1am.

The best and least expensive of the portside restaurants is known locally as Panórios. Peek into the roasting pans at fat stuffed tomatoes, crisp baked eggplant, fresh grilled souvlaki, and other Greek favorites.

Trapatselis Restaurant, Apollonía Road, Adámas. ☎ **22-010.**

Cuisine: GREEK/CONTINENTAL.

Prices: Appetizers 200–900 Drs (85¢–$3.75); main courses 850–1,800 Drs ($3.55–$7.50). No credit cards.

Open: Daily 1–4pm, 7pm–midnight.

This very good full-fledged restaurant, about 100 meters east of the bus stop on the waterfront road, has a much more varied menu, with a large selection of appetizers and continental dishes, brighter lighting, and spiffy waiters. Locals come for the fresh grilled fish that cost 1,200–10,000 Drs ($5–$41.65) per kilo.

EVENING ENTERTAINMENT

Kynigós (☎ **22-349**) is a funky ouzerí on the *paralía.* Kyle thought it was a good place for her sunset ouzo and octopus ritual, but some of the locals were skeptical about foreigners' hanging out with its authentic, somewhat rowdy, seamen crowd.

Adámas has a few portside café/bars, the best places to admire the nightly *vólta* (stroll), and the **Vipera Lebetina Bar** (☎ **22-501**) on the steps uphill behind the small portside tourist information office. The **White Disco** is directly on the town beach, in front of the Venus Village complex.

Folégandros

98 nautical miles SE of Piraeus

ARRIVING/DEPARTING Three ferries a week (five in the high season) stop at Folégandros on the Piráeus, Síkinos, Íos, Santoríni route. Two or three a week stop on the Náxos, Páros, Mílos, Sérifos, Sífnos run. Once a week there's service to Crete (Ághios Nikólaos, Sitía).

ESSENTIALS The **post office** and **OTE,** open weekdays 8am to 3pm, are right off the central square in Chóra. The **police** (☎ **41-249**) are behind nearby. The **Maraki Travel Agency** (☎ **41-273**), on the left just around from the southwest corner of the bus stop square in Chóra, can exchange money, help with travel arrangements, and sell you a map of the island for 600 Drs ($2.50).

Most tourists who know of Folégandros have seen it only when passing its rather forbidding northern coast where precipitous cliffs rise up to almost a thousand feet. Maybe they catch a glimpse of Chóra hovering high up, white and maybe a little forlorn, and probably some imagine how lovely and pristine the little capital is, but so far relatively few have ventured up to experience its austere beauty.

Since Roman times Folégandros has been used as a place of exile, but for the last decade it has become increasingly of the self-imposed sort. Those wanting to get away from the tourist hordes have discovered it, but for the present it remains unspoiled. The fewer than one thousand inhabitants still go about their daily lives of growing barley in terraced fields, raising livestock and fishing, except in the summer, when they welcome visitors from Athens and a growing number of foreign tourists, mostly from Scandinavia and England.

ORIENTATION

Visitors arrive in the unimpressive port of **Karavostássi,** where there's a decent beach and a few hotels and rooms to let. Campers may head south one kilometer to **Livádi Beach.** Most people, however, will jump aboard the bus that is waiting to chug the four kilometers up to **Chóra.**

GETTING AROUND

There are no taxis on the island, no cars for rent, and no reason to rent one, and as yet not even any motorcycles for hire. (Please, please let that continue to be the case!) The bus meets all ferries and has a regular route along the main road that runs along most of the spine of the island eight or nine times a day; the fare is 80 Drs (35¢).

WHAT TO SEE AND DO

Chóra, one of the most beautiful capitals in the Cyclades, would be enough in itself. Above it the handsome all white **Panaghia Church** beckons you to climb the hillside for a closer look and incredible views. Even from the bus stop square the sheer drop of the cliff offers a pretty awesome sight. On the right in the next square you'll find the picture-perfect **Kástro,** built when Marco Sanudo ruled the island in the 13th century and inhabited ever since. The town itself centers on five closely connected squares, along and around which you'll find churches, restaurants, and shops.

South of Chóra about a kilometer is **Águios Elefthérios,** the highest point on the island. Continue west by foot or bus to reach the village of **Áno Meriá,** small farms so widely dispersed that they're barely recognizable as a community. Swimmers will want to get off at the first crossroad and walk down to **Angáli,** the best fine-sand beach on the island, where there are a few tavernas and rooms to let. **Águios Nikólaos,** another good beach, is a couple of kilometers farther west, and yet another four kilometers will bring you to **Livadáki.** (In the summer there's caique service to these beaches from Karavostássi.)

More adventurous sorts may want to make it to the far northwest end of the island to the beach at **Águios Gheórghios,** an hour's walk beyond the last bus stop. The truly intrepid may want to hire a boat and guide to visit **Chrissospiliá,** a cave with stalactites and other curiosities, below the Panaghia Church.

WHERE TO STAY

Beachers may want to stay at Karavostássi, if they like the pebbled beach there. The **Aeolos Beach Hotel** (☎ **0286/41-205**) looks like the best hotel, but it was closed during our too-brief visit; doubles should cost about 10,000 Drs ($41.65). Campers will want to head south to **Livádi Camping** (☎ **0286/41-204**). We recommend you stay in Chóra, where there are also a number of good rooms to let.

Anemomilos Apartments, Chóra, Folégandros 84011. ☎ **0286/41-309.** 17 apts.

Rates: 17,250 Drs ($71.90) for two up to 24,000 Drs ($100) for five. AE, V.

The best and most traditional-looking of the luxury apartments are on the right up from the bus stop. They are all simply elegant, each with its own personality (one especially configured for the handicapped), most with sensational views.

Castro Hotel, Chóra, Folégandros 84011. ☎ **0286/41-230** (or **01/77-81-658** in Athens). Fax 0286/41-230. 10 rms.

Rates: 9,200 Drs ($38.35) single; 11,500 Drs ($47.90). No credit cards.

Our favorite hotel is in the Kástro, built in 1212 and fully renovated in 1992. Of course the rooms are small and your own private bathroom may be down the hall, but they're both faithfully restored and comfortable, and there's nothing like having a window with the ocean right under it 200 meters below. The charming owner, Despo Danassi, makes you feel at home—her family has owned it for five generations—and serves you a homemade breakfast on antique tableware and furniture.

Hotel Odysseus, Chóra, Folégandros 84011. ☎ **0286/41-239.** Fax 0286/41-366. 9 rms (all with bath).

Rates: 6,900 Drs ($28.75) single/double. No credit cards.

The best budget choice is on the west side of town, a few blocks beyond the OTE/ post office, then left. The rooms are simple, quiet, comfortable, and very clean, and the sunsets are splendid.

Polikandia Hotel, Chóra, Folégandros 84011. ☎ **0286/41-322.** Fax 0286/41-323. 31 rms (all with bath).

Rates: 10,400 Drs ($43.35) single; 13,000 Drs ($54.15) double. No credit cards.

This handsome new traditional-style hotel is on the left as you enter town. The rooms are large and comfortable with colorful furnishings, but we saw those dreaded group-tour stickers on the front door.

WHERE TO EAT

Folégandros doesn't yet have many good dining places. Locals recommend the **Pounda,** on the bus-stop square in Chóra, but it felt a little too exposed. A nice English couple recommended **Nikolas,** on the second square, but more for the friendly, informative owner than his "turbo service" and food. We recommend **Piatsa,** on the third square, a simple, family-run taverna, with main courses costing 700–1800 Drs ($2.90–$7.50).

On the far side of town, you'll find the **Bzut Disco,** which wasn't bzuting during our visit, and just before it, on the left, the small and mellow **Kaliteremi Music Bar.**

The Dodecanese

10

THE *DÓDEKA*, OR 12, ISLANDS THAT CONSTITUTE THE DODECANESE (DODEKÁNISSOS) form Greece's far eastern strategic border, within kissing distance of neighboring Turkey. From tiny Kastellórizo in the far south—just look at a map—to Pátmos at the northern end, they span a diverse touristic and geographic landscape that makes for pleasant travel. Like most of the islands, the Dodecanese have been or are actively in the process of being subjugated to the onslaught of European group tourism, continuing a long tradition in Dodecanese history.

From the Asian tribes of Anatolia in antiquity to the Crusaders in the Middle Ages the unfortunate 12 seem to be perennially in the way of this or that conquering horde. It's hardly surprising that these particular islanders, credited with organizing the rebellion against the Turks, are among the most politically minded people in all Greece and have often been leaders in new social movements.

Of all those who overran the islands, the Italians (who occupied the Dodecanese between 1913 and 1943) have left the greatest mark. Many older citizens speak the language fluently and hints of Italian taste crop up in the cuisine and culture of the region. Romans, Venetians, Genoese, and Crusaders constructed most of the islands' magnificent temples and fortresses. It was under Mussolini's direction that ancient and medieval sites on Rhodes and Kos were restored in a particularly Fascist style. Though repeatedly occupied by different nations, the Dodecanese have miraculously remained essentially Greek.

Of the major islands, **Rhodes** is the largest and most developed, with a wall of beach resorts on both sides of the main town that scream, "Miami, Miami." Don't let that put you off; we still love exploring the back lanes of the Old Town. One-and-a-half hours away by ferry is tiny **Sými,** once a secret and now a ballyhooed neoclassical gem that still manages to draw "oohs" and "aaahs" from its many day-tripping and longer-term guests. Nearby and north is **Kos,** which used to be a favorite and is now a Scandinavian colony where visitors just Ping-Pong on the beach-bar axis. **Kálymnos** has made a fairly positive transition from sponge island to tourist enclave. **Léros** is also trying its hand at tourism with mixed results: Some love the seclusion; others find it dreary. When we vacation in Greece it's straight to **Pátmos** we head. Who knows how, but it manages to resist the ravages of tourism while embracing all who visit. And far-off **Kárpathos,** site of the Dodecanese's newest international airport, has just bitten into the apple of group tourism. The "other Dodecanese"—**Kássos** (Cassos), **Chalkí** (Chalkis), **Tílos, Nísiros** (Níssyros), **Astipaléa,** and **Kastellórizo** (Megísti)—are still almost unscathed by foreign invaders. Many can be visited on day excursions from one of the larger neighboring islands, so they make up our section at the end, "Baker's Dozen."

IMPRESSIONS

Rhodes, where history lies sleeping.
—Freya Stark, *Beyond Euphrates,* 1951

In Rhodes the days drop as softly as fruit from trees.

Never has one seen anything like [the island of Kálymnos]. . . . Plane after stiff cubistic plane of pure color. The mind runs up and down the web of vocabulary looking for a word which will do justice to it. In vain.
—Lawrence Durrell, *Reflections on a Marine Venus,* 1953

What's Special About the Dodecanese

Architecture

- The medieval Old Town of Rhodes features the beautifully restored Palace of the Knights, now a fine museum.
- Sými has a picture-postcard waterfront, with traditional, neoclassic seafarers' homes built amphitheatrically up its hills.
- The pristine, but now commercialized, whitewashed stucco village of Líndos, Rhodes, is a national architectural preserve.
- Astipalea's main port and hilltop Venetian-era kastro are surrounded by Cycladic-style cuboid housing.
- Pátmos's Chóra is crowned by the fortified Monastery of St. John, within whose walls is a stunning maze of traditional stucco homes.

Beaches

- Rhodes's half-moon cove of gold sand, in the shadow of the Líndos Acropolis, is one of the most beautiful settings in Greece.
- The long south coast beach of Kefalos on Kos has become a center for windsurfing and sailing.
- The isolated cove at Psilí Ámmos on Pátmos, lined with fine sand and salt pines, is ideal for swimming and sunbathing.

Religion

- The Monastery of St. John and the Holy Cave where St. John the Evangelist wrote the Book of Revelation make Pátmos one of the most important sites of Christian pilgrimage in the world.

Getting to the Dodecanese

The Dodecanese are easily reached from Athens, other Aegean isles, and even Turkey. Car ferries leave every day from Piraeus. Excursion boats (risky in rough weather) and catamaran **hydrofoils** operate almost daily between several of the islands. Though twice the price, hydrofoils are twice as fast (a handy tool for those making day trips), and more stable on high seas. **Excursion boats** operate daily between Rhodes and Marmaris, Turkey, and between Kos and Bodrum, Turkey. **Olympic Airways** has frequent service to Rhodes, Kos, and Leros, and twice weekly flights to Kárpathos, Kassos, and Kastellorizo, as well as connections between Rhodes, Santoríni, Páros, and Mýkonos. An airport is under construction on Kálymnos as well.

Interisland Travel

There is frequent and extensive ferry service between the Dodecanese isles and, less often, between the Dodecanese, Crete, the Cyclades, and the Northeast Aegean islands. See the "Arriving/Departing" section for each island for more specifics; schedules change dramatically before and after the high season.

Seeing the Dodecanese

If you have only one week in which to see the Dodecanese, this would be our recommendation for sampling the best:

Days 1–4 Fly to Rhodes from Athens (or Crete or Mýkonos) and settle into an Old Town hotel. Begin your sightseeing on the Street of the Knights. Take a day trip to the village of Líndos for a look at its Acropolis, the wonderful local architecture, and a swim at its fine beach. Take a day cruise to Sými, a very different architectural treasure trove on an unspoilt island.

Days 5–6 Take the hydrofoil or ferry to Pátmos. From Skála you can hike or take the bus up to the Monastery of St. John in the picturesque Chóra, and visit some of the island's beaches.

Day 7 Take the hydrofoil to Kos or the ferry to Leros; at either island you can connect with direct flights to Athens. If you'd prefer to go by sea, book a private cabin on the Piraeus steamer and enjoy a minicruise.

If you're looking for more of an "off the beaten path" adventure, study our section called "Baker's Dozen." It may be possible to fly to Rhodes and overnight there; take the daily excursion boat from Kamiros Skala to the undeveloped island of Halki; spend a few nights and take an excursion boat to agricultural Tilos; spend a few nights and take another excursion boat to the sponge divers' isle of Sými; spend the night and return by excursion boat to bustling Rhodes.

1 Rhodes

250 nautical miles E of Piraeus

ARRIVING/DEPARTING • By Air **Olympic Airways** offers one flight daily from Iráklio, Crete; three flights daily from Athens; three flights daily from Kárpathos; one flight daily from Kos; four flights weekly from Páros; one flight daily from Mýkonos; three flights weekly from Santoríni. Reservations and ticket information can be obtained from the Olympic Airways Office, Odós Ieroú Lochou 9 (☎ **24-571** or **24-555**). Flights fill quickly, so make reservations early. Taxis cost about 1,400–1,600 Drs ($5.85–$6.60) between the airport and Rhodes town. There's a duty-free shop at Rhodes International Airport to accommodate European charter travelers as well as an information desk with erratic hours.

• By Sea Daily car ferries from Piraeus (it's a grim 18-hour ride) and infrequent service from Rafína (even worse!). There are four ferries weekly to Ághios Nikólaos, Crete, and Santoríni. Several **ferries** weekly ply the Dodecanese waters to Tilos, Nissiros, Halkis, and Kárpathos, while daily ferries service the more popular Sými, Kos, Leros, Kálymnos, and Pátmos. There's a once weekly ferry to Astipalea via Kálymnos. Once weekly you can take a cruise ship to Limassol, Cyprus, and then on to Haifa, Israel. There's a daily ferry (except Sunday) to Marmaris, Turkey, and one to Samós (in the Northeast Aegean group) which continues onto Thessaloníki (northern Greece). Your best bet is to check the EOT office for their printed schedule of weekly departures; they can tell you the travel agents selling tickets to each boat. Ferryboat tickets as well as tickets to Turkey can be purchased from several agencies on Amerikís Street or from the very helpful **Triton Holidays** office near the entrance to the Old Town (see "Getting Around").

There are daily **caique** excursions between Rhodes and Sými for 3,000 Drs ($12.50) return trip, and daily excursions from Kamiros Skala (an east coast port 19 miles south of Rhodes) to Halki.

The stories surrounding the origin and name of Rhodes are among the loveliest in Greek mythology. In the lofty heights of Mt. Olympus, Zeus, after his battle against the giants, was dividing the spoils of his victory among the other gods. Helios, the

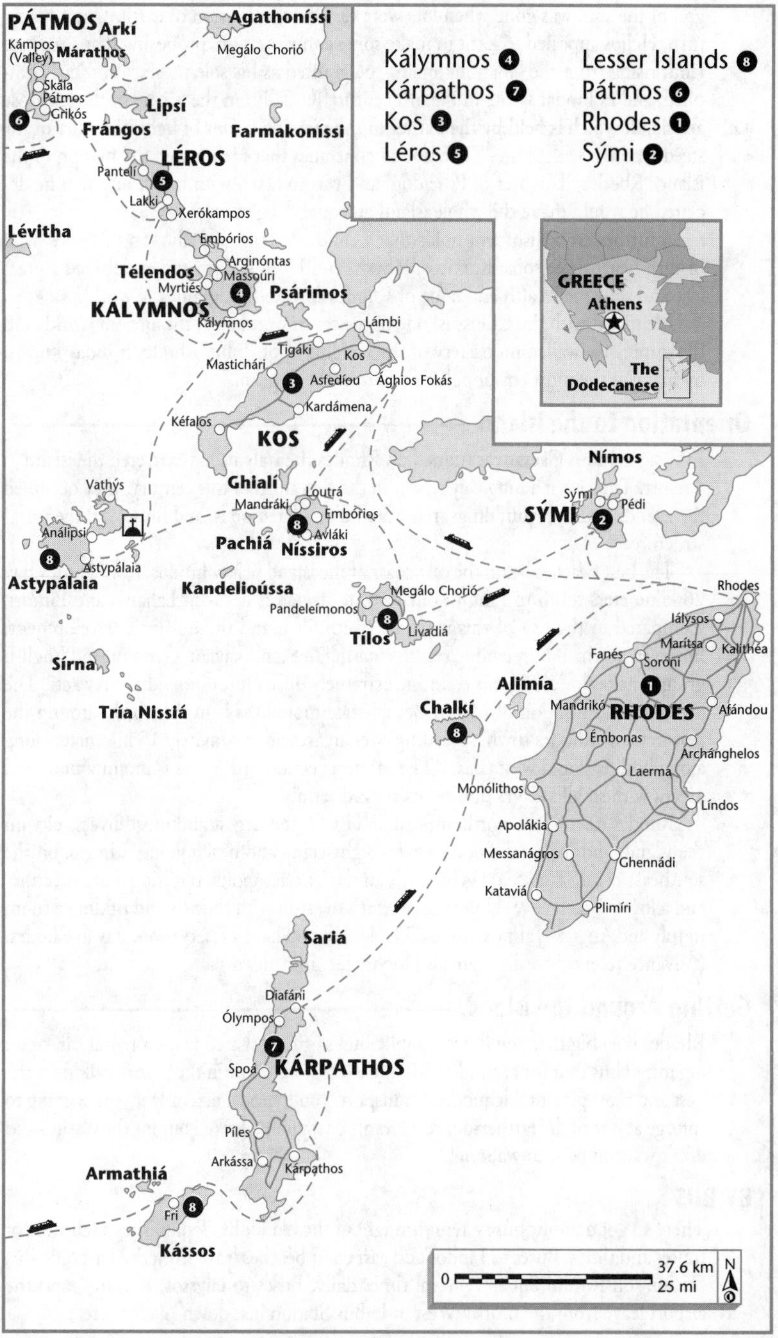

Car Ferry Routes

Monastery

god of the sun, was gone when lots were cast for the division of earth. Upon his return, Helios appealed to Zeus to make some compensation, proposing that a piece of land, rising from the "foaming main," be granted as his sole possession. Zeus complied, and as Pindar wrote in the 5th century B.C., "From the waters of the sea arose an island, which is held by the Father of the piercing beams of light, the ruler of the steed whose breath is fire." The legend continues that Helios wed the nymph of the island, Rhodes, daughter of Poseidon, and was so taken with her beauty that he declared he would make the whole island an equal delight.

A further embellishment holds that a child was born of Helios and Rhodes, who in turn begat three sons: Kamiros, Ialysos, and Lindos. Each son established a great city and thus the wealth and fame of Rhodes spread throughout the world.

Identified with the Colossus, one of the seven wonders of the ancient world, and the impressive walled monastery of the Knights of St. John, Rhodes is today known by many as the most cosmopolitan resort in the Aegean.

Orientation to the Island

Ever since Julius Caesar vacationed on Rhodes the Italians have coveted the island as a resort. They went a long way when, in the first third of this century, they occupied the island, built new buildings, renovated dilapidated ones, and improved the infrastructure.

The best beaches lie on the east coast of the island below Líndos, from Lardos Bay 26 kilometers south to Plimiri; our favorite stretch is between Lahania and Plimiri. Compared to the rest of this woefully overbuilt island there is little development; however, a strip of burgeoning resorts catering to Scandinavian, German, and English groups makes life along this coastline extremely difficult for individual travelers. The greatest concentration of Miami Beach–style monoliths is in the north, around the perimeter of Rhodes town, spreading over an area approximately 15 kilometers long along both east and west coasts. The interior section of Rhodes is mountainous and green, with small villages dotting its rugged terrain.

Rhodes town is the northernmost and by far the largest and most diverse city on the island, and makes the best base for sightseeing and beach going. Lindos, on the southeast coast, is a scenic gem, with an ancient acropolis, traditional architecture, and a lovely beach cove. Unfortunately, it's overrun with tourists and finding a room in July and August is almost impossible. Unless you have a reservation, stay in Rhodes. (Advance reservations here are also highly recommended.)

Getting Around the Island

Rhodes is so big that you'll need public buses, group-shared taxis, a rental car, or an organized bus tour for around-the-island excursions. Within the town, walking is the best and most pleasurable mode of transport; you'll need a taxi only if you're going to splurge at one of the farther-out restaurants or if you're decked out for the Casino and don't want to be seen walking!

BY BUS

There's a good public bus system throughout the island; EOT publishes a schedule of routes and times. Buses to Líndos and east coast beaches leave from the East Side Bus Station, on Rimini Square, several times daily. Buses to Ialyssos, Kamiros, and the airport leave from the nearby West Side Bus Station just down Averof Street.

BY TAXI

In Rhodes city, there's a large, well-organized taxi stand (☎ **27-666** or **64-712;** for radio taxis call **62-029**) in front of Old Town, on the harbor front in Rimini Square. There, posted for all to see and agree upon, are the set fares for sightseeing throughout the island. Since many of the cab drivers speak sightseer English, a few friends can be chauffeured and lectured at a very reasonable cost. Taxis are metered, but fares should not exceed the minimum on short round-the-city jaunts. For longer trips, negotiate cab rentals directly with the drivers.

BY CAR

There are several car-rental companies in each community, and a local travel agent may be able to give you the best price. We've had good luck with **Budget Rent A Car** (☎ **37-756**) and **Rent A Reliable Car** (☎ **0241/22-508,** fax 0241/23-110). They both have three locations, including the airport, but delivered our car to the hotel. There are many rental offices on Odós Oktovriou 28, where you can compare prices, but count on spending anywhere from 15,000 Drs ($62.50) to 24,000 Drs ($100) per day. *Caveat emptor.* Don't just grab the lowest price; make sure you have full insurance coverage and understand the terms!

BY TOUR/CRUISES

There are several **tour operators** featuring nature, archeology, shopping, and beach tours of the island. **Triton Holidays,** near Mandráki Harbor, behind the Bank of Greece, at Odós Plastira 9 (☎ **0241/21-690;** fax 0241/31-625), is one of the largest and best agencies. They also offer a wide variety of day and evening cruises, hiking tours, and excursions within the Dódecanese group and to Turkey. There are new one-day boat trips to Líndos, which leave about 9am from the yacht harbor in Rhodes and return about 6pm (5,000 Drs or $20.85).

About Rhodes City

HISTORY

When the three ancient Doric cities of Ialissos, Lindos, and Kameros banded together in 408 B.C. to create a new capital, they did so to gain even greater access to the rich trading and shipping routes of the Mediterranean and Asia Minor, particularly with Egypt. Their city of Rhodes rapidly flourished under the Dorians, having inherited lucrative commercial contacts and cultural traditions. Great temples were erected on the Acropolis and a wide, straight road was built down to the harbor. A remarkably modern code of law was instituted. The Colossus was built, a symbol of Rhodian strength and wealth. Proud, autocratic Rhodians were extremely independent and commercially minded; nowhere was this more true than in their steadfast opposition to Athens in every major conflict. During the Persian Wars, Rhodes sided with Persia, and in the prolonged Peloponnesian conflict, Rhodes came to the aid of Sparta.

However, Rhodes's authority declined as Rome, once an ally and trading partner, eventually overran and annexed the island. Cassius, one of the assassins of Caesar, orchestrated the forceful and punishing takeover. Not until the early 14th century was Rhodes to emerge again as a major force. The Order of the Knights of St. John of Jerusalem took refuge on Rhodes in 1306 and three years later grabbed control of the island.

For over two centuries Knights from Spain, France, Italy, and England came to join the order, dedicated to returning Jerusalem to the Christian fold. The Knights renovated the huge fortifications over the ancient city and built the inns and castle, the hallmarks of Rhodes. Each "Tongue," or foreign contingent with the monastery, had a headquarters, while the grand master, the life-term leader of the Knights, resided in the palace or castle.

Turkish invaders assaulted the city throughout the residence of the Knights, particularly during the siege by Mehemet II in 1422. By 1522 the Knights' numbers had dwindled to a mere 650, after the furious attacks by Suleyman II's 100,000-man army. The ramparts fell and Süleyman realized his dream of conquering mighty Rhodes.

ORIENTATION

Today, Rhodes City is divided into two sections, the old town, dating from medieval days, and the new town. The **Old Town** is surrounded by the massive walls (nearly eight feet thick) built by the Knights of St. John and overlooks the harbor. The **New Town** surrounds the old on all sides and extends south to meet the resort strip. At its north tip is the town beach in the area called 100 Palms, and nearby Mandraki Harbor, once straddled by the Colossus, is now used as a mooring for private yachts and tour boats.

Walking away from Mandráki on Plastíra Street, you'll come to **Cyprus Square,** where most of the New Town hotels are clustered. Veer left and continue to the park where the mighty fortress begins. Opposite it is the **EOT** office; there is also a **Rhodes Municipal Tourist Office** down the hill at Rimini Square (see "Fast Facts" for information on both).

Fast Facts: Rhodes City

American Express The local American Express agent is Rhodos Tours (☎ **21-010**), at Odós Ammochóstou 23, at the New Market. They're open Monday through Saturday 8:30am to 1:30pm and 5 to 8:30pm.

Banks The National Bank of Greece, on Cyprus Square, keeps extended hours for exchanging currency Monday through Thursday 8am to 2pm and 6 to 8pm; Friday 8am to 1:30pm and 3 to 8:30pm; 8am to 2pm on Saturday, and 9am to noon on Sunday).

Bookstores Both the Academy Bookstore (☎ **20-254**) at Odós Dragoúmi 7, and Moses Cohen (☎ **24-049**) at Odós Theméli 83D have a large selection of foreign language books.

Churches The St. Francis Catholic Church (☎ **23-605**) at Odós Dimokratías 28 has English language services on Saturday and Sunday.

Emergencies For medical emergencies call Rhodes General Hospital (☎ **22-222**) on Erythroú Stavroú Street. For other emergencies call the tourist police (☎ **27-423**) or dial 100.

Laundry/Dry Cleaners There's a self-service laundry called the Lavomatique, at Odós Oktovríou 32. It will take four kilos per load at 800 Drs ($3.35), the dryer is 300 Drs ($1.25), and it's open from 7am to 11pm every day. A dry cleaner is on Dodekanísson Street.

OTE/Telephone The main branch, open daily 6am to midnight, is located at Odós Amerikis 91 in the New Town). There is also a branch just off Simi Square, open daily from 7:30am to 11pm.

Police The police (☎ **23-849**) in Old Town are open from 10am to midnight to handle any complaints of overcharging, theft, swindles, or other price- or goods-related problems. There's a tourist police office (☎ 27-423) on the edge of Old Town, near the port.

Post Office The main branch, open daily from 8am to 2:30pm, is located at Odós Amerikis 91 in the New Town.

Tourist Offices At the EOT office (☎ **23-655**, fax 26-955); open Monday through Friday 7:30am to 3pm), at the intersection of Makaríou and Papágou Streets, you can get advice about the whole island, as well as check on the availability of accommodations. There is also a **Rhodes Municipal Tourist Office** (☎ **35-945**), down the hill at Rimini Square near the port taxi stand. Their high season hours are more substantial: Monday through Friday from 8am to 7pm, and Saturday from 8am to 6pm.

What to See & Do in Rhodes City

The modern-day city of Rhodes has sights dating from every era of its history. Some come to Rhodes just to shop for gold or furs and lap up the sun, and never venture out to sightsee!

If it's activities you want, Rhodes City has them, too. Information on taking **folk dance lessons** can be obtained from the **Old Town Theatre** (☎ **29-085**), where Nelly Dimoglu performs, or by writing the **Traditional Dance Center,** Odós Dekelías 87, Athens 143, Greece (☎ **25-10-80,** in Athens). Classes run from June through the beginning of August, 30 hours per week; each week dances from a different region are studied. There are also shorter classes. Call to check. For more conservative jocks, try the **Rhodes Tennis Club** (☎ **25-705**) in the resort of Elli, or the **Rhodes-Afandau Golf Club** (☎ **51-225**), 19 kilometers south from the port. For sailing and yacht information call the **Rodos Yacht Club** (☎ **23-287**).

EXPLORING THE OLD TOWN

The best introduction to the old walled city is through **Eleftheria (Liberty) Gate,** where you'll come to **Simi Square,** containing ruins of the **temple of Venus,** identified as such by the votive offerings found at the site, and thought to date from the 3d century B.C. The remains of the temple are next to a parking lot (driving hours are restricted in Old Town), which rather diminishes the impact of the few stones and columns still standing. Nevertheless the ruins are a vivid reminder that a great Hellenistic city once stood within these medieval walls.

Simi Square also is home to the **Municipal Art Gallery of Rhodes** (open Monday through Saturday from 8am to 2pm), with additional hours Wednesday from 5 to 8pm) above the Ionian and Popular Bank. One block farther on is the **Museum of Decorative Arts** (open Monday through Friday from 8:30am to 3pm, Saturday, Sunday and holidays 8am to 1pm; admission 600 Drs ($2.50) containing finely made Rhodian objects and crafts. Continue through the gate until you reach the Museum Reproduction Shop (with a precious painted tile of the Madonna above its door), then turn right on Ippiton Street toward the Palace of the Knights.

STREET OF THE KNIGHTS This street (Ippotón, on the maps) is known as the Street of the Knights, and is one of the best preserved and most delightful medieval relics in the world. The 600-meter-long, cobble-paved street was constructed over an ancient pathway that led in a straight line from the Acropolis of Rhodes to the port. In the early 16th century it became the address for most of the inns of each nation, which housed Knights who belonged to the Order of St. John. The inns were used as eating clubs and temporary residences for visiting dignitaries, and their facades reflect the different architectural details of their respective countries.

Begin at the lowest point of the hill (next to the Museum Reproduction Shop), at the Spanish house now used by a bank. Next door is the **Inn of the Order of the Tongue** (language) **of Italy,** built in 1519 (as can be seen in the shield of the order above the door). Then comes the **Palace of the Villiers of the Isle of Adam,** built in 1521, housing the Archeological Service of the Dodecanese. The **Inn of France** now hosts the French Language Institute. Constructed in 1492, it's one of the most ornate of the inns, with the shield of three lilies (fleur-de-lis), royal crown, and that of the Magister d'Aubusson (the cardinal's hat above four crosses) off-center, over the middle door. Typical of the late Gothic period, the architectural and decorative elements are all somewhat asymmetrical, lending grace to the squat building. Opposite these inns is the side of the **Hospital of the Knights,** now the archeological museum (see below).

The church farther on the right is **Aghía Triáda** (open 9am to noon daily), next to the Italian consulate. Above its door are three coats-of-arms: those of France, England, and the pope. Past the arch that spans the street, still on the right, is the **Inn of the Tongue of Provence,** shorter than it once was due to an 1856 explosion. Opposite it on the left is the traditionally Gothic **Inn of the Tongue of Spain,** with vertical columns elongating its facade and a lovely garden behind.

The Inn of France is open daily. The ground floor houses the Institut Français, but you can get a view of its garden and an occasional art show in the 2d floor gallery. The other inns are now used as office space or private residences and are closed to the public.

PALACE OF THE KNIGHTS At the crest of the hill on the right, through the grand gates, is the amazing Palace of the Knights (also known as the Palace of the Grand Masters or Magisters), thought to be the original site of the ancient Temple of Helios. The palace, on Ippiton Street (☎ **23-359**), was neglected by the Turks (they turned it into a prison), and in 1856 was accidentally blown up, along with the Church of St. John. During the Italian occupation the Fascist government undertook the enormous project of reconstructing the castle. Only the stones on the lower part of the building and walls are original; the rest is the work of 20th-century hands. The palace reflects a happy Gothic style of architecture, with large bright windows flooding the interior with light. Inside, offsetting the dark weighty Renaissance furniture is a collection of pastel-colored Hellenistic, Roman, and early Christian mosaics "borrowed" from Italian excavations on neighboring Kos. The intricately painted urns are Japanese and were presented as gifts from Italy's allies across the Pacific. The palace is open Tuesday through Sunday from 8:30am to 3pm; admission is 1,000 Drs ($4.15), half-price for children, Sundays are free.

From the Palace of the Knights, go back down Ippiton Street to Simi Square. The **Church of the Virgin of the Castle** will be on your left and the **Archeology Museum of Rhodes** will be ahead on your right.

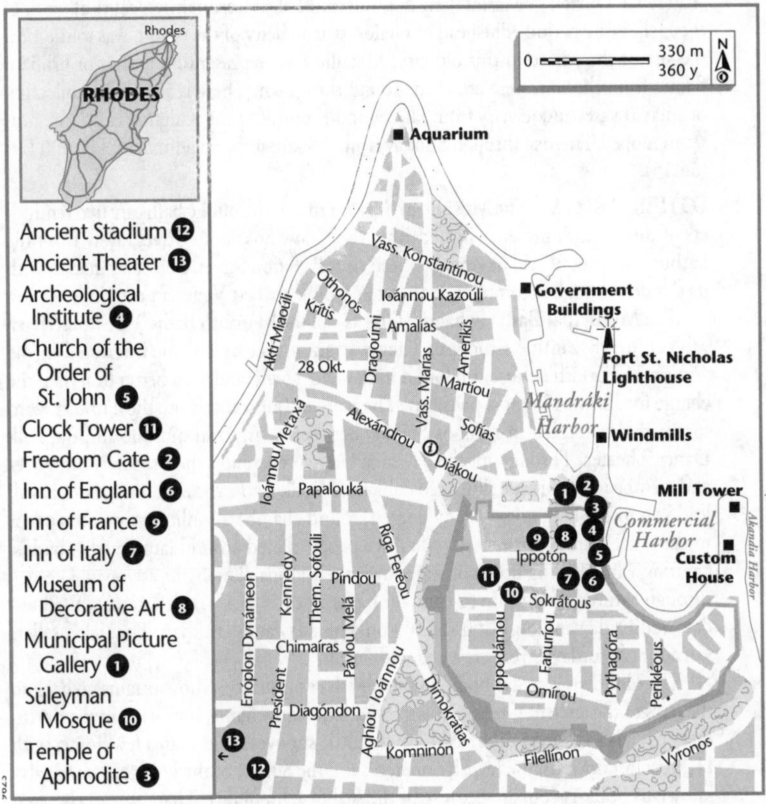

CHURCH OF OUR LADY OF THE CASTLE Formerly the Byzantine Museum of Rhodes, the Church of the Virgin of the Castle (☎ **27-674**) was reopened in 1988, occupying the renovated interior of this 11th-century church (also known as Our Lady of the Castle). Inside is a permanent exhibition of paintings of Rhodes from the early Christian period to the 18th century, including icons, wall paintings, and miniatures. The museum is open daily from 8:30am to 3pm; admission is 500 Drs ($2.08), children and students free.

ARCHEOLOGICAL MUSEUM OF RHODES Opposite you is the medieval hospital, now housing the Archeological Museum of Rhodes, on Apelou Street (☎ **27-657**), with several exquisite Greek sculptures. The first floor is lined with tombstones of knights from the 15th and 16th centuries, many of which are festooned with extravagant coats-of-arms and wonderfully overblown inscriptions. One of the masterpieces of the collection of ancient works is a funeral stele dating from the 5th century B.C. showing Crito, the grieving daughter of Timarista, embracing her mother for the last time. It's an elegant and expressive example of classic Greek art. Equally stunning, on the 2d floor, is the petite statue of Aphrodite, sculpted 400 years later

(Lawrence Durrell's "Marine Venus"), but also an extraordinarily beautiful work of the Hellenistic period. The head of Helios, patron deity of the island, was found near the site of the palace in this old city. Metallic rays, representing flashes of brilliant flames from the sun, were attached around the crown. There is also a fine collection of ancient vases and jewelry from Ialysos and Kamiros in the Knights' Hall. The museum is open Tuesday through Sunday from 8:30am to 3pm; admission is 1,000 Drs ($4.15).

OTHER SIGHTS The **Mosque of Süleyman** and the public baths are two reminders of the Turkish presence in Old Rhodes. Follow Sokratous Street, away from the harbor; the mosque will be straight ahead near Panetiou Street. You can't miss it, with its slender, though incomplete, minaret and pink-striped Venetian exterior.

The **Municipal Baths** (what the Greeks call the "Turkish baths") are housed in a 7th-century Byzantine structure. They warrant a visit by anyone interested in the vestiges of Turkish culture still found in the Old Town, and are a better deal than the charge for showers in most pensions. The hamam (most locals use the Turkish word for "bath") is located in Arionos Square, between a large old mosque and the Folk Dance Theater. Throughout the day men and women enter their separate entrances and disrobe in the private shuttered cubicles. A walk across the cool marble floors will lead you to the bath area—many domed, round chambers sunlit by tiny glass panes in the roof. Through the steam you'll see people seated around large marble basins, chatting while ladling bowls of water over their heads. The baths are open Tuesday through Saturday from 7am to 7pm; the baths cost 850 ($3.55) on Tuesday, Wednesday, and Friday and only 250 ($1.05) on Thursday and Saturday. The ticket sellers warn that Saturday is very crowded with locals.

The old town was also home to the Jewish community, whose origins go back to the days of the ancient Greeks. Much respected as merchants, they lived in the northeast or **Jewish Quarter** of the Old Town. Little survives other than a few homes with Hebrew inscriptions, the Jewish cemetery, and the Square of the Jewish Martyrs (also known as Seahorse Square because of the seahorse fountain). There is a lovely synagogue, where services are held every Friday night; a small black sign in the square shows the way. The synagogue is usually open daily from 10am to 1pm and is located on Dosiadou Street, off the square. This square is dedicated to the thousands of Jews who were rounded up here and sent to their deaths at Auschwitz. If you walk around the residential streets, you'll still see abandoned homes and burnt buildings.

After touring the sites of the old city, a walk around the walls is recommended (the museum operates a daily tour, Monday through Saturday at 2:45pm, beginning at the Palace of the Knights). The fortification has a series of magnificent gates and towers, and is remarkable as an example of a fully intact medieval structure. Admission is 1,000 Drs ($4.15).

EXPLORING THE NEW TOWN

The two major attractions within the confines of the new city are **Mandraki Harbor** and **Mount Smith.** The harbor is perhaps more famous for the legend of the Colossus than its present use. The Colossus, a 90-foot-tall image of Helios, was cast from 304 to 292 B.C., but tumbled down in an earthquake only 66 years after its completion. The shattered giant, one of the seven ancient wonders, lay on the ground for more than 800 years before it was hauled away and eventually carried through the Syrian desert by a caravan of 900 camels. It was probably melted down to make weapons. The exact site of the Colossus has never been firmly established. Myth makers and romantics have placed it on either side of Mandraki Harbor, where mighty ships from Rhodes and foreign ports could pass under its gigantic legs. Recently a psychic led some divers to the harbor, swearing they'd find big chunks of the Colossus. Large pilings were found, but Greece's culture minister denied they were part of the Colossus. Two columns capped by a stag and doe, symbols of Rhodes, mark the supposed location of the Colossus. More serious historians and archeologists place the site farther inland, near the once-standing Church of St. John and temple of Helios (now the Palace of the Grand Masters).

Mandraki also has a Venetian-era watchtower, three picture-postcard windmills, and boats of all varieties, from funky excursion boats to Sými, to space-age hydrofoils, regal sailing vessels, and super-sleek jet-powered yachts.

Mt. Smith is a modest hill named after an English admiral. It's north of the present city and the site of the ancient **Acropolis,** which dates from 408 B.C., which, with Mt. Smith, the north shoreline, and the Old Town, once bordered the city. Traces of its north-south main street have been found under the modern New Zealand Street. On top of Mt. Smith are remnants of temples dedicated to Athena and Zeus Polieus. Archeologists believe that this very large temple complex was easily visible to ships in the Straits of Marmaris, and therefore all treaties and allegiance documents between Rhodes and her warring neighbors were kept here. Below this are the three tall columns and a pediment that remain from the vast Temple of Apollo.

Below the Acropolis is a long **stadium** built into the side of Sandourli Hill. It was reconstructed by the Italians in the early 1940s, though some of the original tiers from the 2d century B.C. can be seen. To its left is the totally reconstructed 800-seat theater once used to teach rhetoric (an art for which Rhodes was well known). In the vicinity are the remains of a gymnasium, and above it near the acropolis, a nymphaeon where caves and water channels indicate that here river goddesses may have been worshiped.

OTHER SIGHTS Modern Rhodes has a number of other diverting attractions. Among them is the **Aquarium,** standing on the northern point of the city, where an amazing variety of Mediterranean marine life is on display. The Aquarium, officially known as the Hydrobiological Institute, is open daily from 9am to 9pm; admission is 375 Drs ($1.50), half price for children. As you walk along the waterside from the Old Town to the Aquarium (see below), you'll see a complex of Italianate buildings. These massive and forbidding-looking structures were put up by the Italians during the Fascist era.

SHOPPING Lest we ignore the favorite pursuit of some readers, note that Rhodes offers lots of window shopping plus the possibility of some good buys. Don't forget to get a receipt; faulty merchandise (particularly jewelry) can sometimes be exchanged with tourist police help.

In the Old Town, look for classic and contemporary gold and silver jewelry almost everywhere. The top of the line Greek designer Ilias LaLaounis has a boutique on Simi or Museum Square. The high-priced, high-quality Alexander Shop, one block from Socratous Street behind the Alexis Restaurant, offers stylish European work, elegant gold and platinum link bracelets and beautifully set precious gems. There are dozens of competitors in the crowded lanes in between. While you're on Socratous, stop in at the traditional Kafeneion Bekir Karakouzos at no. 76 to rest your feet and have a coffee.

For imported leather goods and furs (the former often from nearby Turkey and the latter from Kastoria in northern Greece), stroll down the length of Socratous Street. Antique-ophiles should drop into the Ministry of Culture Museum Reproduction Shop on Ippitou Street, open from 8am to 8pm daily to sell excellent plaster and resin reproductions of favorite sculptures, friezes, tiles, and other works from throughout ancient Greece.

The New Town, especially Makariou Street and the crowded roads around the EOT office, features many European boutiques and well-known franchises. The natural cosmetics company, the Body Shop, is at Odós Makariou 25, easily spotted by the crowd waiting to get in and buy their sunblock and makeup products. Nearby at no. 43 is Benetton, for anyone who forgot their resortwear and is contemplating a night on the town. We also found some great sales along Kyprou Street, with end-of-summer prices on swimsuits, sports shirts, and flashy Greek-made minidresses.

Where to Stay in Rhodes City

Hotels and pensions in the Old Town are cheaper and less sterile than those in modern Rhodes, and there's a special feeling along the dimly lit medieval streets. With all of the following recommendations, reservations are suggested, at least six weeks in advance for the high season. Note that hotels open from late April to mid-October unless otherwise noted, and that rates drop up to 40% in the low season.

The true low-budget traveler will have a hard time in expensive Rhodes. If you can't get into one of the recommendations below, contact EOT for their list of rooms to let or look for one of the small pensions off Platía Martiron Evreon (Square of the Jewish Martyrs), near the harbor between the Aghía Ekaterini and Milon Gates. From the several we inspected, we liked the styleless **Hotel Spot** (☎ **0241/34-737**) at Odós Perikleos 21. It's run by an old couple who told us their nephew said "A spot is a good place to be." There are nine spotless rooms with common baths; rates run 7,150 Drs ($29.80) for two or 8,450 Drs ($35.20) for three. Across the lane at Odós Dimosthenous 21 is the Fantasia Rooms to Let (no phone). For 6,500 Drs ($27.10), two can share a simple room with attached shower in a home overlooking a large, walled garden. The new **Rodos Youth Hostel** in a handsome, restored 400-year-old building at Odós Erghíou (☎ **0241/30-491**) has 50 beds at 1,800 Drs ($7.50), breakfast for 750 Drs ($3.15), a common-use kitchen, hot showers, self-service laundry facility, a bar, and no curfew.

Note: Taxis are required to take passengers *with baggage* into the Old Town if so requested; there is a prohibition against entering this vehicle-free zone only for those *without luggage.* Insist on getting the service you've paid for and resist drivers who want to take you to commission-paying New Town hotels.

IN THE OLD TOWN

Doubles for less than 9,000 Drs ($37.50)

Hotel Kastro, Odós Aríonos 14, 85100 Rhodes. ☎ **0241/20-446.** 12 rms (2 with bath).

Rates: 5,900 Drs ($24.60) single/double without bath; 7,730 Drs ($32.20) single/double with bath. No credit cards.

These simple, clean twin-bedded rooms are a good value. Owner Vasilis Caragiannos sculpts benches and friezes in a medieval style, speaks fluent Italian, and has a dog called Rambo and a turtle called Papandreou. You'll see his artwork in the garden that adjoins the hotel. The taverna next door is occasionally noisy with tourists dancing to electric bouzouki, but it usually closes before midnight.

Maria's Rooms, Odós Menekléous 147-Z, 85100 Rhodes. ☎ **0241/22-169.**
8 rms (3 with bath).

Rates: 7,150 Drs ($29.80) single/double without bath; 8,450 Drs ($35.20) double with bath. No credit cards.

We like this pristine little pension near the Café Bazaar, which for price and quality merits the highest marks. The rooms are sparkling white, squeaky clean, and Maria is a warm and welcoming hostess.

Pension Minos, Odós Omírou 5, 85100 Rhodes. ☎ **0241/31-813.**
17 rms (none with bath).

Rates: 6,900 Drs ($28.75) single/double. No credit cards.

This clean and contemporary pension, though in a soul-less concrete edifice, is one of the best budget choices. Hostess Maria Lenti is an indefatigable cleaner and the airy large rooms with private sinks, the common toilets, and the showers all gleam. We loved the balconied room no. 15 with its glorious view across the Old Town's minarets and domes to the harbor. Go to the minimarket or bakery across the street for a take-out breakfast or snacks, then dine like royalty on the scenic rooftop terrace.

Sunlight Pension, Odós Ippodámou 32, 85100 Rhodes. ☎ **0241/21-435.**
10 rms (all with bath).

Rates: 6,000 Drs ($25) single/double. No credit cards.

The small, modern rooms, each with its own refrigerator, were ultra-clean when we visited and host Stavros Galanis seems intent on maintaining the standard. Downstairs from the guest quarters is a secluded garden and the diminutive Stavros Bar, a place that seems to be a popular late-night meeting ground.

Doubles for Less than 20,000 Drs ($84)

Hotel La Luna, Odós Ierokléous 21, 85100 Rhodes. ☎ **0241/25-856.**
7 rms (none with bath).

Rates (including breakfast): 11,160 Drs ($46.50) single; 14,430 Drs ($60.15) double. No credit cards.

This small, delightful hotel is one block from the taverna-lined Orfeous Street in a quiet residential neighborhood. La Luna has a large, shaded garden with a cozy bar and breakfast tables. The real highlight is the setting of the common bathrooms: Built into this old home is a genuine 300-year-old Turkish bath! Each eclectically decorated room has flower-print wallpaper, and though bathless, all are spacious and bright. Manager Tony Kaymaktsis maintains a fresh, clean and very friendly place, and will regale you with stories of Ben Kingsley's stay during the filming of the British epic *Paschali's Island.*

S. Nikolis Hotel, Odós Ippodámou 61, 85100 Rhodes. ☎ **0241/34-561.**
Fax 0241/32-034. 10 rms. 4 apartments (all with bath). TEL

Rates (including breakfast): 15,600 Drs ($65) single; 19,500 Drs ($81.25) double. AE, EC, MC, V.

This restored lodging is run by Sotiris and Marianne Nikolis. All compact tidy rooms have modern tiled showers, and heaters and blankets if the chilling meltémi begins to blow. In 1990, a 10-ton marble pediment dated to the 2d century was found beneath the medieval foundations in their backyard. After excavations were complete, this garden became the excellent Ancient Market Bar and Restaurant. Upstairs is their marble rooftop terrace overlooking the Old Town, where a delicious breakfast is served daily. They also have attractive, nearby apartments for rent that come with kitchen and are suited to families (rates equal the hotel's but breakfast isn't included), and a honeymoon suite under construction, as well as some simpler rooms to let. Usually open year-round, but call ahead to be sure between November and April.

IN THE NEW TOWN

The modern hotels, even in the New Town, are more expensive in Rhodes than on other islands. Mediocre breakfasts are usually exorbitant, and most bland establishments cater to groups and are rarely available to individual travelers.

Hotel Despo, Odós. Lambráki 40, 85100 Rhodes. ☎ **0241/22-571.**
64 rms (all with bath). TEL

Rates (including breakfast): 15,600 Drs ($65) double. No credit cards.

From the usual Class C fare, this colorful hotel, in the heart of New Town, is one of the best. It's so well managed that the 1950s-era black and white leather furnishings in the lobby don't show any signs of age. Sunny clean rooms have carpeting, modern attached showers and balconies.

International Hotel, Odós Kazoúli 12, 85100 Rhodes. ☎ **0241/24-595.**
Fax 0241/30-221. 42 rms (all with bath).

Rates (including breakfast): 11,000 Drs ($46.05) single; 16,250 Drs ($67.70). V.

A clean, simple, relaxed, and friendly hotel on a quiet street a couple of blocks east of the National Theater, near the beach and tennis courts. There's a nice little bar in the open lobby with fairly inexpensive drinks, soft jazz, and modern Greek music.

Kamiros Hotel, Odós 25 Martíou 1, P.O. Box 45, 85100 Rhodes. ☎ **0241/22-591.**
Fax 0241/22-349. 48 rms (all with bath). A/C MINIBAR TV TEL

Rates (including breakfast): 19,240 Drs ($80.15); 21,775 Drs ($90.75). AE, MC, V.

This recently completely renovated hotel is a bit of a splurge, but it's a good value and a good location, in the heart of town overlooking Mandraki Harbor, just a few blocks from the Old Town. The rooms are large, the bathrooms especially spacious, and double-paned windows make them especially quiet for the central location. The spacious lobby is attractively furnished with large contemporary blue leather sofas and chairs. The buffet breakfast is unusually substantial.

Marieta Pension, Odós 28 Oktovríou, 52, 85100 Rhodes. ☎ **0241/36-396.**
8 rms (all with bath).

Rates: 7,920 Drs ($33) single/double. No credit cards.

The clean, spacious Marieta Pension is a welcome alternative to the overpriced New Town hotels. Hosts Michael and Marietta Potsos ran the Gold Star Supermarket chain in St. Louis for many years. Now they've returned to Rhodes and run a pleasant, home-style pension in a 52-year-old traditional villa. The rooms are huge and high-ceilinged.

Royal Hotel, Odós G. Lambráki 50, 85100 Rhodes. ☎ **0241/24-601.** Fax 0241/33-358.
60 rms (all with bath). TEL

Rates (including breakfast): 13,500 Drs ($56.35) single; 18,000 Drs ($75) double. No credit cards.

Around the corner from the Ionian Bank on a quiet back street, the older Royal has spacious, carpeted rooms with modern tiled private baths. They're a bit worn, but the large balconies and quiet location make this an acceptable choice. The large, comfortable lobby has a bar and a pleasant breakfast lounge.

Where to Eat in Rhodes City

With some effort, well-prepared, tasty, and imaginative meals can be found, but prices vary widely, usually from expensive to outrageous, and restaurateurs continue to swindle tourists by overcharging, underweighing portions, or just not displaying a menu. Unless you're in one of the better restaurants, don't be shy about determining the cost of your meal before you consume it. If you have any problems, keep that receipt and head for the **market police** (☎ **23-849**). Most of the restaurants listed below claim to be open year-round, but experience has taught us that many close some of the time between November and April for a break, repair work, or lack of customers.

IN THE OLD TOWN

The Old Town is crammed with tavernas and restaurants, all hungry for tourist dollars. Hawkers stand in front of eateries and accost passersby—handing out business cards, ushering people in for a look at the kitchen, and finally strong-arming them into sitting down. It's all part of the game. The best way to handle a restaurant bully is to continue walking to one of the restaurants listed below. Lest you think that Old Town restaurants are strictly for tourists, many Rhodians consider this section of town to have some of the best food in the city, particularly for fish, although low-cost seafood feasts are an impossible contradiction.

Dodekanisos, 25 and 45 Platía Evréon Martýron. ☎ **21-634.**

Cuisine: GREEK/SEAFOOD.
Prices: Appetizers 500–3,200 Drs ($2.10–$13.55); main courses 1,500–2,800 Drs ($6.25–$11.65); fish 5,000–14,000 a kilo. AE, MC, V.
Open: Daily 11am–midnight (in winter from 6pm–midnight).

Everything at these tavernas is prepared with care: the grilled chicken is crisp and scented with oregano; the filet of perka is caught daily, and vegetables are fresh, firm, and not oily. Two branches are on opposite sides of the square; the larger specializes in fish, and the smaller, original one caters to locals with a varied grill and homestyle menu. Georgia, a Greek-American friend who's recently moved to Rhodes, sent us here for "great food, great prices." Well said.

Cleo's Restaurant, Odós St. Fanouríou 17. ☎ **28-415.**

Cuisine: ITALIAN. **Reservations:** Recommended in summer.
Prices: Appetizers 600–2,800 Drs ($2.50–$11.65); main courses 1,600–4,500 Drs ($6.65–$18.75). AE, EC, MC, V.
Open: Mon–Sat 7pm–midnight.

This tranquil, white-washed courtyard and two-story interior are found down a narrow lane off the noisy Socratous Street. Excellent Italian and nouvelle European

READERS RECOMMEND

Restaurant Latino, Odós Ippodámou 11. "Just down Ippodámou Street from the S. Nikolis Hotel was a restaurant that I couldn't tear myself away from! I ate there every night. It wasn't extremely pricey (for Rhodes) and the Italian food was amazing."—Heather Howard, Beverly Hills, Calif.

fare is served: the pasta pomodoro mozzarella, their well-seasoned mussels, and tender beef filet are all excellent. Don't miss the light-as-air gourmet desserts.

$ **Kavo d'Oro,** In alley off 41 Sokrátous. ☎ **36-181.**

Cuisine: GREEK/CONTINENTAL.

Prices: Appetizers 500–1,250 Drs ($2.10–$5.20); main courses 800–2,800 Drs ($3.35–$11.65). No credit cards.

Open: Daily 10am–3pm, 6pm–midnight.

Kavo d'Oro is a very reliable and ultra-friendly eatery. This unpretentious little spot offers Greek food just the way we like it: hot and fresh. We started with a delicate taramasaláta, moved to a plate of fried peppers, and then split a stifado and deep-dish moussaka that were both a delight. Before we finished with a fresh fruit platter and coffee, Sophia, the chef's wife, offered us a liqueur on the house. It's a bargain for pricey Rhodes.

★ **Yiannis Taverna,** Odós Appélou 41. ☎ **36-535.**

Cuisine: GREEK.

Prices: Appetizers 250–600 Drs ($1.05–$2.50); main courses 750–2,400 Drs ($3.15–$10). No credit cards.

Open: Daily 9am–midnight.

For a budget Greek meal, visit chef Yiannis' small place on a quiet lane behind the popular Kavo d'Oro. Not every dish is available daily, but the moussaka, stuffed vegetables, and meat dishes that come from a man who spent 14 years in New York's Greek diners are well made and flavorful. Portions are hearty, it's cheap, and the friendly service is a welcome relief from nearby establishments. Their breakfast omelets are a great deal, too!

★ **The Old Story (Palia Istoria).** Odós Mitropóleos 108, at Dendrinous St. ☎ **32-421.**

Cuisine: GREEK. **Reservations:** Recommended in summer.

Prices: Appetizers 900–1,500 Drs ($3.75–$6.25); main courses 2,500–4,200 Drs ($10.40–$17.50). EC, V.

Open: Daily 7pm–midnight.

This is one of the best restaurants in Rhodes, well worth the ten-minute cab ride (or 25-minute walk) into the New Town south of Diagora Stadium. Most of the clientele is Greek, drawn by the subtle cuisine and lack of tourists. We had unusual *mezédes* (appetizers): a finely chopped beet salad, lightly fried zucchini, a true country salad with potatoes, olives, and tomatoes, fried *saganáki* (fried cheese), then a fluffy greens and cheese soufflé, delicious meatless dolmádes, and a moist and tender roast pork with potatoes. A feast indeed!

Manolis Dinoris Fish Taverna, 14A Museum Sq. ☎ **25-824.**

Cuisine: SEAFOOD.

Prices: Appetizers 250–3,500 Drs ($1.05–$14.60); fish from 10,000–18,000 Drs ($41.70–$75) a kilo. AE, EC, MC, V.

Open: Daily noon–3pm, 7pm–midnight.

We happened upon this special place by the Old Town's front gate while hunting for an exhibit sponsored by the municipality. What a treat! Housed in the stables of the 13th-century Knights of St. John's Inn, with vaulting arches and impossibly thick masonry, the building was restored as a restaurant. We tried a full panoply of seafood delights (including their lobster); everything was delicious and fresh. We preferred the quiet garden on the side to the front patio, but in winter there's a roaring fire going indoors at their old stone hearth that makes it very cozy. Open year-round.

IN THE NEW TOWN

There are some good just-for-locals eateries in the New Town, but few with as much style as those in the Old Town. A tourist favorite is the **Mandraki Market Square,** in the agora one block inland from the harbor. There are more than a dozen small outdoor grill restaurants in this circular courtyard; throughout the day lambs are rotating on spits, chickens are roasting over gas fires, and pork is being hacked from roasted torsos to make souvlaki. You'll also find café bars, juice stands, postcards stalls, and other distractions to make this a fun (but not so cheap) lunch spot. Los Angelenos will feel nostalgic for the Farmer's Market!

Aris Taverna, Odós G. Leóntos 4-6. ☎ **32-320.**

Cuisine: GREEK/CONTINENTAL.
Prices: Appetizers 250–1,200 Drs ($1.05–$5), main courses 950–3,500 Drs ($3.95–$14.60). EC.
Open: Daily 10am–11pm.

This favored place around the corner from the Marietta Pension is often crowded with local businesspeople and their out-of-town guests. Kyle liked to order their tuna salad, butter beans, and fried peppers; John likes the heartier *giouvetsi* (here especially tender lamb) or their rich spaghetti bolognaise.

Break Delicatessen, Odós Sof. Venizélou 8. ☎ **34-809.**

Cuisine: FAST FOOD.
Prices: Snacks 250–1,800 Drs ($1.05–$7.50). No credit cards.
Open: Daily 7am–3am.

Two blocks west of EOT off G. Lambráki Street, Break is a New Age fast-food place, actually much nicer and better than you'd imagine. The counter chef huddles over a crêpe grill, turning out a dozen varieties priced as low as $1.50. If you want an inexpensive salad, burger, fried chicken, croissant, spinach pie, or ice cream, it's here—and at all hours!

Yefira Restaurant, Pastida village. ☎ **47-031.**

Cuisine: GREEK.
Prices: Appetizers 350–1,000 Drs ($1.45–$4.15); main courses 1,000–2,600 Drs ($4.15–$10.85). No credit cards.
Open: Mon–Sat 5pm–midnight, Sunday 11am–midnight.

About 15 kms. south (about 3,000 Drs ($12.50) by taxi), inland between Rhodes and the airport, is this fine grill mentioned by all our Rhodian buddies as their favorite dining spot. Go for wonderful mezédes (appetizers) (try the codfish with garlic and potato spread) and then anything that's fresh from the spit; we went wild for the lamb and chicken, but don't ignore the pork souvlaki. This is excellent Greek food in a real Greek village—and at low prices.

Lindos Restaurant, Platía Vass. Pávlou. ☎ **24-421.**

Cuisine: GREEK/INTERNATIONAL.
Prices: Appetizers 350–1,200 Drs ($1.45–$5); main courses 1,000–3,600 Drs ($4.15–$15). No credit cards.
Open: Daily noon–midnight.

This modern restaurant is north of the tourist area of New Town, a ten-minute walk from the port. Though it may not be a familiar haunt for most tourists, it is wildly popular with local residents, who keep the kitchen busy turning out such specialties as roast lamb, moussaka, wonderful Greek and tuna salads, steaks, and grilled chicken.

Evening Entertainment in Rhodes City

Outside of Athens, Rhodes has the most active nighttime scene in Greece. From Greek studs cruising the harbor for bombshell Swedish girls on holiday to the suave and sophisticated rich and near-rich who play high-stakes blackjack in the Casino Grand Hotel, Rhodes by night is brimming with energy.

For a different type of evening, try one of the many outdoor cafés lining the **harborside** of the New Town. There's a string of them under the lit arches outside the Agora (New Market). You'll have a good time watching the Greeks engage in *kamaki,* the ancient sport of girl-chasing (*kamaki,* actually, is Poseidon's trident, but you get the idea). Otherwise, at the north end and inland from the harbor, on G. Estatheadi Street, is the **Dimotikou Cinema,** which often shows American films in English (Greek subtitles). The **Palace Cinema** is south of Old Town on Dimokratias Street, near the stadium.

For entertainment of a strictly adult nature, try walking G. Fanduriou Street in the Old Town. On and around the street you'll find bars, music, and willing company. *The* party-scene street in the New Town is Iróon Politechniou Street; if you don't want to go home alone, this is the street to stroll through, as is the surrounding neighborhood.

LOCAL CULTURAL ENTERTAINMENT

Sound and Light, Odós Papágou, south of Rimini Square, Old Town. ☎ **21-922.**

The Sound and Light (Son et Lumière) presentation dramatizes the life of a youth admitted into the monastery in 1522, the year before Rhodes's downfall to invading Turks. In contrast to Athens's Acropolis show, the dialogue here is more illuminating, though the lighting is unimaginative. Nevertheless, sitting in the lush formal gardens below the palace on a warm evening can be a pleasant and informative experience, and is heartily recommended to those smitten by the medieval Old Town. Twice-nightly performances are scheduled according to season (check the posted schedule) and include one performance in English.

Admission: 1,250 Drs ($5.20).

Traditional Folk Dance Theater, Odós Adronikou, off Arionos Square, Old Town. ☎ **20-157.**

The Greek folk dance show, presented by the Nelly Dimoglou Dance Company, is always lively, filled with color, and totally entertaining. Twenty spirited men and women perform dances from many areas of Greece in colorful, often embroidered, flouncy costumes. The five-man band plays an inspired, varied repertoire, certainly more interesting than the amplified bouzouki emanating from the Old Town's new tavernas. The choreography is excellent, the dancers skillful, and even the set (an open square surrounded by two-dimensional Rhodian houses) is effective—a thoroughly recommended evening. Performances are Monday through Friday evenings at 9:20pm from late May through early October.

Admission: 3,000 Drs ($12.50) adults, 1,500 Drs ($6.25) students.

DISCOS & NIGHTCLUBS

There are at least a hundred **nightclubs** on Rhodes, so you're sure to find one to your taste. We're hesitant to make any specific recommendations because the scene changes so quickly. La Scala, the hottest spot on the coastal Ialysos Road during our last visit, had inexplicably changed its name to **Amazon** (☎ **37-830**), and young Italian studs like those posing in front of it before were walking up and down the street looking for it. **Buzio's Disco,** near the port, was outstandingly garish and sure to help draw a crowd to a lively quarter. Elsewhere in the New Town **le Palais** (☎ **34-219**), on Odós 25 Martíou, was still drawing a lively young crowd on Friday and Saturday nights, but several hipper young locals said they preferred **Plastik** and **Cozy.** The action doesn't start until after 10pm, and the usual admission is 2,500 Drs ($10.40), which includes the first drink.

The Old Town tends to be a bit less wild and loud, so if you're not up for a serious spree, you might find the stylish new **Symposium,** off lively Sokratous. Nearby, at Odós Omirou 70, the **Ancient Market Bar** offers an even more sedate venue for actual conversation; there's even a no-smoking section.

Rhodes sports a variety of Greek nightclubs, where bouzouki bands strum and singers croon. **Minuit Palace** in Ixia and **Melody Palace** (☎ **93-777**) and the **Stork** in Kremasti (near the airport) were considered the best clubs at our visit. The custom, as in many of the top clubs is: When the audience is driven to ecstasy by a heart-wrenching performance, send bunches of flowers and bottles of champagne to the stage. Finally, when the act accelerates into an absolute orgasmic state, the crowd smashes plates with enthusiasm and spontaneity. At both, the international pop entertainers come on at 10pm, the Greek bouzouki kings at midnight. Admission is buried in the exorbitant drink charges (bottles of whisky run about 20,000–30,000 Drs ($83.35–$125); anyone dining should expect to pay 12,000–18,000 Drs ($50–$75) per head.

GAMBLING

Gambling is a popular nighttime activity in Greece. Rumor has it that there's a network of private high-stakes (and illegal) gambling dens scattered throughout the city, much as there is in Iráklio. But for those who want to wager in a less subterranean atmosphere, saunter over to one of Greece's three legal casinos, the **Casino Grand Hotel,** Grand Hotel Astir Palace, Rhodes (☎ **28-098** or **228-109**). It's off Óthonos Amalías Street on the northwest side of New Town. Open daily year round, 8pm to 2am, the casino attracts visitors from around the world. If you have visions of Las Vegas or Atlantic City, you'll find this casino on the small side. Admission is for those 21 years and older only; they'll check your passport. Dress nicely: Closed shoes and, between November and April, jacket and tie are required.

Líndos

Líndos is without question the most picturesque town on the island of Rhodes. Be warned, however, that it is often deluged with tourists; your first view of Líndos will be unforgettable for the wrong reasons. The Archeological Society has control over all development in the village (God bless 'em!), and the traditional white stucco homes, shops, and restaurants form the most unified, classically Greek expression in the Dodecanese. Far too many vehicles are left by a towering, centuries-old plane tree whose roots are enclosed in a pebble-paved bench. Here, next to an ancient fountain with

Arabic script, the old village women in black chatter in the shade, watching hundreds of skimpily clad tourists cross back and forth to the beach below.

Bear right into the maze before you, aim to get lost and you'll find the basis for Líndos's aesthetic reputation. Avoid the Disneyland atmosphere of the high season, and with luck the peasant blouses, ceramic plates, and rock-star posters (David Gilmore of Pink Floyd has a house here) hung along the shopfronts won't distract you from the village's architectural purity.

ORIENTATION

There are two entrances to the town. The first and northernmost leads down a steep hill to the bus stop and taxi stand, then veers downhill to the beach. At this square you'll find the friendly, extremely informative **Tourist Information Kiosk** (☎ **0244/31-428**), where Michalis will help you daily between April 1 and November 1 from 9am to 7:30pm. Here, too, is the commercial heart of the village with the Acropolis above. The rural **clinic** (☎ **31-224**), **post office,** and **OTE** are nearby. The second road leads beyond the town and into the upper village, blessedly removed from the hordes. This is the better area for architecture enthusiasts.

WHAT TO SEE & DO

THE ACROPOLIS Past the bus stop square and donkey stand you'll see "Acropolis" signs. A visit to the superb remains of the Castle of the Knights on a hill above the town will help to orient you. From the east ramparts of the castle you can see the lovely beach at St. Paul's Bay below and more of Rhodes's less-developed eastern coastline.

The Acropolis contains the ruins of one of Rhodes's three Dorian towns (settled by Lindos, one of Helios and Rodon's three grandsons), and within its medieval walls are the impressive remains of the Sanctuary of Athena, with its large Doric portico from the 4th century B.C. St. John's Knights refortified the Acropolis with monumental turreted walls and built a small church to St. John inside (though their best deed was to preserve the ancient ruins still standing). Stones and columns are strewn everywhere, and at the base of the stairs leading to their Byzantine church is a wonderful large relief of a sailing ship, whose indented bridge once held a statue of a priest of Poseidon. From the north and east ramparts you'll have the most wonderful views of new Líndos below, where most of the homes date from the 15th century. Dug into Mt. Krana across the way are caves left by ancient tombs. The Acropolis (☎ **27-674**) is open from 8:30am to 3pm Tuesday through Sunday. Admission is 1,000 Drs ($4.15), half price for children, Sunday free. If you want to conserve your energy for picture taking, a 900 Drs ($3.75)-donkey ride is available at the town's entrance.

OTHER ATTRACTIONS In Líndos, try to stay away from the village's commercial heart. Instead, stroll through the maze of narrow streets, and look for ancient scripts carved in the wooden door lintels. There's the Byzantine Church of the Virgin, **Aghía Panagia,** from 1479. Inside there are intricate frescoes painted by Gregorios of Sými in 1779. The floor is paved *chochlakia,* the Rhodian technique done with pebbles, and here it's a perfect sawtooth pattern of upright black-and-white stones, worn smooth over the centuries. After feeling it, scout out a chaise longue on one of the two beaches encircling the main port to admire the luxury yachts docked at the point.

An elaborate local wedding took place there during our stay. Such glorious lace and embroidery were brought out for the bride and honored guests that afterward it was impossible to consider any of the comparatively primitive lace things for sale in the shops. Embroidery from Rhodes was coveted even in antiquity; it's said that Alexander the Great wore a grand embroidered Rhodian robe into battle at Gaugamila. And in Renaissance Europe, the French ladies used to yearn for a bit of Lindos lace.

WHERE TO STAY & EAT

In the high season (ironically, when the weather is hottest!) 4,000 resident tourists are joined by up to 10,000 day-trippers from Rhodes. Since no hotel construction is permitted, almost all of the old homes have been converted into pensions (called "villas" in the brochures) by English charter companies. However, in the peak season, the local **Tourist Information Kiosk** (☎ **0244/31-428**) has a list of the homes that rent rooms to individuals and will help to place you, though plan to pay 6,000 Drs ($25) to 8,000 Drs ($33.35) a bed in tiny rooms with shared facilities.

Triton Holidays (☎ **0241/21-690**) books six-person villas for 35,000 Drs ($145.85) a day in the low season, including kitchen facilities (reservations are usually made a year in advance). If Lindos is booked or not to your taste, consider the attractive beaches to the south at Pefkas, Lardos, or Kalathos. **Heliousa Travel** (☎ **0244/44-057,** fax 44/041) in Lardos can help you find a room as well as with other travel needs.

Despite the huge number of restaurants in tiny Lindos, we just can't assume the risk of steering you to any in particular. However, on the beach, the huge **Triton Restaurant** would get our nod because you can easily change into your swimsuit in their bathroom, essential for nonresidents who want to splash in the gorgeous water across the way. It's not as overpriced as all the others, and you can eat a decent meal of typical stuffed tomatoes or moussaka for 2,000 Drs ($8.35) and chalk it off to "cabana rental." (There's a wimpy public shower right on the sand.)

Sights Around the Island

The island of Rhodes is known for scenery, and one of the greatest pleasures an around-the-island tour provides is a chance to view some of its wonderful variations. The sights described below, with the exception of Ialysos and Kamiros, are not of significant historical or cultural importance, but if you get bored with relaxing, try some.

Ialysos was the staging ground for the four major powers that were to control the island of Rhodes. The ancient ruins and monastery reflect the presence of two of these groups. The Dorians ousted the Phoenicians from Rhodes in the 10th century B.C. (An oracle had predicted that white ravens and fish swimming in wine would be the final signs before the Phoenicians were annihilated. The Dorians, quick to spot opportunity, painted enough birds and threw enough fish into wine jugs so that the Phoenicians left without raising their arms.) Most of the Dorians left Ialysos for other parts of the island; many settled in the new city of Rhodes. During the 3d to 2d centuries B.C. the Dorians constructed a **temple to Athena** and **Zeus Polius** (similar to those on Mt. Smith), whose ruins are still visible, below the monastery. Walking south of the site will lead you to a well-preserved 4th-century B.C. fountain.

When the Knights of St. John invaded the island, they too started from Ialysos, a minor town by the Byzantine era. They built a small, subterranean chapel decorated with frescoes of Jesus and heroic knights. Their little whitewashed church is built right into the hillside above the Doric temple. Over it, the Italians constructed the **Monastery of Filerimos,** which remains a lovely spot to tour. Finally, Süleyman the Magnificent moved into Ialysos (1522) with his army of 100,000 and used it as a base for his eventual takeover of the island.

The site is open from 8:30am to 3pm Tuesday through Sunday. Proper dress is required, and admission is 500 Drs ($2.10). Ancient Ialysos is 6 km inland from Trianda on the island's northwest coast; public buses leave from Rhodes frequently for the 14-km ride.

The ruins at **Kamiros** are much more extensive than those at nearby Ialysos, perhaps because this city remained an important outpost after 408 B.C., when the new Rhodes was completed. The site is divided into two segments: the upper porch and the lower valley. The porch served as a place of religious practice and provided the height needed for the city's water supply. Climb up to the top and you'll see two swimming-pool-size aqueducts, their walls still lined with a nonporous coating. The Dorians collected water in these basins, assuring themselves a year-round supply. The small valley contains ruins of Greek homes and streets, as well as the foundations of a large temple. The site is in a good enough state of preservation for you to imagine what life in this ancient Doric city was like more than 2,000 years ago.

You should think about wearing swimsuits under your clothes: There is a good stretch of beach across the street from the site, where some rooms to let, a few tavernas, and the bus stop are. The site is open Tuesday through Sunday 8:30am to 3pm. Admission is 500 Drs ($2.10). Kamiros is 34 kms southwest of Rhodes town, with regular bus service.

Petaloúdes is a popular tourist attraction because of the millions of black-and-white-striped butterflies that have overtaken this verdant valley. When resting quietly on flowering plants or leaves, the butterflies are well camouflaged. Only the screaming of parents, the wailing of infants, and the Greek disco/rock blaring out of portable radios disturbs them. Then the sky is filled with a flurry of red, their underbellies exposed as they try to hide from the summer crush. The setting, with its many ponds, bamboo bridges, and rock displays, was too precious for us. (Real butterfly hounds should make it a point to stop on Páros, in the Cyclades, to see the only other Petaloúdes in Greece. There you'll find, as the Greeks call it, *psychopiana,* an elevated state of the mind and heart.) Petaloúdes is 25 km south of Rhodes and inland; it can be reached by public bus but is most easily seen with a guided tour.

Kalithea is an attractive east coast beach resort, 11 km south of Rhodes, celebrated for its medicinal hot springs. The old-fashioned bathing facilities are now closed. On the southwest tip of the island, the stretch from **Plimiri** to **Gennadi** has seen much less development and offers a contrast with most other beaches on the island. If Gennadi's dark sand and stone beach appeals, there are rooms to let and tavernas. Bus service to this part of the island is, at best, infrequent. If you have a car and are making an around-the-island tour, consider the east coast towns of **Monolithos,** with its spectacularly set monastery, and farther north, **Embonas;** there are rooms for rent in both. These are the kind of rural Greek villages that are disappearing on heavily touristed Rhodes.

Excursions to Turkey

Crossing to the Turkish port of Marmaris has become a standard excursion, (There's an 8am hydrofoil in the high season.) Large, comfortable ferryboats return from Turkey to Rhodes daily (three times weekly from mid-October to mid-April). Passport and fee 20,500 Drs or $85.40 for a day trip with a guided tour of Ephesus, or 9,400 Drs or $39.15 for one way passage) should be submitted one day in advance of departure; nearly all travel agencies sell tickets to Turkey. The Turkish Consulate is at 10 Iróon Polytechniou for those who need visas. For additional information on what to see and do on your excursion, consult Tom Brosnahan's *Turkey on $40 a Day.* The guide also lists hotels, restaurants, and transportation options.

2 Sými

Approximately 244 nautical miles E of Piraeus; 6 nautical miles N of Rhodes

ARRIVING/DEPARTING Several excursion boats arrive daily from Rhodes; two boats are owned cooperatively (the *Sými I* and *Sými II*) and are booked locally in Rhodes through **Triton Holidays** (☎ **0241/21-690**). Round-trip tickets are 5,000 Drs ($20.85). Most boats leave at 9am (two or three times weekly in the off-season) from Mandraki Harbor, stop in the main port of Yialós, then continue onto Panormitis Monastery or the beach at Pedi for sightseeing, before returning to Rhodes. There are daily car ferries from Piraeus, two ferries a week to Crete via Kárpathos, and two local ferries weekly to Kálymnos.

ESSENTIALS Tourist services include several travel agents, open Monday through Saturday from 9am to 1pm and 5 to 8pm. We found **Sými Tours** (☎ **0241/71-307,** fax 72-292) at the end of the harbor behind the Ionian Bank. There are a few other banks in Yialos, the port and biggest village. The police, located near the post office and **OTE**, are open 24 hours a day. **OTE** is located about 100 meters behind the *paralía;* it is open weekdays 7:30am to 3pm. The free *Sými News* is a local paper with useful information.

Tiny, rugged Sými is distinguished by a broad sweep of pastel-yellow neoclassical homes that line its two towns: Sými Town (also called Horió) and Yialós, the port. The absence of modern-designed buildings is due to an archeological decree (as in the case of Lindos and Pátmos) that severely regulates the style and methods of construction and restoration for all old and new buildings. Relics of Sými's turn-of-the-century prosperity (from trading and shipbuilding) are the richly ornamented churches scattered over the entire island. Islanders proudly boast that there are so many churches and monasteries that one could worship in a different sanctuary every day of the year.

During the 1940s and 50s, Sými's economy turned on sponges. In the following decades, sailors and fishermen used their skills to service the burgeoning commercial shipping industry. When the maritime business soured, Symians fled abroad to work, leaving their pristine home in the hands of developers. Picture-perfect traditional-style Sými is now the star of many Greek postcards. It's become a magnet for monied Athenians in search of long-term real estate investments, and a highly touted "off the beaten path" resort for European tour groups trying to avoid other tour groups.

Orientation/Getting Around

Ferries and excursion boats usually dock first at hilly Yialós on the barren, rocky northern half of the island. There's a pretty clock tower, on the right as you enter the port. used as a local landmark when defining the maze of vehicle-free lanes and stairs. Yialós is the liveliest village on the island and the goal of most overnighters. Sými's main road leads to Pédi, a developing beach resort one cove east of Yialós, and a new road rises up to Horio, the old capital. The island's 4,000 daily visitors most often take an excursion boat that stops at the major ports. However, there are a few motorbike rental shops in Yialós, three public buses a day between Yialós and Pédi, and a few taxis. (The Yialós-Pédi fare should be about 500 Drs or $2.10). **Sými Tours** (☎ **71-307**) organizes bus tours to the island's few sites. Caiques shuttle people to Emboriós beach from Yialós—at about 300 Drs ($1.70) per person each way—leaving the port when full. Most other beaches can be reached either from Yialós or Pedi by caique: Aghía Marina, Ághios Nikólaos, and Nanú Beach usually have daily connections with the two towns; expect to pay about 1,200 Drs ($5) for a round-trip excursion.

What to See & Do

Sými's southwestern portion is hilly and green; located here is the medieval **Panormítis Monastery,** popular with Greeks as a refuge from modern life. Pater Gabriel presides; young Athenian businessmen speak lovingly of the monk cells and small apartments that can be rented for R & R. (Rates are about 5,000 Drs or $20.85 for a family unit sleeping four with a kitchen and shower.) The whitewashed compound is appreciated both for its verdant, shaded setting and for the 16th-century gem of a church inside. The Taxiarchis Michail of Panormítis boasts icons of St. Michael and St. Gabriel adorned in silver and jewels. The town of **Panormítis Mihaílis** is most lively and interesting during its annual festival in early November, but can be explored year round via local boats or bus tours from Yialós. The hardy can hike there (it's 10 km, about three hours from town) and enjoy a refreshing dip in its sheltered harbor as reward for their labors.

In Yialós, by all means hike the gnarled, chipped stone steps of the *Kalí Stráta*—the wide stairway that ascends to **Horió** ("village"). This picturesque community is filled with images of a Greece in many ways long departed. Heavy-set, wizened old women sweep the whitewashed stone path outside their homes. Occasionally a young girl or boy or a very old man (too old to have left for America or Australia to make his fortune) can be seen retouching the neon blue trim over the doorways and shutters. Nestled between the immaculately kept homes are the abandoned villas, their faded trim and flaking paint lending a wistful air to the village. While young emigres continue to support their parents who inhabit Sými, renovated villas now rent to an increasing number of tourists, and where tourists roam, tavernas, souvenir shops, and bouzouki bars soon follow. Commercialization has hit once-pristine Sými, but for now it's an acceptable level.

There's a small **museum** in Horió that seems to be a conglomeration of the one or two items that each islander considered important enough for public exhibition. You can't miss the blue arrows that point the way; it's open from 9am to 2:30pm Monday through Saturday.

Crowning Horió is the **Church of the Panaghia.** The church is surrounded by a fortified wall, and therefore called a castle. It is adorned with the most glorious frescoes on the island, which can be viewed only when services are held (7 to 8am on weekdays, all morning on Sunday).

Sými is, unfortunately, not blessed with wide sandy beaches, though there's talk of making a fine sand beach at Pedi. Close to Yialós, the main town, are two beaches. The first is called **Nos,** with a 50-foot-long rocky "beach." **Emborios** is a pebble beach a bit farther than Nos (a 15-minute walk west of Yialós); it's a much larger beach and has a taverna as well as the nice new **Niriides Apartments** (☎ **0241/64-303** or **71/784**).

Two local crafts that continue to be practiced on this island are **shipbuilding** and sponge fishing. Walk along the water toward Nos beach and you'll probably see boats under construction or repair. It's a treat to watch the men fashion planed boards into a graceful boat, an old tradition on Sými. It was a boatbuilding center in the days of the Peloponnesian War, when spirited sea battles were waged off Sými's shores.

Sponge fishing is almost a dead industry in Greece, and Sými's industry is no exception. Only a generation ago 2,000 sponge divers worked waters around the island; today only a handful undertake this dangerous work and most do so in the waters around Italy and Africa. Working at depths of 50 to 60 meters (often without gear in the old days), many divers died or were crippled by the turbulent sea and too-rapid depressurization. The few sponges that are harvested, and many more imported from Asia or Florida, are sold at shops along the port. Even if they're not the real thing, they make fabulous, inexpensive gifts to take to friends. Sponges run from a few hundred to several thousand drachmas, depending on size and quality.

Where to Stay

Many tourists bypass hotels for private apartments or houses. Between April and October, rooms for two with shower and kitchen access go for 8,000–9,500 Drs ($33.35–$39.60); more luxurious two-bedroom, villa-style houses with daily maid service rent for 11,500–17,500 Drs ($47.90–$72.90). The best way of tapping into this alternative is to visit **Sými Tours** (☎ **0241/71-307**), located on the left-hand side of the harbor. They also represent two newly renovated villa-hotels, the six-room **Forei Hotel** and the five-room **Hotel Marika,** both above the Clock Tower on the north side of the harbor. At both, rooms with private showers go for 7,000 Drs ($29.15).

Hotel Aliki, Yialós, Sými. ☎ **0241/71-665.** Fax 0241/71-655. 15 rms (all with bath). A/C TEL

Rates (including breakfast): 11,400 Drs ($47.50) single; 15,600 Drs ($65) double. No credit cards.

We recommend this splurge, but with qualifications. The well-restored, traditional Alíki is the standard by which all Sými lodging is judged, with elegantly styled rooms, including some with dramatic, waterfront views. The level of service doesn't quite match the high standard of interior decor. Another of our hesitations relates to the nonview rooms, a poor value if compared with the equally priced seaview rooms. The other hesitation is availability—the Aliki has become a chic overnight getaway from bustling Rhodes; reservations, often months in advance, are required.

Hotel Dorian, Yialós, Sými. ☎ **0241/71-181.** 9 rms (all with bath). TEL

Rates: 10,250 Drs ($42.70) single; 14,500 Drs ($60.40) double. No credit cards.

This very pleasant, traditional style hotel climbs the hill above the Hotel Aliki and offers a very nice, but simple rooms with minimal service. However, prices are good for seaview rooms, many of which have balconies or terraces.

★ **Hotel Village,** Horió, Sými. ☎ **0241/71-800.** 17 rms (all with bath). A/C TEL

Rates (including breakfast): 11,400 Drs ($47.50) single; 14,400 Drs ($60) double. No credit cards.

This hotel, also known as the Chorio, is in the center of the upper town above Yialós and about a 15-minute walk from Pedi. The pastel-gold and blue color hotel, opened to visitors in 1989, is a cluster of small buildings perched high on the shoulder of the hill, blending naturally with the village around it. Rooms are plainly furnished and spotless; some have porches while upper rooms have balconies.

Where to Eat

Family Taverna Meraklis, Yialós. ☎ **71-003.**

Cuisine: GREEK.
Prices: Appetizers 400–1,000 Drs ($1.65–$4.15); main courses 850–2,400 Drs ($3.55–$10). EC, MC, V.
Open: Daily 8am–midnight.

This tiny storefront taverna, hidden on a back lane behind the Ionian and Popular Bank, away from the day-trippers, is welcome more as a respite from the crowds than as a great dining experience. From a limited daily menu, some small fish, stuffed vegetables, meat and mezédes (appetizers) are served, all for moderate prices. Chefs Anna and Sotiris pride themselves on their home cooking, which is most evident in their fresh vegetable dishes.

Taverna Neraida, Town Square, Yialós. ☎ **71-841.**

Cuisine: SEAFOOD.
Prices: Appetizers 300–800 Drs ($1.25–$3.35); main courses 800–2,800 Drs ($3.35–$11.65). No credit cards.
Open: Daily 11am–midnight.

Following our time-proven rule that fish is cheaper far from the port, this homey taverna has the best fresh fish prices (8,000 Drs or $33.35 per kilo) on the island, as well as a wonderful range of mezédes. We're especially fond of the black-eyed pea salad and skordaliá. The grilled daily fish is delicious and the very typical ambience is a treat.

3 Kos

200 nautical miles E of Piraeus

ARRIVING/DEPARTING • By Air **Olympic Airways** has two flights daily from Athens. The airport is in an out-of-the-way inland village 26 km from Kos town, but Olympic provides bus service to and from their office (☎ **28-330**) at Odós Vas. Pavlou 12.

• By Sea Three car ferries run daily from Piraeus via Pátmos, and there is infrequent service from the port of Rafína. Kos is served by daily boats from Rhodes (both car ferries and excursion ships). It's connected to the other Dódecanese by local excursion ships, which include three to five times weekly excursions to Kálymnos, Pátmos, volcanic Nisiros, and Tilos, and occasional steamers to Astipalea and Halki. In summer, there are several caiques daily from the beach of Mastichari to nearby Kálymnos. There are currently a few hydrofoil companies operating almost daily between Kos, Leros, Kálymnos, and Pátmos, two a week to Tilos, and one hydrofoil twice a week to Samos. Tickets are sold at the various travel agencies near the port.

Ferry service to Samos (continuing onto Lesvos and Thessaloníki) is an exhausting 11 hours going by the once-a-week slow boat. As everywhere, double-check schedules with **Tourist Information** in Athens (☎ 143), the **Piraeus Port Authority** (☎ 45-11-311), or the Strintzis Lines (☎ 0294/25-200) in Rafína.

Group tourism has certainly taken its toll on lovely Kos. In the summer, foreign visitors—mostly brought in on cheap package tours—outnumber the island's 30,000 inhabitants nearly two to one, so we recommend you avoid it in the high season. In the spring and fall you'll find Kos still has more than its share of archeological sites, unspoiled beaches, friendly people, and good food. We only wish it were more Greek. (If you're interested in the authenic, you'll have to look hard or elsewhere.)

Since ancient times Kos has been associated with the healing arts and the practice of medicine. Prior to the Dorian settlement of Kos in the 11th-century B.C., Koans established a cult dedicated to the worship of Asclepios, the god of healing and medicine. Asclepios was either a son of Apollo (from whom he acquired his knowledge) or a mortal (perhaps the physician of the Argonauts) who was deified because of his great healing power. An Asclepion, a sanctuary dedicated to the god, was built so the sick could make offerings in order to receive a cure. Throughout the centuries Kos produced many notable doctors, but none more renowned than Hippocrates (born 460 B.C.), the so-called Father of Medicine. He established the first medical school and a canon of medical ethics that is, to this day, the code of doctors throughout the world.

Orientation

Many first-time visitors prefer to settle in the northern port town of Kos, then explore the rich variety of archeological and historical sights and sample the capital's lively nightlife. After examining the beaches on bicycle excursions, long-term visitors move out and find accommodations closer to the golden sand. Our recommendation for beach-goers is to head south to the Ághios Stefanos–Kefalos region on the southwestern side of the island.

Getting Around

Residents of Kos town can easily walk to most sights, and in fact a stroll along the harbor or the busy back streets of the Agora is one of the greatest pleasures offered by the island.

BY BUS

Public bus service is inexpensive (the highest fare is 600 Drs or $2.50 to far-off Kefalos) but infrequent. Buses service all the beach areas, but this is nowhere to get stranded after sunset: A return taxi will be very costly. The KTEL bus station is around the corner from Olympic Airways on Kleopatras Street. Local city buses leave frequently from the EOT office on the port, and pass by local sights such as the Asclepion.

BY BICYCLE/MOPED

A bicycle is the preferable mode of transportation for nearby tanning. You can rent them anywhere for 600 Drs ($2.50) per day, but remember that the best bikes go early, so get there before 9am. Mopeds are great for longer excursions (or for lazier people) and can be rented all over town for 3,000 to 5,000 Drs ($12.50–$20.85).

BY TAXI/CAR

Taxis actually use meters on Kos, and most trips in Kos Town will not even exceed the 300 Drs minimum fare. However, the airport is a 4,000 Drs ($16.70) ride away, and the beaches even more. There is a taxi stand near the Tourist Office; call **23-333** to book a car. Several companies rent cars and Jeeps—including **Avis** (☎ **24-272**) and **Interrent** (☎ **23-315**)—but this is an extravagance unless you do some heavy-duty exploring. Expect to pay 20,000 Drs ($83.30) per day including insurance and fuel.

Essentials

Your first stop should be the very helpful **Municipal Tourism Office** (☎ **24-460**), located at Odós Vas Gheórghio 1, near the east side hydrofoil pier (open 7:30am to

3pm Monday through Friday). The **tourist police** (☎ **22-444**) are open 24 hours daily in the police station on Aktí Miaoúli; you can ask them about available rooms to let. For medical assistance contact the **Hippocrates Hospital,** Odós Ippocratou 32 (☎ **22-300**). The **OTE** is on Vironos Street and the **post office** is on Venizélou Street, both about two blocks from the agora.

What to See & Do

From the time of the Roman Empire to the Allied victory over the Germans in World War II, Kos was occupied and ruled by foreign forces. Nowhere is the legacy of foreign domination more apparent than in the area of the port and capital city, Kos (also called Hora). The town has a network of Greek and Roman excavations, as well as Byzantine remains, Venetian buildings, a medieval castle, and a Turkish Mosque, all within one or two square kilometers of each other. Only five kilometers northwest of Hora is the Asclepion, the most important archeological site on the island. From July to September, you can catch the many art exhibitions, theater, and dance performances funded by the Kos Hippokratia Festival.

Kos's many archeological sites can be seen in one day; consider touring the outdoor sites like the Odeoum, western excavations, agora, and plane tree after seeing the Asclepion, Roman villa, castle, and museum.

A DAY TOUR

The best way to get to all of these sites is by bicycle; if you're hardy (fit for about 12 kilometers of cycling) you can visit everything in a day. Starting from town, take the main road to the intersection of Koritsas, Alexandrou, and Grigoriou Streets, and follow the signs for the Asclepion. You'll pass through the hamlet of **Platani,** also called "Turkish Town," where residents still speak Turkish. It's a great place to stop for an inexpensive snack; you might consider returning for dinner in the quieter evening hours. The **Clarisse Ceramic Factory,** on the left, is a good place to buy souvenirs. You'll know you're nearing the Asclepion when you enter an exquisite cyprus-lined roadway.

ASCLEPION The Asclepion was excavated in the early part of this century, first by the German archeologist Herzog in 1902, then by a team of Italians. The Italians unearthed the lowest of four levels of the terraced site. The second level is the Propylaea, thought to be where the treatment of the sick actually took place (sulfur springs and a Roman-era bath, on the left, were central to the ancients' idea of exorcising disease). This level of the Asclepion (the largest) was bordered by a Doric portico on three sides, and contained many rooms to house visitors and patients. A number of niches and pedestals were found here, as well as statues and other votive offerings. Don't miss the refreshingly cool drinking fountain next to the stairway; it is Pan who, from his shaded enclave, leaps out at the parched visitor. Continue climbing the magnificent stairway to the two upper terraces, both containing temples from the Greek and Roman eras.

In the center of the third level is the **Altar of Asclepion** and two temples, the left one dedicated to Apollo and the right to the original Temple of Asclepion. Pilgrims placed their votive offerings (sometimes of enormous value) in the cella of these temples, prior to therapy. The Ionic temple on the left, with the restored columns, dates from the 1st century B.C., while the Asclepion Temple is from the beginning of the 3d century B.C.

As you ascend the stairs to the highest level, look back toward Turkey and you'll see the 7th-century B.C. ally of Kos, Halikarnassos (present-day Bodrum), part of the Doric Hexapolis uniting Kos, Halikarnassos, and Knidos with the Rhodian cities Lindos, Ialyssos, and Kameros. The fourth story contains the once-monumental 2d-century B.C.. Temple of Asclepion. This huge sanctuary, built in the Doric style of contrasting black and white marble, must have been an awe-inspiring sight, visible for miles around.

The **Asclepion** (☎ **28-763**) is open daily 8:30am to 3pm; admission is 750 Drs ($3.15), half price for students, Sunday free.

WESTERN EXCAVATION Returning to Kos, veer right on Grigoriou Street and proceed until you reach the site of the Western Excavation, on your left; through the tall trees the Odeum is on your right. The Western Excavation, also known as the ancient Greek and Roman city, connects the site by two 3d-century B.C. perpendicular roadways. Follow the road leading away from the Odeum until you come to the large reconstructed building on the right; it was originally thought to be a **nymphaeum** (a place where virgins were readied for the fulfillment of their destiny); later research led archeologists to conclude that it was a public toilet! Nevertheless it's a great toilet, with a superb mosaic floor; you'll have to climb up on the right side of the building to peer inside. Across from the toilet is the **Xystro,** a restored colonnade from a gymnasium dating from the Hellenistic era. If you continue walking along the road you'll come to a covered area that houses a lovely 2d-century A.D. mosaic showing the Judgment of Paris and various Roman deities. The buildings in the center of the site are, like the Xystro, from the 3d century B.C.; you should climb up to discover the fine marble parquet floor and remarkable mosaics (many of which are covered by a thin layer of sand for protection).

Walk back through the site along the road and make a left to arrive at the second part of the site. The remains here date from the Roman and early Christian eras. The highlight is the splendid mosaic in the **House of Europa** (the first on your left) depicting a lovely, terrified-looking Europa being carted away to Crete by Zeus (in the incarnation of a bull) for his pleasure.

ROMAN SITES Cross the modern road and proceed to the **Odeum,** excavated during the Italian occupation of the island in 1929. Many of the sites on the island have exceptional carved marble, and the Roman-era Odeum is no exception. The famous sculpture of Hippocrates (among others) was found in the covered archways at the base of the Odeum.

Continue down the modern road to the restored Roman villa known as **Casa Romana,** adjacent to a Roman bath and a Greek Dionysian temple. Reconstruction of the Roman villa was the work of the Italians who, one can only surmise, were going around the Mediterranean world fixing up ancient edifices to demonstrate the connection between the Great Roman Empire and the newly established Fascist state. It's a fascinating archeological achievement, and presents a unique opportunity to tour a complete Roman villa. Admission is 500 Drs ($2.10), half price for children and free Sunday. It is open Tuesday through Sunday from 8:30am to 3pm.

HIPPOCRATES TREE Follow the Odeum road for three blocks and turn left to see the recently relandscaped ruins of the Dionysian temple. Continue down Pavlou Street, and to the right of the nursery on Kazousi Square you'll find the ancient **Agora,**

a 2d-century B.C market. Walking along the edge of the Agora, toward the harbor, you'll come to Lozia Square. Here you'll find a Turkish mosque and the **plane tree of Hippocrates,** under which he was supposed to have taught his students. The stories about this poor tree have been concocted so as to compare it to the apple tree under which Newton achieved scientific enlightenment. It's extremely unlikely that this tree was alive in the doctor's time, but who knows? Anyway, you can't help feeling for the aged trunk that supports still virile, muscular branches, fortunately propped up with old columns and pedestals.

CASTLE OF THE KNIGHTS Walk across the bridge and you'll be at the Castle of the Knights of Rhodes. When entering this impressive fortress, built in the late 14th century and restored by the Grand Masters d'Aubusson and d'Amboise in the 16th, you'll see fragments of statues, columns, pedestals, and other architectural paraphernalia from ancient times. To some it may look like a tag sale of worn-out classical items, but it underscores a ubiquitous phenomenon in Greece: succeeding generations pulled down existing structures to build new edifices that were more appropriate to the time. You might spot whole doorways taken from houses located in the ancient city, or a giant slice of pure-white Doric column stuck in the middle of an extension wall.

The design of the castle was considered innovative because of its system of inner and outer walls and the numerous subterranean tunnels and rooms that facilitated covert movement within them. As if that weren't enough, the whole fortress was surrounded by a moat. The views of the harbor and beach from the top of the far wall are unsurpassed (but that's why they built it there in the first place!). Admission is 500 Drs ($2.10), half price for students, and free on Sunday. It is open Tuesday through Sunday from 8:30am–3pm.

ARCHEOLOGICAL MUSEUM For those tireless souls who need to see it all in a day, a visit to the Archeological Museum (☎ **28-326**) is the grand finale. The central room contains finely executed 2d-century A.D. mosaics and sculptures found at the House of Europa. The mosaic (completely intact and in color) depicts the two most famous figures in the Koan pantheon, Asclepios and Hippocrates. The "must see" in this museum's excellent collection of Hellenistic and Roman sculpture is the figure of a man assumed to be Hippocrates. Whatever his identity, the statue is a deeply expressive work, showing the pathos of a man who has taken on the suffering of the world. Admission is 500 Drs ($2.10), half price for children, and free Sunday. The museum is open from Tuesday through Sunday from 8:30am–3pm.

SYNAGOGUE As with the other Dodecanese islands, Kos once had a large and influential Jewish population. Today there is but one family that survived the Holocaust and still lives on the island; the few others have emigrated to Israel. What remains of their presence is a synagogue, built in 1935, that was recently bought by the municipality of Kos and restored as a cultural center and office building. Although there are no torahs or other holy objects within the building, it is quite a stately place with a fine courtyard and identifiable religious decor. Inside are stained-glass windows of rather plain though elegant design and a chandelier; there is also a sculpture by Alexandrous Alwyn (see Ziá under Asfendíon, below). (When asked about the building, some neighbors told us that they call it the "*havra,*" or chatter place, because of the custom of congregations reading aloud at their own pace.) The synagogue is open Monday through Friday from 9am to 2:30pm; there are no religious services held in the building.

Where to Stay

Try to arrive in Kos during the morning, or you might find yourself sleeping in the park or on the beach. For those without reservations, your first stop should be the tourist police. Within Kos there are basically three areas for hotels: Lambi Beach to the west, the central area behind the harbor, and the beach on the east side.

Kos Camping (☎ **0242/23-275**) is 2½ kilometers out of town toward the east, opposite a rocky beach in Psalídi. The sleeping bag charge is 1,250 Drs ($5.20) per night, with tents going for an additional 700 Drs ($2.90).

Hotel Affendoulis, Odós Evripilou 1, Kos 85300. ☎ **0242/25-321** or **25-797.**
17 rms (all with bath). TEL

Rates: 7,800 Drs ($32.50) single; 10,500 Drs ($43.75) double. No credit cards.

Our number-one choice is this fine modern hotel on a quiet side street a mere 200 meters from the eastern beach. To begin, this spotless hotel, with its polished marble floors and ultra-white walls, is the domain of the Zikas family, as helpful and gregarious a clan as we found in Kos. We enjoyed sitting (and writing) in the open lobby decorated with more Greek style than usually found in a Class C place. There is a shaded outdoor breakfast area (an additional 800 Drs/$3.35 per person) and a much-used honor-system kitchen for drinks and snacks. The bright, balconied rooms have firm mattresses and are comfortably furnished, again with decorative touches. A good value.

$ **Pension Alexis,** Odós Irodotóu 9, Kos 85300. ☎ **0242/28-798.**
12 rms (none with bath).

Rates: 5,500 Drs ($22.95) single; 6,900 Drs ($28.75) double. No credit cards.

For those on a tight budget, we recommend this inexpensive place at the corner of Omiróu Street. All rooms share common facilities, including a homey kitchen and breakfast area. We particularly liked the spacious upstairs rooms with their clean parquet floors, balconies, and fine views of the harbor. The pension is in the Zikas family home and the feeling of living in a Greek house remains.

Pension Anna, Odós Venizélou 69, Kos 85300. ☎ **0242/23-030.**
18 rms (all with bath). TEL

Rates (including breakfast): 6,250 Drs ($26.05) single; 8,250 Drs ($34.40) double. No credit cards.

If all else fails and you need a room, try the Pension Anna, a simple, family-run place. Rooms are totally plain but comfortable, and the location is fairly quiet and convenient.

Hotel Galini, Platía 3d Septemvríou, Kos 85300. ☎ **0242/23-368.**
31 rms (all with bath). TEL

Rates (including breakfast): 7,800 Drs ($32.50) single; 11,250 Drs ($46.90) double. No credit cards.

This Class C inn is pleasant, but beginning to show the wear and tear of German, Finnish, and Italian tour groups. It's a good choice because of its quiet location in a newly developed quarter of town. Rooms are quite plain but clean.

Hotel Maritina, Odós Vironos 19, Kos 85300. ☎ **0242/23-211.** Fax 0242/26-124.
68 rms (all with bath). MINIBAR TV TEL

Rates (including breakfast): 9,200 Drs ($38.35) single; 14,950 Drs ($62.30) double. AE, DC, MC, V.

This is a fine Class C hotel where last-minute arrivals may find a room, though it's pricey compared to the competition. Rooms overlook a quiet side street in town and are a bit worn from use by several tour groups.

Pension Kalamaki Nitsa, Odós G. Averof 47, Lambi Beach, Kos 85300. ☎ **0242/25-810.** 12 rms (all with bath).

Rates 7,500 Drs ($31.25) single/double. No credit cards.

Across the street from popular Lambi Beach is a simple pension above a liquor store. Rooms are basic but clean and have private showers. Although it's only a short walk to the beach, the sand and water are cleaner a bit farther away from town.

Hotel Theodorou, Odós G. Papandreou, Kos 85300. ☎ **0242/23-363.** 60 rms (all with bath). TEL

Rates (including breakfast): 7,350 Drs ($30.65) single; 11,725 Drs ($48.85) double. No credit cards.

This lively place is a three-story hotel filled with Northern Europeans who seem to be perpetually up for a party. The location is ideal for those in need of a beach only 20 meters from the lobby and close to the town's nightlife. The tariff is on the high side for clean but totally standard Class C accommodations; you're paying for the ever-popular Psalidi Beach.

Where to Eat

In town, the plethora of continental/pizza/burger/ice cream joints is disheartening, but with a little walking you can get a decent meal. Don't forget to try some of the local Kos wines: the dry white Lafkos, the red Appelis, or the light subtle Theokritos retsína.

Arap (Platanio) Taverna, Platinos-Kermetes. ☎ **28-442.**

Cuisine: TURKISH/GREEK.

Prices: Appetizers 350–800 Drs ($1.45–$3.35), main courses 800–1,800 Drs ($3.35–$7.50). No credit cards.

Open: Daily 10am–midnight.

Because of its proximity to Bodrum (Turkey), there are a number of tavernas serving both Turkish and Greek cuisine in this village on the road to the Asklepion, about two kilometers south of town. The best is very popular; among their dishes was a fine *imam biyaldi,* a Turkish stuffed eggplant.

★ **Taverna Mavromatis,** Psalidi Beach. ☎ **22-433.**

Cuisine: GREEK.

Prices: Appetizers 200–2,500 Drs (85¢–$10.40); main courses 800–4,000 Drs ($3.35–$16.70). No credit cards.

Open: Daily 11am–11pm.

One of the best choices in town (it's a 20-minute walk southeast of the ferry port) is the 30-year-old vine- and geranium-covered taverna run by the Mavromati brothers. Their Greek food is what you came to Greece for: melt-in-your-mouth *saganáki,* mint and garlic spiced *souzoukákia,* tender grilled lamb chops, moist beef souvlaki. Prices are reasonable (even for fresh fish) and the gentle music, waves lapping at your feet, and shaded back patio are delightful.

Mores, Themistokleous and Salaminos Streets. ☎ **25-878.**

Cuisine: SEAFOOD.

Prices: Appetizers 450–1,000 Drs ($1.90–$4.15); main courses 900–2,100 Drs ($3.75–$8.75). No credit cards.

$ **Open:** Daily noon–3pm; 6:30–11pm.

We've long favored a little seafood taverna, now gone touristic, which has a menu that offers the usual items plus some that seem wholly original. We loved the spicy and hot (wait, this is Greece!) mussel and shrimp *saganáki,* as well as a fine octopus stifado with richly cooked pearl onions. Don't be put off by the new kitschy pictures—the food is very good and the place is still frequented by locals.

Restaurant Olimpiada, Odó Kleopátras 2. ☎ **23-031.**

Cuisine: GREEK.

Prices: Appetizers 450–900 Drs ($1.90–$3.75); main courses 700–1,600 Drs ($2.90–$6.70). EC, MC, V.

Open: Daily 11am–11pm.

The best value for simple Greek fare is the Olimpiada, around the corner from the Olympic Airways office on Pavlou Street. The food is mostly fresh, flavorful (if not original), and inexpensive, and the staff is remarkably courteous and friendly. The okra in tomato sauce and the several vegetable dishes are the best. Open year-round.

Evening Entertainment

To our minds, the portside cafés opposite the daily excursion boat to Kálymnos are best in the early morning. A much more romantic alternative in the evening is the pricier, luxurious **Rendevous Café,** on the east side. Here you can lounge in a striking modern environment or outdoors on the marble terrace, hold hands, and sip cocktails to the many moods of live piano accompaniment. **Platanos,** across from the Hippocrates Tree, has live jazz—Brazilian guitar the night we visited—after 8pm. If you're interested in something considerably more raucous, wander up nearby Odós Nafkliróu on the northeast side of the Ancient Agora. There are of course many nightspots along the port and a few up Odós Bouboulinas. The lively **Playboy Disco,** Odós Kanári 2 (☎ **22-592**) has an impressive lightshow.

Continue on out Odós Kanári if you're interested in bouzouki music and Greek dancing. Friends recommend the **Aspa** and **Kritika.** We suggest you pick up a copy of *Kos: Where and How* for 400 Drs ($1.70) and let your fingers do the walking.

Around the Island

Although there are many fascinating archeological sites, the reason that most people come to Kos is for its wonderful **beaches.** The island lies on a 45° angle; at its tip, the port of Kos faces due northeast to Bodrum, Turkey.

THE BEACHES

The two best beaches are between Tigaki and Marmari on the north coast and Kefalos and Kardamena on the south. Both can be reached by bus; from Kos town the closer northwest coast beaches are a mere hour's bicycle ride away and considerably more convenient, though very crowded.

If you do want to stay on the northwest side of the island, a good choice is to go farther south to **Mastihari,** a quieter village with its own fine beach and many rooms to let. From Mastihari, small excursion boats make the 30-minute crossing to Kálymnos several times daily.

Tigaki is typical of the beach towns that deal almost exclusively with groups, but it's convenient for day trips, and pleasant. From here there's also regular caique service to Psarimos, a small island off Tigaki that has decent swimming and a taverna on the beach. Marmari is a nearby beach that is a little quieter, but it too has become increasingly popular because of its newfound windsurfing potential.

Not to be overlooked are the beaches to the west of the port town, Kos. **Lambi Beach,** a ten-minute walk from town, is usually packed, but you can take advantage of the many tavernas that line the shore for a nice lunch. On the other side of the harbor to the east are the beaches extending all the way down to the cape of **Ághios Fokas.** These also get crowded, and are lined with the greatest number of beach front hotels. The well-groomed pebble and sand Psalidi Beach is just three kilometers east of the main port, but it may fall victim soon to the construction of a new yacht marina.

ASFENDÍOU (RUSTIC VILLAGES)

The inland villages of **Ziá, Evangelístria,** and **Lagoúdi,** are all part of the Asfendíou region, a 30-minute drive from downtown Kos. These hamlets are situated halfway up the craggy peaks that form the island's geological backbone, placing them in forests of eucalyptus, pine, and fig and olive trees. During spring, the ground is littered with wildflowers of every hue, and the soft aroma of camomile, oregano, mint, and sage perfumes the air. Locals hike these villages during the summer for the cooling breezes blowing across the mountain. There is a wonderful mix of stately churches, crumbling houses, active farms, and new construction, and the people everywhere seemed the friendliest on the island. We loved the quintessentially Greek ambience of this area.

The most efficient way to visit this area is by car, but we prefer taking the public bus, infrequent but cheap, and walking from town to town. In the village of Evangelístria, we happened upon an English artist's studio that is worth a visit. **Alexandrous Alwyn** is known for his bronze sculpture though many of his highly eclectic sketches and paintings are also on display. His work is somewhat like Henry Moore's, only warmer and more expressive, and is set in a lovely courtyard outside of his studio; open daily. Ask any local for directions.

It's almost worth taking the trip solely for the superbly simple dining at the **Sunset Balcony** (**☎ 29-120**), just west of the church in Ziá. We had Heiniken beer and a large plate of more than a dozen *mezédes,* all of which were distinctive and delicious, and after we'd all but licked it clean we finished with near-perfect souvlaki, all for less than $20 each. The sun setting over the Kos plains and the sea with several nearby islands is nearly as remarkable as it is on Santoríni.

SOUTHERN KOS & KÉFALOS

Kardámena is an overdeveloped concrete and sand lot with many, many places to stay; however, we prefer to head south toward the almost connected villages of Ághios Stefanos and Kéfalos. In between these developed areas (and just to the north, as well) is an enormous stretch of sand and stone visited by a mere fraction of tourists who inhabit the town beaches. The names of these beaches running north to south are **Polemi, Magic** (one of the best), **Paradise, Camel, Bubble** (with watersports), and **Sunny.** All are served by frequent bus service from Kos town. The town of **Kéfalos,**

overlooking the sea, used to be a wealthy place that relied more on income brought in by its many sailors and ship captains than by tourism. The seaside is now being rapidly developed, and the village has the largest number of consumer conveniences on the southern part of Kos, including a bank, post office, OTE, tavernas, and shops. It's our beach of choice for those driven out of the main town by mopeds and music bars.

This four-kilometer-long stretch of gray sand and stone lines a gently arced cove running south from Ághios Stefanos (site of the island's Club Mediterranee resort) to the about-to-blossom-resort of Kéfalos. On the mid-stretch of beach, the superorganized **Surfpool Windsurfing School** caters weekly programs to German tour groups, but also rents K2 equipment for beginners or semi-pros by the day. Rates, including wetsuits, are 4,800 Drs ($20) per hour, or 18,000 Drs ($75) for five hours, which can be used up over several days. During the high season, brisk offshore breezes provide swift sailing but few waves, an ideal combination for racing back and forth parallel to the seashore. The colorful presence of so many windsurfers and sailboats (rented at Club Med) make up much of Kéfalos' scenic appeal.

Where to Stay & Eat

Newly developed Kéfalos has many rooms-to-let complexes with little personality, and a few good value hotels. Most of the beachside ones have small restaurants, but we found two casual places on the sand that really appealed. **Restaurant Corner** (☎ **71-223**) in the middle of the beach serves only those specials that take advantage of the day's fish catch (sold at 10,000 Drs or $41.65 per kilo, a bargain for this ambience). The octopus, lightly battered, fried, and served with oregano and lemon is great. **Captain John** (☎ **71-152**) at the south end of the beach has an international menu, and draws the biggest morning crowd with their 8:30am opening and large variety of breakfast eats. Both places serve lunch and dinner daily, have inexpensive food and local wines, and don't accept credit cards.

Hotel Kokolakis, Kéfalos, Kos. ☎ **0242/71-466.** Fax 0242/71-496.
42 rms (all with bath). TEL

Rates (including breakfast): 7,650 Drs ($31.90) single/double. No credit cards.

This was one of the first hotels here, and claims a prime location just off the quiet main street on the beach. Balconied rooms, most overlooking their small pool and the sea, are simple and whitewashed. There's a rattan bar next to the pool (the pool's open to the public at 400 Drs or $1.65) for snacks and drinks, and a lobby lounge and breakfast area. The front desk also rents Jeeps at a good price of 16,000 Drs ($66.65) per day.

Hotel Kordistos, Kéfalos, Kos. ☎ **0242/71-251.** 21 rms (all with bath). TEL

Rates (including breakfast): 6,500 Drs ($27.10) single; 8,500 Drs ($35.40) double. EC, MC, V.

This is another good choice, though quiet sea-facing back rooms overlook some unfinished (illegal), permanently halted construction. The well-kept simple twin-bedded rooms have private showers and small balconies.

Sacallis Inn, Kéfalos, Kos. ☎ **0242/71-010.** 25 rms (all with bath). TEL

Rates (including breakfast): 6,850 Drs ($28.55) single; 8,500 Drs ($35.40) double. V.

Tony and Maria Sacallis recently opened their inn, and we found it spotless, well designed, and very appealing. Large rooms are spic 'n' span, with fresh carpeting, modern facilities, and tiled balconies, most overlooking the picturesque Kastri islet and the azure sea. There's a large beachside patio with a bar and a nice lawn. There's a Greek/continental seaview taverna, and additional rooms are on the way.

Excursions to Turkey

Many visitors to Kos find themselves staring longingly at the Turkish coastline, imagining an excursion into exotic Asia Minor. Boats to Bodrum, Turkey, now leave twice daily from the main harbor; ask the tourist police for ships' agents and schedules. The one-way fare (including "taxes" and "harbor fees") is 7,000 Drs ($29.15); 11,000 Drs ($46) for same-day return and 12,000 Drs ($50) if you stay over and return at a later date. You can usually buy tickets on the boat, though some agents may require submission of your passport and fee one day in advance of your trip. Contact the tourist police regarding any necessary papers, as politically motivated visa regulations and rules change frequently. For additional information on what to see and do, consult Tom Brosnahan's *Turkey on $40 a Day.* The guide also lists hotels, restaurants, and transportation options.

4 Kálymnos

183 nautical miles E of Piraeus

ARRIVING/DEPARTING One car ferry leaves daily via Léros and Pátmos from Piraeus; schedules should be confirmed in Athens at **Tourist Information** (☎ **143**) or at the **Port Authority** (☎ **45-11-311**). There is also a daily boat from Myrties beach to Léros, and irregular service (about five times a week) to Kálymnos from the other Dódecanese islands; in the high season there's twice daily service to Kos and Pátmos. There are once weekly connections to the Cyclades, Pythagorion on Samós, and Iráklio, Crete. Schedules should be checked at the port of departure. Kálymnos is sometimes added to the hydrofoil's schedule during the summer, but you should check with a travel agent as this changes frequently.

ESSENTIALS Midway on the harbor, near the Poseidon statue but set back from the *paralía,* is the **Tourist Information** hut (☎ **29-310** or **23-138**), open daily 8:30am to 1pm and 2 to 7pm to provide information on rooms to let and sightseeing. Along Eleftherios Street (the harbor road) you'll find the **police** (☎ **29-301**), the **National, Commercial** and **Ionian Banks,** and several travel agents, among them the helpful **Kalymnos Tours** (☎ **28-329,** fax 29-656). A few blocks inland from the harbor is the **taxi stand;** there you'll find the **OTE** and the **post office.**

Kálymnos is best known for natural sponges, but the island also offers some out-of-the-way beaches, a few resort developments, and, if you get off the beaten track, peace and quiet rarely found on her better-known neighbors, Rhodes and Kos. The thriving sponge-fishing industry (10% of Greece's total output) used to make Kálymnos refreshingly autonomous; now the industry has fallen on hard times, and limited tourism is being courted by the island as a source of income. To compensate for the losses in the sponge industry, Kalymniots have amassed the largest fishing fleet in Greece, comprising more than a thousand registered ships. At a recent visit, we met a team of Japanese tuna fishermen who were training local anglers.

Unfortunately, like its better-known Dodecanese neighbors, Kálymnos has been hit by the scourge of group tourism. Some of the best hotels in areas that are now overbuilt—such as the beach communities of Massouri and Myrties—are rented by Scandinavian tourist companies for the entire season, making it difficult for the independent traveler. If it's a Greek retreat that you seek in July or August, head farther out to Emborios or to inland villages.

Orientation

Most visitors to Kálymnos come on a day trip from Kos and only have time for a visit to one of the sponge treatment centers (plus a splash at the beach). Orient yourself while you're approaching the harbor at Pothiá, and it becomes obvious that the waterfront, packed with active boats, still dominates life here. To the left, silver-domed spires top the cream-colored **Ághios Nikólaos Church,** a treasure trove of icons and frescoes. Indeed, this is one of the most elaborate churches in the Dodecanese, as it was the object of tribute by the well-to-do sponge fishermen and their families. The barren hillside above the town is capped with a 30-foot-tall cross, standing alone as a beacon to the returning fishermen. To the right, built over the water, is the **Christ Our Savior Church,** whose rotund pink basilica is paired with a tall, slim clock tower.

In the middle of the pier is a modern bronze sculpture of a nude sponge diver, arms raised above his head, who, we suppose, should be viewed upside-down for maximum effect. He's the work of local sculptor Michael Kokkinos, whose many other sculptures pop up in the oddest, most pleasant places.

Getting Around

It's easy to walk around Kálymnos town, but the island itself is large. During the summer there are roughly four **buses** an hour between Pothiá, Myrties, and Massouri. The bus departs from the front of City Hall; buses to Emborios run far less frequently (only three days a week when we were there). **Taxis** pool individuals for a very modest 350 Drs ($1.45) for the beach run; expect to pay 2,400 Drs ($10) for a private cab to Emborios. (See "Around the Island" section below for information on taxi tours.) There are **moped** rental shops aplenty. **Hatzilaou-Mamakas Auto Moto Rent** (☎ **0243/28-990,** fax 29-814), with offices in Pothia, Massouri, and Myrties, has the best selection of vehicles for hire at good prices; a Piaggio Vespa with insurance will cost about 2,500 Drs ($10.40), a Fiat Panda, 12,500 Drs ($52.10).

What to See & Do

You can't leave Kálymnos without learning something about the islanders' nearly extinct occupation—sponges. The industry dates back to 1700 when divers, weighted by a stone belt, would dive 10 to 15 meters down (holding their breath), collecting up to ten sponges per dive. The sponges, animals living in plant-like colonies on rocks at the bottom of the sea, were then cleaned and treated. In 1885 the Skafandre (a primitive diving suit) made it possible for the divers to remain underwater at depths of 30 to 40 meters for nearly an hour! In heavy, rubberized canvas suits, with an air tube attached to a fishbowl helmet, men would walk the sea bottom, cutting sponges with their knives and gathering them with racquet-style baskets. On board, other workers would trample the sponges to squeeze out the dark membrane and milky juices. Each May 10 the ships would depart Kálymnos for the annual harvest, after much celebration, prayer, and a blessing from the high priest of Ághios Nikólaos. On October 30 another festival was held to thank God for those who returned home safely.

The riskiness of this occupation, in which many died or were crippled by the "bends," has reduced the number of divers from several thousand to about 80. Today the fleets sail north to nearby Sámos and Ikariá, or south of Crete to the Libyan Sea, and the men wear modern scuba gear. The export of sponges has declined due to competition from plastic sponges, from the poorer-quality natural sponges processed in the Philippines and Malaysia, and from pollution in the Mediterranean. Nonetheless, on a reduced scale this industry still thrives. Incidentally, many Kalymniots immigrated to Florida after the war, settling in Tampa and Tarpon Springs to continue their trade off the coasts of the Bahamas.

IN POTHIÁ

Astor Workshop of Sea Sponges. ☎ 29-815.

To get to Pothiá's sponge factory, take the stairs at the left of the pier, past the tavernas up into town. About halfway up, a cement path on your right leads to the workshop run by Nick Gourlas. Here you can see each stage of preparation: the sponges' blackish original color, their softening after being beaten with sticks to loosen pebbles and fibers, and the subsequent whitening after a bath in sulfuric acid. Think that's rough? You can watch one of the workers trimming them into a round shape with gardening shears. Sponges here are for sale according to their size and grade. The cheaper unbleached sponges are more durable for cleaning chores; the light ones with big pores are for bathing; the finest-quality smooth ones, with tiny pores, are for sensitive skin and cosmetic use. If you get really turned on by this, the Astor Workshop has inexpensive rooms to rent right upstairs. Next door is the Dorellos Sponge Warehouse, a more up-to-date (less charming) version of the sponge show and tell.

Museum of Kálymnos. ☎ 23-113.

The sponge-fishing industry has left another cultural legacy as well. A typical Kalymniot mansion, once owned by sponge magnate Mr. Vouvalis, has been donated by him to the city as a museum, and it's filled with local archeological finds and personal and business memorabilia. The museum is in the Aghía Triada section, a few blocks (ten minutes' walk) up from the harbor near taxi square. You'll notice that almost every taverna or shop displays a barnacle-encrusted amphora or other ancient sea treasure brought back from the depths by the local fishermen.

Open: Tues–Sun 10am–2pm; entrance is free.

AROUND THE ISLAND

There's more to see on Kálymnos than Pothiá's sponges. A **round-the-island** tour may be taken in a taxi seating four, at about 16,000 Drs ($66.65) for eight hours or 9,000 Drs ($37.50) for four hours. If Spyros or Manolis are available, you'll end up knowing more about Kálymnos than you ever wanted to! **Kálymnos Tours** (**☎ 28-329**) has a bus tour around the island in English twice a week (3,500 Drs or $14.60), round-the-island swim *cum* barbecue cruises, and daily boat trips.

Many of the island's major sites are along the east-west road that bisects the island, and though often scenic, they're not exactly on par with Delphi! Just outside of Pothiá is the small **Castro Chrissocherias,** where a basilica is hidden underneath a fortress. At **Pera Kastro,** above the old capital of Horio, you can see small white chapels clinging like barnacles to the rocky hillside around the remains of a tenth-century fortress. At the island's proudest shrine, the **Church of Jesus of Jerusalem,** are the ruins of a domed basilica and some columns that were built over what is now thought to be the ancient Sanctuary of Apollo.

Where to Stay

If you want to make quiet Kálymnos your headquarters in the Dodecanese, you might stay in Pothiá for a night until you find your own retreat (probably near Myrtiés/Massoúri). Since tourism has only recently arrived, many of the newest and brightest accommodations are to be found in private rooms. Pothiá's **Tourist Information Office** (☎ **0243/29-130**) can point you in the right direction; expect to pay 5,500 Drs ($22.90) for a double with private shower in Pothiá and a little less in the villages. Housing is open mid-April to mid-October unless otherwise noted.

IN POTHIÁ

Olympic Hotel, Pothiá, 85200 Kálymnos. ☎ **0243/28-801.** Fax 0243/29-314.
41 rms (all with bath). TEL

Rates (including breakfast): 7,275 Drs ($30.30) single; 11,675 Drs ($48.65) double. AE, MC, V.

In the Ághios Nikólaos part of town (named for the central church), sits this large, modern, all-white hotel, with four stories and an elevator! Large rooms have tiny bathrooms with showers, but good-sized balconies overlooking the harbor and potentially noisy *paralía.* Breakfast is served in the large, sunny lobby and there's a rooftop terrace for snacks and sunning.

$ **Hotel Panorama,** Ammoudara. Pothiá, 85200 Kálymnos. ☎ **0243/23-138.**
13 rms (all with bath).

Rates: 4,875 Drs ($20.30) single; 6,500 Drs ($27.10) double. No credit cards.

This top-of-the-line choice is located on the heights of central Pothiá above the sponge-factory lane. This sparkling three-tiered hotel is the domain of Themelis and Desiree Koutouzi, who opened their marble and stucco inn in 1989. Lower-level rooms have large patios, while all enjoy a wonderful breeze and fine views over the harbor. It's a good idea to call in advance to have someone meet you at the boat; the walk uphill is fairly strenuous with a large bag in tow.

Hotel Pátmos, Ághios Nikólaos, Pothiá 85200, Kálymnos. ☎ **0243/22-750.**
15 rms (all with bath).

Rates: 2,400 ($10) single; 4,100 Drs ($17.10) double. No credit cards.

Directly behind the Tourist Information hut is this small, aging pension. Its compact, well-tended rooms in the heart of the harbor are managed by the jovial, Greek-only speaking Christos Maragous, who allows guests to keep their rooms until 5pm if they're catching the late boat. Open all year.

Where to Eat

There are several feed-the-day-tripper pizza and moussaka cafés on the central port opposite the excursion ferries, but a short walk to the left side of the harbor will be rewarded by some fine, authentic Greek food.

$ **Afrismeno Kyma Ouzerí/Taverna Kosari,** On the port. ☎ **23-427.**
Cuisine: GREEK.
Prices: Appetizers 300–1,250 Drs ($1.25–$5.20), main courses 900–2,800 Drs ($3.75–$11.65). No credit cards.
Open: Daily 11am–2am.

This friendly taverna/ouzerí plays it both ways with grilled meat and fish, simple *mezédes,* and traditional stews. It's casual but delightful for a seaside lunch. Next to the Fast Food Pantelis, it has its own octopi hanging out to dry. Make sure to order some cooked in the typical Kalymniot way.

Kálymnos Yacht Club [Naftikos Omilos or Nok]. ☎ 29-239.

Cuisine: GREEK.

Prices: Appetizers 200–400 Drs (85¢–$1.65); main courses 600–1,700 Drs ($2.50–$7.10). No credit cards.

Open: Daily 8am–3pm, 6:30–11pm.

One of Pothiá's better eateries and a delightful place to watch the yachts at night is the Kálymnos Yacht Club, an old seafarers' club draped in fishnets with a huge mural of a sponge fisherman (what else?) floating above a background of the city. You can eat a hearty Greek meal of simple, inexpensive fish or meat dishes, surrounded by crusty old Greek sailors and local youngsters. It's the past and future of the island's seafarers. Open year round.

Ouzeri Meris, On the *paraliá* in Christos. No phone.

Cuisine: SEAFOOD MEZEDES.

Prices: Appetizers 400–1,000 Drs ($1.65–$4.15). No credit cards.

Open: Daily 5pm–midnight.

We found a place that had John pining for octopus two months after we returned to New York. You probably won't find this treasure by the octopus painted on its sign; instead, saunter down the *paralía* and look for a place with about 20 octopi drying on a wire above the entrance. You can luxuriate over a plate of grilled octopus *mezédes* and an ouzo, but we were knocked out by the octopus balls, which are made from diced octopus and deep-fried in a light batter. As a cultural aside, the locally correct way to eat grilled octopus is to dip it into ouzo before chewing.

Restaurant Zefteris, Christos Street. **☎ 28-642.**

Cuisine: GREEK.

Prices: Appetizers 400–800 Drs ($1.65–$3.35); main courses 700–1,400 Drs ($2.90–$5.85). No credit cards.

Open: Daily 11:30am–11pm.

When you get really hungry head straight for this restaurant in the Christos section of town, just off the harbor. Their quiet back garden and old-fashioned come-into-our kitchen taverna is a treat. Try the plump *souzoukákia* or huge, freshly made dolmádes. Open year round.

Evening Entertainment

One of Pothiá's better late-night drink and snack spots is **Mike's Piano Bar** (**☎ 29-221**), otherwise known as the **Do-Re-Mi.** This popular rusticated stone lodge seems to attract a cross section of tourists, yachters, and Kalymniots until very late (if you stay late enough, you can try their breakfast menu). You'll find the Do-Re-Mi next to the Tourist Information office, behind the portside Poseidon statue. Nearby is another good social spot called the **Scirocco Café-Bar** (no phone), an open-air nightspot 100 meters west along the waterfront. Scirocco is particularly popular with ferry-watchers because of its fine view of the Piraeus car ferry pier.

Around the Island

Kandoúni is the first sandy part of the Platís Ialos western coast. Ticky-tacky hotels and rooms line this beach and Linaria, the next cove. The narrow, soiled beach is crowded, with strong, direct winds that make it rough for swimming. We say continue north along the oleander-lined road to **Myrtiés,** a gray sand and pebble beach resort below a commercial stretch of road, or better yet, to **Massoúri,** which has undergone transformation into a more classy resort.

MYRTIÉS

Just one kilometer away from Myrtiés across the shimmering crystal blue water is the small island of **Télendos,** with its few houses looking square at this village. Local boats will take you across for 125 Drs (69¢) if you're not up to swimming to it. A favorite Kálymnos folk story tells of a young princess who died so in love with her little island of Télendos that its one hill took her reclined shape; with an active imagination it's possible to see the curve of her hip and the profile of her young face.

Where to Stay and Eat

Atlantis Hotel, Myrtiés 85200, Kálymnos. ☎ **0243/47-497.** 17 rms (all with bath). TEL

Rates: 5,750 Drs ($23.95) single/double. MC, V.

This old-fashioned hotel and restaurant offers the friendliest, homiest service in town. The large terrazzo-floored lobby is decorated with local ceramics and weavings. Bright, large rooms have big bathrooms and new simple furnishings, most of them with a small kitchen and refrigerator; we preferred the second floor rooms with balconies and fine sea views. The popular taverna serves seafood and grilled meats in the evenings.

Hotel Myrsina, Myrtiés 85200, Kálymnos. ☎ **0243/47-997.** 40 rms (all with bath). TEL

Rates: 6,900 Drs ($28.75) single; 8,100 Drs ($33.75) double. EC, MC, V.

This is one of the nicest hotels in this area—newly built, with a large pool and grand sea views. Spacious balconies look over the road to the bay, making the clean but ordinary rooms something special. The bad news is the group hammerlock, so only the odd rooms are available to individuals in the high season.

Themis Hotel, Myrtiés 85200, Kálymnos. ☎ **0243/47-230** or **47-893.** 9 rms (all with bath).

Rates: 5,750 Drs ($23.95); 6,900 Drs ($28.75). No credit cards.

If you like the sound of water lapping beneath your window, you should try this little hotel on the harbor down from the church. The hard-working family that runs it and its busy restaurant spent many years in Montréal. If they're full try the handsome new Zephyros Hotel across the street.

Restaurant Argo, Main street, Myrtiés. ☎ **47-825.**

Cuisine: GREEK.

Prices: Appetizers 220–550 Drs (90¢–$2.30), main courses 900–1,800 Drs ($3.75–$7.50). No credit cards.

Open: Daily 11am–2am.

This simple grill offers a good variety of meat and some fish dishes (ask what's fresh before you commit). The best thing about it is the terrace dining area with stunning bay views.

MASSOÚRI

Massoúri, the best-developed resort on the island, is the next beach north of Myrtiés. Small hotels, private houses, restaurants, and tourist shops crowd the coastal road above a long picturesque rock-and-sand beach. On our last visit we found it among the most pleasant we visited anywhere. The people are friendly, accommodations are excellent, there's plenty of good food and even a little nightlife. Groups do have a lock on most of the rooms in the high season, but in the spring and fall there will be plenty of rooms available. We suggest you save time and even money by contacting **Advance Travel** (☎ **0243/48-148**) on the main street. **Massouri Holidays** (☎ **0243/47-626**) also books some local apartments, as well as exchanging money, selling maps, renting safe deposit boxes, and offering telephone service.

Where to Stay and Eat

Advance Travel and Massouri Holidays book some of Massoúri's 100-odd rooms to let; local apartments in a quiet area rent for 8,000 Drs ($33.35) a night with kitchenette, shower, and twin beds. Other choices are **Niki's Pension** (☎ **0243/47-201**) and **Lina's Studios** (☎ **0243/47-017**), both nearby above the road, commanding fine vistas of the sea and nearby islands. Expect to pay about 6,500 Drs ($27.10) for a double room.

★ **Fatolitis Apartments,** Massoúri 85200, Kálymnos. ☎ **0243/47-615.** 35 rms (all with bath).

Rates: 6,000 Drs ($25) double; 8,000 Drs ($33.35) triple. No credit cards.

This multitiered cluster of small apartments tumbles down from the main road below the cheerful wicker and flower-print decor of the Fatolitis Snack Bar. The family owners run a clean, stylish place with potted plants, large, seaview verandas for lounging, and simple, natural wood furnishings. Two- and three-bed studios have a fridge and kitchenette. A great deal if you can book one!

Hotel Massouri Beach, Massoúri 85200, Kálymnos. ☎ **0243/47-555.** Fax 0243/47-177. 30 rms (all with bath). TEL

Rates (including breakfast): 7,150 Drs ($29.70) single; 9,200 Drs ($38.30) double. EC, MC, V.

This beachside hotel has clean modern rooms, complete with heating and breakfast, a pretty good deal. The hotel has a wonderful seaview terrace and a small bar; make sure to request a seaview room to take advantage of their beachfront location.

Hotel Plaza, Massoúri 85200, Kálymnos. ☎ **0243/47-134.** 63 rms (all with bath). TEL

Rates (including breakfast): 9,200 Drs ($38.35) single; 11,500 Drs ($47.90) double. No credit cards.

We liked the sea-facing doubles and the big pool with its own bar at this large, group-oriented hotel. It's very spacious, with breakfast and dining geared to lots of clients, but it is a quality Class B inn with Class C prices.

Aegean Tavern, Main street, Massoúri. No Phone.

Cuisine: GREEK.

Prices: Appetizers 300–600 Drs ($1.25–$2.50); main courses 700–1,800 Drs ($2.90–$7.50). No credit cards.

Open: Daily noon to midnight.

George Pizanias returned home after many years of operating a Greek restaurant outside Atlanta to open this charming new place above the street, so you miss the passing vehicles and catch the evening breeze. The service is friendly and the food is fresh and somewhat updated, with less oil than usual and attractively presented; we tried standards like a country salad, moussaká and *saganáki*—all superb.

Matheos Restaurant, Main street. Massoúri. ☎ **47-184.**

Cuisine: GREEK.

Prices: Appetizers 250–550 Drs ($1.05–$2.30), main courses 800–2,000 Drs ($3.35–$8.35).

Open: Daily noon–midnight.

This pleasant taverna is above the road on the north side of town, with a bamboo-shaded veranda offering limited bay views. From their freshly made fare, we liked the *skordaliá,* stuffed tomatoes, and various lamb dishes. Friendly service, too.

EMBORIOS

Other areas to explore include the winding mountain road between **Vathí,** where thousands of mandarin trees fill the verdant valley at the head of a fjord, and **Stimeniá.** Everyone will tell you the best beaches accessible by car are between **Arginóntas** (where the frequent public bus ends) and **Emboriós** (along the northwest coast above Massoúri). If you've missed the twice weekly bus from Pothia, or the daily excursion boat from Myrties (it costs 1,500 Drs or $6.25 Drs or $6.70 round-trip per person), from Arginontas you can take a moped (or an older cab) up through the 12-family village of Skalia to Emborios, with its 20 resident families. We spent a magical day in Emborios and the surrounding hills. After dining in a nearly empty taverna on the beach, swimming in clean water, and walking in the craggy hills where few tourists tread, we were convinced that this is the place for long-term visitors to Kálymnos.

Where to Stay and Eat

There are a scattering of rooms to rent, mostly attached to (or upstairs from) a taverna. At our visit, **Harry's Apartments and Restaurant** (☎ **0243/47-434**) was the most sophisticated choice. Both the fine pension and taverna lie close to the bay, around a shaded garden. Each of six apartments has a small kitchen; two should plan to pay 8,500 Drs ($35.40) a night. Call ahead for reservations before you make the trip north. Simpler but cheaper rooms are found at **Pension Pizanias** (☎ **0243/47-277**), attached to the tasty **Restaurant Themis** (☎ **0243/47-277**). Here, eight very simple double rooms are 5,500 Drs ($22.90) a night.

Campers can head south to **Ormós Vlichadion** (accessible only by cab) for a beautiful rock-and-sand beach populated only by one taverna.

5 Léros

171 nautical miles E of Piraeus

ARRIVING/DEPARTING • By Air **Olympic Airways** offers one flight daily between Athens and Léros. Call them in Athens (☎ **96-16-161**) or at their office in Plátanos, Léros (☎ **0247/22-844**) for information.

• By Sea One car ferry leaves daily from Piraeus (it's an 11-hour trip) in the high season; three times weekly year round. There are excursion **boats** every day between the main port of Lakkí and Pátmos, and daily excursions between Kálymnos and Léros, with less frequent caiques to Lipsí, Nísiros, and Astipálea. There is periodic **hydrofoil** service between the small port of Aghía Marína and Pátmos during the high season.

ESSENTIALS Lakkí and Plátanos both have banks, telephone exchanges, and post offices. **DRM Travel and Tourism,** in Aghía Marína (☎ **0247/24-303,** fax 24-303) or Alinda (☎ **0247/23-502**), is an excellent resource for independent travelers. Chris Kokkonis and wife Christine can help with hotel, pension, and villa bookings, and recommend the best local eateries and island tours. They also arrange tours and/or accommodations on Lipsí, Nísiros, Astipálea, and Tílos, as well as Pátmos, Sými, and Ikaría.

You run out of the house without your wallet and when you go back to get it you realize that you've locked the keys inside. One Greek might say to another: "I'm going to buy you a one-way ticket to Léros."

For years isolated Léros, renowned in mythology as the island of Diana, was best known for its mental health hospital. Despite this reputation and Greece's strong military presence here, Léros is now trying to lure tourists to its rocky shores and tranquil bays. The calming, hilly landscape and unaffected lifestyle offer a haven for some; others find the place too tame. We suggest that if you're drawn here, visit on a day excursion or make a stopover on the way to or from Pátmos; you can always move on to the next destination. If you love it, so much the better—just know that Léros is nearly deserted in May, June, and September and absolutely packed in July and August, so make hotel plans accordingly.

Orientation

Most boats call at **Lakkí,** a dull town on the southwestern side of the island. The most visually arresting sights here are the distinctively Fascist buildings lining the harbor. The massive proportions and streamlined shapes recall the presence of Italian troops during the first half of this century (Lakkí's excellent natural harbor was the main port for the Italian Navy in the eastern Mediterranean). Most of the better hotels, beaches, restaurants, and other tourist services can be found only a few kilometers due north, beginning in **Pantéli** (our favorite village), and ending in the gray gravel beach town of **Alínda** (the most developed base for visitors). Midway is **Plátanos,** the capital, a picturesque market town with stately 19th-century homes built on tiers below an impressive Venetian fortress. Boxy, whitewashed, flat-roofed houses cluster around the bustling main square.

A few excursion boats and the occasional hydrofoil dock at **Aghía Marína,** in between Alínda and Plátanos. The airport is in the far north, near Parteni, and close to some of the island's best beaches. At the far southern point of the island is **Xirócampos,** the island's only sanctioned campground and where you can get daily morning excursion boats to **Kálymnos.**

Getting Around

Léros is only 52 sq kms and easy to get around on foot or by bike. There are bicycles and mopeds (for the lazy) for rent in all of the main tourist centers; expect to pay 400 Drs ($1.50) a day for a bike and about five times that for a motorized two-wheeler.

The island's KTEL bus runs approximately every two hours and makes a north-south tour that stops in nearly all of the important tourist centers.

Where to Stay & Eat

We'd suggest staying in Pantéli and using it as the base from which to tour the island. The small beach resorts at Aghía Marína and Alínda are nearly connected and offer a wider and better choice of accommodations and dining though they lack the charm. Avoid the main port of Lakkí; take a taxi into Pantéli or Alínda for more hospitable housing. As mentioned, there is camping at **Xirócampos** (☎ **0247/23-372**) for 800 Drs ($3.35) a night; the campgrounds have hot showers, a dining area with snackbar, and a laundry room.

In central **Plátanos,** there's the quiet family-run **Elefteria Hotel** (☎ **0247/23-550**), with clean comfortable doubles for 4,950 Drs ($20.65).

IN PANTÉLI

There are many rooms to rent above the tavernas at Pantéli's waterfront; most of these places, such as the **Alex, Rena, Kavos,** and **Pantéli,** charge about 5,500 Drs ($22.90) for a double room with private shower, and can be booked through **DRM Travel.**

Pension Afroditi, Pantéli 85400, Léros. ☎ **0247/23-477.** 10 rms (8 with bath).

Rates: 4,600 Drs ($19.15) single; 5,750 Drs ($23.95) double. No credit cards.

Set back from the harbor is this simple ten-room affair, with reasonably clean facilities and a nice garden.

Maria's Taverna, On Pantéli's *paralía.* No phone.

Cuisine: GREEK.
Prices: Appetizers 250–800 Drs ($1.05–$3.35); fish from 10,000 Drs ($41.65) per kilo. No credit cards.
Open: Daily 5–11pm.

Perhaps best of all in Pantéli—you'll know you've found it when you spot the funky advertisement, "Get Down to Maria's." Notwithstanding the sign, the taverna is of the ancient and informal variety. Prices are positively cheap and the food is traditional fish fare.

Savana Bar, On Pantéli beach. ☎ **23-969.**

Cuisine: CONTINENTAL.
Prices: Snacks/desserts 300–800 Drs ($1.25–$3.35). No credit cards.
Open: Daily 8:30am–2am.

This very popular beachside bar serves partygoers a late breakfast of fresh juices, varied coffees, croissants, pancakes, and omelets. As the sun wanes they turn their attention to grilled sandwiches, mixed tropical drinks, and ice cream concoctions.

IN ALINDA

The town beach is fairly attractive and sheltered, but it's also busy and kids on motorbikes do their best to destroy the peace. We suggest you investigate the many good accommodations away from the moto madness. Our suggestions are: the **Ara Hotel** (☎ **0247/24-140,** fax 24-194), at the top of the hill behind the Alinda Hotel, with a swimming pool, 10 studios at 9,000 Drs ($37.50) for two, and eight apartments at 10,125 Drs ($42.15) for three; the **Chrissoula Apartments** (☎ **0247/22-451**), 500 meters off the north end of the beach, with a very nice new swimming pool, 16 studios from 5,750 Drs ($23.95) and nine apartments from 9,200 Drs ($38.35), MC, EC, V accepted; and our favorite even without a pool, **Effie's Apartments**

(☎ **0247/24-459,** fax 23-507), 50 meters off the middle of the beach (ask at the Finikas Taverna), with eight apartments from 9,200 Drs ($38.35), EC and MC accepted.

Alinda Hotel, Alinda 85400, Léros. ☎ **0247/23-266.** 18 rms (13 with bath).

Rates (including breakfast): 4,600 Drs ($19.15) single/double without bath; 6,900 Drs ($28.75) single/double with bath. EC, MC, V.

One of two choices on the *paralía,* but far enough off it for a semblance of quiet. The back rooms face an attractive garden and orchard. The management is friendly and helpful, and there's a good restaurant.

Finikas Taverna, Paralía, Alinda. ☎ **22-695.**

Cuisine: GREEK.
Prices: Appetizers 500–950 Drs ($2.10–$3.95), main courses 850–1,650 Drs ($3.55–$6.90). EC, MC, V.
Open: Daily 9am–11:30pm.

This casual place has checkered tablecloths draping wooden tables at water's edge. You can dine under the shade-providing tamarisks or in the back garden and sample stuffed vegetables, good lamb dishes, and a flavorful *choriatiki.*

Theofilos Cafe/Pizza Restaurant, *Paralía,* Alínda. ☎ **22-497.**

Cuisine: GREEK/CONTINENTAL.
Prices: Appetizers 450–800 Drs ($1.90–$3.35), main courses 800–2,200 Drs ($3.35–$9.15). No credit cards.
Open: Daily noon–11pm.

We had a sumptuous little meal at this white-canopied, outdoor diner overlooking the beach. The menu features delicately prepared moussaka and great pizza (they have a large selection), all at modest prices. Be sure to go inside for a peek at the Theophilos-like painting.

Around the Island

If you feel like exploring but don't have much time, consider a two- to three-hour taxi tour of the island with an English-speaking guide/driver for approximately 7,000 Drs ($29.15). Among its pleasures is a visit to a local beekeeper who sells honey straight from the comb.

If it's a beach you crave, head north to **Blefoúti** where there is also a simple taverna. Near Pantéli (actually, the next cove over) is the less-congested beach at **Vromólithos;** there, too, you'll find a taverna that opens only in the summer months. On the west coast is a delightful little church, **Ághios Isidoros,** built on an outcrop in Gourna Bay; you can reach the well-tended church by way of a causeway.

6 Pátmos

163 nautical miles E of Piraeus

ARRIVING/DEPARTING There is one departure daily from Piraeus; it's a long, sometimes arduous, trip by **steamer.** Check with **Tourist Information** in Athens (☎ **143**) or with the **Piraeus Port Authority** (☎ **45-11-311**) for schedules. There are daily car ferries to Léros, Kálymnos, Kos, and Rhodes. Ferries connect Pátmos to Ikariá four times a week and to Sámos, three times a week to Sámos (both in the Northeast Aegean group). Once a week, the Sámos ferry continues on to Chios, Lésbos,

Límnos, and Thessaloníki. During the high season, smaller and faster excursion boats cruise to Pythagórion, Sámos in less than three hours, making the round trip for 3,800 Drs ($15.80).

The fastest but most expensive method of transport is the **hydrofoil** that services Pátmos four times weekly (almost daily in summer) from Rhodes (4 hours) or Kos (1½ hours), and three times a week from Sámos (1 hour). Your travel time is cut roughly in half, though summertime meltémi winds sometimes prevent them from sailing. Contact Apollon Travel (☎ **0247/31-324**) at the port of Skala for schedules.

ESSENTIALS There is a **Tourist Information office** (☎ **0247/31-666**) in Skala behind the Port Authority around the corner from the post office. They can help with housing on the island, including rooms, hotels, and houses. During summer, they are open Monday through Friday from 9am to 11pm, Saturday and Sunday from 9am to 4pm. The **town police** (☎ **31-303**) can be found upstairs in the main square. The **hospital** (☎ **31-211**) is on the Skala-Chóra Road. The **Apollon** or the more helpful **Astoria Shipping Agencies** on the *paralía* will cash checks throughout working hours (usually until 8pm, including Saturday). The **OTE** is 300 meters from the port behind the main square; it is open Monday through Saturday from 9am–2pm, 5pm–8pm (10pm in summer). The **post office** is on the main square; it is open Monday through Friday from 7:30am to 2pm. *Pátmos Summertime* is a helpful free publication. Patmophiles will want to read resident Tom Stone's *Pátmos,* published by Lycabettus Press, and might be inspired to attend the English language Catholic mass at St. Francis House each Saturday night.

"Dear visitor, the place which you have just entered is sacred."

Thus begins the brochure handed out to all who visit Pátmos's Holy Cave of the Apocalypse, the site where St. John the Evangelist wrote the Book of Revelation. From a distance, Pátmos is all gray stone: barren rocks, no beaches, ascetic, just a rough-hewn pedestal for the huge walled fortress of the Monastery of St. John. Rounding Point Hesmeris reveals the hidden port of Skála, cluttered with bars, tavernas, and hotels. There's a Wild West quality about this small fishing port that's heightened by the gregarious locals who meet the boats. On isolated Pátmos, 12 hours by steamer from Piraeus, 4 hours by hydrofoil from Rhodes, the stagecoach has arrived.

Thousands of Christians make a pilgrimage to the religious shrines of Pátmos annually, but the majority arrive on Mediterranean cruise ships and depart the same day. Any traveler seeking peace and quiet, good-hearted, gentle Greek people, and a disarmingly sophisticated social scene should stick around. Pátmos surprises all who stay long enough for a second look.

History

Since antiquity the isolated, arid island of Pátmos has been considered the "Siberia" of the Mediterranean world. Although many believe that Pátmos's inhabited history began with the founding of the Monastery of St. John in 1088, the island was originally colonized by the people of Caria in Asia Minor, who brought with them their cult worship of Artemis. Unexcavated ruins (from the 6th to 4th centuries B.C.) found on Kastelli Hill include the remains of an ancient acropolis, walls, temples to Apollo and Dionysos, and a hippodrome.

Pátmos's reputation as a "Siberia" fit only for banishment or exile began in the Hellenistic period. It is said that Orestes, son of Agamemnon and Clytemnestra, took refuge on Pátmos after he murdered his mother and her lover to avenge his father's death. Unfortunately, Orestes's lover, Erigone, was the product of his mother's illicit relationship, and the distressed woman brought Orestes to trial when she learned he had murdered her mother. The Erinyes (Furies) pursued Orestes throughout the Aegean until he landed on the isolated island of Pátmos. Orestes was acquitted by the gods, and after founding a temple dedicated to Artemis, left Pátmos to ascend the throne of Argos.

The Romans immortalized the island by sending John the Theologian into exile there in A.D. 96 during the Emperor Domitian's wide-scale persecution of all Christians in the empire. Saint John (in the Book of Revelation) only makes this reference to his sojourn: "I dwelled in an island which is called Patmos, as to preach the word of God and have faith in the martyrdom suffered by Jesus Christ."

For centuries after Saint John's historic visit, Patmians continued to trade with the mainland port of Miletus, their link to Asia Minor, and to adhere to the Artemis cult worship practiced in Ephesus. In 313 the Emperor Constantine officially recognized Christianity. Pátmos fell into relative obscurity, endured devastating raids through the Islamic period, and was eventually retaken by the Byzantine Empire.

In 1088 a devout monk, Christodoulos, went to Alexius I Comnenus to ask permission to found a monastery dedicated to Saint John on the island. Alexius realized the political favor such a bequest could earn him with the already powerful Christian church. The 1088 Chrysobull (Alexius's imperial decree that is still proudly displayed in the monastery) granted to the monks of Christodoulos "the right to be absolute rulers to all eternity." This Chrysobull (it also exempted Pátmos from government taxation or judicial interference and granted the monastery the right to own ships tax-free) shaped the future development of the island.

Pátmos's autonomous religious community flourished. The centuries of Turkish domination that withered Greek culture elsewhere left Pátmos almost untouched. The Monastery of St. John became the finest cultural and theological school in the country, even prospering under the Italian occupation. After World War II Pátmos was reunited with the Greek nation.

Today Pátmos is one of the few Greek islands that has benefited from tourism without having to sell its soul. The monastery's real estate monopoly ensured slow, careful development of the land. The monks never condoned nude or topless sunbathing; this has kept away the more risqué summer tourists. No military construction was permitted, so there is no commercial airport on the island (many foreign residents use Olympic's private helicopter landing pad in Skála). The revenue produced by Holy Land day-trip visitors is enough to keep Skála thriving; the less commercial sections of the island are supported by the elite foreign population. The fortuitous combination of historical and social factors has made Pátmos a unique, unspoiled island "sacred" to many.

A Festival

If you're lucky enough to be in Greece at Easter (late April or early May), try to book a room so that you can witness the **Nipteras.** It's a reenactment of the Last Supper that's only performed on Pátmos, in the square outside the Monastery of St. John, and in Jerusalem. The festivities and holy days extend from the Monday before Easter to the following Tuesday, when there's great feasting and dancing in Xanthos Square.

Orientation

Pátmos has an unusually long tourist season, thanks to the moderating sea breezes that sweep across the island year-round. Most visitors stay at the east coast port of Skála at the island's narrow midriff, where the majority of the island's hotels and rooms are located. To the south, the hilltop Monastery of St. John dominates the port in much the same way that the city of Oz dominated the consciousness of those who lived beneath it.

The jumble of whitewashed homes that cling to the fortress-like walls of this medieval monastery comprise Chóra (or "City"). Chóra has been the island's main town since the 11th century, and it's an architectural delight on the order of Lindos, Rhodes. Anyone visiting the island must explore the hilltop village and its monastery, even if only for the day.

To the left (south) as you leave the ferryboat pier is the uphill road running east to Chóra, and the coastal road running southwest to the family beach resort at Gríkou. To the right (north) of the pier are the Skála town beach and the coastal route leading to the beach resort of **Kámpos.**

Getting Around

The port of Skála is compact enough to walk around with pleasure. Outside of Skála, goat paths lead up and over the many untouristed hillsides to wild, unexpected natural vistas. Hiking around the island will also bring you into contact with the lovely Patmian people, whose deep religious beliefs make them even more hospitable than the average welcoming Greek citizen.

BY BUS

From the ferryboat pier, the island's bus stop is directly ahead, a little to the left, behind the statue of Emmanuel Xanthos. Buses from Skála to Chóra run eight times daily, per the schedule posted next to the stop; the fare is 140 Drs (60¢). (However, we actually enjoyed the 30-minute uphill trek on a rough-stone chariot road to visit the Monastery of St. John.) The entire island has only two other bus routes: to the beach at Kámpos four times daily, and to the beach at Gríkou six times daily.

BY BOAT

Local fishermen turn their caiques into beach shuttles during the summer season, and offer daily excursions to many of the island's private coves. Each night you can walk along the harbor and read the chalkboard destination signs hanging off the stern of every caique. These small boats charge 600 Drs ($2.50) each way to Psiliámos or Lámpi and 350 Drs ($1.45) to Kampos each way.

BY TAXI OR RENTAL CAR

There are **taxis** (☎ **31-225**) available in Skála, next to the post office. However, they're usually grabbed up by the repeat visitors or commuting residents who rush off the ferry before you. If you're interested in nighttime dining in Chóra, for example, walk over or call ahead to book one; fares to Chóra run 700 Drs ($2.90), depending on the time of day and season, plus a 100 Drs fee for radio calls. Sometimes families prefer to rent a car. Sound like you? Contact **Rent A Car Pátmos** (☎ **32-203**) on the port near the post office. Subcompacts start at 14,500 Drs ($60.40).

BY MOPED

Mopeds afford greater freedom of movement. Most Patmion roads are actually paved, so it's not as risky as elsewhere, but exercise caution on the gravel-filled, winding, hilly roads. There are moped rental shops aplenty in Skála; expect to pay 1,800–2,500 Drs ($7.50–$10.40) per day for a single-seater.

What to See & Do

The island's two great Christian monuments, the Monastery of St. John and the Holy Cave of the Apocalypse, are of such historical and artistic significance that they should be seen by everyone visiting Pátmos.

THE MONASTERY OF ST. JOHN

The Monastery of St. John, (☎ **31-234**) was founded in 1088 by the monk Christodoulos. Tall gray stone walls were constructed to protect the hilltop retreat from pirate raids, giving it the appearance of a solid medieval fortress.

Upon crossing the monastery's main threshold, the visitor is transported by the stillness and ethereal calm into a private world. Supported by heavy gray brick columns, the large covered cistern containing holy water in the center of the courtyard (an ideal bench for contemplation) held wine in the days when 200 monks inhabited Chóra. Except on major Greek Orthodox holidays, the monastery's religious activities are not as impressive as its museum-quality collection of manuscripts, religious icons, Byzantine art, and frescoes.

The **Outer Narthex,** to the left of the entrances, is richly painted with 17th-century frescoes depicting traditional tales from the life of St. John (a flashlight is needed for a thorough examination of the dark chapel). Tour guides meet the day-cruise visitors; their anecdotes of monastic life and vivid descriptions of the many parts of the monastery that are now off-limits make joining a tour worthwhile.

For centuries the remarkable collection of more than 13,000 documents in the monastery **library** has drawn scholars to Pátmos. The earliest text is a 6th-century fragment from the Gospel of Saint Mark; on Pátmos there are 33 leaves of this priceless work, which has been divided among museums in Leningrad, Athens, Britain, the Vatican, and Vienna. The 1088 Chrysobull issued by Alexius I Comnenus granting the monastery sovereignty over Pátmos is displayed, as well as an 8th-century text of Job and Codex 33, the 10th-century illustrated manuscript of the discourses of Saint Gregory the Theologian. In the **Treasury** are jewels and icons donated by Catherine II, Peter the Great of Russia, and other dignitaries, and the 4th-century B.C. marble tablet describing Orestes' visit to Pátmos.

After 200 years of tourist abuse (many valuable texts were taken back to Europe by visiting scholars) the library and original Treasury have been closed to view. One may visit the well-secured **Treasury-Library-Museum,** where a sampling of the rich vestments, icons, and religious artifacts belonging to the monastery are displayed.

From the roof (now closed) one can see a spectacular panorama of the Aegean, including the islands of Ikaría and Sámos to the north, Léros, and beyond it, Kálymnos, to the southeast Amorgós, and in the far southwest Santoríni.

The monastery requests that you "Respect the Holy Places, our traditions and our morals by your dignified attire, serious appearance, and your general behavior." Visiting hours change radically according to season, primarily geared to the comings and goings of cruise ships, but we suggest visiting between 9 and 10am (before the ships arrive). Contact Tourist Information (☎ **31-666**) for the current schedule; museum admission is 500 Drs ($2.10).

HOLY CAVE OF THE APOCALYPSE

The Monastery of the Apocalypse (☎ **31-234**) was built at the site of the grotto where Saint John received his revelation from God. Located a five-minute walk below the hilltop monastery, it can be easily visited on the pleasant, vista-filled descent to Skála.

A rousing brochure written by Archimandrite Koutsanellos, Superior of the Cave, provides an excellent description of the religious significance of each niche in the rocks, and the many icons in the cave. The little whitewashed monastery that surrounds the cave was the 18th-century home of the Patmias School, an institute of higher learning unparalleled during the Turkish occupation. A large modern structure built after World War II to accommodate the school and a theological seminary dominates the barren hillside above Skála.

Appropriate attire is required (appropriate means no slacks for women, no shorts for anyone). This dress code applies when visiting any of the island's religious sites, including the several other monasteries and nunneries, which have fine frescoes and religious icons. Those with an interest in the significance of Pátmos in Christian history will be fascinated by Otto Meinardus's *St. John of Pátmos* and the *Seven Churches of the Apocalypse,* published by Lycabettus Press. Opening hours are roughly the same as the Monastery.

The **Simantiri House** (☎ **31-360**) belonged to the family of the same name for eight generations, beginning in 1625. Today this superbly restored Venetian-style Patmian mansion is open to the public, daily from 9am to 3pm and 5 to 8pm, for tours. The best way to find the Simantiri House is to ask for the Zoodochos Pigi Monastery; it's just down the street. Admission costs 350 Drs ($1.45). The Zoodochos Pigi Monastery (☎ **31-256**) is itself a treat to behold; it's open to the public daily from 9am to noon and 3 to 6pm; admission is free.

LOCAL LANDMARKS

If you stay on Pátmos long enough, you'll begin to hear about the hundreds of "must see" sites cherished by the locals. We'll only explain two sites that you're likely to encounter.

A little way out in the harbor, opposite the Patmion Hotel, is a large red buoy that marks **"Devil's Rock."** This submerged plateau is marked not only as a warning to sailors—it keeps sinners on their toes! For here, nearly 2,000 years ago, the Devil used to preach to local citizens by communing with the spirits of their ancestors. The alternate telling of this folktale suggests that the Devil was Kynops, a local magician sent by priests from the temple of Apollo to challenge Saint John's influence. In either case, one day the Devil/Kynops offered to enlighten St. John himself, but when he dove underwater to display his powers, Saint John crossed himself and the Devil was halted there, frozen in stone. Even though this is a convenient fishing perch, today the local fishermen avoid it because "the fish caught off this rock smell funny."

Another local landmark you might be curious about is the wrought-iron fencing that encloses a nondescript flat rock, toward the north end of the waterfront. Devoted Patmians have enclosed the stone slab where Saint John is said to have baptized more than 14,000 converts from among the local population.

Skála

Skála is still small enough that most commercial activity is along the waterfront, with more recent development on the low hill behind the *paralía,* on unpaved back lanes two or three deep. If you walk from the ferry north to the well-marked Astoria Hotel, you'll pass the busy heart of town, **Emmanuel Xanthos Square.** In the maddeningly irregular, whitewashed lanes behind the square are some hotels and shops. From the square north along the waterfront are several small tavernas, hotels, and bars. Behind is the little "neighborhood" of **Nethia,** where some fine hotel rooms to let are located. Ten minutes past Nethia on the path curving up to the right and over the hill is the local beach, **Órmos Melóï.**

WHERE TO STAY

There are not many hotels in Skála, so the best ones require reservations two to three months in advance if you're planning to visit Pátmos at Greek or Christian Easter, or in July or August. Most establishments are open April to late October, according to demand. Last-minute planners should have no trouble finding a room to let in the surrounding hillside; if you're interested in renting a kitchenette apartment or villa on a long-term lease, contact the **Apollon Agency** (☎ **0247/31-356,** fax 0247/31-819) for more information. At the nearby Melóï Beach is the well-situated, popular **Stefanos Camping** (☎ **0247/31-821**), also known as **Patmos' Flowers Camping.** This convenient campground (1.5 km from the port) becomes very crowded in the high season; they charge 1,200 Drs ($5) for tents and 2,000 Drs ($8.35) site rental for two persons.

Hotel Adonis, Skála 85500, Pátmos. ☎ **0247/31-103** (or 01/51-21-035 in Athens). Fax 0247/32-225. 23 rms (all with bath). TEL

Rates (including breakfast): 10,800 Drs ($45) single; 13,400 Drs ($55.85) double. No credit cards.

The Patmian style, white stucco and stone facade, and small rooftop neon sign distinguishes this hotel from the many residences sprouting on the hillside. Fresh, wood-trimmed rooms, with harbor-view balconies (ask for the top floor!) provide quiet and convenient lodging. New tiled bathrooms even have shower curtains. Breakfast is served on the shaded front porch, within scent of the jasmine-covered arbor.

★ **Hotel Australis,** Skála 85500, Pátmos. ☎ **0247/31-576.** 19 rms (all with bath). TEL

Rates (including breakfast): 8,375 Drs ($46.50) single/double. No credit cards.

The welcoming Fokas and Chris Michalis, who spent many years in Australia, run this small, friendly hotel in a blooming hillside oasis that makes it feel like a high-priced villa. The grounds are covered with bright bougainvillea, geraniums, carnations, fuchsias, dahlias, and roses; they were recently featured in *Garden Design* magazine. The pleasant communal porch, where breakfast is served, looks out on the harbor. (Their son Michael has three handsome new studios over his house on the old road to Chóra.)

Blue Bay Hotel, Skála 85500, Pátmos. ☎ **0247/31-165.** Fax 0247-32-303. 22 rms (all with bath). TEL

Rates: 8,000 Drs ($33.35) single; 13,800 Drs ($57.50) double. No credit cards.

Reader Robert H. Smith of El Cerrito, California, wrote to insist we consider this handsome new hotel about 200 meters left from the port. We found it every bit as quiet, immaculate, attractive, and comfortable, and the Karantani family as hospitable, gracious, and helpful as he said. In fact, we found Mr. Smith there again, with his wife and friends; high praise indeed, we think.

Castelli Hotel, Skála 85500, Pátmos. ☎ **0247/31-361.** Fax 0247/31-656. 45 rms (all with bath). TEL

Rates (including breakfast): 9,000 Drs ($37.50) single; 12,500 Drs ($52.10) double. No credit cards.

Guests are accommodated here in two white stucco blocks framed with brown shutters. From wood-trimmed balconies, the striking vista can be enjoyed from your own cushioned wrought iron chairs. Spotless rooms are large with beige tile floors; the common lounge and lobby areas are filled with photographs, flower-print sofas, found seashells, fresh-cut flowers from the surrounding gardens, and other knickknacks of seaside life. Such good care and charm make this a good value.

Hotel Effie, Skála 85500, Pátmos. ☎ **0247/31-298.** Fax 0247/32-700.
35 rms (all with bath). TEL

Rates (including breakfast): 8,000 Drs ($33.35) single; 11,500 Drs ($47.90) double. No credit cards.

Turn left before the Old Harbor Restaurant to find this recently built hotel on the quiet hillside. The rooms are large, light, spare and spotless, with wood-trimmed balconies with somewhat limited views. Owners Effie and Nick make all their guests feel at home and are constantly busy improving the place, with a new garden on its way.

Hotel Ellinis, Skála 85500, Pátmos. ☎ **0247/31-275.** Fax 0247/31-846.
40 rms (all with bath). TEL

Rates: 9,200 Drs ($38.35) single/double. V

Located around the port, next to the Fina Station at the Melóí end of Skála, is this clean Class C lodging, with a fountain in front and a wonderful evening view across the harbor to the illuminated village and sky-high monastery. It's run by Christodoulous Grillis and family, giving the otherwise plain accommodations some familial warmth. The family also keeps 14 rooms to let nearby (6,900 Drs ($28.75) for two).

Romeos Hotel, Skála 85500, Pátmos. ☎ **0247/31-962.** Fax 0247/31-070.
58 rms and 2 suites (all with bath). TEL

Rates (including breakfast): 16,550 Drs ($68.95) single; 21,750 Drs ($90.60) double; 24,000 Drs ($100) suite. EC, MC, V.

Of all of Skála's newer lodgings, this one in the back streets behind the OTE is especially commodious, with the biggest pool on the island and a quiet garden. Run by a Greek-American family, the Romeos has spotless rooms, with woven cotton upholstering, simple decor, and countryside-view balconies bringing sea breezes. Rooms are built like semi-attached bungalows on a series of tiers on Mt. Kastelli. The larger honeymoon suites, with matrimonial beds, full bathtubs, and a small lounge are another option.

★ **Skala Hotel,** Skála 85500, Pátmos. ☎ **0247/31-343.** Fax 0247/31-747.
78 rms (all with bath). TEL

Rates (including breakfast): 10,250 Drs ($42.70) single; 15,500 Drs ($64.60) double. AE, EC, MC, V.

The Skála, located well off the street behind a lush garden overflowing with arresting pink bougainvillea, has aged like a fine wine to become our favorite lodging in this busy town. Annual improvements include the expanding garden, a large pool with an inviting sun deck and bar, a large breakfast buffet, adjustable heat in all guest rooms, additional conference and meeting facilities, and even better and more personalized service. Host Captain Gríllis and his staff offer guests the kind of hospitality one expects on such a sophisticated island. Some rooms have harbor views, but you'll have to put in your request for one in advance, as they're often booked by return guests. Open April through October.

$ **Villa Knossos,** Skála 85500, Pátmos. ☎ **0247/32-189.**
10 rms (all with bath).

Rates: 8,000 Drs ($33.35) single/double. No credit cards.

We're always pleased to find good budget choices on these expensive islands, and this small white villa just off the port is a find! Nicos and Despina Mourtzaki have done an impressive landscaping job, obscuring the simple twin-bedded rooms with purple and pink bougainvillea, potted geraniums, and multicolored hibiscus.

Where to Eat

Because of the many foreign residents and long-term tourists, most restaurants and tavernas cater daily to repeat customers, and we found the food usually moderately priced, well prepared, and graciously served. Listings are open May to September unless noted. Sweet tooths can be satisfied at many local bakeries. The **Edelweiss Pâtisserie** (no phone), one lane behind the *paralía,* stays open late to serve ice cream and sweets to passersby. The traditional **Pratirio Arto,** is on the second square behind the main one, and opens daily except Sunday from 8am to 2pm to sell fresh bread, delicious *tiropitta,* and a variety of dunk-em biscuits. The modern, mirrored **Koumanis Bakery** is Skála's premier sweet palace, with three branches serving fine European and Greek delicacies. They're open daily from 8am to 2pm and 4:30 to 10pm to serve the special Patmian *tiropitta,* a cheese pie baked in a crust like a tart, and many of the island's special cookies. Duty forced us to inquire about one specialty, the half-moon *poungi* which starts with a fragile *kourambiedes* dough, then is filled with a mixture of vermicelli, nuts, and honey. They're a sinfully delicious bargain at 220 Drs (95¢) each.

★ **Arion Cafebar,** *paralía* of Skála. ☎ **31-595.**

Cuisine: CONTINENTAL.

Prices: Snacks/Desserts 180–690 Drs ($1–$3.80). No credit cards.

Open: Daily 8:30am–3am.

Just as day café crowds favor the main square, sunset idlers seem to favor the harbor. The elegant old **Arion** on the port has high ceilings and exposed stone walls. Large old fans stir up a breeze above the long, broad, polished-wood bar. Ornate iron medieval-style wall sconces produce the intimate lighting. Late breakfasts, drinks, snacks, delicious ice cream concoctions, and coffee are served inside and out.

The Balcony (Jimmy's), Chora village. ☎ **32-115.**

Cuisine: GREEK/INTERNATIONAL.

Prices: Appetizers 450–1000 Drs ($1.85–$4.15); main courses 700–2,500 Drs ($2.90–$10.40). No credit cards.

Open: Daily 11am–4pm, 7–11pm.

Near the entrance to the Monastery you'll find this simple place with good food, reasonable prices, friendly management and a great view. Even though we weren't hungry, we thought we ought to try such a convenient place, so we had a fresh village salad with a distinctive cheese, an excellent omelet, and a couple of beers, sat drinking in the scenery, and came away completely satisfied.

Grigoris Grill, Opposite Skála car ferry pier. ☎ **31-515.**

Cuisine: GREEK.

Prices: Appetizers 450–900 Drs ($1.85–$3.75), main courses 900–2,300 Drs ($3.75–$9.60). No credit cards.

Open: Daily 6pm–midnight.

One of Skála's better-known eateries, formerly the center of Patmian chic. We recommend any of the grilled fish or meat dishes, particularly in the low season, when more care and attention are paid to preparation. Well-cooked veal cutlets, large, tender lamb chops, and the swordfish souvlaki are favorites. Gregory's also offers several vegetarian specials.

Olympia Taverna, Chóra village. ☎ **31-543.**

Cuisine: GREEK.
Prices: Appetizers 310–625 Drs ($1.70–$3.50), main courses 700–1,150 Drs ($2.90–$4.80). No credit cards.
Open: Mon–Sat noon–2pm and 6:30–10pm.

This taverna on Theofakosta Square, less frequented by tourists because of its low-key presence, is one of our favorites for traditional Greek home-style cooking. On our last supper we dined on octopus *yiuvetsi,* stuffed aubergine, horta and beet salad, and a sublime slab of cake, all delicious and inexpensive. During the summer they open the roof garden (great views) for open-air dining.

$ **Pantelis Restaurant,** One lane back from Skála port. ☎ **31-230.**

Cuisine: GREEK.
Prices: Appetizers 450–1,000 Drs ($1.90–$4.15), main courses 700–1,700 Drs ($2.90–$7.10). No credit cards.
Open: Daily 11am–11pm.

One of Skála's older establishments serves delicious food at low prices in a comfortable, homey environment. The Pantelis, located right behind the Astoria Hotel, has delicious lightly fried calamari and swordfish kebab, as well as a complement of vegetarian entrées. It's a favorite with locals and stays open to serve the community year-round.

★ **The Patmian House,** Chóra village. ☎ **31-180.**

Cuisine: GREEK/CONTINENTAL. **Reservations:** Recommended.
Prices: Appetizers 480–1,000 Drs ($2–$4.15), main courses 1,200–4,800 Drs ($5–$20) plus 23% tax and service. No credit cards.
Open: Daily 7pm–midnight, June through mid-September.

It shouldn't surprise you that sophisticated Chóra features one of the best and most interesting Greek restaurants in the entire country, one set in a restored 17th-century dwelling on the back lanes behind Xanthos Square, and glowingly reviewed in *Vogue, The Athenian, European Travel & Life* and several German and Australian periodicals. Victor Gouras, a Patmian gourmand who worked at several top New York restaurants, and his talented wife Irene, have created the perfect place for that splurge evening. Young Nick and Alex Gouras take summers off from their jobs at New York's Periyiali and the chic Aureole to help out in the family business. From several superb hors d'oeuvres we recommend Irene's special *taramosaláta,* her gigantes (giant beans) in garlic sauce, *spanakópita,* or the tasty zucchini fritters. The varied selection includes a superb rabbit stifado flavored with juniper berries, a tender, moist lemon chicken, a melt-in-your-mouth veal parmigiana, and a Patmian vegetarian specialty *melitzánes mé revíthia* (an eggplant and chickpea casserole). Ask the Gouras family about any fish, steaks or meat specialties of the day, and don't miss the *diplés,* a honey-dipped roll.

Plaza Kaffeterion, Main Square of Skála. ☎ **31-266.**

Cuisine: CONTINENTAL.
Prices: Snacks/desserts 300–800 Drs ($1.25–$3.35). No credit cards.
Open: Daily 7am–midnight.

Start your day in the lively square across from the post office. This place is the most local in feel, with continental breakfast or a hearty English or American breakfast the favorites. The Plaza is also popular for early evening drinks.

Fish Taverna to Pirofani, Central paralía of Skála. ☎ **31-539.**

Cuisine: SEAFOOD.
Prices: Appetizers 450–2,300 Drs ($1.85–$9.60), main courses 600–1,200 Drs ($2.50–$5). Fish 7,500–8,500 Drs ($31.25–$35.40) a kilo. No credit cards.
Open: Daily noon–3pm, 6pm–11pm.

This is our favorite for seafood, next door to the Skala Hotel. Begin with their special tzatzíki, have grilled melanouri or barboúnia, wine and salad, and it's a Patmian feast! Pirofani, supplied daily by local fishermen, is a casual, portside place for a Saturday night fish fry or grilled lobster.

Around the Island

Other than the towns of Skála and Chóra, most of Pátmos's limited development has centered around the beach areas. Short-term visitors should allow a day to visit Chóra and the Monastery of St. John; after that, the island's exquisite beaches can be explored by foot (as we prefer) or by caique excursions from Skála.

CHÓRA

The narrow, twisted lanes that encircle the monastery are lined with two-meter-tall white stucco walls surrounding the private residences of Chóra's elite international set. Even during siesta the ornately carved brown wood doors rarely open to reveal the elegant, stylish homes within. The town is a minimecca for the wealthy who scorn the splashier resort islands: actors, writers, publishers, diplomats, tycoons, and their friends. Chóra is like Bar Harbor, Newport, Malibu, and Positano; generations may pass, but the houses never change hands. Buyers interested in available villas are carefully (and silently) screened by the current residents. However, Chóra's exclusivity rarely affects the day visitor. The town's streets seem refreshingly deserted, even in the high season.

The wealthy who couldn't get into Chóra have built villas "down below," near the beaches. Their presence and their anonymity add the spice and mystique that make Pátmos such a special island.

Mr. Emanouil J. Fillieras, otherwise known as Manios, presides over the giftshop in the Monastery of St. John, but we also discovered that, as a real estate broker, he

READERS RECOMMEND

Kima Restaurant. *"To reach this really great restaurant, go past the Hotel Australis and turn right as though going to Melóï Beach. A sign on the right just before the beach indicates the short road leading to the restaurant. This is the location for a romantic dinner, with the tabled terrace right on the level of the water. Small boats, some of them off yachts, moor right outside the restaurant. The food is really good and different, with special sauces and plenty of garlic."*—Diane D. Jumet, New York, NY.

arranges rental of private houses (particularly in Chóra) for intermediate- and long-term guests. If you're contemplating spending a few weeks or more on Pátmos (lucky you), and don't mind spending upward of 240,000 Drs ($1,000) a month for a two-bedroom, one-bath villa, give Manios a call at **0247/31-398** or **0247/31-407.**

BEACHES

Pátmos has some very good beaches. The town beach, a sand and pebble patch just 500 meters from the ferryboat pier, offers no privacy; it's usually filled with Greek families who don't mind sunbathing in full view of the clothed tourists who stroll along the waterfront promenade.

The nearby **Melóï Beach,** just a 15-minute walk northeast of Skála, is a little more secluded though not the island's best. At Melóï, virile young Greek men who've come with their tourist girlfriends are likely to be playing cassette tapes of the latest European hits. "NUDITY IS FORBIDDEN" signs are prominently posted, and the locals often complain when this rule is ignored. However, the beachside **Meloi Restaurant** (☎ **31-888**) is a good taverna and a very pleasant place to while away the evening.

It takes a moped, taxi (500 Drs or $2.10), excursion boat (same price as taxi), or sturdy legs (a ten-minute walk from the nearest bus stop) to reach **Agriolivádo Beach,** about three kilometers north of Skála. Along this unspoiled, tranquil sandy cove you'll find one taverna and some efficiency apartments.

KÁMPOS

The next beach cove north of Agriolivádo is **Ormós Kámpos,** a sheltered cove popular with families. Its pale sand and rock beach is shaded by a few pine trees and the water is calm and shallow enough to make it ideal for children. Kámpos village, on the hill above, has about 400 residents and is quite lively in the high season. There are very few rooms-to-let because most overnighters rent homes long term, although a local travel agent may be able to find a room if any of the villas become vacant. **Acrogialo** (☎ **32-590**) is a popular restaurant on the beach that's not expensive. The casual Greek food and service are equally good, and proprietors Vasilis, Panormitis, and their dog and cat are fun to visit. There are also some small tavernas up the hill on Kámpos Square. **Ta Kavourakia,** open from early morning to late, but known for its seafood, has Greek bouzouki music every Saturday night. Two buses ply the Kámpos-Skála road daily, but most residents hop the frequent, inexpensive beach shuttles for the 20-minute ride; taxis cost 1,000 Drs ($4.15).

GRÍKOS

Four kilometers south of Skála is the resort village of **Gríkos,** where many foreigners have built villas for their summer holidays. As you descend from the coast road toward the shores of Grikou Bay, you'll see the islet of Tragonísi, its hills framing the large boulder that sits in the middle of the bay. This is called Kalikatsou, or "cormorant," by the Greeks, because of its appearance at the tip of a narrow, curved spit of land. The natural caves within this rock formation have been enhanced by human hands, leading Patmian author Tom Stone to speculate that monks might have inhabited these caves from the fourth to the seventh centuries, much as they did in Turkey's Cappadocia region.

Gríkos is a long-established resort with a very limited, pleasantly low-key hotel and restaurant scene. If it's lively nightlife you crave, head up toward Chóra to **Aloni Taverna** for Greek dancing late Wednesday and Friday nights or spend your evenings in Skala. There's an okay, family-oriented, pebble and sand beach right in town, with pedalos, windsurfers, sunfish, and canoes for rent. The more private beach is in the cove just south at Petras.

WHERE TO STAY & EAT

Hotel Artemis, Gríkos 85500, Pátmos. ☎ **0247/31-555.** 24 rms (all with bath). A/C TEL

Rates (including breakfast): 8,000 Drs ($33.35) single; 14,250 Drs ($59.40) double. No credit cards.

This is a very nice alternative in the lodging scene, built in traditional style. It's furnished simply with local handcrafts, which lends an air of enchantment to the place. All rooms have balconies facing the water, and there's a TV room and a small bar downstairs adjoining a lush garden, where breakfast is served.

Hotel Gricos Apartments, Gríkos 85500, Pátmos. ☎ **0247/31-294.** Fax 0247/31-783. 21 rms (all with bath).

Rates: 5,675 Drs ($23.65) room with refrigerator; 6,500 Drs ($27.10) room with refrigerator and sink. No credit cards.

Let's put this in the pretty good and quite unusual category, a place where tuneful birds serenade newly arriving tourists in an atrium-style lobby. It's one lane inland from the beach so sea and village views are pretty limited, but you'll get a clean twin-bedded room with some kitchen facilities, at a very good price.

Patmian House Apartments, Gríkos 85500, Pátmos. ☎ **0247/31-180.** 8 villas (all with bath).

Rates: 11,500 Drs ($47.90) two-bedded villa. No credit cards.

The owners of Chóra's chic Patmian House Restaurant maintain eight attached villas and a flowering garden, just a few lanes inland from the beach. Each efficiency apartment has its own cooking facilities and is furnished in a spartan, easy-to-maintain beachhouse manner.

★ **Petra Apartments,** Gríkos 85500, Pátmos. ☎ **0247/31-035.** Fax 0247/32-335 or 01/80-62-697 in Athens. 25 rms, apts (all with bath). TEL

Rates: 15,790 Drs ($65.80) apt. for two; 27,480 Drs ($114.50) apt. for four. No credit cards.

The charming Stergiou family take loving care of our favorite lodging in Gríkos. If the folks aren't home, Christos and his sheepdog Lumpi will happily show you around these stylish apartments, made into one or two bedroom units with small kitchenettes, compact bathrooms, and verandas with wonderful views over Grikou Bay. Each is simply but carefully decorated, with the necessities of home plus some local color. It's a perfect family place, within a five-minute walk of the beach, but with an elegant outdoor bar for the adults. It's popular with Europeans in August, and open only from June 1 to September 10, so early reservations are advised.

Xenia Hotel, Gríkos 85500, Pátmos. ☎ **0247/31-219.** 35 rms (all with bath). TEL

Rates (including breakfast): 17,785 Drs ($49.10) single/double. No credit cards.

The older but well-located Xenia is at the north end of the cove. A couple we met from Amsterdam described it as "the perfect location for a quiet, idyllic, seaside holiday." Many of the spacious but worn doubles overlook the bay and beachside snack bar. A good choice if you want hotel amenities in a beach setting.

Stamatis Restaurant, Gríkos beach. ☎ **31-302.**

Cuisine: GREEK.

Prices: Appetizers 550–1,400 Drs ($2.30–$5.85), main courses 900–1,700 Drs ($3.75–$7.10). No credit cards.

Open: Daily 10am–11pm.

Eleni is the talented chef at the reliable restaurant located adjacent to the pier. The covered terrace is where diners consume prodigious amounts of fresh mullet, traditional Greek entrées (we had fine *pastitsio* and fresh green beans), and drinks overlooking the windsurfers.

LÁMPI & PSILÍ ÁMMOS

To the north of Skála is **Órmos Lámpis,** famous for wonderful striped and patterned smooth stones. The deep earth tones of cream, gray, lilac, and coral are particularly striking when wet, and a small bottle filled with Patmian seawater and Lámpi stones makes an unforgettable souvenir of your stay. Daily excursion caiques which round Cape Geranós take about one hour from Skála, and the round-trip fare is 1,200 Drs ($5); one-way taxi fare is 1,000 Drs ($4.20). The last stop on the Kámpos bus line leaves you about a 15-minute walk away. There are rooms-to-let by the beach at Lámpi and a few tavernas (the Dolphin and the Lampi Beach are both good) for light snacks.

On the other side of the island's southern point is what's universally acclaimed as Pátmos's best beach—the kilometer stretch of **Psilí Ámmos** (Greek for "fine sand"). This protected cove, dotted with shade-giving salt pine trees and tucked in the craggy south coast, provides a special bathing experience. The water is shallow and calm until the afternoon, when breezes can bring waves, truly a rarity in the Aegean! Because it's so isolated (only accessible by caique—day trips from Skála are 1,200 Drs or $5—or by a moped-worthy road then a hike), nude bathing is as condoned as it ever will be on this orthodox island. There is even a small taverna that opens for great home-cooking in the summer.

There are a few less known beaches that are best reached by caique. Among these are the twin pebble and sand coves beyond Kámpos, called **Vayiá** and **Livádi Déla Póthitou.** On the southern end of the island, on the opposite coast from Psilí Ámmos at a narrow crossover point between two bays, are two fine, rarely visited beaches near Gríkos, **Órmos Pétras** and **Órmos Diakoftoú.**

7 Kárpathos

242 nautical miles SE of Piraeus

ARRIVING/DEPARTING • By Air There are three flights weekly from Athens, one flight daily from Rhodes, four flights weekly from Kássos, and one flight weekly from Sitia, Crete. Tickets can be purchased at the Olympic Airways Office (☎ **22-150**) at 25 Martíou and Apodimon Karpathion Streets, on the main square, in Pigádia.

• By Sea Kárpathos is serviced by steamers from Piraeus via Santoríni or Crete two to four times weekly, depending on season. Car ferries connect the island to nearby Kássos and far-off Rhodes three times weekly.

ESSENTIALS Try to share a taxi from the airport or car-pool in the port of Pigádia for taxi tours (quite expensive) around the island. The local bus is the most fun way to travel, but not for those with a time pressure because of its infrequent, unreliable service. The **tourist police** (☎ **22-218**) and local **police** (☎ **22-226**) are housed by the ferryboat pier. The main **post office** and **OTE** are in Pigádia. There's a small **Health Clinic** (☎ **22-228**). Homespun fabrics, lace, and local handcrafts are good value gifts from the island.

The second-largest of the Dodecanese group is a stark contrast to the sophisticated international resort of Rhodes. Because of its relative isolation—midway between Crete and Rhodes, but southwest of the island chain paralleling Turkey—Kárpathos for years remained distinctly its own place. Sadly, the development of an international airport from a former airstrip has brought group tourism to this wild and rugged outpost. Still, a local dialect (peppered with ancient Doric words) still spoken at the village of Olýmpos is so indigenous that even other Karpathians cannot understand it. And, although 95% of the islanders have emigrated to America for study or work during their lifetimes, when on Kárpathos they shed the title "Greek-Americans" and become simply "Karpathians."

Orientation

Lawrence Durrell called Kárpathos "an ideal hide-away." Tourists who moor at the southern port, Kárpathos town or **Pigádia,** will find a sparkling village of chiseled stone houses, whose red terra-cotta-tiled roofs peek above the treetops. Pastel-colored facades are broken by bas reliefs of Doric columns; many of their ornate wrought-iron balconies depict the double eagle symbol of the Byzantine Empire. The southern half of the island—large verdant plains, fruit trees, and trellised vineyards—contrasts with the barren, mountainous reaches of the windblown north. Apéri, a small village ten kilometers north of Pigádia and once capital of the island, features the island's most important monastery and traditional stone homes built on both sides of a flowing stream. **Arkássa,** on the opposite coast, shows signs of the ancient Arkaseia on the bluffs above fruit orchards.

A newly built highway crossing the once-impassable Mt. Kalolimni (3,675 feet) unites Pigádia with the northern port of **Diafáni.** Eight kilometers away, perched on the side of Mt. Profítis Ílias, is the famous village of **Olýmpos.** Ethnologists have studied the oldest settlement on the island to learn more about the roots of contemporary Greek folk tradition. The 600 villagers are said to live 300 years behind the times, and it's a treat to visit this intimate community, although its rarity has already been exploited by locals and visitors. Olympian women wear full cotton skirts and lace-trimmed blouses, covered by a flower print or black apron. Even the faces of the young, swathed in black cotton head scarves, seem timelessly Greek. The old men in their baggy black pants and stiff cotton overshirts continue to farm or herd as always; now many of the young men have gone to Athens or abroad. Olýmpos is more authentic during one of

READERS RECOMMEND

"We took a very nice wooden boat two hours from Kárpathos to Diafáni, and walked around the town for an hour. Women in traditional costumes were baking in an old oven outdoors and gave us hunks of bread. Delicious! The local bus took us to Olympos, quite an isolated place, where they lead very old-fashioned lives. At lunch at the Parthenónas Taverna we had a special macaroni—a dish of the town—then wandered around more. Ólympos is all vertical, and a majority of the houses are empty. Back in Diafáni an old woman was impressed that I was from so far away and gave me a woven-yarn bracelet. A long and very interesting day." —Marvin Cohen, New York, N.Y.

its many festivals. The post-Easter festivities are very colorful and elaborate, involving all the villagers, who wear traditional holiday costumes. Karpathian music is much faster-paced than the bouzouki played elsewhere, and the lively dances are thought to be unique to the island.

Where to Stay

Outside Pigádia, most of the island's villages offer accommodations in rented rooms, an ideal way to share village life.

Karpathos, Odós Dimokratias 25, Pigádia, Kárpathos 85700. ☎ **0245/22-347.** 16 rms (4 with bath).

Rates: 7,375 Drs ($30.75) double without bath, 8,750 Drs ($36.45) double with bath. No credit cards.

Located two blocks from the waterfront, the older Karpathos is a Class D inn. Even the bathless rooms and common toilet and shower facilities are clean, because the place is well run by the Margaritis family.

Porfyris Hotel, Pigádia, Kárpathos 85700. ☎ **0245/22-294.** 22 rms (all with bath).

Rates: 9,000 Drs ($37.50) single/double. No credit cards.

The Porfyris is one of the island's oldest and best choices with a great view toward the port. Their comfortable restaurant serves moderately priced Greek and some continental food (we prefer the local portside tavernas at lunch or dinner).

8 Baker's Dozen

The name "Dodecanese," "Twelve Islands," represents the original number of islands counted. There are hundreds of other small islands tucked in and around the eight better-known ones that we have already discussed. Most are occupied by only a few fishing families, many have no electricity or indoor plumbing, and few are of interest to the average tourist. This section concludes with the five islands that round out one "baker's dozen": Hálki, Tílos, Nísiros, Astipálea, and Kastelórizo.

Hálki, Tílos, and Astipálea do have something in common with Kárpathos—they're all included in a clever English company's brochures for "Greece: The Unspoilt Islands." **Laskarina Holidays** (☎ **0629/822-203** or **824-881,** fax 0629/822-205) at St. Mary's Gate, Wirksworth, Derbyshire DE4 4DQ, Great Britain, offers a number of vacation packages including round-trip airfare from England, and hotels, rooms to let, houses, or villas on several little-developed islands. If this is the Greece you're after, we can't think of a better resource. Their agents on each island may be able to help last-minute arrivals with temporary lodgings.

Getting to these islands is extremely difficult, and in the meltémi-blown seas of summer, often unreliable. We'd recommend contacting the Pireaus Port Authority (☎ **01/45-11-311**) or Athens Tourist Information (☎ **143**) first about ferry schedules. Then you should call **Triton Holidays** in Rhodes (☎ **0241/21-690**), **V Tours** in Kos (☎ **0242/22-340**), (**Kalymnian Shipping** in Kálymnos (☎ **0243/29-612**), or **Astypalea Tours** in Astipalea (☎ **0243/61-328**) for specific information on connections by local boats and privately run excursions.

Kássos

Kássos, three nautical miles southwest of Kárpathos, is separated from her larger neighbor by the treacherous waters of the Karpathian Straits. Forbidding vertical cliffs, which form most of the coastline, have caused Kássos development to be confined to settlements in the northwest. Few inhabitants remain since the first tide emigrated to Egypt to build the Suez Canal; many Kassiots return now only for the holidays. Ironically, every July 7, Kássos commemorates the massacre of its citizens by the Egyptian troops of Ibrahim Pasha, who overran the tiny island in the Ottoman offensive of 1824.

Just one kilometer from the port is the principal town, **Fri.** Peek into any of the fine stone houses and you'll see interiors that have been lavishly decorated with artwork brought home by generations of seafarers. The most popular site on Kássos is the **Sellai Cave,** also called *Hellenokamera,* known for its beautifully colored stalactites. The Pelasgian walls (masonry consisting of large, hand-hewn stones) that surround the grotto once provided the islanders with a refuge from private invaders.

If you didn't bring your yacht, plan to spend a few days—transportation is pretty meager; connect with the **Maritime and Tourist Agency** (☎ **0245/41-323**). Luckily, Fri boasts a Class C hotel just 50 meters from the water's edge. The **Anagennisis Hotel** (☎ **0245/41-495;** fax 0245/41-036), Fri, Kássos 85800, has 10 rooms with balconies and private facilities. Single travelers should count on spending 5,200 Drs ($21.65); two will pay 7,350 Drs ($30.65). Ferries call at Kássos only thrice weekly on their way from Piraeus, Crete, or Rhodes. (Piraeus-bound ferries stop only twice a week.) Desperadoes can hop on one of **Olympic Airway's** twice weekly flights to Kárpathos or Rhodes.

Hálki

Hálki (Chalkis), one of the smallest of the Dódecanese, is most often visited as a day excursion from her larger, glitzier neighbor, Rhodes, just 1½ hours west by ferry from the main port, or 2 hours from Skála Kámiros. Tired of discos, beach umbrellas, casinos, and honking horns? Sharing the life led by the 300 villagers who've remained on the island may bring welcome relief to those who've been "Rhode-ed out."

Caiques pull into the small port of **Emborió,** where you'll find a few outdoor ouzerís, and tavernas serving inexpensive, fresh seafood. This bustling village of sponge divers turned fishermen is built around a stately clock tower, the neoclassic Town Hall, and the beautiful Church of Ághios Nikólaos. Overnighters can find a room to let in many of the traditional pastel stone houses overlooking the water; long-term guests should contact Laskarina Holidays (see above).

A few kilometers' hike above the port is **Chóra,** the island's capital during the 18th and 19th centuries, built around a 15th-century fortress (constructed by the Knights of St. John) to protect villagers from sea-level attack by Turkish pirates. It's a wonderful hike up here, rewarded by vistas toward Rhodes or Kárpathos. Hálki offers some antiquities (including a black mosaic-paved stone path nearly a kilometer long and remains of several temples to Apollo), two Byzantine monasteries, and uncrowded, sandy beaches. **Pondemos,** a ten-minute walk west of Emborio, is a pretty sand and shingle cove with a popular taverna.

Halki can be reached by daily caique from Kamiros Skála, Rhodes, or by steamer from Piraeus, Rhodes, or Kárpathos, twice weekly.

Tílos

Tílos, equidistant (about four hours by ferry) from the much more diversified islands of Kos and Rhodes, gets few foreign visitors and is the least developed for tourism of these outer Dodecanese. Ferries call at the southern port of **Livádia,** the island's most interesting village. Here you'll find a few tavernas, kafenía, the sleepy harbor, and most of the 200 resident Tiliots. Nearby are small, sandy beaches, and several freshwater streams. It's possible to rent rooms in the attractive arcaded houses, which face east to the Turkish coast, but long-term guests should contact Laskarina Holidays (see above).

North is the port of **Megálo Horió,** called **Skála.** It's Tílos's other center of activity (even less here), and a good base from which to hike between the remnants of seven inland Crusader Castles. Crossing the island's spine of pumice stone cliffs created by the long-ago volcanic eruption of Nísiros, you'll come to the Monastery of Ághios Pandelímon, a Byzantine beauty.

There are two car ferries to Tílos from Piraeus or Rhodes weekly, regular excursion boats from Sými or Hálki, and once weekly excursions from Kos.

Nísiros

Nísiros (Nyssiros), a volcanic island south of Kos, is often compared to Santoríni by tourists. **Please note:** A volcano is the only thing these islands have in common! The island is shaped like a Circle-in-the-Square; myths tell of an angry god who threw a plump demon to the earth, perhaps creating the huge pit in the island. **Laki,** the four-kilometer-wide volcano, is rimmed by gray stone hills that fall squarely to the sea. Within dormant Laki are two extinct craters, Alexandros and Polyvotis; flowering almond trees sprout from the rich volcanic soil around them. The rest of Nisiros is predominantly barren, and visitors complain of the fierce heat reflected off the black stone landscape. In fact, tourists are urged to wear leather-soled shoes because plastic sandals and sneakers have been known to melt, adhering their wearers to the ground.

Local sights include a Venetian fortress above the port of **Mandráki;** monasteries clustered among the half dozen villages that rim the volcano; and Pelasgian walls made of black trachyte, remnants of the ancient acropolis near Mandráki. Most tourists go for the volcano. (By the way, a geothermal well has been sunk into the crater to harness the power of the volcano, and there are plans to add as many as four more and export electricity by underwater cable to neighboring Kos and Kálymnos.)

Nísiros is serviced by car ferries from Piraeus, which also call at Astipálea or Rhodes, twice weekly, and by daily excursion caiques from Kos. If you should somehow find yourself there, try the **Hotel Porfyris** (**☎ 0242/31-376**), which has a swimming pool and 38 comfortable rooms, all with bath; doubles cost 8,000 Drs ($33.35).

Astipálea

The butterfly-shaped Astipálea, the westernmost of the Dodecanese, is situated 90 nautical miles from Rhodes. The landscape recalls both Rhodes and neighboring Amorgós, but the architecture is most influenced by the sensual, whitewashed homes of the Cyclades islands. The main village, Astipálea, incorporates the port of Skála or Yialós and the old town of Kástro, with seven Mýkonos-style windmills on a hill above it. The hike uphill to visit them is well worthwhile for the beautiful vista over Maltezána Bay, its many rocky islets, and the sand and shingle beach cove of Livádia.

Astipálea is crowned by a 15th-century Venetian kastro and may remind readers of Pátmos's Chóra (which is dominated by the Monastery of St. John). Within the castle is a well-preserved icon of the Madonna, and above its door is the Quirini family's coat-of-arms. These noble Venetians ruled "Castello," the capital of "Stampalia," from 1207 to 1522.

Today, the island is becoming a summer retreat for wealthy Athenians, who have built coastal villas or occupy many of the port's small cubist homes, now renovated as studios or rooms to let. The beaches also fill up with Greek families on July and

August camping holidays, but there are few hotels to accommodate tourists, all charging about 5,500 Drs ($22.90) for two. At the port is the **Aegeon** (☎ **0243/61-236**), the **Astynea** (☎ **0243/61-209**), the only one open year-round, and across Mich. Karageorgi Street, at no. 24, the **Paradissos** (☎ **0243/61-224**). Anyone interested in a longer stay should contact the English tour company, Laskarina Holidays, mentioned in this section's introduction.

Isolated Astipálea can be reached by the once-weekly (three times weekly in summer) car ferry from Piraeus, which calls first at Páros and Amorgós, and takes 16 hours. There's a once-weekly ferry from Kálymnos (a 5-hour trip) or a once weekly excursion boat (a 3-hour trip). There are also two excursion boats weekly during the summer from Kos.

Kastellórizo

Kastellórizo (Méyisti), made famous by the hit film *Mediterraneo,* remains more important as a symbol of Greek independence than as a tourist attraction. This tiny droplet of stone is 65 miles southeast of Rhodes and less than two miles from the Turkish port of Kas. (There's a lively black market tourist-and-goods trade between the two.) The 250 residents (said to remain only to keep the population above the 200 mark at which the land reverts to Turkey) are totally dependent on supplies brought in from far-off Rhodes.

The name "Kastellórizo" comes from the Venetian occupation of the island, when it was renamed after the red-stone fortress (Castello Rosso) built by the eighth grand master of the Knights of St. John. The Greeks call it Méyisti, the "Biggest." Some will tell you it's because Kastellórizo is the largest among a cluster of tiny islands; others claim that the islanders deserve this title for their bravery in overcoming past misfortunes.

The island has been occupied by at least seven nations, including the Egyptians, Italians, Turks, and Venetians. Even the grand fortress built by St. John's Knights was used as a prison for wayward members of the Order. In 1913 local citizens revolted and quickly came under French control. After World War I the Italians regained the island; during World War II they forced the remaining islanders to evacuate. Kastellórizo was occupied by Allied troops, who drew German bomb attacks; most of the town was burned and pillaged. The few citizens who returned after the war (the island was returned to Greece in 1948) had nothing to come home to.

The port town, now partially rebuilt, is tiered amphitheatrically to the water's edge. The pastel-colored, red tile-roofed houses will remind some of Sými, but here the ornate wooden balconies (vestiges of Turkish influence) overhang the oblong harbor. The sea bottom can easily be seen through the crystal-clear waters. As Kastellorizots occupy themselves only with fishing, the few portside tavernas serve some of the most superb seafood in the Dodecanese.

If sitting over a plate of shrimp or lobster and admiring the Turkish coast gets wearing, stroll over to the harborside mosque. It's been turned into a **museum** of local folklore and handcrafts, and displays some fascinating photographs of the island in her heyday. Otherwise, organize a group to charter a caique for a trip to the east coast "blue grotto" **Parásta.** This fantastic grotto, filled with stalactites and stalagmites, reflects every hue of blue light from its deep waters and has been compared to the one at Capri. Plan a morning trip with your boat captain so you can be in and out of the grotto during low tide, when the overhanging entrance is passable. If you're stuck there you may see why the cave is also called "Fokiali," after the seals which are said to live inside.

In addition to the one licensed hostel, the 17-room **Pension of Dimou Meghistis** (☎ **0241/49-272**) at the port, there are several rooms to let above the *paralía's* shops and tavernas. Kastellórizo can be reached thrice weekly by ferry from Piraeus or Rhodes, or thrice weekly by Olympic Airways flights from Rhodes. When relations are positive between the two countries, there is legal caique service from the Turkish port of Kas for day-trippers only.

11 Central Greece

JUST READING THE LIST OF CHAPTER HEADINGS ALONE SHOULD GIVE YOU THAT classical tingle all tourists seem to get when sightseeing in Central Greece. Imagine Thebes, Delphi, Mt. Parnassus, Thermopylae, and Mt. Olympus. Imagine also Metéora, where James Bond, in *For Your Eyes Only,* dangled off the edge of one of its precariously perched, sky-high monasteries. All these sights and more are described in this chapter.

Fortunately, Central Greece is blessed with a practical and functional transportation infrastructure. To most major sights you'll have a choice of train or bus, and often a plane. Renting a car is still the most efficient way to cram everything in, but the lack of one here won't prove detrimental to your enjoyment of the area's natural and artificial beauties.

There are no weather limitations here either; but we prefer spring or fall, when the tourist crush has decreased to a mere press. In late April and May there's still some snow on the slopes of Parnassus and Olympus and a bevy of wildflowers illuminate the Thessalian Plain. In the dry, hot summer you'll probably be tempted to forget classical sightseeing and instead dive off the mainland directly to the islands. By mid-September things have simmered down, the Greek children are back in school, and Central Greece returns to the relaxed state that makes it so lovable.

Seeing Central Greece

If you have a week, you can combine the best of Central Greece with a beach jaunt to Skiáthos (see Chapter 12, "The Sporades"). Car pooling will give you the most freedom and be much more efficient, but all the sites listed below are serviced by public buses.

Days 1–2 From Athens to Delphi via Thebes. Two nights in Delphi to see the site before or after the crowds go home and go to Óssios Loukás.

Days 3–4 Continue northwest through Lamía and Tríkkala to Kalambáka. Next day see the monasteries at Metéora.

Days 5–7 Head east through Lárissa to Vólos, take ferry to Skiáthos. On the last day, fly or drive back to Athens.

Archeology buffs and those with less time should consider one of the fine guided bus tours departing from Athens. Call Dimitri Cocconi and his staff at **Educational Tours** (☎ **01/89-80-829,** fax 01/89-40-952) for information about their three-day Delphi and Metéora package (62,040 Drs ($258.50) per person, 11,000 Drs ($45.80) single supplement including some meals and hotel) or the popular five day Classical Tour,which goes to Ancient Corinth, Mycenae, Epidaurus, Ancient Olympia in the Peloponnese, then to Delphi and Metéora 83,160 Drs ($346.50) single supplement, 16,500 Drs ($68.75).

1 Boeotia

45 miles NW of Athens and 28 miles SW of Livadiá

GETTING THERE • By Train From Athens's Stathmós **Baríssis,** ten trains depart daily for Thebes or Livadiá. Call **01/36-24-402** for information.

- **By Bus** From Athens's terminal at Odós Liossíon 260, 13 buses depart daily for Thebes (☎ **01/83-17-179**).
- **By Car** Take the Athens-Lamía highway north to Thebes.

What's Special About Central Greece

Historical and Mythological Sites

- Delphi, the ancient oracle, believed to be the earth's "navel." Its archeological site and museum remain the most important repository of classical art in the country.
- The Pass of Thermopylae, where the Spartans' incredibly brave defense, against all odds, in 480 B.C. has been heralded in prose and poetry ever since.
- Mt. Pelion, whose hills are said to be inhabited by Chyron the Centaur, known in mythology for his romantic escapades.
- Mt. Olympus, rising above the Aegean coastline at Litochóro, is celebrated as the home of the ancient gods.

Religious Shrines

- The monastery of Óssios Loukás, built in the 11th century near the site of Delphi, has some of the finest Byzantine mosaics in Greece.
- The monasteries of Metéora, built up on the rock peaks that dot the landscape near Kalambáka, were founded by persecuted monks seeking refuge.

Boeotia (pronounced "Bee-*oh*-sha," in Greek *Viotía*) extends from the Aegean coast to the Pindus range and includes such legendary sights as Mt. Helicon, haunt of the Muses; the Pass of Thermopylae, where the Spartan general Leonidas and his men fell; Aulis, the port used by warships setting sail for Troy; its capital, City of Seven Gates, the legendary Thebes; and most important, nestled at the foot of Mt. Parnassus, the site of the oracle of Delphi. If you do nothing else during your visit to Greece, try to pay a call at one of the most remarkable places on the face of our earth.

Thebes

The journey from Athens to Delphi on the Athens-Lamía highspeed motorway will take you through the heart of Thebes (Thíva or, less commonly, Thívai), the ancient capital of Boeotia. Thebes' prominent position in the classical world has been assured by the literary works surviving from antiquity that treat of it. Works by Aeschylus (*Seven Against Thebes*), Sophocles (*Oedipus Rex*), Seneca (*Oedipus*), and Statius (*The Thebaid*), are all set in Thebes. These works are mainly tragedies. Thebes endured much in those times and in later epochs: Because of the onslaughts, pillages, and wholesale ravaging that it experienced, modern-day Thebes offers the visitor nothing more than a slowly developing city and industrial park. Between the days of Alexander and the liberation from Turkey, Thebes was devastated or razed at least eight times, numbering among its conquerors the Bulgars, Normans, Franks, Lombards, and Turks. No wonder that the city lives on only in books!

The glory of Thebes was reached in the mid-5th century B.C., when it twice defeated mighty Athens in battle; after that the fates turned against it and Thebes was crushed by Sparta (382 B.C.). Between 371 and 362 B.C., Thebes enjoyed an unusual decade of prosperity as an ally of Athens. The invincible city-state developed a new fighting formation called the *phalanx*, the close-knit line of battle, later adopted by Alexander the Great. When Alexander arrived in Thebes in 336 B.C., he flattened the entire city, with one exception—the centuries-old house of the poet Pindar. (Pindar was one of Greece's greatest lyric poets; born near Thebes in 518 B.C., he went to Athens, where he befriended Aeschylus and began to write.)

ORIENTATION

The **bus station** is on Epaminóndou Street, near the square that represents the main part of town. The **railroad station** is on the west side of town, and train riders will probably want to take a **taxi** to reach the Archeological Museum. Once you're at Epaminóndou Square, though, you'll be within walking distance of several local tavernas, the museum, and the Palace of Cadmus (now only a rock-filled lot at Pindárou and Antigónis Streets).

WHAT TO SEE & DO

The **Archeological Museum** (☎ **0262/27913**), at the foot of Pindárou Street, about a five-minute walk from Epaminóndou Square, is small but certainly worthwhile if you're in town. Outside, in a garden of stelae, is an "antique" table made up of columns and sculptural fragments, shaded by a grape arbor, that makes a pleasant picnic spot. Large mosaics mounted outside include an early Christian floor depicting the months of the year as young men bearing gifts. In the first room straight ahead is a collection of Mycenaean *lárnakes* (clay coffins) from 1400–1200 B.C. Excavated at a site near Thebes, this important find revealed a great deal about Mycenaean funeral customs, through both the primitive paintings on the coffins and their contents. This display at Thebes is unique in all of Europe. There is also a unique collection of 40 lapis lazuli cylindrical seals from far-off Mesopotamia, recovered near Thebes. The sculpture room houses votive offerings from the sanctuary of Apollo Ptoios, one of the most famous sanctuaries in ancient Greece.

The museum is open Tuesday through Sunday from 8:30am to 3pm. Admission is 500 Drs ($2.10) for adults, half price for students.

Livádia

Livadiá's one must-see sight can be combined with a café or picnic break in your tour of classical Greece. This special site is the **Trophónios Oracle,** a well-marked spot just one kilometer west off the Athens-Delphi highway. Here, in the scenic **Trophónios Park,** you'll find the **Xenía,** a picturesque and costly café overlooking a stream. In ancient times the stream was called the Fountain of Memory, to refresh those who were to consult the oracle. The Xenía is a popular hangout for Livadians, particularly on weekends and holidays.

While awaiting your order, you can contemplate the importance of this classical site as recorded by Pausanius, author of the original "Hellas on 50 Drachmas a Day" (and a talented Roman scribe). Trophonios was an ancient god of the Underworld whose advice was very popular in the 6th century B.C. As you admire the Fountain of Memory, glance to the left at the large square niche in the cliff. This was the sanctuary of the gods Daimon and Fortune, where pilgrims were fed the flesh of sacrificial victims after a draught of the waters of Lethe, the Fountain of Forgetfulness, which flows beneath it. Having forgotten the past (or, more likely, what he was about to eat), the pilgrim would be primed at the Fountain of Memory. Late in the evening he was annointed with oil and led up to the oracle (thought to be in a gorge of what is now called Mt. Ághios Ilías, behind you), and with honeycakes in each hand, was slid into a coffinlike pit in the floor of the mantic cave. After his revelation the pilgrim was hoisted out feet first, totally dazed, by the priest who would question him and record his impressions.

When you can tear yourself away, head northwest. After 37 km of winding, uphill roads the scenery will grow richer, as rocks and olive trees alternate with prospects over the Gulf of Corinth and an occasional glimpse of Mt. Parnassus. The less picturesque newer highway will bring you right into a charming village called Aráchova.

Aráchova

Just 10 km north of Delphi, the lovely mountain town of Aráchova is perched on the slopes of Mt. Parnassus at 950 meters above sea level. Although the main street suffers from the invasion of the tour buses, a descent or ascent by hand-hewn rock stairs leading from it will take you into another world.

Just as Americans might flock to Vermont in the fall for maple syrup or cheese, so Greeks from the cities come on a long winter weekend to tiny Aráchova for its specialties and nearby skiing. Many small tempting stores that line the main street feature the village's most celebrated products: strong, fragrant red wine (*krassí*); sharp white cheese called *fromaella*; and, most apparent, elegant, finely patterned carpets (*chaliá*).

Several markets display local cheese, wine, and honey in their windows, and souvenir stores are draped with weavings. If this specialty is what has drawn you here, go straight to the shop of **Katína Panagákou** (**☎ 31-743**), Odós Delphi 15, on the south side of main street about 200 meters from the tower. Katína is a superb weaver and her shop features the work of many local artisans. You can purchase new or antique rugs (*chalia*) or weavings. Although her prices are reasonable, quality costs.

There are two holidays that really draw crowds to Aráchova. On St. George's Day, following Easter, the death of the village's patron saint is celebrated with a traditional bacchanalia on the plaza outside the church. The festivities extend over several days and encompass all those who are fortunate enough to be in town.

ORIENTATION

In the height of the tourist season, many readers may prefer to stay overnight in Aráchova when visiting the overcrowded village of Delphi. There are six local **buses** running back and forth between Delphi and Aráchova that stop in front of the Celena Cafeteria across from the main square, where taxis can be found. The **police station** (**☎ 32-004**) is just off the south side of the square, and there's a ski rental shop nearby. The **tourist office,** the **telephone center,** and the **post office** are on Xenía Square, a block off the main square.

WHERE TO STAY

If you're planning to be in Aráchova for the St. George's Day festivities, arrive early or telephone ahead for reservations. One alternative is to stay in a private home, although you will have a problem making reservations. The town has formed a housing co-op and has set prices for a double at 6,600 Drs ($27.50).

IMPRESSIONS

Delphi I should think the Greekest thing of all.
—Henry Adams, 1898

Above these mountains proud Olympus tow'rs.
The parliamental seat of heavenly pow'rs.
—Mary Wortley Montague, *Verses Written in the Chiosk at Pera, Overlooking Constantinople, 1718*

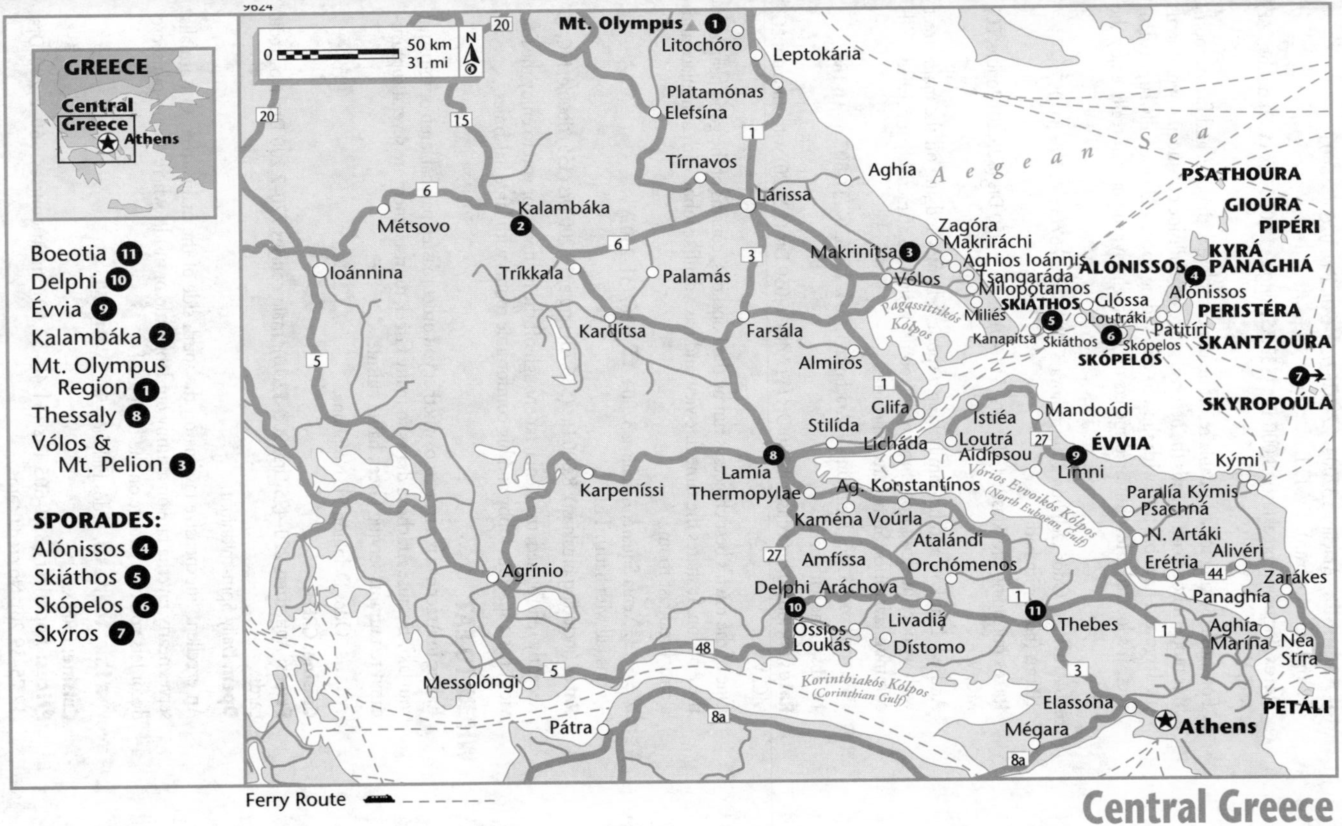

Central Greece

Hotel Anemolia, Aráchova 32004. ☎ **0267/31-640.** Fax: 0261/31640.
52 rms (all with bath). TV TEL

Rates (including breakfast): 8,000 Drs ($33.35) single, 12,000 Drs ($50) double. AE, MC, V.

For those looking for affordable resort luxury complete with sauna and fitness room, this modern hotel commands the best real estate on a hillside outside of town. Rooms are large and have big tubs with showers and sliding doors and especially large balconies. It's located a few hundred meters off the highway, so you can really enjoy the view.

Hotel Apollon, Odós Delphón 20, Aráchova 32004. ☎ **0267/31-427** or **31-057.**
10 rms (none with bath).

Rates (including breakfast): 4,180 Drs ($17.40) single, 6,050 Drs ($25.20) double. EC, MC, V.

Andreas Louskou and his family keep a spotless, homey lodging on the main street with wonderful views from most of its rooms, which are attractively furnished, with common lavatories. Some have balconies.

Hotel Parnassos, Odós Delphón 18, Aráchova 32004. ☎ **0267/31-307** or **31-189.**
10 rms (none with bath).

Rates (including breakfast): 4,180 Drs ($17.40), 6,050 Drs ($25.20) without bath. EC, MC, V.

One of the town's best choices is run by the Louskous, cousins of the good people at the Apollon. It shares the same fine view and has a denlike lobby with a fireplace and a cozy breakfast room.

Xenia Hotel, Xenía Square, Aráchova 32004. ☎ **0267/31-230.**
45 rms (all with bath). TEL

Rates (including breakfast): 8,800 Drs ($36.70) single, 13,200 Drs ($55) double. MC, V.

Recently refurbished, the Xenia, far enough off the highway for you to enjoy the fine view, has a spacious lobby and big comfortable rooms with large balconies.

WHERE TO EAT

Eating in Aráchova is a treat, too, whether you order roasted paschal lamb or the usual souvlaki. Because Aráchova draws so many Greek tourists, there are several sophisticated restaurants serving Greek haute cuisine.

O Karmalis, Odós Delphión 51. No phone.

Cuisine: GREEK.

Prices: Appetizers 220–495 Drs (90¢–$2.10); main courses 770–2,200 Drs. No credit cards.

Open: Daily 5pm–midnight.

An excellent, inexpensive taverna on the south side of the main street, O Karmalis serves hearty taverna fare on a sunny outdoor patio or inside, where the no-nonsense decor lets you concentrate on the food itself.

Taverna Karathanassi, Odós Delphón 56. ☎ **31-360.**

Cuisine: GREEK.

Prices: Appetizers 330–605 Drs ($1.40–$2.50); main courses 660–2,200 Drs ($2.75–$9.20). No credit cards.

Open: Daily 5:30pm–midnight.

Across from the small square where Aráchovan men sit sipping coffee is the family-run Taverna Karathanassi. The friendly chef is eager for guests to enjoy her grilled lamb, veal, or chicken. The moist bread is baked fresh daily and the *choriátiki saláta* (Greek salad) is a meal in itself.

MT. PARNASSUS

The Greek Tourist Organization (EOT) has established a full-service ski resort based at Fterolaka with an altitude of 2,252 meters, a 27-km or 50-minute drive from Aráchova. There are 12 ski runs; beginners get the chair lifts while you more experienced skiers will have to make do with the two upper-level T-bars. There's a ski rental shop, snack bar, cafeteria, and clothes and accessories boutique at the **Fteroláka Center.** The ski center is open from December to April; contact its office (☎ **0234/22-689, 22-693**) for more information. Daily lift tickets can be purchased for under 2,500 Drs ($10.40). The center gives lessons, and you can rent gear (☎ **0267/22-693** for reservations).

In good weather, hikers may want to try the nearly four-hour ascent to the top of Parnassus. The Delphi Youth Hostel has tourist-drawn maps of the route; it suggests hitching a ride to Kelariá and hiking from there. In Athens contact the **Hellenic Federation of Mountaineering** (☎ **01/32-34-555**) for information.

2 Delphi

110 miles NW of Athens

GETTING THERE • By Bus From Athens's terminal at Odós Liossíon 260 (☎ **83-17-096**), five buses leave daily for Delphi.

• By Car Take National Road 1 to Thebes, exit and continue west.

ESSENTIALS The new Delphi **tourist office** (☎ **0265/82-900**), at Odós Friderníkis 44, is open daily from 8am to 3pm—and from 6 to 8pm in July and August—with useful information always posted in the window. The **tourist police** (☎ **89-920**) are at Odós Friderníkis 27, next door to the **post office,** which is open weekdays from 7:30am to 7:30pm, Saturdays from 8am to 2:30pm, and Sundays from 9am to 1pm. The **telephone center** is at Odós Friderníkis 10 and is open from 7:30am to 3:10pm Monday through Saturday, and Sunday from 9am to 2pm. The two **banks** on Friderníkis Street reopen after standard hours from 5 to 7pm during the summer. The main post office and kiosk at the museum change money also.

If there is only one archeological site in Greece that you'll allow yourself to see, it must be the oracle of Delphi. Nowhere will you find more interesting remains, a more beautiful setting, or a better collection of art gathered in the same place. If any of our readers write and tell us they didn't hear the oracle calling, then we can only assume they weren't listening. Delphi is the most mystical and magical site in the entire country.

Getting Around

You can easily walk anywhere within the small town of Delphi (Delfí), including all the sites. The Delphi **bus stop** is next to the Taverna Castri on the west end of the main street. The local bus to Aráchova leaves throughout the day; the fare is 150 Drs (60¢). To get to Óssios Loukás, take a bus to Dístomo (or exit the Athens bus at the highway intersection), then walk 3 km to catch the bus directly to the monastery. (**Be warned** that this is not an easy trip; check the tourist office for current schedules).

From Delphi, you can share a taxi with up to four people for about 9,000 Drs ($37.50), a bargain for the 45-minute scenic drive to Óssios Loukás. (Negotiate the fare before you leave and have the driver wait for you.)

What to See & Do

According to Plutarch, there were two precepts inscribed upon the Delphic oracle: KNOW THYSELF (*Gnóthi seautón*) and NOTHING IN EXCESS (*Medén ágan*), "and upon these all other precepts depend."

Some visitors to Delphi may wonder what they should visit first, the archeological site or the museum. Kyle and many near-experts suggest that one should tour the museum first, arguing that a visit to the museum will orient or enhance one's walk through the remains at the site. John believes one should buy a detailed map or guidebook at the museum and head straight for the site. Then, when you go to the museum, you'll be much happier and more interested in trying to translate those little signs in French that describe the museum artifacts.

It's best to plan your visit to the Delphi Museum and archeological sites at the beginning or end of the day, before or after the tour groups have swamped them.

Delphi Museum, Delphi. ☎ **0265/82-312.**

One of the first things you'll see upon entering the museum is an **omphalós,** a marble cone sculpted to appear as if covered with braided wool. In antiquity Delphi was held to be the center of the world, the "navel" or *omphalos.* On the right-hand wall in the next room is a **frieze** from the treasury of the Sifnians (525 B.C.), depicting the war between the Greeks and the Tartans, the gods at Mt. Olympus, and the war between the gods and the giants.

In the next room you'll find the famous **winged sphynx of the Naxians.** The sphynx—part bird and lion and part woman—stood atop a tall pedestal at the base of the temple of Apollo.

Enter the room with the two still and imposing archaic **kouroi** (600 B.C.); to the right are the remains of sacred offerings found in a secret passage under the temple of Apollo, one of the most exciting exhibits in the museum. The 5th-century B.C. **offerings,** thought to be from one of the Ionian cities because of their style, are made of gold and ivory; because of their value, they were moved, after a 5th-century A.D. fire, from storage in the treasury of the Corinthians to an underground vault. In 1939, French archeologists found at least three life-size figures (of Apollo, Artemis, and possibly Leto) and a huge bull. The bull is made of wood, covered with hammered and cast silver and decorated with gold and ivory. The human figures, now charred, are made of solid ivory. Don't miss the beautiful censer in the corner (it dates from 450 B.C.).

As you return to the main hall, continue through the rooms displaying metopes from the Athenian treasury; admire the forceful imagery of the "Labors of Heracles." The exhibit of remnants and restored sections of the *tholos* from the sanctuary of Athena Pronaea is of particular interest if you have already viewed the extraordinarily beautiful circular building standing below the main site of Delphi.

In the remaining rooms there are three highlights that you should search out. The first is a figure of **Agias,** a star athlete of the 5th-century B.C. He's the best preserved of a group of six related figures, and is thought to be a copy of a bronze executed by Lysippus. The second sculpture of note is the contemplative **Antinoös,** the Greek youth loved and deified by the Roman Emperor Hadrian—he's thought to have drowned

1 Roman Agora (Marketplace)
2 Votive offering of Corfu ("Bull")
3 Votive offering of Athens ("Victory at Marathon")
4 Votive offering of Lacedaemonians
5 Votive offering of Argos ("Seven Against Thebes")
6 Votive offering of Argos ("Descendants")
7 Votive offering of Argos ("The King of Argos")
8 Votive offering of Taras
9 Treasure House of Sikyon
10 Treasure House of Siphnos
11 Treasure House of Megara
12 Treasure House of Thebes
13 Treasure House of Boeotia
14 Treasure House of Potidaea
15 Treasure House of Athens
16 Bouleuterion (Council House)
17 Treasure House of Cnidus (Knidos)
18 Rock of Sibylla
19 Naxian Column
20 Asclepion
21 Portico of the Athenians
22 Treasure House of Corinth
23 Prytaneion (Magistrates' Building)
24 Treasure House of Cyrene
25 Supporting Polygonal Wall
26 Tripod of Plateae
27 Votive offering of Rhodes
28 Grand Altar
29 Spring
30 Temple of Apollo
31 Votive Tripods
32 Treasure House of Acanthus
33 Portico of Attalus
34 Shrine of Neoptolemos
35 Votive offering of Daochos
36 Club of the Cnidians
37 Kassotis Spring
38 Ischegaon–Supporting Wall
39 Votive offering of Krateros
40 Theater
41 Western Portico

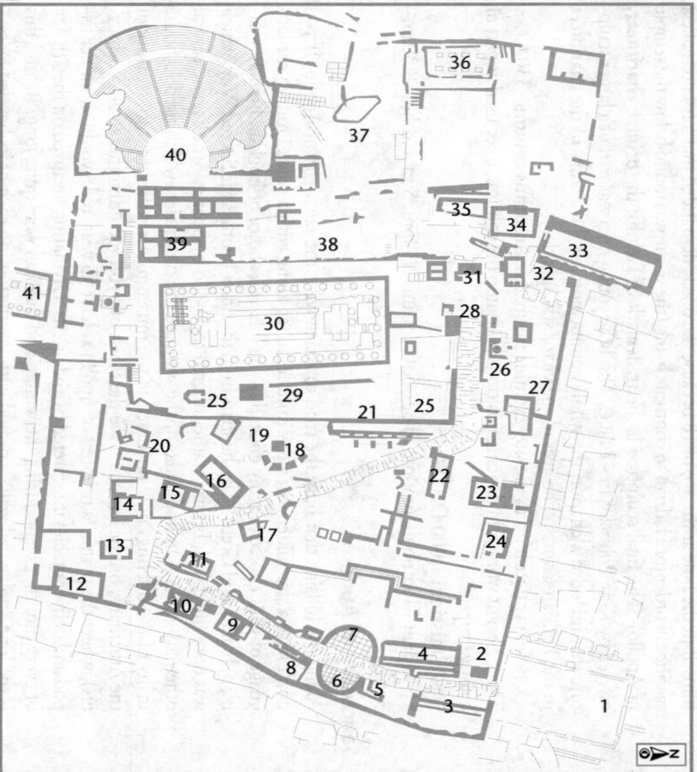

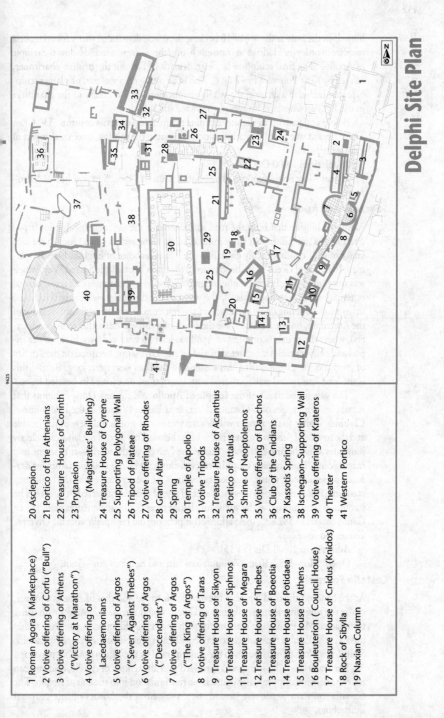

Delphi Site Plan

himself in the Nile at the age of 18 because the oracle demanded that a friend make a sacrifice in order for Hadrian to continue living (the statue was found below the temple of Apollo). The final sculpture is the trademark of Delphi: the **bronze charioteer,** offered by King Polyzalos in 474 B.C. This lithe young man was part of a larger sculpture that included a chariot; the whole commemorated the victory of the charioteer in the Pythian Games. The eyes of the victor still sparkle.

Before you rush off to the site, examine the marble **Acanthus column** (330 B.C.). Three elegant women in dancing positions pose atop the column, once used as part of a votive tripod.

Admission: 1,000 Drs ($4.15).

Open: Mon noon–6:30pm, Tues–Sat 7:30am–7:30pm, Sun and hols 8:30am–3pm.

Sanctuary of Apollo

Along the hillside that hugs the road to Aráchova is the sanctuary of Apollo. If you don't have a site guide, wait a few minutes to tag along with a guided tour in the language of your choice (on any given day you'll have a choice of English, French, German, Italian, and Greek). Up the stairs from the ticket booth is the **Sacred Way,** which was once lined with bronze statues offered to Apollo by Sparta, Arcadia, and several other city-states. On both sides of the walk are the **treasuries,** which used to house many of the offerings now preserved in the museum. After the beautiful treasury of the Athenians, on the left you'll see the **Rock of Sybil** (grandmother of all soothsayers), where the pythia (a priestess of Apollo at least 50 years old) would sit on her tripod and deliver oracles interpreted by the priests. Divination occurred on the 7th day of every month, except during the winter, and the lines were quite long. Behind this is the long "polygonal wall," covered with inscriptions on each of its beveled faces.

The vast foundations of the **temple of Apollo** and the few Doric columns that remain invoke images of his beautiful temple at Bassae (Vásses) in the Peloponnese. Climbing higher to the theater will reward you with a wonderful view of the temple and the temple of Athena Pronaea in the valley below. This view of the landscape clearly illustrates why the ancients chose this as the "navel" of the world—it is serene and magnificent. The compact **amphitheater** at this level held 5,000 spectators for dramatic presentations, music, and poetry readings. At the very top of the site is the long **stadium** (which now hosts theatrical events) one of the best preserved in Greece. The stadium is remembered as the venue for chariot races during the quadrennial Pythian Games (begun in 582 B.C., these athletic competitions did for Apollo what the Olympic Games did for Zeus).

Admission: 1,000 Drs ($4.15).

Open: Mon–Fri 7:30am–7:30pm, Sat–Sun and hols 8:30am—3pm.

Castalia Fountain

At the bend on the road between the temple of Apollo and that of Athena Pronaea, under the huge maple trees, pilgrims to Delphi would cleanse themselves with water from sacred Mt. Parnassus. Walk up the path and at the old fountain you'll see niches carved in the Yambia rock, which contained offerings brought to the nymph of Castalia. Stairs (now blocked off) lead up to the gorge formed by the Yambia and Náfplio crags.

The water from the spring was sprinkled over the temple of Apollo, and you can taste the deliciously pure water yourself—a free initiation into the cult of Apollo. The Castalia fountain is a lovely shaded spot, away from the hordes of international shutterbugs.

Admission: Free.

Open: Daily 24 hours.

Temple of Athena Pronaea

From the roadway, walk five minutes past the Castalia Fountain to the tourist café. Below it are the remains of the **gymnasium,** which had racetracks, boxing and wrestling rings, and baths for training local athletes. Keep walking along the roadway, past the laurels, till you see three white Doric columns, topped with one of the few in situ pediments in Greece. In the relative isolation of the 4th-century B.C. temple of Athena, you can admire the remains of the mysterious, circular **tholos.**

Thought to be the work of master architect Theodoros (ca. 380 B.C.), the tholos was originally composed of 20 outer columns that surrounded ten Corinthian semicolumns, in two tiers. This is the spot from which to admire all the ruins of Delphi, contemplate the oracle's role in the ancient world, and listen to the prophecy of the birds.

Admission: Free.

Open: Daily 7:30am–sunset.

Where to Stay

Delphi is a small mountain village built above and below both sides of its main highway, called Friderîkis Street. Hotels and pensions are cheek to cheek with bookshops, souvenir stands, and expensive tavernas, but there are some excellent places to stay at that make Delphi an ideal base camp for touring this region.

In addition to the following, there are a few budget accommodations on Apóllonos Street, one street uphill from Friderîkis and nearest to the bus stop. **Loúla Sotiríou** (☎ **0265/82-349**) rents four doubles with access to a common bathroom for 4,400 Drs ($18.30) per night. Her pleasant home is on the west end of town, at Odós Apóllonos 84, the last house on the right before the Amaliá Hotel.

Apollon Camping (☎ **0265/82-762**) is basic but is the best-situated campground in the vicinity of Delphi. It's located off the main highway, 2 km south of the village, and offers a swimming pool, a minimarket, a taverna, a café, and tent sites that overlook the mountains, the valley, and the Gulf of Corinth beyond. Rates are 920 Drs ($3.80) per person, 360 Drs ($1.50) per tent.

DOUBLES FOR LESS THAN 5,300 DRS ($22.10)

$ **Delphi Youth Hostel,** Odós Apóllonos 31, Delphi 33054. ☎ **0265/82-286.** 19 rms (none with bath), 100 beds.

Rates: 2,225 Drs ($9.40) bed; 5,225 Drs ($21.80) double. No credit cards.

This hostel is well known on the budget traveler's circuit for its gracious, helpful, and friendly staff and its better-than-average accommodations. You can call or write ahead for reservations. There are three doubles, but the 100 beds are what's really in demand. In high season new arrivals should sign up for a bed between 7:30 and 10am, before sightseeing. The hostel will also put overflow crowds out on the roof for 880 Drs ($3.70).

$ **Pension Odysseus,** Odós Isaía 1, Delphi 33054. ☎ **0265/82-235.** 8 rms (none with bath).

Rates: 3,850 Drs ($16) single; 4,090 Drs ($17.05) double. Showers 385 Drs ($1.60) extra. AE, DC, MC, V.

Located on a small pedestrian street lined with red planters is an ideal pension: low priced and quiet, with fantastic views, clean rooms, and a spacious terrace. The effusive hostess, Toula, encourages her guests to buy food at the local markets and bring it back to enjoy at one of her terrace tables.

DOUBLES FOR LESS THAN 7,400 DRS ($41)

Hotel Aiolos, Odós Frideríkis 23, Delphi 33054. ☎ **0265/82-632.**
29 rms (all with bath).

Rates (including breakfast): 7,476 Drs ($31.15) single; 9,900 Drs ($41.25) double.

This hotel is a good value. The lobby has a lot of old-world charm and big, comfortable chairs. The rooms are quiet, light, and cheerful. They offer excellent views down to the valley carpeted with olive trees and out to the port of Iteá on the Gulf of Corinth.

Hotel Athina, Odós Frideríkis 55, Delphi 33054. ☎ **0265/82-239.**
12 rms (8 with bath).

Rates (including breakfast): 4,850–5,500 Drs ($20.20–$22.90) single; 4,180–6,050 Drs ($17.40–$25.20) double. 20% higher with bath. V.

This small hotel has attractive rooms with superb views from the balconies. Breakfast is an extra 550 Drs ($2.30), served in front of a great view. Manager Nicholas Zinelis speaks English and is very helpful.

Hotel Hermes, Odós Frideríkis 27, Delphi 33054. ☎ **0265/82-318.** Fax 82-639.
30 rms (all with bath). TEL

Rates (including breakfast): 6,800 Drs ($28.30) single; 11,000 Drs ($45.80) double. MC, V.

This charming hotel is built into the hillside on a quiet part of the main street. The lobby is decorated with local weavings, and the top-floor rooms have the same superb view you can enjoy in the pleasant breakfast room. Owners Tony and Nick Droseros happily told us, "Your boss, Arthur Frommer, slept here!"

Hotel Pan, Odós Frideríkis 53, Delphi 33054. ☎ **0265/82-294.**
17 rms (all with bath). TEL

Rates (including breakfast): 5,500 Drs ($22.90) single; 7,990 Drs ($33.30) double. AE, DC, MC, V.

Check in the gift shop near the peaceful south end of the main street for Yannis and Andreas Lefas, hosts of this clean, modern hotel; both speak English well. The lobby is spare, making the most of beautiful maroon marble floors. All rooms share a terrace with a wonderful valley view; the breakfast room is especially charming.

Hotel Sibylla, Odós Frideríkis 19, Delphi 33054. ☎ **0265/82-335.** Fax 0265/83-024.
10 rms (all with bath). TEL

Rates: 4,500 Drs ($18.75) single; 6,200 Drs ($25.80) double.

The lobby is small and very European. The rooms, comfortable but plain, share the same scenic views as the Aiolos and Athina. There's a new in-house travel and exchange desk.

DOUBLES FOR LESS THAN 14,300 DRS ($58.30)

★ **Hotel Olympic,** Odós Frideríkis 57, Delphi 33054. ☎ **0265/82-641.**
Fax 0265/82-639. 25 rms (all with bath). TEL

Rates (including breakfast): 11,550 Drs ($48.10) single; 14,300 Drs ($59.60) double. MC, V.

If it weren't so immaculate, you might take this new hotel as something from a grander, more gracious time. Easily the most beautiful hotel in town, with quality and distinction everywhere: handsome wood, black wrought iron, and sleek dark furnishings contrasting with cool white plaster walls. All this, and a splendid view.

Hotel Panorama, Odós Ossíou Louká 47, Delphi 33054. ☎ **0265/82-061.**
Fax 0265/82-081. 20 rms (all with bath). TEL

Rates (including breakfast): 11,000 Drs ($45.80) single; 13,200 Drs ($55) double. MC, V.

This comfortable inn high on the hill above town offers simple village style with modern amenities—central heat, direct-dial telephones, music, together with warm hospitality. The view is as its name suggests.

Where to Eat

Even with the huge demand put on lunchtime restaurants, there are some fine, reasonably priced meals to be had in the village of Delphi. A note for those who just get going after dinner: Delphi has bars and discothèques on Friderikis Street. If you're in the mood for star gazing, try **Delphi by Night.** If a Greek dance show is more your style, climb the steps to **Katói** in a pretty garden behind the wall at Odós Apóllonos 36, where free lessons are given from 9:30 to 11:30 nightly in fair weather; in winter, classes move indoors to a more intimate and rustic setting with an old-fashioned fireplace.

Isaía Cafeteria Delfi, Odós Isaía 10. ☎ **82-863.**

Cuisine: SNACKS/DESSERTS.
Prices: Snacks/desserts 220–1,650 Drs (90¢–$6.90). No credit cards.
Open: Daily 8am–midnight.

Light meals, snacks, and breakfast are offered at reasonable prices, making this a popular rest stop before or after the museum. This little bar is on the pedestrian lane a few meters down from Apóllonos Street.

Castalia Spring Cafe, near the Oracle. ☎ **82-210.**

Cuisine: CONTINENTAL.
Prices: Snacks 440–880 Drs ($1.80–$3.70); main courses 800–2,200 Drs ($3.30–$9.20). No credit cards.
Open: Daily 8am–11pm; till 1am in summer.

This very pleasant café right at the archeological site, at the entrance to the temple of Athena Pronaiea, offers fresh-squeezed orange juice, sweets, and ice cream while you enjoy the view of the ancient gymnasium and valley below. George Koublis, formerly of the Los Angeles eatery Greek Connection, serves light snacks, moussaká, souvlaki, and salads—and has plans for more.

Taverna Arachova, Odós Friderikis 50. ☎ **82-452.**

Cuisine: GREEK.
Prices: Main courses 880–2,250 Drs ($3.70–$9.40).
Open: Daily 6:30pm–midnight.

This small traditional taverna specializes in fresh veal, beef, lamb, and chicken—much of it raised on Ghiorgos Panagakos's own farm—roasted over charcoal. Don't miss the chips or roast potatoes.

$ **Taverna Vakchos,** Odós Apóllonos 31. ☎ **82-448.**
Cuisine: GREEK.
Prices: Main courses 700–1,800 Drs ($2.90–$7.50); fixed-price daily meals 1,800–2,500 Drs ($7.50–$10.40). V.
Open: Daily 7am–11pm.

You'll find our favorite place next door to the Youth Hostel—its staff recommended it to us, and they should know about budget eating. The Vakchos (Bacchus) is bright, spacious, and no-frills, with gorgeous views and typical taverna fare well prepared and amiably served. Locals still recommend it enthusiastically.

Excursions from Delphi

With Delphi as a base, you can visit Aráchova or Mt. Parnassus (already covered in this chapter), areas of great scenic beauty. Southwest of Delphi is the 11th-century Byzantine monastery of Óssios Loukás; an exquisite chapel in this lovely compound boasts gold-backed mosaics that rival those at Dafní for the affections of Byzantophiles. If you're contemplating breaking up your archeological tour with a refreshing splash in the sea, it's most easily done along the Gulf of Corinth coast. The beaches are not very good, and the best would be all the way west to Náfpaktos, near the Antírio cross-over point for entry into the Peloponnese. For those readers who are proceeding up the eastern coast of Greece to Mt. Pelio, Vólos, or the Sporades, or due north to Metéora and on to Thessaloníki, we'll take you up Boeotia on the Lamía highway.

If you are traveling (as do many of the tours from Athens) from Delphi to the monastery of Óssios Loukás, you'll pass a spot of great importance in Greek literature. Where the road continues straight to Livádia and splits right (south) to Dístomo and Óssios Loukás is thought to be the **triple way,** the crossroads where Oedipus killed his father, King Laius. Oedipus (his name means "swollen foot") was walking from Delphi to Thebes, having received a horrible omen from the oracle that he would kill his father and marry his mother, from whom he had been separated since birth. At this very fork in the road a distraught Oedipus met an older man riding in a royal chariot who refused to let him pass. The man whipped Oedipus and, in defense, Oedipus killed his attacker, fulfilling the first part of the oracle's terrible prophecy.

MONASTERY OF ÓSSIOS LOUKÁS

The church of Óssios Loukás is one of the most ornately decorated and well-designed Byzantine sanctuaries in Greece. Its brilliant gold-backed mosaics and innovative octagonal structure make Óssios Loukás a must for those interested in Byzantium. Set on the slopes of Mt. Helikon, the church is dedicated to the hermit Saint Loukás (not Saint Luke the Apostle), and is part of a larger monastery that is run by four bearded monks.

Óssios Loukás Stiriótis established a kind of medieval oracle, a church known for prophecies and the ascetic life, in A.D. 942. He lived there until his death in 953. Loukás's original church was replaced during the 11th century by Romanós the First, the new church designed as a local variation of Haghía Sophía in Constantinople. Loukás's relics, formerly kept in the Vatican, were moved to the church in 1987, converting the status of the site from a museum to a holy place. Monks screen visitors to ensure that they are wearing the proper attire (no shorts or halter tops); those not dressed appropriately will be provided with a bright orange pajamalike covering.

As you enter the narthex, where the admission fee—550 Drs ($2.30) and postcards are sold, look up and you'll see some of the best and the brightest of the sparkling mosaics. Proceed into the church and turn left at the second niche. When you step up, Loukás will be above you, sporting a helmet and beard, his intense eyes watching over tourists, arms up in resignation. Many of the mosaics, including the one decorating the main dome, were severely damaged or destroyed by an earthquake in 1659. Paintings and frescoes, which in turn were damaged by Turkish troops in the 19th century, replaced the lost mosaics. Notice the lacelike carved marble pillars in front of the altar and the patterns and columns of the marble floors.

We mistakenly entered the monastery from the back and walked down a narrow path (where we were blessed by a monk who was chopping wood) that led to the church and the crypt where old Loukás was originally buried. The crypt contains some interesting and colorful frescoes festooned with graffiti from the ages.

Within the grounds of the monastery is the flagstone "village" of Óssios Loukás, complete with taverna. Don't miss the view of the valley below from the patio. There isn't a sign of modern life (except the road), so the panorama is strictly medieval. The monastery is open 8am to 2pm daily and 4 to 6pm May through September.

Heading North

To work our way back to the north of Boeotia requires returning to the main highway at Amfíssa. Surrounded by mountains and situated on the same plain as Iteá, it serves mostly as a major marketplace for all the local hillside villages. Amfíssa's abundant supply of water, hot temperatures, and flat terrain (easier for watering and makes a more tender olive) make it an ideal area for growing olives! One local resident claimed that the area is planted with over five million olive trees; and if you check your at-home supermarket shelves to see where your salad dressing is made, they could be right. The town is like an oven in summer and remarkably cold in winter, so unless you want to watch the olives grow, we suggest that you move on to the high point of your northward journey.

PASS OF THERMOPYLAE

The mountains (west) will be to your left, the sea (east) to your right, and straight ahead the national highway system has paved its track directly through one of the most famous places of antiquity. Watch for the statue of Leonidas, celebrated Spartan leader, who stands erect, shield and spear in hand, marveling at the amount of vehicular traffic that flows through this strategic pass.

In 480 B.C., when Xerxes and the Persians reached Thermopylae, they realized that to conquer Greece they would have to fight their way through this pass. Leonidas, commander of the Spartan forces and general of all the Greek troops, had 7,300 men stationed in the middle. Weeks of standoff went by, until an Amalian soldier, angry at the confederation, turned traitor and decided to show Xerxes a new back route over the mountains. The traitor, Ephialtes, led the Persian captain to the path over Mt. Phrikion, where they found 1,000 Phocidian troops stationed. The Persian captain, Hydarnes returned at night with 2,000 men, who slew the Phocidians and the next morning emerged on the east side of the pass. As he'd planned with Xerxes, at the appointed hour the attack against the Greek forces began from both sides. Leonidas realized at once what had happened and dismissed most of the troops. He kept with him 700 Thespians, 300 Spartans, and 300 Theban hostages.

Leonidas and his Spartan troops have long been heralded for their bravery on that day. Byron wrote of Greece's 19th-century struggle for independence: "Earth! Render back from out thy breast a remnant of our Spartan dead! Of the three hundred grant but three, to make a new Thermopylae!" (*Don Juan,* Canto III). One terrible aspect of the story recorded by Herodotus tells of the moment when Leonidas himself fell in battle. Savage fighting broke out between the Persians (who hoped to exhibit his body as proof of victory) and the loyal Spartans (who wanted to protect their leader). Two of Xerxes' own brothers were killed in the struggle, and over many deaths the Greeks retook Leonidas's body four times. Of course, soon all the Greeks were slaughtered and Xerxes and his men pushed on to Attica.

Thermopylae means "Hot Gates" in Greek, and the pass was named for the hot springs that flowed through it in antiquity and are now routed to several spas on the east coast. If you've had enough driving for the day, the **Camping Leonidas** grounds are just off the highway, and to the east (about 30 km from the pass), on the coast, the pretty beach resort of **Kaména Voúrla.** The narrow strip of beach is matched across the highway by a row of new white two-story hotels, the architecture of a pleasant middle-class resort overlooking the island of Évvia.

3 Évvia

50 miles N of Athens

GETTING THERE • By Train Several trains run daily to Chalkís from Athens's Stathmós Paríssis. Call **01/36-24-402** for information.

• By Bus There are 16 buses daily to Chalkís from Athens's terminal at Odós Liossíon 260 (☎ **01/83-17-153**).

• By Sea Daily car ferries connect Ághios Nikólaos and Ághios Konstantínos to Chalkís. There are several other frequent car ferries (10–30 daily) from the mainland, connecting Oropoús with Eretría, Grammatikós with Almiropótamos, Arkítsa with Loutrá Aidipsoú, Ághia Marína with Néa Stira, and Rafína with Marmári and Karistos. Call **0294/63-491** for schedules.

• By Car Drive north on National Road 1 to Schimatari, exit and follow signs to Chalkís. The only land bridge, which connects Ághios Minás to Chalkís, extends a mere 210 feet.

The island of Évvia (Euboea) is Athens's equivalent of New York's Long Island. Its proximity and sand beaches make it the place for weekend homes and minivacations. This section is for readers who need a quick break from the Athenian heat. Readers who seek the way to the lesser-known pleasures of Skýros should turn to the section on Kými, the port city nearest to this Sporades isle.

Older Greeks will swear that the island of Évvia was actually part of the mainland until Poseidon (angry over some mortal who'd flirted with a mermaid) took his trident and sliced the Évvia piece off. Since that time long ago the Greeks have done everything possible to reconnect it, while enjoying the benefit of two additional coastlines.

Chalkís

Évvia's capital is Chalkís or, more commonly, Chalkída (from the Greek word for "bronze," *chalkós*), and in antiquity this thriving port was well known for the metalwork it contributed to the sanctuaries at Delphi and Olympia and for the weapons produced during continuous wars. Over the centuries Évvia, in whole or in part, fell under the rule of the Athenians, Spartans, Thebans, Macedonians, Franks, Venetians, and Turks. Meanwhile, its sailors were opening new trade routes for the Hellenic world and founding cities in northern Greece (Calcidice or Chalkidikí), in Italy, and in Asia Minor.

The **Évripos Channel** is the most interesting thing about present-day Chalkís because of its irregular currents, which change direction 7–14 times a day, or sometimes don't change at all, depending on the moon and the season. The rapid shift and brief lulls in between make it very dangerous for boats to pass through, and it's said that Aristotle drowned himself here in frustration at not being able to explain the currents. Today, scientists only guess that the Évripos acts as a sluice between two water levels of the Évvian (Euboean) Channel.

If you arrive by public transport, you'll find the Chalkís **bus station** on Venizélou Street (☎ **0221/22-640** or **22-436**), and the **train station** (☎ **0221/26-250**) nearby. The **archeological museum** is at Odós Venizélou 13, where you can see a small collection of finds, particularly from Erétria. There's also an attractive Turkish mosque near the Évripos Channel bridge. Expensive hotels and cafés line the promenade of Chalkís's harbor, with the restaurants on one side of the street and their café tables overlooking the water on the other side.

Northern Évvia

Signposted as BOREIOS EVVIA (Greek for "Northern Évvia," pronounced *Vórios Évvia*), this area features a medicinal hot-springs spa at **Loutrá Aidípsou.** Many hotels with mineral water bubbling right into the rooms have been built for arthritis and rheumatism sufferers. If this interests you, the Greek Tourist Organization (EOT) in Athens can provide you with more information about it and other Grecian spas. **Límni,** 85 km north of Chalkís, was so picturesque a port that Zeus and Hera got married there, but times have changed: As with all good nearby places, hotels and speedboats have followed in the wake of suntanned Athenian weekenders, and idyllic Límni is no more.

Southern Évvia

Heading, from Chalkís, toward southern Évvia (*Nótios Évvia* in Greek, so don't mistake the "N" in the road sign N. EVVIA for "Northern"!) you'll notice occasional evidence of resort life. Eretria Beach, Holidays in Evvia, and the Golden Beach are all huge, full-service resorts packed with locals on summer weekends. Some 4 km south of town is **Evvia Camping** (☎ **0221/61-081**). Erétria's narrow pebble beach makes it a nice day trip or a convenient weekend away from the Athenian *néfos* (pollution).

Néa Stira is the most efficient ferry crossing (time- and moneywise) if you're driving up to Kými for the ferry to Skýros. There are five ferries daily; fares run 290 Drs ($12.10) per car. If for some inexcusable reason you're stuck here overnight, there's the **Hotel Plaza** (☎ **0224/41-492**)—*no* relation to New York's—with a 24-hour snack bar.

Kými

Kými, 93 km (58 miles) northeast of Chalkís, is the only place on Évvia worthy of a one-night stand. It's a charming mountaintop fishing village, and the explanation for this apparent contradiction is that the plateau it's on is more spacious and hospitable than the narrow coast. Tall, narrow stone houses are stacked in among the pine and fir forests, but everyone finds his way into the main square. Here you'll find the **Hotel Krineion** (☎ **0222/22-287**), a charming, wood-trimmed 50-year-old lodging that's seen a lot of visitors. Large, clean doubles are 6,050 Drs ($25.20). The front rooms have great views. A more modern alternative is the **Hotel Kými** (☎ **0222/22-408**), located up the hill by the post office. Doubles here are 4,400 Drs ($18.30).

The best of Kými's cuisine can be sampled at any of the tavernas off the square. For breakfast there's a bakery below the *platía* (square), where you may also buy picnic supplies for the boat; or try the small *zacharoplastío* (café/pâtisserie) on the square that features Kými's unique all-almond baklavá.

Kými is the birthplace of George Papanicolaou, the doctor who originated the PAP test (PAP for *Pap*anicolcou). His home still stands next to the square. In the surrounding region are several Byzantine churches; the remains of an ancient *kástro* (fort) are 4 km north of the village. The most delightful site is the charming **Folklore Museum of Kými** (filled with sailors' memorabilia, embroidery, costumes, and brought-home treasures), set in a traditional house below the *platía.* It's open daily from 10am to 1pm and 5 to 7:30pm in summer; on Wednesday from 4 to 6pm, and on Saturday, Sunday, and holidays from 10am to 1pm from October to April. Call 22-011 for more information.

PARALÍA KÝMI

A non-town at water's edge, Paralía Kými is one big pier and the few services needed to maintain it. The three boats to Skýros don't leave till the afternoon; and buses stop right in front of the ferry. Tickets for the daily Skýros ferries can be purchased on the day of departure in Paralía Kými; call 0222/22-020 for schedule information. There are also three sailings weekly to Alónissos, Skópelos, and Skíathos. Weather and demand play havoc on sailing schedules from this little port; check in Kými for information on departures to Samothráki (Samothrace), Alexandroúpolis, Kavála, and Vólos (see also the respective sections of this book).

4 Thessaly

Thessaly (Thessalía), the home of Mt. Olympus and other famous peaks in Greek mythology, was regarded as a special place by the ancient Greeks. Olympus, of course, was the abode of the gods; Mt. Pelion was inhabited by frolicking centaurs and wood fairies; and Mt. Ossa was used as a "stepping stone" by the giant Aloadae to reach heaven and try to dethrone the gods. As you drive from Athens, entering Thessaly through the provincial town of Lamía, you're impressed by the change in landscape—the stark contrast between the lowlands and the lofty, scenic heights. In the western part of the Thessalian Plain are the startling *metéora* ("rocks in air"), just outside the provincial capital of Kalambáka. When you see these incredible monoliths towering majestically over the flat plains, you can understand why the ancients—and, later, the Christians—invested this region with religious significance. Consider the miracle-built monasteries that crown these isolated peaks and the awe they inspire.

When you pass through Lamía, notice the medieval castle of the Catalan Duchy (built between 1319 and 1393) towering on the heights above you to the northeast. From this prospect it could guard the narrow waterway curling around Évvia into the mainland ports. Scholars have found that its walls were largely built over the remains of classical ones, proving once again that once a fortress, always a fortress.

An old local through road that wends its way around tavernas, beaches, kids on bicycles, and erratic coastline is a slower, more difficult route compared with the modern toll road, but it's certainly more fun.

5 Vólos & Mt. Pelion

Vólos 196 miles NE of Athens

GETTING THERE • By Train There are seven trains daily from Athens's Stathmós Laríssis (☎ **01/36-24-402**) (three express, which cuts the trip by half an hour). In Vólos call **24-056.** The national railway organization OSE runs six trains daily from Vólos to Thessaloníki, 12 to Lárissa, and one to Kalambáka (for Metéora).

• By Bus There are nine OSE buses daily from Athens's Odós Liossíon (☎ **22-527** in Vólos for schedule information). There are nine KTEL (privately run) buses daily from the station at the corner of Grigoríou Lambráki and Lachaná Streets (☎ **83-17-186** in Athens or **25-527** in Vólos for information), and four KTEL buses daily to Thessaloniki.

• By Sea Ferry tickets to the Sporades can be purchased from the **Sporades Travel Agency,** Odós Argonáfton 32 (☎ **0421/23-400**), or from **George Skouris,** Odós Venizélou 14-26 (☎ **0421/27-204,** fax 0421/30-668)**.** Sailings are twice daily to Skíathos, once daily to Skópelos, daily except Monday to Alónissos, and every Tuesday and Friday to Skýros (12 hours!). Hydrofoil tickets and information are available at **Falcon Tours**, Argonafton 34 **(**☎ **0421/21-626)**.

• By Car From National Road 1 follow Highway 6 (E-87) or 30 east.

ESSENTIALS The Thessaly region **EOT** (Greek Tourist Organization) is on Rígas Feréos Square (Platía Ríga Feréou), open Monday through Friday from 7am to 2:30pm (☎ **0421/23-500** or **36-233**). When it's closed, there is much useful information posted outside on the bulletin board. The **tourist police** (☎ **27-094**), open from 8am to 2:30pm daily, are on the second floor of the police station, at Odós 28 Oktovrióu 179. There are several **banks** around Argonáfton, Iásonos, and Dimitriádos Streets, but none keeps extended hours; travel offices will cash traveler's checks. The **post office** is at Odós Pávlou Melá 67 (about four blocks inland from the port); the telephone center (**OTE**) is nearby, on Venizélou Street, open 24 hours. Emergency **medical assistance** can be obtained at the Vólos Hospital by calling **27-531.**

Several years before the Trojan War, Jason set sail on the *Argo* from his father's kingdom of Iolkos in search of the Golden Fleece. On board with him were 55 sailors, including such luminaries as Theseus, Orpheus, Heracles, Asclepius, Castor, and Pollux. Jason returned from Colchis with the Golden Fleece and the woman who'd helped procure it, the enchantress Medea. Medea was only the first in a long line of romantic conquests that included Hypsiple, queen of Lemnos, and Glauce, daughter of the king of Corinth. When Jason finally abandoned Medea, she killed their two sons and fled to Athens. Her tale is eloquently told by Euripides and Seneca.

High on the slopes of Mt. Pelion (Pílion or, more commonly, Pílio) is Áno Vólos, a hill village where some 18th-century tower houses (similar to the Máni towers in the Peloponnese) still protect inhabitants from raiding pirates. It's thought that this was the ancient Iolkos, and in the wooded forests above it, the cave where Chiron (Cheiron) the Centaur lived. Jason was only one of the remarkable heroes that Chiron schooled in the finer arts. Achilles, Heracles, Asclepius, Aeneas, and Peleus all sat at his hooves (according to Homer) and listened to the wisdom of the half-man, half-horse creature. Although most centaurs were renowned for their bawdy behavior and drunkenness, Chiron was an expert at music, shooting, and the medicinal use of herbs and plants for which Mt. Pelion is still justly famed. (It was he who cut the spear, or **pelios,** from one of the pine trees on Mt. Pelion that saved the life of Achilles.) All the centaurs were known to live in the Pelion region, where they frolicked and wreaked havoc with pretty river nymphs and wood fairies who inhabited the lush, verdant highlands. Their high jinks kept the area from ever becoming overpopulated, and anyone touring one of the most beautiful, scenic regions in Greece will have much to thank them for.

Vólos

These stories from mythology constitute the only appeal that the modern-day city of Vólos will have for many. Because of the devastation of two earthquakes in 1955, today's rows of concrete housing, functional commercial buildings, and an active but unattractive port are what confront the visitor. However, it's the gateway to the Sporades islands of Skíathos, Skópelos, and Alónissos (Skýros is more easily reached from Kými, Évvia). Once touched by Pelion's wooded, fairyland beauty, you may decide to sample these equally blessed, verdant islands and leave the sun-bleached, arid Cyclades to others.

ORIENTATION

Whether you're arriving by train (at Papadiamánti Street) or by bus, you'll be within a five-minute walk of Rígas Feréos Square, the city's tourist center. A sidelong glance will bring the International Pier into view; walk along the waterfront to reach **Argonáfton Street,** a catchy name for the main piers from where the Sporades ferries and hydrofoils leave, and where you'll find the most attractive and expensive hotels and cafés. If you continue on a long walk (25 minutes) east along the water, past Platía Geórgiou (a pleasant park) and past the church of Ághios Konstantínos, you'll come to the **Archeological Museum,** on Athanasáki Street (open Tuesday to Saturday from 8:30am to 3pm, Sundays and holidays 9:30am to 2:30pm. Admission 440 Drs ($1.80), famous for its permanent exhibition of prehistoric finds from throughout Thessaly, as well as painted funerary stelae from the Hellenistic village of Dimítris.

GETTING AROUND

BY BUS From Vólos there are five buses daily to the Kalá Nerá/Miliés/Vizítsa area; at Vizítsa, the bus turns around and continues down to the east coast beaches of Pelion. Miliés is a pleasant, 15-minute walk downhill from Vizítsa. Makrinítsa, Portaria, and Chaniá are easily reached by ten daily buses from Vólos.

BY CAR Renting a car is probably the most convenient way for a group to sightsee in the Mt. Pelion region. We recommend **Europcar,** at Odós Iásonos 79 (☎ **0421/36-238** or **24-381,** fax 0421/24-192); day rates are about 13,475 Drs ($56.15) for a compact car, including tax and mileage.

WHERE TO STAY & EAT

The only place to stay when you're in centaur land is in the hills of Mt. Pelion. Since we understand that there's always someone who will prefer a bed nearest the ferryboat, train, or bus, here are some suggestions.

Hotel Iason, Odós Pávlou Melá 1, Vólos 38001. ☎ **0421/26-075.**
32 rms (12 with bath). TEL

Rates (including breakfast): 5,500 Drs ($22.90) single; 7,700 Drs ($32.10) double. No credit cards.

The best deal around the port is the older Hotel Iáson (Jason). The friendly manager keeps a tidy place, whose spacious rooms have tidy bathrooms and balconies with port views.

Hotel Kipseli, Odós Aghíou Nikoláou 1, Vólos 38001. ☎ **0421/24-420** or **26-020.** 54 rms (34 with bath). TEL

Rates (including breakfast): 7,920 Drs ($33) single; 8,800 Drs ($36.70) double without bath, 9,700 Drs ($40.80) double. No credit cards.

Hotel Kipséli is situated in the upscale section of the Vólos waterfront (to your right as you leave the ferry), where the rooms—some with harbor views—are fine. The people at the front desk are friendly and accommodating. Their cafeteria is also quite good.

Hotel Philippos, Odós Sólonos 9 at Odós Dimitriádos, Vólos 39001. ☎ **0421/37-607.** Fax 0421/395-50. 39 rms (all with bath). TEL

Rates (including breakfast): 7,700 Drs ($32.10) single; 11,330 Drs ($47.20) double. No credit cards.

This recently built addition to the Vólos skyline, two blocks from the port back toward Rígas Feréos Square, has quiet, comfortable rooms, a good breakfast served in an attractive place, and a friendly manager who speaks English.

Picknickers may fare best here. Try the markets along Iásonos (Jason's) Street; it's one block in from the water. The only eatery we can enthusiastically recommend is **Tzafoliás Grill** (☎ 29-626) at Odós Argonáfton 40. A dining suggestion in the unremarkable cuisine culture of Vólos: Try Dímitra retsína—it's locally made and widely acknowledged to be the best in Greece.

Exploring the Pelion Hills

The area around Mt. Pelion is popular with Greeks, who rush up on long winter weekends or for the traditional Easter ceremonies. Leaving Vólos, the air is immediately cooler and fresher, and within minutes the scent of pines and basil eradicates the fumes of commercial industry. You'll find that the farther you climb, especially when you reach the other side of the 5,305-foot massif, the more beautiful and timeless the scenery becomes.

KATICHÓRI

You'll pass through the pretty village of Anakassia on the way to **Katichóri.** Tucked up off the main road are a few traditional, "Pelion-style" houses lining narrow cobblestone streets. Local citizens stroll through their village, skinned lambs ready for roasting tossed over their shoulders, oblivious of the occasional tourist. Right on the side of the road is one of those special places worth coming to for a quiet and peaceful stay in the old Greek style, the **Guest House Matsangou** (☎ **0421/99-380,** fax 35-030). Lily Matsangou's nine rooms are, like the exterior of the mansion, renovated in the traditional Pelion style. High-ceilinged, stucco-walled rooms have wood and flagstone floors, antique handcrafted furnishings, woven rugs, and tall, plush-mattressed beds. Grapevines grow over the trellis-roofed patio that overlooks the Pelion range and pine forests decending into the sea, a view undisturbed by modern life. The Matsangou is open year-round, but Lily requires a minimum booking to open in winter. Doubles with shared bath are 9,900 Drs ($41.25).

PORTARÍA

Some 3 km from Katichóri is **Portaría** (altitude 600 meters), where a 13th-century chapel of the Virgin stands next to a mid-18th-century church of Ághios Nikólaos. A modern Xenía Hotel intrudes on the mansions, whose roofs have been restored to their original gray slate (villagers usually opt for the cheaper, red terra-cotta tiles). Around the picturesque square of this "commercial" center are a small bank, a post office, and some rooms to let. A fountain, dated "1927," offers delicious spring water; it's located at the bend in the road, under the aging plane tree. Portaría is far enough into the mysterious Pelion world to provide endless hikes and walks leading pleasantly to nowhere. And there's an attractive hotel right here. The stone walls of the **Hotel Pelias** (☎ **0421/99-290** and **99-291**, **99-175**) blend well with the quiet village square; inside, contemporary paintings and a handsome fireplace grace the inviting lobby. Doubles with bath and balcony run 11,000 Drs ($45.80) in summer, including breakfast (Visa accepted).

MAKRINÍTSA

Some 17 km from Vólos is **Makrinítsa,** the star village of Pelion. It's the most traditional; centered around the charming Iríni (Peace) Square are three-story mansions, fountains, and spectacular old plane trees (one's so large you can walk into it!). The stone facade of the tiny church of Ághios Ioánnis is decorated with ornate marble plaques. Next to it is a marble fountain where fresh cold water rushes from the mouths of bronze chimeras. Right on the square, facing the church and fountain on one side and the breathtaking valley view on the other, is the Pantheon Café (☎ **99-143**).

Whether you've come to spend the night or not, Makrinítsa is the perfect place to sample the laudable restoration work being done by the Greek government. Three mansions have already been restored and are used as hotels. The **Archontiko Sisilianou** (☎ **0421/99-556**) is located up the cobblestone steps behind the church of Ághios Ioánnis. This mansion has a simple white stucco interior that's enlivened by traditional, dark earth-tone woven fabrics, gray slatted-wood doors and window shutters. Bed-and-breakfast doubles at all three restored *archontiká* are 13,183 Drs ($57.60).

Farther west from Iríni Square is the **Archontiko Mousli** (☎ **0421/99-228**), whose best feature is the immaculate slate-paved patio shaded by plum and plane trees. The tall stone mansion is capped with a second-story façade broken up by old wooden shutters and beautiful stained-glass windowpanes. The **Archontiko Xiradaki** (☎ **0421/99-250**) is below the road on the left before you reach the square.

Our great find was the **Hotel Diomidis** (☎ **0421/99-430** or **99-090,** fax 99-114). Just follow the signs to the Sisilianoú Mansion and you'll walk first into Diomídis' courtyard! The Roútsos have decorated the house cheerfully in traditional Pelion style, and each floor has a floor-length, late-night sitting lounge. Room no. 10 is the double to ask for; it has a balcony overlooking Vólos and the sea, right to the Sporades (8,470 Drs ($35.30) single, 9,680 Drs ($40.30) double.

The souvenir to buy from this region is honey, but nuts and homemade fruit preserves are also widely available and delicious. Makrinítsa is also famous for selling fresh herbs (some 2,000 kinds!) gathered on Mt. Pelion.

Continuing from Portaría through 9 km of chestnut trees, evergreens, and hairpin turns brings us to **Chaniá,** at 1,200 meters, the ski center of the region. You can contact the Ski Center in Agrioléfkes nearby (☎ **96417**) for ski information, or the Mountaineering Club Lodge (☎ **25-696** in Vólos), which sponsors area hikes and climbs. There's a **youth hostel** operating in Chaniá sporadically throughout the year; call **96-416** for information.

MILIÉS

In Pelion, the largest plane tree, the public fountain that sustains its neighbors, the central church, and a few tavernas usually mark the heart of a village. These days there's a news kiosk, a mailbox, sometimes a pay phone, and occasionally a taxi stand or bus stop to complement the facilities.

Miliés, 31 km south of Vólos, is no exception, with an outstanding **library** facing the village square. Two stories of historical volumes reflect the high degree of literacy and learning that has always existed in Pelion. (In the library's bookshop you can purchase a wonderful book of photographs of the region's traditional architecture.) The library is open Tuesday through Saturday from 8am to 1:30pm and 5 to 7pm; Sunday, 10am to 1pm. Next door is the small **town hall** and around the corner, a well-designed **folk museum.** Director Fay Stamatis has documented the family workshops crafting natural dyes, weaving, tin work, and saddleries that still function in Miliés. Opening hours vary but are posted on the front door; 20-minute cassette tours in English are available.

If you're ready to tackle some short local hikes, head down the hill through the village to the ramshackle mill house and abandoned train station. The railway tracks used to service Miliés, Vizítsa, and other villages all the way back to Vólos, and there's some hope that service will be revived. Until then, a stroll along the tracks through these green woods, roaring waterfalls, and gently sloped hills is quite rewarding.

Miliés is a wonderful place to while away time during Greece's dog days of summer. Residents can guide you down the village's stone steps to a well-kept traditional tower with a low wooden door. Knock and your hosts will lead you upstairs to several bedrooms and sitting rooms with polished wooden floors, woven drapes, hooked rugs, lead windows, and finely carved moldings. Many of the eight rooms have fireplaces, all have fresh flowers, and all overlook fields of goats, strolling farmers, rustling pines, and a valley frozen in time. A high-season double costs 13,815 Drs ($57.80). Or you can drive (slowly) down the small, partly paved road right off the hairpin turn as you leave the town to **O Palios Stathmos** (Old Station) **Guesthouse** (☎ **0423/86-425**), a modern, three-story hotel across from the local landmark from which it takes its name; a double with bath costs 10,450 Drs ($43.50).

O Stathmos is also a popular local taverna. They serve the freshest, creamiest tzatzíki we've ever had and the Italian chef makes a tender beef in lemon sauce with herbed peas and crisp potatoes. With the house wine and a fresh salad, this is a real treat for two at 2,750 Drs ($11.50). There's another taverna on the main square, next to the playground, with live music after 10pm nightly.

VIZÍTSA

Vizítsa, west of Miliés, is an even more fulfilling destination, with its own square lined with plane trees, a central fountain, churches, and tavernas. The plus here is the well-organized presence of the national tourist organization EOT, which has opened eight restored mansions and guesthouses for rent. Most are located on the right up from the main road, where signs point to the **Reception Guesthouse** (☎ **0423/86-373**). This reception also serves as the local folk-art museum; so, those passing through should stop in to see their collection of snowshoes, clothing, utensils, and tools. A total of 60 beds are available; doubles with private baths rent for 13,750

Drs ($57.30) including breakfast. The main guesthouse serves breakfast for all in a common dining room as well as a scrumptious baklavá and spirits such as *tsipouro* (strong, locally brewed ouzo).

Among the few inhabited homes are several decrepit mansions with caved-in roofs (a continual problem with slate), broken windows, and eroded stone siding that contrasts vividly with the lovely, restored ones used as hotels. If you go to Vizítsa, don't drink the water gushing down the main stone street to the bus stop. Instead, let the old Vizitsians, sitting at the café/bar in the square above, usher you to another spring. On the way, you can sample the tunes on their aging Greek jukebox.

Exploring the Pelion Beaches

After several kilometers of hairpin turns down from Makrinítsa, a left fork will take you through apple orchards to **Zagóra,** the largest town of Pelion, where traditional and more recent houses are scattered on the hillsides that slope down to the tilled fields in the valley below. Taking the right fork leads to the cutoff for **Ághios Ioánnis,** 7 km away. Every hotel, taverna, and campground in this small, easygoing community is a stone's throw from the water's edge without spoiling its natural beauty. Fresh fish, a lively nightlife, and a sandy beach keep travelers happy, and since it's off the beaten track it may remain this peaceful for a few more years.

The **Captain George Hotel and Bar** (☎ **0426/31-297**) is well known because of its colorful manager, Freddie Kourkouvellos, who spent many years in Boston. Double rooms with bath and American-style breakfast are 11,000 Drs ($45.80). Media freaks will appreciate the phone in every room and availability of TV and VCR with almost-current films. Between them, Captain George's crew speak Chinese, Portuguese, English, and Greek.

A possible splurge in this region would be the **Aloe Hotel** (☎ **0426/31-421**), where well-furnished, comfortable doubles cost 19,250 Drs ($80.20). Hearty meals are served on an elegant stone terrace or inside next to a wall of windows overlooking the sea. On the low end, there are many rooms to let advertised in the village and widely available for about 6,600 Drs ($27.50).

Following the road south brings you through Makrirráchi to Tsangaráda, midway on the Pelion coast and 62 km from Vólos. Trucks of hay tangle up traffic (only one passes at a time); donkeys carrying bundles of wood and old ladies out picking herbs vie for a portion of roadway. **Milopótamos,** 8 km from Tsangaráda as the road forks east, is considered one of the prettiest, unspoiled beach areas of Pelion. It's a broad sandy stretch interrupted at intervals by surf crashing over the rocks. On the hillside, about 2 km from the beach road, is a unique guesthouse, clinging to the cliffs. The **Milopotamos Guesthouse** (☎ **0421/49-203**) has over a dozen double rooms whose balconies face the sea; rates are 7,700 Drs ($32.10) for two. Local residents sent us to their favorite gourmet restaurant—a cookout! We bought fresh fish from near the beach, grabbed a loaf of fresh bread, and headed to the grill to cook it, all the while sipping a fine local retsína and chopping pungent fresh tomatoes and canteloupe.

En Route to Kalambáka

The 60 km between Vólos and Lárissa on the toll motorway pass quickly. Lots of watermelon, heat, and unpaved roads make Lárissa feel like a midwestern cow town on a summer's day—in other words, a place to breeze through. It is a well-connected transportation hub, and there are several recently built hotels, but we think you'd do better to continue on.

TRÍKKALA

From Lárissa, head due west to Tríkkala. Here's another 60 km drive one could do without; however, any route that shortens the way to Kalambáka and the legendary monasteries of Metéora is okay with us. Tríkkala, a friendly town of some interest, is thought to be the birthplace of Asclepius, the god of Medicine. In the southwest part of town, Hellenistic-era walls and Roman baths mark the site of the oldest Asclepion in Greece. The ancient Doris became the Homeric city of Tríkki; it rose near the acropolis built above the Lítheos River. A rather picturesque Venetian fortress sits on St. Nicholas Heights, south of the city, and an old Muslim mosque can be found near the bus station.

GETTING THERE & GETTING AROUND

Buses run from Athens to Tríkkala seven times daily, departing from the terminal at Odós Liossíon 260 (☎ **83-11-434**); between Tríkkala and Lárissa there's a bus every half hour. Bus service to Vólos runs four times daily, to Kalambáka every 20 minutes all day, to Ioánnina two times daily, and to Metéora directly three times daily. There are five **trains** daily which pass through Kardítsa, departing from Athens's Stathmós Laríssis (☎ **01/82-13-882** or **041/236-259** in Lárissa).

WHERE TO STAY & EAT

The **Hotel Lithaeon,** Odós Óthonos 10 (☎ **0431/28-091**), conveniently located at Tríkkala's bus station, is surprisingly pleasant; doubles with breakfast are 8,100 Drs $33. A budget alternative is the small, older **Hotel Palladion,** Odós Výronos 4 (☎ **0431/20-690**), a couple of blocks toward the river, where simple, clean doubles with shared toilet facilities cost 6,785 Drs ($28).

If you're overnighting in Tríkkala, you'll want to find King George Square (Platía Vassiléos Gheorghíou) on the banks of the river for some nightlife, tavernas, and local color. From the bus station, follow the curving riverbed away from the abandoned mosque. The **Panorama Café,** atop the tallest building in town, is a good place for a drink. Our friends recommend **Taverna Psatha,** on Kitrilákis Square, for the best traditional taverna fare.

FROM TRÍKKALA TO KALAMBÁKA

The 29 km of highway left before you reach Kalambáka build up the suspense in a very theatrical fashion. "What could Metéora possibly look like?" you're wondering. Don't worry—when you're getting near Kalambáka the signs will make it all too obvious: CAMPING ROCKS, CAMPING PERILOUS BOULDER, CAMPING WONDERS OF THE EARTH.

6 Kalambáka

220 miles NW of Athens

GETTING THERE • By Train There are six trains daily to Athens (three expresses, which cut the 6-hour trip by two hours) and seven from Athens's Laríssis station (☎ **01/82-13-882**). There are also four trains daily to and from Thessaloníki, and two trains daily to and from Vólos. Tickets can be bought at the Kalambáka station (☎ **22-451**).

• By Bus Seven buses from Athens to Tríkkala departing daily from the terminal at Odós Liossíon 260 (☎ **83-11-434**). Between Tríkkala and Kalambáka there's a bus every 20 minutes all day, and to Metéora directly there's one three times daily. (In Kalambáka ☎ **22-432.**)

• **By Car** From National Road 1 take Highway 6 (E-87) west; or 80 from Lamía Highway 3 north to Néo Monastíri, then take Highway 30 northwest through Kardítsa and Tríkkala.

ESSENTIALS The **police** (☎ **22-109**) can be found near the bus station on Chatzipétrou Street. The **post office** is one block above Central Square. The telephone center (**OTE**) is at Odós Kastakíou 27, on the right on the road to Metéora. Call 22-222 for **medical emergencies.**

In this part of Thessaly the two great mountain ranges of Pindus (Píndos) and Ossa split apart to let the Pínios River flow into the Vale of Tempi, and from there to the sea. Kalambáka, at the foot of the Pindus massif, sits at the point where the Pínios reaches the level valley floor; the unique rock formations of Metéora are thought to be the heavily eroded riverbed of the Pínios dating from a time when it was a much more active and deeper river. It is said that the monks from Metéora believe that during the time of Noah's ark all of Thessaly was under water, which has disappeared as the result of an earthquake. In much the same way that the ark landed on the peak of Mt. Ararat when the waters receded, the persecuted monks of the Convent of Stagón built their churches atop inaccessible pinnacles of time-worn stone. In the 12th century these small religious cells began to draw the devout from all over the Byzantine world, and by the 14th century Metéora was a community of such religious learning, art, and wealth that its only rival was Mt. Áthos. At this point the monks of the monastery of Metéoron (Grand Metéoron, the largest) had freed themselves from the rule of the abbot of the Convent of Stagón and tried to take over control of the other, less influential monasteries in the area. Such in-fighting caused the number of monasteries to decline.

The Turkish occupation of Greece had a favorable effect on Metéora, because Süleyman the Magnificent put strong bishops in charge of Thessaly's ecclesiastical matters. Varlaam and Roussánou were the monasteries that benefited most from the influx of funds and new recruits; their libraries were enriched with new manuscripts, their churches decorated with brilliant frescoes, and their chapels enlarged and refurbished. Over the next few centuries the fortunes of the Metéora monasteries again declined, and now only four (from a high of 24) still function.

Orientation

Kalambáka is a small provincial town, whose main development has occurred in a line along the north-south highway. The monasteries of Metéora are reached via an access road that veers east at the north end of town. Approaching the town from Tríkkala, from the south, you'll pass the campgrounds called Theópetra, International, and Kalambáka (this one's uphill and has better views).

At the south end of the village is a roundabout with several outdoor cafés and small shops circling it; this open area is known as **Rígas Feréos Square.** Within 1 km the main highway runs into another, larger, less commercial area, called **Central Square.** From here the road veers right up to Metéora. The **train station** is just south of town, on the Tríkkala-Ioánnina highway. The **bus station** is up from it at the corner of Plátanos and Oikonómou Streets. There are tavernas on both squares, some hotels near the railroad station, and several hotels in the little streets around Central Square and the road to Metéora, where they can take advantage of the remarkable views.

Getting Around

Kalambáka's **taxi stand** (☎ **22-310**) is on the main street; for about 6,600 Drs ($27.50) you can book a taxi for the 19 km circuit to the six monasteries that are open to visitors, including half an hour's waiting time at each one; the drivers are very knowledgeable. Local buses to Metéora stop at King Paul (Vassiléos Pávlou) Street three times daily, but check with your hotel reception for schedule information.

What to See & Do—The Monasteries of Metéora

If you were to drive the 19 km circular path through the valley of monasteries, you would approach them in this order: Ághios Nikólaos, Roussánou, Metamorphosis or "Grand Metéoron," Óssios Varlaám, Aghía Triás, and Ághios Stéphanos. Below, however, we list them in the order of how important we consider them. Following is some information that will help you plan your tour.

BUS TRANSPORTATION The local Kalambáka bus stops first at the Ághios Nikólaos Monastery. The next and last stop is in front of Metamorphosis (Grand Metéoron); you can walk 150 meters from here to the Óssios Varlaám monastery. To reach the Aghía Triás and Ághios Stéphanos monasteries requires a walk of 5 km along the paved roadway. Buses make this run four times daily; the fare is 225 Drs (95¢). If you don't have a car we recommend taking a taxi around the 19 km circuit for maximum enjoyment.

DRESS CODE MEN IN SHORTS AND WOMEN IN TROUSERS OR SLEEVELESS DRESSES ARE NOT ALLOWED TO ENTER. This sign is posted in front of each monastery and convent, *and the monks are quite serious.*

FOR THE DISABLED The exquisite configuration of Metéora and its monasteries is best appreciated at a distance, but if you want to go inside a monastery, Ághios Stéphanos is the most easily accessible, being just 20 meters across a footbridge (wheelchair capable) from the paved road. The easiest climb up is the three-minute hike to Óssios Varlaám, which has lovely examples of frescoes and religious objects that are found in the others. If you have only a one solid ten-minute hike left in you, then you **must** see the area's largest creation, the Metamorphosis (Grand Metéoron).

Metamorphosis (Grand Metéoron), Kalambáka 42200. ☎ **22-278.**

The first monastery of Metéora was founded by St. Athanássios, a monk from Mt. Áthos, between 1356 and 1372. The church was built atop Platý Líthos (Broad Stone), one of the largest flat-topped rock formations. Metéoron achieved its autonomy and religious authority after the king of Serbia's son became a monk there. The new monk, Joasaf, ensured royal donations to the monastery's coffers, making Metéoron the most wealthy and powerful of the existing units. The sanctuary was enlarged in the middle of the 16th century to the size of the present-day church. It's decorated with colorful frescoes, elaborately carved wood, and an inlaid ivory pedestal for the bishop. Notice the particularly gruesome images in the narthex of the saints being tortured.

The museum is housed in the old dining room, part of the 16th-century addition to the original monastery. The museum contains a collection of rare manuscripts; most are modest illuminations of the Gospel and the Book of St. John, dating from between the 9th and 16th centuries. Next to the museum is the old kitchen that once served meals for the guests of Meteoron Hostel. Leaving the museum and church, turn left at the base of the stairs. A small wooden door with a hole large enough for your head contains a bizarre array of the skulls of monks who served the monastery long ago.

Admission: 440 Drs ($1.85).

Open: Wed–Mon 9am–1pm and 3:20–6pm.

Óssios Varlaám, Kalambáka 42200. ☎ **22-277.**

The monastery of Óssios Varlaám, about 150 meters from Grand Metéoron, is an easier walk up, and well worth a visit. The stone corridors are filled with admonitory signs: DO NOT MAKE NOISE, NO SMOKING, PRIVATE ENTRY; but the lovely flowering garden softens the austerity of the place. The frescoes in the chapel (on the right) were done by Franco Catellano in 1565, 48 years after the monastery's founding by two wealthy brothers from Ioánnina. These frescoes were restored in 1870.

Admission: 330 Drs ($1.40).

Open: Sat–Thurs 9am–1pm and 3:20–6pm.

Águios Nikólaos, Kalambáka 42200. ☎ **22-375.**

The first monastery you'll come to on the road north from Kalambáka (and the first bus stop) is Águios Nikólaos, perched on a lone rock towering above the road. You'll have to climb up there to see it (notice the pulley-and-basket system the monks once used), but the stairs can easily be managed in ten minutes. Halfway up, the path forks; a wonderful painted sign, now faded badly, indicates a young man and woman walking up the stairs to the left and an old hobbled couple with canes using the ramp to the right. (On our last trip, there were two donkey meisters offering to take visitors up for a small fee.)

Águios Nikólaos is no longer inhabited and gets few visitors, making it the nicest of the monasteries because of its intimacy. The monastery was built in 1388 and later expanded. Its small chapel is filled with excellent frescoes by the Cretan School painter Theophánes the Monk (done in 1527), which are low enough for close study. The chapel's ornately painted and carved-wood ceiling is in surprisingly good condition. We heartily recommend Águios Nikólaos to sightseers with energy to spare after Metéoron.

Admission: 330 Drs ($1.40).

Open: Daily 9am–6pm.

Roussánou, Kalambáka 42200. No telephone.

This precariously perched nunnery, open to the public since 1989, was accessible until last year only by a series of ladders. Now there is a path, staircase, and bridge to Roussánou and its bevy of smiling nuns—we suspect that they're delighted to have guests. The monastery is thought to have been built in the late 13th century as a hermitage and has been rebuilt and restored in recent times. It became a monastery by decree in 1545. The highlight here is the 16th-century Cretan frescoes depicting gory scenes of martyred saints. Highly recommended.

Admission: 330 Drs ($1.40).

Open: Daily 9am–1pm and 3–6pm.

Águios Stéphanos, Kalambáka 42200. ☎ **22-279.**

The convent of Águios Stéphanos, a hermitage founded by Jeremias in 1312, is the most southeasternly one open at Metéora. The frescoless church has obviously been renovated, but the presence of a nun studying in the back pews by the old wood stove adds a great deal of ambience. Águios Stéphanos was transformed into a monastery in the 1330s by Emperor Andrónicus III Paleológos. We guess that this monastery is so popular with tour groups because it's directly accessible from the roadway. A small museum inside displays ecclesiastical items such as robes, painted icons, and documents, but you may have to wait in line to get a peek.

Admission: 330 Drs ($1.40).
Open: Tues–Sun 9am–1pm and 3–6pm.

Aghía Triás, Kalambáka 42200. ☎ **22-220.**

The convent of Aghía Triás (Holy Trinity, also Aghía Triáda), founded by the monk Dométios in 1438, is perhaps the most amazing sight of Metéora. Its solitary placement is bewildering. Aghía Triás is approached by 139 steep steps. After you've rested long enough to enter, you can see in the first room the platform, attached to guide wires, that swings out to the nearby plateau to bring back materials and people. Inside, the small chapel is filled with frescoes, which are, sadly, blackened by the smoke from votive candles and the modern heater.

Aghía Triás, on its lone, seemingly inaccessible peak, was the star location of *For Your Eyes Only,* a James Bond movie. The monastery is a superb construction that's best admired from afar, and for most its interior is just not worth the climb.

Admission: 300 Drs ($1.30).
Open: Daily 8am–1pm and 3–6:30pm.

Byzantine Church of the Assumption, Kalambáka 42200. No phone.

This church is worth a visit for anyone spending time in Kalambáka. It's located on the highest street in the village, Koimós Theotókou. The church was built in the 7th century and restored in 1326, and is the only three-aisled basilica of its type other than Haghía Sophía in Istanbul. The worn frescoes inside are the work of the Cretan monk Neóphytos, son of the Theophánes who painted the fine frescoes in the Ághios Nikólaos monastery. Inside is an ancient sun throne, where the bishop and local priests sat to address the congregation. In a corner of the apse, closed to the lay public, are mosaic fragments of a peacock image (perhaps from the Roman era). A brief history of the church, in several languages, is available at the door. When we visited, a local religious holiday was being celebrated and all the women in their traditional black cotton, apron-covered dresses insisted on giving us cookies and servings of a delicious wheat, walnuts, and cinnamon cereal called ***kóliva.*** It was one of those surprise moments that make Greece so delightful.

Where to Stay

Hotel Aeolic Star, Odós Diákou 4, Kalambáka 42200. ☎☎ **0432/22-325.**
Fax 0432/23-031. 18 rms (9 with bath). TEL

Rates (including breakfast): 4,290 to 5,885 Drs ($17.90–$24.50) single; 5,500 to 8,800 Drs ($22.90–$36.70) double with/without bath. No credit cards.

The friendly Papadeli family will make you feel at home above the central square. They don't have a lobby so much as a large living room where you're welcome to join family and friends. The rooms are comfortable and clean, all with balconies, some with views of Metéora.

★ **Hotel Antoniadi,** Odós Trikkálon 148, Kalambáka 42200. ☎ **0432/24-387.**
Fax 0432/24-319. 24 rms (all with bath). TEL

Rates (including breakfast): 8,800 Drs ($36.70) single; 11,500 Drs ($47.90) double. V.

Although it doesn't have views of Metéora, Antoniádi is the best all-around hotel in town, with superior accommodations, a friendly staff, congenial atmosphere, and excellent food in its restaurant—which is recommended even for those not staying there.

Hotel Astoria, Odós Kondíli 93, Kalambáka 42200. ☎ **0432/22-213.**
10 rms (6 with bath).

Rates: 3,300–5,500 Drs ($13.75–$22.90) single with/without bath; 5,500–8,800 Drs ($22.90–$36.70) double. No credit cards.

Astoria is a smaller and older hotel, just half a block up from the train station. Its rooms are large, clean, and comfortable—especially good for a family. The friendly owner, who speaks good English, informed us it was named for the Waldorf Astoria where his father used to work!

Hotel Helvetia, Odós Kastrakíou 45, Kalambáka 42200. ☎ **0432/23-041.**
18 rms (all with bath). TEL

Rates (including breakfast): 7,370 Drs ($30.70) single; 8,850 Drs ($36.90) double with bath. V.

Up the monastery road is the clean, Class C Hotel Helvetia. Its upper-floor rooms have a view across the street to the pockmarked "cave" rocks where many hermits had hidden homes. The Helvetia has pleasant rooms. Christos and Vassiliki Gasos are hosts who encourage camaraderie among guests in their café/bar. Their son often works at the reception desk, and he speaks English.

Hotel Rex, Odós Kastrakíou 11, Kalambáka 42200. ☎ **0432/22-042.** Fax 0432/22-372.
35 rms (all with bath). TEL

Rates (including breakfast): 5,500–7,700 Drs ($22.90–$32.10) double. No credit cards.

The best value is near downtown, on the road to Metéora. It's a quiet hotel, recently repainted (although not as well kept as others in this category), with large rooms, attractive furniture, and the most comfortable beds in town.

Where to Eat

$ **O Kipos Taverna,** Odós Trikkálon. ☎ **23-218.**

Cuisine: GREEK.

Prices: Main courses 770–1,320 Drs ($3.20–$5.50). No cards.

Open: Daily 7:30pm–2am.

This traditional taverna, called The Garden, at the east edge of town, on the road to Tríkkala, is picture perfect. It serves nothing ready-made, and plays authentic Greek music you're welcome to dance to. Its charcoal-broiled chicken is among the best we've ever tasted.

Santa Lucia Pizza, Odós Trikkálon 85. ☎ **23-024.**

Prices: Pizza 1,210–1,870 Drs ($5–$7.80). No credit cards.

Open: Daily 11am–3pm and 5pm–midnight.

If you're hungry for something American (Italian-style), Santa Lucia has 15 kinds of pizza, five kinds of spaghetti, and 10 kinds of salads, as well as Greek dishes—and they deliver.

7 Mt. Olympus Region

GETTING THERE • By Train There are seven **trains** daily to Lárissa or Kateríni, departing from Athens's Stathmós Caríssis (☎ **01/82-13-882**).

• By Bus Four buses to Kateríni (get off at Litochóro) depart daily from Athens's terminal at Odós Liossíon 260 (☎ **83-17-059**); seven buses go daily from Athens to Lárissa (☎ **83-17-109**), where you can catch a frequent local bus to Litochóro.

• **By Car** Take National Road 1 for 70 km north of Lárissa; Litochóro is 10 km east of the highway.

ESSENTIALS Litochóro is the jumping-off point for the climb up Mt. Olympus. The **Federation of Mountaineering and Skiing** has a regional office at Central Square (Kentrikí Platía) (☎ **0352/81-944**) in Litochóro; or you can call the federation in Athens at **0132/34-555.** The federation maintains four refuges on Olympus: one at Spílios Agapitós (altitude 2,100 meters, 22 km from Litochóro); on the eastern face of Olympus at Vryssopoúles (altitude 1,900 meters); a 15-bed refuge at King Paul (altitude 2,700 meters, 1½ hours away from Spílios Agapitós); and at Stavrós (altitude 1,000 meters, 1½ hours from Litochóro), which is maintained by the **Thessaloniki Alpine Club** (☎ **031/224-710**). There are some English-speaking guides available in Litochóro.

From Kalambáka, the road continues west to the picturesque hill village of Métsovo, and 125 km later to Ioánnina. This is the province of Epirus (Ipiros), bounded by the Pindus Range to the east and the Ionian Sea to the west, a region of varied and lush scenic beauty.

There's an active SCENIC ATTRACTION road stop at **Aghía Paraskeví,** where you'll see hundreds of cars parked and Greek men pulling their children and wives by the hand across the busy highway to the shaded rocks and gushing waterfall. A narrow footbridge crosses the river: to one side is a modern chapel; on the other, a pleasant café and souvenir shops selling tokens of Paradise.

Continuing north of the vale, one can't help noticing the near-perfect facade of an impressive castle. It crowns the hill above **Platamónas,** from which it guarded the Gulf of Thermae. The castle was built between 1204 and 1222 by the Crusaders, and was spared by the Turks only because they used it to guard against pirates from the east. About 70 km north of Lárissa is the tiny village of **Litochóro,** at the base of Greece's legendary Mt. Olympus, 2,917 meters high.

Mt. Olympus, the equivalent of Heaven or the Top of the Sky for the ancients, was, of course, home of the gods. Apollodorus and Homer tell of the Gigantomachy, the War between the Giants (sons of Uranus, or Sky, and Gaia, or Earth) and the Olympians. The Giants were the creators of our cosmos, the ordered world created from chaos. Their many sons, the Titans, included the one-eyed monster Cyclops. His brother Cronus eventually led an uprising of Titans to take over leadership of the cosmos. Uranus predicted that someday Cronus too would lose his throne to one of his sons. Each time his wife, Rhea (the Earth Mother), bore him a child, Cronus swallowed it whole to forestall the outcome of Uranus's prediction. Finally, when her sixth child was born, Rhea dressed a large stone in baby clothes and fed it to Cronus. Her hidden son, Zeus, was given to the goat Amalthea, to be raised in Crete. When Zeus reached manhood, his mother helped him to feed a special potion to Cronus, which made him throw up the other five children, all gods, who were ready to do battle. Zeus (with the help of his siblings) took over Cronus's kingdom and established his home on Greece's highest peak, Olympus. Homer describes the attempt made by the Giants to return the attack: "Ossa they strove to set upon Olympus, and upon Ossa leafy Pelion, so that the heavens might be scaled." Zeus had cunningly enlisted the aid of the Cyclops, uncle of Cronus, who forged for him the powerful thunderbolt that became his symbol. Wrote Ovid about the battle's outcome: "Then the omnipotent Father with his thunder made Olympus tremble, and from Ossa hurled Pelion." Thus was Mt. Olympus secured for the gods, and it wasn't until 1913 that a mortal dared to scale its highest peak.

12

The Sporades

GREEKS HAVE BEEN VACATIONING ON THE SPORADES FOR YEARS, ATTRACTED BY fragrant pine trees growing down to the edge of golden sand beaches. Few foreign tourists ventured to any of the Sporades, preferring the well-trodden paths leading to the Cyclades. With so few foreign visitors, prices stayed low and hotels and restaurants remained relatively empty. It was only a matter of time before this idyllic state of affairs would come to an end. Groups began to visit Skiáthos, and later Skópelos. An airport was built on Skiáthos with flights going back and forth from Athens several times a day and, in the summer, up to 50 charter flights a week from Europe; now there are two hydrofoil services linking the islands as well as connecting them to several mainland ports. Still, with all the development and change, nothing has altered the Sporades' most basic appeal. The islands are as lush as ever, with plum, fig, olive, grape, and almond orchards planted in the midst of pine and plane forests. The long crescent-shaped beaches—some sandy, others of polished snow-white stones—are superior to nearly any in the Aegean islands.

Skiáthos and Skópelos are to the Sporades what Rhodes and Kos or Mýkonos and Páros are to their respective groups: the most popular islands, with excellent beaches, chic boutiques, a cosmopolitan following, and great scenic allure. Alónissos is less developed for tourism, but has many of the attractions of its more famous neighbors. Skýros, more remote, is a Cycladic look-alike with whitewashed cube architecture, an arid landscape, and some terrific beaches. It's an ideal destination for those who want to get away from the crowd.

The Sporades have traditionally been one of Greece's best-value destinations, which seemed to maintain lower rates for nearly everything, especially in comparison with the Cyclades and other popular destinations. That has changed. The Sporades, especially Skiáthos and Skópelos, are among the most expensive islands in Greece, yet we still come away feeling that a visit to these Aegean islands represents excellent value for the money.

Seeing the Sporades

As among the Dodecanese and Saronic Gulf islands, so among the Sporades (see the map of Central Greece in Chapter 11) one can go to any island from any other island at almost any time of day. Excursion boats and hydrofoils run constantly from early morning to mid-evening; rarely in the summer will you have to wait more than an hour.

This efficient state of affairs is bolstered by the operation of the **Flying Dolphins,** a fleet of yellow-and-blue Russian-built hydrofoils that fly on the surface of the water at more than twice the speed of a normal ferry, and a competitor from the Nomikos line, the **Ikarus.** The **Ceres Company's** huge new Flying Cat hydrocatamarans are even more comfortable and faster! The cabin is laid out like the interior of an airplane, with bucket seats, fore-and-aft sections, and even food and beverage service in first class.

IMPRESSIONS

The sea is absolutely smooth, sometimes violet, sometimes blue, glistening in patches with a fine grain of silver; and the islands of all sizes . . . seem not to rise out of the water but to be plaqued on it like cuff links on cuffs.

—Edmund Wilson, *Europe Without Baedeker,* 1947

What's Special About the Sporades

Beaches

- The long, broad stretches at Koukounaries and Lalaria beaches on Skiáthos are among Greece's best and most dramatic.
- Skýros has many long, sandy beaches such as Magaziá and Mólos.
- There are many uninhabited islands off Alónissos with virtually empty beaches.

Villages

- Visiting the north coast village of Glossa, on Skópelos, will give you a feeling for one of the Sporades' most traditional island settlements.
- The town of Skópelos is among the most architecturally exquisite in all of Greece.
- Skýros's main town is built in a Cycladic style, with whitewashed pillbox houses arranged in a labyrinth-like layout.
- Alónissos' old town is being restored after it was nearly levelled by an earthquake.

Natural Sights

- Mediterranean seals and dolphins are often seen off the coast of Alónissos.
- Alónissos in the recently established Marine Park reserve is a popular place for hikers and backpackers.
- There are dramatic grottos along the coast of Skiáthos.

If you want to travel through the Sporades at a more leisurely pace, there are many ferry and excursion boats and caiques that connect the various islands as well as several mainland ports.

1 Skiáthos

41 nautical miles from Vólos

ARRIVING/DEPARTING • By Air Olympic Airways offers three flights daily from Athens; contact Olympic information in Athens (☎ **961-6161**) for reservations. There is an Olympic Airways office on Skiáthos (☎ **0427/22-200**), but they have suspended bus service from the airport to the town; expect to pay 1,265 Drs ($5.30) by taxi.

• By Sea Skiáthos can be reached by either ferryboat (3 hours) or hydrofoil (75 minutes) from Vólos or Ághios Konstantínos; there is also ferryboat service from Kymi, on Évvia (5 hours). In the high season, there are four hydrofoils daily from Vólos, three from Ághios Konstantinos, and service from Thessaloníki (3 hours). If you are in Athens, depart from Ághios Konstantínos; but from the north, Vólos is closer and offers the option of a quick side trip to the Mt. Pelion region. Kými makes little sense for going to Skiáthos, unless coming from Skýros. For hydrofoil information, contact the **Ceres Hydrofoil Joint Service** at Piraeus (☎ **453-7107** or **453-6107**), **Skiáthos Holidays** (☎ **0427/22-018** (Skiáthos), Ághios Konstantinos (☎ **0235/31-614**), Thessaloníki (☎ **031/223-811**), or Vólos (☎ **0421/39-786**) for schedules and details. For ferryboat information, contact the **Nomikos North Aegean Lines** in Vólos

(☎ **0421/25-688**). Ferry tickets can be purchased through several local travel agents (Skiáthos information is ☎ **0427/22-216** or **22-209**). Plan your itinerary carefully in order to connect between buses and ferries or hydrofoils.

Renowned as the gem of Greece's most exquisite island group, Skiáthos today retains both its sophisticated and natural allure. For most, that attraction comes from the purity of the water and the fine sand beaches; the most famous, Koukounaries, is considered one of the very best in Greece (we prefer yet another excellent beach, Lalaria, with its magnificent rock formations). Elegant shops, flashy nightlife, excellent restaurants, and well-kept villas and pensions are the glittering amenities created by the booming tourist trade, yet with all of these virtues most Greeks stay on the ferry until Skópelos or Alónissos, two of the Sporades less inundated in the high season by foreign visitors.

If there's any possibility of seeing Skiáthos before or after the period from July 20 to September 20 (when the tourist crush is at its worst), try to do so. If not, the overwhelming demand for accommodations may make your foray into a day trip. But make the effort in any case; if you don't like it or can't find a room, you can always take a hydrofoil to other, less inhabited destinations.

Orientation

Hydrofoils, excursion boats, and ferries dock at the port town called Skiáthos, on the island's southern coast. It lies on the main roadway that links the 12 kilometers of southern resort developments together. Skiáthos's north coast is much more rugged and scenically pure: steep cliffs, pine forests, and rocky hills are its only inhabitants. If you crave the restaurant/shopping/nightlife scene, or you've arrived with reservations at one of the resort communities, we'd recommend setting up a base for exploration in the port town. From here, you can try caique excursions to the island's magnificent beaches or take public buses to different villages. Many families prefer to rent two- to four-bedroom villas outside of the town or overlooking a beach, with only an occasional foray into town.

Skiáthos is a relatively modern town, built in 1830 on two low-lying hills, then reconstructed after heavy German bombardment during World War II. Two-story whitewashed villas with bright red tiled roofs line both sides of the V-shaped harbor, which juts out into the water like a boomerang. At its tip is the lovely little Bourzi, one of many islets that poke up off Skiáthos's coastline (but this one has an elegant café next to the church on its peak). Ferryboats moor at the dock in the center of the harbor. The main street (with cars on it) that shoots up through town is named Papadiamanti, after the island's best-known son, an author who made his fame writing about island life and Greek customs; his style has often been characterized as both vernacular and nontranslatable. (The Papadiamanti villa has been turned into a museum filled with his works and memorabilia; it is open daily from 9:30am to 1pm and 5 to 7:30pm.) On this busy lane you'll find the police, post office, several banks, Olympic Airways, a fine travel agency, and the telephone office (OTE).

On the west flank of the harbor (the left side as you disembark the ferry) are several cheerful outdoor cafés, a few traditionally built small hotels, the excursion caiques that post their beach and island tour schedules on signs over the stern, and in the corner, a staircase leading up to the town's next level. Mounting the stairs above the Oasis Café will lead you to Trion Ierarhon Square, a stone-paved mall next to a church, with many boutiques, bars, and ornate villas around it.

The eastern flank is home to many tourist services as well as a few recommended hotels.

Getting Around

BY BUS For most of the places you'll want to visit, Skiáthos is well equipped with public transportation. From the bus station at the harbor, buses run every half hour between 7:30am to 10:30pm back and forth to Koukounaries, the south coast's most popular beach; the fare is 250 Drs ($1.05). Most of the resorts are on this stretch as well.

BY CAR AND MOPED Two reliable rental car agencies are Creator at 8 Papadiamanti (☎ **22-385**) and the local Avis licensee on the *paralía* (☎ **21-458,** fax 23-289), run by the friendly Yannis Theofanidis. Expect to pay between 13,750 to 18,125 Drs ($57.30–$75.50). Mopeds are available from K. Dioletta Rent a Car, on Papadiamanti Street, starting at 1,000 Drs ($4.20) per day motorbikes from 2,300 Drs ($9.60) a day.

BY SEA The north coast beaches and the historic kastro are most easily reached by caique; these sail frequently from the west side of the harbor to all the sights and cost about 3,000 Drs ($12.50) for the classic around the island excursion that includes stops at Calaria Beach and Kastro.

Fast Facts: Skiáthos

American Express **Mare Nostrum Holidays** at Odós Papadiamanti 21 (☎ **21-463**) is open 8am to 10pm daily.

Banks There are many banks in the town, such as the National Bank of Greece on Papadiamanti Street, open Monday through Friday from 8am to 2pm and 7 to 9pm, Sun 9am to noon, closed Saturday.

Emergencies For medical emergencies contact the Skiáthos Hospital (☎ **22-040**) or the police (☎ **21-111**).

Greek Tourist Organization (EOT) Vólos, a one-hour ride away on the mainland, has the nearest official EOT (☎ **0421/23-500**). They're very knowledgeable about the Sporades, Metéora and the Mt. Pelion region.

Laundry/Dry Cleaners Directly across the street from the bank, on Georg. Panora Street, is the Miele Laundromat, open from 8am to 11pm daily. Along the airport road is **Lido Dry Cleaners,** who also do laundry and have a 24-hour turnaround on cleaning.

Maps Maps of all the Sporades and main towns are available at kiosks and travel agents.

Olympic Airways Olympic Airways (☎ **22-200**) is located on Papadiamanti Street about 200 meters from the port on the right hand side; open Monday through Friday from 9am to 4:45pm; closed Saturday and Sunday.

OTE The OTE (telephone office) is inland from the harbor on Papadiamanti Street and is open from 7:30am to 10pm Monday through Friday; 9am to 2pm and 5 to 10pm Saturday and Sunday.

Police About 200 meters from the harbor on Papadiamanti Street you'll find the police, some of whom speak English (☎ **21-111**).

Post Office Inland from the harbor on Papadiamanti Street is the post office (open from 7:30am to 2pm Monday through Friday, closed Saturday and Sunday); they also exchange money.

Telephones/Telecommunications See OTE above.

Travel Agencies The **Mare Nostrum Holidays Office** (☎ **0427/21-463** or 4; fax 0427/21-793), at Odós Papadiamanti 21, is open from 8am to 10pm daily and books villas, hotels and rooms, sells tickets to many of the around-the-island, hydrofoil and beach caique trips, as well as booking Olympic flights and exchanging currency. We found Katerina Michail-Craig, the managing director, to be helpful, exceedingly well informed and filled with tasteful tips on everything from beaches to restaurants; she also speaks excellent English. **Skiáthos Holidays,** the Flying Dophin agent, is right on the *paralía;* in the high season they have as many as 8 high-speed hydrofoil boats daily to Skópelos and Alónissos and daily excursions to Skýros. Call **0427/22-018** or **22-033** for up-to-date departure schedules. Tickets may be bought at their office or at most travel agencies. The Nomikos Line operates the other hydrofoil service as well as steamers to the other islands. They are located at the base of Papadiamanti Street and the *paralía.*

What to See & Do

Skiáthos's natural attractiveness makes it a perfect island for the outdoors lover. From the port to the northern tip, Kástro is an enjoyable two-hour hike over scrubby brush, rolling green hills, and fields of wildflowers. The northeastern coast is lined with secluded sand-and-pebble beaches accessible only to the hiker or boatsman. If there's one thing Skiáthos is famous for, it's beaches. Through the years, Europeans and Greeks alike have voted with their sandals and umbrellas for Koukanaries, although we prefer the more remote Lalaria. Either way, our point is, head straight for the beaches!

The island is also popular with shoppers, and we've tried to find the most exciting outlets for Greek goodies.

BEACHES

Examining the island's beaches clockwise from the port, we first reach Megáli Amos, the sandy strip below the popular group-tour community of Ftelia, probably the island's least attractive. Ten minutes farther west by bus is Vromolimnos, on the Kalamaki peninsula, a better beach by virtue of being less crowded. There are several small pebble-and-sand patches along the south coast road, but the next big exit for bus takers is Troulos. Many aficionados appreciate the picturesque islets that can be seen right off the coast here.

We prefer the beach next door, the much ballyhooed Koukounariés. The bus gently edges its way uphill (it's so packed with barefoot, bikini-clad tourists that it's a wonder it doesn't tip over) past the Pallas Hotel luxury resort. As the bus descends, it winds around the inland waterway, Lake Strofilias, and then stops at the edge of a fragrant pine forest. The word *koukounariés* means "pine cones" in Greek, and behind this grove of trees is a kilometer-long stretch of fine gold sand in a half-moon-shaped cove. Tucked into the evergreen fold are some changing rooms, a small snack bar, and the concessionaire for windsurfers. The beach is extremely crowded with an easy mix of topless sunbathers, families, and singles, all out to polish their suntans. On the far west side of the cove is the island's Soviet-style, spartan Xenia Hotel, a landmark more than a recommendable lodging (for better accommodations, see "Where to Stay"). Note that there are many lodgings in the area, but because of the intense mosquito activity and ticky-tack construction, we prefer to stay back in town or in a villa.

A short but scenic walk from the Koukounaries bus stop (the end of the line) due west to the tip of the island is to the broad Aghía Elenis cove. This beach is popular for windsurfing, because it's a bit rougher than the south coast beaches but not nearly as gusty as those on the north. Most people head to the two linked beaches, Banana and Bananaki, both local favorites. Here you'll find slightly less crowded strips of sand than Koukounaries but with the same sand, pine trees, rental chairs, and umbrellas (1,043 Drs. or $4.35 a set), windsurfer/jetski rentals and a snack bar or two. If you prefer nude sunbathing, you'll probably feel even more comfortable at Bananaki (the farther one, to your right as the dirt road trail splits); expect to walk 15 to 20 minutes from the Koukounaries bus stop with a fairly steep grade.

Limonaki Xerxes is a nearby cove named for the spot where Xerxes brought in ten triremes to conquer the Hellenic fleet moored at Skiáthos during the Persian Wars. This is also called Mandraki Beach, and is a 20-minute walk up the path opposite the Lake Strofilias bus stop. Mandraki is a pristine and relatively secluded beach for those who crave a quiet spot.

What was once a hefty one-hour walk is now linked by a new road from the bus stop at Troulos Beach that leads to Megas Aselinos, a windy, sandy north coast beach where free camping has taken root. Most of the other north coast beaches are only accessible by boat, the exception being the acceptable Ormos Xanema, a windy, unprotected cove that can be reached by car, driving east from the port town.

Lalaria, on the island's northern tip, near Kástro, is to our minds one of the loveliest beaches in Greece. One of its unique qualities is the Tripia Petra, perforated rock cliffs that jut out into the sea on both sides of the cove. These have been worn through in time by the wind and the waves to form perfect classical archways. From the shore these "portholes" frame a sparkling landscape: While gulls squawk in the distance, you just lie on the gleaming white pebbles, admiring the neon-blue Aegean and cloudless sky through their rounded openings. If you swim through the arches against the brisk meltémi winds, you can play with the echo created inside them. Out in the water is a perfect vantage point to admire the glowing, silver-white pebble beach and jagged white cliffs above it. The water at Lalaria beach is an especially vivid shade of aquamarine because of the highly reflective white pebbles and marble and limestone slabs which coat the sea bottom. There are many naturally carved caves in the cliff wall that lines the beach, providing privacy or shade for those who've had too much exposure. Lalaria can only be reached by caique excursions from the port; the fare is 3,450 Drs. ($14.40) for the so-called around-the-island trip. Excursion boats usually stop at one or more of the other sights described below.

KÁSTRO

In the 16th century, when the Turks overran the island, the inhabitants moved to its northern tip and built a fortress. The village of Kástro remained occupied until 1829. Once joined to firm ground by a swaying drawbridge, this impregnable rock can now be reached by cement stairs. The remains of over 300 houses and 22 churches have mostly fallen to the sea, but two of the churches, with porcelain plates imbedded in their worn stucco facades, still stand. From this prospect there are excellent views to the Kastronísia islet below and the sparkling Aegean. The Kástro can be reached on foot, a two-hour hike from the port. Starting out on the uphill path just west of the harbor will take you by the monasteries of Ághios Fanourias, Ághios Dionisios, and Ághios Athanássios to Panaghía Kardási, where the road officially ends. The lazy can cruise to Kástro or hire mopeds and try Skiáthos's latest roadway, which runs to the north coast from just south of Ftelia.

CAVES

There are several extraordinary caves carved in Skiáthos's rugged coastline, and the caique drivers seem most proud when they take tourists to see them. Along the coast of Pounta on the island's eastern side, opposite Kamini, is Spiliá Kaminári, a huge roofless cave at the water's edge. Farther north is Skotiní Spiliá, a fantastic 20-foot-tall sea cave reached through a narrow crevice in the cliff walls. It's just wide enough for caiques to squeeze through for a close look (the one we took just fit!). Seagulls drift above you in the cave's cool darkness, while below, fish swim down in the 30-foot subsurface portion. This odd pattern of erosion has created spectacular scenery and many sandy coves along the east and north coasts, though none are as beautiful or well sheltered from the meltémi as Lalaria beach.

SHOPPING

Shopping is as good on Skiáthos as on Mýkonos; it's not cheap, but there's some excellent merchandise.

The highlight of the shopping scene, at least as it relates to Greek craft and folk art, is ★ **Archipelago** (☎ **22-163**), adjacent to the Papadiamanti House. This brilliantly put together space is the work of Marcos and Andrea Botsaris, an erudite couple who are among the premier collectors of folk art in the country. The exquisite objects of art and folklore, both old and new, largely come from outside of the Sporades, specifically from Epirus, Macedonia, Thrace, Lesvos, and the Peloponnese, and include costumes, jewelry, sculpture, painting, and all manner of objects. If you visit but one shop, make sure it's Archipelago. Our shopping find last visit was **Aris** (☎ **22-415**), Odós Agliánous 4, where Maria Drakou sells bright, unusual dresses, T-shirts, and short, flirty, washable shirts handpainted with lively floral and abstract patterns.

Gallery Castello, off Papadiamanti Street (☎ **23-100**), is run by Maria Vagena, a woman with an eye for the eclectic: Greek jewelry, ceramics, rugs, weavings and an assortment of objects varying from artistic to the everyday, and old and new, make up the ever-changing inventory. We especially like Maria's taste in antique silver jewelry as well as weavings from Pelion, Epirus, and Crete. Open daily 9:30am to 2pm and 6 to 11pm.

We loved the **Galerie Varsakis** (☎ **22-255**), on Trion Ierarhon Square, for its collection of folk antiques, embroidered bags and linens, rugs from around the world and other collectibles. We found very reasonably priced gifts and window-shopped their superb antiques, and better yet, discovered that Harris, the proprietor, speaks English and is quite an original himself. In the world of look-a-like T-shirt shops, we were pleasantly surprised to find an original, simply called **Island** (☎ **23-377**). This small shop, located on upper Papadiamanti (across from OTE) stocks all-cotton shirts, designed and made in Greece, as well as other casual wear both attractively styled and priced. Open daily 9:30am to 1:30pm and 5:30 to 10:30pm.

Where to Stay

Between July 20 and September 20 it can be literally impossible to find a room in Skiáthos. If you're traveling at this time of year, try phoning ahead from Athens to book a room, or better still, book your accommodations well before you arrive. Many hotels will accept reservations when a deposit equal to one-third of the proposed rent is wired to them through an Athens bank, or if you book through an agency, is secured by check or credit card. (For those of you who make plans in advance, most of these hotels request that reservations by mail be made two or three months prior to the summer season.) If you're getting off the ferry cold and arrive between 8am and 10pm head to **Mare Nostrum Holidays** (☎ **0427/21-463**), up Papadiamanti Street. They'll try to help you secure a place when all else fails.

If you do intend to book lodgings through an agency, expect to pay 7,940 Drs ($74.75) nightly for a first class room, 34,500 Drs ($143.75) for a studio, or 69,000 Drs ($287) on up for a fully equipped three-bedroom villa on the beach. Most of these will be located on or near one of the island's popular beach resorts. Lower cost housing can be found in the town—where we usually stay.

All over the hillside above the eastern harbor are several unlicensed "hotels," which are fairly recently constructed rooms to rent. Inquire from passersby when you're hotel hunting and you'll be surprised at which buildings turn out to be lodgings.

One of our favorite parts of town is the quiet neighborhood on the hill above the bay at the western end of the port. On the winding stairs/street of this area can be found numerous private rooms-to-let. Take a walk and look for the signs, ask the corner merchant, or check with the Vólos EOT office (see Fast Facts: Skiáthos) for their guide to accommodations.

Hotel Akti, Skiáthos 37002. ☎ **0427/22-024.** 14 rms (all with bath). TEL

Rates: 11,500 Drs ($47.90) single; 16,100 Drs ($67.10) double. AE, EC, MC, V.

This thoroughly redone hotel, opened in the summer of 1991, has rooms that, on our inspection, were spotless and tastefully furnished. Our concern here is for its location, set on a fairly noisy, harborfront street. If you're a light sleeper, you'd do well to move on, otherwise the Akti is a gem.

Hotel Athos, Ring Rd., Skiáthos 37002. ☎ and fax **0427/22-477.**
15 rms (all with bath). TEL

Rates: 11,500 Drs ($47.90) single; 16,100 Drs ($67.10) double. AE, EC, MC, V.

A relative newcomer, opening in 1991, the Hotel Athos is located on the fringe of Skiáthos, on the ring road leading to the major beach resorts. This may be an especially attractive place for those who wish to have ready access to the town without the bustle. The rooms, many facing the sea, are spotlessly clean and particularly in the low season, represent good value.

Bourtzi Hotel, Odós Moraitou 8, Skiáthos 37002. ☎ **0427/21-304.** Fax 0427/23-243.
23 rms (all with bath). MINIBAR TEL

Rates: 10,350 Drs ($43.10) single; 11,500 Drs ($47.90) double. No credit cards.

Mostly a group hotel but with a few rooms available to individuals, the Bourtzi Hotel is a quiet and attractive lodging option. We especially like the back, garden-facing rooms and the ever so slightly larger than normal baths. The owners also run the 22-room Pothos Hotel (same ☎), near the Hotel Morfo. The facilities are quite similar to the Bourtzi, and like it, most rooms are contracted to agencies, but if you get stuck you should consider the Pothos.

Karafelas Hotel, Odós Papadiamanti 59, Skiáthos 37002. ☎ **0427/21-235.**
17 rms (all with bath). MINIBAR

Rates: 4,500 Drs ($18.95) single; 8,200 Drs ($34.15) double.

One of the homiest least expensive lodgings is the Karafelas Hotel, though it could be better maintained. Walk away from the port far down on Papadiamanti Street, past the post office, and where the street forks left, just on the left, you'll see the hotel. Ask for a ground floor room in the back garden; what you'll get is your own little villa with two beds, bathroom and shower, a front porch overlooking a garden, and your own clothesline! And the owners are fairly obliging. During the high season, it's a good idea to reserve a room two to three weeks in advance as it's also popular with groups.

Hotel Meltemi, Skiáthos 37002. ☎ **0427/22-493.** Fax 0427/21-294.
18 rms (all with bath). TEL

Rates (including breakfast): 12,800 Drs ($53.35) single; 16,000 Drs ($66.70) double. AE, EC, MC, V.

On the east side of the harbor opposite the many moored yachts, is the modern and comfortable Hotel Meltemi. The Meltemi's spacious rooms all have private baths and may be booked by April, but give them a try; try to reserve at least three weeks in advance. Hosts Yorgo and Giuliana Rigas run a very friendly bar out on the waterside. The front rooms, which face the harbor and have balconies, are noisy.

$ **Hotel Morfo,** Odós Ananiniou 23, Skiáthos 37002. ☎ **0427/21-737.**
Fax 0427/23-222. 17 rms (all with bath). TEL

Rates (including breakfast): 14,000 Drs ($58.30) single; 17,600 Drs ($73.30) double. EC, MC, V.

On a quiet backstreet in the center of town (roughly parallel to the Olympic Airways office) is the tranquil Hotel Morfo. You enter through a small, well-kept garden into a festively decorated lobby. Guest rooms are just a tad better than a Class C hotel. Given the lovely setting, tasteful decor, and friendly staff, we think the Morfo merits a good value lodging award.

Pension Orsa, P.O. Box 3, Skiáthos 37002. ☎ **0427/22-430.** Fax 0427/21-736.
12 rms (all with bath). TEL

Rates: 17,250 Drs. ($71.90) double. MC.

This is one of the best of the rooms-to-let establishments. To get there, walk down the port west past the fish stalls and Jimmy's Bar, go up two flights of stairs, and watch for a recessed courtyard on the left, with a handsome wooden door promising "Orsa, Rooms for Rent." Most of the rooms have windows or balconies overlooking the harbor and the islands beyond. A charming garden terrace is a perfect place for a tranquil breakfast at 780 Drs. ($3.25). Ask for the balcony room on the third floor. **Caution:** Disco music from the nearby Bourtzi nightclub may invade your sleep until the wee hours of the morning, a common problem throughout the islands.

A SPLURGE IN PLATANIAS

★ **Atrium Hotel,** Skiáthos-Platanias Rd., Skiáthos 37002. ☎ **0427/49-345.**
Fax 0427/49-376. 75 rms (all with bath). A/C TEL

Rates (half board): 34,500 Drs ($143.75) single; 47,750 Drs ($198.95) double. AE, EC, MC, V.

This is really a lovely place, built above a tree-lined beach about 15 minutes outside of the town. We loved the swimming pool that overlooks the sea, broad balconies with spectacular views and the fully appointed rooms and facilities. The Atrium also has full watersports gear and a bar and restaurant. There may be better places on the island, but unless you're willing to rent a hugely expensive villa, you'll likely not do as well as a stay at the Atrium.

Where to Eat

The western harbor and the lanes around Papadiamanti Street are lined with medium- and overpriced tavernas and cafés. As is the case with most of the overdeveloped tourist resorts, there is a plethora of ice-cream parlors, fast food stands, minimarkets—you get the picture. This just means that in Skiáthos you'll have to walk a little farther for that genuine Greek meal.

Asprolithos, Mavroghiáli and Koraí Streets, ☎ **23-110.**

Cuisine: GREEK. **Reservations:** Recommended
Prices: Appetizers 345–2,300 Drs ($1.45–$9.60); main courses 1,265–4,600 Drs. ($5.25–$19.15). AE, V.
Open: Daily 7pm–1am.

Walk up Papadiamanti Street, a block past the high school, and turn right for a simply superb meal of light, updated taverna fare. You can get a classic moussaká here if you want to play it safe, or try specialties like artichokes and prawns smothered in cheese. We devoured their snapper baked in wine with wild greens, served with thick french fries that had obviously never seen a freezer. The main dining room is dominated by a handsome stone fireplace, and there are also tables outside where you can catch the breeze. An elegant ambience and friendly service.

Le Bistrot, Martínou Street ☎ **21-627.**

Cuisine: CONTINENTAL. **Reservations:** Recommended.
Prices: Appetizers 750–2,300 Drs ($3.15–$9.60); main courses 1,500–4,000 Drs ($6.25–$16.65). EC, MC, V.
Open: Dinner only 7pm–1am daily.

This intimate, continental restaurant is easily spotted by its twin, across the street, which functions as a bar, overlooking the water. Both the bar and the dining room are lovely spaces. The full-course meals are beautifully prepared from their own stocks and sauces. Swordfish, roast pork, and steamed vegetables should be savored slowly, so there will be room for their delicious desserts.

$ **Carnayio Taverna,** Paralía. ☎ **22-868.**

Cuisine: TAVERNA/SEAFOOD.
Prices: Appetizers 800–2,300 Drs ($3.35–$9.60); main courses 1,250–3,500 Drs ($5.20–$14.60).
Open: Daily dinner only 8pm–1am.

The consensus among Greek-cuisine connoisseurs—of whom we presumptuously consider ourselves—is that the best taverna in Skiáthos is the Carnayio Taverna, located on the waterfront across from the Alkyon Hotel. It's generally packed with local families and we've never gone wrong with any dish served here. Among our favorites over the years are *exohiko,* fish soup, lamb uvetsi, and, of course, grilled fish. The garden setting is sublime, and if you're there late enough, you might be lucky to see a real round of dancing waiters and diners.

Kampoureli Ouzerí, Paralía. ☎ **21-112.**

Cuisine: GREEK.
Prices: Appetizers 350–2,650 Drs ($1.45–$11.05).
Open: Noon–1am.

This ouzerí, toward the ferries on the waterfront, is one of the most "Greek"-style eateries in town, though it caters to a largely nonlocal crowd. You can have the authentic ouzo and octopus combo at 450 Drs ($1.90) or sample their rich supply of cheese pies, fried feta, olives, and other piquant *mezédes* (hors d'oeuvres). This is John's favorite place to while away the evening—lounging over ouzo, munching on light, tasty tidbits (always grilled octopus when it's fresh!), and admiring the beautiful sea views.

Taverna Limanakia, Paralía. ☎ **22-835.**

Cuisine: TAVERNA/SEAFOOD.
Prices: Appetizers 350–1,500 Drs ($1.45–$6.25); main courses 1,150–4,000 Drs ($4.80–$16.65). MC.
Open: Daily dinner only 7pm–midnight.

Very much in the style of its next door neighbor Carnaiyo, the Limanakia serves some of the best taverna and seafood dishes in town. We vacillate about which of the two we prefer, but we've always come away feeling satisfied after a meal in this reliable eatery.

Taverna Mesogia, off Dimitriádou Street ☎ **21-440.**

Cuisine: TAVERNA.
Prices: Appetizers 430–1,000 Drs ($1.80–$4.20); main courses 950–2,530 Drs ($4–$10.50).
Open: Daily 7pm–midnight.

We were taken here by local friends who escape here during the height of the season to get back in touch with their Greek roots. The cuisine is utterly normal taverna style (our favorite dish was the lamb uvetsi), but we, too, were happy to leave the overly saturated harborside diners behind and settle in for a quiet meal. Mesogia is a little tough to find, situated in the midst of the town's most labyrinthine neighborhood, but when you find the very attractive (and good food) Taverna Alexandros, you'll be just a turn or two away.

$ **Stavros Gyros & Souvlaki,** Trión Ierarchón Square. No tel.

Cuisine: GRILL.
Prices: Main courses 575–1,150 Drs. ($2.40–$4.80)
Open: Dinner only 7pm–1am daily.

To the left of the Varsakis Gallery is Stavros', an unassuming souvlaki stand with a green awning, that ranks as one of our favorites in the Sporades. Outside you'll see pine picnic-style tables and a chalkboard menu; for 1,400 Drs. ($5.85) you can appease even the biggest Big Mac attack, though instead of burgers it's souvlaki and lamb chops. Chase them down with soda, beer, wine, or ouzo, order their peasant salad with feta, and you'll be ready to tackle some more sights, and at a price that is unknown (to us, at least) in any other part of the island. Delicious and great value.

READERS RECOMMEND

Taverna Ilias, Skiáthos. ☎ **22-016.** *"My wife and I have traveled extensively in Greece, and the best restaurant we've eaten at anywhere is the Taverna Ilias in Skiáthos. My wife recommends the chicken curry, and I recommend the moussaká, the aroma of which comes right through the crust. The food is great and the service is impeccable."*—Bruce Bassof, Boulder, Colo.

Evening Entertainment

A lot of the Skiáthos scene takes place on the streets: along the waterfront, outside of ice-cream parlors on Papadiamanti Street, and in the lanes behind Trion Ierarhon Square. The rebuilt **Scorpio Disco Club** (☎ **23-208**) is the island's hottest disco, and draws a mixed crowd every night between 10pm and 3am. Drinks serve as the cover charge here; expect to pay 700–1,200 Drs ($2.90–$5) each. The **Banana** is another popular bar catering to the island's foreign clientele.

The hottest and coolest places in town are respectively **La Piscene Club,** about five blocks in from the port (beyond Taverna Stavros on Evangelistrias Street), and **Remezzo,** on the far western end of the port. Both places sizzle; here is where you party down, meet the beautiful people from around the world and have a wild, wild time (at La Piscene) or a sophisticated rendezvous at Remezzo (9:30pm to 4am every night). Where do you take that person you met at Remezzo to speak softly to each other? To the Mythos Bar, right on the harbor next to the ouzerí. The decor is white-with-tufted-seats and sleek without the cost. If you like to have videos with your drinks, try the **Oasis Café** at the western end of the harbor. Here the beer (draft) is only 350 Drs ($1.45) a stein, and if there's a game of any sort being played they'll have it on the tube. Lastly, there is the island's most picturesque (and expensive) late-night retreat, the **Bourtzi Café** located atop the point, jutting out into the harbor (☎ **21-229**). Tawny-haired women, silver foxes, or dashing Greek tycoons hop right off their yachts and onto the Bourtzi's willing barstools. The bar action is great fun to meddle with; the Bourtzi's a good value at cocktail hour, when you can admire their priceless sunset view.

If you're a movie-holic, like us, you'll be glad to know that the Attikon Cinema often has films in English.

2 Skópelos

58 nautical miles from Vólos

ARRIVING/DEPARTING • By Air To reach Skópelos by air, you'll have to fly to nearby Skiáthos and take a hydrofoil or ferry to the northern port of Loutraki (below Glossa) or the popular town of Skópelos.

• By Sea The ferry to Skópelos from Skiáthos takes 90 minutes if you call at Skópelos, or 45 minutes if stopping first at Glossa/Loutraki. The price for a ticket is the same; about 990 Drs ($4.10). Ferry tickets can be purchased at the **Nomikos Lines** office on the left side coming off the dock. The hydrofoil takes 15 minutes to Glossa/Loutraki (4 times daily; 1,380 Drs ($5.75)), 35 minutes to Skópelos (eight times daily; 1,610 Drs ($6.70)). Hydrofoil tickets can be purchased at the port Flying Dolphin office (☎ **22-300** or **22-145**), immediately opposite from the dock; they're open all year and operate as the local Olympic Airways representative.

From Skiáthos you can take the daily scheduled ferry on the Nomikos Lines or hop on one of the many excursion boats. Similarly, it's possible to catch a normal ferry or hydrofoil from Alónissos (seven times daily; 1,380 Drs or $5.75), or ride on one of the excursion boats. Expect to pay a little more on the excursion boats, but if they're not full you can usually negotiate the price. There are infrequent connections to Kými. Check with the **Port Authority** (☎ **22-180**) for current schedules; they change frequently. We felt the extra expense of the hydrofoil was well worth it for hopping from island to island.

ESSENTIALS The **Municipal Tourist Office** of Skópelos (☎ **23-231**) is located on the waterfront, to the left of the pier as you disembark; it is open daily from 9:30am to 10pm in the high season. They dispense information as well as change money and reserve rooms. The only OTE on the island is in Skópelos town; in Glossa, Klima, Moni Evangelistrias, Moni Prodromou, Ormos Agnonda, and Ormos Panormos you can try a kiosk or hotel for telephone service. The post office, which is located on the south side of the port, on the road behind the Bar Alegari, is open Monday through Friday from 8am to 2:30pm.

The English-speaking staff at **Skopelorama** run an excellent travel agency, located next door to the Hotel Eleni on the north end of the port (☎ **0424/22-917** or **23-250;** fax: 0424/23-243); it is open daily from 9am to 1pm and 5 to 10pm. They can help you find a room, exchange money, offer excursions and provide information; they know the island inside out and are really friendly folk. The **National Bank of Greece** and the **Commercial Bank** are on the *paralía;* they are open 8am to 3pm Monday through Thursday, until 1:30pm Friday and 6:30 to 8:30pm Monday through Friday, 10:30am to 2pm Saturday. There's a **police** station in Skópelos town (☎ **22-235**). They can help you find a room as well as handle emergencies. There is a self-service **laundry** (☎ **22-602**) just down the street from the Adonis Hotel, which is open daily except Sunday.

You'll know as soon as your boat pulls into the harbor of Skópelos that you've come to one of Greece's most architecturally pristine islands, on a par with Hydra and Sými. The main town, also called Skópelos, scales the low hills around the harbor and has the same winding, narrow paths that characterize the more famous Cycladic islands to the south. A walk through the back streets and alleyways will delight anyone with an eye for intricately trellised gardens, whitewashed houses with precariously overhanging wooden balconies, and meticulously constructed green and gray slate roofs. Old women sit outside in front of their houses in groups of three and four, knitting and embroidering, the speed of their needles only topped by the velocity of their conversation.

The rest of the island is rich in vegetation, with wind-swept pines growing down to secluded coves, wide beaches, and terraced cliffs of angled rock slabs. The interior is densely planted with fruit and nut orchards. The plums and almonds from Skópelos are legendary, and are integrated into the island's unique cuisine. The coastline, like that of Skiáthos, is punctuated by impressive grottos and bays. A camera is a must.

Orientation

Skópelos has two major towns: Skópelos on the southeast coast, and Glossa, on the northwest coast directly across the Aegean from Skiáthos and a winding three kilometers up the hill from Loutraki, port town to Glossa. The ferries from Alónissos, Skýros, and Kými and most of the hydrofoils and other boats from Skiáthos dock at both Glossa/Loutraki and Skópelos. A good paved road runs due south from Skópelos to the two beaches at Ormós Stafilos, then west and up the beach-filled west coast to the four villages in the north: Klima, Machalas, Glossa, and Loutraki. If you've never been to Skópelos, it's best to find a room in Skópelos town and begin your exploration there; you'll find all of the necessary tourist services, the starting point for many bus and boat excursions, as well as a large group of hotels. After you've acquainted yourself with the balance of the island, you can move to one of the villages or beaches. However, if it's a quieter, purer Greek village you're looking for, use the village of Glossa as your base. Its name means "tongue" in Greek and that's what will be hanging out (which several residents assured us is the origin of the name, though we remain skeptical) if you hike up the steep hill from Loutraki.

Skópelos is built amphitheatrically around a C-shaped harbor. To the right, as you exit the boat, are only a few of Skópelos's 123 churches (which must be an ecclesiastical record for such a small village). The waterfront is lined with banks, cafés, travel agencies, and the like. Interspersed between these prosaic offerings are some truly regal-looking shade trees. Many of the hotels are on the far left (as you leave the dock) end of the *paralía.* There are beaches on both sides of the harbor; Konstantinos beach, on the north end, is a 15-minute walk away. The bus and taxi stand is under a giant plane tree about 200 meters to the left of the dock. Most of the shops and the OTE are up the main street leading off the *paralía.* The back streets are amazingly convoluted; the best plan is to wander up and get to know a few familiar landmarks.

Getting Around

BY BOAT To visit the more isolated beaches, take one of the large excursion boats that visit more secluded beaches in a day and provide a barbecue lunch. These should cost about 10,925 Drs ($45.50) and should be booked a day in advance in the summer months. Excursion boats operate only in the peak season to Glisteri, Glyphoneri, and Sares beaches, for about 1,150 Drs ($4.80). From the port of Agnondas, there are fishing boats traveling to Limanari, one of the island's better beaches.

BY BUS Skópelos is reasonably well served by public transportation. Buses run every half hour in the high season beginning in Skópelos and making stops at Stafilos, Agnodas, Panormos Bay, Melia, Elios, Klima, Glossa, and Loutraki—in other words, nearly anyplace you'd want to go. A typical fare, from Glossa to Skópelos, runs 690 Drs ($2.90).

BY MOPED AND CAR The most convenient way to see the island is to rent a moped at one of the many shops on the port. The cost should be about 2,530 Drs ($10.50) per day. A Jeep at **Motor Tours** (**☎ 22-986**), for example, will run around 20,700 Drs ($86.25), including third-party insurance; expect to pay a few thousand drachmas less for a Fiat Panda.

BY TAXI There is a taxi stand on the southern side of town, near Madro Travel, where cars will shuttle you to any place on the island. A typical fare, from Skópelos to Glossa, runs 4,600 Drs ($19.20).

What to See & Do

As might be expected, Skópelos is much like Skiáthos, with most of the activities and sights taking place outdoors. The whole of Skópelos's 90 square kilometers is prime for hiking, biking, climbing, horseback riding, sailing (ask at the Skópelos travel agencies), and most of all, sunning and swimming. There's a kastro in Skópelos town, as well as numerous churches and monasteries. If you're island-hopping, you might want to take advantage of Skópelos's two ports. The northern port at Loutraki/Glossa is a short jaunt from Skiáthos, while Skópelos town is close to Alónissos. Depending on where you've been and where you're going, consider starting at one end of the island, crossing to the other and moving on to the adjoining island.

Skopelorama (see "Essentials") operates a fine series of excursions such as monasteries by coach, traditional Skópelos, a walking tour of the town, several cruises, and a day trip to Alónissos.

The following is a rundown of the beaches on Skópelos. A 15-minute walk to the north will take you to Ághios Konstantinos, where there are villas and a few places to eat. Sares beach is a short caique ride away from Skópelos town and is much less crowded than the two town beaches. Ormos Stafilos is on the south coast. There is a long and often-packed beach along the sheltered coastal stretch; a 15-minute hike due east will take you to Velanio, Skópelos's nude beach. There is a taverna and a ten-room pension at Stafilos. One of the island's best beaches, Limnonari, can only be reached by caique from Agnondas. The longest beach, and one of the nicest and least crowded, is the enormous stretch between Milia and Panormos, where scruffy pines and shrubs grow down to the sand's edge. There are about six tavernas in Panormos (and the best watersports facilities on Skópelos, the **Beach Boys Club, ☎ 0424/33-496**) and one at Milia. Milia is the better of the two beaches and a favorite on the island. The public bus goes to Milia six times daily and drops you off about half a kilometer above the beach. The best way to go is by car or moped, so you can come and go without waiting for the bus.

For those who stay in Glossa, most of the coastline is craggy, with just a few hard-to-get-to beaches. Among the best places to catch some rays and do a bit of sunning is Ághios Iannis, just beyond Glossa.

SHOPPING

Skópelos has a variety of galleries displaying local photography, ceramics, and jewelry. The Skópelos branch of **Archipelagos** (**☎ 23-127**) is one of the best of these and can be found facing the waterfront near the bus stop. **To Sinnefo** (no tel.) is located in the backstreets, off Velizaríou Street (one of the few named), and specializes in hand-made puppets, mobiles and marionettes. **Nick Rodies,** whose gallery is located next door to Skopelorama (**☎ 22-779**), is from a Skópelos family who've made ceramics for three generations. We loved (and bought) an elegantly shaped black vessel that remains one of our favorites. The studio is open daily from 9am to 1pm and 5 to 11pm.

Where to Stay

Skópelos is nearly as popular as Skiáthos, and because of its increasing flow of tourists several new hotels have cropped up, especially in Skópelos town. If you need advice about one of the in-town hotels or pensions or accommodations available in the outer limits, talk to Skopelorama or the officials at the town hall.

Warning: The hotel classification system, so widely used with consistency on most Greek islands, has been turned topsy-turvy on Skópelos: there are Class D hotels that are more expensive than Class C inns; some Class D rooms are equipped with private showers while a few Class C places have shared facilities. In other words, make sure to look at a room and agree on a price before accepting anything, or you may be unpleasantly surprised. Also, to make matters more confusing, there are really no real street names in the main, older section of town, so you'll have to ask for directions several times before finding your lodging.

New camping facilities have been constructed seven kilometers from Skópelos town on the road above Agnodas Beach. They offer dormitory accommodations with showers for budget prices (no phone yet!).

Hotel Andromahi, Velizaríou Street, Skópelos 37003. **☎ 0424/22-941.**
7 rms (all with bath).
Rates: 8,050 Drs ($33.50) single; 11,000 Drs ($45.83) double. MC, V.

We discovered this traditional style inn while looking for a bakery (we found one, just up the street) and were delighted to take the tour. The Andromahi feels like an old-fashioned bed-and-breakfast with many homey touches and painted furniture. Our only hesitation, and it's fairly serious, is that it's probably pretty noisy in the late evening. Other than that, this is a gem; open all year.

★ **Hotel Denise,** Skópelos 37003. ☎ **0424/22-678.** Fax 0424/22-769. 25 rms (all with bath). A/C MINIBAR TEL

Rates (including breakfast): 13,225 Drs ($55.10) single; 17,940 Drs ($74.75) double. EC, MC, V.

One of the best hotels in Skópelos because of its premier location and clean facilities, Hotel Denise stands atop the village overlooking the town and commands spectacular views of the harbor and Aegean. The Class C (despite a/c and minibar in the room!) Hotel Denise was upgraded during 1991, but it still fits in well with Skópelos's architectural style. Each of the Denise's four stories is ringed by a wide balcony, and the rooms have hardwood floors and furniture; view rooms are among the best in town. As the Denise is very popular, before hiking up the steep road, call for a pickup and to check for room availability; better yet, reserve in advance.

$ **Drosia,** Skópelos 37003. ☎ **0424/22-490.** 10 rms (all with bath). TEL

Rates: 7,245 Drs ($30.20) single; 8,250 Drs ($34.40) double.

This Class D hotel is next to the Denise, atop a hill overlooking the village, with exceptional views. The Drosia is of the same vintage as the Denise but with slightly less expensive and well-equipped rooms. All in all, it represents very good value.

Hotel Eleni, Skópelos 37003. ☎ **0424/22-393.** 37 rms (all with bath). TEL

Rates: 7,475 Drs ($31.10) single; 11,900 Drs ($49.40) double. EC, MC.

The Hotel Eleni is a gracious modern hotel, 100 meters from the waterfront, whose rooms all have balconies. Owner Charlie Hatgidrosis returned from the Bronx to build his establishment after he and his brother operated several pizzerias in New York.

Pension Katarina, Skópelos 37003. ☎ **0424/23-307**. 7 rms (all with bath).

Rates: 10,925 Drs ($45.50) single/double.

A recently built (1991) pension, the attractive Katarina commands a wonderful view of the town from its south side waterfront perch. We much admired the well-kept rose garden as well as the attractively built lobby and guest quarters. The only downside here is that the Katarina is set just a couple of doors from two popular bars. Request a top floor, water-facing view room.

Rania, Skópelos 37003. ☎ **22-486.** 11 rms (all with bath). TEL

Rates: 9,200 Drs ($38.30) single or double.

Down by the waterside, the Rania is just beyond and to the left of the larger, group-oriented Amalia. Very simply furnished rooms have bath, balcony, and phone, and are reasonably well maintained. The Rania is one of the few hotels open year-round.

SPLURGE CHOICES

Hotel Prince Stafilos, Skópelos 37003. ☎ **0424/22-775, 23-011.** Fax 0424/22-825. 70 rms (all with bath). TEL

Rates (including breakfast): 23,575 Drs ($98.20) single; 26,750 Drs ($111.40) double.

For a slightly overpriced splurge in Skópelos, try the Prince Stafilos, on the southern end of the bay. (They will give you a ride from the ferry dock.) The owner, Pelopidas

Tsitsirigos, is also an architect and a welcoming presence behind the desk. All the amenities are here—pool, restaurant, and bars—as well as a large buffet breakfast. We especially like the traditionally inspired decor of the lobby.

Skópelos Village, Skópelos 37003. ☎ **0424/22-517.** Fax 0424/22-958.
36 units (all with bath). MINIBAR TEL

Rates: 23,000 Drs ($95.85) studio; 27,025 Drs ($112.60) apartment.

A special recommendation goes to the Skópelos Village, where each room is actually a duplex apartment equipped with kitchen, private bath, and one or two bedrooms. The villas share a common swimming pool, barbecue, and snack bar where breakfast is served. The buildings are tastefully constructed as "traditional island houses," though we doubt if most island houses share a pool or a barbecue. Each villa can comfortably sleep from two to six people, depending on their feelings about each other.

Where to Eat

There are a number of really good dining options in and around the town as well as a few well-recommended bars.

★ **Anatoli Ouzerí,** Skópelos. No telephone.
Cuisine: GREEK.
Prices: Appetizers 230–690 Drs (95¢–$2.90); main courses 1,150–2,185 Drs ($4.80–$9.10).
Open: Dinner only 9pm–1am.

This diminutive ouzerí deserves little apology for its top of the town location. Make no mistake, you'll have quite a climb to reach Anatolí, but we found the food superb, more than justifying the effort. Our meal featured several delicious *mezédes* (appetizers), including lightly fried green peppers, blackeyed peas with fresh spices, and an exceptional octopus salad. Largely unknown by all other than residents or long-term guests, the Anatoli Ouzerí should be your first stop on the dining trail. If you're in luck, Ghiorgos Xidaris, the rail-thin proprietor/chef, will play his acoustic baglama with accompanists. If you come early or late in the season, bring a sweater. An unqualified treat.

Crêperie Greca, Skópelos. No telephone.
Cuisine: CREPES.
Prices: Appetizers and main courses 575–1,380 Drs ($2.40–$5.75).
Open: Daily noon–3pm and 7pm–2am.

If it's crêpes you've been missing, try Crêperie Greca, across from the Adonis Hotel (on the sloping street up from the waterfront bus stop). Zucchini and cheese, or chicken and mushroom, are the most filling, but for drama try the flaming fruit and cream crêpes, all prepared as if by magic by Greca on a tiny burner near the front door.

Finikas Taverna & Ouzeri, Skópelos. ☎ **23-247.**
Cuisine: GREEK.
Prices: Appetizers 460–2,300 Drs ($1.90–$9.60); main courses 1,495–1,725 Drs ($6.20–$7.20).
Open: Daily dinner only 7:30pm–2am.

Tucked away in the upper backstreets of Skópelos is a picturesque garden taverna/ouzerí dominated by a broad leaf palm. The Finikas may offer Skópelos' most romantic setting, perhaps by dint of its isolated location as well as its lovely garden dining area. Among the many fine dishes we sampled, John's vegetarian urges had him try a wonderful ratatouille, while Kyle's meat craving was satisfied by pork cooked with prunes and apples, a traditional island specialty.

Kymata, Skópelos. ☎ **22-381.**

Cuisine: GREEK.
Prices: Appetizers 345–1,265 Drs ($1.45–$5.30); main courses 1,035–2,875 Drs ($4.30–$12).
Open: 11am–2:30pm and 7pm–midnight.

There are several ordinary tavernas along the waterfront, with Kymata standing out in the crowd. It is the last one to the right of the waterfront, just off the ferry dock. The traditional Greek taverna style food is excellent, so stick with the *tzatzíki/moussaká* type dishes in lieu of the expensive seafood.

Molos Taverna & Ouzeri, Skópelos. ☎ **22-551.**

Cuisine: GREEK.
Prices: Appetizers 400–1,380 Drs ($1.70–$5.75); main courses 2,000–2,560 Drs ($4.55–$10.70).
Open: Daily noon–2:30pm and 6pm–1am.

A very local favorite right near the ferry on the *paralía.* Molos features many specialties, but among them we enjoyed a platter of rofos (a large white fish) and onions; stuffed pork with cheese, garlic and vegetables; *abelourgos* (stuffed chicken with ham, wrapped in grape leaves); and *koukiar,* a slice of thinly cut veal with eggplant, covered with a béchamel sauce. Molos is open all year round.

Spiro's Taverna, Skópelos. ☎ **23-146.**

Cuisine: GREEK.
Prices: Appetizers; main courses 575–2,645 Drs ($2.40–$11).
Open: Daily noon–midnight.

Spiro's Taverna, to the left as you leave the ferry dock, is often packed with a crowd eager for their spit-roasted chicken. This simple outdoor café is popular with locals, expatriates, and travelers alike; open throughout the year.

CAFÉS & SNACK BARS

Platanos Jazz Bar, Skópelos. No telephone.

Cuisine: BAR.
Prices: Appetizers and main courses 600–1,495 Drs ($2.50–$6.20).
Open: 5am–3am.

For everything from breakfast to a late-night drink, try Platanos, the jazz pub, beneath the enormous plane tree just to the left off the ferry dock. Breakfast in the summer starts as early as 5 or 6am for ferry passengers, who can serve themselves German drip-style coffee, fruit salad with nuts and yogurt, and fresh-squeezed orange juice, all for 1,725 Drs ($7.20). Platanos is equally pleasant for evening and late-night drinks (expect to pay about 1,035 Drs ($4.30), all to be enjoyed accompanied by their phenomenal collection of jazz records.

WHERE TO STAY & EAT IN GLOSSA

There are about 100 rooms to rent in Glossa; expect to pay 8,000 Drs ($33.30) for single or double occupancy. The best way to find a room is to visit one of the tavernas or shops and inquire about a vacancy; it's a small town with an informal reservation system. If you can't find a room in Glossa, you can always take a bus or taxi down to Loutraki and check into a pension by the water.

Hotel Atlantes, Glossa. ☎ **0424/33-223, 33-489,** or **33-767.**

10 rms (all with bath). TEL

Rates: 6,210 Drs ($25.90) single; 8,050 Drs ($33.50) double. V.

Its owner and host, Les Chocalas, born in Mississippi but raised here, has returned to his native island after a 30-year absence to build this comfortable hotel, opposite the church on the edge of town. All rooms have baths and balconies looking down on the flower-filled garden or out to sea. If Les has no room in the inn, ask him or George Antoniou at the Pythari Shop (☎ **0424/33-077**) in town for advice on a room-to-let.

Taverna Tagnanti, Glossa. ☎ **33-606** or **33-076.**

Cuisine: GREEK.
Prices: Appetizers 200–850 Drs (80¢–$3.55); main courses 920–2,875 Drs ($3.80–$12).
Open: Daily 7am–midnight.

A seasonal resident sent us to this modest taverna and, since then, we've received several letters from happy readers about the inexpensive food, friendly staff, and spectacular view. The menu is standard taverna style, but we enjoyed everything sampled. The Stamataki and Antoniou families run this and a nearby souvenir shop, Pithari, and if requested, will even help you find a room in town. This is the place to meet, greet, and eat in Glossa.

Evening Entertainment

The night scene isn't nearly as active on Skópelos as on neighboring Skiáthos, but there are still plenty of bars, late night cafés, and discos. Most of the coolest bars are on the far south side of town; **Faiyum** (☎ **22-921**), near the Selini Restaurant, is typical. **Labikos Disco** and **Kirki** are among the hottest places on the island for dancing.

3 Alónissos

62 nautical miles from Vólos

ARRIVING/DEPARTING • By Air The fastest way by air is via Skiáthos with connection by hydrofoil. Although it's possible to arrive from Skýros, there are many fewer boats and it's a much farther trip.

• By Sea Alónissos is on the ferry line with Skiáthos and Skópelos, so during the busy summer months there is daily service. The hydrofoils come and go seven times a day. Excursion boats from Alónisso's neighbors also operate on a daily basis throughout the summer. There's at least one boat a day arriving from either Vólos, Ághios Konstantinos, or Kými (once weekly). In spring and fall service to the island drops off considerably; check with the local **Port Authority** (☎ **65-595**) for the schedule.

ESSENTIALS The **post office** is open from 8am to 2pm Monday through Friday. The **telephone office** (OTE) is directly on the waterfront, but operates only in the summer; hours are from 7:30am to 9pm daily. There is a **doctor** who can handle most emergencies (☎ **65-208**). The local **pharmacy** is on the right-hand road, just off the harbor. **Ikos Travel** (☎ **65-320;** fax 65-321) sells hydrofoil and ferry tickets and can book Olympic Airways flights. They also sell an excellent map, published by the

Association of Hotels and Travel Agents of Alónissios, that is a must if you're planning on exploring the island and if you plan to take one of their many excursions. The **police** have an office in Patitiri (☎ **65-205**).

If recent history is a guide, then Alónissos, the least known and one of the most naturally attractive of the major Sporades, would have to be considered a star-crossed island. For many centuries when Alónissos was a major producer of wine, vineyards covered over one-fourth of the island. Then, in 1950, a blight hit the crop, killing the vines and contaminating the soil. To this day the island is unable to resume any significant farming, although there are olive groves covering the hills. And 1965 was another trying year for Alónissos: A minor earthquake hit the island, damaging the hilltop Byzantine capital. Roofs caved in and many walls cracked, but ironically the real damage was dealt by a military commission sent in to study the situation. Instead of recommending rebuilding the old town, they suggested moving the entire population of the capital to a minor port, Patitíri ("wine press"), and making it a model community. As you might imagine, the substandard housing has created yet another blight on the island. A Canadian film crew even came to Alónissos a few years ago to make a documentary on how not to build a town. However, the Greek island spirit cannot be denied and the waterfront, as you arrive, is a familiar and pleasant blend of tavernas, hotels, and tourist services.

With all this doom and gloom, it's a pleasure to report that luck seems to be turning for underdog Alónissos. Fifteen locals, eager to return to their homes, and a band of Dutch, American, French, German, and English devotees, have moved to old Alónissos to rebuild it, using traditional materials, methods, and designs. Prior to 1990 they even went so far as to forego electricity, rejecting modern comforts and conveniences for some greater psychic connection to the past. Reportedly, most people use electricity only in the bars, tavernas, and shops, but still not at home. Tavernas, bars, and a couple of craft shops have opened in the last few years, and it looks as if the capital may once again regain some of its lost dignity, although locals in Patitiri resent the foreign invasion of their old hometown. It's a complicated world, even in faraway Alónissos.

Orientation

The total population of Alónissos is about 3,000; most people live between Patitíri and the old capital, so you can imagine how little development has taken place on the rest of the island. Actually, that's part of the lure for the many Greek visitors who've been displaced by the foreign invasion on Skiáthos and Skópelos. They used to flock to the Sporades for beautiful beaches, lush vegetation, and uncrowded villages. They still come, but so do boatloads of foreign tourists who have also discovered these special islands. Alónissos is the last frontier for those who long for the good old days of cheap living, deserted beaches, and utterly unsullied scenery (with the obvious exception of the port).

Excursion boats, hydrofoils, and the Nomikos ferry call at Patitíri, on the southern tip of the island. Old Alónissos is connected to Patitíri by the island's only paved road; almost all of the beaches are reached by excursion boats. The vast majority of the island is mountainous and green, with olive trees and pines accounting for much of the foliage.

The harbor in Patitíri, at the bottom of some steeply rising hills, is fairly small. To your right as you disembark from the ferry is a barren hill with the largest number of private rooms to rent, many overlooking the harbor. The waterfront presents the usual mix of cafés, hotels, fish tavernas, and shops. A good place to begin if you're just arriving is the **Ikos Travel Office** (☎ **65-320,** fax 0424/65-321), turn right just off the *paralía.* Panos ("Pakis" to everyone) Athanassiou runs the agency and knows the island and its politics—not to mention good hotels and beaches—as well as anyone. There's a cluster of hotels on the southern side of the port. The port's summertime-only OTE is on the waterfront, while the **post office** is on the main road leading from the port back up into the less attractive part of Patítri and on to old Alónissos. The post office is about a five-minute walk up the road. A short walk will take you through the town and by the Bay of Votsi.

Getting Around

BY BUS For you old Alónissos hands, you'll be happy to hear that the on-again, off-again bus from Patitíri to old Alónissos is back in business with five to six runs per day; the fare is 230 Drs (95¢) one way—tickets may be purchased on board or at Ikos Travel.

BY MOPED & CAR Mopeds and motorcycles are available in Patitíri for 3,450 Drs. ($14.40) per day, depending on the size. A Jeep/truck can be rented for 25,700 Drs ($107.10) per day, including insurance. Be very careful of the torturous mountain roads in the remote, northern parts of the island.

BY TAXI A taxi (☎ **65-573** or **65-425**) from Patitíri to old Alónissos costs 920 Drs ($3.80) each way.

BY BOAT Most of the excursion boats to the nearby beaches leave the port sometime between 9 to 11am for about 805 Drs. roundtrip ($3.35). Ask at Ikos Travel about chartering a boat, or at least convincing a fisher to go to some of the nearby Lesser Sporades. Rental boats are available for approximately 17,250 Drs ($72) per day for a boat with a 9-hp motor.

ON FOOT Our favorite means of transportation leads you on a 30-minute walk up a winding trail through olive groves to a magnificent panorama. The new island map (see "Essentials," above) will show you the route, which begins near the post office. Ask and the way will be shown. The faint-hearted should take a taxi up and walk down. The road from Patitiri to old Alónissos is one of the few paved roads, though there is a large network of dirt and unimproved roads that crisscross the island.

What to See & Do

Most people come to Alónissos to escape the crowds, find a quiet beach, and bliss out. Lofty ambitions all, but the island offers several other interesting diversions that shouldn't be overlooked.

BEACHES

Local water taxis leave in the morning for Marpounda Beach, on the south coast. The beach is a long strip of sand and pebbles, stretching from Výthisma to the hotel beach at Marpoúnda. The other beaches are along the eastern coast. The best beach on the island, Kokkinókastro (Red Castle) Beach, is far out on a point in between two other attractive beaches, Chryssí Miliá and the beach on Tzortzí Bay. Part of the wonder of Kokkinókastro is that there are pottery shards, broken stone slabs, huge carved blocks, and pieces of clay with traces of writing all strewn about, said to be the remains from the ancient city of Íkos. Where else in Greece can one find such a perfect blend of Hellenism and hedonism?

Excursion boats also stop on Peristéra, an islet immediately adjacent to Alónissos. There are fine beaches within 30 minutes walking distance of where the boat docks at Vassilikón.

AROUND THE ISLAND

The coast is pitted with grottos of exceptional beauty, and there are several excursions run by Ikos Travel that take you along the coast. There is a cave in nearby Vótsi, actually a short walk outside of Vótsi in Platsoúka, that is particularly picturesque (it's most accessible on calm days). Alónissos offers opportunities for spear-fishing, skin diving, and underwater explorations of the ruins at Psathoúra and the Byzantine shipwreck at Águios Petros. On Yioúra, you can visit the opening of the so-called Cyclops Cave, where Ulysses is said to have met the Cyclops. Since 1990 the Ministry of Culture has closed the cave for excavation. On Kyratanagia, you can visit a tranquil, scenic monastery. Ikos Travel operates a day trip for 5,625 Drs ($31.25), including lunch.

Increasingly, people are coming to Alónissos to hike, both with and without backpacks, and to watch for sea mammals such as dolphins and seals in the National Marine Park. We've never had the time to do this, but we'll likely do it on our next visit. If you've made the big effort, write to us and share your experiences. Was it worth it? Did you see any Mediterranean seals?

OLD ALÓNISSOS

You can either walk or take a taxi to the old capital. Wear good shoes if you choose to walk; depending on your enthusiasm, it will take 45 minutes to an hour. (There is a footpath shortcut just above the post office.) Once in the village, built in Byzantine times, wander through the streets, climbing to the top. There's a curious mix of exquisitely rebuilt homes, with the same sort of slate roofing seen on Skópelos, and dilapidated and abandoned buildings. A growing community of artisans have set up shop in Old Alónissos, and their wares are exhibited in the little stores along the main path through the village. Old Alónissos is a very quiet corner, isolated from the turmoil of the world; it's a pleasure just to sit on a ledge, look out to the sea, and let your mind wander.

Where to Stay

There are quite a few private homes that rent rooms, and if you're looking to save money they're usually on a par with most of the Class D and some of the Class C hotels and pensions. Expect to pay 5,750–7,000 Drs ($24–$29.10) per person for a room. Most of the rooms are on the north side of the port, such as **Pension Lucy** (☎ **0424/65-016**), run by one of the most gracious hostesses in town; a double runs 6,900 Drs ($28.75). By the time you arrive on Alónissos there may be accommodations available in the old capital. The folks at Ikos Travel can arrange to rent houses that sleep three to four people for 15,000–16,000 Drs ($62.50–$66.70).

Hotel Gorgona, Rousoúm Yialós, Alónissos 37005. ☎ **0424/65-317.** Fax 0424/65-629. 17 rms (all with bath). TEL

Rates: 11,500 Drs ($47.90) single or double. No credit cards.

It would be hard for us not to like a place that has a mural of a mermaid flanking the front door. Throw in the fact that all of the beds have firm, orthopedic matresses, it's in a quiet location, and it's about the cleanest facility in town and you'll understand why we really like the Hotel Gorgona. Request a sea-facing room, and for the price, it's one of the best upper-priced values in town.

Hotel Liadromia, Patitíri, Alónissos 37005. ☎ **0424/65-521.** Fax 0424/65-096. 20 rms (all with bath). TEL

Rates (including breakfast): 14,950 Drs ($62.30) single or double. EC, MC, V.

This is a very nice hotel near the harbor. Many of its rooms have great views, and a roof garden provides an extra treat. The hostess, Maria Thansiou, an Alónissos original, has brought considerable style to this attractive inn. Lace curtains, wall hangings, murals and wrought iron fixtures distinguish this hotel from the usual Class C lodging.

★ **Paradise Hotel,** Alónissos-Magnisías 37005. ☎ **0424/65-213** or **65-160.** Fax 0424/65-161. 31 rms (all with bath). TEL

Rates (including breakfast): 12,995 Drs ($54.15) single; 17,250 Drs ($71.90) double. EC, MC, V.

The Paradise Hotel, run by the gracious and gregarious Kostas, is perched on the rocky shore east of the boat harbor. You'll enjoy late-afternoon drinks on the hotel's pine-shaded terrace overlooking the water-worn rocks or a swim in the clean, clear sea below. The staff will arrange transportation from the dock.

WHERE TO STAY IN STENI VALA

Theodorou Hotel, Stení Vála, Alónissos 37005. ☎ **0424/65-158** or **65-558.** Fax 0424/65-321. 10 rms (all with bath). MINIBAR TEL

Rates: 6,900 Drs ($28.75) single/double.

If you really want to get away from it all, there's the Theodorou Hotel, a basic inn located about halfway up the east coast of the island in Stení Vála. Rooms are very simply furnished and transportation to the hotel is provided by Land Rover or boat. The village is served by two restaurants and a pub.

Where to Eat

Argo, ☎ **65141.**

Cuisine: TAVERNA. **Reservations:** Not required.
Prices: Appetizers 405–1,610 Drs ($1.70–$6.70); main courses 1,305–9,200 Drs ($4.30–$38.30). Fish priced per kilo. No credit cards.
Open: Daily 12pm–2am.

This outdoor taverna has just opened up next door to the Paradise Hotel and has the same eagle-eye view of the rocky eastern shore of the island. In the center of the tables stands a white plaster neoclassical fountain with a goddess that lights up at night—a kitsch fantasy that will delight or dismay, according to your taste. Locals praise the fare, particularly the deep-fried calamari.

★ **Kamaki Ouzerí,** Patitíri. ☎ **65-245.**

Cuisine: GREEK.
Prices: Appetizers 460–2,070 Drs ($1.90–$8.60); main courses 750–3,450 Drs ($3.10–$14.40).
Open: Daily 6pm–1am.

The gregarious Spyros is definitely in charge of the grill as this ultra-popular ouzerí, miraculously not located on the waterfront. A wide selection of *mezédes* (appetizers)

and fresh fish distinguish this fine, but very basic eatery from the more touristed establishments. Probably the best food in town, especially for grilled seafood and fish.

Ouzerí Lefteris, Patitiri. No telephone.

Cuisine: GREEK.
Prices: Appetizers 400–830 Drs ($1.70–$3.45); main courses 725–2,500 Drs ($3–$10.40).
Open: Daily 10am–4pm and 6pm–1am.

We come here for the best bargain in town: an ouzo and hot plate combo, a bargain at 310 Drs ($1.70), including an assortment of *mezédes* (appetizers). The Lefteris also has many other salads, freshly grilled fish, and their delicious house specialty, saganáki shrimp with onions, tomatoes, pepper, mustard, and feta.

WHERE TO EAT IN OLD ALÓNISSOS

Taverna Astrofegia/Mina's Bar, Old Alónissos. ☎ **65-182.**

Cuisine: INTERNATIONAL. **Reservations:** Recommended.
Prices: Appetizers 710 Drs ($3); main courses 1,955 Drs ($8.15).
Open: Daily 6pm–midnight from June 15–Sept 15.

Good food, the island's best nightlife, and stunning views are all to be found at Astrofegia, a.k.a. Mina's Bar, located on the top level of old Alónissos, in a dining area covered by a grape arbor. On any given night you might find a costume/dress-up evening (there's an annual fancy party) set to fifties Greek music, African beats, or Frank Sinatra. The cuisine is international and reasonably priced. We appreciate the fact that owner Iannis Toundas tries to use organic vegetables as much as possible in his many tasty salads.

Paraport Taverna, Old Alónissos. No telephone.

Cuisine: GREEK.
Prices: Appetizers 350–1,000 Drs ($1.45–$4.15); main courses 860–2,500 Drs ($3.60–$10.40).
Open: Daily 9am–2pm and 6pm–1am.

At the top of old Alónissos village is the Paraport, where head chef Ilias and family dole out good standard Greek taverna fare. We pay tribute here to the late Alónissos Blues Band, a mélange of local bouzouki players and European summer residents who lost their lead singer; but their legacy lives on when a local band belts it out once a week or so.

4 Skýros

25 nautical miles from Kými; 118 nautical miles from Piraeus

ARRIVING/DEPARTING • By Air Olympic Airways has five flights a week between Athens and Skýros. The planes are small, so reserve well in advance. The local office is **Skýros Travel** (☎ **0222/91-123** or **91-600**). A taxi from the airport is about 850 Drs ($3.55) per person in a shared cab. A bus meets most flights and goes to Skýros town, Magaziá and sometimes Mólos; the fare is 350 Drs ($1.45).

• By Sea There is only one ferry company serving Skýros, the **Lykomides Co.,** and it is owned by a company whose stockholders are all citizens of Skýros. The old company provided great service in the busy summer months and lousy service in the off-season. So the citizens of Skýros bought their own boat and only allow it to dock at Skýros. During the summers, it runs twice daily from Kými to Skýros (11am and 5pm) and twice daily from Skýros to Kými (8am and 2pm). Off-season, there is one ferry each way, leaving Skýros at 8am and Kými at 5pm. The fare is 1,550 Drs ($8.60).

For schedules to Kými, call **0222/22-020** in Kými. For Skýros ferry schedules, call 0222/91-790 or 91-789. The Lykomides office in Skýros and Kými sell connecting bus tickets to Athens; the fare is 2,550 Drs ($10.65) for the 3½ hour ride.

The **Flying Dolphin** now goes to Skýros five times a week, starting in mid-May, daily in July and August, from Skiáthos, Skópelos and Alónissos. This is easily the most convenient way to go, though pricey compared to the ferry; one-way tickets cost 9,500 Drs ($39.60) for the 4-hour plus Vólos–Skýros commute.

The tricky part of getting to Skýros is the connection with the ferry from the other Sporades islands. The off-season ferry from Skiáthos, Skópelos, Alónossis, and Vólos is scheduled to arrive at Kými at 5pm, but is usually late. It is not uncommon to see the Skýros ferry disappearing on the horizon as your ferry pulls into Kými. Oh well, make the best of the 24-hour layover and get a room in Paralía Kými (See our section on Kými for details).

From Athens, buses run regularly for the three-hour trip to Kými, from which you take a local bus to Paralía Kými. Just make sure of your connection.

The ferries from Kými and Vólos and hydrofoils from the other Sporades dock at Linaria, on the opposite side of the island from the town of Skýros. The island's only bus—sometimes they bring another over from the mainland—will meet the boat and take you over winding, curvy roads to Skýros town for 190 Drs (80¢). Depending on the mood of the driver, the bus will stop at Magazia Beach, immediately below the town next to the Xenia Hotel.

ESSENTIALS The largest tourist office is **Skýros Travel Center** (☎ **0222/91-123** or **91-600;** fax 0222/92-123), next to Skýros Pizza Restaurant in the main market; it is open daily 8am to 2:30pm and 6:30 to 11:30pm. English-speaking Lefteris Trakos is very helpful on many counts, including accommodations, changing money, Olympic Airways flights (he is the local ticket agent), long-distance calls, some interesting bus and boat tours, as well as Flying Dolphin tickets. The **post office** is near the bus square and is open Monday through Friday from 8am to 2pm. There's only one **bank** (with no extended hours), also near the bus square; the best idea is to bring plenty of drachmas. The **telephone office** (OTE) is open Monday through Friday only from 7:30am–3pm, is 50 meters south of the bus stop.

Skýros is an island of wide, fine-sand beaches, attractive whitewashed pillbox architecture, picturesque surroundings, low prices, and relatively few tourists. How can this be? First, it's difficult to get to Skýros. The ferry leaves either from the isolated port of Paralía Kými (with a two-hour boatride to Skýros), on the east coast of Évvia, or from Vólos (or the other Sporades), which is the starting point for a four-hour hydrofoil ride to the island. Second, Greek tourists prefer the other, more thickly forested Sporades, especially Skiáthos. In this matter we disagree with the Greeks. Skýros's scruffy vegetation and stark contrast between sea, sky, and rugged terrain make it all the more dramatic and revealing. Historically, perhaps the biggest damper on tourism had been placed by many Skyriots themselves, who have always been ambivalent, at best, about developing this very traditional island for tourism. As evidence of this, until recently there were only a handful of hotels on the whole island. Since 1990, however, Skýros has seen a miniboom in the accommodations-building business, and with the impending completion of the giant marina, it's setting itself up to become yet another tourist mecca.

In fact, on our last visit in 1994, the island was ready for its first direct charter flight from Switzerland, a harbinger of accelerated change.

None of these obstacles should deter you—be assured that, at least for now, Skýros remains an ideal place for an extended stay.

Orientation

The boats dock at Linariá, on the opposite side of the island from the town of Skýros. The town itself is built on a rocky bluff overlooking the sea.

Skýros looks quite like a typical Cycladic hill town, with whitewashed cube-shaped houses built on top of each other. The streets and paths that are called streets are too narrow for cars and mopeds, so most of the traffic is by foot and hoof. As you alight from the bus at the *platía,* head north toward the center of town and the main tourist services. To get to Magaziá Beach, follow the main street all the way to Rupert Brooke's statue of Immortal Poetry and take the switchbacks down. If in doubt, just follow the dung and you'll end up on the donkey path. (If your load is heavy, take a taxi to Magaziá; it's a hike.) Magaziá is several kilometers long, so if you want to be alone just keep walking.

The most scenic area on the island (with a pebble beach) is Ághios Fokas, on the southern coast near Tris Boukes, at the grave of the poet Rupert Brooke. Locals call it paradise, and like all such places it's extremely difficult to reach. Most Skyrians will suggest walking, but it's a long, hilly hike. To get there, take the bus back to Linariá, stop at the crossroads with Pefkos and begin your hike there.

Among the beaches, far more convenient are Calamitsa, a three-kilometer walk south of Linariá, and closer still is Aherounes, and the two beaches near Skýros, Magaziá and Molos (where there is windsurfing). Roads and an occasional bus, taxi, or private car lead across the Oros Olympos mountains in the center of the island to Atsitsa, where there are a few rooms to rent, and Kirapangia. Archili, once a lovely stretch of sand, is being transformed into a marina capable of receiving giant cruise ships.

History

The island has the kind of history that inspires tales of adventure and romance. During the Byzantine era, the head clerics from Epirus sent ten families to Skýros to serve as governors. With the exception of St. George's Monastery, they were given every inch of land. For hundreds of years these ten families dominated the affairs of Skýros. The island prospered as a safe harbor (in Kalamitsa), and consulates opened from countries near and far. The merchant ships were soon followed by pirates, who pillaged and plundered with reckless abandon. Instead of fighting the pirates, the ruling families went into business with them; the families knew what boats were expected and what they were carrying, and the pirates had the ships and bravado to steal the cargo. This unholy combination worked for only a short while, until the pirates turned their plundering on the islanders. By 1830 though, pirates had ceased to attack the island.

Greek independence reduced the influence of these ruling families. During WWI, these aristocratic families were often without food and were left to trade their ill-gotten booty with the peasant farmers. Chief among these bartered items were sets of dinnerware. Dinner plates from China, Italy, Turkey, Egypt, and other exotic locales became a sign of wealth. Skyrian families made elaborate displays of their newly acquired plates. Whole walls were covered, and by the 1920s local Skyrian craftsmen began making their own plates for the poorer families who couldn't afford the originals.

Carnival of Skýros

The 21-day celebration is highlighted by a four-day period leading up to Lent and the day itself, also known as Katharí Deftéra (Clean Monday). On this day Skýros residents don traditional costumes and perform dances on the *platía.* A special kind of flat bread, *lagana,* is served as well as taramasaláta and other meatless specialties. (Traditionally, vegetarian food is eaten for 40 days leading up to Pascha, Easter).

Prior to this, and culminating on Sunday in the mid-afternoon, are a series of ritual dances and events performed by a core group of bedecked male residents—as in the ancient Greek dramas, the roles for women are played by men. The costumes are a sight: The men wrap 70 pounds of bells around themselves and wear masks, animal skins, and hoods. The rituals tend to be completely pagan in origin and very aggressive.

As the Carnival is celebrated on Skýros, according to local ethnologist Manos Faltaits, there are interesting connections with similar events, celebrated as a shepherd's feast, in Sicily, Bulgaria, Austria, and northern Greece. In those places, the festivities celebrate the victory of shepherds over farmers. In Náoussa, in northern Greece, the village reportedly divides into two factions and throws stones at each other; in other places they battle with wooden swords.

Getting Around

BY BUS The only scheduled run is the Skýros–Linariá shuttle that runs four to five times daily; 185 Drs. (80¢). Skýros Travel has a twice-daily beach excursion bus in the high season.

BY MOPED AND CAR Mopeds and motorcycles are available in Skýros, near the police station or the taxi station, for 4,600 Drs. ($19.20) per day. A Fiat Panda can be rented for about 13,800 Drs. ($57.50) per day, including insurance. The island has a relatively well developed network of roads.

BY TAXI Taxi service between Linariá and Skýros is available but expensive, about 1,840 Drs ($7.70). Rates to other, farther destinations are similarly high.

ON FOOT Skýros is a fine place to hike. The new island map, published by Skýros Travel & Tourism, will show you a number of good routes, and it seems to be pretty accurate. For some sample trips see What to See and Do.

What to See & Do

MUSEUMS

Peek into the doorway of any Skyrian home and nine times out of ten you'll see what looks like a room from a dollhouse: tiny tables from Mt. Athos, and chairs and plates from the island, loads of plates, hanging on the wall. This unusual state of affairs is wonderfully celebrated in the island's two museums, the folk art and archeological museums. The **Faltaits Museum** (**☎ 91-232**) is the private collection of one man, Manos Faltaits, and it's one of the best island folk art museums in Greece. The museum contains a large and varied collection of plates, as well as examples of embroidery, weaving, woodworking, and clothing. We especially like the photographs of the men in traditional costume from Carnival. There's a workshop attached to the museum where young artisans make lovely objets d'art using traditional patterns and materials. The proceeds from the sale of workshop items go to the upkeep of the museum. (The museum also has another shop in the town called **Argo,** on the main street (☎ **92-158**), which is open from 10am to 1pm and 6:30pm to midnight). The folk art museum is open daily in the summer from 10am to 1pm and 5:30 to 8:30pm; in the off-season just ring the bell and someone will open it for you. Admission is free. The nearby **Archeological Museum** (☎ **91-327**) has a small collection of Mycenaean and late Helladic funerary objects, and a room dedicated to the very popular arts of Skýros. This museum is open Tuesday through Sunday from 8:30am to 3pm, and admission is 440 Drs ($1.80).

ATSÍTSA

The northwest quadrant of the island is covered in dense pine forests, spreading down to the rocky shore and opening into gentle bays and coves. This area provides wonderful hiking for sturdy walkers. Take a taxi (3,450 Drs or ($14.40) to Atsitsa. (The cautious will arrange for the taxi to return in five or six hours.) Explore the ruins of the ancient mining operation at Atsitsa, then head south for about four and one half miles to Águios, Fokas, a small bay with a tiny taverna perched right on the water. Kali Orfanou, a gracious hostess, will provide you with the meal of your trip—fresh fish caught that morning in the waters before you, vegetables plucked from the garden for your salad, and her own feta cheese and wine. Stay, swim in the bay, and hike back to your taxi. The ambitious will continue south for seven or eight miles to the main road and catch the bus or hail a taxi. This part is mainly uphill, so walker beware. In case you tire or can't pry yourself away from this secluded paradise, Kali offers two extremely primitive rooms with the view of your dreams, but without electricity or toilets (in the formal sense).

THE WILD HORSES OF SKÝROS

Skýros is the home of a unique breed of wild and very small horses, often compared to the horses depicted on the frieze of the Parthenon. The Meraklides, local Skyrians who care for these rare animals, have moved most of the diminishing breed to the nearby island of Skyriopoulou. Ask around and you might be able to find a Meraklide who'll let you ride one.

SHOPPING

Ergastiri, on the main street, has interesting ceramics, Greek shadow puppets, and a great selection of postcards. For Skyrian plates try the small shop at no. 307, across from Fragoules hardware. Also popular for plates is the studio of **Yiannis Nicholau,** next to the Xenia. He makes all of the plates and also serves as the beer distributor for the island. Good hand-carved wooden chests and chairs made from beech (in the old days it was blackberry wood) can be purchased from Lefteris Avgoklouris, former student of the recently departed master, Baboussis, in Skýros town; his studio is on Konthili Road. (☎ **91-106**), around the corner from the post office. Another fine carver is **Manolios,** in the main market.

EVENING ENTERTAINMENT

If you've gotta dance, try the **Castro Club** in Linariá or the **Skýros Club** in the Skýros Palace Hotel. Aside from these, there are few evening diversions other than bar-hopping on the main street. **Rodon** is best for listening to music, but there isn't any dancing, while the **Calypso** attracts a more refined set of drinkers who appreciate their better-made, pricier cocktails. The **Renaissance** was among the most popular spots on our last trip.

Where to Stay

The whole island has only a few hotels, so most visitors to Skýros take private rooms. The best rooms are in the upper part of the town, away from the bus stop, where women in black dresses accost you with cries of "room, room." Walk beyond the *platía,* up the main street. Women will offer you rooms here so investigate and make your choice. A more efficient procedure is to stop in at **Skýros Travel Center.** Skýros is somewhat more primitive in its facilities than other islands, so before agreeing to anything check out the rooms to ensure they are what you want. Rates for in-town or beach rooms during the high season are about 5,200 Drs ($21); so-called Class A rooms run 5,850 Drs ($24).

★ **Hotel Nefeli,** Skýros 34007. ☎ **0222/91-964.** Fax 0222/92-061.
12 rms (all with bath). TEL

Rates: 9,775 Drs ($40.70) single; 13,800 Drs ($57.50) double. AE, MC, V.

One of the best in-town options is the excellent Hotel Nefeli, built in the modern Skyrian style. Many rooms have fine views, and the large, downstairs lobby is a welcoming space, always filled at breakfast time. As the Nefeli is one of the better choices, you'd do well to reserve in advance.

WHERE TO STAY ON MAGAZIÁ BEACH/MÓLOS

$ **Hotel Angela,** Mólos, Skýros 34007. ☎ **0222/91-764.** Fax 0222/91-555.
14 rms (all with bath). TEL

Rates: 11,500 Drs ($47.90) single or double. No credit cards.

Among the most attractive and well kept abodes in the Molos/Magaziá Beach area is the Hotel Angela. Located adjacent to the sprawling Paradise Hotel complex, we found these clean and tidy rooms the best bet for the money. All rooms have balconies, but because the hotel is set back about 100 meters from the beach, there are only partial sea views. Nevertheless, the facilities and hospitality of the young couple who run the Angela make up for its just-off-the-beach location.

Pension Galeni, Magaziá Beach, Skýros 34007. ☎ **0222/91-379.** 13 rms (all with bath).

Rates: 10,350 Drs ($43.10) single or double.

Near the beach is the small but delightful Pension Galena. They recently upgraded their rooms, so that they now all have private facilities. We like the front (sea facing) rooms on the top floor for their (currently) unobstructed views. The Galeni overlooks one of the cleanest parts of Magaziá—at least it was when we visited!

Paradise Hotel, Mólos, Skýros 34007. ☎ **0222/91-560.** 60 rms (all with bath). TEL

Rates (including breakfast): 13,800 Drs ($57.50) single; 16,100 Drs ($67.10) double in the new building.

At the north end of Magaziá Beach, in the town of Mólos, you'll find the cheery Paradise Hotel. The new building has 20 rooms while the older, more basic facilities are in another 40-room building; prices in this less attractive structure run about 50% less. We suggest staying in the new wing where the rooms are better kept and have much better light. While the hotel is somewhat removed from the main town, there is a taverna on the premises and another down the street.

Xenia, Magaziá Beach, Skýros 34007. ☎ **0222/91-209.** Fax 0222/92-062.
24 rms (all with bath). TEL

Rates (including buffet breakfast): 11,700 Drs ($65) single; 15,600 Drs ($86.70) double. AE, DC, V.

The Xenia, predictably expensive (and recently upgraded), was built right on the beach and occupies, arguably, the best location on Magaziá. In 1989 they added a controversial (and obnoxious-looking) concrete breakwater that is supposed to protect the beach from erosion. The rooms have handsome 1950s-style furniture and big bathrooms with tubs, as well as wonderful balconies and sea views.

WHERE TO STAY ON AHEROUNES BEACH

Pegasus Apartments, Aherounes Beach, Skýros 34007. ☎ **0222/91-552.**
8 rms (all with bath). MINIBAR

Rates: 10,150 Drs ($42.25) studio; 20,250 Drs ($84.50) apartment. EC, MC, V.

The peripatetic Lefteris Trakos built these apartments and studios that are fully equipped and can accommodate small groups, with the former sleeping up to six people while the latter is suitable for two or three. One of the pluses of staying here is the chance to see (and ride, if you're under 15) Katerina, a Skyriot pony.

A SPLURGE CHOICE

Skyros Palace Hotel, Girismata, Skýros 34007. ☎ **0222/91-310.** Fax 0222/92-070.
80 rms (all with bath). A/C TEL

Rates (including breakfast): 15,640 Drs ($65.20) single; 22,540 Drs ($93.90) double. AE, DC, EC, MC, V.

Even though we list this as a splurge, we remain ambivalent about this out-of-the-way resort. Certainly it offers the most luxurious accommodations on the island, with a lovely pool and adjacent bar, planned tennis courts, air-conditioned rooms, and a well-planted garden, but we question the location of the complex. The beach, across the road, is an especially windy, rocky stretch of coastline, with, when we made our inspection, nearly treacherous water. Also, there is nothing else around (at least at the moment), so you'll have to take a 15 to 20 ride into the town for any nighttime action. Still, if you want to get away from it all and have some up-scales amenities to boot, the Skýros Palace Hotel might just be the place to go.

Where to Eat

On our last trip, we sampled some pretty good food, and at very reasonable prices. For starters, we breakfasted daily at **Anemos** (☎ **92-155**), located right on the main drag. You can drink real filtered coffee, eat an omelet and try their freshly squeezed juice. In the evening, the Leventis serve vegetarian pizza. Speaking of pizza, don't overlook the nearby **Skyros Pizza Restaurant** (☎ **91-684**), which serves tasty pies as well as other Greek specialties in huge portions.

The best bakery in town is hidden away up in the hills on the edge of Skýros. Walk up along the stairs to the weird statue of Poetry, bear right up the whitewashed stone path, and ask a local. It's tucked away, but your nose will be your guide (they also sell their bread in the market).

$ **Glaros Restaurant,** Skýros. No tel.

Cuisine: GREEK.
Prices: Appetizers 230–575 Drs (95¢); main courses 700–2,300 Drs ($2.90–$9.60).
Open: Daily 7pm–1am.

This venerable establishment, favored by locals in the busy summer season as a reward for staying open all year, serves from a very small list of traditional taverna fare. We've been regulars at this basic place on nearly every trip to the island over the past ten years and can report that the mousssaká, and so on are as good as ever. Another excellent value place.

$ **Restaurant Kabanero,** Skýros. ☎ **91-240.**

Cuisine: GREEK.
Prices: Appetizers 350–1,000 Drs ($1.45–$4.15); main courses 980–1,400 Drs ($4.10–$5.85).
Open: Daily 6am–midnight.

The Kabanero Restaurant represents one of the best dining values in Skýros. This perpetually busy eatery serves the usual suspects on the Greek menu: mousssaká, stuffed peppers, and tomatoes; fava; various stewed vegetables; as well as meat of all persuasion. We found the preparation up to snuff and prices about 20% less than most of the others in town. A treat.

Marietes Grill, Skýros. ☎ **91-311.**

Cuisine: GREEK.
Prices: Appetizers 220–360 Drs (90¢–$1.50); main courses 860–1,725 Drs ($3.60–$7.20).
Open: Daily 1–3pm and 6am–midnight.

One of the oldest places in town, the Marietes is a second-generation-run grill that is equally popular with locals and travelers. The dining room is as simple as simple gets, so what you go for is the food. Our recommendation here is for the grilled chicken and meats. There is a small sampling of salads.

13

Western Greece

THE IONIAN COASTLINE IS ONE OF THE MAGNIFICENT, UNIQUELY GREEK LANDSCAPES in the country. If you've heard about Corfu's legendary beauty (the setting for Shakespeare's *Tempest*) or read about Odysseus's home, Ithaca, in the *Odyssey,* you may well imagine what divine sights greet those who follow the mainland coast and look out to these verdant, rocky clumps of paradise. The Ionian Sea is as well known for its deep emerald color as the Aegean is for its turquoise hue, and from the elevated coastal highway, you can appreciate its fiery depths.

Epirus (Ípiros) is that mountainous region that begins at the coast and stretches inland, hugging the Pindus range and reaching out to Thessaly on the eastern side. What makes it intriguing are the fiercely independent mountain people who have retained many of their traditional customs, clothing, and building styles.

Seeing Western Greece

Western Greece is usually visited in conjunction with a beach break on the nearby Ionian Islands, or as part of a tour of all northern Greece. (See the map of Western Greece and the Ionian Islands in Chapter 14.) If you have some extra time, we'd recommend driving up the scenic west coast (from the Peloponnese or Athens) and spending a night at the miniresort of Párga. Then continue east to Ioánnina, where you can spend a few nights and absorb its charms slowly. From there, it's a pleasant drive to Métsovo, where hikers especially will enjoy having a few days to explore.

1 Ionian Coast

Igoumenítsa is 295 miles NW of Athens

GETTING THERE • **By Bus** The **bus** to and from Athens runs three times daily on the privately run KTEL lines (☎ **01/51-25-954** in Athens); it's a nine-hour ride. Most other destinations are served by local buses from Igoumenítsa, Ioánnina, and Préveza.

• **By Sea** If you follow our advice, you won't jump your steamer from Italy when it calls at Corfu just to cross over to Igoumenítsa. But if you did, the informative Baláskas Brothers at **Milano Travel** (☎ **0665/23-565**) can answer all your questions; they're located at Odós Aghíon Apostólon 9, opposite the ferry pier, and open 8am to 10:30pm in summer. **John Kantas,** at Odós Aghíon Apostólon 13, is also very helpful. From Igoumenítsa to Corfu: passenger fares are 1,000 Drs ($4.15) per person; for a car and driver the cost is 6,500 Drs ($27.10); ferries depart about 12 times daily.

The **Hellenic-Mediterranean Lines** and **Ventoúris Ferries** run steamers to Brindisi or Bari, in Italy, every two days in July and August from Igoumenítsa; fares range from 10,000 Drs ($41.65) for a seat to 36,000 Drs ($150) for a cabin in the high season. Contact the Milano Travel Office for information, or call the Hellenic-Mediterranean office at 22-180.

• **By Car** From the Peloponnese, drive west on the coast highway, then cross the Gulf of Corinth from Río, near Pátra, and drive northwest along the coast. From Athens, the inland highway north through Livadiá, Tríkkala, and Ioánnina is the quickest route to Igoumenítsa.

ESSENTIALS There are no government tourist offices in this region, so local travel agents are the best source of information.

What's Special About Western Greece

Natural Scenery

- Párga's heart-shaped beach cove lined with fine gold sand is one of the prettiest in the country.
- The Ionian Sea views from the mainland's west coast highway are unforgettable, especially at sunset.
- It's so scenic that Aristotle Onassis and Paul McCartney, two vacationers with access to an unlimited range of possibilities, chose to make their home-away-from-home on Ionian islands.

Traditional Villages

- The island in the lake of Ioánnina, and the city's fortified old town, both contain fine examples of 18th- and 19th-century stucco and stone housing and public buildings.
- Métsovo is a mist-shrouded alpine village whose inhabitants maintain their traditional lifestyle.

The mountains look on Marathon,
And Marathon looks on the sea;
And musing there an hour alone,
I dreamed that Greece might still be free.

The author of those lines from *Don Juan,* Lord Byron, died in Messolónghi in 1824. It's one of those places on Greece's beautiful west coast that even Byron fans could do without.

Messolónghi

Messolónghi was founded 400 years ago after the Evinos River began to silt up, uniting three islets. The shallow lagoons surrounding the town provide excellent fishing and breeding grounds for eel and *avgotáracho* (a local fish roe). Instead of charming, seaside tavernas, which should be serving these local delicacies, Messolónghi features incomplete tract housing overlooking dirty marshland to the sea. From the local army base, hundreds of uniformed soldiers spew forth to roam the streets or crowd the ouzerís.

This town actually does have an interesting, illustrious history. Its inhabitants held out bravely for four years against the Turkish assault in the War of Independence, but in 1826 there was a great massacre and the town was razed by fire. Lord Byron, a champion of Greek liberty, died of a fever at Messolónghi as he took part in the fighting there. For those who've come this far to see **Byron's grave,** it is in the Garden of Heroes, signposted HEROE'S TOMB, just before you enter the town.

IMPRESSIONS

The situation of Messolonghi is not unknown to you. The dykes of Holland when broken down are the deserts of Arabia for dryness in comparison.
—Byron, in a letter, 1824

Lyssanias asks whether the child in Nyla's womb is his.
—Question submitted to the oracle at Dodona, inscribed on a lead tablet found at the site

From Messolónghi north, the road curves inland through verdant fields striped with plastic tents where tobacco is drying. Olives and cypress trees alternate.

Astakós

About 48 km north is the lovely port of **Astakós** with ferry service to Kefalonía and Ithaca. Newer houses line the gentle slope of forested hills that surround this cove. Beautiful 19th-century villas line the broad streets, clogged with taverna tables. The simple quay juts out into the placid water, where an infrequent caique takes passengers to the island of **Kálamos,** farther north. From Astakós, there are daily sailings in summer to **Aghía Efimía** in Kefalonía or Ithaca (☎ **0674/61-487** for schedule information).

WHERE TO STAY & EAT

If you're lulled into spending the night, there are some rooms to let above the storefronts around the town square, or try the **Stratos Hotel** (☎ **0646/41-096**), a relaxed, modern place where comfortable doubles with half tubs with showers and large balconies overlooking the harbor cost 16,000 Drs ($66.65); the cafeteria downstairs serves midday and sunset beverages to the parade of port-watchers.

Astakós has a few tavernas; we liked **Spíros,** on the port, for its fresh fish, stewed vegetable dishes, and baked eggplant.

Mítikas

Mítikas is another charming port on the Ionian coast, 81 km north of Messolónghi. This quiet village has several hotels and a few tavernas, built during the boom times when ferries docked here going to and from Ithaca and Kefalonía. All that's changed. Now, if there's enough interest, local cruise companies from Lefkás circle the nearby Pringiponíssi (four private islands) so that tourists can ogle Skorpiós, the island owned by the late Aristotle Onassis. These boats occasionally stop at Mítikas for lunch.

The friendly inhabitants seem little touched by their brush with tourist fame. They proudly tell Americans of the days when young John Kennedy, Jr. and Onassis used to water-ski off their shores. The calm waters are broken now by fishing boats that bring back their mullet and eels to local tavernas. The most satisfying thing to do in Mítikas is watch life go by. Older women, dressed in black, sweep their patios along the waterfront. Crisply dressed young girls promenade along the main street, holding hands. Old men in dusty blue and gray sit at the café/bars and watch you watch them. Robust young men clean the eels on the long thin stretch of pebble beach, swapping stories about Australia, where they return each winter to earn money for their families in Mítikas.

WHERE TO STAY & EAT

On our last trip we chose to stay at **Gláros Rooms** (☎ **0646/81-240**), across from the church on main street, owned and operated by the friendliest people in town; the son, Miltiádes, speaks English and his wife, Mary, who comes from Toronto, teaches English at the local school. Doubles with shared bath, and some with balconies overlooking the peaceful harbor, cost 4,875 Drs ($20.30). The **Hotel Kymata** (☎ **0646/81-258**), a little farther down the street, has comfortable doubles with bath for 9,100 Drs ($37.90).

The **Glaros Restaurant,** across from the church, has the best food in town. Much of it is grown on the owners' farm.

EN ROUTE TO PRÉVEZA

The Ionian coast banks sharply here, leaving drivers at a 30° angle to admire the fairyland greenery and small stone fragments that appear to have been tossed randomly into the sea. We'd say how poor the road is, but things change so quickly in Greece (where a flooded spring or a frozen winter can cause terrible destruction to macadam paving) that it may look like U.S. 40 when you attempt it. Near the crossover to Lefkás at water's edge are more ramparts from the well-preserved Venetian fortress at **Santa Maura** (built by Giovanni Orsini in 1300).

Near **Vónitsa** there's a well-preserved Byzantine castle so impregnable that it was able to hold out against the Turks until 1479. At **Áktio** (Actium), site of the famous naval battle where the forces of Augustus defeated those of Mark Antony and Cleopatra, there is another break in the road, the entry into the Ambracian Gulf (Amvrakikós Kólpos).

Préveza

Here a very small car ferry shuttles back and forth across the half kilometer waterway from the parking lot of Áktio to the busy, crowded Préveza harbor. For the Áktio–Préveza shuttle, cars are charged 700 Drs ($2.90) and people 90 Drs (38¢) each. There are several pleasant cafés along Préveza's harbor, all in full view of the steady crawl of vehicles waiting for the next shuttle and the nightly *vólta.* The old, narrow back streets of town are a good place to stock up on picnic supplies for your journey.

WHAT TO SEE & DO

For archeology buffs, there's the large, intriguing site of Nikópolis nearby, and veering east, the transportation hub of Árta. **Nikópolis** is 8 km north of Préveza, a Roman town built in A.D. 31 by Emperor Augustus to commemorate his victory at Actium (Aktio). Several walls have survived with triple gates, and you can climb around to see the remains of the temples of Mars (Ares) and Poseidon, part of an aqueduct, and some baths. In the Byzantine period Nikópolis prospered, and the remains of five basilicas can be examined at the site. Unfortunately, their fine mosaic floors are covered with gravel. The foundation wall of the outer city wall is one square mile long and can be found (by the diligent few) above the village of **Smyrtoúla.** Impressions left by Mark Antony's bronze battering rams can still be discerned. The upper part of the Roman theater is visible on the Nikópolis slope; the rest is still beneath it. The museum at the site has more burial monuments; its guard will also open one of the basilicas for you for a tip. The site and museum are open 9am to 3pm daily; the admission fee is 500 Drs ($2.10). Shaded by olives and carpeted with grass, Nikópolis is the right place to be on a sticky August day. Travelers without wheels can catch the local bus from Prevéza to Igoumenítsa or Árta and get off at the site.

Archeology buffs should watch for signs to **Kassópi** on the road north from Préveza to Árta (the local bus passes by). Kassópi is a well-preserved ancient town that was organized according to ideas in Aristotle's *Politics;* it was designed by Hippodamus. Cobbled streets, many with a gutter down the center, were sloped to carry rainwater; about 20 blocks have been laid out in a geometric pattern. The site's guard passes the time between visitors by tending the sheep that inhabit Kassópi and give it such a lived-in feel. The site is open 9am to 3pm daily. The admission fee is 500 Drs ($2.10); half price for students. The view is very impressive from here, but don't pass by this next site, the nearby **Zalónga.**

The men of Zalónga were massacred by the troops of Alí Pashá almost 200 years ago. It was on this cliff at Zalónga that, in 1822, 62 Souliote women, with children in their arms, danced to the edge and stepped off, one by one. A monument celebrates these women, who preferred death to rape or submission to Turkish rule. The monument can be seen high on the mountain from miles away, but steps and a 15-minute walk will lead you there. Just below it is the small chapel of **Ághios Dimítrios,** whose frescoed interior tells the sad story of the women of Soúli.

Árta is the second-largest town in Epirus after Ioánnina, and is known for its bridge, which spans the Arachthos River (it's the oldest stone bridge in Greece). Legend has it that the bridge's builder, in order to make it stand, bricked his wife into one leg. The church of Panaghia Parigorítissa, in the center of town, has been converted into a museum for local finds from Roman and Byzantine times. The church is an interesting 13th-century work; it, the ruins of a temple along Pyrrou Street, the nearby remains of the ancient theater, and a crumbling fortress above the town are the major sights. In Ághios Vassilios and Aghía Theodóra, rare icons and fine frescoes, gifts of the Komnines and Angheli Imperial families, are exhibited.

WHERE TO STAY & EAT

If you decide to stop your wanderings here in Préveza (not our recommendation), try the **Hotel Mínos (☎ 0682/28-424)**, a quiet, family-oriented place where comfortable doubles with bath cost 9,260 Drs ($38.60). Turn right from the ferry and continue along the port about 50 meters, turn left at the little square and find it about 200 meters up on the left.

Even if you're not spending the night, try to eat at **To Delphinaki (☎ 26-130)**, where the specialty is *kolokithokeftédes,* scrumptious zucchini fritters; the fresh fish and fine wine are also a treat. Turn right from the ferry and continue along the port for about 350 meters, where you'll see their sign with a smiling dolphin, turn left and it's about 200 meters up on the right.

EN ROUTE TO PÁRGA

Continuing north from Préveza to Igoumenítsa, this irregular coast still offers some of the best scenery in Greece. The changing light, especially as the day wears on, creates subtle images throughout the drive. As striking as Delphi, the Ionian coast is a region where the magic of that "Greek light" is illuminated.

Beach lovers should continue for 57 km to **Párga,** a very pretty resort that is perfect for R&R—in the low season. You'll find it very built up, to accommodate Corfu's overflow traffic and booked solid by tour groups in the high season, but the two long beach coves that fan out like outstretched wings from its long central quay provide enough room for everyone to enjoy the clean, calm waters.

Párga

The town beach is a scenic stretch of white sand (and a few scattered rocks) with a view over the gorgeous bay. The water is emerald and turquoise, with tiny islands tastefully positioned for even the most discerning tourist. Unfortunately word is out on all this beauty, so rooms are nearly impossible to find in the summer—though you may find them being offered in the spring and fall.

ORIENTATION & INFORMATION

The **police, post office,** and **bus station** are all in the same building at Odós Alexádrou Várga 18, near the big church. If you want to check on the Igoumenítsa sailings for Corfu, there's a telephone center (OTE) uphill of Vasila Street (open 7:30am to 3:10pm Monday to Friday, longer hours in summer). There are several **souvenir shops** that act as banker's agents across from each other in the tiny square. The **West Travel Tourist Office** (☎ **0684/31-223,** fax 31-948), upstairs at Odós Bagga 1, the main pedestrian lane that leads off right coming from square after the church and winds uphill to the fortress, sells ferry and excursion tickets to the local caiques, and can rent cars, book rooms or apartments, and help you with other travel-related problems. Several of the souvenir shops sell snorkels, masks, and fins—snorkeling is the thing to do in this transparent water.

WHAT TO SEE & DO

Small paddleboats are ideal for touring Párga's other nearby coves. Caiques advertise their **excursion trips** on small signs on the quay; our favorite sign advertises DAY TRIP TO HADES, which departs at 9am (does it ever return?). There are several boats running to **Paxí** (1,500 Drs or $6.25) and to the **Nekromantia Cave,** on the River Styx (1,200 Drs or $5).

If you walk up the lane running behind the harbor, the "tost," burger, and disco joints disappear. You can explore the walls of the **Venetian fortress** that straddles Párga's two coves, or cross over and reward yourself with a swim at long, sandy **Váltos beach** (the best locally).

Nekromantío is the most popular day trip from Párga, a site 25 km south at the village of **Messopótamos.** At the ancient grounds of the "Necromantic Oracle" is the estuary of the Acheron River, where the souls of the dead used to board the ferry to Hades. Today you can explore the subterranean lake of **Acherónda** and visit the famous **oracle** at the Ephyros of Thesprotia, recommended to Odysseus for its wise counsel. Excavations have revealed a dark, twisting corridor leading into the main sanctuary, a labyrinth created to remind pilgrims of the tortured wanderings of restless souls in Erebos, the last stop before Hades.

WHERE TO STAY & EAT

New hotels are still being constructed and there are rooms to let all over town and beyond Valtos beach. Shop around and bargain before July or after September 15th.

Our favorite place is the older **Hotel Paradissos** (☎ **0684/31-229,** fax 31-226), at Odós Livadá 33, in the center of town, which has been renovated without losing its charm, attentive service and friendly atmosphere; doubles with bath cost 9,980 Drs ($41.60), and AE, EC, MC, V are accepted. The **Aghios Nektários** (☎ **0684/31-150**), at Odós Aghias Mánnas 36, up the street from the bus station, is also quite acceptable; doubles with bath are 8,450 Drs ($35.20). During our last visit we stayed at the lovely new **Hotel Maistrali** (☎ **0684/31-275**), at 4 Kryonéri Place, just 50 meters from the town beach—they were already fully booked for next July and August—where spacious doubles with bath and balcony cost 9,100 Drs ($37.90).

Walk up to the center of "town" and you'll find **To Kantouni** (no phone) in a niche off Vassilas Street. Under a canvas canopy sit a few tables and chairs; wander into the dark, cool interior of this little storefront and the cook will show you her fare. Everyone says she has the best moussaká in town, and the prices are hard to beat.

The best fresh seafood can be found at **Tzimas (or Four Brothers) Restaurant** (☎ **31-251**), at Odós Anexartisías 63, the last place on the right on the harbor. Climb the pedestrian street to the fortress and continue past it to **Flisvos** (☎ **31-694**), one of the most beautiful outdoor restaurants you'll ever see, with a glorious view and good food at surprisingly reasonable prices. Come to watch the sunset and you won't need reservations.

Igoumenítsa

This west coast city is the jumping-off point for maritime excursions to Corfu and Italy. Fortunately, there is frequent service to these points because there's absolutely nothing to do in the town besides waiting for your ship to come in. The restaurants are generally awful, and if you should be unlucky enough to spend the night, you'll find the hotels vastly overpriced. There are no archeological points within proximity, and the beaches are few (the water in this heavily trafficked channel isn't so great either).

Those coming from Italy with EurailPasses should resist all urges to jump ship unless you're going to travel in northern Greece first. Since the trains don't run to Igoumenítsa, you'll have to pay for a bus; continue on to Pátra, where you can get a train free to Athens or other parts of Greece.

WHERE TO STAY

If you get stuck here, make your way a half kilometer north toward Ioánnina to the gracious **Hotel El Greco** (☎ **0665/22-245**), Odós Ethnikis Anástasis 86, where attractive doubles with bath cost 13,500 Drs ($56.55)—about half what you'd pay closer to the ferry—and credit cards are accepted. The **Hotel Epirus** (☎ **0665/22-504**), Odós Párgas 20—150 meters above the port on the road to Parga—is the only other place we find acceptable; a clean, fairly quiet double with bath costs 11,375 Drs ($47.40).

2 Epirus

Ioánnina is 270 miles NW of Athens or 62 miles E of Igoumenítsa

GETTING THERE • By Air **Olympic Airways** (☎ **26-518**) flies from Ioánnina to Athens twice daily, to Thessaloníki 5 times a week. Their office is on Central Square near the post office; from here a bus departs one hour before flight time for the airport (fare is 200 Drs or 90¢).

• **By Bus** Two buses leave daily for Pátra; call the bus station on Byzaníou Street (☎ **25-014**) for schedules. The bus to Igoumenítsa, which runs every two hours or so, and the bus to Athens or Thessaloníki leave from Zosimadón Street (one block above the intersection of Venizélou and Avéroff Streets). Buses leave every two hours until 10pm for the 7½ hour trip to Athens; call **26-286** for schedule information.

• **By Car** The route along the coast we've described is more scenic and diverse; Highway 5 (E-19) is more direct.

ESSENTIALS The information office of the **Greek Tourist Organization** (EOT) (☎ **0651/25-086**) is on Central (Pýrros) Square, at Odós Zervá 2; it's open from 7:30am to 2:30pm weekdays, with extended hours in the summer.

For a wide selection of foreign language **periodicals**, try Athanasios Daktylithos (☎ **28-005**), Odós Pirsinela 14. You can do **laundry** at Express Wash (☎ **75-215**),

Odós Napoléon Zérvas 86, open Mon–Sat 8am–2pm and 5pm–7pm, 1,725 Drs ($7.25) per load.

The **Robinson Travel Agency,** at Odós 8 Merarchías 10 (☎ **0651/29-402,** fax 0651/25-071), offers a program of outdoor adventures including trekking in the Pindus mountains, gorge hiking, hang-gliding, kayaking, and flora and fauna walks in the Epirus area. The **tourist police** (☎ **25-673**), open 7am to 2pm, are on the first floor, room 10, of the main police station, at 28 Októvriou, no. 11. The **post office** is at no. 3; **the telephone center** (OTE) is next door at Odós 28 Októvriou 4 and is open daily from 7am to midnight.

The capital of Epirus (Ípiros), **Ioánnina** (Yánnina), is a city of nearly 50,000 inhabitants. It's a bustling metropolis with lots of light industry and traffic—not the ideal place for relaxation. However, it boasts a highly regarded university, a picturesque setting on ancient Lake Pamvótis, and several colorful sights associated with its most infamous resident, Ali Pasha. The archeological museum has surprisingly interesting finds from Epirus, including objects related to Zeus's oracle at Dodóni (Dodona). The Aslán Tzamí (mosque), in the city's special old walled-in section near the lake, houses an intriguing collection of folk art and political memorabilia. Some 4 km outside of town, in the village of Pérama, is a spectacular cave, 2 km long, filled with galleries of stalactites and stalagmites that are well lit and fun to explore. And don't leave without visiting Nissí, the islet in Lake Pamvotis (now Lake Ioánnina) where a small community of homes and monasteries has been built; it's one of northern Greece's most colorful and pleasant excursions. Even more important, don't leave the region without a visit to Dodóni, site of an ancient oracle much revered in antiquity, that still speaks to the modern pilgrim who goes with open ears.

From Ioánnina you can work your way through dramatic mountain countryside over the Athamanon range to the traditional hill village of Métsovo, where embroiderers and craftsmen thrive in a foundation-funded, creative environment respectful of their past.

The best way to explore and experience this dramatic region is to rent a car (or take a bus) through the area referred to as **Zagóri** or the **44 Villages.** These mountain hamlets are simple, traditional places, with low-built houses overlooking fertile valleys and rushing waterways. For hikers, there is a 12 km walk through the Víkos Gorge, in Víkos-Aóös National Park. The Robinson Travel Agency in Ióannina offers outdoor excursions in the Epirus area.

Ioánnina

The "village in the lake," as it's known to many, slopes down an acropolis-topped hillside to the banks of tranquil **Lake Ioánnina.** The main road, King George Street, runs into Central (or Pýrros) Square, then becomes Avéroff Street until it bumps into the walled-in fortress that has captured the old city. Along King George Street and around Central Square, there are several hotels, cafés, and tourist services.

From Central Square it's a five-minute walk downhill to explore the walled-in fort, then another five minutes around its perimeter or through an opposite gate out to the shore of Lake Ioánnina. The tall, brown brick **Litharítsia prison** is on a rise in the green park surrounding the old clock tower; this can be used to orient you to nearby Pyrrus Square. Ioánnina's other major artery, **October 28 Street**, runs perpendicular to King George Street from their intersection at Central Square.

WHAT TO SEE & DO

In the **Ioánnina Theater,** there are often performances during the summer of *Ipirótika,* a festival of indigenous songs and dances (with older singers specializing in the popular *dimotiká,* traditional ballads and folk songs), as well as other cultural events. Contact the Greek tourist office (EOT) for more information, including the date of the one-day-only performance of classical theater at Dodóni.

While we're looking at things to do, there's some interesting **shopping** for folk art, hammered copper and tin dishware, jewelry, and trinkets as well as crafts in the old town. Just across from the main gate to the old town there is an interesting little shop filled with what are probably "new" antiquities, some embroidered vests, skirts, and thick, cozy woven socks.

Island in the Lake

A boat leaves the lakeside just left of the old fortress every half hour for the island. The ten-minute trip costs 165 Drs (79¢). The water is too murky with green algae to see much, but you get the impression of plenty of life there.

Nissí (the name means, simply, "island"), was settled in the 17th century by refugees from the Máni in the Peloponnese. Its most colorful inhabitant was the dissident Turkish ruler Ali Pasha, who came in 1820 and took refuge here for two years. After much cajoling, he received a royal pardon from Constantinople (Istanbul), which was just a trick on the Ottoman sultan's part: Troops had been dispatched to Ioánnina to end his command. At their arrival, he shouted, "Stop! What's up?" and was shot dead.

The **Ali Pasha House** is straight up the blessedly car-free pathway of souvenir shops. The holes in its wooden floor are ample evidence of Ali's demise. The "museum" was actually the pre-1820 home of Ali's wife, Vassiliki, who betrayed his presence in the Ághios Panteléimon monastery. The 17th-century monastery next door is closed to visitors, but just behind the Ali Museum is the **Prodrómou Monastery of St. John the Baptist,** built in 1506–1507 and filled with frescoes.

AN ISLAND TOUR Continue back up Souvenir Street; where the other side of the island comes into view is the **Moní Philanthropínon,** built in 1292. If you walk through the richly decorated frescoed church you'll come to the wing used as a "secret school" during the Turkish occupation. It's obvious that the frescoes have been grossly defaced (due to the Muslim taboo against worshipping human images), but are still very much worth seeing. Next door, the **Moní Stratigopoúlou** (11th century) was dedicated to St. Nicholas, whose portrait is inside the first entry. The frescoes are much darker and eroded here. If the door's closed, an old woman in black will open it up for you; expect to give a small contribution. Farther along this path is the **Eleoúsis Monastery,** from the 16th century, which is also closed to the public. Even if you've only got a few hours between buses in Ioánnina, a brief visit to the island and a stop for lunch is well worthwhile.

If you have more time, the island can be circled in a half-hour stroll along a gravel-and-dirt path on the lakefront, a perfect place for jogging too.

Other Attractions

Archeological Museum, March 25 Square (northwest side of City Park). ☎ **24-490.**

A special surprise is the lovely, well-lit, modern museum with many artifacts from Dodóni and other archeological digs in the Epirus region. Pieces include pottery, jewelry, coins, and icons primarily from the 5th to 3d century B.C., when Dodóni

(Dodona) was one of the most important oracles in Greece. A highlight of the museum is the small bronze statuary from Dodóni (its detail intricate and amazing on a boy holding a dove, and a lion spout from a funerary sarcophagus). Outdoor alcoves adjoining the galleries have pieces of the marble pillars and friezes from various neighboring archeological sites.

Admission: 500 Drs ($2.10) adults, half price for students.

Open: Mon, 12:30pm–7pm; Tues–Fri, 8am–7pm; Sat & Sun, 8:30am–3pm.

Folk Art Museum, Odós Michaíl Anghélou 42 ☎ **20-515.**

Good official signs direct you to this small museum. Its growing collection of costumes and various handcrafted objects exemplify the diverse talent of the region.

Admission: 100 Drs. (40¢).

Open: Mon 4:30–8pm, Wed 10am–1pm.

Municipal Popular Art Museum in Aslan Tzami (Mosque), Alexander Noustou St. ☎ **26-356.**

The museum is located on the lake side of the old city, up some cobblestone-paved lanes. Displayed haphazardly in the various prayer areas are some fine local costumes, weapons, old documents, and photos of military men, plus memorabilia from the War of Independence and World War II. The eclectic collection includes some Judaica: three *katubahs* (marriage contracts in Hebrew from 1762) and a gold-embroidered velvet curtain from an old Jewish synagogue in Ioánnina.

Admission: 550 Drs ($2.30) adults half price for students.

Open: Weekdays, 8am–3pm Sat & Sun 9am–3pm.

Vrellis Museum, Mousakai, Epirus. ☎ **55-055.**

We just aren't sure what to say about this wax museum in the nearby town of Mousakai. Residents speak about it reverentially, describing it as a moving tribute to the courage of Epirus's religious and political patriots from the time of the Ottoman occupation until the modern era. However, we experienced this dimly lit, cavelike collection of sometimes grotesque wax figures as the country's number-one kitsch convention. Either way, the Vrellis Museum is still worth seeing; it's best reached by taxi (about 15 minutes) or car; take the road toward Athens some 8 km to Bafra, then turn left and follow the signs.

Admission: Free.

Open: Daily 8:30am–7pm.

Synagogue, 18-B Joseph Elighiá, Old Town. ☎ Avram Negreen at **28-043** or Maurisis Eliazaf at **25-195** or **29-429.**

The Synagogue of Ioánnina is a handsome building located just inside the walls of the old town on Ioustinianoú (Justinian) Street. You'll find it by walking down Avéroff Street and making a quick left after entering the main gate. Continue for about two blocks and it will be on your right. As with others in northern Greece, this religious building is no longer in normal use because most of the local Jewish population was murdered during the German occupation. (There's a Holocaust Memorial nearby, outside the walls, at Karamanlí and Soútsou Streets.) Although the gate will almost certainly be locked, you can gain entrance by contacting one of the gentlemen listed above. (Mr. Negreen runs a small shop at Odós Anexartisías 8 and is usually available to open the synagogue on Wednesday and Saturday afternoons.)

Admission: Free.
Open: Wed and Sat by appointment.

Oracle of Dodóni

Set in a valley amid tall, rugged, gray-blue mountains 21 km south of Ioánnina, Dodóni (Dodona) was the most famous oracle of Zeus, possibly the oldest in Greece. It is now believed that the site was used for religious purposes as early as 2000 B.C.—at first sacred to an earth goddess, Naea, who was supplanted by Zeus in his aspect as god of the sky and weather by about 1200 B.C., although she was still honored as Dione. A large oak near where the earlier sacred oak stood marks the site of the oracle and temple of Zeus. The priests, who, Homer tells us through Achilles' prayer, slept on the ground and never washed their feet, listened to the god's voice in the rustling of the leaves. For centuries, kings and commanders would consult both the oracles at Dodoni and Delphi, hoping that at least one would answer their queries with an answer they liked.

At the site today you'll see a mass of temples with eroded columns, tossed upon each other in serendipitous patterns. The theater, one of the very largest in Greece, is still impressive in its bulk. In the Roman era the first five rows were removed and replaced with a retaining wall for use in gladiator events.

The oracle of Dodoni is open to the public from 8am to 7pm Monday through Friday, from 8:30am to 3pm on Saturday (☎ **82-287**). The admission fee is 440 Drs ($1.80) adults (half price for students). From Ioánnina there's a public bus to Dodoni only twice a day, although there's promise of better service. Taxis from Ioánnina are another option; they charge about 4,800 Drs ($20) round-trip, including waiting time. A theatrical performance is given in the theater once a year, in August, in honor of the Dodona Festivals of antiquity.

WHERE TO STAY

All the main avenues through Ioánnina are terrifically noisy at night, even though most of the hotels were built here. Therefore, although most of the hotels listed below will have odd addresses, they are almost all within a block of a main artery—convenient, but quieter.

Hotel Alexios, Odós Poukevil 14, Ioánnina 45445. ☎ **0651/24-003.** Fax 0651/32071. 92 rms (all with bath). TEL

Rates (including breakfast): 9,900 Drs. ($41.25) single; 13,750 Drs ($57.30) double. No credit cards.

Ioánnina's best value is five blocks from Central (Pýrros) Square up October 28 Street, across from Zalóngou Park. It's modern, clean, pleasant, and quiet, with good views from many of the rooms. We're hoping, however, that the breakfast improves.

Hotel Egnatia, Odós Aravántou 20, at Dagli St., Ioánnina 45445. ☎ **0651/25-667.** Fax 0651/75-060. 52 rms (all with bath). TEL

Rates (including breakfast): 7,700 Drs ($32.10) single; 9,900 Drs ($41.25) double. EC, MC, V.

The Egnatia is on the small, quiet part of Skobourdi Square. Its rooms are plain, but clean; the comfortable lobby is modern with a few rustic touches.

Hotel El Greco, Odós Tsirigótou 8, Ioánnina 45445. ☎ **0651/30-726.** Fax 0651/30-728. 36 rms (all with bath). TEL

Rates (including breakfast): 7,700 Drs ($32.10) single; 10,450 Drs ($43.50) double. No credit cards.

This charming hotel, just off October 28 Street near the bus station, has the friendliest atmosphere in town. There's a cheery breakfast room and parking in back.

Hotel Galaxy, Central (Pýrros) Square, Ioánnina 45221. ☎ **0651/25-056.** 38 rms (all with bath). TEL

Rates (including breakfast): 7,700 Drs ($32.10) single; 12,650 Drs ($52.70) double. No credit cards.

It may be risky to recommend the Hotel Galaxy because it's right on Pýrros Square, but their rooms seemed to be somewhat soundproof. Ask for the lake view.

Hotel Olympic, Odós Melanídi 2, Ioánnina 45220. ☎ **0651/25-147.** Fax 0651/73-008. 44 rms (all with bath). A/C MINIBAR TV TEL

Rates (including breakfast): 11,000 Drs ($45.80) single; 15,400 Drs ($64.20) double. No credit cards.

A tip-top lodging in the center of town off Dodoni Street near 28 Oktovríou, very professionally managed, and one of the more popular, so a reservation is recommended. Guest rooms have double beds and clean and well-lit bathrooms; some include minibars.

Hotel Paris, Odós Tsirigoti 6, Ioánnina 45444. ☎ **0651/20-541.** 55 rms (20 with bath).

Rates: 4,400 Drs ($18.30) single without bath; 6,050 Drs ($25.20) double without bath; 7,700 Drs ($25.20) double with bath. No credit cards.

This budget hotel is down the street from the bus station, near the Hotel El Greco. It's no great shakes, but it's convenient, and well kept, and it has decent shared bathrooms. Some of the rooms with private baths boast tubs, a real bargain.

WHERE TO EAT

The **Atlantic Super Market** at Dodóni and Hatziplepen Streets, just east of Central Square, is the place for picnic supplies. A close facsimile to an A&P, it has three floors of groceries, household goods, hardware, cosmetics, and liquor.

For the best cookies, pastries, and bread, follow Zerbá Street south from Central Square, turn right down the alley at the Bank of Central Greece and find Rapakoúsis Photíos Bakery on the right. The *moustokoloúra,*—a small, flat cake with raisins and sesame seeds—is especially delectable.

Litharitsia Cafeteria, Aghías Marínas and Ghervassíou Streets. ☎ **20-043.**

Cuisine: INTERNATIONAL.

Prices: Snacks 385–990 Drs ($1.60–$4.10), main courses 990–2,400 Drs ($4.10–$10.10). No credit cards.

Open: Daily 11am–1am (depending on season).

Walk east toward the lake from the clock tower and up the stairs to the plaza to find this unique complex made from the Turkish-era prison where Greek insurgents were kept. The prices for snacks and beverages tend to match the elevation, but the view from the rooftop terrace is splendid and well removed from traffic. Downstairs there's a large, handsome dining room with arched windows and rich wood decor, as well as several smaller facilities.

Taverna Gastra, Igoumenítsa Road. No telephone.

Cuisine: GREEK.

Prices: Appetizers 360–550 Drs ($1.50–$2.30), main courses 1,000–3,400 Drs ($4.15–$14.20). No cards.

Open: Daily dusk–midnight.

The highly popular Taverna Gastra is 2 km west of the airport, on the right just before the road branches. A wide variety of well-prepared dishes are served, and dancing is encouraged.

Taverna O Kipos, Odós Karaïskáki 20. ☎ **78-287.**

Cuisine: GREEK.

Prices: Appetizers 150–500 Drs (65¢–$2.10), main courses 1,000–3,200 Drs ($4.15–$13.45). No cards.

Open: Daily dusk–midnight.

This garden taverna (*kípos* means "garden") with traditional decor and music but updated cooking—fresh beef, pork, lamb, veal, and chicken grilled to your taste—won first place during our last visit. The menu is in Greek, but ask for Angelo, the chef/owner, who picked up some English working 14 years in a restaurant in Manhattan.

Taverna O Fomas, Nissí, Lake Ioánnina. ☎ **81-819.**

Cuisine: GREEK/SEAFOOD.

Prices: Main courses 660–1,200 Drs ($2.75–$5), fish from 2,750 Drs ($11.45) per kilo.

Open: Daily from when first customer arrives until last leaves.

Several attractive restaurants greet you as you get off the boat. They're all good—and you can wangle a better price through comparison shopping—but we found this homely, tree-shaded place, about 250 meters along the path to the Ali Pasha Museum, the most inviting, as there were several tables of Greek families enjoying their repast. The trout was tasty, tender, and succulent. For a special treat in season, try the local delicacy, *karavída,* a shellfish that's something between crawfish and lobster.

Métsovo

This is a magical hill village perched at nearly 1,000 meters above sea level, a delightfully refreshing change, like the hill resorts found throughout India and parts of the tropics. Métsovo's position atop a Pindus range hill lures Greeks all summer and on long, holiday winter weekends. Its unique flavor comes in part from the ethnic heritage of its inhabitants, who are Vlachs, originally said to derive from Walachia, in Romania. These former shepherds, who have settled all over the Balkans and beyond, pride themselves on their peaceable community, traditional garb, exquisite weaving, and special cuisine—all of which may be found in Métsovo.

GETTING THERE

Drive 58 km west on Highway 6 (E-87) from Ioánnina or 93 km west from Tríkkala in Thessaly. Two buses from Kalambáka, five buses from Ioánnina, and one bus from Thessaloníki pull into Métsovo's tiny Avéroff Square daily, so you shouldn't find it hard getting here. The only problem is leaving.

INFORMATION

The **police** (☎ **41-233**) here are just the friendly regular town police. The **post office** is on the main street above the square (open 7:30am to 2:30pm weekdays). There are two **banks** on the square—open 8am to 2pm only—but several shops accept traveler's checks and credit cards. You can call **41-111** for **medical assistance.** Contact the **Métsovo Alpine Club** for information on trails and the nearby ski center (☎ **41-249**).

WHAT TO SEE & DO

If you're here on July 26 for the local religious festival, you'll get treated to dancing in the square, as well as traditional costumes (a more elaborately embroidered version of the daily fare), and roasted lamb on publicly shared skewers.

Métsovo's main street provides wonderful shopping for embroidered wool capes, sweaters, carpets, and souvenirs, but you should stick to items indigenous to the north (we've seen embroidered silk blouses from China, synthetic linen tablecloths from Asian factories, and other overpriced junk). Having warned you, we want to rave about the Pratírio Laïkís Téchnis, the **Métsovo Folk Art Cooperative** supported by the Tosítsa Foundation, which runs the folk art museum. The cooperative store is located in the cobblestone paths about 50 meters above the Egnatía Hotel and has a large variety of weavings, embroidery, and charming sculpted wooden dolls. The Laïkís Téchnis's gifted women will also tailor some great-looking clothes to order; if you don't want to look like an extra from the Dora Stratou folk-dance troupe in Athens, they'll whip up a cape, shawl, or suit in heavy hand-carded wool that'll knock 'em out on Fifth Avenue. Another special shop is that of **Ares Talares** (☎ **41-901**), next door to the Egnatía Hotel, where he carries on the family tradition of silversmithing; you'll find superb articles in the local style and exquisite free-form jewelry.

The Tositsa family's mansion has been restored and modernized as a **folk art museum.** Its heavy wood, stucco, and roomy interior is very typical of the *archontiká* seen in the hill country of Mt. Pelion, Kastoriá, and parts of Crete. Simple rooms are filled with decorative woven fabrics or warmth-giving rugs, tapestries, and carpets. The displays are a little too "stagey" for Kyle's tastes, but overall it's an excellent introduction to the best of northern Greek folk craft. The museum is open Wednesday through Friday from 8:30am to 1pm and 4 to 6pm. Admission is 275 Drs ($1.15).

If you're looking for older or newly made, high-quality textiles, be sure to seek out the shop run by **Mr. Boumbas** (☎ **41-522**), located on the main street. The prices are high, but this shop seems to have the best woven goods in Métsovo. For example, we admired an impossibly heavy wool blanket, recently produced, for about $400. Mr. Boumbas doesn't speak much English, but if you *parla Italiano* . . .

You can hike, explore, spend days roaming the hills around here, but don't forget that other Métsovo specialty—cheese. Unfortunately, as charming as the side streets are, the main square, with its two cafés and several cheese shops, is the only turnaround for trucks and buses and gets fume-filled regularly. Zip downhill here to George Avéroff Square to catch your bus; while waiting, sit and watch the traditionally dressed locals stroll and shop for cheese. **Tiropolío** (literally "Cheese Store") is one of many such shops, but it gives out free samples! Smoked cheese is a regional specialty: Try *metsovonay* (which can be stored a long time—good for travelers), *vlachotíri* (made from sheep's milk), or *metsovella* (another, lighter sheep's-milk cheese).

The **Tirokomío** is the local cheese factory, on the right as you enter Métsovo from the west. Go visit it and sample away, but don't forget to search out a bottle of **Kastoghi,** the region's legendary, aged red wine that's sold in single bottles only by those few who collect them (we found a bottle at Stani on the square). The nearby **cathedral of**

Aghía Paraskeví has a carved wood screen, silver chandeliers, and copies of the Ravenna mosaics that are worth a visit.

Have we convinced you to spend the night in this special village?

WHERE TO STAY

Hotels in Métsovo all try very hard to keep in the traditional alpine style of the village. Therefore, our favorite hotels were those that succeeded without getting too kitschy (and with an excellent view over the mist-shrouded mountains).

Hotel Athinae, Métsovo 44200. ☎ **0656/41-332.** 8 rms (5 with bath).

Rates (including breakfast): 4,840 Drs ($20.20) single with/without bath; 6,600 Drs ($27.50) double with bath. No credit cards.

Métsovo's only real budget choice is located above a tavern around the corner from the main square. It's quiet; the rooms are small, but the place is so charming you may soon find this another of its attractive qualities. The owner's sons, Christos and Yannis, speak English and will gladly show you the 16 new family-run rooms with bath just beyond the square.

Egnatia Hotel, 10 Tosítsa Rd., Métsovo 44200. ☎ **0656/41-263.** Fax 0656/41-485. 36 rms (all with bath). TEL

Rates (including breakfast): 8,250 Drs ($34.40) single; 11,000 Drs ($45.80) double. AE, DC, EC, MC, V.

Canaries singing in the lobby are just the start of the award-winning hospitality of this excellent hotel on the quiet main street. The rooms are pleasant and comfortable, with flower-trimmed balconies and splendid views of the hills.

Hotel Bitounis, 25 Tosítsa Rd., Métsovo 44200. ☎ **0656/41-217.** Fax 0656/41-545. 30 rms (all with bath). TEL

Rates (including breakfast): 8,250 Drs ($34.80) single; 11,000 Drs ($45.80) double. AE, V.

The large, comfortable carpeted rooms, most with balconies, overlook the spectacular valley below. The owner's son, Yannis, speaks English. Free parking for guests is a real plus in the summer high season.

Hotel Flokas, Métsovo 44200. ☎ **0656/41-309.** Fax 0656/44-200. 10 rms (all with bath). TEL

Rates (including breakfast): 7,700 Drs ($32.10) single; 9,350 Drs ($39) double. V.

This inn, well above the square on the road leading off right before the bank, has rooms that overlook some red-tile rooftops and the valley below. You're greeted by a dripping fountain and a skylight above the stairs. The rooms have private bath, warm, natural-wood floors, and simple furnishings with traditional decor.

Hotel Galaxias, Métsovo 44200. ☎ **0656/41-124.** 10 rms (9 with bath). TEL

Rates (including breakfast): 13,200 Drs ($55) double. MC, V.

Attached to the excellent Galaxias Restaurant (see "Where to Eat" below) is this equally fine hotel. The decor is standard Métsovo, but there is a quiet, homey feel about the place because of the gracious management of the Barbayanni family. The breakfast room is cozy, but our favorite space here is the garden/café. Not the fanciest lodging in town, but a good value.

Hotel Kassaros, Métsovo 44200. ☎ **0656/41-800.** Fax 0656/41-262.
24 rms (all with bath). TV, TEL

Rates (including breakfast): 8,800 Drs ($36.70) single; 14,000 Drs ($45.80) double. AE, EC, DC, MC, V.

Another fine lodging in the traditional style, on the road leading up just before the square, is Hotel Kassaros. The rooms are spacious, comfortable, and attractive; all have balconies, most with splendid views.

Hotel Victoria, Métsovo 44200. ☎ **0656/41-771** and **41-898.**
57 rms (all with bath). TEL

Rates (including breakfast): 15,216 Drs ($63.40) single; 16,575 Drs ($69.10) double. EC, MC, V.

The newest and largest hotel is on a small road leading off to the left just as you enter the village. The gray-stone first story is topped with a typically whitewashed stucco-and-plaster second story, covered with a red-tile roof. Inside, the gray-slate–paved lobby has big picture windows showing off the exquisite views. Natural-wood beams, furniture, balconies, beds, tables, and chairs give a warm, homey feeling that's enhanced in winter when the tall stone fireplaces are ablaze. The dining room and bar are trimmed with locally produced weavings and rugs.

WHERE TO EAT

Athinae Restaurant, near the square. ☎ **41-332.**

Cuisine: GREEK.
Prices: Main courses 360–1,320 Drs ($1.50–$5.50). No credit cards.
Open: Daily 7am–11pm (depending on season).

María Papapostolou offers down-home cooking Métsovo style, in keeping with her rustic inn and low prices. She has vegetarian dishes as well as grilled meats, but her specialties are a delicious *píta* (mild leeks baked with a cornbread-like crust) and *spetzofái* (meatballs with leeks).

Galaxias Restaurant, just before the square. ☎ **41-202.**

Cuisine: GREEK.
Prices: Appetizers 380–1,000 Drs ($1.60–$4.20); main courses 710–2,000 Drs ($3–$8.35). EC, MC, V.
Open: Daily 7:30am–12am.

With its soaring ceiling and decorations of local antiques, this is easily the handsomest restaurant in town, with the best food. Try the delicious bean soup and the roast goat, as well as the *kokorétsi,* a Métsovo favorite.

Zagóri (Zagória)

No visit to Epirus would be complete without a trip to the dramatic mountainous region of **Zagóri**. Also known collectively as the **Zagorohória,** or the **44 Villages** (though many of them are sadly depopulated), the area is part of the vast Víkos-Aóös National Park system, which means development is strictly curtailed: All buildings must be made of the traditional stone and slate of the Pindus mountains—not a red-tiled roof in sight! As a result, the traditional mountain hamlets seem to have sprouted magically from their surroundings.

The Zagóri villages combine a surprising architectural sophistication with their setting of natural beauty. Square, handsome 18th- and 19th-century gray stone houses overlook rushing waterways, flinty slopes, lush valleys, and the stunning Víkos Gorge, a rocky 10-mile fissure in the earth sometimes compared to the Grand Canyon. These are the wilds of Epirus: wild bear, boar, and wolves are said to inhabit the thickly forested hills but all we ever saw were flocks of sheep and a stray cow or two wandering through cobblestoned streets and tranquil squares.

As with any unspoiled place in the modern world, development is a big political issue here. We've heard several Zagorians bless the sparse bus service that makes their villages less accessible to the masses. The tourists who make it up the mountain tend to be a sophisticated lot, often European or Greek, and they're willing to pay for their quaintness. You may spend as much for a week in Zagóri as in the islands. But we bet you'll come back!

GETTING AROUND

BY BUS Bus service in Zagóri is fairly inadequate: Monday to Friday, two buses make the roundtrip between Ioánnina and Tsepélovo, stopping at Kípi en route. There are two daily buses from Ioánnina to Monodéndri, and one bus that returns, Mon–Fri. There are only three buses a week making the round trip from Ioánnina to Pápingo.

BY CAR The roads are good, if winding, and you can see much of Zagóri in a day by car. One place to go is Budget Rent-A-Car in Ioánnina on Odós Napoléon Zérva 24 (☎ **25-102**). Take the airport road north out of Ioánnina to reach Zagóri and the signs are clearly marked from there. EOT in Ioánnina (☎ **25-086**) gives out free maps.

BY FOOT The Víkos Gorge, from Monodéndri to Pápingo, provides a challenging trek of about eight hours duration. We were warned that though it's perfectly safe for hikers in pairs, one should not go solo, not only because of injury but because there have been a few unpleasant encounters with groups of Albanian immigrants who wander around down there. The friendly, helpful staff at EOT in Ioánnina (☎ **25-086**) provides excellent maps and information about Víkos as does the local mountain club in Megálo Pápingo **(☎ 41-138, 41-230)**, but you can also go with a tour.

ORGANIZED GROUPS Try the old veterans at **Robinson Tours** (☎ **0651/29-402**), long based in Ioánnina, or the resourceful and well-organized **Ares Talares** of the Hotel Egnatia in Métsovo (☎ **0656/41-263**), who has recently started to run excursions here.

KÍPI

On your way to Tsepélovo, be sure to make the detour to Kípi for its famous 16th-century Turkish-style bridges, especially the graceful triple-arched one known as Plakídas.

TSEPÉLOVO

Tsepélovo is 51 km (30 miles) from Ioánnina, built on a slope with charmingly crooked paths, and the few tumbledown houses show up the beautifully preserved ones. One of the more populous **Zagóri** towns, it's an inexpensive base for viewing the area and consequently attracts budget travelers. If you want to spend the night here, try one of the tasteful rustic rooms (6,600 Drs or $27.50 with private bath) in Alexis Gouris's homey guesthouse (☎ **0653/81-214, 81-288**). But you'll have to lock the gate so a stray sheep doesn't get Mr. Gouris's prize roses. Gouris himself, a spry, cultured fellow who learned his English as a translator for NATO, is a wonderful host and a veritable font of information about the area. He recommends one long local hike of about 5 1/2 hours which takes you to Drakólimni (Dragon Lake) and Mt. Astráka (see Pápingos below).

MONODÉNDRI

Monodéndri is where the classic trek through the gorge begins. The town is much celebrated by guidebooks, and it certainly has ravishing views of Víkos, particularly from the lovely 15th-century **Monastery of Aghía Paraskeví** on the lower *platía*, which is in itself not to be missed. If you're not planning to hike, we suggest stopping here for lunch and pushing on to the Pápingos, only about 1 1/2 hour's drive away.

The town is organized around two *platías*, connected by a steep cobblestone path: the upper tier is where the bus stops and where you'll find the **Monodendri Pension & Restaurant** (**☎ 61-233**), which is justly famous for its cheese pies and other delicacies. It's a handsome, modern building interpreting traditional **Zagóri** style, but they wouldn't even let us peek in any of their rooms (all full during our visit). Doubles with private bath cost 8,580 Drs ($35.75). It's best to book ahead.

On the lower *platía,* near the monastery, is the well-run **Vikos Pension** (**☎ 0653/61-323**), which is organized around a garden courtyard. The rooms (8,800 Drs or $36.70 per double, private facilities) are large and furnished in tasteful traditional style with slate floors, but unfortunately none of them have good views.

On your way out of Monodéndri, be sure to make the 4-km (2.4-mile) detour northwest of Monodéndri to the Víkos Balcony, following the signs to Osia. Agoraphobes beware—these are even more spectacular vistas of the gorge and mountains!

THE PÁPINGOS

Megálo (Big) Pápingo and Mikró (Little) Pápingo combine the classic fairytale Zagóri architecture with the area's friendliest ambience and most varied scenery. This is the point at which trekkers emerge from Víkos. You can see both the 600-meter (2,000 foot) drop of the gorge and the twin mesa-shaped peaks of Mt. Gamíla, which tower more than 2,400 meters (8,000 feet) overhead. Megálo Pápingo is a relaxed, sprawling community whose unofficial center is between Koulis's café-bar and Yiorgos's restaurant (**☎ 41-124**) where we had a wonderful meal of fresh, savory broiled chicken, yoghurt as thick as ice cream, and flaky cheese pie for about 2,200 Drs ($19.20). There's a 2-km road that snakes up to tiny Micró Pápingo, with more breathtaking views along the way.

The Greeks love these towns, so it's wise to book ahead, especially for Christmas, Easter, or the dog days of August. There are many options:

A few years ago EOT's four traditional *archontiká* guesthouses in Megálo Pápingo were sold to private owners, and **Guesthouse Astraka** (**☎ 0653/41-693**) is now the only one that still accepts visitors. Unfortunately the furniture and decorations are no longer authentically Zagóri, but the 130-year-old mansion is still gorgeous, with its carved wooden ceilings and other details (11,000 Drs or $45.80 for double with a private bath; MC and EC accepted).

It's a little like staying at your grandmother's, but we adored the few *domátia* (rooms) available next door to Astraka at **Eleni Economides'** old house with its garden courtyard (contact Mrs. Economides through Nikos at Hotel Koulis,

☎ **0653/41-138, 41-115**). The best deal is the small tower with two brass four-poster beds, private bath, and a spectacular mountain view (11,000 Drs. or $45.80) but the other two rooms have details like painted ceilings, family icons, and antique furniture.

Hotel Koulis (☎ **0653/41-138, 41-115**) is a simple, traditional family house where whitewashed doubles with hand-decorated curtains and private baths go for 9,900 Drs or $41.25 (no credit cards). Friendly young Nikos speaks excellent English and knows the local trails like the back of his hand. This is also the home of a well-liked bar-restaurant.

The best-known, most sophisticated hotel in the area, **Saxonis Houses** (☎ **0653/41-615**), draws its clientele from Athens and abroad. Nikos Saxonis (who for many years ran the Greek branch of McCann-Erickson) and his wife, Poli, have artfully restored several small 18th-century buildings, preserving details like fireplaces, built-in beds, and painted ceilings while adding bright accents. Guests rave about the breakfasts of filter coffee, little cakes, and fresh-squeezed orange juice, served in a tranquil rose garden. Doubles go for 20,650 Drs or $86 (no credit cards).

There are many enjoyable hikes of varying intensity in the immediate vicinity, and you don't have to go far to get a great view. The most famous—and strenuous—one takes you up Mt. Astráka to the Gamíla Refuge where you can stay overnight. (To get maps and the key, call the local mountain club in Megálo Pápingo at **41-138, 41-230.**) It's only 1½ hours from Gamíla to Drakólimni (Dragon Lake) and four hours beyond that to Tsepélovo (see above). Other pleasant expeditions include a local swimming hole on the road between the Pápingos. Ask any of the locals to show you the way.

14

The Ionian Islands

FOR THE MODERN TRAVELER, THE IONIAN ISLANDS ARE OFTEN THE GATEWAY TO Greece. Trains, boats, and planes choose this most direct route to deposit visitors, fresh from Europe, into a new land. The cultural transition is least harsh in the Ionians, for if these islands are the most European part of the country, so in many ways are they the least Greek.

Of all the Greek islands, the Ionians are the most fortunate recipients of nature's bounty. All have plentiful rainfall, fertile land, temperate climate, and lush, semitropical scenery. Their strategic position put them in the way of every conqueror set on annexing the wealthy mainland of Greece. As a result, the Islands reflect aspects of many cultures.

Corfu (Kérkyra), one of the great tourist meccas, has always been the gem of the Ionian, the culture and architecture reflecting the elegant styles of the French, Italian, and English conquerors. Tiny **Páxos (Paxí)** and **Antipáxos (Antípaxi)** are small verdant links in the Ionian chain, miniretreats that offer a change of pace from the frenzy of the others. **Lefkáda** (Lefkás) is a large, slowly developing island just a stone's throw away from the mainland, known for its Arts and Letters Festival and embroidery exports. **Ithaca** (Itháki) is the island immortalized by Homer, the birthplace of Odysseus, and the most longed-for home east of Dorothy's Kansas. **Kefalonía** (Kefallinía) is the largest, most self-sustaining of the Ionians; successful sea trade and agriculture have enabled many residents to ignore the recent influx of foreign tourists flocking to see its natural beauties and historic sights. **Zákynthos** is the southernmost island, its proximity to the Peloponnese, pebble beaches, and moderate climate have made it one of the most popular destinations for Greek tourists.

SEEING THE IONIAN ISLANDS

Below we offer our seven-day introduction to Greece for those who are coming from Italy (and are in the mood to keep on going!).

Day 1–3 Disembark in Corfu and sightsee (with an optional day trip to Páxos);

Day 4 Take the ferry to Igoumenítsa on the mainland (two hours), then a public bus along the gorgeous coast of Epirus to Prevéza (two hours); cross over to Lefkáda via the land bridge (20 minutes); traverse the island to the port of Frikes (45 minutes), and overnight at a beachside villa.

Day 5 Take the morning excursion boat directly to Fiskardo, on the north tip of Kefalonía, or take an optional day trip to Vassilikí, Ithaca, returning in the afternoon to Fiskardo. Overnight at a traditional home in Fiskardo.

Day 6 Cross Kefalonía as part of a private taxi tour, stopping at Mýrtos beach and other sights, then spend the night in the capital Argostóli.

Day 7 See Argostóli's museums; then fly direct to Athens or take the ferry to Pátra, after having experienced a taste of the Ionians.

A SPECIAL REQUEST

*An environmental group called the **Monk Seal Project** (tel. **0674/28-084**) has been studying the Mediterranean monk seal or* Monachus monachus, *one of the 12 most endangered species in the world. Almost half of the world's known monk seals live in the Ionian Sea off the coasts of Lefkada, Ithaca, and Kefalonía. Under the auspices of the World Wildlife Fund, the Monk Seal Project has asked all visitors to avoid disturbing the seals in their cave habitats and to report all sightings, with the seal's size, color, markings, and behavior, to them in Fiskardo to further their research and conservation efforts. Let's all help this worthy cause.* Call or write c/o Alíki and Dimítris Panos, Fiskardo, Kefalonía.

What's Special About the Ionian Islands

Architecture

- The stunning Venetian-era housing and *cantouni* of Corfu's Old Town.
- Fiskardo's stucco and wood traditional Ionian housing untouched by the 1953 earthquake that leveled the rest of Kefalonía.

Beaches

- The broad gold sand stretch of Corfu's Águios Gheórghios, still an unspoilt resort area.
- The shimmering white pebble beach at Myrtos, on Kefalonía's west coast, which ranks with us as one of Greece's Top Ten.
- A newly accessible pebble beach below the white rock cliffs at Porto Katsiki, on Lefkáda's west coast. A newcomer to the Top Ten.

Literary Shrines

- Part of Homer's *Odyssey* was set in the Ionians. The island of Ithaca is said to have been his home, and Paleokastrítsa, Corfu is said to have been his final stop before returning.

Museums

- Corfu's Museum of Asiatic Art is a surprisingly broad collection of ceramics, prints, and sculpture from the Orient.
- The Corgialenios Historical and Cultural Museum in Argostóli, Kefalonía has a delightful collection of costumes and displays of 19th-century daily life.

Natural Spectacles

- Every August, the rare loggerhead turtles come to Calamaki Beach on Zákynthos to lay their eggs in the sand.
- The World Wildlife Fund is studying endangered Mediterranean monk seals living in the Ionian waters off Kefalonía, Ithaca, and Lefkáda (see above).

TV and Film Locations

- Billy Wilder's film *Fedora* was shot in several villas on Corfu.
- James Bond's *For Your Eyes Only* was partially shot in Corfu's Achilleion Palace Museum.
- Paul Mazursky's adaptation of Shakespeare's *The Tempest* was filmed in several Corfu villages.

1 Corfu

132 nautical miles from Pátra; 18 nautical miles from Igoumenítsa

ARRIVING/DEPARTING • By Air Olympic Airways offers direct and connecting flights from 35 cities around the world—ranging from Dubai, Johannesburg, Cleveland, or Tripoli. From Athens, there are four flights daily, as well as ten other flights midday throughout the week. For reservations and information, contact the Olympic office in Corfu town at Odós Kapodistríou 20. (☎ **0661/38-694**; open Monday through Saturday from 9am to 4:45pm) or in Athens (☎ **01/96-16-161**).

• **By Sea** Car ferries run from Igoumenítsa 12 times daily between 5am and 10pm (☎ **0661/32-655**). **Kerkira Lines** (☎ **0661/22-991**) has thrice daily service to Igoumenítsa. There are two international ferries daily to and from Brindisi, Italy, run by two companies (☎ **0661/39-747** and **38-089**); plus a daily boat from Ancona, Italy (for information call the **Minoan Line,** ☎ **0661/46-555**, or the **Strintzis Lines,** ☎ **0661/25-232**). All four international lines call daily at Pátra, Peloponnese. Four times daily Monday to Saturday, and once on Sunday, there are excursion boats to the isles of Páxos and Antipáxos (for info call **32-655**). The local tourist information office **(EOT)** has a complete schedule listed in their office, and you can stroll down to the piers and check with the various travel agents as to availability. Ferry tickets to the Greek mainland or to Europe can be purchased from travel agents at the respective ports of departure.

It's ironic that Corfu (Kérkyra, also Corcyra in English) should be the first glimpse of Greece for many travelers; as you'll soon discover, its beauty and culture are unlike anywhere else. Corfu (or Kérkyra as the Greeks call it, after its Dorian name) is a melting pot of its cultures: Italian, French, and British. The Italians have touched the cuisine, art, and language, the French its architecture and education, the British its laws and lifestyle. Some Greeks say the Corfiots are too refined, too European, too cosmopolitan and artistic to be Greek, yet ever since Homer immortalized the island of the hospitable Phaeacians, the Greek people have held Corfu in high regard.

The sumptuous beauty of the island, so unlike the stark-white aridness of the Aegean islands, has drawn visitors for centuries. Most European royalty summered there at one time or another, bringing their native artists and performers with them for entertainment. They left a great cultural legacy which survives in artists such as Dionysos Solomos, the author of the Greek national anthem and a celebrated modern writer.

Homer tells us how Odysseus was washed ashore on the beautiful island of Scheria (thought to be today's Corfu), and with Athena's help, came to meet the Princess Nausicaa. Athena urged Nausicaa in her sleep to launder her clothes in preparation for her wedding day. She went to the river (thought to be the stream at the picturesque modern resort of Paleokastrítsa) with her handmaidens, and when they were done, they began a game of catch ball. Their laughter awoke the bedraggled Odysseus. Although the voyager's appearance frightened off her companions, Nausicaa stayed to hear him out. She encouraged Odysseus to plead with her mother, Queen Arete, for aid in reaching his homeland. Odysseus, still an anonymous traveler, was welcomed

IMPRESSIONS

[The capital of Corfu is] a very clean and rather attractive town. It reminded me of Brighton.
Evelyn Waugh, *Diary,* 1927

[On Zákynthos, the islanders build their houses low] because of the manifold earthquakes which do as much share this island as any other place in the world. The earthquakes are so frequent with them that sometimes they feel ten of them in a month
—George Sandys, *Purchas His Pilgrimes,* 1625

into their home and feasted. After supper, when talk turned to the Trojan War, Odysseus' sorrow caused him to reveal his identity. King Alcinoos and the queen were very moved, and listened to his tales all night. A royal ship was outfitted to transport him back to Ithaca the next day. After depositing him on the shore, the Phaeacians set sail for home. Poseidon was furious that they'd assisted Odysseus, and he turned their vessel into stone. Corfiots claim that the large, free-standing boulder in Paleokastrítsa's harbor is the petrified Phaeacian ship, frozen within sight of the port of Alcinoos.

History

Corfu was first settled by Dorians from Corinth in the 8th century B.C. As Corinth's colony, Corcyra prospered and in time established its own independent settlements on the mainland. Since antiquity, because of its strategic position, Corfu has been the center of countless hostilities. Always resilint after defeat, it remained the prize of the Ionians.

Of its European conquerors, the Venetians, who occupied the island between 1386 and 1797, were perhaps the most influential. They created a titled gentry of Greeks, who, with their Venetian overseers, ruled the peasant "serfs" with a heavy hand. The Venetians fortified the entire island; their Old Fort (to the north, separated from the mainland by the celebrated *contrafossa* or moat) and the New Fort (to the right of the domestic harbor) still greet visitors.

Venetian investments in olive cultivation and the extensive trade with Europe made Corfu even wealthier, attracting the attention of many pirates, and eventually the Turks. They attacked the island several times but failed to conquer it.

By the 18th century the islanders were ready for change. Intellectual Corfiots had been stirred by the ideals of the French Revolution, and when Napoleon sent his fleet to "liberate" the island from the Venetians, the French were welcomed with open arms. In 1799 the Russo-Turkish Alliance wrested Corfu away from the French. A year later, the Treaty of Constantinople declared the creation of the Septinsular Republic (Republic of the Seven Islands), with allegiance to the Ottoman Empire. In 1807, under the Peace of Tilsit between Napoleon and Alexander I of Russia, it was returned to French rule.

When Napoleon fell from power both Austria and Great Britain wanted control over the Ionians. The 1815 Treaty of Paris created the Ionian Republic, a free and independent state under the protectorship of Great Britain. The British installed a legal and educational system (Italian was widely spoken on Corfu until 1851), and an infrastructure and network of roads that served the island well, but quelled local participation in liberation movements springing up throughout the Greek mainland. In 1864 the Ionians became part of the newly founded kingdom of Greece.

Orientation

The sickle-shaped island of Corfu is approximately 600 km in area; within this are more than 300 large and small villages. On Corfu, the traditional blue wooden trim of Greece is more apt to be the green of the Venetians. Though it has undergone tremendous development in the recent past, the acknowledged beauty queen of the island is **Paleokastrítsa.**

If you approach this community from the heavily wooded road running east to Corfu town around the sunset hour, its beauty is still breathtaking. The clear waters, the black rocks that break the still surface of the bay, the misty glow of the evergreens in the dying light are an unforgettable picture. Although tourist development has lessened the appeal of Paleokastrítsa, it's become a much more democratic resort.

The other unique community on the island is the wonderfully picturesque European city of **Corfu.** We found no better place to stay if your interest is in things antique, historical, luxurious, romantic, swinging, fashionable, or gastronomic. European ferries call at the International Port (a 15-minute walk north), Igoumenítsa and Páxos car ferries arrive at the New Port (a 5-minute walk from the Old Town), the airport is 10 minutes away, and the best sightseeing is an arm's length from elegant boutiques, gourmet restaurants, excellent museums, and sophisticated nightlife. If you can afford it, try to rent a car to explore the rest of the island, which is justly famed for its scenic beauties. The eastern coastline, facing Albania and the northern Greek mainland, has been developed à la Miami Beach.

Getting Around

Corfu town and most of the island's major resorts are small enough to walk around in, once you're there. The island itself is too large and too heavily trafficked for walking around; public buses are cheap, fairly efficient, and safer than mopeds. However, we'd encourage hikers to plan a walking trip between the many picturesque hill villages in the island's north.

BY BUS

Around-the-island buses leave from two terminals. Green and cream-colored buses to the distant towns and beaches of Paleokastrítsa, Ághios Gordis, Glyfáda, Kassiópi, Kávos, and other villages leave from the New Fort Station, a large square beneath the Neo Frourio near the New Port. Most run several times daily, with fares ranging from 300 Drs–600 Drs ($1.25–$2.50).

Dark blue buses to the suburbs, nearby villages, and the major sights such as the Achilleion, Ághios Ioánnis, and the resorts of Benítses, Kontokáli, and Dassía, leave from the San Rocco Square station, also called Theotóki Square, at Avramíou and Theotóki Streets, near the post office in the south part of the new town. The no. 2 bus to the well-situated suburb of Kanóni (where the ritzy Hilton and some Class C hotels and restaurants are located) leaves from the Esplanade every half hour, from 7:30am to 10pm. Be sure to ask when the last bus returns, as some service ends as early as 8pm. The blue local buses cost 125 Drs (53¢); tickets are sold on board.

BY TAXI

Taxis usually meet all the ferries; you can catch one outside the Customs House if you're an international traveler, or by the small park if you're exiting the mainland ferry. **Tip:** Travelers arriving at Corfu from Igoumenítsa may be able to hitch a ride from a tourist who's transporting his/her car on this car ferry.

Taxis are easy to find throughout Corfu town, but this expensive transport should be saved for dining out or discoing at one of the seaside resorts. But the taxi problem, serious in Athens and other highly touristed destinations in Greece, is particularly acute on this island. Finding a driver willing to use a meter (and on a legal basis) is as tough as finding inexpensive fresh fish. Below are the posted legal rates (expect a 20% increase during the lifetime of this edition).

LEGAL TAXI RATES

Type	Amount
Minimum	350 Drs ($1.45)
Luggage Supplement	250 Drs ($1.05)
Port or airport supplement	250 Drs ($1.05)
Single mileage tariff (in town)	100 Drs (42¢)
Double mileage tariff (out of town)	150 Drs (63¢)
One way and from 1am to 5am	150 Drs (63¢)
Fares from 5am to 6am	60 Drs (25¢)
If taxi waits	800 Drs ($3.35/hour)
Radio call surcharge	200 Drs (83¢)

Although this table is a good guideline, rates can vary by a factor of ten! Of those drivers who use their meter, some actually doctor it to charge double for a legitimate single-tariff ride. The best advice is to ask a local, nontaxi driver for the approximate fare. Armed with that, and insisting that the driver use the meter, you might get there for close to the official rate. For out-of-town trips, we found it easiest to bargain for a flat rate. We've also heard that the radio taxis (☎ **33-811** or **33-812**) are generally more trustworthy.

SAMPLE TAXI FARES

From Corfu Town	Rate
To airport	1,150 Drs ($4.80)
To international port	1,150 Drs ($4.80)
To Paleokastrítsa	3,450 Drs ($14.35)
To Sidári	4,600 Drs ($19.15)

Note: If you think you've been overcharged, get the driver's identification number and report it immediately to the tourist police. They're reasonably diligent about prosecuting the reckless.

BY CAR

There are several rental-car companies around the island: to be exact, 36 in Corfu town and another 78 around the island, according to the printed list the EOT will gladly hand you when you ask for advice. High-season travelers should definitely pay the extra drachmas for a **Hertz** (four locations; ☎ **38-388**), **Avis** (Odós Ethnikís. Antistáseos 42, ☎ **24-404**) or **Euro Hire** (three locations; ☎ **22-062**); it's easy to reserve one in advance of your arrival. There are also several other companies if you want to shop around; expect to pay from $90–$140 per day, including unlimited mileage and a stiff 18% tax. We had good service from Kostas Ginis at the small **Sunrise Rent A Car** (☎ **44-325** or **33-519**) at Odós Arseníou 1, as well as from **International Rent Cars** (☎ **37-710**) at Odós Kapodistríou 20A.

Tip: Check your hotel reception desk first to see if they can get you a good rate on a rental car.

Western Greece & the Ionian Islands

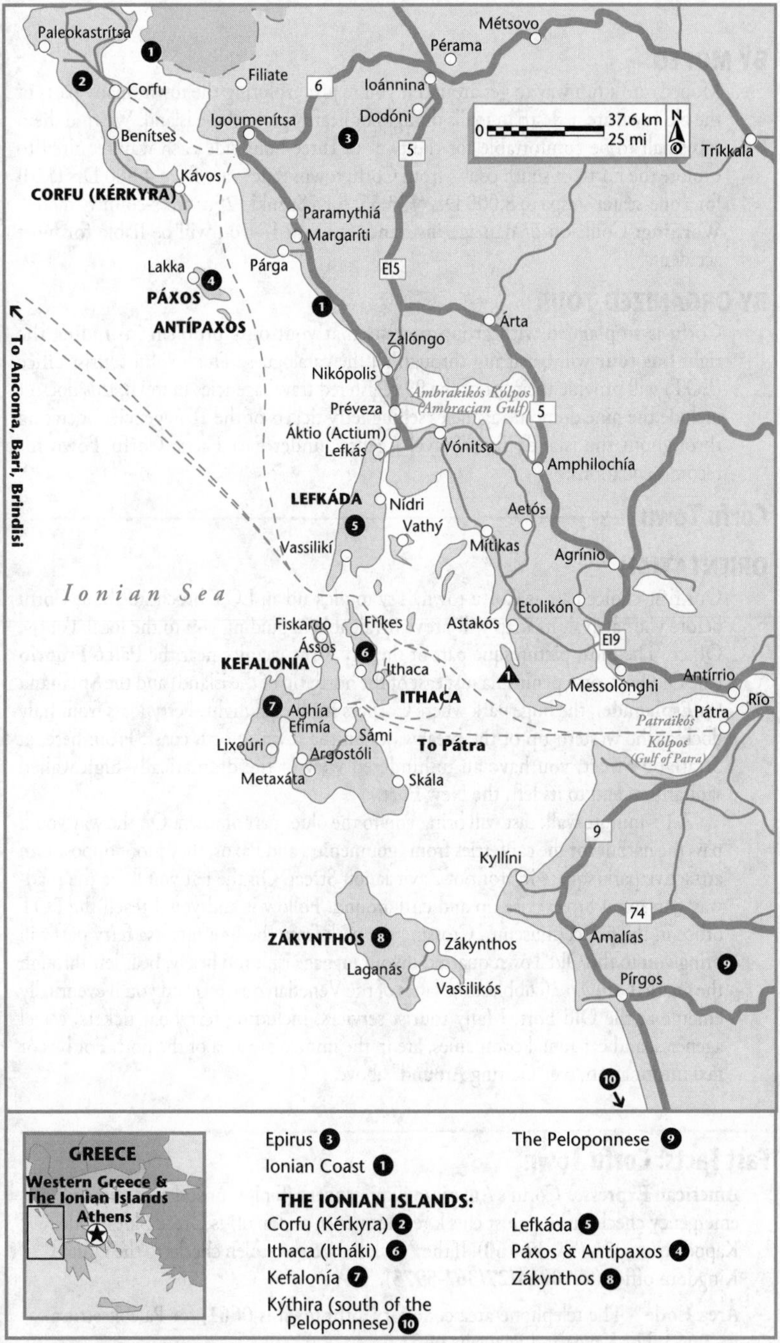

BY MOPED

Mopeds are a fun way to get around if you're just exploring the town (many parts of the old town are pedestrian malls though) or nearby parts of the island. We find them too small to be comfortable for the two- or three-hour ride each way required to explore the north or south coasts from Corfu town. Rates vary from 4,800 Drs ($20) for a one-seater Vespa to 8,000 Drs ($33.35) for a Suzuki 125cc cross-country model. **Warning:** Collision or damage insurance is limited—you will be liable for most accidents.

BY ORGANIZED TOUR

Corfu is so plagued with group tourists that your only problem in finding the right **bus tour** will be sifting through all the catalogues. The helpful tourist office (EOT) will provide their list of the 99 registered travel agencies in town; this doesn't include the nine domestic agencies selling ferry tickets or the 167 agencies operating throughout the island. See "Travel Agents" under Fast Facts: Corfu Town for recommendations.

Corfu Town

ORIENTATION

Our first-choice base is Corfu town. Try to pick up an EOT brochure about Corfu before your arrival; its map will prove invaluable in guiding you to the local Tourist Office. The most picturesque part of the city is the vicinity near the **Paleó Froúrio** (the Old Fort, on a peninsula just east of the north tip of the island) and the **Spianáda** (or **Esplanade**), the huge park where Corfiots stroll each night. Ferryboats from Italy dock at the western tip of the breakwater on the town's north coast. From here, at Stratigou Street, you have an unhindered view of the dramatically high walled sanitarium, and to its left, the **New Fort.**

A 15-minute walk east will bring you to the older part of town. On the way you'll pass the harbor for the car ferries from Igoumenítsa and Páxos; they moor opposite an attractive park/square in front of Zavitsianou Street. On the left you'll see the roadway (Arseníou Street) rise up and curl around. Follow it and you'll reach the EOT office in the palace/museum. Crossing the park from the Igoumenítsa ferry pier will bring you to the Old Town quarter; if your luggage isn't too heavy, bear left through the gnarled *cantouni* (cobblestone lanes of the Venetian quarter) and you'll eventually emerge at the Old Fort. Many tourist services, including ferryboat tickets, travel agencies, and car-rental companies, are in the immediate area of the port. For bus or taxi information, see "Getting Around" above.

Fast Facts: Corfu Town

American Express Corfu's American Express agent (for lost or stolen credit cards, emergency check cashing, lost check replacements, and mail) is Greek Skies, Odós Kapodistríou 20A (☎ **39-160**). If they're closed, report stolen checks to the United Kingdom office (☎ **0044/27/367-5975**).

Area Code The telephone area code for Corfu town is **0661;** for Paleokastrítsa it's **0663.** For Kavos and Páxos its **0662.**

Banks Most banks operate Monday through Thursday from 8am to 2pm, till 1:30pm Friday, though several have extended hours in Corfu town. The National

Bank branch at the Customs House is open to meet ferryboats; the Ionian and Commercial Banks on San Rocco Square have evening hours (5 to 7pm Monday through Friday, 8am through 2pm weekends). The Municipal Tourist Office at the New Port will exchange traveler's checks from 8am to 8pm Monday through Friday, 8am to 2pm Saturday.

Bookstores Xenglossos, Márkou Street off San Rocco Square (☎ **44-044**) is a good shop for foreign language books. The newsstand next to the GPO has a large variety of paperbacks and international newspapers.

Consulates The British consulate (☎ **30-055**) is located at Odós Menekrátous 1 in Corfu Town.

Church Services The Holy Trinity Anglican Church (☎ **31-467**) at Odós Mavíli 21, corner of Zambéli, offers weekly English language services.

Emergencies For medical emergencies, contact the Corfu General Hospital (☎ **45-811**). For general emergencies, dial **100;** for ambulance service dial **166.**

Eyeglasses Optiko is a capable, quick and inexpensive maker/repairer of eyewear, located at Odós Voulgareos 75 near the Town Hall.

Hospitals The Corfu General Hospital (☎ **45-811**) on Konstanta St. is considered the best.

Language Classes Written, literary, and spoken modern Greek is taught each summer at the School of Foreign Languages, Odós Mildiadi Margariti 46, Corfu Town, 49100, ☎ **0661/45-003.** Write or call them for more information.

Luggage There's a luggage storage opposite the New Port, next door to the Commercial Bank, at Odós Avrami 130 (☎ **37-673**).

Newspapers The *Corfu News,* an advertiser-supported yet discriminating judge of Corfu, is free and available in many hotels. The politically conscious *Corfiot* is sold by subscription at 250 Drs ($1.05) per issue. The daily *Athens News* is widely sold and contains local performance schedules.

Police Next door to EOT are the tourist police (☎ **30-265**), who are open daily 7am to 9pm for simple complaints about hotels, taxis, and so on. Theft should be reported to the regular police (☎ **39-575**) at Odós Alexandras 17.

Post Office The central post office (☎ **25-544**) is one block from San Rocco Square at Alexándras Avenue, open 7:30am to 8pm Monday through Friday, 7:30am to 2pm Saturday, 9am to 1:30pm Sunday.

Telephones The main telephone office **(OTE)** is at Odós Mantzárou 9 near the Archeological Museum, open 6am to midnight daily. There is a convenient branch (with international phone directories) at Odós Kapodistriou 34 on the Esplanade, open daily 7:30am to 11pm.

Tourist Office The Greek Tourist Office **(EOT)** (☎ **0661/37-638** or **37-639**, fax 0661/30-298), is at Odós Zavitsianoú 15; the Tourist Information Office is on Platiá Solomoú, near the New Fortress. Open weekdays 9am to 8pm, until 2pm on Saturday from May to October. In the winter months they're open weekdays only 9am to 2:30pm. The Municipal Tourist Office (☎ **0661/42-602**) has a branch at the New Port, inside the Customs House (open daily 7am to 9pm, Sunday 8am to 1pm). There are also branches at the airport (open Friday through Monday 7am to 1pm and 9pm to midnight) and in the village of Kondokali. They offer information and money exchange services during these hours. Be sure to pick up the Tourist Office's free brochure with its up-to-date town map, so you don't need to purchase one.

Travel Agents We found *Greek Skies* (☎ **0661/39-160,** fax 0661/36-161) to be generally useful. Manager Spyros Lemis will book rental cars, confirm flights and assist with hotel reservations. They're located at Odós Kapodistríou 20A on the esplanade; open daily except Sunday. *Charitos Travel,* upstairs at Odós Arseniou 35 (☎ **0661/44-611**, fax 0661/36-825), has long been helpful to Frommer readers for island tours (including mountainbike tours), renting private villas, arranging wedding logistics (true!), and booking top quality hotel rooms at a discount. Charitos runs several bus and boat excursions; for example, a full-day coastal tour stopping at two beaches with a barbecue and wine costs 9,800 Drs ($40.85). The *Corfu Sun Club* (☎ **0661/33-855**, fax 33-100), nearest the ferry port at Odós Arseniou 45-49, advertises itself as the "Accommodations Information Center." They will assist you with a private room on the island, though most bookings require a one week minimum stay. Rates vary from 8,800 Drs ($36.65) for a double with private bath per night, to 80,000 Drs ($333.35) for a two-person "villa" with kitchenette per week. **Crystal Travel,** (☎ **41-090,** fax 42-221). Odós Stratigoú 46, arranges tours, sightseeing, ferry tickets, accommodations and car rentals.

Note: With the sharp rise in development on the island, there has been an increase in the number of tour/travel agencies. Some problems have arisen. If your arrangements through a travel agency prove unsatisfactory, notify the Association of Travel Agents (☎ **21-521**).

WHAT TO SEE & DO

Other than touring and sunning, most activity on this hedonistic island can be individually tailored. Museum and old-stone buffs can go wild at Corfu's two excellent collections; shoppers have high-fashion boutiques in the charming old town quarters; sports enthusiasts have a wide range of enterprise; and you hard-core party animals have bars, clubs, and discos where you can move and groove.

Museums

Archeological Museum, Odós Vraila 1. ☎ 30-680.

The small collection of finds in the archeological museum are well labeled and of surprising interest. The first gallery contains ceramics and a large archaic lion of the late 7th century B.C., found near Menekrates' tomb. In the room behind it is the museum's highlight, the **Gorgo Pediment** from the Doric Temple of Artemis. These sculptures (from the early 6th century B.C.) have been installed in a re-creation of their original setting. The broad features of Gorgo are almost Aztec in style; she's surrounded by her children, Pegasus (the winged horse) and Chrysaor (a young man). One look at her face and you can imagine how she turned men to stone; her children are the offspring of the blood shed when Perseus cut off her head. These sculptures are considered the finest extant works of the archaic period, and represent a bold departure in style for the Corinthian artist who sculpted them. Pegasus was the symbol of Corinth, and the two "leopanthers" (half lion, half panther) depicted flanking both sides of the pediment typify the great attention to detail paid by the artist. The temple's remains were discovered 2 km inland from Mon Repos (formerly the British lord high commissioner's palace). All the sculptures have been installed at the museum, leaving the site of little interest.

Admission: 500 Drs ($2.10) adults, 250 Drs ($1.05) students; Sunday admission free.

Open: Tues–Sun 8:30am–3pm.

Museum of Asiatic Art, Palace of St. Michael and St. George, Corfu Town. ☎ **30-443.**

The Museum of Asiatic Art is located in the Palace of St. Michael and St. George, built as headquarters for this Order of Knights (they recognized English, Ionian, and Maltese subjects for distinguished service). Constructed between 1819 and 1824 after the design of the architect Sir George Whitmore, the palace is a wonderful example of the English neoclassical style seen along the Promenade and throughout the old town. The building is just as much a work of art as the collection it houses.

The collection of Asian art is superb. There are excellent examples of Japanese netsuke and wood-block prints, porcelain, sculpture, and watercolors. In the wing adjoining the elaborate throne room is a large collection of Chinese art, so well labeled that it provides novices with a comprehensive introduction to art, culture, and religion from the Shang Dynasty (1500 B.C.) to the Ching (19th century). The museum is composed principally of the collections of two Greek statesmen who served many years abroad. Like any collection that's been lovingly assembled, the works at the Asian art museum vary in quality, while always exhibiting their former owner's appreciation of other cultures.

Admission: 600 Drs ($2.50) adults, 350 Drs ($1.45) students.

Open: Tues–Sun 8:30am–3pm.

Achilleion Museum, Gastouríou, Corfu. ☎ **56-210.**

In 1890 the Empress Elizabeth of Austria decided to build herself a retreat away from the intrigues of the Hapsburg court. (Remember Romy Schneider as Elizabeth in the German film *Sissy*?) The Achilleion was named after her hero Achilles (whom she identified with her son Rudolph), and many sculptures of him adorn its outdoor garden. She thought of herself as his mother, the dolphin Thetis—hence the many dolphin images throughout the well-maintained grounds and extraordinary interior. Shelf tops, commodes, and mantelpieces are filled with family memorabilia, portraits, and war mementoes. The ground floor has bright murals, frescoes, and a painted ceiling. Wrought-iron handrails sweep up the marble staircase that is supported by 12 gods and goddesses; garish architectural trim, lots of gilt, and a saddle-seated throne of Kaiser Wilhelm II of Germany (who bought the estate for himself after Elizabeth was assassinated by an Italian anarchist) fill the parlor rooms. At night, the Achilleion becomes a gambling casino.

Admission: 400 Drs ($1.65) adult; 200 Drs (85¢) children.

Open: Daily 8am–7pm. **Bus:** Public bus no. 10 from San Rocco Square runs directly to the Achilleion six times daily between 7am and 8pm, and returns four times daily between 7:20am and 8:20pm.

Other Sights

Like many towns in northern Greece, Corfu once had a substantial Jewish population; only 70 people survived the Holocaust out of a population of over 3,000. Today, the only visible sign of the community is a reasonably well preserved **synagogue** built approximately 300 years ago (two other synagogues were destroyed during battles on the island). The synagogue is still in use (every Saturday morning beginning at 9am) and has much of its original ornamentation. Members of the community claim that their ancestors, from Puglia, Italy, brought locally made treasures with them. The display of torah crowns is the most interesting aspect of the Sephardic-style interior. To gain access to the synagogue during the week, call the Jewish Community Center (☎ **38-802**). The synagogue is located on 4th Pakados Velissaríou Street, about two blocks up from the New Fort bus station.

The island's small **Byzantine Museum** is housed in the 16th-century church of Antivouniótissa and contains a fine collection of icons, frescoes, and religious paintings by well-known Greek artists. Artifacts date to the 11th century; a Russian altar cloth donated by Nikifórou Theotóki is of particular interest. The Byzantine Museum (☎ **38-313**) is off Arseníou Street, inland from the Old Fort, and is open Tuesday–Saturday 8:45am–3pm, Sunday 9:30am–2:30pm; admission 625 Drs ($3.50).

The beautifully planted **British Cemetery** is dedicated to the British soldiers and civilians who lost their lives in the Ionian during its term as a British protectorate. The cemetery entrance is on Kolokotróni Street.

A Walk Around Corfu Town

Anyone with at least a day on Corfu should seize the opportunity to walk around its old quarter. If you're coming from the new port (the Igoumenítsa ferry pier), begin by walking along **Arseníou Street,** the road that leads uphill around the point. This walk provides wonderful views of Vidos Island (the one celebs are always trying to purchase), Epirus, on the Greek mainland beyond it, and the Albanian coast up to the north. You'll pass many elegant neoclassical buildings from the various European occupations: notice the French consulate on the corner of Arseníou and Kapodistríou. From this corner you can gauge the layout of the **Old Fort,** on its own rocky point with the yacht-filled Mandraki Harbor beneath it. On the left of Kapodistríou is the palace of St. Michael and St. George, now the EOT office and the Museum of Asiatic Art, and still a fine building to admire. A statue of an Austrian mercenary, by name Schulenberg, who assisted the defense of the island against the Turks stands at the entrance to the fort, a footbridge crossing over the **contrafossa.** This moat is 15 meters deep and 23 to 40 meters wide. On the tip of this fortified outcropping is the tiny **church of St. George.**

Crossing back over the contrafossa brings you to **Dousmáni** Street, the road bisecting the Esplanade. These formal gardens are now used for cricket matches. Continue on Dousmani as it crosses Georgious, the busy thoroughfare with sidewalk cafés along its arcaded west wall, a popular place to relax over ouzo and watch cricketeers or playing children.

The streets behind Dousmáni—Ouidmándou, Voulgaréos, Aghíon Pánton, and Sevastianoú—are full of boutiques, jewelers, souvenir stands, and Greek handcraft stores. The deeper you walk into this old quarter, the more enchanted you'll be. Many little streets never intersect; many alleys are dead ends, and often a gate or fence will lead nowhere. The magic of old Corfu is in the buildings left from its colonial days, when so many cultures left their mark to create this teeming cosmopolitan town.

When you've tired of the Old Town, turn east toward the Esplanade and approach the Old Fort, the site of the nightly *son-et-lumière* (sound-and-light) show. Just below it to the south is Corfu's closest swimming spot, the Yacht Club, and to the north, the old Mandraki Harbor and its glamourous yachts.

At the end of the Esplanade you'll pass the Maitland Rotunda (commemorating Corfu's first lord high commissioner under the British regime), then the Corfu Palace Hotel. At the next corner, Vraila Street, are the archeological museum and the town tennis courts. Keep strolling on King Constantine (Vassiléos Konstantínou) Street, as it parallels the water. In less than 2 km you'll reach **Plage Mon Repos.** The beautifully landscaped grounds were part of the overall concept of Sir Frederick Adam, a British lord high commissioner who built this as his summer residence. Begun in 1831, it soon became known as "Sir Frederick's Folly." When Greece became independent, Mon Repos was used as the summer palace of the Greek royal family, but since the abolition of the monarchy it's been closed to the public. Today, it's a pleasant pebble and sand swimming beach.

Joggers will enjoy the 10-km (6-mile) run to the suburb of Kanoni; others can catch the no. 2 bus. From this scenic area you can overlook, or motorboat to, **Pondikoníssi** (Mouse Island), which has a 12th-century church dedicated to Christ. The smaller and closer islet just supports the convent and church of Vlachernon, reachable from the mainland by a little causeway. The Kanoni peninsula is surrounded by the Ionian Sea on one side and the Chalikiopoulos Lagoon on the other.

Allow about two hours to explore the town; another hour if visiting Kanoni, and another few hours if you enter the museums or go for a swim.

Festivals and Holidays

Corfu's favorite holidays are celebrated in honor of her patron saint, Spýridon, four times a year—on Palm Sunday, Easter Sunday, August 11 (to commemorate the Corfiots' resistance against the Turks in the siege of 1716), and on the first Sunday in November. St. Spýridon is credited with saving the medieval town from the plague in 1630, from the Turks on several occasions, and again during World War II, when a bomb dropped through the roof of his church but didn't explode. In the **Ághios Spyrídon Cathedral,** on Filellínon Street in the old quarter, you can see gold and silver icons and the embalmed body of the saint himself. (It's said that the embalmed body of Spyrídon, a 4th-century bishop of Cyprus, was smuggled from Istanbul and put in a silver casket in his Corfiote church.)

Easter, as it is everywhere in Greece, is a major holiday on Corfu. The biggest night is Holy Saturday, when a processional leads to the Esplanade where the bishop will announce at midnight *"Christos anesti"* (Christ is risen). After his proclamation, the hymns, fireworks, bands, bells, and dancing begin, in time with the turning on of lights everywhere. On Easter Sunday, the feast of roast lamb and wine continues until the afternoon, when everyone goes out again to dance.

Sports and Recreation

Sports enthusiasts will find more variety than on most other islands, with many activities in Corfu town. Interested in playing cricket on the Esplanade? Call the Gymnastikós Sýllogos (Gymnastic Association) about temporary memberships (☎ **32-835**) or the Byron Club (☎ **24-595**). At Vraila Street, near the archeological museum, are the town tennis courts. For information on booking time, contact the Corfu **Tennis Club** (☎ **37-021**) or the Kefalonanduko Tennis Club (☎ **38-040**).

Swimmers can try the fun **Corfu Yacht Club** (☎ **24-759**) beneath the Old Fort, where laps in a roped-off part of the reasonably clean bay cost 200 Drs (83¢) per day. They have a concrete sun deck and a small snack bar at the site. Less than 2 km south (about a 20-minute walk) you'll reach **Plage Mon Repos.** It's not the island's best beach by any means, but it's convenient to the town, and a grand setting for a swim.

Joggers can run in circles on the grassy Esplanade or on pavement for a scenic 10 km (6-mile) run to the suburb of Kanoni. Walkers should buy the *Corfu Book of Walks* filled with strolls and hikes (available at the hard-to-find Ploos Bookshop (☎ **22-694**) at 4, 2d Parod, Theotoki Street in the Old Town), or discuss a possible route between some of the northern villages with the EOT (see "Around the Island" for some ideas). Golfers should head straight to Livadi Tou Ropas (Ropas Valley) on the island's west side, to the **Corfu Golf Club** (☎ **94-220**) on Ermones Road near the village of Vatos. The 18-hole, par 72 course was designed by David Harradine. Green fees run 8,000 Drs ($33.35) per day, or 35,000 Drs ($145.85) per week, plus 2,800 Drs ($11.65) per day for club rental.

WHERE TO STAY

As on Rhodes and Mýkonos, hotels tend to be much more expensive on Corfu than on other, less touristed islands. Happily, some of the older lodgings in and around the Old Town (the most convenient location) have been maintained and provide clean, if spartan, living for moderate prices. There are also some budget hotels around the New Port, and some good choices in the nearby suburbs with reasonable rates. Most hoteliers urge that reservations be made one to two months in advance (particularly at the budget hotels). **Note:** Most hotels operate from April 1 to October 31 unless otherwise noted.

The tourist police are responsible for rooms-to-rent that are government licensed, and will give you the names and phone numbers of available rooms. Contacting a travel agent (see Fast Facts for recommendations) is probably a better idea for last-minute, high season accommodation.

In and Around the Old Town

Hotel Arcadion, Odós Kapodistríou 44, Corfu 49100. ☎ **0661/37-671.**
55 rms (all with bath). TEL

Rates: 10,400 Drs ($43.35) single; 15,600 Drs ($65) double. No credit cards.

This neoclassic hotel is an aging, but good value choice along the Esplanade. It offers a central location, and simple twin-bedded rooms with balconies overlooking the ancient citadel and Mandraki Harbor. The compact single rooms with showers are good value, though the facilities are somewhat worn and the café crowd below can make it noisy in the summer.

Bella Venezia, Odós Zambéli 4, P.O. Box 32, Corfu 49100. ☎ **0661/44-290.**
Fax 0661/20-708. 32 rms (all with bath). A/C TV TEL

Rates: 14,300 Drs ($59.60) single; 20,540 Drs ($85.60) double. AE, DC, V.

This wonderfully restored neoclassic mansion on the fringe of Old Town houses a newly renovated hotel. Large, high-ceilinged rooms, fitted with heaters for year-round guests, have a simple Old World charm that will please traditionalists. Though plainer than the Cavalieri, the well decorated common spaces, attentive service, attractive breakfast patio, and snack kiosk outside make this an excellent value.

Cavalieri Hotel, Odós Kapodistríou 4, Corfu 49100. ☎ **0661/39-041.**
Fax 0661-39-283. 50 rms (all with bath). A/C TV TEL

Rates (including breakfast): 20,800 Drs ($86.65) single; 32,500 Drs ($135.40) double. AE, DC, V.

The Cavalieri, a favorite of the late William Holden and the very-much-alive Joan Collins, overlooks Corfu town and the water. Originally a 17th-century nobleman's mansion belonging to the family of Count Flamburiari, the building was partly bombed during the Second World War. By keeping the facade, this Venetian-style hotel, decorated with antiques and marble, wallpaper and polish, was created. Though the rooms are fairly standard the common spaces are quite attractive in an Old European kind of way. The velvet-upholstered sitting room off the lobby will be your first indication of the continental style yet to come, from the back garden where you'll "take" breakfast to the balconies or colonnaded rooftop bar overlooking the water, to the elegant fixtures and features that abound.

Around Corfu Town and the Suburbs

Archontiko Hotel, Odós Athanasíou 61, Garítsa 49100, Corfu. ☎ **0661/36-850.** Fax 0661/38-294. 10 rms, 10 suites (all with bath). MINIBAR TV TEL

Rates: 13,200 Drs ($55) single; 17,185 Drs ($71.60) double. No credit cards.

Located along the southern seafront road (farther on than the Calypso) is a retro-fitted mansion built in 1903 that still retains some of its original grandeur. Although the floors have been cut up to accommodate a larger number of rooms, many suites are large enough for three to six beds. The first two floors feature frescoed cathedral ceilings (the higher floors have lower ceilings); large rooms, simply decorated, with spotlessly clean modern bathrooms; and common spaces accented with flowers and ancient urns. Breakfast and snacks are served outside under a vine-covered arbor. Although a bit out of the way, the waterside walk is pleasant and the neighborhood is quiet.

Hotel Atlantis, Odós Stratigoú 48 (New Port), Corfu 49100. ☎ **0661/35-560.** Fax 0661/46-480. 61 rms (all with bath). TV TEL

Rates: 11,400 Drs ($47.50) single; 13,600 Drs ($68.35) double. AE, DC, EC, MC, V.

Across from the Customs House in the New Port, a ten-minute walk from the Old Town, the Atlantis is well kept and the staff is friendly and helpful. The buff-colored rooms are spacious and comfortable, with charming prints by the artist Xomeritakis.

Hotel Europa, Odós Gitsiáni 10, Mantoúki, Corfu. ☎ **0661/39-304.** 34 rms (20 with bath).

Rates: 3,900 Drs ($16.25) single without bath, 5,200 Drs ($21.65) single with bath; 6,500 Drs ($27.10) double without bath, 7,800 Drs ($32.50) double with bath. No credit cards.

The cute, homey Hotel Europa is a bit difficult to find, but its isolation from the portside traffic is well worth the minor inconvenience. It's aging but kept clean, with acceptable common toilets and hot water showers. The bright twin-bedded rooms are a good value for this almost "in town" location.

Kontokali Hostel and Campground, Kontokáli, Corfu. ☎ **0661/91-202** or **91-207.** 10 dormitories (none with bath).

Rates: 1,950 Drs ($8.10) bed. Camping: 1,170 Drs ($4.85) per tent plus 1,170 Drs ($4.85) per person. No credit cards.

Corfu's only youth hostel, with four beds per dormitory, is in Kontokali village, about 8 km northeast of town. It has a small kitchen area, though many low-budget travelers prefer the adjacent camping area. Both, unfortunately, are opposite a shallow, dirty-water bathing area. Though twice the price, the in-town budget choices are better value.

Hotel Marina, Anemómilos, Corfu 49100. ☎ **0661/32-783.** 110 rms (all with bath). TEL

Rates: (including breakfast) 17,680 Drs ($73.65) single/double. EC, MC, V.

This newer hotel has bright, comfortable, and quiet rooms directly across the street from Plage Mon Repos, the small but popular sand beach, a 15-minute walk south of

Old Town. Each has a balcony with sea or town views, fresh white stucco walls, marble floors and tiled bathrooms with a full size tub (!) and shower curtains (!). Breakfast is served outdoors in an adjoining garden, and there's a large TV lounge off the lobby. Though a little less convenient than some choices, the Marina is very good value amongst the larger, full-amenity hotels.

Hotel Royal, Odós Figaréto 110, Kanóni, Corfu 49100. ☎ **0661/37-512.** Fax 0661/35-343. 121 rms (all with bath). TEL

Rates (including breakfast): 9,750 Drs ($40.60) single; 12,350 Drs ($51.45) double. No credit cards.

Called the *Vassilikón* in Greek, the Hotel Royal is just not to be believed. Its rooms tower over a marble veranda and three swimming pools, terraced so that each one spills into the one below. Families adore this hydraulic system, which would have made the ancient Romans green with envy. The abundant, glittery decor might be described as wildly ornate or simply modern rococo. Now, what's the catch? Well, the Royal is built on a verdant hillside overlooking the international airport. Was this such a drawback that we couldn't recommend it to you? Luckily, a reader wrote us a rave review of her honeymoon stay at the Royal: "It's next to the Olympic runways, but flights stopped in the evening and during the day we were touring the island, so the noise didn't bother us. When we were at the hotel, it was actually interesting to watch the planes take off." Although flights now run into the wee hours, the Royal is still quite a popular place.

A Splurge Choice

★ **Corfu Hilton,** Nausicaa Street, Box 124, Kanóni, Corfu 49100. ☎ **0661/36-540.** Fax 0661/36-551. 255 rms, 11 suites (all with bath). A/C MINIBAR TEL

Rates: 45,500 Drs ($168.75) single; 54,600 Drs ($227.50) double; from 84,500 Drs ($352.10) suites. (Ask Charitos Travel or the hotel about special packages; at our visit there was 7-day package at $175 per night for two, including half-board plan.) AE, DC, EC, MC, V.

Located in an attractive suburb, this hotel is one of the splashiest resorts in all Greece, making it a first-class splurge. This many-acred complex includes extremely attractive grounds, with a large saltwater outdoor pool (plus an indoor one) and a gorgeous garden set above a tranquil, pebbly beach where even waterskiing is available. Guest quarters are spacious and well appointed with balconies. Sports venues and bowling alleys contribute to the many resort facilities, making this an ideal spot for those wanting to relax in active surroundings. The staff, consistent with our experience with Hilton hotels around the world, is extremely well informed and helpful. Our only warning about this comfortable resort is that it is situated above the extremely active airport. We strongly suggest that you insist on a room overlooking the sea (not the airport side); you'll be rewarded with a better view and a quiet night's sleep. This delightful resort is open year-round.

Dining/Entertainment: As befits a true resort, dining opportunities abound. The Eptanissa Restaurant offers a daily fixed menu for half-board guests, with a special Greek Night buffet on Thursday. There's a poolside restaurant and a beach snack bar. The Eptanissa Grill serves Greek and continental fare in an attractive setting overlooking the gardens; there's a great buffet at breakfast and a salad bar at supper. The Kefi Bar has a pianist nightly after 9pm.

Services: 24-hour room service, concierge, babysitting (with notice), laundry service, minivan to Corfu town.

Facilities: Two swimming pools, watersports, 20% discount at Corfu Golf Club, health club, two tennis courts, jogging track.

WHERE TO EAT

Corfu, perhaps because of its Italian heritage, has some excellent restaurants serving Greek and Italian cuisine. Many pricey, touristy cafés (open mid-April to end of October) are scattered throughout the Old Town, and under the arcaded portico across from the Esplanade. However, several locally known tavernas around the New Port or south of Old Town in Garítsa will show you a traditional Greek meal at its best!

In and Around the Old Town

Restaurant Aegli, Odós Kapodistríou 23. Old Town. ☎ **31-949.**

Cuisine: GREEK/CONTINENTAL.
Prices: Appetizers 900–1,430 Drs ($3.75–$5.95); main courses 1,450–2,600 Drs ($5.95–$10.85). AE, EC, DC, MC, V.
Open: Daily 10:30am–midnight.

This is our favorite of the higher-priced Esplanade cafés. It's very pleasant to sit on their comfy, leather-cushioned chairs and watch life drift by, especially if you're waiting for one of the Aegli's Corfiot specialties. They feature sofrito (a veal in garlic sauce), swordfish, spicy salami, a selection of pastas, and pastitsada (a baked veal in tomato and cheese sauce).

Chambor, Odós Guildford 71, Town Hall Square. Old Town. ☎ **39-031.**

Cuisine: INTERNATIONAL.
Prices: Appetizers 2,340–4,550 Drs ($6–$18.95); main courses 5,200–7,800 Drs ($21.65–$32.50). AE, EC, V.
Open: Mon–Sat 9am–2am; Sun 5pm–2am.

It's not only the stunning setting across from Corfu's illuminated and imposing Town Hall, or the linen, Japanese umbrellas, whole wheat bread and tahini brought with bread plates to your table. Chambor also has an exotic and imaginative menu equal in style to its French Moroccan chef. We began with a mixed appetizer plate of both spinach and eggplant croquettes, saganaki, sausage, tart tzadzíki, and potent taramasaláta, then followed it with a rich, creamy pasta carbonara and a casserole of bream (a local fish) baked with vegetables. After a grated carrot and orange salad, we cleared our plates for the heavenly chocolate mousse. An excellent choice if you need a break from the roughshod presentation and simplicity of most taverna fare.

$ **Giogias Taverna,** Odós Guildford 16, Old Town. ☎ **37-147.**

Cuisine: GREEK.
Prices: Appetizers 390–1,170 Drs ($1.60–$4.85); main courses 1,040–1,950 Drs ($4.35–$8.10). No credit cards.
Open: Daily 11:30am–midnight.

It's becoming increasingly difficult to find a genuine taverna in the Old Town, but this is a typical grill on a humble scale, located one block inland from the Esplanade behind the Olympic Airways office. Here one can sample oregano-scented, fresh grilled lamb, souvlaki, moist barbecued chicken, and numerous other meat specialties for a modest sum. Everything tastes fresh and is obviously cooked with great care. Open year-round.

Taverna Papyrus, Odós Águios Gheodóras 25. Old Town. No phone.

Cuisine: GREEK.

Prices: Appetizers 650–1,170 Drs ($2.70–$4.85); main courses 1,170–2,600 Drs ($4.85–$10.85). No credit cards.

Open: Daily 1–4:30pm and 9pm–1am.

A favorite of students from the nearby Ionian University, this authentic little taverna is tucked into a corner near the Byzantine Museum (it's also known as "Kosta's"; ask a local for directions). In a tiny kitchen, owner Costas turns out delicious and inexpensive Corfiot favorites like veal sofrito. An old-fashioned budget favorite.

Pizza Pete, Odós Arseníou 19. Old Town. ☎ **22-301.**

Cuisine: ITALIAN/GREEK.

Prices: Appetizers 520–1,300 Drs ($2.15–$5.40); main courses 1,430–2,860 Drs ($5.95–$11.90). MC, V.

Open: Daily 9am–3am.

For casual Italian and Greek fare in a scenic, waterside setting, try this outdoor pizzeria on the Old Town promenade, overlooking coveted Vidos Island. New owners Takis and Yiannis still serve "Pizza" Pete's menu of snacks, juices, and milkshakes as well as their own Greek dishes. Early on you can enjoy a full English breakfast (800 Drs or $3.35), or come later to watch the sunset over drinks, their crisp-crust pizza, a late-night café, or ice cream. Their vegetarian pizza (not quite up to Pete's) is topped with fresh peppers, tomatoes, onions, olives, and mushrooms, and their new, homemade, oven-baked moussaká is quite good.

Around Corfu Town and the Suburbs

Bekios Grill, Mantoúki, Corfu Town. ☎ **25-946.**

Cuisine: GREEK.

Prices: Appetizers 325–1,040 Drs ($1.35–$4.35); main courses 1,040–1,950 Drs ($4.35–$8.65). No credit cards.

Open: Daily 8:30pm–1am.

This is a grill restaurant about 500 meters west of the New Port opposite the Port Police, a favorite of Mantouki residents and Corfu Town workers. Most of their fresh meat is sold by the kilo, with roast lamb, grilled pork chops, and roast chicken being the top choices. Their large *choriatiki* and crispy chips go well with everything. We think the modest prices justify the 20-minute, waterfront evening stroll from the Old Town. Open all year.

Ciao, Odós Vlachernón 46, Garitsa. ☎ **26-462.**

Cuisine: ITALIAN.

Prices: Appetizers 520–1,100 Drs ($2.15–$4.60); main courses 1,170–1,950 Drs ($4.85–$8.10). DC, EC, MC, V.

Open: Daily 7pm–2am; closed Mon in winter.

This contemporary bistro behind the Ethniki Stadio (a 20-minute walk south of the Esplanade) is favored by our Corfiot friends for the city's best Italian fare. From their varied selection (18 exotic pastas and 19 varied pizzas), we found the spaghetti carbonara and the ecological pizza (a vegetarian delight) to be particularly good, and appropriately light for an August evening on their outdoor terrace. Our friends rave about their chicken cacciatore and veal marsala.

★ **Iannis Taverna,** Yasson at Sosípatros Street, Anemómilos. ☎ **33-061.**

Cuisine: GREEK.

Prices: Appetizers 520–1,040 Drs ($2.15–$4.35); main courses 975–1,950 Drs ($4.05–$8.10). No credit cards.

Open: Mon–Sat 8pm–1am.

Here, you're forced to enter that most public of Greek enclaves, the kitchen, where the amiable staff will take you on a tour of about 20 courses simmering in pans. The variety, especially in the early evening, is outstanding and each dish is a paradigm of *haute grecque.* The list of offerings changes nightly, so just point and enjoy. On our last visit we sampled a flavorful veal stifado with sweet pearl onions, a picante potato kukya (a variety of bean), and an octopus and potato stew—all delicious. Vegetarians will find at least three dishes nightly. Don't ignore the tasty house krassi, a local vintage. Iannis is open all year and is always packed with the loyal and adoring.

$ **Sossi Fish Taverna,** Mantouki, Corfu Town. No phone.

Cuisine: GREEK

Prices: Appetizers 520–1,100 Drs ($2.15–$4.60); main courses 1,100–$1,950 Drs ($4.60–$8.10). No credit cards.

Open: Daily 8:30pm–midnight.

Mr. Sossi's tiny *psarotaverna* (fish taverna) is a block inland from the waterfront, about 500 meters west of the New Port at the end of the Mantouki bus line. A haven for fish lovers who remember when fishing was Corfu's main enterprise, he serves up fried sardines, bream, and small snapper cooked in affordable stews, soups, and casseroles. Hearty bread, thick tzadzíki, or a very garlic-y *skordalia* sustain diners until the nightly special is ready. It's the place to join cabbies, dock workers, and neighborhood folk in a wholesome, tasty, traditional meal, year round.

Viceroy Indian Restaurant, Nausicaa Street, Kanóni. ☎ **44-656.**

Cuisine: INDIAN. **Reservations:** Recommended in summer.

Prices: Appetizers 925–2,275 Drs ($3.85–$9.50); main courses 1,950–2,730 Drs ($8.10–$11.35).

Open: Daily 7pm–11:30pm.

If you're staying in this district or are looking for a change of taste, this new, highly regarded north Indian restaurant is a piquant choice. Specialties include the lamb korma and chicken chili masala, both well—but not *too hotly*—spiced, fragrant with coriander and curry. The Viceroy Biryani, a rice pilaf with pieces of moist chicken, lamb and prawns, graced with saffron and egg, is a good dish in combination with one of their vegetable curries. The Sri Lankan chef and British management work hard; the service was lacking at our visit but should improve over time.

EVENING ENTERTAINMENT

Recent community laws have established an 11pm noise curfew in Corfu Town, and a more liberal 3am (4am Saturday) curfew outside the town limits. Therefore, most of the noisy, swinging nightlife is centered in the resort complexes, though the town has more than its share of glamour, glitz, and glitter.

Bars and Music Clubs

The **Acteon Bar** is one of the best choices for a budget drink and *mezédes* (appetizers) at sunset. This casual café, about 100 meters south of the Old Fort gate on the waterside, has a first-rate view over Corfu's serene waterway. Later, after you've had dinner and the mandatory walk along the Esplanade, you can stop for a drink or dessert at **Biston Serano,** one of the nicer outdoor cafés, at no. 8 on the Esplanade. There are several other choices within a ten-minute walk south. **The Lobby,** at Odós Kapodistríou 39, is decorated in trompe l'oeil antiquities to contrast with its contemporary pop music track. This is where the bartenders are elegant and fun and the latest American releases play through the night. Nearby, occupying the ground floor of a fading Venetian mansion at Odós Kapodistríou 10, is **Tequila.** Their outdoor terrace is filled with palm trees and café tables shaded by thatch umbrellas, while the dimly lit interior is shrouded in minimalist style and loud New Wave music.

An older, more sophisticated foreign crowd gathers after 5pm in winter at the **Cavalieri Hotel bar,** an English-style wood-panelled and red leather pub off the charming lobby. In summer, most regulars go directly up to the hotel's colonnaded rooftop bar, particularly stunning at sunset. Another option is the elegant piano bar at **Quattro Stagioni,** an attractive, very European bistro on N. Theotoki Street in the Old Town. From 7pm to 2am nightly a pricey menu of light Italian fare is served at the bar or to those enjoying the outdoor café.

Discos and Night Clubs

If action is your modus operandi, head one mile north of the New Port to "Disco Mile," a strip of seven waterside dancing clubs. We saw Greeks, Scandinavians, Germans, Britons, and Australians drinking outside the doors, waiting for clubs to empty so they could take their turn stomping the night away to European and American hits. Most charge a 3,000 Drs ($12.50) cover charge, including one drink, and are open nightly after 10pm (often only Thursday to Saturday night in the low season).

A disco we particularly liked on the waterside Ethnikís Antistáseos was **Apocalipsis** (☎ **40-345**), whose wild limestone "Fall of the Roman Empire" facade really caught our eye. You'll know it by the Olympic Flame burning on its roof. Nearby at Odós Ethnikís Antistáseos 52 is **Hippodrome** (☎ **43-150**), marked by freestanding classical columns draped in gold lamé. Talk to the locals to get their advice on nightclubs and discos so you don't drop your drachmas at last-year's hot spot.

Between Alíkes and Gouvia on the coast road are three of the most popular nightclubs, those super-energized plugged-in bouzouki joints where plate-smashing and Greek crooners dominate the scene. **Esperides** (☎ **38-121**), **Ekati,** and **Corfu By Night** (☎ **38-123**), expensive supper or late drinks clubs, will provide some of the most unforgettable experiences of your stay. The air-conditioned **Adonis** (☎ **91-381**) and **Reflections** (☎ **91-735**), another disco with a British DJ, are both up in Gouvia.

Gambling

The **Corfu Hilton** (☎ **36-540**) is operating in the evening as a year-round casino. Gamblers can play French or American roulette, baccarat, or black jack (bets are a 1,000 Drs ($4.15) minimum, and a 250,000 Drs or $1,042 limit). The casino also offers a bar (to celebrate your winning, we hope), restaurant, and dance floor. The Casino is open daily from 9pm to 2am; minimum age for entry is 21 years. Take your passport.

Family Fare

The **Corfu Festival** has been one of the highlights of the September season for the past few years, presenting internationally acclaimed ballet, opera, dance, and music performances. Check with the EOT upon arrival to confirm the season's schedule of events.

The **Shell Museum,** Odós Solomoú 7–9, is a result of twenty years of roaming and collecting by Mr. Sagias Napolean. Judging from the comments in the visitors' book, it's an unqualified success with kids, as well as adults. Open daily 10am–7pm; admission is 500 Drs ($2.10).

The glass-bottomed **Kalypso Star** (☎ **46-525**) departs for an underwater odyssey from the Old Port in Corfu. Adult fare is 3,500 Drs ($14.60); children 1,750 Drs ($7.30).

The **Danilia Village** is the colonial Williamsburg of Corfu. Within its confines are a traditional Corfiot village, fields for goatherds and shepherds, pottery makers, perfume cells, weavers, wine and olive presses, an Orthodox church, an agricultural museum displaying traditional Greek objects, fields being tilled—in short, everything needed to re-create a day in the life of a 200-year-old Greek village. In the evening the Greek taverna opens, offering a filling meal of local specialties, much free retsina, and loud bouzouki; a troupe of *syrtáki* and *zeibékiko* dancers and musicians will entertain you, and ask you to join in with them. The results can be great fun (remember to bring your camera).

Several tour companies offer excursions to the village, located 8 km northeast of Corfu town, off the Paleokastrítsa road. The average fee is 12,000 Drs ($50), which includes a tour of the grounds, dinner, wine (as much as you want), entertainment, and transportation to and from your hotel. Independents can make reservations directly with Danilia Village—call their in-town office (☎ **36-833**) at Odós Kapodistríou 38—and take the no. 7 bus to Gouviá, then walk 2 kms to the site. It's open Monday through Saturday from 10am to 1pm and 6pm till the action stops (dinner starts at 8:30pm).

There are two **movie theaters** in Corfu town, the Pallas (on Theotóki near San Rocco Square), and the Orpheus (on Akadimías Street, closed in high season).

Paleokastrítsa

Just 26 km due west of Corfu town is the small community of Paleokastrítsa, set high on the rocks above a lovely bay. Several rounded coves line the edges, forming rock-and-pebble beaches. The lure of Paleokastrítsa is the pure transparent water that has drawn fishermen and divers for years. Bathers seeking less crowded areas should walk down to Aghía Triáda beach (a path descends from the clifftop roadway just past Paleokastrítsa Rent a Car) or try some of the less visible pebbley coves around the marina. Of all the other resorts on the island that we cover—Ághios Gheórghios, Sidári, Glyfáda, and Kassiopi—we find Paleokastrítsa to have the most dramatic scenery which, combined with restaurants and nightlife, makes it the top alternative to Corfu Town.

WHAT TO SEE & DO

Since the area's renowned for its scenic beauty, leisurely walks are the best way to take in the sights. About an hour's walk uphill behind the Hotel Odysseus (on a beaten donkey path) is the small village where the Corfiot residents of Paleokastrítsa live. This harbor and its hilltop acropolis, **Angelókastro,** have long been associated with the Phaeacian kingdom of Alcinoos and Arete immortalized by Homer in the *Odyssey.*

A spectacular walk can be made to the **monastery of Panaghías Paleokastrítsas,** above the village. It looks steep, but don't let the path scare you—in actuality it is only about 15 minutes to the top. This is best done at sunset when the view (and the light) is constantly changing. Beautiful little bays and inlets interrupted by lush greenery endow one with a sense of the vitality of Greek monastic life. The monastery itself is still in use and a walk around the top provides the visitor with peaceful gardens and lots of grape arbors to rest under. *Remember:* Women must wear a skirt (it's possible you'll be given one at the door).

Factory outlet fans can satisfy their thirst at **Ceraco Fine Bone China Factory** (☎ **22-650**), on the road to Paleokastrítsa, which sells discontinued patterns and fine-quality seconds. Because the cost of labor is significantly lower here than in other European countries, the prices are unbelievably low for such superior quality goods. They're open six days a week from 9am–5:30pm and accept AE and V.

Hedonists can head halfway back to Corfu town and stop at the **Mavromatis Company** (☎ **22-174**), manufacturers of koum kouat (kumquat) liqueurs. You can sample many of the clear amber fruit liqueurs and brandies, and purchase these special gifts there.

WHERE TO STAY & EAT

Other than the few super-plush hotels on the cliffs, most housing is in group-booked villas or rooms to rent. Unfortunately, the proliferation of groups has made it extremely difficult to find high-season rooms, so call ahead before you venture out here with your luggage. (By the way, some readers may prefer a room farther away from the bay in the height of mosquito season, August).

Oceanis Hotel, Paleokastrítsa, Corfu. ☎ **0663/41-229.** 71 rms (all with bath). TEL

Rates (including breakfast): 19,500 Drs ($81.25) single/double. AE, V.

This huge, Class B inn is one of the larger resorts and usually has some rooms left over for individual travelers. Its spacious modern rooms offer spectacular views throughout the region; many overlook the good-sized swimming pool and panoramic sundeck. The Oceanis also organizes theme nights, Greek night buffets, and poolside barbecues in the high season.

Hotel Apollon-Ermis, Paleokastrítsa, Corfu. ☎/Fax **0663/41-211.** 43 rms (all with bath). TEL

Rates (including breakfast): 6,500 Drs ($27.05) single/double. No credit cards.

This is one of two small hotels owned by the Ionian Yacht Club. The Class C Apóllon-Ermis has green-shuttered double rooms with small balconies overlooking the roadway and town beach. Their ground-floor café is very popular (see below) with beachgoers.

Hotel Zefiros, Box 2, Paleokastrítsa, Corfu. ☎ **0663/41-244.** 15 rms (all with shower).

Rates (including breakfast): 6,600 Drs ($27.50) single; 10,400 Drs ($43.35) double. No credit cards.

This dark-pink hotel next door to the Apollon-Ermis is a decent choice if its sister Yacht Club property is all booked up. The well-kept rooms have showers inside, but have shared toilets outside in the hall. The front-facing rooms have balconies facing the small harbor and town beach.

Rooms to Let

We rented a wonderful room from **George Bakiras** and his wife Eleni (☎ **0663/41-311** or **41-328**), who can be written to at: Michalas, Bakiras, Lakones, Corfu. Look for their sign on the left of the road, 100 meters past the Odyssey Hotel: ROOMS TO LET/GREEN HOUSE/30 M. FROM BEACH/G. BAKIRAS. The Bakiras family's modest bungalow contains eight large doubles; four have kitchenettes and all have private facilities. Their front porch, in this wooded setting, overlooks the marina. Rooms are 7,750 Drs ($32.30) per night, and their hospitality can't be beat. They also now rent nine rooms with kitchenette above the Paleokastrítsa main street, with "superb sea view."

Next door to the Green House at the **Belvedere Restaurant** (☎ **0663/41-583**), which has a great view of Belvedere Cove and good food at reasonable prices, AE, MC, V accepted.

George Michalas has 13 simple rooms, all with private bath, for 8,000 Drs ($33.35) for two. Our favorite thing here is the grape-shaded patio just a few flights of steps above a cove with a rocky beach.

Across the steps from here, still on this embankment below the Odyssey Hotel, is the **Villa Georgina,** c/o Spiros Loulis, Lakones, Paleokastrítsa, Corfu (no phone). The kindly Mr. Loulis rents eight modernized rooms with private shower and bidet; rates are 7,500 Drs ($31.60) per night. The common balcony offers a tough-to-discern sea view through dense evergreen trees. You'll also find other rooms to let tucked up on the wooded hillside above the village's main street. **Camping Paleokastritsa** is set in a densely wooded area about a ten-minute walk east of Ághia Triáda Beach.

Apollon Restaurant, opposite the village beach. ☎ **41-211.**

Cuisine: CONTINENTAL.
Prices: Appetizers 650–1,560 Drs ($2.70–$6.50), main courses 1,300–3,000 Drs ($5.40–$12.50). No credit cards.
Open: Daily 11am–3pm and 7–11pm.

The Apollon, on the ground floor of the Apollon-Ermis Hotel, is the friendliest, best value eatery around the pretty beach area. At lunch you'll find families, barefoot and damp, having thick, extra-cheesey pizzas with myriad toppings. At sunset, the low-volume Greek folk music serenades young couples enjoying cheese pies and a beer. Then about 9:30pm, everyone turns out for their good value daily specials (a four-course meal for 2,200–3,500 Drs ($9.15–$14.60), or hearty portions of Greek and continental fare.

Around the Island

Pagi, a petite, mountaintop village northwest of Paleokastrítsa, is the turning point for buses snaking down the cliff north to the beach at Afionis, or south to the beach at Ághios Geórgios. The hour ride from Corfu Town spent twisting in and out of the shaded, wooded, cool forests and valleys will remind you what all the hoopla was about this island.

ÁGHIOS GHEÓRGHIOS

Órmos Ághios Gheórghios (not to be confused with the St. George's Beach resort area on the southwestern coast) is a spectacular 2 km stretch of pale gold sand curving gently around a broad bay of the same name. Though undergoing rapid small-scale development, for now it remains an idyllic haven from the white concrete hotel strip lining Corfu's better-known beaches.

The far north end of this cove (not connected by road to the mid-beach stretch) is a little-developed area for beach lovers called Afionis. There's a charming set of rooms at the Taverna Afionis, run by George Bardis, formerly of Brighton Beach, New York. The nightly tariff is 6,500 Drs ($27.10) for twin beds and a private bath just a stone's throw from the water. The Taverna Vrahos next door also rents simple rooms. Jump on the "Arilas" bus (twice daily) from Corfu Town to inquire about lodgings; there were no phones yet at our visit.

At the small but much bigger central beach of Ághios Gheórghios, most development is due to **Thompson Holidays** and **Nur Travel,** those enterprising European budget travel companies that stake out new resort turf with their modest "villas." Limited traveler amenities include **Costas Cars and Bikes** (☎ **0663/96-298**) for moped and car hire, and several minimarkets and souvenir shops that double as money changers. Three buses a day make the one-hour trip from the New Port bus terminal.

Where to Stay and Eat

Several of the small hotels and rooms to let complexes claimed they would accept individual travelers from April to June and mid-September to late October, when their contracts with tour operators expired. You can also check for vacancies during the high season.

The **Hotel Belle Hélène,** Ághios Gheórghios Armenadon, 49081 Corfu (☎ **0663/96-201**) is the best of the new beachside lodgings. Good basic rooms, most with sea views, are complimented by a comfortable lounge with a terrace and outdoor pool. The attached continental and Greek restaurant has a Teutonic bias, reflecting Nur Tour's clientele. Their 54 rooms cost 13,000 Drs ($54.15) single or double with breakfast or 20,800 Drs ($86.65) with a half board plan; AE and V credit cards are accepted.

The **Kostas Golden Beach Hotel,** Ághios Gheórghios Pagi, 49081 Corfu (☎ **0663/96-207**) is another mid-beach choice, with 40 modern, balconied rooms and a small, beachside pool. When Thompson Holidays hasn't packed it with Britons on tour, the Golden Beach is another good choice in the same price range. The **Hotel Corfu Star,** Ághios Gheórghios Pagi, 49081 Corfu (☎ **0663/96-210**) is uphill from these and another, cheaper option.

In the central part of the beach there are several rooms to let above a few undistinguished tavernas and near the Arista Market. Prices will average 6,500 Drs ($27.10) for a double with private toilet and shower. The very pleasant **San George Camping** (no phone) is farther uphill on the cliffside; a tent for two will cost 3,250 Drs ($13.55).

Dining highlights include the beachside **Taverna Nafsika** (which has Greek dancing on Friday nights when there are enough people gathered in this tiny outpost to dance) and the **Moonlight Grill Room,** another simple taverna about 500 meters inland on the road back to Pagi.

NORTHWESTERN VILLAGES

Hikers (or drivers with Jeeps) can ascend the steep cliff road for 3 km to Makrádes, then continue another, more level 4 km to Alimatádes, both small villages of stone homes. The dusty lanes are filled with load-bearing donkeys and women carrying bundles of grape leaves on their heads. At periodic roadside stands, couples sell packets of hand-picked oregano, thyme, rosemary, and bay leaves, and bottles of home-brewed red and white wine.

From Pagi, there's also a better quality car road through the north country. Follow the enchanted fern-filled stretch of road that crosses a stone bridge to the traditional hill village of **Vatonies.** Old women with white cloths shading their heads from the sun and black dresses with colorful aprons carry twigs, herbs, and hay for chickens. Drivers coming from Paleokastrítsa can take the turnoff for Doukádes, a tiny, unspoiled mountain village whose square is still filled with goatherds, women in traditional clothes, and aging farmers playing cards. There's one **taverna** in town, a good place to stop and refuel.

The larger road from Kastellani Gyrou leads 12 km north to Sidári. Along its borders are drab, gray-green, ancient gnarled olive trees. The dappled light filtering through the overhead branches makes the lacy black olive nets glow. In all the crannies and valleys are chartreuse ferns and furry moss patches.

SIDÁRI

Sidári was described to us as "paradise," one of the oldest, best-known beauty spots on the island. Folks, it just ain't so. The waters off its small, fine-sand (but not overly clean) beach are shallow and calm. We found better swimming just around the rocky point to the west, an area known to locals as **"Canal d'Amour,"** It's said that all who sail through the eroded half-cave at this point will be able to marry whoever is on their minds at the time. The "Canal d'Amour is ever more picturesque than the bustling, wildly commercialized village. Buses run from Corfu town to Sidári several times daily between 9am and 7:30pm.

Where to Stay and Eat

The best-priced hotels and pensions are monopolized by the travel agencies in the village, but a few said they would do business with individual travelers if they had any extra rooms. Your best bet is to contact the **Kostas Kantarelis Travel Office** (☎ **0663/95-314**) who own a few properties and book several others. In the high season (they're only open, like most of Sidari, from April 15 through October 30), expect to pay 9,750 Drs ($40.60) for a double with private bath, 13,650 Drs ($56.85) for one with a kitchenette in an apartment complex. They also rent cars, mopeds, and bicycles at good prices. You can also ask them about booking the Three Brothers on the main street, or the Hotel Mimosa, another good bet overlooking the beach. Most Sidari hotels have their own restaurants, and there are several undistinguished fast-food parlors on the main street.

NORTHERN COAST

East of the village of Sidári, the north coast roadway disintegrates into a picturesque, backwoods country lane with lots of cabbage and tomato patches. If you detour to **Kanaloúri** you'll be treated to a lovely little village where inhabitants wear traditional homespun cotton clothes. Drivers must watch out for the donkeys who like to swing their bottoms out into the road when they hear a car approach!

The nondescript roadstop of Roda is being developed as the next resort, with construction raging along its narrow, pebble beach. At the coastal boomtown of **Acharávi,** there's a good, sandy beach, but it gets jammed with day trippers from Sidari (out to find an isolated beach) as well as the local sybarites.

The beach at Aghía Ekateríni, known as **Kalamáki Beach,** is a gray sand-and-pebble stretch, as is Ághios Spyrídon, named after Corfu's patron saint. Both have developed with clusters of rooms to let and tavernas, but not until you get to the harbor of Kassiópi do you find the next full-blown resort.

KASSIÓPI

In years past travelers have sung the praises of the charming, sleepy fishing village of Kassiópi. Alas, no more—it's now one long strip of billboards, pizza parlors, discos, souvenir stands, and rooms-to-let, leading to a relatively peaceful, attractive port lined with several tavernas. All the nearby watering holes have narrow rocky banks, though while bathing you get a distant view of Albania. Kassiópi is serviced eight times daily from the New Port bus terminal in Corfu town.

Where to Stay and Eat

If the charter business from England and Holland is off, there may be rooms available at the ubiquitous "villas" in town, where doubles with bath run 6,250 Drs ($26) a night. **Note:** Kassiópi is plagued with strong maistral winds in August and has a short tourist season (most businesses open only from mid-May to the end of October). The **Salco Holidays Tourist Bureau** (☎ **0663/81-317** or **81-437**), off the main square by the harbor, will help you find a room, rent a car, organize a day trip, or rent a motorboat for watersports. They're well organized to entertain tourists locked into 14-day Kassiópi packages, even offering daytrips to Albania!

EASTERN COAST

Between Kassiópi and Corfu town is 36 kilometers of cove and beach-lined coastline. The pretty little, tree-lined port at San Stefanos is a new destination for day trippers, who enjoy lounging at the two tavernas overlooking a cove filled with colorful fishing boats. Most of the housing along the more upscale east coast is in private villas, the best of which are booked by the **CV** (Corfu Villas) **Travel Office** (reach them at Odós Donzelot 7, Corfu 24009, ☎ **0661/24-009**; or 43 Cadogan St., Chelsea, London SW3 2PR, England, ☎ **071/581-0851**). Kouloúra, Kalámi, and Kéntroma are small boating ports farther south with pebbly bathing areas. All are densely packed with tourists who've descended from the brush-covered slopes of villa land to partake of the water. Many of these communities have been written of in Lawrence Durrell's *Prospero's Cell.*

About 20 km north of Corfu Town, the coast road runs high above the water through forests of olive and cypress. The pretty hillside beach community of **Nissáki** has one huge Class A resort, several tavernas, and wooded slopes coated with newly built whitewashed villas. The long, crowded white sand stretch of **Barbáti,** where many water sports are offered, runs south to Pirgi. **Ipsos** is a very commercialized resort area; across the roadway from myriad hotels and rooms is a narrow pebble shore and very placid water. The town float is packed with kids and sunbathers. Looking out to sea, the views of evergreens growing along the waterfront reminded us of New Hampshire.

There are several campsites in this vicinity, until we come to **Dassia,** home of Corfu's own Club Med. At **Komménos** the coast breaks out into a lush spit of land occupied by one of our favorite luxury resort developments, the Daphnila Bay (☎ **0661/91-520**). The coast south from Gouvia has undergone great upheaval and construction to become an undistinguished, budget-group-tour destination.

Pérama is the first community south of the inlet below Corfu town. Many villas to let and hotels crowd the coast road, but some hardy olive trees manage to poke their heads through. Just above Gastouri is **Achillío,** the inland retreat of the wealthy where many of the European royal villas (including the Achilleion of Empress Elizabeth of Austria) can be seen. As in so many wealthy enclaves, the lush overgrowth obscures the sightseers' view of many of the finest homes.

Benítses (12½ km or 15 minutes by bus south of Corfu town), once a scenic fishing village along this coast, has become the island's most jam-packed, democratic beach town. For 2 km of coast road there are lots of bars (including Japanese sing-along-style *karaoke* clubs!), fast-food joints, seafood restaurants, laser and video discos, boutiques, and travel agents. At night it's chaos, but during daylight, there's a lazy summer feel to the action that's very relaxing.

There are a great number of resort hotels all the way down the coast to the once-sleepy beach of **Kávos,** now destroyed by the many boat excursions emanating from Corfu in search of a quiet beach. (There are even daytrips to Páxos, easily seen from the point at Asprókavos.) Along this road (about 20 km south of Corfu Town) are the sister resorts of **Moraitíka** and **Messónghi,** separated by the narrow Messónghi River, both with narrow sand and shingle beaches leading to calm, shallow seas.

WESTERN COAST

From Vrakaniótika village and its fortress, near the site of the island's largest enclosed lagoon, one major road leads down into the narrow tip of Corfu's "tail." Some 7 km south, at the village of Argyrádes, a narrower road veers west to the other Ághios Geórgios, a small beach and sand-lined swimming cove that's favored for weekend outings with the kids. Heading north to the island's mid-point is **Ághios Górdis,** a very popular beach and swimming area, about 40 minutes by public bus from Corfu town.

Most tourists based in Corfu head for **Glyfáda** as a day beach trip, for good reason. Glyfáda is conveniently reached and is one of Corfu's best beaches: it's long, large, there's room for everybody, and the sand is kept remarkably clean. Unfortunately, the recently built Grand Hotel Glyfáda monolith and several new condos dominate the once-rural skyline. The bus from Corfu's New Port terminal runs nine times daily between 7am and 7:30pm to this sandy, active cove.

The hilltop village of Pélekas (above Glyfáda beach) is touted as the place from which to watch the sunset; only on Corfu could this attribute create a full-fledged resort! It's terribly overcrowded, overbuilt, and filled with well-dressed families and coeds; there are as many moped dealers as rooms to let. Yet the half-hour ascent to the top of **Pélekas Hill** to watch the sunset makes your visit here worthwhile. Before the sun goes all the way down, circle the parking area on the hilltop for magnificent views over the entire island and Ionian Sea.

North of Glyfáda there's a one-lane roadway that continues along the coast to **Myrtiotíssas Monastery.** After a visit to this holy place, you can walk down behind it and arrive at a lovely sand beach. Inland from the newly built seaside resort at Ermones is the 18-hole golf course at **Livádi Toú Rópa** (Ropa's Meadow), nestled in a valley near **Vátos** on Ermones Bay.

This agricultural heartland of Corfu is quite remarkable. In the cooler hours of the early evening, the fields fill up with farmers, and you begin to see the true islanders emerge. Old, wind-burnt women in black cotton head scarves just sit out on their stoops, head in hand, contemplating the sky. Wiry old men and young boys and girls comb the countryside, removing olives from the glistening black nets where they've landed. At **Gardelades** you must choose either the left-hand turn to the beautiful Paleokastrítsa Bay or the right-hand turn for Corfu Town.

2 Páxos & Antípaxos

31 nautical miles SE of Corfu; 21 nautical miles W of Igoumenítsa. Antípaxos is 3 nautical miles S of Páxos

ARRIVING/DEPARTING • By Sea Two high-speed boats from Corfu daily. The 1½ hour trip costs 6,000 Drs ($25) round-trip (return coupons can be used after the date of purchase). Two car ferries run Monday through Saturday from Corfu for 1,400 Drs ($5.85) each way, but take three hours and call at Igoumenítsa. The minicruisers *Petrakis* and *Sotirakis* (☎ **0661/38-690**) sail to Páxos and Antipáxos from the beach resorts of Kassiópi (on Corfu's northern tip) and Kávos (on Corfu's southern tip) on regular day trips. The *Rena S II Love Boat* (☎ **0661/25-317**) provides daily service between Páxos and Párga, and other boats provide irregular service from Igoumenítsa and Moltos (all on the mainland). Call the **Gáios Port Authority** (☎ **0662/31-259**) for more information.

ESSENTIALS The area code of both islands is 0662. There is no Tourist Police on Páxos, but the regular **police** (☎ **31-222**) will handle complaints and emergencies. There is a **medical clinic** (☎ (OTE) **31-466**) in Gáios. The telephone office **(OTE)** is located one block behind the main *platía* in Gáios; when we were there last summer they were only open from 7:30am to 3pm Monday through Friday. Several travel agents and two general stores exchange traveler's checks; in the low season they're open Monday through Friday from 8am to 1:30pm (with evening and weekend hours in the high season). There are a handful of **travel agencies** on the island, on the waterfront in Gáios, and in the village of Lakka; all sell boat tickets. In addition, the friendly office of **Paxos Sun Holidays** (☎ **0662/31-201**), one block in from the Gáios waterfront, is an Olympic Airways agent.

Páxos (Paxí), about three hours by car ferry from Corfu, is a popular outing. It's only 10 km long and less than 4 km wide, but its resident fishermen, tiny villages, traditionally dressed women, and lively tavernas provide enough activity to make the trip worthwhile. Yachtsmen love to cruise around Páxos's irregular coastline; others go looking for peace, quiet, and a much-needed change from the hustle-bustle of Corfu.

Páxos is still authentically Greek enough that the truly affable locals wish you a passing "*Yássou!*" or "*Kaliméra!*" along the road. In fact, the whole island has a kind of anachronistic quality to it. Resembling those in small Cycladic villages, Páxos's whitewashed, green shuttered, stucco houses are in contrast to the neoclassic Ionian style found on neighboring islands, and are significantly more modest than their Corfiot cousins. And unlike the other Ionians, the deep silence of Páxos or Antipáxos is more often broken by the crowing of a rooster than by the mechanical buzz of a moped.

Orientation

The island has become something of an antiresort by virtue of rejecting the Corfiot style of development. However, more and more day trippers end up spending the night, to savor the simple local lifestyle, sample excellent seafood in the portside tavernas, and take long walks around the heavily wooded island.

From your first stop, the east coast port of Gáios, you can see the islets of Panaghía, Ághios Nikólaos, and south to Mongoníssi and Kaltsioníssi. Within this main town are a fortress and monastery, site of festivities that spill over from the islet of Panaghía on its holy day, the Day of the Dormition (August 15). Páxos's other cultural highlight is the annual Music Festival. Every September a number of internationally known classical musicians perform in the villages of Lákka and Longós. There is one main north-south road across the island; a few kilometers south is Oxias, known for its mineral springs.

North of Gáios there are several villages and beachside communities—most notably the very quiet, tiny harbor of Longós, and the prettier, more developed Lákka. Longós, 4 km south of Lákka, has rooms to let, with most activity centered around the bus stop or small marina. There is a quiet pebble beach nearby. Lákka, on the northern tip of the island, should be your base if Gáios proves to be too busy. The large, enclosed Lákka Bay is favored by sailors and windsurfers for its calm water and steady breezes. In both communities, Planos Holidays (☎ **31-744**) can arrange for rooms, excursions, and other travel needs.

If you've come this far for a deserted beach, head farther south to the island of **Antípaxos (Antípaxi).** Locals (or at least those who are well traveled) call it the "Barbados of Greece" because of its clean white beach. During the high season boats constantly commute between Gáios and Antípaxos, making the half hour trip to the northwest tip of this tiny island. The picturesque port opens out to a broad cove that's almost corked by another verdant islet that just drifted in too close.

Antípáxos, about one-fourth the size of Páxos, has a population of less than 200. Its chic isolation has nurtured a village with some tavernas and rooms to let. This hilltop village is surrounded by stone walls, taking advantage of the island's most plentiful building material. A few foreign-owned deluxe villas, wired with personal generators and radio phones, are sprinkled around the olive and pine groves. In between are the fine, golden sand beaches the island is noted for.

Getting Around

Walking is our favorite mode of transport, but in the heat of August we'd settle for the island bus, which runs four times a day from Gáios to Lákka, making a stop in Longós. If you want to contribute to the noise pollution, small mopeds and motorbikes of all sizes are available for hire. Contact one of the agencies lining the *paralía* in Gáios, and insist on a helmet.

Day-trippers from Corfu usually opt for a beach visit during their three-hour layover on Páxos. There's an informal taxi stand conveniently located in Gáios's main *platia* (square).

Boats to Antípáxos run many times daily during the high season. Captains normally wait for a full boatload of sun worshippers before setting sail for the brief commute. The cost for a return ticket is 1,000 Drs ($4). Once on Antipáxos, you can walk everywhere.

Where to Stay

Páxos has a hotel (in Gáios) and rooms to let around the island, primarily in Gáios, Longós, and Lákka. Although there are a few rooms to let on Antipáxos, it's impossible to know what might be available without basing yourself in Gáios and commuting over to find out in person.

Páxos Beach Hotel, Gáios, Páxos 49082. ☎ **0662/31-211.** Fax 0662/32-166.
42 rms (all with bath). TEL

Rates (including half board): 14,150 Drs ($58.95) single; 22,100 Drs ($92.10) double. No credit cards.

There is one attractive Class B resort on the island, set in olive groves above a pretty pebble beach. This simple, rustic resort has a good restaurant, bar, TV lounge, and Ping Pong room. Simply furnished, twin-bedded rooms are located in hewn stone bungalows with seaview verandas.

ROOMS TO LET

Most visitors still prefer private rooms, and it's estimated there are about 5,000 private beds; three-quarters of these are in Gáios. High-season, category A private rooms, with bath, run approximately 7,200 Drs ($29.95) for a double, 6,325 Drs ($26.35) for a single. Before and after the impossible-to-find-a-room high season, there is some softness in the market and negotiating power increases, though most places are only open mid-April to October.

If at all possible, contact the **Planos Holidays office** (☎ **0662/31-744** or **31-821;** fax 0662/31-010) in Lákka, Páxos 49082 before your arrival. Their office in the central part of Lákka's *paralía* provides travel information, money exchange, and most importantly, villa and apartment rental information. They are agents for the British firms, the Greek Islands Club and Villa Centre Holidays, and really keep a finger on the pulse of available housing in Gáios, Longós, and Lákka.

As you alight from the boat there may be townspeople offering rooms. Ask to look at the accommodations before making a commitment, unless you're traveling in August; if you are, grab it!

Where to Eat

Restaurant Rex, Gáios. No phone.

Cuisine: SEAFOOD/GREEK.
Prices: Appetizers 500–980 Drs ($2.10–$4.10); main courses 1,150–2,100 Drs ($4.80–$8.75). No credit cards.
Open: Daily noon–10pm.

Residents who want to eat fish head for Restaurant Rex, just off the central *platía.* The restaurant usually offers several fixed-price meals, most prepared with locally caught fish. If it's too jammed with day-trippers, try the Blue Grotto, on the waterfront opposite the Páxos Sun Holidays office.

Taka-Taka, Gáios. ☎ **31-323.**

Cuisine: GREEK.
Prices: Appetizers 500–1,500 Drs ($2.10–$6.25); main courses 1,050–1,400 Drs ($4.35–$5.85). No credit cards.
Open: Daily 11:30am–10pm.

This grill offers a good selection of traditional Greek cuisine, from its quiet setting two blocks behind the *platía.* The specialty is grilled meat and fish, but do try the delicious stuffed tomatoes, shish kebab, or fish courses. One of Taka-Taka's main attractions, other than its friendly proprietor, the food, and its super-clean kitchen (a rarity), is the vine-covered garden dining area.

The favorite tavernas in Lákka at our visit were the **Kapodistrias** and **Souris Taverna,** both inexpensive and centrally located. Locals cited **Nassos, Vassilis,** and **Iannis** as the finest taverna proprietors in Longós, where everyone specializes in fish.

3 Lefkáda

87 nautical miles NW of Pátra; 31 miles S of Igoumenítsa

ARRIVING/DEPARTING • By Air Olympic Airways has daily flights to and from Préveza, a mainland city 25 minutes by bus from Lefkáda. Tickets and information can be obtained from Olympic's Lefkáda town office (☎ **0645/22-430**) or from the

Préveza office at Spiliádou and Bálkou Streets (☎ **0682/28-674**); a bus leaves for Aktion airport 70 minutes before flight time. (Olympic information in Athens is **01/96-16-161.**)

• **By Bus** Four buses daily from Athens's terminal at Odós Kifissoú 100; the 6-hour trip costs 6,325 Drs ($26.35) each way. There are also two express buses daily from Igoumenítsa to Préveza, for those coming from Corfu. Call the Athens (☎ **01/51-33-583**) or Lefkáda (☎ **0645/22-364**) bus terminals for information; reservations are recommended one day in advance.

• **By Sea** The *F/B Meganissi* connects the port of Nidrí, Lefkáda with Fríkes, Ithaca, and Fiskardo, Kefalonía. Call their office in Nidrí (☎ **0645/92-427**), Fríkes (☎ **0674/33-120**), or Fiskardo (☎ **0671/51-478**) for schedules and information. The *F/B Afroditi* connects Vassilikí, Lefkáda with Písso Aetós, Ithaca, and Fiskardo or Sámi on Kefalonía (☎ **0671/22-000**). Additional information can be obtained from the Lefkáda Port Authority (☎ **0645/22-322**).

ESSENTIALS This island's **area code** is 0645. Myriad travel agents exchange currency daily from 9am to 9pm throughout the high season. Post Offices exchange money Monday through Friday from 8:30am to 1pm. **Lefkáda Hospital** (☎ **25-371**) is at Odós Valaoritis 24 in the main town; there's a **health clinic** in Vassilikí (☎ **31-065**). The **island police** (☎ **22-346**) are at Odós Mela 55 in Lefkáda town, with offices in Nidrí (☎ **95-207**) and Vassilikí (☎ **31-012**). In case of emergency, call 22-100. The Lefkáda **telephone office OTE** is near City Hall and is open 24 hours. The Vassilikí OTE, on the village's main street, is open Monday through Saturday from 2:30–11pm, with a portable branch on the harbor in high season, which is open Sunday from 9am to 2pm.

The lyric poetess Sappho, born about 600 B.C. on Lesbos (Lésvos, also called Mytilíni), was considered one of the greatest poets of her age. Plato wrote: "Some say there are nine muses. Sappho of Lesbos makes their number ten." Only fragments remain of her work.

Although Sappho's name is more often associated with her (hotly disputed) love for women, it is a legend of love for a man that links her with Lefkáda. Myth has it that she was in love with Phaon, a boatman who'd been anointed by Aphrodite to become an exquisitely beautiful man. After sweet romance and several love poems, Phaon grew tired of her. Sappho traveled to Lefkáda where for centuries the priests of Apollo had made a devotional leap from cliffs 236 feet high. The Lefkadian Leap (Katapontismós) was thought to cure lovesickness. Sappho threw herself to her death from Kávos tís Kyrás, the white cliffs of Cape Lefkátas.

If you've driven from the mainland over the marshland to Lefkáda, it's easy to appreciate the island's nonisland status. The Corinthians first dug a canal between this semipeninsula and an outcropping of the mainland. North of their link was the site of the Battle of Actium, a tragic naval loss for Mark Anthony that many believe Cleopatra engineered. In either case Augustus ordered that the canal, now silted up, be redug so that he could appreciate his place of victory more easily. In 1300, Orsini built the Santa Maura fortress to safeguard the narrow canal for Lefkáda; in 1807 the Russians (during their brief protectorate of the Ionians) built two fortresses at Acarnania to guard the approach to the canal from the mainland.

For years, this has seemed much ado about nothing, as locals and tourists blithely loaded onto a traditional tow rope–guided raft-ferry for the briefest of floats between the two. Today, there's even a bridge that obviates the need for it, underlining the "nonisland" quality that diminishes Lefkáda's appeal to foreign tourists. However, long sand and pebble beaches on the island's west coast (including the stunning Porto Katsíki, voted one of the Mediterranean's best beaches by Condé Nast's *Traveler* magazine) and the windsurfing potential of Vassilikis Bay (considered the eastern Mediterranean's best) have recently been exploited, both strong attractions for those looking for someplace off the beaten track.

Orientation

The island's main village, Lefkáda (Lefkás), is directly across from the canal, joined through the marshland by a ribbon of paved roadway. Prospects over the silted, marshy lagoon make you turn around and march back into the crowded streets of the market area; these, although recently constructed, are somewhat more interesting. Although visitors will find accommodations most easily in the main town of Lefkás, and the east coast resort of Nidrí is the most tourist-oriented (overly so, in our opinion), we suggest the newly developed south coast village of Vassilikí as a more attractive base camp. Since 1988, when the local government began cutting and paving roads west down the dramatic cliffs of Cape Lefkátas, several stunning beaches have been revealed. The finest is Porto Katsíki, said to be the late Aristotle Onassis's favorite beach until he decided to cart away boatloads of sand to make his own beach on nearby Skorpiós. We're voting it one of Greece's Ten Best Beaches!

Getting Around the Island

If you've arrived from the mainland, the bus station is at the new port alongside Xenia Hotel. Local buses run from here four times daily in a big circle around the island. You'll find the main taxi stand next to the port. Fares are expensive (for example, from Vassilikí to Lefká town, about 34 km, the fare is 4,500 Drs ($18.75); you'll have to ask your hotel to call you one if you're staying outside the main town. If you're into beach exploration, fishing caiques depart daily from Lefká, or Vassilikí for beach cruises and round-the-island jaunts; just check out the signboards posted on their sterns when they come in to moor at night.

You may want to tour the island by Jeep with friends. Rates start at 15,000 Drs ($62.50) per day plus mileage; they're widely available from any local travel agent. Mopeds are available everywhere from about 3,250 Drs ($13.55) per day, but the best west coast beaches are only accessible by rough roads—too challenging for our moped abilities!

The Port of Lefká

The port of Lefká is definitely the busiest town on the island. Its interior is more appealing than the developed coast; the shore facing the mainland is lined with hotels, tourist offices, parking lots, and a wide roadway. Don't miss the marble bust of Aristotle Valaorítis, Greece's national poet, in a small park opposite the bridge. **St. Maura Travel Services** (☎ **0645/25-119**, fax 0645/92-171), operated by John Kalivas and Dionisia Zavitsanou, is a helpful agency one block inland from the port at Odós Dörpfeld 18. They're open from 9am to 2pm and 5 to 10pm daily from April 1 through October 30 with information on rooms, bus or boat tours, money exchange, long-distance phone service, and so on.

WHERE TO STAY

St. Maura Travel Services (see above) can assist you in finding a room-to-let. Doubles with private shower run about 9,500 Drs ($39.60) in town, about 20% less in the villages.

Byzantio Hotel, Odós Dörpfeld 4, Lefkáda 31100. ☎ **0645/22-629.** Fax 0645/24-055. 15 rms (none with bath). TEL

Rates: 5,750 Drs ($23.95) single; 8,625 Drs ($35.95) double. No credit cards.

An old but budget-conscious choice run by Dimitris Vlachos, the Byzantio is homey and pleasant (old photos and prints hang in the hallways). The public areas, communal baths, and toilets are well kept. Both the older and the new wing have high-ceilinged, well-lit rooms that share a long terrace overlooking the harbor. There's also a small bar and TV lounge.

Hotel Lefkas, Odós Panágou 2, Lafkáda 31100. ☎ **0645/23-916.** 93 rms (all with bath). TEL

Rates (including breakfast): 9,775 Drs ($40.70) single; 14,200 Drs ($59.15) double. No credit cards.

This buff-colored hotel is the most visible from the harbor. Its spacious rooms with Muzak and balcony top a marble-lined restaurant, bar, and disco. The style, shape, and enormous floor space make the Lefkás appear less welcoming than it actually is; we found their abundant staff helpful and friendly.

WHERE TO EAT

The island still relies on its agricultural base, so chances are you'll have locally grown olives and cold-pressed olive oil, and farm-raised beef and lamb whenever you dine. Try the grilled lithiri (a local fish) wherever you find it, and don't forget the locally produced Taol or Logothetis wines.

Regantos Taverna. Central Square. No phone.

Cuisine: GREEK.
Prices: Appetizers 460–860 Drs ($1.90–$3.60); main courses 920–2,300 Drs ($3.85–$9.60). No credit cards.
Open: Daily 7–11pm.

Still a Lefkiot's favorite restaurant, this old taverna is loved for its home-style cooking and robust Greek fare, including local salamis and beef dishes that are the island's specialty.

Kostas Taverna, Main Street. No phone.

Cuisine: GREEK.
Prices: Appetizers 350–860 Drs ($1.45–$3.60), main courses 1,050–2,300 Drs ($4.35–$9.60). No credit cards.
Open: Daily noon–10pm.

Kostas Logothetis runs another good taverna near the market. For a quick, inexpensive meal, try their delicious souvlaki or lamb kebabs with garlic-filled *tzatzíki.* The moussaká and grilled squid are also very good.

EVENING ENTERTAINMENT

Nightlife is limited in the village of Lefká. If strolling the harbor on a moonlit night doesn't turn you on, maybe one of the few discos that open up every summer will. Otherwise, head straight for the **Phoenix Cinema,** in summertime, an outdoor affair. It's just around the corner from the yacht marina, beyond the bus station at the harbor. A Greek B-picture thriller will drain your pockets of 750 Drs ($3.15).

Vassilikí

The south coast port of Vassilikí, 34 kms from Lefká town, is our pick for an overnight stay. Though newly built, its small size, bustling harbor and the pebble Pónti beach are very appealing. Development has come to Vassilikí for two reasons: the introduction of ferry service bringing day trippers from Fiskárdo (Kefhalonía) and Fríkes (Ithaca), and the discovery of Ormos Vassilikís's windsurfing potential. It's considered the best windsurfing in the eastern Mediterranean because the deep cove surrounding the bay provides a natural windbreak which guarantees steady west winds yet smooth water. Several European tour operators have filled the hotels and rooms to let with clients on week-long windsurfing packages, who lend a continuity and athletes' seriousness of purpose not usually found at other resorts.

Vassilikí Travel (☎ **0645/31-305**; fax 0645/31-081) is open daily from 9am to 11pm from May 1 through October 30. Vangelis will help you find a room, rent a car or moped, or make long-distance calls. They also offer day cruises with a picnic to Porto Katsíki, the island's best beach, just around Cape Lefkatas, for 1,725 Drs ($7.20), or to Sívota Bay, Skorpiós, and Meganíssi for 3,450 Drs ($14.35). A few kilometers south of town is the pretty beach at Aghio Fili, also served by regular caiques from Vassilikí's port.

Friendly Sarah Goddard at **Samba Tours** (☎ **0645/31-520**, fax 31-522), on the main street, is most helpful. They're open daily 8:30am–9pm and change money, sell ferry tickets, and arrange accommodations, car and yacht rentals.

Windsurfers should contact **Club Vassiliki** (☎ **31-588**) on Vassilikí Beach; their week-long board program runs about 40,000 Drs ($166.65) and can be booked in advance as a tour package with Club Vass, 30 Brackenbury Rd., London W6 0BA, Great Britain (☎ **081/741-4471** or **741-4686**). Day rentals can be arranged locally for 16,000 Drs ($66.65), 2,500 Drs ($10.40) per hour. **Wildwind Sailing Holidays** (☎ **31-588**) has **sailing** programs from Ponti Beach; their local instructors will rent you a catamaran for 7,000 Drs ($29.15) per hour when they're off duty from the package tour students.

WHERE TO STAY

There are a few hotels and hundreds of rooms to let in Vassilikí, but many are booked for the short season (in most places May 15 through October 10) by European tour operators. For assistance and advance reservations (25% deposit requested), contact **Vassiliki Travel** (☎ **0645/31-081**); double rooms with private shower start at 8,000 Drs ($33.35); two-person studios with kitchenette at 9,000 Drs ($37.50), and two-bedroom apartments at 12,500 Drs ($52). **Vassiliki Beach Camping** (☎ **0645/31-308**) is inland from the waterfront behind Ponti Beach.

Hotel Apollo, Vassilikí, Lefkáda 31082. ☎ **0645/31-122.** 34 rms (all with bath). TEL

Rates (including breakfast): 11,500 Drs ($47.90) single; 17,250 Drs ($71.80) double. MC, V.

Simple but spacious, full amenity rooms overlook the marina and beyond it, Ponti Beach, where windsurfers provide a bevy of color. The hotel has a garden restaurant, and a pleasant roof terrace for evening drinks. A good deal plus travel services, such as daily cruises and coach trips.

Hotel Paradise, Vassilikí, Lefkáda 31082. ☎ **0645/31-256.** 15 rms (10 with bath). TEL

Rates: 6,325 Drs ($26.35) single/double without bath; 8,625 Drs ($35.95) single/double with bath. No credit cards.

This is a nice, old-fashioned hotel dating from Vassilikí's pre-boom days. Rooms are bright and very well kept, and the common bathrooms are scrubbed clean. The Paradise's good location and pretty garden make it a very good value; the hotel is open year round.

WHERE TO EAT & NIGHTLIFE

Vassilikí's restaurant scene is growing rapidly, but we can recommend a few special places found on our recent visit. In the evening, the small harbor comes alive with strollers and some good bars. The **Byzantio** is an old stone building on the south side of the port with a post-hippy crowd; the nearby **Zeus** has a slicker, younger crowd of foreigners enjoying its loud rock sound track. **Sam's Place,** just off Pónti Beach, serves a walloping English breakfast called "The Works" (1,300 Drs/$5.40) from 10am–1pm; it closes until 10pm, when it becomes a rocking music bar, with a jam session on Mondays and "Paddy's Night" (Irish music) on Fridays.

Livanakis Kafeneion, on the port. No phone.

Cuisine: SNACKS/COFFEE.
Prices: Snacks 350–1,050 Drs ($1.45–$4.35). No credit cards.
Open: Daily 8am–9pm.

This very old-fashioned portside café has postage stamp–size outdoor tables overlooking the day-excursion boats and fishing caiques. We liked their early breakfast of fresh bread, honey, cheese, and strong Greek coffee (500 Drs or $2.10) so we could watch the locals primping their boats in anticipation of the 10am onslaught of day-trippers. Livanakis serves coffee to old-timers playing *távoli* (backgammon) throughout the day, then gets into ouzo-mode.

Restaurant Miramare, *paralía* near ferry dock. ☎ **31-138.**

Cuisine: GREEK.
Prices: Appetizers 400–980 Drs ($1.65–$4.10); main courses 1,050–2,200 Drs ($4.35–$9.15). No credit cards.
Open: Daily 8:30am–2am.

Miramare has a very welcoming feeling to it, with vine-laden walls and a great view of the sea. The service is friendly and the food delicious. After a very filling meal of chicken, garden-fresh *maroúli* salad, and potatoes, fresh fruit was brought "from the house."

Taverna No Problem, Sivota Bay. ☎ **31-182.**

Cuisine: SEAFOOD.
Prices: Appetizers 350–860 Drs ($1.45–$3.60), fish sold for 4,600–9,200 Drs ($19.20–$38.35) per kilo. No credit cards.
Open: Daily noon–11pm.

This is the best of the row of tavernas lining the yacht marina at beautiful Sivota Bay, just 6 km east of Vassilikí. Day or night, it's worth an excursion to sample their simply prepared, excellent, freshly caught seafood. The fried calamari is tender and light, their *choriátiki saláta* (Greek "peasant" salad) has ripe red tomatoes and lots of olives, their chips are made fresh, and their local fish, particularly the fleshy white lithiri, are wonderfully grilled. A worthwhile excursion, and very well priced for fresh fish.

Nidrí

The eastern coast port of Nidrí (Nydrí), 16 km south of Lefká town, was the island's first resort area because of its picturesque location facing the mainland. Ironically, the port's popularity with sailors and tourists has made these calm waters too polluted and crowded for swimming. Across the placid blue Ionian, you'll see the islet of Madoúri with the cream-colored 18th-century mansion of the poet Aristotelis Valaoritis looking back to the Nidrí's yacht marina. Behind it is tiny green Spárti, and south of it are Skorpídi and Skorpiós (famed home of the Onassis family). Some four nautical miles out is Meganíssi, a much larger island with some beaches and villages for stranded day-trippers. Although Nidrí's waterfront was extended and dozens of gelaterias, cafés, discos, and pizza bars have opened, old women still sit beside the sailing yachts, grilling ears of corn and selling oregano to passersby.

If the hustle-bustle of Nidrí and its myriad group tourists sound appealing, you'll want to contact **Nidri Travel** (☎ **0645/92-514**; fax 0645/92-256) in the center of Nidrí's long main street; open from 7am to 11pm daily. Since there are few hotels, from May to October you should count on them to help you find one of the 1,000 or so rooms to rent in the village. Many rooms are actually in "villas" that European budget-tour operators have constructed to house clients; rates start at 8,000 Drs ($33.35) for doubles with private shower. The office is a wellspring of information on local goings-on, sights, day-tours, and watersports activities planned for the charterettes who live there.

What to See & Do Around the Island

Lefkáda draws many tourists each August to its popular **Festival of Arts and Literature** and **International Festival of Folklore,** two weeks of lectures, folk dances, theater pieces, and exhibitions. If you're here for either festival, August 11 is St. Spýridon's Day, when colorful folk dancing, dining, and singing take place in the inland village of Kariá, 14 kms south of Lefká town. A traditional wedding ceremony is performed in the central square, and locals don festive costumes from Karia's small museum.

In Lefkás, you can shop in the agora for the intricate lacework and embroidery that Lefkadian women are known for. There are no "bargains" among the handmade products, but they are exported to Europe and America, and from the point of view of what you'd pay at home they will seem a bargain. The old **Lefkas Library** has a small costume and folk crafts collection to see. From the port, or from Nidrí or Vassilikí, you can join a fun day cruise, our favorite way to explore the ubiquitous islets of the Ionians. The dense green foliage and stark black rocks that protrude unexpectedly from the calm waters are all scenic hallmarks of a region best appreciated from the water. Don't forget to bring your binoculars to snoop around Skorpios!

The east coast faces directly to the mainland and thus offers sheltered coves and inlets ideal for boating and, in less crowded areas, recreational swimming. At **Nikiana,** about 8 km south of Lefkás town, there's a mild surf. South of Nidrí is a very scenic drive along the curving peninsula which forms Vlichó Bay. Sívota is on the island's southeast tip, facing the larger islet of **Meganíssi.** This peaceful port offers three tavernas (see "Where to Eat" in Vassilikí) at the harbor for a relaxing lunch.

The road network winds west to **Vassilikí;** in 1991, Ponti Beach was the site of the First Panhellenic Funboard championship, an inter-Greece windsurfing meet (call **0645/31-131** for annual dates). From this port, only the daring need hike out to Cape Lefkatas, whose white cliffs invite images of Sappho in her fateful dive. Instead, an inland road north of Vassilikí brings you to Komilio (14 km), a small village where you can catch the newly built coast road down the length of Cape Lefkatas.

About 11 km south is our favorite beach, Porto Katsíki, with two small coffee and snack *kantínas* parked up on the cliffs. It's stiff but glorious walk down to the heavenly gold sand beach cove, certainly one of the best in Greece. Even closer to the Komilio turnoff are the 5-km long **Ghialós,** a deserted sand and pebble beach, and **Grammí,** another fine sand beach accessible only by caique. These areas are destined for the next wave of development.

Kalamítsi is set high on a hill above the west coast; its traditional housing and sea views are well worth a detour if you're on your way to the pretty little resort of **Ághios Nikítas.** You'll first pass **Káthisma,** a long sand beach where, to our chagrin, car traffic is permitted on the sand. It's the best and most easily reached by public bus from Lefkáda town, only 12 km north.

At **Ághios Nikítas** there's a clean beach and rough cold water that experienced sportsmen say is better than at Vassilikí for windsurfing. Information central in this tiny group resort (everything is within 100 meters of the seaside) is **Vantage Travel** (☎ **0645/97-415**). Vantage will book rooms, exchange currency, place long distance calls, arrange a rental car, and generally introduce you to the bustle of clubs, cafés, and shops that have just opened. Ághios Nikítas's best place is the **Odyssey Hotel,** Ághios Nikítas, Lefkáda 31080 (☎ **0645/97-351;** fax 0645/97-421), where 31 bright new rooms, all with shower and phone and some with double beds (!), open onto seaview balconies. They have a popular bar and breakfast lounge. Singles run a 10,350 Drs ($43.15) Drs ($63.90) and doubles 17,250 Drs ($71.90) per night. DC, EC, MC, V are accepted.

4 Ithaca

53 nautical miles NW of Pátra; 82 nautical miles S of Igoumenítsa.

ARRIVING/DEPARTING • By Sea Vathý (Vathí) Ithaca, is served by daily car ferry connections from Pátra via Sámi, Kefalonía on the **Strintizis Lines** (☎ **0674/33-120**); it's a 5-hour ride. Direct service, due to begin in late 1992, from Pátra to Písso Aetós should cut the trip to 3 hours. The poorly run *F/B Afroditi* (☎ **0674/32-104**) sails daily from Vassilikí, Lefkáda, connecting Písso Aetós, Ithaca to Fiskardo and Sámi, on Kefalonía. The *F/B Meganissi* runs from Fríkes, Ithaca, to Fiskardo, then to Nídrí, Lefkáda. More information can be obtained from the Port Authority (☎ **32-909**).

ESSENTIALS The Island's area code is 0674. The **National Bank of Greece** has a branch just off the *paralía,* before you arrive at the *platía;* several nearby travel agents change traveler's checks during extended hours. The **hospital** in Vathý (☎ **32-222**) is 200 meters from the harbor, on the road to Anthoússa. The town **police** (☎ **32-205**) are on the same road, about 500 meters from the port. The post office is midway along the port, open from 7:30am to 2:30 pm weekdays. The telephone center **(OTE)** is a handsome, two-story building on the south side of the harbor; it's open Monday through Saturday from 7:30am to 10pm.

Ithaca (Itháki) is best known as the home of Odysseus, the island that he yearned to return to throughout his journey of ten long and lonely years. From its rugged, stony, uninviting west coast the modern visitor rightly questions why anyone would be anxious to return; inland, Ithaca boasts wildly beautiful rocky hills and verdant pine-covered valleys.

In 1982 a **Festival of Greek Music** was established, a celebration of national culture (held during one month of the summer) on the island of the country's best-loved hero. At present, a new port is being constructed at the isolated beach of Písso Aetós, and smaller ships cruise into the north coast village of Fríkes, both developments designed to increase tourism to the island. Although certain hedonistic pleasures—myriad bars, discotheques, resort hotels, and boutiques—are still a few years away, Ithaca still has most to offer to one who's memorized favorite passages from the *Odyssey* and *Iliad.* Then, guide in hand, you can set off to explore the sights of Homer's world.

Orientation

Ithaca is shaped like an irregular bowtie, and large car ferries must round its cinched waist before attempting to squeeze into a narrow wrinkle of the southern bow. All of these Pátra boats call at Vathí (it means "deep"); as you approach the harbor, the small islet of Lazareto will be on the right. The edifice marked with a sign reading EVERY TRAVELER IS A CITIZEN OF ITHACA was a church in the 17th century and a prison in the 19th century; in 1953 it was a casualty of the earthquake. It is said that Lord Byron, upon arriving at Ithaca, rejected the trek to see Odysseus's home in favor of a swim to colorful Lazareto.

Ithaca's headier days returned in the 19th century, when the nearby cove of Loútsa was the headquarters of a large shipbuilding operation. Today, marine service shops cater to passing yachts. The former fishing village of Fríkes, on the east coast 23 km north of the main port, is the hub for intra-Ionian ferries. It, and nearby *Kióni,* are both picturesque villages where group-booked tourists occupy traditional housing, enjoy small town life and hike to nearby pebble beaches. We found both preferable to Vathí for long-term visitors.

Getting Around

The island's main bus stand is in front of the pharmacy on the Vathý *platía.* Buses circle the island once a day in the low season, and three times a day after July 15. There are travel agencies on the Vathý *paralía* (harbor front), and a few in Fríkes and Kióni that rent mountain bicycles (1,700 Drs. or $7.10 per day) well suited to this hilly place, mopeds (from 5,750 Drs or $23.95 for a two-seater), and cars (starting at 15,000 Drs or $62.50 per day); most accept MC and V credit cards. If you've only got a day on Ithaca, we'd recommend the 3-hour round-the-island tour by taxi with an English-speaking driver. Those stationed at the Vathí taxi stand charge about 10,000 Drs ($41.70). Several travel agents sell intra-Ionian ferry tickets; caique captains in Fríkes and Kióna also organize around-the-island boat excursions.

Vathý

The petal-shaped, amphitheatrically layered port of Vathý or Vathí (also called Itháki) opens out to the sea. Today, the new earth-colored houses reconstructed from the rubble left by the 1953 earthquake surround and frame the small harbor. It may be here that the Phaeacians of Scheria (Corfu) left Odysseus to orient himself before returning to his palace. The town has a small **Archeological Museum** behind the portside OTE (open Wednesday through Monday from 10am to 3pm), good white-stone beaches to the south (daily caiques go to Gidáki for day trips), and the greatest concentration of tourist services on the island.

WHERE TO STAY

As on the rest of the island, Vathý has very few hotels. Most people rent private rooms, easily booked through one of the town's many travel agents. **Polyctor Tours** (☎ **0674/33-120** or fax 0674/33-130) on the main square can help you find a room or house to rent. Rates run 5,750–6,900 Drs ($23.95–$28.75) for two with shared toilet facilities; about 8,000 Drs ($33.35) with private shower. (AE, EC, MC accepted) Things open up from late April to mid-October; rates other than in July and August are usually 30% less.

Hotel Mentor, Vathý, Ithaca 28300. ☎ **0674/32-433.** Fax 0674/32-293.

36 rms (all with bath). TEL

Rates: 8,625 Drs ($35.95) single; 12,650 Drs ($52.70) double; 21,000 Drs ($87.50) four-bed suite. No credit cards.

Of the hotels, the Mentor, on the *paralía,* is the best. This inn with a large roof garden and terrace view of the sunset, is a clean and comfortable establishment. There is small gift shop off the lobby, and a port view taverna, also run by the Livanis family. They also rent apartments above the east side of the port, starting at 12,500 Drs ($52.10) per night, sleeping two, with a kitchenette.

Hotel Odysseus, Vathý, Ithaca 28300. ☎ **0674/32-381.** Fax 0674/32-381.

10 rms (all with bath). TEL

Rates: 11,500 Drs ($47.90) single or double. No credit cards.

The newly built Odysseus is on the quiet residential side of the harbor, a ten-minute walk north of the ferry pier. High-ceilinged rooms with French doors opening out onto harbor-view balconies are our first choice, because there's so little traffic at night to disturb your sleep. There's also a large terrace cafeteria and restaurant for moderate-price Greek fare.

WHERE TO EAT

Tiny Ithaca has two island specialties. The traditional *tserepa*—a chicken, garlic, and tomato dish stewed for hours in a clay oven—seems to have gone the way of Odysseus, in all save the most traditional homes. However, the thick, sweet honey and rice pudding called *ravanai* is still widely sold in Vathý's harborside *zacharoplastía* (pâtisseries), and occasionally in the village tavernas. Also, try the island's vegetable dishes; they're particularly flavorful because of the locally pressed olive oil used for cooking. Note that most places are only open from May to October.

Trehadiri Taverna, Vathý. ☎ **33-066.**

Cuisine: GREEK.
Prices: Appetizers 350–800 Drs ($1.45–$3.35), main courses 860–1,400 Drs ($3.60–$5.85). No credit cards.
Open: Daily 6pm–midnight.

One block in from the port, behind the National Bank, you'll find Gerrys Donjas and his wife whipping up fresh vegetable and meat dishes, including a fragrant eggplant imam, baked with spices, and a tasty moussaká. Don't miss the grilled leg of lamb if available, otherwise try the tender roast veal; both are delicious.

★ **Gregory's Taverna,** Pallo Karabo. ☎ **32-573.**
Cuisine: GREEK.

Prices: Appetizers 350–1,500 Drs ($1.45–$6.25); main courses 860–2,000 Drs ($3.60–$8.35). No credit cards.
Open: Daily 9am–4pm and 6:30pm–1am.

Across from Vathý, on the other side of the harbor (about a 2-km walk east), is the outstanding country-style taverna of Gregory Vlismas. Many diners come by boat from other parts of the island, though we thoroughly enjoyed the 25-minute *vólta* (stroll) from town and found it well worthwhile for their fresh fish, fine Ithacan barrel wine, and homemade Greek specialties. After omelet breakfasts, they continue serving all day, whipping up many a lobster dinner after sundown. You can sit by the water and savor the freshest octopus salad or a grilled fish that was swimming that morning. Have we said it's one of our favorite places?

Around the Island

A car makes a day tour around the island practical and enjoyable; hilly routes climb up and down through rapidly changing countryside, and in the narrow midriff region the deep blue of the sea is ever present. The **Cave of the Nymphs** (Marmarospiliá) is a hike up above the port of Vathý; here, it is said, Odysseus hid the gifts and jewels bestowed upon him by the hospitable Phaeacians. Aëtó, the village at the island's narrowest point, is fondly believed to be the site of Odysseus's own palace; many archeologists differ and offer the port of Polis, on the tip of the island facing west to Fiskárdo, Kefalonía, as the better strategic setting. New excavations are certain to inspire new theories and dash old hopes. The beach at **Ormós Aëtós,** about 15 minutes' drive north of Vathý, is one of the island's prettiest rocky beach coves. This should not be confused with the popular beach at Písso Aëtós, on the west coast of this same spit of land, which is being developed as a car ferry pier.

South of Vathý two prongs of roadway pierce the mountainous southern half of the island. Some 2 km above the port is the larger village of **Perachóri,** a very scenic spot at sunset. Continue from here to reach the monastery of Taxiarchón, known for its El Greco icon, founded in 1693, and dedicated to the patron saint of the island.

Stavrós (17 km from Vathý) has a small Archeological Museum (open Wednesday through Monday from 10am–3pm) and is the hub city for the tiny network of spindly roads that crisscross the northern mass of the island. Near here is the monastery of Katharae, whose belfry provides views over the Bay of Pátra and the Greek mainland to the east. Cypress, oleander, pine, olive, and an odd palm line the hilly terrain. Was this prospect what brought Odysseus to build his kingdom in the north?

FRÍKES & KIÓNI

On the island's northeast coast is the small port of Fríkes, where day-trip boats arrive from Fiskárdo, and just 5 km south (a very scenic 45-minute walk) is the picturesque port of **Kióni,** home to many of the island's seafaring families. Tourism, boat repair, sailing (mostly in the merchant navy), and some fairly minimal agriculture are the people's trades, lending an informal air to everyday life. Both harbors are quiet and clean; the water is so inviting that people swim off the rocks only a few hundred meters from the boats. In addition, there are even better rock and pebble beaches within a ten-minute walk of either port.

Fríkes is less developed, but just a bit busier than Kióni due to the excursion boats that stop here connecting Lefkáda with Kefalonía. The more architecturally pure Kióni (building styles are governed by local preservation laws) has fewer services but more charm.

WHERE TO STAY & EAT

Polyctor Tours (☎ **0674/31-771**) or **Kiki Travel** (☎ **0674/31-728** or **31-387**) overlook the waterfront. Both offices change money, book rooms, and rent apartments, and Polyctor sells ferry tickets. In July and August, finding a room can be a problem; write to these offices well in advance of your trip or plan to stay in Fríkes's only hotel. Two-person apartments with kitchenettes and shower rent for 7,800 Drs to 13,500 Drs ($32.50–$56.25); four-person, two-bedroom houses with verandas start at 24,000 Drs ($100).

Hotel Nostos, Fríkes 28300, Ithaca. ☎ **0674/31-644.** Fax 0674/31-716.

32 rms (all with bath). TEL

Rates (including breakfast): 9,500 Drs ($39.60) single; 14,500 Drs ($60.40) double. No credit cards.

This friendly, top-quality hotel was brought to our attention by readers Patricia and William E. McCulloh of Gambier, Ohio. Hosts Niki and Andreas Anagnostatos are friendly, helpful, and English-speaking. The hotel has the most evocative name on the island for readers of the *Odyssey: Nóstos!*

Fríkes supports the **Votoalo** and **Penelope** tavernas, some snack cafés, and a market (great for picnics). The **Nostos Hotel** (see above) is also known for its fine Greek food.

Kióni overlooks three abandoned windmills topping the hills that enclose the harbor. Not much happens here so the favorite activity (other than swimming, fishing, sailing, or sleeping) is to plant yourself at an outdoor café and soak up the ambience.

There are plenty of rental rooms, but all are booked by travel agents or handled by the Greek Islands Club (an English touring company). **Kioni Vacations** (☎ **0674/31-668** June to October, or off-season in Athens at **01/52-31-462**) can help you find a room (about 12,650 Drs or $52.70 for a two- or three-person studio with kitchenette), rent a moped, or change traveler's checks at their portside office. Ask them if the Greek Islands Club has a vacancy in their **Hotel Kioni;** expect to pay around 14,200 Drs ($59.16) for a double.

The **Sunrise Café** and **Koutsouvelis Taverna** are both on the central harbor, with tables spread over a waterfront terrace. Fried snapper and typical Greek fare are available at each; expect to pay about 3,000 Drs ($12.50) per person for a meal with wine.

5 Kefalonía

71 nautical miles NW of Pátra; 44 nautical miles W of Kyllíni

ARRIVING/DEPARTING • By Air Three flights daily on **Olympic Airways** from Athens. Their office is at Odós R. Vergoti 1 (☎ **28-808**), toward the harbor from the archeological museum.

• By Sea One car ferry daily leaves from Pátra to Sámi (call Pátra information at **061/277-622** or **01/82-36-012** in Athens for schedule information). Two car ferries run weekly from Piraeus to Sámi on the **Minoan Lines,** which continue on to Corfu (☎ **01/75-12-356** in Piraeus for information). From Kyllíni (on the Peloponnese) two or three car ferries daily run to Argostóli (call **0623/92-211** or **01/82-28-198** in Athens for information). The **Hellenic Mediterranean Lines** (☎ **061/42-95-20** in Pátra) has daily departures in summer from Pátra to Kefalonía, then to Brindisi, Italy.

Intra-Ionian Island voyages: from May to October, two boats leave daily from Vassilikí, Lefkás to Písso Aëtós, Ithaca, then to Sámi and Fiskárdo; one boat daily from Fríkes, Ithaca to Aghía Efimia, on the *F/B Afroditi.* For information call **0674/22-456** or **51–462.** Three weekly car ferries run year-round (twice daily in summer) from Nídri, Lefkás to Fríkes, Ithaca, then to Fiskárdo on the *F/B Meganissi.* For information call **0671/51-478** in Argostóli or **0674/51-496** in Fiskárdo. Other information can be obtained from the **Argostóli Port Authority** (☎ **0671/22-224**).

Kefalonía (Kefallinía, also Cefalónia or Cephallonia) is one of Greece's best-kept secrets; a large, unspoiled island with spectacular scenery, beautiful beaches, traditional housing, and excellent wine. Since antiquity it's been an island of prosperous sailors and traders. During each period of foreign occupation, locals took advantage of new ties to Europe to educate their children, import new goods, and learn the ways of new cultures. It's not enough to say that Kefalonians got around; the Juan de Foca Strait off Seattle, Washington, was named after a Kefalonian sailor who joined the Spanish navy! The entire island was leveled by an earthquake in 1953, with the exception of the northernmost village of Fiskardo; after huge waves of emigration, many stayed to rebuild their homes and fields.

With an economy long buoyed by earnings sent home from citizens working abroad, there has been little cause to exploit the island's resources. However, in the last few years the Greek government has taken steps to add tourism to other revenue-producing industries such as agriculture and livestock breeding.

Each summer, this large island draws thousands of visitors, particularly British and Italian ones, who settle into apartments or "villas" with the family, and rent cars for sightseeing and daytrips to the beach. In addition, so many Kefalonians return that there's often not enough room to welcome foreigners. In line with their flush economy, room and board prices are higher than at most comparable islands, and foreign tourists will have little luck bargaining. However, those looking for an island with one of the best beaches in Greece (at Mýrtos), the tastiest white wines (Gentilini and Robola), and superb indigenous architecture (at Fiskardo) should push onward.

Orientation

The odd-shaped island of Kefalonía, the largest of the Ionians, looks rather like a high-heeled shoe with a high tongue reaching up to parallel the shores of Ithaca. Under the instep is the main town, **Argostóli;** directly opposite it on the inside of the heel is the coastal town of **Lixoúri.** Behind the heel and up the inside of the tongue (the west coast of the island) are the best beaches, usually at the foot of spectacular, steep chalk-white cliffs. On the top of the shoe is the island's other port, **Sámi,** a village where most Piraeus and Pátra ferries will leave you, to avoid having to round the "sole" of the island to Argostóli. To our minds, Fiskardo's traditional architecture makes Kefalonía unique, and its fishing port and rocky coves are absolutely charming. Since many tourists may prefer the busyness of Argostóli, we recommend spending a few nights in each port.

Getting Around

BY BUS The privately run KTEL buses (☎ **22-276** or **23-364**) service the entire island; however, it's so big and hilly that it takes forever to get to most places you'll want to go. From Argostóli to Sámi, where the ferryboats arrive, there are four buses daily (two on Sunday). The northbound Fiskardo bus runs only twice daily (once on Sunday) from Argostóli, but its route provides the most exquisite scenery. There are once-daily buses between Sámi and Fiskárdo. There are buses every half hour between 9:30am and 6:45pm to the nearby beaches at Lássi, Makrís Ghialós, and Platís Ghialós. The Argostóli station is on the port at Metaxá Street.

BY TAXI The island's main taxi station is at Valianoú or Central Square in the heart of Argostóli. A four-passenger Mercedes taxi will cost 24,000 Drs ($100) for an around-the-island eight-hour tour. On the way the driver may choose to pick up anyone who flags him down, and then charge them whatever fare seems equitable (this in no way reduces *your* fare!). Meter use is legally compulsory, though rarely practised. Flat rates are agreed upon by all drivers; for example, Airport to Argostóli 1,450 Drs ($6.05), Argostóli to Sámi 4,000 Drs ($16.65), Argostóli to Fiskardo 8,200 Drs ($34.15) or 11,500 Drs ($47.90) round trip, including one-hour waiting time.

BY CAR **Pefanis Rent-a-Car** (☎ **22-338**) has an office off the square at Odós Valianoú 4. Their rates are approximately 16,000 Drs ($67.10) per day for a compact car. There are 20 rental car companies in town, so shop around and book one early. (Most rental cars are taken by visiting ex-islanders.)

BY MOPED Mopeds are too slow to cover much ground, but if you're based in a village and want to explore locally, they can be a lot of fun because the roads on wealthy Kefalonía are very good. In high-priced Argostóli, three-day moped rentals are 12,000–16,000 Drs ($50–$66.65) for a two-seater Vespa; about 50% less by the day.

FERRY The ferryboat to Lixoúri (a fun, 30-minute voyage between two points of land jutting into the Argostolion Gulf) leaves from the northern ferry dock of Argostóli, in front of the Cephallonia Star Hotel. This large car ferry runs 22 times daily; the fare is 200 Drs (83¢). Landlubbers can take a round-about roadway by car or public bus.

Argostóli

The island's capital is an amusing, lively, modern town totally rebuilt after the devastation of the earthquakes of 1953. Greater Argostóli spreads to the main part of the island and connects to the north-south highway. The village proper is on its own spit of land tied to the mainland by the **Trapano Bridge.** This broad causeway was originally built in 1910 by the British C. P. de Bosset in 15 days; two years later it was replaced by masonry. The center portion of the bridge was adorned with a large pyramid dedicated by Kefalonian citizens in gratitude to the "Glory of the British Nation."

ESSENTIALS

ORIENTATION The **Trapano Bridge** is at the south end of the village, off **Metaxá Street,** the harborside road. The bustling **agora** is in this section, running two and three streets in from the water. During the day it's a beehive of activity as trucks unload produce, and fishermen bring their catch into all the shops. This is where you'll see behind-the-scenes Greek life; it's also the best place to get Gentilini or Calliga wines (the island's best-known export and a perfect gift to bring home) and groceries for campers and picnickers.

Walking along the harbor toward the Lixóuri shuttle ferry will bring you to the heart of Argostóli. Two blocks in from the water is **Valianoú Square,** lined with hotels, tavernas, cafés, and shops. In the narrow lanes to the south are travel services and businesses; to the west are the museums and library, and above them, houses banked on a steeply ascending hillside. If you climb over this and descend the other side (a paved roadway winds down), you'll arrive at the excellent but crowded town beaches of **Makrís Ghialós** and **Platís Ghialós.**

INFORMATION The very helpful tourist information office **(EOT)** office, open daily from 8am to 10pm (Monday through Friday till 3pm in the low season), is next to the Port Authority building on the harbor (☎ **0671/22-248** or **24-466**). Dennis Messaris and his multilingual assistant Vassiliki are enthusiastic experts about the island.

FAST FACTS • Area code for Argostóli, Lixoúri, and Skála is 0671; for Sámi and Fiskárdo it's 0674. There are several banks around Valianoú Square open regular hours, plus several commercial *currency exchanges* open daily from 9am to 6pm. The *Argostóli Hospital* (☎ **24-641**) is on Souidías Street. The *OTE* is located behind City Hall, open daily from 7:30am to 11pm. The *post office* is on Lithostrato Street (open Monday through Friday from 7:30am to 2pm, later during August). The *tourist police* (☎ **22-200**) are located one block from the Cephallonia Star Hotel, off the harbor. *Ferry tickets* can be purchased from Argostóli travel agents (Maria at the *Bartholomos Agency,* ☎ **28-853,** fax 22-809, just east of central square is terrific) or at the port in Sámi (where the large car ferries depart). *Filóxenos Travel* (☎ **0671/23-055,** fax 0671/28-114, or **01/57-12-820** in Athens) at Odós G. Vergoti 2 on the southwest corner of the *platía,* rents rooms, books tickets, and runs many island excursions. Owner Paul El-Zery is very helpful. He offers a one-day round-the-island tour for 4,800 Drs ($20), and day trips to Lefkáda or Ithaca.

WHAT TO SEE & DO

One of the island's highlights is the incredible **Corgialenios Historical and Cultural Museum** (☎ **28-221**), located a block above Valianoú Square. Housed on the ground floor of the stately Corgialenios Library, it's an absolute must for everyone visiting the island. It includes a large, superb collection of artisans tools, costumes, European antiquities left by occupiers, and old photographs, maps, and 19th-century articles used throughout the island. One of its most poignant gift items (many excellent lace pieces are for sale) is the collection of black-and-white photos from 1904 depicting Argostóli as it was before the earthquakes. An hour spent in this museum is a better introduction to modern Kefalonian history than reading all the history books combined. It is open Monday through Saturday from 8am to 2pm; admission is 500 Drs ($2.10), free on Friday.

The **Archeological Museum** (☎ **28-300**) is located just south of City Hall. This small but interesting collection was recently closed for renovation, but is slated to reopen for 1995.

Shopping Tips: The **Calliga Vineyards** is open for tours; contact EOT for their current schedule. When present-shopping, buy the fine white "Robola" in a burlap sack with Greek writing and the Calligata wax seal that sells for about 1,600 Drs ($6.65); Calliga Cava is a popular aged red wine for the same price. Oenophiles should note that Kefalonía's Gentilini (it sells for about 3,000 Drs ($16.70 a bottle), is considered one of the very best wines in all of Greece. Tucked away in a remote spot in nearby Minies (just above the airport) is the **Gentilini Vineyard.** The superb quality of this modestly scaled winery is testament to one man's determination to produce a Greek export wine (it's now sold in London!). Spiros and Anna Cosmetatos are the very capable vintners, and informative, gracious, and fascinating hosts. Although they don't run organized tours or wine tastings, if you call ahead (☎ **0671/41-618**) and it's convenient for them, the Cosmetatos will conduct an informal tour of their vineyard.

Other special products for shoppers include Kefalonía's "Golden" brand honey, uniquely rich and tasty for baklavá aficionados, tart quince preserves, and almond pralines!

WHERE TO STAY

Most housing is open from mid-April to late October; **Filóxenos Travel** (☎ **0671/ 23-055,** fax 28-114) is a good source for rooms to rent around the island. In Argostóli, these discreetly marked complexes (geared to house returning Kefaloniots) are usually better value than hotels. We stayed in the modern, sky-blue stucco apartment complex of Chicago expatriates *Jerry and Lákis Zérvos* at Odós Metaxá 3 (☎ **0671/28-919**), one block east of Valianoú Square. Eight spacious, clean doubles with private bath (many with balconies) cost 8,000 Drs ($33.35). **Camping Argostóli Beach** (☎ **0671/23-487**), the closest facility, is north of town in Fanári, on the beach.

Hotel Aenos, Platía Metaxá 11, 28100 Argostóli. ☎ **0671/28-013.** Fax 0671/28-054.
40 rms (all with bath). TEL

Rates (including breakfast): 8,325 Drs ($35.70) single; 13,700 Drs ($57.10) double. AE, DC, EC, MC, V.

This refurbished hotel has cottage cheese-textured ceilings, dark natural-wood furnishings, a picturesque and usable roof garden, and an active outdoor café. The Aenos seems to attract returning Greeks, who are really the soul of its lively, active social life—just check out its café tables overlooking the square!

Hotel Alegro, Odós Choidá 2, 28100 Argostóli. ☎ **0671/22-268.**
16 rms (10 with bath). TEL

Rates: 7,475 Drs ($31.15) double without bath; 9,775 Drs ($40.75) double with bath. No credit cards.

This small older hotel offers convenient but spartan lodgings in the lively town agora. It's a clean pension of small rooms, many with balconies and all with sinks. Singles pay 10% less.

Castello Hotel, Platía Metaxá, 28100 Argostóli. ☎ **0671/28-054.** Fax 0671/23-252.
20 rms (all with bath). TEL

Rates (including breakfast): 8,575 Drs ($35.75) single; 13,700 Drs ($57.10) double. AE, EC, MC, V.

The recently redecorated interior is part pastel chiffon, part go-go moderne: large beige glass globes hang like Christmas tree balls from the lobby ceiling. Renovated doubles are clean and cheery, though rooms overlooking the square can be noisy.

Cephallonia Star, Odós Metaxá 50, 28100 Argostóli. ☎ **0671/23-181.**
Fax 0671/23-180. 47 rms (all with bath). A/C TEL

Rates (including breakfast): 9,775 Drs ($40.70) single; 16,100 Drs ($67.10) double. MC, V.

This older Class C hotel is well kept and a good value. It's centrally located opposite the Lixouri shuttle, and many balconied rooms offer fine views over the water. In August, we found a mobile amusement park set up across the street.

Hotel Ionian Plaza, Vallianoú Square, Argostóli 28100, Kefalonía. ☎ **0671/25-581.** Fax 0671/25-585. 43 rms (all with bath). A/C TV TEL

Rates: 10,900 Drs ($45.40) single; 17,135 Drs ($71.40). MC, V.

Vassilis Vassilatos returned to Argostóli after 15 years in Manhattan and built this impressive hotel and the **Restaurant Palazzino** next to it in the neoclassical Kefalonian style. It's lovely and elegant, with an excellent staff. The rooms are spacious and more than comfortable, well worth the extra drachmas.

A Splurge Choice

White Rocks Hotel and Bungalows, Platís Ghialós, 28100 Argostóli. ☎ **0671/27-167.** Fax 0671/28-332. Telex 312277 WRHC. 102 rms, 60 bungalows (all with bath). A/C MINIBAR TEL

Rates: Low season 20,900 Drs ($116.10) double with breakfast; high season 24,000 Drs ($133.30) double with half board. AE, DC, V.

This splurge hotel, a modern, white stucco place with blue and coral upholstered furnishings, sits in a pine forest on a cliff above two beautiful beaches. The separate, more spacious bungalow units are in the open with a sunset vantage. Top-flight service, the seaview bar and the beach facilities warrant resort prices for those who don't want to cope with staying in town. If an overnight stay is out of the question, stop by their Greek and European food self-service restaurant (open 12:30 to 3:30pm daily) for a pricey, but pleasant break from the northern public beach below.

WHERE TO EAT

There are two fine tavernas in the center of town (one old, one new) plus a number of pastry shops on Valianoú Square. Don't miss the local specialty, a Kefalonian meat pie, a mixture of pork and lamb cooked with rice and a touch of spinach. We found it delicious and nutritious.

Old Plaka, Odós Metaxá 26. ☎ **24-849.**

Cuisine: GREEK.

Prices: Appetizers 400–600 Drs ($1.65–$2.50); main courses 1,100–1,725 Drs ($4.60–$7.20). No credit cards.

Open: Daily 6–11:30pm.

One of the newest taverna/grills and one of the best, it has a superb location opposite the bay at the quiet north end of the port. The open, bright kitchen cries out for inspection; those who respond will discover succulent pork, goat livers, and moist chickens turning on the spit. Add a plate of fresh horta (greens), zucchini and potatoes, and the fine spinach pie and you'll take off for a portside *vólta* very content.

★ **Patsoura's,** Israel Street. ☎ **22-779.**

Cuisine: GREEK.

Prices: Appetizers 400–980 Drs ($1.65–$4.10); main courses 920–1,400 Drs ($3.85–$5.85). No credit cards.

Open: Daily noon–4:30pm and 7–11pm.

This restaurant, about five blocks north of Valianoú Square as you walk along King George (Vassiléos Gheorghíou) Street, is in a fenced-in garden surrounded by chirping cicadas and birds. Smiling chef Christianthou Patsoura runs this tiny gem (really called **Perivoláki,** but no one would know what you were talking about if you got lost). Patsoura cooks up a mean *crasato,* pork cooked in wine that's one of the island's specialties. His aubergine pie is also exceptionally tasty.

Other dining choices are centered around Valianóu Square, our favorite spot for people watching. (At our recent visit, the National Brass Band of Budapest was performing under the stars to entertain us!) Of the many pastry shops, we especially liked **Paloma Pâtisserie** on the east side for its variety of desserts, both European and Greek. **Quick's,** on the north side, is not only that, it's also cheap—you can get burgers, fries, souvlaki, moussaká and ice cream in a bright formica and fluorescent establishment. **Taverna Kalíva** (Cottage) is just off the square, next to Filóxenos Travel, and serves good basic Greek fare and Kefalonian specialties. For fresh fruit, try the minimarket next to the KTEL bus station; there's also a seafood market here before 10am daily.

EVENING ENTERTAINMENT

If spending a night watching American films subtitled in Greek at the **Rex Cinema** (one block north of the square on G. Vergoti Street) doesn't excite you, try the popular café/bar at the **Aenos Hotel** off the square. (The **Mythos Bar** is one of many cafés right on the square that are fun to hang out in.) **The Old Pub House,** one of the few places to survive the earthquake, one block off the square toward the *paralia,* is a favorite watering hole of the cognoscenti, where the music rocks until 2am. The seaside **Limanaki** and the **Kouros Music Bar** are popular discos a little farther on.

Fiskárdo

Fiskárdo, 46 km north of Argostóli, is the one village on Kefalonía that survived the earthquake of 1953 almost totally unharmed. When you come down the hill and turn the corner into its tiny square, you see a tranquil harbor with the hills of Ithaca rising beyond it. The charming village spreads mainly to the right around the C-shaped cove; a lighthouse dots the left side. Flotillas of yachts moor around the bay. It's no wonder people come to dote on this tiny village; it's an architectural gem unlike most left in Greece. And they do come—the winter population of less than 100 swells tenfold with Italians in July and August.

Although there is increasing tourist congestion (particularly during midday, when the daytrip cruises from Lefkáda and Ithaca arrive), a quiet pace prevails among the cherry and fig trees, peaches and apricots. A Doric-columned schoolhouse sits proudly amid stucco villas with colonnaded porticos and overgrown grape arbors. The port is made for idlers, whether you choose to sit in a taverna with ouzo, schmooze with the locals (almost everyone speaks English), or sample the exceptionally clear water. The ambience is so fetching that we were content to loll on the flat rocks at the far end of the cove like the sea lions that populate this area.

The **Ships Agency** (☎ **0674/41-325**) is the center of activity for foreign visitors. From 9am to 10pm daily, they change money, sell excursion boat tickets, provide a metered long distance phone, arrange sail boat charters, and service a lively two table kafeneion off the harbor. **Fiskardo Rent a Car and Moto** (☎ **51-581**) is nearby if you're looking for wheels to hit Myrtos beach.

WHERE TO STAY

Try to stay in Fiskárdo overnight to sample the essence of Greek life, preferably in one of the classic villas or the former Traditional Settlements (government-renovated 150-year-old villas). Each house has been divided into simply-furnished twin or triple bedded rooms with attached showers. Only two of the government-renovated homes, recently returned to their original owners, are still used for private rental. Contact these family owners directly: **Mrs. Athanasia Dendrinou** (☎ **0674/41-326**) or **Mrs. Vasso Palikisianou** (☎ **0674/41-303**) by phone, or by writing them at 28084 Fiskárdo, Kefalonía, Greece, for information on availability and prices. Most of the restored rooms have common baths and charge about 10,350 Drs ($43.15) regardless of season (not open in winter).

Erisos Pension, Fiskárdo 28084. ☎ **01/93-42-992** in Athens. 6 rms (all with bath).

Rates: 12,075 Drs ($50.30) single/double. No credit cards.

Spyridoula Manousardiou has transformed her traditional home just off the port by adding private bathrooms with showers to each tidy, tile-floored room. Aegean blue shutters enclose these bright, high-ceilinged spaces. The flowering bougainvillea shrouding the stone exterior makes this one of the village's prettiest homes.

Fiscardo Philoxenia, Fiskárdo 28084. ☎ **0674/41-319** or **01/56-12-037** in Athens). 6 rms (all with bath).

Rates: 14,200 Drs ($59.15) double or triple. No credit cards.

Makis Kavadias's restored villa is in the heart of the village just behind the Ships Agency. Within the bright green wooden gate are several large, modernized rooms that share a fully equipped, common kitchen. Ask for an upstairs room with a porch overlooking the harbor.

★ **Fiskardona,** Fiskárdo 28084. ☎ **0674/41-316.** 7 rms (all with bath).

Rates: 13,650 Drs ($56.90) single/double; 15,600 Drs ($65) triple. No credit cards.

This yellow-shuttered stone and stucco house sits right behind the port on a tiny square. The gracious Mr. Tzamarelos and his family have rebuilt and modernized this mid-19th-century villa, while maintaining many original architectural details. Front-facing rooms have small balconies overlooking the town (potentially noisy in the high season), and there's a common kitchen, dining area, and TV lounge on the ground floor.

Rooms to Let

EOT, the Greek Tourist Organization, estimates that there are at least 150 private rooms with 400 beds for rent at rates of 8,500 Drs ($35.40) for bathless doubles, 10,250 Drs ($42.70) with bath. We liked the seven simple rooms rented by **Stella Barzouka** (☎ **0674/41-310**) in a newly built, old style house in the village. There are common showers, a large kitchen and a landscaped garden for guest to share. **Makis Market** also represents several four- to six-person apartments with kitchenettes, which rent for about 27,000 Drs ($112.50) per night (25% less in the low season) between April 1 and November 30.

WHERE TO EAT

Choosing a restaurant in Fiskárdo won't be hard. There are only half a dozen tavernas, a few snack shops and two bars, all along the port. You'll get a feel for the style of each; these are our picks.

Dendrino's Restaurant and Grill. Paralía, Fiskárdo. ☎ **41-203.**

Cuisine: GREEK

Prices: Appetizers 500–920 Drs ($2.10–$3.85), main courses 1,300–1,750 Drs ($5.40–$7.20). V.

Open: Daily 11am–midnight.

This is the fanciest and priciest of the local eateries, befitting its location overlooking the yacht harbor. While the food is quite good, we found the toney international crowd a bit too boisterous for a moonlit night. But their Greek standards and fresh fish are very well prepared.

Restaurant Faros. Paralía, Fiskárdo. ☎ **41-277.**

Cuisine: GREEK
Prices: Appetizers 650–920 Drs ($2.65–$3.85), main courses 1,400–1,750 Drs ($5.60–$11.80). V.
Open: Daily 11am–11pm.

This is a friendly portside place with much less of a "scene" than at other tavernas, but with similarly rushed service at supper. Go for a leisurely lunch—we loved their Kefalonian meat pies with a salad. Fresh fish is well priced and excellently prepared.

Breakfast, Drinks, and Dessert

For ice cream (19 flavors), sweets, or yoghurt try **Grace's,** on the *paralía.* Although every establishment fills up with tourists for a drink, ouzo, or coffee at night, **Le Barbare** is the slickest nightspot. It's just off the port in the tiny town square. **Harry's Bar,** no relation to the famed Venetian haunt, and **The Captain's Cabin,** a good pizza, sandwich, and pastry spot, are both popular choices on the port.

Around the Island

If Argostóli is under the "arch" of the high-heel–shaped island, Livathos is the region around the "sole." This prosperous area, heavily striped with narrow, scenic, winding roads, has traditionally been inhabited by wealthy sea captains. **Metaxáta** (where Lord Byron stayed for four months in 1823) is one village with several modern luxury villas. **Kourkoumeláda,** to the south, is the product of one man's faith. After the earthquake of 1953, George Vergotis, a wealthy entrepreneur, rebuilt the entire village and all its former homes by himself. If you sailed east past the lovely sand beach at **Ormos Lourda** to Ormos Katelíou, you'd be near Markópoulos. As its name implies, the city claims to be founded by ancestors of Marco Polo. During the week before the Feast of the Assumption (early August) its citizens are said to catch harmless snakes with black crosses on their heads, which then disappear until the following year.

At the island's "toe" is the village of **Skála,** called Neá Skála by those who've seen the ghost town of half-crumbled houses left over from the earthquake. It's now a budding resort of rooms to let favored by the British.

The east coast's principal port, Sámi looks like a calm, sheltered harbor in a niche of the white cliffs which score the east coast's verdant palisades. The ruins of a 3d-century Roman bath (with its mosaic floor intact) led archeologists to conclude that this was indeed the port of ancient Sámi. About an hour's walk from the town to the point is the **Monastery of Agrilion,** where remnants of a Venetian fort and some walls can be seen. Today Sámi has lost its prime role to the economically better-developed and more lively main town of Argostóli, site of the airport. However, if you're stuck overnight you can find a nice room at the **Castle of Sámi** (☎ **0674/22-656**).

For 20 km north of Sámi there is good road following the east coast. At the 7-km mark you reach the **Melissáni Grotto,** (☎ **22-997**), a large, multicolored cave that encloses a huge underground lake, where you can take a boat ride for 800 Drs ($3.35). For many years it appeared that water flowed backward into the land at Katavóthres, near Argostóli. Now scientists say that in fact this water is flowing due east, through an underwater tunnel into the underground lake at Melissáni.

Farther north is the small village of **Ághios Efimías** (departure point for daily ferries to Fríkes, Ithaca, and to Astakós on the mainland. From here north the coast rises to tall rocky heights and the roadway moves inland to some charming, small villages and finally, to Fiskárdo.

The west coast of Kefalonía has the best beaches on the island and some of its most breathtaking scenery. The main road south from Fiskárdo winds down through sweet little villages to **Ássos** (about 13 km south), where the tongue of Kefalonía's shoe butts out into another small peninsula. Topping it is a Venetian castle from 1595; the buff-colored stones ramble across this acropolis, once used to safeguard Kefalonía's western flank. Within its protective arc is the picturesque port of Ássos, one of the loveliest in Greece. Boxy, pastel-colored houses unified by red tiled roofs are the summer cottages of Greeks and Italians who stroll through the portside in bikinis and diaphanous dresses. The village square is called Platía Parison and is dedicated to the city of Paris for its "generous contribution to the reconstruction of Ássos after the earthquakes of 1953." Everywhere are figs, peaches, flowering oleander, and geraniums.

The drive between Assos and **Ormós Mýrtos** (about 10 km) is one of the prettiest on the island. For your efforts, you're rewarded with a long, wide stretch of fine pearl-colored pebbles and the most Paul Newman–blue waters, with only a scattering of fellow sun worshippers. We voted **Mýrtos Beach** one of Greece's top ten beaches.

South of this, on the green, rugged coast is the **monastery of Kipouréon,** built in 1744. It's still inhabited by the original sect of monks who zealously guard its fine collection of antique icons. Rounding the cape to Lixoúri you'll find many more good beaches, best reached by boat. The newly built resort at **Lixoúri** is easily reached by ferry from the Argostóli pier (see "Getting Around" above). It's a pleasant half-hour minicruise for a day trip to this area's fine, dark sand beaches. Day-trippers may want to rent a scooter from one of the numerous shops along the *paralía* in Lixoúri, particularly if you consider heading northwest to the peninsula's best beach at **Petáni,** on Ortholithías Bay, or south to **Mégas Lákos** and **Kounópetra,** both with good, small pebble beaches.

Seven kilometers south of Lixoúri, on Xi Beach, is the luxurious new **Cephalonia Palace** (☎ **0671/93-190,** fax 92-638), with two restaurants, two bars, a pool, tennis, courts, a minimarket, laundry facilities, and a shuttle bus several times a day to Lixoúri; rooms run from 19,550 Drs ($81.45) for a single to 26,565 Drs ($110.70) for a triple.

At Petáni Beach we found **Angels Efthimiatos,** a former Toronto Maple Leafer who inherited his grandfather's shack on the beach and turned it into a taverna/snack bar that serves grilled food and "traditional" American sandwiches and hamburgers.

6 Zákynthos

53 nautical miles NW of Patras; 18 nautical miles W of Kyllíni

ARRIVING/DEPARTING • By Air One flight daily on *Olympic Airways* leaves from Athens year-round, with additional flights during the summer. For information, contact their office at Odós Roma 16 on Ar. Margou Square (☎ **0695/28-611**), or in Athens (☎ **01/92-92-111**).

• **By Sea** Several *car ferries* make the 1 1/2-hour trip daily from Kyllíni, on the Peloponnese mainland. Call the Kyllíni (☎ **0623/92-211**) or Zákynthos (☎ **0695/22-417**) port authorities for schedule information.

ESSENTIALS The **area code** is 0695 for the entire island. Several travel agents (most are open daily from 9am to 9pm in summer) and the post office (see below) exchange traveler's checks outside of bank hours. The **hospital** (☎ **22-514**) is west of the port. The **tourist police** (☎ **22-550**), on the **paralía** two blocks from the second gas station toward Platía Solomoú, are open from 8am to 2:30pm weekdays. The **police station** is off Lombárdou at Odós Tzouláti 5. The **post office** is at Odós Tertseti 27 at Gouskos Street, west of the Government House, open from 7:30am to 2pm, Monday through Friday. The telephone center, **OTE,** is just east of Platía Solomoú, beyond the museum; it is open 7am to midnight daily.

Zákynthos, or Zánte as it's also known, is the southernmost of the islands in the Ionian Sea (the southernmost of *all the seven* Ionian Islands, Kýthira, is off the southeastern coast of the Peloponnese). At 417 square kilometers, it's the third-largest island after Corfu and Kefalonía, and the closest one to the Peloponnese mainland. Though not as architecturally distinctive as the other Ionians, Zákynthos is popular with Greek visitors looking for a few relaxing days on a not-yet-spoiled-by-tourists resort.

The island, first noted in history by Homer as Yliessa, was settled by Zákynthos, son of Dardanos, king of Troy. In Hellenic times this tiny democracy was wooed by both Athens and Sparta because of its fertile soil and strategic location. In 1204 Zákynthos fell to the Byzantine conquerors and was ruled by a succession of Frankish princes; during this time the kastro, whose ruins reflect the extent of the entire city at that time, was built. In 1484 the Venetians took Zákynthos and ruled it for over 300 years. They began what became one of the nicest legacies of this fertile island: the lucrative cultivation of grapes (made into wine, and, of course, Zante currants). In 1500 the Venetians expanded the city of Zákynthos outside the fortress walls. The narrow streets, open squares, and arcades that form weatherproof promenades along the harbor were designed by the Italians, but date only from 1953. In that year more than 90% of the island's buildings were leveled by a tremendous earthquake that damaged parts of many of the Ionian islands, but which started in Zákynthos. Zantiots are fiercely proud of their artistic sons, and the port's Solomós Museum houses the memorabilia of Dionysos Solomós, Greece's national poet, and Foskolos and Kalvos, two other celebrated poets of the Ionian School.

Orientation

The southern position of Zákynthos in the warm Ionian Sea gives it an especially pleasant climate in the winter; the many sheltered coves on the north end of the island provide cooler water and temperate breezes in the summer.

The island is not as heavily developed as Corfu and doesn't yet cater solely to group tourists; however, British and Scandinavian holiday makers are in very full force, and reservations are required in the summer. Prices have climbed dramatically, reaching parity with the other Ionian resorts. There are several thousand beds to rent privately around the island, and we found staying with a local the best way to vacation inexpensively in this first-class, Greece-for-Greeks resort. The lively port of Zákynthos (Zante) is our recommended base for first-time visitors.

Getting Around

To explore the island, you'll want to start in the port. From here there are frequent **buses** to every corner and beach, and several shops from which to rent **mopeds,** the preferred mode of transport. **Stamatis** (☎ **23-673**), at Odós Filitia 9, is one friendly place; **Moto Sakis** (☎ **23-928**) at Leof. Dimokratis 3, is another; both rent mopeds (don't forget helmets) for about 2,400 Drs ($10) per day. You can rent **bicycles,** too, but the many hills require pretty strong calf muscles! The faster mopeds allow you to fully enjoy the cool pine forests and scent of roses that line every roadway. If you've got a few days to explore, buy a map (500 Drs or $2.10; available everywhere), enabling you to jog, hike, or just plain wander down all the roadways to appreciate the island's beauty.

Zákynthos Town

Zákynthos town is the capital for excellent restaurants, elegant (and expensive!) boutiques, and rousing nightlife—the choice if a few kilometers' walk to the beach is acceptable. There are several small, reasonably priced Greek-style pensions tucked into the back streets, away from the harbor and among the bakeries, markets, and service businesses that the locals use. Several churches crop up in the small alleys and many tree-lined squares, so that a walk through Zákynthos alternates between the screech of mopeds, cars, and hustle-bustle activity and the quiet, shaded relief of monumental churches and plazas.

INFORMATION

There was no municipal or government tourist office at our visit, but you can ask for help at the **Tuo Travel Agency** (☎ **0695/22-255**), at Odós Filita 42, one block west of the harbor opposite the bus station; or at **Potamitis Tours** (☎ **0695/23-118**) at 3 San Marcos Square.

CITY LAYOUT

The harborside lane, **Lombárdou Stráta Marina,** runs between the two spindly arms of manmade breakwater that form the docking area. You'll disembark facing **Platía Solomoú,** where the statue of Solomós dominates the busy port patrol.

The fourth right turn off Venizélou (the main street running inland from Solomoú Square) is **King Constantine (Vassiléos Konstantínou) Street** (also signposted as May 21 Street), the town's main drag for shops, restaurants, café-bars, and markets. This street leads into the 16th-century Platiafaros, or **Ághios Márkos Square** (St. Mark's Square), a rare exception to the post-quake rebuilding. Here you'll find some "fast-food cafés" (the most chic) and on the west side, the Solomós Museum.

Farther up the museum street are several **banks,** and opposite them the island's **taxi stand.** If you take the first left off Venizélou Street onto Filitia Street, in three long blocks you'll come to the **bus station. Note:** Zákynthos has undergone some street-name changing that can cause confusion.

WHAT TO SEE & DO

If it's a rainy day in Zákynthos town, head for the **Solomós Museum** at Odós Vassiléos Konstantínou 6, next to the Ághios Márkos Cathedral. It's open from 9am to 2pm daily for a look at the author's lifelong collection of literary memorabilia. The

Byzantine Museum offers a small, well-presented collection (labeled in Greek and French) of Byzantine-era through 19th-century church paintings from the Ionian School of Art. It's open from 8:30am to 2:30pm Tuesday through Sunday.

The **Cathedral of Águios Dionissios** (St. Denis), across from the harbor on the south end of town) is one of the island's finest because of the wrought-silver casket in which relics of Zákynthos's patron saint repose. Twice a year, on August 24 and December 17, there are processions throughout the town for St. Dionissios, who must pass over streets strewn with myrtle branches.

There are many pricey boutiques at the port, but there is also a **handcrafts cooperative** at Odós Lombárdou 42 (on the *paralía*, or harbor front, with a branch in Volimes), where locally made items are sold. We admired tablecloths, place mats, and curtains, as well as hand-knit sweaters and woven rugs.

There are organized trips beyond the port town. Readers with a SCUBA license might enjoy a dive into the Ionian. **Zante Diving/Driftwood Club** (offices on Lagana Beach, ☎ **0695/51-196**) offers a range of cruise and dive trips off the west coast, where they claim there are more than 1,000 underwater caves to explore. Venturing farther afield, the **Tuo Travel Agency** (☎ **22-255**) offers round-the-island day trips, plus tours to Kefalonía, Olympia, Delphi, Mýcenae, and Athens. Vasilis, our man to see on Zákynthos, also books diving and horseback riding trips.

WHERE TO STAY

We've seen many changes on Zákynthos. Among them are the European tour groups who have recently established a strong presence, locking up many hotels for years in advance. At the same time, Class D and E inns have closed, making it tough for the individual budget traveler. Below are some hotels (open May to October unless otherwise noted) where you have a chance at a room during the high season; however, if everything is booked, march over to the tourist police and request assistance. They'll likely find you accommodations in a private home. Expect to pay about 5,000 Drs ($20.80) for a double room with private bath, 3,750 Drs ($15.60) for shared facilities.

Apollon, Odós Tertséti 30, Zákynthos 27575. ☎ **0695/42-838.**
15 rms (all with bath). TEL

Rates (including breakfast): 8,625 Drs ($35.95) single; 10,900 Drs ($45.40) double. EC, MC, V.

The Apollon is conveniently located a few blocks up from the harbor near the post office. Though central, it's blessedly quiet, with clean, undistinguished rooms and a pleasant breakfast lounge.

Hotel Bitzaro, Odós Dionysíou Roma 46, Zákynthos 27575. ☎ **0695/23-644.**
Fax 0695/23-493. 40 rms (all with bath). TEL

Rates (including breakfast): 10,600 Drs ($44.15) single; 14,950 Drs ($62.30) double. No credit cards.

This attractive family-run hotel is just a few blocks south of Platía Solomoú, far enough away from the port and town traffic. The rooms are comfortable, ultra clean and extremely well maintained. (Try to avoid those nearer the bar, which can get noisy.) The family has recently opened a new hotel at Kalamáki Beach (☎ **0695/25-773**).

Omonoia Hotel, Odós Xanthopoúlou 3, Zákynthos 27575. ☎ **0695/22-113.** 9 rms (all with bath). TEL

Rates: 9,750 Drs ($40.65) double. No credit cards.

The Omonoia is a small, homey place in a peaceful residential neighborhood a few blocks inland from the *paralía.* The rooms are small and dark, but cleanly kept. Open year-round.

Palatino Hotel, Odós Kolokotróni 10, at Kolyva Street, Zákynthos 29100. ☎ **0695/45-400.** Fax 0695/45-400. 30 rms (all with bath). A/C TEL

Rates: 14,400 Drs ($60) single; 17,250 Drs ($71.85) double. AE, DC, EC, MC, V.

A block from the beach you'll find the newest, most comfortable hotel in town—spacious, quietly elegant, cheerful and relaxed. All bathrooms have full bathtubs with shower and shower curtains! Rooms with balconies are the best deal, because the hotel is situated far enough from traffic to be able to enjoy them.

Hotel Phoenix, Platía Solomoú, Zákynthos 27575. ☎ **0695/42-719.** Fax 0695/45-083. 34 rms (all with bath). TEL inland from the ferry pier.

Rates: 7,590 Drs ($31.60) single; 10,695 Drs ($44.55) double. No credit cards.

This has merged with the neighboring Hotel Astoria, and some rooms have balconies overlooking the square. Facilities are clean, spacious, and well furnished.

WHERE TO EAT

Zákynthos's greatest concentration of pizza joints, snack cafés, and restaurants is in Ághios Márkos Square. Most serve a variety of Greek courses and Italian-inspired pasta, and are open quite late at night.

Café Olympia, Odós Alexándrou Roma 3. ☎ **28-747.**

Cuisine: SNACKS/DESSERTS.
Prices: Main courses 300–600 Drs ($1.25–$2.50). No credit cards.
Open: Daily 7am–10pm.

For breakfast, we sleepwalked to Café Olympia, opposite the Platía Solomoú and the Government House. Cheese pies, yogurt, Greek coffee, butter biscuits, and other treats awaited us each morning—and we always left only little bit poorer.

The Clock, Odós Vassiléos Konstantínou 11. ☎ **23-587.**

Cuisine: INTERNATIONAL.
Prices: Appetizers 460–980 Drs ($1.90–$4.10); main courses 1,050–1,725 Drs ($4.35–$7.20). No credit cards.
Open: Mon–Sat 9am–2pm and 6:30–11:30pm; Sun only evenings.

A good, inexpensive "restaurant, steak house, café bar, pizza" is how The Clock (*Tó Rolói*) describes itself, and this family-run place lives up to its claim. Some Englishmen weary of "breakfest complet" extolled the virtues of The Clock's bacon and eggs, but we like it for lunch and dinner. Their large and varied menu will satisfy meat lovers and vegetarians alike, at moderate prices. The chefs deserve praise for serving hot (not tepid) food.

Orea Hellas, Odós Ioánnou Logothétou 11. ☎ **28-622.**

Cuisine: GREEK. **Reservations:** Recommended weekends in summer.
Prices: Appetizers 460–920 Drs ($1.90–$3.85); main courses 1,100–2,070 Drs ($4.58–$8.60).

Open: Daily 7am–1am.

Orea Hellas (Fair Hellas) is a sentimental favorite with Zantiotes, set in the heart of what was the restaurant district before the earthquake of 1953. Host Takis Kefalinos is a friendly and excellent chef. The small indoor restaurant (open all year) is decorated with turn-of-the-century prints of Zante; across the street is an outdoor lot, lit with Christmas tree lights, that opens at dinner for food and live music. One of Hellas's best dishes is *sáltsa,* an island specialty that's something like a beef goulash. The lamb, with big, rice-flake-like noodles, is very tasty, and the loin of pork is one of the best-sellers. Add a carafe of *krassí* (wine), and life can't be beat!

Tres Jolie, Odós Dennis Stefánou 15. ☎ **24-621.**

Cuisine: SNACKS/DESSERTS

Prices: Snacks 350–600 Drs ($1.45–$2.50). No credit cards.

Open: Daily 9am–9pm.

You'll find this new little place by walking south from the government building on Alex. Roma and turning left toward the harbor. Pretty as its name suggests, with delicious sandwiches, pastries, confections, and ice creams made on the spot. Everything's fresh daily as they sell out by midafternoon!

Zohios, Odós Psarón 9. No phone.

Cuisine: GREEK.

Prices: Appetizers 400–600 Drs ($1.65–$2.50); main courses 980–1,150 Drs ($4.10–$4.80). No credit cards.

Open: Daily 8pm–1am

This is a traditional taverna favored by locals, just off El. Venizélou and Dessila behind the little green square. A typical moussaká, sautéed vegetables (try the stuffed tomatoes or eggplant), some pasta dishes, and fried seafood are particularly good and inexpensive.

EVENING ENTERTAINMENT

Zákynthos really comes alive at night. The harborside promenade fills with Greeks out for their nightly *vólta,* taking a slow turn around the port to relish the cool evening breezes. Particularly popular with the younger set is the **Ship Inn,** located on the *paralía* near the tourist police office. Inside at the bar and clustered out front you'll find teenage and early-twenties Greek mopeders downing beer.

The two most popular discos near the town are within close proximity to one another along the road to Argassi. **Video Disco** is the newer, therefore superior by local standards. **Argassi** is just a bit farther on and ranks a close second.

Film buffs will appreciate the town's two outdoor, vine-covered cinemas. The **Cine Lux** is across from the EOT town beach near the Bitzaro Hotel. The other is right in town on the *paralía.* Film time begins when the sun goes down.

Around the Island

While on Zákynthos, explore. You just may find a beach resort that can lure you away from the gourmet fare in the beachless port town. Our friend Nick Galifopoulos recommended his favorite beach (which is in his hometown), but we found that **Alíkes** to be truly the prettiest white sand beach on the island.

Alíkes is 10 km north of Zákynthos town, along an inland road that winds up around the verdant hills through vineyards and olive groves. Along the uncrowded beach you'll find a few hotels. The Tsoukalas brothers (guess where they've lived abroad?) run the **Montreal Hotel,** Alíkes 29090, Zákynthos (☎ **0695/83-241**). All 31 bright, clean rooms, angled to face the sea, overlook the lefkas trees. They shade the hotel's seaside café, where you can rent a canoe for under $4 an hour. Bed and breakfast singles cost 9,775 Drs ($40.70); doubles run 12,650 Drs ($60).

Tsilivi Beach is another beach area which developed just four kilometers north of the port, in the village of Planos. In August, the most preferable location on the island is undoubtedly **Kalamáki Beach,** where the Crystal Beach Hotel offers a bird's-eye view of the famous loggerhead turtles, which come late each evening during the month to lay their eggs on the shore. The **Crystal Beach** (☎ **0695/22-774**) is only one of two that managed to get a license during the years when everyone thought turtle footprints were just tractor marks. The World Wildlife Fund has established a "biogenic reserve" at Kalamáki to protect the turtles, which were only discovered nine years ago by locals. Besides attracting curious tourists, the turtles actually serve a secondary purpose: they eat jellyfish, making the waters safer for swimming. If you decide to stay, one of the Crystal Beach's 58 doubles with shower cost 14,400 Drs ($60).

South of Zákynthos town the island becomes heavily wooded with pine and olive forests. At **Cape Ghérakas,** there is little building other than a few older hotels and some tavernas. There are turtledoves and hidden coves filled with crafty fishermen who are always alert for the movement of fish. Going back toward the city there are many ROOM TO LET signs among the olive groves decked out with laundry lines and fields filled with grazing cows. There are also several all-amenity, Class C hotels in the resort areas of **Vassilikós** and **Argássi.** In Argássi, the traditionally styled and furnished 60-room **Hotel Levante** (☎ **0695/22-833**) is the most attractive; doubles with private facilities cost 13,500 Drs ($56.25).

Last, and least in our opinion, is the fully developed **Laganás Beach,** where large hotels provide accommodations for foreign tour groups (this resort is its own little world). There are Jeeps on the beach, tavernas, snackbars, and pizzerias as well as a notable lack of charm. Nevertheless, if you find yourself stranded in Laganás Beach as part of a budget package, go out and explore the rest of the island. The verdant countryside will convince you why the Venetians dubbed Zákynthos the "Flower of the Levante."

Northern Greece

15

MACEDONIA'S CAPITAL IS THESSALONÍKI, GREECE'S SECOND-LARGEST CITY AND THE port named in antiquity after Alexander the Great's half-sister. Yet Macedonia also includes the Chalkidiki peninsula, one of Greece's most scenic resorts and host to Mt. Athos, a totally independent religious community over 1,000 years old.

There are great Hellenic-era antiquities at Pella, Vergina, and Veria; Roman ruins at Philippi and Amfipolis; and one of the world's great museums in Thessaloníki. Macedonia was one of the wealthiest members of the Hellenic Federation more than 2,000 years ago, and still prospers in agriculture, industry, and trade today. The fur industry of Kastoria, the tobacco of Kavala, the shipping of Thessaloníki are the kind of growth industries that will keep Greece alive forever. Unlike so many of the islands or the southern cities which survive on tourism generated by past deeds, much of Macedonia, and Thrace, too, can live on its own. Visiting them becomes an exploration into the heart and soul of modern Greece. Thrace, because of its high Muslim population, smoothly bridges the cultural gap that might exist at the border of two countries with such a volatile past and provides a good introduction to Turkey.

Macedonia, for many, will always be known as the land of Alexander the Great. It is the land that nourished his ambitious dreams until, a young man in his 20s, he took up the reins of his assassinated father, Philip II, and set out to subdue all Greece. However coarse and provincial, it was Macedonia, rather than cosmopolitan Athens, that inspired this conqueror, who created, as Constantine Cavafy says in his poem "In the Year 200 B.C.," "the great new Hellenic world . . . with our far-flung supremacy and our common Greek language, which we carried as far as . . . the Indians."

Seeing Northern Greece

If you only have three or four days to spare, spend your time based in Thessaloníki, one of our favorite Greek metropolises. We'd recommend a half-day bus tour to Pella (38 km northwest, the birthplace of Alexander the Great and a fascinating site and museum) and an afternoon in the Archeological Museum; and then a full-day walking tour of the city itself, its Byzantine and Roman sights, cafés, shops, and waterfront.

The next day you can take a guided bus tour across Halkidikí, then cruise around the holy peninsula of Mt. Áthos to admire the monasteries. History buffs will want to take another expertly guided day trip to the archeological sites that illuminate Macedonia's past. If by this time you crave a beach, head east to Kavala to catch the ferries for the Northeast Aegean island of Thassos.

IMPRESSIONS

The monasteries [on Mt. Athos] are like so many little fortresses in the midst of the most sublime solitude.

The dogs . . . in many parts of Macedonia wear body clothes, and these animals afforded us the last remaining traces of the Macedonian costume.

—E. D. Clarke, *Travels in Various Countries,* 1818

What's Special About Northern Greece

Historical Sites

- The birthplace of Mustafa Kemal Ataturk, founder of modern Turkey, is an intriguing house museum in Thessaloníki.
- The Greek Orthodox Monasteries on Mt. Áthos contain the world's finest collection of Byzantine religious artifacts.
- Thessaloníki has an amazing assortment of Byzantine churches, including the 8th-century Aghia Sophia.
- Kavala's Panaghia Hill district features the family home of Muhammad Ali in a neighborhood of traditional Turkish housing.
- Thessaloníki's superb archeological museum and the excavations at Vergina, Veria, Pella, and Dion provide a fascinating look at the life and times of Alexander the Great and his father, Philip II.

1 Thessaloníki

335 miles N of Athens

GETTING THERE • By Plane **Olympic Airways** has several daily flights to and from most European capitals and major American cities. Lufthansa Airlines has daily service from Frankfurt. There are six flights daily to Athens, five weekly to Ioánnina, one flight daily to Límnos and Lesvos, twice weekly to Rhodes or Iráklio, Crete, and once weekly to Chaniá, Crete. The Olympic office is at Odós Komninón 1. A bus runs between the train station and the airport (the bus fare is 125 Drs or 50¢). There is a tourist police station, a Greek tourist information (EOT) office (☎ **471-170**), and a duty-free shop at the airport for international travelers. Call **230-240** in Thessaloníki or **01/981-1201** in Athens for Olympic schedule information.

• By Train Trains arrive at the Thessaloníki station on Monastiríou Street (call **276-382** or **517-517** for information), a world unto itself. All day and night trains are pulling in from throughout Greece, all the European cities (lots of EurailPasses go through here!), and from Turkey and east to Asia. The Information Booth is open daily to meet all trains; if they're out of maps, study the mural map of the city outside. There are two banks, a post office, and a telephone center (OTE), all open daily, located to the right as you exit. The luggage storage (the only official one in all of Thessaloníki) is open 24 hours and charges 220 Drs (90¢) per piece until midnight each day.

There are two trains daily to Istanbul. You get your money's worth in scenery as you tear through Thrace for the 18-hour ride; the 1994 fare was 12,650 Drs ($52.70) in coach class. There's a special express train that shuttles back and forth to Athens four times a day, cutting the 12-hour journey in half; one way fare is 9,400 Drs ($39.15).

• By Bus There are eight buses daily from the terminal in Athens at Odós Kifíssou 100; the 8-hour trip costs 5,500 Drs ($22.90) each way; call **01/51-48-856** for reservations.

The consolidated **bus station** we were promised had not materialized on our last visit, but most are near the train station. Buses to Athens leave from Monastiríou 65; those to Pella, Édessa, Vólos, and Kastoriá leave from Anageniseos 22; those to Flórina from Anageniseos 42; for Véria for 26 Oktovriou 10. Check with EOT for additional details.

The OSE bus lines has a special Thessaloníki to Istanbul twice daily bus (the trip is 14 hours long and the fare is 12,000 Drs ($50.40)) and in the high season (if there's enough demand) there are express buses from Athens to Thessaloníki to Brussels, London, Perugia, Berlin, and Amsterdam. Check with OSE (☎ **538-416**) at the train station for more information.

• **By Boat** There are three car ferries per week between Thessaloníki and Skiáthos or Skópelos, once a week to Alónissos; call **01/41-78-084** for schedules and information. There's also infrequent service to Limnos, Lesvos, and Chios, and occasionally to the Dodecanese islands.

• **By Hydrofoil** The **Ceres Hydrofoil Company** in Piraeus (☎ **01/45-37-107** in Athens; ☎ **031/534-376** in Thessaloníki) offers daily service in summer between Thessaloníki and the Sporades, including Skiáthos, Skópelos, and Alónissos. The cruise between Thessaloníki and Skiáthos, for example, takes about three hours.

We dreaded going to Salonica after everything we'd heard about it, but were delighted with the city when we arrived. Yes, there's some air pollution, but the winds often carry it away; the harbor isn't pristine—what busy port is?—and it is a little smelly, but you soon get used to it; and the traffic whizzes past, but at least it's moving. Give it a chance and you'll find it one of the most cosmopolitan cities in Europe, full of vital, attractive, friendly people enjoying good shops, sights aplenty, excellent food, and a vibrant, varied nightlife.

In recent years Albanian and Serbian immigrants have thrown their culture and energy into the brew.

One of the city's many charms is that it isn't touristed-out. People won't eye you with contempt or as the next mark for a pitch, there are no rows of tacky souvenir stalls, and not a single T-shirt reading "I [heart] Thessaloníki"—though there are obviously a great many people who love it.

History

Greece's second-largest city and third-largest port is the capital of Alexander's country, a city founded as recently as 316 B.C. by the Macedonian General Kassandros. Just two decades earlier King Philip had won a decisive victory for his Thessalian allies at the Plain of Crocus; the daughter (Alexander's half-sister) born to him that year was named Thessaloníki ("Thessalian Victory") to commemorate it. When she was wed to General Kassandros, the city given to them as a home was renamed after her.

During the Roman occupation the Via Egnatia was paved as a through road between Rome, on the Adriatic coast, and Constantinople, capital of the Byzantine Empire. (Egnatia Street is still one of Thessaloníki's major arteries, paralleling the sea.) Under the Romans it became the most powerful city of northern Greece. Cicero had been exiled here; Antony and Octavius were welcomed in 42 B.C. after the Battle at Philippi, where Brutus and Cassius, conspirators against Julius Caesar, met their deaths. In gratitude, they made Thessaloníki a free city. Politarchs, or magistrates, were elected from the people to govern this Roman city, now independent like Athens.

Saint Paul arrived in about A.D. 49. From the Acts of the Apostles we're told: "They came to Thessaloníka, where there was a synagogue of the Jews. . . . And Paul went in, as was his custom, and for three weeks he argued with them from the scriptures . . . and some of them were persuaded, and joined Paul and Silas; as did a great many of the devout Greeks and not a few of the leading women." After he was forced to leave the city, he wrote his "Letter to the Thessalonians" to the newly converted Christians of Thessaloníki. (The Jewish population at that time, called the Romaniote, spoke Greek and traced their lineage to the days of Alexander's mission to Jerusalem in 333 B.C.)

In A.D. 306 the Emperor Galerius had Saint Dimitrios, the city's patron, put to death, a deed that caused many years of bloodshed throughout the Goth's occupation. By the seventh century, Thessaloníki was one of the greatest Byzantine cities and enjoyed a rare prosperity. In 1430 the Turkish forces of Murad II laid siege to the city; the Turks continued to rule here until 1912.

The expulsions of Jews from Spain during the reigns of Ferdinand V and Isabella (late 15th to early 16th centuries) caused nearly 20,000 to settle in Thessaloníki alone. By the time of the German invasion of Greece we know the Jewish population was over 60,000, and more than 35 synagogues were in use. (The very few Jews who survived World War II still speak Ladino, the old Sephardic tongue from their Basque homeland.)

Most of the architectural and artistic legacy of the Turkish occupation was eradicated by the Greeks, although two minarets and some hamams (Turkish baths) still stand. In this century alone, Thessaloníki has suffered terrible fires and severe bombings, yet something from each era has survived to sustain the patchwork whole we see today. From the Roman era there is the Arch of Galerius; then the great Byzantine chapels, mosaics, and frescoes; the White Tower on the harbor, a 16th-century Ottoman fortification; a stone on the waterfront that marks where King George I was assassinated by a Greek madman; some exquisite neoclassical office buildings and art deco apartments; the parklike exhibition grounds of the International Trade Fair begun in 1926 (which now draws over a million traders in mid-September); the tiered communications tower that dominates the field opposite the Archeological Museum. Thessaloníki's Aristotle University complex was built after the war over the old Jewish Cemetery.

Today the city is best known as a Byzantine city, for the wealth of art and architecture that remained from the centuries when Thessaloníki was second only to Constantinople. Recent archeological excavations at Dervéni and Vérgina (site of King Philip's tomb) have turned up such remarkable artifacts from the Macedonian period that we consider Thessaloníki most notable for its Archeological Museum and nearby sites.

Orientation

Don't be startled to find that this city of over half a million feels as large and bewildering as Athens. Those arriving by train or bus will be at the west end of the city, near Monastiríou Street, which in a few blocks becomes Egnatía Street. You'll confine most of your sightseeing to the rectangular area (about a 20-minute walk east) bordered by Egnatía Street on the north; Venizélou and Dragoúmi Streets, which end at Eleftherías Square, to the west; Níkis Street (Leofóros Vassiléos Konstantínou), the harborside avenue, on the south; and the park, Archeological Museum, and exhibition grounds to the east. **Platía Aristitélous** is a central meeting grounds on the waterfront at Níkis Street.

While you're here, walk over to the waterfront: to the left you'll see Thessaloníki's famous landmark, the **White Tower,** recently converted into a museum of local archeological finds and Byzantine treasures. From there, a five-minute walk inland on N. Germanou Street will bring you to the **Archeological Museum** and the exhibition grounds behind it. To the right of Platía Aristotélous is **Eleftheria Square** and the large pier for commercial vessels and the Sporadic North Aegean islands ferry. Between the port and the train and bus station, there are several budget hotels.

Lathóthika, the area to the west of Eleftherías Square, in from the waterfront, was once the red-light district, but recent regentrification has filled it with chic tavernas, bars, and restaurants.

If you walk straight up through the square to Aristotélous Street, the second intersection is Ermoú Street. There are several hotels to the left and the famed 8th-century, domed cruciform-shaped **Aghia Sophia Church.** The next major intersection north is Egnatía Street, for more than 2,000 years a major thoroughfare. Egnatía Street has become so noisy that it's impossible to recommend the older hotels seen everywhere along it.

To the right, at the intersection of Aristotélous and Egnatía Streets, you can look east to the third-century Arch of Galerius. Straight ahead, across Egnatía, is **Dikastirion Square.** On the left are the arched windows and dusty-brown brick of the 11th-century Panaghia Halkeon Cathedral; on the right is the Roman Exedra. Dikastírion Square serves as the bus terminal for most of the local Thessaloníki bus lines.

Getting Around

Thessaloníki is the major transportation hub for all vehicular, air, train, and water traffic in Macedonia and Thrace. Thousands of Europeans pour through Greece's northern borders with Yugoslavia and Bulgaria every July and August, though recent unrest in these countries has diminished traffic considerably.

BY CAR

If you've driven into Thessaloníki, good luck finding a parking space downtown. Many of the new hotels have parking lots and charge 660 Drs ($2.75) to 1,320 Drs ($5.50) a day for parking; there is a free parking lot near the White Tower and Archeological Museum. To explore Thessaloníki, park your car and walk, or sample the public bus system.

Driving is the easiest way to reach the popular seaside suburb of **Thermae,** just southeast of the city and somewhat comparable to Athens's Glyfáda. There are some excellent fish restaurants and "hot" outdoor discos in Thermae. **Panorama,** just 12km from the city center, is another popular suburb, quiet and prettier, with classy hotels, restaurants, cafés, and street life.

Renting a car is the most convenient way (and because of increased bus fares, a good value for two or more people) to explore the Alexander country. There's an **Avis** office (☎ **227-126**) at Odós Níkis 3 and at the airport; a **Hertz** office (☎ **277-787**) at Odós Venizélou 4 and at the airport (☎ **473-952**); a **Europcar** office at Odós G. Papandreou 5 (☎ **826-333,** fax 826-205) and at the airport (☎ **473-508**); as well as smaller, local rental companies. A compact car will cost about 20,570 Drs ($85.70), including insurance, per day. It's cheaper to make a reservation in the U.S.

BY BUS

City buses run regularly along the major streets; the fare is 82 Drs (35¢). Regional buses to Pella, Veria, Vergína, Kavala, and Metéora leave from the constellation terminal near the train station. Call **513-734** or EOT, the tourist office, for information.

Fast Facts: Thessaloníki

American Express The American Express bank, Odós Tsimiskí 19 (☎ **272-791**) Monday through Friday, 8am to 1:30pm is where you can cash or replace traveler's checks and pick up mail.

Banks The National Bank of Greece, Odós Tsimiskí 11, has extended hours from 8am to 1pm and 6 to 8pm, Monday through Friday; 8am to 2pm on Saturday; and 8am to 12pm on Sunday and holidays.

Kapa Bureau d'Echange (☎ **280-145**), Odós Egnatía 49-51, with slightly less-favorable rates of exchange, is open every day 8:30am–8:30pm.

Bookstores Foreign-language periodicals can be found at several kiosks near the port or Aristotélous Square, but the best selection can be found at Malliaris Kaisia, at Odós Aristotélous 9. This excellent bookstore also has a wide selection of regional maps, guidebooks, phrasebooks, tawdry romance novels, cardboard foldup models of Greek temples, and stationery and other supplies. They are open from 9am to 9pm daily. Molhos on Tsimiskí and Dragoúmi have a similar selection, including books about Mt. Áthos.

Consulates The American consulate (☎ **266-121**) is at Odós Níkis 59 (open 9am to 12pm Tuesday and Thursday) and the British vice consulate is at Odós Venizélou 8 (☎ **278-006**).

Emergencies Call **166** for medical emergencies; the Thessaloníki Red Cross is near the port, by the bus station.

Hairdressers Antigone (☎**266-012**), Odós Tsimiskí 90, second floor, open Mon–Sat, offers great cuts for 11,000 Drs ($46). They also do perms, dyes, and facials.

Laundry Bianca Laundry (☎ **209-602**), Odós Antioniadou 3, open Mon–Fri 8am–2pm, charges 1,725 Drs ($7.20) per load.

Ministries The Ministry of Northern Greece, Dikitríou Square (☎ **270-092**), is the place to apply for and pick up permits to visit the holy site of Mt. Áthos.

Post Office The central post office, open 7:30am to 8pm daily, where you can also change money, is off Aristotélous Street at Odós Tsimiskí 28.

Telephone Center [OTE] The OTE, open 24 hours a day, is at Karalou and Ermou streets.

Tourist Information On Platía Aristotélous you'll find the EOT at no. 8 (☎ **031/271-888**)—probably the best, friendliest and most helpful in Greece—open weekdays from 8am to 8pm Monday through Friday, Saturday, and Sunday until 2pm.

What to See & Do

If you're only in Thessaloníki for one hour, and it costs you $50 to get there and back, we still say the Archeological Museum and its contents are an unforgettable, not-to-be-missed, once-in-a-lifetime experience. Continuing excavations at Vergína (site of Philip of Macedon's Royal Tomb) have added such lustrous displays to this well laid out, lit, and maintained museum that anyone should be able to enjoy it.

THE ARCHEOLOGICAL MUSEUM

The Archeological Museum (☎ **830–538**), on YMCA Square (Platía Hanth), two blocks up from the White Tower at the intersection of Angelaki and Tsimiskí Streets, is organized in two circles: the inner galleries are dedicated to recent finds from Sindos; the outer circle is most of the older portion of the museum. A new wing houses the magnificent finds at Derveni and Vergína.

The Sindos wing, opened in 1982, displays 6th- to 5th-century B.C. examples of gold hair ornaments, jewelry, filigree pendants, dollhouse-size tables and chairs, and some delicate miniature glass amphoras. Most of these tombs were found underwater, so all metal other than gold was badly damaged. The buried warrior's golden face mask and helmet from 520 B.C. are particularly impressive. One case has gold-filigree pomegranates the size of a baby's fingernail, but carved in such detail that you can't imagine anyone's fingers being small enough to create it.

In the next galleries there are grave steles from Veria and fine marble statues from the ancient Agora of Thessaloníki, from around the 1st to 2d centuries A.D. In the central gallery you'll find a fascinating display devoted to 2,300 years of Thessaloníki daily life, including a striking 3d-century mosaic from a local house. In the fourth gallery there's a bold, strong sculpture of Emperor Augustus, still obviously very much in control even if frozen in stone.

At Derveni, gold and bronze from the last half of the 4th century B.C., as well as ornate silverwork burial gifts, were found. In the beginning of the gallery are finds from a royal tomb at Katerini and from Thermi and Stavroupolis. But the real prizes are from Vergina, the first great capital of Macedonia, birthplace of King Philip II. Excavations in the late 1970s unearthed one of the most important archeological finds since the Tut tombs, the royal tomb of Philip himself, untouched in 2,100 years. The riches of the find are staggering, none more so than the exquisite crown of the great king. The solid gold funerary box is another example of the fine level of craftsmanship of the Macedonians; even the bones of Philip are displayed, providing an eerie experience for the viewer. Imagine the man that was Philip—a great leader, warrior, king—now a set of surprisingly small bones that today are far overshadowed by the splendor of the objects found with him in the royal tomb. This is a gallery not to be missed. Professor Andronicos's museum guide is great and a must for the quality of the reproductions!

The museum is open Monday from 10:30am to 7pm, Tuesday to Friday from 8am to 7pm, and Saturday and Sunday from 8:30am to 3pm. Admission costs 1,100 Drs ($4.60), free on Sunday. Video, 330 Drs ($1.40) extra. Professor Andronicos's museum guide is 1,100 Drs ($4.60).

OTHER MUSEUMS

There are other interesting stops in Thessaloníki.

White Tower (Historical and Art Museum of Thessaloníki), Lefkos Piŕgos Square. ☎ **267-832.**

The White Tower, also called the Bloody Tower (Lefkos Pirgos) because it was the site of a Turkish massacre of Christian soldiers, was built in the early 16th century after designs by the renowned Ottoman architect, Sinan. The interior has been recently renovated to house local archeological finds and Byzantine treasures. Take time to visit the display downstairs before you climb the broad stone stairs that spiral up and around inside the cool cylinder and lead to five small display floors. Marble architectural ornaments, column fragments, mosaics, 4th- to 5th-century tombs with wall paintings, and Byzantine jewelry, coins and religious paintings fill the vaulted coves and wonderful low-ceilinged galleries. Don't miss the small side rooms you have to stoop to enter and especially the two enameled, carved gold Byzantine bracelets on the third floor. The top is usually open for a good view of the city.

Admission: 550 Drs ($2.30).

Open: Mon 12:30–7pm, Tues–Fri 8am–7pm, Sat–Sun 8:30am–3pm. **Transportation/Directions:** On the waterfront, two blocks west of archeological museum.

Macedonian Folk and Ethnographic Museum, Odós Vassilias Olgas 68.
☎ **830-591.**

This museum exhibits items connected with the pre-industrial era of northern Greece. There are myriad ornaments, weapons, and household items. We particularly liked the costumes and folk arts displays.

Admission: 550 Drs ($2.30).

Open: Fri–Wed 9:30am–2pm. **Transportation/Directions:** One block inland from harbor, two long blocks south of Archeological Museum.

A WALKING TOUR OF THESSALONÍKI

Our walking tour begins with a quick coffee on Thessaloníki's most attractive square, **Platía Aristotelous.** The platía opens up to Níkis Street, the waterfront drive along the city's busy port. Make a left on the portside avenue and proceed until you come to the **White Tower,** a symbol of medieval Thessaloníki and now, a museum. Continue up Vassileos Georgiou; to your left, two blocks east of the White Tower, is the **Archeological Museum.** At this point you might want to stop for a look at what is fast becoming Greece's premier collection.

To continue with the walking tour, turn left on Angelaki, and after five blocks, turn left on Egnatía until reaching the massive **Arch of Galerius,** now shrouded in scaffolding. The arch was constructed in A.D. 303 to commemorate the Roman victories of Emperor Galerius over forces in Persia, Armenia, and Asia Minor. The reliefs, which portray the battle with the Persians, have been badly eroded, though the arch is still impressive. Walk through it, continuing to the domed **Rotunda.** Built only a few years after the arch, the Rotunda served as a mausoleum for the emperor. Later it was converted to a Christian sanctuary and decorated with masterful mosaics. In 1590 it was converted into a mosque and remained in use under the Ottomans until 1912.

EOT expects a renovated Rotunda to be open to the public in the summer of 1995! Line up to view the finely executed mosaics within.

The next stop will be of particular interest for those coming from or headed to Turkey. Walk north from the Rotunda, away from Egnatía, until you reach the next main avenue, Aghios Dimitriou. Continue to the right along Dimitriou a couple of blocks up to the Turkish consulate (it's the "compound" on the corner of Aghios Pavlou Street), and next door, the **birthplace of Mustafa Kemal Atatürk.** Born in 1881,

Ataturk is revered in Turkey as the father of the modern nation. All political parties in Turkey, from anarchist to totalitarian, rally behind the teachings and ideals of Ataturk. The house (open from 9am to noon, Monday through Friday) contains historical photos, Turkish-style furniture, and other paraphernalia. Apply to the Turkish consulate for entry to this fascinating site. Don't be alarmed if they request your passport as a "deposit"; it's the price you'll pay for "security" precautions.

Return to Egnatía and cross the street, to the subterranean **Church of the Metamorphosi** (in between the two parallel streets that run perpendicular to Germanou). This one isn't on the normal tour route, but we liked it for its sunken, listing foundation and the perfectly preserved Byzantine brick-and-tile exterior. (If you've stopped at the church and are looking for a bite to eat, try the **Koumparakia Restaurant,** which overlooks this tiny sanctuary.)

Two blocks down, on diagonally running Patriorhou Ioakim, is one of Thessaloníki's most important Byzantine churches, **Aghía Sophía.** Constructed in the eighth century, Aghía Sophía marked an important turning point in Western architecture by incorporating the Oriental cupola and a cruciform style over the older basilica form. When the Ottomans ruled Thessaloníki, the church was converted to a mosque. The interior mosaics, including a figure of Christ enthroned on a rainbow and surrounded by the Apostles and olive trees, date from the 11th century.

Return to Egnatía, turn left, and make a right on Aghía Sophía Street to the **Panagia Achiropiitos.** The name means "Our Lady not done (that is, painted) by (human) hands," referring to the icon that is said to have miraculously appeared at this, one of the oldest Byzantine churches in Thessaloníki (fifth century). The mosaics on the upper walls and finely filtered light from the arched windows are reason enough to take a quick look inside (opening hours are erratic).

Continue up Egnatía, turning right at the bus station and following the road two blocks to the **Roman Agora** and **theater.** Thessaloníki was the Roman capital of the Macedonian province, and one of the most significant cities in the empire. The large square contains the few remains of what was once a center of Roman activity; a theater, vestiges of the water system, and a solitary column are all that survive. Above the northern perimeter of the market is a small, shaded park that's ideal for a rest, picnic, or cool drink.

For those who may be disappointed that so many of the famous churches are closed or under scaffolding, consider taking an out-of-the-way interlude in this otherwise geographically concentrated walking tour. The eventual destination is **Ossios David,** a 5th-century church with mosaics of the Vision of Ezekiel. The location is Epimenidou (the "old town," much like Pláka in Athens), and instead of giving you detailed directions on how to get there (difficult), we'll give some general guidelines. Walk away from the direction of Egnatía, crossing Águios Dimitriou and past the huge reconstructed church of Ághios Dimitrios (stop in if you're touring on Sunday; they have baptismal ceremonies all morning long and it's quite an experience!). Continue in the same direction up Ághios Nikólaos Street and veer right onto Epimenidou. Somewhere in that neighborhood is tiny Aghia David. Ask any passerby for exact directions.

Return to the Platía Dikastirion on Egnatía and the 11th-century **Panaghia Halkeon.** According to an inscription the church was built in 1028. If such a thing is possible, the Panagia Halkeon could be characterized as a "seductive" sanctuary, with soft Byzantine curves and domes and highly articulated doorways.

Alternating brick, mortar, and stone add a subtle pattern to the church's classical design.

Walk down Venizélou back toward the platía and you'll pass the **Bedestan,** or Ottoman bazaar, still filled with jewelers. You'll see the main shopping streets, where shoes and clothes are often a bargain. Our recommendation is to complete the tour by returning to Aristotélous *platía,* ordering a fresh, delicious Greek lemonade—and congratulating yourself on seeing the best of Thessaloníki.

Where to Stay

In Thessaloníki there are more older hotels in the budget-price range and more new ones in the business expense-account range. This probably reflects the surge of visitors who arrive each August and September for the International Trade Fair; during the Trade Fair (when demand is high) many hotels raise their prices by 15% to 20% or make continental breakfast compulsory. Another drawback in the Thessaloníki hotel scene is that many of the city's budget hotels are in neighborhoods that have become intolerably noisy in recent years. So although some of our recommendations mean that you'll have to walk an extra few blocks to sightsee, at least you'll be getting enough sleep to enjoy it.

The most popular of the nearby campgrounds on a beach (the water is polluted at the commercial port) is Aghía Triáda, where the EOT has organized campgrounds (☎ **0392/51-360**).

AROUND DIIKITIRÍOU SQUARE

This area, once a quiet enclave of professional people, fashionable shops and government offices, remains pleasant but marred by an ugly excavation. Locals complain about Albanian immigrants in a nearby park, though it looked peaceful enough to us. Some good-value hotels can still be found here.

Hotel Bill, Odós Amvrossíou 16, Thessaloníki 56230. ☎ **031/537-666.**
21 rms (all with bath). TEL

Rates: 4,730 Drs ($19.70) single; 7,150 Drs ($29.80) double. No credit cards.

An excellent value, with balconies and baths in some of the large clean double rooms that compete with much pricier establishments. Kyle slept well here!

Hotel Esperia, Odós Olympou 58, Thessaloníki 54631. ☎ **031/269-321.**
Fax 031/269-457. 70 rms (all with bath). A/C TV TEL

Rates (including breakfast): 15,147 Drs ($63.11) single; 16,962 Drs ($70.68) double. No credit cards.

The rooms are carpeted, each has a large tiled bathtub, and the front balconies overlook the classical Ministry of Northern Greece building. Newly refurbished, it offers very high quality and a friendly staff. When you exit the hotel, two blocks to the right you'll find the ruins of the Roman agora and across the street, the café favored by off-duty policemen and bus drivers.

Park Hotel, Odós Dragoumi 81, Thessaloníki 54630. ☎ **031/524-121.**
Fax 031/524-193. 56 rms (all with bath). A/C TEL

Rates (including breakfast): 13,750 Drs ($57.30) single; 15,400 Drs ($64.20) double. V.

This hotel has a large modern lobby and bar that come as close to a Hilton as you'll find in this price range. Spacious rooms have air conditioning and music; many have refrigerators and television.

NEAR THE PORT

The port is always Kyle's first choice of where to stay, and in Thessaloníki it's the nicest area!

Hotel Continental, Odós Komninou 5, Thessaloníki 54624. ☎ **031/277-553.**
39 rms (15 with bath and A/C). TEL

Rates: 4,950 Drs ($20.60) single without bath; 11,000 Drs ($45.80) double with bath. No credit cards.

A block off the water between Eleftherias and Aristotélous Squares, it's "continental" on the outside only. Inside it's ordinary, but clean and quiet—except for the TV blaring in the little lobby.

Hotel Luxemburg, Odós Komninou 6, Thessaloníki 54624. ☎ **031/278-449.**
29 rms (6 with bath).

Rates: 4,100 Drs ($17.10) single without bath; 6,800 Drs ($28.20) double with bath. No cards.

You won't believe the prices when you see the spiffy Beaux-Arts exterior. The rooms (except for the ceilings) don't live up to the promise, but they're clean, quiet, and comfortable—and, presently at least, the best value in town.

Hotel Tourist, Odós Mitropoléos 21, Thessaloníki 54624. ☎ **031/276-335.**
Fax 031/229-796. 37 rms (all with bath). TEL

Rates: 8,470 Drs ($35.30) single without bath; 10,230 Drs ($42.60) double with bath. No credit cards.

The exterior of this old-fashioned hotel on a fairly quiet street has been recently renovated, and the lobby is spare with an attractive glass-doored cage elevator, though the desk man is a little short on charm. The halls are spacious, as are most of the rooms, with high molded ceilings.

YWCA, Odós Mitropoléos 18, Thessaloníki 54624. ☎ **031/276-144.** 65 beds.

Rates: Not yet available.

The YWCA, an old favorite, was moving to new quarters during our last visit; we hope they're as cozy and pleasant as the old ones were.

NEAR THE RAILROAD AND BUS STATIONS

Though not our favorite neighborhood, the area near the railroad station (leading into Egnatía) may be convenient for late-night bus or train arrivals, even though our other hotel recommendations are all within a five-minute 1000 Drs ($4.15) cab ride or 20-minute walk of the railroad station.

Hotel Rex, Odós Monastiríou 39, Thessaloníki 54627. ☎ **031/517-051.**
59 rms (22 with bath). TEL

Rates: 7,700 Drs ($29.20) single without bath; 10,450 Drs ($43.50) double with bath. No credit cards.

Across the street and one long block to the left of the station, its third-floor sun roof has an urban sort of charm, but its captive clientele hasn't done much for the manners of the staff.

Hotel Vergina, Odós Monastiríou 19, Thessaloníki 54627. ☎ **031/516-021.** Fax 031/529-308. 133 rms (all with bath). A/C TEL

Rates (including breakfast): 16,500 Drs ($68.70) single; 19,745 Drs ($82.30) double. AE, MC, V.

Down the road a bit from the station, this well-managed eight-story, white concrete edifice has pleasant, spacious rooms with balconies—a few with telephones, televisions, and ceiling fans.

NEAR EGNATÍA STREET

As befits any inn astride a through road in operation for thousands of years, the hotels along busy Egnatía Street are, if nothing else, very convenient, but above all, noisy.

Hotel Acropol, Tandalidou 4. ☎ **031/536-170.** 30 rooms (none with bath). TEL

Rates: 4,400 Drs ($18) single; 4,950 Drs ($20.60) double.

This modest, budget hotel is around the corner from Egnatía—and a bit removed from the noise—with an attractive vine hanging over the entranceway. Large rooms with their own sinks are drab but clean, and the shared bathrooms are immaculate, with real bathtubs. The Acropol is no beauty. What makes it special is the owners, the Hatjitheodorou family, who are all outstandingly helpful, friendly, and understanding of the weary traveler.

Hotel Amalia, Odós Ermoú 33, ☎ **031/268-321.** Fax 233-356. 66 rooms, all with private bath. TEL

Rates: 10,230 Drs ($42.60) single; 13,090 Drs ($54.50) double.

This modern hotel was recommended to us by locals. It's not a bad value for the large, bright, blue and white rooms, many of which have balconies. Although it's right on Ermoú, the thick glass windows seem to provide some insulation against noise.

Hotel Ariston, Odós Diikitiriou 5, Thessaloníki 54623. ☎ **031/519-630.** 35 rms (11 with bath). TEL

Rates: 6,600 Drs ($27.50) single without bath; 11,000 Drs ($45.85) double with bath. No credit cards.

This older hotel is about 50 meters northeast of where four other streets intersect at Democracy Square. (The street signs read Karaóli and Dimitríou, and some maps label it Churchill, but everyone still calls it Diikitiríou.) Some of the bathless rooms have strange, amusing "Murphy"-style pull-out showerstalls, others are American-style, with the toilet outside in the hall. It's an adventure staying at the Ariston, so if you don't like what you're led to, ask for something else; they're very accommodating.

Hotel Augustus, Odós Svorónou 4, ☎ **031/522-550, 522-955.** 20 rooms, all with shared bath.

Rates: 4,400 Drs ($18) single; 4,950 Drs ($20.60) double.

You'll recognize this beaux arts–style building near Platía Dimokratía by its handsome flatiron shape. The interior doesn't live up to its ornate facade, but the plain rooms are clean, recently renovated, and come with their own sinks. Shared bathrooms are well maintained. The Augustus is just off the Egnatía, so it manages to escape the incessant traffic roar.

Youth Hostel, Odós Svólou 44, Thessaloníki 56224. ☎ **031/225-946.**

Rates: 1,650 Drs ($6.90) bed in double or triple dorm. No credit cards.

The manager of this co-ed hostel near the Archeological Museum is helpful when he's there (8:30am to noon and 7pm to midnight), but there's no linen or cooking facilities. Hot water for showers is available only in the evenings, and the bedrooms are closed from noon to 5:30pm for cleaning—not sleeping!

Where to Eat

There's a *joie de vivre* among the Salonicans that makes dining out in this cosmopolitan city an unexpected pleasure. There are many tried-and-true restaurants that the International Trade Fair has kept alive, as well as many inexpensive, simple tavernas and grills, and westernized fast-food chains that a traveler in any budget range can afford.

NEAR THE PORT

You'll find most of the older and better eateries as well as some glitzy new ones near the harbor and Aristotélous Square. One block up from Aristotélous Square on the right you'll find the **Terkenlis Bakery and Confectionary** at Odós Tsimiskí 30, with the best pastries and sweets in town, probably in Macedonia and possibly in all Greece.

Clochard, Odós Koromilá 4. ☎ **239-805.**

Cuisine: INTERNATIONAL. **Reservations:** Recommended.

Prices: Appetizers 500–1,800 Drs ($2.10–$7.40); main courses 1,320–4,000 Drs ($5.40–$16.70). DC.

Open: Daily 8pm–2pm; Sat noon–3pm.

As you'd expect from the name the accent is on the French in this *très chic* piano bar on a small street one block off the harbor in the center of town, which serves only the very best meats and fresh fish in season grilled to perfection in it international kitchen. You'll want to dress up for this very sophisticated restaurant.

Olympos-Naoussa, Odós Níkis 5. ☎ **275-715.**

Cuisine: CONTINENTAL. **Reservations:** Recommended.

Prices: Appetizers 480–690 Drs ($2–$2.90); main courses 590–1,390 Drs ($2.50–$5.80). No credit cards.

Open: Mon–Fri 12–4pm.

Just down the street from the port, traditional continental cuisine is served in this elegant, older restaurant that caters to the suit, tie, and grandmother crowd. We recommend the *midia tiganita,* a local specialty of fried mussels. The service is good, even when busy and there is also less formal, outdoor seating.

Rogotis Restaurant Grill, Odós Venizélou 8. ☎ **277-694.**

Cuisine: GREEK/CONTINENTAL.

Prices: Appetizers 770–1,000 ($3.20–$4.20); main courses 990–3,100 Drs ($4.10–$12.92). AE, DC, EC, MC.

Open: Mon, Wed, Sat 10:30am–5:30pm; Tues, Thurs, Fri 10:30am–11:30pm.

This old-fashioned, dark-wood taverna is just off Eleftherias Square. Known by its former street address but actually named Souzoukákia, it has a large and interesting menu with varied *mezédes* (appetizers), meat dishes, grilled and skewered fish, and a tasty, ground veal souzoukákia that's made daily.

Stratis, Odós Níkis 19. ☎ **279-353.**

Cuisine: GREEK. **Reservations:** Recommended.

Prices: Appetizers 240–1,309 Drs ($1–$5.40); main courses 990–3,000 Drs ($4.10–$12.50). AE, V.

Open: Daily noon–midnight.

This very attractive, low-key restaurant across from the harbor has a varied, traditional Greek menu: lots of meats, excellent imported wines, seafood specialties, and a range of excellently prepared and displayed *mezédes* (the traditional array of appetizer-size portions of piquant foods, best had with ouzo or wine). The regionally produced Corona white wine is particularly good.

Ta Nicia, Odós Prox. Koromilá 13. ☎ **285-991.**

Cuisine: SEAFOOD. **Reservations:** Recommended.

Prices: Appetizers 550–2,530 Drs ($2.30–$10.50); main courses 1,980–3,300 Drs ($8.25–$13.75). AE, EC, MC, V.

Open: Daily noon–5pm, 8pm–1am.

If you didn't know the name means "the islands," you might think it had something to do with Nice—only nicer—because there is something a little French about this intimate little place a block off the harbor, where the best seafood in town is prepared in a *nouvelle* Greek manner all its own. You won't often find mussels, crab, and cuttlefish cooked so originally or served with such simple elegance. If you're lucky you might find walnut pie or quince baked in white wine for dessert.

Totis Cafe Pâtisserie, Odós Aghías Sophías 2. ☎ **265-330.**

Cuisine: SNACKS/DESSERTS.

Prices: Desserts 640–1,320 Drs ($2.70–$5.50), coffee 605–990 Drs ($2.50–$4.10). No credit cards.

Open: Daily 8am–2am.

For light snacks, heavy ice-cream sundaes, and tart fresh lemonade try the Totis Café at the corner of Vass. Konstantinou. Its comfy, leather-plush chairs are often filled with postcard writers, children, weary parents, and youngsters in love. It's not cheap, but it's alive and lots of fun.

Zythos, Odós Katoúni 5, ☎ **540-284.**

Cuisine: GREEK. **Reservations:** Not required.

Prices: Appetizers 605–1,650 Drs ($2.50–$6.90); main courses 825–2,530 Drs ($10.54). No credit cards.

Open: daily: 7am–1am.

This popular restaurant was one of the first to open in Lathóthika, the newly hip area west of Eleftherias Square. There are four other fine dining choices right on Odós Katoúni, but this was the one we fell in love with. Zythos has airy wooden tables and canvas chairs on the street outside, an elegant interior of high ceilings, little wooden café tables and tiled floors, and pleasant, low-key service. But the inventive, delicious food is the real drawing point. We loved their deep-fried mushroom fritters and cheese-stuffed squid, and devoured a chicken souvlaki plate of tender skewers wrapped in smoky bacon.

NEAR THE ARCHEOLOGICAL MUSEUM

Impero Pizza, Odós Smírnis 12. ☎ **239-103.**

Prices: Main courses 440–1,870 Drs ($1.80–$7.80). No credit cards.
Open: Daily 9am–4pm, 6pm–3am.

Just up the street from the U.S. consulate (at Odós Nikis 59) you'll find this little café that serves delicious pizza. Resident Yanks claim that it's the best in town—and who knows more about pizza? Besides which, they speak English, thanks much to the American music they play.

Ta Koubarakia, Odós Egnatía 140. ☎ **271-905** or **268-442.**

Cuisine: GREEK.
Prices: Appetizers 330–600 Drs ($1.40–$2.50); main courses 1,200–2,300 Drs ($5–$9.60). No credit cards.
Open: Mon–Sat noon–4pm, 8pm–12am.

This café, centrally located for day-tour walkers across Egnatía and west from the Arch of Galerius, behind the Sunken Byzantine Church, is always filled with Greeks licking their lips over the excellent grilled calamari and broiled whole fish. If you can't read the menu, politely venture inside this very clean little place and choose from their fresh, attractive selection.

Tiffany's, Odós Iktínou 3. ☎ **274-022.**

Cuisine: GREEK.
Prices: Appetizers 330–1,375 Drs ($1.40–$5.70); main courses 1,080–3,950 Drs ($4.50–$16.40). No credit cards.
Open: Daily noon–midnight.

No breakfast, but lunch and dinner are exceptional at this attractive outdoor and indoor taverna on a quiet, shaded pedestrian mall, just a five-minute walk from the Archeological Museum, in the shopping district. We suggest their tangy *magiritsa* (lamb liver with egg and lemon soup), *ambelophylla* (their delicious variation of stuffed vine leaves), and *kolokythakia yemista* (squash stuffed with minced meat in egg and lemon sauce).

Evening Entertainment

The liveliest and most varied night life in Thessaloníki can be found late nights along and off the harbor, in what the locals call the center of town, especially along and around Proxenou Koromila Street. We recommend two restaurants on the quieter west end, but if you're looking for something a little wilder meander east toward the White Tower; you could enjoy just watching others enjoy themselves. **Divus Dancing Hall** (☎ **286-067**), Odós Proxenou Koromila 51, pretty much lives up to its name after 10pm. During our last visit the hottest spot was **P.O.** (☎ **273-030**) at Odós Níkis 77, where the local young people were enjoying themselves immensely to American music. **Aroma** (☎ **284-858**), Odós Nikis 63, is a smart-looking cafeteria during the day, but after 9pm it's a chic nightclub.

The big hit with us on our last trip was **Milos** (☎ **525-968**), Odós Gheorghíou 56, an old mill and satellite building transformed into an entertainment complex with an art gallery, theater, several excellent restaurants, bars, and live music clubs that range from classical to heavy metal. It's west of the center of town, best reached by taxi; the fare should be about 1,100 Drs ($4.60) one way.

The bar scene changes seasonally, so this year's picks may be next year's duds. The summer disco crowd moves outdoors and out of town, on the road just past the airport, where presumably the decibel level won't disturb sleeping planes. The favorites were **Boudroum, Evergreen** and **Kaos,** but don't take our word for it; ask around. Most are open June through September and charge about 1,700 Drs ($7.20) for admission and one drink. It's about a 12 km 1,300 Drs ($5.50) cab ride to get there, but don't bother going before 11pm because the crowds are still at the bars.

If you're up for a nighttime *vólta,* that leisurely Greek saunter, there's no better place to do it than along the harbor in front of Aristotélous Square. Beyond the White Tower you can escape the traffic and be romanced by the moon and the waves, or at least entertained by others enjoying romance and various other quiet amusements. If you wander west to the waterfront around the commercial and ferryboat pier, and particularly up to the region of Polytechniou and 26 Otovriou Streets, you'll find some colorful ladies of the night, along with clubs, bars, and neon signs.

To escape reality, sample the cinemas near the White Tower. The **Aristoteleion** (☎ **232-557**), at Ethnikis Aminis Plaza 2, is a grand old 1,000-seat palace that plays recent American films in full Dolby stereo. Farther east at Odós Níkis 73 is the **Cinema Pallaso** (☎ **278-515**), for recent European fare and schlock American B-movies. Both the **White Tower** on N. Germanou Street and the **Dimotiko Teatro Kipou** have outdoor performances (check with EOT for schedules).

2 Chalkidikí & Mt. Áthos

GETTING THERE • By Bus Polígiros (69 kilometers from Thessaloníki) and other communities are serviced by regular buses from the Thessaloníki station (☎ **513-734**) at Odós 26 Oktovriou 100.

Chalkidiki (Halkidikí), the three-fingered peninsula settled centuries ago by sailors from Chalkís in Évvia, is revered by the Greeks for its lush pine forests and gold sand beaches. Now, however, most of the forests have been cut back to make way for the condos and the narrow beach strips are so overcrowded that it's hard to tell the sand from the flesh.

Kassándra, the westernmost (left, on a map) finger of the peninsula was the first to be developed. The roads throughout are packed with condominiums and vacation villas for Thessalonikans, and there are hotels or mega-resort complexes for European group tourists around each sandy strip.

Sithonía, the middle finger, has a more densely forested interior and a very rugged and beautiful coastline, whose few sand beaches have been much less developed. Campers will find ample opportunities along the west coast, especially at Nikitas, Tripotamos, and Pórto Koufó. Along the east coast there are campsites at the beaches of Sárti, Ághios Sikiás, and Kalamítsi, and as always, rooms to let along the coast road and in the larger inland villages such as Sikiá. Sithonia's biggest resort complex is at Néos Marmarás, now renamed Pórto Carras after its developer. He planted one million grape vines, almond trees, orange and grapefruit groves, and flowering bushes after filling in a mosquito-breeding lake at this picturesque site. Besides its three hotels—the Meliton, the Sithonia Beach, and the slightly more modest Village Inn—Mr. Carras built a marina, several swimming pools, tennis courts, and an 18-hole golf course.

The eastern (or right) finger of Chalkidiki is **Mt. Áthos** (Ágion Óros, the Holy Mountain), the independent Greek Orthodox state revered by the Greeks. The 20 monasteries of this most scenically beautiful of the fingers are closed to women visitors, and will only allow ten men ashore each day to visit (see the Mt. Áthos section below on information regarding permits). You can visit Ouranopoli (the closest "open" city) by bus, but this small village gets inundated with day-trippers who join the Round-Áthos Cruises and will not provide the spiritual experience that women readers might seek. Instead, you'd do well to join a Mt. Áthos day trip or quietly explore Ierissos (the ancient Acanthos), Gomati, or Megáli Panagia on your own. Also of interest in the eastern sector is Arnea, a mountain town whose women are known for hand-weaving, making shopping for fabrics and flokati rugs a real treat. Aristotle, the great philosopher, was born in nearby Stagira, where he lived for several years until heading north to tutor King Philip of Macedon's son, Alexander.

What to See & Do

You can take the public bus to Polígiros, the capital of Chalkidiki, but unfortunately the drive doesn't take you through any of the beautiful scenery for which the peninsula is justly famed. **Polígiros** has become a good-sized modern town of little interest to most tourists, save for the **Archeological Museum** near its north end. Museum and archeology fans will find the collection of primitive clay figurines from the 5th century B.C., and the Picasso-esque style of painting on the black figure vases particularly pleasing. For the cognoscenti, there are fragments from the Sanctuary of Zeus Ammon near Kallithéa on the Kassandra finger and finds from the ancient city of Acanthos (at Ierissos), where Aristotle taught. The museum is open Tuesday through Sunday from 8:30am to 3pm. Admission is 550 Drs ($2.30).

If this is as far as you'll get in Chalkidiki, and you have the energy, a hike up *Profitis Ilías hill* provides a wonderful prospect. West of Polígiros is the village of **Petralona,** famous for its natural cave, where a skull and some remains were found indicating habitation by a primeval man more than 700,000 years old (the first tourist?). The cave is filled with colorful stalagmites and stalactites and the paleontological museum at the site is quite interesting; open daily from 9am to 6pm Petralona can be reached twice daily by bus via Néa Kalikrátia and is also the object of many local day tours.

For those with only a day, we'd recommend one of the **Mt. Athos cruise** excursions that originate in Thessaloníki. As offered by **Doucas Tours (☎ 031/224-100)**, Odós Venizélou 8 on Platía Eleftherias, this day trip costs 10,500 Drs ($43.80) for a coach tour across Chalkidiki to Órmos Panagía on the central finger of Sithonia, then a cruise along the west coast of Athos to Ouranópolis (see below).

If you'll have an opportunity to visit other resorts in Greece (such as the Ionian islands, the western coast south of Ioannina, and much of the Peloponnese), which offer the same lovely combination of green forests and sand beaches, we'd suggest you avoid the crowded Chalkidiki resorts.

Mt. Áthos

The monastic community inhabiting 20 monasteries and 700 related houses perched on the Holy Mountain has remained untouched by time since St. Anathasios founded the Lávra Monastery in A.D. 963. At its peak, Áthos had 40,000 monks; the Crusaders sold 39,000 of them into slavery. Today, Mt. Áthos is an independent religious state that's not even part of Greece: The monks follow their own Orthodox calendar (whose year begins 17 days after ours); their time zone is four hours later than at Ouranopolis, the nearest lay community. In the 1981 census, Áthos had 1,500 residents; only 20 or 25 monks still live at each of the open monasteries.

Many of the customs practiced at Mt. Áthos are unique, but the basic precepts of the Orthodox religion are the same as those studied at Tínos, Pátmos, and Metéora (Greece's other religious enclaves). The Orthodox service you'll hear on Áthos is the same you'd hear in Moscow, Bucharest, or Sofia. Visitors with some knowledge of the Orthodox faith will gain tremendously from their conversations with the monks, all of whom are well educated and speak several languages. The Bibles, icons, frescoes, and religious art displayed in the monasteries make up one of the best collections of its kind in the world.

Laymen (no women) can get permission to stay for up to four days on the Holy Mountain. Days are spent hiking between the monasteries and exploring the lush, forested, and flowering countryside. By sunset you must reach the monastery where you'll spend the night because then doors are locked. The monks farm (they grow their own food), study and pray in the early morning, and sleep in the afternoon. Nights are spent dining, and talking with the few guests they receive. Meals consist of locally grown eggplant, onions, olives, and bread, with the occasional tomato, cucumber, or fresh fish (if one is caught). The monks will offer you wine and their homemade ouzo to soften the sudden austerity the lay visitor meets.

Of the 20 monasteries that are open, **Lávra,** the oldest and one of the few that hasn't been rebuilt, is the most architecturally pure. Fortress walls surround this stone, wood-trimmed Byzantine compound. The **Monastery of Símonos Pétras** is perched on top of a 6,700-foot-high cliff, where Simon built it in the mid-14th century. It was rebuilt by the Serbians, and after a 1581 fire, was restored by funds from the Orthodox faithful of Bucharest. Between 1821 and 1891 it was closed by the Turks (Mt. Áthos as a whole remained fairly autonomous under the Turkish occupation), and in 1891 suffered another fire that destroyed the library. Like many monasteries, Simonos Petras boasts such treasures as the left hand of Saint Magdalene and the hand of Saint Dionysios of Zakynthos.

The 13th-century **Monastery of St. Gregory** was deserted in 1500, rebuilt by the governor of Moldovlahia, and burned down in 1761. It was restored and its church dedicated to St Nicholas. At St. Gregory are the two legs and right palm of St Anastasia Romaia, as well as beautiful icons and frescoes in the church. The **Monastery of Zográphou** is famous for its library, which contains early ecclesiastical codes and 66 codes on parchment of 16th- to 19th-century Byzantine music. Fortunately, a 1976 fire that destroyed one wing left the library unharmed.

The 12th-century **Monastery of Panteleímon** has been called the Russian monastery since the 14th century, when it was rebuilt with Serbian and Byzantine funds after a fire. After Greek monks abandoned it for one near the coast, a Russian abbot was elected, and for 100 years the main mass has been given in Russian and Greek. The 19th-century influx of Russian Orthodoxy has left its mark visually on all the monasteries that have been partially rebuilt or restored since that time. (Recent interest expressed by the patriarch of Moscow is said to somewhat concern the Greek government.) In 1963 the Holy Mountain celebrated its first millennium of religious occupation, an event that brought the unique Mt. Áthos to the attention of the world.

GETTING TO ÁTHOS

Only ten foreign male lay visitors are granted permission to remain overnight on Mt. Áthos each night. It is suggested that interested parties make application three to four months in advance of their planned arrival; a dated entry permit will then be issued. To obtain the permit, you must send a letter, including: details of your passport (or a photocopy); personal or professional information, including why you want to visit Mt. Áthos; a declaration of your "intention to be a pilgrim"; and a letter of recommendation from your consulate. Address the letter to the Ministry of Northern Greece, Dükitiriou Square, 54623 Thessaloníki. They will preapply for you, requesting your dates. Applicants in Athens may contact EOT or the Ministry of Foreign Affairs, who will then forward your request to the Thessaloníki office. Interested readers in religious professions should apply to the Ecumenical Patriarchate, Istanbul, Turkey, in a letter noting their religious background.

Once you've been notified in writing that your request has been granted and your date is issued, you'll have to pick up your permit personally from the Ministry of Northern Greece on Ághios Dimitriou Street, which is open only Monday through Friday. To reach Mt. Áthos, take a bus from Odós Karakassi 68, Thessaloníki, to Ouranopolis on Chalkidiki. There is one boat a day to Dafní (2 hours), the harbor of Mt. Áthos. You must show your letter of permission to board the boat. From Dafní, you can take the bus 12 kilometers uphill to Karyes, the administrative capital of Áthos. There, you'll present your letter for a Diamonitirion, a pass enabling you to visit other monasteries. There is no charge for room or board at any of them, but the boat trip and pass will cost about $60.

Note: Women should not even try to win this battle; **Doucas Tours** (☎ **031/224-100** or **269-984** in Thessaloníki) and others have organized well-guided day cruises around the Holy Mountain for 12,000 Drs ($50).

3 In Alexander the Great Country

From Thessaloníki 38 miles W to Vergína; 42 miles W to Veria; 21 miles NW to Pella; 48 miles S to Dion

GETTING THERE/GETTING AROUND • By Bus Although each of the sites can be reached by public **bus** from Thessaloníki's west side KTEL stations, we found the schedules too limited to permit viewing more than one or two on any given day. Bus fares to the many connecting points between Pella, Véria, Vergína, and Dión cost $6–$9 each and add up quickly.

• **By Car** Two or more travelers can see more in less time by **renting** a car from one of the many companies in Thessaloníki. Rates run about $85 a day, including insurance.

• **By Organized Tour** Many travelers prefer the ease and expert narration that comes with a guided bus tour. The tourist information office (EOT) in Thessaloníki maintains a list of tour agents in the area who offer such excursions. Among the many, is **Doucas Tours,** Odós Venizélou 8 (☎ **269-984,** fax: 031/286-610), one of the largest operators in this area. In 1994 they offered an Alexander the Great Tour, including visits to Pella, Edessa, Véria, and Vergína every Tuesday at a cost of 9,790 Drs ($40.80). Their day trip to the newly excavated site and museum at Dion left every Saturday and cost 8,800 Drs ($36.70). Doucas also offered a Friday trip to

Philippi, Kavala, and Amphipolis (see section 4, "Exploring Macedonia," below), which cost 8,800 Drs ($36.70).

Hesiod traces the settlement of Macedonia to the descendants of Makednos and Magnes, sons of Zeus who populated the region after about 2000 B.C. These Makedniam tribes spread southward to the Pieria Mountains in the Pindus range, eventually moving over the next thousand years into the Peloponnese as Dorian peoples. Herodotus called the Makednia a "wide-wandering" Greek race, accurately foreshadowing the goals and eventual triumph of Macedonia's most celebrated son, Alexander.

Historians believe that King Perdikkas first founded the Macedonian capital at Vergína in the 7th century B.C. It was known as Aigaes in antiquity. East of the present-day city of Vergína, on both sides of the national highway, are small mounds that have contributed a great deal of information about dress, burial customs, and the weaponry and tools manufactured by these families. Archeologists found that some mounds had been opened and reused later during the Hellenistic era by Macedonian settlers. Frenchman Leon Heuzey began excavating at Vergína in 1861, thinking that it was probably the small Macedonian village of Balla. Over the years archeologists uncovered a Macedonian tomb (found in 1937) and a royal palace, both thought to date from the early 3d century B.C. In 1959 Professors Bakalakis and Andronicos joined the team of Greek archeologists and historians at the site. In the early 1970s they began to feel that this excavation at Vergína might not be Balla at all, but rather the first great Macedonian capital, Aigaes, birthplace of King Philip II. In 1977 Professor Andronicos made the most envied find of the century—he discovered what has come to be considered the Royal Tomb of Philip II. And most astonishing of all, the tomb had never been plundered!

Vérgina

The wealth of gold funerary objects discovered at Vergína needs no explanation, for this spectacular event took the world by surprise and has received a huge amount of publicity. What may be less well known is that finally, in 1982, Professor Andronicos found the first row of seats of an ancient theater. "This is the sort of thing we archeologists and historians dream about. The theater established a direct link with King Philip and his death," said Professor Andronicos, who for many years fought the doubts others had about the importance of the Vérgina site. "We know that King Philip II was killed by one of his seven bodyguards while attending the wedding of daughter Cleopatra in the theater of Aigaes."

The **royal tomb** that has yielded such wealth is in the midst of excavation and study, and may not be opened to the general public for several years. One can visit the Macedonian tomb and royal palace near the modern-day village of Vérgina, and see from above the early stages of excavation at the theater.

The **Macedonian tomb** has been partially cleared from under the mound of soil that was piled over it in antiquity to thwart vandals. Unfortunately, it didn't work. When the huge white marble doors were pushed aside, the tomb was empty. The facade is almost perfectly intact; four Ionic semicolumns in relief grace the entry. Through the grated, modern iron protective gate you can see the halves of the marble sealing doors, carved in relief to resemble wood joined by metal studs. If you bring a flashlight, you can see to the right the damaged remains of the marble throne.

The **royal palace** is thought to have been built for King Antigonas Gonatas, who preceded Philip by almost half a century. Although the knee-high remains are difficult to appreciate, what immediately strikes the visitor is the palace's size: it's 144.5 by 94.5 meters. The central courtyard, whose walls of buff-colored Poros stone can be discerned, once had 60 Doric columns. Archeologists have found traces of several badly damaged mosaics, and have come to the conclusion that early Christian squatters at the site may have been offended by the nudity or religious frolicking portrayed in some; the only intact mosaics are of floral patterns and geometric designs. Along with the obviously high level of artistry, scholars have determined that there was great architectural and engineering sophistication in Macedonia at the time. Even in the largest palace rooms, no trace of internal support columns has been found, indicating a technical expertise capable of designing walls to hold the weight of the heavy, tiled roofs.

The partially uncovered **theater** can be viewed in the plains below the hillside palace. The site of the tombs and royal palace are open Tuesday through Sunday from 8:30am to 3pm.

Véria

Fifteen kilometers northwest of Vérgina, and the largest nearby town to make bus connections to the site, Véria is better known for its Byzantine-era churches than for remains of the Roman era. Some are housed in its **museum** (open 9am to 5pm daily), with exquisite painted stelae, pottery, and figurines from Vérgina and exceptionally high quality finds from the Macedonian tomb at Lefkádia. Véria was later one of two Macedonian capitals during the reform period of Emperor Diocletian (3d century A.D.). The **Cathedral of St. John Theologos** and the **Church of Christ** display some fine frescoes from the later Byzantine period.

Before we head east to the second Macedonian capital, Pella, we'll note some other sites south of Thessaloníki. There is very little of interest at Pidna, but recent finds at the site of Dión may one day prove to be as exciting as those at Vergína.

Dión

About 80 km south of Thessaloníki, at the foot of the magnificent Mt. Olympus, is the village of Dión. Recent excavations have revealed that this was an important religious center for worship of the gods of the sacred mount. King Philip II celebrated his victories here, and his son, Alexander the Great, came to sacrifice to Zeus to bless his famous expedition. The selection of this site for such important worship is no mystery, for the landscape is very blessed. Springs pour out of the hills and run down to the nearby sea. The thunderstorms that were thought to be the god's battles roll off the mountain and across the oak groves of Dión, lending credence to the legends that grew around it.

Much progress has been made in the excavations in recent years, filling the new museum with some very fine works. As you reach the town of Dión, turn down a small road toward the sea to the east, and you'll pass a small, badly preserved theater on the right. About half a kilometer farther is the main part of the site, to the left. There are ancient paved roads running by stores, workshops, an odeon, and the well-preserved foundations of public baths. The short, standing pillars supported the floor under which heated air would flow. Across the modern road is the Temple of Demeter, where finds date to 500 B.C. Farther down the public road on your right, is the most interesting part of the area. Under six feet of water, archeologists found an intact sanctuary of Isis, the Egyptian goddess. Water and mud heaved into place by an earthquake had protected it from vandals for centuries. Rich finds of sculpture were uncovered still standing in place, including the wonderful cult statue of Aphrodite that stands in the museum. A copy sits in the reeds and water that have partially reclaimed the temple, although the foundations are still clearly visible.

The Dión Museum is on the same road as the archeological site, but back in the quiet village. The brand-new building (with scholarly teams cataloging recent finds out back) contains tasteful displays of very exciting finds from the site. The sculptural works, votive offerings from throughout the ancient world, are especially impressive, particularly the cult statue of Aphrodite found underwater in the Temple of Isis. Upstairs is a collection of household items, including surgical tools, dentist's instruments, and rusted iron nails used in house construction.

The Archeological Museum and site of Dión are open daily from 8am to 7pm, 8:30am to 3pm on Sunday, and 12:30 to 7pm on Monday; admission is 550 Drs ($2.30) for both.

Pélla

At the end of the 5th century B.C. the Macedonian capital had moved from Aigaes to Pella. It was traditional in the Macedonian culture to bury royalty in the ancient capital (a tradition that Alexander, who died in Babylon and was buried in Alexandria, was not to fulfill). This probably explains why Philip's tomb was found at Aigaes. King Philip II ruled his kingdom from Pella, and from here launched more successful military missions than the Greek world had ever seen. The city-states south of the Thermopylae Pass would soon come to know the high degree of civilization achieved in Macedonia. King Philip was an early exponent of Panhellenism, a concept of Greek unity for mutual protection and prosperity that had been proclaimed by Gorgias, Lysias, and then directly to Philip himself in the famous *Philippos* (as well as to the kings of Sparta and Syracuse), by Isokrates. When Philip, after defeating the combined southern Greek forces at the Battle of Chaironeia (338 B.C.), called for peace and unity against the common Persian foe, he was on the verge of realizing this goal. On the eve of his death (two short years later) Philip was proclaimed head of the Hellenic Federation; he'd achieved an alliance with the Corinthian League, which represented all the southern city-states and most of the Aegean islands. The Molossian Kingdom in west-central Greece and Thessaly were his subject allies. In his own right he'd taken control of the entire northern Balkan region—the stage was set for Alexander.

ALEXANDER THE GREAT

From Plutarch's *Parallel Lives* we've learned a great deal about Philip and Alexander. Even as a young boy, Philip's favored son, a pupil of the wisest tutor of the day, Aristotle, was aware of his strengths. Plutarch writes: "Being nimble and light-footed, his father encouraged him to run in the Olympic Race. 'Yes,' said he, 'if there were any kings there to run with me.'" As a young man Alexander was trained in the sophisticated military tactics and weaponry that the great minds of Philip's court had invented. "Whenever Alexander heard Philip had taken any town of importance, or won any signal victory, instead of rejoicing at it altogether, he would tell his companions that his father would anticipate everything, and leave him and them no opportunities of performing great and illustrious actions." His impatience to lead is legendary; the case of the Gordion Knot tied by Gordius, father of the king of Phrygia, is only one example. Alexander, knowing the legend that whosoever untied the complicated knot would rule over all of Asia, cut it in two with his sword. Plutarch tells us: "Alexander wept when he heard from Anaxarchus that there was an infinite number of worlds; and his friends asking him if any accident had befallen him, he returns this answer: 'Do you not think it a matter worthy of lamentation that when there is such a vast multitude of them, we have not yet conquered one?'"

Alexander (who lived from 356 to 323 B.C.) gathered together the troops his father had readied for him. Allied with a newly unified Greece, he marched east across Persia all the way to the banks of the Indus River in India, conquering all and spreading the arts, ideals, traditions, and language of the Greeks. To his everlasting credit, he admired the peoples he subjugated, and remained to live among them the rest of his life. Just as Ionic columns have turned up in Pakistan and Iraq, Far Eastern religious cults found expression in some areas of southern Greece. It's said that 10,000 of his officers married Eastern women; the young man who'd been schooled by Aristotle to keep an open mind to all thoughts and all men was greatly taken by the beauties and wisdom of the East. After his death the Macedonians only held onto their own kingdom until 168 B.C., when the Romans defeated them at the Battle of Pidna, but Alexander's legacy will never be forgotten.

THE ARCHEOLOGICAL SITE OF PELLA

The small site and its few remains have led scholars to speculate on the great wealth and high standard of living achieved by its inhabitants. Graceful fluted Ionic columns still stand within the large areas of beautiful crafted mosaics. The site is only part of the Macedonian capital that Alexander had enlarged according to a master urban plan. In the museum there's a small display of statuary, pottery, and jewelry excavated at the site. The late 4th-century mosaics not *in situ* have been carefully reconstructed and placed here. The museum and site are open from 8:30am to 3pm Tuesday through Sunday. Admission to both site and museum is 440 Drs ($1.80).

MODERN PELLA & ENVIRONS

In the modern town of Pella there are several moderately priced tavernas and shops. The 51-room **Hotel Avra (☎ 0384/91-300)**, in nearby Aridea, is a modern, comfortable, lodging favored by tour groups for its proximity to the site. Many tourists working their way west to Epirus prefer to move onward through the picturesque metropolis of **Édessa,** known for its cascading waterfalls and its Byzantine-era bridge that was one link in the Romans' Egnatía Way.

The two archeological sites that have offered us the richest artifacts displayed in the Thessaloníki Museum are Sindos and Derveni. There is little to see at **Dervéni** (10 km east of Thessaloníki on the Kavala highway) or at **Sindos** (23 km west), where a treasure-filled cemetery spanning centuries was found when excavating a site for a new factory in the industrial zone. In both areas, archeological work continues.

4 Exploring Macedonia

322 miles NW of Athens; 131 miles W of Thessaloníki

GETTING THERE • By Plane Two flights weekly leave from Athens. **Olympic Airways (☎ 22-275)** is on Odós Meg. Alexandrou 15.

• **By Train** The nearest major railroad station is in Flórina; there are two trains daily from Athens (☎ **82-13-882** for information.).

• **By Bus** Two buses daily depart from Athens's terminal at Odós Kifíssou 100 for the 11-hour ride to Kastoriá; phone **51-29-308** for schedule information in Athens or **0467/83-455** in Kastoriá.

ESSENTIALS Contact the Kastoriá **town hall** (☎ **22-312**) for local tourist information. The **area code** is 0467. The local **police** (☎ **23-333**) are at Odós Gramou 25. If you have time, visit the fine Byzantine icons at the Church of Ághios Spýridon (☎ **26-649**).

Readers continuing west (hopefully not in the bitter cold winter) will reach first the prefecture of Flórina, then that of Kastoriá. **Flórina,** once home to rebel Greek forces, borders on the Albanian and Yugoslav borders, giving it a somewhat more ethnic feel than is evidenced in the hill country farther south. It's a verdant region dotted by small cold-water lakes; ice skating is a popular winter activity. In the northwest area tranquil **Lake Préspa** is actually the larger Megáli Préspa and tiny Mikrí Préspa, two bodies of water separated by a very narrow land bridge at the village of Lemos. Both are partially Greek and partly Albanian; Megáli Préspa also has the (possibly unique) distinction of being part Yugoslavian as well. In any case this region of shallow, marshy wetlands has for centuries been an active breeding ground for wildlife and birds. Since 1977 the region around Mikri Prespa has been a National Wildlife Preserve, most noted for its over 185 different species of birds. Mikri Prespa numbers among its happy inhabitants two types of endangered pelicans and some of Europe's rare cormorants.

The city of Kastoria, center of Greece's fur-producing region, is set on a promontory jutting into the still gray-blue (smelly and polluted) waters of Lake Orestias (or Kastoria). Because of its influential position as a successful trading center, it is graced with an extraordinarily large number of Byzantine churches and well-dressed inhabitants who cruise the city's hilly streets in BMW's and Mercedes. More than 70 churches from the Byzantine and later eras are tucked in between typical Macedonian *arhontiko* (mansions). Many of these mansions have large, open fireplaces and their own exceptional frescoes. The excellent **Kastoria Folklore Museum,** housed in the Nerantzis Aivazis mansion, a traditional-style house on Kapetan Lazarou Street, has interesting displays of locally produced embroideries and, of course, a history of the fur trade. It is open Tuesday through Sunday from 9:30am to 12:30pm and 2 to 6pm. Admission: 220 Drs (90¢).

Kastoriá also has a new Byzantine Museum with a collection of ikons drawn from its many *archontiká*. Unfortunately it was closed on our last visit. It's located near the Xenia Hotel, open Tues–Sun, 8:30am–2:30pm, and admission is free. Kastoria's fur trade is based on its skilled craftspeople ("trimmers"), who can take small pieces of furs, or ends, and stitch them together to form a whole cloth, from which lower priced coats are sewn. In several factories you can watch as leftovers imported from European and Scandinavian furriers are melded together to form blankets and carpets. "Stop and shop" is what we say for Kastoria: Furs here are cheaper than anywhere else.

Kastoria is also a lovely place to stroll. On the west side of the lake, near the Hotel Kastoria, is a weeping-willow-lined lane that attracts walkers, cyclists, fishers, and just plain folks. If you climb up the heights of the town, you'll be rewarded with a fine view that reminded us of a northern Italian lake town. Kastoria has spawned a unique, squared-off paddle boat for making your way around the lake; these funny-looking vessels are available for rent by the hour for a few drachmas.

While you're waiting for your plane, train, or bus, walk over to Van Fleet Square, where the timeless outdoor tavernas and idling backgammon players show no evidence of living with a fur trade that's a $100-million-a-year industry. (By the way, the square is named after the U.S. General Van Fleet, who spoke there when U.S. troops were helping push back the Communist forces from this region into Albania in 1949.)

WHERE TO STAY

Europa Hotel, Odós Ághios Athanasiou 8, Kastoria 52100, Kastorias. ☎ **0467/23-826.**
36 rms (all with bath). TEL

Rates: 8,140 Drs ($33.90) single; 10,055 Drs ($41.90) double. EC, MC, V.

These well-kept rooms have partial views of the lake and are a good choice if everything else is booked.

Hotel Orestion, Platía Davaki 1, Kastoria 52100, ☎ **0467/22-257.**
20 rms (all with bath). TEL

Rates: 8,530 Drs ($35.50) single; 10,664 Drs ($44.40) double. V.

This clean and comfortable hostel is located above Platía Davaki. Standard double rooms are well kept by the friendly proprietors. A bar and breakfast room is open year round.

Hotel Tsamis, Odós Koromila 3, Dispilio 52100, Kastorias. ☎ **0467/85-334.**
Fax 0467/85-777. 81 rms (all with bath). TEL

Rates (including breakfast): 11,880 Drs ($49.50) single; 16,940 Drs ($70.60) double. V.

We found this newly renovated lodging on the National road leading from the south on our last visit. It's a modern three-story inn with carefully tended grounds, willows leading down to its own dock, and spectacular views of the lake and town. The stone lobby has a fireplace that in the colder months is particularly welcoming. The nicely decorated guest rooms have lakeview balconies; prices are on the high side but an excellent value.

WHERE TO EAT

Dining is best done by walking along the lakefront and stopping in the various cafés.

Rendezvous Café/Bar, on Lake Kastoriá. ☎ **24-793.**

Cuisine: SNACKS/DESSERTS.
Prices: 350–1,210 Drs ($1.45–$5). No credit cards.
Open: Daily 11am–12:30am.

Pizza, snacks, and bars are the norm at the Rendezvous Café/Bar. What a wild place: a bubbling fountain in front with foaming soap suds, pink tablecloths, pink neon, pink curtains, and, if you dare go inside, pink everything else to give the Rendezvous that "in the pink" ambience. They serve great coffee drinks and ice cream.

Taverna Michalis, Flórina highway. No phone.

Cuisine: GREEK.
Prices: Appetizers 605–1,320 Drs ($2.50–$5.50); main courses 935–2,200 Drs ($3.90–$9.20). No credit cards.
Open: Daily 6:30pm–12am.

Everyone's favorite country taverna is on the road leading north to Flórina. They're open year round, so items change according to season. The roast meats and stuffed vegetables are especially good.

East Through Macedonia

Let's turn eastward from Thessaloníki and look at the Macedonia that becomes more Oriental in flavor every kilometer east we go. The scenic way to Dráma is along the Kavala highway that hugs northern Chalkidiki; passing **Lake Koronia** and **Lake Volvi** will demonstrate how easily an island could have been made of Chalkidiki had the two lakes been joined! North of Lake Koronia is the famous village of **Langádas** where each May 21 the Festival of the Anastenarides is held. Local firewalkers will come out and dance on blazing embers in honor of Saints Konstantinos and Eléni. (There's not much here on other days of the year.) On the north side of Lake Volvi is the hamlet of **Filadelfia,** one of many Greek cities called "Brotherly Love."

Amfipolis, a new village on the site of an ancient, prosperous mineral-mining town, is noted for its Byzantine church and for the remarkable marble Lion Statue found in the riverbed of the flowing Strimon River. The Strimon, which contributed to the rich mineral deposits sought after by Thracian, Roman, and Athenian alike, also preserved for us the remnants of a large wooden bridge from the 5th century, which has recently been brought up from its bottom.

The roads leading to **Dráma,** called the "Plain of Gold" for its late afternoon amber light, are often lined with shade-giving poplar and elm trees. The plain was the battleground for a 5th-century B.C. defeat of Athens by the more powerful Macedonian forces, yet very little of interest remains from antiquity. Consider a lunch break in one of Drama's pretty public gardens. If you're not prepared to picnic, there's a small taverna, on its own little island in the middle of the healthy Aghía Varvara springs that bubble up in downtown Drama.

Philippi

Depending on whether you're a Romaphile or a Christianophile you'll say Philippi is best known for (a) the Battle of Philippi or (b) the site where Saint Paul preached his first sermon on Christianity. In 42 B.C., Mark Antony and Octavius met Caesar's assassins on the Plain of Philippi (Brutus's fleet had arrived at Kavála) and defeated them soundly, causing Brutus and Cassius to commit suicide. After their victory, Mark Antony and Octavius committed great sums of money to renewing Philippi, and most of its fascinating archeological site dates from this period of largesse. They granted Philippi the status of a Roman colony and a garrison guarding the Via Egnatia and its language, laws, and coinage followed the Roman model.

In the Acts of the Apostles, we read about Saint Paul's visit to Philippi, probably about A.D. 49: "We went to Philippi, which is the leading city of the district of Macedonia, and a Roman colony. . . . On the sabbath day we went outside the gate to the riverside, where we supposed there was a place of prayer; and we sat down and spoke to the women who had come together." Paul and Silas set up a church in the house of Lydia, one of the women laundering who'd accepted Paul's words and been baptized. Their troubles were caused by a young prophetess who was trying to disclaim the preacher. Impatiently, Paul exorcised the spirit that enabled her to prophecy, a radical disability for one gainfully employed as a seer. In any case it is said that her supporters and "agents" demanded that Paul be jailed for interfering with their livelihood. A small crypt in the Roman forum is supposed to be the cell where Paul and Silas were imprisoned.

WHAT TO SEE & DO—THE ARCHEOLOGICAL SITE

As you enter Philippi, the site's entrance and museum are on the left of the main road. The **Propylon** has been restored and welcomes visitors. The largest part of the site is the **forum** or agora (on the south side), where there are remains of the arcade that once spanned three sides. There are remnants of a Roman bath, but a much more impressive plumbing feat are the 50 marble seats still in place in the **public toilets** at the southeastern end of the agora. At the north end, finely preserved stairs lead up to a terrace and portico. A bold, hewn-brick arch on top of rectangular columns is the striking remains of a 6th-century basilica. The tawny-colored stone and acanthus leaf-trimmed columns were made up from the Roman-era palaestra and forum, destroyed in clearing the land for the chapel. The smaller basilica A, as it's called, is near the ruins of the theater.

The **theater** dates from the 4th century B.C. and was actively used in Philip's time for the presentation of dramatic works. In the 3d century A.D. it was converted to a gladiator's arena; wild animal exits and entrances and a guardrail for the spectator seating were added at that time. The theater has been somewhat restored, and during the summer a Historic Drama Festival is held there (you can check with the EOT for schedule information).

The small **Archeological Museum** (☎ **051/516-251**) at the site exhibits finds from the Neolithic period (Dikili-Tach and Sitagri regions) and from the Hellenic and Roman eras, when Philippi was at its prime. The Museum of Philippi (also spelled Filippi) is open from 8:30am to 3pm Tuesday through Sunday. The site is open daily 9am to 5pm. The admission fee for the museum and the site is 450 Drs ($1.90) each. To get to Philippi from Kavala, take the Drama bus from the KTEL station, which leaves every 20 minutes. Ask the driver to let you off at "Archaia Philipi"; the half-hour ride costs 440 Drs ($1.80).

5 Kavála

107 miles E of Thessaloníki; 106 miles W of Alexandroupolis; 285 miles W of Istanbul

GETTING THERE • By Plane Ten Olympic flights per week daily from Athens. The **Olympic Airways** office is at Odós Ethnikis Antistasseos 8 (☎ **051/836-639**). The airport bus, costing 275 Drs ($1.15), leaves their office 90 minutes before flight time.

• By Train The nearest train station is 30 kilometers in Dráma; it's serviced several times daily from Athens and from Thessaloníki. Contact the OSE in Dráma **(0521/32-444),** in Athens (☎ **01/52-22-491**) or Thessaloníki (☎ **031/276-382** or **517-517**) for information.

• By Bus Two buses daily from Athens's terminal at Odós Kifíssou 100 (☎ **01/51-29-363**) to Dráma or Kávala (11 hours). KTEL buses run along the Via Egnatía (built in the mid-second century from Rome to Constantinople) from Thessaloníki every hour. The KTEL bus station for buses to Philippi (Dráma), Thessaloníki, Athens, and other eastern destinations is on Mitropolous Street, about a block up from the harbor.

• **By Ferry** The tourist information office **EOT (☎ 051/222-425)** has ferry schedule information about boats to Limnos (twice weekly), Lesvos, and Chíos (once weekly), Kymi, Évvia (infrequently), and Thassos (eight times daily).

ESSENTIALS The **EOT** office (**☎ 051/222-425**) is at Odós Filellínon 5, at Eleftherias Square. They're open during the summer Monday through Friday from 7am to 7pm, Saturday 8am to 2pm, and closed Sunday; they close by 2pm during the winter. You can buy tickets there to the annual summer-long Drama Festivals held on the island of Thassos and in the ancient theater at Philippi; check with them for schedules and show times. The **tourist police** (**☎ 222-905**) are in the police station at Odós Omonias 119. Besides the **banks** on the square, the Macedonia Thrace Bank on Omonias and P. Mela Streets is open extra hours, from 6am to 7:45pm daily and from 10am to 12:45pm on Saturday in summer. The **post office**—open Monday through Friday from 7:30am to 8pm—is at Erithrou Stavrou and Mitropolitou, near the bus station. **OTE** is nearby, at Averof and Ethnikis Antistasis, and open daily 7am–midnight.

For English-language periodicals, try the selection at Papadogianis Books, Odós Omonías 46, across the square from EOT.

Located on the slopes of Mt. Simvolon over an area occupied at least as long as 3,000 years ago, the modern port of Kavála rests on the remains of the ancient port of Neapolis. Contemporary concrete-block housing descends from the west, fascinating wood and stucco, traditional Turkish-blend villas descend from the east; the new meets a modern pier for the Thassos ferries and the old meets the original crescent-shaped port and breakwater installed for the Piraeus ferries. From the impressive hilltop remains of the Byzantine fortress, one can appreciate the amphitheatrical design of the city. The 16th-century Kamares Aqueduct commissioned by Süleyman the Magnificent still dominates the central part of town. If you confine your stay in Kavala to the old Panaghia quarter, colored by its residents' Turkish heritage, and to the scenic port lined with cafés and shops, you'll have the best possible time in this otherwise industrial and commercialized city.

Besides its successful fishing industry, Kavála is the central market town for the area and Thrace's large tobacco industry. The scented leaves used in "Oriental" tobaccos have been farmed by Anatolian peoples in the Kavala area for centuries, and their integration into the community is one of the more intriguing aspects of this cross-over region.

Orientation

Kavala is the midway point between Thessaloníki and Istanbul (there's a huge "460 KMS" sign on the harbor). The town you will want to know is all within a quarter mile of the port. The long-distance **ferries** arrive at the east end of the harbor, beneath the old Panaghia quarter on the hill. **Buses** arrive one block up from the west end of the harbor. **Erithrou Stavrou Street** is the main thoroughfare, running east-west next to the fishing-boat docks and intersecting Koudouriotou Street, which runs up the hill next to the Panaghia quarter. **Eftherias Square** is one block above the middle of the port. The higher-priced hotels are on Erithrou Stavrou Street and Venizélou Street, which runs parallel one block north; the budget hotels are on either side of Eftherias Square.

What to See & Do

There are two museums worthy of mention in Kavála. The handsome modern **Archeological Museum** (☎ **222-335**), on the west side of the waterfront, attractively displays a full spectrum of finds including some particularly beautiful jewelry, fine vases, and excellently crafted terra-cotta figurines from Amfipolis (a prosperous mining town near Thessaloníki), Avdira, Neapolis (the ancient Kavála), and Philippi (open Tuesday through Sunday 8:30am to 3:30pm). There's also a small **folk art museum** (☎ **227-820**). Admission is 440 Drs. ($1.80). There's a big bazaar Saturday mornings near the Archeological Museum with an amazing array of merchandise.

On the east side of the harbor, up on Panaghia Hill, is the **home of Muhammed Ali** (the ancient one). This traditional-style Turkish house was where Ali, founder of the Egyptian dynasty that ended with King Farouk, was born in 1769. It's maintained courtesy of the Egyptian government, who also own and are partially restoring the **Imaret** down the hill, also built by Muhammed Ali. This was a priests' school combined with a poorhouse, which at times housed and fed up to 300 people. It's a wonderful, sprawling piece of Islamic architecture, and inside you'll find the highly popular **Refreshments Imaret** (☎ **836-286**), open daily 11am to 3am, down under cool white arches around a lush garden, where you can sip something cool, listen to exotic music and drift away for a while. Beautiful and soothing anytime, but at its most enchanting at dusk.

Muhammed Ali should inspire you (especially those of you continuing east into Turkey) to explore the narrow, cobblestone lanes of the Turkish Panaghia district.

Where to Stay

The EOT **Batis Campgrounds** (☎ **051/243-051**) at Kavála Beach is a luxurious watersports/resort-style camping area.

George Alvanos Rooms to Let, Odós Athenemiou 35, Kavála 65403.
☎ **051/288-412, 221-781.** 5 rooms (all with shared bath).

Rates: 2,750 Drs ($11.50) single; 3,850 Drs ($16) double. No credit cards.

These are currently the only rooms to let in the Panaghia, Kavála's old Turkish quarter, and by far the best budget value in town: immaculate, airy, and cheerful, with a clothesline available. The two bathrooms are also very clean and pleasant. The Alvanoses give you a key to the house and disappear upstairs for the rest of your visit, though they are perfectly willing to make recommendations or suggestions if you give them a shout. These rooms go quickly, so call in advance. Ask for a double with the seaview.

Hotel Galaxy, Odós Venizélou 27, Kavála 65302. ☎ **051/224-521.** Fax 051/226-754. 150 rms (all with bath). A/C TEL

Rates (including breakfast): 12,980 Drs ($54.10) single; 18,700 Drs. ($77.90) double. AE, DC, EC, MC, V.

This superior hotel has balconies that face directly over the brightly painted caiques south to the hills of Thassos, with the Castle up on the left. There's a roof garden (great view!), restaurant, bar, and air-conditioned rooms, some with big bathtubs and minibars. It's popular with the "Saint Paul in Greece" tour groups—St. Paul landed at the ancient port of Neapolis on his way to Philippi—but it's so big you can almost always find a room.

Hotel Nefeli, Odós Erythroú Stavroú (Red Cross) 50, Kavála 65403. ☎ **051/227-441.** Fax 051/227-440. 100 rms (all with bath). TEL

Rates: 10,450 Drs ($43.50) single; 13,200 Drs ($55) double. EC, MC, V.

We stayed here across from the park near the archeological museum during our last visit and found it quite satisfactory. Outside on the street gets rather lively in the evenings, but inside remains quiet. The rooms are simple and spacious, and the Acropolis-view roof garden competes favorably with pricier neighbors.

Panorama Hotel, Odós Venizélou 26C, Kavála 65403. ☎ **051/224-205, 229-711.** 54 rms (16 with bath). TEL

Rates (including breakfast): 7,700 Drs ($32.08) single; 9,350 Drs ($38.50) double; 20% more for private shower.

This hotel is just down and across the street from the Galaxy but prices are much more reasonable. Nothing special to look at, but the location is convenient and the management is friendly and helpful.

Parthenon Hotel, Odós Spetsón 14, Kavála 65403. ☎ **051/223-205.** 12 rms (none with bath).

Rates: 3,500 Drs ($14.60) single; 5,000 Drs ($20.80) double.

The only budget hotel we can suggest has flowered coverlets, wallpaper, and couches that create a strange, almost-Oriental decor in this balconied, high-ceilinged, creaky-floored abode. Shared baths are big, old but clean, and we enjoyed our stay.

Where to Eat

You should stick to seafood in Kavala, so it's best to head down to Venizélou Street and stroll the harbor. In the newer part of town you'll have a wide variety of stylish, portside cafés and fast-food and souvlaki places.

Kiriakos Taverna, Odós Perigali 14. ☎ **222-494.**

Cuisine: GREEK/INTERNATIONAL/SEAFOOD.
Prices: Main courses 1,870–3,000 Drs ($7.80–$12.80). No credit cards.
Open: Daily 10am–5pm, 8pm–2am.

Near the stadium, on the right about a kilometer from the center of town on the road to Alexandroupoli, overlooking the beach is a fine place for *xifias* (swordfish) and fried *midia* (oysters).

Panos Zafira, Platía Karaoli-Dimitriou 20. ☎ **227-978.**

Cuisine: SEAFOOD.
Prices: Main courses 440–2,200 Drs ($1.80–$9.20); fish 7,700–12,000 Drs ($32.10–$50) per kilo. V.
Open: Daily noon–midnight.

On the east side of the harbour along with several others you'll find this popular place known for grilled calamari and small local fish—*marides* (blackfish), *kotsomoures* (red), and *gavros* (fresh anchovies)—which are cheaper than most other seafood.

Pavlidi Bakery, Odós The. Poulidou 5. ☎ **223-589.**

Prices: 45–385 Drs (20¢–$1.60). No credit cards.
Open: Daily 8am–8pm.

Since 1923 this *artopoleo,* on the left just as you start the climb to the Castle and Panaghia, has been baking *spanakópita, tiropita, milopita* (apple turnovers that go fast), whole-wheat and sesame breads, and a number of delicious sweets. They have fruit juice and soft drinks, if you want to make a meal.

Taverna O Faros, Odós Theo. Poulidou 25. ☎ **838-987.**

Cuisine: GREEK/SEAFOOD.
Prices: Appetizers 300–550 Drs ($1.40–$2.30); main courses 880–2,200 Drs ($3.70–$9.20). No credit cards.
Open: Daily noon–12:30am.

Have the day's catch fried or broiled and served with a wedge of lime or savor exceptionally well-prepared Greek fare over some of the hearty, regional Limnos white wine at "The Lighthouse." At this special taverna high on the main street of Panaghia across from the Imaret, you can watch the neighbors stroll as you enjoy warm hospitality and special ambience as well as superb food.

6 Thrace–Alexandroúpolis

213 miles E of Thessaloníki; 179 miles W of Istanbul

GETTING THERE • By Plane There are ten flights weekly from Athens. **Olympic Airways,** Odós Ellis 6, is at the corner of Koleti Street. Call **0551/26-207** or **28-653** for information.

• By Train Four trains leave daily from Athens's Laríssis station (☎ **0551/26-212**) make the 17-hour ride to Alexandroúpolis, with stops at Dráma and Komotini. From Alexandroúpolis—the OSE (☎ **26-395**) is on the east side of town on the *paralía*—one train leaves nightly for Istanbul; the 10-hour ride costs 5,500 Drs ($22.90).

• By Bus Two buses leave daily to Thrace from Athens's terminal at Odós Kifíssou 100; call **01/51-32-084** for information. Daily five buses leave for Kavála from the Snack Shop at Odós Erithrou Stavrou 28, near the Oceanis Hotel. The Alexandroúpolis KTEL station is at Odós Venizélou 36, a block north of main street, but the bus to Istanbul leaves from the train station—purchase your ticket ($28) there well in advance—usually at 10am daily for the 7-hour trip.

• By Ferry The ticket agent for the **Samothraki ferry** (which runs four times a week) is one short block from the harbor esplanade, on Kypou Street; call **26-721** for schedule information. Contact the port authority (☎ **0551/26-468**) for more information.

ESSENTIALS The **Municipal Tourist Office** (☎ **0551/24-998**) is three blocks behind the lighthouse, at Leof. Dimokratis 306, open Monday through Friday from 8am to 2pm. The **tourist police** (☎ **37-411**) are at Odós Karatskaki 6, two blocks off the *paralía* near the lighthouse. The **post office** is on the *paralía* two blocks west of the lighthouse. The telephone center OTE is at Ioakim Kavri and Venizelou Streets, east of bus station, and is open daily from 6am to midnight.

The coastal road swings inland as you cross the Néstos River and heads north to the fascinating village of **Xánthi,** 63 km from Kavála. This is a tobacco town, but here it's grown, not just traded and shipped, and the fragrance is everywhere. Many of the villagers are traditionally dressed in Turkish peasant clothes of baggy black trousers, full skirts, and headdresses. The women who wear white bandannas are Pomaki, descendants of the Bulgarian hill people who were converted to Islam from Christianity. Some 70 km farther east, in **Komotiní,** the locals are dressed in traditional garb, too, but here the head-clothes are black and the faces are pure Turkish. Komotinis are Musulmani, Muslims of direct Turkish descent. In Komotiní worship is carried out five times daily in the 450-year-old New Mosque.

Nearly one-fourth of Thrace's population is Muslim, in a country where more than 90% of the population shares the Orthodox faith. This story goes back to the years after World War I when the Greeks developed their *megali idea* of uniting all the areas with an Orthodox population once again under the Greek flag, perhaps reestablishing a great capital at Constantinople. They invaded the weakened Ottoman Empire and got nearly as far as Ankara before they were repulsed by the furious Turks. Since anyone of Orthodox faith in Anatolia now feared for their lives, they fled (more than a million) into neighboring Greece, increasing its population by more than 20%. Under the Treaty of Lausanne the western part of Thrace was given to the Greek nation in 1923. In the last decade the government has made a big push to industrialize this region. The borders shared with Bulgaria and Turkey ensure that it will always be heavily fortified as a strategic military outpost. Villages such as Xanthi and Komotini are of the past; Alexandroúpolis is of the future.

What to See & Do

There isn't much to see in **Alexandroúpolis,** a pleasant little seaport. The nearby cave at Makri is pushed by tour operators as the famed cave where Odysseus met the Cyclops and defeated him. Every August there's a Wine Festival; in February a Hunter's Week (the thing to do in this rugged region) is celebrated near the city. At nearby Pithion the OSE train will be rerouted for its trip to the Turkish border. Drivers and hitchhikers will head for the land border at Kastanee to cross into Edirne, Turkey.

Local buses go to several nearby **beaches,** making for an easy day excursion. Another day trip through pretty, unspoiled scenery is through the **Evros Valley** region, paralleling the Turkish border north from Alexandroupolis. In **Didymótichon,** the double row of walls, ten towers, three gates, a reservoir, and food storage cells of an imposing Byzantine castle can still be seen. It was one of the most important Byzantine cities, home to both the Emperor Iannis Paleologos and to Sultan Beyazit.

Where to Stay

If you're here waiting for the Samothraki ferry (and it's hard not to be if that's where you're going or coming from) you'll probably want a place to stay. Our first choice is the **EOT Campground** (☎ **0551/26-225**), just one kilometer outside town, overlooking the water. It can accommodate up to 900 persons, but call ahead to find out how crowded it will be.

If you want to stay in town, look along Dimokratías Street.

Hotel Alex, Leof. Dimokratías 294, Alexandroúpoli 68100. ☎ **0551/26-302** and **28-400.** 28 rms (all with bath). TEL

Rates: 4,840 Drs ($20.20) single; 6,930 Drs ($28.90) double. No credit cards.

The rooms are small and modestly furnished but carpeted and comfortable. Though it's on the main street downtown the front rooms are quiet because they have new double-paned windows—part of recent remodeling that's also added a bar/cafeteria.

Park Hotel, Leof. Dimokratías 458, Alexandroúpoli 68100. ☎ **0551/28-607.** 24 rms (all with bath). TEL

Rates (including breakfast): 8,470 Drs ($35.30) single; 10,230 Drs ($42.60) double. No credit cards.

On the west side of town across from a very nice park, with a few trees and shrubs of its own, this little suburban hotel suits its name quite well. The lobby is especially homelike, with a big fireplace, comfy furnishings, and white curtains trimmed with local tatting that looks especially made for it. The rooms are attractive and comfortable, all with balconies that can be enjoyed.

Where to Eat

When in Alexandroúpolis, try *lagos* (hare) and the locally produced telemes cheese.

Klimateria, Odós Kyprou 14. ☎ **26-288.**

Cuisine: GREEK/TURKISH/SEAFOOD.
Prices: Appetizers 275–495 Drs ($1.15–$2.05); main courses 825–1,375 Drs ($3.45–$5.70). No credit cards.
Open: Daily 7am–1am.

This is a popular taverna on a small square a block off the *paralía,* near the train station, where you can sample a spicier-than-usual moussaká with a delicious hunk of Greek bread. The Turkish influence can be tasted in the cuisine here. (Just wait till you get to Istanbul!) Their lamb and beef dishes are also flavorful; try the *katsikaki* (baked goat).

16

The Northeastern Aegean Islands

THE ISLANDS THAT COMPRISE THE NORTHEASTERN AEGEAN GROUP, THE LEAST visited of any of the Aegean islands, can be further divided into the eastern islands of Sámos, Chíos, and Lésvos (Mytilíni) and the northern islands, including Límnos, Samothráki, and Thássos. The division reflects both physical and cultural differences.

The better-known eastern islands are more autonomous; they all share a cultural (and transportation) connection with Turkey, reflecting that country's exotic, Asian heritage. The smaller northern islands, though less visited by foreigners, in July and August become extensions or weekend resorts of Thessaloníki and the larger mainland cities.

Seeing the Northeastern Aegean Islands

The Northeastern Aegean islands are spread out and rather difficult to hop between; therefore, we recommend you limit your ambitions if you only have a week to travel.

Days 1–4 Fly from Athens to Samós and make your base Sámos town. Make sure to see Pythagórion, the Eupalínos Tunnel, the Archeological Museum and at least one of the island's beaches. Take a day trip to the incredible archeological site at Ephesus, Turkey, one of the Seven Wonders of the Ancient World.

Days 5–7 Take a ferry to Chíos and arrange accommodations in the village of Mestá. Use your time to take buses around to see Pírgi and the island's beaches. Fly back to Athens.

1 Sámos

174 nautical miles NE of Piraeus

ARRIVING/DEPARTING • By Air Three flights leave daily from Athens via **Olympic Airways.** Their office (☎ **0273/27-237**) is at the corner of Kanari and Smyrnis Streets in Sámos town, or at Odós Lykourgos 90 (☎ **61-213**) in Pythagórion. From the airport, you can take a taxi to Samós town (2,500 Drs or $13.90) or Pythagórion (1,000 Drs or $5.60), then catch a public bus to other parts of the island.

• By Sea There are daily boats (sometimes two) from Piraeus to Samós town and Karlóvassi in the high season. Pythagórion is connected to Chíos four times weekly, to Ikaría three times, and to Lésvos, Límnos, or Rhodes twice weekly. Five times a week there are car ferries to Páros, four times to Léros, Kálymnos, or Kos, twice weekly to Náxos, and once to Mýkonos. In summer there's hydrofoil service to Chíos and Lésvos from Sámos town. Smaller excursion boats leave Pythagório for Pátmos four times weekly (this can be a rough trip!); the larger, smoother-sailing steamers go three times a week. There are once weekly sailings to Kavála and Thessaloníki on the mainland; call the Piraeus (☎ **45-11-311**) or Sámos (☎ **0273/27-318**) or Pythagório (☎ **0273/61-225**) port authorities for schedule information.

During the 6th-century B.C., in the glory days of the Ionian civilization, Sámos was heralded for its rich contribution to art, architecture, and science. The island's favorite son, Pythagoras, is the most notable in a long list of luminaries (including the philosopher Epicurus, Aesop of *Fables* fame, and the mathematician Aristarchos) who brought Sámos honor and fame. Herodotus, in his *History,* devoted a large portion of his historical writing to Sámos.

Sámos is mountainous and green; its peaks are the highest in the Aegean islands and sections of the scenic interior are as thickly forested as one finds in the region.

What's Special About the Northeastern Aegean Islands

Archeology

- The Eupálinos Tunnel, built in the 6th century B.C., is one of the most remarkable engineering feats of the ancient world.
- The restored amphitheater on Thássos is the venue for superb classical Greek theater productions each summer.

Culture and Lifestyle

- The Women's Agricultural Tourist Cooperatives on Chíos and Lésvos place tourists in rural family homes to learn about the local lifestyle.
- Pírgi, on Chíos, is a tiny traditional village completely painted in geometric and Op Art gray-and-white patterns—the only one like it in Greece.
- In Mestá, Chíos, you can live as the natives used to, in a walled-in village of pastel stucco homes, many of them restored as studio apartments.

Because Sámos is one of the closest Greek islands to Turkey, it is a particularly convenient crossover point for those who want to visit Ephesus—one of the most important archeological sites in Asia Minor. We'd recommend a brief stay to see Sámos's historic sites, combined with an excursion to the unforgettable splendor of Ephesus.

Orientation

The large, almond-shaped Sámos has three ports. The ferries from Piraeus and the Cyclades normally stop at both Sámos (northeast coast) and Karlóvassi (northwest coast). Sámos town (sometimes called Vathí) is an old port that has undergone extensive development but remains an essentially Greek town with lots of commerce and color. **Karlóvassi** is the most Greek in feeling of Sámos's major towns, with a friendly harbor, nearby beaches, and a scattering of hotels, though it's only convenient for those heading to Marathókampos beach. The Dodecanese and Chíos ferries land at **Pythagório,** a picturesque village on the southeast coast that was the ancient capital of the island. Nearby are the Eupalínos Tunnel, the huge, ancient Heraion and the airport. However, because it's the best base for sightseeing it is excessively crowded with tour groups (said to occupy more than 80% of the port's buildings!).

For years Kokkári was the island's most unspoiled resort, but now it's overrun with tourists who prefer less touristy villages. All along the north coast, the pebble beaches, though plagued by strong winds, are also undergoing intense development. This fate awaits Marathokámpos, once our favorite south coast beach. Midway on the north

IMPRESSIONS

Love's lyric fount of glee
Rose in marbled Mytilene
Channeled by the purple sea.

—Oliver St. John Gogarty, "The Isles of Greece: Lesbos," *Collected Poems,* 1951

The [Ottoman] pasha reasoned with the people of Sámos upon the propriety of their paying for a Turkish frigate which was wrecked upon their territory, "because the accident would not have happened unless their island had been in the way."

—E. D Clarke, *Travels in Various Countries,* 1818

coast road between Kokkári and Karlóvassi is the Platanákia region of villages set on steeply terraced hills and valleys where grow Sámos's famous muscadine grapes—from which muscat wine is made.

Getting Around

BY BUS There's good public transportation on Sámos; the Sámos town bus terminal (☎ **27-262**) is inland on Kanári Street. The bus travels 13 times a day between Sámos town and Pythagório for the 20-minute trip. Buses go to Kokkári and the inland village of Mytilíni seven times a day. There are four buses daily from Pythagorion to Iréo (near the Heraion); call for schedules (☎ **27-262**).

BY PRIVATE CAR/TAXI The most common taxi fare, from Sámos to Pythagório, costs 2,200 Drs ($9.15). You can book an all-day taxi for an around-the-island tour. Count on paying about 3,200 Drs ($13.50) per hour or 20,000 Drs ($83.30) for a full day by negotiating with a driver at one of the portside taxi stands, or booking by phone (☎ **28-404** in Sámos or **61-450** in Pythagorion).

We recommend **Aramis Rent a Motorbike-Car** (☎ **0273/23-253;** fax 23-620), 200 meters left from the harbor in Sámos town and near the bus station in Pythagório (☎ **0273/62-267**) for the best prices and selection. Expect to pay about $65 per day. There are plenty of other agencies, so shop around. You'll probably find them cheaper in Sámos town than elsewhere.

BY BICYCLE OR MOPED You can also rent a bicycle or moped in Sámos from several shops near the central square. In Pythagório, **Nicos Rent a Motor Bike** (☎ **61-094**) on Lykourgos Street rents both. His rates include helmets: bicycles rent for 1,200 Drs ($5), Vespas for 2,600 Drs ($10.85), and two-person mopeds for 4,400 Drs ($18.40) a day.

BY BOAT Excursion boats from the Pythagório harbor go to Psilí Ámmos beach daily, and to the island of Ikaría three times weekly. There is a popular day cruise to the sandy beach on Samiopoula ("small island"), where there is a taverna and rooms to let.

What to See & Do

Sámos has a lot to offer, but you will have to travel out of the way to discover the truly special spots. Before you make plans for your island hop, inquire whether the Eupalínos Tunnel is open. If it is, and you have any interest in archeology or engineering, it alone will justify a special visit to Sámos.

IN & AROUND PYTHAGÓRIO

This ancient village and harbor is named after the most notable of all Samians, Pythagoras, who is still studied ("Reason is immortal, all else mortal") by students for his theories about geometry and mathematics and their relation to the other disciplines. Aesop was one of Pythagoras's contemporaries, and it is he who penned such expressions as "appearances often are deceiving," "slow and steady wins the race," "familiarity breeds contempt," and "any excuse will serve a tyrant" (the last being particularly applicable to his times). Under the autocrat Polycrates, two engineering marvels were added to Sámos's infrastructure. The first is the **harbor** at Pythagório and the three-mile wall built around it, the second is the **Eupalínos** (or Eupalinian) **Tunnel.** Columns from the city fortifications and an unexcavated theater are visible

The Northeastern Aegean Islands

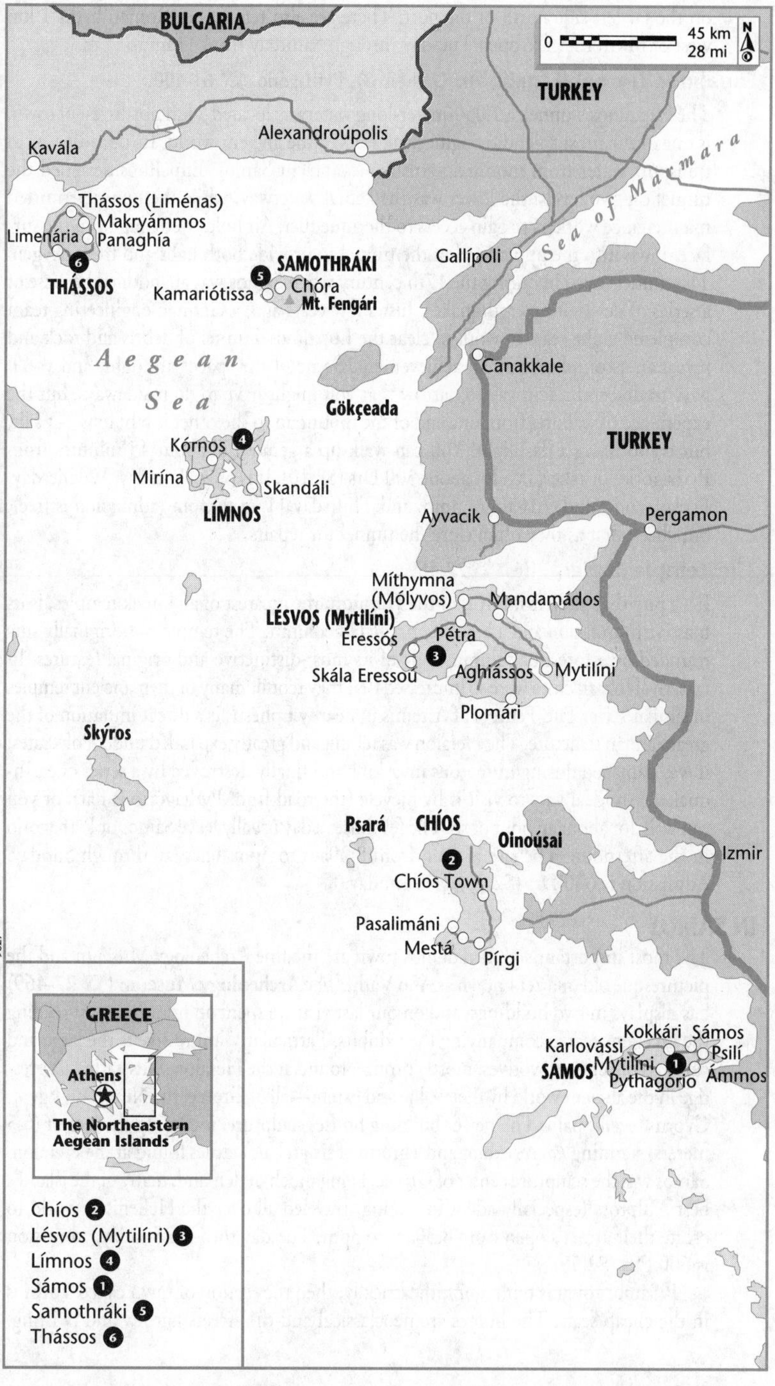
BULGARIA
TURKEY
0
45 km
28 mi
N
Alexandroúpolis
Kavála
Sea of Marmara
Thássos (Liménas)
Makryámmos
Limenária
Panaghía
THÁSSOS
SAMOTHRÁKI
Kamariótissa
Chóra
Mt. Fengári
Gallípoli
Canakkale
Aegean Sea
Gökçeada
TURKEY
Kórnos
Mirína
Skandáli
LÍMNOS
Ayvacik
Pergamon
Míthymna (Mólyvos)
Mandamádos
LÉSVOS (Mytilíni)
Eressós
Pétra
Skála Eressoú
Aghiássos
Mytilíni
Plomári
Skýros
Psará
CHÍOS
Oinoúsai
Izmir
Chíos Town
Pasalimáni
Mestá
Pírgi
Kokkári
Sámos
Karlovássi
Psilí
SÁMOS
Mytilíni
Pythagório
Ámmos
GREECE
Athens
The Northeastern Aegean Islands
Chíos 2
Lésvos (Mytilíni) 3
Límnos 4
Sámos 1
Samothráki 5
Thássos 6

on the far left side north of the port. There are also remains of Roman baths 1 km west of town; they are open Tuesday through Saturday from 11am to 2pm.

Eupalínos Tunnel (Efpalinion Orygma), Pythagório. ☎ **61-400.**

The Eupalínos Tunnel, a 1,050-meter-long waterway located 2 km northwest of town, is one of the most splendid engineering feats of the ancient world. Its purpose was to transport water from mountain streams to ancient Sámos. Eupalínos designed the tunnel on two levels: the lower was the actual waterway, while the upper permitted maintenance workers to gain access to the aqueduct. Air holes were dug from the surface down into the upper level of the tunnel to provide both light and fresh oxygen. The tunnel caved in during the 17th century when Sámos was abandoned because of a series of devastating earthquakes. Just a few years ago, a German engineering team completed eight years of work to clear the Eupalínos Tunnel of debris and rock and reveal an astounding human achievement. Some of the spaces are tight, and you'll have to descend a stairway so narrow that you might have to do it sideways, but the experience of walking from one end of the mountain to the other is fabulous—it's lit, but try to bring a flashlight! You can walk up a gentle hill about 45 minutes from Pythagório, or take a taxi for about 500 Drs ($2.10). It is open Tuesday, Wednesday, Friday, and Sunday 10am to 3pm, and Thursday 11am to 3pm (admission is free), but check first as they often close the tunnel for repairs.

The Temple of Hera, Iréo. ☎ **27-469.**

It's a pity that all that survives of the **Heraion,** the greatest of all Greek temples, is its massive foundation and a lone reconstructed column. The temple was originally surrounded by a forest of columns, one of its most distinctive and original features. In fact, rival Ionian cities were so impressed that they rebuilt many of their ancient temples in similar style. The Temple of Artemis in nearby Ephesus is a direct imitation of the great Samian structure. The Heraion was rebuilt and greatly expanded under Polycrates; it was damaged during numerous invasions and finally destroyed by a series of earthquakes. An ideal way to visit is by bicycle (the road from Pythagório is flat), or you can walk for about an hour or so. The few buses a day usually leave Sámos or Pythagório in the afternoon. The site is open from 8:30am to 3pm Tuesday through Sunday. Admission is 600 Drs ($2.50), free Sunday.

IN SÁMOS

The most important sights in Sámos town are the fine Archeology Museum and the picturesque old quarter known as Ano Vathí. The **Archeology Museum** (☎ **27-469**) has displays in two buildings, and on our last visit we spent an hour here just reading the excellent text accompanying the exhibits. Particularly impressive is the large and various collection of votives, mostly bronze, found at the Heraion, illustrating its prestige in the ancient world by their value and extent—all of Greece, the Near East, Egypt, Cyprus, even Spain. The newer building houses sculpture, including the largest (5.5 meters) standing *kouros* extant and a group of six archaic statues found at the Heraion. Sámos was the sculpture center of Greece; being much in demand, many of the island's best sculptors (especially adept in casting) traveled all over the Hellenistic world to create their art. It's open from 8:30am to 3pm, Tuesday through Sunday; admission is 600 Drs ($2.50).

If Sámos town is built amphitheatrically, then the section of town called **Vathí** is in the cheap seats. The homes are neoclassical and the streets narrow and twisting.

Vathí is in direct contrast to the town below; up in this quiet village there are few cars, motorcycles, tourist buses, or hotels. It's a residential area that retains a lot of its original character—a nice place to wander about.

AROUND THE ISLAND

Sámos has the best-known paleontological remains in Greece, mostly from Stephanidis Valley, near **Mitilíni.** Many of the finds excavated in this area are on display in the **paleontological museum** (☎ **51-205**), open Monday through Saturday from 8:30am to 2pm and 6 to 7:30pm; admission is 400 Drs ($1.65). There is bus service to **Mitilíni** three times a day from Sámos or Pythagório.

Kokkári is a short bus ride away from Sámos town on the north coast. Up until a decade ago it was a traditional Greek fishing village with small cobbled back streets, a few tavernas, and off in the distance, green, brush-covered hills. Today, small hotels, pensions, and rooms-to-let occupy many of the town's older homes. People come to Kokkári for the line of **beaches** that extend westward to Avlákia; they're made of large gray sand and pebbles and are fairly wide. Be forewarned that the winds on this side of the island are notorious; you may have to move on to sunbathe comfortably.

Samians have dubbed Platanákia, an interior corner of their island off the north coast road, "Paradise." Here, densely wooded valleys give way to terraced hills and mountain hamlets. To visit, take the Sámos road toward Ághios Konstantínos. At about the 18-km point from Sámos town there is a left turn to Aïdónia (meaning "nightingales") and Manolátes.

Oenophiles should stop at the **Paradisos Restaurant** (☎ **94-208**), which is a large garden café located just at the Manolátes turnoff from the coast highway. Your host, Mr. Folas, who worked in vineyards many years, makes his own wine from the excellent Samian grapes. Mrs. Folas's *tirópita* (fresh baked after 7pm) is made from local goat's milk and butter and wrapped in a flaky pastry. Paradisos is open daily for lunch and dinner, and now has a few rooms to let.

About 15 minutes up the winding country road to Manolates, totally wooded with evergreens and lulled by the sound of a running stream, are two more "country" tavernas. Near **Aïdónia** is a clear mountain spring that attracts scores of songbirds and is a delightful watering and washing spot.

We prefer the peaceful, half-hour hike uphill if you have the stamina, but a car road now also takes you right to Manolátes. You'll be rewarded by sky-high views of the steeply tiered grapevines growing over the foothills of Mt. Ámbelos (1,140 meters high) down to the deep-blue sea. The small and picturesque hamlet of Manolátes is a typical Samian village, with stucco homes and red-tiled roofs. The narrow cobblestone streets are so steep that you may find yourself bending forward to avoid falling backward. Manolátes has a simple taverna, and a small snackbar deeper in the pedestrian lanes with panoramic views.

Beaches

There are beaches near Sámos town, the closest and best being **Plaz Gagoú,** and on the east side of the port, the beach at **Kalámi.** There's an excellent beach at **Potámi,** on the far western end of the island, near Karlóvassi.

The most rapidly developing part of the coastline is on **Marathókampos Bay** along the extreme southwestern shore. A long, but narrow, rock and pebble beach, several tavernas, and a mushrooming number of hotels, pensions, and windsurfers fill the once-tiny village of **Órmos Marathókampos.**

Closer to Pythagorio are the resort beaches extending from **Iréo** east. Lots of luxury hotels, restaurants, beach cabanas, and watersports facilities have sprouted up under the din of the nearby airport. A better grade of beach (but crowded) is at *Psilí Ámmos,* about 5 km from Pythagorio (by excursion boat) on the south coast and 10 km from Sámos. There's occasional bus service to **Psilí Ámmos** from Sámos town. Another popular beach excursion is a visit to **Samiopoula,** a boat ride away to an excellent and usually uncrowded island beach (although there are also some rooms to rent).

Pythagório

ESSENTIALS The multitalented Pythagório Town's Tourist Office (☎ **0273/61-022**) is on the main street, Lykoúrgo Logothétou Street, one block up from the harbor; open daily from 8am to 10pm for assistance with rooms, changing money, making long distance calls, and so on. The local **police** (☎ **61-333**) are also on the main street to handle problems or emergencies. Samina Travel has an office on the port in Pythagório (☎ **61-583**); see the friendly Pavlo for advice. The **post office** is four blocks up from the harbor on the main street; the **OTE** is on the *paralía* near the pier. Alex Stavrides runs a laundromat off the main street on the church street; it's open 9am to 9pm daily, till 11pm in summer.

The **bus station** (actually just a couple of benches under a tree) is, like nearly everything else, on the busy main street, on the left, five or six blocks up from the harbor.

WHERE TO STAY

Pythagório is almost completely at the service of European tour groups. If you land there roomless, head for the Town's tourist office, one block off the *paralía* on the main street, for help with finding one of the many private rooms (approximately 6,250 Drs or $34.70 for a double room with private bath), catch the bus to Sámos town, or inquire at Rhenia Tours (☎ **61-589**) or Samina Travel (☎ **61-583**). These facilities claim to be open April 15 to October 31 unless otherwise noted.

$ **Hotel Alexandra,** Odós Metamorphoseus 11, Pythagório 83103. ☎ **0273/61-429.** 12 rms (8 with bath).

Rates: 4,875 Drs ($20.30) double without bath; 5,900 Drs ($24.70) double with bath. No credit cards.

This is a quiet pocket of good value, a small hotel on a tranquil lane near the church run by the kind and friendly Manolaros family. The upstairs rooms are plain and newer, with private bath, while the downstairs rooms are old-fashioned, with high ceilings and a shared bath. All will enjoy the wonderfully planted, lovingly tended shade garden and the company of Dimitri and his son John. Excellent value.

Hotel Evripili, Pythagório 83103. ☎ **0273/61-407.** 10 rms (all with bath).

Rates (including breakfast): 6,500 Drs ($27.10) single; 8,100 Drs ($33.75). No credit cards.

This 400-year-old stone mansion, across the lane from the new Hotel Labito, has been converted into compact, comfortable guest rooms, most with balconies. Although Austrian tour groups often fill the place in July and August, between April and late October you can check downstairs in the cozy basement breakfast lounge about room availability.

Captain Fragoulis, Pythagório 83103. ☎ **0273/61-473.** 9 rms (all with bath).

Rates (including breakfast): 5,500 Drs ($22.90) single; 8,150 Drs ($33.95) double. No credit cards.

This personal little pension has a mostly rustic stone facade and a wonderful view of Pythagório from its location on the road back to Sámos. The good Captain's son-in-law is an artist and he's lent his touch to the decor of this well-maintained hostelry.

George Sandalis Hotel, Pythagório 83103. ☎ **0273/61-691.** 14 rms (all with bath).

Rates (including breakfast): 7,500 Drs ($31.25) single; 10,500 Drs ($43.60) double. No credit cards.

Also above the town, this homey establishment has very tastefully decorated rooms, balconies with French doors (rear rooms face quiet hills), and a lovely flower garden. A reader who spent Greek Easter here assures us that this special inn had the cleanest rooms he had found on his tour. The friendly Sandalises spent many years in Chicago and are gracious hosts.

Hotel Hera II, Pythagório 83103. ☎ **0273/61-319.** Fax 0273/61-196.
7 rms (all with bath). A/C TEL

Rates (including breakfast): 14,425 Drs ($60.55) single; 16,275 Drs ($67.80) double. No credit cards.

Hotel Hera II (a favorite with in-the-know locals) is one of the most luxe hotels, situated on the hillside on the road back to Sámos. Behind the white marble is a small, luxurious neo-Baroque villa with drop dead views over the harbor below. Rooms with piped-in music are elegantly simple and the service (other than during July and August, when group-booked tourists take over) is first-rate.

★ **Hotel Labito,** Pythagório 83103. ☎ **0273/61-086.** Fax 0273/61-085.
69 rms (all with bath). A/C TEL

Rates: 12,825 Drs ($53.45) single; 15,065 Drs ($62.75) double. No credit cards.

This wonderful new hotel, designed to resemble rows of two-story Samian mansions painted in classic lemon-yellow with green and white trim, are a welcome addition to the heart of the village. Set just two lanes behind the port, it's in an ideally quiet and convenient location. The marble lobby, simply decorated indoor and terrace breakfast and bar areas, and the matched pastel pink or blue room furnishings add a touch of luxury rarely seen in a Class C hotel. Our top value choice in town.

Hotel Olympiada, Pythagório 83103. ☎ **0273/61-490.** 10 rms (all with bath). TEL

Rates: 4,800 Drs ($26.70) single; 9,315 Drs ($38.80) double. No credit cards.

This attractive, newly built hotel has pleasant plantings and a good view from its perch next to the pricey Hotel Hera II. Although it's about a 15-minute walk from the *paralía* (a steep uphill if you have luggage), the well-kept rooms are good value.

WHERE TO EAT

There are a few places to recommend, although prices at this resort are higher than what you'd pay in Sámos town.

Esperides Restaurant, Pythagório. ☎ **61-767.**

Cuisine: INTERNATIONAL. **Reservations:** Recommended in summer.
Prices: Appetizers 400–1,200 Drs ($1.65–$5), main courses 1,000–3,500 Drs ($4.15–$14.60). No credit cards.
Open: Daily 6pm–midnight in summer; noon–midnight rest of year.

This pleasant, walled garden is a few blocks inland from the port, and west of the main street. There are uniformed waiters and a dressier crowd. The variety of continental and Greek dishes is well presented and will appeal to a wide variety of palettes. We resented the frozen french fries served with their tasty baked chicken, but the meats and vegetables are fresh.

The Family House, Pythagório. No phone.

Cuisine: GREEK/CONTINENTAL.

Prices: Appetizers 500–2,400 Drs ($2.10–$10), main courses 650–3,500 Drs ($2.70–$14.60). No credit cards.

Open: Daily 6pm–midnight.

A more casual garden, enlivened by Christmas tree lights strung through some white-washed citrus trees, can be found a block east of the main street below the main church. The Greek food is tasty and not overcooked, and there's a respectable selection of pasta and seafood dishes for those who shun moussaká.

Restaurant Pythagora, Paralía. ☎ **61-371.**

Cuisine: GREEK.

Prices: Appetizers 450–1,000 Drs ($1.90–$4.15), main courses 1,200–2,800 Drs ($5–$11.65). No credit cards.

Open: Daily 11am–1am.

Of the many portside cafés, this is favored for its freshly made Greek specialties, a good selection of continental alternatives, and the gorgeous view of the harbor.

$ **I Varka,** Paralía. No phone.

Cuisine: SEAFOOD.

Prices: Appetizers 240–1,000 Drs ($1–$4.15), main courses 1,000–3,000 Drs ($4.15–$12.50). No credit cards.

Open: Daily May–Oct noon–midnight. Only 6pm–midnight in July–Aug.

The community of Pythagório has funded this ouzerí/taverna (pronounced *Ee Várka,* "The Boat") in a garden of salt pines at the south end of the port. Delicious fresh fish and grilled meats, and a surprising variety of *mezédes* (appetizers) are produced in the small kitchen built within a dry-docked fishing boat. The grilled octopus, strung up on a line to dry, and the pink barboúnia or clear gray mullet, all cooked to perfection over a charcoal grill, are the true standouts of a meal here.

Fast Facts: Sámos Town

Banks Sámos has a branch of the National Bank of Greece on the port (open from 8am to 2pm Monday through Thursday, till 1:30pm Friday). Several travel agents change money at a less favorable rate but stay open daily from 8am to 10pm.

Consulates There is a British Consulate on Sofouli Street in Sámos town (☎ **27-314**). Call them for information regarding hours and services.

Emergencies In Sámos, call the local police at **22-100** all hours of the day.

Hospitals The hospital (☎ **27-407** or **27-426**) is in Sámos town.

Laundry There are two laundromats within two blocks of the tourist office (EOT) office, including the Lavomatique (☎ **28-833**), which sells washer and dryer coupons at the news kiosk on the main square.

OTE The OTE is on Platía Iróon (Heroes' Square), across from the municipal garden (open daily, 24 hours).

Police The police station (☎ **27-333**) is near the Credit Bank at the south end of the OTE.

Post Office It's across the street from the OTE.

Telephone/telecommunications See OTE, above.

Tourist Offices The Sámos EOT Office (☎ **0273/28-530** or **28-582**) is a half block in from the port, one lane from the main square. It's open daily from 8am to 2:30pm, with extended hours (daily 7:30am to 10pm) in the high season. This EOT is manned by local people who are very helpful and informative; they won't make room reservations by phone but will help you find accommodation once you're at their office.

Travel Agencies International Travel (☎ **0273/23-605**; fax 0273/27-955), the agency nearest the port in Sámos town, is one of the best and friendliest; they can help you with all travel arrangements, find accommodations, change money at good rates and store your luggage for free. Samina Travel, up the harbor road at Odós Sofoúli 67 (☎ **0273/28-841**; fax **0273/23-616**), in Sámos town at the port, is also helpful and can change money and assist you in arranging day trips and plane tickets. Pythagoras Tours (☎ **0273/27-240**), on the port in Sámos, is one of many that sell ferryboat tickets to Piraeus, Ikaría, and Lésvos.

WHERE TO STAY

Sámos town is usually mostly booked by European tour groups during July and August. Ask EOT for their help with finding one of the many private rooms (approximately 8,000 Drs or $33.35) for a double room with private bath), or inquire at Samina Travel (☎ **28-841**). Facilities claim to be open April 15 to October 31 unless otherwise noted.

Aeolis Hotel, Odós Sofoúli 33, Sámos 83100. ☎ **0273/24-316.** Fax 0273/28-063. 57 rms (all with bath). A/C

Rates (including breakfast): 10,350 ($43.15) single; 15,525 Drs ($64.70). MC, V.

This attractive hotel is easily the best on the port. Even the front rooms are quiet, as the windows are double paned. The friendly owners take excellent care of it and are planning to add a swimming pool and jacuzzi on the top floor.

Pension Avli, Odós Lykoúrgou, Sámos 83100. ☎ **0273/22-939.** 20 rms (10 with bath).

Rates: 4,000 Drs ($16.65) single/double without bath; 5,700 Drs ($23.70) single/double with bath. No credit cards.

This is our favorite pension on the island, a lovely, restored Samian convent (complete with crypt) with a grand marble courtyard filled with plants and breakfast tables. Spyros tends his home well; the 10 bathless rooms are as large as you'd expect, simple but spotless, and have their own water closet. The common showers are down the hall. His modernized rooms with private bath are often reserved for groups, but you can inquire about their availability.

Emily Hotel, Odós Grámmou and Odós 11 Noemvríou, Sámos 83100. ☎ **0273/28-24-691.** 18 rms (all with bath). A/C TEL

Prices (including breakfast): 10,350 Drs ($43.15) single; 14,375 Drs ($59.90). AE, V.

You'll find this charming new hotel on the right several blocks up from the port on the small street between the Samos Hotel and the Catholic Church. The rooms are spacious, attractively furnished and especially quiet, most with their own balcony.

★ **Hotel Paradise,** Odós Kanári 21, Sámos 83100. ☎ **0273/23-911.** Fax 0273/28-754. 48 rms. 2 suites (all with bath). A/C TEL

Rates (including breakfast): 12,650 Drs ($52.70) single; 13,800 Drs ($57.50) double. EC, V.

This is a bright and sparkling addition to Sámos town—a stylish hotel with verdant grounds surrounding a large swimming pool set in their back garden. It's a convenient mid-village location, tranquil and a bit removed from the tourist crush but booked fairly solid by groups. There's a large snack bar, evening cocktail bar and pretty breakfast room. We love the cool blue, tastefully decorated rooms with homey, usable balconies, and a real bath tub. The large, bright suites have the same rough-stucco, country cottage feel plus an additional seating area.

Pythagoras Hotel, Odós Kalámi, Sámos 83100. ☎ **0273/28-422.** Fax 0273/27-955. 17 rms (all with bath).

Rates: 4,370 Drs ($18.20) single; 6,325 Drs ($26.35). MC, V.

We tried this older family hotel about 500 meters left from the port on the way to the town beach. It was plain but comfortable, and from our seaside room all we could hear was the surf and birds singing in the trees. The neighborhood café downstairs serves a good, inexpensive breakfast.

Hotel Samos, Odós Sofoúli 11, Sámos 83100. ☎ **0273/28-378.** Fax 0273/23-771. 105 rms (all with bath). TEL

Rates (including breakfast): 8,000 Drs ($33.35) single; 10,300 Drs ($42.95) double. EC, MC, V.

This comfortable lodge is the closest to the ferry with a popular café bar out front. The facade has been restored to resemble that of a classic Samian-style mansion, with such interior amenities as an elevator and wall-to-wall carpeting. Spacious, simple rooms are super-clean with first-rate service. We recommend the rooms in the back of the hotel, which are quieter and have larger balconies. All in all, a good bargain.

Sibylla Hotel, Platía Aghíou Nikoláou. Sámos 83100. ☎ **0273/22-396.** 20 rms (all with bath).

Rates: 4,375 Drs ($24.30) single; 7,250 Drs ($40.30) double. No credit cards.

This pretty hotel a couple of blocks in from the middle of the port, off the northwest corner of St. Nicholas Square, is popular with tour groups but a good choice if you can get a room. All are sparkling clean, designed in the old villa style of the local mansions (actually, the building originally served as a tobacco factory).

WHERE TO EAT

The real specialty on Sámos isn't the food (mostly tourist-quality, mediocre, and expensive), it's the wine; as Byron exclaimed, "Fill high the bowl with Samian wine!" The wine that most people (those used to California and French wines) prefer is a dry white called Samaina. There's also a relatively dry delicious rosé called Fokianos. The Greeks go wild over the sweet wines, and when we say sweet . . . These wines have names like Nectar, Dux, and Anthemis. Almost any restaurant on the island will serve one or all of these wines, and you really ought to try a bottle.

Christos Taverna, Platía Aghíou Nikoláou. ☎ **24-792.**

Cuisine: GREEK.

Prices: Appetizers 400–1,000 Drs ($1.65–$4.15); main courses 600–2,000 Drs ($2.50–$8.30). No credit cards.

Open: Daily 11am–11pm.

GREEK FOOD TO REMEMBER, a sign says. "Sure," we thought—but we'd tarried too long at the museum and it was the only place open. We played it safe with a Greek salad and stuffed eggplant—excellent and each a meal in itself. An English family told us our choice was the best meal they, too, had had. We came back several times and remember clearly how good it was!

$ **Gregoris Grill,** Smyrnis Street. ☎ **22-718.**

Cuisine: GREEK.

Prices: Appetizers 300–650 Drs ($1.25–$2.70); main courses 600–1,800 Drs ($2.50–$7.50). No credit cards.

Open: Daily 7–11:30pm.

We recently returned to this grill, 100 meters up from the *paralía* around the corner from the Olympic Airways office, and can report that this is still a first-class place. It isn't much to look at but the lamb chops were luscious and everything was cooked just right. The service is ultra-friendly (they don't speak English) and prices are cheap. Highly recommended, for a great value, typical taverna dinner.

Restaurant Medusa, Odós Sofoúli 25. ☎ **23-501.**

Cuisine: INTERNATIONAL.

Prices: Appetizers 575–2,000 Drs ($2.40–$8.35); main courses 1,400–2,800 Drs ($5.85–$11.65). No credit cards.

Open: Daily 9am–1am.

This very popular café/restaurant serves a huge variety of snack foods including pizza, sweet and savoury crêpes, grilled meats and fish, pasta, salads, and even some Greek standards. Though a bit pricey, particularly for drinks, the Medusa's portside views, Greek pop music track, and interesting, well-prepared food make it the favorite of our Samian friends.

Pergola Restaurant, Sámos Town. ☎ **28-794.**

Cuisine: CONTINENTAL.

Prices: Appetizers 700–2,500 Drs ($2.90–$10.40), main courses 800–2,900 Drs ($3.35–$12.10). EC, MC, V.

Open: Daily 6pm–midnight.

This isolated garden of lemon and pomegranate trees is in an undeveloped neighborhood one long block from the bus station away from the port. Locals like the Pergola for a splurge meal, opting for their filet marsala, house spaghetti, or seasonal specials prepared with European tastebuds in mind. A pleasant change from the typical taverna.

Kokkári

Kokkári, off-season, is a fishing village built up around a scalloped shore that boasts many waterside cafés, chic boutiques, small, pebble beaches, and pedestrian bridges and walkways. Its small-scale commercialism—though dense—is very appealing, and draws hordes competing for its few rooms and hotels in the summer months.

WHERE TO STAY & EAT

The Tourist Office (☎ **0273/92-333**) will do their best to place you; expect to pay 5,725 Drs ($23.85) for a room with bath, 4,875 Drs ($20.30) without. Most hotels willing to subrent a group-tour booked room to individuals will cost at least 10,000 Drs ($41.65) for two. The large deluxe **Hotel Arion** on the edge of town, with doubles for 17,500 Drs ($72.90), is a place sure to satisfy the splurge urge in some of our readers.

From the many rooms-to-let we looked at, we can recommend the simple twin-bedded rooms, with private toilet and shower (some with balconies), handled by the **Café Manos** (☎ **0273/92-217**) on the west end of the waterfront. They manage a small, brown-shuttered building and around the corner from it, the **Pension Christos,** both inland just off the east end of the waterfront. The newly built **Sophia Rooms-to-Let** (☎ **0273/92-431**) is above the west waterfront, so rear-facing water-view rooms will be the quietest. Both places charge 4,800 Drs ($20) for a single or double room.

Hotel Olympia Beach, Kokkári 83100. ☎ **0273/92-353.** Fax 0273/92-457.
11 rms (all with bath). TEL

Rates (including breakfast): 11,500 Drs ($47.90) single/double. No credit cards.

This is a bright, clean place overlooking the beach that is often booked by Euro-groups. If you do stay here, try to secure a sea-facing room, or you might find the road noise disturbing. The same management has recently built the **Hotel Olympia Village** (☎ **0273/92-420**) on the road into Kokkári. Though the facilities are nice, we didn't find the location as appealing.

★ **Taverna Avgo Tou Kokora**, Kokkári. ☎ **92-113.**

Cuisine: GREEK.

Prices: Appetizers 500–1,400 Drs ($2.10–$5.85); main courses 1,200–2,650 Drs ($5–$11.05). No credit cards.

Open: Daily noon–1am.

Locals rave about this chic seaside café with a refreshingly diverse menu and a postcard-perfect setting. (Its fanciful name means "Cock's Egg.") You'll find the island's biggest assortment of *mezédes* (appetizers) as well as a variety of grilled meats and fish, and of course, several dishes playing on the name of the establishment.

Evening Entertainment

The best discos in Sámos town are out of town on the road to Mitilini, **Metropolis,** which is big, loud and has a pool; **Zorba's,** for bouzouki; and the **Totem Disco,** 3 km from town on the main road to Pythagorio. The in place in town is the **In Music Bar,** near the central square, and there are several other bars of various kinds on the lanes just off the port.

Nightlife in Pythagório is much more restrained. The **San Lorenzo,** above the port on the Sámos road, and **Labito,** on the village's back lanes, are considered two of the island's best discos.

Excursions to Turkey

During the high season there are usually two boats a day between Sámos and Kuşadasi, Turkey, a popular, well-developed resort 20 minutes from the magnificent archeological site at Ephesus. One-way trip to Kuşadasi runs 12,000 Drs ($50), while a round-trip ticket (including a guided tour of Ephesus and a same-day return) costs 19,500 Drs ($81.25). If you decide to buy a round-trip ticket but wish to stay in Turkey for longer than a day, you'll have to pay an extra port tax. Many travel agencies sell tickets to Turkey, with boats departing from both Sámos town and Pythagório.

For additional information on what to see and do once you arrive in Turkey, consult Frommer's *Turkey on $40 a Day,* by Tom Brosnahan. The guide also lists hotels, restaurants, and transportation options.

2 Chíos

153 nautical miles NE of Piraeus

ARRIVING/DEPARTING • By Air Four flights leave daily from Athens. The **Olympic Airways** office is in the middle of the port road (☎ **24-515**).

• By Sea One **car ferry** leaves daily for Piraeus via Sámos, continuing onto Lésvos and once a week to Thessaloníki, Kavála, and the Dodecanese. Excursion boats service Chíos from Pythagorio, Sámos four times weekly. Check with the **Chíos Port Authority** (☎ **0271/44-432**) for current schedules and prices.

ESSENTIALS There is a **Tourist Information Office,** Odós Kanari 18 (☎ **0271/44-389**), in the City Hall of Chíos. They are very helpful and will assist you in finding a reasonably priced room. Open daily in summer 7am to 2:30pm and 6am Monday through Friday; 10am to 1:30pm on Saturday, 10 to 12pm on Sunday. The **tourist police** (☎ **44-427**) are headquartered at Odós Neorion 35. Another mine of information on the harbor, at Leof. Aegean 84, is **Chios Tours** (☎ **0271/29-444**), open daily to assist with a room search and possibly a discount. Chios Tours organizes excursions around the island, to Çeşme, Turkey, and to Sámos and can make or confirm international air reservations—all in all, a top-notch shop. Chios Tours or the Tourist Office will change money after the portside banks' normal hours. The **post office** and **OTE** are a block off the harbor on the right side.

Chíos (Híos) offers the adventurous visitor remote, sandy coves, intact medieval villages (where one can rent a room in a 700-year-old house!) excellent fishing, a diverse landscape, and an undisputed identity as a true shipowner's island. The elite families that control Greece's private shipping empires tend to congregate behind high stone fences on secluded islands; a point of pride for locals. The names Onassis (who came to the island from Smyrna during the massive population exchange between Greece and Turkey), Livanos, Karas, Pateros, and Chandris are only part of Chíos's modern-day pantheon.

The declining merchant navy employs the majority of the work force. The home-grown mastic industry produces millions in revenue from Chiclets and other gum products. Compared to the more familiar and heavily trampled Greek islands, and despite Scandinavian, Dutch, and German tour groups, tourism is, economically speaking, a relative sidelight. Chíos remains an ideal destination for those who want to escape the hordes and one of the most exotic places from which to cross over to Turkey.

Orientation

Boats dock at **Chíos town,** the largest on the island and a thriving, refreshingly Greek port filled with Greeks. Late-19th-century mansions (and some dating as far back as the 14th century) in various states of repair, line the coast road on the outskirts of town. There are beaches on nearly every coast of Chíos. The black-stone beach at **Emborios,** on the southern tip of the island, is magnificent, as is the western coast pebble cove at Trachiliou.

The most interesting villages, dating from medieval times, are **Pírgi** and **Mestá.** Both are in the mastic region, in the southern half of Chíos, so named because of the gum trees that still grow in the countryside—mastic in the Phoenician language was *chio,* which may account for the island's name. Pírgi is known throughout Greece for the distinctive gray-and-white geometric designs that decorate the facades of most of the village buildings. Mestá, and many of the hamlets surrounding it (including **Olýmpi** and **Véssa**), are architectural gems; these villages' two-story stone-and-mortar houses are linked by narrow vaulted streets and quiet *platíes* (squares).

Although no one knows for sure where Homer was born, most historians believe that he was from Chíos. The "Stone of Homer," where the blind poet was supposed to have sat when he composed his legendary works, is outside Vrodados in a grove of olive trees, at the ancient site of the Temple of Cybele and Rhea.

Getting Around

BY BUS All buses leave from Chíos town; the blue buses serve local destinations, green buses the more remote locales. There are four buses a day to Mesta (330 Drs or $1.40), eight a day to Pírgi (330 Drs or $1.40), five to Kardamilla, and only two buses a week to Volissos.

BY TAXI If you arrive by plane, count on taking a cab into town. Taxis to and from the airport are about 1,100 Drs ($4.60) for the 7-km ride. They're easily found at the port; fares run 3,300 Drs ($13.75) to Pírgi, and 4,400 Drs ($18.30) to Mesta.

BY CAR This is a large island, and fun to explore, so car-pooling really pays off. If you wish to rent a car, try **Vassilakis Brothers Rent-A-Car,** Odós Evgenias Handri 3 (☎ **23-205,** fax: 25-659). They also have an office at the airport (☎ **27-582**) and in Karfas (☎ **32-284**). Compact cars rent for about 13,200 Drs ($55) per day, but make sure to inquire about the specific terms of insurance.

BY MOPED Chíos is a great place for moped riding, with good roads and terrific scenery. There are several moped-rental shops on the port. A fully insured Honda 50, suitable for two, runs 3,850 Drs ($16) per day; expect to pay a few hundred less for a moped.

What to See & Do

Greeks come to Chíos for weeks at a time to take advantage of its many secluded beaches, scenic countryside and villages, and interesting cultural sites.

BEACHES

Beginning with the best, **Embórios** is a small fishing village built around a volcanically formed cove. The water appears black from the dark smooth stones on the ocean floor. Men wade knee-deep to catch squid and pry off crustaceans while snorkelers explore the colorful seabed. If you walk past the small man-made black-pebble beach that's filled with families, just over those rocks to your right is a beach that will knock your socks off. Walking on the black rocks feels and sounds like marching through a room filled with marbles, the sound reverberating against the rough volcanic cliff behind. The panorama of the beach, slightly curving coastline, and distant sea is heaven on earth. Yes, we are fond of this beach! There are regular buses from Chíos town or from Pírgi (8 kms away) to Embórios, or you can try hitching along the main highway from Chíos.

Up the coast, about 2 km, is a white-stone beach at **Komí.** If the best is on the far southern point of the island, it follows that second best should be on the extreme northern coast. **Nagos** is another seaside village that offers some great black-sand beaches. Most people go to the beach right near the town, but it can sometimes become crowded. The secret is to hike to the two small beaches a little to the east—take the small road behind the white house near the windmill and you'll get there. To get to Nagos you'll have to take the Kardamilla bus and hope that it'll continue the 5 km to the beach. If not, you can usually get a ride by waving down a private car.

On the west coast of Chíos, directly across from the main town, are a series of coves and beaches between Ormos Elinatas and Ormos Trachiliou. One cove, about 2 km north of the town of Lithion, has a long stretch of fine white pebbles and stones and serves as a nude beach; south of it is the slightly more developed cove above Lithion. If you intend to go to the west coast, consider renting a car or moped for the long, winding road, because there is only infrequent bus service to Lithion.

There are quite a few beaches near Chíos town. To the south is **Bella Vista,** a sandy beach that's often crowded. There's a sandy beach at **Karfás,** and a shallow bay. To the north, at **Vrondádos,** are two pebble beaches, one public, the other private, but open for a 275 Drs ($1.15) fee.

AROUND THE ISLAND

If your tour around the island takes you to the interior sections, you'll likely encounter huge swaths of the landscape that have been burned. This is from a series of calamitous fires that spread throughout the island during 1988.

The two most interesting excursions are to the mastic villages, including Véssa, Armólia, Pírgi, Olýmpi, and Mestá, and to Anávatos and Néa Moní, the 11th-century monastery in the center of the island. **Pírgi** is the only village in Greece decorated with such a distinctive white-and-gray motif. From the main *platía* the view is like some strange Neo Geo or Op Art dream with the geometric patterns taking on a life of their own. The men who sit at the outdoor cafés don't seem to be fazed at all. The irony is that of all villages in Greece, Pírgi is where the majority of coffee-shop owners in New York City come from. Just off the main square in Pírgi is the 12th-century Byzantine chapel of Ághioi Apóstoloi, built in the style of the earlier Néa Moní. It's a tiny jewel, with 17th-century frescoes still in good condition.

Mestá is very different from Pírgi. This remarkable 14th-century "fortress" village was built inside a system of walls, with corner towers and iron gates to fend off invaders. The meter-thick, attached walls of the houses create a labyrinthine maze of streets that will charm, delight, and disorient you. Though many young people have moved away, life is thriving in Mestá thanks to the many renovation projects. The arch-roofed houses that have withstood centuries of earthquakes reveal interiors of remarkable grace. Life is slow and quiet here—Kyle couldn't tear herself away to update the rest of the island for three days!

There are two beautiful churches; the newer one (it's 120 years old) is the fourth-largest and one of the wealthiest in Greece. Its ornate frescoes, massive chandeliers, and lovely icons make it worth a stop on your trip through the main square. The older church, Paleós Taxiarchis, is buried deep in the village; the gatekeeper lives across the street. Its Byzantine frescoes have been revealed beneath the plaster that covered them during its use as a Turkish mosque. Both churches are dedicated to the patron saints of the village, Michael and Gabriel.

Chíos is ringed by several private islets that are served by charter boats, if you want a local travel agent to arrange a day trip. The most famous of these is **Oinousai** (Inoússes) an 18-square-kilometer island that is home to 30 multimillionaire families who are said to control 25% of Greece's 2,700 registered-vessel merchant fleet. Constantine Lemos, who supposedly grosses a million dollars a day, is only one among many who form the tightly knit society on Oinousai. The social life on this private isle is rumored to be as wild as anything in Greece. Daily excursion boats ply the short distance between Chíos and Inousses for beach, fish, and island tours. Chíos Tours can arrange such a day trip for about 6,050 Drs ($25.20).

Five nuns live a quieter life at **Néa Moní,** a medieval (11th-century) church built by craftsmen brought over from Turkey. It's one of Greece's prettiest monasteries, with an octagonal chapel that is highlighted by exquisite mosaics: Marble white, azure blue, and ruby red dominate the glittering field of gold tiles. If you've arrived from Turkey and visited the Kariye Camii in Istanbul, the high quality and style of these mosaics should be familiar (though the work in Istanbul is more recent this was restored after an 1881 earthquake). These at Néa Moní are the best of their kind, on par with those at Ossios Loukas and Dafní. Be sure to look into the cistern (bring a flashlight), a cavernous vaulted room with columns, to your right as you come through the main gate. The small chapel at the entrance to the monastery is dedicated to the martyrs of the 1822 massacre by the Turks (who also damaged the monastery itself). The skulls and bones are the victims themselves. There are only a few buses each week (check the schedule at the station) to Néa Moní; you may have to take a moped, car, or taxi. It's open daily except from 1 to 4pm (the nuns' nap) and after 8pm.

Where to Stay

If you're just arriving on Chíos, it might make sense to find accommodations in the town before setting off for one of the island's many special villages (prettier and cheaper, though you'll need your own transportation to sightsee). Chíos town has a large number of private rooms; you can expect to pay 5,550 Drs ($30.80) for two. Contact the Tourist Office for references.

Pension Giannis, Odós Livanoú 48-50, 82100 Chíos. ☎ **0271/27-433.**
13 rms (10 with bath).

Rates: 6,050 Drs ($25.20) single/double without bath; 8,800 Drs ($36.70) single/double with bath. No credit cards.

It's half past midnight, you just got off the ferry from Piraeus or Sámos, don't have a room, and the town is dead. What do you do? Walk straight ahead, away from the port, and into this pleasant pension. It's not a bad value, the rooms are clean and fine, and the garden behind it is a treat.

Hotel Diana, Odós Venizélou 92, 82100 Chíos. ☎ **0271/24-656.** Fax 0271/26-748.
51 rms (all with bath). A/C TEL

Rates (including breakfast): 8,800 Drs ($36.70) single; 11,000 Drs ($45.80) double. EC, MC, V.

This is an aging Class C-inn, one block in from the port. The rooms have showers and are comfortable and clean, with terrazzo floors. There is a lobby breakfast room, but even better, a rooftop bar. Open year round.

★ **Hotel Kyma,** Odós Chandrís 1. 82100 Chíos. ☎ **0271/44-500.** Fax 0271/44-600. 59 rms (all with bath). A/C TEL

Rates (including breakfast): 11,220 Drs ($46.75) single; 14,520 Drs ($60.50) double. No credit cards.

Our favorite in-town lodging was built in 1917 as a private villa for John Livanos—you'll notice the lovely portrait of Mrs. Livanos on the ceiling in the ground floor. Though the hotel is of historic interest (the treaty with Turkey was signed in the Kyma in 1922) most of the architectural details, other than in the lobby area and breakfast room, are gone; all rooms have been renovated in a modern style. On the positive side, many rooms have views of the sea, a few have wildly enervating whirlpool baths, and the management, under the smart direction of host Theo Spordilis, is capable and helpful to a fault. And that's not all. We enjoyed one of our best breakfasts in Greece here, complete with Chíos oranges, thick yogurt, tea and coffee of all varieties, and more fresh fruit.

OUTSIDE OF CHÍOS TOWN

Karfas, 7 km south of Chíos town around Cape Aghía Eléni, is an exploding tourist resort. Its fine sandy beach is lined with expensive Greek all-inclusive holiday hotels. There are also a great many rooms and apartments for rent in the Vrondatos beach area north of Chíos town. Contact Tourist Information or Chíos Tours (☎ **0271/29-444**) for specific recommendations.

Golden Sand Hotel, P.O. Box 32, Karfás 82100, Chíos. ☎ **0271/32-080.** Fax 0271/31-700. 108 rms (all with bath). A/C MINIBAR TEL

Rates: 15,730 Drs ($65.50) single; 20,900 Drs ($87.10) double, depending on season. AE, EC, MC, V.

The Golden Sand is one of the earliest Karfas beach resorts, an attractive, group-oriented, two-story lodge with a large roof deck and marble floors throughout. This Class A establishment also has a large pool, its own private beach, satellite TV and radio in large guest rooms, and a spacious, airy breakfast area. There's even a beauty salon and kids' playground! The resort opens from May to October, but between mid-June and mid-September a compulsory half board plan is in effect, adding 2,750 Drs ($11.45) per person, per day, to the high season rates above.

TRADITIONAL VILLAGES

There are a few villages in Greece that seem timeless; built in centuries past, life appears to have changed little in the intervening years. Many are outdoor architectural museums, studied and appreciated for their unique styles of construction, but unfortunately abandoned by the younger members of the community. Mestá, 36 km northwest of Chíos town, is just such a village, and fortunately, the Greek government acquired 33 old abandoned homes to protect them from further deterioration. Four of these homes, originally built over 500 years ago, have been restored and opened by EOT as part of its Traditional Settlements Program. The wonderful Dimitri Pipidis (☎ **0271/76-319**) manages the four houses (total of eight rooms) and each comes equipped with a kitchen, bathroom, and enough sleeping space for two to six people. The price is determined by the number of beds: for one bed, 7,700 Drs ($32.10); two beds, 8,800 Drs ($36.70); and three beds, 10,000 Drs ($41.70).

If there is no answer at the Mestá number, just drive to the village—Dimitri's office is on the center *platía.* If the houses are booked, Dimitri will assist you in finding one of the many private rooms in Mestá. A typical room runs 6,600 Drs ($27.50) depending on the house and season. For the high season, make your reservations early, a must in the busy summer months.

There are also private rooms for rent in Pírgi, though it's so busy with day trippers that we found Mesta much more relaxing. One such place is **Astra Rooms** (☎ **0271/71-149**) where very simple, bathless rooms go for 2,420 Drs ($10.10) a bed per night. Astra is located one block off the main *platía*, where several businesses offer nearby rooms to let.

In Pasalimani, around the corner from the petit harbor, there is a wonderfully rustic inn called the **Mikro Castello** (☎ **0271/28-743**), which is a handmade four-room treasure trove of carved wood sculpture. Each room has a platform bed, fireplace, and rudimentary kitchen gear. We've visited twice and are always taken with it. A room for two, including breakfast, costs 8,800 Drs ($36.70); no credit cards accepted.

In the other mastic villages the only accommodation may be a room in the home of a local family. The **Women's Agricultural-Tourist Cooperative of Chíos,** like their counterpart on Lésvos, offers a program enabling tourists to share the life of local farm families in very simple (primitive) farmhouses. Their members offer 65 bathless rooms in the towns of Mestá, Pírgi, Armolia, or Olýmpi. You can enjoy this 3,960 Drs ($16.50) for one; 5,500 Drs ($22.90) for two, plus an additional 660 Drs ($2.75) for breakfast. Though not required, you can cook, or work in the fields with your host. In any of the villages, except Mestá, we think it's the best choice. For reservations, write to the cooperative at Pirgi 82102, Chíos, Greece, or call **0271/72-496.** The office is open all year.

For the traveler with latent hermetic tendencies, visit Psará, a small island 18 nautical miles off the west coast of Chíos, where rooms are offered in a restored 17th-century parliament building, with the same price scale as the Mestá houses. Call them (☎ **0274/61-293** or **0251/27-908** in Lésvos) for information. There is ferry service to Psará from Chíos three times a week.

Where to Eat

Our cognoscenti friends on Chíos prefer to take a short drive, south or north, for fine cuisine. Starting with the beaches, **Giamos** on Karfas beach is known as a good outlet for meat courses. If you're in **Embório** or **Pasalimáni** make sure to try the fish and squid. Both villages are known for their seafood, and you can watch the fishers bring in their catch right in front of your table. The same is true just north of **Vrondados** at the **Ormos Lo Restaurant** near the public beach.

Apolaisi, Aghía Ermióni Village. ☎ **31-359.**

Cuisine: SEAFOOD.

Prices: Appetizers 600–1,320 Drs ($2.45–$5.50); fish from 9,350 Drs ($39) per kilo. No credit cards.

Open: Daily 5pm–midnight.

One or two kilometers south is a delightful fish taverna run by Yiorgo Karanikola. We spent a lovely evening, on a candlelit terrace above the harbor, dining on fried calamari, grilled fish, and an assortment of salads while fishers below were taking their boats out for their night's work. You'll need to take a taxi to get to Apolaisi; plan on a 10- to 15-minute ride.

Chíos Marine Club, Odós Nenitoúsi 1. ☎ **23-184.**

Cuisine: GREEK.

Prices: Appetizers 270–1,320 Drs ($1.10–$5.50), main courses 550–2,750 Drs ($2.30–$11.50). EC, MC, V.
Open: Daily noon–2am.

This is a good, if simple, taverna right in town, with a Greek and the pasta-meats-fish variety to please all in your crowd. Try their galeos (a local fish) grilled, or their bamies, an okra dish.

Iviskos, Central Square. No phone.

Cuisine: CONTINENTAL.
Prices: Snacks/desserts 350–2,500 Drs ($1.45–$10.40) No credit cards.
Open: Daily 7am–2am.

Not only does Iviskos serve wonderful bread with their 7am breakfast, but they also serve a dynamite Black Forest cake until 2am. This is the place for light eats and people-watching. Picnickers and shoppers can also head two blocks in from the port to the main *platía,* where you'll find bakers, butchers, produce vendors, and so. For more of a hearty soup-to-nuts meal, try the tavernas clustered on the right side of the port.

Theodosiou Ouzerí, Paralía, Chíos. No phone.

Cuisine: GREEK.
Prices: Appetizers 385–3,080 Drs ($1.60–$12.80) No credit cards.
Open: Daily 5–midnight.

In the evening, many residents prefer to pull up a streetside chair at a café along the water and sip an ouzo or slurp a chocolate sundae. Of the many cafés on the *paralía* we like Theodosiou Ouzerí, located on the far right side of the port, both for the scene and its menu.

Paradise (Yiorgo Passa's), Langada Village. ☎ **74-218.**

Cuisine: SEAFOOD.
Prices: Appetizers 594–2,530 Drs ($2.50–$10.50); fish from 9,350 Drs ($39) per kilo. No credit cards.
Open: Daily 11am–2am.

About 20 km north of Chíos is a fantastic dining venue—a fishing village with a strip of five or six outdoor fish taverns lining the harbor. Of those that we sampled, we prefer the food prepared by Yiorgo Passa at his Paradise Snackbar. His place is the first on the left as you walk down to the waterfront. Prices are low, portions generous, and the ambience delicious. **Note:** There are evening dinner cruises to Langada from Chíos; check with Chíos Tours about the schedule and prices.

Excursions to Turkey

During the summer there are daily departures to Çeşme, Turkey, from the port of Chíos. The round-trip price is about 14,000 Drs ($58.30), including a bus tour of the city of Izmir, or a two-hour bus ride and tour of Ephesus and all taxes. In the other months boats run less frequently; check with the portside travel agents such as Chíos Tours. **Note:** Çeşme is a 45-minute bus ride from Izmir on the Aegean coast, where buses run frequently to Istanbul and all the coastal cities including Ephesus.

For additional information on what to see and do once you arrive in Turkey, consult Frommer's *Turkey on $40 a Day,* by Tom Brosnahan. The guide also lists hotels, restaurants, and transportation options.

3 Lésvos (Mytilíni)

188 nautical miles NE of Piraeus

ARRIVING/DEPARTING • By Air Three flights leave daily from Athens, ten flights weekly from Thessaloníki. Olympic Airways (☎ **28-660**) has an office at Odós Kavetsou 44, about 200 meters south of Aghia Irinis park (walk up from the harbor and turn left); with an airport bus to meet flights 330 Drs ($1.40).

• By Sea One boat daily calls from Piraeus, stopping at Chíos and one boat weekly from Rafina. Two boats call weekly from Kavála, stopping at Límnos; one boat weekly from Thessaloniki, stopping at Límnos and daily boats to Chíos. Ask EOT about ferry service to Alexandroúpoli and Samothráki, and the hydrofoil service to Kavála, Límnos, and Chíos, both of which are supposed to be regularized by 1995. Call the **Maritime Co.** (**0251/23-720**) or the **port police** (☎ **0251/28-647**) for current schedules.

Generally speaking, always double-check schedules in Lésvos (unreliable even for Greece). Also, many of the ferries to Mytilíni are scheduled to arrive at midnight, but are as late as 2:30am. The late boats are not necessarily met by people with *domátia* (rooms to let), so do be sure to call ahead for accommodation. If you're stuck, you can always wake up the nightclerk at the Hotel Sappho, midway down the *paralía* at Koundourióti 31 (☎ **22-888**), where doubles go for 9,900 Drs ($41.25).

ESSENTIALS The EOT is at Odós Aristarhou 6 (☎ **0251/42-511;** fax 0251/42-512) on the port in Mytilíni. They're open daily from 8am to 2pm with extended hours in the high season and have a complete listing of hotels, pensions, and rooms throughout the island, and are willing to make calls for you for accommodations in Mytilíni. The **tourist police** (☎ **22-776**) are located on the *paralía.* The **Vostanio Hospital** (☎ **43-777**) on Votsani Street will take care of emergencies. The **post office** is next door to the OTE, both a long block up from the harbor on Vournazon near the park. The telephone **area code** for Mytilíni is 0251, for Molyvos/Mithymna and Eressós it's 0253, and for Plomari it's 0252. For **laundry,** the Lavomatique (☎ **42-570**), across from the bus station at Venizelou and Smirnis, offers quick, cheap, friendly service every day and even has evening hours; expect to pay 2,200 Drs ($9.20) to wash and dry a load.

It's impossible to think about Lésvos (also called Lésbos or Mytilíni) without the island's two most obvious, and related, associations: the love of women for women and the great classical poet Sappho, whom Plato dubbed the Tenth Muse. Legends abound about the origin of the former, some suggesting that it developed as a cult or college devoted to Aphrodite (possibly founded by Sappho), others theorizing that the island became "lesbian" when the Athenians wreaked vengeance on its inhabitants, after a failed rebellion, by murdering all of its men. As for Sappho, she is an equal mystery because so little of her writing has survived. What is known is that she lived in the 7th century B.C. and was born in the village of Eressos on the western part of the island. She wrote openly about love and desire, of men and women: "Love's unbound my limbs and set me shaking,/A demon bittersweet and my unmaking." Sappho's tragic legend of love began with her unrequited passion for Phaon, an attractive younger man, whom Sappho followed across the sea to the mainland. When he finally rejected her in Lefkada, Sappho flung herself over the white cliffs and plunged to her death.

That Lésvos was an artistic center is without dispute (there is still a festival each May called "The Week of Prose and Arts"), but it was most famous in ancient times for its academies and symposia. Theophrastus, director of the Athens Academy, was from Lésvos—both Aristotle and Plato went to Lésvos to teach and study. The maxims "Know thyself" and "Nothing in excess," inscribed on the Temple at Delphi, were taken from the writings of Pitticus, one of the Seven Sages of Greece and a tyrant of Lésvos. The philosopher Epicurus came to Lésvos from Sámos to study and write: "Pleasure is our first and kindred good," which is something that one who has lived on the lovely island of Lésvos has the privilege to say.

Today, the island's face is changing because of the growing number of British tourists—read: groups—especially the northern town of Mólyvos, one of the loveliest parts of the island.

Orientation

Lésvos, Greece's third-largest island, is shaped something like a rounded triangle with two inland bays fed by the Aegean through a pair of south coastal channels.

Mytilíni (and the airport) are on the southeastern corner of the triangle, just across from Ayvalik, on the Turkish coast. The east coast road, leading up to **Mandamádos,** is the most scenic on the island; olive and fruit trees grow down to the water's edge and thermal springs form warm pools that attract bathers. **Mólyvos** (formerly called Míthymna), at the northern tip of the triangle, is a castle-crowned village with stone and pink-pastel stucco mansions capped by red-tile roofs. The town overlooks the sea, its modest harbor, and flanking pebble beaches overflowing with sunners and swimmers. Seven kilometers south of Mólyvos is the enterprising village of **Pétra,** where the Women's Agricultural-Tourist Cooperative program welcomes visitors to live in local homes.

The paved road to Mólyvos meets the west-bound road at *Kaloní,* a sardine center 4 km north of Lésvos's largest inland body of water. The western half of the island is the least visited; sandy beaches run the length of the coast from Sígri to Skála Eressoú. The villages on this part of Lésvos are as serene as one finds on the island.

Plomári is 40 kilometers southwest of Mytilíni. It's a village very much like Mithymna, but with a significant twist: Plomari is one of Greece's major ouzo centers. If you're there when the potent drink is being distilled your nose will catch the fennel scent wafting in the breeze.

Getting Around

BY BUS AND TAXI Mytilíni has an expensive and infrequent bus system with daily service in summer: to Kaloní or Mólyvos (four times), to Mandamádos (once), Plomari (four times), and to Eressos and Sigri (once). The round-the-island KTEL buses can be caught at the south end of the port behind the Argo Hotel. Lésvos is a big island (a taxi to Mólyvos costs 8,800 Drs ($36.70) one way, 11,000 Drs. ($45.80) to Eressos or Sigri), better suited to cars and buses than mopeds. The city bus station and taxi stand are on the port near the Popular Art (folk) Museum.

BY CAR There are many car-rental offices on the port in Mytilíni; **Europcar** (☎ **0251/43-311**) has offices in Mytilíni and a desk at the airport (☎ **0251/61-200**). Expect to pay 14,300 Drs ($59.60) a day without gas for a Fiat Panda.

BY BOAT **Aeolic Cruises** (☎ **0251/23-960,** fax: 0251/43-694) offers daily boat excursions around the island during the high season from their portside office.

Mytilíni

Mytilíni's sophisticated, big-city ambience is most akin to Thessaloníki than any other Aegean backwater. Unlike most of the country, Lesviots know that they're Europeans, and they feel that they share with the continent a rich cultural legacy. Though Mytilíni is not to everyone's taste, we confess to a sneaking soft spot for its chic style and gloomily imposing architecture. Even if you're looking for white cubes over a dazzling sea, we suggest sticking around town long enough to take in the best sights, especially the excellent Theophilos Museum in nearby Variá, the port, and the ornate, peaked dome Church of St. Therapon. The port street, or Prokymaia, is **Koundourióti Street,** the most important area of the city for tourists, with nearly all services and shops, while Ermoú Street, parallel to the harbor, is the main commercial thoroughfare. There are many grand old garden villas scattered around town, especially near the archeological museum, west of the port. To the north, toward the fortress, Mytilíni's crumbling ochre backstreets contain a mix of traditional coffeehouses, artisans, and food vendors, along with stylish new jewelry, antiques and clothing stores.

WHAT TO SEE & DO

In addition to the following, don't overlook the well-preserved Roman aqueduct thought to have been built in the 2d century. This impressive edifice is located near Moria, a short distance from Mytilíni.

Museums

Behind the dock is the new **Archeological Museum** of Mytilíni, at Odós Eftalíou 7 (☎ **28-032**), with a fine sculpture collection. The museum exhibits finds from the Bronze Age up to the Hellenistic era from Therme and Molyvos, including the latest excavations, and a rich selection of mosaics, sculpture, and tablets. Open Tuesday through Sunday from 8:30am to 3pm; admission is 500 Drs ($2.10).

The **Popular Art Museum,** Koundourióti Street (☎ **41-844**) is in a small white house in the center of the port. Its current curator and guide, Ioanna, will give you a wonderful tour of its fine embroideries, eccentric pottery (much of which came from Cannakale, Turkey), costumes, and historical documents. Open Monday through Saturday 8:30am to 2pm; admission is 250 Drs ($1.05).

About 3 km south, in Variá, is the former house—now a museum—of folk artist Hatzmichail Theóphilos (1868-1934), who emigrated from the Mt. Pelio region to paint on his home island. His watercolors of ordinary people, daily life, and local landscapes are widely celebrated, and they are also exhibited at the Museum of Folk Art in Pláka, in Athens. The museum itself is comprised of a series of rooms hung floor to ceiling with Theophilos's extraordinary canvases. Be sure to take in the photographs showing Theophilos dressed as Alexander the Great; he used to travel around Greece dressed as the fallen soldier and would pose little costumed boys as his minions! Be sure to make it to this collection. It is open Tuesday through Sunday from 9am to 1pm and 4:30 to 8pm; admission is 250 Drs ($1.05).

Other Collections

The mildly compelling Teriad Library and Museum of Modern Art is adjacent to the Theophilos Museum, in the home of the noted art critic Stratis Eleftheriadis-Teriad. Copies of his published works, including the *Minotaure* and *Verve* magazines, as well as his personal collection of works by Picasso, Matisse, and other modern artists are displayed. It is open Tuesday through Sunday from 9am to 1pm and 5 to 8pm; admission is 500 Drs ($2.10).

There is also a Traditional House of Mytilíni (☎ **28-550**) in front of the cathedral in the center of Mytilíni town, whose interior has been restored and furnished in a 19th-century style. Admission is by appointment only, with Mrs. Vlahou Marika, owner of this private collection.

WHERE TO STAY

Mytilíni is cursed with a large number of older hotels on the port that are hardly worth mentioning. Instead, we suggest taking a visit to the helpful EOT office and inquiring about the availability of private rooms.

Hotel Erato, Odós Vostani 2, Mytilíni 81100. ☎ **0251/41-160.**

22 rms (all with bath). TEL

Rates: 6,600 Drs ($27.50) single; 9,000 Drs ($37.50) double. EC, MC, V.

This four-story lodging was converted from a medical clinic. Bright rooms with scrubbed-clean bath and balcony go for a reasonable rate. Most of the rooms that we inspected seemed pretty quiet for such a central location. Open all year round.

Salina's Garden, Odós Fokeas 7-9, Mytilíni 81100. ☎ **0251/42973.**

8 rooms (2 with bath).

Rates: 4,950 Drs ($20.65) single; 6,600 Drs ($27.50) double. No credit cards.

These clean, rustic rooms, ranged around a lovely garden, are not far from the old fortress in town. There is no Salina here, just a friendly, English-speaking Greek family who create a relaxed, mellow atmosphere very popular with budget travelers. They also rent motorbikes for a reasonable price. This place fills up fast, so call ahead.

WHERE TO EAT

Mytilíni, with its youthful, somewhat avant-garde population, has even more portside cafés and tavernas than your average bustling harbor town. At the southern end of the port (opposite the new docks) are several small **ouzerís,** specializing in grilled octopus, squid, shrimp, and local fish. Small portions of *tzatzíki, patátes,* and olives accompany wine or one of the many types of ouzo from Plomari. The cluster of chairs around the small lighthouse at the point is the most scenic (as well as the windiest) of these places. For *après* ouzo there are several cafés, but on soccer night it's almost impossible to get a seat.

Arapis Grill, Paralía. No phone.

Cuisine: GREEK.

Prices: Appetizers 275–1,100 Drs ($1.15–$4.60), main courses 550–2,750 Drs ($2.10–$11.45). No credit cards.

Open: Daily 11:30am–11:30pm.

This taverna, located mid-port near the Sappho Hotel, is one of the better grills around, with particularly good beef dishes. Try any of their tender souvlaki, or the lamb with potatoes.

Around the Island

Many visitors to Lésvos prefer to stay in Mólyvos, up on the north coast, and take excursions from there. Alternatively one could do the same thing from the south coast village of Plomari, but it has been taken over by groups. The Cooperative Tourism and Travel Agency (☎ **21-329**, fax 0251/41-268) at Odós Konstantinoupóleos 5, next to the bus station, will help you find rooms in any of the island's rural areas.

If you want to disappear into Lésvos's seductive landscape, head to the west, where fewer visitors tread. The long coast road, which sometimes veers inland through olive groves, has a series of less-than-inviting pebble and stone beaches; however, if you feel like stopping for a fish lunch, we can recommend the harbors at Panaghiouda, Pyrgi Thermis, and Skala Mistegnon.

Before we go on, a few good words should be said in support of the lovely port town of **Skála Sykaminiá** and, closer to Mólyvos, **Eftálou** (the birthplace of author Arghýris Eftálou and the site of a famous thermal bath). These two are simple villages, with unpretentious architecture, natural allure, and the deliberate pace of life that marks Greek peasant life.

MÓLYVOS (MÍTHYMNA) & THE NORTH

The legend told most often about Mólyvos concerns Arion, a 7th-century-B.C. poet-musician and contemporary of Sappho. Apollo told Arion in a dream that the sailors who were returning him to Lésvos were going to kill him for the prize he had won in a music contest. The events unfolded as Apollo had prophesied, and when Arion was granted one last wish, he asked the sailors if he could play his lyre. They consented and Arion, at the very last moment, played and jumped into the sea. He was picked up by a school of appreciative dolphins, who carried him on their backs to the shores at Mólyvos. Historians believe that part of the story is based on fact.

Although there are now altogether too many souvenir shops selling genuine plastic neon-green backscratchers and the like, the village is still a wonderful place to soak up a lot of Greek atmosphere: the men who live in cafés, studying their ouzo, the bright, colorful geraniums and roses that decorate balconies and sills, the unfathomable layout of streets, alleyways, and passages, and the women, always working, who have a special place on Lésvos. In Mólyvos, you can wander up to the Genoese fortress, stroll along the port, or swim at the local pebble beaches.

Where to Stay

One place to start in Mólyvos is the **Tourist Information Office** (☎ **0253/71-347**)—they maintain a list of private rooms to rent, many of which are up on the hill near the ochre-colored castle. A Class A room in Mólyvos typically starts at 6,000 Drs ($27.50).

Hotel-Bungalows Delfinia, Mólyvos 81108. ☎ **0253/71-315.** Fax 0253/71-524. 65 rms, 57 bungalows (all with bath). MINIBAR (in bungalows) TEL

Rates (including breakfast): 14,014 Drs ($58.40) single; 19,250 Drs ($80.20) double; 27,500 Drs ($114.60) for bungalow with half-board plan. AE, DC, V.

This contemporary white stucco and gray stone resort, in a panoramic setting above the port and beach, is not a bad value in full-service hotels. Piped-in music, minibars, room service, and one-day laundry can go a long way toward making a vacation special. Though the rooms are simple, there's a salt water swimming pool, table tennis, snack bar, basketball, volleyball, and tennis facilities. There's also heating because it's open year round.

Nicholas Prokopiou Rooms To Let, Odós Eftaliótou 22, Mólyvos 81108. ☎ **0253/71-403.** 4 rms (none with bath).

Rates: 5,500 Drs ($22.90) double; 6,600 Drs ($27.50) triple. No credit cards.

We found a lovely unnamed stone house in the old part of town that had rooms. For a modest sum, one gets a clean double-bedded room, kitchen facilities, and the pleasure of dining in a secluded, verdant garden.

Sea Horse Pension, Mólyvos 81108. ☎ **0253/71-320.** Fax (0253) 71-374.
14 rms (all with bath).

Rates (including breakfast): 6,900 Drs ($28.75) single; 7,900 Drs ($32.90) double. No credit cards.

There are a cluster of recently built Class C style group hotels set below the old town, near the beach. Among them is this smaller, homier pension, *Thalássio Álogo* in Greek, where the friendly manager Stergios keeps tidy rooms with good views. There's also a restaurant and an in-house travel agency.

Where to Eat

As for dining, Mólyvos has quite a few good possibilities. Two of the best are:

Melinda's, Mólyvos. ☎ **71-787.**

Cuisine: INTERNATIONAL.
Prices: Appetizers 275–720 Drs ($1.15–$3); main courses 915–2,520 Drs ($3.80–$10.50). No credit cards.
Open: Daily 7pm–1am.

This restaurant offers a scrumptious vegetarian menu (they also serve meat entrées). Our favorites are carrot-and-currant salad, brown rice, vegetable-and-hazelnut salad, and nut roast with a spicy sauce. Needless to say, this isn't a Greek place, but we like the food, service, and ambience.

Tropicana, Mólyvos. ☎ **71-869.**

Cuisine: CONTINENTAL.
Prices: Snacks/desserts 350–2,300 Drs ($1.50–$9.60). No credit cards.
Open: Daily 8am–1am.

After lunch or dinner, we suggest strolling up into the old town to sip a cappuccino, have a tuna salad, or nibble on a dish of ice cream. The ambience is sublime: an outdoor café under a plane tree where the sounds of classical music smoothly stir the soul. Hari Procoplou runs the place, having moved back from Los Angeles where he learned the secrets of ice creamery.

Evening Entertainment

A wonderful selection of foreign language books and visiting foreigners is found nightly at Estravagario, around the corner from the post office (☎ **71-824**).

Nighttime in Mólyvos revolves around bars, and bars there are plenty. Among the hottest spots when we last visited were **Perlita** and **Gotaluzi. Koukos** is supposed to attract a largely gay following, while a local favorite, the **Castro Bar,** has been known to host an active pick-up scene.

If you're still with us, you're about to hear of one of our favorite new spots in all of Greece. On the road to Eftalou past the Sappho Tours office (about a ten-minute walk outside of central Mólyvos) is a sign that points to an olive grove. **Vangelis Bouzouki** (no telephone) is the destination, and to get there you'll have to walk another 500 meters through the orchard until you reach a clearing. There, amidst gnarly olive trees and a few stray sheep, is the site of Mólyvos's top acoustic bouzouki club.

A circular cement dance floor is surrounded by clumps of café tables. Forget the food, but imbibe on ouzo and some late night *mezédes* (appetizers) and sit back to enjoy the show.

Excursions

Two of the more interesting excursions from Mólyvos are visits to **Pétra,** a fishing village just a few kilometers south with an enormous rock in its center, and **Mandamados,** a village known for the manufacture of *koumaria,* ceramic vases that magically keep water cool even in scorching heat. In Pétra, the **Committee for the Equal Rights of the Two Sexes** started a housing program to place visitors in 50 local homes, where they can help in the fields, in the kitchens, or in the local women's handicraft cooperative. The **Women's Agricultural-Tourist Cooperative of Pétra** (☎ **0253/41-238,** fax 0253/41-309) has a reception area in the village; stop in to find a room with breakfast, or try their popular restaurant (open daily in summer for lunch or dinner). Rates are fixed at 6,380 Drs ($26.60) single with bath, 7,480 Drs ($31.20) double.

If it's beaches you want, consider Pétra as a base. **Anaxos Beach,** a short distance from town, is a dark sandy crescent with a scattering of tavernas and private rooms, and is the best in the immediate area. The most pleasant part of the beach is to the west; you'll have to walk to get there. **Riga's Restaurant** (☎ **41-405**) is a local favorite in Pétra, serving supper to locals year-round.

PLOMARI & THE SOUTH

Located on the south coast, Plomari is another sleepy, tiered fishing village that has been able to accept tourist development without completely selling its soul. The village has a very different architectural appeal than Mólyvos but also offers winding streets, mysterious passageways, outdoor cafés, a scenic harbor, and a relaxed pace that will make you wonder how you could have lived any other way. Plomari is especially known for its potent ouzo (the Ouzo Festival is held each July) as well as fresh shrimp, red hot peppers, and locally produced mushrooms.

In Mytilíni the **Cooperative Tourism & Travel Agency** (☎ **025-21-329**) has a list of rooms for rent in the area.

We liked **Pension Lida** (☎ **0251/44320**), located in two handsome old villas right in town, where doubles with sea view and private bath are 7,150 Drs ($30), including breakfast in a little garden balcony.

Plomari's in-town beaches are fine for swimming, but travel a few kilometers east to **Ághios Isódoros** for better water, a long pebble beach, and a growing number of pensions and condos. Due west on Lésvos's south coast is the popular sand beach at **Vatera** that's 8 km long, 30 meters wide, and often jammed; keep walking and you're bound to find an empty spot. For a really great fish meal, take the first right turn past Ághios Isídoros and go about two miles to the town of Aghía Varvára. Fresh swordfish steaks are 1,650 Drs ($7) per person at **Blue Sea** (☎ **32-834**), where you sit under the stars, right beside the unspoiled rocky coastline. There are also a few rooms available here.

A really enjoyable day trip is to the rural hamlet of **Agiassos** (as seen in Mytilíni's Popular Art Museum, 23 km north), where local craftsmen still turn out their ceramicware by hand. The town, built up on the foothills of Mt. Olympus, consists of traditional gray stone houses whose wooden "Turkish" (Ottoman) balconies are covered in flowering vines, narrow cobblestone lanes, and modest churches.

It's best reached from Mytilíni, though there is a very bad road from Plomári and you can share a taxi (5,500 Drs. or $22.88) for the one-hour, 25-km ride.

SKALA ERESSÓS & THE WEST

Eressós, the winter village, and its summery neighbor, **Skála Eressós** (4 km south), have become a full-blown resort. The main reason has nothing to do with Eressós being the birthplace of Sappho—or the lesbian community that makes pilgrimages there—but is due to the fact that it is the best beach on Lésvos, a wide, wonderful, dark-sand stretch. A long stretch of sandy beaches and coves extends north from there to Sigri. When you return from the beach to the village you can visit the archeology museum, behind the Church of St. Andrew, the Byzantine-era fortress (closed Monday), or the fifth-century basilica, Ághios Andreas.

A few who stay in this area prefer the village of Eressos, but most people reside at the beach. In Mytilíni, the **Cooperative Tourism & Travel Agency** (☎ **21-329**) has a list of available rooms. If you choose to stay at the beach there's a lot of summer-home construction and some rooms to let.

We enjoyed dining along the water, and found one good place to the far left as you face the sea. The **Arion Restaurant,** otherwise known as The Boy on the Dolphin (☎ **53-384**) serves a delicious vegetarian moussaká and other Greek specialties with a vaguely English touch; it's open for lunch and dinner.

Here's a little tidbit: If you need beach supplies or food for a picnic, stop in at the food/variety store on the road in Skala leading up to Eressos. Look at the man behind the counter, notice the sign outside, and think about who ran for president against George Bush in 1988. Yes, you are at the **Dukakis Super Market** with none other than the cousin of the former Governor of Massachusetts, Mike D.; Lésvos is the family home in Greece.

Excursions to Turkey

Although few Americans heading to Lésvos realize there's a direct connection to Turkey via the port of Ayvalik, about 30,000 tourists make the crossing annually. During the high season, ships to Turkey sail daily except Sunday. Tickets for the Turkish boats are sold by **Aeolic Cruises Travel Agency** (☎ **23-960**) on the port in Mytilíni for about 14,300 Drs ($59.60) round-trip; submit your passport one day in advance of departure. Ayvalik, a densely wooded fishing village, makes a refreshing base camp from which to tour Pergamum or ancient Troy. An all-inclusive tour to Pergamum with lunch, bus, and round-trip boat fare costs about $70.

For additional information about Turkey, consult *Frommer's Turkey on $40 a Day,* by Tom Brosnahan.

4 Límnos

186 nautical miles NE of Piraeus

ARRIVING/DEPARTING • By Air Olympic Airways has three flights daily to Límnos from Athens, and one flight daily from Thessaloníki. Olympic Airways (☎ **0254/22-078**) is on Garofalidi Street, in Mirina. Their airport bus departs 90 minutes before flight time and costs 220 Drs. (90¢).

• **By Sea** Getting to Límnos isn't much of a problem from northern Greece. It's connected by boat to Kavála four times weekly, to Lésvos three times weekly, and to

Chíos, Samothráki, Alexandroúpoli, the Dodecanese, and the Évvian port of Kymi infrequently. The schedule changes often, so you'll have to contact the **Límnos Port Authority** (☎ **0254/22-225**) or the port authority (or travel agency) from your point of origin.

ESSENTIALS There is a **tourist police** (☎ **22-201**), an OTE, and **post office** in the main port of Mírina.

The rough, jagged rocks that enclose Límnos's port, Mírina, suggest a volcanic antecedent, perhaps related to the Olympian god of iron and fire, Hephaestus. Born ugly and lame, Hephaestus was cast out by his father Zeus, and as Milton wrote, was "Dropt from the zenith like a falling star, on Lemnos, the Aegean isle." Here he fashioned shields and spears for the Olympians and created a race of cast-gold robotic maidens who stoked the fiery furnace that caused volcanic disturbances. Another tale says that Aphrodite once made the island's women repulsive to their husbands because the men had favored Hephaestus over her during the couple's tempestuous marriage. The ignored and angry women ultimately slaughtered all the men—they poisoned their wine, slit their throats, and tossed them into the sea. For a while Lésvos was inhabited only by women, until the *Argo* and its manly crew pulled into Límnos's snug harbor to repopulate the island.

Mírina

The Venetians controlled Límnos during the Middle Ages from their base at the main port of Mírina (Mýrina). The vast castle and fortifications on the left hill above the harbor are today balanced by a lovely white chapel on the right hill. Few tourists visit windswept Límnos, yet during antiquity its soil was thought to have healing power, and exports were strictly regulated. Today the most sought-after but rarely exported product of Límnos is its delicious wine.

The best activity in sleepy Mírina is to go to the beach. There are two excellent **beaches** within a few kilometers south of the port: **Platí** is the closer of the two, but **Thános** is less crowded. The port is lined with a clean sand beach, but why not make the extra effort (you already have if you've made it to Límnos) and day-trip to the above destinations. You can rent a bicycle in town, or a car if you decide to explore further.

WHERE TO STAY

Aktaeon, Odós Arvanitáki, Mírina 81400. ☎ **0254/22-258.** 14 rms (12 with bath).

Rates: 3,850 Drs ($16) single without bath; 8,800 Drs ($36.70) double without bath, 11,000 Drs ($45.80) double with bath. No credit cards.

The Aktaeon, on the *paralía,* a smaller, well-maintained hotel with some charm, is open year round. Private rooms are available, but you'll have to bargain, because the Limniots will often double the "expected" rate for the few tourists they meet. The best seaside taverna is behind the sheltered fishing boat mooring.

Hotel Sevdalis, Odós Garofalídou 6, Mírina 81400. ☎ **0254/22-303.** Fax 0254/22-382. 36 rms (all with bath). A/C TEL

Rates: 9,240 Drs ($38.50) single; 14,850 Drs ($61.90) double. No credit cards.

The standard rooms at this Class C hotel are about 200 meters from the beach. There's a lounge with TV and a bar for guests.

A SPLURGE CHOICE

Akti Mirina, Mírina 81400. ☎ **0254/22-681.** Fax 0254/22-382.
125 bungalows (all with bath). A/C MINIBAR TEL

Rates: 19,500–79,350 Drs ($81.25–$330.65) double bungalows; 73,600–128,000 Drs ($306.65–$533.35) suites. AE, EC, MC, V.

One kilometer west of town around the fortified hill is this complex of luxurious, exorbitantly priced bungalows that dominate the scene with their three restaurants, several bars, a private beach, a heated sea-water swimming pool, seasports, minigolf, and tennis facilities, and the wonderful climbing rocks along the shore. These plush amenities and a modern convention center are responsible for attracting more tourists to the island than any other Limniot asset.

5 Samothráki

30 nautical miles S of Alexandroúpolis

ARRIVING/DEPARTING • By Air **Olympic Airways** offers daily flights between Athens and Alexandroúpolis or Kavála (both on the mainland), a handy way to save ferry time!

• By Sea Samothráki is served six times weekly by **steamer** from Alexandroúpolis (☎ **0551/26-721** for information). There are infrequent ferries to Kavála. Contact the local port authority (☎ **0551/41-305**) for the current schedule.

ESSENTIALS There's a **bank, OTE** (the telephone **area code** is 0551), and **post office** in the village, plus a modest offering of private rooms. **Note:** Samothráki, although a Northeast Aegean island, is now part of the district of Thrace.

Samothráki (Samothrace) is a forbidding place. Not only is it a very windy, rocky, mountainous island with a port that's nearly impossible to navigate (there really is no natural harbor). In ancient times the ultra-secretive Mysteries were practiced here—with a vague suggestion of human sacrifice. Even Samothráki's Mt. Moon (Fengari), one of the highest in the region, has a name that resonates with darkness and the unknown. Other than for religious pilgrimages, few people ever visited the island; it successfully avoided the invasions and disasters that befell the other Aegean islands. The situation remains much the same today: Samothráki has staved off yet another army—the legions of tourism.

Like Mílos, the island is closely associated with a particular piece of sculpture, the forthright *Winged Victory (Nike) of Samothrace* on display in the Louvre. The 4th-century B.C. statue was commissioned by Demetrius Polyocretes—who was the patron of the Colossus of Rhodes—for his victory over Ptolemy in Egypt. It was found 2,100 years later, in the middle of the 19th century, by the French consul, who somehow spirited the masterpiece off the island and back to Paris. Excavations at the site of the mysteries, the temple of the Great Gods near Palaeopolis, began in 1938 when an archeological team from the United States uncovered the foundations of a complex of temples and initiation sanctuaries. The **Arisinoe Rotunda** (dedicated by one of the Ptolemies' wives) is a circular building on the order of the tholos at Delphi and the largest structure of its kind in Greece.

The mysteries date back prior to the Greek settlement of the islands, and may have originated as a Phoenician rite celebrating the cult of the Cabeiri. Herodotus claimed that the Cabeiri were a race of dwarfs who protected the fields, but modern writers believe they were a group of fertility gods. The initiation rites of the Cabeiric mysteries were reinterpreted by the Greeks, and such notables as Philip of Macedonia and his wife-to-be, Olympias, journeyed to Samothráki to take part in the ritual.

Around the Island

Boats arrive at the port of **Kamariótissa,** where you may be met by a dinghy that will take you ashore. There's a Class C hotel on the harbor, the **Niki Beach** (☎ **0551/41-561**), with 38 double rooms with private bath at 11,275 Drs ($47). You'd be advised to move on up to the central mountains. The bus (which stops at the major villages in the summer) will stop at the base of the Mountain of the Moon, where **Chora,** the capital, was built to discourage pirates from attacking—how could they! Above the village is a Byzantine fort that seems superfluous in this remote outpost.

The bus from Chóra (it's a pleasant 4-km walk downhill) also stops in **Paleópolis,** the site of the Mysteries, an excavation, and a museum. Similar to the museum on Mílos, there's a French-made cast of the *Winged Victory,* as well as objects found at the site.

It's possible to climb the 1,600-meter Mt. Fengari, but consult the local police about the conditions on the slopes; the mountain is covered with snow for much of the year. From the peak of the mountain there's a fine view of Turkey, and it's said that Poseidon sat atop the crest to watch the battle at Troy.

6 Thássos

14 nautical miles S of Kavála

ARRIVING/DEPARTING • By Air If you're pressed for time, consider the twice-daily flights between Kavála and Athens. There is an **Olympic Airways** office (☎ **0593/22-546**) in the port of Limenas.

• By Sea **Steamers** from Kavala (☎ **224-472**) make the 70-minute trip to Skála Prínos (the northwest port) up to eight times a day in summer. From Keramoti on the mainland (☎ **223-716**), only 35 minutes to Liménas, there are eight departures a day, with two boats continuing from Liménas to Skála Prínos before returning to Kavála.

ESSENTIALS The *local police, bus station,* and the *Commercial Bank of Greece* are all on the port in Liménas (Thássos town). The *tourist police* (☎ **22-500**) are open daily during the summer months. Check with the portside **Katha Travel** (☎ **0593/22-546**), open daily, for general information, and with *Prinos Travel* (☎ **0593/71-152**) in Skála Prínos about Kavála, Límnos, and Samothráki where they have branch offices. Both the police and Katha have lists of available private rooms as well as current bus and ferry schedules. The **OTE** and **post office**, both in town, are on the street behind the port.

Thássos is the northernmost island in the Aegean, off the Macedonian coast near Kavála (now incorporated in the district of Macedonia). Unlike Límnos and Samothráki, Thássos is a wooded, green island with broad sandy beaches and a few Greek- and Roman-era archeological sites.

The island has always had a wealth of natural reserves. Marble was quarried by the Parians when they ruled Thássos—and along with other minerals is still being exploited.

Herodotus claimed that there were active gold mines on the island when he visited in the 5th century B.C. There are none today, but oil was recently discovered off the coast, proving once again that the rich get richer.

Most visitors come to Thássos on weekends from nearby Kavála or as the first island encountered on the drive from Europe or Turkey.

Orientation

Thássos is a small round island with hilly coastal plains and a mountainous interior abounding with plane, chestnut, fir, almond, olive, and pine trees. Much of it was charred by several devastating fires in 1988. Ferries from Kavála dock at the northwest town of Skála Prínos; from Keramoti at the northeast coast town and capital, **Liménas** or **Thássos.** The remnants of an ancient acropolis, harbor, fortifications, and theater are centered around Liménas. A coastal road, with olive trees and tobacco plants on one side and the turquoise sea on the other, completely encircles the island, passing the excellent east coast beaches from **Chryssí Ammoudiá** to **Chryssí Aktí.** Megálos Prínos and Mikrós Prínos, about 4 km inland from the Kavála ferry pier, are traditional mountain villages. Many of the centuries-old houses display intricately carved wood panels. The west coast road continues down to the extreme south coast to the resort town of **Limenariá.** Tacky shops, cafés, new rooms-to-let, and pastel-colored houses line the waterfront.

Getting Around

The Skála Prínos to Liménas and the Liménas to Limenaria buses run hourly in the high season; the KTEL **bus** station is next to the Commercial Bank. The **Prinos Travel** office (☎ **0593/71-202;** fax 0593/71-152) in Skála Prínos handles all tourist needs in town, including rental cars. In Liménas, there's a **Thassos Rent A Car** office (☎ **22-535**), but we easily toured the island by **moped** and they're widely available.

Around the Island

The main reason to go to Liménas is for the archeological ruins. Of greatest interest is the poorly rebuilt ancient theater, where Greek plays are performed each July and August. The agora, acropolis, and other ancient ruins are situated within walking distance; signs mark the way to most of these sites.

Finds from Thássos's rich past are on display at the **museum,** two blocks southeast of the port (across from the church). The highlight of the collection is a giant kouros carrying a ram, dating from the 6th century B.C., when Thássos was something of a sculpture center. The museum is open from 8:45am to 3pm Tuesday through Sunday; admission is 500 Drs ($2.10).

LIMÉNAS

Liménas is the most developed town on the island, but unless you're thirsting for discos and souvenir shops, you're better off setting up base at the tranquil port of Skála Prínos or near one of the fine east coast beaches (there are rooms everywhere). The nearest **beach,** aside from the private beach at Makryammos, is 4 km to the west at **Glyfáda.** There are better, less crowded beaches at **Chryssí Ammoudiá** and **Chryssí Aktí,** 10 km from Liménas and a short but winding bus ride from the inland villages of **Potamiá** and **Panaghía.**

If you do stay in Liménas you'll have a large offering of rooms from which to choose. Harbor-view doubles can be found at the upgraded, eight-room

Astir (☎ **0593/22-160**) for 5,175 Drs ($21.55) per night, or at the **Angelika** (☎ **0593/22-387**), where 26 rooms for two including private bath cost 7,150 Drs ($29.80). Both are on the *paralía* and are open year round.

SKÁLA PRÍNOS

As an alternative to staying in Liménas, we prefer staying in Skála Prínos, another ferryboat pier but with significantly less commercial development. The half-kilometer-long town is lined with beaches, both to the east and west.

Where to Stay & Eat

Elektra Hotel, Skála Prínos 64004. ☎ **0593/71-374.** 30 rms (all with bath). TEL

Rates (including breakfast): 5,500 Drs ($22.90) single; 9,900 Drs ($41.20) double. No credit cards.

On the west side of the beach (on the right as you disembark from the ferry) is the biggest and best-looking hotel in this little town. It has its own restaurant and bar and pool; rooms are clean white with attractive furnishings. Balconies overlook a small shipyard where wooden fishing vessels are constructed.

Hotel Prinos, Skála Prínos 64004. ☎ **0593/71-327** or **71-620.** 16 rms (all with bath).

Rates: 3,850 Drs ($16) single; 5,500 Drs ($22.90) double. No credit cards.

Our first choice on the Prínos beach is this hotel, whose proprietress gave us a very warm welcome. Spotless, balconied doubles with modern showers overlook the ferry activity and sunrise. Though simpler than the Elektra, we like its homey ambience.

Taverna Delfini, Skála Prínos. ☎ **71-341.**

Cuisine: Greek.
Prices: Main courses 935–2,200 Drs ($3.90–$9.20). No credit cards.
Open: Daily 10am–11pm.

Next door to the Hotel Prinos is our favorite taverna in northern Greece, a modest, plain white building with cheerful blue trim. At the superb **Delphini,** fresh fish (particularly red mullet) and a huge variety of local vegetables are cooked to perfection.

Appendix

A Basic Greek Vocabulary

Greek is relatively easy to pronounce. Every syllable in a word is uttered as written, and words of more than one syllable almost always have a stress accent. The pronunciation guide on the next page is intended to aid you as you go over the basic words and phrases listed in this appendix. While your pronunciation may not be perfect, you'll find that people in Greece will quickly warm to you if you try to speak to them in their own language.

The transliteration of Greek into English presents a special problem, because there is no recognized standard system to go by. Thus, for example, the island of ΑΙΓΙΝΑ is variously spelled Aegina, Aiyina, and Egina, while the name ΓΕΩΡΓΙΟΣ shows up in English as Georgios, Gheorghios, and Yeoryios, to cite only some of the variants. So, don't be surprised if you see a street or town spelled differently on your map or on a signpost. (If you can read the Greek, you have the game won!)

GREEK ALPHABET	NAME	TRANSLITERATION	PRONUNCIATION
Α, α	álfa	a	f*a*ther
Β, β	víta	v	e*va*de
Γ, γ	gámma	gh *or* y	*y*es
Δ, δ	délta	d *or* dh	*th*en
Ε, ε	épsilon	e	*e*gg
Ζ, ζ	zíta	z	*z*one
Η, η	íta	i	mach*i*ne
Θ, θ	thíta	th	*th*in
		i	*is*
Ι, ι	yóta	y (semi-consonantal)	nat*i*on
Κ, κ	káppa	k	*k*ey
Λ, λ	lámbda	l	*l*amb
Μ, μ	mí	m	*m*other
Ν, ν	ní	n	*n*et
Ξ, ξ	xí	x	a*x*e
Ο, ο	ómikron	o	*o*ver
Π, π	pí	p	*p*et
Ρ, ρ	ró	r	bu*rr*o (with a slight trill)
Σ, σ, ς*	sígma	s	*s*ee
Τ, τ	táf	t	*t*op
Υ, υ	ípsilon	y *or* i	p*y*ramid
Φ, φ	fí	f *or* ph	*ph*ilosophy
Χ, χ	chí	ch *or* h	Scottish lo*ch* or German *ich*
Ψ, ψ	psí	ps	la*ps*e
Ω, ω	oméga	o	*o*ver (but slightly longer)

*The letter ς occurs only at the end of a word; σ occurs elsewhere in a word. For example: σεισμός "earthquake."

DIPHTHONGS	TRANSLITERATION	PRONUNCIATION
ΑΙ, αι	ai, ae, *or* e	like *e* above
ΕΙ, ει / ΟΙ, οι	i	like *i* above
ΟΥ, ου	ou	L*ou*vre
ΑΥ, αυ	av before vowels and some consonants af before other consonants	*av*ert *af*firm
ΕΥ, ευ	ev before vowels and some consonants ef before other consonants	l*ev*el l*ef*t

DOUBLE CONSONANTS	TRANSLITERATION	PRONUNCIATION
ΓΓ, γγ / ΓΚ, γκ	ng nasalised	a*ng*le
ΜΠ, μπ	b	*b*ar
ΝΤ, ντ	d (at the beginning of a word) nd (in the middle of a word)	*d*andy da*nd*y
ΤΣ, τσ	ts	hit*s*

WORDS & PHRASES

Airport	**Aerodrómio**
Automobile	**Aftokínito**
Avenue	**Leofóros**
Bad	**Kakós,-kí,-kó***
Bank	**Trápeza**
The bill, please.	**Tón logaryazmó(n), parakaló.**
Breakfast	**Proinó**
Bus	**Leoforío**
Can you tell me?	**Boríte ná moú píte?**
Car	**Amáxi**
Cheap	**Ft(h)inó**
Church	**Ekklissía**
Closed	**Klistós, stí, stó***
Coast	**Aktí**
Coffeehouse	**Kafenío**
Cold	**Kríos,-a,-o***
Dinner	**Vradinó**
Does anyone speak English?	**Milál kanís angliká?**
Excuse me.	**Signómi(n).**
Expensive	**Akrivós, -í,-ó***
Farewell!	**Stó ka-ló!** (*to person leaving*)
Glad to meet you.	**Chéro polí.****
Good	**Kalós, lí, ló***
Good-bye	**Adío or chérete****
Good evening	**Kalispéra**
Good health (cheers)!	**Stín (i)yá sas** *or* **Yá-mas!**
Good morning	**Kaliméra**
Good night	**Kaliníchta****
Hello!	**Yássas** *or* **chérete!****
Here	**Edó**
Hot	**Zestós, -stí, -stó***
Hotel	**Xenodochío****
How are you?	**Tí kánete** *or* **Pós íst(h)e?**
How far?	**Pósso makriá?**
How long?	**Póssi óra** *or* **Pósso(n) keró?**
How much is it?	**Pósso káni?**
I am from New York.	**Íme apó tí(n) Néa(n) Iórki.**
I am lost or I have lost the way.	**Écho chathí** *or* **Écho chási tón drómo(n).****
I'm sorry, but I don't speak Greek (well).	**Lipoúme, allá dén miláo elliniká (kalá).**
I don't understand, please repeat it.	**Dén katalavéno, péste to páli, sás parakaló.**

*Masculine ending -os, feminine ending -a or -i, neuter ending -o.

**Remember, *ch* should be pronounced as in Scottish *loch* or German *ich,* not as in the word *church.*

I want to go to the airport.	**Thélo ná páo stó aerodrómio.**
I want a glass of beer.	**Thélo éna potíri bíra.**
It's (not) all right.	**(Dén) íne en dáxi.**
Left (direction)	**Aristerá**
Ladies' room	**Ghinekón**
Lunch	**Messimerianó**
Map	**Chártis****
Market (place)	**Agorá**
Men's room	**Andrón**
Mr.	**Kýrios**
Mrs.	**Kyría**
Miss	**Despinís**
My name is . . .	**Onomázome . . .**
New	**Kenoúryos, -ya, -yo***
No	**Óchi****
Old	**Paleós, -leá, -leó*** ***(pronounce palyós, -lyá, -lyó)***
Open	**Anichtós, -chtí, -chtó***
Pâtisserie	**Zacharoplastío****
Pharmacy	**Farmakío**
Please	**Parakaló**
Please call a taxi (for me).	**Parakaló, fonáxte éna taxi (yá ména).**
Post office	**Tachidromío****
Restaurant	**Estiatório**
Restroom	**Tó méros *or* I toualétta**
Right (direction)	**Dexiá**
Saint	**Ághios, aghía, *(plural)* ághi-i *(abbreviated* ag.*)***
Shore	**Paralía**
Square	**Platía**
Street	**Odós**
Show me on the map.	**Díxte mou stó(n) chárti.****
Station (bus, train)	**Stathmós (leoforíou, trénou)**
Stop (bus)	**Stási(s) (leoforíou)**
Telephone	**Tiléfono**
Temple (of Athena, Zeus)	**Naós (Athinás, Diós)**
Thank you (very much).	**Efcharistó (polí)****
Today	**Símera**
Tomorrow	**Ávrio**
Very nice	**Polí oréos, -a, -o***
Very well	**Polí kalá *or* En dáxi**
What?	**Tí?**
What time is it?	**Tí ôra íne?**
What's your name?	**Pós onomázest(h)e?**

*Masculine ending -os, feminine ending -a or -i, neuter ending -o.

**Remember, *ch* should be pronounced as in Scottish *loch* or German *ich,* not as in the word *church.*

Where is . . . ?	**Poú íne...?**
Why?	**Yatí?**

NUMBERS

0	**Midén**	17	**Dekaeftá**	151	**Ekatón penínda éna**
1	**Éna**	18	**Dekaoktó**	152	**Ekatón penínda dío**
2	**Dío**	19	**Dekaenyá**	200	**Diakóssya**
3	**Tría**	20	**Íkossi**	300	**Triakóssya**
4	**Téssera**	21	**Íkossi éna**	400	**Tetrakóssya**
5	**Pénde**	22	**Íkossi dío**	500	**Pendakóssya**
6	**Éxi**	30	**Triánda**	600	**Exakóssya**
7	**Eftá**	40	**Saránda**	700	**Eftakóssya**
8	**Októ**	50	**Penínda**	800	**Oktakóssya**
9	**Enyá**	60	**Exínda**	900	**Enyakóssya**
10	**Déka**	70	**Evdomínda**	1,000	**Chílya***
11	**Éndeka**	80	**Ogdónda**	2,000	**Dío chilyádes***
12	**Dódeka**	90	**Enenínda**	3,000	**Trís chilyádes***
13	**Dekatría**	100	**Ekató(n)**	4,000	**Tésseris chilyádes***
14	**Dekatéssera**	101	**Ekatón éna**	5,000	**Pénde chilyádes***
15	**Dekapénde**	102	**Ekatón dío**		
16	**Dekaéxi**	150	**Ekatón penínda**		

CALENDAR

Monday	**Deftéra**	Friday	**Paraskeví**
Tuesday	**Tríti**	Saturday	**Sávvato**
Wednesday	**Tetárti**	Sunday	**Kiriakí**
Thursday	**Pémpti**		

January	**Ianouários**	July	**Ioúlios**
February	**Fevrouários**	August	**Ávgoustos**
March	**Mártios**	September	**Septémvrios**
April	**Aprílios**	October	**Októvrios**
May	**Máios**	November	**Noémvrios**
June	**Ioúnios**	December	**Dekémvrios**

*Remember, *ch* should be pronounced as in Scottish *loch* or German *ich*, not as in the word *church*.

MENU TERMS

Hors d'Oeuvres—Orektiká

Choriátiki saláta "Village" salad ("Greek" salad to us)
Chórta Dandelion salad
Domátes yemistés mé rízi Tomatoes stuffed with rice
Melitzanosaláta Eggplant salad
Piperiés yemistés Stuffed green peppers
Saganáki Grilled cheese
Spanokópita Spinach pie
Taramosaláta Fish roe with mayonnaise
Tirópita Cheese pie
Tzatzíki Yogurt-cucumber-garlic dip

Fish—Psári

Astakós (ladolémono) Lobster (with oil-and-lemon sauce)
Bakaliáro (skordaliá) Cod (with garlic)
Barboúnia (skáras) Red mullet (grilled)
Garídes Shrimp
Glóssa (tiganití) Sole (fried)
Kalamarákia (tiganitá) Squid (fried)
Kalamarákia (yemistá) Squid (stuffed)
Karavídes Crayfish
Oktapódi Octopus
Soupiés yemistés (Stuffed cuttlefish)
Tsípoura Dorado

Meats—Kréas

Arní avgolémono Lamb with lemon sauce
Arní soúvlas Spit-roasted lamb
Arní yiouvétsi Baked lamb with orzo
Brizóla chiriní Pork steak or chop
Brizóla moscharísia Beef or veal steak
Dolmadákia Stuffed vine leaves
Keftedes Fried meatballs
Kotópoulo soúvlas Spit-roasted chicken
Kotópoulo yemistó Stuffed chicken
Loukánika Spiced sausages
Moussaká Meat and eggplant
Païdákia Lamb chops
Piláfi rízi Rice pilaf
Souvláki Lamb (sometimes veal) on the skewer
Youvarlákia Boiled meatballs with rice

B The Metric System

Length

1 millimeter (mm) = .04 inches (*or* less than $^{1}/_{16}$ in.)
1 centimeter (cm) = .39 inches (*or* just under $^{1}/_{2}$ in.)
1 meter (m) = 39 inches (*or* about 1.1 yards)
1 kilometer (km) = .62 miles (or about $^{2}/_{3}$ of a mile)

To convert kilometers to miles, multiply the number of kilometers by .62. Also use to convert kilometers per hour (kmph) to miles per hour (m.p.h.).
To convert miles to kilometers, multiply the number of miles by 1.61. Also use to convert from m.p.h. to kmph.

Capacity

1 liter (l) = 33.92 fluid ounces = 2.1 pints = 1.06 quarts = .26 U.S. gallons
1 Imperial gallon = 1.2 U.S. gallons

To convert liters to U.S. gallons, multiply the number of liters by .26.
To convert U.S. gallons to liters, multiply the number of gallons by 3.79.
To convert Imperial gallons to U.S. gallons, multiply the number of Imperial gallons by 1.2.
To convert U.S. gallons to Imperial gallons, multiply the number of U.S. gallons by .83.

Weight

1 gram (g) = .035 ounces (*or* about a paperclip's weight)
1 kilogram (kg) = 35.2 ounces = 2.2 pounds
1 metric ton = 2,205 pounds = 1.1 short ton

To convert kilograms to pounds, multiply the number of kilograms by 2.2.
To convert pounds to kilograms, multiply the number of pounds by .45.

Temperature

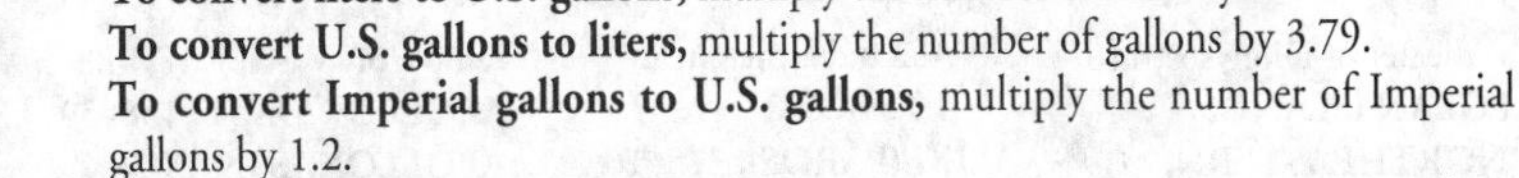

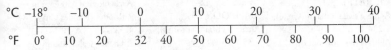

To convert degrees Celsius to degrees Fahrenheit, multiply °C by 9, divide by 5, and add 32 (example: 20°C × $^{9}/_{5}$ + 32 = 68°F).
To convert degrees Fahrenheit to degrees Celsius, subtract 32 from °F, multiply by 5, then divide by 9 (example: 85°F – 32 × $^{5}/_{9}$ = 29.4°C).

Index

Now Save Money On All Your Travels By Joining FROMMER'S™ TRAVEL BOOK CLUB The World's Best Travel Guides At Membership Prices!

mmer's Travel Book Club is your ticket to successful travel! Open up a world of travel information and simplify your vel planning when you join ranks with thousands of value-conscious travelers who are members of the Frommer's *avel Book Club.* Join today and you'll be entitled to all the privileges that come from belonging to the club that offers a travel guides for less to more than 100 destinations worldwide. **Annual membership is only $25.00 (U.S.) or 5.00 (Canada/Foreign).**

The Advantages of Membership:

1. Your choice of **three free** books (any **two** Frommer's Comprehensive Guides, Frommer's $-A-Day Guides, Frommer's Walking Tours or Frommer's Family Guides—plus **one** Frommer's City Guide, Frommer's City $-A-Day Guide or Frommer's Touring Guide).
2. Your own subscription to the **TRIPS & TRAVEL** quarterly newsletter.
3. You're entitled to a **30% discount** on your order of any additional books offered by the club.
4. You're offered (at a small additional fee) our **Domestic Trip-Routing Kits.**

Our **Trips & Travel** quarterly newsletter offers practical information on the best buys in travel, the "hottest" cation spots, the latest travel trends, world-class events and much, much more.

Our **Domestic Trip-Routing Kits** are available for any North American destination. We'll send you a detailed ap highlighting the best route to take to your destination—you can request direct or scenic routes.

Here's all you have to do to join:

nd in your membership fee of $25.00 ($35.00 Canada/Foreign) with your name and address on the form below ong with your selections as part of your membership package to the address listed below. Remember to check off ur three free books.

If you would like to order additional books, please select the books you would like and send a check for the total nount (please add sales tax in the states noted below), plus $2.00 per book for shipping and handling ($3.00 Canada/ reign) to the address listed below.

FROMMER'S TRAVEL BOOK CLUB
P.O. Box 473
Mt. Morris, IL 61054-0473
(815) 734-1104

[ ] **YES!** I want to take advantage of this opportunity to join Frommer's Travel Book Club.

[ ] My check is enclosed. Dollar amount enclosed______________*
(all payments in U.S. funds only)

Name ____

Address ____

City ______________________ State ____________ Zip ____________

Phone (   ) ________________ (In case we have a question regarding your order).

All orders must be prepaid.

o ensure that all orders are processed efficiently, please apply sales tax in the following areas: CA, CT, FL, IL, IN, NJ, Y, PA, TN, WA and CANADA.

With membership, shipping & handling will be paid by Frommer's Travel Book Club for the three FREE books you elect as part of your membership. Please add $2.00 per book for shipping & handling for any additional books purchased $3.00 Canada/Foreign).

llow 4-6 weeks for delivery for all items. Prices of books, membership fee, and publication dates are subject to change ithout notice. All orders are subject to acceptance and availability.

Please send me the books checked below:

FROMMER'S COMPREHENSIVE GUIDES

(Guides listing facilities from budget to deluxe, with emphasis on the medium-priced)

	Retail Price	Code
☐ Acapulco/Ixtapa/Taxco, 2nd Edition	$13.95	C157
☐ Alaska '94-'95	$17.00	C131
☐ Arizona '95 (Avail. 3/95)	$14.95	C166
☐ Australia '94'-'95	$18.00	C147
☐ Austria, 6th Edition	$16.95	C162
☐ Bahamas '94-'95	$17.00	C121
☐ Belgium/Holland/ Luxembourg '93-'94	$18.00	C106
☐ Bermuda '94-'95	$15.00	C122
☐ Brazil, 3rd Edition	$20.00	C111
☐ California '95	$16.95	C164
☐ Canada '94-'95	$19.00	C145
☐ Caribbean '95	$18.00	C148
☐ Carolinas/Georgia, 2nd Edition	$17.00	C128
☐ Colorado, 2nd Edition	$16.00	C143
☐ Costa Rica '95	$13.95	C161
☐ Cruises '95-'96	$19.00	C150
☐ Delaware/Maryland '94-'95	$15.00	C136
☐ England '95	$17.95	C159
☐ Florida '95	$18.00	C152
☐ France '94-'95	$20.00	C132
☐ Germany '95	$18.95	C158
☐ Ireland, 1st Edition (Avail. 3/95)	$16.95	C168
☐ Italy '95	$18.95	C160

	Retail Price	Coc
☐ Jamaica/Barbados, 2nd Edition	$15.00	C14
☐ Japan '94-'95	$19.00	C14
☐ Maui, 1st Edition	$14.00	C15
☐ Nepal, 2nd Edition	$18.00	C12
☐ New England '95	$16.95	C16
☐ New Mexico, 3rd Edition (Avail. 3/95)	$14.95	C16
☐ New York State '94-'95	$19.00	C13
☐ Northwest, 5th Edition	$17.00	C14
☐ Portugal '94-'95	$17.00	C14
☐ Puerto Rico '95-'96	$14.00	C15
☐ Puerto Vallarta/ Manzanillo/Guadalajara '94-'95	$14.00	C13
☐ Scandinavia, 16th Edition (Avail. 3/95)	$19.95	C16
☐ Scotland '94-'95	$17.00	C14
☐ South Pacific '94-'95	$20.00	C13
☐ Spain, 16th Edition	$16.95	C16
☐ Switzerland/ Liechtenstein '94-'95	$19.00	C13
☐ Thailand, 2nd Edition	$17.95	C15
☐ U.S.A., 4th Edition	$18.95	C15
☐ Virgin Islands '94-'95	$13.00	C12
☐ Virginia '94-'95	$14.00	C14
☐ Yucatan, 2nd Edition	$13.95	C15

FROMMER'S $-A-DAY GUIDES

(Guides to low-cost tourist accommodations and facilities)

	Retail Price	Code
☐ Australia on $45 '95-'96	$18.00	D122
☐ Costa Rica/Guatemala/ Belize on $35, 3rd Edition	$15.95	D126
☐ Eastern Europe on $30, 5th Edition	$16.95	D129
☐ England on $60 '95	$17.95	D128
☐ Europe on $50 '95	$17.95	D127
☐ Greece on $45 '93-'94	$19.00	D100
☐ Hawaii on $75 '95	$16.95	D124
☐ Ireland on $45 '94-'95	$17.00	D118

	Retail Price	Code
☐ Israel on $45, 15th Edition	$16.95	D130
☐ Mexico on $45 '95	$16.95	D125
☐ New York on $70 '94-'95	$16.00	D121
☐ New Zealand on $45 '93-'94	$18.00	D103
☐ South America on $40, 16th Edition	$18.95	D123
☐ Washington, D.C. on $50 '94-'95	$17.00	D120

FROMMER'S CITY $-A-DAY GUIDES

	Retail Price	Code
Berlin on $40 '94-'95	$12.00	D111
London on $45 '94-'95	$12.00	D114
Madrid on $50 '94-'95	$13.00	D119
Paris on $50 '94-'95	$12.00	D117

FROMMER'S FAMILY GUIDES

(Guides listing information on kid-friendly hotels, restaurants, activities and attractions)

	Retail Price	Code
California with Kids	$18.00	F100
Los Angeles with Kids	$17.00	F103
New York City with Kids	$18.00	F101
San Francisco with Kids	$17.00	F104
Washington, D.C. with Kids	$17.00	F102

FROMMER'S CITY GUIDES

(Pocket-size guides to sightseeing and tourist accommodations and facilities in all price ranges)

	Retail Price	Code
Amsterdam '93-'94	$13.00	S110
Athens, 10th Edition (Avail. 3/95)	$12.95	S174
Atlanta '95	$12.95	S161
Atlantic City/Cape May, 5th Edition	$13.00	S130
Bangkok, 2nd Edition	$12.95	S147
Barcelona '93-'94	$13.00	S115
Berlin, 3rd Edition	$12.95	S162
Boston '95	$12.95	S160
Budapest, 1st Edition	$13.00	S139
Chicago '95	$12.95	S169
Denver/Boulder/Colorado Springs, 3rd Edition	$12.95	S154
Dublin, 2nd Edition	$12.95	S157
Hong Kong '94-'95	$13.00	S140
Honolulu/Oahu '95	$12.95	S151
Las Vegas '95	$12.95	S163
London '95	$12.95	S156
Los Angeles '95	$12.95	S164
Madrid/Costa del Sol, 2nd Edition	$12.95	S165
Mexico City, 1st Edition	$12.95	S170
Miami '95-'96	$12.95	S149
Minneapolis/St. Paul, 4th Edition	$12.95	S159
Montreal/Quebec City '95	$11.95	S166
Nashville/Memphis, 1st Edition	$13.00	S141
New Orleans '95	$12.95	S148
New York '95	$12.95	S152
Orlando '95	$13.00	S145
Paris '95	$12.95	S150
Philadelphia, 8th Edition	$12.95	S167
Prague '94-'95	$13.00	S143
Rome, 10th Edition	$12.95	S168
St. Louis/Kansas City, 2nd Edition	$13.00	S127
San Diego '95	$12.95	S158
San Francisco '95	$12.95	S155
Santa Fe/Taos/Albuquerque '95 (Avail. 2/95)	$12.95	S172
Seattle/Portland '94-'95	$13.00	S137
Sydney, 4th Edition	$12.95	S171
Tampa/St. Petersburg, 3rd Edition	$13.00	S146
Tokyo '94-'95	$13.00	S144
Toronto '95 (Avail. 3/95)	$12.95	S173
Vancouver/Victoria '94-'95	$13.00	S142
Washington, D.C. '95	$12.95	S153

FROMMER'S WALKING TOURS

(Companion guides that point out the places and pleasures that make a city unique)

	Retail Price	Code
☐ Berlin	$12.00	W100
☐ Chicago	$12.00	W107
☐ England's Favorite Cities	$12.00	W108
☐ London	$12.00	W101
☐ Montreal/Quebec City	$12.00	W106

	Retail Price	Cod
☐ New York	$12.00	W10
☐ Paris	$12.00	W10
☐ San Francisco	$12.00	W10
☐ Washington, D.C.	$12.00	W10

SPECIAL EDITIONS

	Retail Price	Code
☐ Bed & Breakfast Southwest	$16.00	P100
☐ Bed & Breakfast Great American Cities	$16.00	P104
☐ Caribbean Hideaways	$16.00	P103

	Retail Price	Cod
☐ National Park Guide, 29th Edition	$17.00	P10
☐ Where to Stay U.S.A., 11th Edition	$15.00	P10

FROMMER'S TOURING GUIDES

(Color-illustrated guides that include walking tours, cultural and historic sites, and practical information)

	Retail Price	Code
☐ Amsterdam	$11.00	T001
☐ Barcelona	$14.00	T015
☐ Brazil	$11.00	T003
☐ Hong Kong/Singapore/ Macau	$11.00	T006
☐ London	$13.00	T007

	Retail Price	Code
☐ New York	$11.00	T008
☐ Rome	$11.00	T010
☐ Tokyo	$15.00	T016
☐ Turkey	$11.00	T013
☐ Venice	$9.00	T014

Please note: If the availability of a book is several months away, we may have back issues of guides to that particular destination. Call customer service at (815) 734-1104.